WHERE to SKI AND Snowboard 2002

The Reuters Guide
to the World's Best Winter Sports Resorts

What do the world's top 350,000 traders have in common?
(Apart from bags of money.)

Get the cost of this book refunded when you book your next holiday!
If you book your next winter sports holiday through the specialist travel agency Ski Solutions, you can get the cost of this book knocked off the bill.

There's no catch. Ski Solutions sells the complete range of package holidays offered by UK bonded tour operators. And if that choice isn't enough, they can tailor-make a holiday just for you.

At the back of the book are two vouchers. When you make your booking, tell Ski Solutions you want to claim this refund. Send one voucher to Ski Solutions, and the other to us. That's all you have to do.

Ski Solutions are on 020 7471 7700.

Get the next edition free! by sending us resort reports
We are always grateful for feedback on the resorts our readers visit. The 100 most useful reports earn a free copy of the 2003 edition, in advance of publication in September 2002.

Send resort reports via our web site at:
www.snow-zone.co.uk
or send an e-mail message to:
reports@snow-zone.co.uk
or write to:
Where to Ski and Snowboard
FREEPOST
The Old Forge
Norton St Philip
Bath
BA2 7ZZ

WHERE *to* SKI AND Snowboard 2002

The Reuters Guide
to the World's Best Winter Sports Resorts

Edited by
Chris Gill
and
Dave Watts

Published in Great Britain by
NortonWood Publishing
The Old Forge
Norton St Philip
Bath BA2 7LW
United Kingdom

tel 01373 835208
fax 01373 834106
e-mail mailbox@snow-zone.co.uk

This edition published 2001

10 9 8 7 6 5 4 3 2 1

ISBN 0 9536371 2 3

A CIP catalogue entry for this book is available from the British Library.

Editors Chris Gill and Dave Watts
Assistant editors Martin Hall, Mandy Crook, Minnie Burlton, Catherine Weakley, Emma Morris, Melanie Papworth
Australia/NZ editor Bronwen Gora
Contributors Chris Allan, Alan Coulson, Nicky Holford, James Hooke, Tim Perry, Adam Ruck, Helena Wiesner, Ian Porter
Advertising manager Sam Palmer

Design by Fox Design Consultants
Production by Guide Editors
Contents photos
by Snowpix.com / Chris Gill
Production manager Ian Stratford
Proof-reader Sally Vince
Printed and bound in Italy
by Conti Tipocolor

Book trade sales are handled by
Portfolio Books Ltd
Unit 5 Perivale Industrial Park
Horsenden Lane South
Greenford UB6 7RL
tel 020 8997 9000
fax 020 8997 9097
e-mail sales@portfoliobooks.com

Individual copies of the book can be bought by credit card from www.amazon.co.uk or through our own web site at:
www.snow-zone.co.uk
or by phoning:
01373 835208

WHERE to SKI AND Snowboard 2002

Contents

Resort chapters

SHERIDAN HOTEL

About this book

it's simply the best

We believe that *Where to Ski and Snowboard* is the best guide to ski and snowboard resorts that you can buy. Here's why:

• By making the most of technology we are able to go to press as late as mid-July and bring the book **up to date for the season ahead** – the 2001/02 season. To see what we mean, check out our What's new chapter, crammed with new resort developments.

• To help you compile a shortlist of resorts, we work hard to make our information **reader-friendly**, with cost ratings, star-ratings for the main aspects of each resort, and crystal-clear lists of resort plus-points and minus-points at the start of each chapter.

• We don't hesitate to express **critical views**. We learned our craft at Consumers' Association, where Chris became editor of *Holiday Which?* magazine and Dave became editor of *Which?* itself – so a consumerist attitude comes naturally to us.

• Our resort chapters give an **unrivalled level of detail** – including scale plans showing the extent and layout of each major resort, as well as all the facts you need to have at your fingertips.

• We use colour printing fully, including not only maps but also photographs, carefully chosen so that you can see for yourself what different resorts are like. In this edition we've really pulled out the stops: second-division resorts that used to get one-page chapters now get two-page chapters so that every resort can have colour graphics – so we now have **25% more photographs and 50% more mountain maps** than last year.

Our ability to keep on developing and improving *Where to Ski and Snowboard* is largely due to the continuing support of our advertisers – many of whom have been with us since the first edition in 1994 – and of Reuters, who first sponsored the book last year. We are grateful for that support, which has given us the confidence to make bigger-than-ever investments in this new edition.

We are uncompromising in our commitment to helping you, our readers, to make an informed choice; we're confident that you'll find this edition the best yet.

Enjoy your skiing and riding this season.

Chris Gill and Dave Watts
Norton St Philip, 11 July 2001

Get this edition FREE!

We reckon *Where to Ski and Snowboard* is a bargain at only £15.99. But if you plan to take a winter sports holiday this winter or the next, you can buy the book safe in the knowledge that you can get the cost of it refunded. See page 16.

Issues of the season

the editors have their say

HERE COMES THE EURO

From 1 January 2002 the euro will become the official currency of most of the main Alpine countries, including France, Austria and Italy (but not Switzerland). Euro coins and notes will replace French francs, schillings and lire. The old currencies will cease to be legal tender (ie businesses will no longer have to accept them) on various dates in January and February – each country is making its own rules. So if you have stocks of these 'old' currencies in your desk drawer, take an early trip and spend them or cash them in for pounds or euros at the bank. (For a while you will still be able to change the withdrawn currencies for euros at banks in the relevant countries.)

The exchange rates between the local currencies and the euro have been fixed for a couple of years now. One euro is worth about 6.6 French francs, 13.8 schillings or 1,940 lire.

EASY PRICE COMPARISONS

One benefit of the euro is that you will be able to make price comparisons more easily. Below are prices for a six-day lift pass for various resorts (also converted into pounds at the euro's mid-July 2001 value – approximately 60p). On the right, for comparison, are prices for a few non-euro countries converted into pounds at mid-July's exchange rate.

France		
Serre-Chevalier	150	£90
Trois Vallées	182	£109
Austria		
St Anton	171	£103
Soll	143	£86
Italy		
Courmayeur	161	£97
Sauze d'Oulx	137	£82
Andorra		
Soldeu	123*	£74*

Switzerland	
Grindelwald	£102*
Zermatt	£128*
US	
Heavenly	£223*
Vail	£250*
Canada	
Banff	£170
Whistler	£163*

* 2000/01 prices; other prices are for 2001/02

Since we last did a comparison like this (for the 1996/97 season) virtually all the European costs have gone down in terms of pounds (because of the strength of the pound against European currencies). But costs in North America have soared because the American and Canadian dollars have strengthened against the pound.

ANDORRA: A REVISED VIEW

If your idea of Andorra is that it's a country of resorts resembling construction sites populated by yobs reeling under the influence of duty-free vodka, and that its ski areas are primitive and suitable only for beginners, you're way behind the times – as we were, before a tour last winter. Yes, the construction sites still exist. Yes, there are still lively bars full of young people. But these factors don't dominate the resorts as they did 10 or 20 years ago. Another revelation is the mountains, which now offer state-of-the-art lift systems, grooming and snowmaking, as well as the excellent British-oriented ski schools that the place is famous for. We were, in a word, impressed.

We'd be even more impressed if the warring parishes that control the Soldeu and Pas de la Casa lift companies could bring themselves to agree on a shared lift pass. The two lift networks are only yards apart – as our introduction to Andorra shows (page 608), the two even share a piste, with huge signs at the bottom to direct you to the correct lift. But to use both areas you have to buy two passes. Bananas!

THE TEMPERATURE'S RISING

Last winter was one of the warmest that we have experienced in the Alps, with a lot of rain rather than snow. In early January at over 2200m above Zermatt it was raining at around midnight as we walked back to our hotel. In mid-March it was raining at over 3000m in the French Alps. Dreadful conditions. When we were in western Canada in February, the story was the same wherever we went: 'This is the worst winter for snowfall anyone can remember.'

It looks like global warming is taking its toll on ski resorts. Since 1850 Alpine glaciers have lost about a third of their surface area and about half their volume. This year the United Nations Panel on Climate Change said that the Alps are warming up faster than the rest of the world, and a German professor of geosciences predicted that global warming 'could push the snowline up from 1200m to 1800m'. Whatever that means, a shift of 600m in the altitude at which snow is reliably found would spell big trouble for many low resorts – including well-known names such as Kitzbühel, Grindelwald, Megève and Gstaad.

Equally worrying are the changes in the permafrost (permanently frozen earth that currently occurs above 2500m in the Alps). When that melts it leaves areas liable to disastrous mudslides, as happened in Italy's Aosta valley region last summer. And in some places cable-car stations and mountain restaurants have been built on permafrost. Experts are worried about the Corvatsch cable-car station at St Moritz, for example; they plan to anchor the foundations, but they may have to rebuild it elsewhere in a few years' time. Just up the road in Pontresina, a 13m-high wall the length of the village is being built to protect it from landslides caused by melting permafrost.

So enjoy your skiing and boarding while the snow lasts. And use our snow reliability ratings to plan where to go. We'd be very hesitant about booking a holiday far in advance in any resort that gets less than a 3-star rating.

LOST IN ADMIRATION – NOT

This season, as every season, we have on countless occasions found ourselves lost on the pistes of the Alps. This isn't because we are useless at finding our way, or because we go out unprepared. It's because so many resorts force us to rely on signs and maps that are simply rubbish. We have been banging on about the lunatic signs and inadequate maps in Verbier for years, but there are lots of other resorts where problems arise, especially when visibility is poor.

In a white-out at Serre-Chevalier (shortly after one of us fell head first off the side of a badly marked catwalk), we lost our way so completely that we ended up climbing up a piste in order to be sure of getting back from one sector to another. In Clavière, our navigation was thrown completely when we skied under a chair-lift that we weren't expecting. Explanation: the piste map didn't show the new lift (amazingly enough, it also didn't show another lift that had been built the previous year). In La Clusaz, in cloud, we made three attempts to find our way from the Aiguille sector to the run for La Balme, taking instructions from lifties not once but twice.

These are problems resulting from mediocre signs and maps. Different problems are going to arise in the Swiss resort of Flims, which has adopted a bizarre new system of run grading which involves (for example) the most difficult runs being graded green with black diamonds. Mad, bad and dangerous. Think again, Flims.

TALES OF THE ESF

Every French resort has a branch of the Ecole du Ski Français (ESF). This is effectively a French trade union that has been instrumental in keeping out competition, especially from British ski instructors. As well as having ridiculous rules about qualifying as a ski instructor (which include a test of ski racing but do not include a test of ability to communicate adequately), ESF members have been accused of outrageous behaviour in some resorts, such as sealing up rival schools' office doors with glue. We continue to get a steady flow of complaints about ESF instructors. In the last few seasons these include instructors:

- teaching snowboarding when they are themselves beginners with only a few hours' experience
- taking one of your editors off-piste on the basis that avalanche risk was low when in fact it was high
- losing two of a touring group and calmly heading for a mountain refuge, when the two who were lost did not know where they were meant to be staying the night and did not speak French
- having to borrow a piste map to find the way
- abandoning or losing children on the slopes.

This kind of behaviour is not just unprofessional, it's dangerous. These reports lead us to humbly suggest that the ESF would be better engaged in raising standards among its own members than obstructing fair competition.

THE 35-HOUR WEEK SHUTS SKI LIFTS

In spring, the sun soon gets hot, and the slopes can suffer and become slushy by mid-morning. So it makes sense to get up the mountain early to enjoy the best of the snow. In North America the lifts usually start at 8.30 (and you can often ride up earlier on an 'early bird' pass and have the pistes to yourself for a while). In Zermatt you can start heading up at 8am. But in Europe's most expensive resort, Courchevel, you can't start using your lift pass until 9am. 'Why not?' we asked. 'No demand,' we were told. 'Not true,' we replied, 'look at the people queueing each morning for the lifts to open.' 'Well, okay,' they said, 'the real reason is that France now has a 35-hour week by law and opening more hours would mean putting on another shift.' The same sort of thinking results in some Austrian lift systems closing shortly after 4pm even on a March afternoon with hours of sunlight left. At least American resorts (which close even earlier) have the excuse that they have huge areas of gladed slopes to patrol – though we believe it is an excuse, not a reason.

Highlights of the season

the editors reminisce

Our annual editorial introduction (a few pages back) tends to focus more on what's wrong with the skiing experience than on what's right. You won't be surprised to hear that on the whole we enjoy the time we are obliged to spend on the slopes each winter, so we thought we would give a few pages over to the more enjoyable business of reflecting on the days that went right. You'll see that many of these reflect the very strange weather of the 2000/01 season – showing that, when you go skiing or boarding, whatever the weather you can have a great time.

HITTING THE SLOPES BEFORE CHRISTMAS

I don't know about you, but as the season approaches I long to get back on the slopes. Except in a handful of resorts, that means waiting until Christmas as far as the Alps are concerned. That's why the first week in December saw me and 100 *Daily Mail Ski & Snowboard* magazine readers on the slopes of Whistler, on Canada's west coast. Whistler is renowned for its cloudy weather, with snow on the mountain and rain in the village. But this was Whistler's driest start to a season for years. The locals complained about the lack of snow. But virtually everyone in our group had a great time. Seven days of sunshine (in three previous visits I'd had only one day of sun) and well-groomed trails meant that, although only a fraction of the 7,000 acres of terrain was open, we had a great start to the season. We are planning to go back this year; if you'd like to join us, call Ski Independence on 0870 555 0555. *DW*

EUROPE'S BEST OFF-PISTE?

On a two-day trip to Italy's Monterosa region, day one was ruined by Europe's strangest winter for ages – the mountain was shrouded in fog from top to bottom. But at night the fog turned to snow; when daybreak came, the skies were brilliant blue and fresh snow lay thick on the trees. It was Sunday, and it seemed like the whole of Milan and Turin was driving in to tiny Champoluc where I was staying. I met my guides, Simon from tour operator Ski 2, local girl Tiziana and mountain guide Claudio. We headed up and it was mayhem; the pistes were packed with Italians hurtling down, pausing only to scream into their mobile phones. I was convinced the day was going to be ruined by the crowds. How wrong I was.

We headed up to Passo dei Salati, above Gressoney, and down an off-piste route towards Alagna – a lovely deserted run of over 1000m vertical – in perfect light powder. A chair-lift followed by a tiny cable-car took us to Punta Indren at 3260m. On the way up in the cable-car you can see just a few of the couloirs, cliffs and steep, steep descents that account for Alagna's growing cult reputation among experts. But time constraints meant they were not for us today. Instead we headed off back towards Gressoney, starting with a long traverse, then down into a fabulous ski-anywhere bowl, making fresh tracks wherever we chose. Any intermediate could manage this terrain on the right free-ride skis. But the place was deserted: we skied for 30 minutes without seeing a soul. In Val-d'Isère or Verbier the whole mountain would have been tracked out hours before. But the hordes of Italians stuck to the pistes. It was simply magical.

Then it was back to the Hotel California and the sounds of the Byrds, Dylan, Presley, Baez, The Doors, and more. A perfect day. *DW*

BABES IN THE WOODS

Most of the skiing I have done with my kids has been on high, open slopes in resorts like Courchevel, Chamonix and Verbier, where the runs below the tree line haven't been very attractive for young kids. But last Easter we had a holiday in Les Arcs. We again spent most of our days on open slopes – but there were notable exceptions. We were holidaying with friends, and altogether our kids numbered seven. The kids quickly discovered that the forest runs above Peisey-Vallandry, perfectly enjoyable in themselves, also had a secret ingredient: hundreds of opportunities to dive off into the woods over bumps and hollows and around a few trees, before rejoining the piste. They weren't going fast (usually) and they were all wearing helmets, so we were able to put aside the obvious parental worries. The kids had the time of their lives – all the more enjoyable because none of the grown-ups had the courage to follow them along the narrow, winding paths they took so easily in their stride. *CG*

THE JOYS OF GETTING HIGH

It was raining over most of the Alps in early March. It was certainly raining in Austria, where I was. But I was lucky enough to be staying near the Hintertux glacier, where powerful new gondolas whisk you up from 1500m to 3250m in less than 20 minutes. The rain turned to snow before we hit 2000m. By the time we were at the top there was a foot of fresh snow on the piste and we had a delightful time cruising around in powder despite the limited visibility. The area has one of Europe's best glaciers; it offers year-round skiing and riding and has extensive terrain that's considerably steeper than usual for a glacier. And, now that it has new high-capacity lifts, the horrendous lift queues that used to blight it have disappeared. It's a bleak place to stay but a great place to ski or board. *DW*

A LOUSY DAY IN A ZERMATT HUT

We were staying up the mountain at the newly reopened and extended Riffelalp Resort hotel, which has its own private trains to take you home after a night out in town. Astonishingly, when we strolled home from the station along the snow-covered path around midnight it was raining – this was in early January, at over 2200m. The next day we ventured out, but conditions were miserable: the piste by the hotel was sheet ice, there was fog higher up and rain lower down. A nightmare. But we were in Zermatt, home of the world's best mountain restaurants. The obvious thing to do was lunch. We rang the best of the lot – Zum See, a tiny, charming, rustic hut just off the run back to the village from the Klein Matterhorn area. They could fit us in at 2.30, they said. So we skied around in the rain (stopping for the odd refreshment and to dry out), ravenous in expectation. We eventually got a table at about 3pm, sharing with a jolly bunch of people who had been there for three hours already.

We took their recommendation for a good-value claret and ordered from the appetising menu – spicy prawns, lamb fillet, Argentinian beef, all kinds of salad ... It was delicious – and astonishing that such fabulous ingredients should be cooked so well in cramped conditions in an unpretentious old cow shed halfway up a mountain. Then there was pudding – only one dessert of the day left (it's best to reserve one when you book, they are so popular) but plenty more to choose from. Coffee, schnapps, and it was time to leave – sliding back to Zermatt in the dark. *DW*

CLIMBING THROUGH THE CLOUDS

It was a grey, damp Saturday in January. My brother Tony and I had arranged to meet a friend, Mark, in La Clusaz – one of the lowest major resorts in the French Alps. As we drove up from Lake Annecy towards La Clusaz, the car thermometer stubbornly refused to drop towards zero, and the occasional drizzle became more persistent. Maybe it would be snowing higher up, but we weren't convinced.

We made our rendezvous successfully, and reckoned the best chance of snow rather than rain was on La Clusaz's highest slopes, at La Balme. The car park at the gondola station was almost empty – the usual weekend crowds no doubt deterred by the dreary weather – and we walked straight on to the gondola. There wasn't a lot of chat in the cabin; we all thought we were in for a damp day. Then, shortly before the top gondola station at 1900m, everything changed: we burst into brilliant sunshine and blue skies.

The chair-lift above the gondola serves a superb open bowl of over 600m vertical, with two winding red pistes and vast areas of friendly off-piste terrain. The bowl faces due west, and the south-facing flank was nicely softened when we ventured on to it after a few blasts down the pistes. Because the crowds had stayed at home, we had more space than anyone has a right to expect this close to Geneva on a Saturday – and a truly memorable morning before moving on to do our editorial duty and explore some of the lower trails. *CG*

THE WORST SNOW FOR DECADES? WHO CARES?

We undertook a short tour of resorts in western Canada last season, and you could say that we picked the wrong season to do it. When we were there in February, there was gloom everywhere; all that varied, as we went from resort to resort, were the estimates of exactly how long it was since snow had been in such short supply. So was the trip a complete waste of time? Far from it.

On our first morning, in Fernie, we were out of the door on time for breakfast, only to be given the bad news by the resort's PR lady – that much of the best skiing simply wasn't accessible, because the top drag-lift giving access to it was dangling uselessly in mid-air, the snow surface being about three metres lower than usual.

But our guide for the morning thought we might find some decent skiing in the newly developed Timber and Currie bowls, so off we went, rather gloomily, up the Timber fast quad. And as we rose up the mountain our spirits rose in parallel. The snow looked ... well, it looked good. And it was: we went on to have a great day's powder skiing, riding the higher White Pass quad repeatedly and enjoying knee-deep untracked snow on the black diamond runs in both bowls – the kind of conditions that we dream about finding in the Alps.

In the rest of our stay, our exploration of every resort was to some extent restricted by shortage of snow. But we also had some fabulous skiing, both on prepared trails and in deep snow. In brand new Kicking Horse, as in Fernie, large areas of the mountain were closed – but in the high bowls there was again excellent powder. Which gives you some idea of what it's like over there in a good snow year. *CG*

What's new?

lifts and snow for 2002

The main news from the resorts of Europe and North America.

AUSTRIA

The new Ski Alliance Amadé joint lift pass covers over 275 lifts in more than 30 ski resorts in eastern Austria: the Gastein valley and Grossarl; Salzburger Sportwelt (main areas: Flachau/ Wagrain/ St Johann and Zauchensee/ Kleinarl); Hochkönigs Winterreich (Maria Alm and neighbours). Buses, trains and road tolls between the resorts are also covered by the pass.

ALPBACH The Muldenlift drags up to Gmahkopf are being replaced by a chair-lift. And, at nearby Reith, a new eight-person gondola replaces the single-seater chair to the top of the mountain.

BAD GASTEIN The parallel Weitmoser drags on Schlossalm are being replaced by a six-pack.

ELLMAU 2000/01 saw a second six-pack to the Hartkaiser-Brandstadl area and another one was installed between Ellmau and Scheffau.

HINTERTUX-MAYRHOFEN Last season saw a gondola replace the old double chair-lift from the Hintertux base area, and the world's highest jumbo gondola was installed from 2660m to 3250m. For 2001/02 the Eggalm/Rastkogel area above Lanersbach is being linked with Mayrhofen's slopes, via a new six-pack from Rastkogel and a new 150-person cable-car from the Mayrhofen slopes. All this will mean a 40% increase in Mayrhofen's terrain to a total of 143km. In the existing Mayrhofen area the old double chair up to Schafskopf will be replaced by a six-pack for 2001/02. Another new six-pack will be built in this area, opening up new runs.

ISCHGL For 2001/02 another fast eight-seater chair replaces a slow three-seater to Idjoch. Last season saw a quad upgraded to an eight-seater and another quad and six-pack installed to replace existing T-bars on the Ischgl side. Over in Samnaun, yet another six-pack replaced a T-bar. More snowmaking was also installed.

LECH For 2000/01 the Rüfikopf cable-car was modernised with new panoramic cabins, and the restaurant at the top refurbished. The Zuger Hochlicht cable-car was taken out of service.

MONTAFON A six-pack and a quad chair are being installed in the Silvretta Nova area for 2001/02. A six-pack will replace the T-bar to the top of Grüneck at Golm, and an eight-seater chair replaces the parallel T-bars in the Seebliga area on Hochjoch.

OBERGURGL A new eight-seater gondola from Hochgurgl up to Wurmkogl is planned for 2001/02. In the Gaisberg sector, a quad chair-lift replaces the Übungs drag-lift; and a six-pack replaces the Steinmann and Sattel drag-lifts.

SAALBACH-HINTERGLEMM For 2000/01 two lifts on the south-facing slopes above Hinterglemm were replaced by fast chairs.

SCHLADMING The old gondola from Haus was upgraded to an eight-seater last season. The slow double chair-lift from Rohrmoos on Hochwurzen was also replaced, by a fast six-pack.

Sölden A new gondola was installed last season on the Tiefenbach glacier. Also new was a six-pack from Langegg to the Rotkoglhütte.

Söll For 2000/01 the old single-seat chair to the Hohe Salve was replaced by an eight-seater gondola from Hochsöll. In Hopfgarten, a queue-prone T-bar was replaced by an eight-seater chair.

St Anton There's a new eight-person gondola from Nasserein to Gampen and a new fast quad from east of the central village to Fang. The old funicular has been demolished, widening the home run.

St Johann For 2001/02 the old single-person chair from Oberndorf will be replaced by an eight-seater gondola.

Westendorf Two T-bars at the top, up to Fleiding and Gampen, are being replaced by quad chairs for the 2001/02 season.

Wildschönau For 2001/02 the old Hahnkopf and Kothkaser drag-lifts on Schatzberg are being replaced by a new six-pack.

Zell am See For 2001/02, a quad chair will replace a T-bar up to Schmittenhöhe on the Sonnkogel side and snowmaking will cover 70% of the lower slopes. In Kaprun, a giant gondola will replace the funicular which suffered the tragic fire last year. It will eventually end at the Alpincenter at the top of the defunct funicular. But for 2001/02 only the first stage will be in place, ending near the top of the existing gondola. So for 2001/02 everyone will have to take a solitary fast quad to the main slopes from the top of the gondolas – expect huge queues.

France

As we went to press the Mont Blanc tunnel, closed since the tragic fire in 1999, was officially due to reopen in the autumn of 2001. But the project has been delayed several times and locals predict that it won't open until December at the earliest, and maybe not until after the 2001/02 season.

Alpe-d'Huez For 2000/01, new developments included a second stage to the Marmottes gondola, the replacement of the old Chatelard drag-lift to Auris by a two-seater chair, a lift from the Villard-Reculas car park up to the fast chair, increased capacity of the Alpette gondola at Oz, and a second automatic snowmaking plant. Plans for 2001/02 include replacement of the glacier double chair by a quad starting lower down on the glacier, and increased capacity on the first stage of the Marmottes gondola.

Avoriaz/Morzine For 2000/01 the gondola from Ardent to Les Lindarets was upgraded to increase its capacity. For 2001/02 another six-pack will replace the double drag from Les Lindarets up to Avoriaz. A new piste will be built at the top to join the existing runs down to Les Lindarets. In Morzine, the Belvédère and Mouilles double chairs were replaced by quads for 2000/01, and the area at the top of the Pleney gondola was rebuilt to make reaching the other lifts easier. More snowmaking was installed.

Chamonix The Charlanon drag, completing the Flégère-Brévent link, was upgraded to a fast quad last season.

Châtel In 2000/01 the three-person chair from Les Combes to Cornebois was replaced by a high-speed quad.

Les Contamines A new gondola on the back side of the mountain, from Belleville to La Ruelle, replaced the old chair-lift for 2000/01.

Courchevel For 2000/01 the slow chair from Les Creux to La Vizelle was replaced by a six-pack and the start of the Creux Noir chair was moved up the mountain to avoid congestion at Les Creux. For

2001/02 a new six-pack will replace the long Pralong drag-lift from the beginner slopes above 1850. Another six-pack will replace three drag-lifts in 1650, making the journey to Signal from 1850 quicker.

Les Deux-Alpes The old Jandri 3 gondola from mid-mountain to the glacier was dismantled last season. A new eight-seater chair, to replace the original gondola, should be ready for 2001/02.

Flaine France's first fast eight-seater chair was installed for 2000/01, from the village at Flaine Forêt to Les Grands Vans. We understood that a new gondola would be in place for 2001/02, going from Samoëns village to Samoëns 1600, but as this page went to press we heard that it has been delayed. A new fast quad from Morillon 1100 will serve the Bergin run.

Les Menuires For 2001/02, a new six-pack will go from the centre of the village to mid-mountain, and another new fast six-seater up to Mont de la Chambre and the links with Méribel and Val-Thorens. The top section of the rickety old gondola that used to be the main way up will be demolished.

Méribel For 2001/02, the slow old Plan des Mains chair, from the bottom of Mont Vallon up to the Plattières gondola, will be replaced by a six-pack.

Montgenèvre For 2000/01, a new chair-lift from the top of the Gimont valley up to Col Saurel opened up a new area of slopes.

La Plagne For 2000/01, the queue-prone Grande Rochette gondola from Plagne-Centre was replaced by a new gondola with three times the capacity. 2001/02 will see more snowmaking. The Biolley two-seater chair-lift from Plagne Centre and the two-seater from Plagne 1800 to Aime-la-Plagne are being upgraded to quads.

Risoul/vars 2001/02 will see a new six-pack from Risoul up to the top of Peyrefolle. In Vars, snowmaking is being extended.

Serre-Chevalier For 2001/02 a new six-pack will replace the parallel Prorel drag-lifts, linking the Chantemerle section to the Briançon slopes. And snowmaking is being doubled.

Val-d'Isère 2000/01 saw a new high-speed chair replace the defunct Cascade and Pissaillas chairs on the Pissaillas glacier. For 2001/02 the old Bellevarde cable-car is being replaced by a giant gondola. And the Glacier chair, an essential link from Solaise towards the Col de L'Iseran and the Pissaillas glacier, is being upgraded to a six-pack.

Valmorel For 2000/01 a new quad chair-lift was built from the Col de Madeleine up to the Beaudin sector. The Prariond chair in the Mottet section was also new last year, with its blue run of the same name.

Val-thorens For 2001/02 a new jumbo gondola will start from the bottom of the gondola towards Caron and take you to near the Col de la Montée du Fond, ending the need to walk to the Maurienne side (the Fourth Valley). Two new successive quads in the Fourth Valley will take you from Plan Bouchet at the top of the gondola up from the Maurienne valley to Pointe du Bouchet and three new runs.

Italy

Turin has been chosen to host the 2006 Olympic Winter Games; most of the Alpine events will be held at Sansicario and Sestriere, with the freestyle competitions at Sauze d'Oulx.

Bormio A new fast quad is to replace the Isabella chair from Bormio 2000 next season. Bormio has been chosen to host the World Alpine Ski Championships in 2005.

Cervinia There's a new piste down into Zermatt from the top of the fast chair-lifts to the Swiss border.

Livigno A new six-pack from Valfin on the Mottolino slopes to the top of Monte della Neve has opened up a couple of new black runs.

Madonna di Campiglio A fast quad from the valley floor to Pradalago replaced two old chairs last season. A new bridge with a magic carpet links Grostè to Pradalago. Snowmaking has been extended.

Monterosa Ski The area is in the middle of an ambitious programme to link Alagna properly by lifts and piste to Gressoney (the link has in the past involved skiing off-piste). For 2000/01 the ancient cable-car out of Alagna was replaced by a new gondola to Pianalunga, followed by a new chair-lift, which takes you to the top cable-car (still tiny and ancient) up to Punta Indren. 2000/01 also saw new fast chairs and more snowmaking at Antagnod and Orsia.

Selva/Sella Ronda For 2000/01 a new fast quad replaced the drag from Piz Seteur, in Plan de Gralba, up to Passo Sella. And in Canazei, two chairs on Belvedere were upgraded – to a six-pack and a quad. There's also a new gondola up to Col Pradat in Colfosco's local area, and a new quad chair at Bufaure di Sotto in Val di Fassa. The Marmolada glacier is now included in the Dolomiti Superski pass.

Switzerland

Arosa For 2000/01 the new Carmenna fast quad replaced two old lifts from mid-mountain to near the top of the Weisshorn.

Champéry The old Grand Paradis and Planachaux double chairs are being replaced by six-packs.

Davos For 2000/01 the Dorftälli drag to Weissfluhjoch was replaced by a six-pack starting at the mid-station of the funicular railway. Plans to replace the railway have been abandoned.

St Moritz The World Alpine Ski Championships are to be held in St Moritz in 2003. For 2001/02 on Corviglia, the Plateau Nair T-bar from Marguns will be replaced by a fast quad.

Verbier The first two stages of the gondola from Le Châble to Les Attelas, via Verbier and Les Ruinettes, will be upgraded for 2001/02.

Villars For 2001/02 a six-seater chair will link from La Rasse to Chaux Ronde, replacing a drag and slow chair.

United States

California

Heavenly The new eight-person gondola from the centre of South Lake Tahoe to the middle of Heavenly's slopes is now open. Work on the pedestrian village around the new gondola base is under way. Two new gladed runs are opening for 2001/02 in the upper Nevada area off Skyline Trail.

Lake Tahoe At Squaw, work on a new base village is progressing. The first phase should be ready for 2001/02.

Mammoth Mountain Work has started on a new car-free village at the core of Mammoth Lakes, eventually with a gondola link to the slopes. A six-pack has replaced the two lifts up from Juniper Springs.

Colorado

Aspen After 54 years as a skiers-only mountain, snowboarding is now allowed on Aspen Mountain. At Highlands, even more steep terrain is to be added in Highland Bowl, and the base lodge at Highlands Village is ready.

Copper Mountain The new car-free resort centre is now open.

Keystone 2000/01 saw a new six-pack on the back side of Keystone Mountain – speeding up the return from North Peak.

Telluride For 2001/02 three new fast chairs will open an extra 733 acres of terrain (a massive 70% increase in the area of Telluride's slopes) and 20 new runs in Prospect Bowl. A new mountain restaurant with a Ute Indian theme (teepees etc) is also planned.

Vail The 2000/01 season saw another fast quad and another 125 acres of terrain in Blue Sky Basin. Snowmaking has been upgraded.

Winter Park The first phase of the slope-side village is now complete.

Utah

Alta-Snowbird For 2001/02, Alta is installing its first fast quad to replace the slow triple Sugarloaf lift. From the top of this you will be able to ski down into Snowbird's Mineral Basin to access the whole of Snowbird's terrain as well on a joint area lift pass. A second fast quad in Mineral Basin will bring you back. The joint area will cover 4,700 acres, making it the biggest lift-linked area in Utah and one of the biggest in the US. The resorts will keep separate ownership and operation, and Alta is still refusing to allow snowboarding.

The Canyons For 2000/01 an open-air gondola opened from the parking area to the resort village and the new Dreamscape quad chair accessed the area's eighth mountain and 300 acres of new terrain. For 2001/02 a new triple chair between Dreamscape and Peak 5 opens five new intermediate trails.

Deer Valley A new day lodge at the bottom of the Empire and Ruby lifts will be open for 2001/02. The Quincy triple chair will be replaced by a high-speed quad. And snowmaking will be increased.

Snowbasin A new base lodge and skier services lodge will be ready for 2001/02. And there will be two plush new mountain restaurants. A new access road reduces the journey time from Salt Lake City.

The Rest of the West

Jackson Hole For 2000/01, the old Union Pass surface lift to the base area from the Hobacks was replaced by a quad chair. Another quad was built from the Moose Creek condo area of Teton Village to the Union Pass chair. In nearby Grand Targhee, 500 acres of former snowcat skiing will be served by a fast quad for 2001/02.

New England

Smugglers' Notch Snowmaking was extended by 40% for 2000/01 and a new water reservoir will increase the capacity further for 2001/02. Four new trails opened on Sterling Mountain last season and two more are planned for 2001/02.

Canada

Western Canada

Banff For 2001/02 Sunshine's old access gondola will be replaced by a new eight-seater, almost doubling the capacity and cutting the journey time to Sunshine Village to under 13 minutes. For 2000/01 the Wolverine fast quad replaced the old Wheeler chair and another quad replaced the Fireweed T-bar.

Big White Last season saw the opening of the new Happy Valley adventure area, with huge tubing hill, linked to the village by a new eight-person gondola. 2001/02 will see four new black trails off the Ridge Rocket chair.

Fernie The Bear T-bar was replaced by a fast quad for 2000/01, improving access to both Lizard and Cedar Bowls.

Jasper A new quad chair-lift from mid-mountain to Eagle Ridge will open up twenty new runs for the 2001/02 season, and provide a more direct route to the Knob chair-lift.

Kicking horse The resort started operating last season, 2000/01. As this page goes to press it is confirmed that the chair-lift to Blue Heaven and the first developments at the mountain village will not be in place until 2002/03.

Lake Louise For 2000/01 the Glacier chair from the base was replaced by an additional fast quad.

Panorama For 2000/01 new expert terrain was opened in Taynton Bowl. A new open-air gondola connects the lower and upper villages.

Eastern Canada

Tremblant A new beginner area by the village is planned for 2001/02.

Andorra

Pal-Arinsal 2000/01 saw the resorts of Pal and Arinsal become one. The new link is via a 50-person cable-car from Coll de la Botella in Pal to the top of the Arinsal slopes. Snowmaking was also extended.

Pas de la Casa For 2000/01 the Font Negre drag above Pas de la Casa was replaced by a six-pack. Two drags to Grau Roig from Encamp have also been upgraded to a six-pack. 2001/02 will see the expansion of the Pas de la Casa beginner area and new snowmaking.

Soldeu The new gondola from Canillo to El Forn is now open. There's a new beginner area at the top, and a new fast quad continues up to Portella, and the Soldeu El Tarter slopes. The Espiolets beginner area has been improved and snowmaking has been extended. For 2001/02, the Riba Escorxada beginners' area is being improved and further additions to the Espiolets beginner area are planned. Artificial snowmaking is to be extended.

Spain

Baqueira-Beret For 2000/01 a new fast chair and drag opened up the area facing the main Beret slopes. And a new chair in the Bonaigua sector has opened up two new blue runs. Snowmaking has increased.

Sweden

Åre For 2001/02 there will be two new red and two new blue slopes (all with snowmaking) in the central area above the town.

Scotland

Cairngorm The long-awaited funicular railway at Cairngorm will be ready for 2001/02.

by Chris Gill

All-inclusive holidays *come home on-budget*

There's a lot involved in a winter sports holiday. Lots of things to arrange, lots of things to go wrong, lots of things to pay for. Maybe that's why many of us go for package holidays in the winter when we arrange things for ourselves in the summer. If accommodation, meals and flights are taken care of, that only leaves the equipment, the lift pass and the lessons to arrange, and the expensive drinks and lunches to budget for. But it is possible to simplify things further – and even to remove, largely, the need for a drinks and lunch budget. How? By going with a company that packages some or all of these things.

Club Med is the big name in this game, and one it's difficult to escape, such is the scale of its operation. The brightly painted extension to Aime la Plagne? It's Club Med. The place with the swooping roofs in Arc 2000? The twin round tower blocks in Sestriere? The grand old Palace hotel in Villars? Ditto Wengen? They're all Club Med 'villages'.

The 'village' terminology is presumably meant to strike a chord with Club Med's summer clientele. The company (which has just celebrated its 50th birthday) started out running all-inclusive summer holidays, and they do take place in something like self-contained holiday villages. The ski 'villages' are really hotels with ski shops and crèches in the basement.

The great majority of the ski villages are in France (it's a French company), but Club Med has taken over a handful of old hotels in Swiss resorts and also now has villages in Italy – Sestriere and Cervinia – and in Colorado – Crested Butte and Copper Mountain.

Because Club Med apparently can't be bothered to deal with flights to anywhere other than Geneva and Turin, the villages in the southern French Alps are sold in Britain without flights. Others include flights, and all include insurance.

But perhaps the defining characteristic of the Club Med package is that it includes all meals, including beer and wine – and because this is a French operation lunch is just as serious a meal as dinner. In most villages, lunch is taken back at base (most are high resorts where this is not a problem) but in some – Chamonix and three Swiss resorts – Club Med has taken over a mountain restaurant where your included lunch can be had.

Clearly, the full-board formula has its attractions. Well, it has one attraction: that your lunch (and accompanying drinks) are paid for. You have to weigh against this the fact that most of the villages are in resorts with big lift networks where in the normal course of events you wouldn't be heading back to base for lunch every day – beginners apart, many people would be planning on having lunch savouring the views on a remote mountaintop or in some equally remote village in another valley.

Generally, Club Med includes your lift pass and tuition (the Méribel villages are an exception). Some do only half-day tuition, but most do full day. Skiing or boarding equipment costs extra, but is available on-site in all villages except Flaine – so at least you don't have to schlepp around the resort. They carry a range of kit, including performance skis.

Most villages have childcare facilities, and for many Club Med fans these are at the heart of the formula. There is a mini club in 20 of the villages (included in the holiday cost) for ages 4 to 13; the deal includes dinner and evening entertainment until 9pm. Of those 20, five have a petit club for ages 2 to 4, and of those three have a baby club for ages 4 months to 2 years; these facilities cost extra.

A handful of villages welcome children but make no special provision for them. Club Med recommends these for couples and singles. And two villages are 'Adults Only' – open only to those over 18, recommended for singles. It was to one of these – Val-Thorens – that a pal and I went a couple of seasons back for a taste of the Club Med recipe. (The other is in Copper Mountain.)

We went in early December, when Val-Thorens was only half-open, Courchevel was just waking up and Méribel was pretty much still asleep. First clue as to how Club Med makes money: the place was full, even at that stage of the season.

There was a pretty international crowd, although naturally French-dominated. There were very few Brits – there were only five of us on the transfer minibus from Geneva, and the village has 180 rooms – a lot of Israelis, quite a few Dutch, the occasional Russian. So it wasn't difficult to find dinner tables where English rather than French was the lingua franca. In what is apparently a standard Club Med arrangement, meals were taken at big round tables for eight people, and you just cruised around until you found a likely looking bunch of companions. Bottles of house wine were freely distributed by waiters, and beer was on tap. All the food was served via buffets,

SNOWPIX.COM / CHRIS GILL

Val-Thorens is one of the small number of resorts offered by both Club Med and Equity Total Ski ↓

the most popular bits of which generated queues at peak times. The food – with an exotic theme on some evenings – was pretty good, though not exactly a highlight of the day. It was no penance to skip the lunch at base occasionally and splash out on a restaurant meal, and when an invitation came our way late in the week to dine out in smart restaurant elsewhere in the village, we weren't slow to accept.

We joined the free ski classes most days and wound up in a friendly French-speaking advanced group with a Gitane-smoking ESF instructor who spoke good English when his failing respiratory system permitted him to speak at all. We had a lot of fun. He took us off-piste in what I later discovered to be dangerous circumstances, but that's ESF instructors for you.

Val-Thorens is a 'three-trident' village, the most common kind on the Club Med rating scale. Two-trident places are simpler, and generally have only half-day ski school. Four-trident places offer 'comfort and facilities of the highest standard'; there are three in Méribel, and others in Tignes, Val-d'Isère and St Moritz.

The other major programme that can be described as all-inclusive is that of Equity Total Ski, which recently celebrated a decade's operation. This company's pricing is a lot simpler than Club Med's. All their holiday prices include the cost of your lift pass, equipment hire and insurance. And they all include either tuition or guiding around the slopes (it varies by resort – you don't have a choice). On the other hand, they don't include lunch, or drinks with dinner – so two serious budget variables are introduced into the equation.

The Equity Total accommodation is less uniform. The programme falls roughly into two halves. They offer a moderate number of Austrian and French resorts, in which they generally run their own chalets or hotels, and sometimes offer other hotels too. Then, in a larger number of Italian resorts, they offer two or three standard hotels that may be shared with other companies' clients. The resorts are a mix of established big names – Val-Thorens, Mayrhofen, Sauze d'Oulx – and smaller, less well-known places such as Le Corbier, St Michael and Sansicario. It's strong on 'back-door' resorts attached to major ski areas – St-Martin-de-Belleville for the Trois Vallées, Leogang for Saalbach-Hinterglemm, Valtournenche for Cervinia.

The third source of all-in packages that I'm aware of is Interski – or Interski Classics, the brand this 17-year-old operator introduced a couple of seasons back to distinguish its 'adults and families' programme from its bread-and-butter school/college groups programme. Interski specialises in three resorts in the Aosta valley – Courmayeur, La Thuile and (particularly) Pila, a purpose-built resort with a fair-sized mountain above the big town of Aosta. Interski's accommodation is in Aosta; a gondola takes clients up to the Pila slopes in 18 minutes.

The main Interski product is fully inclusive, making good use of the fact that the company has its own stock of equipment and runs its own ski school – claimed to be the biggest such operation in the Alps, with a mix of British BASI-qualified instructors and 'hand-picked maestri' from the local Italian schools. With over 300 instructors, it can have few rivals.

Interski Classics package prices are not so comprehensive: they don't include tuition or equipment, although both can be added at reasonable supplementary cost. But as well as the usual half-board accommodation and travel (by coach or by air), prices do include vouchers for snack lunches, lift pass and insurance.

There is no better way to entertain major clients, senior staff or key journalists than to take them for a day's sailing on a yacht like *Azzurra*...

by **Dave Watts**

Equipment revolution

new gear means more fun

Ski and snowboard equipment is changing more quickly than ever before. Every year a major technical breakthrough is made which makes riding mountains easier and more fun. Over the last few years skis have got shorter, wider and more shaped. Free-ride skis have multiplied and New School twin-tip skiers are now outshining snowboarders in fun-parks. For the 2001/02 season, major advances in bindings and mounting systems have been made to give you a smoother ride and new skis have been developed to help you have more fun. The days of the agonising ill-fitting ski boot have long gone. Now nearly all boots have special custom fit liners that mould to the shape of your foot. And this season even sees the introduction of soft ski boots – hi-tech versions of the leather boots your granddad used to wear.

Prices in the UK are now as competitive as in Europe. Readers used to get annoyed when they bought gear in the UK and then found it on sale significantly cheaper in ski resorts. That has changed as a result of manufacturers pricing in euros and UK retailers being determined to match European prices. And if you buy in North America, remember that you'll have to pay duty and VAT when you bring your gear back to the UK.

Some retailers have price-match guarantees. Snow + Rock, for example, offers a price pledge that it will refund the difference if you find you can buy something cheaper abroad (within time limits).

GETTING SOFT

Over the last few years nearly every manufacturer has introduced custom fit inner boots across all or part of its range. Normally, the inner boots are heated up and then automatically mould to the shape of your foot when you put it in. You can also buy separate inner boots called Zip Fit, made of cork and oil. These mould to the shape of your foot, last for ages and can be swapped from boot to boot if you change your boots or demo a new pair. I have heard good reports of them but have not tried them myself yet.

The big news for 2001/02 is that there will be some soft boots on sale. Yes, soft boots for skiers, not boarders. Rossignol has launched a range of three SOFT boots where your foot goes into a comfortable soft, leather-like boot that fits into a stiff 'Cockpit' frame, which gives the good lateral and rear support needed for performance skiing but which does not confine you in a full traditional wrap-around plastic ski boot. The clips and buckles go over the soft boot, not the hard plastic – indeed the top 'buckle' is merely a Velcro tightener. The range goes from the high-performance SOFT 1 with a Cowhide

↑ Left: Salomon and Rossignol have both brought out soft ski boots for this season

Right: Lange has a rear release system boot designed to prevent anterior cruciate ligament damage

boot (as used by Rossi's free-ride team) to the SOFT 3 aimed more at a first-time buyer/intermediate rider.

Salomon also has a soft boot. The Verse AF is a lace-up boot similar to lace-up snowboard boots, with just two buckles on the upper part of the boot. There are men's and women's versions, aimed primarily at intermediate skiers looking for comfort.

Lange is launching its revolutionary RRS (rear release system) boots on the European market after introducing it in the US last year. It is designed to prevent the fastest-growing serious skiing injury – anterior cruciate ligament damage – and works by a catch on the rear of the boot releasing and allowing the boot to hinge backwards to remove pressure on the ligament at the front of the knee during a backward leaning fall or near fall.

Nordica has introduced a new range of boots, the F Line Tech, for intermediate skiers who consider comfort to be king. The boot incorporates the ingenious Slide-In system that lets you slide your foot into the boot hands free. It works by the pressure of your foot causing the two outer shell flaps to move forward.

SMOOTH RIDE

Traditional bindings are mounted on to the surface of the ski and prevent the ski from flexing naturally – they create a 'flat spot' under your boot. With the new carving and more shaped free-ride skis it is important that the ski flexes naturally if you are to get the best out of them, carve your turns and get maximum edge grip. Last season Salomon launched its new Pilot system, where the binding is attached to the sides rather than the top of the skis through specially drilled holes, allowing the ski to flex naturally and giving quicker edge grip and transmission of power from boot to ski. For 2001/02 the Pilot system has been extended to most of the Salomon ski range.

Volkl has a new Motion System with rails on the ski which a Marker binding slides on to and is fixed by just one screw. I tried this system on a demo version of their top free-ride ski the Volkl Vertigo Motion and thought it was phenomenal – perfect response and a really smooth ride. Atomic uses a single track that runs down the middle of its skis to attach its new Device bindings. Retailers need to

Two of the new binding systems designed to allow the ski to flex and carve naturally: the Atomic Device (left) and the Volkl Motion →

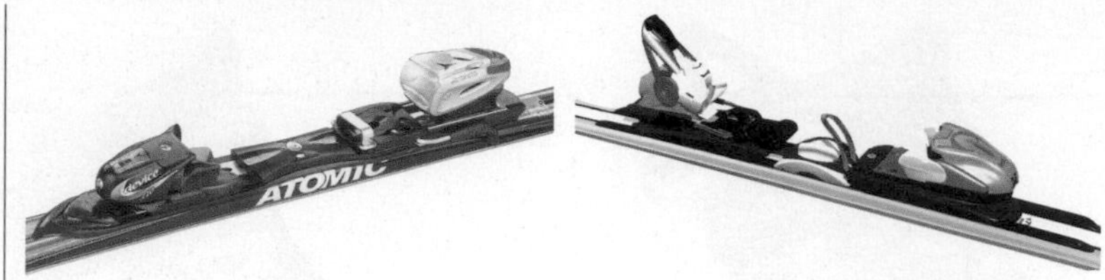

slide the toe and heel sections into position and then, like Volkl's bindings, tighten with one screw.

Some of the other manufacturers' developments are based on plates that fit on to the skis and have various devices such as springs that allow the plate and therefore the ski to flex naturally. They have pre-drilled holes for bindings to fit into. Rossignol has a Power Propulsion System, Dynastar has an Autodrive floating plate and Fischer has its Accelerator plate that work in this way.

The classic Salomon X-Scream (left) is still going strong but will face stiff competition from new skis such as the Volkl Vertigo Motion (right) this season ↓

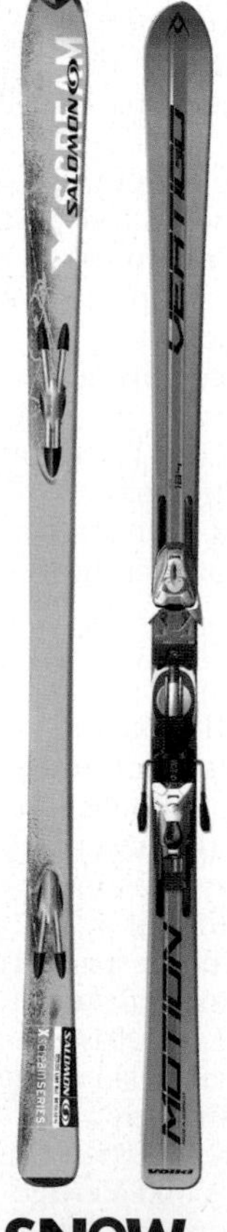

FREE-RIDE AND NEW SCHOOL RULE

Most manufacturers are extending their free-ride range. Free-ride skis are wider and more shaped than conventional skis, so that they float in powder, cut through the crud off-piste and carve like a dream on piste. Just as rear-entry boots became extinct a few years ago, traditional skinny skis are now dead. Classic free-ride skis for the last few seasons have been the Salomon X-Scream range and the Rossignol Bandit XX. Both these are still on sale (with improvements, of course, say the manufacturers). And this year I predict they will face stiff competition from the Volkl Vertigo Motion that I mentioned in the bindings section. I also loved the Volant Gravity free-ride ski – sadly not widely available in the UK.

A couple of seasons ago Salomon took the market by storm when it introduced its Teneighty twin-tip ski, which is great in the half-pipe and fun-park throwing flips and 360s, but also performs well on piste and floats like a dream in powder and crud off the groomed terrain. Last season Salomon was joined by pretty much every major manufacturer, who all brought out their own all-terrain twin-tips. For 2001/02, Salomon has a new Pocket Rocket aimed at 'guys going jumping in the backcountry', as one of their reps put it. It is a Teneighty-like twin tip but much wider and designed for sick off-piste tricks. Even bigger and longer are the expert, extreme back country skis designed for heli-skiing in Alaska and the like (as well as leaving casually outside bars in Chamonix and Val d'Isère) such as Salomon's AK (Alaska ... geddit?) Rocket, K2's AK Launcher and Fischer's Alltrax Big Stix.

Rossignol has new Free zb (known as 'Frisbee') twin-tip skis aimed at the piste as well as off-piste rider who wants to look cool.

The most eccentric twin tip for next season is the Head Mad Trix, which comes with a pre-mounted binding, which they say was invented one day after dinner by Olympic freestyle gold medallist Jonny Mosely. He wanted something that would work well for Big Mountain free-ride and for Big Air tricks including landing or taking off fakie (ie switch, ie backwards). The Mad Trix is a twin-tip which is wide at one end and narrower at the other, with a binding that you can flip around. Set one way the wide section of the ski is at the front, ideal for Big Mountain free-riding. Unclip the binding, swivel it around and reclip it, and the wide section is at the back and the binding 4cm further forward, ideal for fakie Big Air manoeuvres.

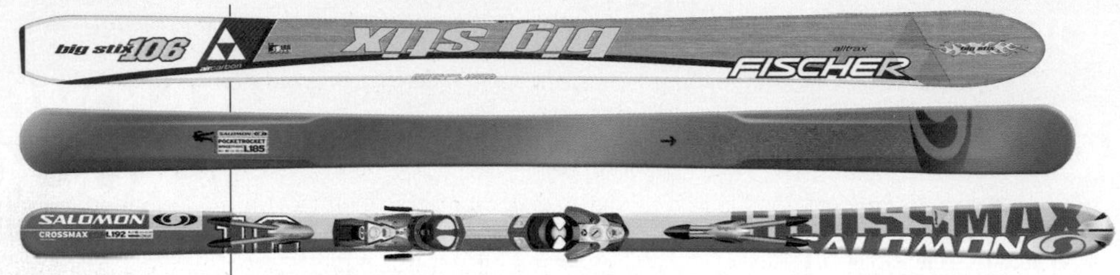

↑ From the top: Fischer Big Stix are designed for extreme heli-skiing in powder; Salomon's new Pocket Rockets are for throwing tricks in the powder; and Salomon's Crossmax range is for Skiercross and carving on piste

Other developments on the ski front include K2's abandonment of one of the best gimmicks of recent years – the flashing red light that showed the piezo-electric cell derived from Stealth bomber technology was working, dampening down vibrations and ensuring a smoother ride. They say their new MOD technology means this is no longer necessary. (I've heard it also saves them $50 per pair of skis!)

Salomon have a new Crossmax carving range of skis, ideal for skiercross races as well as all-round on-piste carving. Again, I tried these last winter and loved them.

All the major manufacturers now have at least one pair of skiboards in their range – defined as less than a metre long and with fixed rather than releasing safety bindings. They take very little time to get to grips with and provide a totally different on-snow thrill. Whilst all manufacturers have a cruisey carving skiboard that will take the first-time snow visitor around the mountain by the second day, there are also specialist skiboards aimed at in-line skaters and skiers who want to outdo snowboarders for flash tricks in the terrain parks. New small manufacturers like Line are leading the way.

GET ON BOARD

One of the delights of snowboarding is that soft boots are the norm (hard boots similar to conventional ski boots used to be common among European riders but they are now all but extinct). Soft boots are a complete contrast to conventional ski boots and give you a great sense of freedom. Don't expect a completely 'soft' experience, though – the boots are becoming ever stiffer to give you more support. This coming season sees more advances, especially in fit, comfort and convenience, from all the major manufacturers such as Burton, Salomon, Northwave, Vans, Ride and K2. If you're looking to buy boots, watch out for all the little gadgets that make things easier – such as a place to tuck your laces after you've tightened them and a locking system that holds laces in place half way through tightening.

With soft boots, the traditional way to attach your feet to the board is with straps that are part of the binding – again these have been changed over the years to make them much easier to use, with further improvements this coming season for response, power, comfort, support and ease of getting them on and off. Personally, as relative beginners to snowboarding, we prefer step-in bindings where your boot clicks into the binding rather in the same way that a ski boot does. Fit is very important with all boots, but even more so with step-ins – it pays to buy them a little tight since loose boots can cause pain when riding. Find a knowledgeable shop assistant and ask advice. Again this season sees further improvements in the comfort, performance and convenience of step-in boots.

As a halfway house Flow bindings are a good option – there's just one big strap over the top of your boot, and once that's set in place you just have to drop the back of the binding to get in and out. For next year Flow has an entry-level combination of Transfer boots and FL3 freeX bindings for £180. It's often worth shopping around for deals like this – some manufacturers do them for the whole set of board, boots and bindings.

With boards my recommended type for relative beginners is an easy to ride 'free-ride' board. These are designed for all-mountain use and many of the big-name manufacturers such as Salomon, Burton and Nitro have these for around £200 – even wide boards, specially designed for all those size 11 wearers out there. They are good boards too, benefiting from all the technology that's been developed in higher level boards, but being less stiff and so more forgiving.

Other options for more advanced riders are 'freestyle' boards (for doing tricks and riding half-pipes), Alpine 'freecarve' boards and 'race' boards. For advanced free-riders, one of the most innovative things on the board front this season is K2's integrated Recon Riser system, which raises riders a little above the board. It should mean that riders with bigger feet can ride narrower boards, which are quicker edge to edge, and that smaller footed riders can get more leverage and so more power to their edges.

BODY FACTOR

To make the most of all this fabulous new equipment you need to be fit and injury-free. A few years ago Snow + Rock started a special Body Factor unit, which I can personally recommend. After suffering a bad back for ages and seeing various physios locally, the osteopath at Body Factor sorted me out in just three sessions. They specialise in treating sports injuries and also do fitness assessments and have an alignment programme. There are Body Factor units at Snow + Rock's Covent Garden and Surrey (M25) superstores. For details or an appointment call 01932 564364.

Flow makes convenient entry snowboard bindings and this year has a combination of Transfer boots and FL3 freeX bindings for £180 ↓

Get your money back

And get your ski insurance FREE!

You can reclaim the price of Where to Ski and Snowboard and get free ski insurance for up to two people when you book a winter sports holiday for the 2001/02 or 2002/03 seasons. All you have to do is book the holiday through the specialist ski travel agency Ski Solutions.

Ski Solutions is Britain's original and leading ski travel agency. You can buy whatever kind of holiday you want through them.

Ski Solutions sells the package holidays offered by all the bonded tour operators in Britain (apart from the very few who are direct-sell only). And if that isn't enough choice, they can tailor-make a holiday, based on any form of travel and any kind of accommodation. No one is better placed to find you what you want than Ski Solutions.

Phone Ski Solutions on

020 7471 7700

Making a claim

Claiming your refund and free insurance is easy. At the back of the book are two vouchers. When you make your definite booking, tell Ski Solutions that you want to take up this offer. Cut out the vouchers and send one to Ski Solutions and the other to Where to Ski and Snowboard (the addresses are on the vouchers).

free!

Get next year's edition FREE

There are too many resorts for us to visit them all every year, and too many hotels, bars and mountain restaurants for us to see. So we are very keen to encourage more readers to send in reports on their holiday experiences. As usual, we'll be giving 100 copies of the next edition to the writers of the best reports.

There are five main kinds of feedback we need:
- what you particularly **liked and disliked** about the resort
- what aspects of the resort came as a **surprise** to you
- your other suggestions for **changes to our evaluation** of the resort – changes we should make to the ratings, verdicts, descriptions etc
- your experience of **queues** and other weaknesses in the lift system, and of the **ski school** and associated childcare arrangements
- your feedback on **individual facilities** in the resort – the hotels, bars, restaurants (including mountain restaurants), nightspots, equipment shops, sports facilities etc.

You can send your reports to us in three ways. In order of preference, they are:
- by e-mail to: reports@snow-zone.co.uk (don't forget to give us your mailing address)
- printed on paper, word-processed
- handwritten on a form that we can provide.

Where to Ski and Snowboard, FREEPOST, The Old Forge, Norton St Philip, Bath BA2 7ZZ

by Chris Gill

Family holidays

which ones work best?

Every autumn, a farcical process takes place in the Gill household. It consists of my pleading with my kids to go on a skiing holiday in a few months' time – preferably at Christmas. Or to look at it another way, pleading to be allowed to blow ever-escalating amounts of money on them. It's the kind of thing that can easily lead parents of my generation (if you see what I mean) into a Pythonesque rant about how privileged our children are. 'Spoilt brats! When I were a lad, nearest we got to holidays was being allowed out of t'pit into t'daylight for a couple of hours on Christmas Day!' That kind of thing.

Both kids have been taken to the mountains most winters since they were babies, and have been on skis since the age of four. Laura, now ten, seems to me to have a passably good time when we go skiing – though I can see that ski resorts will really register on her coolometer only when she's old enough to gain access to the Farm Club (next winter, to judge by her increasingly effective use of cosmetics). Alex (now 13) has a whale of a time, skiing at speeds I choose not to match and only rarely colliding with anything (sadly, usually his sister). Yet, come the following autumn, neither of them seems to have a fond memory left of last winter's treat, or any inclination to repeat it. They get taken to places like Verbier, Courchevel and Chamonix, and given the choice they'd rather be in Somerset.

Still, I usually succeed, and am allowed to spend the aforementioned amounts of money. And this year we did two unusual things: we rented an apartment instead of going to a catered chalet, and we went at Easter instead of Christmas or January. Good calls? Read on.

TO CATER, OR NOT TO CATER?

I got hooked on the catered chalet holiday at an early stage in my skiing career – year two, if memory serves – and for the fifteen years or so from then until the arrival of children I rarely took any other kind of ski holiday. So it was perfectly natural that as soon as Alex was safely portable I persuaded my wife Val that we should take him off to a chalet equipped with nannies who could minister to him all day. In those days, that pretty much meant going with Ski Esprit, an operation started in the early 1980s by the late Bob Moore (not at the time a father himself) to exploit what he rightly perceived to be a gap in the market. Our holiday in Montchavin went without a hitch, and we were hooked.

We've since had countless chalet holidays (with Esprit, as it is now known, and with others) that have reinforced the view that this kind of holiday has two great attractions. The first is that chalet-based childcare run by UK tour operators is as hassle-free as it could be. (We had one or two tearful morning partings in the early days – but usually by mid-morning I was my usual cheerful self again.) The second is that in a fair-sized chalet there is a good chance that your children will find compatible companions to have snowball fights with, and so on.

We have had the occasional apartment-based holiday in the past, but that was in America. Apartments in the States are simply in a

different league from most of those in the Alps. I know, there have always been spacious and comfortable apartments to be found in Switzerland, and doubtless elsewhere. But the sad fact is that the great bulk of Alpine self-catering accommodation on the package market is pretty cramped. In the States, the apartments are always spacious, comfortably furnished and thoroughly equipped. Alex and Laura still haven't got over the apartment in Smugglers' Notch – not the swankiest of American resorts – that had TVs not only in the living room and each bedroom, but also suspended above the hot-tub in the master bathroom.

But things are changing, slowly. In resorts like La Plagne and Les Arcs, owners are being encouraged to amalgamate adjacent apartments to create units that can give a family more than just sleeping space. And new apartments are being built with more style as well as space. On our recent trip, we stayed in the new MGM development above Arc 1800. The apartments are scarcely luxurious – there is nowhere comfortable to sit, for heaven's sake – but in practice we and our friends in other apartments got on just fine.

And our needs, of course, have changed. If they get their way, as they usually do, Alex and Laura are now old enough to spend their days and their evenings with us, so the need for childcare has disappeared, while the freedom of having your own apartment rather than sharing a chalet is becoming an advantage as the kids get older.

We didn't take our self-catering too seriously, quickly settling into a rhythm of eating in and eating out on alternate nights – and on two nights when we ate in we cheated by resorting to the excellent pizzas from the little takeaway joint in the same development. We were able to identify enough family-friendly restaurants in Arc 1800 to see out the week; but if you are there for a fortnight you might find yourself running out of options. All in all, we found the apartment-based formula very successful, and wouldn't hesitate to do it again, now that we don't need childcare.

WINTER OR SPRING?

Personally, I'm a winter skier. Of course, spring has its advantages, including off-piste spring snow – and on modern skis I even enjoy skiing slush. But basically I like crisp days, squeaky-cold snow that doesn't freeze into ice cubes overnight, and dark evenings. Apart from any other considerations, many resort villages that seem acceptably jolly under cover of snow and darkness at 5pm in January seem seriously tacky when their scruffy pot-holed streets are exposed to the glare of the spring sun at 5pm in April.

But I hadn't thought about the merits of later holidays for kids. On this most recent holiday in Les Arcs, the light evenings meant

that the kids could enjoy hours of play out on the snow before supper without any concern that they might be difficult to track down when the time came to drag them indoors. Our apartment in Les Arcs was on the ground floor, right beside the piste, which meant the kids could stay outside until the sun went down, building and demolishing snowmen or sliding down the hill on plastic trays without getting out of sight, and then just troop in across our little terrace. In January, they would have been kicking their heels inside, cursing the TV for its lack of a cartoon channel.

TAKE YOUR CHOICE

Whether you like the idea of a catered chalet or of self-catering, there are plenty of tour operators to choose from.

A couple of seasons ago I had a very enjoyable day exploring Puy-St-Vincent, an underrated small resort in the southern French Alps, and earmarked it for a family visit some time. Snowbizz is a one-resort operation that has up to now had a virtual monopoly on the resort in the UK. Its comprehensive childcare arrangements include ski-guiding for children, and evening amusements at a modest charge. Accommodation is in apartments. A highly experienced reporter this year, with kids of 8 and 9, calls Snowbizz 'the best operator I have travelled with', despite criticisms of his apartment.

The Snowbizz monopoly has been broken this year by none other than Esprit. The family specialist has undergone something of a renaissance this year, since it passed into the hands of Peter Dyer, who built up Crystal to something approaching its present size. It is no surprise to find that the company is becoming less family oriented, with a much expanded programme of 'ordinary' holidays in a much bigger range of countries and resorts. But there are still 9 resorts in which the familiar Esprit childcare facilities are offered.

Ski Famille is another small operator concentrating on a single French resort – Les Gets, linked to Morzine, in the northern Alps. The company has several catered chalets, generally with special bedrooms for the children. There is comprehensive free day care. Another small family specialist is Ski Hillwood, with its own childcare facilities in Les Gets, Söll and Argentière.

Many chalet operators that you wouldn't call family specialists nevertheless offer lots of options. One of the most impressive is Mark Warner, with nine chalet-hotels in big-name resorts equipped with nurseries. Laura cut her snowman-building teeth in one of these. We've also enjoyed staying with Simply Ski. We haven't used the childcare they offer in Verbier, Courchevel and La Plagne, but while staying in Courchevel 1300 with Esprit we have seen contented children being safely shepherded around by Simply Ski nannies. Lotus Supertravel is an example of a major chalet operator that can provide nannies in all of its French resorts.

These days, practically all tour operators have responded to the demand for family holidays, including the bigger mass-market operators doing hotel as well as chalet holidays. Neilson runs its own kids' clubs in half a dozen resorts in the Alps and Norway, for example. Crystal has nurseries in a dozen French and Italian resorts, and a nanny service in a dozen more French and Austrian ones.

For a clear picture of the childcare facilities of Alpine hotels, in particular, Made to Measure is a good starting point. This company's specialist family department is staffed by skiing mothers who have experienced for themselves the joys of taking children skiing.

by **Dave Watts**

Something for the weekend

the quick fix break

A weekend away with just one day off work can give you three great days on the slopes, leaving you with the feeling of having been away for ages and returning to work feeling really refreshed. And it does not need to cost you an arm and a leg.

My favourite weekend away was my first, many seasons ago in April in Chamonix. Spring had arrived and the snow had been melting. We flew into Geneva on Thursday night, arriving at the hotel around midnight. When we awoke it was winter again and snowing like crazy. So we abandoned plans to go up Mont Blanc and went instead to the tree-lined, sheltered slopes of Les Houches, a few minutes' drive away and had a fabulous time playing in the powder. The next day we ventured through the Mont Blanc tunnel and skied the perfectly groomed pistes and untracked powder of Courmayeur under brilliant blue skies. It was just what dreams are made of. On Sunday we split up – some of us went up the Grands Montets, above Argentière and skied its infamous off-piste routes, while others opted for the epic 24km Vallée Blanche run down Mont Blanc. We met up for one last beer before heading off for our 8pm flight home and back to the office on Monday morning.

Since then I have been on countless other weekend jaunts. I have loved them all; but the Chamonix trip remains my favourite. Why? Simply because it was my first. I had been sceptical of weekends away, as being too short, too dependent on the weather and too expensive. But I was wrong on all counts. When I got back from Chamonix I felt exhilarated and as if I had been away for a week. If you go for just three or four days you pack a lot into the limited period and the contrast with the environment back home is marked. We experienced different extremes of weather and enjoyed them all – the secret to this is to choose the right resort, which has slopes which can be enjoyable whatever the weather. And weekends away don't have to break the bank – you can get packages for under £300.

ARRANGING THE WEEKEND

The key to making the most of your time is to catch late flights each way – so it helps if you live near a suitable airport. Swissair has well-timed flights for both Geneva and Zürich from Heathrow (but book early as the late flights are very popular). EasyJet has suitable flights from both Luton and Liverpool to Geneva. Alitalia has good flights to Milan and Venice.

We don't recommend flying to Munich if you are travelling out on a Friday or back on a Sunday – the queues on the motorway can be horrendous as the whole of Munich seems to go weekend skiing and the airport is on the far side of the city from the Alps. Similarly, allow plenty of time if you are driving back to Lyon airport on a Sunday evening – we encountered very heavy traffic after leaving Courchevel in what we thought had been good time.

Booking a rental car or taxi in advance is usually cheaper than arranging one after you arrive. Several tour operators can arrange that as part of a complete weekend package. Taxis can be ridiculously expensive compared with the cost of renting a car. For example, expect to pay over £200 each way between Geneva airport and Courchevel by taxi – a small car for the weekend would be much less than the one-way taxi price. In our experience train and bus times between airports and resorts are more suitable for week-long visitors than for weekenders looking for maximum time on the slopes.

Using a weekend specialist, such as one of those advertising in this chapter, makes sense if you don't want the hassle of making your own arrangements or renting a car. They know the best resorts to go to, can arrange transfers by their own staff or through local companies, and have special deals with hotels that do them good room rates or that might not otherwise take weekend bookings. Some of them have weekend chalet accommodation too. Some also arrange special weekend courses (eg with off-piste guides or even heli-skiing weekends). And local tour operator representatives and contacts can save valuable time arranging lift passes (beware of big weekend queues on Saturday and Sunday mornings) and equipment hire and advise on local restaurants and other facilities.

Several operators do a lot of 'corporate' business: fixing weekend breaks for companies that want a conference away from the office, or want to reward successful employees or loyal customers.

CHOOSING A RESORT

As for choosing a resort, there are various considerations. Many people think they should go for a resort within a short drive of your arrival airport. But by definition, resorts close to major airports are close to large numbers of people poised to hit the slopes on fine weekends, which can mean queues for the lifts, crowds on the slopes and competition for hotel beds. But these days most resorts are within striking distance of a major airport and an hour's extra transfer time is not really that much if it gets you to quieter slopes.

Resorts close to Geneva include Chamonix, St Gervais, Megève and Les Contamines (all in the Mont Blanc area and sharing an area lift pass), Flaine and La Clusaz in France, and Villars and Les Diablerets in Switzerland. All these are within an hour or so of Geneva by car. Verbier and Crans-Montana in Switzerland are a bit further, as are the Three Valleys and other Tarentaise resorts – even Val-d'Isère can be reached in under three hours now – and Morzine and the Portes du Soleil resorts in France.

Flying to Zürich opens up lots of other possibilities. Flims, Davos and Klosters are the nearest big resorts, and the less-well-known resorts of Engelberg and Andermatt are within easy reach. St Anton and Lech in Austria are within striking distance, as are the resorts of the Montafon valley.

In Italy, Courmayeur is a popular and attractive weekend destination. If the Mont Blanc tunnel is open (see Courmayeur chapter) it is easily accessible from Geneva – but while the tunnel is shut Turin is the nearest international airport. Resorts such as Sauze d'Oulx and Sestriere are also easily accessible from Turin.

Unless you are booking at short notice when you know the snow is good, we'd be tempted to avoid low resorts such as Megève and Villars – unless you have transport to get you to more snowsure slopes. And because you don't want your whole weekend ruined by a white-out if it snows all the time, we'd also be tempted to avoid very high resorts where the skiing is entirely above the tree line – which would rule out places such as Tignes and Val-Thorens in France, Obergurgl in Austria and Cervinia in Italy.

WHAT ABOUT PRICE?

The cost can vary enormously. The flight and transfer or car hire are the expensive fixed costs and obviously make a weekend proportionately more expensive than a full week. But as we said before, you do get three days' skiing (half a full week) for only one day off work, and the three days makes a substantial break. A four-night break is, of course even better – it only costs two days off work and means you can travel out and back on Thursday and Monday evenings (quieter than Fridays and Sundays).

In general, through a good specialist tour operator, you can expect to pay £300 to £350 a head for flights, car hire and a double room in a 3-star hotel for three nights, assuming two people sharing. With lift passes and meals you could be looking at £450 to £500. For a 4-star hotel add another £100 or so.

SCOTT

by **Dave Watts and Chris Gill**

Ski courses

improving your skiing

If you would like to improve your skiing, we recommend trying one of the increasing number of specialist ski improvement courses that are run by qualified British instructors. Some of these are provided by ski schools made up mainly of British instructors and can be booked up on the spot as well as in advance. Others are intended for advance bookers and transport and accommodation can often be arranged too. Whichever way you choose, the bottom line is that you are no longer stuck with the group or private lessons that the local ski schools have to offer.

Optimum is the name of a business run by Martin and Deirdre Rowe out of the charming Chalet Tarentaise which they renovated themselves. It has a cosy rustic living room and bar and fairly basic bedrooms (all with shower, though) and is in the tiny hamlet of Le Pré, near Villaroger, with a chair-lift into and slope home from the Les Arcs skiing. Martin used to run the highly regarded British section of the ski school at Soldeu in Andorra before starting his own courses. Now he employs his own top British ski coaches. Groups are a maximum of eight and most courses are designed to help skiers get off a learning plateau, with video analysis twice a week. They can arrange heli-skiing and run occasional weeks where you ski different resorts daily. We can vouch personally for the chalet, the food and the free-flowing wine – and we have had glowing reports of the courses. If you don't want to take a course (or have friends who don't want to) there's no problem staying in the chalet and having a normal holiday.

Triple 8 Ski Systems courses are run in Tignes by BASI-qualified instructors led by Hugh Pelling. They offer five-day Personal Performance Clinics (two-and-a-half hours a day) with no more than six in a class, a session spent on snowblades and digital video analysis, with two additional feedback sessions after skiing ends. They also have a five-day Family Package with parents and children developing their skills together and they offer a Skier Alignment service to ensure your body and equipment are working as efficiently together as possible. They can arrange catered chalet accommodation in one of the few real chalets in Tignes and self-catered apartments.

Warren Smith is a dynamic British ski instructor who runs a Ski Academy in Verbier. He runs courses for private groups and special week-long mogul, carving and powder/free-ride camps. His is one of the few schools to run new school freestyle clinics where you can learn the new school tricks on twin-tip skis in the fun-park and half-pipe. He also runs summer courses on the Tignes glacier (call 01442 266449 or visit www.warrensmith-skisynergy.com).

New Generation is a school

which started as Le Ski school in Courchevel 1650, linked to the tour operator of the same name – but has now branched out into Courchevel 1850 and Méribel too. It consists of highly qualified young British instructors committed to giving clients enjoyment as well as technique. We have nothing but rave reviews about them: 'Young and highly motivated. Adapt teaching to the clients' needs, not ski school dogma,' 'I've taken five group classes now and not had a bad one ... this school is one reason I keep coming back to 1650,' 'I did a check-up clinic (two afternoons for £45 total) – very helpful, small group, personal attention, kept us busy.' As well as normal courses they offer Check Up Clinics and Freeride Clinics, each with a maximum of six people. For contact details see the Méribel chapter.

Other highly regarded courses are taught in various resorts by The Ski Company, run by Sally Chapman and Phil Smith, both BASI trainers. The five-day courses are mostly for all-round performance, but they also have special weeks such as off-piste, slalom or carving. Call 0870 2412085 for details.

One of the longest-established British instructors running his own clinics is Ali Ross, who was preaching carving techniques long before the new carving skis came on the scene. We have personal experience of the value of Ali's clinics, particularly in dealing with heavy snow and in helping intermediates to tackle deep snow. His clinics are run in Tignes and can be booked through Ski Solutions, who can fix your accommodation too.

Two other highly regarded British schools in the Alps are Supreme based in Courchevel 1850 and the British Alpine Ski School (BASS) who have branches in Morzine, Les Gets and Avoriaz. Both employ well-qualified British instructors.

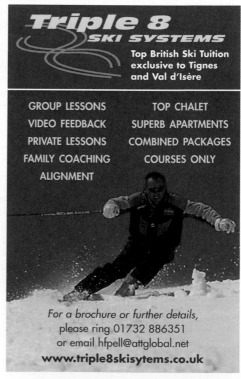

by Chris Gill

Avalanche danger

be aware of the risks

Memories are fading of the tragic winter of 1998/99, when freak snowfalls resulted in twice the normal number of avalanche deaths in Austria (because of the single horrendous incident at Galtür, when a major part of the village was demolished) and deaths in France and Switzerland that were 50% up on the norm. But the risk of avalanche is always there. In the major Alpine countries, avalanche deaths in 1998/99 totalled 142; the following season, with no such newsworthy incidents, they totalled 101; and when the figures are all in for last season they will doubtless amount to a similar result – the average over the last 15 years is 99 deaths. Here's some guidance on how to avoid joining the statistics.

Key fact 1: in the Alps, people skiing and boarding outside the controlled pistes account for the great bulk of the avalanche accidents and deaths.

The Austrian and French statistics distinguish between people going off-piste and people touring – presumably on the basis of whether they have used lifts to get up the mountain. In Austria, deaths among those touring (ie those making their way through the mountains unaided) outnumber those using lifts to go off-piste by five to two. In France, the numbers of mortalities in these two groups are much more balanced, and in some years it's those going off-piste who dominate the statistics. The important thing is that the problem arises outside the controlled pistes.

Key fact 2: avalanches rarely hit pistes.

They do hit pistes occasionally. For example, in November 1992 an avalanche hit a group of 10 skiers on an open piste in Savoie and killed seven of them. But such incidents are exceptional. There have been only two other deaths on French pistes in the last decade, and three in Austria. There are much more serious risks you could worry about than this, such as the car journey to Gatwick.

Key fact 3: out-of-bounds skiing in North America is just as dangerous as off-piste skiing in the Alps.

Avalanche deaths in the US average a fairly modest 19 per year – fourth in the international league, fractionally above Italy and below France, Austria and Switzerland. The biggest single group of fatalities in the States is people riding snowmobiles – a group that scarcely exists in Europe; take them out of the US figures and you're left with fewer than 15 deaths a year, exactly half the French figure. But then 'out-of-bounds' or 'back-country' skiing isn't done on anything like the scale that off-piste skiing is done in the Alps. The skiing mountains over there may not seem as obviously dangerous as the Alps, but when you step outside the ski area boundary you are in dangerous terrain.

Reflectors to make use of the Recco Rescue System are built in to some brands of clothing and now into some models of Atomic ski boots – and you can buy stick-on versions for other boots. The detectors (the expensive bit of the system) are in use in most resorts ↓

Key fact 4: North American resorts, however, do offer the one way to ski 'off-piste' deep snow without risk of avalanche.

American resorts take responsibility for a lot more steep, avalanche-prone terrain than European resorts do – if it's inside the resort boundary, it's the resort's responsibility. Yet in the last 15 years there have been only three deaths from avalanches in American ski areas – two in 1985/86 and one in early 1999, when a slide at Jackson Hole swept a snowboarder over a cliff to his death.

It's difficult to over-emphasise the importance of this to the competent British skier or rider who has had enough of crowded pistes and is itching to take on terrain that is more challenging and less densely populated. In the Alps, you have to go to the trouble and cost of arranging guidance and the necessary kit to help you deal with an avalanche – and still you risk being one of the 100 killed each year. In contrast, the exciting in-bounds steeps of places such as Aspen-Snowmass and Snowbird can be explored with confidence.

Key fact 4: the great bulk of the avalanches that cause deaths do not occur spontaneously, but are caused by the victims.

In the last decade, over 80% of the avalanches in France resulting in death or injury were triggered, by those involved in the accident. This statistic is clearly connected to another, which is that 80% of the avalanches were of the slab variety, starting from a fracture across the slope rather than a point. It's the weight of the skier or rider on the slope that causes the fracture and starts the avalanche. In some years, the proportion of injurious avalanches reckoned to be slab slides triggered by skiers and riders approaches 100% of the total.

Key fact 5: young men are particularly prone to taking risks with avalanches.

US statistics show that most avalanche deaths occur in the group that is at high risk of accidental death in general: 70% of fatalities are males in their late teens to late 20s. This same group has 74% of all fatal road accidents. If you're in that group, perhaps you should acknowledge that you're prone to excessive risk-taking, and start taking special care instead.

Key fact 6: you are responsible for your own safety.

A couple of years back I learned this important lesson. The content of the lesson was familiar, but I had never really absorbed it – never really made it a part of my approach. I was skiing in an advanced group with an instructor from Val-Thorens. During the week there was a fair amount of fresh snow, and the link with Méribel and Courchevel was closed. When it reopened, a suggestion that we should head off for Courchevel for the day was cheerfully received. We stuck to the pistes on the way over but on the way down into Courchevel our instructor suggested that we traverse out to our left to ski an off-piste slope under La Saulire. We weren't equipped with transceivers or any other special precautions. 'What's the avalanche risk?' I asked. 'Oh, it's low – one or two,' said the instructor. Off we went. Later, after I had split from the party to spend the night with friends in Courchevel, I noticed a warning sign, saying the avalanche hazard was not one or two, but four. I checked with the ski patrol; it was indeed four. That's four – 'high' – on a scale of five.

Key fact 7: if you are hit by an avalanche, you need to be rescued quickly if you're going to survive.

Some of those who are hit by avalanches are killed by the force of the slide, or are quickly suffocated. Many survive the immediate impact, but are buried in the debris. In these circumstances, minutes count: most people who survive are found and pulled out within 15 minutes of the avalanche. The chances of survival decline rapidly thereafter. In practice, what this means is that you need to be equipped to maximise the chance of being found quickly if you're buried.

If you are making major off-piste expeditions – 'back-country' ski touring, or doing long runs away from the nearest lift system – everyone in the party should be fully prepared for avalanche rescue and survival. This means having both the right equipment – crucially, radio transceivers so that those not buried can locate those who are – and appropriate training in its use. Make sure you get some practice as well as the theory – it isn't easy.

If you are going off-piste within or close to a lift network, it's likely that any avalanche will trigger the resort rescue services, and in those circumstances you can hope that a more rapid and precise system for locating buried people will swing into action: the Recco Rescue System.

Most resorts covered in this book are now equipped with Recco detectors, and many have several portable detectors distributed around the slopes for speedy rescue. Some helicopter rescue services, which cover many resorts, also carry Recco detectors. Under each resort covered in this book, in the Mountain facts section, we tell you if Recco detectors are in use.

To take advantage of the system, you need to be equipped with Recco reflectors. The detectors emit a directional radio signal. When the signal hits a Recco reflector, even under 10m of snow, the frequency is doubled and sent back to the receiver in the detector. The trained operator can then instantly pinpoint the buried victim. Detectors can easily be used from helicopters searching for victims.

Recco reflectors are small, inconspicuous and cheap – and require no batteries or other maintenance. Reflectors are built in to some brands of clothing (and now some Atomic boots – see photo). Failing that, you can buy self-adhesive ones to stick on your boots for only £12.95 a pair – a price not worth bothering about for something that may save your life. They are offered at half price when you buy a new pair of ski (or snowboard) boots from Snow + Rock.

The Swiss Alpine Club, Swiss Air Rescue and the Federal Institute for the Study of Snow and Avalanches in Davos have recommended that all skiers and snowboarders should wear Recco reflectors. We agree.

by Chris Gill

Luxury chalets

the ultimate holiday

For some people, holidays mean hotels, with staff on hand to mix the martinis and carry the bags. For others, in contrast, there is nothing to match the complete privacy of renting a holiday home where there are no intrusions. But for many British skiers the uniquely British institution called the catered chalet is the definitive form of Alpine accommodation.

Twenty-five years ago, when I was taking my first chalet holidays, the expression 'luxury chalet' would have been a contradiction in terms. The catered chalet business didn't do luxury. It was only in the late 1980s that one or two companies realised that you could offer a luxury experience without having the fleets of bellboys and room-service waiters that hotels are obliged to lay on. All you had to do was provide comfortable and stylish accommodation, good food and wine, and a little bit of personal service – not a lot, but just enough to make the customer feel the staff are there to do something other than have a good time.

The new formula worked, and works, probably better than anyone would have expected, and has now spread widely.

FINDING YOUR DREAM CHALET

You can find isolated luxury chalets in all sorts of places, from Austria to Aspen, but the breed in general is still not widespread: most are concentrated in the more upmarket French mega-resorts of Méribel, Courchevel and Val-d'Isère.

The greatest concentration is found in Méribel, particularly in the hands of long-time local specialist Meriski. This company, more than any other, illustrates the transformation of the chalet business. A decade ago it was a run-of-the-mill chalet operation, but then it successfully repositioned itself upmarket, and now has range of 16 impressively comfortable chalets, most of which can be considered luxury properties.

One of our favourites is the four-bedroom Iberis. The splendidly spacious and tastefully furnished pine-panelled sitting room has huge floor-to-ceiling windows. There's an extravagantly luxurious master bedroom, complete with walk-in wardrobe and jacuzzi bath. Mira Belum is another captivating place, with an interesting split-level living space. More recently acquired chalets that we haven't visited include Liandon, only 200m from the piste, and three newly built ones in the Mussillon area, designed to give splendid views from their top-floor sitting rooms; Marielene and Mariefleur will be joined by a third similar chalet this winter.

The Ski Company Ltd is perhaps the most upmarket of all the established luxury chalet operators, and has an increasingly serious presence in Méribel. Its eight-bedroom Lodge de Burgin is one of the most spectacularly impressive chalets we have seen. It has an enormous, beautifully furnished living room with several different sitting areas and a wall of windows looking over to the pistes across the valley. The Génépi next door is very similar, but with a jacuzzi bath in every room and an outdoor hot-tub. Introduced for last season was a pair of similarly smart five-bedroom chalets, Aurore and Boreale. The big news for this season is completion of the outdoor heated swimming pool that these properties share, along with the existing hot-tub.

The pick of Scott Dunn Ski's four properties in Méribel is the Grand Ours, with its six bedrooms spread over three floors and the sunny living room/balcony on the middle one.

The famously luxurious chalet Brames is back on the market through Descent International. This is the grandest chalet I have visited in Méribel, with two-storey living room and some beautiful bedrooms, and a glorious setting with a southerly view up the valley towards Mont Vallon.

If you like the idea of luxury but want to keep the cost down, consider staying down in the old village of Les Allues, served by the gondola up from Brides-les-Bains. Bonne Neige has two tempting properties here. Their original is Les Allodis – a converted barn at the foot of the run back to the village. This place makes a real change from the modern properties that dominate in Méribel – all beams and antique furniture, but with modern conveniences including underfloor heating, boot dryers in the ski room, a sauna/jet shower suite and an outdoor hot-tub. A newer acquisition is the modern chalet St Joseph, a spacious, stone and timber chalet with superb views over the Bozel valley towards Champagny.

Courchevel is well established as the smartest resort in France, and clearly doesn't lack smart chalets – but relatively few of them find their way on to the UK package market. My current favourite is Lotus Supertravel's five-bedroom chalet Founets, which has a lovely high-ceilinged sitting/dining room and a great position only yards from both the Bellecôte piste and the Bergerie bar-restaurant. Supertravel's Eboulis and Maisonnée chalets are worth looking at, too.

FlexiSki's five-bedroom chalet Anemone is beautifully rustic, and one of Courchevel's originals. Last season they added the recently built but otherwise similar Vizelle.

Scott Dunn Ski has several properties. In a league of its own (and about 50% more expensive than anything else in Scott Dunn's programme) is the five-bedroom Alaska, complete with indoor

THE CHALET HOLIDAY IN ITS ORIGINAL FORM

The catered chalet holiday is a uniquely British idea. Tour operators install their own cooks and housekeepers in private chalets which they take over for the season. They package them with travel on the UK market, normally offering half-board, sometimes with some provision for a snack lunch. Dinner is a no-choice affair at a communal table, including wine unlimited in quantity but not quality. You can either book a whole chalet (the smallest typically sleep around six or eight) or book space in a larger chalet that you share with whoever else turns up.

In the early days of the 1960s and 70s, taking a chalet holiday meant roughing it in creaky old buildings, putting up with spartan furniture and paper-thin walls, and with six or more people sharing a bathroom. And the chalet girl – always a girl, back then – was often straight out of college or finishing school, and more intent on having a fun season on the slopes than preparing gourmet meals. Happily, things have changed for the better in recent years.

swimming pool. That apart, the most impressive is a very grand apartment with wonderful views, the Cristal de Roche penthouse, just a few yards from the heart of Courchevel 1850. Two other fine chalet-apartments are the brand-new Pralong units, right opposite the button lift of the same name. Coblette has a steam room and is right on the Chenus piste.

In Val-d'Isère, Scott Dunn has an exciting development this season – Eagle's Nest, an extraordinary chalet complete with an indoor jetstream pool, sauna and steam room, and all floors linked by a lift. The top floor is entirely given over to living space with the sitting area opening on to a large south-facing balcony. Both the sitting area and the dining area have the warm feel of old wood and open fires. Eagle's Nest is well situated in the exclusive Les Carats area, just 100m from the edge of La Face and only five minutes' walk from the village.

Scott Dunn Ski has several other good properties in Val, the most impressive being the Abri du Houard, also in Les Carats, right by the piste. Eight people can wallow luxuriously in 360 square metres of living space – a central fireplace separates the dining and sitting room area which has plenty of comfortable sofas and floor to ceiling windows offering spectacular views across the valley. There is a sauna, hot-tub and table-tennis room. New for last season is chalet Sanville, with a glorious galleried living room with huge beams and an impressive stone fireplace. Views from the rear of the chalet look down to the village. There is a sauna on the lower ground floor.

The Ski Company Ltd has an impressive enclave of four modern luxury chalets right out at the southern extremity of the resort, with massive, well-furnished living rooms, huge windows and splendid views. YSE's Mountain Lodges are an old favourite, offering no picture windows but splendidly atmospheric and comfortable living rooms, with stone walls and ample leather sofas.

Verbier is with some justification thought of as the chalet capital of the Alps but, here again, there are relatively few luxury properties on the UK market. The Ski Company Ltd's chalet Goodwood is much the best I have seen – a fabulously comfortable and stylish place in a great position, tucked away down a side street a few yards from the main square, a bearable walk from the Medran lift station. Flexiski's Bouvreuil is not so grand, but tastefully rustic, and close to Medran.

The big news in Verbier this season is the Residence 'L' offered by Descent International. In a high position on the Savoleyres side of Verbier, this sounds like a rival for the Goodwood. It has two sitting rooms, study, sauna, steam room, massage room, cinema, games room, terrace with outdoor hot-tub, and a 'well-stocked' wine cellar.

Sadly, luxury chalets have never been common in Zermatt. Scott Dunn has some excellent apartments. And Ski Total's chalet Palazzo is a beautifully converted old farm building in the heart of the village, with a generous sitting room and sunny terrace.

In Austria, St Anton is probably the main chalet resort. FlexiSki, Simply Ski and Mark Warner all have upmarket chalet hotels here, but if you want a change from Alpine kitsch take a look at Lotus Supertravel's architect-designed Bergspitze.

Drive to the Alps

and ski where you please

by **Chris Allan**

The days when driving from Britain to the Alps was the preserve of the most intrepid of motorists have long gone. The advent of the Channel Tunnel and the improvements made to the motorway networks in northern France and the Alps have made life much, much easier for the growing number of Brits who decide to drive down. You can now get to most resorts easily in a day. The advantages? It's less hassle, it gives you tremendous freedom once you're in the Alps and it can save money.

If you've never tried driving to the Alps, you don't know what you're missing. For a start, it simplifies the whole business of getting all your kit from here to there: you just load up at one end and unload at the other, without tangling with airport trolleys. If you're taking your family or going self-catering, just think of all the extra things you can cram in that you'd otherwise have to leave behind. You also don't have the hassle of the downsides of flying, especially on charter flights, such as inconvenient flight times, hanging around at airports, checking in early, waiting for transfer coaches, and so on.

But for us, the freedom factor is the key. If the snow's bad in your resort, if the lift queues are horrendous or if the resort you've plumped for is a let-down, car drivers can try somewhere else.

Another plus-point is that you can extend the standard six-day holiday by two days while taking only one extra day off work. We do it by crossing the Channel early on a Friday morning and returning nine days later on the Sunday evening. Of course, you need accommodation for the Friday night on the way out, and for the Saturday night on the way back. On the trip out, we often take advantage of this to spend a day in a different resort before moving on to our final destination late on the Saturday. You could stop off in Valmorel before going on to the Three Valleys, for example, or at Verbier or Crans-Montana before going on to Saas Fee or Zermatt. You can also choose to stay in cheaper accommodation in the valleys rather than in the resorts (in Moûtiers, for example, if you are going to Valmorel for the day, or in Le Châble if you are going to Verbier).

After a full day on the slopes on the final Saturday, driving towards the Channel for a few hours before stopping for the night means you won't find Sunday's journey too demanding, and you'll even have time for a traditional French Sunday lunch if you book an early evening crossing.

AS YOU LIKE IT

If you fancy visiting several resorts, you can use one as a base and make day-trips when it suits you. This way, you can still take advantage of tour operator prices and get a discount for driving. The discount varies and may depend on whether you go in high or low season – but you can expect to get from around £70 to £130 per person, which often includes the Channel crossings.

The key to turning this kind of holiday into a success is to go for a base that offers easy road access to other resorts. Our suggestions for France are in a separate chapter. A good choice in Austria is the Tirol:

WINTER TYRES

For several seasons now we have used Snowtrac tyres made by a specialist Dutch company, Vredestein, and been very happy with them, both on-snow and off. They are made in common car sizes from 135/80 R13 up to 205/60 R15, and are usually available from stock. The UK warehouse is in Wellingborough. **t** 01933 677770

the resorts east of Innsbruck offer many options for day-trippers. Söll is a convenient base for exploring resorts such as Alpbach and Kitzbühel. Further east, you can use Zell am See as a base to visit Bad Gastein and Saalbach, while Flachau is convenient for visiting the resorts covered by the Top Tauern lift pass, such as Schladming. Western Austria is not ideal for this sort of holiday, but from St Anton you could make day-trips to Lech, Zürs, Ischgl and Serfaus.

You could consider resorts on the Swiss side of the Portes du Soleil, such as Morgins and Champéry, as a base for trips to resorts such as Verbier, Crans-Montana and Chamonix, as well as visiting the Portes du Soleil resorts. Although eastern Switzerland provides more of a challenge to day-trippers, you might find that it's well worth the effort. Lenzerheide is about the best choice of base camp. Flims, Arosa, Davos and St Moritz are all within striking distance. From St Moritz you could even go over to Livigno in Italy.

Because many resorts are so remote, Italy isn't easily recommendable for day-trippers.

AROUND THE ALPS IN SEVEN DAYS

If you want to see as much of the Alps as possible, consider making a Grand Tour by car, moving every day or two to a different resort and enjoying the complete freedom of going where you want, when you want. Out of high season there's no need to book accommodation before you go. So you can decide at the last minute which part of the Alps and which countries to visit – where the snow is best, perhaps.

A touring holiday doesn't mean you'll be spending more time on the road than on the piste – provided you plan your route carefully. An hour's drive after the lifts have shut is all it need take.

Many of the areas that are great for day-trippers are also worth considering if you're going on tour. These include western Austria and the Tirol. Take western Austria, for example; you could start with Lech, Zürs and St Anton, move on to Serfaus and Ischgl, then go down to Obergurgl, perhaps stopping at Sölden on the way.

Italy is far more suitable for tourers than day-trippers provided you're prepared to put up with some slow drives on winding passes. You could start in Livigno, drive to Bormio and then to the Dolomites, visiting Madonna di Campiglio and Selva, and finish your Italian expedition in Cortina.

Eastern Switzerland also offers a very attractive touring holiday. You could start in Davos/ Klosters, take in Lenzerheide and Arosa and end up in Flims. You could even include St Moritz with a little extra driving. Again in Switzerland, you could easily combine several resorts in the Bernese Oberland – Gstaad, Adelboden, Grindelwald and Lauterbrunnen, where trains go up to Wengen and Mürren.

There's no need to confine yourself to

This map should help you plan your route to the Alps. All the main routes from the Channel and all the routes up into the mountains funnel through three 'gateways', picked out on the map in larger type – Mâcon, Basel and Ulm. Decide which gateway suits your destination, and pick a route to it. Occasionally, different Channel ports will lead you to use different gateways.

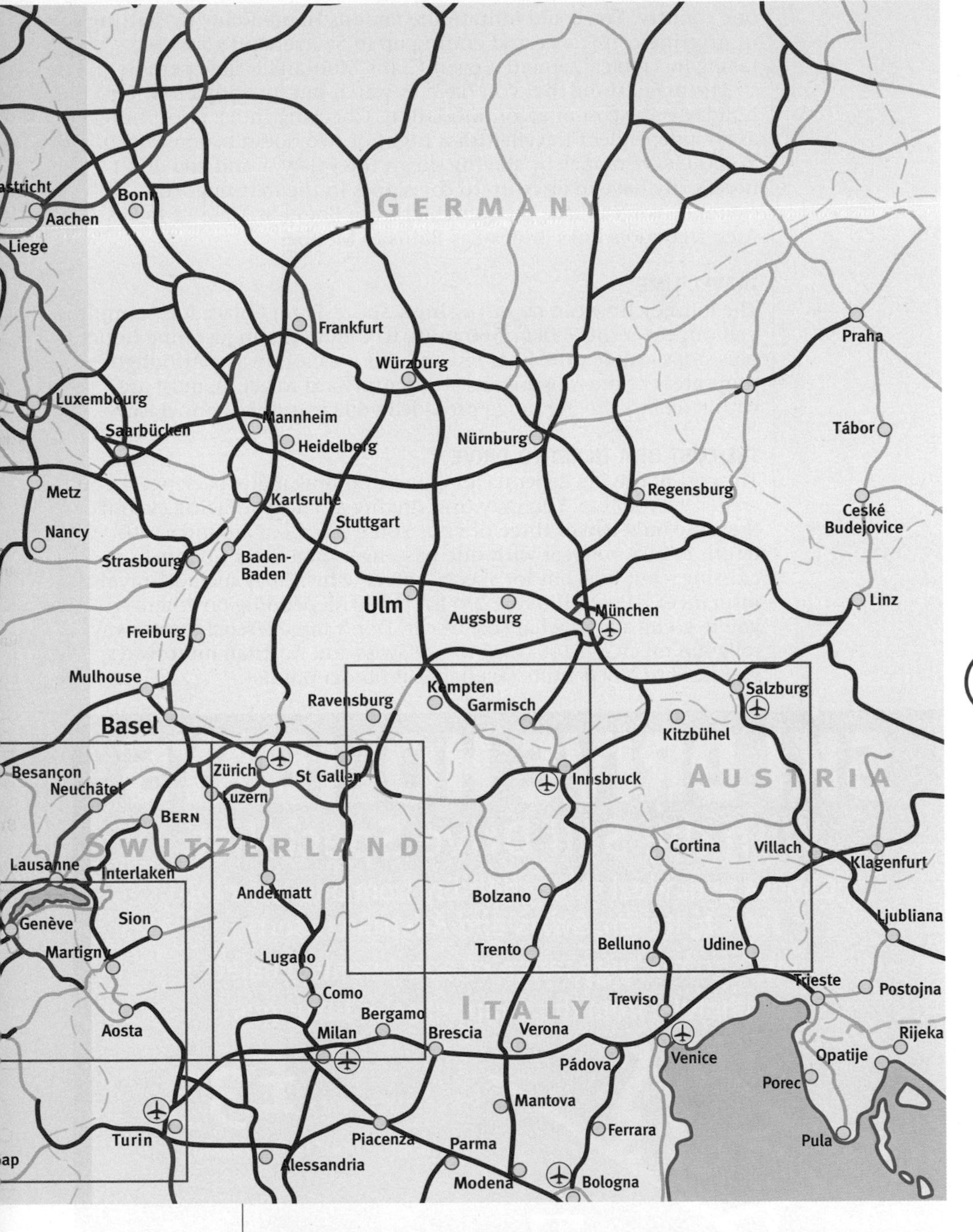

The boxes on the map correspond to the areas covered by the more detailed maps at the start of the main country sections of the book:
Austria page 92
France page 190
Italy page 348
Switzerland page 396.

one country. You could imitate the famous Haute-Route by starting in Argentière in France and ending up in Switzerland's Saas-Fee, taking in Verbier, Zermatt – even Crans-Montana if time permits.

The major thing that you have to watch out for with a touring holiday is the cost of accommodation. Checking into a resort hotel as an independent traveller for a night or two doesn't come cheap. You can save money by staying down the valley – and you don't necessarily have to drive up to the slopes in the morning. For example, you can take the funicular from Bourg-St-Maurice to Les Arcs; a gondola links Brides-Les-Bains to Méribel.

TRAVEL TIME

The journey time can be surprisingly short. From Calais, for example, you can cover the 900km/560 miles to Chamonix in just nine hours plus stops – all but the final few miles is on motorways. Although some areas of the Alps are less straightforward to get to, most are within a day's driving range provided you cross the Channel early.

THE COST OF A TICKET TO DRIVE

The cost of driving depends, of course, on how many passengers you cram into your car. You may find driving as cheap as flying even if there are only two or three of you. You'll pay from around £130 return to take your car with one passenger on a short Channel crossing – but look out for special offers (which may include travel insurance). Allow £100 to £200 for petrol, depending on where you're going and in what sort of car. Don't forget French motorway tolls – as much as £100. And to use Swiss and Austrian motorways you need to buy permits (available at border points).

by **Chris Gill**

Drive to the French Alps *to make the most of them*

If you've read the preceding chapter, you'll have gathered that we are keen on driving to thc Alps. But we're particularly keen on driving to the French Alps. The drive is a relatively short one, whereas many of the transfers from Geneva airport are relatively long. And the route from the Channel is through France rather than Germany, which for Francophiles like us means it's a pleasant prospect rather than a grim one.

TRAVEL TIME

The French Alps are the number-one destination for British car-borne skiers. The journey time is surprisingly short. From Calais, for example, you can comfortably cover the 900km/560 miles to Chamonix in about nine hours plus stops – with the exception of the final few miles, the whole journey is on motorways. And except on peak weekends the traffic is relatively light.

With some southern exceptions, all the resorts of the French Alps are within a day's driving range, provided you cross the Channel early in the day (or overnight). And the weekend traffic jams that used to make such a nightmare (for drivers and coach passengers alike) of the journey from Albertville to the Tarentaise resorts are pretty much a thing of the past, except on peak-season Saturdays and in bad weather, thanks to road improvements.

DAY-TRIP BASES

Most people driving to the French Alps do it simply because they find it a more relaxing way to get themselves, their kit and perhaps their kids to their chosen resort. But, as we have explained in the previous chapter, having a car opens up different kinds of holiday for the more adventurous. Day-tripping, for example.

In the southern French Alps, Serre-Chevalier and Montgenèvre are ideal bases for day-tripping. They are within easy reach of one another, and Montgenèvre is at one end of the Milky Way lift network, which includes Sauze d'Oulx and Sestriere in Italy – you can drive on to them or reach them by lift and piste. On the French side of the border, a few miles south, Puy-St-Vincent is an underrated

resort that is well worth a visit – as is Risoul, a little further south. The major resorts of Alpe-d'Huez and Les Deux-Alpes are also within range, as is the cult off-piste resort of La Grave.

The Chamonix valley is an ideal destination for day-trippers. The Mont-Blanc lift pass covers Chamonix, Les Contamines, Megève and others. Flaine and its satellites are fairly accessible – and so are Verbier in Switzerland, if the intervening passes are open, and Courmayeur in Italy, if the Mont Blanc tunnel is open. You could stay in a valley town, or base yourself in a relatively cheap resort such as St-Gervais.

MOVING ON

A look at the map in this chapter shows that a different approach will pay dividends in the Tarentaise region of France. Practically all the resorts here – from Valmorel to Val-d'Isère – are found at the end of long winding roads up from the main valley. You could visit them all from a base such as Aime, but it would be hard work. If instead you stayed in a different resort each night, moving on from one to the next in the early evening, you could have the trip of a lifetime. Imagine a week in which you could explore the Three Valleys, La Plagne, Les Arcs and Val-d'Isère/Tignes.

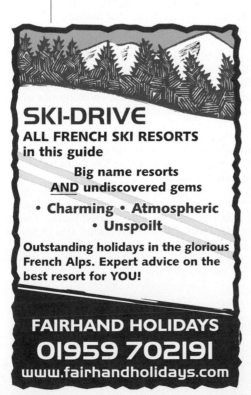

GETTING THERE

The map in our Driving to the Alps chapter shows the main routes across France to the Alps. Whatever route you prefer across the Channel, the gateway to the French Alps is Mâcon and the initial target is Beaune. If you're taking the short crossing to Calais, Boulogne or Dunkirk, the route is via Reims, Troyes and Dijon. From Le Havre or Caen your route sounds even simpler: the A13 to Paris then the A6 south. But you have to get through or around Paris. The most direct way around the city is the notorious périphérique – a hectic, multi-lane urban motorway close to the centre, with exits every few hundred yards. But this is not the quickest route if it is jammed with traffic. The more reliable alternative is to take a series of motorways and dual carriageways through the south-west fringes of Greater Paris. The route (or one of the routes – there are a couple of variants) is signed, but not easy to follow without a detailed map and a good navigator to shout instructions.

MAKING THE MOST OF THE TRIP

The journey across France can be a holiday in itself. Here are some suggestions for stopovers en route.

Arras

One plan we sometimes employ is to cross the Channel quite late in the day and to stop for the night an hour or so into France. Our favourite spot, without doubt, is Arras – an astonishing little town with two central squares surrounded by ornate arcades.

Paris

What better way to celebrate the start or end of your French holiday than with a slap-up meal in a Parisian restaurant? Don't be afraid to tangle with the Paris traffic – just be ready to use your horn. For comfortable modern rooms with the great convenience of a secure garage, we use the Mercure Tour Eiffel hotel.

Disneyland

If you have kids of the right age, you will already know about this. If the budget will stand it, we'd recommend blowing some of it on staying at the theme park in the Newport Bay Club hotel.

Burgundy and points south

On the way back, we like to spend a last day on the slopes and then drive for two or three hours. Mâcon has a reasonable choice of hotels and restaurants, including the Michelin-starred Pierre. Tournus has several star hotel-restaurants. Chalon-sur-Saône and Dijon have plenty of choice.

by **Dave Watts**

Flying to the Alps

cheap deals galore

EasyJet started the first cheap scheduled flights to the Alps by flying to Geneva in the 1997/98 season. They still have the biggest range of flights on offer but have now been joined by three other cut-price airlines. And this competition has made the bigger, established airlines smarten up their acts and offer some competitive deals. This is great news for independent skiers or riders, who can now get flights for under £100, rent a car for a week for under £200 (£50 each between four) and have affordable holidays they arrange themselves.

I have used three of the cheap airlines quite often – EasyJet, Buzz and Go – over the last three seasons. All three were usually pretty much on time, and their no-frills service and pay-as-you-eat food is all you need on a short flight of 90 minutes or less. They are particularly convenient for me because I live only 20 minutes from Stansted and 40 from Luton, the airports they operate from. From Heathrow I have mainly used Swissair, which has well-timed flights for weekend or short-break trips and offers competitive fares through agents if you book a package. It may also be cheaper than the 'cheap' airlines when flights start to get full and 'cheap' prices rise.

By the time we went to press, most of the airlines had not firmed up their programmes for the 2001/02 season. What we talk about here is what applied last season.

All the cheap airlines are ticketless, and none of them works through travel agents. You book direct with the airline and they are increasingly trying to encourage bookings on the internet rather than by telephone because it is cheaper for them. There's usually a discount of a few pounds for booking on the Web and you may not be able to book in any other way (with EasyJet, for example, bookings for more than a month in advance can only be made on the Web). You pay by credit card and either print out your own confirmation (if you book on the Web) or may receive it in the post or by fax. But all you need is a confirmation number; there are no tickets. Prices vary according to demand, and in general the cheapest flights (which they quote in their adverts) are for midweek flights early or late in the day, booked months in advance. As a flight fills up, the prices charged go up. But you may also get a bargain by booking at the last minute if the flight is not full. At their lowest, prices can be as little as £40 return; at their peak they can be well over £200 return.

Policies about flexibility vary. EasyJet's prices are made up of a price for the outward journey and another for the return leg – you can book either journey separately or book both and add the two fares together. If you book and then want to change the date or time of your flight (or even the name of the passenger), you pay an administration fee and any difference between the fares. Such changes can be made up to an hour before the original scheduled flight departure time. Buzz, on the other hand, offers a 'Done Deal' fare, where you cannot make any changes after you've booked, or a (very much more expensive) flexible fare which allows you to change

AIRLINE CONTACT DETAILS

Phone numbers for the major airlines are listed on page 657.

your flight without charge. And if you try to book a one-way flight they quote the full return flexible fare – just like a standard scheduled airline might do. Go's cheapest 'Saver' fares are available only if your journeys span a Saturday night – another common scheduled airline requirement.

Watch out for unexpected extras which are creeping in. For example, there is often a £3 charge for paying by credit card (rather than charge or payment card). Policies on carrying skis and boards and on excess baggage vary. With Buzz last season you had to pre-book them and pay an extra £12 and even then they counted as part of the 25kg baggage allowance. On a Go flight last season the 20kg weight limit was 'being strictly enforced by management because they make money out of it', I was told by an apologetic check-in lady, who charged me £4 for each extra kilo (on the return from Munich, they didn't bother). Most people with skis and boots are going to exceed a 20kg limit. With Buzz the year before, four of us were travelling together, and had packed stuff communally. In total we were within the weight limit, but the check-in staff insisted that we checked in separately and had our luggage weighed individually. This meant scrabbling about in the check-in area, repacking to even out weights as far as possible. And we still ended up having to pay a bit in excess baggage. Ridiculous (and a rip-off).

Last season EasyJet had several flights a day from Luton to both Geneva and Zürich. It also flew from Liverpool and Gatwick to Geneva. And it had flights from Luton and Liverpool to Nice (great for a weekend in Isola 2000), Barcelona (handy for Andorra) and Malaga (for Sierra Nevada in Spain).

Go flew from Stansted to Lyon (good for most French resorts), Munich (handy for Austria), Milan (for Italian resorts), Barcelona and Malaga. Buzz (a subsidiary of KLM) flew from Stansted to Lyon, Milan, Toulouse (for Andorra) and, on Saturdays only, to Chambéry (closer than Lyon for most French resorts) and Geneva. Ryanair went from Stansted to Turin (nearer than Milan for western Italian resorts), Venice, Carcassonne and Perpignan (both for Andorra and the Pyrenees) and St-Etienne (40 minutes south-west of Lyon and within striking distance of the French Alps).

Swissair operated several direct flights a day from Heathrow and Manchester to Zürich and from Heathrow to Geneva, and are likely to continue to do so. Late flights (8pm or later) to and from Heathrow to both Geneva and Zürich make short breaks particularly easy if you live in the south-east – but book well in advance as these late flights are very popular. Crossair (a Swissair subsidiary) have useful flights on Saturdays to Sion, less than half an hour's transfer to, for example, Nendaz (for Verbier's slopes) and Crans-Montana, and a bit further to Saas-Fee, Zermatt and Verbier.

Alitalia has eight flights a day direct from Heathrow to Milan, which gives access to many of the Italian resorts. Three direct flights a day from Gatwick to Venice are handy for the Dolomite resorts and once a day they fly from Gatwick to Turin (nearer than Milan for the western Italian resorts such as Courmayeur and Sauze d'Oulx).

by **Martin Hall**

Travel by train
it can be less of a strain

Taking the train to the Alps can be a great way to get more time on the slopes without taking more time off work. You can leave on Friday night, arriving in your resort on Saturday morning, and return on the following Saturday night, arriving back home on the Sunday – eight days' skiing for five days out of the office. Even if you opt for a different service that doesn't deliver the eight-day week, travelling by train is one of the most restful ways to get to the Alps – provided your journeys to and from the railway stations at either end are not too stressful.

The most popular train destination, with several different direct and indirect services, is the Tarentaise valley in France. You can step off the train in Bourg-St-Maurice and on to a funicular straight up to Arc 1600, and there are quick bus transfers to the other famous mega-resorts of this region – Val-d'Isère, Tignes, La Plagne, Courchevel and Méribel, with slightly longer transfers to Les Menuires and Val-Thorens.

But you can travel by train, one way or another, to many other resorts. And many traditional resorts, especially in Switzerland, are on the rail network and therefore reachable without resorting to buses. How many times you'll have to change trains is another matter.

DIRECT TRAIN SERVICES TO THE FRENCH ALPS

Since 1997, Eurostar has offered a truly direct service to the Alps – you board the train at London Waterloo or Ashford in Kent and disembark at Moûtiers or Bourg-St-Maurice in the Tarentaise valley, without changing trains en route. The special winter services run from New Year through to the end of April. Last season, standard return tickets cost £169 for the overnight service and £189 for the daytime one, but seats can also be booked as part of a package holiday. The overnight service affords you two extra days' skiing or boarding – it leaves on Friday night, arriving early on Saturday morning, and returns late Saturday evening, arriving back in London on Sunday morning. The service uses standard Eurostar carriages with no special sleeping arrangements – you just doze (or not) in your seat. The daytime service gives you no more than the standard six days on the slopes: both outward and return services leave on Saturday morning, arriving late afternoon. The outbound service also stops at Ashford, in Kent, and Aime (between Moûtiers and Bourg-St-Maurice). The return service doesn't stop at Aime.

All the other train services to the Alps involve a change somewhere along the line, but they can still be fairly convenient and also allow for extra time on the slopes. Unlike Eurostar, many of the other services are equipped with sleeping compartments.

The Snowtrain is another weekly overnight service to the Tarentaise giving an eight-day week on the slopes, but it starts from Calais. It runs throughout the winter season, leaving Calais on Friday night and arriving in the Alps the following morning – first stop is Chambéry, then Moûtiers, Aime, and finally Bourg-St-Maurice. For the return journey you leave the Alps on Saturday evening, arriving in Calais early on Sunday morning. You cross the Channel by ferry from Dover (you can pay a supplement for a coach transfer from

London or make your own arrangements and travel as a foot passenger). The train works on a charter basis and can be booked only through UK tour operators – they have allocated spaces on each service. Overnight amenities include on-board couchettes (six drop-down berths to a compartment) and a disco/bar. Beware, it can get very noisy and crowded. It is possible to book a compartment for the exclusive use of four or five people on both legs of the journey.

There is a similar Friday night sleeper service to the Tarentaise starting from Paris. You take the Eurostar to Paris from London Waterloo and change trains at Paris Gare du Nord for an overnight service to the Alps. The return journey leaves the Alps on Saturday evening, arriving in Paris early on Sunday morning. The service starts at about £200 return including couchettes. Several tour operators offer this service as part of an overall package.

There are a number of indirect services available on the French railway throughout the week but most mean crossing Paris from the Gare du Nord to the Gare de Lyon – the change of station is not difficult, with a direct metro, regular buses and plenty of taxis at your disposal. Indirect services to many Alpine destinations via Brussels or Lille also run every day of the week and involve only a change of platform. This can be easier than going via Paris, and the timing of the slower overnight services via Brussels may be more suitable for some holidaymakers; the services tend to be less frequent and are often more expensive, but are worth considering at peak dates.

Motorail (or autotrain) is another option, getting your car to the Alps without having to drive it. The services are not cheap, but the train takes a lot of the strain out of long journeys and saves on hotel and petrol costs, as well as substantial extra mileage on your car. Most services run overnight, with a choice of couchette or sleeper accommodation. Vehicles are usually loaded one hour before departure and are available for pick up half an hour after arrival. You should book your trip well in advance – at least 80 days in advance is recommended on most services. The main motorail/autotrain options of interest to British skiers are the French railway services from Paris to Briançon, Lyon, St-Gervais and Geneva. The Belgian railway runs services from Brussels to Milan and Venice and to Villach and Salzburg, in Austria.

Choosing your resort

get it right first time

Most people get to go skiing or boarding only once or twice a year – and then only for a week at a time. So choosing the right resort is crucially important. This book is designed to help you get it right first time. Here is some advice on how to use our information to best effect – particularly for the benefit of readers with relatively narrow experience of different resorts. Chamonix, Châtel and Courchevel are all French resorts, but they are as similar as chalk and Camembert.

Lots of factors need to be taken into account. The weight you attach to each of them depends on your own personal preferences, and on the make-up of the group you are going on holiday with. On page 87 you'll find 20 shortlists of resorts which are outstanding in various key respects.

Each resort chapter is organised in the same way, to help you choose the right resort. This short introduction takes you through the structure and what you will find under each heading we use.

WHICH RESORT?

We start each chapter with a one-line verdict, in which we aim to sum up the resort in a few words. If you like the sound of it, you might want to go next to our What it Costs rating, in the margin. These ratings, ranging from ① to ⑥, reflect the total cost of a week's holiday from Britain, including a typical package of flights plus half-board accommodation, a lift pass and meals and drinks on the spot. As you might expect with a six-point scale, 3 means on the low side of average, 4 means on the high side. Further on in the margin copy we give the cost of lift passes in local currency; these are for the 2001/02 season if the resort had decided prices by the time we went to press, otherwise we use the 2000/01 prices. Below the What it Costs rating, in the How it Rates section, we rate each resort from 11 points of view – the more stars the better. (All these star ratings are brought together in one chart, which follows this chapter.) Still looking at the information in the margin, in most chapters we have a What's New section; this is likely to be of most use and interest in resorts you already know.

For major resorts, the next things to look at are our lists of the main good and bad points about the resort and its slopes, picked out with ⊕ and ⊖. These lists are followed by a summary in **bold type**, in which we've aimed to weigh up the pros and cons, coming off the fence and giving our view of who might like it. These sections should give you a good idea of whether the resort is likely to suit *you,* and whether you should read our detailed analysis of it.

You'll know by now whether this is, for example, a high, hideous, purpose-built resort with superb, snowsure slopes for all standards of skier or boarder but absolutely no nightlife, or whether it's a pretty, traditional village with gentle wooded skiing, ideal for beginners if only there was some snow. We then look at each aspect in more detail.

THE RESORT

Resorts vary enormously in character and charm. At the extremes of the range are the handful of really hideous modern apartment-block resorts thrown up in France in the 1960s – step forward, Les Menuires and Flaine – and the captivating old traffic-free mountain villages of which Switzerland has an unfair number. But it isn't simply a question of old versus new. Some purpose-built places (such as Valmorel) can have a much friendlier feel than some traditional resorts with big blocky buildings (eg Davos). And some places can be remarkably strung out (eg Vail) whereas others are surprisingly compact (eg Wengen).

The landscape can have an important impact – whether the resort is at the bottom of a narrow, shady valley (eg Ischgl) or on a sunny shelf with panoramic views (eg Crans-Montana). Some places are working towns as well as ski resorts (eg Bormio). Some are full of bars, discos and shops (eg St Anton). Others are peaceful backwaters (eg Arabba). Traffic may choke the streets (eg Sölden). Or the village may be traffic-free (eg Mürren).

In this first section of each chapter, we try to sort out the character of the place for you. Later, in the Staying There section, we tell you more about the hotels, restaurants, bars and so on.

THE MOUNTAINS

The slopes Some mountains and lift networks are vast and complex, while others are much smaller and lacking variation. The description here tells you how the area divides up into different sectors and how the links between them work.

Snow reliability This is a crucial factor for many people, and one which varies enormously. In some resorts you don't have to worry at all about a lack of snow, while others (including some very big names) are notorious for treating their paying guests to ice, mud and slush. Whether a resort is likely to have decent snow on its slopes normally depends on the height, the direction most of the slopes face (north good, south bad), its snow record and how much artificial snow it has. But bear in mind that in the Alps high resorts tend to have rocky terrain where the runs will need more snow than those on the pasture land of lower resorts. Many resorts have increased their snowmaking capacity in recent years and we list the latest amount they claim to have in Mountain Facts and comment on it in the Snow reliability text. Bear in mind that snowmaking can operate only if temperatures are low enough (typically –2°C or less), so it's much more useful in midwinter than in spring.

For experts, intermediates, beginners Most (though not all) resorts have something to offer beginners, but relatively few will keep an expert happy for a week's holiday. As for intermediates, whether a resort will suit you really depends on your standard and inclinations. Places such as Cervinia and Obergurgl are ideal for those who want easy cruising runs, but have little to offer intermediates looking for more challenge. Others, such as Sölden and Val-d'Isère, may intimidate the less confident intermediate who doesn't know the area well. Some, such as the Trois Vallées and Portes du Soleil, have vast amounts of terrain so that you can cover different ground each day. But some other well-known names, such as Obergurgl, Courmayeur, Livigno, and many of the American resorts, have surprisingly small areas of pistes.

For cross-country We don't pretend that this is a guide for avid cross-country skiers. But if you or one of your group wants to try it, our summary here will help you gauge whether the resort is worth considering or whether it is a washout. It looks not just at the amount of cross-country available but also at its scenic beauty and whether or not the tracks are likely to have decent snow (many are at low altitude).

Queues Another key factor. Most resorts have improved their lift systems enormously in the last 10 years, and monster queues are largely a thing of the past. Crowding on the pistes is more of a worry in many resorts, and we mention problems of this kind here. On our piste maps, note that we mark with a chair only high-speed chairs that shift large numbers of people. Lifts not marked with a symbol are slow chairs or drag-lifts.

Mountain restaurants Here's a subject that divides people clearly into two opposing camps. To some, having a decent lunch in civilised surroundings – either in the sun, contemplating amazing scenery, or in a cosy hut, sheltered from the elements – makes or breaks their holiday. Others regard a prolonged midday stop as a waste of valuable skiing time, as well as valuable spending money. We are firmly in the former camp. We get very disheartened by places with miserable restaurants and miserable food (eg some resorts in America); and there are some resorts that we go to regularly partly because of the cosy huts and excellent cuisine (eg Zermatt).

Schools and guides This is an area where we rely heavily on readers' reports of their own or their friends' experiences. The only way to judge a ski school is by trying it. Reports on schools are always extremely valuable and frequently record disappointment.

Facilities for children If you need crèche facilities, don't go to Italy. In other countries, facilities for looking after and teaching children can vary enormously between resorts. We say what is available in each resort, including what's on offer from UK tour operators – often the most attractive option for Brits. But, again, to be of real help we need reports from people who've used the facilities.

SNOWBOARDING

The Mountains section applies to both skiers and snowboarders. But because certain things are important to snowboarding that aren't relevant (or aren't as relevant) to skiing, we also include a special assessment for snowboarders. This covers issues such as whether the slopes present special attractions or problems (eg flat sections that snowboarders have to 'scoot' along), whether there is a good fun-park and half-pipe, how much you can expect to have to use drag-lifts and whether you'll find specialist snowboard schools and shops and lively snowboard bars in the resort.

STAYING THERE

How to go The basic choice is between catered chalets, hotels and self-catering accommodation. The catered chalet holiday remains a peculiarly British phenomenon. A tour operator takes over a chalet (or a hotel in some cases), staffs it with young Brits (or Antipodeans), fills it with British guests, provides half-board and free wine, and lets you drink your duty-free booze without hassle. You can take over a complete chalet, or share one with other groups. It is a relatively economical way of visiting the expensive top resorts.

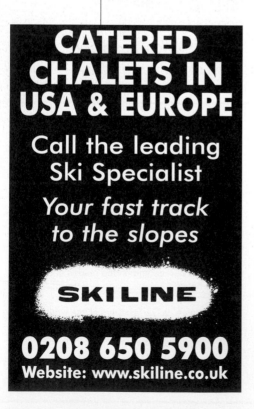

Get next year's edition free

There are too many hotels, nightspots and mountain restaurants for us to see them all every year – so we need reports on your holiday experiences. As usual, the 100 best reports will earn copies of next year's edition.

We want to know:

- what you particularly **liked and disliked** about the resort
- what aspects of the resort came as a **surprise** to you
- your suggestions for **changes to our evaluation** of the resort
- your experience of lift **queues** and of the **ski school** and associated childcare
- your feedback on other **individual facilities** – hotels, bars, restaurants etc.

e-mail: reports@snow-zone.co.uk
mail: our address is at the front of the book; we'll send a form if you like.

Hotels, of course, can vary a lot but, especially in France and Switzerland, can work out very expensive. In North America, watch out for supplements: rooms are often capable of sleeping four, and UK tour operators are inclined to base their standard brochure prices on the assumption that you fill all available bed spaces.

Apartments can be very economical but French ones, in particular, tend to be very small – it's not unusual for brochure prices to be based on four people sleeping in a one-room studio, for example. To be comfortable, pay extra for under-occupancy.

We also look at what's available for independent travellers who want to fix their own hotels or self-catering accommodation. With hotels we've given each a price rating from ① to ⑤ – the more coins, the pricier the hotel.

Staying up the mountain / down the valley If there are interesting options for staying on the slopes above the resort village or in valley towns below it, we've picked them out. The former is often good for avoiding early-morning scrums for the lifts, the latter for cutting costs considerably.

Eating out The range of restaurants varies widely. Even some big resorts, such as Les Arcs, may have little choice because most of the clientele stay in their apartments or chalets. Others, such as Val-d'Isère, have a huge range available, including national and regional cuisine, pizzas, fondues and international fare. American resorts generally have an excellent range of restaurants – most people eat out. This is an area where we rely a lot on reporters recommending restaurants that were good last season – and we are often able to recommend some out-of-the-way restaurants that you might not otherwise find (eg in the Les Arcs and Saas-Fee chapters).

Après-ski Tastes and styles vary enormously. Most resorts have pleasant places in which to have an immediate post-skiing beer or hot chocolate. Some then go dead. Others have noisy bars and discos until the early hours. And, especially in Austrian resorts, there may be a lot of events such as tobogganing and bowling that are organised by British tour operator reps. We are largely dependent for this section on hearing from reporters who are keen après-skiers.

Off the slopes This is largely aimed at assessing how suitable a resort is for someone who doesn't intend to use the slopes – a non-skiing spouse or elderly relative or friend, for example. In some resorts, such as most French purpose-built places, there is really nothing to amuse them. In others, such as Seefeld in Austria, there are more people walking, skating, curling and swimming than there are people skiing or boarding. Excursion possibilities vary widely. And there are great variations in the practicality of meeting skiers and boarders for lunch up the mountain.

Resort ratings at a glance

The following six pages bring together the ratings we give each resort for 11 key characteristics. You'll find these ratings at the start of each resort chapter too. Use the tables here to compare resorts directly for the aspects that are most important to you. You'll be able to see at a glance which resorts come out top and bottom of the pile.

AUSTRIA

	Alpbach	Bad Gastein	Ellmau	Hintertux	Ischgl	Kitzbühel	Lech
Page	95	97	104	107	115	120	126
Snow	**	***	**	*****	****	**	****
Extent	*	****	****	**	****	****	****
Experts	*	***	*	***	***	***	****
Intermediates	**	****	****	***	****	****	****
Beginners	****	**	****	*	**	**	****
Convenience	**	**	***	**	***	**	***
Queues	***	***	****	***	***	**	***
Restaurants	***	****	**	**	**	****	**
Scenery	***	***	***	***	***	***	***
Resort charm	*****	***	***	***	****	****	****
Off-slope	***	****	***	*	***	*****	***

	Mayrhofen	Obergurgl	Obertauern	Saalbach-Hinterglemm	Schladming	Sölden	Söll
Page	134	142	147	149	156	160	162
Snow	***	*****	****	***	***	*****	**
Extent	***	**	**	***	***	***	****
Experts	*	**	***	**	**	***	*
Intermediates	***	***	****	****	****	****	****
Beginners	**	****	*****	***	****	**	***
Convenience	*	****	****	****	***	***	**
Queues	*	*****	****	***	****	***	***
Restaurants	****	**	***	****	****	***	**
Scenery	***	***	***	***	***	***	***
Resort charm	***	****	**	****	****	**	***
Off-slope	****	**	**	**	****	**	**

	St Anton	St Johann in Tirol	Westendorf	Wildschönau	Zell am See
Page	169	177	179	181	184
Snow	****	**	**	**	**
Extent	****	**	*	*	**
Experts	*****	*	*	*	**
Intermediates	***	***	**	**	***
Beginners	*	****	****	****	***
Convenience	***	***	***	***	**
Queues	**	***	****	****	**
Restaurants	***	****	***	**	***
Scenery	***	***	***	***	***
Resort charm	****	***	****	***	***
Off-slope	***	***	**	**	****

FRANCE

	Alpe-d'Huez	Les Arcs	Avoriaz	Chamonix	Châtel	La Clusaz	Les Contamines
Page	193	202	208	212	220	225	231
Snow	****	****	***	****	**	**	****
Extent	****	***	*****	***	*****	***	**
Experts	****	****	***	*****	***	***	**
Intermediates	****	****	****	**	****	****	***
Beginners	*****	****	****	*	**	****	***
Convenience	****	****	****	*	**	***	**
Queues	****	***	**	**	***	***	***
Restaurants	****	**	****	**	***	****	****
Scenery	****	***	***	*****	***	****	***
Resort charm	*	*	**	****	***	****	****
Off-slope	***	*	*	*****	**	***	**

	Courchevel	Les Deux-Alpes	Flaine	La Grave	Megève	Les Menuires	Méribel
Page	234	242	247	253	258	264	267
Snow	****	****	****	***	**	****	****
Extent	*****	***	****	**	*****	*****	*****
Experts	****	****	****	*****	**	****	****
Intermediates	*****	**	*****	*	****	*****	*****
Beginners	*****	***	*****	*	***	***	***
Convenience	****	***	*****	***	**	*****	***
Queues	****	**	****	****	****	****	****
Restaurants	****	**	**	**	*****	***	****
Scenery	***	****	****	****	***	***	***
Resort charm	**	**	*	***	****	*	***
Off-slope	***	**	*	*	****	*	***

	Montgenèvre	Morzine	La Plagne	Puy-St-Vincent	Risoul	La Rosière	Serre-Chevalier
Page	277	281	287	297	299	302	304
Snow	****	**	****	***	***	***	****
Extent	****	*****	****	**	***	***	****
Experts	**	***	***	***	**	**	***
Intermediates	****	****	*****	***	****	***	****
Beginners	*****	***	*****	***	****	*****	****
Convenience	****	**	*****	*****	****	***	***
Queues	****	***	**	****	****	***	***
Restaurants	**	***	**	***	***	*	***
Scenery	***	***	****	***	***	***	****
Resort charm	***	***	*	**	**	***	***
Off-slope	*	***	*	*	*	*	**

FRANCE (continued) – ITALY

	Ste-Foy	St-Martin-de-Belleville	La Tania	Tignes	Val-d'Isère	Valmorel	Val-Thorens
Page	310	312	315	318	326	336	341
Snow	***	***	***	*****	*****	***	*****
Extent	*	*****	*****	*****	*****	***	*****
Experts	****	****	****	*****	*****	**	****
Intermediates	***	*****	*****	*****	*****	****	*****
Beginners	**	***	**	**	***	*****	****
Convenience	***	***	****	****	***	*****	*****
Queues	*****	****	****	****	****	****	***
Restaurants	*	****	****	**	**	**	****
Scenery	***	***	***	***	***	***	***
Resort charm	***	****	***	**	***	****	**
Off-slope	*	*	*	*	**	**	**

	ITALY Bormio	Cervinia	Cortina d'Ampezzo	Courmayeur	Livigno	Madonna di Campiglio	Monterosa Ski
Page	350	352	357	362	367	371	373
Snow	***	*****	***	****	****	***	***
Extent	**	***	***	**	**	***	****
Experts	*	*	**	***	**	**	***
Intermediates	***	****	***	****	***	****	****
Beginners	**	*****	*****	**	****	****	**
Convenience	***	***	*	*	**	**	****
Queues	***	***	***	****	****	***	****
Restaurants	****	***	****	****	***	****	**
Scenery	***	****	*****	****	***	****	****
Resort charm	****	**	****	****	***	***	***
Off-slope	****	*	*****	***	**	***	*

	Sauze d'Oulx	Selva	Sestriere	La Thuile
Page	376	381	389	391
Snow	**	****	***	****
Extent	*****	*****	****	***
Experts	**	***	***	**
Intermediates	****	*****	****	****
Beginners	**	****	***	****
Convenience	**	***	****	***
Queues	***	***	***	****
Restaurants	***	****	**	*
Scenery	***	*****	***	***
Resort charm	**	***	*	***
Off-slope	*	***	*	**

SWITZERLAND – UNITED STATES

	Adelboden	Andermatt	Arosa	Champéry	Crans-Montana	Davos	Flims	Grindelwald
Page	399	401	403	405	407	412	419	424
Snow	**	****	***	**	**	****	***	**
Extent	***	*	**	*****	***	*****	****	***
Experts	**	****	*	***	**	****	***	**
Intermediates	***	**	***	****	****	*****	*****	*****
Beginners	****	*	****	**	***	**	****	***
Convenience	***	***	***	*	**	**	***	**
Queues	***	**	****	****	***	**	***	**
Restaurants	**	*	****	***	***	***	***	***
Scenery	***	***	***	****	****	****	***	*****
Resort charm	****	****	**	****	**	**	***	****
Off-slope	****	**	****	***	****	*****	***	****

	Gstaad	Mürren	Saas-Fee	St Moritz	Verbier	Villars	Wengen	Zermatt
Page	428	430	434	439	445	454	456	461
Snow	*	***	*****	****	***	**	**	****
Extent	****	*	**	*****	*****	**	***	****
Experts	**	***	***	****	*****	**	**	*****
Intermediates	***	***	****	****	***	***	****	****
Beginners	***	**	*****	**	**	****	***	*
Convenience	*	***	***	**	**	***	***	*
Queues	***	***	***	**	***	***	***	***
Restaurants	***	**	***	****	***	***	****	*****
Scenery	***	*****	****	****	****	***	*****	*****
Resort charm	****	*****	*****	*	***	****	*****	*****
Off-slope	****	***	****	*****	***	****	****	****

	CALIFORNIA			COLORADO				
	Heavenly	Mammoth		Aspen	Beaver Cr'k	Breckenridge	Copper Mountain	Crested Butte
Page	474	481		486	493	495	500	502
Snow	****	****		*****	*****	*****	*****	****
Extent	***	***		****	***	**	**	**
Experts	***	****		*****	****	****	****	****
Intermediates	****	****		*****	****	****	****	***
Beginners	****	****		*****	*****	****	****	****
Convenience	*	**		**	****	***	****	***
Queues	****	****		****	*****	****	****	*****
Restaurants	*	*		****	**	**	*	*
Scenery	****	***		***	***	***	***	***
Resort charm	*	**		****	***	***	**	****
Off-slope	**	*		****	***	***	*	**

UNITED STATES (continued)

	Keystone	Steamboat	Telluride	Vail	Winter Park
Page	504	509	514	516	522
Snow	*****	****	****	*****	*****
Extent	**	***	**	****	***
Experts	***	***	****	****	****
Intermediates	****	****	***	*****	****
Beginners	****	*****	*****	*****	*****
Convenience	**	***	****	***	***
Queues	****	****	*****	**	****
Restaurants	***	***	*	**	***
Scenery	***	***	****	***	***
Resort charm	**	**	****	***	**
Off-slope	**	**	**	***	*

UTAH

	Alta	The Canyons	Deer Valley	Park City	Snowbasin	Snowbird
Page	529	531	533	535	540	542
Snow	*****	****	****	****	*****	*****
Extent	***	***	**	***	***	***
Experts	*****	***	***	****	****	*****
Intermediates	***	***	****	****	****	***
Beginners	***	***	****	****	**	**
Convenience	****	****	****	***	*	*****
Queues	***	****	****	****	*****	**
Restaurants	**	***	****	**	*	*
Scenery	****	***	***	***	****	***
Resort charm	**	**	***	***	**	*
Off-slope	*	**	**	***	*	*

	REST OF THE WEST Big Sky	Jackson	Sun Valley	NEW ENGLAND Killington	Smugglers'	Stowe	Sunday River
Page	546	548	553	558	562	565	567
Snow	****	****	***	***	***	***	***
Extent	***	***	***	**	*	*	**
Experts	*****	*****	***	***	***	***	**
Intermediates	****	**	****	***	***	****	****
Beginners	****	***	***	****	****	****	****
Convenience	****	***	**	*	*****	*	***
Queues	*****	***	****	****	****	****	****
Restaurants	*	*	****	*	*	**	***
Scenery	***	***	***	***	***	***	***
Resort charm	**	****	***	**	**	****	**
Off-slope	**	***	***	*	*	*	*

CANADA – AND THE REST

WESTERN CANADA

	Banff	Big White	Fernie	Jasper	Kicking Horse	Lake Louise	Panorama	Whistler
Page	573	580	582	586	588	590	595	597
Snow	****	****	****	****	****	****	***	****
Extent	****	***	***	*	***	****	**	****
Experts	****	*****	*****	**	****	****	****	*****
Intermediates	****	****	**	**	***	****	***	*****
Beginners	***	****	****	****	***	***	****	****
Convenience	*	****	****	*	*	*	****	****
Queues	****	*****	****	****	*****	****	****	***
Restaurants	***	*	*	**	**	**	*	**
Scenery	****	***	****	***	***	*****	***	***
Resort charm	***	**	**	***	*	***	**	***
Off-slope	*****	**	**	***	*	****	*	**

EASTERN CANADA / ANDORRA / SPAIN

	EASTERN CANADA Tremblant	ANDORRA Arinsal	ANDORRA Pas de la Casa	ANDORRA Soldeu	SPAIN Baqueira
Page	606	612	614	616	621
Snow	****	***	***	***	***
Extent	**	*	***	**	***
Experts	***	*	*	*	***
Intermediates	***	**	***	***	****
Beginners	****	***	****	****	**
Convenience	****	***	****	***	***
Queues	***	***	***	***	***
Restaurants	**	**	***	*	**
Scenery	***	***	**	***	***
Resort charm	****	*	*	*	**
Off-slope	***	*	*	*	*

NORWAY / SWEDEN / NEW ZEALAND

	NORWAY Hemsedal	SWEDEN Åre	NEW ZEALAND Queenstown
Page	631	634	644
Snow	****	***	**
Extent	*	**	*
Experts	**	**	***
Intermediates	****	****	***
Beginners	***	****	***
Convenience	**	***	*
Queues	****	****	***
Restaurants	*	***	*
Scenery	**	***	****
Resort charm	**	***	**
Off-slope	*	***	*****

Resort shortlists

To streamline the job of spotting the ideal resort for your own holiday, here are lists of the best ten or so resorts for 20 different categories. Some lists embrace European and North American resorts, but most we've confined to Europe, because America has too many qualifying resorts (eg for beginners) or because America does things differently, making comparisons invalid (eg for off-piste).

SOMETHING FOR EVERYONE

Resorts with everything from reassuring nursery slopes to real challenges for experts

Alpe-d'Huez, France p193
Les Arcs, France p202
Aspen-Snowmass, Colorado p486
Courchevel, France p234
Flaine, France p247
Mammoth, California p481
Vail, Colorado p516
Val-d'Isère, France p326
Whistler, Canada p597
Winter Park, Colorado p522

INTERNATIONAL OVERSIGHTS

Resorts that deserve as much attention as the ones we go back to every year, but don't seem to get it

Alta, Utah p529
Andermatt, Switzerland p401
Bad Gastein, Austria p97
Big Sky, Montana p546
Flims-Laax, Switzerland p419
Ischgl, Austria p115
Monterosa Ski, Italy p373
Risoul, France p299
Sun Valley, Idaho p553
Telluride, Colorado p514

RELIABLE SNOW IN THE ALPS

Alpine resorts with good snow records or lots of snowmaking, and high or north-facing slopes

Argentière, France p212
Cervinia, Italy p352
Courchevel, France p234
Hintertux, Austria p107
Lech/Zürs, Austria p126
Obergurgl, Austria p142
Saas-Fee, Switzerland p434
Val-d'Isère/Tignes, France pp326/318
Val-Thorens, France p341
Zermatt, Switzerland p461

OFF-PISTE WONDERS

Alpine resorts where, with the right guidance and equipment, you can have the time of your life

Alpe-d'Huez, France p193
Andermatt, Switzerland p401
Argentière/Chamonix, France p212
Davos/Klosters, Switzerland p412
La Grave, France p253
Lech/Zürs, Austria p126
Monterosa Ski, Italy p373
St Anton, Austria p169
Val-d'Isère/Tignes, France pp326/318
Verbier, Switzerland p445

POWDER PARADISES

Resorts with the snow, the terrain and (ideally) the lack of crowds that make for powder perfection

Alta/Snowbird, Utah pp529/542
Andermatt, Switzerland p401
Aspen-Snowmass, Colorado p486
Berthoud Pass, Colorado p522
Big Sky, Montana p546
Fernie, Canada p582
Grand Targhee, Wyoming p548
La Grave, France p253
Jackson Hole, Wyoming p548
Kicking Horse, Canada p588
Monterosa Ski, Italy, p373
Snowbasin, Utah p540
Ste-Foy, France p310

BLACK RUNS

Resorts with steep, mogully, lift-served slopes within the safety of the piste network

Alta/Snowbird, Utah pp529/542
Andermatt, Switzerland p401
Argentière/Chamonix, France p212
Aspen-Snowmass, Colorado p486
Beaver Creek, Colorado p493
Courchevel, France p234
Jackson Hole, Wyoming p548
Whistler, Canada p597
Winter Park, Colorado p522
Zermatt, Switzerland p461

CHOPAHOLICS

Resorts where you can quit the conventional lift network and have a day riding helicopters or cats

Aspen-Snowmass, Colorado p486
Crested Butte, Colorado p502
Fernie, Canada p582
Grand Targhee, Wyoming p548
Lech/Zürs, Austria p126
Monterosa Ski, Italy p373
Panorama, Canada p595
Verbier, Switzerland p445
Whistler, Canada p597
Zermatt, Switzerland p461

HIGH-MILEAGE PISTE-BASHING

Extensive intermediate slopes with big lift networks

Alpe-d'Huez, France p193
Davos/Klosters, Switzerland p412
Flims/Laax, Switzerland p419
Milky Way: Sauze d'Oulx (Italy), Montgenèvre (France) pp376/277
La Plagne, France p287
Portes du Soleil, France/Switz p295
Selva/Sella Ronda, Italy p381
Trois Vallées, France p324
Val-d'Isère/Tignes, France pp326/318
Whistler, Canada p597

MOTORWAY CRUISING

Long, gentle, super-smooth pistes to bolster the frail confidence of those not long off the nursery slope

Les Arcs, France p202
Aspen-Snowmass, Colorado p486
Breckenridge, Colorado p495
Cervinia, Italy p352
Cortina, Italy p357
Courchevel, France p234
Megève, France p258
La Plagne, France p287
La Thuile, Italy p391
Vail, Colorado p516

RESORTS FOR BEGINNERS

European resorts with gentle, snowsure nursery slopes and easy longer runs to progress to

Alpe-d'Huez, France p193
Les Arcs, France p202
Cervinia, Italy p352
Courchevel, France p234
Flaine, France p247
Montgenèvre, France p277
Pamporovo, Bulgaria p623
La Plagne, France p287
Saas-Fee, Switzerland p434
Soldeu, Andorra p616

MODERN CONVENIENCE

Alpine resorts where there's plenty of slope-side accommodation to make life easy

Les Arcs, France p202
Avoriaz, France p208
Courchevel, France p234
Flaine, France p247
Les Menuires, France p264
Obertauern, Austria p147
La Plagne, France p287
Puy-St-Vincent, France, p297
Valmorel, France p336
Val-Thorens, France p341

WEATHERPROOF SLOPES

Alpine resorts with snowsure slopes if the sun shines, and trees in case it doesn't

Les Arcs, France p202
Courchevel, France p234
Courmayeur, Italy p362
Flims, Switzerland p419
Montchavin/Les Coches, France p287
Schladming, Austria p156
Selva, Italy p381
Serre-Chevalier, France p304
Sestriere, Italy p389
La Thuile, Italy p391

BACK-DOOR RESORTS

Cute little Alpine villages linked to big, bold ski areas, giving you the best of two different worlds

Les Brévières (Tignes), France p318
Les Carroz (Flaine), France p247
Champagny (La Plagne), France p287
Leogang (Saalbach), Austria p149
Montchavin (La Plagne), France p287
Peisey (Les Arcs), France p202
Le Pré (Les Arcs), France p202
St-Martin (Three Valleys), France p312
Stuben (St Anton), Austria p169
Vaujany (Alpe-d'Huez), France p193

SNOWSURE BUT SIMPATICO

Alpine resorts with high-rise slopes, but low-rise, traditional-style buildings

Andermatt, Switzerland p401
Arabba, Italy p381
Argentière, France p212
Les Contamines, France p231
Ischgl, Austria p115
Lech/Zürs, Austria p126
Monterosa Ski, Italy p373
Obergurgl, Austria p142
Saas-Fee, Switzerland p434
Zermatt, Switzerland p461

SPECIALLY FOR FAMILIES

Alpine resorts where you can easily find accommodation surrounded by snow, not by traffic and fumes

Les Arcs, France p202
Avoriaz, France p208
Flaine, France p247
Lech, Austria p126
Montchavin (La Plagne), France p287
Mürren, Switzerland p430
Risoul, France p299
Saas-Fee, Switzerland p434
Valmorel, France p336
Wengen, Switzerland p456

SPECIAL MOUNTAIN RESTAURANTS

Alpine resorts where the mountain restaurants can really add an extra dimension to your holiday

Alpe-d'Huez, France p193
La Clusaz, France p225
Courmayeur, Italy p362
Kitzbühel, Austria p120
Megève, France p258
St Johann in Tirol, Austria p177
St Moritz, Switzerland p439
Selva, Italy p381
Söll, Austria p162
Zermatt, Switzerland p461

DRAMATIC SCENERY

Resorts where the mountains are not just high and snowy, but spectacularly scenic too

Chamonix, France p212
Cortina, Italy p357
Courmayeur, Italy p362
Heavenly, California p474
Jungfrau resorts (Grindelwald, Mürren, Wengen), Switzerland pp424/430/456
Lake Louise, Canada p590
Saas-Fee, Switzerland p434
St Moritz, Switzerland p439
Selva, Italy p381
Zermatt, Switzerland p461

VILLAGE CHARM

Resorts with traditional character that enriches your holiday – from mountain villages to mining towns

Alpbach, Austria p95
Champéry, Switzerland p405
Courmayeur, Italy p362
Crested Butte, Colorado p502
Lech, Austria p126
Mürren, Switzerland p430
Saas-Fee, Switzerland p434
Telluride, Colorado p514
Wengen, Switzerland p456
Zermatt, Switzerland p461

LIVELY NIGHTLIFE

European resorts where you'll have no difficulty finding somewhere to boogy, and someone to do it with

Chamonix, France p212
Ischgl, Austria p115
Kitzbühel, Austria p120
Saalbach, Austria p149
St Anton, Austria p169
Sauze d'Oulx, Italy p376
Sölden, Austria p160
Pas de la Casa, Andorra p614
Val-d'Isère, France p326
Verbier, Switzerland p445

OTHER AMUSEMENTS

Alpine resorts where those not interested in skiing or boarding can still find plenty to do

Bad Gastein, Austria p97
Chamonix, France p212
Cortina, Italy p357
Davos, Switzerland p412
Gstaad, Switzerland p428
Innsbruck, Austria p111
Kitzbühel, Austria p120
Megève, France p258
St Moritz, Switzerland p439
Zell am See, Austria p184

Resort chapters explained

FINDING A RESORT
The bulk of the book consists of chapters devoted to individual major resorts, some also covering minor resorts that share the same lift system. These chapters are ordered alphabetically and grouped by country – first, the four major Alpine countries in alphabetical order; then the US and Canada (where resorts are grouped by states or regions); then minor European countries; then Australasia.

There's a **chapter-by-chapter listing** in the detailed Contents at the start of the book.

Short cuts to the resorts that might suit you are provided by a table of comparative **star-ratings** and a series of **shortlists** of resorts with particular merits. To find these, just turn back a few pages towards the front of the book.

At the back of the book is an **index** to the resort chapters, combined with a **directory** giving basic information on hundreds of other minor resorts. Where the resort you are looking up is a minor resort covered in a chapter devoted mainly to a bigger resort, the page reference will take you to the start of that chapter, not to the page on which the minor resort is described.

There's further guidance on using our information in the chapter on Choosing your resort – designed to be helpful particularly to people with narrow experience of resorts, who may not appreciate how big the differences can be.

READING A CHAPTER
The **cost** of visiting each resort is rated on a scale of one to six – ① to ⑥ – reflecting the typical cost of a one-week trip based on a half-board package from the UK, plus a lift pass and an allowance for lunch in mountain restaurants. We assume two people sharing a room – even in the US, where package prices are often based on four people sharing.

Star-ratings summarise our view of the resort in 11 respects, including how well it suits different standards of skier/boarder. The more stars, the better.

We give phone and fax numbers and internet addresses of the **tourist office** (and we now give phone numbers for recommended hotels, too).

The UK tour operators offering **package holidays** in each resort are listed in the index at the back of the book, not in the main chapters.

Our **mountain maps** show the resorts' own gradings of runs – so those for the US and Canada show green, blue and black runs, and no red ones (unlike Europe). On some maps we also follow the North American convention of using black diamonds to indicate open expert terrain where the runs are not precisely defined. We do not distinguish single-diamond terrain from the steeper double-diamond terrain.

We show all the lifts on the mountain, including any definitely planned for construction for the coming seasons. We use the following symbols to identify **fast or high-capacity lifts**:

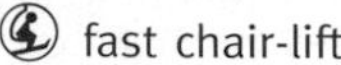
fast chair-lift

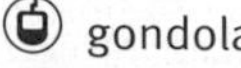
gondola

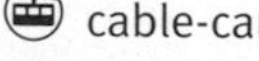
cable-car

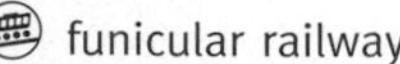
funicular railway

Austria

Austria is a completely different holiday experience from the other Alpine countries. If you have never been there you will notice a huge difference – many people who discover it fall in love with it and never want to go anywhere else. One essential ingredient is that the partying is as important as the skiing or riding in most Austrian resorts – après-ski starts early and finishes late. The other essential ingredient is the nature of the villages. There are none of the monstrous purpose-built block resorts of France and a few big resorts such as St Anton. But essentially Austria is the land of cute little villages clustered around onion-domed churches; of friendly wooded mountains, reassuring to beginners and timid intermediates in a way that bleak snowfields and craggy peaks will never be; of friendly, welcoming people who don't find it demeaning to speak their guests' language; and of jolly beer-fuelled après-ski action, starting in many resorts in mid-afternoon with dancing in on-mountain restaurants and going on as long as you have the legs for it. And Austrian resorts have (rather belatedly) made great strides in their attempt to catch up on the snowmaking front – most have radically increased their snowmaking capacity in recent years. In midwinter, especially, lack of snow generally goes hand in hand with low night-time temperatures, even at low altitudes, and snowmaking comes into its own.

It's the après-ski that strikes most first-time visitors as being Austria's unique selling point. The few French resorts that have lively après-ski are dominated by British or Scandinavian holidaymakers (and resort workers and ski-bums). The French are noticeable by their absence and you could be in London or Stockholm rather than France.

But Austrian après-ski remains very Austrian. Huge quantities of beer and schnapps are drunk, German is the predominant language and German drinking songs are common. So is incredibly loud Europop music. People pack into mountain restaurants at the end of the day and dance in their ski boots on the dance floor, on the tables, on the bar, on the roof beams, wherever there's room. There are open-air ice bars on the mountain, umbrella bars and countless transparent 'igloos' in which to shelter from bad weather. In many

ISCHGL TOURIST OFFICE

One of the Austrian resorts that has it all – nightlife, charm and good snowy slopes ↓

resorts the bands don't stop playing or the DJs working until darkness falls, when the happy punters slide off down the mountain in the dark to find another watering hole in town. After dinner the drinking and dancing starts again – for those who take time out for dinner, that is.

Of course, not all Austrian resorts conform to this image. But lots of big name ones with the best and most extensive slopes do. St Anton, Saalbach-Hinterglemm, Ischgl and Zell am See for example, fit this bill.

One thing that all Austrian resorts have in common is reliably comfortable accommodation – whether it's in four-star hotels with pools, saunas and spas, or in great-value family-run guest houses, of which Austria has thousands. The accommodation scene is very

much dominated by hotels and guest houses; catered chalets and self-catered apartments are in general much less widely available (though there are one or two resorts, such as St Anton and Kitzbühel, where catered chalets are more easily come by).

Most Austrian resorts are real, friendly villages on valley floors, with skiing and boarding on the wooded slopes above them. They have expanded enormously since the war, but practically all the development has been in traditional chalet style, and the villages generally look good even without the snow that is the saving grace of many French and even some Swiss resorts. Unlike Courchevel and Verbier, many Tirolean resorts are as busy in August as in February.

Outside the big-name resorts the skiing is often quite limited. There are many Austrian resorts that a keen skier could explore fully

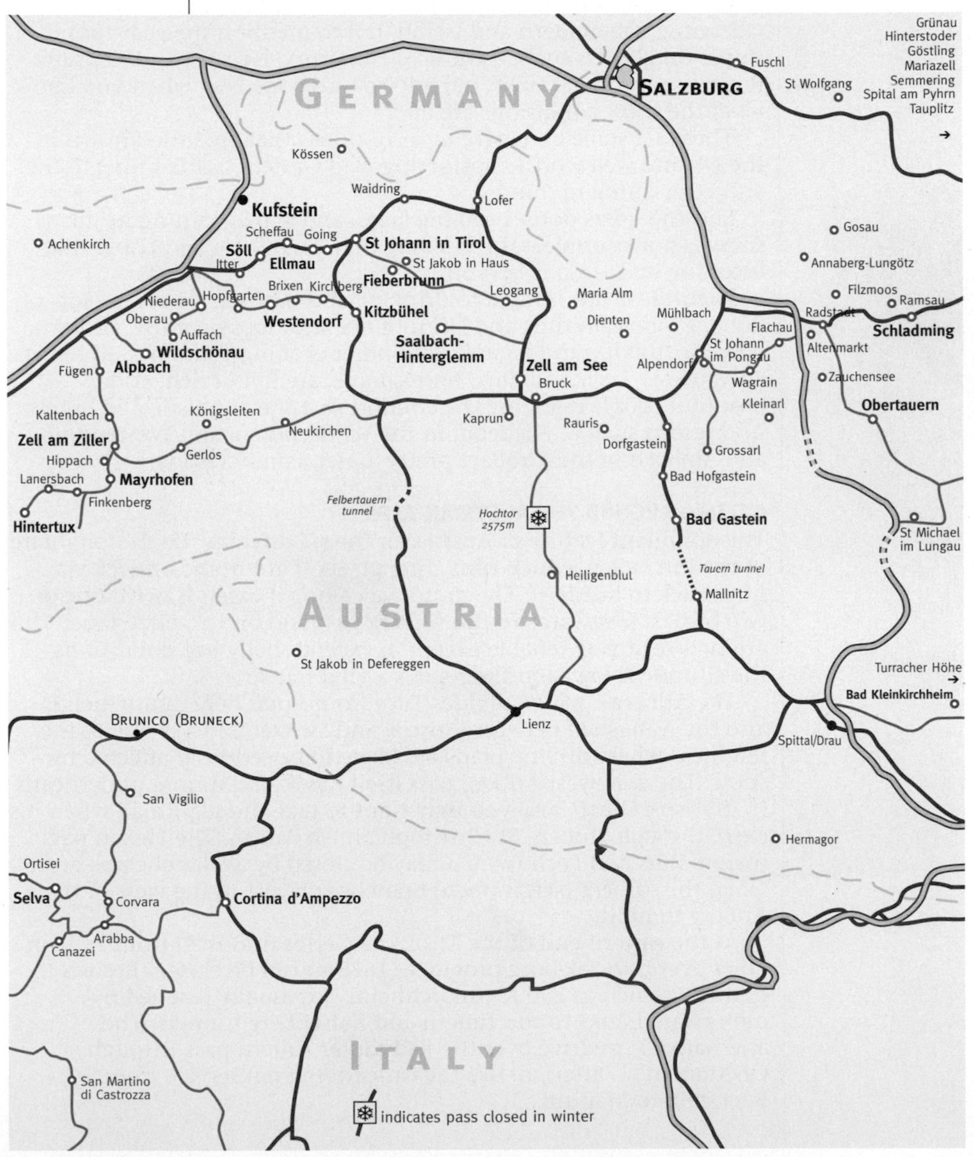

in half a day. Those who start their skiing careers in such resorts may not be worried by this; those who have tried the bigger areas of France and developed a taste for them may find the list of acceptable Austrian resorts quite a short one.

Unfortunately, several of the resorts on that shortlist bring you up against another problem – low altitude, and therefore poor snow conditions. Kitzbühel is at 760m, Söll at 700m, Zell am See at 775m. The top heights of Austrian resorts are relatively low, too – typically 1800m to 2000m; as we have noted above, snowmaking is becoming more widespread, but it works only when the conditions are right.

The resorts of the Arlberg area, at the western end of the Tirol – St Anton, Lech and Zürs – stand apart from these concerns, with excellent snow records and extensive skiing. And there are other resorts where you can be reasonably confident of good snow, such as Obergurgl, Obertauern and Ischgl, not to mention the year-round slopes on glaciers such as those at Hintertux, Neustift and Kaprun. But for most other resorts our advice is to book late, when you know what the snow conditions are like.

There are some extensive areas of slopes that are little-known in the UK and well worth considering. Bad Gastein, Schladming, Ischgl and Lech spring to mind.

Snowboarders don't need big areas; and snowboarding in slushy snow is not as unpleasant as skiing in it. So it's not surprising that boarding in Austria is booming.

Nightlife is not limited to drinking and dancing. There are lots of floodlit toboggan runs and UK tour operator reps organise Tirolean, bowling, fondue and karaoke and other evenings. And not all resorts are raucous. Lech and Zürs, for example, are full of rich, cool, beautiful people enjoying the comfort of 4-star sophisticated hotels. And resorts such as Niederau in the Wildschönau and Westendorf and Alpbach in the Tirol are pretty, quiet, family resorts.

GETTING AROUND THE AUSTRIAN ALPS

The dominant feature of Austria for the ski driver is the thoroughfare of the Inn valley, which runs through the Tirol from Landeck via Innsbruck to Kufstein. The motorway along it extends, with one or two breaks, westwards to the Arlberg pass and on to Switzerland. This artery is relatively reliable except in exceptionally bad conditions – the altitude is low, and the road is a vital transport link.

The Arlberg – which divides Tirol from Vorarlberg, but which is also the watershed between Austria and Switzerland – is one of the few areas where driving plans are likely to be seriously affected by snow. The east–west Arlberg pass itself has a long tunnel underneath it; this isn't cheap, and you may want to take the high road when it's clear, through Stuben, St Christoph and St Anton. The Flexen pass road to Zürs and Lech (which may be closed by avalanche risk even when the Arlberg pass is open) branches off just to the west of the Arlberg summit.

At the eastern end of the Tirol, the Gerlos pass road from Zell am Ziller over into Salzburg province (1628m) can be closed. Resorts in Carinthia, such as Bad Kleinkirchheim, are usually reached by motorway thanks to the Tauern and Katschberg tunnels. The alternative is to drive over the Radstädter Tauern pass through Obertauern (1740m), or use the car-carrying rail service from Böckstein to Mallnitz.

Alpbach 1000m

Traditional charm for those who like familiar slopes

WHAT IT COSTS

HOW IT RATES

The slopes	
Snow	**
Extent	*
Experts	*
Intermediates	**
Beginners	****
Convenience	**
Queues	***
Restaurants	***
The rest	
Scenery	***
Resort charm	*****
Off-slope	***

What's new

The Brandegg T-bar was replaced by a four-seater chair-lift last season. New snowmaking has been installed from the gondola mid-station to the base. This piste has also been rerouted.

An eight-person gondola to replace the one-seater chair to the top of Reith should be ready for 2001/02. A new chair-lift to replace the Muldenlift drags behind Gmahkopf is also planned.

Plans for a lift link between Alpbach and Reith, and another one linking with Schatzberg in the Wildschönau area, are still on the drawing board. More immediate are plans for a high-speed chair-lift to replace the long Pöglbahn II double chair-lift from above Inneralpbach up to the Gmahkopf ridge area.

- ⊕ Charming traditional village with a relaxed atmosphere
- ⊕ Good, varied, intermediate terrain, not without challenges for experts
- ⊕ Handy central nursery slopes
- ⊕ Short transfers from Innsbruck
- ⊕ Several other worthwhile resorts within day-trip distance

- ⊖ Limited slopes
- ⊖ Main slopes are a shuttle-bus-ride away from the centre
- ⊖ Few long easy runs for beginners to progress to
- ⊖ Low altitude means lower slopes can suffer from poor snow – though a north-facing aspect and increased snowmaking have helped

Alpbach is an old British favourite – there is even a British club, the Alpbach Visitors. It is exceptionally pretty and friendly – 'it has great character and atmosphere,' says one visitor – and its small mountain is not without interest, even for experts. It's the kind of place that inspires loyalty in its visitors – a recent reporter who has been going for 19 years claims only junior status.

THE RESORT

Alpbach is near the head of a valley, looking south across it towards the Wiedersbergerhorn, where most of the slopes are to be found. It's captivating both in summer and winter, and has won awards for its outstanding beauty. Traditional chalets crowd around the little church, and open snowfields (including the nursery slopes) are only a few steps away.

Alpbach is small, but not necessarily convenient. The main village is the place to stay for atmosphere and après-ski, but involves using a free shuttle-bus to and from Achenwirt, 1.5km away, where the main gondola goes up to Hornboden. The backwater hamlet of Inneralpbach (about 1.5km south-east of Alpbach itself) is much more convenient for the slopes, with its own lifts up to the central ridge at Gmahkopf – just above Hornboden.

The Inn valley is a few miles north, and trips east to Kitzbühel or west to Innsbruck are possible. The Hintertux and Stubaier glaciers are within reach.

THE MOUNTAIN

Alpbach's slopes, on two flanks of the Wiedersbergerhorn, are small and simple. Piste grooming is excellent.

Slopes Chair-lifts and drags serve the open, north-facing slopes above the tree line, with black runs following the lift lines and reds (and a single blue) take less direct routes. The runs are mostly of 200m to 400m vertical, but

MOUNTAIN FACTS

Altitude	670m-2025m
Lifts	19
Pistes	45km
Blue	15%
Red	70%
Black	15%
Artificial snow	25km

Phone numbers
From elsewhere in Austria add the prefix 05336.
From abroad use the prefix +43 5336.

TOURIST OFFICE

Postcode A-6236
t +43 (5336) 600-0
f 600-200
info@alpbach.at
www.alpbach.at

ALPBACH TOURIST OFFICE

The village is a cosy cluster of wooden chalets ↓

you get 500m down the second stage of the gondola, and a full 1000m when snow is good enough to ski to valley level. Behind Gmahkopf is a short west-facing slope where a new chair-lift is being built to replace the two short Muldenlift drags. The small area at Reith (about 3km down the valley from Achenwirt) is on the lift pass. A new eight-seat gondola is due to open here for 2001/02.

Snow reliability Alpbach cannot claim great snow reliability; but at least most slopes face north. The village nursery slope and, increasingly, other runs have artificial snow. New snowmaking and piste rerouting on the home run down to the gondola base station should have improved conditions on what has been described as an 'icy and tricky run'.

Snowboarding There's some good free-riding terrain and a half-pipe near the top of the main gondola.

Experts Alpbach isn't ideal, but the reds and the three blacks are not without challenge, and runs of 1000m vertical are not to be sniffed at. There are a number of off-piste routes to the valley, short tours are offered, and the schools apparently take the top classes off-piste.

Intermediates There is fine intermediate terrain; the problem is that it's limited. This resort is for practising technique on familiar slopes, not high mileage.

Beginners Beginners love the sunny nursery slopes beside the village. But higher slopes are not ideal for confidence-building: most longer runs are graded red (there's one blue).

Cross-country 24km of pretty cross-country trails rise up beyond Inneralpbach; the most testing is about 8km long and climbs 300m.

Queues Serious queues are rare, thanks to the efficient gondola and the recent chair-lift upgrades. The resort does attract some weekend trade.

Mountain restaurants The area has squeezed in many mountain restaurants. Recommended are the Hornboden at the top of the gondola, the cosy Böglalm above Inneralpbach, the Kolberhof, and the Asthütte (Kafner Ast) for the sun. Achenwirt, at the lift base, doesn't really count as a mountain restaurant, but it is enthusiastically recommended.

Schools and guides Alpbach and Alpbach Aktiv are the two main ski schools. We have had excellent reports on both in the past, but the Alpbach school currently enjoys better support. Both take children.

Facilities for children Babysitters can be arranged by the tourist office.

STAYING THERE

How to go Hotels and pensions dominate in UK packages.

Hotels Of the smart 4-star places, the Alpbacherhof (5237) and ancient Böglerhof (5227-0) get most votes. But simpler Haus Thomas (5944) – 'very clean ... you feel like part of the family' – and Haus Angelika (5339) are recommended by visitors. The Alphof (5371) is 'excellent', as long as your room is not above the disco.

Self-catering Some self-catering is available via the tourist office and the Alpbach Visitors Club.

Eating out The Reblaus, and hotels Jakober, Berghof and Post ('superb', says a recent report) are popular, as is the Wiedersbergerhorn in Inneralpbach – worth a taxi-ride. The Rossmoos Inn is also recommended for its lively Tirolean evenings and 'superb' food.

Après-ski At peak times this is typically Tirolean, with lots of noisy tea-time beer-swilling in the bars of central hotels such as the Jakober and the Post. In the evening the Waschkuchl Pub is good for a drink. The Birdy Pub and Weinstadl disco have late-night dancing.

Off the slopes Activities include pretty walks and trips to Innsbruck. There's also an indoor swimming pool and an outdoor ice-skating rink.

Bad Gastein 1080m

Spa-town resort with extensive slopes

WHAT IT COSTS

HOW IT RATES

The slopes

Snow	***
Extent	****
Experts	***
Intermediates	****
Beginners	**
Convenience	**
Queues	***
Restaurants	****

The rest

Scenery	***
Resort charm	***
Off-slope	****

- ➕ Four separate, varied areas with a huge number of slopes both above and below the tree line
- ➕ Great for confident intermediates, with lots of long, challenging reds – and great cruising and carving in the Schlossalm sector
- ➕ More reliable snow than in most low-altitude Austrian resorts, with high Sportgastein area as back-up
- ➕ Lots of good, atmospheric, traditional mountain restaurants
- ➕ Plenty of off-slope facilities, many related to its origins as a spa resort
- ➕ New Ski Alliance Amadé lift pass covers wide range of nearby resorts

- ➖ Unless you have a car, you need to choose your location with care or budget for a lot of pricey taxi rides – the lift bases are widely spread and using the public transport can be time-consuming and frustrating
- ➖ Spa-town atmosphere is not to everyone's taste, and downtown Bad Gastein can suffer from local traffic on the narrow streets; more spacious Bad Hofgastein is a better base for many people
- ➖ Near-beginners and timid intermediates must be wary of leaving the Schlossalm sector

The Gastein valley isn't widely known internationally. It deserves better: it's a great resort for competent intermediates who are happy on genuine red runs, and the list of drawbacks we've identified above is short.

With its grand hotels, trinket shops and cramped, steep setting, central Bad Gastein itself is a far cry from your standard chalet-style Austrian village. You might prefer it. If not, staying out of the centre near the lifts offers a more normal winter-sports holiday experience, and both Bad Hofgastein and Dorfgastein, down the valley, are equally well worth considering as a base.

To make the most of the valley, you need a car. With five spread-out mountains, of which only two are linked, the valley needs a top-notch public transport system, and it doesn't have one – travelling from one end of the valley to the other can take over an hour and may involve a couple of changes.

What's new

For 2000/01 the old chair-lift from the Graukogel base up to the mid-mountain station was replaced by a faster double chair-lift with a moving carpet loading system.

2001/02 will see the replacement of both of Schlossalm's Weitmoser parallel T-bars by a new six-pack.

For 2001/02, the old Gastein ski pass has been replaced by the new Ski Alliance Amadé joint lift pass – see separate box on lift passes.

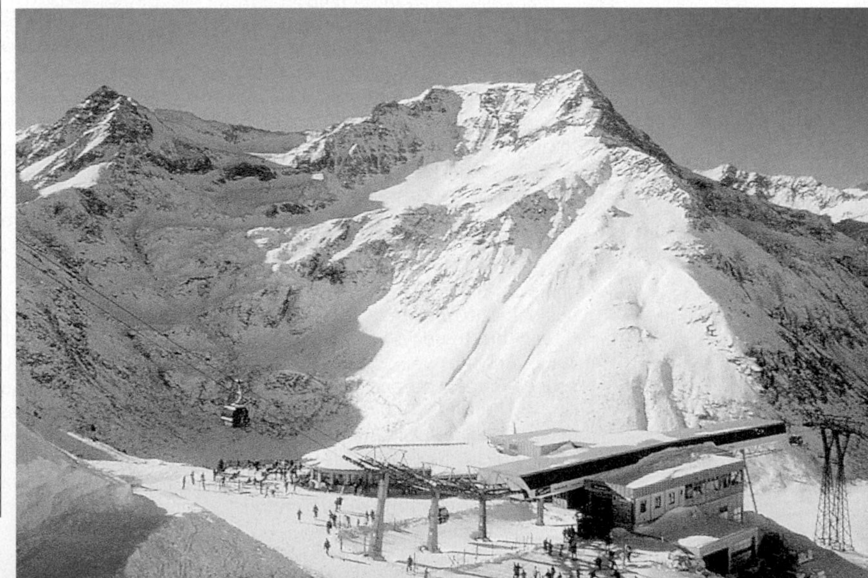

BAD GASTEIN TOURIST OFFICE

Many of the slopes are above the tree-line – though there is a healthy amount of vertical below it ➔

MOUNTAIN FACTS

Figures relate to the Gastein valley and Grossarl areas only

Altitude	840m-2685m
Lifts	51
Pistes	200km
Blue	24%
Red	66%
Black	10%
Artificial snow	60km

Recco detectors used

LIFT PASSES

2001/02 prices in euros

Ski Alliance Amadé Ski Pass

The new joint lift pass covers over 275 lifts in more than 30 ski resorts in this part of Austria: the Gastein valley and Grossarl; Salzburger Sportwelt (main areas: Flachau/ Wagrain/ St Johann and Zauchensee/ Kleinarl); Hochkönigs Winterreich (Maria Alm and neighbours). Buses, trains and road tolls between the resorts are covered by the pass.

Main pass
1-day pass 32
(low season 29)
6-day pass 150
(low-season 140)

Children
Under 15: 6-day pass 75
(low season 70)
15–19: 6-day pass 140
Under 6: free pass

Notes Morning and afternoon tickets are also available (as are tickets from 11am, 1pm and 2pm on). 1½-day and 2½-day tickets are also possible.

The resort 

Bad Gastein sits near the head of eastern Austria's Gastein valley. It is an old spa that had its heyday many years ago; it has now spread widely, but still has a compact core. Here, a bizarre combination of buildings (smart, modern, hotel-shopping-casino complex; baroque town hall; concrete multi-storey car park) are laid out in a cramped horseshoe, set in what is virtually a gorge, complete with waterfall crashing beneath the main street. It mainly attracts a quite formal German/Austrian clientele. The main road and railway bypass the centre – though it can still get choked with local traffic.

Up the hill above the centre of the town, beside the railway, is a modern suburb with more of a ski-resort feel. For easy access to the slopes, this is the place to be – a gondola gives direct access to Stubnerkogel. On the other side of the town is a second mountain, Graukogel, accessed by a chair-lift starting a bus-ride from the centre.

A few km down the valley is Bad Hofgastein – also a spa, but a more modern and less stuffy-feeling village in an open setting on the wide valley floor. The slopes of Schlossalm – linked to Stubnerkogel via the intervening valley of Angertal – are accessed by a funicular from the outskirts of Bad Hofgastein. But you need a bus to get to it from the wrong side of the sprawling resort.

Dorfgastein is a more relaxed and rustic village a little further down the valley. Dorfgastein has its own extensive slopes, accessed by chair-lifts starting well outside the village, linked with the slopes of Grossarl in the next valley to the east.

Sportgastein is a separate sector, at the head of the Gastein valley, with little in the way of resort development.

Buses and trains covered by the lift pass run between the villages and lift stations. There is a confusing range of bus services running at least hourly throughout the day, half-hourly on some routes at peak times; this sounds inadequate, and reporters confirm that it is. A car is most definitely an asset if you want to get around easily.

The new Ski Alliance Amadé lift pass covers over 30 resorts in five areas in

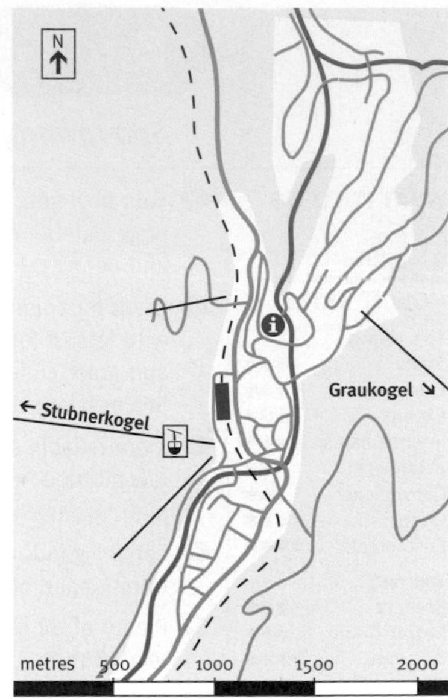

eastern Austria – see margin. The linked resorts of Alpendorf, Wagrain and Flachau are easily reached by a regular train service to St Johann im Pongau, near Alpendorf. From there it's a short hop to the parallel linked area of Kleinarl, Flachauwinkl and Zauchensee. Further afield but worth a visit is Schladming (also linked by rail but involving at least one change). Drivers can also visit Maria Alm, to the north of the Gastein valley.

Also worth visiting but not included on the lift pass are Zell am See (easily reached by rail) and snowsure Obertauern and Kaprun.

The mountains

Most of the runs are on the open slopes above the tree line, though there are runs to the lift stations at valley level. The terrain is generally quite challenging without being at all extreme – only on Schlossalm is there an extensive area of genuinely easy slopes.

THE SLOPES
Extensive but fragmented

Most people based in Bad Gastein or Bad Hofgastein naturally spend most of their time on the extensive slopes of the main mountains, Stubnerkogel and Schlossalm.

Stubnerkogel is the more challenging mountain, with blue runs forced to take roundabout routes.

boarding *The Gastein valley is starting to embrace boarding, at least on the slopes. There's a snowboard park with a half-pipe at Haitzingalm on Schlossalm, and the valley plays host to lots of specialist snowboard events. The area is not ideal for beginners – there are few easy slopes and there's still a fairly high proportion of drag-lifts (unavoidable when making the link between Bad Hofgastein and Bad Gastein, and between Dorfgastein and Grossarl). There's a fair bit to do in the evenings, but it's not as lively and as boarder-friendly as a lot of other Austrian resorts.*

There are runs in all directions from the peak giving about 500m vertical on the open slopes above the tree line and rather more in the woods below it.

Schlossalm is better suited to timid skiers, with drags and chair-lifts serving a wide area of gentle runs above mid-mountain. But the top lifts lead to some challenging terrain, and the Kleine Scharte cable-car takes you up a serious 750m vertical. The runs from Schlossalm down into Angertal are south-facing and low, but well covered by snowmaking, and there is always the option of riding down in the new gondola that serves this mountainside.

The separate and much smaller **Graukogel** is a steep, straightforward mountain. With pistes running through the forest, the area is a great asset in bad weather and quiet at other times.

The higher, more exposed slopes of **Sportgastein**, 9km south of Bad Gastein, have the best snow in the area and are served by an eight-person two-stage gondola; the descent totals an impressive 1065m, but there are few pistes – basically, variants on the long run back down to the main lift.

Down the valley, the extensive slopes of **Dorfgastein** and **Grossarl**, linked via Kreuzkogel, offer a good choice of runs arranged in three tiers – though there is no easy run to the valley. This area is unjustly neglected by those staying further up the valley.

SNOW RELIABILITY

Good for a low-altitude resort

Although the area is of typically Austrian low altitude, this part of the Alps has a relatively good snow record and there is a battery of snowmakers in crucial sections. There are a lot of lifts and runs above mid-station height, and the higher sector of Sportgastein is an important fallback.

FOR EXPERTS
More fast cruises than challenge

There are few black runs but there are long, testing reds with steepish terrain for fast cruising or mogul-bashing, depending on the conditions.

Graukogel has the World Cup slopes, and provides some challenge on its upper slopes. The other main sectors have plenty of opportunities to go off-piste, with or without hiking.

Sportgastein is worth the trip – there are off-piste possibilities on the front of the mountain, and a long off-piste trail off the back drops almost 1500m from Kreuzkogel to Heilstollen in the valley (on the bus route). Remember to check the bus times carefully or a long wait (or walk) could await you at the bottom. On the sunny opposite shoulder a reader reports 'enormous' fields of corn snow in spring.

Dorfgastein has the least demanding slopes in the area, but there is a fine black run from mid-mountain to the village.

FOR INTERMEDIATES
Not for leisurely cruisers

Good intermediates will love all the areas on the lift pass – more than enough to keep you happy for a week. A particular delight is the beautiful 8km red run, well away from the lifts, from Höhe Scharte down to Bad Hofgastein. The open north-facing slopes of Stubnerkogel down into Angertal are good, for both interest and snow-cover – try the red down to Hartlgut at the end of the day and a train-ride home after a few beers. The same is true of the Graukogel runs.

For early intermediates, the area as a whole is uncomfortably challenging. But Grossarl (linked to Dorfgastein) and Schlossalm are less demanding than other sectors, and the open bowl around the main cluster of restaurants at Schlossalm is splendid cruising (and carving) territory.

FOR BEGINNERS
Unsuitable slopes

Nursery slopes are dotted around the valley, but none combines convenience with reassuringly gentle gradients. The transition to longer runs is not an easy one, either.

FOR CROSS-COUNTRY
Extensive, but low and scattered

There are an impressive 90km of trails, but all are along the valley floor, making only the small loop at Sportgastein reasonably reliable for snow. Another drawback is the scattered nature of the loops. Bad Hofgastein is by far the best base for cross-country skiing, with long trails stretching almost to Bad Gastein.

QUEUES
Buses can be a problem

There are few problems outside the peak season in late February. The powerful gondola at Sportgastein put paid to the queues that used to arise when conditions were poor elsewhere. Morning queues to get out of the

SCHOOLS/GUIDES

2000/01 prices in euros

Bad Gastein
Manager Werner Pflaum
Classes 6 days
5hr: 10am-3pm, 1hr lunch; 3hr: 1pm-4pm
6 full days: 123
Private lessons
55 min
36 for 55 min; each additional person 9

Luigi
Manager Luigi Kravanja
Classes 6 days
5hr: 10am-3pm with 1hr lunch
6 full days: 113
Children's classes
Adults with children full-day: 36
3 full-days: 98
Private lessons
1hr or full-day
33 for 1hr; each additional person 18

CHILDCARE

Both ski schools run ski kindergartens.

There is a kindergarten at the Grüner Baum hotel, taking children aged 3 to 8, from 9.30 to 4pm. Skiing is available, with a special lift.

Bad Gastein phone numbers
From elsewhere in Austria add the prefix 06434.
From abroad use the prefix +43 6434.

valley and for the Bad Hofgastein mid-station cable-car are the worst. Peak period queues for the valley buses may be the biggest problem.

MOUNTAIN RESTAURANTS
One of the pleasures of this area

Numerous atmospheric, traditional huts are dotted around. Good value and good food are the norm. Bad Gastein's places are more expensive than those in the rest of the valley. The Jungerstube has been recommended for its 'atmosphere and traditional food'.

Bad Hofgastein's smart Kleine Scharte at Schlossalm has a large terrace, plus yodelling! Jolly places include Aeroplanstadl on the 8km Höhe Scharte run, Hamburger Skiheim again at Schlossalm (with 'barbecue in the snow') and the Panoramastube in Dorfgastein. The Wengeralm, also above Dorf, is a cosy, upmarket refuge with a good terrace. We've had good reports of the restaurants at Sportgastein.

SCHOOLS AND GUIDES
English widely spoken

The two schools have good reputations (for their English as well as the tuition). But we lack recent reports.

FACILITIES FOR CHILDREN
Reasonable

With its fragmented areas and rather serious slopes, Bad Gastein hardly seems an ideal resort for small children, but there are facilities for all-day care, of which the ski kindergarten at the Grüner Baum sounds the most inviting. There's a new 'Fun Centre' with a variety of activities for kids at the top of the Stubnerkogel gondola.

Staying there

HOW TO GO
Packages mainly to hotels

Although apartments make up nearly 15% of the total beds available, British tour operators sell mainly hotel-based packages.

Chalets The nearest thing to a catered chalet is Ski Miquel's Tannenburg, a traditional-style old hotel run as a chalet-hotel. It is a short walk from the gondola and we've had good reports of its 'good atmosphere, very pleasant communal rooms and bar, and large en-suite bedrooms'; one reporter 'couldn't praise the food highly enough' and 'would definitely return'.

Hotels This is an upmarket spa resort, and it has lots of smart hotels with good spa facilities – there are almost as many 4-star places as 3-star ones.

((((5) **Elisabethpark** (2551-0) Luxury hotel popular with Brits looking for excellent facilities, style, comfort and formality. Poorly placed for the slopes, but does run a courtesy bus.

(((4) **Salzburger Hof** (2037-0) 4-star with excellent spa facilities, a longish walk from the village gondola.

(((4) **Wildbad** (6434 3761) Luxurious 4-star within reasonable walking distance of the main lift.

(((4) **Schillerhof** (2581) Reliable 3-star in good position, opposite Graukogel lift.

(((4) **Grüner Baum** (2516-0) Splendidly secluded Relais & Châteaux place, tucked away in the Kötschachtal.

((3) **Mozart** (2686-0) Well placed for buses. Good, filling food.

((3) **Alpenblick** (2062-0) Good value, informal 3-star; well placed for the slopes.

Self-catering Plenty of apartments are available for rent but you have to book them directly.

EATING OUT
Something for most tastes

There is a fair range of restaurants, including surprisingly fine Chinese and seafood places. The Bellevue Alm, a short way up Stubnerkogel, is one of the liveliest places to eat at (it's a half-hour walk from the centre of Bad Gastein or you can take the private chair-lift up) – there's a weekly folklore evening with traditional food and dancing. The à la carte menus at the 3-star hotels Nussdorferhof and Mozart are good value. The Medeterran in the town centre has also been recommended.

APRES-SKI
Varied, but no oom-pah-pah

There are elegant tea rooms, sophisticated dances, numerous bars, discos and casinos, but the general ambience is rather subdued. This part of Austria has not imported the informal Tirolean-style 'oom-pah-pah' jollity. There is tea-dancing at the Bellevue Alm though. The Elisabethpark, Salzburger Hof, Weismayr, Eden and Lindenhof bars are all pleasant for a quiet drink. The Hexenhaüsl is a more informal little wooden schnapps bar.

↑ Grand hotel and spa buildings in the centre, chalets on the outskirts

BAD GASTEIN TOURIST OFFICE

GETTING THERE

Air Salzburg, transfer 2hr. Linz or Munich, transfer 3½hr.

Rail Mainline station in resort.

ACTIVITIES

Indoor Fitness centre (swimming, sauna, gym), thermal baths, squash, tennis, bowling, indoor golf, darts, casino, museum, theatre, concerts

Outdoor Natural ice rinks (skating and curling), sleigh rides, horse-riding, ice-climbing, toboggan runs, snow bikes, 35km cleared paths

TOURIST OFFICE

Postcode A-5640
t +43 (6434) 25310
f 253137
info@gastein.com
www.gastein.com

Haegglom's has live music, gets full of young Swedes and is 'brilliant', says a reporter. The Bunny Bar is more sophisticated than its name suggests.

The Gatz and High Life are the main clubs. The casino gives you a generous amount of free chips, so those with will power and/or luck can have a surprisingly inexpensive couple of hours there. Bowling and a casino trip are likely to be organised by tour operator reps.

OFF THE SLOPES

Great variety of things to do

Provided you don't mind the style of the place, Bad Gastein has a lot to offer off the slopes, whether you're active or not. The spas are supposed to have a regenerative effect thanks to the high radon content. The Gastein Healing Gallery is a highlight – a train takes you down into an old gold-digging tunnel where you can lie on benches inhaling radon in steam-room-like heat and humidity for a couple of hours. We find all this a bit strange: radon is a radioactive, carcinogenic gas, and we spend a fortune keeping it out of our homes in the UK. The Rock Pool is a large indoor pool hewn out of the rock, heated naturally by hot springs.

Meeting up the mountain is no problem for pedestrians, though getting to the best mountain restaurants isn't easy.

There are organised coach trips to Kitzbühel, Salzburg and Goldegg Castle, and trains run to the resorts of Zell am See and St Johann im Pongau.

Bad Hofgastein 860m

Bad Hofgastein is a sizeable, quiet, old spa village set spaciously in a broad section of the valley. It has an impressive Gothic church, traditional-style buildings, elegant quiet hotels, narrow alleys and a babbling brook. Everything is kept in pristine order.

THE RESORT

Although rather sprawling, the village has a pleasant pedestrianised area which acts as a central focus. Because of the spa 'cures' there's a relatively high number of people just pottering about during the day, notably at the curling rinks in Kurpark. The place looks very pretty in the evenings, under the soft glow of its lamps. The large spa building, the Kurzentrum, is rather a blot on the landscape.

The best location to stay is in the pedestrian zone, which is relatively handy for most things including the slopes. A high proportion of hotels are a long walk from the lift station – but there is a shuttle-bus.

THE MOUNTAINS

The Schlossalm sector above Bad Hofgastein is linked to the Stubnerkogel area via the Angertal valley, forming the largest body of slopes in the valley.

The slopes Bad Hofgastein's main access lift is a short funicular that takes you up to a mid-station at Kitzstein, above which most of the slopes are found. Here, you have a choice between a cable-car or two-stage chair up to Schlossalm.

Snowboarding The blue runs between Schlossalm and Angertal form the largest network of beginner runs in the area, however you need to negotiate a few drag-lifts to ride them all.

Snow reliability Snowmaking is fairly extensive up to 2050m. But the low altitude of the town means that snow-cover down to the bottom is unreliable.

Experts There are no real challenges on the local pistes but there is ample opportunity to go off-piste.

Intermediates Good intermediates will enjoy the local slopes, especially the long red run from Hohe Scharte back down to town.

Beginners If you stay in Bad Hofgastein, you'll have to catch a bus to the limited nursery area over at Angertal.

Cross-country Bad Hofgastein makes a fine base for cross-country when its lengthy valley-floor trails have snow.
Queues Both the funicular and the much lower capacity cable-car above it can generate big queues (30 minutes in the rush hour during peak season is not unusual). At such times, the chair is an obvious alternative to the cable-car and there's closed circuit TV at the funicular base station which shows you the situation up at the cable-car.
Mountain restaurants The Schlossalm area boasts some of the best mountain huts in the valley (see earlier section).
Schools and guides We have received complimentary reports of the ski schools in the past, but haven't heard from recent visitors.
Facilities for children The Angertal school runs the village ski kindergarten, which can be very inconvenient for parents. Lack of many English-speaking children to play with may be another drawback.

STAYING THERE

How to go Bad Hofgastein is essentially a hotel resort. The hotels tend to be large and of good quality, and many have their own fine spa facilities. Some are within easy walking distance of the funicular, a few provide courtesy transport, and most of the rest are close to bus stops.
Hotels The Palace Gastein (6715-0) is a big 4-star with superb leisure facilities, including pool and thermal baths. The elegant Germania (6232-0) is similarly comfortable.

The high-quality Norica (8391-0) is atypically modern in design, but is well positioned in the pedestrian zone. The Alpina (8475-0) is another well located 4-star, five minutes from the slopes. The Astoria (6277-0) is well appointed but quite poorly positioned and doesn't supply courtesy transport.

The Kurpark (6301) has been recommended for its good food, service and central location.
Self-catering Accommodation can be organised through the tourist office.
Eating out There is a good range of restaurants, and many hotels offer good formal dining. The Moserkeller is an intimate restaurant, and Pension Maier one of the better informal places. The Pyrkerhöhe, on the slopes just above town, is worth an evening excursion, and Da Dino is a popular pizza and pasta place.

Après-ski It is very quiet by Austrian standards. Some reporters have been disappointed; others have loved the peacefulness. There are, however, a few animated places around. The Picolo ice bar in the centre of town is lively immediately after the lifts close. Evergreen has a friendly atmosphere. Visions is a spacious modern disco, while Match Box and C'est la Vie have loud music and are full of teenagers.

Most of Bad Hofgastein's clientele prefer something more sedate. Café Weitmoser is an historic little castle popular for its cakes at tea-time. The outdoor bar of the Osterreichischer Hof is a pleasant spot to catch the last of the sun. Another atmospheric tea-time rendezvous is the Tennishalle. Later, the West End bar is a cosy place for a quiet drink. The Glocknerkeller in Hotel Zum Toni and the Rondo bar in Hotel Kärnten have live music in a low-key ambience.

The Bad Gastein casino provides taxis to and from Bad Hofgastein.
Off the slopes The Kurzentrum is at the centre of things, and is arguably an even more impressive spa facility than that of Bad Gastein. It has a splendid thermal pool, and offers a range of therapies. Other off-slope amenities include artificial and natural ice skating, indoor tennis, squash, sleigh rides. There are lovely walks.

Dorfgastein 830m

Those who prefer not to stay in large, commercialised villages should consider Dorfgastein. Prices are lower, and the atmosphere is friendlier and more informal – a contrast to its rather cold setting, sheltered from the sun.

The extensive slopes are more suitable for early intermediates than the steeps above Bad Gastein. Runs are long and varied, amid lovely scenery. Unfortunately the low-altitude nursery slopes can be cold and icy. Bad Hofgastein's funicular is 15 minutes away by bus.

There are a few shops and après-ski places, a short walk or bus-ride from the slopes. Café St Ruperb is a nice village pizzeria. The Kirchenwirt (7251) and Römerhof (7777) are comfortable hotels, while Pension Skihausl (7516) is cheaper, does good food, and is next to the slopes.

There is an outdoor heated pool with sauna-solarium, a bowling alley and a ski kindergarten.

Bad Hofgastein phone numbers
From elsewhere in Austria add the prefix 06432.
From abroad use the prefix +43 6432.

Dorfgastein phone numbers
From elsewhere in Austria add the prefix 06433.
From abroad use the prefix +43 6433.

Ellmau 800m

A quiet base from which to access the extensive Ski Welt area

WHAT IT COSTS

HOW IT RATES

The slopes

Snow	**
Extent	****
Experts	*
Intermediates	****
Beginners	****
Convenience	***
Queues	****
Restaurants	**

The rest

Scenery	***
Resort charm	***
Off-slope	***

- ⊕ Part of Ski Welt, Austria's largest linked ski and snowboard area
- ⊕ Pretty, easy slopes
- ⊕ Excellent nursery slopes (but snow reliability can be a problem)
- ⊕ Massive recent investment in snowmaking has paid off
- ⊕ Cheap by Austrian standards
- ⊕ Quiet, charming family resort – more appealing than neighbouring Söll

- ⊖ Poor natural snow record but increased snowmaking does compensate
- ⊖ Village a bus-ride from slopes
- ⊖ Mostly short runs and little for experts or good intermediates
- ⊖ Lack of nightlife other than rep-organised events
- ⊖ Ski Welt slopes can get busy at weekends and in high season

Like nearby Söll, Ellmau gives access to the large Ski Welt circuit, with good slopes for early intermediates. The resort is a pleasant, quiet alternative to Söll, and offers more amenities than other neighbours such as Scheffau.

Although Ellmau's natural snow record is poor, continuing investment in snowmakers has made a big difference. The snow may not always be in tip-top condition, but at least there'll be some. The new chairs that replace drags at Hartkaiser make it possible to move around the mountain a bit quicker now, though of course the runs will still be short.

MOUNTAIN FACTS

Altitude	620m-1830m
Lifts	93
Pistes	250km
Blue	43%
Red	48%
Black	9%
Artificial snow	130km

THE RESORT

Ellmau sits at the north-eastern corner of the Ski Welt, between St Johann and Wörgl. Although a sizeable resort, and becoming more commercialised each year, it remains quiet, with traditional chalet-style buildings, welcoming bars and shops, and a picturesque old church. Buses around the resort, necessary if you stay in the village, attract complaint for being infrequent.

Make sure you get an Ellmau guest card entitling you to various discounts, including to the Kaiserbad leisure centre.

THE MOUNTAINS

The Ski Welt is the largest mountain circuit in Austria. It links Going, Scheffau, Söll, Itter, Hopfgarten and Brixen. Most runs are not difficult, but

↑ If you find the Ski Welt circuit this quiet and with this much fresh snow, send us an e-mail and we'll fly out and join you

SKI WELT

What's new

The snowmaking capacity in the Ski Welt has been hugely increased in recent years. It now covers 130km of pistes (over half the pistes in the Ski Welt) and is the largest snowmaking facility anywhere in Austria. Almost all the pistes in the Ellmau–Going sector now have snowmaking.

For 2000/01 a high-speed six-seater chair-lift replaced a T-bar up to the Hartkaiser–Brandstadl area. This joins another six-pack that was installed for the previous season.

Another six-person chair replaced a T-bar on the link between Ellmau and Scheffau.

we receive complaints that it is slow to get about, due to the number of short connecting runs and the piste map. Westendorf is covered by the Ski Welt pass, though its local slopes are not linked. Kitzbühel, Waidring, Fieberbrunn and St Johann are in easy reach for day trips and covered by the Kitzbüheler Alpenskipass.

Slopes Ellmau is close to the best slopes in the area, above Scheffau. The funicular railway on the edge of the village takes you up to Hartkaiser, from where a fine long red (a favourite with reporters) leads down to Blaiken (Scheffau's lift station). A choice of gondola or two-stage chair goes back to Brandstadl, the start of three varied, long alternatives back to Blaiken.

Immediately beyond Brandstadl, the slopes become rather bitty; an array of short runs and lifts link Brandstadl to Zinsberg. From Zinsberg, excellent, long, south-facing pistes lead down to Brixen. Then it's a short bus-ride to Westendorf's pleasant separate area. Part-way down to Brixen you can head towards Söll, or by conquering the Hohe Salve get access to a long, west-facing run to Hopfgarten.

Ellmau and Going share a pleasant little area of slopes on Astberg, slightly apart from the rest of the area, and well suited to the unadventurous and families. One piste leads to the funicular for access to the rest of Ski Welt. The main Astberg chair is rather inconveniently positioned, midway between Ellmau and Going.

Snow reliability With a low average height, and important links that get a lot of sun, the snowmaking that the Ski Welt has installed is essential. And the Ellmau–Going sector now claims almost all its slopes are covered by snowmaking. This can, of course, only be used when it is cold enough and it cannot prevent slush and icy patches forming. The north-facing Eiberg area above Scheffau holds its snow well.

Snowboarding Ellmau is a good place to try boarding as the local slopes are easy. For decent boarders it is more limited, but there is a fun-park and quarter-pipe near Söll.

Experts There's a steep plunge off the Hohe Salve summit, and a little mogul field between Brandstadl and Neualm, but the area isn't really suitable except for those prepared to seek out off-

LIFT PASSES

2001/02 prices in euros

Ski Welt Wilder Kaiser-Brixental
Covers all lifts in the Wilder Kaiser-Brixental area from Going to Westendorf, and the ski-bus.

Main pass
1-day pass 29
6-day pass 143

Children
Under 16: 6-day pass 81
Under 6: free pass

Short-term passes
Single ascent on some lifts, passes from 11am, noon 2pm to the end of the day.

Alternative periods
5 in 7 days, 7 in 10 days, 10 in 14 days.

Alternative passes
Söll pass available (6-day pass for adults 117, for children 68) covers 12 lifts, 34km piste). Kitzbüheler Alpen-skipass covers five large ski areas – Schneewinkel (including St Johann), Ski Region Kitzbühel, Ski Welt Wilder Kaiser, Bergbahnen Wildschönau and Alpbachtal (adult 6-day 160).

CHILDCARE

Ist school has a playroom open from 9am. Hartkaiser school opened a ski nursery last season. Top school welcomes children and provides lunchtime care on request. There is also a village non-skiing kindergarten.

Phone numbers
From elsewhere in Austria add the prefix 05358.
From abroad use the prefix +43 5358.

TOURIST OFFICE

Postcode A-6352
t +43 (5358) 2301
f 3443
ellmau@netway.at
www.ellmau.com

piste opportunities. The ski route from Brandstadl down to Scheffau is a highlight and you can go off-piste with a guide from Brandstadl to Söll.
Intermediates With good snow, the Ski Welt is a paradise for early intermediates and those who love easy cruising. There are lots of blue runs and many of the reds deserve a blue grading. It is a big area and you get a feeling of travelling around. The main challenge is when the snow isn't perfect – ice and slush can make even gentle slopes seem tricky. In general the most difficult slopes are those from the mid-stations to the valleys. For timid intermediates the easy slopes of Astberg are on hand to Ellmau guests.
Beginners Ellmau has an array of good nursery slopes, now covered by snowmaking. The main ones are at the Going end, but there are some by the road to the funicular. The Astberg chair opens up a more snowsure plateau at altitude. The Brandstadl–Hartkaiser area has a section of short, easy runs, and a nice long piste running the length of the funicular which even near-beginners can manage.
Cross-country When there is snow, there are long, quite challenging trails, but trails at altitude are lacking.
Queues Continued introduction of new lifts has greatly improved this once queue-prone area.
Mountain restaurants The smaller places are fairly consistent in providing good-value food in pleasant surroundings, but the larger restaurants should be avoided. The Rübezahl above Ellmau is our favourite in the whole Ski Welt and the hut at Neualm has also been recommended. The larger self-service restaurants are functional (the Jochstube at Eiberg is an exception) and suffer queues. Going is a good spot for a quiet lunch.
Schools and guides The three schools have good reputations – except that classes can be very large. We had a good report about the Top School this year: 'Both our six-year-old and our adult friend were very pleased with the service and the way they progressed.' As well as the main schools there are mountaineering schools that organise tours in the Wilder Kaiser and the Kitzbühel mountains.
Facilities for children Ellmau is an attractive resort for families. Kindergarten facilities seem to be satisfactory and include fun ideas such as a mini train to the lifts. We have had no recent reports, however.

STAYING THERE

Ellmau has a compact centre, but its accommodation is scattered, and the bus service unreliable. Hotel position is quite important, so make sure you cater for your needs when booking.
How to go Ellmau is essentially a hotel and pension resort, though there are apartments that can be booked locally.
Hotels Bär (2395) is an elegant but relaxed Relais & Châteaux chalet, but twice the price of any other hotel. Hochfilzer (2501) is central, well equipped (it has an outdoor hot-tub) and popular with reporters.
Self-catering There is a wide variety. The Landhof apartments (with pool and sauna) were highly praised by a recent reporter: 'An absolute treasure.'
Après-ski The rep-organised events include bowling, sleigh rides, Tirolean folklore and inner-tubing, but there is little else. The Memory bar and Dorfstüberl are favourites, though both are very quiet.
Eating out The hotel Hochfilzer has a reputation for good food and the Café Bettina, midway between the funicular and town, is good for afternoon coffee and cakes.
Off the slopes The Kaiserbad leisure centre is good. There are many excursions available, including Innsbruck, Salzburg, Rattenburg and Vitipeno. St Johann in Tirol is a nice little town only a few miles away by bus. Valley walks are spoilt by the busy main road.

Going 775m

Going is a tiny, attractively rustic village, well placed for the limited but quiet slopes of the Astberg and for the vast area of nursery slopes between here and Ellmau. Prices are low, but it's not an ideal place for covering the whole of the Ski Welt on the cheap.

Going is ideal for families looking for a quiet time, particularly if they have a car for transport to Scheffau or St Johann when the Astberg's low runs have poor snow.

Hintertux 1500m

Powerful new lifts and excellent snow in a bleak setting

WHAT IT COSTS

3

HOW IT RATES

The slopes	
Snow	*****
Extent	**
Experts	***
Intermediates	***
Beginners	*
Convenience	**
Queues	***
Restaurants	**
The rest	
Scenery	***
Resort charm	***
Off-slope	*

- ⊕ One of the best glaciers in the world, with some great runs for experts and intermediates on guaranteed good snow
- ⊕ Some excellent off-piste opportunities
- ⊕ Series of high-speed gondolas have speeded up access to the skiing
- ⊕ Ziller Valley lift pass covers other nearby resorts, including Mayrhofen
- ⊕ Short transfers from Innsbruck

- ⊖ Tiny village in bleak setting
- ⊖ Little to do off the slopes
- ⊖ Not really suitable for beginners
- ⊖ Inadequate mountain restaurants

Hintertux has one of the best glaciers in the world and its slopes are open 365 days a year. It's popular with national ski teams for summer training. In winter, it provides guaranteed good snow even when lower resorts are suffering badly. The village itself is small, with few diversions. The traditional old villages of Madseit and Juns are pleasant, but Lanersbach is a more attractive option.

MOUNTAIN FACTS

for Hintertux, Eggalm and Rastkogel

Altitude	1300m-3250m
Lifts	34
Pistes	125km
Blue	30%
Red	56%
Black	14%
Artificial snow	15km

THE RESORT

Tiny Hintertux is bleakly set at the end of the Tux valley. Ringed by steep mountains except to the north, the village is often in shade. It is little more than a small collection of hotels and guest houses; there is another, smaller group of hotels near the lifts, which lie a 15-minute walk away from the village, across a car park that fills with day-visitors' cars and coaches, especially when snow is poor in lower resorts. Lanersbach, the largest of the villages in the valley, is 5km down the road. It has its own ski area, which has a new link with Mayrhofen's area (see separate chapter), and a regular free shuttle-bus to Hintertux.

THE MOUNTAINS

Hintertux's slopes are fairly extensive and, for a glacier, surprisingly challenging. We revisited it last season when it was raining in lower resorts and had a great time skiing powder.

Slopes A series of speedy new gondolas now takes you in three stages from the base at 1500m to the top of the glacier at 3250m in under 20 minutes. Two gondolas go from the base to Sommerbergalm. From here two more gondolas, including a 24-person jumbo, go up to Tuxer Ferner Haus, beside the glacier. Then a short slope takes you down to a further 24-person gondola, which whisks you up to Gefrorene Wand ('frozen face') at 3250m. From Sommerbergalm, a fast quad chair serves the slopes below Tuxer Joch; from the top of this sector, an excellent secluded off-piste run goes down to the base station. Between the top of the glacier and Tuxer Ferner Haus there are further chairs and drag-lifts to play on and links across to another 1000m-vertical chain of lifts below Grosser Kaserer on the west. Behind Gefrorene Wand is the area's one sunny piste served by a triple chair. Descent to the valley involves a short ascent to Sommerbergalm on the way, now achieved by a six-seater chair-lift.

The Ziller Super Ski pass covers all the lifts and buses in the Ziller valley.

TVB TUX / J P FANKHAUSER

In good conditions you can ski down to the village from the glacier – a huge descent ↓

What's new

Hintertux has invested millions in its lift system in recent years. For 2001/02 the big news is a link between the Eggalm/Rastkogel area above Lanersbach with Mayrhofen's slopes, via a high-speed six-seater chair from Rastkogel and with a new 150-person cable-car and a new piste to bring you back. This transforms the attraction of tiny Lanersbach as a place to stay by opening up 143km of lift-linked pistes.

This follows powerful new gondolas on the Hintertux glacier for the 2000/01 season which now whisk you from the base at 1500m to the top of the glacier at 3250m in under 20 minutes. These include the world's highest jumbo gondola, holding 24 people, going from 2660m to 3250m and a new eight-person gondola from the base area.

Snowboarding There is Europe's highest World Cup half-pipe on the glacier (a popular hang-out throughout the summer), and a fun-park. There are also some great off-piste opportunities.
Snow reliability Snow does not come more reliable than this. Even off the glacier, the other slopes are high and face north, making for very reliable snow-cover. The runs from Tuxer Ferner Haus down to Sommerbergalm have snowmaking as well.
Experts There is more to amuse experts here than on any other glacier, with a couple of serious black runs at glacier level and steep slopes and ungroomed ski routes beneath.
Intermediates The area particularly suits good or aggressive intermediates. The long runs down from Gefrorene Wand and Kaserer are fun. And there is a pleasant, tree-lined ski route to the valley from Sommerbergalm and another from Tuxer Joch. Moderate intermediates will love the glacier.
Beginners This is not a resort for beginners. But there are nursery slopes down the valley at Madseit and Juns.
Cross-country There are 20km of cross-country trails, alongside the Tux creek, between Madseit and Lanersbach.
Queues There used to be huge queues at Hintertux when snow was poor elsewhere. The splendid new lifts have largely solved this problem – but we have had one reporter complaining that there was a 'frightening' unruly crush with 'no queue management' for the jumbo gondola when the chair-lifts were closed by high winds. The main runs can get crowded, when it is best to head over to the quieter Keserer lifts and runs.
Mountain restaurants The inadequate mountain restaurants tend to get very crowded and the big self-service places lack charm. The 90-year-old Spannagelhaus is an exception and there are great views from the Gletscherhütte, at the top.
Schools and guides The ski school has a good reputation.
Facilities for children There's a children's section of the ski school, and Lanersbach has a nursery.

STAYING THERE

How to go Most hotels are large and comfortable and have spa facilities, but there are also more modest pensions.
Hotels Close to lifts are the 4-star Neuhintertux (8580) and Vierjahreszeiten (8525). We stayed in the Hintertuxerhof (85300) a short walk away and found it welcoming, with good food, sauna and steam room.

Gletscher BUS
Ski & Glacier World Zillertal 3000
59 cable cars and ski lifts - 214 km of ski runs
• New! Ski Zillertal 3000: Eggalm - Rastkogel - Penken
have now joined to form the largest all-in-one
ski area in the Ziller Valley
• Hintertux Glacier with 365 days of the best ski fun
im Zillertal
Tux
1300 - 3250 m
www.tux.at
Winter all-in packages
for seven nights including six days of Super Ski Pass and
Tux sportbus until 2 a.m. per person:
Half-board *** from € 444 and Bed and breakfast*** from € 340,-
Tux Tourist Office, A-6293 Tux
Tel. ++43/(0)5287/8506, Fax 8508
www.tux.at with search for available rooms
info@tux.at
OLPERER
3476 m
KL. KASERER
GEFRORENE WAND-SPITZE
3288 m
HINTERTUXER GLETSCHER
Tuxer-Ferner-Haus
2660 m
LÄRMSTANGE
FRAUENWAND
Tuxer Joch
HORNSPITZ
2648 m
HOHER RIFFLER
3221 m
Schlegeis-Stausee
Spannagelhaus
2531 m
Tuxer Joch-Hütte
2313 m
ZEMMGRUND
GRÜNBERG
2867 m
Sommerbergalm
2100 m
GRÜBLSPITZ
2395 m
Breitlahner
FLACHSPITZE
2246 m
Bichlalm
FLOITENGRUND
Hintertux
EGGALM
2239 m
SCHEIDEGG
2030 m
Madseit
Ginzling
PENKENJOCH 2095 m
TUXER TAL
TUX-Lanersbach
Lattenalm
Vordertanersbach
WANGLSPITZE
Gemais
NEW!
RASTKOGEL
2760 m
Lämmerbichl
Finkenberg
Wiesenhof
1930 m
GERENTSBERG
Mayrhofen
Hochschwendberg
MARCHKOPF
VOGELFREI Werbeagentur, Mayrhofen

Phone numbers
From elsewhere in Austria add the prefix 05287.
From abroad use the prefix +43 5287.

TOURIST OFFICE

Postcode A-6293
t +43 (5287) 8506
f 8508
info@tux.at
www.tux.at

Pensions Kössler (87490) and Willeiter (87492) are in the heart of the village.
Self-catering There are plenty of apartments.
Eating out Restaurants are mainly hotel-based. The Vierjahreszeiten cafe is pleasant and informal.
Après-ski Nightlife is quiet, though there are some bars and discos in the valley and a night bus between Lanersbach and Hintertux runs until 2am. The Rindererhof has a lively tea dance and a new après-ski bar is due to open at the bottom of the gondola.
Off the slopes The spa facilities are excellent but, in general, you're much better off in Mayrhofen if you don't want to use the slopes.

Lanersbach 1300m

The attraction of staying in Lanersbach and neighbouring Vorderlanersbach will be transformed by the new link for 2001/02 from the Rastkogel slopes above Vorderlanersbach directly into Mayrhofen's ski area. There are also regular free buses to Hintertux.

THE RESORT

Lanersbach is an attractive, spacious, traditional village spoilt only a little by the busy road up to Hintertux, which passes the main lift. Happily, the quiet centre near the pretty church is bypassed by the road, yet within walking distance of the gondola up to Eggalm. The village is small and uncommercialised, but it has all you need in a resort. And prices are relatively low. Vorderlanersbach is even smaller with a gondola up to the Rastkogel area.
Slopes The slopes of Eggalm, accessed by the gondola from Lanersbach, have a high point of 2300m at Beil, and a small network of pleasantly varied, mostly wooded pistes served by three other lifts and leading back to the village and across to Vorderlanersbach. From there you can take the Rastkogel gondola, which gives access to the new high-speed, six-person chair-lift link with Mayrhofen's slopes. The area is also served by two old, slow chairs and two T-bars and reaches 2500m. There is no slope directly back to the village, but there is a piste that leads to a chair-lift in the Eggalm sector.
Snow reliability Snow conditions are usually good, at least in early season; by Austrian standards, these are high slopes and there is some snowmaking on Eggalm, but the Vorderlanersbach sector, in particular, gets a lot of sun.
Snowboarding The Mayrhofen and Hintertux pipes and parks are easily accessed and floodlit boarding using the Hinterangerlift is popular.
Experts There are no pistes to challenge experts, but there is a fine off-piste route starting a short walk from Beil and finishing at the village.
Intermediates From 2001/02, there will be Mayrhofen's slopes as well the local ones to enjoy – 143km in total.
Beginners Both areas have nursery slopes but there are no ideal progression slopes.
Cross-country These are the best bases in the area for cross-country.
Queues Up to now the areas have been delightfully deserted. Whether hordes coming over from Mayrhofen will change that remains to be seen.
Mountain restaurants These are delightfully quiet.
Schools and guides The Lanersbach school now has a new rival in Luggi's, but we lack reports on either.
Facilities for children The non-ski nursery takes children from age two, the schools from four. Lanersbach is generally child-friendly, though a lack of other English-speaking children to play with could be a problem.

STAYING THERE

How to go Lanersbach is essentially a hotel resort.
Hotels The Lanersbachherof (87256) is a good 4-star with pool, sauna, steam and hot-tub close to the lifts, but it is also on the main road. The cheaper 3-star Pinzger (87541) and Alpengruss (87293) are similarly situated. In Vorderlanersbach the 3-star Kirchlerhof (8560) has 'comfortable rooms and excellent food' says a reporter.
Self-catering Quite a lot available.
Eating out Restaurants are mainly hotel-based.
Après-ski Nightlife is quiet by Austrian standards but there is a disco or two. We enjoyed the jolly Hühnerstall in Lanersbach (an old wooden building with traditional Austrian music) and the ancient wine bar in Vorderlanersbach.
Off the slopes Off-slope facilities are fairly good considering the size of the resort. Some hotels have pools, hot-tubs and fitness rooms open to non-residents. There is a tennis centre which also has squash and bowling. Mayrhofen is a worthwhile excursion and Salzburg is just within range.

Innsbruck 575m

A cultured city base for a range of little ski resorts

WHAT IT COSTS

3

Innsbruck is not a ski resort in the usual sense. It is an historic university city of 130,000 inhabitants, with a vibrant cultural life, set at a major Alpine crossroads, and a major tourist destination in summer. Its local slopes are of local interest. But the city has twice hosted the Olympic Winter Games, and it lies at the heart of a little group of resorts that share a lift pass and are accessible by efficient bus services. Among them, as it happens, is one of the three or four best glacier areas in the Alps – the Stubaier Gletscher.

MOUNTAIN FACTS

Altitude	575m-3210m
Lifts	63
Pistes	130km
Blue	35%
Red	42%
Black	23%
Artificial snow	34km

The Inn valley is a broad, flat-bottomed trench hereabouts, but Innsbruck manages to fill it from side to side. It is a sizeable city, and as you would expect from its Olympic background it has an excellent range of winter sports facilities, as well as a captivating car-free medieval core. It has smart modern shopping areas, trendy bars and restaurants, museums (including, of course, one devoted to the Olympics), concert halls, theatres, a zoo and other attractions that you might seek out on a summer holiday, but normally wouldn't expect to find when going skiing.

Winter diversions off the slopes include 300km of cross-country trails, some at valley level but others appreciably above it; curling and skating at the Olympic centre, including public ice-hockey sessions; several toboggan runs totalling 50km, the longest (above Birgitz) an impressive 10km and 960m vertical; and rides on a four-man bob at Igls.

Not the least of the attractions of staying in such a place is that you don't pay ski resort prices for anything.

There are hotels, inns and guest-houses of every standard and style, with 3-star and 4-star hotels forming the nucleus. Among the more distinctive hotels are the grand 5-star Europa Tyrol (5931), the ancient 4-star Goldener Adler (571111) and the 3-star Weisses Kreuz (59479), in the central pedestrian zone, and the 4-star art nouveau Best Western Neue Post (59476).

As well as the traditional Austrian restaurants there's a wide choice of Italian ones, plus a smattering of more exotic alternatives from Mexican to Japanese.

There is an impressive 1400m vertical of slopes on the south-facing slopes of **Seegrube-Nordkette**. The focus of the slopes at Seegrube (1905m) is reached by cable-car rising 1050m from Hungerburg on the outskirts of the city (with buses and a

There are great views from the top of Igls's slopes →

INNSBRUCK TOURISMUS / MICHAEL GILHAUS

Innsbruck & Igls phone numbers
From elsewhere in Austria add the prefix 0512.
From abroad use the prefix +43 512.

LIFT PASSES

2001/02 prices in euros

Innsbruck Gletscher Skipass
covers Seegrube–Nordkette, Patscherkofel (Igls), Axamer Lizum, Glungezer (Tulfes), Schlick 2000 (Fulpmes), Stubaier Gletscher
6-day pass 141 for adults
113 for over 60s
85 for children aged 7 to 15

Super-Ski pass
covers all the above plus one day in the Arlberg (St Anton) and one day in Kitzbühel
5 days out of 6 pass (2000/01 prices)
175 for adults
120 for children aged 7 to 15

funicular up to the cable-car departure station). Although there are red runs to the valley, the snow is not reliable. You go up here expecting to ski the red runs of 370m vertical below Seegrube, served by a chair-lift. A further stage of the cable-car rises 350m vertical to access the Karinne ski route, which is said to be fearsomely steep (up to 70 per cent gradient). You can ski it with a guide and collect not only a T-shirt but a certificate to prove you did it.

But for visitors, if not for residents, skiing usually means heading for the opposite side of the Inn trench, to east or west of the side valley that runs southwards towards the Brenner pass and Italy. The Brenner road is a major pipeline for goods and tourists travelling between Germany and Italy, and opens up the possibility of excursions to the resorts of the Dolomites, such as Selva.

The standard Innsbruck lift pass covers the lifts in all the resorts dealt with here, except Seefeld. The extraordinary Super-Skipass includes days in Kitzbühel to the east and St Anton to the west. Free ski-bus services run to and from all the lift-pass-covered areas, but only at the beginning and end of the day. A car makes life in general more convenient, especially if you are staying in one of the outlying villages rather than in downtown Innsbruck.

There are snowboard parks in the Seegrube and Axamer Lizum sectors, and at Schlick 2000 and the Stubaier Gletscher.

IGLS 900m

Igls seems almost a suburb of Innsbruck – the city trams run out to the village – but really it is a resort in its own right. Its famous downhill race course is an excellent piste.

The village of Igls is small and quiet, with not much in the way of diversions apart from the beautiful walks, the Olympic bob run and the tea shops. You can stay in Igls, and a couple of UK operators sell packages to its comfortable hotels. Most are small and concentrated in the centre of the village, a bit of a walk from the cable-car station. An exception is the family-run 5-star Sporthotel (377241), which occupies the prime site, centrally placed between the tram station and the cable-car station: 'Excellent facilities, good food and nice bar' said a reporter this year.

The skiing on Patscherkofel revolves around the excellent, varied, long red run that formed the men's downhill course in 1976, when Franz Klammer took ski racing (and the Olympic gold medal) by storm. There is a blue-run variation on this run, and off-piste possibilities. A cable-car rises 1050m from the village (and you can take it down if the lower runs are poor or shut). At the top, a chair rises a further 275m to the summit offering wonderful views over Innsbruck. A fast quad and a couple of drags serve slopes below the cable-car station. There is a short beginner lift at village level, and another a short bus-ride up the hill. We have received mixed reports on the grooming of the trails however.

In general the resort is very suitable for families with good easy slopes at village level.

Après-ski is quiet and the Pub is the only place with much life.

AXAMER LIZUM 1580m

The mountain outpost of the Inn-side village of Axams is a simple ski station and nothing more, but it does have some good slopes and reliable snow conditions.

Axamer Lizum could scarcely offer a sharper contrast to Igls. If offers much more varied slopes and a network of lifts, with the base station at a much higher altitude. The slopes here hosted all the Olympic Alpine events in 1976 except the men's downhill (which was at Igls), and this is the standard local venue for weekend sport – hence the huge car park which is the most

↑ Axams is the nearest village to Axamer Lizum, where most of the 1976 Olympic Alpine events were held

INNSBRUCK TOURISMUS / MICHAEL GILHAUS

Axams phone numbers
From elsewhere in Austria add the prefix 05234.
From abroad use the prefix +43 5234.

Neustift phone numbers
From elsewhere in Austria add the prefix 05226.
From abroad use the prefix +43 5226.

prominent feature of the 'resort'.

You can stay up here – there is a 4-star hotel at the lift base, the Lizumerhof (68244) – but it's difficult to see why you would want to. (If you want a holiday in a skiing service station with nothing to amuse you in the evenings, you might as well go somewhere that has rather more extensive slopes than these.)

The main slopes on Hoadl and Pleisen are blues and reds, almost entirely above the trees but otherwise nicely varied. The vertical of the main east-facing slopes above the main lift station is 'only' 700m, but for good skiers at least there is the possibility of a 1300m descent at the end of the day from Pleisen to the outskirts of Axams – an easy 6.5km black run.

On the opposite side of the base station, a chair-lift serves a fairly easy black slope. Beyond it are links to the slopes above Mutters, but the lifts here are closed for 2001/02 – see below.

There is accommodation not far away at lower altitude in Axams – including four 3-star hotels – and in other nearby villages such as Götzens (one 4-star hotel, two 3-star gasthofs) and Birgitz (two 3-star hotels).

INNSBRUCK TOURISMUS / MICHAEL GILHAUS

The historic city of Innsbruck makes an interesting, relatively cheap base from which to try the varied nearby slopes ↓

STUBAIER GLETSCHER 1750m

The Stubaier Gletscher is one of the best glacier ski and snowboard areas in the world and you can visit here in summer as well as winter. The nearest place to stay is picturesque Neustift, 20km away and served by regular buses.

The glacier is accessed by two alternative two-stage gondolas from the huge car park at Mutterberg (1750m). On the glacier a variety of chair- and drag-lifts allow fabulous high altitude cruising on blue and red runs, which normally have excellent snow on slopes between 3200m and 2300m. A lovely 10km ungroomed ski-route down via a deserted bowl takes you down to the valley – or if you start at the top, a descent of about 14km and 1450m vertical is possible. There is also good off-piste on the glacier to be explored with a guide.

A new 100m half-pipe has been installed on the glacier for this season and continued improvements to the lift have virtually eliminated what used to be enormous queues.

Neustift is an attractive Tirolean village halfway along the Stubai valley, with the main road bypassing the village centre. It has a small area of local slopes but what you go for is the glacier. There are lots of 4- and 3-star hotels in the village – the Sonnhof (2224) has been recommended by reporters. Most of the restaurants are hotel-based – reporters recommend Bellefonte's pizzas and the atmospheric Hoferwirt.

FULPMES 935m

Fulpmes is a sizeable village between Innsbruck and Neustift, on the way to the Stubaier Gletscher, with a fair-sized ski area of its own called Schlick 2000.

A two-stage gondola leads to a series of chair- and drag-lifts serving a few mainly short blue and red runs on the 2230m Sennjoch. There are also a couple of tougher ungroomed ski-routes and a fun-park.

MUTTERS 830m

Almost as close to Innsbruck as Igls, Mutters is a charming rustic village at the foot of long slopes of 900m vertical. Its slopes are likely to be closed this season and re-opened for the 2002/03 season.

Four new lifts are being built here, including a new access lift from just outside the village. They now look

Seefeld phone numbers
From elsewhere in Austria add the prefix 05212.
From abroad use the prefix +43 5212.

Tulfes phone numbers
From elsewhere in Austria add the prefix 05223.
From abroad use the prefix +43 5223.

INNSBRUCK TOURIST OFFICE

Postcode A-6021 Innsbruck, Burggraben 3
t +43 (512) 59850
f 59850-7
info@innsbruck.tvb.co.at
www.innsbruck-tourismus.com

← Innsbruck is surrounded by pretty villages in delightful settings
INNSBRUCK TOURISMUS / MICHAEL GILHAUS

unlikely to open until the 2002/03 season. They will serve a couple of long red runs and one long blue right back to the valley as well as shorter runs near the top of the mountain. There are also a couple of good long toboggan runs.

The half-dozen hotels in the village divide equally into 3-star and 4-star categories. There is a lively après-ski scene and great off-slope facilities including tennis courts, saunas, skating rinks and 40 curling lanes.

TULFES 920m

Tulfes gets rather overshadowed by the Olympic resorts of Igls and Axamer Lizum, but it has some worthwhile runs.
The runs are on the north-facing slopes of Glungezer. A chair-lift from a car park above the village serves red and blue runs of 600m vertical. This leads to a drag up to the tree line serving a red run of 500m vertical. And this in turn leads to two drags serving open red runs from the top height of 2305m – almost 1400m above the village.

Like Igls, the village sits on the shelf on the south side of the Inn valley. There are a dozen hotels and gasthofs, with the pick of them probably being the 3-star Neuwirt (78309).

SEEFELD 1200m

Seefeld is a pretty all-round winter holiday resort with highly recommended cross-country trails and off-slope activities, and a couple of small, separate areas of downhill slopes.
A classic postwar Tirolean tourist development, Seefeld is well designed in traditional Tirolean style, with a large pedestrian-only centre.

Seefeld's slopes are divided into two main sectors – Gschwandtkopf and Rosshütte. Both are on the outskirts and reached from most hotels by a regular free shuttle-bus.

Gschwandtkopf is a rounded hill with 300m of intermediate vertical down two main slopes, while Rosshütte is more extensive and has a fun-park and half-pipe. The top of Rosshütte can be reached by a funicular to 1800m and then a cable car to 2100m and runs end up in adjacent Hermannstall. From Rosshütte two new six-seater chairs go to the shoulder of Härmelekopf at 2050m – an improvement on the old cable-car, allowing repeated runs as well as the long red run down.

Rosshütte has some seriously steep off-piste challenges for experts and will offer intermediates an interesting day out from Innsbruck – but the terrain is of no interest for a week's stay. The nursery slopes in the central village are broad and gentle, with extensive snowmaking facilities.

Seefeld's 200km of excellent cross-country trails are some of the best in Europe and are one reason why Innsbruck has been able to hold the Winter Olympics twice and, more recently, the Nordic World Championships.

Seefeld is a very pleasant place to stay if you want a comfortable relaxed time without much downhill skiing or riding. Lots of people come here and don't venture onto the slopes. The upmarket nature of the resort is reflected in the hotels – there are seven 5-stars and almost 30 4-stars. On our last visit we stayed at the 4-star Hiltpolt (2253), which was very comfortable with good food.

Ischgl 1400m

The most underrated resort we know. Cute, snowsure, wild

WHAT IT COSTS

(5)

HOW IT RATES

The slopes	
Snow	****
Extent	****
Experts	***
Intermediates	****
Beginners	**
Convenience	***
Queues	***
Restaurants	**
The rest	
Scenery	***
Resort charm	****
Off-slope	***

What's new

The lift system is being continuously improved and now boasts three gondolas and 14 high-speed chair-lifts. For 2001/02 another high-speed eight-seater chair replaces a slow three-seater to Idjoch. Parking facilities at the base area will also be greatly increased. Last season saw a quad upgraded to an eight-seater and another quad and six-pack installed to replace existing T-bars on the Ischgl side. Over in Samnaun, yet another six-pack replaced a T-bar.

More snowmaking was installed and the Idalp-Panorama and Höllboden restaurants were rebuilt and expanded.

The resort has introduced a unique refund service if the road to and from it is shut because of avalanche danger. Alternative accommodation will be paid for as long as the road is closed.

- ⊕ Charming old Tirolean village, expanded in sympathetic fashion
- ⊕ High slopes with reliable snow
- ⊕ Lots of good intermediate runs, extending over the Swiss border to duty-free Samnaun
- ⊕ Impressive lift system
- ⊕ Very lively après-ski

- ⊖ Not ideal for beginners, for various reasons
- ⊖ Few tough runs for experts
- ⊖ A few T-bars still to be eradicated
- ⊖ Few British tour operators go there
- ⊖ Wild après-ski may not be to everyone's taste

Ischgl receives rave reviews from almost every reader who goes there but remains hardly heard of on the British market. It combines a pretty, largely traffic-free, traditional Tirolean village with extensive intermediate slopes, the most efficient lift system in Austria, some of the most reliable snow in Austria and some of the liveliest après-ski. Although there are some good-value basic pensions, it is dominated by pricey, upmarket hotels and is popular with Germans and Scandinavians. The après-ski needs to be seen to be believed – scantily clad dancing girls on the bars of plush 4-star hotels, live music in many bars, and lots of clubs. The resort is quite trendy and attracts top-draw entertainers for end-of-season open-air concerts – Elton John, Diana Ross, Madonna, Bon Jovi, Tina Turner, Bob Dylan, Rod Stewart and, last season, Sting.

The resort 

The village is in the long, narrow Paznaun valley and the lower, steep, north-facing slopes and the village get almost no sun in early season.

The main street is virtually traffic-free, with architecture that is a mixture of original buildings, traditional Tirolean-style hotels and shops and more recent additions built in the local style. The village is long and narrow, but you can walk from one end to the other in 10 minutes or so.

But it's far from flat – and the ups and downs can be quite treacherous. There's now an underground moving walkway (as in airports) from the centre of town to the Fimba gondola, which cuts out some nasty hills.

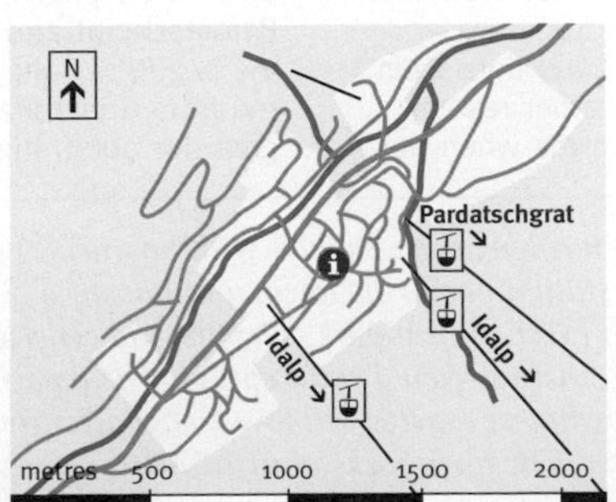

There's a selection of lively bars, an excellent sports centre and a fair number of shops to stroll round. But early evening drunks can be intrusive.

The mountains

Ischgl is a fair-sized, relatively high, snowsure area ideal for intermediates. Most pistes are red, with very few black or easy blue runs. Being able to pop over to duty-free Samnaun in Switzerland adds spice to the area. The local lift pass covers Samnaun and the more expensive Silvretta pass covers this area plus Galtür, and smaller Kappl and See – all linked by an infrequent bus service. Visiting St Anton is easy with a car.

THE SLOPES
Cross-border cruising

The main slopes start at the top of three gondolas. From both ends of the village you can get up to the sunny **Idalp** plateau, where the schools and guides meet. At the east end of town the third gondola goes about 300m higher to Pardatschgrat, from where it's an easy run down to Idalp – with the alternative of testing red and black runs towards Ischgl. Lifts radiate from

← Most of Ischgl's slopes face north or north-west, so the snow keeps in excellent condition

ISCHGL TOURIST OFFICE

LIFT PASSES

2001/02 prices in euros

VIP Skipass
Covers all lifts in Ischgl and Samnaun and local buses.

Main pass
1-day pass 37
6-day pass 159

Senior citizens
Over 60: 6-day pass 126

Children
Under 16: 6-day pass 95
Under 7: free pass

Short-term passes
Single and multi-ascent passes for main lifts; half-day pass from 11.30 (28); trial pass from 2pm (17).

Alternative periods
5 skiing days in 7, 10 days in 14.

Notes VIP Skipass is available to those staying in Ischgl, Samnaun or Mathon only on presentation of a guest card. Discounts for physically disabled and groups. Credit cards are not accepted at the lift pass office.

Alternative passes
Silvretta ski pass covers Ischgl, Samnaun, Galtür, Kappl and See (adult 6-day 186), 66 lifts and use of ski-bus; See is 15km away.

Idalp, leading to a wide variety of mainly north-west- and west-facing intermediate runs. Idalp is the hub of the slopes and can get very crowded, especially at ski school meeting time and the end of the day.

A short piste brings you to the lifts serving the **Höllenkar** bowl, leading up to the area's south-western extremity at Palinkopf. There are further lifts beyond Höllenkar, on the Fimbatal.

The mountain ridge above Idalp forms the border with Switzerland. On the Swiss side the hub of activity is **Alp Trida**, surrounded by south- and east-facing runs with great views. From here an enjoyable, scenic red run goes down to tiny Compatsch, from where there is a bus to Ravaisch – for the cable-car back – and Samnaun.

From the Palinkopf area there is a very beautiful run to Samnaun itself, down an unspoilt valley. It is not difficult, but doesn't always have ideal snow conditions and is prone to closure because of avalanche risk.

SNOW RELIABILITY
Very good

All the slopes, except the runs back to the resort, are above 2000m and much of those on the Ischgl side are north-west- or north-facing. So snow conditions are often good here even when they're poor in other resorts (which can lead to crowds when bus-loads of visitors arrive from lower resorts). There is snowmaking on some runs all the way from Idjoch to Ischgl.

FOR EXPERTS
Not much on-piste challenge

Ischgl can't compare with nearby St Anton for exciting slopes, and some of the runs marked black on the piste map barely deserve their rating. But there is plenty of beautiful off-piste to be found with a guide – and because there are few experts around, it doesn't get tracked out quickly. The wooded lower slopes of the Fimbatal are delightful in a snowstorm.

The best steep piste is the Fimba Nord run from Pardatschgrat towards Ischgl. If snow is poor near the bottom, you can do the top half of this repeatedly by catching the gondola at the mid-station. A variant will take you down a black to Velilltal, with return by chair-lift or, conditions permitting, an unpisted ski-route back to Ischgl.

FOR INTERMEDIATES
Something for everyone

Most of the slopes are wide, forgiving and ideal for intermediates (though the high slopes can be windswept and bleak in bad weather). The extent and quality of the slopes have impressed all our intermediate reporters this year.

At the tough end of the spectrum our favourite runs are those from Palinkopf down to Gampenalp and on along the valley to the secluded restaurant at Bodenalp. You can do the top of these runs repeatedly, taking the chair-lift back up from Gampenalp.

There are also interesting and challenging black runs down the Hollspitz chair, and from both the top and bottom of the drag-lift from Idjoch up to Greitspitz. The reds from Pardatschgrat and Velillscharte down the beautiful valley to Velilltal and the red from Greitspitz into Switzerland are great for quiet, high-speed cruising.

boarding *Ischgl has long been popular with boarders. Between Idalp, the main station above the town, and Idjoch, a chair-ride further up, is a big half-pipe and excellent fun-park. The lifts are generally boarder-friendly; where there is a drag, there's often a chair option. The area is well suited to beginners and intermediates; experts will love Ischgl after fresh snow, but nearby St Anton is even better. The town rocks at night, with some very lively bars.*

MOUNTAIN FACTS

Altitude 1400m-2870m	
Lifts	42
Pistes	200km
Blue	25%
Red	60%
Black	15%
Artificial snow	48km
Recco detectors used	

For easier motorway cruising, there is lots of choice, including the Swiss side, where the runs from the border down to Alp Trida should prove ideal. So should the runs that take you back to Idalp on the return journey. But there are frequent moans from intermediates about the red runs down to Ischgl itself; neither is easy, conditions can be tricky, and it can be worryingly crowded at the end of the day with too many people skiing beyond their ability (perhaps helped by a schnapps or two too many).

FOR BEGINNERS
Not ideal
Beginners go up the mountain to Idalp, where there are good, sunny, snowsure nursery slopes and a short beginners' drag-lift. The blue runs on the east side of the bowl offer pleasant progression for fast learners. But away from this area there are few runs that are ideal for the near-beginner. You'd do better to learn elsewhere and come to Ischgl as an intermediate.

FOR CROSS-COUNTRY
Plenty in the valley
There is 48km of cross-country track in the Paznaun valley between Ischgl, Galtür and Wirl. This tends to be pretty sunless, especially in early season, and is away from the main slopes, which makes meeting downhillers for lunch rather inconvenient. We've also seen people doing cross-country high up in the Fimbatal, towards Gampenalp, though this isn't an official trail. Galtür is a better choice for cross-country skiers, with 60km of loops.

QUEUES
An amazing transformation
Ischgl used to be renowned for its queues. But three gondolas now transport 6,700 people an hour out of the village and once on the mountain, high-speed chairs whizz you around. The double-decker cable-car from Samnaun has cut the queues there. The one remaining bottleneck is getting back to Idjoch from Alp Trida on the Swiss side at peak times.

MOUNTAIN RESTAURANTS
Much improved
Mountain restaurants tend to be crowded but quite good quality, with over half now offering table-service. The Paznauner Taya, above Bodenalp, is an attractive, rustic chalet, but it gets very crowded. There is table-service upstairs and often a band playing on the terrace. Down in Fimbatal is the Bodenalpe, a quieter, rustic restaurant (with table-service).

The main restaurant at Idalp has a big self-service cafeteria, and a good table-service alternative (with a sunny outdoor terrace with splendid views).

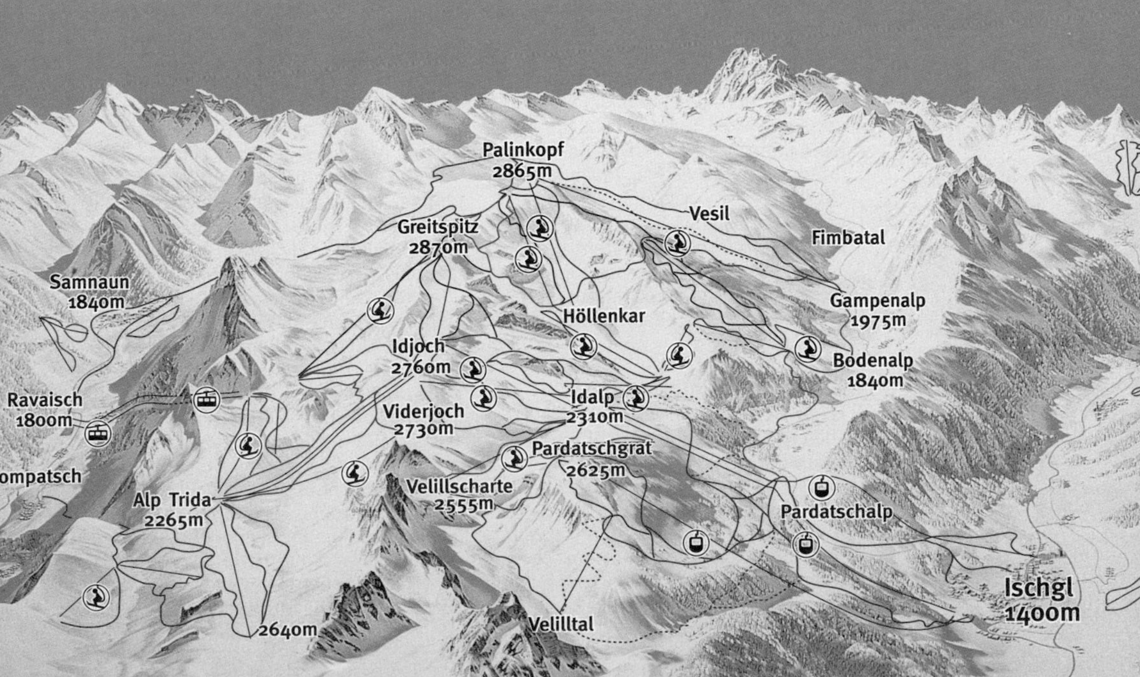

The sunny Idalp plateau is the hub of the slopes – gondolas from both ends of the village meet here, as do the ski schools, and it's a popular lunch and drinking spot, too ➔

ISCHGL TOURIST OFFICE

SCHOOLS/GUIDES

2001/02 prices in euros

Ischgl-Silvretta
Classes 6 days
4hr: 10.30-12.30 and 1.30-3.30
5 full days: 145
Children's classes
Ages: from 6
6 full days including lunch: 145
Private lessons
Half- (2hr) or full-day (4hr) 105 for half-day; each additional person 15

Ischgl phone numbers
From elsewhere in Austria add the prefix 05444.
From abroad use the prefix +43 5444.

CHILDCARE

The childcare facilities are all up the mountain at Idalp. There's a ski kindergarten for children aged 3 to 5; from age 5 they go into a slightly more demanding regime in an 'adventure garden'; lunch is included in both arrangements, which are open 6 days a week. Toilet-trained children can be left at a non-ski nursery; lunch is available.

There's also a smaller, crowded self-service nearby. The restaurant at Pardatschgrat tends to be quieter. The pizzeria at Schwarzwand has been recommended by a recent reporter.

The restaurants on the Swiss side at Alp Trida are pleasant. The Alp Bella has been recommended for a quiet time. The Marmotte has pricey table-service as well as self-service and a huge, sunny terrace. We have had a report of the remote Heidelberghütte towing lunchers 5km to it behind a snowmobile: 'A memorable trip.'

SCHOOLS AND GUIDES
Good despite language problems

The school meets up at Idalp and starts very late (10.30 to 12.30 and 1.30 to 3.30) – perhaps to allow people to get over their hangovers from the nightlife! We've had a rave report of both adult and children's classes. 'Mixed language but the best instruction I've ever had,' said an adult intermediate. 'Mixed language but excellent – very patient and small group. Can stay with class through lunch,' said a satisfied parent.

As well as normal lessons the school organises off-piste tours – this area is one of the best in the Alps for touring.

FACILITIES FOR CHILDREN
High-altitude options

The childcare facilities are all up at Idalp, but we have no first-hand reports of the service they provide. We have, however, heard from reporters who both stayed at hotel Sonne with six-month-old babies and were delighted with the private baby minder the hotel arranged.

Staying there

On or near the main street or near the Pardatsch gondola are the best places to stay. The main lift stations are an easy walk, après-ski is on your doorstep and the village tunnel now makes getting around quick and safe. Beware of accommodation across the bypass road a long way from the lifts.

HOW TO GO
Few packages

Very few British tour operators now feature Ischgl – mainly because they find it difficult to get firm allocations of affordable accommodation.

Hotels There is a good selection from luxurious and expensive to basic B&Bs.

((((5 **Trofana Royal** (600) One of Austria's most luxurious hotels, with prices to match. Sumptuous spa facilities.

((((5 **Madlein** (5226) Convenient, modern family-run chalet. Pool, sauna, steam room. Nightclub and disco.

((((5 **Elisabeth** (5411) Right by the Pardatsch gondola with lively après-ski, pool, sauna and steam room.

((((5 **Solaria** (5205) Near the Madlein and just as luxurious, but with a 'friendly family atmosphere'.

((((5 **Piz Tasna** (5277) Up hill behind church: 'Quiet location, friendly, lovely views over village, excellent food.'

(((4 **Sonne** (5302) Highly rated by reporters. In the centre of the village. Lively stube. Sauna, hot-tub, solarium.

((3 **Jägerhof** (5206) 'Jewel of a hotel' says reporter this year. Friendly, good food, large rooms. Sauna and steam.

((3 **Astoria** (5220) Comfortable B&B hotel that faces the Silvretta gondola.

((3 **Christine** (5346) Probably the best B&B in town. Near the centre of town.

GETTING THERE

Air Innsbruck, transfer 1½hr. Zürich, transfer 3hr. Munich, transfer 3hr.

Rail Landeck (30km); frequent buses from station.

ACTIVITIES

Indoor Silvretta Centre (bowling, billiards, swimming pool, sauna, steam baths, solarium), museum, library, gallery, tennis courts
Outdoor Curling, skating, sleigh rides, hiking tours, 7km floodlit toboggan run

Galtür phone numbers
From elsewhere in Austria add the prefix 05443.
From abroad use the prefix +43 5443.

TOURIST OFFICE

Postcode A-6561
t +43 (5444) 5266
f 5636
info@ischgl.com
www.ischgl.com

(3) **Erna** (5555) Small, central B&B. Firmly recommended by a reporter who has holidayed in Ischgl 20 times.
(2) **Alpenrose** (5255) Popular, good-value pension with 'basic rooms and food' close to Pardatschgratbahn.
(2) **Dorfschmeide** (5769) Small, central B&B recommended by reporter.
Self-catering Some attractive apartments are available.

EATING OUT
Plenty of choice

Our favourite places for dinner are the traditional Austrian restaurants and stubes, of which there's a wide choice. The Goldener Adler probably serves the best food around and has a splendid traditional dining room. The Wippas stube in the Sonne is lively and serves good food. For pizza try the Nona or the Trofana-Alm, which is as much a bar as a restaurant, and for fondue the Kitzloch with its galleried tables overlooking the dance floor. La Bamba is a restaurant-bar serving Mexican specialities. The Grillalm, Salner and Tirol are also popular eateries.

APRES-SKI
Very lively

Ischgl is one of the liveliest resorts in the Alps, from early afternoon on. Lots of revellers are still in their ski boots late in the evening.

The Shatzi bar of the hotel Elisabeth by the Pardatschgratbahn is the place to head for after your last run – indoor and outdoor bars and scantily clad dancing girls. Niki's Stadl across the road is a great place to sing along to live versions of the local Austrian hits. The Kitzloch is said to have lost out a bit to these two places – but had dancing on tables and congas last time we were there. The Trofana Alm is the place to head for near the Silvrettabahn. The Post hotel with its casino also has a busy outdoor bar beneath a giant umbrella. The Sunn-Alm at the hotel Sonne gets crowded and has live music. The Kuhstahl under the Sporthotel Silvretta and Fire & Ice over the road are both lively all evening. Guxa and Allegra liven up after dinner and the Golden Eagle is 'good for live bands'. The dancing girls from the Elisabeth move to the Wunderbar club at the hotel Madlein in the evenings and wear even less. Our favourite club was the place underneath the hotel Post, which has ancient Roman theme decor.

OFF THE SLOPES
No sun but a nice pool

The village gets little sun in the middle of winter, and the resort is best suited to those keen to hit the slopes. But there's no shortage of off-slope activities. There are 24km of marked walks, a 7km floodlit toboggan run and a splendid sports centre.

It's easy to get around the valley by bus. But meeting on the slopes for lunch, except at the tops of the gondolas, is a problem for pedestrians.

STAYING DOWN THE VALLEY
Too far without a car

Ischgl is fairly isolated. Landeck is the nearest big town. It has good shopping and is well positioned for trips to the surrounding resorts, including Serfaus, Nauders, Sölden and St Anton.

Galtür 1585m

Galtür has hit the headlines in recent years because of avalanche disasters, but the village centre has been rebuilt and fortified against further avalanches since the 1999 disaster.

It is a charming, peaceful, traditional village clustered around a pretty little church, amid impressive mountain scenery. Quieter, sunnier and cheaper than Ischgl, it is a good base for a quiet family holiday. There are good 3-star and 4-star hotels – the Almhof (8253), Ballunspitz (8214) and Flüchthorn (8202) have been recommended. The nightlife is quiet, but there are a couple of jolly bars.

Galtür's own slopes are not particularly challenging, but its black runs are ideal for intermediates and there are fine nursery slopes plus plenty of 'graduation' pistes for improvers. The school has a high reputation – and we've had a good report about its teaching of children.

If you intend to visit Ischgl a lot, bear in mind that the bus service isn't very frequent and finishes early.

Off-slope facilities are limited, but there's a natural ice rink and a sports centre with pool, tennis and squash.

Samnaun 1840m

Samnaun is a small, quiet village and its duty-free status makes it a useful stopover for restocking on booze and tobacco. A reporter warns that most duty-free outlets are closed on Sunday.

Kitzbühel 760m

Wonderful town and extensive slopes, but unreliable snow

WHAT IT COSTS

3

HOW IT RATES

The slopes	
Snow	**
Extent	****
Experts	***
Intermediates	****
Beginners	**
Convenience	**
Queues	**
Restaurants	****
The rest	
Scenery	***
Resort charm	****
Off-slope	*****

- ⊕ Large, attractive, varied slopes offering a sensation of travel both on- and off-piste
- ⊕ Beautiful medieval town centre
- ⊕ Vibrant nightlife
- ⊕ Plenty of off-slope amenities, both for the sporty and the not-so-sporty
- ⊕ A surprisingly large amount of cheap and cheerful accommodation
- ⊕ Jolly mountain restaurants

- ⊖ Unreliable snow especially on lower slopes (though increasing amount of snowmaking)
- ⊖ Surprisingly little expert terrain
- ⊖ Disjointed slopes, with quite a lot of bussing to get around them
- ⊖ Disappointing nursery area
- ⊖ Crowded pistes

Kitzbühel is an impressive name to drop in the pub. Its Hahnenkamm race-course is the most spectacular and challenging on the World Cup downhill circuit, helping the resort to cultivate a reputation as a special place. But the race course is untypical of Kitzbühel and often its slopes are icy, slushy or just bare. We have visited Kitz countless times, and rarely found decent snow on the lower slopes. It does of course get good snow at times and has invested serious money in snowmaking (not least to prevent its famous race being cancelled due to lack of snow, with all the resulting bad publicity). But Kitzbühel's low altitude means that its problems won't go away.

The resort has a beautiful old traffic-free centre complete with cobbled streets and lovely buildings. It has expensive, elegant hotels but there is also a huge amount of inexpensive hotel and guest-house accommodation, which attracts low-budget visitors, many of whom are young and like to party in its famous après-ski haunts.

What's new

Recent years have seen a massive investment in much-needed snowmaking. And several T-bars have been replaced by high-speed quads.

The resort

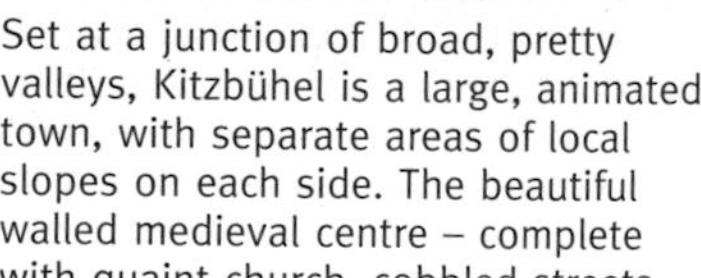

Set at a junction of broad, pretty valleys, Kitzbühel is a large, animated town, with separate areas of local slopes on each side. The beautiful walled medieval centre – complete with quaint church, cobbled streets and attractively painted buildings – is traffic-free during the day and a compelling place to stay.

But the much-publicised old town is only a small part of Kitzbühel; the resort spreads widely, and busy roads surround the old town reducing the charm factor somewhat.

Visitors used to peaceful little Austrian villages are likely to be disappointed by its urban nature. But for those who like it, the sophisticated,

MOUNTAIN FACTS

Altitude	800m-2000m
Lifts	60
Pistes	158km
Blue	50%
Red	42%
Black	8%
Artificial snow	57km
Recco detectors used	

Kitzbüheler Horn
Ecking
Maurach
Streifalm
Hahnenkamm
metres 500 1000 1500 2000 2500 3000 3500 4000

LIFT PASSES

2001/02 prices in euros

Kitzbühel
Covers all lifts in Kitzbühel, Kirchberg, Jochberg, Pass Thurn, Bichlalm and Aschau, linking buses, and swimming pool.

Main pass
1-day pass 32
6-day pass 155
(low season 143)

Senior citizens
Over 60: 6-day pass 124
Over 80: 6-day pass 86

Children
Under 19: 6-day pass 124
Under 15: 6-day pass 86
Under 6: free pass

Short-term passes
Single ascent tickets for the major lifts; hourly refunds on day tickets; day tickets can be bought in half-hourly steps from 11am.

Notes 5% reduction for groups of over 15 people. The season pass is valid in Gstaad.

Alternative passes
Kitzbüheler Alpen-skipass covers five large ski areas – Schneewinkl (St Johann), Ski Region Kitzbühel, Ski Welt Wilder Kaiser, Bergbahnen Wildschönau and Alpbachtal (adult 6-day 160).

glitzy, towny ambience and swanky shops and cafes are what 'make' Kitzbühel.

The bus service around town and to the outlying slopes has been highly praised by a regular visitor: 'More buses now, and extra ones at busy times.' But having a car is useful for visiting lots of other resorts covered by the Kitzbüheler Alpenskipass. It is also handy for visiting Salzburg and Innsbruck, though you can reach these by train too (there's a station in town).

The mountains

Snow and lift queues permitting, the mountain suits intermediates well. Although experts can find things to do, there are many better places for them. Kitz's total area is large, and includes access to sizeable Kirchberg.

THE SLOPES
Big but bitty

Kitzbühel's slopes are divided into four areas – three sizeable and one much smaller. Two of the major areas are connected by piste (almost) in one direction only.

The **Hahnenkamm** is by far the largest, and accessible from the town. It is reached via a gondola or two chair-lifts, from the top of which a choice of steep and gentle runs lead down into Ehrenbachgraben; from there several chair-lifts fan out. One takes you to the gentle peak of Steinbergkogel, the high point of the sector. Beyond is the slightly lower peak of Pengelstein. On the far side of Pengelstein several long runs lead down to the west of the resort; shuttle-buses link their end-points at Aschau and Skirast with Obwiesen, Kirchberg and Kitz. Another lift from Ehrenbachgraben goes up to Ehrenbachhöhe, the focal point of the sector, linked by lifts and runs to Kirchberg and Klausen, on the road between Kitzbühel and Kirchberg.

Pengelstein is the start of the 'ski safari' route to the higher area of **Jochberg–Pass Thurn**. The piste from Pengelstein finishes at Trampelpfad, a short walk or taxi-ride from the Jochberg lifts. A parallel piste from Steinbergkogel ends at Hechenmoos – more than a walk from Jochberg, but you can get the shuttle-bus from here. Jochberg–Pass Thurn is well worth the excursion, with better snow and fewer crowds than the local slopes – but runs are short and there are lots of T-bars. Pass Thurn is the terminus of the shuttle-bus, where it is worth ending the day to ensure a bus seat.

The very small **Bichlalm** area is of little interest except for getting away from the crowds, sampling the restaurants and working on your suntan. When conditions are good, the top station (Stuckkogel) accesses an off-piste route to Fieberbrunn.

The **Kitzbüheler Horn** is equally sunny, with repercussions on snow-cover, but many slopes are above the 1270m-high mid-station, accessed by a modern gondola starting close to the railway station, but some way from the centre. The second stage leads to the sunny Trattalm bowl at around 1660m, but the alternative cable-car takes you up to the summit of the Horn, from

KITZBÜHEL TOURIST OFFICE

Mountain restaurants and extensive views are two of Kitzbühel's delights →

where a fine, solitary east-facing piste leads down into the Raintal on the far side, with a chair-lift returning to the ridge. There are widely spread blue, red and black runs back towards town.

The piste map has recently been greatly improved by the addition of altitudes and mountain restaurants. And a reporter praised 'the Bergbahn Info people in bright jackets at the main lift stations, who offer accurate advice on closures, directions etc'.

SNOW RELIABILITY
More snowmaking now
In a normal year, snow on the lower slopes can be thin or non-existent at times (though the snow at the top is often okay). The problem is that Kitzbühel's slopes have one of the lowest average heights in the Alps. The expansion of snowmaking in recent years has improved matters when it's cold enough to make snow – major runs right down to Kitzbühel, Kirchberg, Klausen and Jochberg are covered. But many slopes still remain unprotected. The best plan is to book late when snow-cover is known to be good. Otherwise, take a car for snow-searching excursions.

FOR EXPERTS
Plan to go off-piste
Steep pistes are concentrated in the ring of runs down into the bowl of Ehrenbachgraben, the most direct of which are challenging mogul fields. Nearby is the Streif red, the basis for the famous Hahnenkamm Downhill race – see the feature panel opposite. When conditions allow, there is plenty of off-piste potential – some of it safely close to pistes, some requiring a guide.

boarding *Kitzbühel was slow off the mark with boarding, keeping to its image of World Cup Downhill venue/skier party town. However, things have changed, and now there is a half-pipe, fun-park and boarder-cross course on the Kitzbüheler Horn, an area with few drag-lifts. Many lifts in the main area are drags, but all major lifts are gondolas and chair-lifts – the area suits beginners and intermediates well. The town is lively at night, with plenty of bars and clubs; the Londoner Pub is the main place with boarder appeal.*

The Hahnenkamm Downhill

Kitzbühel's Hahnenkamm Downhill race, held in mid-January each year, is the toughest as well as one of the most famous on the World Cup circuit. On the race weekend the town is packed and there is a real carnival atmosphere, with bands, people in traditional costumes and huge (and loud) cowbells everywhere.

The race itself starts with a steep icy section before you hit the famous Mausfalle and Steilhang, where even Franz Klammer used to get worried. The course (now thankfully served by snow-guns) starts near the top of the new gondola and drops 860m to finish amid the noise and celebrations right on the edge of town. Ordinary mortals can try all but the steepest parts of the course after the race weekend, whenever the snow is good enough – it's an unpisted red ski route mostly. We tried it last season and found it steep and tricky in parts going slowly – it must be terrifying at race speeds of 80mph or more. The course is normally closed from the start of the season until after the race.

FOR INTERMEDIATES
Lots of alternatives

The Hahnenkamm area is prime intermediate terrain. Good intermediates will want to do the World Cup downhill run, of course. And the long 1000m-vertical blue to Klausen from Ehrenbachhöhe is also satisfying. The long runs down to the Kirchberg–Aschau road make a fine end to the day; earlier, they are rather spoilt by the lack of return lifts.

The east-facing Raintal run on the Horn is an excellent slope for good intermediates to hone their skills on.

The runs above Jochberg are particularly good for mixed abilities. Less adventurous types have some fine runs either side of Pengelstein, including the safari route and the Hieslegg piste above Aschau. The short, high runs at the top of the Pass Thurn area are ideal if you're more timid. There are also easy reds down to both Pass Thurn and Jochberg. Much of the Horn and Bichlalm is good cruising.

FOR BEGINNERS
Not ideal

The Hahnenkamm nursery slopes are no more than adequate, and prone to poor snow conditions. The Horn has a high, sunny nursery-like section, and precocious learners will soon be cruising home from there on the long Hagstein piste. There are plenty of other easy runs to progress to.

FOR CROSS-COUNTRY
Plentiful but low

There are nearly 35km of trails dotted about, but all are at valley level and prone to lack of snow. When the snow is good, try the quiet Reith area.

QUEUES
Still a drawback

Replacing the old Hahnenkamm cable-car with a speedy six-person gondola has vastly reduced morning queues. However, once up the mountain there are some bottlenecks at slow old chairs and drags. But we did have a report of a 'queue-free week during the February half-term' last season. Both the Horn and the Hahnenkamm can have overcrowded pistes. We have also received complaints from reporters about the warning signs for avalanche danger and closed or icy pistes being in German only.

MOUNTAIN RESTAURANTS
A highlight

'One of the reasons we keep going back,' says one of our Kitz regulars. There are many restaurants, now thankfully marked on the piste map. Avoid the large self-service places and stick to the smaller huts. On the Horn the Hornköpfl-Hütte has good food and sunny terraces. Alpenhaus is good for a lively lunch, the Gipfelhaus (recently renovated) is quieter with 'good views and food'. The 'busy' Alderhütte has

Kitzbühel phone numbers
From elsewhere in Austria add the prefix 05356.
From abroad use the prefix +43 5356.

SCHOOLS/GUIDES

2001/02 prices in euros

Hahnenkamm
Classes 6 days
4hr: 2hr am and pm
6 full days 116
Children's classes
Ages: up to 14
6 full days 134
Private lessons
On request.

Kitzbüheler Horn
Classes 6 days
4hr: 2hr am and pm
6 full days 120
Children's classes
6 full days 130
Private lessons
On request.

Red Devils
Classes 6 days
4hr: 2hr am and pm
6 full days 116
Children's classes
Ages: 4 to 11
6 full days 134
Private lessons
On request.

Total
Classes 6 days
4hr: 9.30-11.30 and 1pm-3pm
6 full days 127
Children's classes
Ages: 4 to 11
6 full days 127
Private lessons
On request.

CHILDCARE

Most schools cater for small children, offering lunchtime supervision as well as tuition on baby slopes – generally from age 3. There is no non-ski nursery, but babysitters and nannies can be hired.

GETTING THERE

Air Salzburg, transfer 1½hr. Munich, transfer 2hr. Innsbruck, transfer 1½hr.

Rail Mainline station in resort. Postbus every 15 min from station.

also been recommended. The Bichlalm in the next-door sector is also good if you want some peace. At Jochberg–Pass Thurn the Jägerwurzhütte and Trattenbachalm are recommended, and Panoramaalm has great views. The Steinbergkogel, Sonnbühel, Ochsalm, Seidalm, Fleckalm and Brandseit in the Hahnenkamm sector are good – and there are many others. The pricey Hochkitzbühel table-service restaurant at the top of the gondola has good food, but service is 'not brilliant'.

SCHOOLS AND GUIDES
Off-piste guiding a bargain

There are now half-a-dozen competing schools. The original school, Rudi Sailer's famous Red Devils, got a scathing review from a reporter this year – when an instructor told a nervous woman to 'get down now', then left her after she fell. In contrast to the 200-strong Red Devils, the other schools emphasise their small scale and personal nature. The Total school is the best established of these and includes video analysis. A reporter says: 'Never seen so many British instructors. Good reports all round.'

FACILITIES FOR CHILDREN
Not an ideal choice

Provided your children are able and willing to take classes, you can deposit them at any of the schools. The Total school has supervision until 5pm.

Staying there

The size of Kitz makes choice of location important. The old town is charming, and gives you most options. It's reasonably equidistant from the two main lift stations either side of town – both are within walking distance. However, the Hahnenkamm is very much the larger (and more snowsure) of the two areas, and many visitors prefer to be close to its gondola. But the Hahnenkamm nursery slopes are often lacking in snow, and then novices are taken up the Horn.

HOW TO GO
Mainly hotels and pensions

Kitz is essentially a hotel resort.
Chalets A few tour operators run chalet-hotels here.
Hotels There is an enormous choice, especially of 4-star and 3-star hotels.
((((5 **Tennerhof** (63181) Luxuriously converted farmhouse in big garden with renowned restaurant. Beautiful panelled rooms.
((((5 **Schloss Lebenberg** (6901) Modernised 'castle' with smart pool, and free shuttle-bus to make up for secluded but inconvenient location. Free nursery for kids aged 3-plus.
(((4 **Weisses Rössl** (625410) Smartly traditional exclusive 5-star aparthotel, recently refurbished.
(((4 **Goldener Grief** (64311) Historic inn, elegantly renovated; vaulted lobby-sitting area, panelled bar, casino.
(((4 **Jägerwirt** (6981) Modern chalet with 'helpful staff and wonderful food'. Not ideally placed.
((3 **Schweizerhof** (62735) Comfortable chalet right by Hahnenkamm gondola.
((3 **Maria Theresia** (64711) Big, comfortable modern chalet.
((3 **Hahnenhof** (62582) Small and traditional, with rustic charm.
((3 **Strasshofer** (62285) An old favourite with a regular reporter – 'central, family-run, friendly, good food, quiet rooms at back'.
1 **Mühlbergerhof** (62835) Small, friendly pension in good position.
Self-catering Although there are plenty of apartments in Kitz, very few are available through tour operators. Many of the best (and best-positioned) places are attached to hotels.

EATING OUT
Something for everyone

There is a wide range of restaurants to suit all pockets, including pizzerias and fast food outlets (even McDonald's). Some 4-star hotels have excellent restaurants; Zur Tenne ('top class hotel and food') and Maria Theresia have been recommended by reporters. But the Unterberger Stuben ('excellent but expensive' says a reporter) vies with Schwedenkapelle for the 'best in town' award. Good, cheaper places include the Huberbräu-Stüberl, Sportstüberl and Zinnkrug. Goldene Gams has both a traditional Austrian dining room and one serving modern Italian and French food. On Fridays and Saturdays you can dine at the top of the Hahnenkamm gondola.

APRES-SKI
A main attraction

Nightlife is a great selling point of Kitz. There's something for all tastes, from throbbing bars full of teenagers to quiet little places, nice cafes full of calories and self-consciously smart spots for fur-coat flaunting.

ACTIVITIES

Indoor Aquarena Centre (2 pools, 2 slides, sauna, solarium, mud baths, aerated baths, underwater massage) – free entry with lift pass, indoor tennis hall, 2 squash courts, fitness centre, beauty centre, bridge, indoor riding school, local theatre, library, museum, chess club, casino, three-screen cinema.

Outdoor Ice rink (curling and skating), horse-riding, sleigh rides, toboggan run, ballooning, ski-bobs, flying school, wildlife park, hang-gliding, paragliding, 40km of cleared walking paths (free guided tours), copper mine tours

TOURIST OFFICE

Postcode A-6370
t +43 (5356) 621550
f 62307
info@kitzbuehel.com
www.kitzbuehel.com

Kirchberg phone numbers
From elsewhere in Austria add the prefix 05357.
From abroad use the prefix +43 5357.

Much of the action starts quite late; immediately after the slopes close the town is jolly without being much livelier than many other Tirolean resorts – try the Mockingstube, near the gondola, which often has live music. Cafes Praxmair, Kortschak and Langer are among the most atmospheric tea-time places for cakes and pastries. Stamperl is a very lively bar. Later the lively Big Ben British pub, American-style Highways bar and Das Lichtl (with thousands of lights hanging from the ceiling) get packed. Seppi's Pub is recommended for sport on TV, pizzas and the eccentric owner with his 'huge moustache'. Royal, Olympia and Take 5 are the main discos. The Londoner Pub is the loudest, most crowded, smokiest place in town, with sing-along and dance-along music; you often have to queue to be allowed in as other people leave.

Tour reps organise plenty of the usual events, and there's also a casino for more formal entertainment. A reporter says there's 'table dancing at the Go Go Bar Café Romantica 2km out of town – we weren't tempted.'

OFF THE SLOPES

Plenty to do

The Aquarena leisure centre is covered by the lift pass and is very impressive, with two pools, sauna, solarium and various health activities. There's a museum, which was refurbished last season, and many concerts are organised. The railway also affords plenty of scope for excursions (eg to Salzburg and Innsbruck) and reps organise coach trips.

KITZBÜHEL TOURIST OFFICE

Kitzbühel's beautiful medieval centre is the nicest place to stay ↓

Kirchberg 850m

THE RESORT

Kirchberg is a large, spread out, lively village. If you stay in the village centre, it's a bus-ride to both the lifts up to the main slopes. If you stay near the lifts, don't expect nightlife.

THE MOUNTAIN

Slopes A gondola at Klausen on the road towards Kitzbühel takes you up into the main slopes that Kirchberg shares with Kitzbühel. The alternative route via three successive chair-lifts starts a bus-ride in the opposite direction. The separate small Gaisberg area is on the other side of the valley.
Snow reliability Under 100m higher than neighbouring Kitzbühel, Kirchberg suffers from the same unreliable snow.
Snowboarding Boarders might prefer Kitzbühel for the fun-park on the Horn.
Experts Few challenging slopes.
Intermediates The main slopes it shares with Kitzbühel are ideal for intermediates when snow is good.
Beginners There's a beginner lift and area at the foot of the Gaisberg slopes.
Cross-country Plenty of trails, but all at valley level so can be affected by lack of snow. The area above Aschau is said to be particularly good and there is a night-time track on Lake Schwarz.
Queues As with Kitzbühel poor snow conditions can cause overcrowding.
Mountain restaurants There are some good local huts.
Schools and guides There are three schools but we lack recent reports.
Facilities for children There are non-ski and ski kindergartens.

STAYING THERE

How to go There's a wide choice of chalet-style hotels and pensions.
Hotels The 4-star Klausen (2128) is close to the main gondola and has its own après-ski bar, the Sporthotel Tyrol (2787) is a bit out of the village centre with pool and spa facilities.
Self-catering There is some available.
Après-ski There's a good toboggan run on Gaisberg. Nightlife is very lively both in bars and in discos. Good bars include the traditionally Austrian Kupferstubn, the Boomerang, the Londoner (with frequent live music), Gismo and Fuchslokal.
Off the slopes A few of the hotels have swimming pools, saunas and solariums.

Lech 1450m

Charming luxury for the beautiful people

WHAT IT COSTS

6

HOW IT RATES

The slopes	
Snow	****
Extent	****
Experts	****
Intermediates	****
Beginners	****
Convenience	***
Queues	***
Restaurants	**
The rest	
Scenery	***
Resort charm	****
Off-slope	***

What's new

A couple of years ago a new hands-free electronic lift pass system was introduced for the whole Arlberg region. And over the last few years a number of high-speed chair-lifts replaced slower ones. Pavements were also widened and roads narrowed in the centre of the village.

For 2000/01 the Rüfikopf cable-car was modernised with new panoramic cabins and the restaurant at the top refurbished. The Hasensprung chair had a moving carpet installed to speed loading. The Zuger Hochlicht cable-car was taken out of service.

- Picturesque Alpine village
- Fair-sized, largely intermediate piste network plus good off-piste terrain
- Easy access to the tougher slopes of St Anton and other Arlberg resorts
- Sunny slopes with excellent snow record and extensive snowmaking
- Lively après-ski scene
- Very chic resort, with some very comfortable hotels

- Very expensive, and credit cards not always accepted by hotels, shops, restaurants or lift pass office
- Surprising dearth of atmospheric mountain restaurants other than in the mini-resort of Oberlech
- Very few tough pistes
- Blue runs back to the village are rather steep for nervous novices
- Still a few antiquated lifts

Lech and its higher neighbour Zürs are the most glamorous and expensive resorts in Austria. Their shared slopes could fairly easily be linked with those of St Anton – but then their rich and royal visitors would be forced to mingle with the hoi polloi from their equally famous but less exclusive neighbour.

Lech is for those who don't mind fur coats, do like well-groomed, snowsure, cruising pistes, and are content to enjoy a winter holiday in pampered comfort and style in a traditional Alpine village. There are challenging slopes available (mainly off-piste) and the tougher slopes of St Anton are only a short bus- or car-ride away. But it is the part-timer, who enjoys the après and the strolling as much as the winter sports, who will get the most out of the resort. It helps to have a deep pocket.

The resort

Like other glitz-and-glamour resorts, such as Courchevel and Zermatt, Lech and Zürs attract some visitors who simply want to be seen, but they also have great attractions for the rest of us.

The clientele is largely German and Austrian, with very few Brits. The fur coat count is one of the highest in the Alps. And it helps to be able to afford a helicopter transfer out: Lech lies in a high valley reachable in winter only by driving over the Flexen Pass from Stuben (Zürs is just below the top). This road can be closed for days on end after an exceptional snowfall.

The village offers cosy old-world Austrian charm with modern convenience. While some of the best hotels are right in the centre, they are not obtrusive. The village remains picturesque despite its growth and popularity – there is a domed church and covered wooden bridge over the gurgling river that runs down one side of the main street; on the other side are enticing and pricey shops. In good weather the centre is a picture of open-air cafes, dancing in the street and a fashion show of fur coats and horse-drawn carriages, with good views of the mountains on all sides.

The top hotels are owned by a few families and have large numbers of regular guests who come back year after year.

Oberlech is a small, traffic-free collection of 4-star hotels and chalets set on the piste above Lech and served by a cable-car which works until 1am, allowing access to Lech's much livelier nightlife and shopping. If you stay there, luggage is delivered efficiently from Lech to your hotel via underground tunnels, leaving you unburdened for the short, snowy walk from the cable-car.

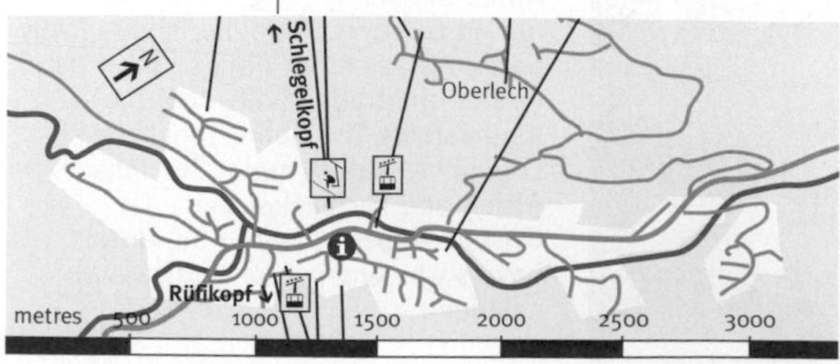

There is a huge amount of easily accessed off-piste in the high bowls above Lech →

LECH TOURISM

MOUNTAIN FACTS

Altitude 1450m-2660m

Arlberg region

Lifts	83
Pistes	260km
Blue	25%
Red	50%
Black	25%
Artificial snow	65km

Recco detectors used

LIFT PASSES

2001/02 prices in euros

Arlberg Ski pass
Covers all St Anton, St Christoph, Lech, Zürs and Stuben lifts, and linking bus between Rauz and Zürs.

Main pass
1-day pass 37
6-day pass 171

Senior citizens
Over 65: 6-day pass 146

Children
Under 15: 6-day pass 103

Short-term passes
Single ascent tickets on some lifts throughout Arlberg. Half-day tickets (adults 28) from noon, afternoon 'taster' tickets (16) from 3pm. Day tickets have by-the-hour reimbursement.

Notes Main pass also covers Klösterle (10 lifts), 7km west of Stuben. Discounts during wedel, firn and snow crystal weeks. Senior citizen pass for women over 60.

Zug is a hamlet, 3km from Lech, which connects with the Lech–Oberlech area. The small amount of accommodation is mostly bed and breakfast with one 4-star hotel, the Rote Wand, which serves the best Kaiserschmarren (a delicious chopped pancake and fruit dessert) in the Arlberg. From Lech, Zug makes a good night out: you can take a horse-drawn sleigh for a fondue at the Rote Wand, Klösterle or Auerhahn, followed by a visit to the Rote Wand disco.

As well as Lech and Zürs, the Arlberg lift pass covers St Anton, St Christoph and Stuben, all reachable by car or bus.

The mountains

Lech and Zürs are working hard on improving their links. There are still some old two-seaters, but new fast chairs have improved the network considerably in recent years. The runs, with a lot of gentle wide blues and reds, flatter leisurely cruisers and suit most of the clientele. For such an up-market resort the piste map is surprisingly unclear – see remarks in the St Anton chapter.

THE SLOPES
One-way traffic

The main slopes centre on **Oberlech**, 300m above Lech, and are reached from the village by chair-lifts as well as the cable-car. The wide, open pistes are perfect for intermediates and there is also lots of off-piste potential for experts. **Zuger Hochlicht** is the highest point of this sector and views from here, and Kriegerhorn below, are stunning. As at St Anton, the toughest runs here are now classed as 'ski routes' or 'high-alpine touring routes' rather than pistes, with all the resulting confusion (see the St Anton chapter). The only way down to Zug, for example, is by one of the ski routes.

The linked Lech–Zürs–Lech circuit can be done only in a clockwise direction. To get to Zürs you take the **Rüfikopf** cable-car from the centre of Lech. From the top there are long cruisey pistes, via a couple of lifts, down to Zürs. In school holidays and other busy periods the linking lifts and runs on the circuit can get crowded.

All the slopes at Zürs are above the tree-line, with two areas on either side of the village. The more difficult runs are off the top of **Trittkopf** – on the

boarding *Lech's upper-crust image has not stood in the way of its snowboarding development, and it continues to improve its facilities. Chairs and cable-cars, with hardly any drags, and perfectly manicured pistes make the area ideal for beginner and intermediate boarders – lessons are with the local ski school. There's also a good fun-park above the town at the Schlegelkopf, with jumps, a boarder-cross and a half-pipe. More confident boarders should hire a guide and track some powder. The town slips back to being an up-market ski destination in the evenings – bars tend to be in 4-star hotels populated by 'beautiful people'.*

A LITTLE HISTORY

The first settlers in Lech came from the Valais region of Switzerland in the 11th century. Skiing started in the early 1900s. The Lech ski school was founded in 1925 and the first T-bar was built in 1939. Patrick Ortlieb, Olympic Downhill champion at Albertville in 1992, was born and learned his skiing in Oberlech.

same side as the runs down from Lech. On the other side of the valley, chairs go up to **Seekopf** and **Zürsersee** with intermediate runs down. There's a chair up to **Muggengrat** (at 2450m the highest point of the Zürs area) from below Zürsersee. This has a blue run back under it and a lovely long red away from all the lifts back down to Zürs. But most people head for the Madloch chair. This accesses the long ski route all the way back to Lech. You can peel off part-way down and head for Zug and the chair-lift up to the Kriegerhorn above Oberlech.

SNOW RELIABILITY

One of Austria's best

Lech and Zürs both get a lot of snow, but Austrian weather station records show a big difference between them despite their proximity. Lech gets an average of almost 8m of snow between December and March, almost twice as much as St Anton and three times as much as Kitzbühel, but Zürs gets half as much again as Lech. The altitude is high by Austrian resort standards and there is excellent snowmaking on Lech's sunny lower slopes.

This combination, together with excellent grooming, means that the Lech–Zürs area normally has good coverage from December until April. And the snow is frequently better here than on St Anton's predominantly south-facing slopes.

FOR EXPERTS

Off-piste is main attraction

There are only two black pistes on the map, although there are the two types of off-piste route referred to above. The official recommendation is to visit these with a ski instructor or guide, though many ignore the advice. But experts will get a lot more out of the area if they do have a guide, as there is plenty of excellent off-piste other than the marked ski routes, much of it accessed by long traverses. Especially in fresh snow, it can be wonderful. A recent reporter found the lack of demanding runs that you can tackle on your own quite limited.

Many of the best runs start from the Steinmähder chair, which finishes just below Zuger Hochlicht. Some routes involve a short climb to access bowls of untracked powder. From the Kriegerhorn there are shorter off-piste runs down towards Lech and a very

scenic long ski route down to Zug. Most runs, however, are south- or west-facing and can suffer from getting a lot of sun.

At the end of the season, when the snow is deep and settled, the off-piste off the shoulder of the Wöstertäli from the top of the Rüfikopf cable-car down to Lech can be superb. There are also good runs from the top of the Trittkopf cable-car in the Zürs sector, including a tricky one above the Flexen Pass down to Stuben.

Experts will also enjoy cruising some of the steeper red runs and will want to visit St Anton during the week, where there are more challenging pistes as well as more off-piste.

Heli-lifts are available to a couple of remote spots.

FOR INTERMEDIATES

Flattering variety for all

The pistes in the Oberlech area are nearly all immaculately groomed blue runs, the upper ones above the trees, the lower ones in wide swathes cut through them. It is ideal territory for leisurely cruisers not wanting surprises. And even early intermediates will be able to take on the circuit to Zürs and back, the only significant red involved being the beautiful long (and not at all difficult) 'ski route' back to Lech from the top of the Madloch chair in Zürs.

More adventurous intermediates should take the fast Steinmähder chair to just below Zuger Hochlicht and from there take the scenic red run all the way to Zug (the latter part on a 'ski route' rather than a piste). And if you feel ready to have a stab at some off-piste, Lech is a good place to try it.

Zürs has many more interesting red runs, on both sides of the valley. We particularly like the west-facing reds down from the Trittkopf cable-car and the usually quiet red run back to Zürs from the Muggengrat chair, which starts in a steep bowl.

FOR BEGINNERS

Easy slopes in all areas

The main nursery slopes are in Oberlech, but there is also a nice isolated area in the village dedicated purely to beginners. There are good, easy runs to progress to, both above and below Oberlech.

LECH TOURISM

The picturesque main street has a gurgling river running between it and the slopes ↓

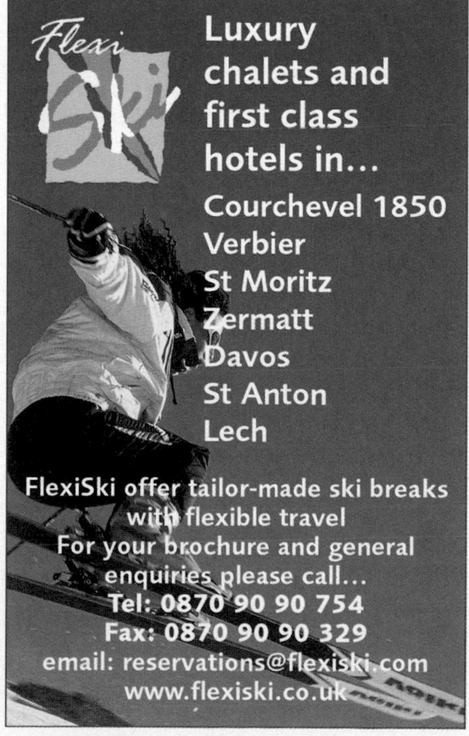

SCHOOLS/GUIDES

2000/01 prices in euros

Lech and Oberlech

Classes 6 days
4hr: 10am-noon and 1pm-3pm
6 full days 146

Children's classes
Ages: 3½ to 13
6 full days 134

Private lessons
Full day only
175 for 1 day; each additional person 15

CHILDCARE

There are ski kindergartens in Lech, Zürs and Oberlech taking children from age 3, from 9am to 4.30.

GETTING THERE

Air Zürich, transfer 2½hr. Innsbruck, transfer 1½hr.

Rail Langen (15km); 9 buses daily from station, buses connect with international trains.

Phone numbers
From elsewhere in Austria add the prefix 05583.
From abroad use the prefix +43 5583.

FOR CROSS-COUNTRY
Picturesque valley trail
There are two cross-country trails in Lech. The longer one is 15km; it begins in the centre of town and leads through the beautiful Zug valley, following the Lech river and ending up outside Zug. The other begins behind the church and goes to Stubenbach (another hamlet in the Lech area). In Zürs there is a 3km track starting at Zürs and going to the Flexen Pass. This starts at 1600m and climbs to 1800m.

QUEUES
No recent complaints
The region proudly boasts that it limits numbers on the slopes to 14,000 a day for a more enjoyable experience, and there have been significant lift improvements in recent years. On our last visit we thought traffic on the circuit through Zürs, particularly, has improved thanks to the fast Zürsersee quad chair-lift which has relieved pressure on the Seekopf chair. But there are one or two remaining problems – notably the Schlegelkopf fast quad out of Lech. The crucial Madloch chair at the top of the Zürs area must still generate queues of people on the one-way circuit going to Lech and so must the cable-cars. But recent reporters have not complained of any problems.

MOUNTAIN RESTAURANTS
Few atmospheric places
There are surprisingly few cosy Alpine restaurants in the area. A jolly area for lunch is at Oberlech, where there are several big sunny terraces set prettily around the piste; our favourite is the Goldener Berg (which has also been highly recommended by a recent reporter). Quite often you'll find a live band playing outside one of the restaurants.

One of the best mountain restaurants is Seekopf (reached by the Seekopf chair-lift) which has a lovely sun terrace. The traditional Schröfli Alm, not marked on the piste map but just above the bottom of the Seekopf lift, is a pleasant traditional chalet. Also popular is the self-service Palmenalpe above Zug, but it does get very crowded. The Mohnenfluh, at the top of the Lech nursery lift, does 'excellent' food.

Many people go back to the villages for lunch. For a gourmet blow-out in Zürs, Chesa Verde in the hotel Edelweiss and the hotel Hirlanda's restaurant both feature in the Gault-Millau gourmet's guide (as does the Arlberg in Lech), and the Lorünser does a 'magnificent' buffet. The hotel Rote Wand in Zug serves more casual fare. Café Schneider in Lech serves good local dishes. Hus Nr 8, at the end of the route back from Zürs, is 300 years old and has good traditional food.

SCHOOLS AND GUIDES
Excellent in parts
The ski schools of Lech, Oberlech and Zürs all have good reputations and the instructors speak good English. Group lessons are divided into no fewer than 10 ability levels. One past visitor enjoyed 'the best tuition I have ever had'. In peak periods, you should book both instructors and guides well in advance, however, as many are hired regularly every year by an exclusive clientele.

FACILITIES FOR CHILDREN
Oberlech's fine, but expensive
Oberlech does make an excellent choice for families who can afford it, particularly as it's so convenient for the slopes. The Sonnenburg and the Goldener Berg have in-house kindergartens. Reporters tell us the Oberlech school is great for children, with small classes, good English spoken and lunch offered.

Staying there

Lech is big enough for some of the cheaper accommodation to be quite a walk from the lifts. Unless you're heavily into nightlife, staying up in Oberlech is very attractive.

HOW TO GO
Surprising variety
There is quite a variety of accommodation from luxury hotels through to simple but spotless B&Bs.
Hotels There are three 5-star hotels, over 30 4-star and countless more modest places.
(((((5) **Arlberg** (2134) Patronised by royalty and celebrities. Elegantly rustic chalet, centrally placed. Pool.
(((((5) **Post** (2206) Lovely old Relais & Chateaux place on main street with pool and sauna.
((((4) **Krone** (2551) One of the oldest buildings in the village, in a prime spot by the river.
((((4) **Tannbergerhof** (2202) Splendidly

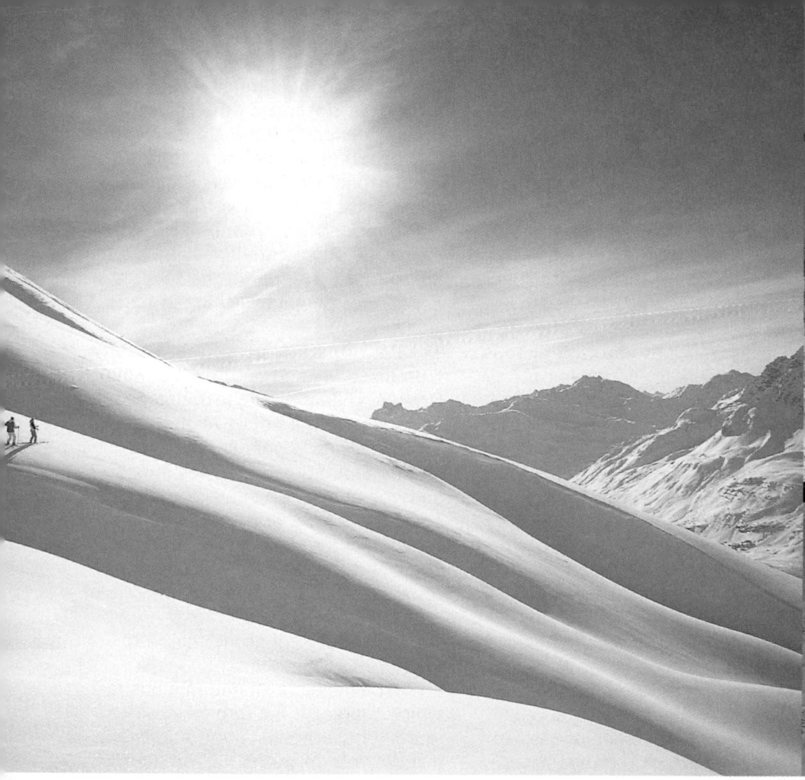

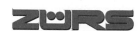

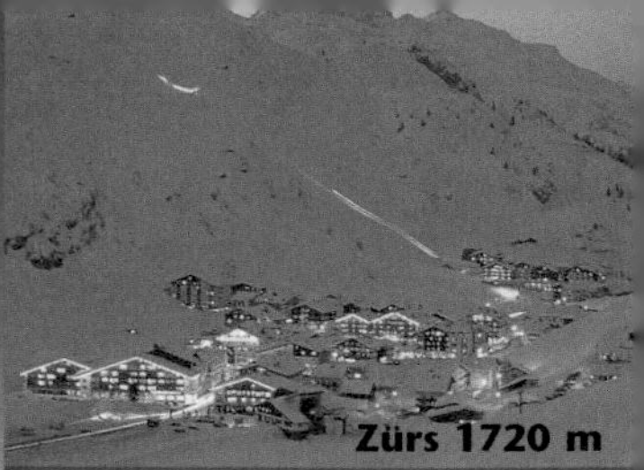
Zürs 1720 m

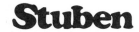

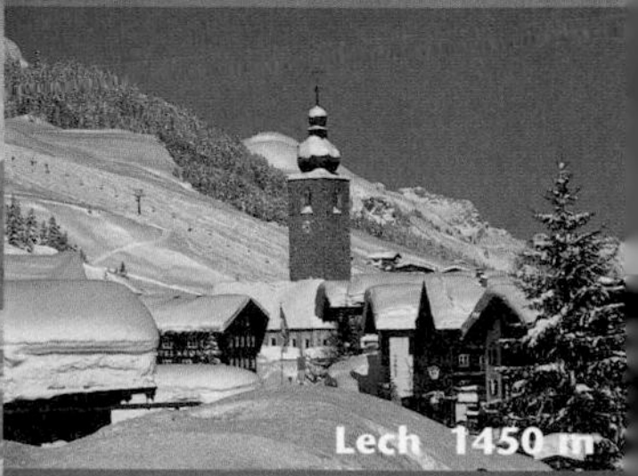
Lech 1450 m

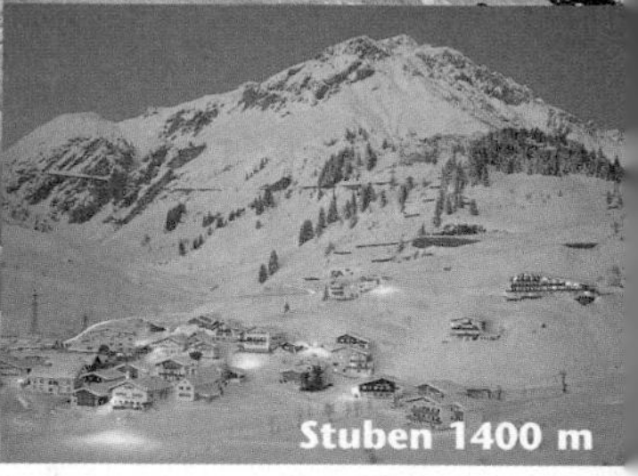
Stuben 1400 m

ACTIVITIES

Indoor Tennis, hotel swimming pools and saunas, squash, museum, art gallery, hotel spas
Outdoor 30km of cleared walking paths, toboggan run (from Oberlech), artificial ice rink (skating, curling), sleigh rides, billiards, helicopter rides

Lech and Zürs phone numbers
From elsewhere in Austria add the prefix 05583.
From abroad use the prefix +43 5583.

TOURIST OFFICE

Postcode A-6764
t +43 (5583) 21610
f 3155
info@lech-zuers.at
www.lech-zuers.at

atmospheric inn on main street, with outdoor bar and hugely popular disco (tea-time as well as later). Pool.
(((④ **Haldenhof** (2444) Friendly and well run, with antiques and a fine collection of prints and paintings.
(((④ **Burg Vital** (Oberlech) (2291-930) 'Excellent – no criticism,' says a reporter this year of this plush luxury hotel with pool, sauna and squash.
(((④ **Burg** (2291-0) Sister hotel of Burg Vital – same facilities and with famous outdoor umbrella bar by cable-car.
(((④ **Sonnenburg** (Oberlech) (2147) Luxury on-piste chalet (popular for lunch). Good children's facilities. Pool.
(((④ **Monzabon** (2104) Excellent restaurant and wine cellar. Pool.
(② **Haus Angerhof** (2418) Beautiful ancient pension, with wood panels and quaint little windows.
(② **Haus Fernsicht** (2432) Pension with spa facilities.
(② **Haus Rudboden** (2220) Right by the nursery slopes.
Self-catering There is lots available to independent bookers.
Chalets There are a couple of catered chalets run by British tour operators.

EATING OUT
Not necessarily expensive

There are over 50 restaurants in Lech, nearly all of them in hotels. For reasonably priced meals try the Montana, which serves French cuisine and has an excellent wine cellar, the Krone, Ambrosius (above a shopping arcade), or the Post, which serves Austrian nouvelle-type food. The Madlochblick has a typically Austrian restaurant, very cosy with good solid food. Hus Nr 8 is one of the best non-hotel restaurants (see mountain restaurants) and does good fondue. For pasta and other Italian fare there is Pizzeria Charly. In Oberlech there is a good fondue at the Alte Goldener Berg, a tavern built in 1432. In Zug the Rote Wand is excellent for fondues and a good night out. Also try the Alphorn, the Klösterle and the Olympia.

A reporter recommends Gasthaus Älpele near Zug, 3km from the road – up the valley on the cross-country route, for its atmosphere and good food. Transport is arranged by the restaurant in the form of covered wagons attached to a snowcat.

APRES-SKI
Good but pricey

The umbrella bar of the Burg hotel at Oberlech is popular immediately after the slopes close, as is the champagne bar in Oberlech's Hotel Montana. Then the 'beautiful people' head for the Hotel Krone's ice bar which has a lovely setting by the river, or to the outdoor bar of the Tannbergerhof. Inside the Tannbergerhof, there's a tea dance disco. The bar in the Strolz store is good for people-watching in bad weather.

Later on, the Arlberg Hotel's Scotch Club disco (owned and run by former Olympic champion, Egon Zimmermann), and those in the hotels Almhof-Schneider and Krone liven up. The latter's Side Step specialises in 60s and 70s music. S'Pfefferkörndl is a good place for a drink, and you can get a steak or pizza there until late. The smart, modern-style Fux bar and restaurant has live music and is one of the latest trendy places.

For a change of scene, the Rote Wand in Zug has a disco.

Taxi James is a shared minibus taxi, which charges a flat fare for any journey in Lech/Zürs – you phone and it picks you up within half an hour.

OFF THE SLOPES
Poseurs' paradise

Many visitors to Lech don't indulge in sports. If you're armed with limitless funds the shopping possibilities are enticing, and the main street is often filled with fur-clad browsers. Strolz's plush emporium in the centre of town is a good place to up the rate at which you're spending euros.

It's easy for pedestrians to get to Oberlech or Zug to meet friends for lunch on the slopes – or for skiers and boarders to get back to the village. The village outdoor bars make ideal posing positions – but make sure you are immaculately groomed or you'll feel out of place. An excursion to St Anton, to see how the other half live, is possible, though Lech clientele may feel more at home getting off the bus at chic St Christoph. For the more active there are 30km of walking paths and a variety of sporting activities – the walk along the river to Zug is especially beautiful.

Zürs 1720m

Ten minutes' drive towards St Anton from Lech, Zürs is almost on the Flexen Pass, with good snow virtually guaranteed. Zürs was a tiny hamlet

Stuben phone numbers
From elsewhere in Austria add the prefix 05582.
From abroad use the prefix +43 5582.

ZÜRS TOURIST OFFICE

Zürs and Lech are set in a high valley (a dead end in winter) and the access road can be closed for days after exceptional snowfalls ↓

used only for farming during the summer until (in the late 1890s) the Flexen Pass road was built and Zürs began to develop, entering the winter sports scene in the early 20th century.

The village is even more exclusive than Lech, with no hotels of less than 3-star standing, and a dozen 4-star and 5-star hotels around which life revolves. But the opulence is less overt here. There are few shops. Nightlife is quiet. There's a disco in the Edelweiss hotel (26620) and a piano bar in the Alpenhof (2191). Mathie's-Stüble and Kaminstüble are worth trying, as is Vernissage, at the Skiclub Alpenrose (22710), which is reported to be the best nightspot in town. Serious dining means the Zürserhof (25130) and the Lorünser (22540); make sure your wallet will stand a visit before you go – credit cards are not accepted. For something cheaper, try spaghetti in the basement of the Edelweiss. Princess Caroline (who stays at the Lorünser) once managed this here at 5am. All phone numbers given are for 4- or 5-star hotels.

Zürs has its own school, but many of the instructors are booked for the entire season by regular clients, and more than 80% of them are hired privately. The resort also has its own kindergarten.

Stuben 1405m

Stuben is linked by lifts and pistes to St Anton, but is on the Vorarlberg side of the Arlberg pass (St Anton is over in the Tirol). There are infrequent but timetabled buses between the village and Lech and Zürs.

Dating back to the 13th century, Stuben is a small, unspoilt village where personal service and quiet friendliness are the order of the day. Modern developments are kept to a minimum. The only concessions to the new era are a few unobtrusive hotels, a school, two or three bars, a couple of banks and a few little shops. The old church and traditional buildings, usually snow-covered, make Stuben a really charming Alpine village.

The north-facing local slopes retain snow well, though the queue-free but slow village chair can be a cold ride. A quicker and warmer way to get to St Anton in the morning, if you have a car, is to drive down the road to Rauz.

Stuben has sunny nursery slopes separate from the main slopes, but lack of progression runs make it unsuitable for beginners. Evenings are quiet, but several places have a pleasant atmosphere. The charming old Post (7610) is a very comfortable 4-star renowned for its fine restaurant.

Mayrhofen 630m

Bigger means better for 2002

WHAT IT COSTS

HOW IT RATES

The slopes

Snow	***
Extent	***
Experts	*
Intermediates	***
Beginners	**
Convenience	*
Queues	*
Restaurants	****

The rest

Scenery	***
Resort charm	***
Off-slope	****

What's new

Massive investment in lifts in recent years includes new high-capacity gondolas out of town and from Hippach and high-speed chairs on the mountain.

2001/02 will see a new 150-person cable-car from the slopes to link with Rastkogel above Vorderlanersbach, previously a bus-ride away. This area links to the Eggalm area above Lanersbach. The link back will be by a new high-speed six-pack. All this will mean a 40% increase in Mayrhofen's terrain to a total of 143km.

Back in the existing Mayrhofen area the old double chair up to Schafskopf will be replaced by a high-speed six-pack for 2001/02. Another new six-pack will be built in this area, opening up new runs.

- ⊕ New lifts for 2001/02 will increase local terrain by 40%
- ⊕ Snowsure by Tirol standards, plus the Hintertux glacier nearby
- ⊕ Various nearby areas on the same lift pass, and reached by free bus
- ⊕ Lively après-ski – though it's easily avoided if you prefer peace
- ⊕ Excellent children's amenities
- ⊕ Wide range of off-slope facilities

- ⊖ Two widely separated areas of slopes and no runs back to the village itself from the main area
- ⊖ Best beginner area served by a queue-prone cable-car, itself a longish walk or bus-ride from town
- ⊖ Slopes can be crowded, with some long lift queues
- ⊖ Mainly short runs
- ⊖ Little to challenge experts

Mayrhofen has long been a British favourite. Many young or youngish visitors like it for its lively nightlife. But it's also an excellent family resort, with highly regarded kindergartens and ski schools and a fun pool with special children's area. The liveliest of the nightlife is confined to a few very popular places, easily avoided by families.

Two new lifts for the 2001/02 season will link Mayrhofen's existing slopes with those of Lanersbach and Vorderlanersbach, increasing the local pistes by around 40% and giving some much needed longer runs – most of the existing runs are very short (typically 300m to 400m vertical). Intermediates who are willing to travel around on the free buses can have an enjoyably varied week visiting different ski areas on the Ziller valley lift pass, including the excellent glacier up at Hintertux. But if you plan to spend a lot of time at the glacier, consider staying in Lanersbach, described in the Hintertux chapter.

Despite recent lift improvements, Mayrhofen itself is not a convenient resort – the main lift station is at one end of town and you have to catch the lift down as well as up, or end up a bus-ride from town.

The resort 

Mayrhofen is a fairly large resort sitting in the flat-bottomed Zillertal. Most shops, bars and restaurants are on the one main, long, largely pedestrianised, street, with hotels and pensions spread over a wider area. As the village has grown, architecture has been kept traditional.

Despite its reputation for lively après-ski, Mayrhofen is not dominated by lager louts. They exist, but tend to gather in a few easily avoided bars. The central hotels are mainly slightly upmarket, and overall the resort feels pleasantly civilised.

The Penken lift station is towards one end of the main street, while the Ahorn cable-car is out in the suburbs, about 1km from the centre. The free bus service is frequent and efficient, though it finishes early (5pm).

MAYRHOFEN TOURIST BOARD / K HRUSCHKA

Mayrhofen is prettily set in a wide valley, with mountains on three sides →

MOUNTAIN FACTS

Altitude	630m-2500m
Lifts	45
Pistes	143km
Blue	29%
Red	59%
Black	12%
Artificial snow	78km

LIFT PASSES

2001/02 prices in euros

Mayrhofen/Zillertal
Coverage depends on period – see notes.

Main pass
1-day pass 28
6-day pass (including glacier) 159

Children
15 to 18: 6-day pass (including glacier) 127
6 to 14: 6-day pass (including glacier) 95.50
Under 6: free pass

Short-term passes
Passes available from 11am, noon and 2pm.

Alternative periods
Zillertaler ski pass available for 4 days' skiing in 6, 5 days in 7, 6 days in 7 and 10 days in 14.

Notes Up to 3-day passes covers Penken, Horberg-Gerent, Ahorn, Rastkogel and Eggalm areas only; 4-day and over includes all 149 Ziller valley lifts (including Hintertux glacier), 478km of piste, ski-bus and railway.

Alternative passes
Zillertaler ski pass also available without Hintertux glacier (6 days 132 for adults, 106 for 15- to 18-year olds, 79 for 6- to 14-year olds).

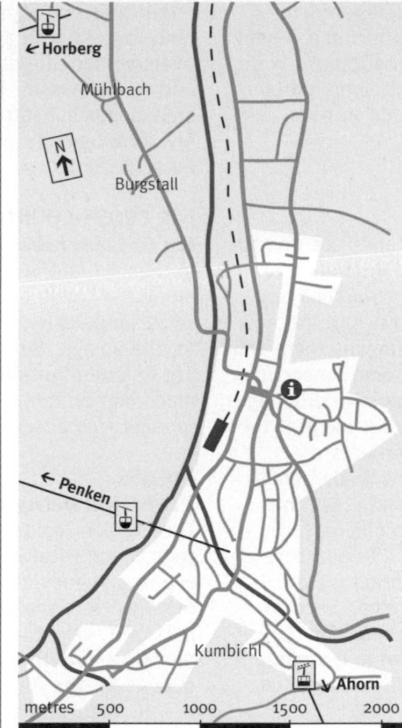

The mountains

Of Mayrhofen's two areas of slopes Penken/Rastkogel/Eggalm is mainly suitable for intermediates, and Ahorn mainly for beginners. Neither has much for experts. A frequent free bus serves other resorts covered by the pass, notably Hintertux and Gerlos – but we hear you may need to be up early to beat the queues. If you buy a lift pass in advance through a tour operator, make sure it covers the Hintertux glacier. Signposting and marking of runs is good.

THE SLOPES
Highly inconvenient

Lifts to the two main sectors are a longish walk or a bus-ride apart, and you often have to take them down as well as up. The largest area is **Penken,** accessed by the main jumbo gondola from one end of town. It is also accessible via the (new for last season) 8-person Hippach gondola, a bus-ride away and by the gondolas from Finkenberg and Vorderlanersbach in the Hintertux valley. You cannot get back to Mayrhofen on snow – you either catch the main gondola down or, if cover is good, you can get back to both Finkenberg and Hippach on snow (the Finkenberg piste is a path, graded red, and there's an unpisted ski-route to Hippach). The Penken area will link via a new cable-car from the 2001/02 season with the **Rastkogel** and **Eggalm** areas previously accessible only by the valley bus, forming a linked area of 128km of pistes – see What's New and the Hintertux chapter.

The only trail from the mountains to Mayrhofen (the outskirts of it) is a winding run down from **Ahorn** (black on the map), so moving between mountains or lunching in the village means a serious waste of slope time.

SNOW RELIABILITY
Good by Austrian standards

Although the highest lift goes no higher than 2500m, the area is reasonably good for snow-cover because (apart from the unreliable valley runs) all of Mayrhofen's slopes are above 1580m. Snowmaking covers nearly all the main slopes in the Penken/Horberg/Gerent area. And there is one of the best glaciers in the Alps within day-trip range, at Hintertux.

FOR EXPERTS
Not ideal

Mayrhofen itself doesn't have much for experts. But there are worthwhile challenges to be found, including off-piste areas, you can go touring, and reporters staying here and visiting the other resorts on the valley lift pass have been more than happy. The long unpisted trail to Hippach is the only

boarding *Mayrhofen is not ideal for learning to snowboard – the nursery slopes are inconvenient and the lifts are mainly drags. For intermediates though, the slopes are good and the gondolas and chair-lifts mean that few drags have to be negotiated. There is a fun-park and a half-pipe, where the British Championships have been held for the last two seasons, in the Penken area. More advanced riders will enjoy the Hintertux glacier, further up the valley – it's a boarder-friendly place (except for the drag-lifts), with Europe's highest World Cup half-pipe and some good off-piste possibilities. Budget prices and lively nightlife make Mayrhofen a popular boarder destination.*

SKI CLUB of Great Britain
Ski Club Rep Resort
skiclub.co.uk
020 8410 2000
skiers@skiclub.co.uk

testing local slope, and is rarely in good order – as a report from a repeat visitor testifies: 'Snow conditions were the best I've known, yet some parts were extremely tricky due to poor snow cover.'

FOR INTERMEDIATES
On the tough side

Most of Mayrhofen's slopes are on the steep side of the usual intermediate range and so great for confident or competent intermediates. And the new expansion for 2001/02 means there will be more of them and some longer runs too, making the area more interesting for avid piste-bashers. But most of the runs in the main Penken area are short. And there are few really gentle blue runs, making the area less than ideal for nervous intermediates. Overcrowding of many lifts and runs can add to the intimidation factor.

If you're willing to travel, each of the main mountains covered by the Ziller valley pass is large and varied enough for an interesting day out.

FOR BEGINNERS
Overrated: big drawbacks

Despite its reputation for teaching, Mayrhofen is not ideal for beginners. The Ahorn nursery slopes are excellent – high, extensive and sunny – but it's a rather tiresome journey to reach them (and to get home again). The overcrowded slopes and restaurants add to the hassle. The Penken nursery area is less satisfactory. And there are few long blues to progress to from the nursery slopes.

FOR CROSS-COUNTRY
Go to Lanersbach

In theory there is a fine 20km trail along the valley to Zell am Ziller, plus small loops conveniently in, or close to, the village. But snow at 600m is not reliable. Vorderlanersbach has a much higher, more snowsure trail running to Madseit.

QUEUES
Problems being tackled

The Penken jumbo-gondola opened in 1995, theoretically ending morning and evening queues among the worst in the Alps. But one peak-period visitor tells of a 'disorganised scrum' for boarding. And there are still lengthy queues for the Ahorn cable-car.

The increased capacity of both the Penken and Hornberg lifts from the valley means the slopes can now get very crowded, causing queues for some lifts. Slow, old lifts are being quickly replaced by fast new ones but that has added to the crowds on the

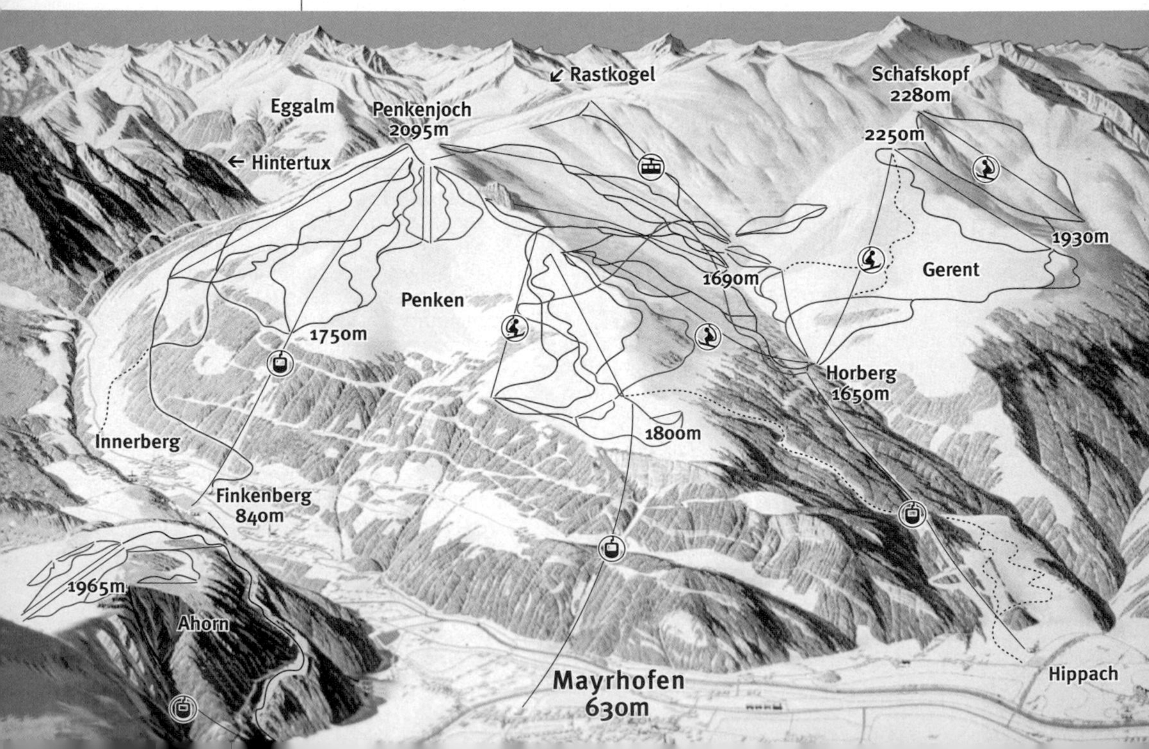

SCHOOLS/GUIDES

Mayrhofen Red Profis
2001/02 prices in euros
Classes 5 days
2½hr: 10am-12.30 or 1pm-3.30
5 half days 89
Children's classes
Ages: 4 to 14
6 full days 158
Private lessons
Hourly and daily
36 for 1hr; each additional person 14

Mayrhofen Total
2000/01 prices in euros
Classes 6 days
4hr: 10am-noon and 1pm-3pm
6 full days 115
Children's classes
Ages: 4 to 14
6 full days including lunch 172
Private lessons
Hourly and daily
40 for 1hr

Mount Everest
2000/01 prices in euros
Classes 6 days
4hr: 10am-noon and 1pm-3pm
6 full days 112
Children's classes
Ages: 5 to 14
6 full days including lunch 169
Private lessons
Hourly
36 for 1hr; each additional person 15

Phone numbers
From elsewhere in Austria add the prefix 05285.
From abroad use the prefix +43 5285.

CHILDCARE

All three ski schools run children's classes for children aged 4 to 14 where lunch is provided. Two of them run ski kindergartens for children aged 1 to 4.

Wuppy's Kinderland non-skiing nursery at the fun pool complex takes children aged 3 months to 7 years, 9am to 5pm, Monday to Friday.

pistes. The new expansion into the previously quiet Rastkogel and Eggalm areas may dissipate the crowds and solve this problem. Buses to and from the more out-of-town gondolas are often crowded, especially the Finkenberg one, which also serves Hintertux.

MOUNTAIN RESTAURANTS
Plenty of them

Most of Penken's many mountain restaurants are attractive and serve good-value food but can get crowded– Vroni's is highly recommended. The tiny Hiatamadl hut serves simple, wholesome home-cooked food. The Schneekar restaurant at the top of the Gerent section has been recommended. To get away from the crowds try the restaurants on Eggalm. The Ahorn's restaurants are inadequate for the hordes using them.

SCHOOLS AND GUIDES
Excellent reputation

Mayrhofen's popularity is founded on its three schools and a high proportion of guests take lessons. We have received many positive reports over the years and one recent reporter was delighted with her two-day private lesson with the Total school.

FACILITIES FOR CHILDREN
Good but inconvenient

Mayrhofen has put childcare at the centre of its pitch, and all the facilities are excellent. But you may prefer to take your offspring to resorts where they don't have to be bussed around and ferried up and down the mountain.

Staying there 

The village is rather long and sprawling, and the lift stations are at one end of it. Although there is a free bus service, location is important. The original centre, around the market, church, tourist office and bus/railway stations, is now on the edge of things. The most convenient area is on the main street, as close as possible to the Penken gondola station.

HOW TO GO
Plenty of mainstream packages

There is a wide choice of hotel holidays available from UK tour operators, but few catered chalets.
Hotels There are dozens of cheap pensions, but most British visitors stay in the larger, better hotels. Most of the hotels packaged by UK tour operators are centrally located close to village amenities, a walk from the Penken gondola. One reporter warns that it can be a bit noisy near the centre of the resort.

(5) **Elisabeth** (6767) The resort's only 5-star hotel, an opulent chalet in a fair position near the post office.
(4) **Manni's** (63301-0) Well-placed, smartly done out; pool.
(4) **Kramerwirt** (6700) Lovely Tirolean hotel simply oozing character. A recent visitor reports 'friendly and helpful staff, comfortable rooms, varied and interesting half-board menu'.
(3) **Strass** (6705) Best placed of the 4-stars, very close to the Penken gondola. Lively bars, disco, fitness centre, solarium, pool and children's playroom, but rooms lack style.
(3) **Rose** (62229) Well placed, a few minutes' walk from the centre. Good food.
(3) **Neue Post** (62131) Convenient family-run 4-star on the main street – 'good food and nice big rooms'.
(3) **Waldheim** (62211) Smallish, cosy 3-star gasthof, not far from the Penken lift.
(3) **St Georg** (62792-0) Poorly positioned for amenities, but ideal for those wanting a multi-facility quality hotel in peaceful surroundings.
(3) **Jägerhof** (62540) Another peaceful hotel with good facilities, mid-way between the two lifts.
(1) **Claudia** (62361), **Monika** (62178) Cheap little twin guest houses in a good position.
(1) **Kumbichl** (62371), **Kumbichlhof** (62458) Adjoining pensions, next to the Ahorn cable-car.

EATING OUT
Wide choice

Most visitors are on half-board, but there is a large choice of restaurants catering for most tastes and budgets. The Hotel Rose has a particularly good, informal restaurant. The restaurants in the Kramerwirt, Neuhaus ('excellent standards of food and service'), and Gasthaus Ländenhof are also recommended. Manni's is good for pizzas ('a genuine pleasure to eat there') and Kaiser Brundl, opposite the Neuhaus, has been recommended for its extensive menu (traditional and international dishes) and good food, though one reporter complained of appalling service on one occasion.

GETTING THERE

Air Salzburg, transfer 3hr. Munich, transfer 2½hr. Innsbruck, transfer 1hr.

Rail Local line through to resort; regular buses from station.

ACTIVITIES

Indoor Bowling, adventure pool, 2 hotel pools open to the public, massage, sauna, squash, fitness centre, indoor tennis centre at Hotel Berghof (3 courts, coaching available), indoor riding-school, pool and billiards, cinema

Outdoor Ice-skating rink, curling, horse-riding, horse sleigh rides, 45km cleared paths, hang-gliding, paragliding, tobogganing (2 runs of 2.5km), snowrafting

TOURIST OFFICE

Postcode A-6290
t +43 (5285) 6760
f 6760 33
mayrhofen@zillertal.tirol.at
www.mayrhofen.com

Wirthaus zum Griena is a 'wonderful old wooden building offering traditional farmhouse cuisine'.

APRES-SKI
Lively but not rowdy

Nightlife is a great selling point. Mayrhofen has all the standard Tirolean-style entertainments, such as folk dancing, bier kellers and tea dances, along with bowling, sleigh rides, tobogganing, but also some seriously lively bars and discos.

At close of play, the Happy End umbrella bar, at the top of the Penken gondola, is lively and the Ice bar, in the hotel Strass (near the Penken gondola base station), gets packed out. Micky's is another recommended après-ski bar.

Some of the other bars in the Strass are rocking places later on – the Lobby bar has live music and the Sport's Arena club has a good atmosphere. Mo's American theme bar and Scotland Yard are also popular with reporters. The Schlussel disco can be 'wild'. Try Am Kamin (in the hotel Elisabeth) if you're after more Manhattan than Mayrhofen. The Neue Post bar and the Passage are recommended for a quiet drink.

OFF THE SLOPES
Good for all

The village travel agency arranges trips to Italy, and Innsbruck is easily reached by train. There are also good walks and sports amenities, including the swimming pool complex – with saunas, solariums and lots of other fun features. Pedestrians have no trouble getting up the mountain to meet friends for lunch.

Finkenberg 840m

Finkenberg is a much smaller, quieter village than Mayrhofen.

THE RESORT

Finkenberg is no more than a collection of traditional-style hotels, bars, cafes and private homes spread along the busy, steep main road between Mayrhofen and Lanersbach. Most hotels are within walking distance of the gondola, and many of the more distant ones run minibuses to the lift station.

THE MOUNTAIN

Finkenberg shares Mayrhofen's main Penken slopes. The gondola up to Ahorn is a short bus-ride away.

Slopes A gondola gives good direct access to the Penken slopes.

Snow reliability The local slopes are not as well-endowed with snowmaking as Mayrhofen's.

Snowboarding There are no special facilities.

Experts Not much challenge, though we did find a black run not marked on the piste map.

Intermediates The whole newly expanded area opens up from the top of the gondola.

Beginners The village nursery slope, given good snow, means beginners do not need to buy the full lift pass. But it's a sunless spot, and good conditions are far from certain.

Cross-country Cross-country skiers have to get a bus up to Lanersbach.

Queues The gondola gives queue-free access to the Penken.

Mountain restaurants See the recommendations given for Mayrhofen.

Schools and guides There are two schools. The Finkenberg School has a particularly good reputation.

Facilities for children There's a non-ski crèche, and the ski nursery takes children from age four.

STAYING THERE

How to go A couple of tour operators go there.

Hotels There are a fair number. The Sporthotel Stock (6775) has great spa facilities and is owned by the family of the famous former downhill champion Leonard Stock.

Eating out Restaurants are mostly hotel-based.

Après-ski Finkenberg is quiet in the evenings. The main après-ski spots are the Laterndl Pub and Finkennest, and there are rep-organised events such as tobogganing and bowling. Mayrhofen is a short taxi-ride away.

Off the slopes Swimming, curling and ice-skating are available, and the local walks have been recommended.

Montafon 650m–1430m

Extensive slopes, well off the beaten package path

WHAT IT COSTS

The 40km-long Montafon valley contains no less than eleven resorts and five main lift systems. Packages from the UK are few (accommodation on a serious scale is not easy to find), but for the independent traveller the valley is well worth a look – especially the Silvretta Nova area (linking Gaschurn and St Gallenkirch) and high, tiny, isolated Gargellen.

What's new

Last year saw the installation of new snowmaking on Golm, with snow-guns all the way down to the Vandans gondola base station.

A new six-pack and a quad chair-lift are being installed in the Silvretta Nova area for next season. Other developments include a new six-pack to replace the T-bar to the top of Grüneck at Golm, and a new eight-seater chair-lift to replace the parallel T-bars in the Seebliga area on Hochjoch – two new red runs and a blue are also being added here.

The Montafon is neglected by the UK travel trade, partly because of its location in Vorarlberg, west of the Arlberg pass – easy enough to reach from Zürich (and from the German motorways), but not so easy from the standard Austrian charter airport of Salzburg. More importantly, the valley lacks the large hotels that mainstream UK tour operators apparently need.

The valley runs south-east from the medieval city of Bludenz – parallel with the nearby Swiss border. The first sizeable community you come to is Vandans, linked to its own ski area by gondola. Next are Schruns, at the foot of one of the major lift networks, and Tschagguns, across the valley. Further up are St Gallenkirch and Gaschurn, at opposite ends of the other major area. Up a side valley to the south of St Gallenkirch is Gargellen, close to the Swiss border – a tiny village, but quite widely known in Britain.

The valley road goes on up to Partenen, where it climbs steeply to Bielerhöhe and the Silvrettasee dam at about 2000m, at the foot of glaciers and Piz Buin (of suncream fame) – the highest peak in the Vorarlberg at 3312m. In summer you can drive over the pass to Galtür and Ischgl. In winter Bielerhöhe is a great launch pad for ski-tours, and there are high, snowsure cross-country trails totalling 20km on and around the frozen lake. You get there by taking a cable-car from Partenen to Trominier, and then a mini-bus – free with the area lift pass.

There are more ordinary cross-country trails along the valley, and an 11km woodland trail at Kristberg (1440m), above Silbertal – up a side valley to the east of Schruns. Trails total 100km.

The shared valley lift pass covers the respectable post-bus service and the Bludenz-Schruns trains, as well as the 62 lifts – so exploration of the valley does not require a car.

The top heights hereabouts – going from 2000m to 2400m – are no match

ALPENSZENE MONTAFON

Schruns is a towny little place, but there are rustic villages to stay in as well →

MOUNTAIN FACTS

Altitude	700m-2395m
Lifts	62
Pistes	209km
Blue	54%
Red	32%
Black	14%
Artificial snow	62km

Gargellen phone numbers
From elsewhere in Austria add the prefix 05557.
From abroad use the prefix +43 5557.

ALPENSZENE MONTAFON

Extensive slopes, above and below the tree line ↓

for the nearby Arlberg resorts; but there is plenty of skiing above the mid-mountain lift stations at around 1500m, and most of the slopes are not excessively sunny, so snow reliability (aided by snowmaking on quite a big scale) is reasonable. Practically all of the pistes are accurately graded blue or red, but there are plentiful off-piste opportunities (including 37km of 'ski routes'). There are snowboard fun-parks in most sectors and a half-pipe at Silvretta Nova.

The Montafon ski school operates in each of the different ski areas – once you've bought your vouchers, you can chop and change between the schools in the different areas if you wish. The schools operate eight ski kindergartens in the valley – taking children from age three.

Tobogganing is popular, and there are several runs on the different mountains – the Silvretta Nova's 6km floodlit run down to the Gortipohl lift base being the most impressive.

GARGELLEN 1425m

Gargellen is a real backwater – a tiny village tucked up a side valley, with a small but varied piste network on Schafberg that is blissfully quiet.

The new eight-person gondola from the village up to the Schafberg slopes seems rather out of place in this tiny collection of hotels and guest houses, huddled in the bottom of a steep-sided, narrow valley. The runs it takes you to are gentle, with not much to choose between the blues and reds; but there is lots of off-piste terrain, and a couple of excellent away-from-the-lifts runs at the extremities of the area. There are three pleasant mountain restaurants, including two rustic huts at the tree line – the Obwaldhütte and the Kessekhütte. The former holds a weekly après-ski party after the lifts close, followed by a torchlit descent. (Slide shows and bridge are more typical evening entertainments.) There are several pistes to the valley, and with care you can ski to the door of the hotel Madrisa (6331) among others. Behind the hotel is a rather steep nursery slope. The altitude of the village (the highest in the valley) and north-east facing slopes make for reasonable snow reliability despite the lack of artificial backup.

A special feature is the day-tour around the Madrisa – a small-scale off-piste adventure taking you over to Klosters in Switzerland. It involves a 300m climb, but is otherwise easy.

SCHRUNS 700m

Schruns is the most rounded resort in the valley – a towny little place, with the shops in its car-free centre catering for locals and for summer tourists.

A cable-car and gondola go up from points outside the village into the Hochjoch slopes, now accessible also from the Silbertal around the side of the mountain. Above the trees is a fair-sized area of easy blue runs, with the occasional red alternative. There are restaurants at strategic points – the Wormser Hütte is a climbing refuge with 'stunning' views. Parents can leave their kids under supervision at the huge new NTC Dreamland children's facility at the top of the cable-car, by the new skier services building. The blue run from Kreuzjoch back to Schruns is about 12km long and over 1600m vertical. Snow-guns cover the long home-run from the top of the cable-car at 1850m all the way back down to town.

Easily accessible across the valley are the limited slopes of Grabs, above the rather formless village of Tschagguns, and the more extensive area of Golm, where a gondola goes from Vandans up to a handful of chairs and drags serving easy slopes above the trees, and offering a vertical

descent of over 1400m. Newly installed snowmaking has improved the cover on the single red run to the Vandans valley station. The children's ski area at the kindergarten near the gondola base has also benefited from new snowmaking.

As you are reminded at every opportunity, Ernest Hemingway ensconced himself in Schruns in 1925/26, and his favourite drinking table in the hotel Taube (72384) is still there to be admired. The Löwen (7141) and the Alpenhof Messmer (726640) are elegant, well-equipped 4-stars with big pools, the former a hub of the après-ski scene.

GASCHURN / ST GALLENKIRCH 900m
Silvretta Nova is the biggest lift and piste network in the valley. As a result, Germans' cars fill to overflowing the huge car parks at the valley lift stations. Gaschurn is an attractive place to stay.
The two main resorts here are quite different. Whereas St Gallenkirch is strung along the main road and spoilt by traffic, Gaschurn is a pleasant village, bypassed by the valley traffic, with the wood-shingled Posthotel Rössle (83330) in the centre.

The lift network covers two parallel ridges running north–south, with most of the runs on their east- and west-facing flanks. The slopes are accessed from three points along the valley. A gondola from Gaschurn takes you up to a choice of chairs rising up to the east ridge, while another gondola from St Gallenkirch goes up to Valisera on the west ridge. A chair-lift to Garfrescha followed by another chair gives access to the central valley from Gortipohl – on the road between the two resorts.

This is the most challenging area in the valley, with as many red as blue runs, and an occasional nominal black. Most of the slopes are above the tree line, typically offering 300m or 400m vertical.

There is lots of off-piste potential, including some seriously challenging (and quite dangerous) slopes down into the central valley.

There are lots of mountain restaurants, many impressive in different ways. At the top of the east ridge is the state-of-the-art Nova Stoba, with seats for over 1,500 people in 17 different rooms catering for different markets, including splendid panelled rooms with table-service. The big terrace bar gets seriously boisterous. At the top of the other ridge is the splendidly woody Valisera Hüsli.

There is snowmaking on one-third of the slopes, with artificial cover down to the valley stations at Gortipohl and St Gallenkirch.

Schruns phone numbers
From elsewhere in Austria add the prefix 05556.
From abroad use the prefix +43 5556.

Gaschurn phone numbers
From elsewhere in Austria add the prefix 05558.
From abroad use the prefix +43 5558.

TOURIST OFFICE
Postcode A-6780
t +43 (5556) 722530
f 74856
info@montafon.at
www.montafon.at

Obergurgl 1930m

High, snowsure slopes with loyal clientele

WHAT IT COSTS

HOW IT RATES

The slopes

Snow	*****
Extent	**
Experts	**
Intermediates	***
Beginners	****
Convenience	****
Queues	*****
Restaurants	**

The rest

Scenery	***
Resort charm	****
Off-slope	**

- ⊕ Glaciers apart, one of the Alps' most reliable resorts for snow – especially good for a late-season holiday
- ⊕ Excellent area for beginners, timid intermediates and families
- ⊕ Mainly queue- and crowd-free
- ⊕ Retains village charm despite modern development
- ⊕ Jolly tea-time après-ski
- ⊕ Obergurgl and Hochgurgl slopes are now linked by gondola

- ⊖ Small area with no tough pistes
- ⊖ Very bleak setting, with few sheltered slopes for bad weather
- ⊖ Few off-slope amenities except in hotels
- ⊖ Quiet nightlife by Austrian standards
- ⊖ For a small Austrian resort, rather expensive

A loyal band of visitors go back every year to Obergurgl or Hochgurgl, booking a year in advance in recognition of the limited supply of beds. They love the high, snowsure, easy intermediate slopes, the end-of-the-valley seclusion and the civilised atmosphere in the comfortable, expensive hotels.

Sceptics say that the villages and the slopes are too limited. They have a point. If we're going to a bleak, high, snowsure resort where there is nothing to do but ski or board, we'd rather go somewhere with rather more skiing or boarding to do (like Tignes, for example).

What's new

The resort is planning three new lifts for 2001/02: a new eight-seater gondola from Hochgurgl up to Wurmkogl; in the Gaisberg sector, a four-seater chair-lift replacing the Übungs drag-lift; and a six-pack in place of the Steinmann and Sattel drag-lifts.

Guests can now buy their passes at hotel reception desks – credit cards are still not accepted at the lift office.

Snowmaking was also extended last season.

There's a new casino at the Hochwirst hotel. And there's a new 24hr internet accommodation booking service.

The resort

Obergurgl is based on a traditional old village, set in a remote, bleak spot, the dead end of a long road up past Sölden. It is the highest parish in Austria and is usually under a blanket of snow from November until May. The surrounding mountains are bleak, with an array of avalanche barriers giving them a forbidding appearance.

Hochgurgl, a bus-ride (or gondola-ride) away across the mountainside, is little more than a handful of hotels at the foot of its own slopes.

Obergurgl has no through traffic and few day visitors. The village centre is mainly traffic-free, and entirely so at night. Village atmosphere is jolly during the day and immediately after the slopes close, but can be subdued later at night; there are some nightspots, but most people stay in their hotels. The resort is popular with British families and well-heeled groups looking for a relaxing winter break.

Despite its small size, this is a village of parts. At the northern entrance to the resort is a cluster of hotels near the main Festkogel gondola, which takes you to all the local slopes. This area is good for getting to the slopes and for ease of access by car, but it's a long walk or a shuttle-bus from the village centre and the nursery slopes. The road then passes another group of hotels around the ice rink, up the hillside to the east (beware steep, sometimes treacherous walks to and from other amenities). The village proper starts with an attractive little square with church, fountain, and the original village hotel (the Edelweiss und Gurgl). Just above are the Rosskar and Gaisberg chair-lifts to the local slopes. Drivers have underground parking bang in the centre of town.

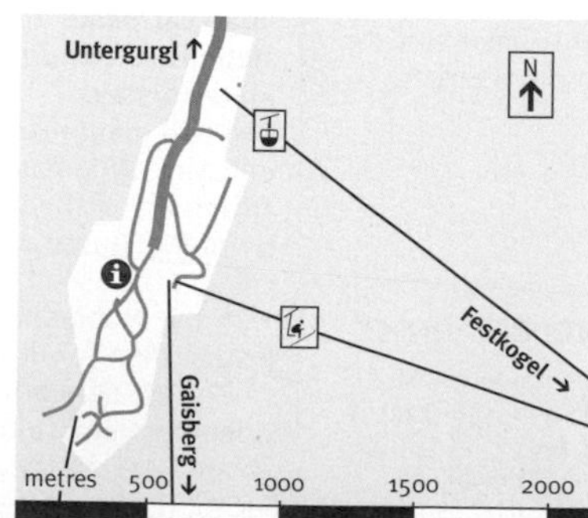

Hochgurgl is high, small and isolated →

OBERGURGL TO

Hochgurgl, despite its location on the slopes at 2150m, is not conveniently arranged. From practically all the half-dozen hotels you have to negotiate roads and/or staircases to get to or from the snow. Hochgurgl is even quieter than Obergurgl at night.

For a day out, it's a short bus or car trip to Sölden (good, quite steep and extensive intermediate slopes), and a long car trip to Kühtai (a worthwhile high area near Innsbruck). Much closer is the tiny touring launch-pad of Vent.

The mountains

The slopes of Obergurgl and Hochgurgl are about 4km apart but are now directly linked by gondola, as well as by road. Even so, the slopes are still surprisingly limited, and lacking interest or challenge for adventurous intermediates or experts. You don't get the sense of travel, as you do in bigger Alpine resorts.

Most of the slopes are very exposed and there are very few woodland runs to head to in poor conditions. Wind and white-outs can shut the lifts and, especially in early season, severe cold can curtail enthusiasm.

The lift pass is quite expensive for the relatively small area.

THE SLOPES
Limited cruising

Obergurgl is the smaller of the two linked areas. It is in two sections, well linked by piste in one direction, more loosely in the other. The gondola and the Rosskar fast quad chair-lift from the village go to the higher Festkogl area. This is served by two drags and a chair up to 3035m (you can join the Rosskar lift at its mid-station too). From here you can head back to the gondola base or over to Gaisberg, with its high point of 2670m at Hohe Mut, reached by a long, slow chair. Two new high capacity chair-lifts are replacing the three drag-lifts here for 2001/02. A chair up from Obergurgl's village square provides the other link on to the Gaisberg slopes.

MOUNTAIN FACTS

Altitude	1800m-3080m
Lifts	23
Pistes	110km
Blue	32%
Red	50%
Black	18%
Artificial snow	25km

boarding *Obergurgl is a traditional ski destination, attracting an affluent and (dare we say it?) 'older' clientele. But the resort is actually pretty good for snowboarding. There's a fun-park and quarter pipe on the Festkogl in Obergurgl and a half-pipe on the Wurmkogl in Hochgurgl. Beginners will be pleased to find that much of the resort can be covered without having to ride drag-lifts. And there's also some off-piste potential for more advanced riders. Evenings tend to be a bit tame but Sölden, 20 minutes by road, has stacks of lively bars.*

The Top Express gondola is the obvious way to travel to **Hochgurgl** during the day. But there is still the alternative of a regular and reliable free shuttle-bus to Untergurgl. From there, a chair-lift goes up to Hochgurgl (also reachable by car, or by bus – once daily). From this season a new eight-person gondola will go up from here to the high point of Wurmkogl (3080m), replacing a chain of old chair-lifts. From Wurmkogl there are spectacular views of the Dolomites. A separate chair-lift from mid-mountain serves runs on the shoulder of Schermerspitze, and there are drag-lifts serving other mid-mountain slopes to north and sound of the main axis.

A single tree-lined run leads down from Hochgurgl to the bottom of the Untergurgl chair.

SNOW RELIABILITY
Excellent

Obergurgl has high slopes and is arguably the most snowsure of Europe's non-glacier resorts – even without its snowmaking, which is now impressively extensive. It has a justifiably popular mid-December white week, and regular late-season visitors who book well in advance.

FOR EXPERTS
Not generally recommendable

There is a fair amount of enjoyable off-piste to be found with a guide – especially from Obergurgl – and the top school groups often go off-piste when there is little avalanche danger. This is a well-known area for ski touring, and we have reports of very challenging expeditions on the glaciers at the head of the valley.

The most challenging official piste is the Hohe Mut mogul field beneath the slow, old chair-lift at Gaisberg. But this is often irritatingly awkward rather than pleasurable, being icy, worn and difficult to follow in places. Other blacks are rather overgraded – they could easily be red – and there are few challenges. Experts will soon tire of cruising the mainly short runs, no matter how powdery the snow.

FOR INTERMEDIATES
Good but limited

There is some perfect intermediate terrain here, made even better by the normally flattering snow conditions. The problem is, there's not much of it. Keen piste-bashers will quickly tire of travelling the same runs and be itching to catch the bus to Sölden, down the valley – unfortunately, there is no pass-sharing arrangement.

Hochgurgl has the bigger area of easy runs, and these make good cruising. For more challenging intermediate runs, head to the Vorderer Wurmkogellift, on the right as you look at the mountain. Less confident intermediates may find the woodland piste down from Hochgurgl to the bus stop at Untergurgl tricky.

The Obergurgl area has more red than blue runs but most offer no great challenge to a confident intermediate. There is some easy cruising around mid-mountain on the Festkogel. The blue run from the top of the Festkogel gondola down to the village, via the Gaisberg sector, is one of the longest cruises in the area. And there's another long enjoyable run down the length of the gondola, with a scenic off-piste variant in the adjoining valley.

LIFT PASSES

2001/02 prices in euros

Obergurgl ski pass
Covers all lifts in Obergurgl and Hochgurgl, and local ski-bus.

Beginners Lift pass or points card.

Main pass
1-day pass 35.5
6-day pass 171.5
(low season 151)

Senior citizens
Over 60: 6-day pass 104.5

Children
Under 16: 6-day pass 104.5
Under 8: free pass

Short-term passes
Half-day (from 11am, noon, 1pm or 2pm).

Alternative periods
5 days' skiing in 7 and 11 days' skiing in 14 passes available.

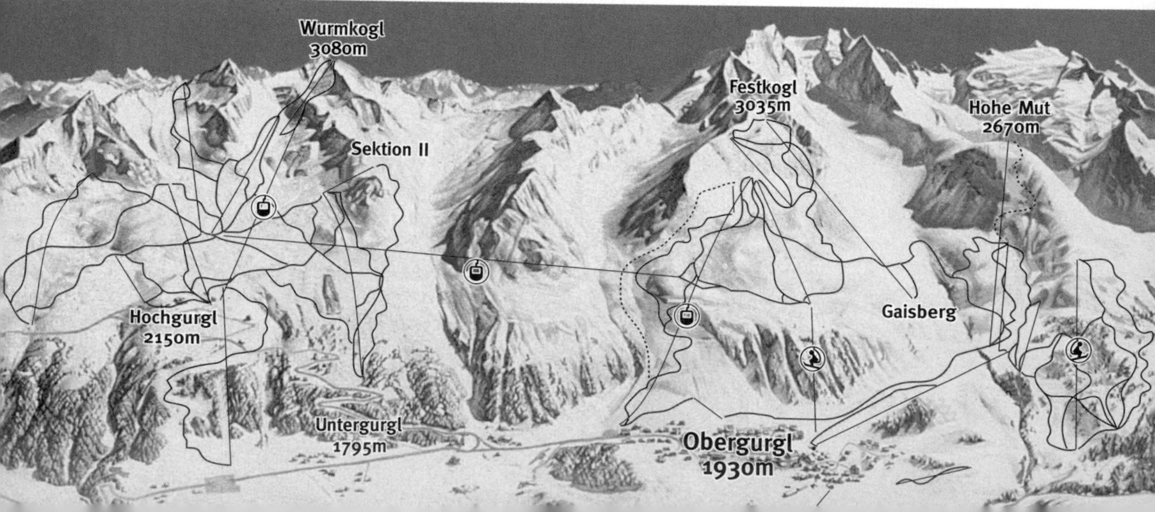

SCHOOLS/GUIDES

2001/02 prices in euros

Obergurgl
Classes 6 days
4hr: 10am-noon and 2pm-4pm
6 full days 143
Children's classes
Ages: from 5
6 full days including lunch 143
Private lessons
Half and full day
167 for full day
106 for half day; each additional person 8.

Hochgurgl
Classes 6 days
4hr: 10am-noon and 2pm-4pm
6 full days 143
Children's classes
Ages: from 5
6 full days 143
Private lessons
Hourly, half and full day
55 for 1hr, for 1 or 2 people; each additional person 15.
109 for half day, for 1 or 2 people; each additional person 15

CHILDCARE

The ski schools at Obergurgl and Hochgurgl take children over the age of 5. Children can join the ski kindergarten from age of 3.

The village kindergarten in Obergurgl also takes children from the age of 3.

The Alpina, Austria and Hochfirst hotels (among others) have in-house kindergartens.

In the Gaisberg area, there are very easy runs in front of the Nederhütte and back towards town. The bottom drag-lifts here serve very short but sometimes surprisingly tricky and bumpy runs.

FOR BEGINNERS
Fine for first-timers or improvers

The inconveniently situated Mahdstuhl nursery slope above Obergurgl is adequate for complete beginners. And the Gaisberg run – under the chair out of the village – and the wide blue run next to the Übungslift can be completed as soon as a modicum of control is achieved.

Near beginners can travel from the top of the four-person Wurmkogl chair to Hochgurgl village (600m vertical) without any problems. However, a recent reporter complained that the Hochgurgl nursery slopes are inconveniently placed for complete beginners to have to walk to.

The quality of the snow makes the area a good (but relatively expensive) choice for beginners compared with most lower Austrian resorts.

CROSS-COUNTRY
Limited but snowsure

Three small loops, one each at Obergurgl, Untergurgl and Hochgurgl, give just 12km of trail. All are relatively snowsure and pleasantly situated. Tuition is available.

QUEUES
Some peak-time bottlenecks

The resort is too remote to attract day trippers, and its authorities do not encourage 'bussing-in' when lower villages are struggling for snow. So major lift queues are rare – even at Christmas and New Year.

We have reports of short queues for the village lifts at the start of ski school but these tend to clear quickly (though one February half-term visitor tells of half-hour waits for the Rosskar lift as classes re-assemble after lunch). Queues for the gondola to Obergurgl can also build up late in the day as people start to head back home.

The same half-term reporter also came across several piste bottlenecks, especially around the Nederhütte – possibly due to poor visibility higher up the mountain at the time. The blue runs from the top of the Wurmkogl lift and the long blue from the Festkogl to the village can also get crowded.

MOUNTAIN RESTAURANTS
Little choice

Compared with most Austrian resorts, mountain huts are neither numerous nor very special. At Gaisberg the Nederhütte is jolly, and David's Skihütte is friendly, cheerful and good value. The 'traditional and welcoming' Schönwieshütte, a 10-minute walk from the piste, has excellent views, as does the small hut at the top of the Hohe Mut chair. At Hochgurgl, the tiny hut at Wurmkogl has stunning views into Italy and basic food. Many people return to one village or the other for lunch – some of the hotel restaurants have sun terraces.

SCHOOLS AND GUIDES
Mainly good news

We've had nothing but good reports of the Obergurgl school in the last couple of years, with good English spoken and excellent tuition and organisation: 'highly efficient, very thorough testing of pupils before being put into a class', 'big effort to make school fun'. Class sizes are normally between 8 and 12 though we have received reports telling of 15 to a class at busy times.

FACILITIES FOR CHILDREN
Check out your hotel

Children's ski classes start at 5 years and children from age 3 can join Bobo's ski-kindergarten. There is also a non-skiing kindergarten for kids aged 3 and up. There's lunchtime supervision for ski school and kindergarten children alike. Many hotels offer childcare of one sort or another, and the Alpina has been particularly recommended.

Staying there 

HOW TO GO
Plenty of good hotels

Most package accommodation is in hotels and pensions, but there are a number of comfortable apartments. Demand for rooms in Obergurgl exceeds supply, and for once it is true that you should book early to avoid disappointment.

Hotels Obergurgl's accommodation is of high quality: most hotels are 4-stars, and none is less than a 3-star. Hochgurgl's hotels include the most luxurious one in the area (the hotel Hochgurgl). Within each rating, hotels are uniformly comfortable. Couples at the Deutschmann and at the Alpina

GETTING THERE

Air Innsbruck, transfer 2hr. Salzburg, transfer 3hr. Munich, transfer 4hr.

Rail Train to Ötz; regular buses from station, transfer 1½hr.

Phone numbers
From elsewhere in Austria add the prefix 05256.
From abroad use the prefix +43 5256.

ACTIVITIES

Indoor Swimming pool (at Hotel Muhle, open to the public), saunas, whirlpools, steam baths, massage, bowling, pool and billiards, squash, table tennis
Outdoor Natural skating rink (open in the evenings), sleigh rides, snow-shoe outings

TOURIST OFFICE

Postcode A-6456
t +43 (5256) 6466
f 6353
info@obergurgl.com
www.obergurgl.com

have rightly been surprised to be asked to share a table.

A cheaper option is to stay down the valley in Untergurgl, where the 4-star Jadghof is recommended. It's worth remembering that some hotels still don't accept credit cards.

((((4) **Edelweiss und Gurgl** (6223) The focal hotel – biggest, oldest, one of the most appealing; on the central square, near the main lifts. Pool.

((((4) **Alpina de Luxe** (600) Big, smart chalet with excellent children's facilities. Pool.

((((4) **Hochfirst** (63250) Recommended by recent reporter. Good spa facilities, comfortable, four or five minutes from gondola.

((((4) **Jenewein** (6203) Recently refurbished, friendly staff, excellent food; good central position next to main lift.

((((4) **Berggasthof Gamper** (6545) Best rooms very comfortable, good food. Far end of town, past the square.

((((4) **Crystal** (6454) If you don't mind the ocean-liner appearance, it's one of the best near the Festkogl lift.

((((4) **Deutschmann** (6594) Popular choice with good food and facilities. Next to the Festkogel lift.

(((3) **Fender** (6316) Good all-rounder with friendly staff; central.

(((3) **Wiesental** (6263) Comfortable, well situated, good value.

(((3) **Granat-Schlössl** (6363) Amusing pseudo-castle, surprisingly affordable.

((2) **Alpenblume** (6278) Good B&B hotel, well-placed for Festkogl lift.

((2) **Haus Gurgl** (6533) B&B near Festkogl lift; friendly, pizzeria, same owners as Edelweiss und Gurgl.

Hochgurgl has equally good hotels.

(((((5) **Hochgurgl** (6265) The only 5-star in the area. Luxurious, with pool.

(((3) **Sporthotel Ideal** (6290) Well situated for access to the slopes. Pool.

(((3) **Laurin** (6227) Well equipped, traditional rooms, excellent food.

Self-catering The Lohmann is a high-standard large modern apartment block, well placed for the slopes, less so for the village centre below. The 3-star Pirchhütt has apartments close to the Festkogl gondola, and the Wiesental hotel has more central ones.

EATING OUT

Wide choice, limited range

Hotel dining rooms and à la carte restaurants dominate. The independent Pic Nic and Krumpn's Stadl are recommended. The Belmonte and the Romantika at the hotel Madeleine are popular pizzerias. Hotel Alpina has a particularly good reputation for its food – though a recent report says the Gotthard-Zeist and Hochfirst are 'just as good as the renowned Alpina'. The restaurant at the Berggasthof Gamper is pleasantly cosy. The two restaurants in the Edelweiss und Gurgl are reportedly 'superb'. Nederhütte and David's Skihütte up the mountain are both open in the evenings. Remember, credit cards are not accepted everywhere.

APRES-SKI

Lively early, quiet later

Obergurgl is more animated in the evening than you might expect. The Nederhütte mountain restaurant has lively tea dancing – you have to ski home afterwards though. All of the bars at the base of the Rosskar and Gaisberg lifts are popular at close of play – the Umbrella Bar outside the Edelweiss hotel is particularly busy in good weather. The Hexenkuchl at the Jenewein is also popular.

Later on, the crowded Krumpn's Stadl barn is the liveliest place in town with live music on alternate nights – it's also recommended for its fondues. The Josl, Jenewein and Edelweiss, and Gurgl hotels have atmospheric bars. The Bajazzo is a more sophisticated late-night haunt. The Edelweissbar and Austriakeller are discos (the latter with karaoke). There's now a casino at the Hochfirst.

Hochgurgl is very quiet at night except for Toni's Almhütte bar in the Olymp Sporthotel – one of three places with live music. There's also the African Bar disco.

OFF THE SLOPES

Very limited

There isn't much to do during the day, with few shops and limited public facilities. Innsbruck is over two hours away by post-bus. Sölden (20 minutes away) has a leisure centre and shopping facilities. Pedestrians can walk to restaurants in the Gaisberg area to meet friends for lunch and there are 11km of hiking paths. Many of the larger hotels have leisure facilities, though these are generally closed to non-residents – the Hochfirst health suite has been recommended.

Obertauern 1740m

Small but varied area, with great snow record

WHAT IT COSTS

5

HOW IT RATES

The slopes

Snow	****
Extent	**
Experts	***
Intermediates	****
Beginners	*****
Convenience	****
Queues	****
Restaurants	***

The rest

Scenery	***
Resort charm	**
Off-slope	**

What's new

Last season the Kurvenlift T-bar up to the Edelweisshutte was replaced by a new fast quad, the Edelweissbahn.

- ⊕ Excellent snow record
- ⊕ Well-linked, user-friendly circuit
- ⊕ Slopes for all standards
- ⊕ Good modern lift system
- ⊕ Good mountain restaurants
- ⊕ Lively après-ski scene
- ⊕ Short transfer from Salzburg

- ⊖ Village lacks traditional charm
- ⊖ Slopes have limited vertical and short runs
- ⊖ Lifts and snow can suffer from exposure to high winds

If you like the après-ski jollity of Austria but have a hankering for the good snow of high French resorts, Obertauern could be just what you're looking for. The terrain is a bit limited by French standards, and the village is no Alpbach. But it's a lot prettier than Flaine – and if you've grown up on slush and ice in lower Austrian resorts moving up 1000m will be a revelation.

THE RESORT

In the land of postcard resorts grown out of rustic villages, Obertauern is different – a mainly modern development at the top of the Tauern pass road. Built in (high-rise) chalet style, it's not unattractive – but it lacks a central focus of shops and bars.

THE MOUNTAINS

The slopes and lifts form a ring around the village. The Tauern pass road divides them into two unequal parts; that apart, the slopes are well linked to make a user-friendly circuit that can be travelled clockwise or anticlockwise in a couple of hours. Visitors used to big areas will soon start to feel they have seen it all. Vertical range is limited, and runs are short – most major lifts are in the 200m to 400m vertical range. Reporters complain about the piste map (which, unlike ours, takes a bird's eye view) and about poor piste marking that complicates navigation in bad weather.

Slopes Most pistes are on the sunny slopes to the north of the road and village: a wide, many-faceted basin of mostly gentle runs, some combining steepish mogulled pitches with long schusses. The slopes on the other side of the road – on Gamsleitenspitze, to the south-west – have some of Obertauern's most difficult runs.

Snowboarding There is a fun-park at

The steep slopes on the south side of the village get some morning sun, but are mainly shady ➔

TVB OBERTAUERN

MOUNTAIN FACTS

Altitude	1630m-2315m
Lifts	29
Pistes	120km
Blue	50%
Red	35%
Black	15%
Artificial snow	70km

Phone numbers
From elsewhere in Austria add the prefix 06456.
From abroad use the prefix +43 6456.

TOURIST OFFICE

Postcode A-5562
t +43 (6456) 7252
f 7515
info@ski-obertauern.com
www.ski-obertauern.com

the mid-mountain lift junction of Hochalm.

Snow reliability The resort's key attraction is the exceptional snow reliability of its high bowl. But it is often windy, which can mean lifts close and snow blows away.

Experts Experts naturally incline towards the genuinely steep pistes and off-piste runs from the Gamsleiten chair, but it is prone to closure. For more challenge, join an off-piste guided group.

Intermediates Most of Obertauern's circuit is of intermediate difficulty. Stay low for easier pistes, or try the tougher runs higher up. The major mid-mountain lift base of the northern slopes is Hochalm, from where the Seekareck and Panorama chairs take you to challenging, often mogully runs. The chair to Hundskogel leads to a red and a black. And over at the Plattenkar quad there are two splendid reds.

Beginners Obertauern has very good nursery slopes, close to the village. After the first couple of lessons you can go up the mountain, because the Schaidberg chair leads to a drag-lift serving a high-altitude beginners' slope and there is an easy run to get you back to the village.

Cross-country There are 17km of trails in the heart of the resort.

Queues When neighbouring resorts are not sharing Obertauern's good snow, non-residents arrive by the bus-load. However, the lift system is modern and impressive and is continually being upgraded. Seven new lifts in the last few years – including a six-pack on Schaidberg – are helping to eliminate the queues of the past and our most recent reporters experienced no serious queues.

Mountain restaurants Mountain restaurants are plentiful and good, but crowded. The smaller huts are more atmospheric ('Often full of groups of Germans singing,' says a reporter). The old Lürzer Alm at village level has been praised.

Schools and guides There are six schools. We have good reports of the Skischule Krallinger, despite large classes at peak times.

Facilities for children Most of the schools – including the Krallinger – take children.

STAYING THERE

How to go Two major British tour operators offer packages here.

Hotels Practically all accommodation is in hotels (mostly 3-star and 4-star) and guest houses. The following hotels have all been recommended: Petersbühel (7235); Enzian (7207-0); Steiner (7306); Das Schütz (7204-0); Edelweiss (7245); Gamsleiten (7286); and Alpina (73360).

Eating out The choices are mostly hotels (the Enzian is recommended) and the busy après-ski bars at the foot of the north-side lifts. The Hochalm restaurant at the top of the Grünwaldkopf quad sometimes serves early-evening meals.

Après-ski Obertauern has a lively and varied après-ski scene. The Latsch'n Alm has a terrace, music and dancing and is good at tea-time. Later, try the Lürzer Alm, which has farmyard-style decor and a disco. The Taverne has various bars, a pizzeria and disco.

Off the slopes There's an excellent, large sports centre – with fitness room, tennis, squash and badminton, but no pool – but there's little else to do in the village in bad weather. However, Salzburg is an easy trip.

For lunch with friends, energetic non-skiers can get to the Kringsalm restaurant on foot.

Saalbach-Hinterglemm 1000m

Attractive villages, lively nightlife and good intermediate runs

WHAT IT COSTS

4

HOW IT RATES

The slopes

Snow	***
Extent	***
Experts	**
Intermediates	****
Beginners	***
Convenience	****
Queues	***
Restaurants	****

The rest

Scenery	***
Resort charm	****
Off-slope	**

What's new

In 2000/01 two lifts on the south-facing slopes above Hinterglemm were replaced by high-speed chairs with bubbles for protection in cold weather. A six-seater replaced a slow old double chair to Spieleckkogel and a four-seater replaced a T-bar to Reiterkogel.

More snowmaking facilities were also installed on the Schattberg pistes.

- ➕ Large, well-linked, intermediate circuit with open and tree-lined runs
- ➕ Saalbach is a big but pleasant, affluent village, lively at night
- ➕ Village main streets largely traffic-free
- ➕ Atmospheric mountain restaurants all over the mountain
- ➕ Sunny slopes
- ➕ Large snowmaking installation and excellent piste maintenance

- ➖ Large number of low, south-facing slopes that suffer from the sun
- ➖ Not much for experts
- ➖ Nursery slopes in Saalbach are not ideal – sunny, and busy in parts
- ➖ Saalbach spreads along the valley and some rooms are far from central
- ➖ Hinterglemm sprawls along a long street with no real centre
- ➖ Can get rowdy at night

Like many Austrian resorts Saalbach-Hinterglemm has a pretty, traditional-style village and very lively nightlife, but unlike many it combines this with a very extensive circuit of slopes on both sides of a valley, and runs are linked by an efficient modern lift system. Its slopes resemble a French resort more than a traditional Austrian one – with the added advantage of excellent traditional mountain restaurants dotted around.

The main downside is the snow. Although it has impressive snowmaking, one side of the valley faces south and these slopes, especially the lower ones, deteriorate quickly in good weather.

Saalbach's après-ski is very lively – and can get rowdy – and is dominated by Scandinavian and German visitors. It rocks from 3pm until the early hours non-stop. There are also large parties of British schoolchildren around at times.

The resort

Saalbach and Hinterglemm, their centres 4km apart, expanded along a narrow dead-end valley floor until, a few years ago, they adopted a single identity. Their slopes are spread across north- and south-facing mountainsides, with lifts and runs connecting the villages via both sides.

Saalbach is one of the most attractive winter villages in Austria. Wedged into the narrow valley, with pisted slopes coming right down to the traffic-free

SAALBACH-HINTERGLEMM TOURIST OFFICE

A perfect view looking towards Hinterglemm of the circuit's sunny south-facing slopes →

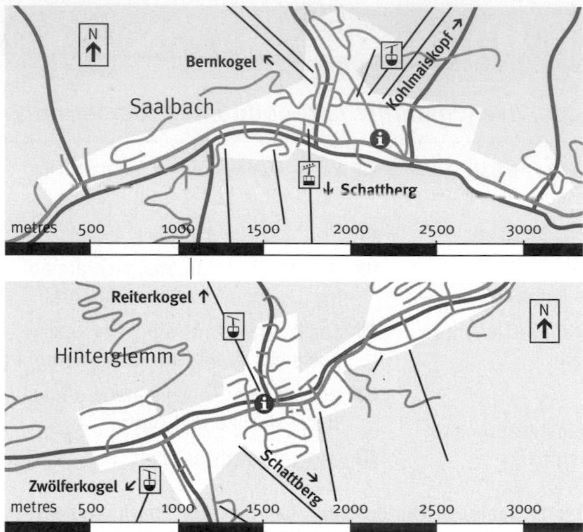

village centre, its traditional-style buildings are huddled together around a classic onion-domed church. Most buildings are modern reproductions – the main exceptions are the Post Inn and the church – and the result is pretty close to Austrian charm with French convenience.

Saalbach is a strange mixture. The attractive, largely traffic-free, main street is lined with expensive, upmarket hotels, restaurants and shops, festooned with fairy lights, but further out there are more cheap and cheerful pensions. The clientele are similarly mixed, with rich BMW and Mercedes drivers rubbing shoulders in the bars and clubs with teenagers (including British school kids) looking for a good time.

Hinterglemm is a more scattered, less appealing collection of hotels and holiday homes, with a small, virtually traffic-free zone in the centre. It offers a cheaper, though not inexpensive, alternative to Saalbach, with far better access to the north-facing slopes.

Several resorts in Salzburg province are reachable by road – including Bad Hofgastein, Kaprun and Zell am See, the last a short bus-ride away.

The mountains

The slopes form a 'circus' almost exclusively suitable for intermediates, much of it on lightly wooded slopes. Few runs are likely either to bore the aggressive intermediate or worry the timid one. There are sufficient open sections and changes of pitch and direction to give pistes variety, but not many genuinely black pistes.

THE SLOPES

User-friendly circuit

The complete circuit of the valley can only be travelled anticlockwise – going clockwise, at Vorderglemm there is no way up the slope on the opposite side of the valley. You can do a truncated clockwise circuit, crossing to the south side of the valley at Saalbach itself. The valley floor is very narrow, so there is very little walking necessary when changing sides. Where you end up at the end of the day is not important because of the excellent bus service, which runs every 20 minutes.

A good deal of the south-facing slopes is above 1400m, albeit with rather short runs. Five sectors can be identified – from west to east, **Hochalm**, **Reiterkogel**, **Bernkogel**, **Kohlmaiskopf** and **Wildenkarkogel**. The last connects via Schönleitenhütte to Leogang – a small, high, open area, leading to a long, narrow, north-facing slope down to Leogang village, broadening towards the bottom. An eight-person gondola brings you most of the way back.

The connections across Saalbach-Hinterglemm's south-facing slopes work well: when traversing the whole hillside you need to descend to the valley floor only once, in whichever direction you go. At Saalbach a very short walk across the main street gets you from the Bernkogel piste to the Kohlmaiskopf lift and vice versa. Both these runs are well endowed with snowmakers to ensure the link normally remains open, and there is a

boarding *Saalbach is great for boarding. Slopes are extensive, lifts are mainly chairs and gondolas (though there are some connecting drags), and there are pistes to appeal to beginners, intermediates and experts alike. For experienced boarders there's good off-piste terrain, a large half-pipe on the Bernkogel above Saalbach, another below Hochalm and a fun-park on the north-facing slopes just above Hinterglemm. There are also dedicated 'carving' zones for boarders and skiers. And the nightlife is some of the liveliest in Europe.*

LIFT PASSES

2001/02 prices in euros

Saalbach-Hinterglemm-Leogang
Covers all the lifts in Saalbach, Hinterglemm and Leogang, and the ski-bus.

Main pass
1-day pass 33
6-day pass 155
(low season 140)

Senior citizens
Over 60: 6-day pass 140

Children
Under 19: 6-day pass 140
Under 14: 6-day pass 78
Under 5: free pass

Short-term passes
Reduced price passes in the morning from 9am to 12.30, and in the afternoon after 11.45.

Notes Can pay extra 10 euros for free use of indoor pool in Hinterglemm. Sun ticket for pedestrians: 7-day pass 51 Euros. Points cards for beginners.
Senior citizen pass for men and women over 60.

MOUNTAIN FACTS

Altitude	930m-2095m
Lifts	52
Pistes	200km
Blue	50%
Red	33%
Black	17%
Artificial snow	30km
Recco detectors used	

choice of lifts going up, including a multi-cabin cable-way to Kohlmaiskopf.

The north-facing slopes are different in character – two distinct mountains, with long runs from both to the valley. Access from Saalbach is by a solitary, queue-prone cable-car to **Schattberg**. The high, open, sunny slopes behind the peak are now served by a fast quad chair.

From Schattberg, long runs go down to Saalbach village, Vorderglemm and Hinterglemm. From the latter, lifts go not only to Schattberg but also to the other north-facing mountain, **Zwölferkogel**, served by a two-stage eight-person gondola. Drags serve open slopes on the sunny side of the peak, and a high-capacity gondola provides a link from the south-facing Hochalm area.

SNOW RELIABILITY
Better than most of the Tirol

Saalbach's array of snowmakers cover several main runs on the lower half of the mountain, on both sides of the valley. The resort also claims to be in a 'snow pocket'. Good piste maintenance helps to keep the slopes in the best possible condition, but an altitude range of 930m to 2100m is only a slight advance on Kitzbühel. As 60% of runs face south, Saalbach suffers when the sun comes out. Both north and south sides can develop icy patches, as we found on our last January visit.

FOR EXPERTS
Little steep stuff

There are few testing slopes. Off-piste guides are available, but snow conditions and forest tend to limit the potential. The north-facing slopes are steeper than those on the south-facing side of the valley. The long (4km) run beneath the length of the Schattberg cable-car is the only truly black run – a fine fast bash first thing in the morning if it has been groomed. The other long black from Zwölferkogel is really a red with just a couple of short, steeper pitches. The World Cup downhill run from Zwölferkogel is interesting, as is the 5km Schattberg West–Hinterglemm red (and its scenic 'ski route' variant).

FOR INTERMEDIATES
Paradise

This area is ideal for both the great British piste-basher, eager to clock up the miles, and the more leisurely

cruiser. The south-facing pistes have mainly been cut through the pine forest at an angle, allowing movement across the area on easy runs.

For those looking for more of a challenge, the most direct routes down from Hochalm, Reiterkogel, Kohlmaiskopf and Hochwartalm are good fun. All the south-facing slopes are uniformly pleasant and, as a result, everyone tends to be fairly evenly distributed over them. Only the delightful blue from Bernkogel to Saalbach gets really crowded at times. The alternative long ski route is very pleasant, taking you through forest and meadows.

The north-facing area has some more challenging runs, and a section of relatively high, open slopes around Zwölferkogel, which often have good snow. None of the black runs is beyond an adventurous intermediate, while the long pretty cruise from Limbergalm to Vorderglemm gets you away from lifts for most of the time and is particularly quiet and pleasant first thing in the morning.

Our favourite intermediate run was the long cruise down on excellent north-facing snow to Leogang – over 1000m of vertical.

FOR BEGINNERS
Best for improvers

Saalbach's two nursery slopes are very well positioned for convenience, right next to the village centre. But they are both south-facing, and the upper one gets a lot of intermediate traffic taking a short cut between the Kohlmaiskopf and Bernkogel areas. The lower one is very small, but the lift is free.

Alternatives are trips to the short, easy runs at Bernkogel and Schattberg. There is also a little slope at the foot of the Schattberg but the schools seem loath to use it – so it's great for pottering about on your own at lunchtime. It's rather sunless and a little steeper than the other nursery areas, but perfectly usable.

Hinterglemm's spacious nursery area is separate from the main slopes. Being north-facing, it is much more reliable for snow later on in the season, but it consequently misses out on the sun in mid-winter.

There are lots of easy blue runs to move on to, especially on the south-facing side of the valley.

FOR CROSS-COUNTRY
Go to Zell am See

Trails run beside the road along the valley floor from Saalbach to Vorderglemm and between Hinterglemm and the valley end at Lindlingalm. In mid-winter these trails get very little sun, and are not very exciting. The countryside beyond nearby Zell am See offers more scope.

QUEUES
Busy, but only one long delay

The Schattberg cable-car is an obvious problem, with waiting routine at peak periods. Otherwise, much depends on snow conditions. When all runs are in good shape there are few problems, other than small morning peak queues to leave Saalbach. If the snow is poor, the Bernkogel chair and the following drag get very busy, as do any lifts servicing the better snow.

Saalbach-Hinterglemm does not get as overrun at weekends as other Tirolean resorts – it's less accessible for the Munich hordes than the Ski Welt area and its neighbours.

MOUNTAIN RESTAURANTS
Excellent quality and quantity

The whole area is liberally scattered with attractive little huts that serve good food. Many have pleasant rustic interiors and a lively ambience.

On the south-facing slopes, the Panorama on the Kohlmaiskopf slope, Waleggeralm on Hochalm and Turneralm close to Bründelkopf serve particularly good food. The little Bernkogelalm hut, overlooking Saalbach, has a great atmosphere. Reporters recommend the Reider Alm adjacent to the beginner slopes ('table-service and very prompt') and the Bärnalm near the top of the Bernkogel chair ('good food, good value'). The Wildenkarkogel Hütte has a big terrace and possibly the loudest mountain-top music we've heard, with resident DJ from mid-morning.

On the north-facing slopes, the Bergstadl halfway down the red run from Schattberg West has stunning views and good food. Ellmaualm, at the bottom of the Zwölferkogel's upper slopes, is a quiet, sunny retreat with good food and 'palatial loos'. The 12er Treff umbrella bar at the top of the Zwölferkogel gondola is good for lounging in the sun. The Simalalm at the base of the Limbergalm quad chair is 'great for the sun and the views'.

SCHOOLS/GUIDES

2001/02 prices in euros

Fürstauer

Classes 6 days
4hr: 10am-noon and 1pm-3pm
1 full day 44
6 full days 129

Children's classes
Ages: from 5
1 full day 44
6 full days 129

Private lessons
2hr and full-day
94 for 2hr, for 1 or 2 people; each additional person 10.

Snowboard classes
Half-day 50
6 half-days 137
3hr: 9am-noon or 1pm-4pm
1 half day 43
6 half days 145

Wolfgang Zink

Classes 6 days
4hr: 10am-noon and 1pm-3pm
1 full day 45
6 full days 123

Private lessons
2hrs and full-day
87 for 2hrs, for 1 to 2 people; each additional person 7.

Snowboard classes
3hr: 9am-noon or 1pm-4pm
3 half days 95

CHILDCARE

Some ski schools take children from age 4 or 5 and can provide lunchtime care.

Several hotels have nurseries, and some in Hinterglemm are open to non-residents.

Phone numbers
From elsewhere in Austria add the prefix 06541.
From abroad use the prefix +43 6541.

GETTING THERE

Air Salzburg, transfer 2hr. Munich, transfer 3½hr.

Rail Zell am See; hourly buses from station, transfer 40 min.

SCHOOLS AND GUIDES

An excess of choice

We're all in favour of competition between schools but visitors to Saalbach-Hinterglemm may feel that they are faced with rather too much of this good thing, with eight or nine to choose from. We have had good reports of the Wolf and Zink schools and the 'excellent' Snowboard Academy.

FACILITIES FOR CHILDREN

Hinterglemm tries harder

Saalbach doesn't go out of its way to sell itself to families, although it does have a ski kindergarten. Hinterglemm has some good hotel-based nursery facilities – the one at the Theresia is reportedly excellent.

Staying there

The walk to lifts from Saalbach's central hotels is minimal. But Saalbach has seen a fair amount of expansion in recent years, and many of the cheaper hotels are in the least convenient part of the village. In Hinterglemm, position isn't so important. Most of the accommodation is near a lift.

HOW TO GO

Cheerful doesn't mean cheap

Chalets We are aware of a few 'club hotels' but Saalbach isn't really a chalet resort.

Hotels There are a large number of hotels in both villages, mainly 3-star and above. Be aware that some central hotels are affected by disco noise.

Saalbach

((((4 **Alpenhotel** (6666) Luxurious, with open-fire lounge, disco, small pool.

((((4 **Berger's Sporthotel** (6577) Liveliest of the top hotels, with a daily tea dance, and disco. Good pool.

((((4 **Kendler** (6225-0) Position second to none, right next to the Bernkogel chair. Classy, expensive, good food.

((((4 **Saalbacher Hof** (7111-0) Retains a friendly feel despite its large size.

(((3 **Haider** (6228) Best-positioned of the 3-stars, right next to the main lifts.

(((3 **Kristiana** (6253) Near enough to lifts but away from night-time noise. 'Excellent food.' Sauna, steam bath.

(((3 **König** (6384) Cheaper 3-star and more basic rooms.

Hinterglemm

((((4 **Theresia** (7414-0) Hinterglemm's top hotel, and one of the best for families. Out towards Saalbach, but nursery slopes nearby. Pool.

(((3 **Wolf** (6346-0) Small but well-equipped 4-star in the the nursery-sharing scheme. 'Especially good' food, excellent position. Pool.

((2 **Haus Ameshofer** (8119) Beside piste at Reiterkogel lift. 'Great value ski-in, ski-out B&B,' says a reporter.

Self-catering There's a big choice of apartments for independent travellers.

EATING OUT

Wide choice of hotel restaurants

Saalbach-Hinterglemm is essentially a half-board resort, with relatively few non-hotel restaurants. Peter's restaurant, at the top of Saalbach's main street, is atmospheric and serves excellent meat dishes cooked on hot stones. The Wallner Pizzeria on the main street is good value. The Auwirt hotel on the outskirts of Saalbach has a good à la carte restaurant.

APRES-SKI

It rocks from early on

Après-ski is very lively and can get very wild from mid-afternoon until the early hours. In Saalbach the rustic Hinterhagalm at the top of the main nursery slope is packed by 3.30. When it closes around 6pm, the crowds slide down to Bauer's Skialm and try to get into the already heaving old cow shed to continue drinking and dancing. The tiny Zum Turn (next door to the church and cemetery) is an atmospheric former medieval jail that also gets packed around 4pm with many who are still there at 11pm.

Later on, The Pub on the main road out of town is packed with young Brits enjoying the karaoke. The Neuhaus Taverne and Crazy Bear have live music. Bobby's Bar is cheap, often full of British school kids, has bowling and serves Guinness. Kings Disco livens up after midnight. The Panther Bar has jungle decor, discreet music and well-

ACTIVITIES

Indoor Swimming pools, sauna, massage, solarium, bowling, billiards, tennis (Hinterglemm), squash

Outdoor Floodlit tobogganing, sleigh rides, skating, ice hockey, curling, 35km of cleared paths, paragliding

TOURIST OFFICE

Postcode A-5753
t +43 (6541) 680068
f 680069
contact@saalbach.com
www.saalbach.com

Leogang phone numbers
From elsewhere in Austria add the prefix 06583.
From abroad use the prefix +43 6583.

heeled clientele. Zum Herrn'Karl, Hellis and Bergers are also popular. Arena disco has go-go dancers and is very popular. A reader recommends the Burgeralm as '3km up the toboggan track, marvellous atmosphere and reindeer steaks before a 1am descent'.

In Hinterglemm there are a number of ice bars which are busy straight after the lifts close, including the Gute Stube of Hotel Dorfschmiede in the centre of town with loud music blasting out and people spilling into the street. The Tanzkimmel is an open, glass-fronted bar with a dance floor, next door to the Londoner, which is the biggest attraction later on – live and disco music, smart, friendly. The Hexenhausl near the Zwölferkogel gondola gets packed and has an animated model of a witch revealing her undergarments. A similar fascination with moving models is demonstrated at the rustic Goasstall just above town by the piste down from Sportalm, where a model goat is equally revealing (and where real goats graze behind glass near the men's loo). Bla Bla is small, modern and smart, with reasonable prices. The Alm Bar has good music and some dancing.

Tour operator reps organise tobogganing, sleigh rides and bowling.

OFF THE SLOPES

Surprisingly little to do

Saalbach is not very entertaining if you're not into winter sports. There are few shops other than supermarkets and equipment places. Walks tend to be restricted to the paths alongside the cold cross-country trails or along the Saalbach toboggan run to Spielberghs. But there are excursions to Kitzbühel and Salzburg.

Leogang 800m

A much less expensive alternative to Saalbach-Hinterglemm.

THE RESORT

Leogang is an attractive, although rather scattered, quiet, farming community-cum-mountain resort, better placed than Saalbach for those with cars wanting to visit other resorts.

THE MOUNTAIN

The village is linked to the eastern end of the Saalbach-Hinterglemm ski circuit, rather out on a spur.

Slopes A gondola from Hütten takes you into the ski area. The local slopes tend to be delightfully quiet being off the main circuit.

Snow reliability The local slopes have some of the best snow in the region, being north- and east-facing, with snowmaking on the run home.

Snowboarding The whole area is great for boarding and there's a half-pipe here, though Leogang nightlife is deadly dull compared with Saalbach.

Experts Not much challenge here, except trying to get round the whole circuit and home again in a day.

Intermediates Great long red run cruise home from the top of the gondola. Plus the whole Saalbach-Hinterglemm circuit to explore.

Beginners Good nursery slopes by the village, and short runs to progress to.

Cross-country The best in the area. There are 25km of trails, plus a panoramic high-altitude trail which links through to other resorts.

Queues No local problems.

Mountain restaurants A couple of good local huts.

Schools and guides Leogang Altenberger school has a high reputation – 'excellent service and tuition; highly recommended'.

Facilities for children There is a non-ski crèche, and children can start school at four years old.

STAYING THERE

It's best to stay at Hütten, near the lift.

Chalets Equity Total Ski and Snowboard runs a catered chalet in a converted farmhouse close to the gondola. Visitors report comfort and character with great catering and entertainment.

Hotels The luxury Krallerhof (8246-0) has its own nursery lift, which can be used to get across to the main lift station. The 4-star Salzburgerhof (7310-0) is one of the best-placed hotels with sauna and steam, within a two-minute walk of the gondola.

Self-catering There are quiet apartments available.

Eating out Restaurants are hotel-based. The Krallerhof has the excellent food you would expect. The much cheaper Gasthof Hüttwirt has a high reputation for Austrian home cooking.

Après-ski The rustic old chalet Kralleralm is very much the focal tea-time and evening rendezvous.

Off the slopes Excursions to Salzburg are possible.

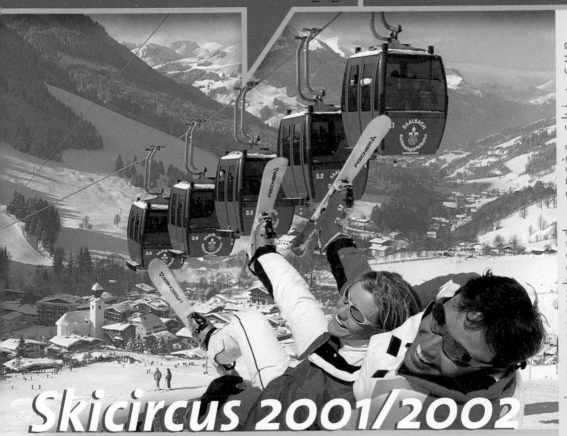

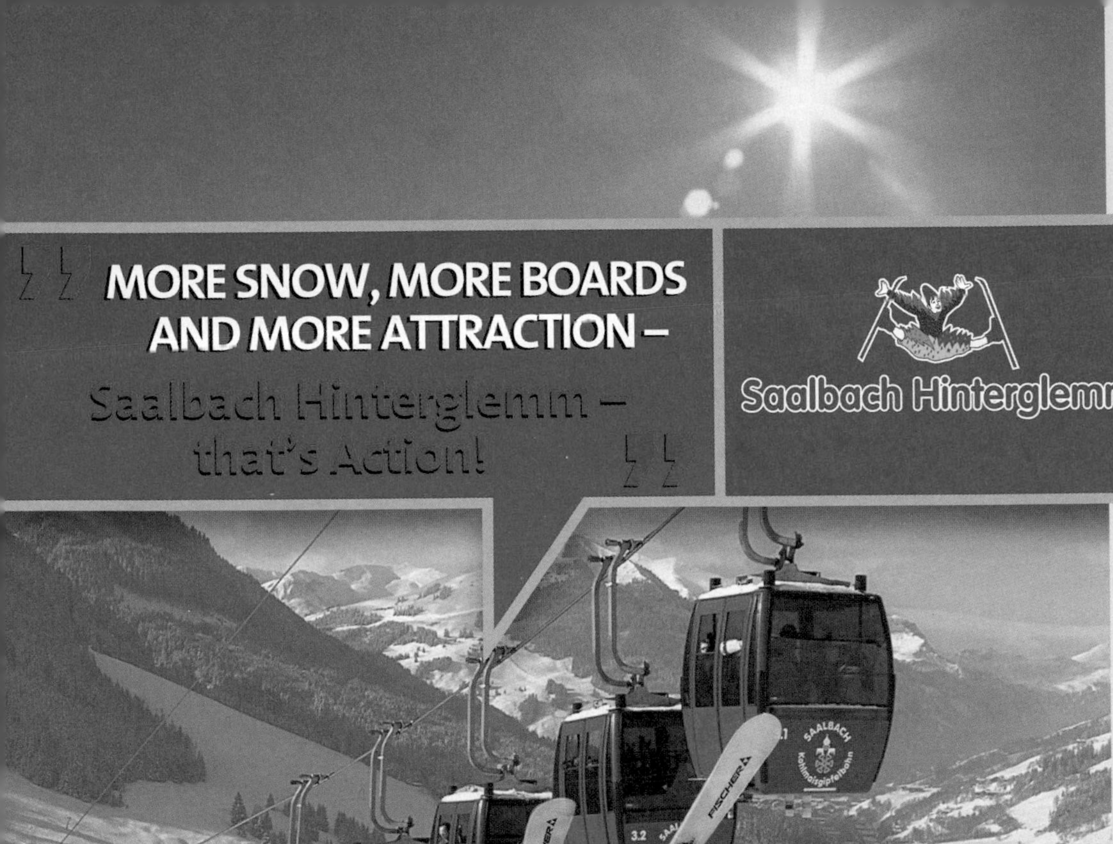
"MORE SNOW, MORE BOARDS AND MORE ATTRACTION –
Saalbach Hinterglemm – that's Action!"
Saalbach Hinterglemm
SAALBACH
Skicircus 2001/2002

Schladming 745m

Pretty old town with extensive intermediate slopes

WHAT IT COSTS

3

HOW IT RATES

The slopes

Snow	***
Extent	***
Experts	**
Intermediates	****
Beginners	****
Convenience	***
Queues	****
Restaurants	****

The rest

Scenery	***
Resort charm	****
Off-slope	****

- ⊕ New lifts have linked extensive but previously fragmented slopes
- ⊕ Excellent slopes for intermediates
- ⊕ Extensive snowmaking operation and superb piste maintenance
- ⊕ Very sheltered slopes, among trees
- ⊕ Lots of good mountain restaurants
- ⊕ Charming town with friendly people and a life independent of tourism
- ⊕ New Ski Alliance Amadé lift pass covers wide range of nearby resorts

- ⊖ Nursery slopes (at Rohrmoos) are inconvenient unless you stay beside them – and beginners are expected to pay for a full lift pass
- ⊖ Very little to entertain experts, on or off-piste
- ⊖ Slopes lack variety – one mountain is much like the others
- ⊖ Most runs are north-facing, so can be cold and shady in early season

Since its four previously separate mountains were linked by lifts and pistes, Schladming has been able to compete with major resorts that are better known internationally. A keen intermediate who wants to make the most of the links can get a real sense of travelling around on the snow. And as the list of plus-points suggests, we see many attractions in the place.

If you like your slopes to be reassuringly consistent, Schladming has a strong claim on your attention. If on the other hand you like the spice of variety and the thrill of a serious challenge, you might find it all rather tame.

What's new

The old gondola from Haus was upgraded to an eight-seater last season – eliminating the queues here. The slow double chair-lift from Rohrmoos on Hochwurzen was also replaced, by a fast six-person chair.

For 2001/02, the new Ski Alliance Amadé joint lift pass is being introduced, covering more than 30 ski resorts in this part of Austria.

The resort

The old town of Schladming has a long skiing tradition – and it's well known to armchair skiers, having hosted World Cup races for many years.

The town sits at the foot of Planai, one of four mountains that are now linked by lifts and pistes to offer 115km of runs. A gondola starting close to the centre goes most of the way up. A couple of km to the east is the small, rustic village of Haus, where a cable-car and gondola go up to the highest of the four linked mountains, Hauser Kaibling. From the western suburbs of Schladming there are chair-lifts back towards Planai and on towards the next mountain to the west, Hochwurzen. The latter chain of lifts passes through Rohrmoos, a quiet, scattered village set on what is effectively a giant nursery slope.

The town (it is definitely not a village) has a charming, traffic-free main square, prettily lit at night, around which you'll find most of the shops, restaurants and bars (and some appealing hotels). The busy main road bypasses the town and is separated from it by a river. Much of the accommodation is close to the centre, which is where we'd recommend staying – just a few minutes' walk from the Planai gondola. But some (mostly cheaper) hotels and most apartments are on the outskirts. The modern sports centre and tennis halls are near the Sporthotel Royer, five minutes'

SCHLADMING TOURIST OFFICE

← Woodland runs of easy red gradient are the norm on all four linked mountains

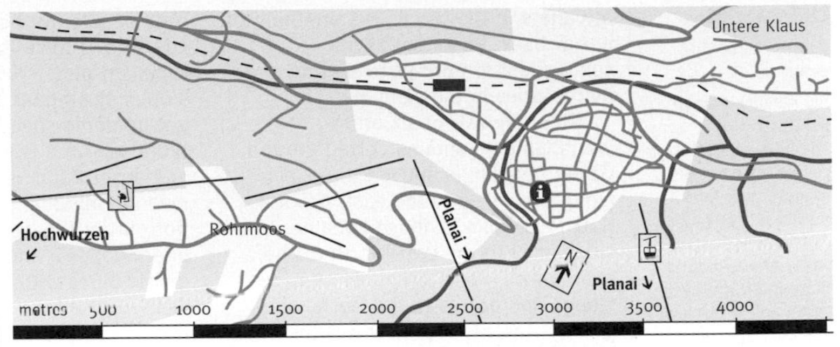

MOUNTAIN FACTS

Figures relate to the whole Sportregion Schladming-Ramsau/ Dachstein area

Altitude	745m-2015m
Lifts	88
Pistes	167km
Blue	29%
Red	61%
Black	10%
Artificial snow	100%
Recco detectors used	

walk from the centre. Rohrmoos makes an excellent base for beginners who aren't looking for lively nightlife. Haus is preferable for those looking for more of a village atmosphere.

Despite the recently created links, it's still quicker to get to a particular hill by car, taxi or the 'very efficient' ski-bus along the valley.

The new Ski Alliance Amadé lift pass covers over 30 partially or wholly linked resorts in this part of Austria. Trips to Bad Gastein are feasible by rail but include at least one change. Drivers can also visit Wagrain/Flachau, Kleinarl and Maria Alm. Snowsure Obertauern is not far away but is not included on the lift pass.

The mountains

Most pistes are on the wooded north-facing slopes above the main valley, with some going into the side valleys higher up, and there are some open slopes above the trees. The views from the limited Dachstein glacier (a 45-minute bus-ride) are superb.

THE SLOPES

Four linked sectors – and more

Each of the linked sectors is quite a serious mountain with a variety of lifts and runs to play on. **Planai** and **Hauser Kaibling** are linked at altitude via the high, wooded bowl between them. In contrast, the links with **Hochwurzen** and the fourth linked mountain, **Reiteralm,** are at valley level. So although the links offer the ability to travel around, getting around the whole area can take time – and involves skiing some runs you wouldn't choose to descend for fun. Although from Schladming it's perfectly practical to get to Hauser Kaibling or Hochwurzen, if you want to spend time on Reiteralm it's more practical to get the bus, or a taxi, to the lift base at Pichl or Gleiming. The link between Planai and Hochwurzen involves riding a lift through a tunnel, whichever way you are travelling.

All the mountains have fairly similar terrain, with mainly red runs of much the same pitch down through heavily wooded north-facing slopes. The lack

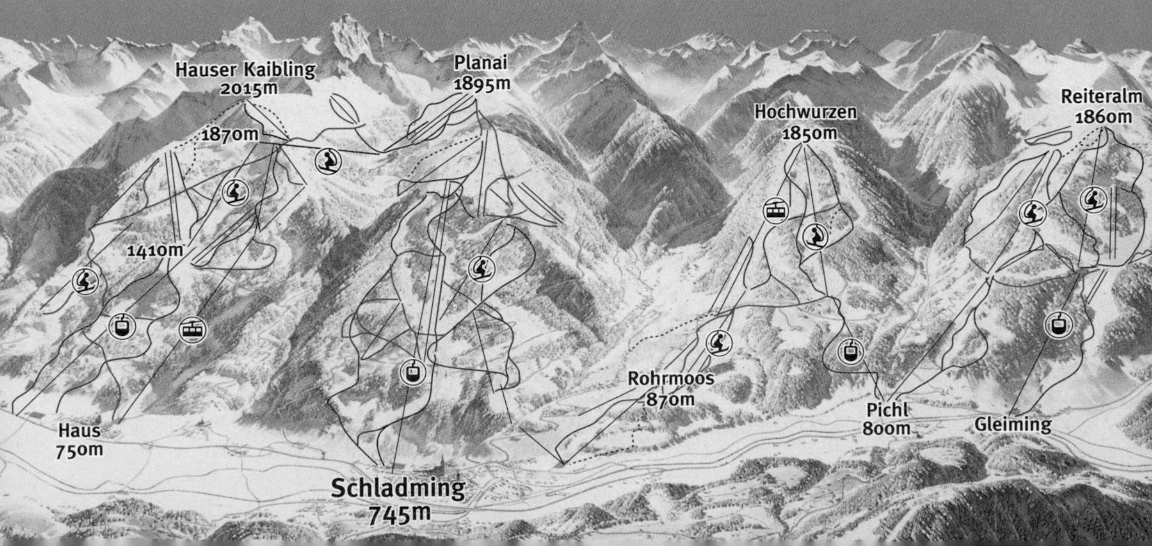

LIFT PASSES

2001/02 prices in euros

Ski Alliance Amadé Ski Pass

The new joint lift pass covers over 275 lifts in more than 30 ski resorts in this part of Austria: the Gastein valley and Grossarl; Salzburger Sportwelt (main areas: Flachau/ Wagrain/ St Johann and Zauchensee/ Kleinarl); Hochkönigs Winterreich (Maria Alm and neighbours). Buses, trains and road tolls between the resorts are covered by the pass.

Main pass

1-day pass 32
(low season 29)
6-day pass 150
(low-season 140)

Children

Under 15: 6-day pass 75
(low season 70)
15-19: 6-day pass 140
Under 6: free pass

Notes Morning and afternoon tickets are also available (as are tickets from 11am, 1pm and 2pm on). 1½-day and 2½-day tickets are also possible.

SCHOOLS/GUIDES

2000/01 prices in euros

Tritscher and Hopl-Planai

Classes 5 days
4hr: 2hr am and pm
5 full days: 109

Children's classes

Ages: from 4
5 full days: 145

Private lessons

1hr, 2½hr or 4½hr
38 for 1hr; each additional person 12

Snowboard School Gerfried Schuller

Classes 5 days
5 full days: 116

Children's classes

Ages: from 5

Private lessons

1hr or 4hr
36 for 1hr; each additional person 7.

of variety in the slopes is something of a drawback. Reporters have complained of poor piste signing and inaccuracies in the piste map.

There are five or six other identifiable mountains dotted around. Galsterbergalm is above Pruggern, along the valley to the east, beyond Haus. Fageralm is above Forstau, up a side valley to the east. North of the main valley, Ramsau has its own low slopes and access to the Dachstein glacier. And near Gröbming is the small area of Stoderzinken.

SNOW RELIABILITY
Excellent in cold weather

Schladming's impressive snowmaking operation makes it a particularly good choice for early holidays; and the northerly orientation of the slopes and superb maintenance help keep the slopes in better shape than in some neighbouring resorts. They claim 100% artificial snow-cover, and certainly the main runs to the valley have full cover. Be wary of the steep bottom part of the World Cup downhill run back to town – it can get extremely icy. The best natural snow is usually found on Reiteralm and Hochwurzen.

FOR EXPERTS
Strictly intermediate stuff

Schladming's status as a World Cup downhill venue doesn't make it macho. The steep black finish to the Men's Downhill course and the moderate mogul runs at the top of Planai and Hauser Kaibling are the only really challenging slopes. Hauser Kaibling's off-piste is good, although limited.

FOR INTERMEDIATES
Red runs rule

The area is ideal for intermediate cruising. The majority of runs are graded red but it's often difficult to distinguish them from the blues.

The open sections at the top of Planai and Hauser Kaibling have some more challenging slopes. And the two World Cup pistes, and the red that runs parallel to the Haus downhill course, are ideal for fast intermediates. Excellent piste grooming and quiet slopes at off-peak times allow you to get up some speed – the Women's World Cup run is great fun.

Hauser Kaibling has a lovely meandering blue running from top to bottom for the less confident intermediates, and Reiteralm has some gentle blues with good snow. Runs are well groomed, so intermediates will find the slopes generally flattering.

FOR BEGINNERS
Good slopes but poorly sited

Complete beginners generally start on the extensive but low-altitude Rohrmoos nursery area – fine if you are based there, not if you're not. Another novice area near the top of Planai is more convenient for most people and has better snow.

FOR CROSS-COUNTRY
Extensive network of trails

Given sufficient snow-cover, there are 300km of trails in the region. The 1999 World Cross-country Championships were held at nearby Ramsau. There are local loops along the main valley floor and in the valleys between Planai and Hochwurzen. Further afield there are more snowsure trails at Stoderzinken.

QUEUES
Only valley bottlenecks

The Planai gondola can suffer delays on peak-season mornings, but there are few other problems. The new gondola at Haus has relieved the pressure there, though the four-person chair at the top – essential for getting to Planai – still generates queues. The Reiteralm gondola is ancient and slow.

MOUNTAIN RESTAURANTS
Plenty of nice places

There are plenty of attractive rustic restaurants in all sectors, though Planai probably has the edge. Onkel Willi's is popular for its live music, open fire, indoor nooks and crannies

---

boarding *Schladming is popular with boarders. Most lifts on the spread-out mountains are gondolas or chairs, with some short drags around. There are two fun-parks and half-pipes on the main linked area, with another fun-park on the Galsterbergalm. The Blue Tomato snowboard shop also runs the specialist snowboard school. The area is ideal for beginners and intermediates, except when the lower slopes are icy, though there are few exciting challenges for expert boarders bar the off-piste tree runs. Nightlife can be quite lively.*

---

and large terrace, Mitterhausalm is good, and the Schladminger Hütte at the top of the Planai gondola has 'great food'. The Knapplhof at Hauser Kaibling is full of ski racing mementos.

SCHOOLS AND GUIDES
Satisfaction likely
There are two schools, and the only recent reports are on the Tritscher school: 'I was the only English speaker in the group but the instructor spoke good English and repeated everything,' says one. Boarders are well catered for by a specialist school.

FACILITIES FOR CHILDREN
Rohrmoos is the place
The extensive gentle slopes of Rohrmoos are ideal for building up youngsters' confidence. The nursery here takes children from 18 months.

Staying there

HOW TO GO
Packages means hotels
Packaged accommodation is in hotels and pensions, but there are plenty of apartments for independent travellers.
Hotels Most of the accommodation is in modestly priced pensions but there are also a few more upmarket hotels.
((((4 **Sporthotel Royer** (200) Big, smart and comfortable, a few minutes' walk from the main Planai lift. Pool.
(((3 **Alte Post** (22571) Characterful old inn with great position on the main square. Very good food, but some rooms are rather small by 4-star standards. 'Excellent value' says a recent reporter.
(((3 **Zum Stadttor** (24525) Similarly priced, although less charming and well placed. 'Comfortable with excellent food,' says a reporter.
(((3 **Neue Post** (22105) Large rooms, friendly, good food, central.
(((3 **Schladmingerhof** (23525) Bright, modern chalet in peaceful position, out in Untere Klaus.
Self-catering Haus Girik (22663) is the best-positioned apartment house in town, close to the gondola.

EATING OUT
Some good places
Fritzi's Gasthaus is highly recommended by readers. Other recommendations include the Kirchenwirt hotel ('excellent home cooking'), Giovanni's (for pizza), Gasthof Brunner ('good value'), Talbachschenke ('good grills and atmosphere') and Lisi's Landhausstüberl. Hotels Neue and Alte Post are 'good but pricey'.

APRES-SKI
Varied and quite lively
Some of the mountain restaurants are lively at the end of the afternoon, but reporters agree that down in the town there's a disappointing lack of teatime animation. Charly's Treff (with umbrella bar) opposite the Planai gondola is the main exception (and has great photos of local hero Arnold Schwarzenegger inside). The Siglu (in a big plastic igloo-like bubble) also reportedly rocks from 3pm until late.

There is, however, no lack of options later on – a reporter found that many of the central bars open later on and stay open until dawn if necessary. Popular spots include the local brewpub Schwalbenbräu and Café Zauberkistl (translated as Magic Box), where the owner regularly performs conjuring tricks. Das Beisl is a smart, beautiful bar attracting a varied age group. Hanglbar has wooden decor and middle-of-the-road music and occasional karaoke. Ferry's Pub has a nautical theme, loud music and a quiet room at the rear. La Porta gets very crowded and has live music. The Gondl-Treff has an international football theme, with big-screen TV. The Sonderbar is a disco with international DJs and three bars.

OFF THE SLOPES
Good for all but walkers
Non-skiers are fairly well catered for. Some mountain restaurants are easily reached on foot. The town shops and museum are worth a look. Train trips to Salzburg are easy. Buses run to the old walled town of Radstadt. There's a public pool and ice rink.

Haus 750m

Haus is a real village with a life of its own. It has a fair amount of accommodation plus its own ski schools and kindergartens. The user-friendly nursery area is handily situated between town and the gondola station. There's a railway station, so excursions are easy, but off-slope activities and nightlife are very limited. Hotel prices are generally lower than in Schladming. Hotel Gürtl has been recommended for 'good food and ambience'.

CHILDCARE

At Rohrmoos the nursery takes children from 18 months.

Children in ski school can be looked after all day.

GETTING THERE

Air Salzburg, transfer $1\frac{1}{2}$hr.

Rail Mainline station in resort.

ACTIVITIES

Indoor Swimming, sauna, bowling, indoor tennis court, squash, museum
Outdoor Ice skating, curling, 8km floodlit toboggan run, sleigh rides, 50km of cleared paths in the Schladming and surrounding area, paragliding

Phone numbers
From elsewhere in Austria add the prefix 03687.
From abroad use the prefix +43 3687.

TOURIST OFFICE

Postcode A-8970
t +43 (3687) 222680
f 24138
touristoffice@schladming.com
www.schladming.com

Sölden 1380m

Good, extensive intermediate slopes with throbbing nightlife

WHAT IT COSTS

(4)

HOW IT RATES

The slopes

Snow	*****
Extent	***
Experts	***
Intermediates	****
Beginners	**
Convenience	***
Queues	***
Restaurants	***

The rest

Scenery	***
Resort charm	**
Off-slope	**

What's new

Previously closed in winter, in recent years Sölden's glaciers have been opened up to winter visitors by a series of fast new lifts – 'the golden gate to the glacier'. A new gondola was installed last season on the Tiefenbach glacier. Also new was a six-pack from Langegg – in the valley separating the two local sectors – to the Rotkoglhütte, greatly speeding access to the Rotkogl slopes for people based at the other end of the resort.

There is a new garage by the Giggijoch gondola with parking spaces for 600 cars.

The 2-seater Heidebahn chair from Gaislachalm up to the Gaislachkogl sector is being replaced by a fast quad for next season.

- ⊕ Excellent snow reliability, with access to two glaciers
- ⊕ Fairly extensive network of slopes suited to adventurous intermediates
- ⊕ Continually improving lift system
- ⊕ Very lively nightlife
- ⊕ Short transfers and day trips to nearby Innsbruck

- ⊖ Sprawling, traffic-filled village
- ⊖ Spread-out village means some central hotels are inconvenient for the two main lifts
- ⊖ Inconvenient beginners' slopes
- ⊖ Drink-fuelled nightlife too rowdy for many visitors
- ⊖ Limited off-slope activities

Sölden has invested massively in new lifts to link its home slopes, which suit adventurous intermediates best, with snowsure runs on the Rettenbach and Tiefenbach glaciers. This is very good news – the Tiefenbach, in particular, is a serious 2km-long slope – and may be enough to establish this quite impressive resort on the international market at last.

THE RESORT

Despite its traditional Tirolean-style buildings and tree-filled valley, Sölden is no beauty: it is a large, traffic-filled place that sprawls along both sides of a river and main road (particularly busy at weekends). The resort attracts a young, lively crowd – mostly Dutch and German – bent on partying.

Gondolas from opposite ends of town go up to Sölden's home slopes – Gaislachkogl and Giggijoch. Staying in a hamlet near one of these lifts gets you away from the noisy main street (an efficient free shuttle-bus service runs between the two base stations). Or you could stay in tiny, remote Hochsölden (2090m), up on the Giggijoch slopes, provided evening isolation doesn't worry you.

THE MOUNTAINS

The two similar-sized sectors are linked by chair-lifts out of the Rettenbachtal that separates them. The Rettenbach and Tiefenbach glaciers – 15km away by road, and until recently closed in winter – are now connected by a series of fast lifts from Rotkogl.

Slopes The Gaislachkogl runs are almost entirely red or black, but there are several blue runs around Giggijoch. Both main sectors have red runs through trees to the village.

The Rettenbach and Tiefenbach glacier slopes are gentler – blues and reds – and rise from 2685m to 3250m.

Piste marking and grooming are reportedly 'very good'.

Snow reliability Most of the area is over 2100m – a good height for Austria – and north-east-facing, so the slopes are generally reliable for snow. Now that there is access to the glaciers, Sölden is one of the best Alpine bets.

Snowboarding There are fun-parks and half-pipes at Giggijoch and on the Rettenbach glacier.

Experts Sölden's pistes have little to challenge experts – three widely separated chair-lifts serve the only half-serious black runs. But off-piste is another story: there is a mountain guides' office in Sölden and there are extensive off-piste possibilities on both main mountains – particularly from the top of Gaislachkogl to the mid-station. And at the top of the valley is one of the Alps' premier touring areas.

Intermediates Most of Sölden's main slopes are red runs ideal for adventurous intermediates. There are several easy blacks, and the long, quiet piste down to Gaislachalm – floodlit on Wednesday nights – is ideal for high-speed cruising. Giggijoch and Rotkogl are good if you prefer a more moderate pace, but Sölden is not really for timid types.

Beginners The beginners' slopes are situated inconveniently – just above the village at Innerwald – and prone to poor snow. Near-beginners can use the blues at Giggijoch.

Cross-country There are a couple of uninspiring cross-country loops by the river, plus small areas at Zwieselstein and Vent. The saving grace is altitude.

MOUNTAIN FACTS

Altitude 1380m-3250m	
Lifts	34
Pistes	141km
Blue	32%
Red	52%
Black	16%
Artificial snow	27km
Recco detectors used	

Phone numbers
From elsewhere in Austria add the prefix 05254.
From abroad use the prefix +43 5254.

TOURIST OFFICE

Postcode A-6450
t +43 (5254) 5100
f 510520
info@soelden.com
www.soelden.com

Queues Recent upgrades have done away with most of the queues, though one visitor reported late-afternoon bottlenecks for the return links from the glaciers.

Mountain restaurants The restaurants have improved in recent years, partly because they have increased in capacity. The self-service places around Giggijoch get very crowded. Gampealm, in the Rettenbachtal, is an atmospheric old hut. The Gaislachalm area is your best bet for avoiding the masses – the self-service Silbertal is recommended.

Schools and guides The only reports we have of the three ski schools tell of small class sizes.

Facilities for children There is no proper day-care nursery for children, but baby-sitters can be arranged. Children aged three and up can join the ski kindergarten. There are special lift pass deals for families.

STAYING THERE

How to go Sölden doesn't generally feature in UK packages. However, there is plenty of accommodation available through the tourist office.

Hotels Sölden has some good hotels. The 5-star Central (22600) is the best and one of the biggest in town. The 4-star Regina (2301), by the Gaislachkogl lift is heartily recommended by a recent reporter. The Arno B&B (2488) on the piste above the Giggijoch lift, and Gasthof Grüner (2214) in Ausserwald are also recommended. Self-catering apartments at the Posthäusl (31380) are good quality.

Eating out Café Hubertus caters for everything from snacks to full meals. The Nudeltopf and Corso are the best pizzerias, and the Hotel Birkenhof's restaurant is pleasantly traditional. S'Pfandl, and Hermann's – up the hill a little at the hamlet of See – are recommended.

Après-ski Sölden's après-ski is notorious. It starts up the mountain, notably at Giggijoch. The resort is full of bars, live bands and throbbing discos. It gets very loud and very rowdy. Even our keenest après-ski reporter was shocked on his last visit: 'Lots of drunks urinating and smashing glasses in the street. There is table dancing and striptease at Rodelhütte, and Lawine has great theme nights if you are into latex and leather.' Phillip's ice bar and disco are also popular and noisy. Somewhat tamer are the nightly toboggan evenings, with drinking and dancing before an exciting 6km floodlit run back to town from the Gaislachalm mountain restaurant.

Off the slopes There's a new sports centre and swimming pool complex, and an ice rink, too. Trips to Innsbruck and Igls are possible.

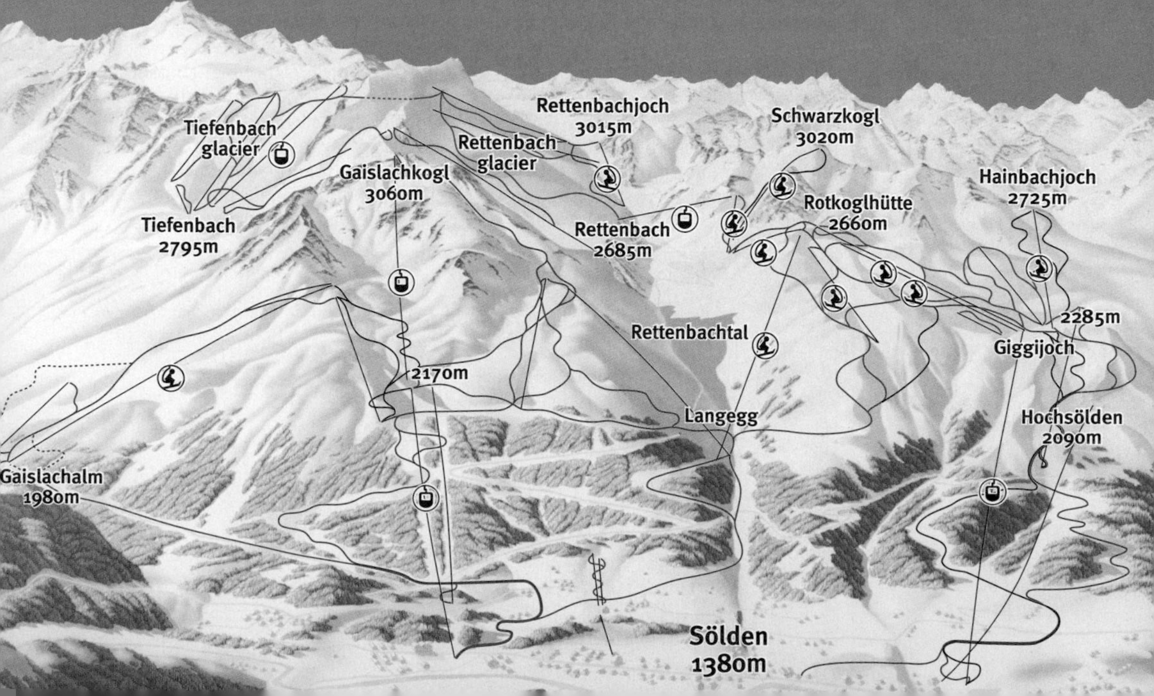

Söll 700m

Small, lively village with large, easy ski and snowboard area

WHAT IT COSTS

HOW IT RATES

The slopes

Snow	**
Extent	****
Experts	*
Intermediates	****
Beginners	***
Convenience	**
Queues	***
Restaurants	**

The rest

Scenery	***
Resort charm	***
Off-slope	**

What's new

The snowmaking capacity in the Ski Welt has been hugely increased in recent years. It now covers 130km of pistes (over half the pistes in the Ski Welt) and is the largest snowmaking facility anywhere in Austria.

For 2000/01 the old single-seat chair to the Hohe Salve was replaced by a fast eight-seater gondola from Hochsöll, giving much quicker access to the steepest runs and to the Hopfgarten and Brixen areas (via a link that got new snowmaking for 2000/01, too).

In Hopfgarten, a queue-prone T-bar (a key link on the Ski Welt circuit) was replaced by an eight-seater chair.

- ⊕ Part of Ski Welt, Austria's largest linked ski and snowboard area
- ⊕ Local slopes are the highest and steepest in the Ski Welt and north-facing so keep their snow well
- ⊕ Massive recent investment in snowmaking has paid off
- ⊕ Plenty of cheap and cheerful pensions for those on a budget
- ⊕ Pretty village with lively après-ski

- ⊖ Poor natural snow record
- ⊖ Long walk or infrequent bus-ride to the lifts
- ⊖ Little for experts or good intermediates
- ⊖ Ski Welt slopes can get busy at weekends and in high season
- ⊖ Local slopes are the most crowded in the Ski Welt
- ⊖ Mostly short runs in local sector

Söll has long been popular with groups of British beginners and intermediates. Its pretty scenery, gentle slopes, small attractive traditional village, good-value accommodation and lively nightlife attract a mixture of young singles looking for a fun time and families looking for a quiet time. In the 1980s it gained notoriety as prime lager-lout territory; it still has some loud bars but has calmed down a lot. Many visitors find the village surprisingly small and are disappointed by the distance between it and the slopes (and by the bus service).

Until recently its main drawback has always been snow – or lack of it. Because of its low altitude and sunny slopes, pistes have often been slushy or bare, not just in Söll but also throughout the extensive Ski Welt circuit it is part of. But this problem has been tackled by a massive investment in snowmaking and half of the Ski Welt's 250km of piste are now covered by snowmaking – more than in any other Austrian ski area. This ensures the region's main pistes and links stay open, though it can't prevent slush and ice developing.

When the snow is good Söll can be a great place for a holiday, cruising the attractive and undemanding pistes of Austria's largest linked area.

The resort

Söll is a small, pretty, friendly village – much smaller than you might expect by its reputation; you can explore it in a few minutes and there aren't many shops. New buildings are traditional in design and there's a huge church near the centre which, according to a recent reporter, is well worth a visit at dusk as the graveyard is lit with candles. The pretty scenery adds to Söll's charm, and it benefits from being off the main road through the Tirol.

SKI WELT

If you are lucky and get fresh snow like this, the Ski Welt is an intermediates' paradise →

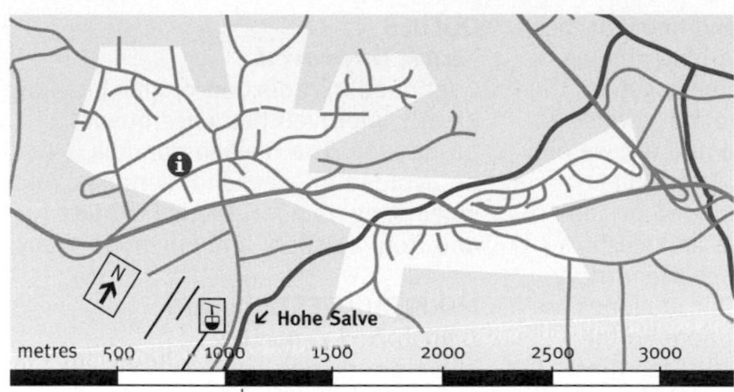

MOUNTAIN FACTS

Altitude	620m-1830m
Lifts	93
Pistes	250km
Blue	43%
Red	48%
Black	9%
Artificial snow	130km

LIFT PASSES

2001/02 prices in euros

Ski Welt Wilder Kaiser–Brixental
Covers all lifts in the Wilder Kaiser-Brixental area from Going to Westendorf, and the ski-bus.

Beginners Points tickets (100 points 300). Most beginner lifts cost from 3 to 10 points.

Main pass
1-day pass 29
6-day pass 143

Children
Under 16: 6-day pass 81
Under 6: free pass

Short-term passes
Single ascent on some lifts, passes from 11am, noon 2pm to the end of the day.

Alternative periods
5 in 7 days, 7 in 10 days, 10 in 14 days.

Alternative passes
Söll pass available (6-day pass for adults 117, for children 68), covers 12 lifts, 34km piste). Kitzbüheler Alpen-skipass covers five large ski areas – Schneewinkel (St Johann), Ski Region Kitzbühel, Ski Welt Wilder Kaiser, Bergbahnen Wildschönau and Alpbachtal (adult 6-day 160).

The slopes are a bus- or taxi-ride or a 15-minute walk from the centre, the other side of a busy road with a pedestrian tunnel underneath. The bus service has been criticised by most reporters as being too infrequent. Some accommodation is further away, though there is some near the lifts too.

The mountains

The Ski Welt is the largest linked area in Austria, but that doesn't make it a Trois Vallées. It covers Hopfgarten, Brixen, Scheffau and Ellmau, but is basically a typically small, low, pastoral Austrian hill multiplied several times. One section is much like another, and most slopes best suit early to average intermediates. Runs are short and scenery attractive rather than stunning – although the panoramic views from the Hohe Salve are impressive on a clear day.

Westendorf is separate, but covered by the area pass. The Kitzbüheler Alpenskipass also covers many other resorts easily reached by car including Kitzbühel, Schneewinkel (includes St Johann, Fieberbrunn, Steinplatte, Waidring), Niederau and Alpbach – an impressive total of 260 lifts and 680km of pistes.

THE SLOPES
Short run network

A gondola takes all but complete beginners up to the shelf of Hochsöll, where there are a couple of short lifts and connections in several directions.

An eight-person gondola (new for last season) takes you to the high point of Hohe Salve. From here there are stunning views and runs down to Kälbersalve and Hopfgarten via Rigi. Rigi can also be reached by alternative chairs and pistes without going to Hohe Salve – to which it is itself linked by chairs. Rigi is also the start of runs down to Itter. From Kälbersalve you can head down south-facing runs to Brixen or up to Zinsberg and Eiberg and towards the north-facing runs in the Ellmau sector.

A quicker way to Ellmau without taking as many south-facing slopes is by taking a cable-car from Hochsöll.

The whole area is vast and will easily keep an early or average intermediate amused for a week.

We have had lots of criticism of the piste map by recent reporters: 'Direction of runs/lifts and the links not clear' and 'Piste map did not correspond with lift numbers – generally a very bad map.'

SNOW RELIABILITY
Artificial help saves the day

With a very low average height, and important links that get a lot of sun, the snowmaking that the Ski Welt has installed in recent seasons is essential. At 125km and covering half the area's pistes, it is one of Austria's biggest artificial snow installations. We were there in January 1999, before any major snowfalls, and snowmaking was keeping the links open well. It did not, however, prevent slush and icy patches forming – usually slush on south-facing slopes, ice on north-facing ones.

FOR EXPERTS
Not a lot

The black run from Hohe Salve towards Hochsöll and the black run alongside the Brixen gondola are the only challenging pistes. There are further blacks in Scheffau and Ellmau, but most experts will need to seek amusement off-piste – from Scheffau's Brandstadl down to Söll, for example.

FOR INTERMEDIATES
Mainly easy runs

With good snow, the Ski Welt is a paradise for early intermediates and those who love easy cruising. There

boarding *Söll is a good place to try out boarding: slopes are gentle and there are plenty of gondolas and chairs. For decent boarders it's more limited – the slopes of the Ski Welt are tame. But there is a fun-park and quarter-pipe near Hochsöll and lots of lively bars in the evening.*

SCHOOLS/GUIDES

2000/01 prices in euros

Söll-Hochsöll

Classes 5 days
2hr or 4hr: 10am-noon and 1.30-3.30
5 full days: 104

Children's classes
Ages: 5 to 14
5 full days: 100

Private lessons
Hourly or full day (4hr)
36 for 1hr; each additional person 13

Austria

Classes 6 days
4hr: 10am-noon and 1.30-3.30
5 full days: 95

Children's classes
Ages: 5 to 14
5 full days: 91

Private lessons
Hourly or daily
35 for 1hr; each additional person 11

ProSöll

Classes 5 days
4hr: 10am-noon and 1.30-3.30
5 full days: 104

Children's classes
Ages: 5 to 14
(younger than 5 years on request)
5 full days: 100

Private lessons
Hourly or daily
36 for 1hr; each additional person 13

are lots of blue runs and many of the reds in truth deserve a blue grading. It is a big area and you really get a feeling of travelling around – we skied it for two days in 1999 and felt we only scratched the surface. The main challenge you may find is when the snow isn't perfect – ice and slush can make even gentle slopes seem tricky. In general the most difficult slopes are those from the mid-stations to the valleys: the most direct of the runs between Brandstadl and Blaiken, the pistes down to Brixen and the red run from Hochsöll back to Söll, for example. Higher up, the red from Hohe Salve to Rigi is a good cruise on relatively good snow.

FOR BEGINNERS

Excellent when snow is good

The big area of nursery slopes between the main road and the gondola station is ideal when snow is abundant – gentle, spacious, uncrowded and free from good skiers whizzing past. But it can get icy or slushy. In poor snow the Hochsöll area is used. Near-beginners and fast learners can get home to the bottom station when the narrow blue from Hochsöll is not too icy.

FOR CROSS-COUNTRY

Neighbouring villages are better

Söll has 35km of local trails but they are less interesting than those between Hopfgarten and Kelchsau or the ones around and beyond Ellmau. Lack of snow-cover is a big problem.

QUEUES

Much improved

Continued introduction of new lifts has greatly improved this once queue-prone area. The Blaiken gondola is to be avoided on weekend mornings. And when snow is poor, the linking lifts to and from Zinsberg and Eiberg get busy.

MOUNTAIN RESTAURANTS

Good, but crowded

There are quite a few jolly little chalets dotted about, but we received a few complaints of insufficient seating and long queues this year. The atmospheric Stockalm (a converted cow shed), Kraftalm and Grundalm are all near Hochsöll. The Alpenrose, near the top of Hohe Salve, has a good sun terrace, generous portions and reasonable prices. Further afield, the Neualm, halfway down to Blaiken, is one of the best huts in the Ski Welt. The nearby Brantlalm has been recommended for lovely views. The Jochstubn at Eiberg is self-service but has a good atmosphere and excellent Tiroler Gröstl. The Filzalm above Brixen is a good place for a quick drink on the way back from the circuit. But our favourite is the Rübezahl above Ellmau – very rustic with wooden carvings, low doors, several rooms and good food.

SCHOOLS AND GUIDES

Three competing schools

The Austria school and the bigger Söll-Hochsöll school have fairly good reputations. But we had a recent report of an 'instructor with little patience'.

CHILDCARE

The ski schools take children from age 5 in special snow-gardens on the nursery slopes from 9.45 to 4pm. Once they progress to Hochsöll, care has to be arranged with the instructor.

Next to the main ski kindergarten, the Söll Hochsöll school operates a Mini Club for children aged 3 to 5 from 9.45 to 4pm.

GETTING THERE

Air Salzburg, transfer 2hr. Innsbruck, transfer 1½hr.

Rail Wörgl (13km) or Kufstein (15km); bus to resort.

Söll phone numbers
From elsewhere in Austria add the prefix 05333.
From abroad use the prefix +43 5333.

ACTIVITIES

Indoor Swimming, sauna, solarium, massage, bowling, squash
Outdoor Natural ice rink (skating, curling), sleigh rides, 3km floodlit ski and toboggan runs, paragliding, hang-gliding

FACILITIES FOR CHILDREN
Fast becoming a family resort

Söll has fairly wide-ranging facilities – the Söll-Hochsöll ski kindergarten, a Mini Club, which looks after children aged three to five who don't want to spend all day on the slopes, and a special kids-only drag and slope on the opposite side of the village to the main lifts. Reports welcome.

Staying there 

There is some accommodation out near the lifts but most is in or around the village centre – a free ski-bus-ride from the slopes. Being on the edge of town nearest the lifts is the best for those who are prepared to walk to the slopes. The other side of town has the advantage that you can board the bus there before it gets too crowded. Be aware that some guest houses are literally miles from the centre and lifts, and that the ski-bus does not serve every nook and cranny of this sprawling community.

HOW TO GO
Mostly cheap, cheerful gasthofs

There is a wide choice of simple gasthofs, pensions and B&Bs, and an adequate amount of better-quality hotel accommodation – mainly 3-star. Söll is not a big catered chalet resort, but there are a couple of big 'club hotels' run by British tour operators.

Hotels

(3) **Greil** (5289) The only 4-star – attractive place, but out of the centre on the wrong side for the lifts and pool.

(3) **Postwirt** (5081) Attractive, central old 3-star with own bar and separate stube.

(3) **Bergland** (5484) Small 3-star, well placed midway between the village and lifts.

(3) **Panorama** (5309) 3-star far from lifts but with own bus stop; wonderful views; pleasant rooms; best cakes around.

(3) **Tulpe** (5223) Next to the lifts.

(2) **Feldwebel** (5224) Central 2-star.

(2) **Schirast** (5544) Next to the lifts.

(2) **Garni-Tenne** (5387) B&B gasthof between centre and main road.

Self-catering The central Ferienhotel Schindlhaus has nice accommodation, though the best apartments in town are attached to the Bergland hotel.

↑ Gentle, rolling, wooded slopes and lots of them is what the Ski Welt is all about

SKI WELT

EATING OUT
A fair choice

Some of the best restaurants are in hotels. The Greil and Postwirt are good, but the Schindlhaus is said to be the best. Giovanni does excellent pizzas, while other places worth a visit include the Dorfstub'n and the Venezia, which received a glowing report from one guest last season.

APRES-SKI
Still some very loud bars

Söll is not as raucous as it used to be, but it's still very lively and a lot of places have live music. Pub 15 is a bit of a sleazy remnant of the old days, but is lively. The Whisky Mühle is a large disco that can get a little rowdy, especially after other bars close. The Postkeller sometimes has a singalong. Buffalo's Western Saloon is popular. There's a floodlit piste and separate toboggan run – both from top to bottom of the gondola. And for a romantic evening you can hire the Gerhard Berger VIP gondola, complete with leather upholstery, curtains and a champagne bucket.

OFF THE SLOPES
Not bad for a small village

You could spend a happy day in the wonderfully equipped Panoramabad: taking a sauna, swimming, lounging

TOURIST OFFICE

Postcode A-6306
t +43 (5333) 5216
f 6180
info@soell.com
www.soell.com

about. The large baroque church would be the pride of many tourist towns. There are numerous coach excursions, including trips to Salzburg, Innsbruck and even Vipiteno over in Italy.

Hopfgarten 620m

Hopfgarten is an unspoilt, friendly and traditional resort tucked away several kilometres from the busy Wörgl road.

THE RESORT

The village is a good size: small enough to be intimate, large enough to have plenty of off-slope amenities. Most hotels are within five minutes' walk of the chair-lift to Rigi.

THE MOUNTAIN

Hopfgarten offers queue-free access to Rigi and Hohe Salve – the high point of the Ski Welt.

Slopes When snow is good, the runs down to Hopfgarten and the nearby villages of Brixen and Itter are some of the best in the Ski Welt. But the fine, and relatively snowsure, runs above Scheffau are irksomely distant.

For a change of scene, and perhaps less crowded pistes, take a bus to Westendorf (see separate chapter) or Kelchsau, both on the Ski Welt pass.

Snow reliability The resort's great weakness is the poor snow quality on the south-west-facing home slope.

Snowboarding A fun-park near Hochsöll can be accessed from the Hohe Salve above Hopfgarten.

Experts Experts should venture off-piste for excitement.

Intermediates The whole Ski Welt is great for intermediates.

Beginners There is a convenient beginners' slope in the village, but it is sunny as well as low, so lack of snow-cover is likely to mean excursions up the mountain to the higher blue runs – at the cost of a lift pass.

Cross-country Hopfgarten is one of the best cross-country bases in the area. There are fine trails to Kelchsau (11km) and Niederau (15km), and the Itter–Bocking loop (15km) starts nearby. Westendorf's trails are close.

Queues There's only a two-person chair out of the village, so queues can be a problem in the morning.

Mountain restaurants See Söll.

Schools and guides Partly because Hopfgarten seems to attract large numbers of Australians, English is widely spoken in the two schools.

Hopfgarten phone numbers
From elsewhere in Austria add the prefix 05335.
From abroad use the prefix +43 5335.

Facilities for children Hopfgarten is a family resort, with a nursery and ski kindergarten.

STAYING THERE

How to go Cheap and cheerful gasthofs, pensions and little private B&Bs are the norm here.

Hotels The exceptions to the rule are the comfortable 4-star hotels Hopfgarten (3920) with pool, and Sporthotel Fuchs (2420), both well placed for the main lift.

Eating out Most of the restaurants are hotel-based, but there are exceptions, including a Chinese and a pizzeria.

Après-ski Après-ski is generally quiet, though a lively holiday can usually be ensured if you go with Aussie-dominated Contiki Travel.

Off the slopes Off-slope amenities include swimming, riding, bowling, skating, tobogganing and paragliding. The railway makes trips to Salzburg, Innsbruck and Kitzbühel possible.

Brixen 800m

It may not be pretty, but it has a queue-free, high-capacity gondola up to the main Ski Welt slopes.

THE RESORT

Brixen im Thale is a very scattered roadside village at the south-east edge of the Ski Welt, close to Westendorf. The main hotels are near the railway station, a bus-ride from the lifts.

THE MOUNTAIN

When snow is good, Brixen has some of the best slopes in the Ski Welt.

Slopes All three runs leading down under the gondola are fine runs in different ways: an unpisted route and a black and a red with snowmaking. There's a small area of north-facing runs, including nursery slopes, on the other side of the village at Kandleralm.

Snow reliability A chain of snowmakers on the main south-facing piste helps to preserve the snow as long as possible.

Snowboarding See Söll..

Experts The black run alongside the Brixen gondola is one of the only challenging pistes in the area.

Intermediates Some challenging local slopes for intermediates to tackle.

Beginners The nursery slopes are secluded and shady, but meeting up with friends for lunch is a hassle – the area is a bus-ride from the village.

Brixen phone numbers
From elsewhere in Austria add the prefix 05334.
From abroad use the prefix +43 5334.

Cross-country Snow permitting, Brixen is one of the best cross-country villages in the Ski Welt. There is a long trail to Kirchberg, and more leisurely loops that circumnavigate nearby Westendorf. A 5km loop up the mountain at Hochbrixen provides fine views and fairly reliable snow.
Queues New lifts have improved the once queue-prone area.
Mountain restaurants The Filzalm above Brixen has been recommended.
Schools and guides The ski school runs the usual group classes, and mini-groups for five to seven people.
Facilities for children Brixen is not as suitable as other Ski Welt resorts, but it has an all-day ski kindergarten with optional lunchtime supervision.

STAYING THERE

How to go There are plenty of hotels and pensions.
Hotels The hotel Alpenhof (88320) and the Sporthotel (8191) are both 4-star hotels with pools.
Eating out Restaurants are mainly in hotels.
Après-ski Après-ski is quiet, but livelier Westendorf is a short taxi-ride.
Off the slopes Off-slope activities include tennis, hotel-based spa facilities and days out to Salzburg, Innsbruck and Kitzbühel. A free bus runs to Westendorf every 45 minutes.

Scheffau 745m

This is one of the most attractive of the Ski Welt villages.

THE RESORT

Scheffau is a rustic little place complete with pretty white church. It is spacious yet not sprawling, and has a definite centre. It is tucked away a kilometre off the busy main Wörgl road, which increases its charm at the cost of slope convenience: the Ski Welt lifts are at Blaiken, on the opposite side of the main road. If convenience is all important to you, you have the option of staying in Blaiken, where there are several more hotels.

THE MOUNTAIN

Scheffau is well placed for the Ski Welt's best (and most central and snowsure) section of pistes.
Slopes A gondola and parallel two-stage chair give rapid and generally queue-free access directly to Brandstadl and the whole Ski Welt.

Scheffau phone numbers
From elsewhere in Austria add the prefix 05358.
From abroad use the prefix +43 5358.

Snow reliability Nearby Eiberg is the place to go when snow is poor.
Experts The pistes above Blaiken are some of the longest and steepest in the Ski Welt.
Intermediates This is as good a base as any in the area.
Beginners The nursery slope is in the village, and is adequate when snow-cover is good enough. But this location means absolute beginners will be separated from those on the main Ski Welt slopes, and makes Scheffau a poor choice for mixed-ability parties – though one regular visitor finds even real beginners can make it up to Brandstadl by the end of the week.
Cross-country See Ellmau chapter.
Queues There can be weekend queues for the gondola. At such times the two-stage valley chair can be a useful alternative – though the VIP pass for Scheffau guests means you can slide past day trippers in the queue.
Mountain restaurants See Ellmau.
Schools and guides The school is well regarded, but groups can be large.
Facilities for children Both the ski kindergarten and non-ski nursery have good reputations.

STAYING THERE

How to go Four major operators offer packages here.
Hotels The 4-star Kaiser (8000) and 3-star Alpin (8556-0) are the best hotels and both have pool, sauna and steam room. The Wilder Kaiser (8118), Waldhof (8122) and Blaiken (8126) are good value gasthofs near the Blaiken gondola.
Eating out There aren't many village restaurants, and those staying in B&B places are advised to book tables.
Après-ski Après-ski is unlikely to draw Blaiken residents up the hill. The usual rep-organised events such as bowling and tobogganing are available.
Off the slopes Walking apart, there is little to do. Tour operators organise trips to Innsbruck and Salzburg.

Itter 700m

Itter is a tiny village halfway around the mountain between Söll and Hopfgarten, with nursery slopes close to hand and a gondola just outside the village into the Ski Welt, via Hochsöll.

There's a hotel and half a dozen gasthofs and B&Bs. The school has a hire shop, and when conditions are good this is a good beginners' resort.

St Anton 1305m

Non-stop on- and off-slope action and pretty village base

WHAT IT COSTS

5

HOW IT RATES

The slopes

Snow	****
Extent	****
Experts	*****
Intermediates	***
Beginners	*
Convenience	***
Queues	**
Restaurants	***

The rest

Scenery	***
Resort charm	****
Off-slope	***

MOUNTAIN FACTS

Altitude 1305m-2650m

Arlberg region

Lifts	83
Pistes	260km
Blue	25%
Red	50%
Black	25%
Artificial snow	65km

Recco detectors used

- ⊕ Extensive slopes for adventurous intermediates and experts
- ⊕ Heavy snowfalls, backed up by snowmakers, generally give good cover despite sunny slopes
- ⊕ Much-improved lift system has greatly reduced queuing problems
- ⊕ Very lively après-ski
- ⊕ Despite resort expansion, village retains distinct Tirolean charm

- ⊖ Slopes not ideal for beginners or timid intermediates
- ⊖ Most of the tough stuff is off piste
- ⊖ Pistes can get very crowded
- ⊖ Surprisingly little to amuse non-slope-users
- ⊖ Nightlife can get rowdy, with noisy drunks in the early hours

St Anton has, along with Wengen and Mürren, a strong British tradition. From the 1920s, successive generations learned to ski here, adopting the distinctive 'feet together' Arlberg style. Sir Arnold Lunn helped start the Kandahar race here in 1928, and the resort has remained popular with good British skiers ever since. It has also become one of the world's Meccas for ski bums. That's a reflection of the wonderful, tough off-piste runs available in the bowls below the Valluga – the best that Austria has to offer. In good snow conditions they are superb. Sadly, conditions are often less than perfect except just after a fresh snowfall, because of their south-facing aspect. But, if you are lucky with the snow you'll have the time of your life. There's a lot to offer adventurous intermediates too, both locally and at Lech and Zürs, a short bus-ride away.

There are lots of lively discos and bars, which keep going from 3pm to 2am. The resort is ideal for the hard-drinking, disco-loving, keen-for-action holidaymaker who can stand the pace of getting to bed late and being up for the first lift – it's not for those who like a quiet life and gentle, uncrowded pistes.

Major improvements for last season's Alpine Skiing World Championships has left St Anton with much improved lifts from the resort, a smart new swimming pool and conference centre and a less intrusive railway line.

The resort 

St Anton is at the foot of the road up to the Arlberg pass, at the eastern end of a lift network that spreads across to St Christoph and above the pass to Rauz and Stuben. The resort is a long, sprawling mixture of traditional and modern buildings crammed into a narrow valley. It used to be sandwiched between a busy road and the mainline railway – but the railway was moved before the start of the 2000/01 World Championship season, and this area will now be landscaped into a park and ice rink.

It is an attractively bustling place, full of life, colour and noise. Although it is crowded and commercialised, St Anton is full of character, and its traffic-free main street retains Alpine charm and traditional-style buildings.

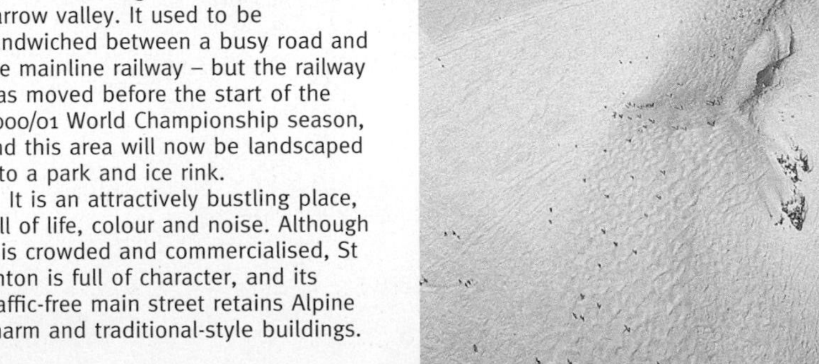

TVB ST ANTON AM ARLBERG

It is the high ungroomed bowls that good skiers and riders come for – but they are far from deserted →

What's new

Major work for the 2001 World Championships benefited the resort enormously. A new eight-person gondola from Nasserein to Gampen has reduced the pressure on the central lifts and made Nasserein a good place to stay for a quieter time. The Fang high-speed quad from east of the central village has improved access for much accommodation too. These lifts have allowed the demolition of the old funicular, making the home piste wider. The railway line and station were moved to the outskirts of the town and the area is to be landscaped into a park with ice rink. For 2001/02 the Arlberg-well.com centre, initially constructed for the World Championships, will be redeveloped to include an indoor pool, flume and waterfall, children's pool, outdoor pool, sauna and seminar and conference rooms.

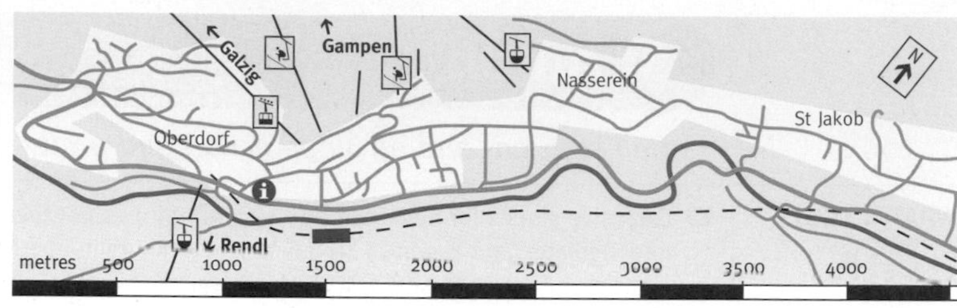

The resort's main slopes start with a central cable-car into the Valluga area and a gondola and chair-lifts into Kapall. On the other side of the main road (served by free buses) a gondola goes to the Rendl area.

If you want to go further afield, regular buses go to Zürs, Lech and the less well-known Klösterle-Sonnenkopf area (which we had a rave review of), and are all covered by the Arlberg lift pass. These buses can get busy and a reporter complained this year of 'a bit of a scrum' and lack of organisation collecting payment and storing skis. Serfaus, Nauders, Ischgl and Sölden are also feasible outings by car.

The mountains

St Anton vies with Val-d'Isère for the title of 'resort with most undergraded slopes'. There are plenty of red pistes that would be black in many other resorts, and plenty of blues that would be red. A few years ago, there were no black pistes on the map. Now there are two, which have been regraded from red. There are many other very popular steep runs marked on the piste map, but they are given off-piste status. Some are classified as 'high-alpine touring routes' – this means they are not marked, not groomed, not patrolled and not protected from avalanche danger. There are also some 'ski routes'. These have some markers, are groomed occasionally in part, but are not patrolled and are protected from avalanches only 'in the immediate vicinity of the markers'.

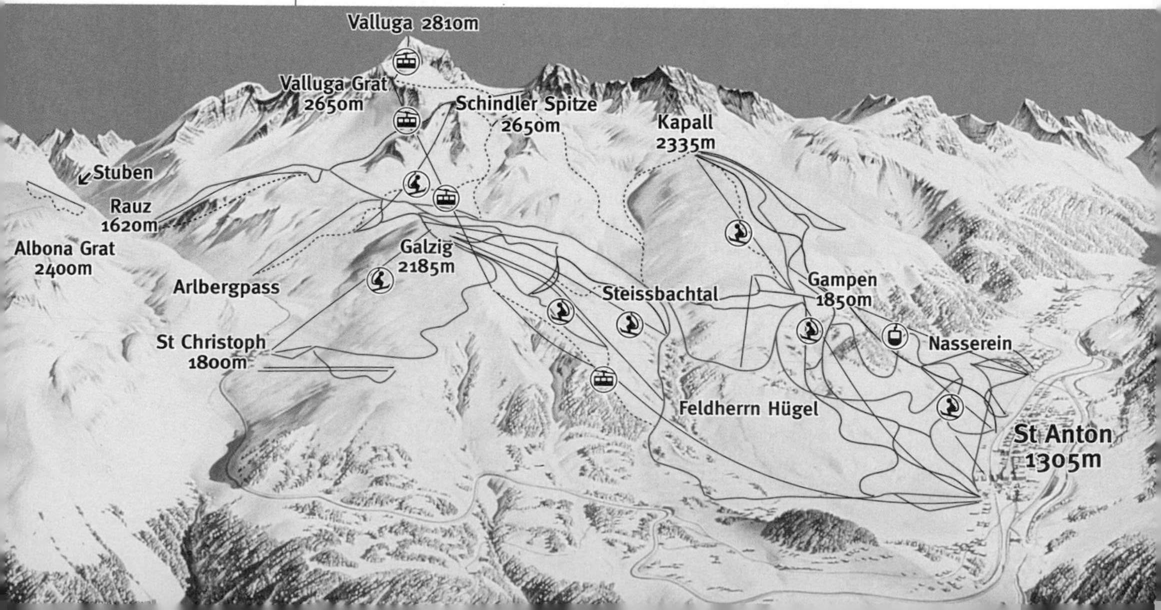

The piste map says that high-alpine touring routes require 'extensive mountain experience' and 'are only recommended when accompanied by an authorised guide'. Ski routes are recommended only for people with 'alpine experience or with a ski instructor'. And yet between them these grades of run cover most of the best runs for experts. And they are commonly used by holidaymakers without the services of an instructor or guide. One visitor commented, 'The lack of marked black runs is discouraging. When we were there the routes of the old black runs were clear and well used. It is entirely unreasonable to expect everyone to take guides on these routes, and it seems irresponsible to ignore the fact that people will go on them. They run the risk of alienating those who want to move off red runs but are not quite ready to take on anything and everything. On some of the ski routes there were snow-guns. This doesn't fit with the theory that you are on your own.' A couple of years ago, a reporter told a worrying tale of being badly lost on an avalanched ski route that was not marked as closed at the start. But on our recent visits we found some ski route areas clearly roped off and marked closed in times of extreme avalanche danger – so it looks as if things might be improving in this respect.

The Arlberg region piste map is rather inadequate. One reporter commented on the poor clarity of the maps with the 'size of print being too small and the lengths and directions of the runs being unclear, which can be both misleading and dangerous'. Fortunately the on-mountain maps and signs are clearer. But reporters have complained of poor piste grooming and one of a blue run that was closed part way down with no prior warning, forcing him to take novices down the only alternative – a steep ungroomed run. Reporters have found the local cable TV, showing the state of some of the pistes and queues, very useful.

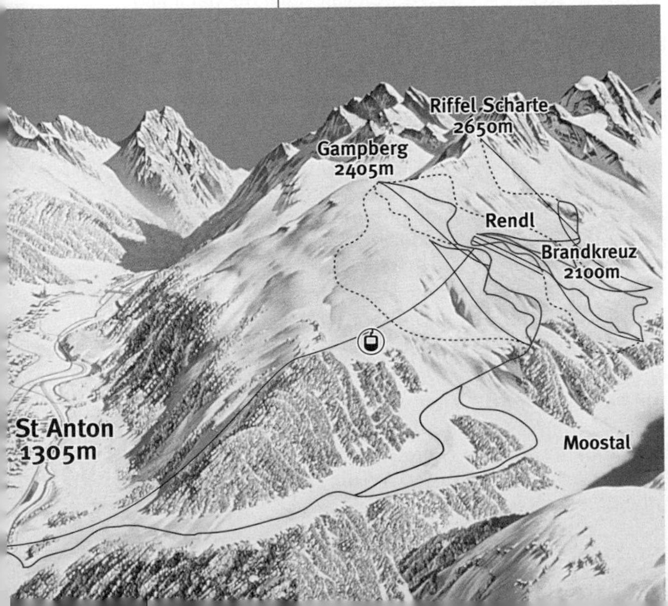

THE SLOPES

Large linked area

St Anton's slopes are made up of several sectors, all except one of which are linked, on a predominantly south-facing mountain.

From the centre, there's a two-stage cable-car up to **Galzig** and then **Valluga**, and a high-speed quad up to **Gampen**. From Gampen, pistes lead back to St Anton and Nasserein, or in the opposite direction across to the links with the Valluga–Galzig area. Or you can go up higher to **Kapall** on the fast six-pack and head down ski routes or good cruising blues and reds.

A new eight-person gondola from Nasserein to Gampen opened last season. This is great for Nasserein residents and can also be reached by taking the relatively new Fang chair between the central lifts and Nasserein.

The high-speed quad that links Gampen to **Galzig** brings you out just above the mid-station of the cable-car up from St Anton. From here you can travel in most directions, including back to town, down to **St Christoph** (from where there's a high-speed quad back up) or back to the link between Galzig and Gampen (a slow chair can take you back to Gampen). At peak periods the pistes down from Galzig are some of the most crowded we've come across.

From Galzig you can get up to St Anton's most famous slopes, the bowls below the **Valluga**, by taking the second stage of the cable-car or going up the Schindlergrat three-person chair, which delivers you to the same height but on a different peak. There's a tiny third stage of the Valluga cable-car which takes you up to 2810m, but this is mainly for sightseeing. The only run down from there is off the back, off-piste to Zürs. You are not allowed to take skis or a board up the lift without a guide.

From both the second stage of the cable-car and the Schindlergrat chair, you can take the long, beautiful but very busy red run to Rauz, at the western end of St Anton's own slopes. From Rauz you cross the road and go along to Stuben, where a slow two-stage chair-lift takes you to the quiet, mainly north-facing **Albona** area.

The final area, **Rendl**, is separate and reached by gondola from just outside town (there are free buses from the village, but it's only a short

LIFT PASSES

2001/02 prices in euros

Arlberg Ski Pass Covers all St Anton, St Christoph, Lech, Zürs and Stuben lifts, and linking bus between Rauz and Zürs.

Beginners Limited pass covering beginners' lifts.

Main pass
1-day pass 37
6-day pass 171
(low season 154)

Senior citizens
Over 65: 6-day pass 146

Children
Under 15: 6-day pass 103

Short-term passes
Single ascent tickets on some lifts throughout Arlberg. Half-day tickets (adults 28) from noon, afternoon 'taster' tickets (16) from 3pm.

Note Main pass also covers Klösterle (10 lifts), 7km west of Stuben. Discounts during wedel, firn and snow crystal weeks. Senior citizen pass for women over 60.

walk). A number of lifts serve the west-facing runs at the top here, with a single north-facing piste returning to the gondola bottom station.

SNOW RELIABILITY

Generally very good cover

If the weather is coming from the west or north-west (as it often is), the Arlberg gets it first, and as a result St Anton and its neighbours get heavy falls of snow. They often have much better conditions than other resorts of a similar height, and we've had great fresh powder here as late as mid-April in recent years. But many of the slopes face south or south-east, causing icy or heavy conditions at times. It's vital to time your runs off the Valluga to get decent conditions.

The lower runs are now well equipped with artificial snowmaking, which ensures the home runs remain open (but not necessarily enjoyable).

FOR EXPERTS

One of the world's great areas

St Anton vies with Chamonix, Val-d'Isère and a handful of others for the affections of experts. It has some of the most consistently challenging and extensive slopes in the world. The jewel in the crown is the variety of off-piste in the bowls beneath the Valluga – see feature panel opposite. Lower down, very difficult trails lead off in almost every direction from the Galzig summit. Osthang is an extremely tough, long mogul field that leads down to Feldherrn Hügel. Not much less challenging are trails down to Steissbachtal, St Christoph and past Maiensee towards the road. These lower runs can be doubly tricky if the snow has been hit by the sun.

The World Championship courses are between Kapall, Gampen and town, and the previously red Fang run has been regraded black since the championships. There are countless opportunities for going off-piste in the Kapall–Gampen area, including the beautiful Schöngraben unmarked route to Nasserein.

The Rendl area across the road has plenty of open space beneath the top lifts and, with an accompanying guide, there is some delightful fun to be had off the back of this ridge.

The Albona mountain above Stuben has north-facing slopes that hold powder well and some wonderful, deserted off-piste descents including beautifully long runs down to Langen (where you can catch the train) and back to St Anton. These are, however, 'high-alpine touring runs' and should be taken seriously. One of our reporters particularly liked the Klösterle/Sonnenkopf area down-valley from Stuben for its excellent off-piste route to Langen.

On top of all this, bear in mind that many of the red runs on the piste map are long and challenging, too.

The ultimate challenge, though, is

boarding *Though steeped in skiing tradition, St Anton is moving with the times and improving facilities for boarders. Although we don't really recommend it to beginners, it is one of the best free-ride areas in the world, with lots of steep terrain and natural hits. There is a fun-park and 100m half-pipe on Rendl. There are still a few T-bars around but fast chair-lifts are now the main ways around the mountains. Tuition is provided by the ski schools and the Snowboard Academy (part of the Arlberg school). A book could be written about the almost legendary nightlife.*

The Valluga runs

The off-piste runs in the huge bowl beneath the summit of the Valluga, and reached by either the Schindlergrat chair or the second stage of the Valluga cable-car, are justifiably world famous. In good snow, this whole area is an off-piste delight for experts.

Except immediately after a fresh snowfall, you can see tracks going all over the mountain – and some of the descents look terrifying. There are two main ski routes down marked on the piste map – both long, steep, often mogulled descents. The Schindlerkar is the first you come to and it divides into two – the Schindlerkar gulley being the steeper option. For the second, wider and somewhat easier, Mattun run, you traverse further at the top. Both these feed down into the Steissbachtal gulley where there are lifts back up to Galzig and Gampen. The Schweinströge starts off in the same direction as the red run to Rauz, but you traverse the shoulder of the Schindler Spitze and down a narrow gulley.

perhaps to go with a guide off the back of the third stage of the Valluga. The initial pitch is very, very steep (if you fall you die, type of pitch). But once you have negotiated that, the run down to Zürs is very beautiful and usually deserted.

FOR INTERMEDIATES

Some real challenges

St Anton is well suited to good, adventurous intermediates. They will be able to try the Mattun run and the easier version of the Schindlerkar run from Valluga Grat (see feature panel on previous page). The run from Schindler Spitze to Rauz is very long (over 1000m vertical), tiring, varied and ideal for good (and fit) intermediates. Alternatively, turn off from this part way down and take the – usually very crowded – Steissbachtal to the lifts back to Galzig.

The Kapall–Gampen section is also interesting, with sporty bumps among trees on the lower half. From Kapall to

SCHOOLS/GUIDES

2001/02 prices in euros

Arlberg
Manager Richard Walter
Classes 6 days
4½hr: 2½hr am and 2hr pm, from 9.30
6 full days 181
Children's classes
Ages: 4 to 14
6 full days including lunch 186
Private lessons
Half or full day
192 for full day; each additional person 16

2000/01 prices in euros

St Anton
Manager Franz Klimmer
Classes 6 days
4½hr: 9.30-noon and 1pm-3pm
6 full days 174
Children's classes
Ages: 5 to 14
6 full days 125
Private lessons
Half or full day
182 for full day; each additional person 15

town (over 1000m vertical), following the men's downhill run is fun.

Less adventurous intermediates will find St Anton less to their taste. There are few easy cruising pistes. The most obvious are the short blues on Galzig and the Steissbachtal (aka 'Happy Valley'). These are reasonably gentle but get uncomfortably crowded, particularly at peak times. The blue to St Christoph is generally quieter. The narrowish blues between Kapall and Gampen can have some challenging bumps. Intermediates looking for easy cruising will find the best by taking the bus to Lech.

In the Rendl area a variety of trails suitable for good and moderate intermediates criss-cross, including a lovely long tree-lined run (over 1000m vertical from the top) back to the valley gondola station. This is the best run in the whole area when visibility is poor, though it has some quite awkward sections.

FOR BEGINNERS
Far from ideal

St Anton has supposedly better nursery slopes now, near the new Fang lift. But there are no easy, uncrowded runs for beginners to progress to. Experts and intermediates who are desperate to visit the Arlberg, but are taking novices on holiday would be better off staying in Lech or Zürs and taking the bus to Rauz when they want to try St Anton.

FOR CROSS-COUNTRY
Limited interest

St Anton is not really a cross-country resort. There are a couple of uninspiring trails near town, another at St Jakob 3km away, and a pretty trail through trees along the Ferwalltal to the foot of the Albona area. There is also a tiny little loop at St Christoph.

Snow conditions are usually good and trails total around 35km.

QUEUES
Improved, but still a problem

Queues are not the problem they once were, since the replacement of several lifts by high-speed chairs. But they can still be tiresome in peak season and at weekends. There are useful 'singles lines' at some lifts which enable you to cut the queues if you don't mind who you ride with – with taped announcements in several languages urging people to fill the chairs.

Perhaps worse than the queues in busy periods are the crowded trails that you'll encounter – we were there one March weekend and had to continuously look all round before making a turn to make sure we didn't hit anyone; we could have done with wing mirrors. And even in January, the Steissbachtal was uncomfortably crowded.

MOUNTAIN RESTAURANTS
Plenty of choice

Look out for the little table-service huts, which have much more going for them than the characterless cafeterias. Two of the best are just above town, the Sennhütte and Rodelhütte. The Rendl Beach is also worth a visit. The S'Gräbli was highly recommended by a recent reporter. The Mooserwirt serves typical Austrian food; the Krazy Kanguruh burgers, pizzas and snacks. The goulash soup at the Taps Bar next to Krazy Kanguruh has been recommended, and the Kaminstube gets beautiful sunset views.

Lunching in St Christoph or Stuben is also a useful idea. The St Christoph choices include the atmospheric Hospiz Alm (though we continue to receive reports of poor restaurant service), where you can sit in a slide which delivers you to the lavatories, the good value Almbar just above it, and Traxl's ice bar at the Maiensee Hotel. Reporters say that in Stuben the views from the Albonagrathütte are worth the short walk to get to it, that the Albona is quiet and friendly and that there are a couple of cosy places in the village for a good, quiet lunch, including the Berghaus just behind the church.

SCHOOLS AND GUIDES
Mixed reports

The relatively new St Anton school has brought much-needed competition to the Arlberg school. But we've had conflicting reports on the Arlberg school. 'Complete beginner group much too big despite our complaints and we learned more from our friends,' said one reporter. 'Superb teaching meant our novices had a great time and one was tackling red runs by the end of the week,' said another. 'Everyone in my chalet was very happy with the Arlberg school, with relatively small classes and good English,' says our most recent report.

Reporters who have hired a guide to the off-piste at the top of the Valluga have had a great day. And we ourselves have skied with excellent off-piste guides on the main ski area.

FACILITIES FOR CHILDREN
Getting better

St Anton might not seem an obvious resort for family holidays, but the resort works hard to accommodate families' needs: the youth centre attached to the Arlberg school is excellent, and the special slopes both for tots (at the bottom) and bigger infants (up at Gampen) are well done. Also the new Arlberg-well.com centre should keep children entertained with its pools, flumes and waterfall.

Staying there

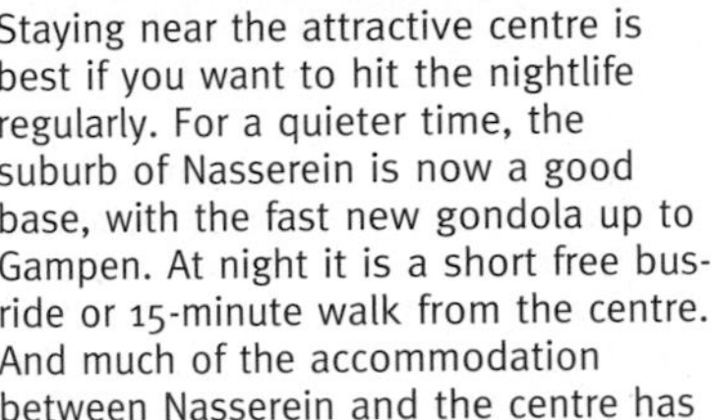

Staying near the attractive centre is best if you want to hit the nightlife regularly. For a quieter time, the suburb of Nasserein is now a good base, with the fast new gondola up to Gampen. At night it is a short free bus-ride or 15-minute walk from the centre. And much of the accommodation between Nasserein and the centre has been made much more convenient by the new Fang chair.

St Anton spreads up the hill to the west of the centre, towards the Arlberg pass. Places up here in and beyond Oberdorf can be 20 minutes' walk from the centre – but quite convenient for the slopes, if snow-cover is good.

HOW TO GO
Austria's main chalet resort

There's a wide range of places to stay, from quality hotels to cheap and cheerful pensions and apartments. What sets St Anton apart from other Austrian resorts for Brits is the number of chalets, which are fairly expensive, though few are particularly luxurious and many are well away from the centre up the hill or at Nasserein.

Chalets The chalets in the centre are virtually all apartment-based.

Hotels There is one 5-star hotel and lots of 4- and 3-stars and B&Bs.

(((((5) **St Antoner Hof** (2910) Best in town, but its position on the bypass is less than ideal. Pool.

((((4) **Schwarzer Adler** (2244-0) Centuries-old inn on main street. Widely varying bedrooms.

((((4) **Alte Post** (2553) Atmospheric place on main street with lively après-ski bar. Endorsed by a reporter.

((((4) **Neue Post** (2213) Comfortable if

uninspiring 4-star at the centre of affairs, close to both lifts and nightlife.

((((4) **Kertess** (2005) Charmingly furnished, further up the hill. Pool.

((((4) **Sport** (3111) Central position, with varied bedrooms, good food. Pool.

(((3) **Grischuna** (2304) Welcoming family-run place in peaceful position up the hill west of the town; close to the slopes, five minutes to the cable-car.

(((3) **Goldenes Kreuz** (22110) A comfortable B&B hotel halfway to Nasserein, ideal for cruising home.

Self-catering There are plenty of apartments available but package deals are few and far between.

STAYING DOWN THE VALLEY
Nice and quiet

Beyond Nasserein is the more complete village of St Jakob. It can be reached on snow, but is dependent on the free shuttle-bus in the morning.

Pettneu is a quiet village further down the valley, with slopes that most suit beginners. It's best for drivers.

EATING OUT
Mostly informal

You live fast and eat hard to make up for it in St Anton. Plain, filling fare is the norm, with numerous places such as the Fuhrmannstube, Trödlerstube and the Reselehof and Alt St Anton in Nasserein serving big portions of traditional Austrian food. A reporter recommends Dixies for pizza, pasta, steaks and fish, and Bobo's serves good Mexican. An atmospheric place for dinner is the wood-panelled Museum, where as well as enjoying upmarket food and wine, you can learn the history of the resort. The toboggan run is floodlit and lift-served a couple of nights a week, and you can stop off at the Rodelalm above Nasserein for traditional food, beer and schnapps – booking is essential.

CHILDCARE

The kindergarten at the Kinderwelt (2526) takes toilet-trained children aged 30 months to 14 years, from 9.30 to 3.30. Ski tuition with the Arlberg ski school in a special snow-garden is available for children aged 4.

GETTING THERE

Air Innsbruck, transfer 1½hr. Zürich, transfer 3hr.

Rail Mainline station in resort.

ACTIVITIES

Indoor Swimming pool (also hotel pools open to the public, with sauna and massage), tennis, squash, bowling, museum, cinema in Vallugasaal

Outdoor Swimming pool, 15km of cleared walks, natural skating rink (skating, curling), sleigh rides, tobogganing, paragliding

Phone numbers

From elsewhere in Austria add the prefix 05446.

From abroad use the prefix +43 5446.

TOURIST OFFICE

Postcode A-6580
t +43 (5446) 22690
f 2532
st.anton@netway.at
www.stantonamarlberg.com

St Christoph is a collection of exclusive hotels and restaurants set high up by the Arlberg pass – convenient for the slopes but deadly quiet at night ➔

TVB ST ANTON AM ARLBERG

APRES-SKI

Throbbing till late

St Anton's bars rock from mid-afternoon until the early hours. A collection of bars on the slopes above town get packed by 3pm. The Krazy Kanguruh is probably the most famous. But, a bit lower down, the Mooserwirt and the S'Gräbli, opposite each other, are equally lively – live bands most days and dancing on the beams in ski boots. All this is followed by a slide down the piste in the dark. The bars in town are in full swing by 4pm, too. Most are lively with loud music – only sophisticates looking for a quieter more relaxed time are less well provided for. The Underground bar has a great atmosphere and live music, but gets packed. The Piccadilly pub and Hazienda are equally popular. Recent reporters enjoyed the atmosphere at Scotty's, Jacksy's, Pub 37 and Funky Chicken. For late-night dancing, Kartouche and the Stanton in the centre of town are the key places.

OFF THE SLOPES

Not very relaxing

St Anton is a sprawling resort, with little to offer non-slope users. Many of the most attractive mountain huts are not readily accessible by lift for pedestrians. The centre is lively with a fair selection of shops. The new Arlberg-well.com centre (see What's New) is a welcome addition. Getting by bus to the other Arlberg resorts is easy. Lech would arguably be a better, if pricier, base, with more to do. It's easy to visit Innsbruck by train.

St Christoph 1800m

A small, exclusive collection of hotels, restaurants and bars right by the Arlberg Pass, with drag-lifts for local slopes and a high-speed quad chair-lift to the heart of St Anton's slopes. It's home to Austria's elite academy for ski instructors. Good for a nice lunch, it's expensive and deadly quiet to stay in. The most expensive hotel of all is the huge 5-star Arlberg-Hospiz.

St Johann in Tirol 650m

Relax on easy runs with plenty of pit stops

WHAT IT COSTS

HOW IT RATES

The slopes

Snow	**
Extent	**
Experts	*
Intermediates	***
Beginners	****
Convenience	***
Queues	***
Restaurants	****

The rest

Scenery	***
Resort charm	***
Off-slope	***

What's new

For 2001/02 the old single-person chair from Oberndorf will be replaced by an eight-seater gondola, greatly improving access for day trippers and taking pressure off the main village gondola.

In recent years a lot more snowmaking has been installed and it now covers almost half the slopes.

MOUNTAIN FACTS

Altitude	670m-1700m
Lifts	17
Pistes	60km
Blue	41%
Red	47%
Black	12%
Artificial snow	28km

- ⊕ Charming traffic-free centre
- ⊕ Lots of mountain restaurants
- ⊕ Plenty of off-slope activities
- ⊕ Easy to visit neighbouring resorts
- ⊕ Good ski and snowboard schools
- ⊕ Few Brits by Tirol standards
- ⊕ Ideal for beginners and intermediates
- ⊕ Good snow record

- ⊖ Very small area, with little to interest experts or keen piste-bashing intermediates
- ⊖ Weekend crowds from Germany
- ⊖ Can be especially busy when nearby resorts with less reliable snow are suffering

This charming resort is an attractive place for beginners and leisurely part-timers who like to spend as much time pottering about having drinks and lunch as they do actually cruising the slopes. Keener and more proficient skiers and boarders will soon get bored unless they are prepared to visit surrounding resorts such as Kitzbühel and the Ski Welt (all covered under the Kitzbüheler Alpen ski pass). There are a surprising number of lively bars in town, too.

THE RESORT

St Johann is a sizeable town with a life other than as a resort. The attractive traffic-free centre is wedged between a railway track, main roads and rivers. The five-minute walk from central hotels to the main lift includes a level crossing and walking beside a busy road. But the village gondola does access the whole mountain.

St Johann has some sprawling suburbs. Lifts at the hamlet of Eichenhof to the east are convenient for the slopes, but it's a trek along a busy road to the centre of town. A new gondola will start from Oberndorf, to the west for the 2001/02 season.

The local pass covers several other resorts and the Kitzbüheler Alpen pass covers the whole region. Kitzbühel itself is only 10 minutes by car or train.

THE MOUNTAIN

St Johann's local slopes are on the north-facing side of the Kitzbüheler Horn – the 'back' side of Kitzbühel's 'second' and smallest mountain.

Slopes The main access lift from the village is a gondola, which transports you to the top of the slopes at **Harschbichl** with a mid-station at Angereralm. From the top, a choice of north-facing pistes lead back through the trees towards town. The slopes on the top half of the mountain are reds, while those below the gondola mid-station are wide blue runs. Two chair-lifts and the mid-station of the gondola allow you to 'yo-yo' the upper part of the mountain. There are more chairs and drags lower down. There is also a sunnier sector of west-facing pistes that can be accessed from the top or

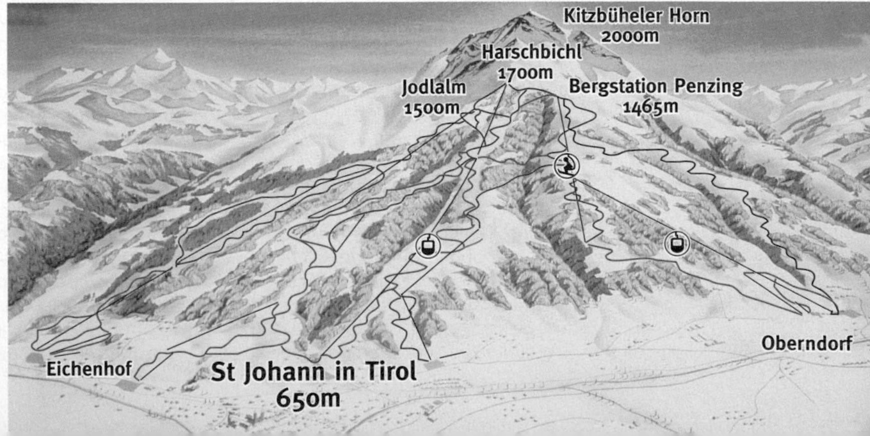

LIFT PASSES

2001/02 prices in euros

St Johann lift pass
Beginners Points card and half-day passes for nursery drags.
Main pass
1-day pass 27
6-day pass 140
Passes of 3 days or more cover Kirchdorf, Waidring and Fieberbrunn, too
Short-term passes
Am till 12.30; pm from noon; 'late sleeper' from 11am; 'try out' from 2pm.
Alternative periods
5 in 6, 11 in 13 days.
Alternative pass
Kitzbüheler Alpen-skipass: 5 large areas – Schneewinkel, Ski Region Kitzbühel, Ski Welt, Bergbahnen Wildschönau and Alpbachtal (adult 6-day 160).

Phone numbers
From elsewhere in Austria add the prefix 05352.
From abroad use the prefix +43 5352.

TOURIST OFFICE

Postcode A-6380
t +43 (5352) 63335
f 65200
info@st.johann.tirol.at
www.st.johann.tirol.at

the mid-station and which lead down to a car park just above Oberndorf, from which a new eight-seater gondola will depart this season.
Snow reliability St Johann gets more snow than neighbouring Kitzbühel and the Ski Welt, and this, together with its largely north-facing slopes, means that it often has better conditions. It also has substantial snowmaking.
Snowboarding St Johann has a fun-park, half-pipe, jumps area and a carving course.
Experts There is nothing here to challenge an expert. The long black run on the piste map is really a moderate red – and the snow suffers from the strong afternoon sun.
Intermediates The slopes are varied. But keen piste-bashers will ski them all in a day and are likely to want to go on to explore nearby resorts. Decent intermediates have a fairly direct-running piste between Harschbichl and town and the black mentioned above. There are some easier red runs on the top part of the mountain, but the best (3a and 4b) are served by long drags or a slow, old chair. The Penzing piste is served by a high-speed quad chair. The less adventurous are better off getting off the village gondola at the mid-station and taking gentle pistes down from there.
Beginners The main nursery slopes are excellent. The slopes served by the first stage of the village gondola make good runs to progress to – though the last part just above the village is a bit steep for some. Every year we hear from happy beginners; this year one said: 'Superb. I could not have picked a better place to learn to ski and have already booked for next year.'
Cross-country Given good snow, St Johann is one of the best cross-country resorts in Austria. The wide variety of trails totals 75km.
Queues Rare except at peak times. The new gondola should ease the pressure on the existing one, but may lead to queues for some of the slow old lifts above Eichenhof.
Mountain restaurants With 14 restaurants spread over just 60km of piste, St Johann must have the densest array of huts of any sizeable resort in Europe. Our favourite is the Angerer Alm, just above the gondola mid-station. It serves excellent local food and has the most amazing wine cellar. The Besgeigeralm is a lovely rustic restaurant on the Oberndorf side.
Schools and guides The St Johann and Eichenhof schools have a good reputation for tuition and friendliness. One beginner reporter this year said, 'Our instructor was English and by the end of the week I could ski from the top to the bottom of the mountain.'
Facilities for children The village nursery, geared to the needs of workers rather than visitors, offers exceptionally long hours. We have no recent reports of how this works in practice.

STAYING THERE

Most accommodation is central, in or close to the traffic-free zone. But hotels beyond the railway track close to the lifts are best for the slopes.
How to go British tour operators concentrate on hotels plus a few pensions, but there are numerous apartments available.
Hotels All hotels are 3- or 4-star. The 4-stars are best placed for the slopes. There are dozens of B&B pensions. The 4-star Sporthotel Austria (62507) is near the lift, with pool, sauna and steam. The Post (62230) is a 13th-century inn on the main street. 'By far the nicest,' says a resort regular. Fischer (62332) is central and 'friendly, with good food'. Kaiserblick (62442) is a modest B&B in a quiet spot.
Self-catering The Alpenblick (expensive), Gratterer (mid-range) and Helfereich (very cheap) are some of the best-situated apartments.
Après-ski Ice bars and tea dancing greet you as you come off the slopes. Max's ice bar, at the bottom of the main piste, has friendly service, music and a large umbrella. Jagglebach, on the main street, is popular day and night. Platzl is a comfortable late-night bar with excellent service. La Scala is the main disco. Tour reps organise sleigh rides, and tobogganing and the resort itself puts on an event most evenings.
Eating out The restaurants stick mostly to good old-fashioned Austrian cooking. The Huber-Bräu is a working brewery where you taste local beers before moving on to good food – but it closes early. The Bären specialises in Tirolean dishes, while the Lemberg serves international and Austrian fare. For a special meal, locals recommend the Ambiente. The Rialto does good pizza and the Hasianco Mexican and pizza.
Off the slopes A public pool, indoor tennis, artificial ice rink, curling and 40km of cleared walks. Or you can take the train to Salzburg or Innsbruck.

Westendorf 800m

Lively, friendly resort with access to the Ski Welt

WHAT IT COSTS

HOW IT RATES

The slopes

Snow	**
Extent	*
Experts	*
Intermediates	**
Beginners	****
Convenience	***
Queues	****
Restaurants	***

The rest

Scenery	***
Resort charm	****
Off-slope	**

What's new

Two T-bars at the top, up to Fleiding and Gampen are being replaced by quad chairs for the 2001/02 season.

MOUNTAIN FACTS

Altitude	800m-1890m
Lifts	13
Pistes	45km
Blue	38%
Red	62%
Black	0%
Artificial snow	23km
Recco detectors used	

- + Charming traditional Tirolean village
- + Access to the extensive Ski Welt circuit via nearby Brixen
- + Good local beginners' slopes
- + Jolly if rather limited après-ski scene
- + Fairly short transfers and day trips to Innsbruck

- − Limited local slopes
- − Lack of challenges for experts
- − Poor natural snow record, though half of the pistes now benefit from artificial back-up

Westendorf is on the Ski Welt lift pass (Austria's biggest lift-linked ski and snowboard area – see chapters on Söll and Ellmau). But the main circuit is a short bus-ride away. The resort has its own beginner and intermediate slopes and its prettiness and friendliness win many repeat visitors.

THE RESORT

Westendorf is a small Tirolean village with a charming main street and attractive onion-domed church (it was awarded 'Europe's most beautiful village' in the European Floral Competition a couple of years ago).

THE MOUNTAINS

The local slopes are small, but you can get into the Ski Welt circuit easily via a bus to Brixen and then a gondola.

Slopes A two-stage gondola takes you to Talkaser (1760m), from where one main north-west-facing red run goes back to the resort (with blue options on the lower half). Short west- and east-facing pistes at the top run below the peaks of Choralpe, Fleiding and Gampen. A couple of red runs from Fleiding go down past the lifts to hamlets served by buses.

Snow reliability Westendorf's snow reliability is a bit better than some other Ski Welt resorts and over half its pistes are now covered by snowmaking.

Snowboarding There's a good fun-park with a half-pipe.

Experts No real challenges and no black runs.

Intermediates Nearly all the local terrain is intermediate and there is the whole of the Ski Welt to explore, which has mile after mile of great intermediate runs.

Beginners Extensive village nursery slopes are Westendorf's pride and joy. And there are a couple of easy blues higher up to progress to.

Cross-country There are 30km of local cross-country trails along the valley but snow-cover is erratic.

TOURISMUSVERBAND WESTENDORF

Westendorf's picture-postcard pretty main street →

Westendorf has its own small area of intermediate terrain and a short bus-ride takes you to the main Ski Welt circuit →

TOURISMUSVERBAND WESTENDORF

Queues Given good conditions, queues are rare, and far less of a problem than in the main Ski Welt area. If poor weather closes the upper lifts, queues can become long.

Mountain restaurants Alpenrosenhütte is woody and warm, with good food; Brechhornhaus is quiet; Gassnerhof is good but you have to catch a bus back to town.

Schools and guides The three ski schools have quite good reputations, though classes can be over-large. One reporter tells of her teenage son's 'excellent' private lesson with the Top school: 'He's been skiing since he was three, but this was a revelation.' Another praises the Westendorf school: 'Teachers very good, good value, great prize-giving in town hall.'

Facilities for children Westendorf sells itself as a family resort. Both the crèche and the ski kindergarten are open all day.

STAYING THERE

The centre is close to the village nursery slopes and a five-minute walk from the main gondola on the edge of the village.

Hotels There are central 4-star hotels – the Jakobwirt (6245) and the 'excellent' Schermer (6268) – and a dozen 3-star ones. The 3-star Post (6202) is 'good value, right in the centre, few facilities except rooms, dining room and bar'. Many reporters stay in more modest guest houses. Haus Wetti (6348) is popular and away from the church bells. Pension Ingeborg (6577) has been highly recommended and is next to the gondola.

Self-catering The Schermerhof apartments are of good quality.

Eating out Most of the best restaurants are in hotels – the Schermer, Mesnerwirt, Post and Jakobwirt are good. The Wasselhof and Klingler have also been recommended. Booking ahead is advisable. Get a taxi to Berggasthof Stimlach for a good evening out.

Après-ski Nightlife is lively but it's a small place with limited options. The One for the Road Bar and Liftstüberl, at the bottom of the gondola, are packed at the end of the day. The Moskito Bar has live music and theme nights but is said by a (42-year-old) reporter to be 'a bit of a dive'. The Village Pub, next to the hotel Post, is very popular and sells draught Guinness. The Cr@zy Pub is popular with locals, with music, pool, darts, table-football and a bowling alley.

Off the slopes There are excursions by rail or bus to Innsbruck, Salzburg and Kitzbühel. Walks and sleigh rides are very pretty.

Phone numbers
From elsewhere in Austria add the prefix 05334.
From abroad use the prefix +43 5334.

TOURIST OFFICE

Postcode A-6363
t +43 (5334) 6230
f 2390
westendorf@netway.at
www.westendorf.com

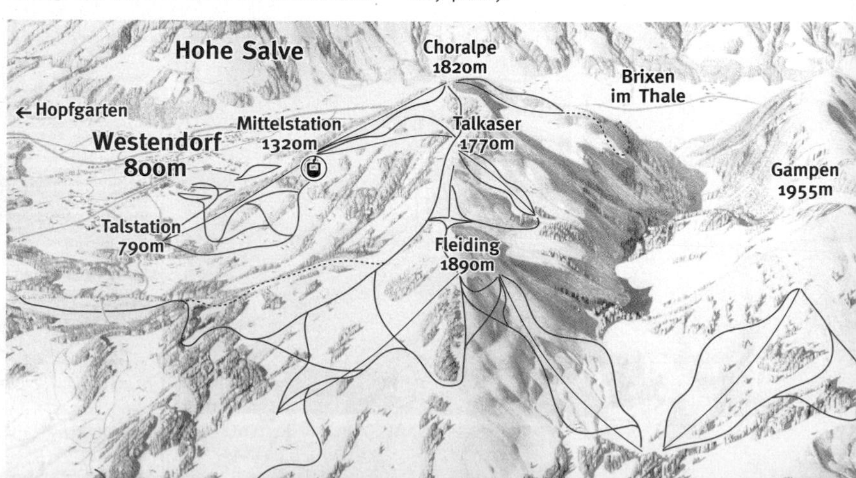

Wildschönau 830m

Niederau and neighbours – family resorts with friendly slopes

WHAT IT COSTS

HOW IT RATES

The slopes

Snow	**
Extent	*
Experts	*
Intermediates	**
Beginners	****
Convenience	***
Queues	****
Restaurants	**

The rest

Scenery	***
Resort charm	***
Off-slope	**

What's new

For 2001/02 the old Hahnkopf and Kothkaser drag-lifts on Schatzberg are being replaced by a new six-pack.

Plans for a lift link between Schatzberg and Alpbach are still on the drawing board – the proposed link would greatly improve the appeal of both areas.

MOUNTAIN FACTS

Altitude	830m-1900m
Lifts	29
Pistes	42km
Blue	35%
Red	56%
Black	9%
Artificial snow	8km

- ➕ Attractive, traditional family-friendly villages
- ➕ Good nursery slopes at Niederau and Oberau
- ➕ Jolly après-ski scene
- ➖ Shuttle buses or a drive between three separate ski areas
- ➖ Limited slopes in separate areas
- ➖ Poor snow reliability but snowmaking is increasing

Wildschönau is the dramatic-sounding brand name adopted by a group of attractive small resorts in the Tirol – Niederau, Oberau and Auffach. The slopes may be limited, but the resorts suit families looking for a friendly, unsophisticated but civilised atmosphere.

THE RESORTS

Niederau is the main resort; it's a spread-out little place, with a cluster of restaurants and shops around the gondola station forming the nearest thing to a focal point – but few hotels are more than five minutes' walk from a main lift. Auffach, 7km away, is a smaller village but has the area's highest and most extensive slopes. On a low col between the two is Oberau – almost as big as Niederau and the valley's administrative and cultural centre. The villages are unspoilt, with traditional chalet-style buildings; roads are quiet, except on Saturdays; and the valley setting is lovely.

THE MOUNTAINS

Niederau's slopes are spread over a wooded mountainside that rises no higher than 1600m. The slopes at Auffach go higher, above the tree line.

Slopes The main lift from Niederau is an eight-person gondola to Markbachjoch. A few minutes' walk away is the alternative chair-lift, and above it a steep drag to the high point of Lanerköpfl (1600m). Beginner runs at the bottom of the mountain are served by several short drag-lifts.

A reliable half-hourly bus (free) goes to Auffach. Its sunny east-facing area, consisting almost entirely of red runs, goes up to Schatzberg at 1900m, with a vertical of 1000m. The main lift up is a two-stage gondola. Drags and a six-pack serve the top runs.

The Kitzbüheler Alpen ski pass covers resorts in the Schneewinkel, Kitzbühel ski region, Ski Welt, and Alpbachtal as well.

Snowboarding There's a half-pipe and a fun-park on Schatzberg and a boarder-cross in Niederau.

Queues There are few queues in either of the main areas.

Snow reliability The low altitude means that snow reliability is relatively poor – and if you can't use all the runs back to Niederau, the piste area there is tiny. Auffach is a better bet, with most of its runs above mid-mountain. Snow-making has been increased in recent years and is now quite extensive. The valley has won awards for its piste grooming.

Experts The several black pistes are

TOURISMUSVERBAND WILDSCHÖNAU

The setting is not particularly 'wild' but adequately 'schön' →

Phone numbers
From elsewhere in Austria add the prefix 05339.
From abroad use the prefix +43 5339.

short and not severe, so are unlikely to hold the interest for long. There are off-piste routes to be found, though – the Gern route, from the top of Schatzberg down a deserted valley to the road a little way from Auffach, is marked on the piste map.
Intermediates Niederau's ungroomed gulley black runs are too awkward for most intermediates. The red runs generally merit their status, but don't add up to a lot. Auffach has more intermediate terrain, and the long main piste, from the top of Schatzberg to the village, is attractive.
Beginners There are excellent nursery slopes at the top and bottom of Niederau's main slopes, but the low ones don't get much sun in midwinter. Auffach has a slope just above the village. Oberau has its own nursery slopes, with a short black run above them. There are more beginner slopes along the hillside at Roggenboden. A real problem is the lack of really easy longer runs to go on to.
Cross-country The 30km of cross-country trails along the valley are good when snow is abundant.
Mountain restaurants These are scarce but good, causing lunchtime queues as ski schools take a break. Many people lunch in the villages.
Schools and guides The ski schools have good reputations but classes can be large.
Facilities for children The kindergarten and nursery take kids from age two.

STAYING THERE

How to go There are a number of attractive hotels and guest houses in the three main villages – many with pools. Several major operators run packages to Niederau and Oberau.
Hotels In Niederau the 4-star Sonnschein (8353) is reportedly the best hotel. The Austria (8188) is another central recommendation. The Schneeberger (8225) and Staffler (8222) are well-placed guesthouses. Haus Jochum (8240) is a spacious, comfortable self-catering close to the Tennladen drag. In Oberau is the oldest hotel in the valley – the 3-star Kellerwirt (8116), dating from 1200.
Eating out The restaurants at hotels Alpenland and Wastl-Hof in Niederau have been recommended.
Après-ski Niederau has a nice balance of après-ski, neither too noisy for families nor too quiet for the young and lively. Bobo's Treff umbrella bar is popular at tea-time. Later, the Almbar is lively, as is the Cave-Bar under the Hotel Staffler. The Drift-Inn bar at Thomson's Hotel Vicky is also popular.

The other villages are quieter, once the tea-time jollity is over for the night. There are good toboggan runs.
Off the slopes There are excellent sleigh rides, horse-riding, organised walks and the Slow Train Wildschönau – on wheels not rails. Several hotel pools are open to the public and at Auffach there's a 3.5km toboggan run. Excursions to Innsbruck are possible.

TOURIST OFFICE
Postcode A-6311
t +43 (5339) 8255
f 2433
info@wildschoenau.tirol.at
www.wildschoenau.com

Zell am See 755m

Charming lakeside town, varied slopes and glacier option

WHAT IT COSTS

3

HOW IT RATES

The slopes

Snow	**
Extent	**
Experts	**
Intermediates	***
Beginners	***
Convenience	**
Queues	**
Restaurants	***

The rest

Scenery	***
Resort charm	***
Off-slope	****

What's new

For 2001/02 in Kaprun, an additional gondola holding 24 people in each cabin will replace the funicular which suffered the tragic fire in autumn 2000. It will run parallel with and end at the existing gondola's top station for 2001/02 and be extended to the Alpincenter at the top of the defunct funicular for 2002/03. So for 2001/02 everyone will have to take a solitary high-speed quad chair to get to the main slopes from the top of the gondola – expect huge queues. But the following year, access queues should improve – the capacity of the new gondola will be 66% greater than the funicular (which will never be re-opened to the public).

In Zell am See for 2001/02, a quad chair will replace a T-bar up to Schmittenhöhe on the Sonnkogel side and snow-making will cover 70% of the lower slopes.

- + Pretty, tree-lined slopes with great views down to the lake
- + Lively, but not rowdy, nightlife
- + Charming old town centre with beautiful lakeside setting
- + Lots to do off the slopes
- + Huge range of cross-country trails
- + Kaprun glacier nearby
- + Varied terrain including a couple of steep black runs

- − Sunny, low slopes often have poor conditions despite snowmakers, which makes the area more limited
- − Trek to lifts from much of the accommodation, and sometimes crowded buses
- − Less suitable for beginners than most small Austrian resorts
- − The Kaprun glacier gets horrendous queues when it is most needed

Zell am See is an unusual resort – not a rustic village like most of its small Austrian competitors, but a lakeside town with a charming old centre that seems more geared to summer than winter visitors. It's a pleasant place, and – since a tunnel now takes through traffic to Schüttdorf – not plagued by traffic.

Zell's slopes have a lot of variety and challenging terrain for a small area, but not enough to keep a keen intermediate or better happy for long, especially if, as some reporters have found, there's a lack of snow. Zell is very near the Kaprun glacier, but so are many low-altitude resorts, all of which run buses there if snow is in short supply. The result can be horrendous queues.

Zell makes an attractive base for holidaymakers who enjoy travelling around. Having a car makes it easy to visit numerous other resorts – including Saalbach-Hinterglemm, Bad Gastein-Bad Hofgastein, Wagrain, Schladming and Obertauern.

The resort 

Zell am See is a long-established, year-round resort town set between a large lake and a mountain. Its charming, traffic-free medieval centre is on a flat promontory, and the resort has grown up around this attractive core. A gondola at the edge of town goes up one arm of the horseshoe-shaped mountain, but Zell's cable-cars are 2km away. Access by another gondola at Schüttdorf is 3km away. Most places to stay are a fair walk from the town gondola. Out by the cable-car station there is some accommodation, too.

You can also stay in Schüttdorf. Some of the accommodation here is close to the gondola (which goes directly to the highest part of the slopes), but the place is less appealing than Zell itself, especially for nightlife.

The mountains

Despite claims to the contrary, the extent of Zell's horseshoe of slopes is not large and the area is best suited to

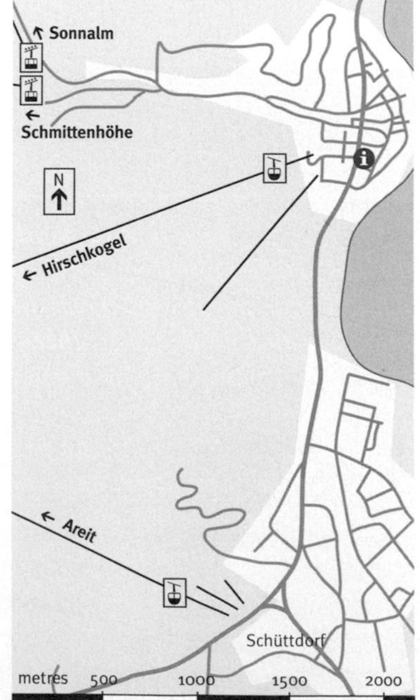

↑ Zell am See on the far side of the lake with pistes coming down into it

ZELL AM SEE TOURIST OFFICE

intermediates. The easiest runs are along the ridge, with steeper pistes heading down to the valley. Kaprun's snowsure glacier slopes are only a few minutes by bus; Saalbach and Bad Hofgastein are easily reached by bus and train respectively and, at a push, Wagrain, Schladming and Obertauern are car trips.

THE SLOPES
Varied but limited

The town gondola takes you to Mittelstation. From there it's either an easy or a steep run to the valley cable-car station. Or you can take a chair up to Hirschkogel to meet the gondola up from Schüttdorf – which you can ride up further and then take a T-bar to the Schmittenhöhe top-station. This is also where the main valley floor cable-car brings you. A gentle cruise and a single short drag-lift moves you to Sonnkogel. Here several routes lead down to Sonnalm mid-station – where another cable-car from the valley arrives. A black piste runs from here to the valley floor. At the end of the day you can take a gentle piste from the top (Schmittenhöhe) cable-car back to town or ride one of the cars down.

SNOW RELIABILITY
Good snowmaking, but lots of sun

Zell am See's slopes get so much sun the snow can suffer as a result. Lots of slopes are now well covered by snow-guns, including the sunny home run to Schüttdorf and 70% of the lower slopes. But though reporters have seen 'lots of snowmaking in evidence', slush, ice and closed runs have still marred their holidays. The Kaprun glacier is snowsure, but expect long queues there (and for buses to get there) when snow is short elsewhere.

MOUNTAIN FACTS

Altitude	760m-2000m
Lifts	56
Pistes	130km
Blue	43%
Red	38%
Black	19%
Artificial snow	40km

Recco detectors used

LIFT PASSES

2001/02 prices in euros

Europa–Sportregion Kaprun–Zell am See
Covers all lifts in Zell and Kaprun, and buses between them.

Beginners Points card or limited pass.

Main pass
1-day pass 33
6-day pass 155
(low season 140)

Children
Under 15: 6 days: 78
Under 6: free pass

Short-term passes
Half-day pass from 11.30 for Zell only.

Alternative periods
5 in 7 days and 10 in 14 days.

Notes Day pass valid at Zell am See only.

boarding *Zell is well suited to boarders. There's a high proportion of chairs, gondolas and cable-cars and a fun-park and half-pipe. You'll also find plenty of life in the evenings. The Kaprun glacier also has a half-pipe and fun-park, with powder in its wide, open bowl. But it also has a high proportion of drag-lifts – some beginners we heard from 'had to do a lot of walking'.*

FOR EXPERTS
Several blacks, but still limited

Zell has more steep slopes than most resorts this size, but can't entertain an expert for a week. When we were last there it was fabulous speeding down the immaculately groomed black runs 13 and 14 – they were deserted first thing. However, as a reporter points out, 'they are more like French reds'. Off-piste opportunities are limited.

FOR INTERMEDIATES
Bits and pieces for most grades

Good intermediates have a choice of fine, long runs, but this is not a place for mileage. All blacks are within a brave intermediate's capability, and there's a lovely cruising run between Areit and Schüttdorf when conditions are good. Some Sonnkogel pistes are also suitable. The timid can cruise the ridge all day on quiet, attractive runs, or head past Mittelstation to Zell's cable-cars on an easy blue. Kaprun's snowsure glacier runs are also good 'especially piste 3 for early intermediates'.

ZELL AM SEE TOURIST OFFICE

The slopes along the ridge from the top station to Schüttdorf are the easiest in the area ↓

FOR BEGINNERS
Two low nursery areas

There are small nursery slopes at the cable-car area and at Schüttdorf, both covered by snow-guns. Near-beginners and fast learners have plenty of short, easy runs at Schmittenhöhe, Breiteck and Areit. Some are used by complete beginners when snow conditions are poor lower down, but it means buying a lift pass.

FOR CROSS-COUNTRY
Excellent if snow allows

The valley floor has extensive trails, including a superb area on the Kaprun golf course. At altitude there are just two short loops, one at the top of the Kaprun glacier, and the other at the top of the Zell gondola.

QUEUES
Not normally a problem

Zell am See doesn't have many problems except at peak times, when the Schmittenhöhe cable-cars are generally the worst hit. A recent visitor found that getting to Schmittenhöhe via the Sonnalm cable-car is quieter.

When snow is poor there are few daytime queues at Zell – many people are away queueing at Kaprun – but getting down by lift at the end of the day can involve delays.

MOUNTAIN RESTAURANTS
Plenty of little refuges

There are plenty of cosy, atmospheric huts. Among the best are Glocknerhaus, Kettingalm, Areitalm ('superb, freshly made strudel'), Pinzgauer and Brieteckalm. The Berghotel at Schmittenhöhe is good, but expensive. Its bar with loud music is lively (see Après-Ski). Over at the top of the Kaprun glacier the Aussichsrestaurant gets busy, but 'has wonderful views and quite good food'.

SCHOOLS/GUIDES

2000/01 prices in euros

Zell am See

Classes 6 days
10am-noon, 1pm-3pm
5 full days: 125

Children's classes
Ages: from 4
5 full days: 125

Private lessons
Hourly: 44 for 1hr

CHILDCARE

The schools take children from age 4 and offer lunch-time care. The Areitbahn school runs a snow kindergarten from age 3, 9am to 4.30.

The village nursery is Ursula Zink (56343), which takes children from age 3, from 9.30 to 3.30.

GETTING THERE

Air Salzburg, transfer 2hr. Munich, transfer 3hr.

Rail Station in resort.

Phone numbers
From elsewhere in Austria add the prefix 06542.
From abroad use the prefix +43 6542.

ACTIVITIES

Indoor Swimming, sauna, solarium, fitness centre, spa, tennis, squash, bowling, museum, art gallery, cinema, library, massage, ice skating

Outdoor Riding, skating, curling, floodlit toboggan runs, plane flights, sleigh rides, shooting range, swimming (Kaprun), ice-sailing, ice-surfing, tubing

SCHOOLS AND GUIDES
A wide choice

There is a choice of schools in both Zell am See and Kaprun. A reporter found boarding lessons from the main Zell school to be 'well-organised', though classes were a bit large, and English not always spoken fluently. There are also specialist cross-country centres at Schüttdorf and at Kaprun.

FACILITIES FOR CHILDREN
Schüttdorf's the place

We have no recent reports on the childcare provisions, but staying in Schüttdorf has the advantage of direct gondola access to the Areitalm snow-kindergarten, and the Ursula Zink nursery is at Zeller-Moos, just outside Schüttdorf. There's a children's adventure park on the mountain.

Staying there

Choice of location is tricky, and we have three favourite strategies. Stay in a beautiful lakeside setting (which gets you on the shuttle-bus before it's too crowded); at the upper edge of the town centre (walking distance from the Zell gondola); or near the cable-car stations at the end of the valley.

Schüttdorf has easy access to the top of the mountain, but it is a characterless dormitory with little else going for it. Though closer to Kaprun, this is, perversely, a drawback unless you have a car. Trying to get on a glacier bus is tough, as they tend to be full when they leave Zell. Families wishing to use the Areitalm nursery and cross-country skiers stand to gain most from staying in Schüttdorf.

HOW TO GO
Choose charm or convenience

Lots of hotels, pensions and apartments.

Hotels A broad range of hotels (more 4- than 3-stars) and guest-houses.

((((4) **Salzburgerhof** (7650) Best in town – the only 5-star. Nearer lake than gondola, but has courtesy bus and pool.

((((4) **Tirolerhof** (7720) Excellent 4-star in old town. Good pool, hot tub and steam room. 'Food good, staff very friendly.'

((((4) **Eichenhof** (47201) On the outskirts of town, but popular and with a minibus service, great food and lake views.

((((4) **Alpin** (7690) Modern 4-star chalet next to the Zell gondola.

((((4) **Zum Hirschen** (7740) Comfortable 4-star, easy walk to gondola. Sauna, steam, splash pool, popular bar.

((((4) **Schwebebahn** (724610) Attractive 4-star in secluded setting by cable-cars.

(((3) **Berner** (779) 4-star by the Zell gondola.

((2) **Hubertus** (72427) B&B near Zell gondola.

((2) **Margarete** (72724) B&B next to cable-car.

Self-catering The budget Karger Christine apartments are near the Zell gondola. Apartment Hofer is mid-range and close to the Ebenberg lift (linking to the gondola, but no boarders allowed). More comfortable are the 3-star Diana and Seilergasse (both in the old centre) and the Mirabell, which is close to the Zell gondola.

STAYING UP THE MOUNTAIN
Three options

As well as the Berghotel (72489) at the top of the Schmittenhöhe cable-car, the Breiteckalm (73419) and Sonnalm (73262) restaurants have rooms.

EATING OUT
Plenty of choice

Zell has more non-hotel places than is usual in a small Austrian resort. The Ampere is quiet and sophisticated; Giuseppe's is a popular Italian with excellent food; and Kupferkessel and Traubenstüberl both do wholesome regional dishes. There are Chinese restaurants in Zell and Schüttdorf. Car drivers can try the good value Finkawirt, across the lake at Prielau, or the excellent Erlhof.

APRES-SKI
Plenty for all tastes

Après-ski is lively and varied, with tea dances and high-calorie cafes, plus bars and discos a-plenty. When it's sunny, Schnapps Hans ice bar outside the Berghotel at Schmittenhöhe really buzzes, with 'great music, a crazy DJ and dancing on tables and on the bar. All ages loved it.' The Diele disco bar rocks; Crazy Daisy on the main road has two crowded bars and 'the group loved it' says one reporter. Evergreen has a live band and 60s and 70s music. The Viva disco allows no under 18s; one reader proclaimed it 'excellent'. Or try the smart Hirschkeller, the cave-like Lebzelter Keller and the Sportstuberl with old ski photos on the walls.

TOURIST OFFICE

Postcode A-5700
t +43 (6542) 770
f 72032
zell@gold.at
www.zellamsee.com

Kaprun phone numbers
From elsewhere in Austria add the prefix 06547.
From abroad use the prefix +43 6547.

OFF THE SLOPES

Spoilt for choice

There is plenty to do in this year-round resort. The train trip to Salzburg is a must, Kitzbühel is also well worth a visit and Innsbruck is within reach.

You can often walk across the frozen lake to Thumersbach, plus there are good sports facilities, a motor museum, sleigh rides and flights.

Kaprun 785m

THE RESORT

Kaprun is a spacious and quite lively village with lots of Tirolean charm.

THE MOUNTAIN

There is a small area of slopes on the outskirts of the village at Maiskogel best suited to early intermediates, and a separate nursery area. But most people will want to spend most of their time on the slopes of the nearby Kitzsteinhorn glacier or on Zell am See's slopes. Both are a busy bus-ride away.

Slopes Investigations into last year's tragic fire on the funicular are still taking place and if it ever re-opens it will be for materials only, not for people. To take the strain a new 24-person gondola (Gletscherjet) has been built to run parallel with the existing eight-person gondola. The first stage of the project will be completed for 2001/02 and the Gletscherjet will start at the bottom station and run to Langwiedboden where it will be met by the quad chair. The second stage, which will take the gondola up to the Alpincenter (2450m) and main slopes, is due to be completed for 2002/03. The main slopes are in a big bowl above served by several T-bars and a couple of chairs. The area above the top of the Alpincenter is open for summer skiing and riding and is particularly good for an early pre-Christmas or late post-Easter break.

Snow reliability Snow is nearly always good. And with new snowmaking facilities from the Alpincenter at 2450m to the top station of the Gratbahn at 2700m due to be finished for 2001/02, it should be even better.

Queues For 2001/02, before the second stage of the new gondola is built, expect huge queues at the quad chair at the top of the two access gondolas. Queues elsewhere on the mountain can be bad when crowds are bussed in if snow is poor in lower resorts.

Mountain restaurants There are a couple of decent mountain restaurants – one at the Alpincenter and another by the top of the gondolas.

Après-ski Nightlife is quiet, but the Baum and Nindl bars are lively.

Eating out Good restaurants include the Dorfstadl, the Bella Musica and the Schlemmerstuberl.

Snowboarding There's a fun-park on the glacier and some excellent natural half-pipes.

Experts There's little to challenge experts except for some good off-piste; the one slightly tough piste starts at the very top.

Intermediates Pistes are mainly gentle blues and reds and make for great easy cruising on usually good snow. From just below the top of the quad chair there is an entertaining red run down to the bottom of the chair. This is our favourite run on the mountain. But queues for the chair in the morning and crowds on the run in the afternoon may make it less pleasant for 2001/02 until the second stage of the new gondola is built.

Beginners There are a couple of nursery slopes in the village and gentle blues on the glacier to progress to.

Cross-country The Kaprun golf course is superb, but at altitude there is just one short loop at the top of the glacier.

Schools and guides There are several ski schools offering the usual classes.

Facilities for children All of the schools offer children's classes and there's a kindergarten in the village.

STAYING THERE

How to go There are some catered chalets and chalet-hotels.

Hotels The Orgler (8205), Mitteregger (8207) and Tauernhof (8235), are among the best hotels.

Off the slopes Off-slope activities are good, and include a fine sports centre with outdoor rapids.

France overtook Austria as the most popular destination for British skiers and snowboarders some years ago, and it is by far the most popular country with our readers. It's not difficult to see why. France has the biggest lift-and-piste networks in the world; for those who like to cover as many miles in a day as possible, these are unrivalled. Most of these big areas are also at high altitude, ensuring high-quality snow for a long season. And French mountains offer a mixture of some of the toughest, wildest slopes in the Alps, and some of the longest, gentlest and most convenient beginner runs.

French resort villages can't be quite so uniformly recommended; but, equally, they don't all conform to the standard image of soulless, purpose-built service stations, thrown up without concern for appearance during the boom of the 1960s and 70s.

The French resorts we flock to are big names where prices are never going to seem low; but when the pound was down near 7 francs they seemed criminally high. As we go to press in June 2001, you can still roughly divide French francs by 10 to get pounds – a level at which most French resort prices seem bearable. (Of course, once the franc is dead and replaced by the euro, the conversion won't be so simple.)

Towards the front of the book there is a special chapter on driving to the French Alps – increasingly popular, especially with people going self-catering. The northern French Alps are easy to get to by car, and comfortable apartments are becoming more common as the French continue their retreat from the short-sighted ways of the 1960s.

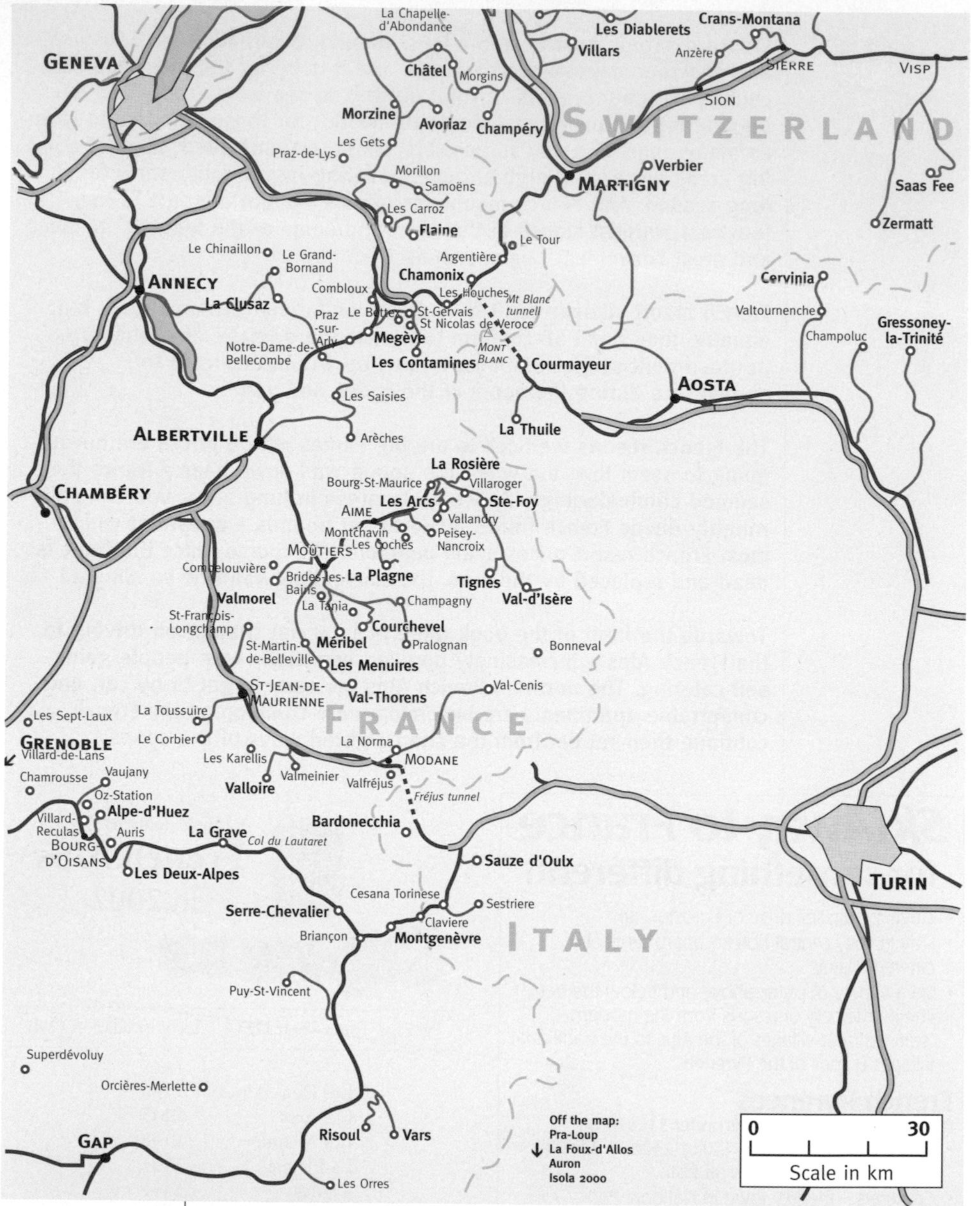

Getting around the French Alps

Pick the right gateway – Geneva, Chambéry or Grenoble – and you can hardly go wrong. The approach to Serre-Chevalier and Montgenèvre involves the 2058m Col du Lauteret; but the road is a major one and kept clear of snow or reopened quickly after a fall. Crossing the French–Swiss border between Chamonix and Verbier involves two closure-prone passes – the Montets and the Forclaz. When necessary, one-way traffic runs beside the tracks through the rail tunnel beneath the passes. The Mont-Blanc tunnel from Chamonix to Courmayeur is unlikely to reopen this season.

French purpose-built resorts are all about snow. The is the great motorway terrain on Bellevarde, above Val-d'Isère but just as easily reached from Tignes ➔

SNOWPIX.COM / CHRIS GILL

ANY STYLE OF RESORT YOU LIKE

The main drawback to France, hinted at above, is the monstrous architecture of some of the purpose-built resorts. But not all French resorts are hideous. Certainly, France has its fair share of Alpine eyesores, chief among them Les Menuires, central La Plagne, Flaine, Tignes, Isola 2000 and Les Arcs. The redeeming features of places like these are the splendid quality of the slopes they serve, the reliability and quality of the snow, and the amazing slope-side convenience of most of the accommodation.

But the French have learnt the lesson that new development doesn't have to be tasteless to be convenient – look at Valmorel, Belle Plagne and Les Coches, for example, and the newer parts of Isola 2000 or Flaine. Val-Thorens, always one of the more acceptable new resorts, is being extended sensitively, too.

If you prefer, there are genuinely old mountain villages to stay in, linked directly to the big lift networks. These are not usually as convenient for the slopes, but they give you a feel of being in France rather than a winter-holiday factory. Examples include Montchavin or Champagny for La Plagne, Vaujany for Alpe-d'Huez, St-Martin-de-

Belleville for the Trois Vallées and Les Carroz, Morillon or Samoëns (a short drive from the slopes) for Flaine. There are also old villages with their own slopes that have developed as resorts while retaining some or all of their rustic ambience – such as Serre-Chevalier and La Clusaz. Megève deserves a special mention – an exceptionally charming little town combining rustic style with luxury and sophistication; shame about the traffic.

And France has Alpine centres with a long mountaineering and skiing history. Chief among these is Chamonix, which sits in the shadow of Mont Blanc, Europe's highest peak, and is the centre of the most radical off-piste terrain in the Alps. Chamonix is a big, bustling town, where skiing and boarding go on alongside tourism in general. At the opposite end of the vacation spectrum is tiny La Grave, at the foot of mountains that are almost as impressive – the highest within France – but with only a few simple hotels.

France has advantages in the gastronomic stakes. While many of its mountain restaurants serve fast food, most also do at least a plat du jour that is in a different league from what you'll find in Austria or the US. It is generally possible to find somewhere to get a half-decent lunch and to have it served at your table, rather than queuing repeatedly for every element of your meal. In the evening, most resorts have restaurants serving good, traditional, French food as well as regional specialities. And the wine is decent and affordable.

Many French resorts (though not all) have suffered from a lack of nightlife, but things have changed in recent years. In resorts dominated by apartments with few international visitors, there may still be very little going on after dinner, but places like Méribel are now distinctly lively in the evening. (It should also be said that nightlife isn't important to many British holidaymakers. Most of our reporting readers say they can't recommend nightspots because all they want to do after dinner is to fall into bed.)

France is unusual among European countries in helping visitors decide which runs to try by using four grades of piste instead of the usual three – a system of which we heartily approve. The very easiest runs are graded green and, except in Val-d'Isère, they are reliably gentle. Since it's relative novices who care most about choosing just the right sort of terrain to build confidence, this is an excellent idea that other countries ought to follow. Blue, red and black follow in the normal way.

Alpe-d'Huez 1860m

An impressive all-rounder; just a pity it faces south

WHAT IT COSTS

(5)

HOW IT RATES

The slopes

Snow	****
Extent	****
Experts	****
Intermediates	****
Beginners	*****
Convenience	****
Queues	****
Restaurants	****

The rest

Scenery	****
Resort charm	*
Off-slope	***

What's new

For 2000/01, a second stage was added to the Marmottes gondola, greatly speeding up access to some excellent challenging terrain. The tricky old Chatelard drag-lift up to Auris was replaced by a two-seater chair. And a lift from the Villard-Reculas car park up to the fast chair-lift was installed. The capacity of the Alpette gondola at Oz was also increased. And a second automatic snowmaking plant was installed.

Plans for 2001/02 include replacement of the glacier double chair by a quad starting lower down on the glacier. The capacity of the Marmottes 1 gondola is being increased. Snowmaking on the Rif Nel nursery slope to les Bergers is being installed.

The proposed 3-star hotel in Les Bergers should now be ready for 2001/02.

- ⊕ Extensive, high, sunny slopes, split interestingly into various sectors
- ⊕ Huge snowmaking installation to keep runs open despite the sun
- ⊕ Vast, gentle, sunny nursery slopes right next to the resort
- ⊕ Efficient, modern lift system, with few long waits
- ⊕ Grand views of the peaks in the Ecrins national park
- ⊕ Some good, surprisingly rustic mountain restaurants
- ⊕ Short walks to and from the slopes
- ⊕ More animated than most purpose-built resorts
- ⊕ Pleasant alternative bases in outlying villages and satellites

- ⊖ In late season the many south-facing runs can be icy early in the day and slushy in the afternoon
- ⊖ Some main intermediate runs get badly overcrowded in high season
- ⊖ Many of the tough runs are very high, and inaccessible or very tricky in bad weather
- ⊖ Practically no woodland runs to retreat to in bad weather
- ⊖ Run gradings tend to understate difficulty
- ⊖ Messy, sprawling resort with a hotchpotch of architectural styles, no central focus and very little charm

There are few places to rival Alpe-d'Huez for extent and variety of terrain – in good conditions, it's one of our favourites. But, in late season at least, despite an ever-expanding snowmaking network, the 'island in the sun' suffers from the very thing it advertises: strong sun means that ice can make mornings miserably hard work, however alluring the prospect of slushy moguls in the afternoons.

The village has few fans, but if you don't like the sound of it you always have the alternative of staying in rustic Vaujany (with its mighty cable-car) or Villard-Reculas, or more modern Oz and Auris.

The resort 

Alpe-d'Huez is a large village spread across an open mountainside, high above the Romanche valley, east of Grenoble. It was one of the venues for the 1968 Grenoble Winter Olympics, and then grew quickly in a seemingly unplanned way. Its buildings come in all shapes, sizes and designs (including a futuristic church which hosts weekly organ concerts) – and many now look scruffy and in need of renovation. It is a large, amorphous resort; the nearest thing to a central focus is the main Avenue des Jeux in the middle, where you'll find the swimming pool, ice skating and some of the shops, bars and restaurants. The rest of the resort spreads out in a triangle, with lift stations at two of the apexes.

AGENCE NUTS / OT ALPE D'HUEZ

The bowl immediately above the village has something for everyone, from beginner to expert – with the bonus of great views →

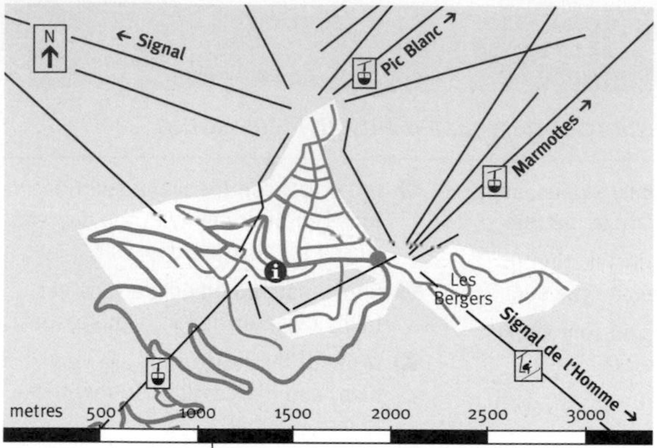

The bus service around the resort is free with the main Visalp lift pass, and there's a handy but slow bucket lift (with a piste beneath it) running through the resort to get everyone up to the main lifts at the top.

A short distance from the main body of the resort (and linked by chair-lift) are the 'hamlets' – apartment blocks, mainly – of Les Bergers and L'Eclose. Les Bergers, at the eastern entrance to the resort is convenient for the slopes (with its own nursery area), but it's a trek from most of the other resort facilities There are a couple of bar/ restaurants and several shops near the slopes. L'Eclose, to the south of the main village, is the least convenient location and has even less to offer than Les Bergers.

There is accommodation down the hill in Huez, linked by lift to the resort.

Staying close to one of the gondolas is useful. Or else it's worth being near the village bucket-lift, though it is closed in the evenings.

Outings by road are feasible to other resorts covered on a week's lift pass, including Serre-Chevalier, Les Deux-Alpes, Puy-St-Vincent and Montgenèvre. You can do a day-trip to Les Deux-Alpes by helicopter for a surprisingly modest fee.

The mountains

Alpe-d'Huez is a big-league resort, ranking alongside giants like Val-d'Isère or La Plagne for the extent and variety of its slopes. The piste grading is unreliable; although it occasionally overstates difficulty, it more often does the opposite. A couple of runs have been regraded in the past few years, but the Signal runs are still a regular source of complaints.

THE SLOPES

Several well-linked areas

The slopes can be divided into four main sectors, with good connections between them.

The biggest sector is directly above the village, on the slopes of **Pic Blanc**. There is sport here for everyone, from excellent tough pitches at the top to vast, gentle beginner slopes at the bottom. The huge Grandes Rousses gondola, otherwise known as the DMC (a reference to its clever technology), goes up in two stages from the top of the village to 2700m. Above it, a cable-car goes up to 3330m on Pic Blanc itself – the top of the Sarenne glacier – where the runs are genuinely black. A lower area of testing runs at Clocher de Macle, previously accessed by a slow chair, is much more attractive now that it is served by the recently extended Marmottes gondola.

The Sarenne gorge separates the main resort area from **Signal de l'Homme**. A spectacular down-and-up fast chair-lift accesses this area from the Bergers part of the village. From the top you can take excellent north-facing slopes back down towards the gorge, or head south to Auris or west to the old hamlet of Chatelard. The return from here is now by a new double chair-lift, instead of the famously tricky drag-lift of old.

On the other side of town from Signal de l'Homme is the small **Signal** sector, reached by drag-lifts next to the main gondola or by a couple of chairs lower down. Runs go down the other side of the hill to the old village of Villard-Reculas. Happily, the 1km-long Signal blue run is now floodlit three nights a week.

The **Vaujany-Oz** sector consists largely of north-west-facing slopes, accessible from Alpe-d'Huez via good red runs from either the mid-station or the top of the big gondola. At the heart of this sector is Alpette, the mid-station of the two-stage cable-car from Vaujany. From here a disastrously sunny red goes down to Oz, and a much more reliable blue goes north to the Vaujany home slopes around Montfrais. The links back to Alpe-d'Huez are made by the top cable-car from Alpette, or a gondola from Oz.

Since a piste was created from below Alpette to Enversin, just below Vaujany, an on-piste descent of 2200m has been possible – not the biggest vertical in the Alps, but not far short.

LIFT PASSES

2001/02 prices in euros

Grandes Rousses
Covers all lifts in Alpe-d'Huez, Auris, Oz, Vaujany and Villard-Reculas.

Beginners Daily lift passes for reduced areas. Beginner pass covers 11 lifts (10), Altitude 2000 covers 26 lifts (17.5).

Main pass
1-day pass 32.5
6-day pass 168

Senior citizens
Over 60: 6-day pass 119
Over 70: free pass

Children
Under 16: 6-day pass 119
Under 5: free pass

Notes Pass for 6 days or more includes one day's skiing at each of the Grande Galaxie resorts (Les Deux Alpes, Serre-Chevalier, Puy-St-Vincent and the Milky Way) and free entrance to the sports centre.

Alternative passes
Passes for Auris only (15 lifts), Oz-Vaujany only (20 lifts), Villard-Reculas only (8 lifts), and Altitude 2000 (26 lifts). Beginners passes for the outlying villages are available.

MOUNTAIN FACTS

Altitude	1120m-3320m
Lifts	86
Pistes	230km
Green	35%
Blue	27%
Red	25%
Black	13%
Artificial snow	53km
Recco detectors used	

The area does offer the longest piste in the Alps – the 16km Sarenne on the back of the Pic Blanc (see the special feature box).

SNOW RELIABILITY
Affected by the sun

Alpe-d'Huez is unique among major purpose-built resorts in the Alps in having mainly south- or south-west-facing slopes. The strong southern sun means that in late season conditions may alternate between slush and ice on most of the area, with some of the lower runs being closed altogether. There are shady slopes above Vaujany and at Signal de l'Homme – and there is a small glacier area on the Pic Blanc, open in summer, but too small to pin all your hopes on in the winter. Overall, the orientation of the slopes is a real drawback of the area as a whole.

In more wintry circumstances the runs are relatively snowsure, and the natural stuff is backed up by extensive snowmaking, covering the main runs above Alpe-d'Huez, Vaujany and Oz. An impressive number of snow-guns – 700-odd – covers 53km of runs.

FOR EXPERTS
Plenty of blacks and off-piste

This is an excellent resort for experts, with long and testing black runs (and reds that ought to be black) as well as serious off-piste options.

The slope beneath the Pic Blanc cable-car, usually an impressive mogul-field, is reached by a 300m tunnel from the back side of the mountain. The tunnel exit was altered last season, supposedly creating a less awkward start to the actual slope; but it is still tricky. The slope itself is of ordinary black steepness, but can be very hard in the mornings because it gets a lot of sun. The run splits up part-way down – a couple of variants take you to the Lac Blanc two-seater chair back up to the Pic Blanc cable-car.

The long Sarenne run on the back of the Pic Blanc is described in a special feature box. There are several off-piste variants. There are also other very long off-piste descents over the bigger glaciers to the north and east, with verticals of 1900m to 2200m, for which guidance is essential. Some end up in Vaujany, others in Clavans (where you need a taxi back), others in more remote spots where you need a helicopter back.

There is good off-piste in several other sectors, too – notably from Signal towards Villard-Reculas and Huez – and from Signal de l'Homme in various directions; the slopes above Auris are a particular favourite of locals. And there's abundant off-piste on the lower half of the mountain that is excellent in good snow conditions, including lovely runs through scattered trees at the extreme northern edge of the area above Vaujany. The piste map indicates some of the main off-piste

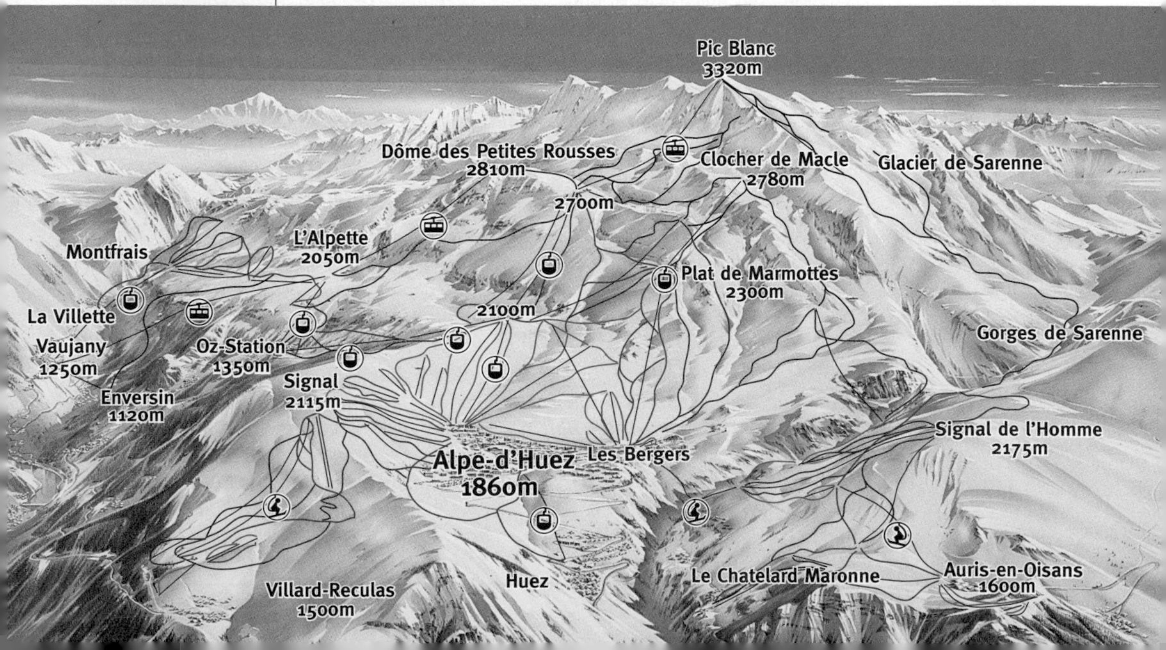

Pic Blanc
3320m
Dôme des Petites Rousses
2810m
Clocher de Macle
2780m
Glacier de Sarenne
2700m
L'Alpette
2050m
Montfrais
Plat de Marmottes
2300m
La Villette
2100m
Vaujany
1250m
Oz-Station
1350m
Gorges de Sarenne
Signal
2115m
Enversin
1120m
Signal de l'Homme
2175m
Alpe-d'Huez
1860m
Les Bergers
Le Chatelard
Maronne
Auris-en-Oisans
1600m
Huez
Villard-Reculas
1500m

routes, but don't be tempted to do them without a guide.

Some of the upper red pistes are tough enough to give experts a challenge. These include the Canyon and Balme runs accessed by the Lièvre Blanc chair-lift from the gondola mid-station – runs which are unprepared and south-facing (late in the day, perhaps best tackled on a board), and steep enough to be graded black in many resorts. Above this, the Marmottes II gondola (which replaced the old Clocher chair last season) serves another series of steep black runs from Clocher de Macle including the beautiful, long, lonely Combe Charbonniere.

FOR INTERMEDIATES
Fine selection of runs

Good intermediates have a fine selection of runs all over the area. In good snow conditions the variety of runs is difficult to beat. Every section has some challenging red runs to test the adventurous intermediate. The most challenging are the Canyon and Balme runs, mentioned previously. There are lovely long runs down to Oz and to Vaujany. The off-piste among the trees above Vaujany, mentioned earlier, is a good place to start your off-piste career in good snow. The Villard-Reculas and Signal de l'Homme sectors also have long challenging reds. The Chamois red from the top of the gondola down to the mid-station is beautiful but quite narrow, and miserable when busy and icy. Fearless intermediates should enjoy most of the super-long black runs from Pic Blanc.

For less ambitious intermediates, there are usually blue alternatives. The main Couloir blue from the top of the big gondola is a lovely run, well served by snowmakers, but it does get scarily crowded at times.

There are some great cruising runs above Vaujany; but it's not easy for early intermediates to get over to the Vaujany sector from Alpe-d'Huez. The blue down to the mid-station of the Vaujany gondola is picturesque and well served by snowmaking.

Early intermediates will also enjoy the gentle slopes leading back to Alpe-d'Huez from the main mountain, and the Signal sector.

FOR BEGINNERS
Good facilities

The large network of green runs immediately above the village is as good a nursery area as you will find anywhere – its only flaw is that it carries a lot of through-traffic. A large area embracing half a dozen runs has been declared a low-speed zone protégée, but the restriction is not policed and so doesn't achieve much. Add to the quality of the slopes the convenience, availability of good tuition, a special lift pass covering 11 lifts and usually reliable snow, and Alpe-d'Huez is difficult to beat. There's another good beginners' area with gentle green runs at the top of the Vaujany gondola, and small slopes in Oz and Auris.

THE LONGEST PISTE IN THE ALPS – AND IT'S BLACK??

It's no surprise that most ski runs that are seriously steep are also seriously short. Look at the exceptionally long runs in the Alps, and they tend to be graded blue, or red at the most. The Parsenn runs above Klosters, for example – typically 12km to 15km long – are manageable in your first week. Even Chamonix's famously long Vallée Blanche off-piste run doesn't include steepness in its attractions.

So you could be forgiven for being sceptical about the 'black' Sarenne run from the top of the Pic Blanc to the Sarenne gorge that separates the resort from the Signal de l'Homme sector. Even though the vertical is an impressive 2000m, a run 16km in length means an average gradient of only 11 per cent – typical of a blue run. Macho-hype on the part of the lift company, presumably?

Not quite. The Sarenne is a run of two halves. The bottom half is virtually flat (boarders beware) but the top half is a genuine black – a demanding and highly satisfying run (with stunning views) that any keen, competent skier will enjoy. The main challenge is the steep mogul-field starting just below the top lift station; after that, things are much gentler, even before you get to the really flat bit. The run gets a lot of sun, so pick your time with care – there's nothing worse than a sunny run with no sun.

↑ The main blue run from the DMC gondola gets extremely busy

SNOWPIX.COM / CHRIS GILL

A much greater problem than lift queues over much of the area is that the main pistes can be unbearably crowded. The runs in the outlying satellites tend to be less crowded in peak periods.

FOR CROSS-COUNTRY

High-level and convenient

There are 50km of trails, with three loops of varying degrees of difficulty, all at around 2000m and consequently relatively snowsure. All trails are within the Alpine domain and a cross-country user's pass costs about 28 euros.

QUEUES

Generally few problems

Even in French holiday periods, the modern lift system ensures there are few long hold-ups. Queues can build up for the gondolas out of the village, but the DMC shifts its queue impressively quickly. And the capacity of the Marmottes I is being increased for 2001/02, which should shorten waiting times next season. With the recently installed Lièvre Blanc quad and the new Marmottes II gondola, one of the old troublespots has been eliminated. The downside is that the Clocher de Macle area is no longer so secluded.

The small Pic Blanc cable-car is still queue-prone and is often closed by bad weather. Although they may not cause queues, there are lots of old drag-lifts dotted around. The small two-seater Lac Blanc chair-lift, back up to the Pic Blanc cable-car from the bottom of two of the black runs down from the Tunnel, gets very congested – though this can be avoided by taking an alternative variant.

MOUNTAIN RESTAURANTS

Some excellent rustic huts

Mountain restaurants are generally good – even self-service places are welcoming, and there are many more rustic places with table-service than you'd expect to find in French purpose-built resorts. One of our favourites is the cosy little Chalet du Lac Besson, on one of the cross-country loops north of the big gondola mid-station – the route to it now has piste status (the Boulevard des Lacs blue), but is no easier to follow in practice.

The pretty Forêt de Maronne hotel at Chatelard, below Signal de l'Homme, is delightful and has a good choice of traditional French cuisine. The Combe Haute, at the foot of the Chalvet chair in the gorge towards the end of the Sarenne run, is welcoming but gets very busy. The Hermine, at the base of the Fontfroide lift, is recommended for basic but good-value food. The terrace of the Perce-Neige, just below the Oz-Poutran gondola mid-station, attracts crowds. The Plage des Neiges at the top of the nursery slopes is one of the best places available to beginners. The Bergerie at Villard-Reculas has good views and is highly recommended by reporters. The Alpette and Super Signal places are also worth a visit. Chantebise 2100, at the DMC mid-station, offers slick and cheerful table service. The Cabane du Poutat, halfway down from Plat de Marmottes, is recommended for good food and service. Back in the village, lunch on the terrace at the Hotel Christina – by the top of the bucket lifts – is a pleasant option.

The restaurants in the Oz and Vaujany sectors tend to be cheaper. At Montfrais, Les Airelles is a rustic hut,

boarding *The resort suits experienced boarders well – the extent and variety of the mountains mean that there's a lot of good free-riding to be had. And, if there's good snow, the off-piste is vast and varied and well worth checking out with a guide. There's also a good fun-park and a half-pipe near the main lift base as well as in Auris. Unfortunately for beginners, the main nursery slopes are almost all accessed by drag-lifts, but these can be avoided once a modicum of control has been achieved. Planète Surf is the main snowboard shop and there are several cool bars to visit – the Freeride Café is recommended.*

SCHOOLS/GUIDES

2001/02 prices in euros

ESF
Classes 6 days
5½hr: 9.25-12.25 and 2.20-4.50
6 full days: 145
Children's classes
Ages: 4 to 16
6 full days: 130
Private lessons
(2000/01 prices)
Hourly. 29 for 1hr, for 1 or 2 people

2000/01 prices in euros

International
Classes 6 days
2½hr am, 2hr pm
6 full days: 202
Children's classes
Ages: 3 to 12
6 full days: 169
Private lessons
Hourly
30 for 1hr, for 1 or 2 people

CHILDCARE

The main schools run ski kindergartens

At Les Bergers the ESF Club des Oursons (0476 803169), takes children from age 4 during ski school hours.

The Eterlous day care centre (0476 806785), in Les Bergers, has a private slope area and takes children aged 2 to 11 all day.

Les Crapouilloux day care centre (0476 113923), next to the tourist information office, takes kids from 2 to 11.

The International school (0476 804277) runs the Baby-Club for children aged 3 to 4, and the Club des Marmottes for those aged 4 to 12.

The Club Med nursery takes children from 4, with or without tuition.

Phone numbers
From abroad use the prefix +33 and omit the initial '0' of the phone number.

built into the rock, with a roaring log fire, atmospheric music and excellent, good-value food.

SCHOOLS AND GUIDES
Contrasting views of the schools

We have a couple of reasonable reports on the ESF, which has apparently improved its act recently, 'good spoken English and good level of instruction'. However, class sizes are seemingly on the big side and we have witnessed classes of 12 students or more. Another recent report indicates that the International school operation has become a bit chaotic of late.

As usual, the best reports are saved for Masterclass, an independent operation run by private British instructor Stuart Adamson: 'We cannot praise him too highly.' Class sizes are limited to eight. Advance booking during high season is advised. The Bureau des Guides also has a good reputation.

FACILITIES FOR CHILDREN
Mixed reports

We've had rave reviews in the past of the International school's classes for children ('started the week nervously snowploughing down greens, ended up skiing parallel down reds ... only three in the class'). Reports on the ESF, on the other hand, have been mixed. Les Crapouilloux day care centre is recommended.

Staying there

HOW TO GO
Something of everything

Chalets There are not many classic chalets in Alpe-d'Huez, but there are quite a few chalet-hotels run by tour operators. Some could do with renovation.

Hotels There are more hotels than is usual in a high French resort, and there's a clear downmarket bias, with more 1-stars than 2- or 3-stars, and only two 4-stars. There is a huge Club Med at Les Bergers.

((((4 **Royal Ours Blanc** (0476 803550) Central. Luxurious, with lots of warm wood. Good food. Superb fitness centre. Free minibus to the lifts.

(((3 **Au Chamois d'Or** (0476 803132) Good facilities, modern rooms, one of the best restaurants in town and well placed for main gondola.

(((3 **Cimes** (0476 803431) South-facing rooms, excellent food; close to cross-resort lift and pistes.

(((3 **Grandes Rousses** (0476 803311) Comfortable but a bit dated and worn around the edges; close to lifts.

((2 **Mariandre** (0476 806603) Comfortable hotel with good food, recommended by readers. Some small rooms. Next to the bucket lift.

((2 **Gentianes** (0476 803576) Close to the Sarenne gondola in Les Bergers; a range of rooms, the best comfortable.

Self-catering There is an enormous choice of apartments available. The Pierre et Vacances residence near the Marmottes gondola in Les Bergers offers a high standard of accommodation with good facilities.

EATING OUT
Good value

Alpe-d'Huez has dozens of restaurants, some of high quality; many offer good value by French resort standards. The Crémaillère, at the bottom end of town, is highly recommended by a frequent visitor. Au P'tit Creux gets a similarly positive review for excellent food, ambience and value. The 'outstanding' Génépi is a friendly old place with good cuisine. The Pomme de Pin is also very popular. The Fromagerie, Rabelais and Edelweiss are others worth a try. And the Origan and Pinocchio pizzerias serve good, wholesome Italian fare.

APRES-SKI
Getting better all the time

The resort gets more animated each year and there's now a wide range of bars on offer, some of which get fairly lively later on. One complaint is that they are widely dispersed, making pub crawls fairly time consuming.

Of the British-run bars, the Roadhouse in Crystal's Hotel Vallée Blanche and the Underground in Neilson's Hotel Chamois are

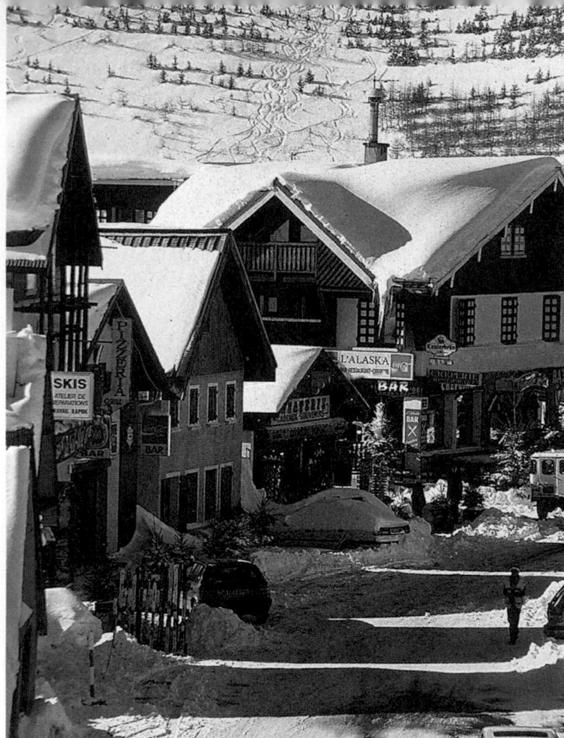

↑ There is a corner of the village that looks quite cute

AGENCE NUTS / OT ALPE D'HUEZ

GETTING THERE

Air Lyon, transfer 3hr. Geneva, transfer 4hr. Grenoble, transfer 1½hr.

Rail Grenoble (63km); daily buses from station.

ACTIVITIES

Indoor Sports centre (tennis, gym, squash, aerobics, climbing wall), library, cinema, swimming pool, billiards, bridge
Outdoor Artificial skating rink (skating and curling), 30km of cleared paths, outdoor swimming pool, hang-gliding, paragliding, all-terrain carts, quad-bikes

TOURIST OFFICE

Postcode 38750
t +33 476 114444
f 476 806954
info@alpedhuez.com
www.alpedhuez.com

established favourites. O'Sharkey's and the Pacific (sister bar to the one in Val d'Isère) are also popular. Smithy's does good Tex-Mex food and can get pretty rowdy late on.

The little Avalanche bar is popular with locals and visitors alike, and often has live music. The P'tit Bar de l'Alpe takes some beating for atmosphere, and also has live music. The Sporting is a large but friendly French rendezvous with a live band. The Etalon and Freeride cafes are also popular. And the Dutch-run Melting Pot does good tapas and is great for a relaxed drink, as is the Zoo.

The Stage One and Igloo discos liven up whenever the French are in town en masse.

OFF THE SLOPES

Good by purpose-built standards

There is a wide range of facilities, including a new indoor pool, an open-air pool (boxer-style cozzies not allowed), Olympic-size ice rink and splendid sports centre. There's also an ice-driving school. Shops are numerous, but limited in range. The helicopter excursion to Les Deux-Alpes is amusing. It's a pity that the better mountain restaurants aren't easily accessible to pedestrians.

Vaujany 1250m

THE RESORT

Vaujany is a small village perched on the hillside opposite its own sector of the domain. Hydro-electric riches have financed huge continuing investment. There's a giant 160-person cable-car (that whisks you into the heart of the Alpe-d'Huez lift system), a superb new sports centre, a huge snowmaking installation and apparently plans for a monorail within the village. Eventually, they are going to run out of things to buy. There are some tasteful new developments up the mountainside. A mile or two up the valley is the even smaller and more rustic hamlet of La Villette (just one tiny bar-restaurant).

THE MOUNTAINS

Although no slopes reach Vaujany itself, it is in practice a good base – its own slopes are not far away, and access to Alpe-d'Huez is speedy.
Slopes There are no village slopes, so even complete beginners have to ride the gondola to Montfrais, which has a mid-station at La Villette. There's a run back to La Villette, but you normally have to ride from there down to Vaujany. The alternative is the Fare black piste, ending below the village at a short lift.
Snowboarding Although there are some good nursery slopes here, beginners will have difficulty negotiating the main drag-lift up towards Alpette. And there's no easy route across to the main Alpe d'Huez sector except by riding down lifts.
Snow reliability A large snowmaking network and shady slopes help the area keep its snow-cover for longer.
Experts The huge cable-car offers quick queue-free access up towards Lac Blanc and the Pic Blanc cable-car up to the resort high-point and the main body of expert terrain. Local challenges include some off-piste runs through the trees and a couple of black runs too.
Intermediates There's a nice variety of cruising runs in the local sector and the lack of crowds is a real bonus. A special lift pass covering 20 lifts in Oz and Vaujany is available.
Beginners There are some good nursery slopes at the top of the gondola and there are some nice cruisy blues to progress to. Complete beginners can buy a special pass that covers the three Enversin lifts and one on Montfrais.

CHALET LA SOURCE *www.lasource.f9.co.uk* TEL & FAX 01707 655988

↑ VILLARD-RECULAS

Situated in the picturesque village of Villard-Reculas – an alpine secret in a spectacular setting with fast links to some of the best skiing in Europe.

La Source is a spacious, luxury-catered, owner-managed chalet offering accommodation for 2 to 14 people, and is perfect for those who appreciate imaginative cuisine and fine wine, with efficient and friendly service. La Source provides free airport transfers, local minibus and ski guiding.

email: lasourcefrance@cs.com

CHALET LA SOURCE ↑

Ski PEAK

VAUJANY

VAUJANY

LA VILLETTE-MONTFRAIS

Quality accommodation & service from one resort specialists with excellent travel arrangements, child care and ski-guiding.

Tel: 01428 741144 **www.skipeak.com**

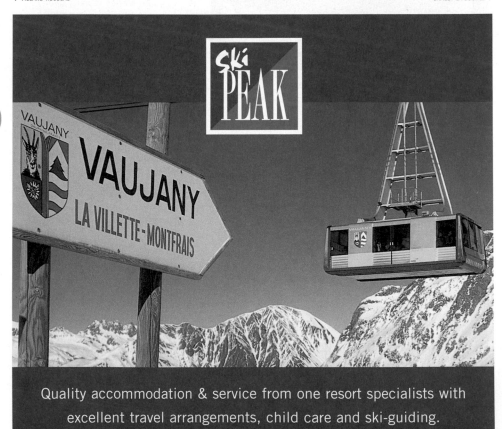

Cross-country The 20km loop between Alpette and Alpe d'Huez is the most snowsure circuit in the area.
Queues Vaujany gets some day visitors, but is generally a quiet spot. We've never seen the cable-car full.
Mountain restaurants The Airelles is probably the most atmospheric.
Schools and guides Vaujany has its own ski school – reports have all been very positive.
Facilities for children There's a big day nursery by the lift station.

STAYING THERE
How to go There's a handful of simple hotels in Vaujany.
Chalets Ski Peak has comfortable, tastefully decorated catered chalets in Vaujany and La Villette. A minibus service for guests is available.
Hotels The Rissiou is run by a British tour operator (Ski Peak) and is well situated for access to the cable-car. It has a popular bar, a pleasant dining room that serves excellent French cuisine (and good inexpensive wines), and fairly basic bedrooms. The staff are friendly and efficient. The hotel Cîmes (0476 798550), over the road, is another option but is less rustic.
Eating out There are a couple of restaurants in the village.
Après-ski The bar at the Rissiou is popular and frequented by the locals. The Cîmes is useful for a change of bar scenery. And the Etendard, by the lift station, has a lively après-ski bar. There are two nightclubs.
Off the slopes As well as the excellent sports centre, there's an open-air ice rink, well-stocked sports shop, small supermarket, and a few chickens wandering the streets.

Oz-en-Oisans 1350m

The purpose-built ski station above the attractive old village of Oz-en-Oisans apparently now takes its parent's name. The village has the basics – ski school, sports shops, nursery slopes, several bar-restaurants and a supermarket. There's also a large underground car park. A couple of large apartment blocks – built in a sympathetic style, with much use of wood and stone – stand between the two gondolas to make up the focus of the resort. Attractive new chalets have recently sprung up behind the centre and more development is planned. A small hotel is under construction. To quote one recent visitor, Oz is now 'taking off'. But another complains that there is still no nightlife. The main run home is liberally endowed with snow-guns, but it needs to be.

Auris 1600m

Auris is a series of wood-clad, chalet-style apartment blocks with a few shops, bars and restaurants, pleasantly set close to the thickest woodland in the area. It's a fine family resort, with everything close to hand, including a nursery and a ski kindergarten. There's also a ski school. Beneath it is the original old village, complete with attractive, traditional buildings, a church and all but one of the resort's hotels. Staying here with a car you can drive up to the local lifts or make excursions to neighbouring resorts such as Serre-Chevalier.

Unsurprisingly, evenings are quiet, with a handful of bar-restaurants to choose from. The Beau Site (0476 800639), which looks like an apartment block, is the only hotel in the upper village. A couple of miles down the hill, the traditional Auberge de la Forêt (0476 800601) gives you a feel of 'real' rural France.

Access to the slopes of Alpe-d'Huez is no problem, but there are plenty of local slopes to explore, for which there is a special lift pass, covering 15 lifts and 45km of piste. Most of the sport is intermediate, though Auris is also the best of the local hamlets for beginners.

Villard-Reculas 1500m

Villard is a secluded village, complete with an old church, set on a small shelf wedged between an expanse of open snowfields above and tree-filled hillsides below. Following the installation of a fast quad chair up to Signal (and the main Alpe d'Huez sector) a couple of years back, the village is becoming more popular as an access point and it is now beginning to find its feet as a 'resort'. Its 500 beds are mainly in self-catering apartments and chalets, though there is one 2-star hotel. There is a supermarket and a couple of bars and restaurants.

The local slopes have something for everyone, and there is now an ESF branch here. Snowmaking on the often icy and patchy home runs down to the village is planned for next season. A crèche is also planned.

Les Arcs 1600m-2000m

Purpose-built for a holiday on the slopes – and little else

WHAT IT COSTS

5

HOW IT RATES

The slopes

Snow	****
Extent	***
Experts	****
Intermediates	****
Beginners	****
Convenience	****
Queues	***
Restaurants	**

The rest

Scenery	***
Resort charm	*
Off-slope	*

What's new

Not much is happening on the lift front right now, presumably because of the imminent expense of the long-awaited link between the Les Arcs and La Plagne slopes. It is expected to be open for the 2002/03 season – a double-decker cable-car linking Plan-Peisey to Montchavin in only four minutes. The result will be the world's third biggest linked ski area.

- ⊕ Easy access to the slopes from most (but not all) of the apartments
- ⊕ A wide range of runs to suit intermediates and experts
- ⊕ Few serious queues
- ⊕ Excellent woodland runs, mainly above Plan Peisey and Vallandry
- ⊕ Opportunity for skiing beginners to learn by the évolutif method
- ⊕ Very easy rail access from UK
- ⊕ Splendid views of Mont Blanc massif
- ⊕ Glowing recent reports of friendly locals – unusual for French resorts

- ⊖ Main village centres range from the charmless to the positively tacky
- ⊖ Few off-slope diversions
- ⊖ Not the best resort for confidence-building green runs
- ⊖ Still lots of slow old chair-lifts and drag-lifts
- ⊖ Very quiet in the evenings, and limited choice of bars/restaurants
- ⊖ Some apartments are quite a walk from the nearest lifts
- ⊖ Nearly all the accommodation is in apartments – there's a limited choice of alternatives

Les Arcs is a classic purpose-built French resort, with all the usual advantages and drawbacks. If altitude and a short walk from front door to lift base are your priorities – and not village charm or animation – put it on the short-list. A further attraction for some is that direct rail services to Bourg-St-Maurice connect with a funicular that takes you straight to Arc 1600 (though not to the other two Arcs).

The terrain isn't in quite the same league as the Three Valleys, La Plagne or Val-d'Isère/Tignes for sheer extent, but within its slightly smaller area it contains an impressive variety, including some of the longest descents in the Alps, plenty of steep stuff, and a very attractive area of woodland runs at one end of the area. For a keen mixed-ability group, it is a strong candidate.

The resort

Les Arcs is made up of three modern resort units, linked by road, high above the railway terminus town of Bourg-St-Maurice. The three villages have a lot in common: like many such resorts, they are purpose-built, apartment-dominated places, offering doorstep access to the snow with no traffic hazards, but lacking Alpine charm, off-slope activities, and evening animation. But reporters repeatedly comment on the friendliness of the natives.

Arc 1600 was the original Arc (it opened in December 1968). It has the advantage of a funicular railway up from Bourg-St-Maurice funicular, giving easy access from Paris and the UK by train. Above the village, a trio of chair-lifts fan out over the lower half of the slopes, leading to links to the other Arcs. 1600 is set in the trees and has a friendly, small-scale atmosphere; and it enjoys good views along the valley and towards Mont Blanc. The central area is particularly good for families: uncrowded, compact, and set on even ground. But things are even quieter here at night than during the day.

Much the largest of the three 'villages' is Arc 1800. It has three sections, though the boundaries are indistinct. Charvet and Villards are small, scruffy shopping centres, mostly open-air but still managing to seem as claustrophobic as the indoor arcades of neighbouring La Plagne. Both are dominated by apartment blocks the size of ocean liners (getting to the shops or the lifts may involve a much longer walk inside your apartment building than outside it). More pleasant on the eye is Charmettoger, with smaller, wood-clad buildings nestling among trees. Villards is the central component, and it's from here that the lifts depart – chair-lifts to mid-mountain, and the big Transarc gondola to Col de la Chal at the head of the Arc 2000 valley.

MOUNTAIN FACTS

Altitude	1200m-3225m
Lifts	76
Pistes	200km
Green	8%
Blue	45%
Red	33%
Black	14%
Artificial snow	12km

Recco detectors used

LIFT PASSES

2000/01 prices in euros

Massif Aiguille Grive–Aiguille Rouge
Covers all lifts in Les Arcs and Peisey-Nancroix, including funicular from Bourg-St-Maurice.

Beginners Five free lifts; one in 1600 and two each in 1800 and 2000.

Main pass
1-day pass 35
6-day pass 167

Senior citizens
Over 60: 6-day pass 142
Over 75: free pass

Children
Under 14: 6-day pass 142
Under 7: free pass

Short-term passes
Half-day afternoon (adult 25). Half-day (am or pm) passes for each area (adult 18). Single and return tickets on most lifts for walkers.

Notes All passes over 1 day cover La Plagne and allow 1 day in La Rosière–La Thuile and Tignes–Val-d'Isère. 6-day pass and over allows one day each in the 3V, Pralognan-la-Vanoise and Les Saises. 5% reduction on presentation of previous season's pass.

Alternative passes
1- and 2-day passes (165, 305) are available; one covers Arc 2000 and Villaroger (21 lifts), the other Arc 1600 and 1800 (38 lifts).

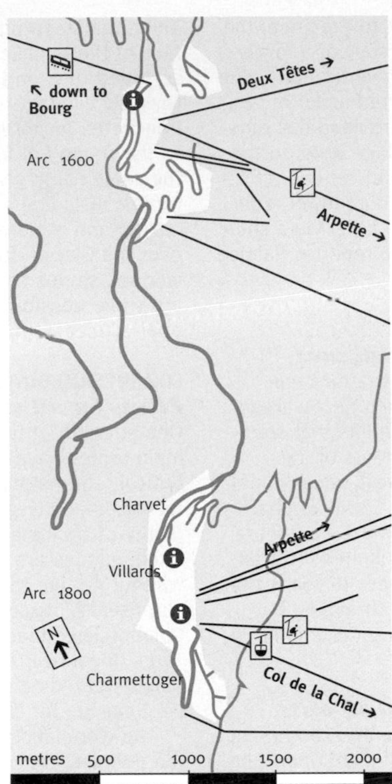

Arc 1800 is spreading up the hillside, with more excellent apartments coming on to the market in Le Chantel.

Arc 2000 is just a few hotels, apartment blocks and the Club Med, huddled together in a bleak spot, with little to commend it but immediate access to the highest, toughest skiing. There is only a handful of restaurants and shops – and it's a serious bus-ride to Arc 1600. A swanky new development known as Arc 1950 or La Daille d'Arc 2000 is now planned for construction just below the original village by the Canadian company Intrawest, which if it comes off may be much more compelling. There are lifts all around 2000, but the main one now is the Varet gondola up towards the Aiguille Rouge.

At the southern end of the area, linked by pistes but reachable by road only by descending to the valley, is Peisey-Vallandry. Vallandry and Plan-Peisey are the key components of this composite resort – recently developed lift-base resorts above the old village of Peisey, which has a bucket lift up to Plan-Peisey. Vallandry is reportedly a bit more lively than 'very quiet' Plan-Peisey. Chair-lifts go up from both bases to mid-mountain. The long-awaited cable-car link with Montchavin and La Plagne will be built here.

There are a couple of alternative places to stay down in the valley at the other, northern end of the ski area – see the end of this chapter.

The mountains

Les Arcs' piste network is not huge. But its terrain is notably varied; it has plenty of runs suitable for experts as well as beginners and intermediates, and a good mixture of high, snowsure slopes and accessible low-level woodland runs ideal for bad weather.

THE SLOPES
Well planned, and varied

The slopes are very well laid out, and moving around is quick and easy – though direction-finding can be a problem at times.

Arc 1600 and Arc 1800 share a west-facing mountainside laced with runs leading down to one or other village. At the southern end is an area of woodland runs – unusually extensive for a high French area – down to Plan-Peisey and Vallandry.

From various points on the ridge above 1600 and 1800 you can head down into the Arc 2000 bowl. On the opposite side of this bowl, lifts take you to the highest runs of the area, from the Aiguille Rouge and the Grand Col. As well as a variety of steep north-

boarding *Les Arcs calls itself 'the home of the snowboard'. Local boy Regis Rolland played a big part in popularising the sport (not least with his 'Apocalypse Snow' movies), and the resort is constantly developing its boarding facilities. Some boarders are doubtless attracted by the budget self-catering accommodation, but also by the great mix of terrain served mainly by boarder-friendly lifts (though getting around can involve some long traverses on near-flat catwalks). Arc 2000 and Vallandry have great smooth runs for beginners and carvers, but some of the blues at 2000 are too flat for comfort. There's a park and half-pipe, and a couple of specialist board schools and shops.*

SCHOOLS/GUIDES

2000/01 prices in euros

ESF
Classes 6 days
3hr am or pm
6 half-days 105
Children's classes
Ages: 3 to 14
6 half-days: 105
Private lessons
Hourly
29 for 1hr, for 1 or 2 people

Other schools
Arc Aventures (ESI)
Virages
Tip-Top (based in Bourg-St-Maurice)

west-facing runs back to Arc 2000, the Aiguille Rouge is the start of a lovely long run (over 2000m vertical and 7km long) right down to the hamlet of Le Pré near Villaroger. Arc 2000 has runs descending below village level, to the lift-base, restaurant and car-park at Pré-St-Esprit, about 200m lower. You can reach Le Pré from here, via a short drag-lift (although one reporter claimed it is often closed).

SNOW RELIABILITY
Good – plenty of high runs

A high percentage of the runs are above 2000m and when necessary you can stay high by using lifts that start around that altitude. Most of the slopes face roughly west, which is not ideal. Those from the Col de la Chal and the long runs down to Le Pré are north-facing. There is limited artificial snow on some runs back to 1600, 1800 and Peisey-Vallandry. Grooming has struck us and readers as 'economical'.

FOR EXPERTS
Challenges on- and off-piste

Les Arcs has a lot to offer experts – at least when the high lifts are open (the Aiguille Rouge cable-car, in particular, is often shut in bad weather).

There are a number of truly black pistes above Arc 2000, and a couple in other areas. After a narrow shelf near the top, the Aiguille Rouge–Le Pré run is superb, with remarkably varying terrain throughout its vertical drop of over 2000m. There is also a great deal of off-piste potential, in various parts.

There are steep pitches on the front face of the Aiguille Rouge, and secluded runs on the back side, towards Villaroger – the Combe de l'Anchette, for example. A short climb to the Grand Col from the chair-lift of the same name gives access to several routes, including a quite serious couloir and a more roundabout route over the Glacier du Grand Col. The wooded slopes above 1600 are another attractive possibility – and there are open slopes all over the mountain.

FOR INTERMEDIATES
Plenty for all standards

One strength of the area is that most main routes have easy and more difficult alternatives, making it good for mixed-ability groups. There are plenty of challenges, yet less confident intermediates are able to move around without getting too many nasty surprises. An exception is the solitary Comborcières black from Les Deux Têtes down to Pré-St-Esprit. This long mogul field justifies its rating and can be great fun for strong intermediates.

The woodland runs at either end of the domain, above Vallandry and Le Pré, and the bumpy Cachette red down to 1600, are also good for better intermediates. Those who enjoy speed will like the Vallandry area: its well groomed runs are remarkably uncrowded much of the time. Good intermediates can enjoy the Aiguille Rouge–Le Pré run (with red and blue detours available to avoid the toughest bits of the black piste).

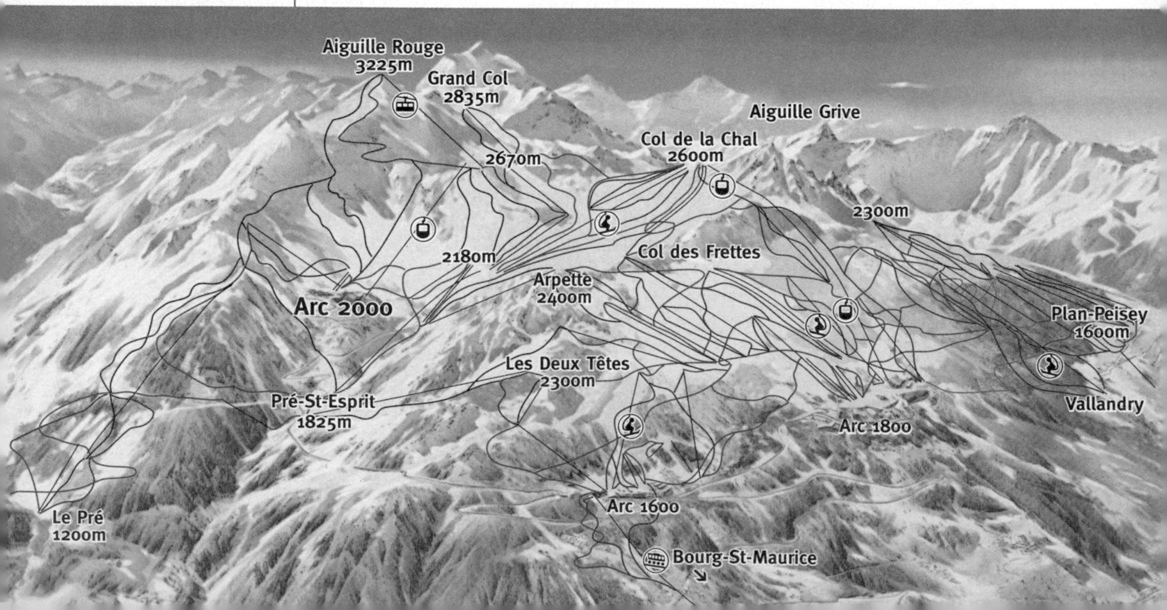

CHILDCARE

The ESF branches in all three stations take children from 3. The International school's Club Poussin in 1800 starts at 4.

At Arc 1600 the Garderie at the Hotel de la Cachette (0479 077050) runs three clubs for children from 4 months to 11 years, from 8.30 to 6pm, with ski lessons available.

At Arc 1800 various schemes running from 8.45 to 5.45 are offered by the Pommes de Pin (0479 041530). The Nurserie takes children aged 1 to 3, the Garderie those aged 3 to 6, and children aged 3 to 9 can have lessons through the two clubs based at the Garderie.

At Arc 2000 Les Marmottons (0479 076425) takes children aged 2 to 6 from 8.30 to 5.45, with lessons for those aged 3 to 6.

The Club Med (2000) has full childcare facilities – this is one of their 'family villages'.

The lower half of the mountainside is good for mixed-ability groups, with a choice of routes through the trees. The red runs down from Arpette and Col des Frettes towards 1800 are quite steep but usually well groomed.

Cautious intermediates have plenty of blue cruising terrain. Many of the runs around 2000 are rather bland and prone to overcrowding. The blues above 1800 are attractive but busy. A favourite blue of ours is Renard, high above Vallandry, usually with excellent snow.

FOR BEGINNERS
1800 best for complete novices

There are nursery slopes conveniently situated just above all three villages. The ones at Arc 1600 are rather steep, while those at 2000 get crowded with intermediate through-traffic at times. The sunny, spacious runs at 1800 are best. There is a lack of attractive long green runs to move on to – La Forêt, above Vallandry, is just a winding woodland path. But the Mont Blanc above 1600 is a beautiful gentle blue, and you can take the gondola up to Col de la Chal and enjoy good snow on the easy runs towards 2000.

FOR CROSS-COUNTRY
Very boring locally

Short trails, mostly on roads, close to all three villages, is all you can expect unless you travel down to the Nancroix valley's 40km of pleasant trails.

QUEUES
Few problems now

Reporters have few complaints about queues except in one or two places. In sunny weather, Arc 2000 attracts the crowds and there may be non-trivial queues for either the gondola or the chair to Col de la Chal. In bad weather, it's the lifts serving the woodland slopes above Vallandry that cause the problem. There are sometimes lengthy waits for the Aiguille Rouge cable-car. A bigger problem than queues is the time taken riding slow old chair-lifts, some of them very long. At holiday times overcrowded pistes can be a problem, too.

MOUNTAIN RESTAURANTS
An adequate choice

Lunch isn't generally a highlight of the day unless you head for the hamlets at the extremes of the area. At the north end, the 500-year-old Belliou la Fumée at Pré-St-Esprit is charmingly rustic. La Ferme and Aiguille Rouge down at Le Pré are both friendly, with good food. Chez Léa in Le Planay serves simple food in rustic surroundings. At the south end, a five-minute taxi-ride from Vallandry will bring you to the Ancolie (0479 079320), a delightful auberge with superb Savoyarde food. Or take the bucket lift down to Peisey and head for the Ormelune, which does 'the best cheese fondue', and perhaps proper food too.

The restaurants dotted around the main slopes are mainly unremarkable. But the little Blanche Murée, just down from the Transarc mid-station, is consistently recommended – 'friendly service, fantastic food, reasonable prices' says one report this year. The Arpette is mainly notable for its wide range of dishes. The restaurant at Col de la Chal has fabulous views.

It is easy to get back to the main villages, where prices are lower.

SCHOOL AND GUIDES
Ski évolutif recommended

The ESF here is renowned for being the first in Europe to teach ski évolutif, where you start by learning parallel turns on short skis, gradually moving on to longer skis. We have a report this year of one beginner who astonished his experienced friends by 'doing perfect parallel turns on steep reds by the end of the week'. Private boarding lessons with the ESF have also been 'very highly recommended'. The International school (Arc Aventures) has impressed reporters over the years: 'Good instruction with English well spoken.' We have had glowing reports of the Optimum ski courses, using British instructors, based in a catered chalet in Le Pré. There are mountain guides available in the main villages.

FACILITIES FOR CHILDREN
Good reports

We have received good reports on the Pommes de Pin facilities in Arc 1800 – 'great care and attention', 'patient approach to teaching'. Comments on children's ski classes are favourable, too – 'nearly all instructors spoke English', 'classes went smoothly'.

Staying there

GETTING THERE

Air Geneva, transfer 3½hr. Lyon, transfer 3½hr. Chambéry, transfer 2½hr.

Rail Bourg-St-Maurice; frequent buses and direct funicular to resort.

Phone numbers
From abroad use the prefix +33 and omit the initial '0' of the phone number.

UK Representative
Erna Low Consultants
9 Reece Mews
London SW7 3HE
t 020 7584 2841
f 020 7589 9531
info@ernalow.co.uk
www.ernalow.co.uk

HOW TO GO
Apartments rule

Over three-quarters of the resort beds are in apartments. There is a Club Med 'village' at Arc 2000.

Chalets There are hardly any catered chalet holidays in Les Arcs but there are in the lower villages.

Hotels The choice of hotels in Les Arcs is gradually widening, particularly at the upper end of the market. All-in packages of full-board accommodation and lift pass can be attractive.

((((4 **Mercure Coralia** (1800) (0479 076500) Newish, and locally judged to be worth four stars rather than its actual three.

(((3 **Golf** (1800) (0479 414343) A pricey 3-star; the best in Les Arcs, with recently renovated rooms, sauna, gym, kindergarten and covered parking.

(((3 **La Cachette** (1600) (0479 077050) Smartly renovated in the mid-1990s, with something of the style of an American resort hotel. But it can be 'dominated by kids' says one reporter.

((2 **Aiguille Rouge** (2000) (0479 075707) Daily free ski guiding.

Self-catering The apartments are mostly tight on space, so paying extra for under-occupancy is a sound investment. The recently built Alpages du Chantel apartments (bookable through Erna Low), are exceptionally attractive, comfortable and spacious by French standards, with a pool, sauna and gym. Set high above Charvet, they are very convenient for skiing but very inconvenient for everything else – and the planned lift up to them has been blocked by objections from residents of Charvet. The Ruitor apartments, set among trees between Villards and Charmettoger, are reported to be 'excellent in all respects'. L'Aiguille Grive has been recommended for spacious apartments and excellent slope access.

EATING OUT
Reasonable choice in Arc 1800

In Arc 1600 and 2000 there are very few restaurants, none of them discussed here. 1800 has a choice of about 15 restaurants; an ad-based (so not comprehensive) guide is given away locally. Le Petit Zinc restaurant in the Hotel du Golf has haute cuisine and high prices; it has a Friday evening seafood buffet. The Gargantus is a good informal place, although very cramped. Readers have been satisfied by 'enormous portions' at L'Equipage and 'good solid meals' at the Triangle Noir. Casa Mia is an excellent all-rounder with exceptionally friendly service. The Mountain Café does much more than the Tex-Mex it advertises, and copes well with big family parties. A popular outing is to drive half-way down the mountain to the welcoming and woody Bois de Lune at Montvenix, which has perhaps the best food in the area (booking advised – 0479 071792).

APRES-SKI
Arc 1800 is the place to be

1800 is the liveliest centre, though even so one reporter calls is 'very, very quiet'. The J.O. bar is open until the early hours and has a friendly atmosphere with live music. The friendly Red Hot Saloon has bar games and 'surprisingly good live music' some nights. The Fairway disco keeps rocking until 4 most mornings and the Apokalypse 'isn't terrible'. The cinemas at 1800 and 1600 have English-language films once or twice a week. In 1600 the bar opposite (and belonging to) the Hotel La Cachette

ACTIVITIES

Indoor Squash (3 courts 1800), Chinese gymnastics, saunas (1600, 1800), solaria, multi-gym (1800), cinemas, amusement arcades, music, concert halls, fencing (2000), bowling (1800)

Outdoor Natural skating rinks (1800 and 2000), floodlit skiing, speed skiing (2000), ski-jump, climbing wall (1800), organised snow-shoe outings, 10km cleared paths (1800 and 1600), hang-gliding, horse-riding, sleigh rides, helicopter rides to Italy, ice grotto, paint balling

TOURIST OFFICE

Postcode 73706
t +33 479 071257
f 479 074596
lesarcs@lesarcs.com
www.lesarcs.com

has games machines, pool and live bands, and can be quite lively even in low season. The Red Rock in 2000 is 'good for youngsters but too busy for grown-ups'.

OFF THE SLOPES

Very poor

Les Arcs is not the place for an off-the-slopes holiday. There is very little to do; it doesn't even have a swimming pool. The main options available are a shopping trip to Bourg-St-Maurice (cheaper for buying ski equipment), preferably on Saturday for the market, and a few walks – nice ones up the Nancroix valley.

Bourg-St-Maurice 840m

Bourg-St-Maurice is a real French town, with cheaper hotels and restaurants and easy access to other resorts for day trips. The funicular goes straight to Arc 1600 in seven minutes. Hostellerie du Pt-St-Bernard has been reported to be a reasonable 2-star hotel. You can leave your skis or board and boots at a ski shop next to the bottom of the funicular, run by a British couple.

Le Pré 1200m

A charming, quiet, rustic little hamlet with a chair-lift up towards Arc 2000. It has a couple of small bars and restaurants. British operator Optimum has a beautiful old chalet here that the owners, Martin and Deirdre Rowe, renovated and run themselves. We can personally vouch for fabulous food, free-flowing wine, jolly bar and basic but adequate bedrooms; and the ski courses they run (Martin used to run the ski school in Andorra) have received rave reviews from reporters. But Le Pré is not at all suitable for beginners.

Peisey-Vallandry 1550m

Peisey-Vallandry is a cluster of five small villages. Peisey, linked by bucket lift to Plan-Peisey, dates back to AD1000, and its most striking feature is the fine baroque church. The other, mostly old, buildings house a small selection of shops, restaurants and bars. The hotel Vanoise in Plan-Peisey is repeatedly recommended by readers for its position, food and 'extremely friendly and helpful staff'.

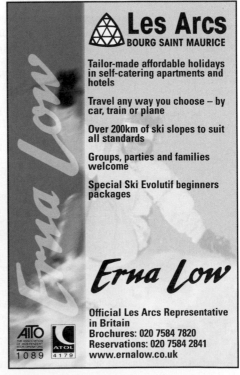

Avoriaz 1800m

The best base on the Portes du Soleil circuit for snow

WHAT IT COSTS

5

HOW IT RATES

The slopes

Snow	***
Extent	*****
Experts	***
Intermediates	****
Beginners	****
Convenience	****
Queues	**
Restaurants	****

The rest

Scenery	***
Resort charm	**
Off-slope	*

What's new

Recent years have seen substantial investment in high-speed chairs (including some six-seaters) which have greatly reduced lift queue problems.

For 2001/02 another high-speed, six-seater chair will replace the double drag from Les Lindarets up to Avoriaz, cutting the queues at this bad bottleneck. A new piste will be built at the top to join the existing runs down to Les Lindarets.

For 2000/01 the gondola from Ardent to Les Lindarets was upgraded to increase its capacity and the car park was also extended.

MOUNTAIN FACTS

for Portes du Soleil

Altitude	975m-2350m
Lifts	206
Pistes	650km
Green	13%
Blue	38%
Red	39%
Black	10%
Art. snow	252 acres
Recco detectors used	

- ⊕ Good position on the main Portes du Soleil circuit, giving access to very extensive, quite varied runs for all grades from novices to experts
- ⊕ Generally has the best snow in the Portes du Soleil
- ⊕ Accommodation right on the slopes
- ⊕ Resort-level snow and ski-through, car-free village give Alpine ambience
- ⊕ Good children's facilities

- ⊖ Much of Portes du Soleil area is low for a major French area, with resulting risk of poor snow or bare slopes lower down
- ⊖ Still a couple of lift bottlenecks and (especially in local Avoriaz area) some crowded pistes
- ⊖ Non-traditional architecture, which some find ugly
- ⊖ Little to do off the slopes
- ⊖ Few hotels or chalets

For access to the impressive Portes du Soleil piste network, Avoriaz has clear attractions. In a low-altitude area where snow is not reliable, it has the best there is – on relatively high, north-facing slopes of varying difficulty, including some of the most challenging terrain in the Portes du Soleil.

But there are drawbacks. First, the character of the village: we don't mind sleeping in purpose-built resorts to get instant access to high-altitude snow, but there is no really high-altitude terrain here. The Portes du Soleil has several attractive low-altitude villages, and we'd rather be based in one. Secondly, cost: Châtel and Morzine are cheap by French standards; Avoriaz is not. Queues can be a nuisance too, but they affect those exploring the Portes du Soleil from other bases as much as they affect those based in Avoriaz – more so, in fact.

The resort 

Avoriaz is a purpose-built, traffic-free resort perched above a dramatic, sheer rock face. From the edge of town horse-drawn sleighs or snow-cats transport people and luggage to the accommodation – or you can borrow a sledge for a small deposit and transport your own! Traffic can be intrusive and fast moving but the problem of horse mess has been cut since they now wear 'nappies' and staff on snowmobiles scoop up what escapes! Cars are left in pay-for outdoor or underground parking – a reporter advises the latter to avoid a chaotic departure if it snows (it took him three hours). You can book your space in advance.

The village is set on quite a slope, but chair-lifts and elevators in buildings mean moving around is no problem except when paths are icy. Pistes, lifts and off-slope activities are close to virtually all accommodation.

The village is all angular, dark, wood-clad, high-rise buildings, mostly apartments. The place at least has a distinct style, unlike the dreary cuboid blocks of Flaine and Les Menuires.

But the compact snow-covered village has a friendly Alpine feel despite the architecture. The evenings are not especially lively, but reporters have enjoyed the 'brilliant parade in half-term week, with a superb fire-eating display' in the past.

Avoriaz is above the valley resort of Morzine, to which it is linked by gondola (but not by piste). It also has good links to Châtel in one direction and Champéry in the other. Car trips are possible to Flaine and Chamonix.

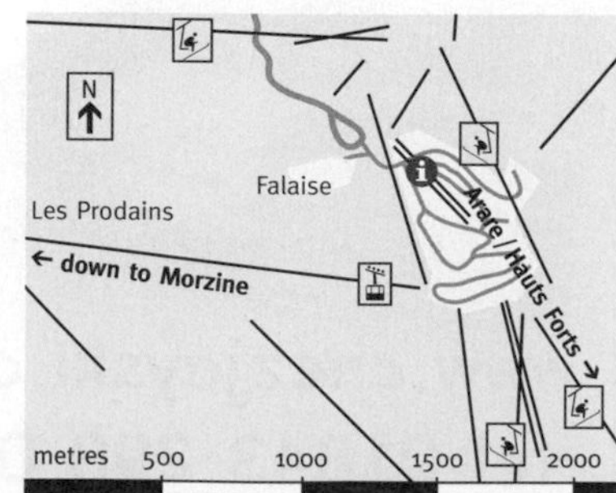

LIFT PASSES

2001/02 prices in euros

Portes du Soleil
Covers all lifts in all 12 resorts, and shuttle-buses.

Main pass
1-day pass 33
6-day pass 159

Senior citizens
Over 60: 6-day pass 127

Children
Under 16: 6-day pass 107
Under 5: free pass

Alternative passes
Day pass for Avoriaz lifts only: 27.
Beginner's day pass (limited area): 17.
Snowboarder pass for fun-park and a few other areas: 20 per day; 6-day pass 92.

The mountains

The slopes closest to Avoriaz are bleak and treeless, but snowsure. They suit all grades from novice to expert and give quick access to the toughest runs in the Portes du Soleil. The whole circuit is easily done by intermediates of all abilities – and the booklet-style piste map makes for easy navigation. Reporters have also commented favourably on the system of Discovery Routes around the Portes du Soleil – choose an alpine animal that suits your ability and follow the signs displaying it. The circuit breaks down at Châtel, where you have to get a (frequent) shuttle-bus. The slopes of Morzine and Les Gets, accessed from the far side of Morzine, are part of the Portes du Soleil but not on the core circuit. An electronic lift pass was introduced for 1999/2000, so you can now keep your pass in your pocket.

THE SLOPES
Short runs and plenty of them

The village has lifts and pistes fanning out in all directions. Staying in Avoriaz assures the comfort of riding mostly chairs – some other parts of the Portes du Soleil (especially on the Swiss side) have a lot of drags. Facing the village are the slopes of **Arare-Hauts Forts** and, when snow conditions allow, there are long, steep runs down to Les Prodains.

The lifts off to the left go to the **Chavanette** sector on the Swiss border – a broad, undulating bowl. Beyond the border is the infamous Swiss Wall – a long, impressive mogul slope with a tricky start, but not the terror it is cracked up to be unless it's icy (it gets a lot of sun). Lots of people doing the circuit (or returning to Champéry) ride the chair down. At the bottom of the Wall is the open terrain of Planachaux, above Champéry, with links to the still bigger open area around Les Crosets and Champoussin. There are several ways to return, but the most amusing is the chair up the Wall, with a great view of people struggling down it.

Taking a lift up from Avoriaz (or traversing from some of the highest accommodation) to the ridge behind the village is the way to the **Lindarets-Brocheaux** valley, from where lifts and runs in the excellent Linga sector lead to Châtel. Getting back is a matter of retracing your steps, although there are several options from Lindarets.

Morgins is the resort opposite Avoriaz on the circuit, and the state of the snow may encourage you to travel anti-clockwise rather than clockwise, so as to avoid the low, south-facing slopes down from Bec de Corbeau.

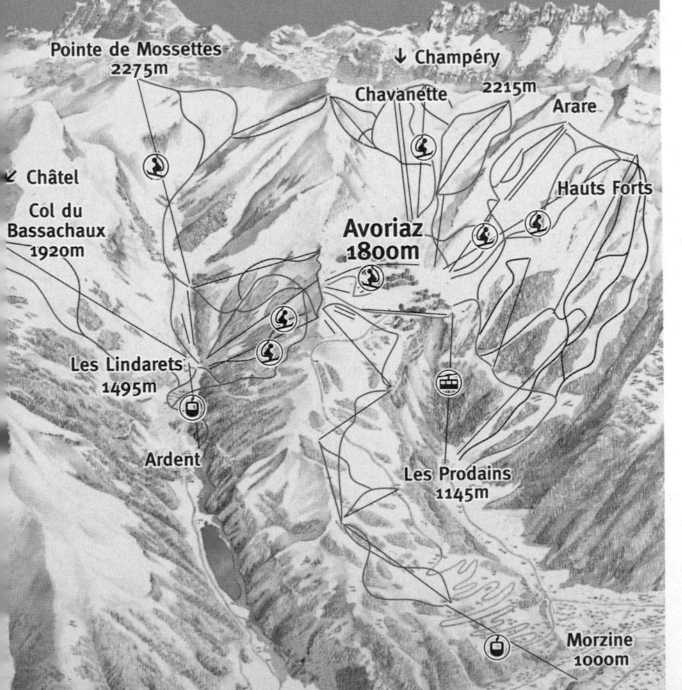

SNOW RELIABILITY
High resort, low slopes

Although Avoriaz town is high, its slopes don't go much higher – and some parts of the Portes du Soleil circuit are much lower. Considering their altitude, the north-facing slopes below Hauts Forts hold snow well. In general, the snow in Avoriaz is usually much better than over the border on the south-facing Swiss slopes.

Piste maintenance is 'erratic and it is quite common for runs not to be groomed overnight,' says a reporter. Snow-guns have been introduced in some areas, including on some blacks.

FOR EXPERTS
Several testing runs

Tough terrain is rather dotted about. The challenging runs down from Hauts Forts to Prodains (including a World Cup downhill) are excellent. There is a tough red, and several long, truly black runs, one of which cuts through trees – useful in poor weather. Two chair-lifts serve the lower runs, which snow-guns help to keep open. The Swiss Wall at

SCHOOLS/GUIDES

2001/02 prices in euros

ESF

Classes 6 days
5hr: 2½hr am and pm
6 full days: 130

Children's classes
Ages: 4 to 11
6 full days: 115

Private lessons
1hr, 1½hr or 2hr
29 for 1hr, for 1 to 2 people; 35 for 3 to 6

L'Ecole de Glisse

Classes 6 days
2hr, am or pm
6 half-days: 91

Private lessons
1hr or 2hr
32 for 1hr; 59 for 2hr

CHILDCARE

Les P'tits Loups (0450 740038) takes children aged 3 months to 5, from 9am to 6pm; indoor and outdoor games, and so on. You have to book in advance.

The Village des Enfants (0450 740446) takes children aged 3 to 16, from 9am to 5.30.

The Club Med in Avoriaz is one of their 'family villages', with comprehensive childcare facilities.

GETTING THERE

Air Geneva, transfer 2hr.

Rail Cluses (42km) or Thonon (45km); bus and cable-car to resort.

Chavanette will naturally be on your agenda, and Châtel is well worth a trip. The black runs off the Swiss side of Mossette and Pointe de l'Au are worth trying. It's not a great area for off-piste adventures, but a recent reporter who visited in less than ideal conditions hired a 'very good' ESF guide who found 'great powder and off piste and took us away from the crowds'.

FOR INTERMEDIATES
Virtually the whole area

Although some sections lack variety, the Portes du Soleil is excellent for all grades of intermediates when snow is in good supply. Timid types not worried about pretty surroundings need not leave the Avoriaz sector; Arare and Chavanette are gentle, spacious and above the tree-line bowls. The Lindarets area and on down to Ardent is also easy, with pretty runs through the trees. Champoussin has a lot of easy runs, reached without too much difficulty via Les Crosets and Pointe de l'Au. Better intermediates have virtually the whole area at their disposal. The runs down to Pré-la-Joux and L'Essert on the way to Châtel, and those either side of Morgins, are particularly attractive. The long, sunny runs down to Grand-Paradis near Champéry are a must when snow conditions allow; they offer great views. Good intermediates may want to take on the Wall, but the chair to Pointe de Mossette from Les Brocheaux is an easier route to Champéry.

FOR BEGINNERS
Convenient and good for snow

The nursery slopes seem small in relation to the size of the resort, but are adequate because so many visitors are intermediates. The slopes are sunny, yet good for snow, and link well to longer, easy runs.

FOR CROSS-COUNTRY
Varied, with some blacks

There are 45km of trails, a third graded black, mainly between Avoriaz and Super-Morzine, with other fine trails down to Lindarets and around Montriond. The only drawback is that several trails are not loops, but 'out and back' routes.

QUEUES
Main problems now gone

The queues for the lifts to Arare and Chavanette have been more or less eliminated by high-speed lifts. And for 2001/02 the bottleneck at Les Lindarets to get back to Avoriaz should be eliminated by a new six-pack. Peak times will still see queues to get out of Les Lindarets towards Châtel though. Weekends can be busy as people pour into their holiday apartments. Crowds on the pistes (especially around the village) can be worse than queues for the lifts, with care having to be taken to avoid collisions.

MOUNTAIN RESTAURANTS
Good choice over the hill

The charming, rustic chalets in the hamlet of Les Lindarets are one of the great concentrations of mountain restaurants in the Alps. A particular Lindarets favourite of ours is the Crémaillière which has wonderful chanterelle mushrooms and great atmosphere. La Pomme de Pin is recommended for its warm welcome and friendly service. The rustic La Grenuille du Marais near the top of the gondola up from Morzine has good value food, good views and atmosphere. L'Abricotine, with table service, at Les Brocheaux and Chavanette at the top of the Swiss Wall have also been recommended. As has Le Yéti, at the top of town: 'Has a terrace with a great view of a huge ski jump (which sees lots of action).'

boarding *Avoriaz has always encouraged snowboarding, opening France's first fun-park in 1993. There's now an excellent 1.5km fun-park and half-pipe – served by three lifts – and a special pass for those whose only interest is riding them. There's a specialist snowboard school and a snowboard village for children aged 6 to 16. A micro fun-park specially for children opened a couple of seasons ago. There's a Big Air competition on the plateau every Wednesday and Chalet Snowboard has a couple of chalets at Les Prodains. Only a few (mainly avoidable) drags are left after the lift upgrades. The blocks of self-catering accommodation may suit the budget boarder willing to pack people in. Nightlife revolves around the couple of bars that manage an atmosphere.*

↑ You can step straight on to the snow from all Avoriaz apartments

SNOWPIX.COM / CHRIS GILL

Phone numbers
From abroad use the prefix +33 and omit the initial ‘o’ of the phone number.

ACTIVITIES

Indoor Health centre ‘Altiform’ (sauna, gym, hot-tub), squash, Turkish baths, cinema, bowling
Outdoor Paragliding, hang-gliding, snow-shoe excursions, ice diving, floodlit tobogganing, dog-sleigh rides, walking paths, sleigh rides, skating, snow-scooter excursions, helicopter flights

TOURIST OFFICE

Postcode 74110
t +33 450 740211
f 450 741825
info@avoriaz.com
www.avoriaz.com

SCHOOLS AND GUIDES
Try BASS
The ESF has a good reputation, but classes can be large. The British Alpine Ski School has British instructors and has been highly recommended, especially for ‘quite excellent children’s lessons. Bookings are taken at Le Tavaillon bar in the high street’. Emery is a specialist snowboard school.

FACILITIES FOR CHILDREN
‘Annie Famose delivers’
The Village des Enfants, run by ex-downhill champ Annie Famose, is a key part of the family appeal of Avoriaz. Its facilities are excellent – a chalet full of activities and special slopes complete with Disney characters for children aged 3 to 16. There’s a snowboard village too, with special terrain, jumps etc. Car-free Avoriaz must be one of the safest villages in the Alps, but there are still sleighs, skiers, and snowcats to watch out for. Not to mention other tobogganing kids.

Staying there 

The main consideration in this steep village is whether you want to go out at night. By day you can get around by using chair-lifts, but at night it’s a walk uphill – or nip in and out of apartment blocks using internal lifts.

HOW TO GO
Self-catering dominates
Alternatives to apartments are few.
Chalets There are several available, comfortable and attractive but mainly designed for small family groups.
Hotels There is not much choice of hotels, but there is a Club Med village.
((③ **Dromonts** (0450 740811) The original Avoriaz construction in the resort centre, renovated for 2000/01.
(② **Falaise** (0450 742600) At the top of the village; encourages families.
Self-catering Some of the better apartments are in the Falaise area by the resort entrance. Reporters have said that some apartments badly need refurbishing – a real problem hopefully being addressed, since the resort is giving owners incentives to do them up.

EATING OUT
Good; booking essential
There are more than 30 restaurants. The hotel Dromont’s Table du Marché has a celebrity chef and excellent French cuisine. L’Igloo is also good. Le Bistro is recommended as ‘good food at good value’. L’Ortolan is friendly and good value. You can buy meal vouchers for seven evening meals in a range of five good restaurants. ‘Restricted menu but excellent value,’ says a reporter.

APRES-SKI
Lively, but not much choice
A few bars have a good atmosphere, particularly in happy hour. Le Choucas and The Place are lively and have bands, Le Tavaillon (popular with Brits because tour op reps meet there) has a football theme and Le Fantastique is worth a visit. Midnight Express club (free entry, pricey drinks) is popular.

OFF THE SLOPES
Not much at the resort
Those not interested in the slopes are better off in Morzine, which has more shops and sports facilities – though Avoriaz does have the Altiform Fitness Centre, with saunas and hot-tubs.

Chamonix 1035m

High drama among Europe's highest peaks

WHAT IT COSTS

HOW IT RATES

The slopes

Snow	****
Extent	***
Experts	*****
Intermediates	**
Beginners	*
Convenience	*
Queues	**
Restaurants	**

The rest

Scenery	*****
Resort charm	****
Off-slope	*****

- A lot of very tough terrain, especially off-piste
- Amazing cable-car to the Aiguille du Midi, leading to the famous (not so tough) Vallée Blanche
- Amazing views of peaks and glaciers
- Town steeped in Alpine traditions, with lots to do off the slopes
- Well-organised and extensive cross-country trail system
- Easy access by road, rail and air

- Several separate mountains: mixed ability groups are likely to have to split up, and the bus service is far from perfect – we always take a car
- Pistes in each individual area are quite limited
- Runs down to the valley floor are often closed due to lack of snow
- Popularity means crowds and queues, and lots of road traffic
- Bad weather can shut the best runs

Chamonix could not be more different from the archetypal high-altitude French resort. Unless you are based next to one mountain and stick to it, you have to drive or take a bus each day – although the cable-car now linking Le Brévent to La Flégère has improved things a little. There is all sorts of terrain, but it offers more to interest the expert than anyone else, and to make the most of the area you need a mountain guide rather than a piste map. Chamonix is neither convenient nor conventional.

But it is special. The Chamonix valley cuts deeply through Europe's highest mountains and glaciers. The views are stunning and the runs are everything really tough runs should be – not only steep, but high and long. If you like your snow and scenery on the wild side, give Chamonix a try. But be warned: there are those who try it and never go home – lots of them.

MOUNTAIN FACTS

Altitude	1035m-3840m
Lifts	49
Pistes	152km
Green	21%
Blue	31%
Red	35%
Black	13%
Artificial snow	9km
Recco detectors used	

The resort

Chamonix is a long established tourist town that over the years has spread for miles along its valley in the shadow of Mont Blanc – the scale map below is one of the biggest in these pages.

On either side of the centre, just within walking distance of it, are lifts to two of the dozen slope areas in the valley – the famous cable-car to the Aiguille du Midi, and a gondola to Le Brévent. Also on the fringe of the centre is the nursery slope of Les Planards. All the other lift bases involve drives or bus-rides – the nearest being the cable-car to La Flégère at the village of Les Praz.

Chamonix is a bustling town with scores of hotels and restaurants, visitors all year round and a lively Saturday market. The car-free centre of town is full of atmosphere, with cobbled streets and squares, beautiful old buildings and a fast-running river. Not everything is rosy: unsightly

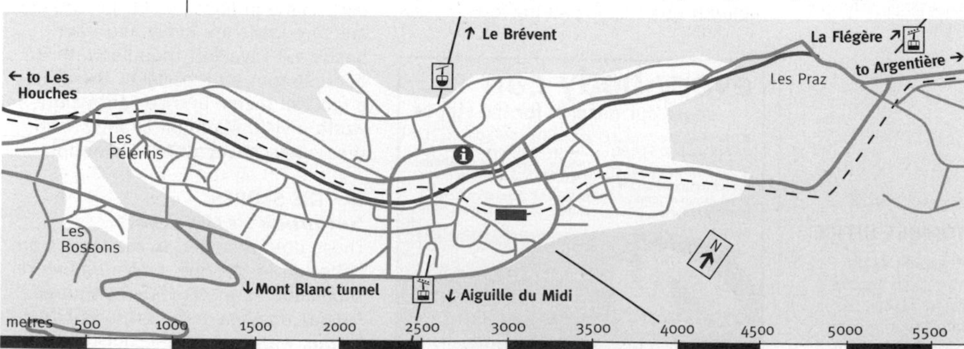

Downtown Chamonix is one of the most diverting ski towns, with a wide choice of shops and restaurants →

OT CHAMONIX-MONT BLANC

What's new

As we went to press the Mont Blanc tunnel, closed since the tragic fire in 1999, was officially due to re-open in the autumn of 2001. But the project has been delayed several times and locals predict that it won't open until December at the earliest, and maybe not until after the 2001/02 season.

The Charlanon drag, completing the Flégère-Brévent link, was upgraded to a fast quad last season. And a new mountain restaurant, La Bergerie, opened at Planpraz, on Le Brévent. There's also a new parking area at Le Brévent.

modern buildings have been built on to the periphery (especially near the Aiguille du Midi cable-car station), some of the lovely old buildings have been allowed to fall into disrepair, and at busy times traffic clogs the streets around the pedestrianised centre. The town squares and pavement cafes are busy most of the day with shoppers and sightseers sipping drinks and staring at the glaciers above. It all makes for a very agreeable and 'cosmopolitan' feel, though the dominant language is English.

Chamonix's shops deal in everything from high-tech equipment to tacky souvenirs. But reporters often comment on the number and excellence of the former, and Chamonix remains essentially a town for mountain people rather than poseurs.

Strung out for 20km along the Chamonix valley are several separate lift systems, some with attached villages, from Les Houches at one end to Argentière and Le Tour at the other. Regular buses link the lift stations and villages (there's an evening service too) but can get very crowded and aren't always reliable. Like many reporters, we rate a car as essential. A car also means you can get easily to other resorts covered by the Mont Blanc pass, such as Megève and Les Contamines. (Courmayeur in Italy will again be a practical proposition if the Mont Blanc tunnel reopens for 2001/02.)

The obvious place to stay is in Chamonix itself – it's central, has all the amenities you could want and some of the slopes are close at hand. For those who intend to spend most of their time in one particular area such as Argentière, Le Tour or Les Houches, staying nearby obviously makes sense. Whatever the choice, no location is convenient for everything.

The mountains

Once you get over the fact that the place is hopelessly disconnected, you come to appreciate the upside – that Chamonix has a good variety of slopes available, and that each of the different areas is worth exploring.

THE SLOPES

Very fragmented

If you really like getting about, the Mont Blanc lift pass covers 11 resorts, 25 mountains, over 200 lifts and 700km of piste. It covers resorts far

beyond the Chamonix valley – including St-Gervais, Megève, Les Contamines, and even Courmayeur in Italy.

The areas within the Chamonix valley – there are 11 in total – are either small, low, beginners' areas or are much higher up on the valley side, with cable-car or gondola access from the valley floor. If you are used to skiing from the door in more modern resorts, this may all seem very tedious.

The modern six-seater gondola for **Le Brévent** departs a short, steep walk from the centre of town, and the cable-car above takes you to the summit at 2525m. At **La Flégère**, like Le Brévent, the runs are mainly between 1900m and 2450m, and the views of Mont Blanc are worth the price of the lift pass. A new, fast chair recently replaced the old Trappe, and the 50-person cable-car linking La Flégère and Le Brévent makes this side of the valley more user-friendly – though reporters have said it's subject to frequent closure in high winds.

There have been improvements to the system at **Les Grands Montets** above Argentière, including increased snowmaking and remodelled runs, but much of the best terrain is still accessed by a cable-car of relatively low capacity. This costs extra to ride – though two free rides are included in a six-day pass – but still attracts queues.

LIFT PASSES

2001/02 prices in euros

Cham'Ski pass
Covers all areas in the Chamonix Valley and the bus services between them, except Les Houches. Includes a day in Courmayeur.

Beginners Cham'Start 6-day pass covers all valley floor lifts (82), Cham'Baby 6-day pass covers the same for 4- to 11-year-olds (60). You can buy day extensions to higher lifts.

Main pass
1-day pass 40
6-day pass 168

Senior citizens
Over 60: 6-day pass 143

Children
12 to 15:
6-day pass 143
Under 12: 6-day pass 118
Under 4: free pass

Notes 6-day passes include two ascents on the Grands Montets cable-car. Additional ascents cost extra (5 for 1 ascent, 73 for 20).

Alternative passes
Ski-pass Mont Blanc covers lifts in the 13 resorts of the Mont Blanc area (762km of piste) and Courmayeur in Italy (6 days 200 for adults, 140 for children).

boarding *Chamonix is a place of pilgrimage for advanced boarders, but not the best place to learn. Head for Argentière and the Grands Montets for the hairiest action – the fun-park and half-pipe host regular competitions. There's also a natural half-pipe/gulley at Le Tour. Most of the ski areas are equipped mainly with cable-cars, gondolas and chairs, though there are quite a few drags at Le Tour. If you do the Vallée Blanche, be warned: the usual route is flat in places. If you're ready to tackle tougher off-piste, check out former British Champ Neil McNab's excellent Extreme Backcountry Camps (www.mcnab.co.uk). Staying in the town itself will certainly guarantee satisfactory nightlife.*

Le Tour, already quite extensive, doubled in size recently with the addition of new runs – an 8km blue, a red and a black – above Vallorcine (which will eventually be linked by lift).

One of the valley-floor areas, Les Bossons, is open for floodlit skiing three nights a week.

The valley piste map is not sufficiently detailed to use for navigation. Use the little Cham'Ski handbook, which includes all of the local area piste maps with brief descriptions of each run and assessments of suitability for different standards of ability.

Most of our reporters have been more impressed than they expected with the piste grooming, but not with the signposting of the runs, or with 'rather antiquated chairs and drags'.

SNOW RELIABILITY
Good high up; poor low down

The top runs on the north-facing slopes above Argentière are almost guaranteed to have good snow, and the season normally lasts well into May. The risk of finding the top lift shut because of bad weather is more of a worry (and is the excuse for not including the lift on the main pass). The Col de Balme area above Le Tour has a snowy location and a good late-season record. The largely south-facing slopes of Brévent and Flégère suffer in warm weather, and runs to the resort are often closed. There's snowmaking on the Bochard piste on Les Grands Montets as well as some of the smaller areas. Several of the beginners' areas need snow-cover down to the valley floor to be operational.

FOR EXPERTS
One of the great resorts

Les Grands Montets above Argentière is justifiably renowned for its extensive steep terrain. To get the best out of the area you really need to have a local guide. Without one you either stick to the relatively small number of pistes or you put your life at risk.

The Grands Montets cable-car takes you up to 3235m; if you've got the legs and lungs, climb the 121 steep metal steps to the observation platform (3275m) and take in the stunning views. (But beware: it's 200 more steps down from the cable-car before you hit the snow.)

The ungroomed black pistes from here – Point de Vue and Pylones – are long and exhilarating. The Point de Vue sails right by some dramatic sections of glacier, with marvellous views of the crevasses. The off-piste routes from the top are numerous and often dangerous; the Pas de Chèvre route is serious stuff, eventually joining the Vallée Blanche run. There are many routes down the Argentière glacier.

The Bochard gondola serves a testing red and a moderate black.

Alternatively, head directly down the Combe de la Pendant bowl for 1000m vertical of wild, unpisted mountainside. The continuation down the valley side to Le Lavancher is equally testing; it suffers frequently from lack of snow on the steep bits.

At Le Brévent there's more to test experts than the piste map suggests – there are a number of variations on the runs down from the summit. Some are steep and prone to ice, and the couloir routes are very steep and very narrow. The runs in the sunny Col de La Charlanon are uncrowded and include one marked red run and lots of excellent off-piste if the snow is good.

At La Flégère there are several good off-piste routes – in the Combe Lachenal, crossed by the linking cable-car, for example – and a pretty tough run back to the village when snow-cover permits. Le Tour boasts little tough terrain on-piste but there are good off-piste routes from the high points to the village and over the back towards Vallorcine or into Switzerland.

FOR INTERMEDIATES

It's worth trying it all

For less confident intermediates, the best areas are at the two extreme ends of the Chamonix valley. The Col de Balme area above Le Tour is good for easy cruising and usually free from crowds. And the slopes of the separate Prarion–Bellevue system above Les Houches are mostly gentle tree-lined blue and red runs, very unlikely to intimidate anyone – a good area for building confidence.

More adventurous intermediates will also want to try the other three main areas, though they may find the Grands Montets tough going (and crowded). The bulk of the terrain at Le Brévent and La Flégère provides a sensible mix of blue and red runs; at Le Brévent the slopes have been redesigned to achieve this. If the weather is good, book a guide and do the Vallée Blanche (see feature box).

A day trip to Courmayeur has traditionally made an interesting change of scene, especially when the weather's bad. It will become practical again if the Mont Blanc tunnel reopens for the forthcoming season.

FOR BEGINNERS

Best if there's snow in the valley

If there is snow low down, the nursery lifts at La Vormaine, Les Chosalets, Les Planards and Le Savoy are fine for teaching first-timers; learners will not be bothered by speed-merchants. The Planards and Glacier du Mont Blanc lifts both benefit from snowmaking.

SCHOOLS/GUIDES

2000/01 prices in euros

ESF

In both Chamonix and Argentière

Classes 6 days

5hr: am and pm

6 full days: 183

Children's classes

Ages: 4 to 12

6 days: 9.30-5pm, including supervised lunch: 212

Private lessons

1hr, 2hr, half- or full day

37 for 1hr, for 1 or 2 people; 43 for 3 to 5 people

CHILDCARE

The ESF runs ordinary classes for children aged 6 to 12. For children aged 4 to 6 there are lessons in a snow-garden. And children in either category can be looked after all day (and amused when not on the slopes) from 8.30 to 5pm.

The day-care centre at the Maison pour Tous (0450 533668) takes children aged 18 months to 6 years from 7.45 to noon and 2pm to 5.30.

The Panda Club takes children aged 10 months to 12 years. There is a crèche in Chamonix that takes children from 10 months (0450 558612). Older babies are taken here or to Argentière (0450 540476), where the club has its own slopes, open to children aged 3 or more.

Some of the more expensive hotels will provide child-minding. Club Med has comprehensive in-house arrangements – their place here is one of their 'family villages', with a crèche taking babies from 4 months.

But the slopes on the south side of the valley can be dark and cold in winter. And the separation of beginners' slopes from the rest inhibits the transition to real runs, and makes lunchtime meetings of mixed groups impractical. Better to learn elsewhere, and come to Chamonix when you can appreciate the tough terrain.

FOR CROSS-COUNTRY
A good network of trails

Most of the 42km of prepared trails lie along the valley between Chamonix and Argentière. There are green, blue, red and black loop sections and the full tour from Chamonix to Argentière and back is 32km. All these trails are fairly low and fade fast in spring sun.

QUEUES
Fewer problems

There are still long queues for the top cable-car on Les Grands Montets. When they reach 30 minutes a booking system operates, so you can keep moving until it's your turn to ride.

At close of play, the lifts from the high-altitude areas to the valley floor get busy – especially the cable-cars.

In poor weather Les Houches is most likely to be open. The queues for the Bellevue cable-car can be bad.

MOUNTAIN RESTAURANTS
Stunning views – not much else

The restaurants are a source of disappointment for many reporters – 'packed, pricey and soulless' was a recent description. The Panoramic at the top of Brévent enjoys the best views. The food's fine but the place is dull. Altitude 2000 provides table-service at rip-off prices. The new Bergerie at Planpraz – built in wood and stone – with self- and table-service has been recommended. There's a plain self-service joint at La Flégère.

On the Grands Montets the Plan Joran serves good food and does table- and self-service. The restaurant at Lognan has been smartly renovated. The rustic Chalet-Refuge du Lognan, off the beaten track overlooking the Argentière glacier, has marvellous food. Book in advance to guarantee a full menu.

The restaurants in the Prarion-Bellevue area at Les Houches are pleasant and good value.

SCHOOLS AND GUIDES
The place to try something new

The schools here are particularly strong in specialist fields – off-piste, glacier and couloir skiing, ski touring, snowboarding and cross-country. English-speaking instructors are plentiful. One second-

THE VALLÉE BLANCHE

This is a trip you do for the stunning scenery rather than the challenge of the run, which (although exceptionally long) is easy – well within the capability of the average intermediate. But be prepared for extreme cold at the top, for flat and uphill sections on the way down, and for hordes of people – going early on a weekday gives you the best chance of avoiding the worst of the crowds. Go in a guided group – despite the ease of the runs, dangerous crevasses lurk to swallow those not in the know. Book your guide or sign up for a group trip the day before at the Maison de la Montagne or other ski school offices.

The amazing Aiguille du Midi cable-car takes you to 3840m. Across the bridge from the arrival station on the Piton Nord is the Piton Central; the view of Mont Blanc from the cafe a stair-climb higher should not be missed – and gives you the opportunity to adjust to the dizzying altitude. A tunnel delivers you to the infamous ridge-walk down to the start of the run. There is a fixed guide-rope, and many parties rope up for this walk. You may still feel envious of those strolling nonchalantly down in crampons; you may wish you'd stayed in bed.

After that the run seems a doddle; mostly effortless gliding down gentle slopes with only the occasional steeper, choppy section to deal with. So stop often and enjoy the surroundings fully. The views of the ice, the crevasses and seracs – and the spectacular mountains beyond – are simply mind-blowing. There are variants on the classic route, all more difficult and hazardous – the 'Vraie Vallée' and 'Envers du Plan' among them. Snow conditions may mean cutting short the full 24km run down to Chamonix, in which case you catch a train from the station at Montenvers (1910m). A short climb and gondola link the glacier to the station.

week skier did report large classes and unimaginative teaching by the Evolution 2 school though, though another near beginner had an 'excellent' private lesson with them. At the Maison de la Montagne in Chamonix is the main ESF office and the HQ of the Compagnie des Guides, which has taken visitors to the mountains for 150 years.

Competition is provided by a number of smaller, independent guiding and teaching outfits, and there are many qualified British guides here.

FACILITIES FOR CHILDREN

Better than they were

The Panda Club is used by quite a few British visitors and reports have been enthusiastic. The Argentière base can be inconvenient for meeting up with children for the afternoons. The Club Med crèche seems to go down well too. UK tour operator Ski Esprit has chalets here, with a nursery in the Cairn chalet-hotel. Links with the ESF mean classes run just for Ski Esprit children.

Beware of children being kept on the valley nursery slopes for the convenience of the school when they really should be getting some miles under their skis.

Staying there

HOW TO GO

Any way you like

There is all sorts of accommodation, and lots of it.

Chalets Many are run by small outfits that cater for this specialist market. Quality tends to be high and value for money good. Collineige has a large selection – all very comfortable. We've had good reports of Bigfoot's chalets and 'Mercedes mini-vans to run you to and from the slopes'. Cheaper places are offered by HuSki (who also run a minibus service) and big tour operators such as Crystal and Inghams. Childcare specialist Ski Esprit has three places, including the excellent Cairn in Les Praz – built as a three-star hotel in 1992, and blessed with good bedrooms and bathrooms. Simply Ski has a centrally located catered chalet hotel, which is bookable for weekend breaks.

Hotels The place is full of hotels, many modestly priced, and the vast majority small, with fewer than 30 rooms. Hotel bookings for a day or two are easy to arrange since Chamonix's peak season is summer. There's a Club Med 'village'.

SNOWPIX.COM / CHRIS GILL

One of the delights of the Brévent and Flégère areas is their great views across the valley to peaks like the Grands Montets ↓

GETTING THERE

Air Geneva, transfer 1½hr. Lyon, transfer 3½hr.

Rail Station in resort, on the St Gervais-Le Fayet/Vallorcine line.

Direct TGV link from Paris on Friday evenings and weekends.

Phone numbers
From abroad use the prefix +33 and omit the initial '0' of the phone number.

(4) **Albert 1er** (0450 530509) Smart, traditional chalet-style hotel with 'truly excellent food' (two Michelin stars, Gault-Millau rating). Recent visitors loved the new half-indoor, half-outdoor swimming pool.
(4) **Auberge du Bois Prin** (0450 533351) A small modern chalet with a big reputation; great views; bit of a hike into town; closer to Le Brévent.
(4) **Mont-Blanc** (0450 530564) Central, luxurious.
(4) **Jeu de Paume** (Lavancher) (0450 540376) Alpine satellite of a chic Parisian hotel: a beautifully furnished modern chalet half-way to Argentière.
(3) **Alpina** (0450 534777) Much the biggest in town: modernist–functional place just north of centre.
(3) **Labrador** (Les Praz) (0450 559009) Scandinavian-style chalet close to the Flégère lift. Good restaurant.
(3) **Sapinière** (0450 530763) Traditional hotel with good French food, run by long-established Chamonix family. Reasonable site on the Brévent side of town. Recommended by recent visitors.
(3) **Vallée Blanche** (0450 530450) Smart low-priced 3-star B&B hotel, handy for centre and Aiguille du Midi.
(2) **L'Arve** (0450 530231) By the river, just off the main street; small newly decorated rooms.
(2) **Richemond** (0450 530885) Now rather faded and old-fashioned, but with good public areas.
(2) **Pointe Isabelle** (0450 531287) Not pretty, but central location; friendly staff, good plain food, well-equipped bedrooms.
(2) **Roma** Simple but satisfactory B&B hotel in hassle-free location on south side of centre; friendly patron.
(1) **Faucigny** (0450 530117) Cottage-style; in centre.
Self-catering Many properties in UK package brochures are typically in convenient but cramped and charmless blocks in Chamonix Sud. The Balcons du Savoy (0450 553232) look much better, are well situated and have use of a swimming pool, steam room and solarium. The Splendid & Golf apartments in Les Praz (0450 559601) are charming and close to the Flégère cable-car. Erna Low has some luxury places available.

EATING OUT
Plenty of quality places

The good hotels all have good restaurants – the Eden at Les Praz and Bois Prin in Chamonix are first-rate – and there are many other good places to eat. The Sarpé is a lovely 'mountain' restaurant and The Impossible is rustic but smart and features good regional dishes. Recent visitors have especially recommended Le Panier des Quatre Saisons ('Excellent food at reasonable prices. Wonderful atmosphere') and Le Crochon ('Good Savoyard fare, plus some varied and innovative dishes'). The Monchu is also good for Savoyard specialities. A recent reporter raves about the Cabane restaurant next to the Labrador hotel in Les Praz. There are a number of ethnic restaurants – Mexican, Spanish, Japanese, Chinese etc – and lots of brasseries and cafes.

ACTIVITIES

Indoor Sports complex (sports hall, gym, table tennis), indoor skating and curling rinks, ice hockey, swimming pool with giant water slide, saunas, six indoor tennis courts, two squash courts, fitness centre, Alpine museum, casino, three cinemas, library, 10-pin bowling, climbing wall
Outdoor Ski-jumping, snow-shoe outings, mountain biking, hang-gliding, paragliding, flying excursions, heli-skiing, ice skating

TOURIST OFFICE

Postcode 74400
t +33 450 530024
f 450 535890
info@chamonix.com
www.chamonix.com

APRES-SKI
Lots of bars and music

Many of the bars around the pedestrianised centre of Chamonix get busy for a couple of hours at sundown – none more so than the Choucas video bar. During the evening, The Pub, Wild Wallaby's, the Mill Street bar and the Bar du Moulin are busy. The Queen Vic gets the vote of one recent reporter for being 'nice and dark and dingy with a snug, pool table, good music and Beamish on tap'. There's a lively variety of nightclubs and discos. The Choucas (again), and Dick's Tea bar are popular. The Cantina sometimes has live music and is open late. There are plenty of bars and brasseries for a quieter drink too.

OFF THE SLOPES
An excellent choice

There's more off-slope activity here than in many resorts. Excursion possibilities include Annecy and Geneva, plus Courmayeur and Turin. The Alpine Museum is 'excellent and very interesting' and there are good sports facilities. The sports centre and 'excellent' swimming pool have been renovated after flood damage.

Argentière 1240m

The old village is in a lovely setting towards the head of the valley – the Glacier d'Argentière pokes down towards it and the Aiguille du Midi and Mont Blanc still dominate the scene down the valley. There's a fair bit of modern development but it still has a rustic appeal. Le Tour, just beyond Argentière, is quiet and picturesque.

A number of the hotels are simple, inexpensive and handy for the village centre – less so for the slopes – but the Grands-Montets (0450 540666) is a large chalet-style building, right next to the piste and the Panda Club for children. The family-run Montana (0450 541499) is recommended for 'lovely rooms, excellent food'.

Restaurants and bars are informal and inexpensive. The Office is the happening place in Argentière, from breakfast till late. The Savoy bar is the British/colonial ex-pat haunt.

Les Houches 1010m

Les Houches, 6km from Chamonix, is not on the valley pass, but is covered by the regional Mont Blanc pass. It's a pleasant village, sitting in the shade of the looming Mont Blanc massif – shady and cold in midwinter. There is an old core with a pretty church, but modern developments in chalet style have spread along the road up to Chamonix.

The area above Les Houches is served by a cable-car to **Bellevue** and a gondola to **Prarion**, the high-point at 1900m. Runs on the back of the mountain towards St-Gervais, and blue, red and black runs of 900m vertical down to Les Houches, make this the biggest single area of prepared runs in the Chamonix valley.

The almost entirely wooded slopes are popular when bad weather or the risk of avalanches closes other areas.

In good weather the slopes are quiet, and the views superb from the several attractive mountain restaurants. It is good for families, beginners and intermediates, with easy runs at the top of the mountain. Snow-cover on the lower slopes is not reliable, but there is a fair amount of snowmaking.

The village is quiet at night, but there are some pleasant bars and good restaurants. Recent visitors enjoyed staying in the Hotel du Bois (0450 545035), with its 'helpful staff and excellent restaurant – Le Caprice' and 'a good local band in the bar on Saturday'. Buses run in and out of Chamonix all evening.

Châtel 1200m

A distinctively French base for touring the Portes du Soleil

WHAT IT COSTS

3

HOW IT RATES

The slopes	
Snow	**
Extent	*****
Experts	***
Intermediates	****
Beginners	**
Convenience	**
Queues	***
Restaurants	***
The rest	
Scenery	***
Resort charm	***
Off-slope	**

- \+ Very extensive, pretty, intermediate terrain – the Portes du Soleil
- \+ Wide range of cheap and cheerful, good-value accommodation
- \+ Easily reached – close to Geneva, and one of the shortest drives from the Channel
- \+ Pleasant, lively, French-dominated old village, still quite rustic in parts
- \+ Local slopes relatively queue-free
- \+ Good views

- − Both resort and top of skiing are low for a French resort, with resulting risk of poor snow – though extended snowmaking has helped
- − Bus or gondola ride to most snowsure nursery slopes
- − Queues can be a problem in parts of the Portes du Soleil circuit, particularly at weekends
- − Village traffic can be congested at weekends and in peak season

Like neighbouring Morzine, Châtel offers a blend of attractions that is uncommon in France – an old village with plenty of facilities, cheap accommodation by French standards, and a large ski area on the doorstep. Châtel's original rustic charm has been largely eroded by expansion in recent years, but some of it remains, and the resort has one obvious advantage over smoother Morzine: it is part of the main Portes du Soleil circuit.

The circuit actually breaks down at Châtel, but this works in the village's favour. Whereas those doing the circuit from other resorts have the inconvenience of waiting for a bus mid-circuit, Châtel residents have the advantage of being able to time their bus-rides to avoid waits and queues. Those mainly interested in the local slopes should also consider Châtel. For confident intermediates, Châtel's Linga has few equals in the Portes du Soleil, while the nearby Torgon section has arguably the best views. The Chapelle d'Abondance slopes are pleasantly uncrowded at weekends. Châtel has become more beginner-friendly with nursery slopes at Super-Châtel and Pré-la-Joux, though these are a lift or bus-ride away.

What's new

For 2001/02 there will be a new boardercross course and fun-park built in the Linga area.

In 2000/01 the three-person chair from Les Combes to Cornebois was replaced by a high-speed quad. Improvements were made to some pistes and to buses, roads and the ice rink. More avalanche protection equipment was installed.

The resort 

Châtel lies near the head of the wooded Dranse valley, at the north-eastern limit of the French–Swiss Portes du Soleil ski circuit.

It is a much expanded and now quite large but nonetheless attractive old village. New unpretentious chalet-style hotels and apartments rub shoulders with old farmhouses where cattle still live in winter.

Although there is a definite centre, the village sprawls along the road in from lake Geneva and the diverging roads out – up the hillside towards Morgins and along the valley towards the Linga and Pré-la-Joux lifts.

Lots of visitors take cars and the centre can get clogged with traffic during the evening rush-hour – more so at weekends. Street parking is difficult but there is (pay-for) underground parking and day car parks at Linga and Pré-la-

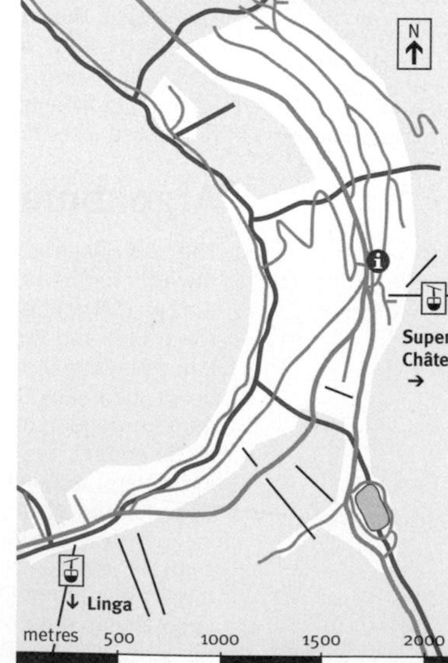

MOUNTAIN FACTS

for Portes du Soleil

Altitude	975m-2350m
Lifts	206
Pistes	650km
Green	13%
Blue	38%
Red	39%
Black	10%
Art. snow	252 acres
Recco detectors used	

LIFT PASSES

2001/02 prices in euros

Portes du Soleil
Covers all lifts in all 12 resorts, and shuttle-buses.

Main pass
1-day pass 33
6-day pass 159

Senior citizens
Over 60: 6-day pass 127

Children
Under 16: 6-day pass 107
Under 5: free pass

Short-term passes
Morning/afternoon passes for the Portes du Soleil (both 25), and for Châtel only (both 18 – 2000/01 price).

Alternative periods
5 non-consecutive-days pass for Châtel only (adult 112 – 2000/01 price).

Alternative passes
Châtel pass covers 51 lifts in Châtel, Linga, Super-Châtel, Torgon, Barbossine, and the link to Morgins (adult 6-day pass 114 – 2000/01 price).

Joux. Other main French Portes du Soleil resorts – Avoriaz, Morzine – are easy to reach on skis or board, but not by road.

A few kilometres down the valley is the rustic village of La Chapelle-d'Abondance (see end of chapter).

The mountains

The Portes du Soleil is classic intermediate terrain, and Châtel's local slopes are very much in character. Confident intermediates, in particular, will find lots to enjoy in the Linga and Plaine Dranse sectors. If you travel the Portes du Soleil circuit the booklet-style piste map makes for easy navigation. Reporters have also commented favourably on the recently introduced system of Discovery Routes guiding you around the Portes du Soleil – choose an alpine animal that suits your ability and follow the signs displaying it. An electronic lift pass was introduced for 1999, so you can now keep your pass in your pocket.

THE SLOPES
The circuit breaks down here

Châtel sits between two sectors of the Portes du Soleil circuit – linked together by an 'excellent, practically continuous', free bus service. **Super-Châtel** is directly above the village – an area of easy, open and lightly wooded beginner slopes, accessed by a choice of gondola or two-stage chair. From here you can cross the Swiss border, either to quiet Torgon or clockwise around the Portes du Soleil to Morgins, Champoussin and Champéry, before going back into France above Avoriaz.

Linga is a bus-ride away. For intermediates and better, the area has some of the most interesting runs in the Portes du Soleil, the best of them leading back towards Châtel. The fastest way to Avoriaz is to stay on the bus at Linga and go to Pré-la-Joux. From here a high-speed quad goes direct to Plaine Dranse; then it's one more lift and run to Les Lindarets, where there's a choice of lifts to Avoriaz.

SNOW RELIABILITY
The main drawback

The main drawback of the Portes du Soleil is that it is low, so snow quality can suffer when it's warm. Châtel is at only 1200m (600m lower than Avoriaz) and some runs home can be tricky or shut, especially from Super-Châtel. But a lot of snowmaking has been installed at Super-Châtel and on runs down from Linga and to Pré-la-Joux. These last two are mainly north-facing and

boarding *Avoriaz is the hardcore destination in the Portes du Soleil. But Châtel is not a bad place to learn or to go to as a budget option or as part of a mixed group of skiers and boarders. Most local lifts are gondolas or chairs and there's a fun-park, half-pipe and boardercross course at Super-Châtel. The Linga area has good varied terrain and off-piste possibilities – and will have a boardercross course and fun-park this year. There are a couple of lively bars.*

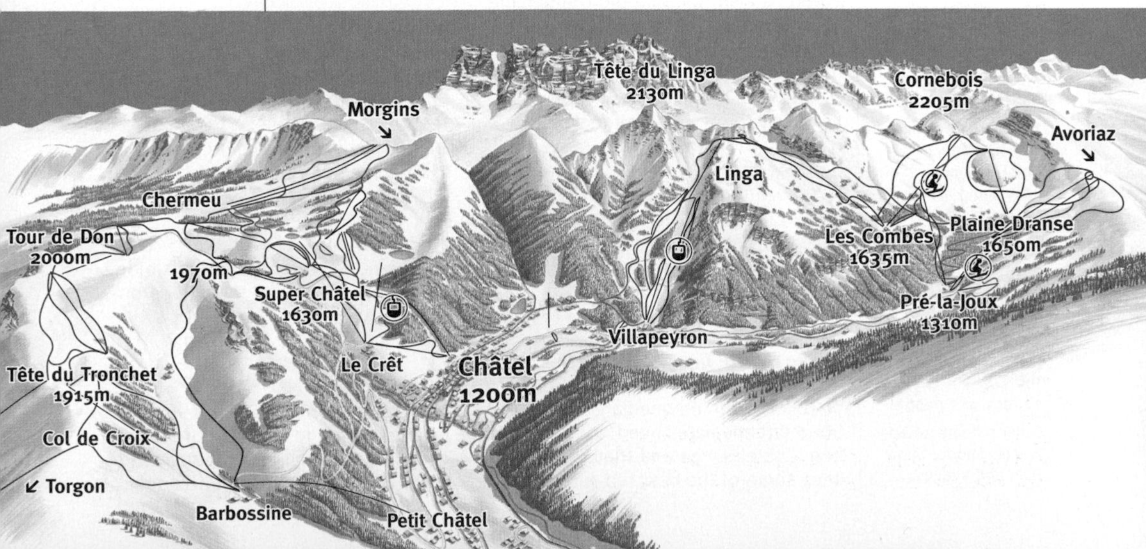

SCHOOLS/GUIDES

2001/02 prices in euros

ESF
Classes 6 days
2½hr am or pm
6 half-days: 96
Children's classes
Ages: 5 to 16
6 half-days: 95
Private lessons
1hr or 1½hr
29 for 1hr, for 1 or 2 people

International
Classes 6 days
3hr: 9am-noon or 2pm-5pm; 2hr: noon-2pm
6 mornings: 102
Children's classes
Ages: from 8
6 afternoons: 108
Private lessons
1hr or 2hr
33 for 1hr, each additional person 5

Stages Henri Gonon
Courses can include 6 days' accommodation, pass and 5 half-days' tuition (2000/01 prices)
Classes 5 days
3hr per day
5 days: 95
Children's classes
Ages: 7 to 16
5 days: 83
Private lessons
1hr
22 for 1 or 2 people

Other schools include: Francis Sports, Snow Ride and Virages.

generally have the best local snow – a regular visitor tells us there is often good snow at Pré-la-Joux till May. But another told us of snow being like a 'damp pudding' in March and pistes to Morgins and Les Lindarets being closed.

FOR EXPERTS
Some challenges

The best steep runs – on and off-piste – are in the Linga and Pré-la-Joux area. Beneath the Linga gondola and chair, there's a pleasant mix of open and wooded ground which follows the fall line fairly directly. And there's a mogul field between Cornebois and Plaine Dranse which has been described as 'steeper and narrower than the infamous Swiss Wall' in Avoriaz. An unpisted trail from Super-Châtel towards the village is also fun. And the challenging Hauts Forts sector beyond Avoriaz is within reach. There's also a great off-piste route from Tête du Linga down the valley of La Leiche – but you need a guide. Two pistes recently created off the Rochassons ridge are both steep and kept well groomed.

Pierre Tardival's Extreme Clinics are held in Châtel and he doesn't seem to have any problem finding local, steep off-piste terrain (this is the man who climbed and skied Everest!).

FOR INTERMEDIATES
Some of the best runs in the area

When conditions are right the Portes du Soleil is an intermediate's paradise. Good intermediates need not go far from Châtel; Linga and Plaine Dranse have some of the best red runs on the circuit. But the Champéry-Avoriaz sector also beckons. The moderately skilled can do the circuit without problem, and will particularly enjoy runs around Les Lindarets and Morgins. Even timid types can do the circuit, provided they take one or two short-cuts and ride chairs down trickier bits. The chair from Les Lindarets to Pointe de Mossette leads to a red run into the Swiss area, which is a lot easier than the 'Swiss Wall' from Chavanette and also speeds up a journey round the circuit.

Leaving aside attempts to complete the circuit in both directions, there are rewarding out-and-back expeditions to be made clockwise to the wide open snowfields above Champoussin, beyond Morgins, and anticlockwise to the Hauts-Forts runs above Avoriaz.

FOR BEGINNERS
Go to Pré-la-Joux

The most snowsure beginners' area is at Pré-la-Joux ('I loved it,' says a reporter), but you need to catch a bus there. There's also Super-Châtel or the low village nursery slopes.

FOR CROSS-COUNTRY
Pretty, if low, trails

There are plenty of pretty trails along the river and through the woods on the lower slopes of Linga, but snow-cover can be a problem.

QUEUES
Bottlenecks being eased

Queues to get to Avoriaz have been eased by the high-speed quad at Pré-la-Joux. But there are still a couple of

← Châtel is a sprawling village with a good bus link between its central gondola and the Linga slopes (pictured here), served by another gondola

JEAN-FRANÇOIS VUARAND

bottlenecks further afield, which tend to be worse at weekends (although we do have reports of little queuing even during half-term and New Year). At Les Lindarets, in particular, there is often a lengthy wait for the chair-lift to the Rochassons ridge on the way back to Châtel; but the queue the other way up to Avoriaz should be eliminated for 2001/02 by the new six-pack – see Avoriaz chapter. You can face queues to get down from Super-Châtel if the slope back is shut by poor snow.

MOUNTAIN RESTAURANTS
Some quite good local huts

Atmospheric chalets can be found, notably at Plaine Dranse (Le Bois Prin, Chez Crépy, Tân o Marmottes and Chez Denis have been recommended). In the Linga area La Ferme des Pistes gets the thumbs up. The Perdrix Blanche at Pré-la-Joux scarcely counts as a mountain restaurant, but is an attractive (if pricey) spot for lunch. It does get busy as there's nowhere else. At Super-Châtel the Portes du Soleil at the foot of the Coqs drags is much better than the big place at the top of the gondola. The Escale Blanche is worth a visit.

CHILDCARE

The ESF's ski kindergarten is for children from age 4.

Le Village des Marmottons takes children from 2 to 8, from 8.30 to 5.30, with ski tuition for those aged 3 up.

Henri Gonon takes children over 6, as does the Ski and Surf International School and Snow Ride.

Francis Sports caters for 3 to 8 year olds at the Pitchounes.

SCHOOLS AND GUIDES
Plenty of choice

There are now six ski and snowboard schools in Châtel. The International school has been recommended by a reporter and the ESF came in for praise this year for their 'very helpful and customer-focused instructors'. Ian McGarry, whose courses have received glowing reports from reporters, will be working with the ESF for part of this year. Bookings can be discussed directly (+35 312 859139), or via the ESF. Those tempted to join Pierre Tardival's Extreme Clinics, also bookable through Ski McGarry, should take the 'extreme' part seriously.

FACILITIES FOR CHILDREN
Increasingly sympathetic

The Marmottons nursery (now with their own snowmaking machine) has good facilities, including toboggans, painting, music and videos, and children are reportedly happy there. Francis Sports ski school have their own nursery area with a drag lift and chalet at Linga: 'Very organised, convenient and reasonably priced'. The ESF has had good reports: 'Small groups with excellent English spoken.'

Staying there

A central position gives you the advantage of getting on the ski-bus to the outlying lifts before it gets very crowded and simplifies après-ski outings. But there is accommodation near the Linga lift if that's the priority.

HOW TO GO
A wide choice, including chalets

Although this is emphatically a French resort, packages from Britain are no problem to track down.

Chalets A fair number of UK operators have places here, including some Châtel specialists.

Hotels Practically all of the hotels are 2-stars, mostly friendly chalets, wooden or at least partly wood-clad. None of the 3-stars is particularly well placed. Les Cornettes in La Chapelle (see end of chapter) is an interesting alternative.

(((3 **Macchi** (0450 732412) Modern chalet, most central of the 3-stars.

(((3 **Fleur de Neige** (0450 732010) Well-maintained, welcoming chalet on edge of centre; Grive Gourmande restaurant does about the best food in town.

Phone numbers
From abroad use the prefix +33 and omit the initial '0' of the phone number.

GETTING THERE

Air Geneva, transfer 1½hr.

Rail Thonon les Bains (42km).

ACTIVITIES

Indoor Swimming pool, bowling, cinema, library

Outdoor Skating rink, horse-drawn carriage rides, helicopter rides, dog-sledding, snow-shoe excursions, farm visits, toboggan run, floodlit skiing at Linga

TOURIST OFFICE

Postcode 74390
t +33 450 732244
f 450 732287
touristoffice@chatel.com
www.chatel.com

③ **Lion d'Or** (0450 813440) In centre, 'basic rooms, good atmosphere'.
② **Belalp** (0450 732439) Very comfortable, with excellent food.
① **Kandahar** (0450 733060) One for peace-lovers: a Logis by the river, a walkable distance from the centre.
① **Rhododendrons** (0450 732404) 'Great service, friendly, comfortable, clean.'

Self-catering Many of the better places are available through Châtel and self-drive specialists. The Gelinotte (out of town but near the Linga lifts and children's village) and Les Erines (central and close to the Super-Châtel gondola) look good. The Flèche d'Or apartments are not well positioned for lifts or shops. The Aveniers is right by the Linga gondola. A couple of reporters have mentioned Châtel's supermarkets are small and over-crowded – worth shopping on the way if you're driving.

EATING OUT
Fair selection

There is an adequate number and range of restaurants. Les Cornettes in La Chapelle-d'Abondance is one of our favourites – amazingly good-value menus with excellent food (but 'disappointing puddings' comments one reporter). The Vieux Four, in an old farm building, has a reputation for the best steaks in Châtel. The Fleur de Neige hotel has a good restaurant and Le Fiacre is also popular. The Perrier serves Savoyard specialities. La Ripaille, almost opposite the Linga gondola, was highly recommended by a past reporter, especially for its fish.

APRES-SKI
All down to bars

Châtel is getting livelier, especially at weekends. The Tunnel bar is very popular with the British and has a DJ or live music every night. The Isba has apparently slightly fallen from grace since its supremo moved on last season to run the new and very popular English-pub-style Avalanche. La Godille – close to the Super-Châtel gondola and busy at tea-time – has a more French feel. The bar in the hotel Soldanelles is also pretty lively. The bowling alley, La Vielle Grange, also has a good bar. The Jean'Club disco at the Super-Châtel bubble is busy at weekends, and there's also the Lagon Bleu in the same area. A reporter has recommended the Saf disco in Morgins.

OFF THE SLOPES
Better to stay in Morzine

Those with a car have some entertaining excursions available: Geneva, Thonon and Evian. Otherwise there is little to do but take some pleasant walks along the river, or visit the cheese factory and the two cinemas. The tourist office organises daily events for non-slope users. But those not using the slopes would find more to do in Morzine. The Portes du Soleil as a whole is less than ideal for those not using the slopes who like to meet their more active friends for lunch: skiers and boarders are likely to be above at some distant resort at lunchtime.

La Chapelle-d'Abondance 1010m

This unspoilt, rustic farming community, complete with old church and friendly locals, is 5km along a beautiful valley from Châtel. 'A car and a bit of French is virtually essential,' says a reporter this year. It's had its own quiet little north-facing area of easy wooded runs for some years, but has more recently been put on the Portes du Soleil map by a gondola and three chair-lifts that now link it to Torgon in Switzerland and, from there, Super-Châtel. This section is only a spur of the Portes du Soleil circuit. But, taken together with Chapelle's own little area, it is worth exploring – good at weekends when Châtel gets crowded and 'excellent for beginners'.

Nightlife is virtually non-existent – just a few quiet bars, a cinema and torchlit descents.

The hotel Cornettes is an amazing 2-star with 2-star rooms but 4-star facilities, including an indoor pool, sauna, steam room, hot-tubs, excellent restaurant (see Eating Out) and atmospheric bar. Look out for showcases with puppets and dolls and eccentric touches, such as ancient old doors that unexpectedly open automatically. It has been run by the Trincaz family since 1894. The Alpage and Chabi are other hotel options. The Airelles apartments have received a favourable report.

La Clusaz–Le Grand-Bornand

Great for late-booking Francophiles

WHAT IT COSTS

HOW IT RATES

The slopes

Snow	**
Extent	***
Experts	***
Intermediates	****
Beginners	****
Convenience	***
Queues	***
Restaurants	****

The rest

Scenery	****
Resort charm	****
Off-slope	***

- ➕ Mountain villages in a scenic setting, retaining traditional character
- ➕ Extensive, interesting slopes – pistes best for beginners and intermediates
- ➕ Very French atmosphere
- ➕ Very short transfer time from Geneva and easy to reach by car from UK
- ➕ Attractive mountain restaurants
- ➕ Good cross-country trails
- ➕ Slopes at La Clusaz and Le Grand-Bornand linked by shuttle-bus

- ➖ Snow conditions unreliable because of low altitude (by French standards)
- ➖ Not many challenging pistes for experts – though there are good off-piste runs
- ➖ Busy at weekends

Few other major French resorts are based around what are still, essentially, genuine mountain villages that exude rustic charm and Gallic atmosphere. Combine that with over 200km of largely intermediate slopes, above and below the tree line, spread over five linked sectors in La Clusaz and the separate Le Grand-Bornand area, and there's a good basis for an enjoyable, relaxed week.

The area's one big problem is its height, or lack of it. Snowmaking has been installed in recent years and is continually increased, but it's still on a modest scale, and of course makes no difference in mild weather. So pre-booking a holiday here remains, as in other low resorts, a slightly risky business.

What's new

In La Clusaz, the drag-lift at the top of l'Aiguille was replaced by a quad chair-lift with a magic carpet last season.

New snowmaking was installed at the base of the Balme area.

In Le Grand-Bornand, the capacity of the Terres Rouges chair was upgraded with the installation of a magic carpet. And the snowmaking network was further extended.

Next season will see the replacement of the Lachat chair, to the resort high point, by a new six-pack, and the development of a new black run on the north-east side of the mountain.

The resort

La Clusaz was once frequented almost entirely by the French. But it has developed into a major international resort – summer and winter. As one of the most accessible resorts from Geneva and Annecy, it's good for short transfers, but it does get crowded, and there can be weekend traffic jams.

The village is built beside a fast-flowing stream at the junction of a number of narrow wooded valleys, and has had to grow in a rather rambling and sprawling way, with roads running in a confusing mixture of directions. But, unlike so many French resorts, La Clusaz has retained the charm of a genuine mountain village. (It's the kind of place that is as attractive in summer as under a blanket of snow in winter.)

In the centre is a large old church, and other original old stone and wood buildings; and, for the most part, the new buildings have been built in chalet style and blend in well. Les Etages is a much smaller centre of accommodation above the main town, where two of the mountain sectors meet.

La Clusaz has a friendly feel to it. The villagers welcome visitors every Monday evening in the main square with vin chaud and a variety of local cheeses. There's a weekly market, tempting food shops and a wide choice of typically French bars.

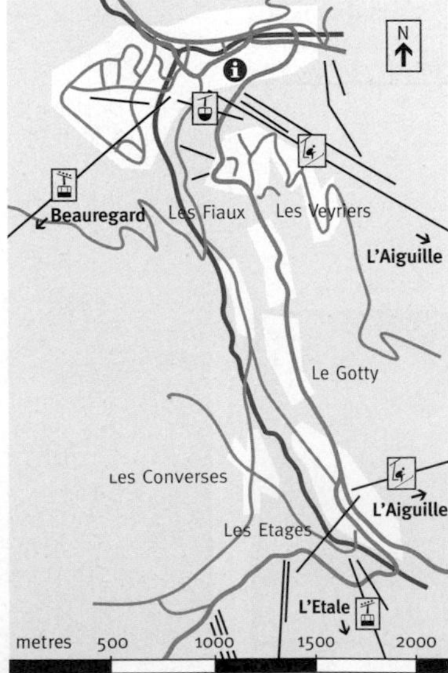

MOUNTAIN FACTS

La Clusaz

Altitude	1100m-2500m
Lifts	56
Pistes	132km
Green	29%
Blue	32%
Red	29%
Black	10%
Art. snow	50 acres
Recco detectors used	

Le Grand-Bornand

Altitude	1000m-2100m
Lifts	39
Pistes	82km
Green	32%
Blue	36%
Red	26%
Black	6%
Art. snow	99 acres
Recco detectors used	

For much of the season La Clusaz is a quiet and peaceful place for a holiday. But in peak season and at weekends the place gets packed out with French and Swiss families.

Le Grand-Bornand, covered by the Aravis lift pass, is an even more charming village than La Clusaz, with even more sense that it remains a mountain community. This is partly because most of the development as a winter sports resort has gone on up the road at the satellite village of Le Chinaillon, which has been developed in chalet style. Le Grand-Bornand and La Clusaz are linked by a free 10-minute bus-ride and buses run every 30 minutes during the day – these become more erratic in peak time traffic. Le Grand-Bornand has quite extensive slopes and is well worth exploring for a day or two or considering as an alternative, quieter base.

If you are taking a car, you might also consider basing yourself at **St-Jean-de-Sixt** – a small hamlet midway between La Clusaz and Le Grand-Bornand, with a small slope nearby, mainly used for sledging.

The mountains 

Like the village, the slopes at **La Clusaz** are rather spread out – which makes them all the more interesting (and scenic). There are five main areas, each connecting with at least one other. At **Le Grand-Bornand** the slopes spread out along the mountainside and can be accessed from either the village or Le Chinaillon up the road.

The Aravis pass, covering the lifts of both resorts, costs very little more than the La Clusaz pass, but is a fair bit more than the Grand-Bornand one.

THE SLOPES

Pretty and varied

Several points in **La Clusaz** have lifts giving access to the predominantly west- and north-west facing slopes of **L'Aiguille**. Links between this sector and the slightly higher and shadier slopes of **La Balme** area have improved massively in recent years: a long red and a black piste have replaced the off-piste route from L'Aiguille towards La Balme, and last season a new gondola opened in the opposite direction, taking you up from the base of La Balme to Cote 2000 on

LIFT PASSES

2000/01 prices in euros

Aravis pass
Covers La Clusaz and Le Grand-Bornand
Main pass
6 days 133 (116 low season)
Senior citizens
Over 60: 6 days 113
Over 75: free pass
Children
Under 15: 6 days 102
Under 5: free pass

La Clusaz pass
All lifts in La Clusaz.
Main pass
1-day pass 24
6-day pass 125
(low season 105)
Senior citizens
Over 60: 6-days 102
Over 75: free pass
Children
Under 15: 6-days 91
Under 5: free pass

Le Grand-Bornand pass
All lifts in Le Grand-Bornand.
Main pass
1-day pass 22
6-day pass 107
(low season 96)
Senior citizens
Over 60: 6 days 101
(low season 91)
Over 75: free pass
Children
Under 16: 6 days 88
Under 5: free pass

L'Aiguille and cutting out the need to take a long, flat run back to La Clusaz. La Balme is a splendid, varied area with good lifts (a high-capacity gondola from the bottom linking to a quad chair); from the top there are wonderful views towards Mont Blanc.

Going the other way from L'Aiguille leads you to **L'Etale** via another choice of easy runs and the Transval cable-car, which shuttles people between the two areas. From the bottom of L'Etale, you can head back along another path to the village and the cable-car up to the fourth sector of **Beauregard** which, as the name implies, has splendid views and catches a lot of sunshine.

From the top of Beauregard you can link via another easy piste and a two-way chair-lift with the fifth area of **Manigod**. From here you can move on to L'Etale.

The main village at **Le Grand-Bornand** has two gondolas on the outskirts up to a gentle open area of easy runs (including nursery slopes) lying between 1400m and 1500m. Chairs fan out above this point, one going up to the 2100m high point of **Le Lachat,** where there are serious red and black runs. Other lifts and runs go across the mountainside to the slopes above **Le Chinaillon** (1300m). Here there is a broad, open mountainside with a row of chairs and drags serving blue and red slopes, and links to the rest of the domain – a wide area of blue and red runs.

SNOW RELIABILITY

Variable because of low altitude

Most of the runs are west- or north-west facing and tend to keep their snow fairly well, even though most of the area is below 2000m. The best snow is usually on the north-west-

boarding *Snowboarding is popular in La Clusaz, and although there are still a lot of drag-lifts, most are avoidable. There are some good nursery slopes, served by chair-lifts, for beginners, and great cruising runs to progress to. La Balme is a great natural playground for good free-riders. There's a fun-park and a half-pipe on Aiguille and another in Le Grand-Bornand. During the week the resorts are fairly quiet, but La Clusaz livens up at the weekend.*

↑ Dramatic mountains and traditional chalet-style villages add up to an attractive resort

OT LA CLUSAZ / MP ROUGE-PULLON

SCHOOLS/GUIDES

2001/02 prices in euros

ESF

Classes 6 days
4hr: 9.30-11.30, 2.45-4.45
5 full days: 131

Children's classes
Ages: 5 to 12
5 full days: 119

Private lessons
Hourly
30 for 1 to 3 people;
42 for 4 or 5 people

Sno Academie

Classes
3½ hr a day
5 days: 116

Private Lessons
1 or 2 people:
2hr 58
3 or 4 people:
2hr 72

facing slopes at La Balme, where a lift takes you up to 2500m. La Clusaz itself is only just over 1000m and, in late season, the runs back can be dependent on artificial snow – of which there is now virtually blanket coverage. However, the long paths linking La Balme and l'Etale to the village are devoid of snow guns and can suffer from lack of snow. The main lifts to Beauregard and Crêt du Merle will carry people down as well as up. You can also ride the gondolas down to Le Grand-Bornand and the runs above Chinaillon have extensive snowmaking facilities.

FOR EXPERTS
Plenty to do, especially off-piste

The piste map doesn't seem to have a lot to offer experts, but the home resort of 1992 Olympic bumps champion Edgar Grospiron is not without challenges. Most of the sectors present off-piste variants to the pistes, and there are more serious adventures to undertake – all the more attractive for being ignored by most visitors.

The best terrain is at La Balme, where there are several fairly challenging pistes above mid-mountain. The black Vraille run, which leads to the speed skiing slope, is seriously steep. On the opposite side of the sector, the entirely off-piste Combe de Bellachat can be reached.

The Noire run down the face of Beauregard can be tricky in poor snow and is often closed. The Tetras on L'Etale and the Mur Edgar bumps run, below Crêt du Loup on L'Aiguille have been regraded as blacks, and rightly so. L'Aiguille has a good off-piste run down the neglected Combe de Borderan, and the piste map now shows the long new Lapiaz black run down the Combe de Fernuy – a continuation of the awkward black down from Cote 2000 to the parallel running Fernuy red.

In Le Grand-Bornand the steepest runs, including the black Noire du Lachat, go from the top of Le Lachat.

FOR INTERMEDIATES
Good if snow is good

Most intermediates will love La Clusaz if the snow conditions are good. Early intermediates will delight in the gentle slopes at the top of Beauregard and over on La Croix-Fry at Manigod, where there's a network of gentle tree-lined runs. And they'll be able to travel all over the area on the gentle, green linking pistes, where poling or walking is more likely to be a problem than any fears about steepness.

L'Etale and L'Aiguille have more challenging but wide blue runs.

More adventurous intermediates will prefer the steeper red slopes and good snow of La Balme and the long linking red down the Combe du Fernuy from L'Aiguille.

Le Grand-Bornand is full of good cruising blue and red intermediate runs

CHILDCARE

The ESF runs a ski kindergarten for children aged 5 to 12.

The two all-day kindergartens in La Clusaz operate 8.30 to 6pm. The Club des Mouflets (0450 326957) takes non-skiing children from 8 months to 4½ years. The Champions' Club (0450 326950) takes children 3½ to 6.

Le Grand-Bornand kindergarten takes children from 3 months.

stretching in both directions above Le Chinaillon – well worth a visit for a day or two if you are staying in La Clusaz. Most visitors we hear from neglect Le Grand-Bornand and are missing out because of that.

FOR BEGINNERS
Splendid beginner slopes

There is a nursery slope at village level at La Clusaz, and a couple of others just above it, but the best nursery slopes are up the mountain at the top of the Beauregard cable-car and at Crêt du Merle. The Beauregard area has lovely gentle blue runs to progress to, including one long run around the mountain right back to the village. There are also some greens at Le Grand-Bornand and St-Jean-de-Sixt.

FOR CROSS-COUNTRY
Excellent

The region has much better cross-country facilities than many resorts, with around 70km of loops of varying difficulty. One good area is near the Lac des Confins, reached by bus. There's also a lovely sunny area at the top of the Beauregard cable-car. At Le Grand-Bornand there are extensive trails in the Vallée du Bouchet and towards Le Chinaillon. And there are further trails at St-Jean-de-Sixt.

QUEUES
Not a problem

Lift queues aren't a problem, except on peak weekends or if the lower slopes are shut because of snow shortage. The chair lifts up the front face of L'Aiguille are the main weekend black spots – avoidable by taking other routes.

MOUNTAIN RESTAURANTS
High standard

Mountain restaurants are one of the area's strong points. There are lots of them and, for the most part, they are rustic and charming, and serve good, reasonably priced – often Savoyard – food. We have had excellent reports on the Télémark above the chair lift to L'Etale and Les Chenons at the bottom of La Balme. There are several other good restaurants higher up in the Aiguille sector, of which the Bercail is said to be the best. Chez Arthur at Crêt du Merle has a calm little table-service restaurant tucked away behind the busy self-service. The restaurant at Beauregard by the cross-country trail is sunny and peaceful, with good views. The Relais de L'Aiguille at Crêt du Loup and Le Neve at Le Rosay on Le Grand-Bornand are also recommended. The Vieille Ferme at Merdassier (see Eating out) is also open at lunchtime.

SCHOOLS AND GUIDES
Mixed reports

There are tales of large classes and poor instruction in ESF group lessons, but we've heard from some satisfied customers too – especially those who took private lessons. According to reports, the smaller Sno Academie – with smaller class sizes – is much more reliable.

GETTING THERE

Air Geneva, transfer 1½hr. Lyon, transfer 2½hr.

ACTIVITIES

Indoor Various hotels have saunas, massage, hot-tub, weights rooms, aerobics, sun beds and swimming pools
Outdoor Ice skating, paragliding, micro-light flights, snow-shoe excursions, ice carts, winter walks, horse-drawn carriage rides, quad-bikes, swimming pool.

Phone numbers
From abroad use the prefix +33 and omit the initial '0' of the phone number.

TOURIST OFFICES

La Clusaz

Postcode 74220
t +33 450 326500
f 450 326501
infos@laclusaz.com
www.laclusaz.com

Le Grand-Bornand

Postcode 74450
t +33 450 027800
f 450 027801
infos@legrandbornand.com
www.legrandbornand.com

St-Jean-de-Sixt

Postcode 74450
t +33 450 027014
f 450 027878
infos@saintjeandesixt.com
www.saintjeandesixt.com

Vallées des Aravis

Postcode 74450
t +33 450 027874
f 450 023851
infos@aravis.com
www.aravis.com

FACILITIES FOR CHILDREN
Good – in theory

We have had mixed reports about the kindergarten in La Clusaz and none about those in Le Grand-Bornand. Generally, however, the resorts are places where families can feel at home.

Staying there

HOW TO GO
Decreasing choice of packages

Few of the big UK tour operators go to La Clusaz, but there's a fair choice of packages from smaller operators, some of whom go to Le Grand-Bornand too. The drive from the Channel and the transfer from Geneva airport are both among the shortest for any resort.

Chalets There are some chalets, including some charmingly rustic ones.

Hotels Small, friendly 2-star family hotels are the mainstay of the area; luxury is not an option here.

((3 **Carlina** (0450 024348) A reporter says it's the best; central with pool and grounds.

((3 **Beauregard** (450 326800) Comfortable; on the fringe of the village. Pool. 'Fantastic for families, excellent food,' says a recent reporter.

((3 **Alp'Hôtel** (0450 024006) Comfortable modern chalet close to the centre, with one of the better restaurants. Pool.

((3 **Alpen Roc** (0450 025896) Big but stylish, central and comfortable, although one reporter said his room was 'very cramped'. Pool.

((3 **Saytels** (0450 022016) Only 3-star in Le Grand-Bornand. Close to church.

((3 **Cimes** (0450 270038) 3-star in Le Chinaillon.

((2 **Aravis** (0450 026031) Traditional place with 'dated' rooms but 'great' food, in la Clusaz centre, close to lifts.

((2 **L'Alpage de Tante Pauline** (0450 026328) Dinky chalet at foot of L'Etale slopes (bus stop outside).

Self-catering There's quite a good choice, including self-catering chalets as well as apartments. Some are out of town and best for those with a car.

EATING OUT
Good choice

There's a wide choice of restaurants, some a short drive away, including the Vieux Chalet, which is one of our favourites – good food and service in a splendid, creaky old chalet. It has a nice sunny terrace for a lunchtime blowout too. The St Joseph at the Alp'Hotel is regarded as the best restaurant in La Clusaz. L'Ecuelle is the place to go for Savoyard specialities. La Cordee and L'Outa are simple places giving great value for money. At the other end of the price scale is the more formal Symphonie restaurant in the hotel Beauregard – highly recommended by a recent reporter.

We're told some of the best food in the area is at the Ferme du Lormay in la Vallée du Bouchet, about 5km on from Le Grand-Bornand. But another reporter rates the Vieille Ferme at Merdassier his favourite place in the Alps – an old farm building with 'serious food, classy staff, perfect atmosphere'. Le Foly, overlooking the Lac des Confins, is a firm favourite with both tourists and locals alike.

APRES-SKI
La Clusaz getting livelier

These resorts have always seemed to us typically quiet French family places, with the difference that La Clusaz is definitely the the place to stay for a livelier time – especially at the weekend. Les Caves du Paccaly, in the centre of La Clusaz, is a new place with woody decor and live music. Le Pressoir is a focal bar, popular for sports videos. Pub le Salto is run by an English couple and has Sky TV and draught Guinness. The Bali bar is a more French central recommendation. The Ecluse disco has a glass dance floor with a floodlit stream running beneath it. The Caffe Inn has DJs or live music, and Club 18 rocks, often with live bands.

OFF THE SLOPES
Some diversions

The villages are pleasant. It's easy for pedestrians to get around the valley by bus and to get up to several mountain restaurants for lunch. There are good walks along the valleys, and a day trip to the beautiful lakeside town of Annecy is possible.

STAYING UP THE MOUNTAIN
Cheap and panoramic

The Relais de l'Aiguille at Crêt du Loup has five adequate bedrooms that are about the cheapest in the resort. And there are no fewer than three places to stay at the top of Beauregard.

Les Contamines 1160m

An unusual blend of village charm and reliable snow

WHAT IT COSTS

HOW IT RATES

The slopes

Snow	****
Extent	**
Experts	**
Intermediates	***
Beginners	***
Convenience	**
Queues	***
Restaurants	****

The rest

Scenery	***
Resort charm	****
Off-slope	**

MOUNTAIN FACTS

Altitude	1165m-2485m
Lifts	26
Pistes	120km
Green/Blue	37%
Red	40%
Black	23%
Artificial snow	3km
Recco detectors used	

- ✚ Traditional, unspoilt French village
- ✚ Fair-sized intermediate area
- ✚ Good snow record for its height
- ✚ Lift pass covers several nearby resorts, easily reachable by road

- ━ Limited scope for experts, and not ideal for beginners
- ━ Quiet nightlife
- ━ Lifts a bus-ride from main village
- ━ Can be some lengthy queues

Only a few miles from the fur coats of Megève and the ice-axes of Chamonix, Les Contamines is a charming contrast to both, with pretty wooden chalets, impressive old churches, a weekly market in the village square and prices more typical of rural France than of international resorts. Its position at the shoulder of Mont Blanc gives it an enviable snow record. What more could you want?

THE RESORT

The core of the village is compact, but the resort as a whole spreads widely, with chalets dotted over a 3km stretch of the valley, and the main access lift is 1km from the centre. There is accommodation by the lift at Le Lay but most people prefer to stay in the charming village centre and drive or take the shuttle-bus to the lifts. A car is useful, but the main Mont Blanc lift pass option covers the local buses, as well as the lifts of Chamonix and Megève (among others).

THE MOUNTAINS

Most of the slopes are above the tree line, though the runs down from Signal are bordered by trees (as is the run from La Ruelle down to Belleville). The front and back sectors are covered on different sides of the piste map and amount to a respectable 120km of piste.

Slopes From Le Lay a two-stage gondola climbs up to the slopes at Signal. Another gondola leads to the Etape mid-station from a car park a little further up the valley. Above these, a sizeable network of open, largely north-east-facing pistes fans

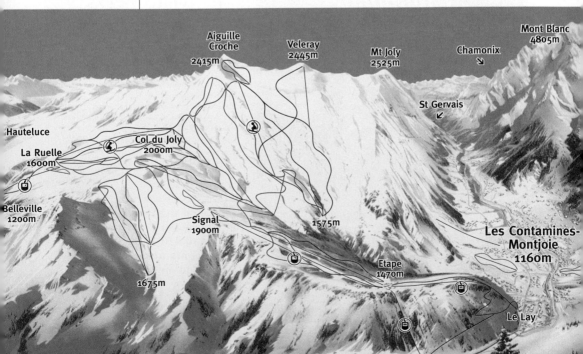

There are some grand views from the slopes →

OT LES CONTAMINES

What's new

A new 16-person gondola on the back side of the mountain, from Belleville to La Ruelle, replaced the old chair-lift for 2000/01.
A new crèche, next to the ESF kindergarten, opened last season. And a branch of the Ecole de Ski Internationale has also opened.

Nine new signed winter walking paths and a permanent toboggan run have also been created. Next season will see the introduction of a new non-consecutive ski pass for Les Contamines–Hauteluce.

out, with lifts approaching 2500m in two places. You can drop over the ridge at Col du Joly (2000m) to a series of south-west-facing runs down to La Ruelle (1600m), with a single red run going on down to Belleville (1200m) and the road to the village of Hauteluce, 7km away. From Belleville, a new 16-person gondola has replaced the old chair-lift back up to La Ruelle. A high-speed chair-lift takes you the rest of the way back up to Col du Joly.
Snowboarding There is a fun-park and half-pipe on the Tierces slope, accessed by the fast Tierces chair-lift.
Snow reliability Many of the shady runs on the Contamines side are above 1700m, and the resort has a justifiable reputation for good snow conditions, said to be the result of proximity to Mont Blanc. There's snowmaking on the home runs from Signal down to the gondola bases. But in late season, you may have to ride the gondolas down from the Etape mid-station.
Experts The steep western section has black runs, which are enjoyable but not terribly challenging for experts. The main attraction is the substantial and varied off-piste terrain – taking a guide is advisable. You can also visit

the other resorts on the Mont Blanc lift pass – notably Chamonix.
Intermediates The black runs are manageable for good intermediates. Other runs are ideal for people of average ability, with some of the best from the gondola's top station to its mid-station. Given good snow, the south-facing runs down to La Ruelle are a delight.

Phone numbers
From abroad use the prefix +33 and omit the initial 'o' of the phone number.

TOURIST OFFICE

Postcode 74170
t +33 450 470158
f 450 470954
info@
lescontamines.com
www.lescontamines.com

Beginners In good snow, the village nursery area is adequate for beginners. There are other areas at the mid-station and the top of the gondola, but no long greens to progress to.

Cross-country There are trails of varying difficulty totalling 29km. One of the loops is floodlit twice weekly.

Queues Peak-period queues in the morning can be a problem, especially if people are bussed in from other resorts with less snow. In such circumstances, it might be worth taking the Gorge gondola instead, though bottlenecks also occur at the mid-station where the two gondolas meet for the second stage up to Signal.

Mountain restaurants There are quite a few lovely rustic mountain restaurants – not all of which are marked on the piste map. La Ferme de la Ruelle is a jolly barn and Chalet du Col du Joly has great views. Best of all are two cosy chalets – Roselette and Bûche Croisée.

Schools and guides We have had mixed reports on the ESF – some parents thought their children's classes too strict and overcrowded. However, our most recent reports are positive. Excursions are offered, including a guided trip to the famous Vallée Blanche. The new International school opened last season, and there are also two guiding companies.

Facilities for children The new all-day village crèche, next to the central Loyers nursery slopes, takes children from one to seven years. Children can join ski school from age three.

STAYING THERE

How to go A couple of operators run catered chalets here, and there are a dozen modest hotels.

Hotels The best hotel is the 3-star Chemenaz (0450 470244) at Le Lay; though convenient for the slopes, this uninspiring spot has few other merits.

Eating out There are various restaurants and crêperies in town for eating out. Recommendations include Le Husky, l'Auberge du Barattet, L'Op Traken and Le Savoisien for traditional Savoie specialities – the last is one of the best regarded restaurants in the village.

Après-ski Après-ski is quiet, but there are several bars, some with live jazz on later, others that get a reasonable crowd at tea-time. There's also a disco for those looking for late-night entertainment.

Off the slopes There are good walks, a toboggan run and a natural ice rink, but St-Gervais, Megève and Chamonix have more to offer.

Courchevel 1300m-1850m

Gourmet skiing and boarding – and it needn't cost a fortune

WHAT IT COSTS

HOW IT RATES

The slopes

Snow	****
Extent	*****
Experts	****
Intermediates	*****
Beginners	*****
Convenience	****
Queues	****
Restaurants	****

The rest

Scenery	***
Resort charm	**
Off-slope	***

What's new

For 2001/02 a new high-speed six-seater chair will replace the long Pralong drag-lift from the beginner slopes above 1850, speeding up the journey to 1650 and to La Vizelle via the high-speed Suisse chair. Another new high-speed six-pack will replace three drag-lifts in 1650, making the journey to Signal and access to the underused red runs in that area from the 1850 area much quicker.

They are also adding to their grooming capacity with the aim of grooming two-thirds of all pistes each night.

For 2000/01 the slow chair from Les Creux to La Vizelle was replaced by a high-speed six-seater and the start of the Creux Noir chair was moved up the mountain to avoid congestion at Les Creux and so that the lift serves only the steeper upper slopes of the red piste down.

- ➕ Extensive, varied local terrain to suit everyone from beginners to experts – plus the rest of the Three Valleys
- ➕ Great easy runs for near-beginners
- ➕ Lots of slope-side accommodation
- ➕ Impressive, continuously updated lift system, particularly above 1850
- ➕ Excellent piste maintenance, and widespread use of snowmakers
- ➕ Wooded setting is pretty, and useful in bad weather
- ➕ Choice of four very different villages
- ➕ Some great restaurants, and good après-ski by French standards

- ➖ Some pistes get unpleasantly busy (but they can be avoided)
- ➖ Rather soulless villages with intrusive traffic in places
- ➖ 1850 has some of the most expensive hotels, bars and mountain restaurants in the Alps (prices in the other villages are much lower)
- ➖ Losing a little of its very French feel as more and more British visitors discover its attractions
- ➖ Little to do away from the slopes (during the day, at least)

Courchevel 1850 – the highest of the five components of this big resort – is the favourite Alpine hangout of the Paris jet set, who fly directly in to the mini-airport in the middle of the slopes. Its top hotels and restaurants are among the best in the Alps, and the most expensive. But don't be put off: a holiday here doesn't have to cost a fortune (especially in the lower villages), the atmosphere is not particularly exclusive, and the slopes are excellent. Courchevel is the most extensive and varied sector of the whole Three Valleys, with everything from long gentle greens to steep couloirs. Many visitors never leave the Courchevel sector; but there is good access to the rest of the Three Valleys, too.

Le Praz is an overgrown, but still pleasant village, 1550 is quieter and good for families, 1650 has more of an old village atmosphere than it seems from the drive through, and the posh bits of 1850 are stylishly woody. But overall the resort is no beauty. Well, nothing's perfect. Courchevel's long list of merits is enough to attract more and more Brits, but it remains much more French than Méribel, over the hill, as well as having better snow.

The resort

Courchevel is made up of four varied villages, most known by their altitudes. A road winds up the hill, linking Le Praz (1300), 1550 and 1650 to 1850; free buses run between the villages.

1850 is the largest village, and the focal point of the area. It has the main lifts to the Three Valleys connections and most of the nightlife and shops. It's conspicuously upmarket, with some very smooth hotels on the slopes just above the village centre and among the trees of Jardin Alpin. There's also a spreading area of smart private chalets. However, the centre of the village is a bit of a messy sprawl.

While some readers 'couldn't afford a second week', others say, 'It's not as upmarket as it's made out to be.' You can pay through the nose to eat, drink and stay, but more affordable places are not impossible to find.

The main road cuts through **1650** but there's also an attractive old village centre, lively bars and quietly situated chalets. Its local slopes (whose main access is an escalator-served gondola) are relatively peaceful. 1650 isn't the most convenient base for the rest of the Three Valleys, but a day trip to Val-Thorens is well within reach, and 1650 is 'a pleasant start and end to the day'.

1550 is a quiet dormitory, a gondola ride from 1850. It has the advantage of having essentially the same position as 1850, with cheaper accommodation and restaurants. But it's a long trip to 1850 by road if you want to go there in the evening. Some accommodation is a fair distance from the gondola.

Le Praz (or 1300) was once a traditional village set amid woodland. Still attractive, its charm has been undermined by expansion triggered by the 1992 Olympics, including the Olympic ski jump. It's quiet, 'excellent for children', with good links to 1850, and has tree-lined slopes on its doorstep for bad weather days. Near-beginners face rides down as well as up: the pistes back to the village are red and black, and at this altitude snow conditions are often poor.

Champagny is an easy road outing, giving access to the La Plagne area.

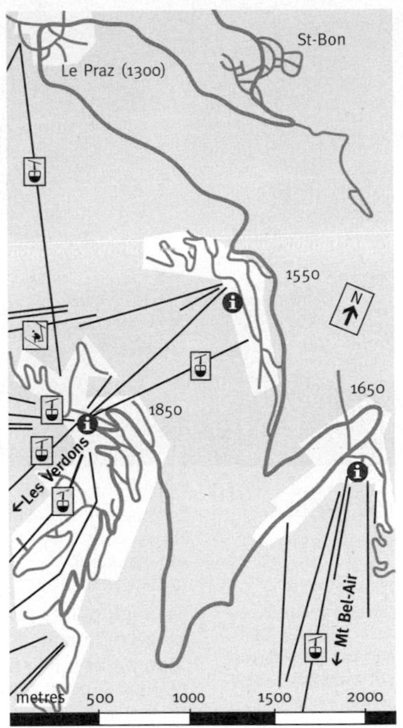

The mountains

MOUNTAIN FACTS

For the Three Valleys

Altitude	1300m-3200m
Lifts	200
Pistes	600km
Green	17%
Blue	34%
Red	37%
Black	12%
Artificial snow	90km
Recco detectors used	

The local slopes are so well linked that Courchevel is essentially just one big network. The central 1850 area is suitable for all; wooded Le Praz suits experts best; while 1650 has mainly fairly easy slopes. Runs lead back to all the villages, but the runs to Le Praz are prone to close with lack of snow. Piste maintenance is superb and daily maps of which runs have been groomed overnight are available at major lift stations (a great idea which all American resorts adopt but which is very rare in Europe). Snowmakers are abundant and the major lifts are modern, fast and comfortable – though there are a number of ancient drag-lifts, too. The area is also very well laid out. The main complaints we've had is that some slopes get busier than expected (but these can be avoided) and that the piste map is too small to be clear (though it is cleverly designed to show the whole of the vast Three Valleys on one map).

Many reporters recommend buying only a Courchevel pass ('I was still finding new runs after two weeks') and buying daily extensions when you want to try the rest of the Three Valleys.

THE SLOPES

Huge variety to suit everyone

A network of lifts and pistes spreads out from **1850**, which is very much the focal point of the area. The main axis is the Verdons gondola, leading to a second gondola to **La Vizelle** and a nearly parallel cable-car up to **La Saulire**. Both

COURCHEVEL TOURIST OFFICE

The Grand Couloir (on the left) is officially a black piste; and there is lots of excellent off-piste nearby too →

1550 (in the foreground) is a short trip from 1850 (above it) by gondola or piste but a long trip by road ↑

COURCHEVEL TOURIST OFFICE

LIFT PASSES

2001/02 prices in euros

Three Valleys
Covers all lifts in Courchevel, La Tania, Méribel, Val-Thorens, Les Menuires and St-Martin-de-Belleville.

Beginners 11 free lifts in the Courchevel valley.

Main pass
1-day pass 37
6-day pass 182

Senior citizens
Over 60: 6-day pass 146
Over 70: 6-day pass 91
Over 75: free pass

Children
Under 17: 6-day pass 137
Under 10: 118
Under 5: free pass

Short-term passes
Half-day (from 12.30) for Courchevel valley (adult 23) and the Three Valleys (adult 28).

Notes 6-day pass and over valid for one day each in Tignes-Val-d'Isère, La Plagne-Les Arcs, Pralognan-la-Vanoise and Les Saisies. Reductions for families.

Alternative passes
Vallée de Courchevel pass covers 67 lifts and 150km of piste around Courchevel and La Tania (adult 6-day 148. One-day extension for Three Valleys, 17).

the high points give access to a wide range of intermediate and advanced terrain (including a number of couloirs), Méribel and all points to Val-Thorens. You can also get over to 1650 from here.

To the right looking up from 1850 the Chenus gondola goes towards a second departure point for Méribel, the **Col de la Loze**. Easy and intermediate runs go back to 1850, with more difficult runs in the woods above **La Tania** (see separate chapter) and **Le Praz** – splendid slopes when snow is in good supply.

To the left of the Verdons gondola is the Jardin Alpin gondola, which leads to some great beginner terrain, and serves the higher hotels and runs until 8pm. It also gives access to 1650.

1650 offers a good mix of beginner and intermediate slopes. Getting to and from Méribel and the rest of the Three Valleys involves slightly more effort than from the rest of Courchevel, since you have to go up and down another valley, but you can always catch the bus from 1850 if you run late on the way back.

SNOW RELIABILITY
Very good

The combination of Courchevel's orientation (its slopes are north- or north-east-facing), its height, an abundance of snowmakers and excellent piste maintenance usually guarantees good snow down to at least the 1850 and 1650 villages. On countless visits we have found that the snow is usually much better than in neighbouring Méribel, whose slopes gets more direct sun.

FOR EXPERTS
Some black gems

There is plenty to interest experts, even without the rest of the Three Valleys.

The most obvious expert runs are the couloirs you can see on the right near the top of the Saulire cable-car. These used to be black pistes (some of the steepest in Europe). But last season's piste map reclassified the Téléphérique (seriously narrow) and Emille Alais as itinéraires. The Grand Couloir is the widest and easiest and remains an official piste – but you have to traverse further along the narrow bumpy, precipitous access ridge to reach it.

There is a lot of steep terrain, on- and off-piste, on the shady slopes of La Vizelle, both towards Verdons and towards the link with 1650. Some of the reds on La Vizelle verge on black steepness and the black M piste is surprisingly little used. If you love moguls, don't miss the top of the black Suisses. Chanrossa, which comes towards 1850 from the top of 1650, is quite difficult – the off-piste just next to it is tougher. For a change of scene and a test of stamina, a couple of long (700m vertical), genuinely steep blacks cut through the trees down to Le Praz.

There is plenty of off-piste terrain to try with a guide and a bit of climbing – high, north-facing slopes right at the top of the 1650 sector, for example (the Vallée des Avals is a great run). Also ask about the mysterious Hidden Valley in 1650, and the huge bowl accessed from the Creux Noir chair.

FOR INTERMEDIATES

Paradise for all levels

The Three Valleys is the greatest intermediate playground in the world, but all grades of intermediates will love Courchevel's local slopes too.

Above 1650 novices have the wonderful long runs of Pyramide and Grand Bosses. Gentle blues such as Biollay in 1850 are fine, gentle slopes, leading to the two easy home runs on either side of the Jardin Alpin.

Those of average ability can handle most red runs without difficulty. Our favourite is the long, sweeping Combe de la Saulire from top to bottom of the cable-car. Very pleasant first thing, when it's well groomed and free of crowds, it's a different story at the end of the day – cut up snow and crowded. Creux, behind La Vizelle, is another splendid, fast long red (it gets bumpy though, and crowded with ski school groups). Marmottes from the top of Vizelle is quieter and more challenging.

The runs from Bouc Blanc through the trees towards La Tania are great – long, rolling cruises 'guaranteed to put a smile on your face'. The top of this section also has fine red runs down to 1850 and 1550, with easier blues alongside. Over at 1650, the reds on Mt Bel Air and Signal are excellent, if

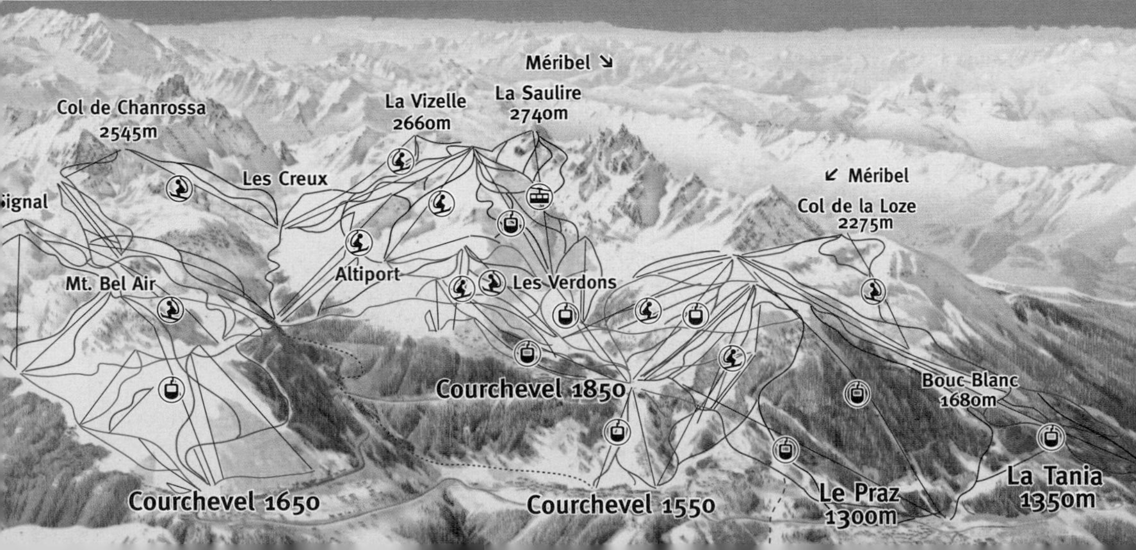

SCHOOLS/GUIDES

2000/01 prices in euros

ESF in 1850
Classes
6 full days:
Adults: 190
Children: 150
Children's classes
Ages: from 3
1 full day: 45
Private lessons
2½hr morning, 2hr lunchtime, 2½hr afternoon, 7hr full day
212 to 252 for full day.

ESF in 1650
Classes 6 days
6 full days: 125
Children's classes
Ages: from 3
Private lessons
9.15-4.45
244 for full day

ESF in 1550
Classes 6 days
Adults: 198
Children's classes
6 days, 183. Ages from 3 to 5

Ski Academie
Classes 5 days
2½hr: am
5 mornings: 115
Children's classes
Ages: from 4
5 mornings: 100

Ski Supreme 1850
2001/02 prices
Classes 12hr course 143
Children's classes
12hr course 135
Private lessons
1hr 55

New Generation
2000/01 prices in sterling
Classes 10 hr £90
Freeride clinic
7½hrs £85
Check Up clinic
4 hours £50
Private lessons
2 hours £75 for 1 to 2 people, £15 per additional person

boarding *For an upmarket resort, Courchevel goes out of its way to attract boarders. There's a fun-park and a half-pipe just below 1850 and the Verdons terrain park (all for skiers as well as boarders) just above 1850. Except above 1650, it's easy to get around the Three Valleys using chairs and gondolas. The big snowboard hangout is 'Prends ta luge et tire toi', a combined shop/bar/Internet cafe in the centre of 1850.*

short, and usually quiet (though this may change with the new six-pack for 2001/02 – see What's new).

FOR BEGINNERS

Great graduation runs

There are excellent nursery slopes above both 1650 and 1850. At the former, lessons are likely to begin on the short drags close to the village, but quick learners will soon be able to go from close to the top of the 1650 area all the way down to the village. The best nursery area at 1850 is at Pralong, above the village, near the airstrip. A green path links this area with chairs to 1650, so adventurous novices have the opportunity to move far afield. The Bellecôte green run down into 1850 is an excellent, long, gentle slope – but does get crowded. It is served by the Jardin Alpin gondola, and a drag which is one of 13 free beginner lifts in Courchevel. 1550 and Le Praz have small nursery areas, but most people go up to 1850 for its more reliable snow.

FOR CROSS-COUNTRY

Long wooded trails

Courchevel has a total of 66km of trails, the most in the Three Valleys. Le Praz is the most suitable village, with trails through the woods towards 1550, 1850 and Méribel. Given enough snow, there are also loops around the village.

QUEUES

There are always alternatives

Even at New Year and Easter, when 1850 in particular positively teems with people, queues are minimal, thanks to the excellence of the lift system. The Chenus, Verdons and Jardin Alpin gondolas have all had their capacity increased over the past few years, improving these old bottlenecks. However, as one reader points out, 'there can be a build-up at 1850 for the gondolas'. At such times 'it's best to avoid skiing back to 1850'. For example, try using the Plantrey chair, below 1850, or the Coqs chair, above it, to get over to Loze, Le Praz and La Tania. The Biollay chair is very popular with the ski school (who get priority) and can also be worth avoiding. Queues for the huge Saulire cable-car have been all but eliminated by the upgrading of the parallel Vizelle gondola.

MOUNTAIN RESTAURANTS

Good but can be very expensive

Mountain restaurants are plentiful and pleasant by French standards, but it is sensible to check the prices and book for table-service restaurants.

The big Chalet de Pierres, on the Verdons piste just above 1850, is one of the highlights if you're inclined to extravagance – a comfortable, smooth place in traditional style, doing excellent food (including superb cakes) with high, high prices. Only a little way behind this for price comes the Cap Horn, near the airstrip. If you're feeling really flush, take a trip down to Bistrot du Praz at Le Praz for a blowout on a bad-weather day (treat yourself to the 'degustation de foie gras chaud'). The Bergerie on the Bellecôte piste is where the 'beautiful people' hang out.

For a good-value lunch above 1850 try the busy Altibar, with a fine terrace, good food and both self-service and table-service sections. The Verdons is well placed for piste-watching and La Soucoupe is an atmospheric self-service place, now with table-service upstairs too. The Panoramic at the top of Saulire was one of our favourites but was gutted by fire and closed for the 2000/01 season. Behind the main lift station at 1850 the Telemark terrace is a great suntrap, with good pizzas.

CHILDCARE

There are kindergartens in 1850 (0479 080847) and 1650 (0479 083369) which take children from age 18 months, until 5pm. The ESF branches in all main parts of the resort have ski kindergartens.

GETTING THERE

Air Geneva, transfer 3½hr. Lyon, transfer 3½hr. Chambéry, transfer 2½hr. Direct flights to Courchevel altiport from London at weekends only (contact tourist office for details). Also scheduled flights from Geneva to Courchevel.

Rail Moûtiers (24km); transfer by bus or taxi.

In 1650, Mont Bel-Air, at the top of the gondola, is our favourite Courchevel restaurant, with good food, friendly and efficient table-service, and a splendid tiered terrace. The Portetta hotel at the bottom has a good late-season sun terrace too. Down in 1550 try the Cortona – 'great pizza'.

SCHOOLS AND GUIDES
Size is everything

Courchevel's branches of the ESF add up to the largest ski school in Europe, with a total of almost 500 instructors. We've had bad reports on ESF 1850 in the past but this year a reporter says, 'They did a good job with a 17-year-old beginner in our party.' Another says, 'The jardin'd'enfants of the ESF at 1850 was disorganised, with oversized classes and rude and arrogant staff. But our 7 and 10 year olds enjoyed their mainstream lessons.' A Bureau des Guides runs all-day off-piste excursions.

Ski Academie, an independent group of French instructors, was 'excellent for our 7 and 9 year olds,' says another reporter.

Supreme in 1850 is owned and staffed by British instructors and we've had good reports: 'Excellent. Our Scottish instructor was the best ever!'

New Generation is a school that started as Le Ski school in 1650, linked to the tour operator of the same name – but has now branched out into 1850 and Méribel too. It consists of highly qualified young British instructors committed to giving clients enjoyment as well as technique. We have nothing but rave reviews about them: 'Young and highly motivated. Adapt teaching to the clients' needs, not ski school dogma', 'I've taken five group classes now and not had a bad one ... this school is one reason I keep coming back to 1650', 'I did a check-up clinic (two afternoons for £45 total) – very helpful, small group, personal attention, kept us busy'. For contact details see p273 of Méribel chapter.

FACILITIES FOR CHILDREN
Lots of chalet-based options

There is a ski kindergarten in 1850 – but see comment under Schools.

Several tour operators run their own crèches using British nannies – an alternative that many families have found attractive.

Staying there

1850 is the swanky place, with the best hotels and chalets, the biggest choice of restaurants and nightlife and the jet set. 1650 is better value, 1550 is quiet and good for families. Le Praz is quiet and good value.

In all the resorts except Le Praz, there is lots of accommodation close to the lifts and runs. The prime place to stay is close to the main lift station at 1850, or on runs leading down to it.

HOW TO GO
Value chalets and apartments

Huge numbers of British tour operators go to Courchevel, with a wide choice of accommodation.

Chalets There are plenty of chalets available from dozens of UK tour operators, including some very comfortable ones and a few that are genuinely luxurious. As usual in a French resort with a stock of ageing hotel buildings, there are also some chalet hotels run by UK tour operators.

In 1850, FlexiSki has two chalets, including the refurbished Vizelle on the Bellecôte piste. Scott Dunn has several upscale places. Simply Ski has highly regarded childcare in their fine Le Praz chalets. Lotus Supertravel has a number of luxurious 'superchalets' with upscale food and wines and free massages – we have stayed in the

Phone numbers
From abroad use the prefix +33 and omit the initial '0' of the phone number.

splendid Chalet Founets a couple of times. Thomson's refurbished flagship St Louis chalet hotel is in a great position just across from the Bellecôte piste. Crystal's club hotel New Solarium is in the pretty Jardin Alpin.

In 1650 Le Ski has 11 good value chalets, including the brand new Rikiki on the piste.

Hotels There are nearly 50 hotels in Courchevel, mostly at 1850 – including more 4-stars than anywhere else in France except Paris.

((((5 **Bellecôte** (1850) (0479 081019) Our favourite among the more swanky places – it offers some Alpine atmosphere as well as sheer luxury.

((((5 **Mélezin** (1850) (0479 080133) Superbly stylish and luxurious – and in an ideal position beside the bottom of the Bellecôte home slope.

((((5 **Carlina** (1850) (0479 080030) Luxury piste-side pad, next to Mélezin.

((((5 **Byblos des Neiges** (1850) (0479 009800) Next to first stop on Jardin Alpin gondola; spacious public rooms, good pool, sauna, steam complex.

(((4 **Grandes Alpes** (1850) (0479 080335) On piste next to main lifts.

(((4 **Rond Point** (1850) (0479 080433) Family atmosphere, central position.

((3 **Croisette** (1850) (0479 080900) Next to main lifts; recently refurbished. It contains the popular Le Jump bar.

((3 **Courcheneige** (1850) (0479 080259) Pleasantly informal chalet in quiet position on the piste above the resort, with popular lunchtime terrace.

((3 **Ducs de Savoie** (1850) (0479 080300) Pleasant, wood-built; well placed for skiing to the door, but only five minutes' walk from centre.

((3 **Sivoliere** (1850) (0479 080833) No beauty, but comfortable (though small lounge), pleasantly set among pines.

((3 **Golf** (1650) (0479 009292) Rather impersonal 3-star, in a superb position on the piste next to the gondola.

((3 **Ancolies** (1550) (0479 082766) 'A real find,' said a US visitor impressed by the friendly staff and excellent food.

(2 **Edelweiss** (1650) (0479 082658) Simple, but 'great value', we're told.

(2 **Peupliers** (1300) (0479 084147) Well placed and cheap by local standards.

SNOWPIX.COM / CHRIS GILL

Two of Courchevel's splendid mountain restaurants: the pricey Cap Horn (front) and the better value Altibar – both by the airstrip ↓

ACTIVITIES

Indoor Artificial skating rink, climbing wall, bridge, chess, squash, swimming and saunas (hotels), gymnasium, health and fitness centres (swimming pools, sauna, steam-room, hot-tub, water therapy, weight-training, massage), bowling, exhibitions (galleries in 1850 and 1650), cinema, games rooms, billiards, language courses

Outdoor Hang-gliding, paragliding, flying lessons, parachuting, floodlit skiing, ski jumping, snow-shoe excursions, dog-sledding, snowmobile rides, 35km cleared paths, 2km toboggan run, curling, ice-climbing, flight excursions

TOURIST OFFICE

Postcode 73122
t +33 479 080029
f 479 081563
pro@courchevel.com
www.courchevel.com

Self-catering There's a large selection of apartments, though high-season dates can sell out early. Some UK tour operators (including Erna Low) have places in the smart and central Forum complex in 1850. As with all French apartments, check room dimensions and book a place advertised for more people than there are in your party.

EATING OUT
Pick your price

There are a lot of good, very pricey French restaurants in Courchevel. Among the best, and priciest, are Le Chabichou (though a reporter calls it 'over-rated') and Le Bateau Ivre in 1850 – both with two Michelin stars. The 'friendly' Berçail also has a high reputation, notably for seafood. Other recommendations for Savoyard food include the cosy La Saulire (booking essential) and La Fromagerie, the good-value L'Arbé, La Cloche ('good atmosphere') and Le Mazot – 'very traditional'. La Cendrée is a 'wonderful Italian'. The Smalto and Strada are good for pizza. Still in 1850, La Potinière does good, cheap pizzas, steaks and pasta. La Locomotive has a railway theme and a varied menu and Hotel Les Tovets has 'reasonable prices and delicious food'.

In 1550, L'Oeil du Boeuf is good for grills. La Cortona does good-value pizza.

In 1650 the Eterlou, Montagne and Le Petit Savoyard (all in the little square) do good traditional Savoyard food and cheaper pizza and pasta. In Le Praz, Bistrot du Praz is pricey but excellent – see 'Mountain restaurants'. Le Yaca is small and 'very French'.

APRES-SKI
1850 has most variety

If you want lots of nightlife, it's got to be 1850. But it doesn't have the same loud Brit-oriented scene as Méribel complains one reporter. There are some exclusive nightclubs, such as La Grange and Les Caves, with top Paris cabaret acts and sky-high prices. The popular Kalico has DJs and cocktails and gets packed. The Bergerie does themed evenings – food, music, entertainment (but prices are high). The down-to-earth Bar L'Equipe seems to be readers' top nightspot.

Le Jump at the foot of the main slope is the place to be as the lifts close but it does get packed. El Gringo has theme nights. La Saulire (aka Jacques), Tee-Jay's and the cheap and cheerful Potinière are also popular.

Cinemas in 1850 and 1650 and La Tania sometimes show English-speaking films.

In 1650 Le Bubble is the hub, has satellite TV and internet access. Cheap bar prices, happy hour, strong Mutzig beer, with frequent live music it has a largely British clientele. Signal, on the main street, is quieter, has great views at the back and shuts at 9pm or so. Rocky's is popular with young Brits and has satellite TV and loud music. Au Plouc is a tiny French bar. The Space Bar has pool, games and live music.

In 1550 the Chanrossa bar is British-dominated, with occasional live music, the Taverne 'French and friendly'.

OFF THE SLOPES
1850 isn't bad

The Forum sports centre in 1850 includes a climbing wall in the shopping centre – good for spectating too. There are a fair number of shops in 1850 and excellent markets at most levels. There's a fun ice-driving circuit and an ice-climbing structure. A pedestrian lift pass for the gondolas and buses in Courchevel and Méribel makes it easy for non-slope users to get around the area and meet companions for lunch on the slopes. And you can take joyrides from the altiport and try to spot friends below.

Les Deux-Alpes 1650m

Twin attractions of snow and fun

WHAT IT COSTS

4

HOW IT RATES

The slopes

Snow	****
Extent	***
Experts	****
Intermediates	**
Beginners	***
Convenience	***
Queues	**
Restaurants	**

The rest

Scenery	****
Resort charm	**
Off-slope	**

- ⊕ High, snowsure slopes, including an extensive glacier area
- ⊕ Varied high-mountain terrain, from motorway cruising to seriously steep blacks and off-piste slopes
- ⊕ Efficient, modern lift system
- ⊕ Excellent, sunny nursery slopes
- ⊕ Stunning views of the Ecrins peaks
- ⊕ Lively, varied nightlife
- ⊕ Wide choice of hotels

- ⊖ Piste network modest by French mega-resort standards – we're sceptical about the claimed 200km – and badly congested in places
- ⊖ Only one easy run back to the resort – a busy zig-zag path; others are red or black, and often ruined by sun
- ⊖ Virtually no woodland runs
- ⊖ Spread-out, traffic-choked resort
- ⊖ Few appealing mountain restaurants

We have a love–hate relationship with Les Deux-Alpes. We quite like the buzz of the town – arriving here is a bit like driving into Las Vegas from the Nevada desert – and we understand the appeal of its vibrant nightlife. We love the high-Alpine feel of its main mountain, and the good snow to be found on the north-facing runs in the middle of the mountain. But we're very unimpressed by the extent of those slopes, and we hate the piste congestion that results when most of the town's 35,000 visitors are crammed on to them. Crowding apart, keen intermediates spoilt by high-mileage French mega-resorts (and not up to the excellent off-piste) will simply find the usable area of slopes rather small.

What's new

The old Jandri 3 gondola from mid-mountain to the glacier was dismantled last season, putting extra pressure on the second stage of the Jandri express. A new eight-seater chair, to replace the original gondola, should be ready to relieve the resultant bottlenecks for 2001/02.

The resort 

Les Deux-Alpes is a narrow village sitting on a high, remote col. Access is from the Grenoble-Briançon road to the north or by gondola from Venosc. The village is a long, sprawling collection of hotels, apartments, bars and shops, most lining the busy main street and the parallel street that completes the one-way traffic system. Although there is no centre as such, and lifts are spread fairly evenly along the village, a couple of focal points are evident.

The resort has grown haphazardly over the years, and there is a wide range of building styles, from old chalets through monstrous 1960s blocks to more sympathetic recent developments. France does have worse-looking resorts, though not many. Fans point out that it looks better as you drive out than as you drive in, because all the apartment buildings have their balconies facing the remote southern end of the resort.

OT LES DEUX-ALPES

It's a long, long town, and ideally you don't want to be stuck out at the northern (right-hand) end 

MOUNTAIN FACTS

Altitude 1300m-3570m	
Lifts	58
Pistes	200km
Green	24%
Blue	39%
Red	24%
Black	13%
Art. snow	59 acres
Recco detectors used	

LIFT PASSES

2001/02 prices in euros

Super ski pass
Covers all lifts in Les Deux-Alpes, entry to swimming pool and skating rink.

Beginners 4 free lifts

Main pass
1-day pass 31
6-day pass 150
(low season 135)

Senior citizens
Over 60: 6-day pass 113 (low season 101)
Over 75: free pass

Children
Under 13: 6-day pass 113 (low season 101)
Under 5: free pass

Short-term passes
Half day passes available.

Notes 6-day pass includes one day's skiing in Alpe-d'Huez, Serre-Chevalier, Puy-St-Vincent and the Milky Way.

Alternative passes
2 limited area passes: 'Ski sympa' covers 21 lifts (15 per day), 'Grand ski' covers 32 lifts (25 per day). Les 2 Alpes/La Grave (39 per day) or an 8 euro supplement for this with a two-day or longer pass.

N
Village
Jandri Express
Diable
down to Venosc
metres 500 1000 1500 2000

The lively ambience helps to distract you from the look of the place.

Alpe de Venosc, at the southern end of town, has many of the nightspots and hotels, the most character, the fewest cars, the best shops and the Diable gondola up to the tough terrain around Tête Moute. More generally useful is the Jandri Express from the middle of the resort, where there is a popular outdoor ice rink and some good restaurants and bars. The village straggles north from here, becoming less convenient the further you go.

The free shuttle-bus service saves on some very long walks from one end of town to the other.

The six-day pass covers a day in each of Alpe-d'Huez, Serre-Chevalier, Puy-St-Vincent and the Milky Way resorts from Montgenèvre to Sauze d'Oulx. All are easily reached by car, road conditions permitting. Helicopter trips to Alpe-d'Huez are good value at around 55 euros for a return trip. One recent reporter describes it as a 'must'. More economical is the shuttle-bus service on Wednesdays (15 euros for the round trip).

The mountains

For a big resort, Les Deux-Alpes has a disappointingly small piste area, despite recent improvements. Although extremely long and tall (it rises almost 2000m) the main sector is also very narrow, with just a few runs on the upper part of the mountain, served by a few long, efficient lifts.

THE SLOPES

Long, narrow and fragmented

The western **Pied Moutet** side of Les Deux-Alpes is relatively little-used, although recent improvements in the lift system and more artificial snow-cover have helped to entice more people to the area. It is served by lifts from various parts of town but reaches only 2100m. As well as the short runs back to town which get the morning sun, there's an attractive, longer north-facing red run down through the trees to the small village of Bons. This is one of only two tree-lined runs in Les Deux-Alpes – the other going down to another low village, Mont-de-Lans, and reachable from either sector.

On the eastern side of the resort, the broad, steep slope immediately above it offers a series of relatively short, testing runs, down to the nursery slopes ranged at the bottom. Most of these runs are classified as black, and rightly so: they aren't groomed and are usually mogulled, and often icy when not softened by the afternoon sun. As a result, many visitors are forced to take the gondolas or the long winding green back down in order to avoid the tricky home runs.

The ridge of **Les Crêtes** above the village has lifts and gentle runs along it, and behind it lies the deep, steep Combe de Thuit. Lifts span the combe to the main mid-mountain station at 2600m, at the foot of the slopes on **La Toura**. The middle section of the mountain, above and below this point, is made up primarily of blue cruising runs and is very narrow. At one point, there is essentially just a single run down the mountain – a broad ledge skirting the Combe de Thuit back to Les Crêtes. There is also the alternative of taking the roundabout (ie partly flat) blue Gours run to the bottom of the combe, where a chair-lift takes you up to Les Crêtes. This pleasant run passes the base of the Fée chair, serving an isolated (and neglected) black run.

The top **Glacier du Mont de Lans** section, served by drag-lifts and the warmer underground funicular, has some fine, very easy runs which afford great views and are ideal for beginners and the less adventurous. You can go from the top here all the way down to Mont-de-Lans – a descent of 2268m vertical which, as far as we know, is the world's biggest on-piste vertical. A walk (or snowcat tow) in the opposite direction takes you over to the splendid La Grave area (a supplement is charged for the lifts).

SNOW RELIABILITY
Excellent on higher slopes

The snow on the higher slopes is normally very good, even in a poor winter – one of the main reasons for Les Deux-Alpes' popularity. Above 2200m most of the runs are north-facing, and the top glacier section guarantees good snow. You should worry more about bad weather shutting the lifts, or extremely low temperatures at the top, than about snow shortage. But the runs just above the village face west, so they get a lot of afternoon sun and can be icy at the beginning and end of the day. Artificial snow on some of the lower slopes helps keep them usable.

FOR EXPERTS
Off-piste is the main attraction

With good snow and weather conditions, the area offers wonderful off-piste sport. There are several good off-piste runs within the lift network, including a number of variations from underneath the top stage of the Jandri Express down to the Thuit chair-lift. The best-known ones are marked on the piste map. The Fée chair built a few years ago opened up new off-piste possibilities into the Combe de Thuit. There are also more serious routes that end well outside the lift network, with verticals of over 2000m.

The Super Diable chair-lift, from the top of the Diable gondola, serves the steepest black run around. The brave can also try off-piste variations here between the rocks.

If the conditions are right, an outing across the glacier to the largely off-piste slopes of La Grave is a must.

FOR INTERMEDIATES
Limited cruising

Les Deux-Alpes can disappoint keen intermediates. A lot of the runs are either rather tough – some of the blues could be reds – or boringly bland. The steep runs just above the resort put off many. As one of our reporters (who classes himself as an 'advanced' skier)

SCHOOLS/GUIDES

2000/01 prices in euros

ESF
Classes 6 days
$2\frac{3}{4}$hr am or pm
6 mornings: 115
Children's classes
Ages: 6 to 12
6 mornings: 96
Private lessons
2hr over lunchtime or full day Sunday
29 for 1hr, for 1 to 3 people

International St-Christophe
Classes 6 days
$2\frac{1}{2}$hr am or pm
6 mornings: 109
Children's classes
Ages: 6 to 12
6 mornings: 86
Private lessons
1hr over lunchtime
30 for 1hr, for 1 to 4 people

European Ski School
Classes 6 days
2hr am or pm
Children's classes
Private lessons

CHILDCARE

Both ski schools run kindergartens on more-or-less identical terms – taking children aged 4 to 6 until 5pm. The ESF (0476 792121) is slightly more expensive and does lunch only on request, but starts at 9.15, whereas the ESI de St Christophe (0476 790421) starts at 9.30. The Crèche du Village offers an excellent service for babies from 6 months to 2 years, from 8.30 to 5.30.
The Garderie du Bonhomme de Neige is for children aged 2 to 6 years.
A list of babysitters is available from the tourist office.

boarding *Les Deux-Alpes has been catering for snowboarders for years, and has built up an excellent reputation. There's a specialist school and lots of boarder-friendly facilities. There's a fun-park with a boarder-cross, a half-pipe, music and a barbecue higher up the mountain in the Toura sector, where most of the lifts are chairs. This is relocated up to the glacier in the summer (access is by T-bar or funicular), which is where the Mondial du Snowboard competition is hosted each year. There's even a kids' park and the ESF offer freestyle classes, using trampolines and a huge air-bag to practise on. There's some great off-piste in the local area for free-riders and the link to La Grave offers some of the best off-piste terrain in the world for advanced riders – a guide is recommended. With cheap and plentiful accommodation, and noisy, lively nightlife in the bars and discos, it's a well-deserved reputation.*

said, 'I myself fell from top to bottom. I was lucky. A girl in a different group broke her back. You cannot afford to be complacent here.'

The runs higher up generally have good snow, and aggressive intermediates can enjoy great fast cruising, especially on the mainly north-facing pistes served by the chair-lifts off to the sides. You can often pick gentle or steeper terrain in these bowls as you wish, but avid piste-bashers will explore all there is to offer in a couple of days. Many visitors take the opportunity of excursions to Alpe-d'Huez and Serre-Chevalier.

Less confident intermediates will love the quality of the snow and the gentleness of most of the runs on the upper mountain. Their problem might lie in finding the pistes too crowded, especially if snow is poor in other resorts and people are bussed in. At the end of the day, you can ride the Jandri Express down or take the long winding green back to town.

FOR BEGINNERS
Good slopes

The nursery slopes beside the village are spacious and gentle. The run along the ridge above them is excellent, too. The glacier also has a fine array of very easy slopes – but bear in mind that bad weather can close the lifts.

FOR CROSS-COUNTRY
Needs very low-altitude snow

There are three small, widely dispersed areas. La Petite Alpe, near the entrance to the village, has a couple of snowsure but very short trails. Given good snow, Venosc (950m), reached by a gondola down, has the only worthwhile picturesque ones. Total trail distance is 20km. You can ski the Mont de Lans glacier with a qualified guide.

QUEUES
Can be a problem

Les Deux-Alpes has a great deal of hardware to keep queues minimal. But the village is large, and queues at the mid-morning peak can be 'diabolically' long for the Jandri Express and Diable gondolas. The Jandri queue moves quickly and the new eight-seater chair from the mid-station to the glacier should get rid of the bottleneck for the second stage. Problems can also occur when people are bussed in when snow is in short supply. The top lifts are prone to closure if it's windy, putting pressure on the lower lifts. A recent visitor reported queues for the gondolas back to the village when large numbers of people declined to tackle the tricky blacks or the busy green run back down. The narrow mid-section of the mountain, particularly the Grand Nord blue run, is a real bottleneck late in the day.

MOUNTAIN RESTAURANTS
On the up

There are mountain restaurants at all the major lift junctions, but they are generally pretty poor. La Pastorale, at the top of the Diable gondola, was for years the only recommendable place. But a few years ago the choice was doubled by the construction of the splendid Chalet de la Toura, in the middle of the domain at about 2600m, with a big terrace, a welcoming woody interior and efficient, if somewhat expensive, table-service. The Panoramic has been recommended.

SCHOOLS AND GUIDES
One of the better ESFs

The ski schools have a fairly good reputation for standards of tuition and English, although class sizes can be large. A recent report claims the

GETTING THERE

Air Lyon, transfer 3½hr. Grenoble, transfer 2hr. Chambéry, transfer 3hr. Geneva, transfer 4½hr.

Rail Grenoble (70km); 4 daily buses from station.

Phone numbers
From abroad use the prefix +33 and omit the initial '0' of the phone number.

ACTIVITIES

Indoor 2 sports centres; Club Forme (squash, swimming pool, sauna, hot-tub), Tanking Centre (flotation chambers, physiotherapy, pressotherapy, sauna, hot-tub, Turkish baths)

Outdoor Ice skating, swimming pool, ice driving lessons, ice gliders (dodgems), snow-shoe excursions

TOURIST OFFICE

Postcode 38860
t +33 476 792200
f 476 790138
les2alp@les2alpes.com
www.les2alpes.com

European school was 'not very helpful'. There are several specialist courses available, as well as off-piste tours and trips to other resorts.

FACILITIES FOR CHILDREN
Fine for babies

Babies from six months to two years old can safely be entrusted to the village crèche. The kindergarten takes kids from two to six years, and there are chalet-based alternatives run by UK tour operators. There are also four free T-bars for children at the village level.

Staying there

HOW TO GO
Wide range of packages

Les Deux-Alpes has something for most tastes, including that rarity in high-altitude French resorts, reasonably priced hotels.

Chalets There are a number of catered chalet packages available from UK tour operators, but some use apartments.

Hotels There are over 30 hotels, of which the majority are 2-star or below.

(((3) **Bérangère** (0476 792411) Smartest in town, although dreary to look at, with an excellent restaurant and pool; on-piste, at less convenient north end of resort.

((2) **Mariande** (0476 805060) Highly recommended, especially for its 'excellent' five-course dinners. At Venosc end of resort.

((2) **Chalet Mounier** (0476 805690) Smartly modernised. Good reputation for its food, and well placed for the Diable bubble and nightlife.

((2) **Souleil'or** (0476 792469) Looks like a lift station, but pleasant and comfortable, and well placed for the Jandri Express gondola. The rooms and food are reportedly 'fantastic'.

((2) **Brunerie** (0476 792223) 'Basic and cheerful', large 2-star with plenty of parking and quite well positioned.

Self-catering Many of the apartments are stuck out at the north end of the resort – well worth avoiding.

EATING OUT
Plenty of choice

The hotel Bérangère has an excellent restaurant and the Chalet Mounier has a high reputation. La Petite Marmite has good food and atmosphere at reasonable prices. Bel'Auberge does classic French and is 'quite superb' – advance booking is advised. La Patate, Le Dahu and Crêpes à Gogo are also recommended. Visitors on a budget can get a relatively cheap Italian meal at either La Vetrata or La Spaghetteria.

APRES-SKI
Unsophisticated fun

Les Deux-Alpes is one of the liveliest of French resorts, with plenty of bars, several of which stay open until the early hours. The Rodéo has a mechanical bucking bronco which attracts great numbers of rowdy après-skiers. Mike's and the Windsor are other noisy British enclaves. Corrigans, Smokey Joe's and Le Baron are recommended. Bar Brésilien has 'great music and tremendous atmosphere – teeming with Brits and Italians'. The Avalanche is the most popular of the discos. There are quieter places too – the 'cosy' Bleuets is recommended.

The resort has contrived a couple of ways of dining at altitude – you can snowmobile to the glacier and back, eating on the way (you're allowed one glass of wine), or at full moon you can ski or board back to town after dinner (accompanied by ski patrollers).

OFF THE SLOPES
Not recommended

Les Deux-Alpes is not a particularly good choice for people not hitting the slopes. It is quiet during the day, the shopping is uninspiring and the village is rather cut off, with little public transport for excursions. The pretty valley village of Venosc is well worth a visit by gondola, and you can take a scenic helicopter flight to Alpe-d'Huez (though there's even less to amuse you there). For the active there are plenty of sports facilities (including a 'very good pool') and lots of scenic walks. Several of the mountain restaurants are accessible to pedestrians – a good thing, as skiers and boarders will be very reluctant to descend the icy lower slopes to the village for lunch. Snowcat tours across the glacier provide wonderful views.

STAYING DOWN THE VALLEY
Worth considering

Close to the foot of the final ascent to Les Deux-Alpes are two near-ideal places for anyone thinking of travelling around to Alpe-d'Huez, La Grave and Serre-Chevalier, both Logis de France – the cheerful Cassini (0476 800410) at Le Freney, and the even more appealing Panoramique (0476 800625), at Mizoën.

Flaine 1600m

Wonderful ski area; bleak buildings but cute alternatives

WHAT IT COSTS

3

HOW IT RATES

The slopes

Snow	****
Extent	****
Experts	****
Intermediates	*****
Beginners	*****
Convenience	*****
Queues	****
Restaurants	**

The rest

Scenery	****
Resort charm	*
Off-slope	*

What's new

For 2001/02, a new eight-seater gondola – the Grand Massif Express – will take you from Samoëns village to Samoëns 1600 in just eight minutes. This will greatly increase the attraction of Samoëns as a base because the lift into the slopes will no longer be a bus- or car-ride away.

A new high-speed quad from Morillon 1100 will serve the the Bergin run.

There will also be a new footpath between Flaine Forêt and Flaine Forum.

Over the last few years there has been huge investment in new high-speed lifts, including France's first high-speed eight-seater chair from the village at Flaine Forêt to Les Grands Vans for 2000/01.

In the longer term, there may be a new village development by Canadian company Intrawest at Vernant or close to the nearby lake.

- + Big, varied area, with off-piste challenges for experts as well as extensive intermediate terrain
- + Huge recent investment in new lifts
- + Reliable snow in the main bowl
- + Compact, convenient, mainly car-free village, right on the slopes
- + Alternative of staying in traditional villages elsewhere in ski area
- + Excellent facilities for children
- + Scenic setting, and glorious views
- + Very close to Geneva airport

- − Bleak 1960s Bauhaus buildings are architecturally listed – but not to everyone's taste
- − Main Flaine bowl has only a few short runs below the tree line, so bad weather can be a problem
- − Links from one area to another are prone to closure by high winds
- − No proper hotels in Flaine itself – only club hotels and apartments
- − Not much nightlife
- − Little to do off the slopes

So long as you don't care about the uncompromising architecture or narrow range of nightlife, Flaine has a lot going for it. It has slopes that intermediates will love, and lots of them – the area deservedly calls itself the Grand Massif and is the third biggest area of linked slopes in France. It also caters well for beginners, with free access to nursery slope lifts – and the ski school has improved in recent years too. There is also challenging terrain for experts – particularly for those prepared to take guidance and go off-piste. Many visitors, especially those with children, love it.

The hotels have now all become club hotels run by tour operators such as Club Med and Crystal. The only alternative is to rent an apartment. But we increasingly receive reports from satisfied guests who choose to stay in the more traditional outlying villages such as Samoëns, Morillon and Les Carroz. The only problems are that these lower villages may suffer poor snow conditions and that links with the high Flaine bowl may be cut off in bad weather.

The resort 

We have to say we fall in the group that does not find Bauhaus architecture attractive. The concrete massifs that are Flaine's buildings were conceived in the sixties as 'an example of the application of the principle of shadow and light'. They look particularly shocking from the approach road – a mass of blocks nestling at the bottom of the impressive snowy bowl. From the slopes they are less obtrusive, blending into the rocky grey hillside. For us, the outdoor sculptures by Picasso, Vasarely and Dubuffet do little to improve Flaine's austere ambience.

In common with other French Alpine

PHOTOZOOM FLAINE

The scenic grandeur of Flaine's spectacular setting is quite a contrast to its stark Bauhaus architecture →

MOUNTAIN FACTS

Altitude	700m-2480m
Lifts	75
Pistes	260km
Green	12%
Blue	41%
Red	38%
Black	9%
Artificial snow	25%
Recco detectors used	

LIFT PASSES

2001/02 prices in euros

Grand Massif
Covers all the lifts in Flaine, Les Carroz, Morillon, Samoëns and Sixt.

Beginners Four free lifts. Ski pass for beginners covers three more lifts (13 per day for adults, 9 for children aged 5-11, 10 for 12-15-year-olds).

Main pass
1-day pass 30
6-day pass 151

Senior citizens
Over 60: 6-day pass 127
Over 75: free pass

Children
Under 12: 6-day pass 110
Under 5: free pass

Notes Discount on all ski-passes for 12-15-year-olds: 6-day 119.

Alternative passes
Flaine area only (1-day pass 26 for adults, 21 for children)

Short-term passes
A half-day Flaine area only from 11.30 costs 24 for adults, 19 for children aged 12-15 and 17 for those aged 5-11.

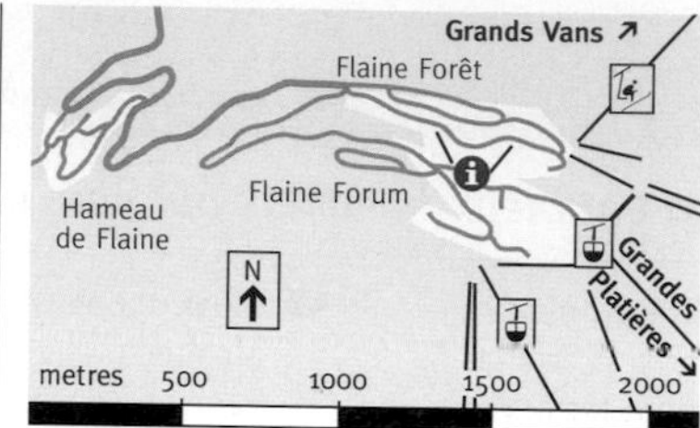

purpose-built resorts, Flaine has improved its looks in recent years. The relatively new development of Hameau-de-Flaine is built in a much more attractive chalet style – but is inconveniently situated a good 15-minute walk or a short bus-ride from the slopes. Fortunately, the regular bus service is 'excellent'.

In Flaine proper, everything is close by: supermarket, sports hire shops, ski schools, main lifts out etc. The resort itself is also easy to get to – only 70km from Geneva, and about 90 minutes from the airport.

There are two parts to the main resort. The club hotels, and some apartments, are set in the lower part, Forum. The focus of this area is a snow-covered square with buildings on three sides, the open fourth side blending with the slopes. Flaine Forêt, up the hillside and linked by lift, has its own bars and shops and most of the apartment accommodation.

There are children all over the place; they are catered for with play areas, and the resort is supposed to be traffic-free. This has become rather lax, in fact, and there is a fair amount of traffic; but the central Forum itself, leading to the pistes, is pretty safe.

There are long-term plans to expand Flaine's bed base significantly. Intrawest (a Canadian company that owns Whistler and other resorts with attractive villages) is now part owner of Flaine so let's hope they bring their flair for attractive development here.

It is possible to visit Chamonix by road, and get to Italy easily when the Mont Blanc tunnel is open.

The mountains

With its 260km of pistes, the Grand Massif claims to be the third largest resort in France (behind the Three Valleys and Espace Killy – the Franco-Swiss Portes du Soleil doesn't count). Certainly it is a genuinely impressive area, with plenty of scope for any standard of skier or boarder, provided you can get to all of it – the greater part of the domain lies outside the main Flaine bowl and there are some fairly low altitude slopes.

THE SLOPES

A big white playground

The day begins for most people at the **Grandes Platières** jumbo gondola, which speeds you in a single stage up the north face of the Flaine bowl to the high-point of the Grand Massif, and a magnificent view of Mont Blanc.

Most of the runs are reds (though there are some blues curling away to the right as you look down the mountain, and one direct black). There are essentially four or five main ways down the barren, treeless, rolling terrain back to Flaine, or to chairs in the middle of the wilderness going back to the summit.

On the far right, the easy 14km, picturesque Cascades blue run (one of the longest in the Alps) leads away from the lift system behind the Tête Pelouse and down to the outskirts of Sixt at 770m (giving a vertical drop of over 1700m). There is no lift back but there is a regular shuttle-bus service to the lifts at Samoëns or Morillon. Sixt has its own little west-facing area offering red and black slopes of 700m vertical – and is now linked to the Cascades run by drag-lift.

On the other side of the Tête Pelouse, a broad cat-walk leads to the experts-only **Gers** bowl. At the bottom, a flat trail links with the Cascades run.

Back at Platières, the alternative is to head left down the long red Méphisto (many of the runs in this

boarding *Flaine suits boarders quite well – there's lots of varied terrain and plenty of off-piste with interesting nooks and crannies, including woods outside the main bowl. The key lifts are all now chairs or gondolas – with few unavoidable drag-lifts. There's a big fun-park (called the JAM Park – standing for Jib and Air Maniacs) just below Les Grands Vans. The ESF runs a special 'Mini surf park' for kids, a great idea for a family-oriented resort like this. BlackSide is the local specialist shop, in the central Forum.*

area have diabolic names – Lucifer, Belzebuth etc) to the **Aujon** area. This opens up another sector of the bowl, again mostly red runs but with some blues further down. The lower slopes here are used as slalom courses. This sector is also reachable by gondola or drag-lifts from below the resort.

The pistes in the Flaine bowl are mostly punchy medium-length runs. For a collection of longer cruises, head out of the bowl via the Grands Vans chair (a new high-speed eight-seater for 2000/01), reached from Forum by means of a slow bucket lift (aka télébenne). From the top, you go over the edge of the bowl and have a choice of three different resorts to head towards, each with its own lifts and runs. Getting around this bowl below Les Grands Vans was made much quicker a couple of years ago by three new high-speed chair-lifts.

The lie of the land is complicated, and the piste map does not represent it clearly. In good snow there is a choice of blues and reds winding down to **Les Carroz** or **Morillon**, the latter with a half-way point at 1100m. While there is a choice of blue, red and black runs on the top section above **Samoëns 1600**, the runs below here to Vercland are testing blacks and reds.

Arrival back in Flaine can cause a problem: some reporters have said that it's difficult to get between the top of the resort and Forum. The trick is to loop round away from the buildings and approach from under the gondola – or catch the bucket down.

This season we have had reports of lifts breaking down too often and being too easily closed because of high winds, cutting off links with the lower villages. The very clear piste signs have, however, been praised.

SNOW RELIABILITY

Usually keeps its whiteness

The main part of Flaine's slopes lie on the wide north- and north-west-facing flank of the Grandes Platières. Its direction, along with a decent height, means that it keeps the snow it receives. There is snowmaking on the greater part of the Aujon sector and on the nursery slopes. The runs towards Samoëns 1600 and Morillon 1100 are north-facing too, and some lower parts have snowmaking, but below here can be tricky or impossible. The Les Carroz runs are west-facing and can suffer from strong afternoon sun, but one of the runs has snowmaking. Recent reports have indicated a marked improvement in grooming.

Les Grandes Platières
2480m
Tête Pelouse
Tête des Lindars
Tête de Véret
2315m
Aujon
2035m
Sixt
…r à Cheval
Gers
1715m
Les Grands
Vans
2205m
Flaine
1600m
Vernant
Tête des Saix
2120m
Les Molliets
Sixt
1900m
1500m
Samoëns Village
720m
Samoëns
1600m
Les Carroz
1140m
Vercland
Morillon
1100m
Morillon
700m

SCHOOLS/GUIDES

2001/02 prices in euros

International

Classes 6 days 3hr per day
6 days 109

Children's classes
Ages: 6 to 12
6 days 86

Private lessons
1hr, 2hr or full day
30 for 1hr, for 1 to 2 people

ESF

2001/02 prices

Classes 6 days for 3hr per day
6 days: 105

Children's classes
Ages: 5 to 12
6 days 80

Private lessons
26 for 1hr, for 1 or 2 people

Flaine Super Ski
Advanced skiers only
0450 908288

Independent instructors
Hired by the day, hour or week; contact Guy Pezet
0450 478454

Phone numbers
From abroad use the prefix +33 and omit the initial '0' of the phone number.

FOR EXPERTS

Great fun with guidance

Flaine's family-friendly reputation tends to obscure the fact that it has some seriously testing terrain. But much of it is off-piste and, although some of Flaine's off-piste runs look like they can safely be explored without guidance, this impression is mistaken. The Flaine bowl is riddled with rock crevasses and potholes, and should be treated with the same caution that you would use on a glacier. There have been some tragic cases of off-piste skiers coming across nasty surprises, including a British skier falling to his death only yards from the piste.

All the black pistes on the map deserve their grading. The Diamant Noir, down the line of the main gondola, is a testing 850m descent, tricky because of moguls, narrowness and other people rather than because of great steepness; the first pitch is the steepest, with spectators applauding from the overhead chair-lift.

To the left of the Diamant Noir as you look down are several short but steep off-piste routes through the crags of the Grandes Platières.

The Lindars Nord chair serves a shorter slope that often has the best snow in the area, and some seriously steep gradients if you look for them.

The Gers drag-lift, outside the main bowl beyond Tête Pelouse, serves great expert-only terrain. The piste going down the right of the drag is a proper black, but by departing from it you can find slopes of up to 45°. To the left of the drag is the impressive main Gers bowl – a great horseshoe of about 550m vertical, powder or moguls top to bottom, all off-piste. You can choose your gradient, from steep to very steep. As you look down the bowl, you can see more adventurous ways into the bowl from the Grands Vans and Tête de Veret lifts.

There are further serious pistes on the top lifts above Samoëns 1600.

Touring is a possibility behind the Grandes Platières, and there are some scenic off-piste routes from which you can be retrieved by helicopter – such as the Combe des Foges, next to Gers.

FOR INTERMEDIATES

Something for everyone

Flaine is ideal for confident intermediates, with a great variety of pistes (and usually the bonus of good snow conditions, at least above Flaine itself). The diabolically named reds that dominate the Flaine bowl are not really as hellish as their names imply – they tend to gain their status from short steep sections rather than overall difficulty, and they're great for improving technique. There are gentler cruises from the top of the mountain – Cristal, taking you to the Perdrix chair, or Serpentine, all the way home. The blues at Aujon are excellent for confidence-building, but the drag serving them is not.

The connections with the slopes outside the main bowl are graded blue but at least one blue-run reporter has found them tricky. Once outside the bowl, all intermediates will enjoy the long tree-lined runs down to Les Carroz, as long as the snow is good. The Morillon slopes are also excellent intermediate terrain.

FOR BEGINNERS

Very good

There are excellent nursery slopes right by the village, served by free lifts which make a pass unnecessary until you are ready to go higher up the mountain. There are no long green runs to progress to in the Flaine bowl – there is one above Morillon – but there are one or two gentle blues (see 'For intermediates').

CROSS-COUNTRY

Very fragmented

The Grand Massif claims 64km of cross-country tracks but only about 10km of that total is around Flaine itself. The majority is on the valley floor and dependent on low snow. There are extensive tracks between Morillon and Les Carroz, with some tough uphill sections. Samoëns 1600 has its own tracks and makes the best base for cross-country enthusiasts.

QUEUES

Few real problems

The massive recent investment in new lifts has eliminated the main trouble-spots. When the resort is full, the Grandes Platières gondola is prone to queues at the start of the day, but it is an efficient lift and the queue moves quickly. Reporters say other queues are usually small, although some of the lifts are still somewhat antiquated, and the area does suffer a weekend influx because of its proximity to Geneva.

One reporter also said queues can be bad when the lifts out of the Flaine

CHILDCARE

Both schools operate ski kindergartens. The ESF's Rabbit Club (0450 908100) takes children aged 3 to 12, until 5pm. The SEI's Green Mouse Club (0450 908441) takes children aged 3 to 12, until 5pm. Club Med Flaine (0450 908166) has a nursery for babies aged from 4 months. The ESF's Rabbit Club will pick up children from Club Med for lessons, and deliver them at the end of the class. There is also an independent nursery, the Petits Loups (0450 908782) for children aged from 6 months to 4 years.

GETTING THERE

Air Geneva, transfer 1½hr.

Rail Cluses (30km); regular bus service.

bowl are shut due to high winds or when the weather is warm and the lower resorts have poor snow.

MOUNTAIN RESTAURANTS
Back to base, or quit the bowl

In the Flaine bowl, there are few restaurants above the resort's upper outskirts. The Blanchot, at the bottom of the Serpentine run, is popular and rustic, with basic food, but it can get very crowded.

At Forum level, across the piste from the gondola, is a pair of chalets containing the welcoming Michet, with very good Savoyard food and table service, and the self-service Eloge – friendly but with very limited food (lasagne and croque monsieurs recommended by one reporter). Up at Forêt level, Chalet Bissac has a good atmosphere, traditional decor and excellent plain food. The nearby Cascade is self-service, with a good terrace. The Chalet L'Epicéa near the end of the Faust piste has a rustic atmosphere, terrace and rave reviews (including 'Greek specialities').

Outside the Flaine bowl, we loved the remote Chalet du Lac de Gers (book in advance and ring for a snowcat to tow you up from part way down the Cascades run) – simple food but splendid isolation and views of the frozen lake. Reporters recommend the Igloo above Morillon, the Chalet des Molliets beside the road up from Les Carroz and the Oreade at the top of the gondola from Les Carroz.

SCHOOLS AND GUIDES
Getting better

The few reports we've had in recent years on the ESF have been mixed. But this season reporters have praised the International school ('took time to assess people ... I would use them again') and the small specialist Super Ski school ('small class sizes, good instruction'). Nouvelle Dimension in Les Carroz and the ESF children's private lessons in Samoëns were both described as 'excellent'.

FACILITIES FOR CHILDREN
Parents' paradise?

Flaine prides itself on being a family resort, and the number of English-speaking children around is a bonus.

Club Med Flaine has good childcare facilities open to residents only. The Petits Loups nursery takes children from 6 months to 4 years. Some other accommodation units have kids' clubs.

Staying there

As a purpose-built resort, Flaine is convenient regardless of where you stay, except in Hameau-de-Flaine.

HOW TO GO
Plenty of apartments

Accommodation is overwhelmingly in self-catering apartments.

Chalets There are few catered chalet options, but they include a couple of attractively traditional Scandinavian-style huts in Hameau. Crystal have taken over the Hotel Totem to run as a club hotel from the 2001/02 season.

Hotels There are no longer any normal hotels in Flaine – you'll have to settle for a tour operator-run club hotel or go to one of the lower, more traditional villages.

Self-catering The best apartments are out at Hameau. In Flaine Forêt, the recently renovated Forêt and Grand Massif apartment buildings are attractively woody inside and there are hotel facilities such as a restaurant, bar and kindergarten.

ACTIVITIES

Indoor Top Form centre (swimming pool complex with sauna, solarium, gymnasium, massage), arts and crafts gallery, cinema, auditorium, concerts, indoor climbing wall, cultural centre with library (some books in English)
Outdoor Natural ice rink, snow-shoe excursions, hang-gliding, paragliding paraskiing, helicopter rides, snow scooters, high mountain outings, ice-driving car circuit

UK Representative

Erna Low Consultants
9 Reece Mews
London SW7 3HE
t 020 7584 2841
f 020 7589 9531
info@ernalow.co.uk
www.ernalow.co.uk

TOURIST OFFICE

Postcode 74300
t +33 450 908001
f 450 908626
flaine@laposte.fr
www.flaine.com

PHOTOZOOM FLAINE

The Flaine bowl seen from the approach road above ↓

EATING OUT
Not many stars

The Perdrix Noire in Forêt is a good bet – smart, busy but friendly. Its bar is also popular. The Michet (see 'Mountain restaurants') is open in the evening. The Trattoria is a good Italian, Chez la Jeanne the best pizza restaurant. Chez Daniel offers a good range of Savoyard specialities, and has also been recommended for lunchtime crêpes and galettes. The Cîmes Rock is 'excellent, but it's best to go early because it gets very busy' (see below).

APRES-SKI
Signs of life

Recent reports suggest that the après-ski scene is picking up. The resort is no longer limited to family groups, and some bars show signs of life.

The White Grouse pub is boisterous: extreme sports videos compete with rock music and punters trying to get pints in before the end of happy hour.

Later, the more French Cîmes Rock is liveliest, with bands or karaoke. The 'seedy' Diamant Noir pool hall is open late, the Chaintre disco later.

OFF THE SLOPES
Curse of the purpose-built

As with most purpose-built resorts, there are few walks, and no town to explore. Not recommended for people who don't want to hit the slopes. But there is a great ice-driving circuit where you can take a spin (literally) in your own car or, more sensibly, have a lesson in theirs (as we did). Snowmobile tours and the weekly torchlight descent are popular, and there's a cinema, gymnasium and swimming pool.

Les Carroz 1140m

This is a spacious, sunny, traditional, family resort where life revolves around the village square with its pavement cafes and interesting little shops. It has a lived-in feel of a real French village, with more animation than Flaine – 'a delight' says a recent visitor, who recommends the 3-star hotel Arbaron (0450 900267) for food, service and views. Also highly recommended is the 2-star Bois de la Char (0450 900618): 'It is perfectly situated beside the piste. The food was good, the staff friendly and it was excellent value for money.'

The gondola and chair-lift go straight into the Grand Massif area, but there's a steep 300m walk up from the centre – the nursery drag is a help.

Apartments make up a high percentage of the beds available.

The ski school's torchlit descent is apparently 'not to be missed' – it starts off with fireworks and ends with vin chaud and live jazz in the square.

Samoëns 720m

This is the only resort in France to be listed as a 'Monument Historique'. Medieval fountains, rustic old buildings, an ancient church – it's all there, although one recent reporter feels that it doesn't add up to a more charming village than Les Contamines, say. Despite the village's recent growth on the outskirts, the traditional-style bars and restaurants still give you a feel for 'real' rural France. A reporter recommends the Pizzeria Louisiana for its wood oven pizzas and 'highly alcoholic' ice creams. Another praises Chalet Fleurie ('five courses – 90 francs given 24 hours' notice') and Chardon Bleu, both a car-ride away in Verchaix.

A new gondola straight from village to the slopes should be open for the 2001/02 season, cutting out the need to take a bus to and from the lift. The local terrain is generally testing and on the whole best suited to confident skiers – though there is a good beginners' area at Samoëns 1600.

Morillon 700m

Not quite in the Samoëns league, but still a pretty rustic village, Morillon makes an excellent base, with an efficient gondola (and a road) up to the mid-mountain mini-resort of Morillon 1100. Up here there is a large and 'delightful' ski kindergarten plus good slopes for adult beginners and brand new apartments right on the piste – it's 'dead as a dodo in the evenings', though, says a reporter.

La Grave 1450m

A superb mountain for good skiers and free-riders

WHAT IT COSTS

3

HOW IT RATES

The slopes

Snow	***
Extent	**
Experts	*****
Intermediates	*
Beginners	*
Convenience	***
Queues	****
Restaurants	**

The rest

Scenery	****
Resort charm	***
Off-slope	*

- ⊕ Legendary off-piste mountain
- ⊕ Usually crowd-free
- ⊕ Usually good snow conditions, with powder higher up
- ⊕ Link to Les Deux-Alpes
- ⊕ Good base for touring nearby resorts

- ⊖ Rather drab, charmless village
- ⊖ Poor weather spells regular lift closures – on average, two days per week
- ⊖ Suitable for experts only, despite some easy slopes at altitude
- ⊖ Nothing to do off the slopes

La Grave enjoys legendary status among experts. It's a quiet old village with around 500 visitor beds and just one serious lift – a small stop–start gondola serving a high, wild and predominantly off-piste mountainside. The result: an exciting, refreshingly crowd-free area. Strictly, you ought to have a guide, but in good weather hundreds of people risk it and go it alone. When the weather shuts the lift, you can head for Alpe-d'Huez, Les Deux-Alpes or Serre-Chevalier.

What's new

La Grave does not change much, and that is half the charm of the place.

THE RESORT

La Grave is an unspoilt mountaineering village set on a steep hillside facing the impressive glaciers of majestic La Meije. It's rather drab, and the busy road through to Briançon doesn't help. But it still has a rustic feel, and prices in the handful of small hotels, food shops and bars are low by resort standards.

The village is small and most accommodation is convenient for the central lift station.

Storms close the slopes on average two days a week – so a car is useful for access to other resorts nearby.

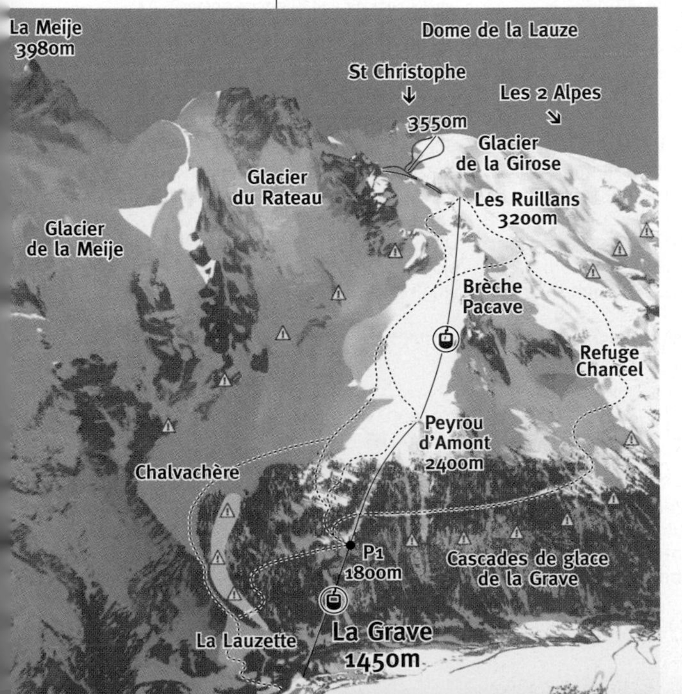

THE MOUNTAIN

A slow two-stage 'pulse' gondola (with an extra station at a pylon halfway up the lower stage) ascends into the slopes and finishes at 3200m. Above that, a short walk and a drag-lift give access to a second drag serving twin blue runs on a glacier slope of about 350m vertical – from here you can ski to Les Deux-Alpes. But the reason that people come here is to explore the legendary slopes back towards La Grave. These slopes offer no defined, patrolled, avalanche-protected pistes – but there are two marked itinéraires (with several variations now indicated on the 'piste' map) of 1400m vertical down to the pylon lift station at 1800m. Top to bottom, the mountain offers a vertical of 2150m.

Slopes The Chancel route is mostly of red-run gradient; the Vallons de la Meije is more testing but not too steep. People do take these routes without a guide or avalanche protection equipment, but we couldn't possibly recommend it.

There are many more demanding runs away from the itinéraires, including couloirs that range from the straightforward to the seriously hazardous, and long descents from the glacier to the valley road below the village, with return by taxi, bus, or strategically parked car. The dangers are considerable, and guidance is

MOUNTAIN FACTS

Altitude	1400m-3550m
Lifts	4
Pistes	5km
Green/Blue	100%

The 'difficulty' figure relates to on-piste; practically all the skiing – at least 90% – is off-piste

Artificial snow	0km

Recco detectors used

Phone numbers
From abroad use the prefix +33 and omit the initial '0' of the phone number.

TOURIST OFFICE

Postcode 05320
t +33 476 799005
f 476 799165
ot.la.meije@wanadoo.fr
www.la.meije.com

essential. You can also descend southwards to St-Christoph, returning by bus and the lifts of Les Deux-Alpes.

Snow reliability The chances of powder snow on the high, north-facing slopes are good, but there are essentially no pistes to fall back on if conditions are tricky. The biggest worry is poor weather keeping the mountain closed for several days at a time.

Experts La Grave's uncrowded off-piste slopes have earnt it cult status among hard-core skiers. Only experts should contemplate a stay here – and then only if prepared to deal with bad weather by sitting tight or struggling over the Col du Lautaret to the woods of Serre-Chevalier.

Intermediates The itinéraires get tracked into a piste-like state, and adventurous intermediates could tackle the Chancel. But the three blue runs at the top of the gondola won't keep anyone occupied for long. The valley stations of Villar d'Arène and Lautaret, around 3km and 8km to the east respectively, and Chazelet, 3km to the north-west, offer very limited slopes with a handful of intermediate and beginner runs.

Beginners Novices tricked into coming here can go up the valley to the beginner slopes at Le Chazelet.

Snowboarding There are no special facilities for boarders, but advanced free-riders will be in their element on the open off-piste powder.

Cross-country There is a total of 30km of loops in the area.

Queues There are short queues only at weekends – at the bottom station first thing, and at the mid-station later.

Mountain restaurants Surprisingly, there are three decent mountain restaurants; the best is the refuge on the Chancel itinéraire (see photo).

Schools and guides There are a dozen or so guides in the village, offering a wide range of services through their bureau.

Facilities for children Babysitting can be arranged through the tourist office.

STAYING THERE

How to go There are several simple hotels.

Hotels The Edelweiss (0476 799093) is a comfortable, friendly 2-star with a cosy bar and restaurant.

Self-catering Self-catering accommodation is bookable through the tourist office.

Eating out Most people eat in their hotels, though there are alternatives.

↑ As well as fabulous views the refuge Chancel does a decent lunch, despite the fact that all ingredients and waste have to be backpacked in and out. Drop in during the morning to find out what's cooking and place your order.

SNOWPIX.COM / CHRIS GILL

Après-ski The standard tea-time après-ski gathering place is the central Glaciers bar, known to habitués as chez Marcel. O'Neill's Irish pub and Le Vieux Guide are busy later. The Candy bar is another option.

Off the slopes Anyone not using the slopes will find La Grave much too small and quiet.

Maurienne valley

Everything from cute old villages to 1960s monstrosities

WHAT IT COSTS

What's new

VALLOIRE

A fast quad from Valmeinier 1800 to Les Inversins was installed for 2000/01. A blue run from Le Grand Plateau – Valloire's highest point – has created an extra link between the two resorts. More snowmaking was also installed, and next season will see more again.

VALFRÉJUS

A new lift pass for Valfréjus, Aussois and La Norma (165km) was introduced last year. More snowmaking is planned for 2001/02.

VAL-CENIS

A new six-pack replaced the Solert drag-lift last season. A new red piste runs from here down to the new Cardinal two-seater chair-lift, which accesses a new blue run. A second snow park was built and snowmaking was extended by 1.5km. A new public swimming pool and ice rink were built in Lanslevillard.

Go to the southern extremity of the Val-Thorens pistes or set off ski-touring northwards from La Grave, and you come to the same place: the Maurienne valley – a great curving trench cut by a river appropriately called the Arc. This backwater has over 20 winter resorts, ranging from pleasant old valley villages to convenience resorts purpose-built in the 1960s. What they have in common is piste and lift networks that are rather limited in size, prices that are low by French resort standards and participation in a special five-day pass deal that allows you to visit a different resort each day. The three resorts covered below are the pick of the crop; the others are in our directory at the back of the book.

Many of these resorts are close enough to be linked – and in the boom years of the 1970s grand plans were formulated to link Valfréjus with Valmeinier and Valloire to the west, and with Bardonecchia in Italy. Valfréjus even painted 'Bardonecchia' on its gondola cabins. But the linking lifts were never built.

A trip to the Maurienne can also include a visit to Europe's highest resort and some of its best snow: Orelle (a non-village in the valley bottom) has a big gondola up to the Val-Thorens lift network.

VALLOIRE 1430m

Valloire is the best known of the Maurienne resorts internationally, and it offers the most extensive slopes, shared with the twin stations of Valmeinier 1500 and 1800. The village has a rustic French feel to it and retains a life as a farming community.

THE RESORT

The resort is quite a drive up from the valley. Despite considerable development, it has retained a feeling of 'real' France, complete with impressive old church, crêperies, fromageries, reasonable prices, villagey atmosphere – including a street market – and friendly locals.

THE MOUNTAIN

The 150km of piste are spread over three similar-sized, sectors, two above Valloire and the third above the separate resort of Valmeinier in the next valley.

Slopes The sectors accessible from Valloire are Sétaz – shady slopes, part open and part wooded, served by gondola to Thimel at mid-mountain – and Crey du Quart – broad, open, west-facing slopes reachable from the village by chair-lift or gondola, or from Sétaz by chair-lift. Black, blue and green runs from Crey du Quart provide links to the two parts of Valmeinier (1500 and 1800) and so to the open west-facing slopes beyond. Each of these sectors is respectable, with top heights in the range 2400m to 2600m and verticals of around 1000m The slopes are almost entirely of intermediate difficulty; Les Karellis (a 45-minute drive) is better for more taxing runs (and for superior snow and scenery). A recent reporter complained about piste map inaccuracies.

Snow reliability Reliable snow-cover is not a strong point. Despite snow-guns on many of the lower slopes, ensuring that most of the area is reliably accessible, some important links – notably the runs down to Valmeinier 1500 from Crey du Quart – can suffer terribly from poor snow. Our recent reporter found these closed in mid-February. The largely north-facing tree runs in the Sétaz area hold their snow well. Grooming is reportedly good.

Snowboarding There's a fun-park with a half-pipe and a boarder-cross course on the Valloire slopes and the extent of the terrain means that there is a fair bit of good free-riding to do. Novices beware: the return from Valmeinier includes some essential drag-lifts.

Experts Sétaz has several black runs, but they don't represent a challenge for experts – the mogul field down to Valmeinier 1500 is steeper.

Intermediates There are plenty of intermediate options in all three sectors. The Crey du Quart section is particularly good for an easy day.

Beginners There are limited village

Phone numbers
From abroad use the prefix +33 and omit the initial '0' of the phone number.

FRANCE

MOUNTAIN FACTS

Valloire/Valmeinier

Altitude	1430m-2595m
Lifts	36
Pistes	150km
Green/Blue	52%
Red	37%
Black	11%
Artificial snow	10km
Recco detectors used	

Valfréjus

Altitude	1550m-2735m
Lifts	12
Pistes	52km
Green/Blue	70%
Red	10%
Black	20%
Artificial snow	none
Recco detectors used	

Val-Cenis

Altitude	1400m-2800m
Lifts	22
Pistes	80km
Green	21%
Blue	23%
Red	42%
Black	14%
Artificial snow	10km
Recco detectors used	

nursery areas but better slopes up the mountain on Sétaz and Crey du Quart.
Cross-country There are 25km of cross-country trails.
Queues There are few bottlenecks given good snow, but they do occur when lower slopes become patchy.
Mountain restaurants Mountain restaurants are in short supply but of good quality. The Thimel and Les Mérégers are recommended, though descending to the village for lunch may be the best option.
Schools and guides The Valloire school has been described as 'excellent', with 'good spoken English'.
Facilities for children The Aiglons nursery takes children from six months to six years.

STAYING THERE

How to go There's a fair choice of hotel and apartment accommodation.
Hotels The 3-star Grand (0479 590095) and 2-star Christiania (0479 590057) are recommended hotels, and both are well placed.
Eating out Most of the restaurants are pizza and fondue joints. The Gastilleur has the best French cuisine in town.
Après-ski Après-ski is fairly quiet but picks up at the weekend. The Irish pub gets 'packed, with great atmosphere'.
Off the slopes There's an ice rink and some walking paths, but not a lot else.

VALFREJUS 1550m

Valfréjus is a small and unusual modern resort – built in the woods, with most of the slopes higher up above the tree line.

THE RESORT

The resort is a compact and quite pleasant affair, built on a narrow, shady shelf, with woods all around. There are several apartment blocks grouped around the main lift station, and chalets dotted around the hillside.

THE MOUNTAIN There are runs of all grades back through the trees towards the village, but the focus of the slopes is Plateau d'Arrondaz, at 2200m, reached by gondola and a slightly lower chair-lift.
Slopes Above Plateau d'Arrondaz are steep, open slopes – genuine bumpy blacks, with excellent snow – on Punta Bagna (2735m), served by the second stage of the gondola, and gentler blue runs from Col d'Arrondaz (2455m). From both the top and the col there are also sunny intermediate runs to Le Pas du Roc on the back side of the hill, with chair-lifts back to both high points or the option of the glorious long away-from-the-lifts blue Jeu run (with off-piste variations and some narrow paths along the way) to the village – almost 1200m vertical.
Snow reliability Snow-cover in the main open area is pretty reliable, but artificial assistance on the lower runs to the village is urgently required.
Snowboarding There's a new natural fun-park and some good off-piste potential. Beginners can get around without having to negotiate any drags.
Experts There is good off-piste sport above the main plateau and heli-skiing over the border in Italy is available.
Intermediates Within the small area, there is something for everyone. Near-beginners might welcome more easy blues, but it would be a good place for a confident intermediate to get in some serious practice on good snow.
Beginners There are nursery slopes at mid-mountain and village level.
Cross-country There is only a small 2km loop up at Plateau d'Arondaz.
Queues A recent visitor reported no real problems though the Pas du Roc chairs are very slow.
Mountain restaurants The 'basic' Punta Bagna, at the top of the gondola, has superb views, and the Bergerie at the mid-station has table-service inside and out.
Schools and guides Tuition is by the ESF and the International school.
Facilities for children The crèche takes babies from three months to three years. Two nurseries take children from three to six.

STAYING THERE

How to go There are three hotels and eight tourist residences in the resort.
Hotels The 2-star Valfréjus (0492 126212) and 2-star Auberge du Charmaix (0479 052728); both are central and have pleasant restaurants.
Eating out The Chic-Choc serves decent Italian food and the Arolle is recommended.
Après-ski Après-ski is limited – the Snow Club, the Bois Brûlé and the Javana are the liveliest bars.
Off the slopes Activities are limited.

↑ Valfréjus has fine challenging slopes above mid-mountain

SNOWPIX.COM / CHRIS GILL

TOURIST OFFICES

Valloire

Postcode 73450
t +33 479 590396
f 479 590966
infos@valloire.net
www.valloire.net

Valmeinier

Postcode 73450
t +33 479 595369
f 479 592005
info@valmeinier.com
www.valmeinier.com

Valfréjus

Postcode 73500
t +33 479 053383
f 479 051367
valfre@club-internet.fr
www.valfrejus.com

Val-Cenis

Postcode 73480
t +33 479 052366
f 479 058217
info@valcenis.com
www.valcenis.com

VAL-CENIS 1400m

Val-Cenis is a marketing concept rather than a place. It comprises two pleasant villages in the Haute Maurienne, the high and remote part of the valley.

THE RESORT

Lanslebourg is a long, linear place, spreading along the Route Nationale 6 (a dead end in winter, when the road over the Col du Mont-Cenis is closed and becomes a piste). It's pleasant enough, but no great beauty. A few km up the valley, and linked by bus, Lanslevillard is more captivating – off the road, randomly arranged, rustic, and split into three.

THE MOUNTAIN

There are lifts up into the north-facing slopes from a number of points along the valley, including Lanslebourg and three points in Lanslevillard. The main one, a gondola, starts between the two villages, on the fringes of Lanslevillard. The lift pass also covers the 35km of slopes in Termignon-la-Vanoise (10 minutes by bus) and allows a free day in one of the other Maurienne resorts.

Slopes Above mid-mountain is a good range of open runs to suit every standard, served by chairs and drags. Below mid-mountain all the runs are prettily wooded – there is usually an easy blue or green alternative to the various red runs back down as well.

Snow reliability Most of the runs are north-facing and there is artificial back-up on the protected tree runs back to each of the base stations.

Snowboarding Beginners should stay in Lanslevillard to avoid some long access drags. There are two fun-parks.

Experts There is ample off-piste but little else to challenge experts. From the top station at 2800m, there is a good, mogulled black down the shady front face and a sunny isolated black over the back to the Col.

Intermediates There are intermediate runs all over the mountain allowing for some top-to-bottom cruises of up to 1400m vertical. A visit to Termignon's mainly easy slopes is highly recommended by 'impressed' reporters, but beware of two 'savage drag-lifts'.

Beginners There are easy runs by the base stations and winding through the forest – including a splendid green following the hairpin road from the Col.

Cross-country There are 6km of free trails locally and a further 80km of trails higher up at Bessans, a few kilometres up the valley.

Queues The new six-pack shifts the queues at the top of the main gondola very efficiently.

Mountain restaurants The rustic La Fema at mid-mountain has been recommended, as has the Mélèzes at the gondola base.

Schools and guides We have no recent reports on the local ESF.

Facilities for children The two village nurseries take kids from six months.

STAYING THERE

How to go There are modest hotels in both villages.

Hotels The best is the 3-star Alpazur (0479 059369). The food is also recommended.

Eating out There is a reasonable range of modest eating-out alternatives with a dozen restaurants in each village. Chez Renée et Dodo, in Lanslebourg, is recommended for local specialities.

Après-ski Après-ski is quiet but there are a couple of discos open till late.

Off the slopes There is not a lot for non-skiers. There's a new leisure centre in Lanslevillard, with a pool, and an artificial ice rink. And there are various walking paths to explore.

Megève 1100m

One of the traditional old winter holiday towns

WHAT IT COSTS

(5)

HOW IT RATES

The slopes

Snow	**
Extent	*****
Experts	**
Intermediates	****
Beginners	***
Convenience	**
Queues	****
Restaurants	*****

The rest

Scenery	***
Resort charm	****
Off-slope	****

- ⊕ Extensive slopes, with miles of easy pistes, ideal for intermediates
- ⊕ Scenic setting, with splendid views
- ⊕ Charming old village centre, with very swanky shopping
- ⊕ Some lovely luxury hotels
- ⊕ Gourmet mountain lunches in attractive surroundings
- ⊕ Excellent cross-country trails, including some at altitude
- ⊕ Different lift pass options cover other worthwhile resorts nearby
- ⊕ Great for weekends – cooperative hotels and close to Geneva
- ⊕ If it snows, deserted mountains
- ⊕ Plenty to do off the slopes

- ⊖ With most of the slopes below 2000m there's a risk of poor snow, especially on runs to the village – although the grassy terrain does not need a thick covering and snowmaking has improved a lot
- ⊖ Three separate mountains, two linked by lift but not by piste and the third not linked at all
- ⊖ Not many challenging pistes – the few blacks are not extreme – but good off-piste potential
- ⊖ Traffic jams and fumes at weekends and peak season

What's new

The resort has appointed fifty local representative ambassadors to provide visitors with information both on the slopes and around the village.

A new magic carpet lift was installed at the Princesse ski kindergarten.

Next season will see the introduction of a new hands-free lift pass system.

Megève is the essence of rustic chic. It has a medieval heart, but it was, in a way, the original purpose-built French ski resort – conceived in the 1920s as a French alternative to Switzerland's St Moritz. And although Courchevel took over as France's most fashionable winter sports resort ages ago, Megève's sumptuous hotels and chalets still attract plenty of 'beautiful people' with fur coats and fat wallets. Happily, you don't need either to enjoy it.

The risk of poor snow still makes us nervous about booking way ahead; but it is certainly true that a few inches of snow is enough to give skiable cover on the grassy slopes. And the list of plus-points above is as long as they come.

The resort

Megève is in a lovely sunny setting and has a beautifully preserved traditional medieval centre, which is pedestrianised and comes complete with open-air ice rink, horse-drawn sleighs, cobbled streets and a fine church. Lots of smart food, clothing, jewellery, and antique and gift shops add to the chic atmosphere.

The main Albertville–Chamonix road bypasses the centre, and there are expensive underground car parks. But the resort's clientele arrives mainly by car and the resulting traffic jams and fumes are a major problem. It's worst at weekends, but can be serious every afternoon in high season.

The clientele are mainly well-heeled French couples and families, who come here as much for an all-round winter holiday and for the people-watching potential as for the slopes themselves. The nightlife is, as you'd expect, smart rather than lively.

A gondola within walking distance of central Megève gives direct access to one of the three mountains,

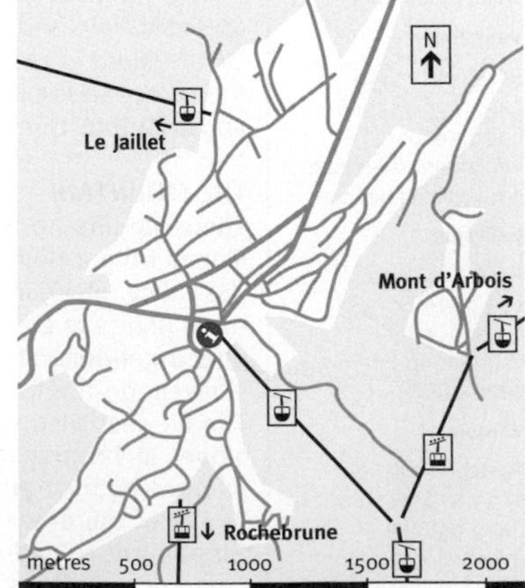

Wherever there's a lift station, there's a restaurant →

MEGEVE TOURIST OFFICE

MOUNTAIN FACTS

Altitude	850m-2355m
Lifts	79
Pistes	300km
Green	17%
Blue	30%
Red	40%
Black	13%
Art. snow	160 acres

Recco detectors used

LIFT PASSES

2000/01 prices in euros

Evasion Mont Blanc
Covers all lifts on Rochebrune, Mont d'Arbois, St-Gervais, Le Bettex, St-Nicolas, Le Jaillet, Combloux, Les Contamines and Bellevue.

Beginners Pay by the ride.

Main pass
1-day pass 29
6-day pass 136
(low season 121)

Senior citizens
Over 60: 6-day pass 121

Children
Under 13: 6-day pass 102
Under 5: free pass

Short-term passes
Half-day pass available in the afternoon.

Alternative passes
Mont Blanc pass covers all lifts in the resorts of the Mont Blanc area (700km of piste and 190 lifts) and the buses between them, plus Courmayeur in Italy 6 days out of 6 (6 days 183 for adults and 128 for children). Jaco pass valid for Le Jaillet, Christomet and Combloux.

Rochebrune. This sector can also be reached directly by a small cable-car from the southern edge of town. The main lifts for the bigger Mont d'Arbois sector start from an elevated suburb of the resort – though there is also a link from Rochebrune. The third sector, Le Jaillet, starts some way out on the north-west fringes of the town.

Staying close to one of the main lifts makes a lot of sense. Some accommodation is a long walk from the lifts and the free bus services are not super-convenient.

The mountains

The three different mountains provide predominantly easy intermediate cruising, much of it prettily set in the woods. But there are tough runs to be found, and large areas of off-piste that are neglected by most visitors. The wooded slopes make it a great resort to head for in poor weather.

There is a variety of different lift passes available, the widest-ranging covering Les Contamines, Les Houches and Chamonix. A car is handy for visiting other resorts included on the various passes.

Plans to create a super ski area linking Megève, St-Gervais, Praz-sur-Arly, Nôtre-Dame-de-Bellecombe, Les Saisies, Flumet, Hauteluce and Crest-Voland, and eventually Les Contamines and Les Houches are under way. The first stage, two new chairs linking Megève and Praz-sur-Arly, should be ready for 2002/03. The whole area, labelled 'Espace Diamant', should cover 600km of pistes, making it one of the largest ski areas in the world.

THE SLOPES
Pretty but low

Two of the three areas of slopes are linked by lift, though not by piste.

The biggest, highest and most varied sector is **Mont d'Arbois,** accessible not only from the town but also by a gondola from La Princesse, way out to the north-east of town. It offers some wooded slopes but is mainly open, especially higher up.

Most of the slopes face more-or-less west, but there are north-east-facing slopes to Le Bettex and on down to St-Gervais. A two-stage gondola returns you to the top, with a mid-station at Le Bettex. You can work your way over to Mont Joux and up to the small Mont Joly area – Megève's highest slopes (2355m). And from there you can descend to the backwater village of St-Nicolas-de-Véroce; chair-lifts bring you back to Mont Joux. Directly behind Mont Joly, further up the same valley

boarding *Boarding doesn't really fit with Megève's traditional, rather staid, upmarket image. But there is a fun-park and a half-pipe on Mont Joux – and free-riders will find lots of untracked off-piste powder for a few days after new snowfalls. It's a good place to try boarding for the first time, with plenty of fairly wide, gentle runs and a lot of chair-lifts and gondolas; though there are a fair number of drag-lifts, they are generally avoidable. Nightlife tends to be rather sophisticated, but there are a few noisy bars as well.*

as St-Nicolas-de-Véroce, is the substantial resort of Les Contamines. You can get to it off-piste and a proper lift-and-piste link is envisaged.

From the Mont d'Arbois lift base, the Rocharbois cable-car goes across the valley to **Rochebrune**. Alpette is the starting point for Megève's historic downhill course. A network of gentle, wooded, north-east-facing slopes, served by drags and chair-lifts, lead across to the high-point of Côte 2000.

The third area, and much the quietest, is **Le Jaillet**, accessed by gondola from just outside the north-west edge of town. From the top of the gondola are predominantly easy, east-facing pistes. The high point is Christomet, served by a long chair-lift. In the other directions, a series of long, tree-lined runs and lifts serves the area above Combloux.

Reporters claim that piste grading is inconsistent and that less advanced skiers should not be too complacent.

SNOW RELIABILITY
The area's main weakness

The problem is that the slopes are low, with very few runs above 2000m, and partly sunny – the Megève side of Mont d'Arbois gets the afternoon sun. So in a poor snow year, or in a warm spell, snow-cover and quality on the lower slopes can suffer badly – in which case you may need to ride the lifts back down.

Fortunately, the grassy slopes don't need much depth of snow, and the resort has made great strides in tackling this weakness, expanding its snowmaking network to 170 snow-guns at the last count. Some runs are now entirely covered, including the long red Olympique run at Rochebrune. There is also a high standard of piste grooming.

FOR EXPERTS
Off-piste is the main attraction

The Mont Joly and Mont Joux sections offer the steepest slopes. The top chair here serves a genuinely black run, and the slightly lower Epaule chair has some steep runs back down and also accesses some good off-piste runs, as well as pistes, down to St-Nicolas.

The steep area beneath the second stage of the Princesse gondola can be a play area of powder runs among the trees. Côte 2000 has a small section of steep runs, including some off-piste.

The black run under the Christomet chair is no longer on the map and, given decent snow, could be a good spot to practise off-piste technique.

FOR INTERMEDIATES
Superb if the snow is good

Good intermediates will enjoy the Mont d'Arbois area best. The black runs below the Princesse gondola are perfectly manageable. The runs served by the Grand Vorasset drag and the most direct route between Mont

Mont Joly 2355m
Cote 2000
Alpette 1870m
Mont Joux 1960m
Altiport
Christom 1855m
Rochebrune 1755m
Praz sur Arly
Mont d'Arbois 1840m
St-Nicolas-de-Véroce 1150m
Le Jaillet 1580m
Megève 1100m
Le Bettex 1380m
1755m
St-Gervais 850m
La Princesse
Combloux

SCHOOLS/GUIDES

2000/01 prices in euros

ESF

Classes 6 days
4hr 9.30-11.30 and 3pm-5pm
6 afternoons 87

Children's classes
Ages: 5 to 12
6 afternoons: 78

Private lessons
Hourly or daily
32 for 1hr, for 1 or 2 people.
All-day classes are available.

International

Classes 5 mornings
2hr 10am-12.30: 108

Children's classes
Ages: 4 to 12
6 mornings: 119

Private lessons
Hourly or daily
1 to 5 people: 1 hr 38

CHILDCARE

There are three kindergartens dotted around the sprawling resort, all offering skiing. Age limits and hours vary. Caboche (0450 589765) at the Caboche gondola station: ages 3 to 10, until 5pm. Meg'Loisirs (0450 587784) is a comprehensive nursery: ages 3 to 6, until 6pm. Princesse (0450 930086), out at the Princesse gondola: ages 2½ to 6, until 6pm.

d'Arbois and Le Bettex are also interesting. Similarly testing are the steepest of the Jaillet sector pistes.

It's a great area for the less confident. A number of comfortable runs lead down to Le Bettex and La Princesse from Mont d'Arbois, while nearby Mont Joux accesses long, problem-free runs to St-Nicolas. Alpette and Côte 2000 are also suitable.

Even the timid can get a great deal of mileage in. All main valley-level lifts have easy routes down to them (although the Milloz piste to the Princesse mid-station is a little steep). There are some particularly good, long, gentle cruises between Mont Joux and Megève via Mont d'Arbois. But in all sectors, you'll find easy, blue runs.

FOR BEGINNERS
Good choice of nursery areas

There are beginner slopes dotted all around at valley level, and more snowsure ones at altitude on each of the main mountains. There are also plenty of very easy longer green runs to progress to.

FOR CROSS-COUNTRY
An excellent area

There are 75km of varied trails spread throughout the area. Some are at altitude (1300m–1550m), making lunchtime meetings with Alpine skiers or walkers simple.

QUEUES
Few weekday problems

Megève is relatively queue-free during the week, except at peak holiday time. But school holidays and sunny Sunday crowds can mean some delays. The Lanchettes drag between Côte 2000 and the rest of the Rochebrune slopes gets oversubscribed – as does the gondola linking the two mountains. Overcrowded pistes at Mont Joux and Mont d'Arbois can also be a problem. Go out in falling snow and you'll have the mountain to yourself.

MOUNTAIN RESTAURANTS
The long lunch lives

Megève is one of the great gourmet lunch destinations. Many of the 30 restaurants have table-service and many of the terraces have magnificent views. Not surprisingly, they can be pricey. Booking ahead is advisable.

The Mont d'Arbois area is particularly well endowed. There are two suave places still owned by the Rothschilds, original promoters of Megève, both popular with poseurs with small dogs and fur coats – the Club House and the Idéal Sports. The Igloo, with wonderful views of Mont Blanc, has both self-service and table-service sections – recent reports of the self-service section are disappointing.

Above St-Nicolas are several little chalets offering great charm and good food at modest prices as well as glorious views.

At the base of the Mont Joux lift, Chez Marie du Rosay is recommended. On the back side of the hill, at Les Communailles, the Alpage was a key factor in one reader's decision to go back to Megève.

At the foot of the Côte 2000 slopes is a former farm, popular for its atmosphere, friendly service and good quality; Radaz, up the slope a little, enjoys better views and is similarly cosy, but the service can be slack.

Alpette, atop the Rochebrune ridge, offers excellent all-round views outside, a comfortable lounge inside.

SCHOOLS AND GUIDES
Adventurous

The two schools offer expeditions to the Vallée Blanche and heli-skiing (in Italy) as well as conventional tuition. The International school appears to be more popular with readers than its rival, the ESF. A recent reporter found the ESF children's classes to be inefficient, with impatient instructors.

FACILITIES FOR CHILDREN
Language problems

A comfortable low-altitude resort like Megève attracts lots of families who can afford day care. The facilities seem impressive – the kindergartens offer a wide range of activities as an alternative to the slopes. Lack of English-speaking staff (and companions) could be a drawback.

↑ It's a low-rise town, but don't count on skiing to the door
MEGEVE TOURIST OFFICE

Phone numbers
From abroad use the prefix +33 and omit the initial '0' of the phone number.

GETTING THERE

Air Geneva, transfer 1hr. Lyon, transfer 2½hr.

Rail Sallanches (13km); regular buses from station.

Staying there

HOW TO GO
Few packages

Relatively few British tour operators go to Megève, but there is an impressive range of accommodation.

Chalets A few UK tour operators offer catered chalets. For a cheap and very cheerful base, you won't do better than Stanford's Sylvana – a creaky, unpretentious old hotel, reachable on skis, now run along chalet lines. Superb food when we visited. This year they are offering another similar property, the Rond Point, in the centre.

Hotels Megève offers a range of exceptionally stylish and welcoming hotels. There are simpler places, too.

((((4 **Mont Blanc** (0450 210202) Megève's traditional leading hotel – elegant and fashionable. Right in the centre, and close to the main gondola.

((((4 **Chalet du Mont d'Arbois** (0450 212503) Prettily decorated, former Rothschild family home, now a Relais & Châteaux hotel in a secluded position above town, near the Mont d'Arbois gondola.

((((4 **Fer à Cheval** (0450 213039) French rustic-chic at its best, with a warmly welcoming wood-and-stone interior and excellent food. Close to the centre.

(((3 **Au Coin du Feu** (0450 210494) 'Very well managed' chalet midway between Rochebrune and Chamois lifts.

(((3 **Grange d'Arly** (0450 587788) Wrong side of the road, but still quite close to the centre and beautifully furnished.

(((3 **Ferme Hôtel Duvillard** (0450 211462) Smartly restored farmhouse, perfectly positioned for the slopes, at the foot of the Mont d'Arbois gondola.

((2 **Gai Soleil** (0450 210070) Comfortable family-run place – five minutes' walk from the centre of town and the main gondola.

((2 **Mourets** (0450 210476) Poor location but repeatedly recommended by readers: 'basic but spacious accommodation with good food and wonderful views'; 'excellent hosts'.

Self-catering There are some very comfortable and well positioned apartments available – not cheap.

EATING OUT
Very French

Megève naturally has lots of high-quality, expensive restaurants – many of which are recommended in the top

ACTIVITIES

Indoor 'Palais des Sports' (climbing wall, swimming pool, sauna, solarium, skating, gym), judo, classical and contemporary dance classes, music lessons, bridge, tennis, bowling, archery, language classes, museum, library, cinemas, pottery, casino, concert and play hall, body-building hall, curling, tennis
Outdoor 50km of cleared paths, snow-shoe excursions, skating rink, riding, sleigh rides, plane and helicopter trips, paragliding, hot-air ballooning, horse-riding, rock-climbing, ice driving, mountaineering

TOURIST OFFICE

Postcode 74120
t +33 450 212728
f 450 930309
megeve@megeve.com
www.megeve.com

restaurant guides. The restaurants in all the best hotels – eg the Fermes de Marie, Chalet du Mont d'Arbois and Mont Blanc – are excellent but extremely expensive. Les Flocons de Sel, although quite pricey, is highly recommended for its quality and service. Michel Gaudin is one of the best in town – with very good-value set menus. The Taverne du Mont d'Arbois is a lovely woody chalet at the foot of the Mont d'Arbois lifts.

Some reporters wish for more variety of cuisine. The Phnom-Penh is one of the few possibilities. Mama Mia is a popular Italian restaurant though recent reports are mixed. The Pallas is recommended for burgers and pizzas.

APRES-SKI
Bit of a gamble?

The only recent reporter who has taken an interest in such things – and who was there in high season – reckons there is a shortage of lively après-ski bars. The Chamois has been recommended. The Puck is an atmospheric locals' bar, while Harry's Bar is an informal British rendezvous, popular for its wide range of beers, a weekly live band, karaoke and satellite TV. The casino, opened a few seasons ago, has more slot machines than blackjack tables. The Club de Jazz (aka Les 5 Rues) is something of an institution – a very popular, if rather expensive, jazz club-cum-cocktail bar, that gets some big-name musicians.

OFF THE SLOPES
Lots to do

There is something for most tastes, with an excellent sports centre, an outdoor ice rink, plenty of outdoor activities and a weekly market. Trips to Annecy and Chamonix are possible. And St-Gervais is worth visiting for a spa treatment. Walks are excellent, with 50km of marked paths, many at altitude. There is a special map of the paths, graded for difficulty. Meeting friends on the slopes for lunch is easy.

STAYING UP THE MOUNTAIN
Several possibilities

As well as mid-mountain Le Bettex (see St-Gervais), there are hotels further up on the slopes, near the summit of Mont d'Arbois. One is the 3-star Igloo (0450 930584), another the 2-star Chez la Tante (0450 213130).

St-Gervais 850m

St-Gervais is a handsome 19th-century spa town set in a narrow river gorge, halfway between Megève and Chamonix, at the entrance to the side-valley leading up to St-Nicolas and Les Contamines. It has direct access to the Mont d'Arbois slopes via a 20-person gondola from just outside the town.

It's a pleasant place to explore, with interesting food shops and cosy bars. Among its diversions are thermal baths and an Olympic skating rink. Prices are noticeably lower than over the hill in Megève. Two hotels convenient for the gondola are the Hostellerie du Nerey (0450 934521), a pleasantly traditional 2-star, and the 3-star Carlina (0450 934110), best in town. At the gondola mid-station is Le Bettex (1380m), a small collection of hotels, private chalets and new apartments, conveniently situated for the runs but with little evening animation.

You can go up on the opposite side of St-Gervais on a rack-and-pinion railway which in 1904 was intended to go all the way to the top of Mont Blanc but actually takes you to the slopes of Les Houches (see Chamonix chapter). Given enough snow, you can descend to St-Gervais off-piste.

Its position makes St-Gervais a good base for touring the different resorts covered by the Mont Blanc regional lift pass.

Other resorts

Praz-sur-Arly and Notre-Dame-de-Bellecombe are much cheaper options for independent car travellers – they are not part of the Megève lift network. Praz (1035m) is a small, quiet place, but has hotels, restaurants, bars, sports club, ski school and ski kindergarten. It has fair-sized slopes of its own, with short, mainly easy, north-facing runs. Notre-Dame (1130m) is further along the road past Praz, a pleasant village with mainly apartment accommodation, simple hotels, and several bars and restaurants. It has its own varied, pretty area.

St-Nicolas-de-Véroce is part of the lift network, and has a handful of simple small hotels.

One reporter spent a very rewarding few days based at the hotel Terminus (0450 936800) in Le Fayet, below St-Gervais, travelling to a different resort each day by coach.

Les Menuires 1850m

Great slopes but horrendous buildings

WHAT IT COSTS

4

HOW IT RATES

The slopes

Snow	****
Extent	*****
Experts	****
Intermediates	*****
Beginners	***
Convenience	*****
Queues	****
Restaurants	***

The rest

Scenery	***
Resort charm	*
Off-slope	*

What's new

For 2001/02, a new high-speed six-person chair-lift will go from the centre of the village to mid-mountain, to be met by another new high-speed six-seater, which will whizz you to Mont de la Chambre and the links with Méribel and Val Thorens. This will eliminate queues for the rickety old gondola that used to be the main way up (the bottom section will still exist but the top section will be demolished).

Over the last few years all new building has been traditional Savoyard chalet-style (stone and wood) and several luxury developments have been built (with swimming pools, saunas etc). The latest for 2001/02 will form the new Hameau des Marmottes at Preyerand in the centre and the Chalets de l'Adonis in the Bruyères area.

The shopping centre in La Croisette will be given a facelift.

- ⊕ Probably the cheapest place to stay in the famously extensive Three Valleys area – biggest in the world
- ⊕ Some great local slopes
- ⊕ Extensive artificial snowmaking
- ⊕ Lots of slope-side accommodation
- ⊕ Trying hard to smarten the place up

- ⊖ Possibly the ugliest resort in the Alps, but gradually improving
- ⊖ Main intermediate and beginner slopes get a lot of sun
- ⊖ No woodland slopes
- ⊖ Nursery slopes are busy as well as overexposed to the sun

Les Menuires is trying hard to lose its reputation as the carbuncle of the Alps (see the What's New section for developments). But, whatever you may think of its appearance, it is certainly the bargain base for the Trois Vallées, with the bonus of immediate access to the excellent, challenging slopes on La Masse, rarely used by visitors from the other valleys.

The resort

The resort is trying hard to lose its reputation as one of the ugliest in the Alps. But there is no getting away from the fact that the buildings that form the original centre of the resort, La Croisette, are simply horrendous – the worst examples of huge buildings being thrown up in the building boom of the 1960s and early 70s. They look particularly vile when approached along the path from the St-Martin and Méribel directions. The main centre has a claustrophobic indoor shopping complex (which we are told is being given a facelift). It is just a shame they cannot tear down the centre and start again. Newer outposts such as Reberty and Les Bruyères are much better. And all new building is now in traditional Savoyard (stone and wood) style and there are some luxury developments. The new outposts have their own shops and bars. Some pleasant bar and restaurant terraces face the slopes.

Three Valleys lift passes for six days or more also give you a day in Val-d'Isère/Tignes, La Plagne or Les Arcs.

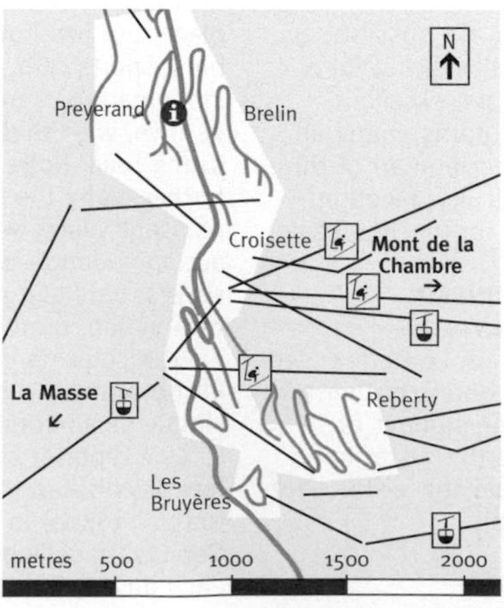

The mountains

Les Menuires has two main attractions: La Masse, a challenging and neglected mountain; and the swift links to the rest of the Trois Vallées.

THE SLOPES

A good base for the Trois Vallées

Les Menuires and St-Martin-de-Belleville share a local area with 160km of runs and 43 lifts. The west-facing slopes have the vast bulk of the runs. The two new high-speed six-packs for 2001/02 will take you up from La Croisette to **Mont de la Chambre**, from where you can head back south to Val-Thorens or east over the ridge to the Méribel slopes. Chairs and drags serve the local slopes, and you can head north to the old village of St-Martin.

The north-east-facing slopes of **La Masse** (2805m) usually have excellent snow on the top half and are served by a two-stage high-capacity gondola.

SNOW RELIABILITY

Cover guaranteed but not quality

La Masse's height and orientation ensure good snow for a long season. The opposite, west-facing slopes are supplied with abundant artificial snow (the resort boasts 323 snow-guns). But

MOUNTAIN FACTS

for the Three Valleys

Altitude 1300m-3200m	
Lifts	200
Pistes	600km
Green	17%
Blue	34%
Red	37%
Black	12%
Artificial snow	90km
Recco detectors used	

LIFT PASSES

2001/02 prices in euros

Three Valleys
See Méribel chapter.

Alternative passes
Vallée des Belleville pass covers 72 lifts and 300km piste in Val-Thorens, Les Menuires and St-Martin (adult 6-day 170). Les Menuires and St-Martin pass covers 43 lifts and 160km of piste (adult 6-day 147).

SCHOOLS/GUIDES

2001/02 prices in euros

ESF
Classes 6 half days: adult: from 95
Children's classes
Ages: up to 12
6 half days: from 86
Private lessons
Hourly 33 for 1 or 2 people

boarding *Les Menuires gets a fair number of boarding visitors – not surprising since it gives relatively economical access to such a huge area of terrain. There is plenty here for every style of rider. Lots of chairs and gondolas in the massive lift system make for comfortable travel, but be warned – there are some flattish sections of piste to negotiate in places. And we'd certainly recommend beginners to go somewhere with more secluded nursery slopes and better snow. There's a fun-park with a half-pipe just above the main village.*

although cover there is guaranteed – so long as the weather is cold enough to make snow – the snow lower down is often icy or slushy.

FOR EXPERTS
Hidden treasures

La Masse has some of the steepest and quietest pistes in the Trois Vallées – most people doing the 'circuit' skip it. Long reds and a black come down beneath the top stage of the gondola. Other steep blacks, usually mogulled, are the Dame Blanche and Lac Noir.

From the top there are also some marvellously scenic off-piste runs, some sporadically marked as itinéraires, others requiring guidance. The wide, sweeping, but not too steep, Vallon du Lou goes towards Val-Thorens. Others go in the opposite direction to various villages from which you need transport back, but the Les Yvoses run takes you back to the lifts.

There's easy access to the rest of the Trois Vallées: within an hour of your door are the steepest slopes of Méribel or Val-Thorens. Courchevel doesn't take much longer.

FOR INTERMEDIATES
600km of pistes to choose from

With good snow, you may find little reason for leaving the local slopes, which are virtually all blue and red. But because most slopes face west, the snow is often better elsewhere in the Trois Vallées. This is paradise for intermediates who like to travel. You can approach Méribel from five different peaks on the ridge. Even a second- or third-timer should have no problem cruising from valley to valley. In poor snow conditions the attractions of Val-Thorens become evident, and there's blue as well as red-run access.

FOR BEGINNERS
Try elsewhere

Although there are wide and gentle slopes for beginners and a special beginner's lift pass, we think you'd be better off in a resort that has more of a real Alpine atmosphere and is easier on the eye. While others can get away from Les Menuires into beautiful Alpine scenery, beginners are stuck with it. The snow quality on the nursery slopes is a worry, and the blue slopes above the resort can get extremely crowded.

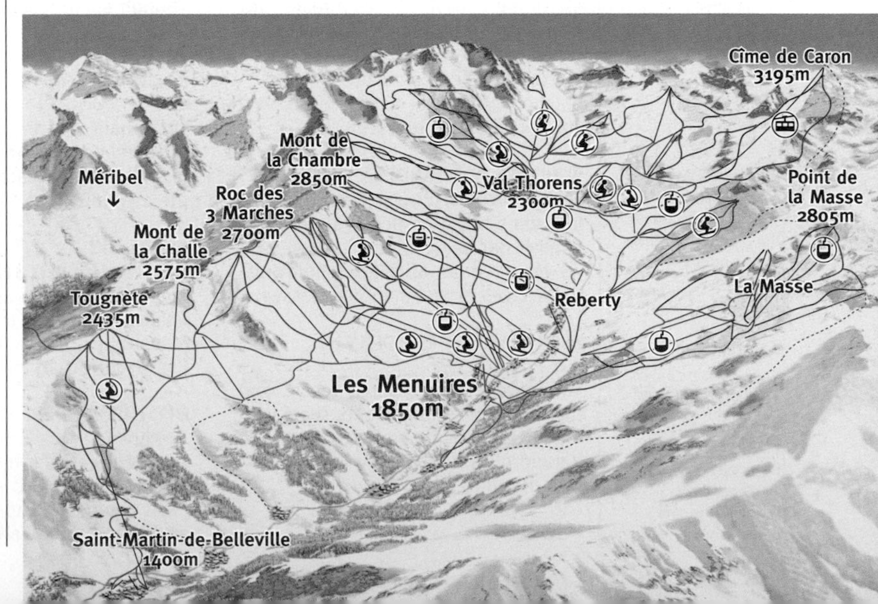

CHILDCARE

The ESF-run Village des Schtroumpfs (0479 006379) takes children aged 3 months to 12 years. It has a nursery for babies, a Baby Club for toddlers and a leisure centre for older children, with activities and ski lessons for children aged 2½ or more.

At Reberty-les-Bruyères, the Marmottons offers similar facilities, but no nursery.

GETTING THERE

Air Geneva, transfer 3½hr. Lyon, transfer 3½hr. Chambéry, transfer 2½hr.

Rail Moûtiers (27km); regular buses from station.

ACTIVITIES

Indoor Library, cinema, fitness centres, sauna
Outdoor Two outdoor heated swimming pools, microlight flights, hang-gliding, guided walks, snow-scooters, artificial skating rink, snow-shoe excursions, paragliding, guided tours, tubing.

Phone numbers
From abroad use the prefix +33 and omit the initial '0' of the phone number.

TOURIST OFFICE

Postcode 73440
t +33 479 007300
f 479 007506
lesmenuires@lesmenuires.com
www.lesmenuires.com

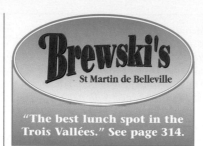

FOR CROSS-COUNTRY
Valley hike
There are 28km of prepared trails along the valley floor between St-Martin and halfway between Les Menuires and Val-Thorens.

QUEUES
Big bottleneck goes
There could be big queues for the old gondola to Mont de la Chambre from La Croisette, especially when it broke down. The new high-speed six-packs for 2000/01 will eliminate that problem. There are few other local queues.

MOUNTAIN RESTAURANTS
A surprisingly atmospheric place
L'Etoile on the left of the main piste as you go down to La Croisette is one of the nicest stops in the Trois Vallées – a rustic old hut with smart terrace and good food served by waiters in berets and traditional dress. The restaurant at the top of the first stage of the La Masse gondola is fairly pleasant. But a lot of people prefer to head for the restaurants of the old village of St-Martin-de-Belleville – Les Airelles and Brewski's are recommended by reporters. The Bouitte, in nearby St-Marcel, is a serious restaurant. It's reachable off-piste, and they'll drive you to the lifts after lunch.

SCHOOLS AND GUIDES
Overcome language barrier
Reports tend to be positive, despite English not being widely spoken, and we have reports of children enjoying themselves in multinational classes.

FACILITIES FOR CHILDREN
All-embracing
This is very much a family resort, and the childcare arrangements seem well organised. The general view is that it is a good place for children to be introduced to the snow.

Staying there 

Despite the fact that the resort is designed for convenient access to the slopes, you may wish to think about location. The central area around La Croisette is best for shops and après-ski. But the 'village' has several more attractive parts with fewer facilities, such as Reberty and Les Bruyères, and overall is well over 1km in length.

HOW TO GO
Budget packages
Some big UK tour operators have a fair selection of hotels and apartments. We know of no catered chalets. There is a Club Med above Reberty.
Hotels None of the hotels are above 3-star grading.
((③ **Ours Blanc** (0479 006166) Best in town: a wood-clad, chalet-style 3-star on the slopes above Reberty 1850.
((③ **Latitudes** (0479 007510) 3-star on the lower fringe of Les Bruyères.
(② **Menuire** (0479 006033) Neat, well equipped place on southern fringe of the resort; but we have had some negative reports.
Self-catering The older apartments are cheap and small. But the newer ones are more attractive, spacious and luxurious. The Montagnettes and Alpages, both in Reberty, are among the best, the latter being an MGM development with a pool.

EATING OUT
Good authentic French cuisine
Though some restaurants lack atmosphere, there's no shortage of good food, including Savoyard specialities. Alternatives include Italian and Tex-Mex. The restaurant in the Ours Blanc and the rustic Ruade are recommended by reporters. L'Etoile (see Mountain Restaurants) is open in the evenings too.

APRES-SKI
Improving but still very limited
There isn't a huge après-ski scene. The Challenge bar has live music and La Mousse is popular. The Liberty and Passeport discos pick up later on.

OFF THE SLOPES
Forget it
Les Menuires is a resort for keen piste-bashers wanting to explore the world's most extensive slopes, though there are some pretty walks.

Méribel 1400m-1700m

The best-looking base for the wonderful Three Valleys

WHAT IT COSTS

6

HOW IT RATES

The slopes

Snow	****
Extent	*****
Experts	****
Intermediates	*****
Beginners	***
Convenience	***
Queues	****
Restaurants	****

The rest

Scenery	***
Resort charm	***
Off-slope	***

What's new

For 2001/02, one of the few remaining bottlenecks in the Three Valleys will be sorted. The slow old Plan des Mains chair, from the bottom of Mont Vallon up to the Plattières gondola will be replaced by a high-speed six-seater chair. This chair is essential for those headed for Méribel and Courchevel from Mont Vallon or Val Thorens, who want to avoid the skate or pole along the alternative flat path to Mottaret.

The last couple of years has seen new eight- and six-seater high-speed chair-lifts in the Altiport area.

For 2000/01, a drag-lift was installed in the floodlit Corbey slalom stadium. The snowpark at Arpasson was extended.

- ⊕ In the centre of the biggest linked piste network in the world – ideal for intermediates who love covering the miles, but plenty for experts, too
- ⊕ Modern, constantly improved lift system means little queueing and rapid access to all slopes
- ⊕ Good piste grooming and snowmaking
- ⊕ Village purpose-built in pleasing chalet-style architecture

- ⊖ Not the best snow in the Three Valleys, and pistes can get busy
- ⊖ Main village spread out, straggling along a long, winding road, with much of the accommodation well away from the slopes
- ⊖ Expensive
- ⊖ Méribel–Mottaret and Méribel Village satellites are rather lifeless
- ⊖ Not the place to go for real French atmosphere – too many Brits

For keen piste-bashers who dislike tacky purpose-built resorts, Méribel is difficult to beat. It is slap in the middle of the Three Valleys – the biggest interlinked winter sports area in the world. With 200 lifts and 600km of pistes, and endless off-piste possibilities, it is difficult to be bored in a fortnight here. The orientation of Méribel's local slopes mean its snow is often not as good as in Courchevel and Val-Thorens. But its Mont Vallon area keeps its snow well and it is quick and easy to get to every part of the Three Valleys.

Méribel is built entirely in tasteful chalet-style, with wood-cladding everywhere. And the centre is very pleasant with raised walkways by the shops above the one-way road. The village has grown rapidly in recent years – at least partly because of its popularity on the British market. Chalets (many of them luxurious) have been built further and further from the pistes and many tour operators run mini-buses to and from the slopes. English is more commonly heard than French on the slopes and in the bars (many of which are British run). It remains decidedly up-market and it's not cheap. We've recently had complaints from new visitors of 'hooray Henry Brits' and pistes so crowded that they are for 'fans of the M25'. But regular visitors love it and wouldn't be seen anywhere else. And we still have a soft spot for it (one of us learned to ski here).

SNOWPIX.COM / CHRIS GILL

Méribel now spreads right along the mountainside, well away from its original centre (near the right of this pic) →

The resort

Méribel occupies the central valley of the Three Valleys system and consists of two main resort villages.

The original resort of Méribel-les-Allues (now simply known as Méribel) is built on a single steepish west-facing hillside with the home piste running down beside it to the main lift stations at the valley bottom. All the buildings are wood-clad, low-rise and chalet style, making this one of the most tastefully designed of French purpose-built resorts. A road winds up from the village centre at about 1400m to the Rond Point des Pistes at about 1650m, and goes on through woods to the outpost of the altiport (an airport with snow-covered runway for little planes with skis) at around 1700m.

The resort was founded by a Brit, Peter Lindsay, in 1938, and has retained a strong British presence ever since. It has grown enormously over recent years, and although some accommodation is right on the piste, much of the newer building is more than a walk away. One clear exception is Belvédère, an upmarket enclave built on the opposite side of the home piste (there's a tunnel for road access). There are collections of shops and restaurants at a couple of points on the road through the resort – Altitude 1600 and Plateau de Morel. The hotels and apartments of Altiport enjoy splendid isolation in the woods, and are convenient for some of the slopes.

The satellite village of Méribel-Mottaret was developed in the early 1970s. The original development was beside the piste on the east-facing slope, but in recent years the resort has spread up the opposite hillside and further up the valley. Both sides are served by lifts for pedestrians – but the gondola up to the original village

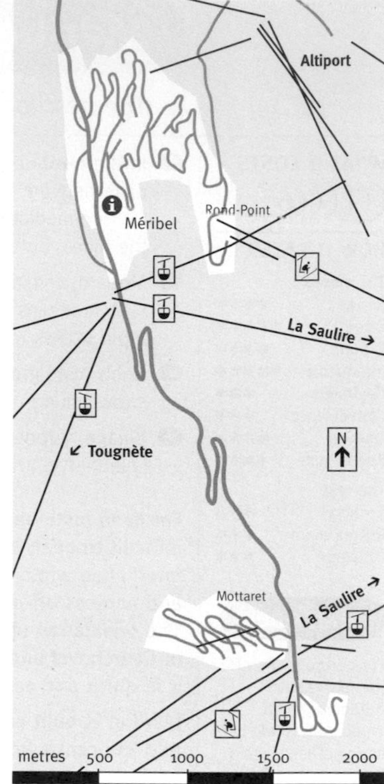

stops at 7.30 and it's a long, tiring walk up. Mottaret looks modern, despite wood-cladding on its apartment blocks. Even so, it's more attractive than many other resorts built for slope-side convenience. It has many fewer shops and bars and much less après-ski than Méribel, but reporters have found it makes a pleasant change, and enjoyed the convenience.

For the Olympics, a new gondola was built from Brides-les-Bains, an old spa town way down in the valley, which served as the Olympic Village for the games, up to Méribel. There's a mid-station at the old village of Les

MOUNTAIN FACTS

for the Three Valleys

Altitude	1300m-3200m
Lifts	200
Pistes	600km
Green	17%
Blue	34%
Red	37%
Black	12%
Artificial snow	90km
Recco detectors used	

Allues. Méribel-Village is a new development between Méribel and La Tania, with a chair-lift up to Altiport. There are some luxury chalets and apartments here but little else – no bars or restaurants in 2000/01.

The mountains

It's keen piste-bashers who will get the best out of what Méribel has to offer. There's endless cruising to be had, as well as challenging terrain. The lift system is generally very efficient and is planned to cut out walks and climbs. Piste grading is not always reliable, however – reporters found 'some blues more difficult than some reds'.

To appreciate the merits of the whole Three Valleys region you'll need to read the entries for Courchevel, Les Menuires and Val-Thorens, too. Lift passes for six days or more also give you a day in Val-d'Isère–Tignes (an hour and a half away), La Plagne or Les Arcs (an hour or so away).

THE SLOPES

Highly efficient lift system

The Méribel valley runs north–south. On the eastern side, gondolas leave both Méribel and Mottaret for **La Saulire** at around 2700m. From here you can head back down towards either village or down the other side of the ridge towards Courchevel.

From Méribel a gondola rises to **Tougnète**, on the western side of the valley, from where you can get down to Les Menuires or St-Martin-de-Belleville. You can also head for Mottaret from here. From there, a fast chair then a drag take you to another entry point for the Les Menuires runs.

The Mottaret area has seen rapid mechanisation over the last decade. The **Plattières** gondola rises up the valley to the south, ending at yet another entry point to the Les Menuires area. To the east of this is the big stand-up gondola to the top of **Mont Vallon** at nearly 3000m. There are wonderful views from the top. A fast quad from near this area goes south up to **Mont de la Chambre**, giving direct access to Val-Thorens.

SNOW RELIABILITY

Not the best in the Three Valleys

Méribel's slopes aren't the highest in the Three Valleys, and they mainly face east or west, getting the full force of the morning or afternoon sun. So snow conditions are often better elsewhere. And grooming seems to be rather better in neighbouring Courchevel.

The lower runs now have substantial snowmaking and lack of snow is rarely a problem, but ice or slush at the end of the day can be. The west-facing La Saulire side gets the afternoon sun, and conditions deteriorate here first – but then you can always go over to Courchevel. The north-west-facing slopes above Altiport generally have decent snow.

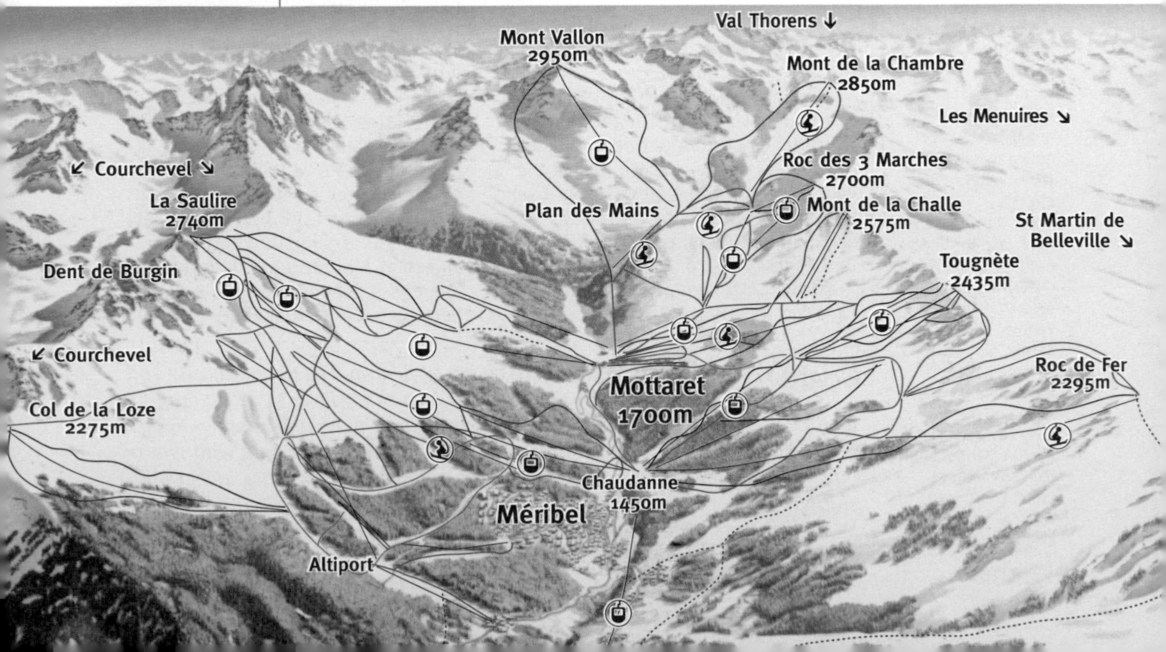

LIFT PASSES

2001/02 prices in euros

Three Valleys
Covers all lifts in Courchevel, La Tania, Méribel, Val-Thorens, Les Menuires and St-Martin-de-Belleville.

Beginners Two free lifts in Méribel-Mottaret and two in Méribel; reduced price lift pass with beginners' lessons.

Main pass
1-day pass 37
6-day pass 182

Senior citizens
Over 60: 6-day pass 146
Over 70: 6-day pass 91
Over 75: free pass

Children
Under 17: 6-day pass 137
Under 10: 118
Under 5: free pass

Short-term passes
Half-day passes (from 12.30) available for Vallée de Méribel (adult 23), Méribel Alpina (adult 20) and Three Valleys (adult 28).

Notes 6-day pass and over valid for one day each in Tignes-Val-d'Isère, La Plagne-Les Arcs, Pralognan-la-Vanoise and Les Saisies. Reductions for families.

Alternative passes
Vallée de Méribel pass covers 150km of runs in Méribel and Méribel-Mottaret (adult 6-day 148). One day Three Valleys extension 17).

At the southern end of the valley, towards Les Menuires and Val-Thorens, a lot of runs are north-facing and keep their snow well, as do the runs on Mont Vallon.

FOR EXPERTS
Exciting choices

The size of the Three Valleys means experts are well catered for. In the Méribel valley, head for Mont Vallon. The long, steep, Combe du Vallon run here is graded red; it's a wonderful long fast cruise when groomed, but presents plenty of challenge when mogulled. And there's a beautiful itinéraire (not marked on the piste map) in the next valley to the main pistes, leading back to the bottom of the gondola.

The slopes down from the top of the Val-Thorens sector were all off-piste when we old hands first visited Méribel. Since the new lifts were installed up here, there are two pistes back from Val-Thorens, but still plenty of opportunity for getting off-piste in the wide open bowls.

A good mogul run is down the side of the double Roc de Tougne drag-lift which leads up to Mont de la Challe. And there is a steep black run all the way down the Tougnète gondola back to Méribel. Apart from a shallow section near the mid-station, it's unrelenting most of the way.

At the north end of the valley the Face run was built for the women's downhill in the 1992 Olympics. Served by a fast quad, it's a splendid cruise when freshly groomed, and you can terrify yourself just by imagining what it must be like to go straight down.

Nothing on the Saulire side is as steep or as demanding as on the other side of the valley. The Mauduit red run used to be black, however.

Throughout the area there are good off-piste opportunities. The ESF runs excellent-value guided groups.

FOR INTERMEDIATES
Paradise found

Méribel and the rest of the Three Valleys is a paradise for intermediates; there are few other resorts where a keen piste-basher can cover so many miles so easily. Virtually every slope in the region has a good intermediate run down it, and to describe them would take a book in itself.

For less adventurous intermediates, the run from the second station of the Plattières gondola back to Mottaret is ideal, and used a lot by the ski school. It is a gentle, north-facing, cruising run and is generally in good condition.

Even early intermediates should find the runs over into the other valleys well within their capabilities, opening up further vast amounts of intermediate runs. Go to Courchevel or Val-Thorens for the better snow.

Virtually all the pistes on both sides of the Méribel valley will suit more advanced intermediates. Most of the reds are on the difficult side.

FOR BEGINNERS
Not ideal

Méribel isn't ideal for beginners. The resort lacks good nursery slopes set apart from the main areas. There is a small one at Rond Point, mainly used by the children's ski school.

The best area for beginners is at Altiport, accessible direct from the village at Altitude 1600 by chair-lift. There is a gentle out-of-the-way area here that can be treated as a nursery

boarding *Méribel is increasingly boarder-oriented. The terrain locally and further afield has lots to offer, you rarely have to take a drag-lift, and there's one fun-park with half-pipe, two quarter-pipes and boarder-cross below the second stage of the Plattières gondola, and another park with quarter-pipe and trick course near the Arpasson drag above the Tougnète gondola mid-station. The resort hosts a number of big-air and boarder-cross competitions. Specialist shops include Board Brains, Exodus and the Quiksilver snowboard shop, and you're bound to feel at home in at least one of the lively bars.*

slope. And you can progress to one of the best and most attractively situated green pistes we know, the Blanchot – long, gentle, wide and tree-lined, with little through-traffic.

FOR CROSS-COUNTRY
Scenic routes
The main area is in the woods near Altiport. There is about 17km of prepared track here, a pleasant introduction to those who want to try cross-country for the first time. There's also a loop around Lake Tueda, in the nature reserve, and for the more experienced an 8km itinéraire from Altiport to Courchevel.

QUEUES
Easily avoided
Huge lift investment over the years has paid off in making the area virtually queue-free most of the time, despite the huge numbers of people. The last big bottleneck at Plan des Mains will be eliminated for 2001/02 – see What's new. The excellent lift network means that if you do find a queue, there is usually an alternative quieter route you can take. The Plattières gondola at Mottaret can get crowded at ski school time, when the schools gets priority – take the alternative Combes high-speed chair.

MOUNTAIN RESTAURANTS
Lots of choice but not cheap
There is lots of choice, but most places get very busy. You might want to take lunch early or late. The self-service Pierres Plates, at the top of the Saulire gondolas, has magnificent views, but the food and atmosphere are nothing special. Chardonnet, at the mid-station of the Mottaret gondola, has table-service and excellent food but is expensive. Rhododendrons, at the top of the Altiport drag, has a modern but atmospheric wooden dining room and

SNOWPIX.COM / CHRIS GILL

From the Tougnète slopes on the far side of the Méribel valley you can go down to the village, to Mottaret, to St-Martin or to Les Menuires ↓

↑ The north-facing slopes above Altiport (see runway at top left of pic) keep their snow well

SNOWPIX.COM / CHRIS GILL

SCHOOLS/GUIDES

2001/02 prices in euros

ESF
in Méribel and Méribel-Mottaret
Classes Adults
6 full days: 195
Children's classes
Ages: 5 to 13
6 full days: 156
Private lessons
1½hr from 47 for 1 or 2 people, 58 for 3 or 4 people
International section
In Méribel and Méribel-Mottaret
Classes Adults
6 mornings of 2½hr: 120
Children's classes
Ages: 5 to 13
6 mornings of 2½hr: 110

New Generation
2000/01 prices in sterling
Classes 10 hr £90
Freeride clinic
7½hr £90
Check Up clinic
4hr £50
Private lessons
2hr £75 for 1 or 2 people, £15 per additional person

'reasonable, plentiful food'. The Altiport hotel has a great outdoor buffet in good weather and the 'best tarts in town' but, again, is expensive. Les Crêtes, below the top of the Tougnète gondola, is a cosy family-run hut with a terrace, has good service and is one of smallest mountain restaurants in the Three Valleys. La Sitelle, above the first section of the Plattières gondola, has decent self-service food and magnificent views towards Mont Vallon. Les Castors, at the main Méribel lift station, scarcely counts as a mountain restaurant, but earns praise for good, affordable food including 'exquisite' carbonara.

SCHOOLS AND GUIDES
No shortage of instructors

The main schools all have English-speaking instructors.

The ESF is by far the biggest, with over 300 instructors. It has a special international section with instructors speaking good English. Recent reports have been mixed, but we've heard tales of instructors behaving more like guides, and abilities being too mixed within a class. One reporter said the instructor was 'rude, arrogant and unhelpful' and gave 'poor tuition'.

The ESF offers useful alternatives to standard classes, such as off-piste groups, heli-skiing on the French/Italian border and 'Ski Discovery' tours of the Three Valleys.

Magic in Motion used to get rave reviews. 'Classes small, English spoken well, we were all pleased with our progress', was typical. But this year we received mixed reviews. One reporter said she and the rest of the group found their instructor very difficult to understand, resulting in him guiding more than instructing; while another claims their beginner group was abandoned at the altiport as the instructor rushed off to his next class.

For 2001/02 New Generation school (which uses only top British instructors and has built up an excellent reputation in Courchevel) is starting a Méribel operation – see the Courchevel chapter for readers' reports and the advert opposite for advance booking details.

FACILITIES FOR CHILDREN
Lots of choice

Despite our fat file of reports on Méribel, none deals first-hand with the resort's childcare facilities. Several chalet operators, like Meriski and Crystal, run their own crèches.

CHILDCARE

The ESF runs P'tits Loups kindergartens at both Méribel and Méribel-Mottaret, with snow-gardens (lifts, inflatable characters etc) for children aged 3 to 5. Open 9am to 5pm.

Les Saturnins in the Olympic Centre building in Méribel takes children aged 18 months to 3 years, offering indoor games and handicrafts, sledging and other outdoor activities.

GETTING THERE

Air Geneva, transfer 3½hr. Lyon, transfer 3½hr. Chambéry, transfer 2½hr.

Rail Moûtiers (18km); regular buses to Méribel.

Staying there

Pick where you stay with care. For easy access to the piste, Mottaret is hard to beat. For those who prefer chalets and a villagey ambience, the best place is around or just above the village centre of Méribel. Check how far you will be from the piste – lots of places are a long hike up. You can hire a ski locker near the main lifts. Local buses are free (though some readers complain they are inadequate), and many UK tour operators run their own minibus services to and from the lifts.

HOW TO GO

Huge choice but few bargains

Package holidays are easy to find, both with big UK tour operators and smaller Méribel specialists. There is a Club Med at Rond-Point.

Chalets Méribel has more chalets dedicated to the British market than any other resort and over 50 operators offering them. What really distinguishes Méribel is the range of luxurious chalets, with drivers who whisk you to and from the slopes. Méribel specialist Meriski has 16 luxury chalets, some among our own favourites. Scott Dunn Ski has four individually designed, spacious chalets full of creature comforts. If money is no object, try one of The Ski Company's four luxury chalets (two of which share an outdoor pool and hot tub) or Descent International's Brames (which you have to take over as one group of up to 20 at a cost of around £30,000 a week).

Of the few chalet-hotels, Mark Warner's Bellevue is handy for the Morel lift and 'adults only' outside school holidays. They also have the Tarentaise in Mottaret. Ski Olympic has the Parc Alpin at Méribel 1600.

Hotels Méribel has some excellent hotels, but they're not cheap.

((((5) **Antares** (0479 232823) Best in town; beside the piste at Belvedere. Ambitious cooking. Pool, fitness, etc.

((((5) **Chalet** (0479 232823) Luxurious, beautifully furnished wooden chalet at Belvedere, with lovely rooms and all mod cons – outdoor pool, fitness, etc.

(((4) **Grand Coeur** (0479 086003) Our favourite almost-affordable hotel in Méribel. Just above the village centre. Welcoming, mature building with plush lounge. Magnificent food. Huge hot-tub, sauna, etc.

Phone numbers
From abroad use the prefix +33 and omit the initial '0' of the phone number.

(4) **Altiport** (0479 085754) Modern and luxurious hotel, isolated at the foot of the Altiport lifts. Convenient for Courchevel, not for Val-Thorens.
(4) **Mont Vallon** (0479 004400) The best hotel at Mottaret; good food, and excellently situated for the Three Valleys pistes. Pool, sauna, hot-tub, squash, fitness room, etc.
(4) **Chaudanne** (0479 086176) One of the oldest Méribel hotels, renovated a few years ago, with a sports centre. But a recent reporter says it has 'tiny rooms, tacky decor and arrogant staff'.
(3) **Adray Télébar** (0479 086026) Welcoming piste-side chalet with pretty, rustic rooms, good food and popular sun terrace.
(2) **Roc** (0479 086416) A good value B&B hotel, in the centre, with a bar-restaurant and crêperie below.
Self-catering There is a huge number of apartments and chalets to let in both Méribel and Mottaret. Make sure that the place you book is conveniently situated and has enough space.

EATING OUT
Fair choice

There is a reasonable selection of restaurants, from ambitious French cuisine to relatively cheap pizza and pasta. For the best food in town, in plush surroundings, there are top hotels – Cassiopée in the Antares, Grand Coeur ('so pleased, we ate there several times'), Allodis and Chaudanne. Other recommendations include: Chez Kiki – 'good food and atmosphere'; Jardin d'Hiver – 'great char grills'; Les Castors – 'best French fare'; La Taverne – 'surprisingly good'; the Tremplin – 'friendly service, booking essential, reasonably priced'; and the Cactus Café – 'good food, makes children welcome'.

Alternatives include the Galette, the Glacier, the Refuge, the Cava, Plantin and Cro Magnon – all popular for raclette and fondue. A reporter recommends the Crocodile in the Hameau at Mottaret. Scott's does good American-style food, and there's even a Pizza Express for the homesick.

ALPINE ACTION *www.alpine-action.co.uk* T 01903 761986 F 01903 766007

Méribel

Chalet Mont Vallon (10 pers)
Chalet Ariondaz (10 pers)

La Tania, Courchevel

Chalet L'Oustal (10 pers)
Chalet Cote Coeur (14 pers)
Chalet Jamais Bleu (12 pers)
Chalet Hanneke (14 pers)

- Great locations – all en suite.
- Free ski guiding – group and child discounts.
- Packed lunches available.
- Superb service from our friendly staff throughout your holiday.

Our brochure can be viewed at:
www.alpine-action.co.uk
Alternatively call our office.

MERISKI *www.meriski.co.uk* T 01451 843100 F 01451 844799

MERISKI

The Méribel Specialist

- 16 luxury chalets
- All bedrooms en suite
- Superb cuisine
- High level of customer care
- Dedicated crèche and MeriKids club
- Chauffeured minibuses
- Heathrow and Manchester flights

← CHALET MIRA BELUM

SIMPLY SKI *Chalet specialist* T 020 8541 2209 *www.simplyski.co.uk*

Simply Ski offers four well appointed chalets in Méribel, sleeping 12–22 people. The largest, Chalet Rousillon, is Simply Ski's 'Simply Select' chalet in Méribel and is located in one of the resort's best locations with views across the valley.

Simply Ski is also able to offer a pre-booking facility for lift passes, ski-hire and ski school so that everything is arranged ready for your arrival. As ever, Simply Ski chalets come with the promise of superb service before, during and after your holiday.

CHALET ROUSILLON →

At Les Allues, the Croix Jean-Claude serves (eventually) good-value French food in a pretty dining room.

APRES-SKI
Méribel rocks – loudly

Méribel's après-ski revolves around British-run places and some readers complain there's nowhere to go if you don't like loud pubs. Dick's Tea Bar is now well established but is remote from the slopes. At close of play it's the piste-side Rond Point that's packed – happy hour starts around 4pm – and has live music. Jack's, with a sun terrace, is also very popular.

The ring of bars around the main square do good business at tea-time. La Taverne (run by the same company that owns Dick's Tea Bar) gets packed. Just across the square is The Pub, with videos, pool and sometimes a band. The Capricorne attracts a cosmopolitan crowd and Le Refuge (down the road towards the lifts) is that rare thing in Méribel: a place where you'll be understood if you use your French.

Later on, live music brings in the crowds at The Pub, Artichaud and Rond Point. There is late dancing at Scott's (next to The Pub) and, of course, there's Dick's Tea Bar (free entry and sub-disco drinks prices until 11.30). Last season Pizza Express (above Dick's and under the same ownership, had a fabulous Beatles tribute band every Monday). El Poncho's serves Mexican dishes and Desperados (beer mixed with tequila).

In Mottaret the bars at the foot of the pistes get packed at tea-time – Rastro and DownTown are the most popular, though reporters say that Zig Zag has lower prices. Later on, Plein Soleil sometimes has live music, and the Rastro disco gets going.

Both villages have a cinema.

OFF THE SLOPES
Flight of fancy

Méribel is not really a resort for people who want to languish in the village, but it is not unattractive. There's a good public swimming pool and an Olympic ice rink. You can also take joyrides in the little planes that operate from the altiport.

The pedestrian's lift pass covers all the gondolas, cable-cars and buses in the Méribel and Courchevel valleys, and makes it very easy for pedestrians to meet friends for lunch.

STAYING DOWN THE VALLEY
A few choices

If you want a quiet time, some UK tour operators have places in the old village of **Les Allues**, down the road from the resort and connected by the gondola up from Brides-les-Bains. There are a couple of bars and a good-value, well renovated hotel – the Croix Jean-Claude (0479 086105). Rooms are small, though, and a reporter says the service is poor.

Brides-les-Bains is an old spa town that served as the Olympic village in 1992. It is very cheap compared with the higher resorts and has some simple hotels, shops and a casino. But it's dead in the evening. And the long gondola ride to and from Méribel is tedious and can be cold. If you are driving, it makes a good base for visiting other resorts.

The new development of **Méribel-Village** is linked by chair-lift to the Altiport area with a blue run back. There's not much to do in this quiet little place (no bar or restaurant last season). Having a car is advisable to reach nearby La Tania or Méribel proper as buses are infrequent. One reporter described the bus service to and from Méribel as 'appalling', with 'no bus after 9.40pm, and long queues in the mornings. A car is vital.'

ACTIVITIES

Indoor Parc Olympique Méribel (skating rink, swimming pool), Forme Méribel (spa, sauna, gym, bowling, billiards, climbing wall), library, bridge, fitness centres, hot-tub, two cinemas, concert hall

Outdoor Flying lessons and excursions, snow-mobiles, snow-shoe excursions, para-gliding, 20km of cleared paths, motor-trikes, sleigh rides, hot air balloon

TOURIST OFFICE

Postcode 73551
t +33 479 086001
f 479 005961
info@meribel.net
www.meribel.net

Montgenèvre 1850m

Not a pretty pass, but an admirably snowy one

WHAT IT COSTS

3

HOW IT RATES

The slopes	
Snow	****
Extent	****
Experts	**
Intermediates	****
Beginners	*****
Convenience	****
Queues	****
Restaurants	**
The rest	
Scenery	***
Resort charm	***
Off-slope	*

- ⊕ Good, convenient nursery slopes, with easy progression to longer runs
- ⊕ Few queues on weekdays, unless people are bussing from other resorts with poor snow
- ⊕ A lot of accommodation close to the slopes, and some right on them
- ⊕ Good snow record, and local slopes largely north-facing – often the best snow in the Milky Way area
- ⊕ Great potential for car drivers to explore other nearby resorts

- ⊖ Poor base for exploring the Italian Milky Way resorts if you don't have a car
- ⊖ Slow lifts and short runs can be irritating
- ⊖ Busy road lined by tatty bars reduces village charm and family appeal – crossing can be tricky
- ⊖ Little to do off the slopes
- ⊖ Little to challenge experts on-piste

Montgenèvre is set at one end of the big Milky Way network, reaching over into Italy. It's a time-consuming trek to Sestriere and Sauze d'Oulx at the far end. But it's much quicker by car, which also facilitates day trips to other French resorts such as Serre-Chevalier and La Grave. And you'll probably find the best snow for miles on the local slopes shared between Montgenèvre and Clavière (in Italy, but only a few yards down the road).

The village is quite pleasant once you get away from the main road. Sadly, you can't avoid it altogether if you want to make use of the bigger area of slopes on the south side of the pass. But most visitors seem to come to terms with it, and don't find that it ruins their enjoyment.

What's new

A new chair-lift was installed last season at the top of the Gimont valley up to Col Saurel (2410m). The lift has opened up a new area, with a red run down to join the Colletto Verde run.

An additional 4.5km of artificial snowmaking was installed in the main sector for last season.

The resort

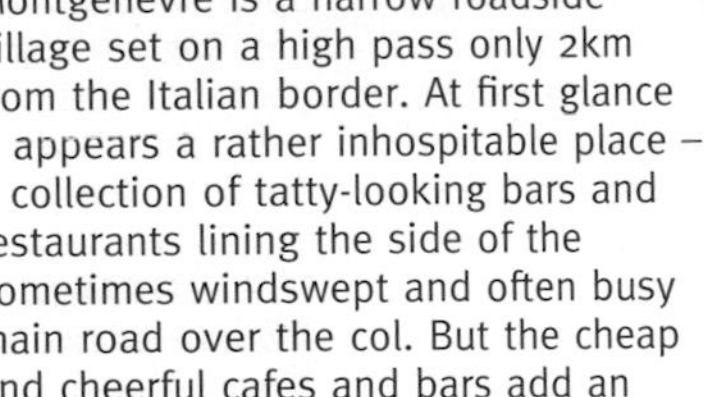

Montgenèvre is a narrow roadside village set on a high pass only 2km from the Italian border. At first glance it appears a rather inhospitable place – a collection of tatty-looking bars and restaurants lining the side of the sometimes windswept and often busy main road over the col. But the cheap and cheerful cafes and bars add an animated atmosphere sometimes missing from French resorts. And tucked away off the main road is a charming old village, complete with quaint church and friendly natives. The place gets a lot of snow, which also accentuates the charm factor.

The slopes are convenient, despite the road; most of the accommodation is less than five minutes from a lift. The main ones are gondolas from opposite ends of the village. On the village side of the road are the south-facing slopes of Le Chalvet. The more extensive north-facing slopes of Les Anges and Le Querelay are across the main road, with the nursery slopes at the bottom. Both sectors have piste

SNOWPIX.COM / CHRIS GILL

The village faces south, with the small Chalvet sector rising to the north →

LIFT PASSES

2000/01 prices in euros

Montgenèvre
Covers Montgenèvre lifts only.

Beginners One free drag-lift. Points cards available. 'Petit Réseau' day pass covers 7 lifts (adult 15, child 12).
Skiing by the hour is available (3-, 4- or 5-hour 'à la carte' passes).

Main pass
1-day pass 21
6-day pass 104

Senior citizens
Over 60: 6-day pass 89
Over 70: free pass

Children
Under 12: 6-day pass 89
Under 8: free pass

Short-term passes
Single ascent for foot passengers of Le Chalvet or Chalmettes (adult 5).

Notes 6-day pass and over allows free days at Alpe-d'Huez, Les Deux-Alpes, Puy-St-Vincent and Serre-Chevalier. Reductions for families.
Extensions by the day to main pass for the Voie Lactée (adult 12).

Alternative passes
Montgenèvre-Monts de la Lune (Clavière) (adults 22 per day, children 18 per day).
Voie Lactée (Milky Way) covers Montgenèvre, Clavière, Cesana, Sansicario, Sauze d'Oulx, Grangesises, Borgata, Sestriere – 400km (adults 37 per day).

CHILDCARE

The Halte Garderie takes children aged 6 months to 6 years, from 9am to 5.30. Meals you provide can be administered.

The ESF's kindergarten takes children aged 3 to 5.

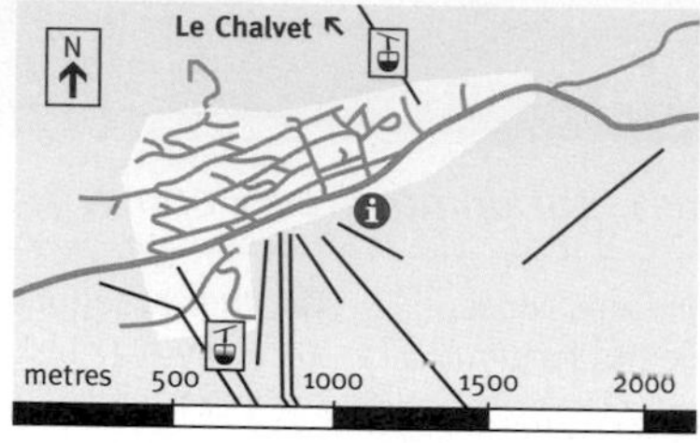

links with Clavière, gateway to the other Italian resorts of the Milky Way – mainly Sansicario, Sestriere and Sauze d'Oulx.

There are hotels, chalets and apartments available, all of which are cheap and cheerful places. Don't expect to find much luxury here. Location is becoming more important as the village expands – some of the newer accommodation is uphill, away from the slopes – though there is a free shuttle-bus.

The best way to get to other resorts and enjoy some time there is to travel by car. Serre-Chevalier and Puy-St-Vincent, with lift pass sharing arrangements, are also easily reached by car, and well worth an outing each. Different lift pass options cater for most requirements.

The mountains

Montgenèvre's local slopes are best suited to leisurely intermediates, with lots of easy cruising on blues and greens, both above and in the woods.

Run gradings on the local area and Milky Way piste maps differ and can be confusing – however, none of the blacks are much more than a tough red.

THE SLOPES
Nicely varied

The major north-facing Les Anges sector offers easy intermediate slopes above the mid-mountain gondola station, with more of a mix of runs lower down. It has a high-altitude link via Collet Vert (reached by a quad chair) to the slopes above Clavière, in Italy (covered on the Monts de la Lune lift pass). This whole area around the border is attractively broken up by rocky outcrops and woods. The runs of the sunny Chalvet sector are mainly on open slopes above its mid-mountain gondola station. When conditions permit, a long blue run from Col de l'Alpet in this sector goes down to Clavière, for access to Italy.

SNOW RELIABILITY
Excellent locally

Montgenèvre has a generally excellent snow record, receiving dumps from westerly storms funnelling up the valley. The high north-facing slopes naturally keep their snow better than the south-facing area but both have snowmaking on the main village-bound pistes.

FOR EXPERTS
Limited, except for off-piste

There are very few challenging pistes in the Montgenèvre–Clavière–Cesana sectors. Many of the runs are overgraded on the map. There is, however, ample opportunity for off-piste excursions, and heli-skiing on the Italian side when conditions are right.

The remote north-east-facing bowl beyond the Col de l'Alpet on the Chalvet side is superb in good snow and has black and red pistes, too. The open section between La Montanina and Sagna Longa on the Italian side is another good powder area. Those with a car should visit Sestriere for the most challenging runs.

FOR INTERMEDIATES
Plenty of cruising terrain

The overgraded blacks are just right for adventurous intermediates, though none holds the interest for very long. The pleasantly narrow tree-lined runs to Clavière from Pian del Sole, the steepest of the routes down in the Chalvet sector and the runs off the back of Col de l'Alpet are all fine in small doses.

boarding *There's plenty to attract boarders to Montgenèvre. There are good local beginner slopes and long runs on varied terrain for intermediates. The only real drawback is that many of the lifts in the area are drags, and you will have to use them to get around – getting over to Sestriere and back involves lots (and a flat green run to skate along as well). There's a fun-park on the lower slopes, and there are some excellent off-piste areas for more advanced boarders. Snow Box is the local specialist shop.*

MOUNTAIN FACTS

Altitude 1850m-2680m	
Lifts	39
Pistes	100km
Green	15%
Blue	27%
Red	39%
Black	19%
Artificial snow	10km
Recco detectors used	

The following figures relate to the whole Milky Way area

Altitude 1390m-2825m	
Lifts	92
Pistes	400km
Blue	12%
Red	67%
Black	21%
Artificial snow	75km

SCHOOLS/GUIDES

2000/01 prices in euros

ESF

Classes 6 half days mornings or afternoons
1 half day: 16
6 half days: 84

Children's classes
Ages: Up to 12
1 half day: 15
6 half days: 79

Private lessons
Hourly or daily
27 for 1hr; for 2 or 3 people 33

Average intermediates will enjoy the red runs, though most are short. On the major sector, both the runs from Collet Vert – one into Italy and one back into France – can be great fun.

Getting to Cesana via the lovely sweeping run starting at the top of the Serra Granet double-drag, and heading home from from Pian del Sole, is easier than the gradings suggest, and can be tackled by less adventurous intermediates, who also have a wealth of cruising terrain high up at the top of the Les Anges sector. These are served by several upper lifts, but you have the option of continuing right down to town. These long, gentle runs are wonderfully flattering cruises.

Further afield, the run down to Clavière from the top of the Gimont drags, on the Italian side, is a beautifully gentle cruise.

FOR BEGINNERS
Good for novices and improvers

There is a fine selection of convenient nursery slopes with reliable snow at the foot of the north-facing area. Progression to longer runs could not be easier, with a very easy blue starting at Les Anges (2460m), leading on to a green and finishing at the roadside 600m below.

FOR CROSS-COUNTRY
Having a car widens horizons

Montgenèvre is the best of the Milky Way resorts for cross-country enthusiasts, but it's useful to have a car. The two local trails, totalling 25km, offer quite a bit of variety, but a further 75km of track starts in Les Alberts, 8km away in the Clarée valley.

QUEUES
No problems most of the time

The slopes are wonderfully uncrowded during weekdays, provided surrounding resorts have snow. Some lifts become crowded at weekends and when nearby Bardonecchia is lacking snow. And queues for the two gondolas out of the village can occur first thing. Links with Italy have improved and are improving still, but many of the lifts are old and slow.

MOUNTAIN RESTAURANTS
Head for Italy

Restaurants are in very short supply locally. Most people travel back to the village for lunch. The Ca del Sol cafe-bar does a good pizza. There are several nice spots in Italy.

SCHOOLS AND GUIDES
Encouraging reports

Recent reports on the ESF are positive – the most recent positively glowing ('great instructor, good with kids').

FACILITIES FOR CHILDREN
Pity about the traffic

The intrusive main road apart, Montgenèvre would seem a fine family resort. Reports on the school's children's classes continue to be complimentary of both class size and spoken English.

GETTING THERE

Air Turin, transfer 2hr. Grenoble, transfer 3hr. Lyon, transfer 4½hr.

Rail Briançon (15km) or Oulx (20km); 5 or 6 buses per day to Briançon from station.

Phone numbers
From abroad use the prefix +33 and omit the initial '0' of the phone number.

ACTIVITIES

Indoor Library, cinema
Outdoor Natural skating rink, paragliding, snow-scooters, sledge runs, heli-skiing

TOURIST OFFICE

Postcode 05100
t +33 492 215252
f 492 219245
office.tourisme.montgenevre@wanadoo.fr
www.montgenevre.com

Staying there

HOW TO GO
Limited choice
UK tour operators concentrate on cheap and cheerful catered chalets, though some apartments are also available and a few operators also package hotels.

Hotels There are a handful of simple places offering good value.

(2) **Valérie** (0492 219002) Central rustic old 3-star.

(2) **Napoléon** (0492 219204) 3-star on the roadside.

(1) **L'Alpet** (0492 219006) Basic 2-star near the centre.

(1) **Chalet des Sports** (0492 219017) About the cheapest hotel rooms in the Alps.

(1) **Le Boom** (0492 219835) Cheap and cheerful place with tiny rooms near the village centre.

Self-catering Résidences La Ferme d'Augustin (0442 030457) are simple, ski-to-the-door apartments on the fringes of the main north-facing slopes, five minutes' walk (across the piste) from town.

EATING OUT
Cheap and cheerful
There are a dozen places to choose from. The Ca del Sol and Le Cesar have been recommended by reporters. The Estable and Transalpin serve good-value traditional fare. Chez Pierrot and the Jamy have an authentic French feel. The 3-star Napoléon is the only hotel with a restaurant open to non-residents – a pizzeria. A trip to Clavière is worthwhile – reporters have testified to the excellence of the restaurants.

APRES-SKI
Mainly bars, but fun
The range is limited. Le Graal is a friendly, unsophisticated place; the Ca del Sol bar is a cosy place with an open fire. Pub Chaberton is also recommended. The little Blue Light disco is popular. The Refuge, La Crepouse and the Jamy are the focal cafe-bars at tea-time.

OFF THE SLOPES
Very limited
There is a weekly market and you can walk the cross-country routes, but the main diversion is a bus-trip to the beautiful old town of Briançon.

STAYING IN OTHER RESORTS
Only for the dedicated
Cesana and Clavière are small villages with few facilities. Cesana is a 15-minute walk from its lifts. Clavière's nursery slope is small and steep but usually uncrowded and snow-reliable. Both resorts are best for dedicated intermediates keen to make the most of the Milky Way slopes without much après-ski.

SNOWPIX.COM / CHRIS GILL

← You get a clear view of the open slopes of Les Anges from the sunny restaurant terrace at mid-mountain on Le Chalvet

Morzine 1000m

A lively, year-round resort linked by lift to the Portes du Soleil

WHAT IT COSTS

4

HOW IT RATES

The slopes	
Snow	**
Extent	*****
Experts	***
Intermediates	****
Beginners	***
Convenience	**
Queues	***
Restaurants	***
The rest	
Scenery	***
Resort charm	***
Off-slope	***

What's new

For 2000/01 the gondola up from Ardent to above Les Lindarets was upgraded to increase its capacity and the car park was also extended. In the local area, the Belvédère and Mouilles double chairs were replaced by quads and the area at the top of the Pleney gondola was rebuilt to make reaching the other lifts easier. More snowmaking was installed in the area of the Fys chair runs down to town, to improve links to Nyon.

MOUNTAIN FACTS

for Portes du Soleil

Altitude	975m-2350m
Lifts	206
Pistes	650km
Green	13%
Blue	38%
Red	39%
Black	10%
Art. snow	252 acres
Recco detectors used	

- ⊕ Part of the vast Portes du Soleil lift network
- ⊕ Larger local piste area than other Portes du Soleil resorts
- ⊕ Good nightlife by French standards
- ⊕ Quite attractive old town – a stark contrast to Avoriaz
- ⊕ One of the easiest drives from the Channel (a car is very useful here)
- ⊕ Few queues locally (but see minus points)

- ⊖ Takes a while to get to Avoriaz and main Portes du Soleil circuit
- ⊖ Bus-ride or long walk to lifts from much of the accommodation
- ⊖ Low altitude means there is an enduring risk of poor snow, though increased snowmaking has helped
- ⊖ Low altitude or inconvenient nursery slopes
- ⊖ Not a great resort for experts
- ⊖ Weekend crowds

Morzine is a long-established French resort, popular for its easy road access, traditional atmosphere and gentle tree-filled slopes, where children do not get lost and bad weather rarely causes problems. For keen piste-bashers wanting to travel the Portes du Soleil circuit, the main drawback to staying in central Morzine is having to take a bus and cable-car or several lifts to get to Avoriaz and the main circuit. Morzine's local slopes can suffer from poor snow.

Such problems can be avoided by taking a car. The little-used Ardent gondola, a short drive from Morzine, gives access to a clockwise circuit via Châtel, missing out often crowded Avoriaz. If local snow is poor, you can visit nearby Flaine by car, which is better than Avoriaz at coping with crowds looking for snow.

The resort

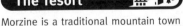

Morzine is a traditional mountain town sprawling amorphously on both sides of a river gorge. Under a blanket of snow, its chalet-style buildings look charming, and in spring the village quickly takes on a spruce appearance.

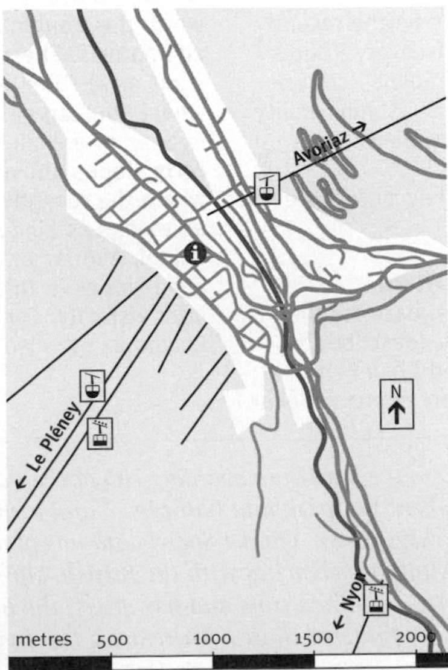

The old centre is next to the river, but most resort amenities are clustered higher up around the Le Pléney lifts. Accommodation is widely scattered, and a good multi-route bus service links all parts of the town to outlying lifts, including those for Avoriaz.

Morzine is a family resort, and village ambience tends to be fairly subdued. Our view that the resort suits car drivers is widely shared. Roads are busy, but parking problems have been somewhat relieved by new car parks built for last season near Pléney.

The mountains

The local slopes suit intermediates well, with excellent areas for beginners and near-beginners too: 'More variety than expected,' said one recent visitor. 1999/2000 saw the introduction of an electronic lift pass system, so you can now keep your pass in your pocket – hold on to the card for a discount next time you visit. Reporters have

↑ Gentle, pretty wooded slopes is what Morzine is all about – and if you get fresh snow like this, count yourself lucky

OT MORZINE / G LANSARD

commented favourably on the recently launched system of Discovery Routes around the Portes du Soleil – choose an alpine animal that suits your ability and follow the signs displaying it around the circuit.

There is floodlit skiing once a week.

THE SLOPES
No need to go far afield

Morzine is not an ideal base for the Portes du Soleil circuit (described in the Avoriaz, Châtel and Champéry chapters). But it has an extensive local area, shared with Les Gets.

A cable-car and parallel gondola rise from the edge of central Morzine to **Le Pléney**, where numerous routes return to the valley, including a run down to Les Fys – a quiet junction of chairs which access **Nyon** and, in the opposite direction, the ridge separating Morzine from the **Les Gets** slopes. Nyon can also be accessed by cable-car, situated a bus-ride from Morzine, and is connected to the slopes of Les Gets higher up the valley that separates the two, with a lift up from Le Grand Pré to Le Ranfolly. The Nyon sector has two peaks – Pointe de Nyon and Chamossière – accessible from Nyon and Le Grand Pré respectively.

From Le Ranfolly you can descend directly to Morzine without using a lift. To get to Morzine from the slopes above Les Gets you go first to the mid-mountain lift junction of Les Chavannes, then to the Folliets chair which takes you up to Le Pléney.

Beyond Les Gets is another small but worthwhile sector, on Mont Chéry. The short walk or 'petit train' shuttle through the village from the base of Chavannes takes about five minutes.

One means of access to the main Portes du Soleil circuit on the opposite side of the valley from Pléney is via a gondola from near the centre of town – another handy 'petit train' shuttle service runs between this and the Le Pléney lifts. The gondola takes you up to **Super-Morzine**, and a series of pistes and lifts lead to Avoriaz. A recent reporter found this route 'not worth the trouble', preferring the alternatives. These are a bus-ride or short drive to either Les Prodains (from where you can get a cable-car to Avoriaz or a chair-lift into the **Hauts Forts** slopes above it) or to Ardent, where the recently renovated gondola accesses Les Lindarets for lifts towards Châtel, Avoriaz or Champéry. The tree-lined slopes in this area are good in poor visibility. Car trips to Flaine and Chamonix are also feasible.

---

boarding *Avoriaz is the hard-core boarding HQ of the Portes du Soleil, with an excellent fun-park and half-pipe – and a special pass for those whose only interest is riding them. Chalet Snowboard has places here, and former British Champ Becci Malthouse teaches with the British Alpine Ski & Snowboard school. With interesting, tree-lined runs and few drags, the local Morzine slopes are good for beginners and intermediates. There are a few lively bars.*

LIFT PASSES

2001/02 prices in euros

Portes du Soleil
Covers all lifts in all 12 resorts, and shuttle buses.

Main pass
1-day pass 33
6-day pass 159

Senior citizens
Over 60: 6-day pass 127

Children
Under 16: 6-day pass 107
Under 5: free pass

Short-term passes
Half-day pass for Portes de Soleil (adult 25).
Also for Super-Morzine-Avoriaz (adult 22) and Morzine-Gets (adult 18).

Notes Discounts for groups of 13 or more and holders of the Carte Neige.

Alternative passes
Morzine-Les Gets pass covers 85 lifts (adult 6-day 118, child 88).

SNOW RELIABILITY

Poor

Morzine has a very low average height, and when snow disappears from the valley, the local slopes become very small and unconnected. There is some snowmaking, most noticeably on runs linking Nyon and Le Pléney, and on the reds and blues back to town. Les Gets recently benefited from extended snowmaking – but more is needed.

FOR EXPERTS

Limited on-piste

The run down from Pointe de Nyon is challenging, but for piste challenges the cable-car at Les Prodains is the place to head for, taking you up to Avoriaz. The Hauts Forts black runs, including the World Cup downhill course, are excellent. The above-the-tree-line slopes of Chamossière offer some of the best off-piste possibilities, and Mont Chéry is also well worth exploring. We've also had reports of great off-piste off the back of Col du Fornet down towards the Vallée de la Manche (but you'd need a guide).

FOR INTERMEDIATES

Something for everyone

Good intermediates will enjoy the challenging reds and blacks down from the Chamossière and Pointe de Nyon high points. Mont Chéry at Les Gets has some fine steepish runs.

Those of average ability have a great choice, though most runs are rather short. Le Ranfolly accesses a series of good cruisers on the Les Gets side of the ridge, and a nice piste back to Le Grand Pré. Le Pléney has a compact network of pistes that are ideal for groups with mixed abilities: mainly moderate intermediate runs, but with some easier alternatives for the more timid, and a single challenging route for the aggressive. Nyon's slopes are rather bitty for those not up to at least the Chamossière runs.

Less experienced intermediates have lots of options on Le Pléney, including a snow-gun-covered cruise from the top to the main lift station. Heading from Le Ranfolly to Le Grand Pré is also a nice run. And the slopes down to Les Gets from Le Pléney are easy when conditions allow (they face south).

And, of course, there is the whole of the Portes du Soleil circuit to explore by going up the opposite side of the valley to Avoriaz or Les Lindarets.

FOR BEGINNERS

Good for novices and improvers

The village nursery slopes are wide,

flat and convenient, and benefit from snow-guns. Fast learners have the inconvenience that the slightly longer, steeper runs are over at Nyon. However, adventurous novices also have the option of easy pistes around Le Pléney. Near-beginners can get over to Les Gets via Le Pléney, and return via Le Ranfolly.

FOR CROSS-COUNTRY
Good variety

There is a wide variety of cross-country trails, not all at valley level. The best section is in the pretty Vallée de la Manche beside the Nyon mountain up to the Lac de Mines d'Or where there is a good restaurant. The Pléney-Chavannes loop is pleasant and relatively snow-reliable.

CHILDCARE

The Halte Garderie l'Outa (0450 792600) takes children aged 2 months to 6 years, from 8.30 to 6pm. From age 3 they can have one-hour introductory lessons. Les Pingouins Malins takes children aged 4 to 12, with ESF instruction and lunch provided (half or full days).

QUEUES
Few problems when snow is good

Queues are not a problem in the local area. The Nyon cable-car and Belvédère chair-lift (Le Pléney) are weekend bottlenecks. Queues to and from Avoriaz are much improved in recent times, but are still bad when snow is in short supply.

MOUNTAIN RESTAURANTS
Within reach of some good huts

The nice little place at the foot of the d'Atray chair is perhaps the best local hut. On the Avoriaz side, Les Lindarets, Les Marmottes and Plaine Dranse are not too far and have some good restaurants. Pommes de Pin at the top of the télécabine d'Ardent is friendly with reasonably priced food. The Restaurant des Crêtes de Zore above Super-Morzine is good.

SCHOOLS/GUIDES

2001/02 prices in euros
ESF
Classes 6 days
5hr: 9.30-noon and 2.30-5pm; 2½hr: am or pm
6 half-days: 107
Private lessons
Hourly
30 for 1 or 2 people
Children's classes
Ages: 7 to 12
6 full days including lunch: 290

SCHOOLS AND GUIDES
British ski school here

The British Alpine Ski & Snowboard School, featuring BASI-qualified instructors, is based in Morzine and Les Gets and we have good reports on the tuition. Reports on the ESF are generally good except for some complaints about class sizes.

FACILITIES FOR CHILDREN
Lots of possibilities

The facilities of the Outa crèche are quite impressive, but we've received reports of poor spoken English and low staff ratios. A new childcare centre, Les Pingouins Malins, opened last season, but we have no reports. The Dérêches Farm offers days learning about animals, snowshoeing and tobogganing. A recent reporter's three and five year olds were both happy with the ESF, making 'rapid progress with friendly, attentive instructors'. Ski Esprit's facilities are good, with in-chalet crèches, an afternoon Snow Club for children attending morning ski school and their own tuition scheme. Ski Famille and Ski Hillwood are other family specialists, based in Les Gets.

Staying there

As the extensive network of bus routes implies, Morzine is a town where getting from A to B can be tricky. It is well worth making sure that your accommodation is near the lifts that you expect to be using, which for most visitors means the gondola and cable-car to Le Pléney, gondola to Super-Morzine or cable-car to Avoriaz.

HOW TO GO
Good-value hotels and chalets

The tour operator market concentrates on hotels and chalets. Independent travellers have a wider choice, notably of apartments.

Chalets There's a wide choice, with something to suit all tastes and tour operators ranging from the smallest to the biggest. Position varies enormously: you can be in the centre

Phone numbers
From abroad use the prefix +33 and omit the initial '0' of the phone number.

GETTING THERE

Air Geneva, transfer 1½hr. Lyon, transfer 3½hr.

Rail Cluses or Thonon (30km); regular bus connections to resort.

ACTIVITIES

Indoor Skating, bowling, cinemas, massage, table tennis, fitness track
Outdoor Horse-riding, sleigh rides, snow-shoe classes, artificial climbing wall, tennis, paragliding

TOURIST OFFICE

Postcode 74110
t +33 450 747272
f 450 790348
touristoffice@morzine-avoriaz.com
www.morzine.com

of town or right on the edge of the slopes; many are on the outskirts, however, without either convenience.
Hotels The range of hotel accommodation is wider than it at first appears – the handful of 3-star hotels includes some quite smooth ones. But the core of the resort is its modest accommodation – dozens of 2-stars and quite a lot of 1-stars. If there is a resort with more hotels in the Logis de France group, we have yet to find it.
((((4 **Dahu** (0450 791369) Upmarket 3-star; elegant public areas and good restaurant and pool. Some distance from all lifts and public buses except the Ardent route, but private shuttle.
((((4 **Airelles** (0450 747121) Central 3-star close to Pléney lifts and Prodains and Nyon bus routes. Good pool.
((((4 **Champs Fleuris** (0450 791444) Comfy 3-star next to Pléney lifts. Pool.
(((3 **Tremplin** (0450 791231) Also next to the lifts; 'friendly staff, good food'.
(((3 **Bergerie** (0450 791369) Rustic, old-fashioned chalet with a few rooms and many more studios, in centre. Friendly staff. Pool and gym.
((2 **Côtes** (0450 790996) Simple, upwardly-mobile 2-star, with more studios than rooms. Pool compensates for poor position on the edge of town.
((2 **Equipe** (0450 791143) One of the best 2-stars; next to the Pléney lift.
Self-catering The Télémark apartments are high quality, and close to the Super-Morzine gondola. We're told those by the Prodains cable-car are excellent.

EATING OUT
A fine choice
Morzine is scarcely a gourmet's resort, but it has a wide choice of good restaurants. The expensive La Chamade has high-quality French cuisine, Café Chaud is popular and atmospheric, and does good fondue, Les Airelles has a fine restaurant (Les Jardins d'Ulysse), known for its hot buffets, and Le Dahu also has good food. The L'Etale is an excellent, atmospheric pizza joint, bedecked in hundreds of different football scarves, also serving local specialities – booking is advisable. Reporters also recommend Clin d'Oeil, Le Don Camillo, the Gavottes, La Grange and the Combe á Zore.

APRES-SKI
One of the livelier French resorts
Nightlife is good by French standards. Le Dixie gets animated, with Eurosport, MTV, a great little cellar bar and some live music. At the Crépuscule, near the Pléney lifts, dancing on the tables in ski boots to deafening music seems compulsory at après time. Just below, the Cavern is popular with resort staff; the Buddha, with cosy Asian decor, is great for a quieter drink. The tiny Sherpa, on the outskirts of town, is also worth a try. L'Opéra, The Paradis du Laury's and La Caverne (a ten-pin bowling alley-cum-disco-cum-pool-hall-cum-bar) are the late night haunts. Taxis to outlying accommodation are said to be difficult to come by in the small hours. There are two cinemas.

OFF THE SLOPES
Quite good; excursions possible
There is an excellent ice rink, which stages ice hockey matches and skating galas. Some hotels have pools which non-residents can pay to use. Buses run to Thonon for shopping, and car owners can drive to Geneva, Annecy or Montreux. There are lots of very pretty walks, and other activities include horse-drawn sleigh rides, horse-riding, paragliding and a cheese factory visit.

Les Gets 1170m

Decent children's facilities, French ambience, convenience, nice village restaurants, fine nursery slopes and reasonable prices make Les Gets a good choice for families and many others. Several reporters said that it feels tucked away and rather secret. But it's a major trek to get into the main Portes du Soleil circuit on snow.

THE RESORT
Les Gets is a little old village of mainly traditional chalet buildings, 6km from Morzine. Although the village has a scattered appearance, most facilities are conveniently close to the main lift station. It is on a through-road, but traffic does not intrude too much. It is fairly quiet in the evenings except at weekends when the atmosphere becomes more chic.

The local pass covers all Les Gets, Nyon and Pléney lifts, saves a fair bit on a Portes du Soleil pass, and is worth considering by less experienced skiers and riders if the snow is good.

THE MOUNTAINS
Les Gets is not an ideal base for the Portes du Soleil, but its local slopes have far more pistes than any of the resorts on the circuit.

Phone numbers
From abroad use the prefix +33 and omit the initial '0' of the phone number.

TOURIST OFFICE

Postcode 74260
t +33 450 758080
f 797690
lesgets@lesgets.com
www.lesgets.com

Slopes As well as the local slopes that are linked to Morzine (see earlier in chapter), Les Gets has runs on Mont Chéry, accessed by gondola and parallel chair. The front slopes face south-east – bad news at this altitude; but the other two flanks are shadier.
Snowboarding The local Les Gets and Morzine slopes are good for beginners and intermediates. Experts are catered for by the excellent fun-park in Avoriaz.
Snow reliability Despite having a slightly higher elevation than Morzine, snow conditions can again be erratic. Fifty snow-guns were installed recently, improving cover back to the resort.
Experts Black runs from the Chéry Nord chair are steep and challenging in parts.
Intermediates High-mileage piste-bashers will enjoy cruising the Portes du Soleil circuit, and the local slopes are not bad for the less adventurous.
Beginners The village nursery slopes are convenient, but there are better, more snowsure ones up at Chavannes. Progression is simple, with a very easy run between Chavannes and the resort and pleasant greens from La Rosta and to La Turche, mean confident novices can cover some miles.
Cross-country Morzine is better, with an excellent array of trails. But Les Gets has 46km of good varied loops on Mont Chéry and Les Chavannes.
Queues Provided there's good snow, not much of a problem, though weekend crowds are a drawback.
Mountain restaurants See Morzine.
Schools and guides We've had mixed reports of the ESF, with tales of 'instructors shouting at our four-year-olds in French' but also of children enjoying 'a great instructor'. Beginners should, if conditions are less than perfect, try to have lessons at Chavannes.
Facilities for children There is a non-ski nursery for children aged three months to three years, and two ski kindergartens. Ski Espace's 'Ile des Enfants' is reputedly the better of the two. ESF's Club Fantaski has been criticised for inattentive supervision. Tour operators Ski Famille and Ski Hillwood have been recommended.

STAYING THERE

How to go Many visitors stay in private chalets, quite a few of which are on the British market in catered form. Most are pleasant, comfy, no-frills places.
Hotels All the hotels are 3-star and below, mostly cheap and cheerful old 2-stars. The 3-star Crychar (0450 758050), 100m from central Les Gets at the foot of the slopes, is one of the best. The 2-star Alpen Sports (0450 758055) is a friendly, family run hotel – 'excellent food and good value for money' says a reporter. We've also had good reports of the the Nagano (0450 797146) and the Marmotte (0450 758033) – both 3-star.
Self-catering The tourist office has a long list of apartments, but there are surprisingly few on the UK market.
Eating out Les Gets has a wide variety of places to eat – including Le Boomerang, with an Australian flavour. Most hotels have good restaurants. The Tyrol and the Schuss are good for pizza. The rustic Vieux Chêne, for Savoyard specialities; the Flambeau and Tourbillon are also recommended.
Après-ski Après-ski is quiet, especially on weekdays. The Pub Irlandaise and Prings, an English-owned pub, get very busy, and Bar les Copeaux has been recommended. The Igloo and Havana Noche are popular discos.
Off the slopes There's a well-equipped fitness centre with a pool, and an artificial ice rink. Outings to Geneva, Lausanne and Montreux are possible.

La Plagne 1800m-2100m

A variety of villages spread across a vast playground

WHAT IT COSTS

(5)

HOW IT RATES

The slopes

Snow	****
Extent	****
Experts	***
Intermediates	*****
Beginners	*****
Convenience	*****
Queues	**
Restaurants	**

The rest

Scenery	****
Resort charm	*
Off-slope	*

What's new

For 2000/01, the queue-prone Grande Rochette gondola from Plagne-Centre was replaced by a new twin-cable gondola with three times the capacity. A 3-star hotel, Les Balcons, opened in Belle-Plagne.

2001/02 will see more snowmaking above outlying villages. The Jean-Luc Crétier slalom course will be equipped with new snowmaking and floodlighting. The Biolley two-seater chair-lift from Plagne Centre and the 1800 two-seater from Plagne 1800 to Aime-la-Plagne are being upgraded to quads.

The planned link to Les Arcs may be ready for 2002/03, but it may slide to 2003/04.

- ⊕ Extensive intermediate slopes, plus plentiful off-piste terrain
- ⊕ Good nursery slopes
- ⊕ High and fairly snowsure – and blessed with some grand views
- ⊕ Purpose-built resort units are convenient for the slopes, and some are not unpleasant
- ⊕ Attractive, traditional-style villages lower down share the slopes
- ⊕ Wooded runs of lower resorts are useful in poor weather
- ⊕ Good cross-country trails

- ⊖ Still some serious lift bottlenecks
- ⊖ Pistes in the main bowl don't have much to offer experts
- ⊖ Lower villages can suffer from poor snow – Champagny especially
- ⊖ Unattractive architecture in some of the higher resort units
- ⊖ Not many green runs for nervous beginners to go on to – though some blues are very easy
- ⊖ Nightlife very limited

In terms of size, La Plagne's terrain and lift network ranks alongside those of Val-d'Isère/Tignes and the Trois Vallées, yet the resort doesn't enjoy the same status. What it lacks is the macho factor: it has very few black runs, and scores of blues. For most intermediates that is, of course, just the ticket – a friendly area, offering a sensation of travel between the widely spread resort villages. And in fact the place is fine for experts who are prepared to head off-piste.

The resort is part-way through a major programme of investment in new lifts. That's very welcome, but it reflects the fact that the lift system is still a weakness. The lifts to Roche de Mio and the Bellecôte glacier, in particular, are just inadequate, and there is no immediate sign of replacements.

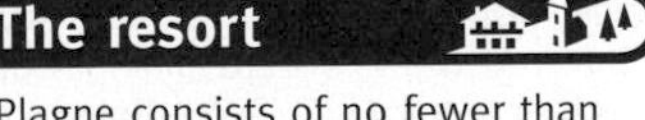

The resort

La Plagne consists of no fewer than ten separate 'villages'; six are purpose-built at altitude in the main bowl, on or above the tree line and linked by road, lifts and pistes; the other four are dotted around outside the bowl.

Even the core resorts vary considerably in style and character. The first to be built, in the 1960s, was Plagne-Centre, at around 2000m – still the focal point for shops and après-ski. Typical of its time, it consists of ugly blocks with dreary indoor 'malls' that house a reasonable selection of shops, bars and restaurants. Some new developments just above Plagne-Centre are more pleasing to the eye.

Lifts radiate from Centre to all sides of the bowl, the major one being the big new twin-cable gondola to Grande

SNOWPIX.COM / CHRIS GILL

Plagne-Centre: brutal on the outside, claustrophobic on the inside →

MOUNTAIN FACTS

Altitude 1250m-3250m	
Lifts	111
Pistes	215km
Green	9%
Blue	58%
Red	28%
Black	5%
Art. snow	50 acres
Recco detectors used	

LIFT PASSES

2001/02 prices in euros

La Plagne
Covers all lifts in La Plagne and Champagny-en-Vanoise.

Beginners Free baby-lift in each centre.

Main pass
1-day pass 35
6-day pass 167

Senior citizens
Over 60: 6-day pass 142
Over 72: free pass

Children
Under 14: 6-day pass 123
Under 5: free pass

Short-term passes
Half-day pass (26).
Single ascent on inter-area links.

Notes Standard 6-day pass and over allows one day each in Les Arcs, Tignes-Val-d'Isère, the Three Valleys, Pralognan-la-Vanoise and Les Saisies.
5% discount on presentation of a La Plagne pass in your name from the last two seasons.
Family discounts are also available.

Alternative passes
Village area passes available for Montchavin-Les Coches, Plagne Montalbert, or Champagny.
Limited 'Discovery' passes in each area.

Rochette. Another is a cable-car up to the even more obtrusive 'village' of Aime-la-Plagne – a group of monolithic blocks that attract derisory comments from most reporters.

Below these two, and a bit of a backwater, is Plagne 1800, where the buildings are small-scale and chalet-style, and many are indeed individual chalets that find their way on to the UK package market.

A little way above Plagne-Centre is the newest development, Plagne-Soleil, still small as yet, but with its own shops and some attractive new chalets. This area is officially attached to Plagne-Villages, which is a rather strung-out but otherwise attractive collection of small-scale apartments and chalets in traditional style, handy for the slopes but for nothing else.

The two other core resort units are a bus-ride away, on the other side of a low hill. The large apartment buildings of Plagne-Bellecôte form a wall at the foot of the slopes down to it. Some way above it is Belle-Plagne – as its name suggests, easy on the eye, with a Disneyesque neo-Savoyard look, and complete with entirely underground parking. Reporters have complained of exhaustion when moving between the different levels in Belle Plagne; the bars and other facilities are concentrated in the lower part.

Then there are the lower resorts in the valleys outside the bowl. At the northern extremity of the area are the old village of Montchavin and its recently developed neighbour Les Coches. At the southern extremity, not far from Courchevel, is the village of Champagny. And at the western extremity is the modern development of Montalbert. For a description of each, see the end of this chapter.

The efficient, free bus system between the core resorts within the bowl runs until after midnight and allows you to explore the après-ski in different areas – the lifts between some of the villages also run late into the evening. The outlying villages are effectively isolated in the evenings.

Day trips to Les Arcs are easy, trips to Val-d'Isère, Tignes or the Three Valleys more time-consuming – all are covered for one day each with a six-day pass.

The mountains

The majority of the slopes in the main bowl are above the tree line, though there are trees dotted around most of the resort centres. The slopes outside the bowl are open at the top but descend into woodland. The exposed glacier slopes on Bellecôte, to the west of the main bowl, rise up to 3250m. The gondola is prone to closure by high winds or poor weather and the drags are normally shut in winter.

THE SLOPES
Multi-centred; can be confusing

La Plagne boasts 215km of pistes over a wide area that can be broken down into seven distinct but interlinked sectors. From Plagne-Centre you can take a lift up to **Biolley**, from where you can head back to Centre, to Aime-la-Plagne or down gentle runs to **Montalbert**, from where you ride several successive lifts back up. But the main lift out of Plagne-Centre leads up to **Grande Rochette**. From here there are good sweeping runs back down and an easier one over to Plagne-Bellecôte, or you can drop over the back into the predominantly south-facing **Champagny** sector (from which a lift arrives back up at Grande Rochette and another brings you out much further east). From the Champagny sector there are great views over to Courchevel, across the valley.

From Plagne-Bellecôte and Belle-

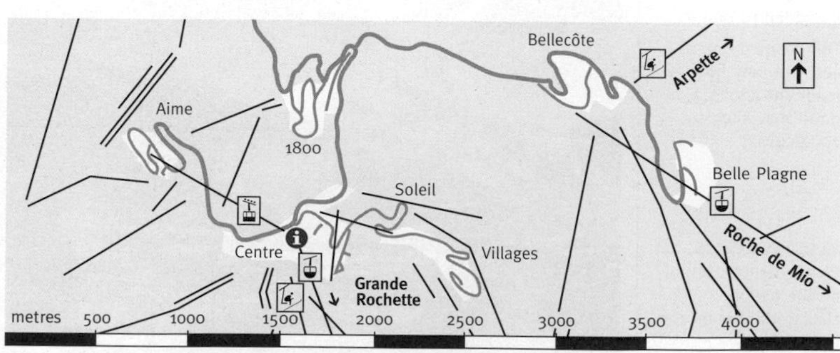

Plagne, a gondola heads up to **Roche de Mio**, where runs spread out in all directions – towards La Plagne, Champagny or **Montchavin/Les Coches.** Montchavin/Les Coches can also be reached by taking a chair from Plagne-Bellecôte. From Roche de Mio you can also take a gondola down to Col de la Chiaupe (there are no runs in that direction) then up to the **Bellecôte glacier**, start of some of the steepest slopes in the area. In good snow there is an easy off-piste run from the foot of Bellecôte at 2300m to Les Bauches, and the Montchavin slopes. Otherwise, you have to return to Roche de Mio.

The special 'evasion' map identifies five circuits of varying difficulty.

Several reporters have indicated that run grading is inconsistent; some runs are more difficult than their grading would suggest, while others are 'flattering'.

SNOW RELIABILITY

Good except in low-lying villages

Most of La Plagne's runs are snowsure, being at altitudes between 2000m and 2700m on the largely north-facing open slopes above the purpose-built centres.

Runs down to the valley resorts can cause more problems, and you may have to take the lifts at times. This is particularly true of Champagny, where the two home runs are both south-facing. The runs down to Les Coches and Montchavin are north-facing and have artificial snow – these, and a few runs around Montalbert and Plagne-Bellecôte, are the main ones with artificial cover in the area, although the network is continually expanding.

FOR EXPERTS

A few good blacks and off-piste

In theory there are two potentially great black runs from Bellecôte to the chair-lift up to the gondola mid-station at Col de la Chiaupe – both beautiful long runs with a vertical of some 1000m that take you away from the lift system. But these are often closed due to too much or too little snow.

The long Emile Allais down from above Aime-la-Plagne through the forest, finishing at 1400m, is graded black only at its final stage. With a couple of drag-lifts taking you back up, it is little used, although north-facing and very enjoyable in good snow. The shorter Coqs and Morbleu runs in the

SNOWPIX.COM / CHRIS GILL

Aime-la-Plagne (on the skyline) isn't a 60s relic – it has expanded in recent years ↓

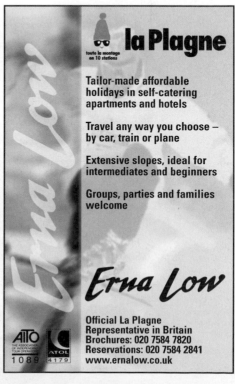

same sector are seriously steep.

The long, sweeping Mont de la Guerre red, with a 1250m vertical from La Grande Rochette–Les Verdons to Champagny, is also a beautiful run in good snow (a rare event).

There are other good long reds to cruise around on. But experts will get the best out of La Plagne if they hire a guide and explore the vast off-piste potential – which takes longer to get tracked out than in more 'macho' resorts. There are popular off-piste variants on the aforementioned black runs from Bellecôte down to Les Bauches (a drop of over 1400m). You can also head down off-piste to Peisey-Nancroix and take the lifts up to the Les Arcs slopes. Another beautiful and out-of-the-way off-piste run from Bellecôte is over the Col du Nant glacier towards Champagny-le-Haut.

In fresh snow, those who enjoy picking their way through woods in search of fresh light powder will not be disappointed by the forests above Montchavin and Montalbert.

FOR INTERMEDIATES
Great variety

Virtually the whole of La Plagne's area is a paradise for intermediates, with blue and red runs wherever you look. Your main choice will be whether to settle for one area for the day and explore it thoroughly, or just cruise around the pistes that form the main arteries of the network.

For early intermediates there are plenty of gentle blue motorway pistes in the main La Plagne bowl, and a long, interesting run from Roche de Mio back to Belle Plagne, Les Inversins (involving a tunnel). The blue runs either side of Arpette, on the Montchavin side of the main bowl, are glorious cruises. In poor weather the best place to be is in the trees on the gentle runs leading down to Montalbert. The easiest way over to Champagny is from the Roche de Mio area rather than from Grande Rochette.

Better intermediates have lots of delightful long red runs to try. Roche de Mio to Les Bauches is a drop of 900m (the second half of this run is marked as a black). There are challenging red mogul pitches down from the glacier to the Col de la Chiaupe mid-station. And the main La Plagne bowl has enjoyable reds in all sectors. The Champagny sector has a couple of tough reds – Kamikaze and Hara-Kiri – leading from Grande Rochette. The Mont de la Guerre red is a satisfying run for adventurous intermediates.

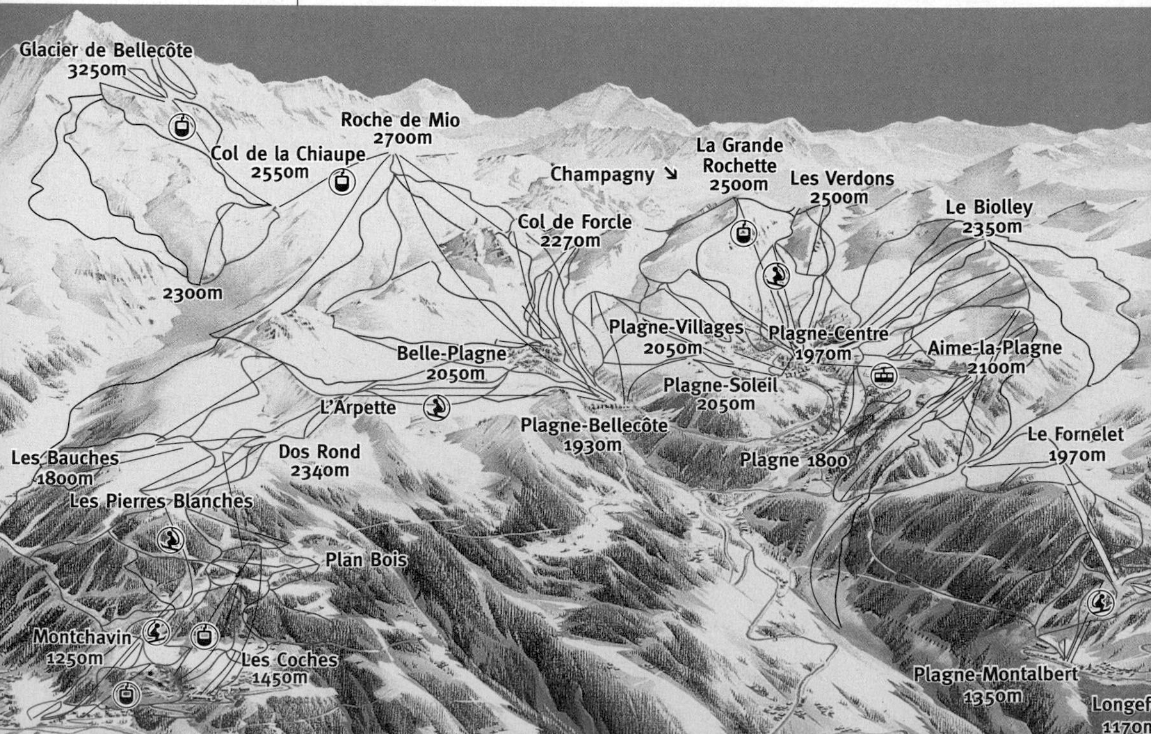

FOR BEGINNERS

Excellent facilities for the novice

La Plagne is a good place to learn, with generally good snow and above-average facilities for beginners, especially children. Each of the main centres has nursery slopes on its doorstep. There's a free drag-lift in each resort as well. There are no long green runs to progress to, but no shortage of easy blues. One reporter felt that the runs back into Plagne 1800 were a bit difficult for novices.

CROSS-COUNTRY

Open and wooded trails

There are 90km of prepared and marked cross-country pistes in La Plagne and its surrounding satellites. The most beautiful of these are the 30km of winding track set out in the sunny valley around Champagny-le-Haut. The north-facing areas have more wooded trails that link the various centres. There is a 25km route above Montchavin/Les Coches and an 18km route above Montalbert. Plagne Bellecôte, Belle Plagne and Plagne Villages are similarly linked by a less arduous, 12km route. Each of the trails has a beginners' circuit. Access is free (except at Champagny). A recent visitor points out that getting to the outlying loops can be time-consuming.

QUEUES

Bottlenecks in high season

When the resort is full there can be big queues to get out of the high-altitude centres at the start of the day. The old gondola from Plagne-Bellecôte via Belle-Plagne to Roche de Mio is still a bad bottleneck, despite the alternative ways available. The higher gondola is also oversubscribed when snow is poor lower down. The new gondola from Plagne-Centre to Grande Rochette has treble the capacity of the original, and shifts the queues impressively quickly. Two six-packs on the top slopes of the Champagny sector have greatly improved the links on that side. The fast Arpette chair from Plagne-Bellecôte towards Montchavin still causes queues, and there are several other lifts that can generate queues

boarding *La Plagne offers some pretty good terrain for all standards of rider – there's a good mix of long, easy runs and high, open slopes with some fantastic off-piste variations that should be done with a guide. Whether on- or off-piste, be prepared for some flat areas, though. There are fun-parks at Plagne-Bellecôte, Belle-Plagne and above Montchavin–Les Coches. The broad, gentle pistes are ideal for beginners and carvers (crowds permitting). Most lifts are gondolas or chairs, though there are still some difficult-to-avoid drag-lifts.*

CHILDCARE

There are ESF ski kindergartens in all the high resort units, generally taking children from age 3. The ESF also runs all-day nurseries in most of the villages, mostly taking children aged 2 to 6 (18 months to 3 years in Belle Plagne). In Centre, independent nursery Marie Christine does much the same.

In Montchavin and Les Coches very young skiers go to the Nursery Club, the ESF taking over at age 4.

that you can't avoid, once you've descended to them – at Les Bauches for example. Crowds on the pistes are as much of a problem as lift queues, particularly above Bellecôte in the afternoon.

MOUNTAIN RESTAURANTS

An improving choice

Mountain restaurants are numerous, varied and crowded only in peak periods, as many people prefer to descend to one of the resorts – particularly Champagny or Montchavin/ Les Coches – at the end of the morning. Le Val Sante at Les Bauches is recommended. As are the Pierres Blanches, the Carroley, Plan Bois and Les Preizes on the Montchavin/Les Coches slopes. Two great rustic restaurants in which to hole up in poor weather for a long lunch of Savoyard dishes are Le Sauget, above Montchavin, and Au Bon Vieux Temps, just below Aime-la-Plagne. Reservations may be required at either. Chalet des Colosses above Plagne Bellecôte is also highly recommended, as is Roc des Blanchets at the top of the Champagny gondola – friendly staff, both table- and self-service, beautiful views over to Courchevel from the terrace and good basic cooking. The little Breton cafe at the bottom of the Quillis lift at the start of the Levasset piste and the Borseliers (lower down) have also been highly recommended. The Forperet, above Montalbert, is also popular.

SCHOOLS/GUIDES

2001/02 prices in euros

ESF
Schools in all centres. Prices vary; those for Plagne Centre are given here
Classes 6 days
2½hr, 3hr, 5hr, 6hr, depending on centre, day and season
6 full days: 150
Children's classes
Ages: Up to 13 or 16 depending on village
6 full days: 131
Private lessons
1hr, 1½hr, 2hr
30 for 1hr

Eric Laboureix
In Belle-Plagne
Classes 6 days
am or pm
6 half days: 170
Children's classes
Ages: Up to 14
6 full days: 166
Private lessons
Hourly
31 for 1hr

Oxygène
Private school in Plagne-Centre
Classes 6 days
am or pm
6 full days: 144
Children's classes
Ages: Up to 14
6 full days: 144
Private lessons
Hourly
32 for 1hr

Evolution 2
Private school in Montchavin
Classes 5 days
5 days (3hr): 84
Children's classes
5 days (3hr): 76
Private lessons
Hourly
29 for 1hr

Antenne Handicap
Private lessons for the disabled
31 for 1hr

Phone numbers
From abroad use the prefix +33 and omit the initial '0' of the phone number.

SCHOOLS AND GUIDES

Better alternatives to ESF

Each centre has its own ESF school, offering classes for all standards. Groups can be much too large (a recent visitor reports seeing classes of up to 20 students) and instructors speak English of varying standard. But reports about private tuition are generally positive. However, the consensus seems to be that the alternatives are preferable. The Oxygène school in Plagne-Centre continues to impress reporters. One recent report has nothing but praise for the sympathetic instructors and management of El Pro in Belle-Plagne. We have had good reports on Evolution 2 (based in Montchavin) – 'wonderful', says the parent of one junior pupil. Antenne Handicap offers private lessons for skiers with any kind of disability.

FACILITIES FOR CHILDREN

Good choice

Children are well catered for with facilities in each of the villages. The nursery at Belle-Plagne is 'excellent, with good English spoken'. However, one recent reporter complained that her daughter was the only English speaker in her ESF class. The Club Med at Aime-la-Plagne is one of their 'family' villages. Several UK chalet operators run child-care services.

Staying there

HOW TO GO

Plenty of packages

For a resort that is very apartment-dominated, there is a surprising number of attractive chalets available through British tour operators. There are few hotels, but there are some attractive, simple 2-stars in the lower villages. There is a Club Med 'village' at Aime-la-Plagne. Accommodation in the outlying satellite resorts is described at the end of the chapter. A reporter suggests checking the resort website for special promotional deals.

Chalets There's a large number available – the majority are fairly simple, small, and located in 1800.

Hotels There are very few, all of 2-star or 3-star grading.

② **Balcons** (0479 557655) Brand new 3-star at Belle Plagne. Pool.

② **Eldorador** (0479 091209) Adequate hotel in Belle-Plagne – 'excellent food', according to several visitors.

② **Terra Nova** (0479 557900) Big, new, 120-room 3-star hotel in Plagne-Centre.

Self-catering La Plagne is the ultimate apartment resort, but communal facilities are generally poor. Fortunately, many tour operators have allocations in the above-average Pierre et Vacances apartments in Belle-Plagne. The MGM apartments in Aime-la-Plagne were recently described as 'a real treat'. Two new 4-star residences – in Aime-La-Plagne and Plagne-Villages should also improve the general standard.

EATING OUT

Nothing fancy

Throughout the resort there is a good range of casual restaurants including pizzerias and traditional Savoyard places serving raclettes and fondue.

Reader recommendations in Plagne-Centre include La Métairie ('the most enjoyable we've encountered in the Alps') and Le Bec Fin. In Plagne-Villages, La Chevrette is recommended for pizzas and steaks. A recent reporter described his pizza at the Loup Garrou, next to the chair-lift in Plagne 1800, as 'the best he had ever tasted'. Au Bon Vieux Temps (see also under Mountain restaurants) at Aime-la-Plagne is open in the evening, though a recent reporter was disappointed by his meal.

In Plagne-Bellecôte, La Ferme and Chalet des Colosses are recommended for Savoyard specialities. Le Matafan in Belle-Plagne is popular for Savoyard dishes (at lunch as well as dinner). The Cloche, Pappagone pizzeria and Maître Kanter have also been recommended.

APRES-SKI

Bars, bars, bars

Though fairly quiet during low season, La Plagne has a wide range of après-ski catering particularly for the younger crowd. In Belle-Plagne, Mat's and the

GETTING THERE

Air Geneva, transfer 3½hr. Lyon, transfer 3½hr. Chambéry, transfer 2½hr.

Rail Aime (18km) and Bourg-St-Maurice (35km) (Eurostar service to Bourg-St-Maurice and Aime available); frequent buses from station.

ACTIVITIES

Indoor Sauna and solarium in most centres, skating (Bellecôte and Aime-la-Plagne), squash (1800), fitness centres (Belle-Plagne, 1800, Centre, Bellecôte), cinemas, bowling

Outdoor Heated swimming pool (Bellecôte), bob-sleigh (La Roche), 30km marked walks, paragliding, skidoos, climbing, skating, hang-gliding, snow-shoe excursions, dog sleigh tours

UK Representative

Erna Low Consultants
9 Reece Mews
London SW7 3HE
t 020 7584 2841
f 020 7589 9531
info@ernalow.co.uk
www.ernalow.co.uk

TOURIST OFFICE

Postcode 73211
t +33 479 097979
f 479 097010
ot.laplagne@wanadoo.fr
www.la-plagne.com

Cheyenne are the main bars. The new Maître Kanter is also recommended. The King Café and the Luna are the liveliest bars in Plagne-Centre, and sometimes have live music. Plagne 1800 is fairly quiet at night – the Couleur Café and La Mine are popular. The Lincoln Pub in Plagne-Soleil is recommended. Plagne-Bellecôte is very limited at night, with only one real bar – Showtime. Aime-la-Plagne is also quiet. Neal's (Plagne-Centre), Le Jet 73 (Plagne-Bellecôte) and Le Saloon (Belle-Plagne) are the main discos recommended by local chalet staff.

OFF THE SLOPES
OK for the active

As well as the sports and fitness facilities, winter walks along marked trails in the March and April sunshine are particularly pleasant. It's also easy to get up the mountain on the gondolas, which both have restaurants at the top. The Olympic bob-sleigh run is a popular evening activity (see feature box). Excursions are limited.

STAYING IN THE LOWER RESORTS
A good plan

Montchavin (1250m) is a relatively unspoilt old farming community where wooden barns and sheds are much in evidence. Restaurant terraces set in orchards at the foot of the slopes add to the scene. There are adequate shops, a kindergarten and a school. Reaching the La Plagne slopes involves a series of lifts; but the local slopes have quite a bit to offer – the local lift pass covers 30km of mostly easy, pretty, sheltered runs, well endowed with snowmakers, with nursery slopes at village level and up at Plan Bois. Those who do venture further afield can return from Roche de Mio in one lovely long swoop (partly black). The more usual way home involves some of the trickiest blue runs we have encountered. Après-ski is quiet, but the village doesn't lack atmosphere and has a couple of nice little bars and a cinema. The Bellecôte hotel (0479 078330) is convenient for the slopes.

Les Coches (1450m) is only a walk away, and shares the same slopes. It is a sympathetically designed modern mini-resort that several reporters have liked for its 'small, quiet and friendly' feel and its traffic-free centre. It has its own school and kindergarten. The Last One pub is good for après-ski, with a big screen TV and regular live bands. La Poze and la Taverne du Monchu are recommended for eating out.

Montalbert (1350m) is a traditional but much expanded village with quicker access into the main area – though it's a long way from here across to the Bellecôte glacier. The local slopes are easy and wooded – a useful insurance against bad visibility. The Aigle Rouge (0479 555105) is a simple hotel.

Champagny-en-Vanoise (1250m) is a charming village in a pretty, wooded setting, with its modern expansion done sensitively. Champagny is better placed than any of the other outlying villages for access into the main bowl – and well placed for an outing by taxi or car to Courchevel (or the beautiful Vanoise national park with its 500km of marked walking paths). Given good snow, there are lovely runs home from above Plagne-Centre but their southerly orientation means you may have to get a gondola instead. There are several hotels, of which the two best are both in the Logis de France consortium. The Glières (0479 550552) is a rustic old hotel with varied rooms, a friendly welcome and good food. L'Ancolie (0479 550500) is smarter, with modern facilities, 'high quality food and smiling staff'; it is very convenient for the gondola. The village is quiet in the evenings.

TRY THE OLYMPIC BOB-SLEIGH RUN

If the thrills of a day on the slopes aren't enough, you can round it off by having a go on the 1992 Winter Olympics bob-sleigh run. The floodlit 1.5km run drops 125m and has 19 bends. You can go in a proper four-man 'taxi-bob' (70 euros in 2000/01 – certain nights of the week only) or in a special padded driverless bob raft (30 euros). Most people find the bob raft's 80kph quite thrilling enough.

With the taxi-bob, you are one of three passengers wedged in behind the driver. You reach a maximum speed of 110kph and the pressure in turns can be as high as 3g – be sure your physical state is up to it. You must be over 18. Additional insurance is available (yours may not be valid).

Portes du Soleil

Low altitude cross-border cruising

The Portes du Soleil vies with the Trois Vallées for the title of World's Largest Ski Area, but its slopes are very different from those of Méribel, Courchevel, Val-Thorens and neighbours. The Portes du Soleil's slopes are spread out over a large area and most of them are part of an extensive circuit straddling the French–Swiss border; you can travel the circuit in either direction, with a short bus-ride needed only at Châtel. There are smaller areas to explore slightly off the main circuit. The runs are great for keen intermediates who like to travel long distances and through different resorts. There are few of the tightly packed networks of runs that encourage you to stay put in one area – though there are exceptions in one or two places. The area also has some nice rustic mountain restaurants, serving good food in pleasant, sunny settings.

The lifts throughout the area have been improved in recent years with several new high-speed chair-lifts eliminating some bad bottlenecks. But the slopes are low by French standards, with top heights in the range 2000m to 2300m and good snow is far from assured (though snowmaking has been expanded in recent years). When the snow is good you can have a great time racing all over the circuit (as we did in fresh powder on our last visit). But the slopes can get very crowded, especially at weekends and in the Avoriaz area.

Purpose-built Avoriaz (page 208) has the most snowsure slopes and is especially good for families, with a big

snow-garden right in the heart of the car-free village. But its local slopes do get crowded, especially at weekends when crowds pour in from nearby Geneva, and prices are rather high by local standards. The other French resort on the main circuit is Châtel (page 220). Given good snow, it has some of the best runs in the area. It is an old and quite characterful village, but it's a busy, traffic-jammed place. It has a couple of good beginner areas both at resort level and up the mountain. Morzine (page 281) is close to Avoriaz. It is linked by lift but there's no piste all the way back to town. It's a summer as well as a winter resort – a pleasant, bustling little town with good shops and restaurants, busy traffic and long walks to the lifts from much of the accommodation. The local slopes are extensive, and linked to those of the slightly higher, quieter, traditional village of Les Gets (page 285). But they are low and good snow is certainly not assured. You can use Morzine as a base to ski the main Portes du Soleil circuit, but it's not ideal. Les Gets is even further off the main circuit.

On the Swiss side Champéry (page 405) is a classic charming, attractive Swiss village – but again just off the main circuit. You have to take a cable-car down from the main slopes as well as up to them or, if there is enough snow, a bus from a piste which ends out of town. Champéry used to be very popular with British tour operators but now few go there.

Champoussin and Les Crosets are purpose-built mini-resorts set on the very extensive open slopes between Champéry and Morgins, with fairly direct links over to Avoriaz. Morgins, in contrast to Champéry, has excellent village slopes – but they are low and very sunny, and although its more serious local runs are enjoyable and prettily wooded, they are also limited in extent.

On a spur off the main circuit are the resorts of La Chapelle d'Abondance (which has one of our favourite hotel-restaurants) in France and Torgon in Switzerland (which has splendid views over Lake Geneva). This area can be reached from above the Super-Châtel area and is usually quiet even when the rest of the circuit is packed.

SNOWPIX.COM / CHRIS GILL

Lifts spread out in all directions from Avoriaz ↓

Puy-St-Vincent 1400–1600m

Underrated little modern resort with some serious slopes

WHAT IT COSTS

HOW IT RATES

The slopes

Snow	***
Extent	**
Experts	***
Intermediates	***
Beginners	***
Convenience	*****
Queues	****
Restaurants	***

The rest

Scenery	***
Resort charm	**
Off-slope	*

What's new

A new blue run – the Tournoux – was planned for last season but will, in fact, be in place for 2001/02.

MOUNTAIN FACTS

Altitude	1400m-2700m
Lifts	16
Pistes	62km
Green	16%
Blue	37%
Red	41%
Black	6%
Artificial snow	10km
Recco detectors used	

- ⊕ Mostly convenient purpose-built resort that isn't too hideous
- ⊕ Good variety of slopes with challenges for all standards
- ⊕ Reasonable snow reliability
- ⊕ Low prices by resort standards
- ⊕ Friendly locals
- ⊕ Some great cross-country routes

- ⊖ Limited area by Alpine standards
- ⊖ Some accommodation is inconveniently located
- ⊖ Upper village has only apartment-based accommodation
- ⊖ Limited après-ski
- ⊖ Not a lot to do off the slopes

Puy-St-Vincent's ski area may be limited, but we like it a lot – more, to be honest, than we expected before we went. It offers a decent vertical and a lot of variety, including steep stuff. Provided you pick your spot with care, it makes an attractive choice for a family holiday.

THE RESORT

Puy-St-Vincent proper is an old mountain village, not far south-west of Briançon. The modern resort of PSV is a two-part affair – the minor part, Station 1400, is just along the mountainside at 1400m; the major part, Station 1600, is a few hairpins (or a chair-lift ride) further up (yes, at 1600m), and there are buildings in various styles dotted around the mountainside. Purpose-built and compact it may be, but 1600 (where most of the accommodation is located) is not perfectly laid out; beware walks to the lifts. We – and a recent reporter – found PSV friendly ('even the lift operators') and well run.

THE MOUNTAINS

Within its small area, PSV packs in a lot of variety, with runs of all colours from green to black that justify their gradings.

Slopes There are gentle slopes between the two villages, but most of the runs are above 1600. A fast quad goes up to the tree line at around 2000m. Entertaining red runs go back down, and a green takes a less direct route. The main higher lift is a long chair to 2700m, serving excellent open slopes of red and genuine black steepness. The shorter Rocher Noir drag serves another steep slope, but also accesses splendid cruising runs that curl around the eastern edge of the area. These runs are also accessed by a fast quad chair from just below 1600. The six-day Galaxie pass covers a series of major resorts beyond Briançon. More to the point for most visitors, it also covers a day's skiing above the valley hamlet of Pelvoux, 10 minutes' drive away. This area has blue, red and black runs, often used for race training, and a vertical of over 1000m served by a chair and a drag.

SNOWPIX.COM / CHRIS GILL

The main monolith at the foot of the lifts is unusual – boldly styled to resemble a mountain range, and largely finished in white →

Phone numbers
From abroad use the prefix +33 and omit the initial '0' of the phone number.

TOURIST OFFICE

Postcode 05290
t +33 492 233580
f 492 234523
courrier@puysaintvincent.net
www.puysaintvincent.com

Snowboarding There is a floodlit fun-park with half-pipe at 1600, but boarders are not allowed on the Rocher Noir drag-lift.
Snow reliability The slopes face north-east and are reasonably reliable for snow. In the 2000/01 season snowmaking was increased so that it now covers one run down to 1400 and several above 1600.
Experts The black runs are short but genuinely challenging for experts, and there are off-piste routes to be tackled with guidance. There are itinéraires outside the piste network, including one to the valley bottom.
Intermediates Provided the limited extent doesn't worry you, it's an excellent area for intermediates who welcome a challenge – but there aren't many very easy runs.
Beginners Beginners should be happy on either of the nursery slopes, and on the long green run from 2000m.
Cross-country There are splendid routes between 1400m and 1700m, ranging from green to black difficulty.
Queues Queues are rare and only form during exceptionally busy periods.
Mountain restaurants There is a modern but pleasantly woody and reasonably priced restaurant at mid-mountain, but in good weather the sunny terraces down at 1600 are the natural place to head for.
Schools and guides You have a choice of French and International ski schools, and a British tour operator, Snowbizz, has its own school, which a reader recommends; it provides free guiding in the afternoons, as well as 'good instruction' in small groups.
Facilities for children There are nurseries in both villages, and both schools run ski kindergartens.

STAYING THERE

How to go A number of British operators offer accommodation here.
Hotels There are four cheap hotels in 1400, but none in 1600.
Self-catering 1600 consists entirely of apartments, and there are more in 1400. A reporter found his valley-facing Pendine 2 apartment convenient for the lifts but cramped in contrast to the larger, piste-facing apartments.
Après-ski Après-ski is focused around the handful of bar-restaurants in each village.
Eating out The bar-restaurants in each village are the main dining options – a recent reporter recommends Le Petit Chamois at 1600: 'Excellent food; good service, reasonable prices.'
Off the slopes Snow-shoe expeditions and paragliding are possible, as well as floodlit sledging and outdoor ice skating (weather permitting). There is a cinema showing English-speaking films.

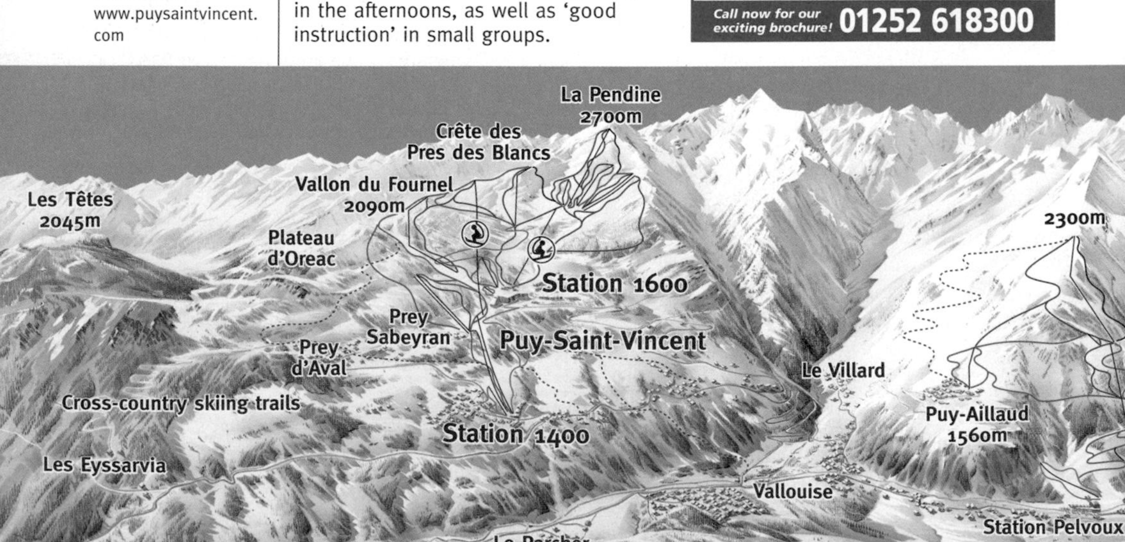

Risoul 1850m

Villagey modern resort in an attractive southern setting

WHAT IT COSTS

3

HOW IT RATES

The slopes

Snow	***
Extent	***
Experts	**
Intermediates	****
Beginners	****
Convenience	****
Queues	****
Restaurants	***

The rest

Scenery	***
Resort charm	**
Off-slope	*

What's new

A new tourist residence opened in Risoul for 2000/01. There were a couple of new ones in Vars as well. And snowmaking was extended on the Olympique and Bouisset runs in the Vars sector. The capacity of the high-speed Escondus lift out of Vars has also been increased.

2001/02 will see a new six-pack from Risoul up to the top of Peyrefolle. In Vars, snowmaking is being extended to the top of the Olympique run as well as the Combe Froide area.

Plans for a new fast quad chair-lift from Valbelle, on the Risoul side, to the Pic de Chabrières, and the replacement of the Sibieres and Peyrol drag-lifts with chair-lifts are on hold till 2002.

- ⊕ One of the more attractive and convenient purpose-built resorts
- ⊕ Scenic slopes linked with Vars add up to a fair-sized area
- ⊕ High resort with reasonable snow reliability
- ⊕ Good resort for beginners, early intermediates and families
- ⊕ Plenty of good-value places to eat

- ⊖ Not many modern lifts – lots of long drag-lifts
- ⊖ Not too much to challenge expert skiers and boarders
- ⊖ Limited après-ski
- ⊖ Little to do off the slopes

Slowly but surely the international market is waking up to the merits of the southern French Alps. Were they nearer Geneva, Risoul and its linked neighbour Vars would be as well known as Les Arcs and Flaine. The village of Risoul is a lot more attractive than either.

THE RESORT

Risoul, purpose-built in the late 1970s, is a quiet, apartment-based resort, popular with families. Set among the trees, with excellent views over the Ecrins national park, it is made up of wood-clad buildings – mostly bulky, but with some concessions to traditional style. It has a busy little main street which surprisingly is very far from traffic-free. But the village meets the mountain in classic style with an array of sunny restaurant terraces facing the slopes. Several reporters have commented on the friendliness of the natives. The village does not offer a very impressive array of resort amenities. Airport transfers (usually from Turin) are not short.

THE MOUNTAINS

Together with neighbouring Vars, the area amounts to one of the biggest domains in the southern French Alps – the combined area is marketed as the Forêt Blanche.

Slopes The slopes, mainly north-facing, spread over several minor peaks and bowls, and connect with the sunnier slopes of neighbouring Vars via the Pointe de Razis (2570m) and the lower Col des Saluces. Plans to install a new fast quad from Valbelle up to the Pic de Chabrières above Vars, the area's highest point at 2750m – providing a third access link between the two – have been put on hold until 2002. The upper slopes are open, but those leading back into Risoul are attractively

SNOWPIX.COM / CHRIS GILL

→ There are lots of places for lunch at the foot of the slopes

MOUNTAIN FACTS

These figures relate to the entire Forêt Blanche ski area

Altitude	1660m-2750m
Lifts	56
Pistes	180km
Green	18%
Blue	37%
Red	35%
Black	10%
Artificial snow	29km
Recco detectors used	

wooded, and good for bad-weather days. Recent improvements in the lift system, including the introduction of some fast chairs, mean that the link can now be made in both directions without having to ride any drag-lifts. Nevertheless, reporters still complain that the system as a whole has too many 'long and steep' drag-lifts. Piste grooming is reportedly poor.

Snow reliability Risoul's slopes are all above 1850m and mostly north-facing, so despite its southerly position snow reliability is reasonably good. Snowmaking is fairly extensive and more is planned. Visitors recommend going over to the east-facing Vars slopes for the morning sun, and returning to Risoul in the afternoon.

Experts The pistes in general do not offer much to interest experts. However, Risoul's main top stations access a couple of steepish descents. And there are some good off-piste opportunities if you have a guide.

Intermediates The whole area is best suited to intermediates, with some good reds and blues in both sectors. Almost all Risoul's runs return to the village, making it difficult to get lost in even the worst conditions. So intermediate children can be let off the leash without much worry.

Beginners Risoul's local area boasts some good, convenient, nursery slopes with a free lift, and a lot of easy longer pistes to move on to.

Cross country There are 45km of cross-country trails in the whole domain, of which 20km are in Risoul itself. A trail through the Peyrol forest links the two resorts together.

Snowboarding There is a lot of good free-riding to be done throughout the whole area, although beginners might find the large proportion of drag-lifts a problem. There is a good fun-park with a half-pipe near the village base, and there are weekly competitions and demonstration sessions.

Queues Outside French school holidays, Risoul has impressively quiet slopes. There may be queues to get out of the village in the morning.

Mountain restaurants The mountain restaurants have increased in quantity and quality – the new Tetras is a stylish chalet and the Refuge de Valbelle is recommended; but most people return to the village terraces.

Schools and guides We have had mainly positive reports on the ESF and Internationale schools, but our most recent reporter describes his private ESF instruction as 'most indifferent'.

Facilities for children Risoul is very much a family resort. It provides an all-day nursery for children over six months. Both ski schools operate ski kindergartens, slightly above the village, reached by a child-friendly lift. One parent reckons many other drags have a dangerous 'whiplash' effect.

STAYING THERE

How to go Most visitors stay in self-catering apartments, but there are a few hotels and more chalets are becoming available from UK operators.

Hotels The Chardon Bleu (0492 460727) is handy for the slopes. You can also stay overnight at the Tetras mountain refuge (0492 460983) at 2000m.

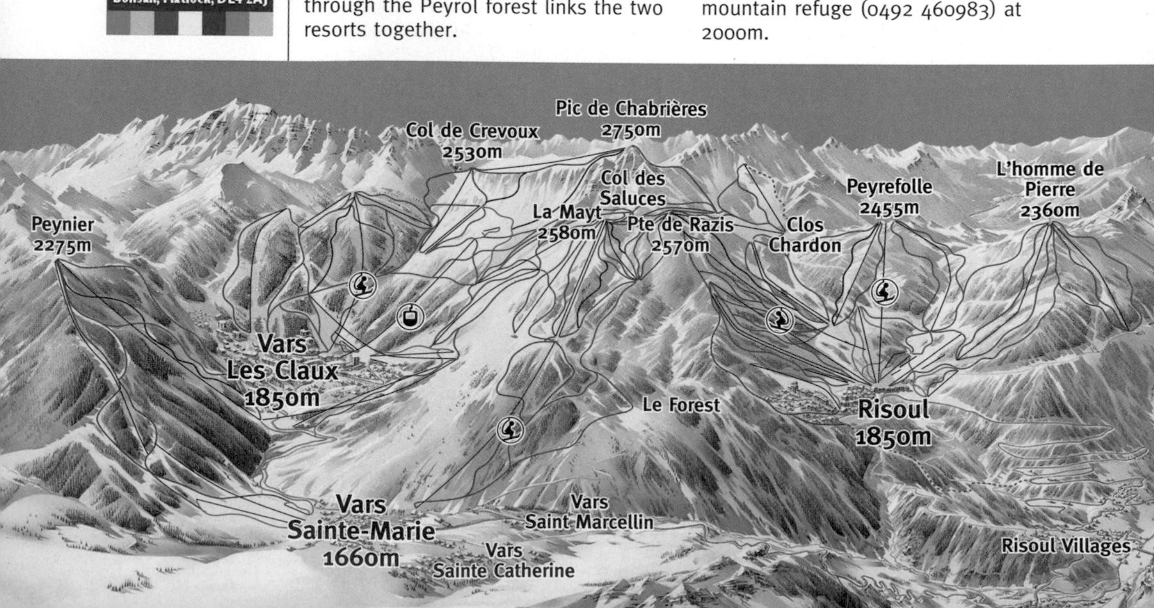

Self-catering The Constellation Forêt Blanche apartments are adequate but cramped.

Eating out There's plenty of choice for eating out, from pizzerias to good French food, and it's mostly good value – the Ecureuil and the Snowboard cafe, at the foot of the slopes, have been highly recommended. More expensive is the Assiette Gourmande.

Après-ski Après-ski is limited to a cinema and a few fairly quiet bars. The best are the Licorne, Cimbro, Chérine, L'Ecureuil and Yeti – the liveliest and full of Scandinavians.

Off the slopes There is little to do; excursions to Briançon are possible.

TOURIST OFFICE

Postcode 05600
t +33 492 460260
f 492 460123
o.t.risoul@wanadoo.fr
www.risoul.com

Phone numbers
From abroad use the prefix +33 and omit the initial '0' of the phone number.

Vars 1850m

THE RESORT

Vars includes several small, old villages on or near the road running southwards towards the 2110m Col de Vars. But for winter visitors it mainly consists of purpose-built Vars-les-Claux, higher up the road. The resort has convenience and reasonable prices in common with Risoul, but is bigger and has far more in the way of amenities. There are a lot of block-like apartments, but Les Claux is not a complete eyesore, thanks mainly to surrounding woodland. There are two centres: the original, and a geographical one where the main gondola starts, with most of the accommodation and shopping, and Point Show – a collection of bars, restaurants and shops, 10 minutes' walk away at another main lift station.

THE MOUNTAINS

There are slopes on both sides of the village, linked by pistes and by chair-lift at the lower end of Les Claux. Lifts also run up from both sides of Ste-Marie (1660m), lower down the mountain.

Slopes The wooded, west-facing Peynier area is the smaller sector, and reaches only 2275m – though there are good long descents down to Les Claux and Ste-Marie. The main slopes are in an east-facing bowl beneath the Pic de Chabrières (2750m) with direct links to the Risoul slopes at the top and at the Col des Saluces. There's a speed skiing course at the top (you can have a go, via the ski school). Beneath it are easy runs, open at the top but descending into trees, with red runs either side.

TOURIST OFFICE

Postcode 05560
t +33 492 465131
f 492 465654
vars.ot@pacwan.fr
www.vars-ski.com

Snow reliability The main slopes get the morning sun, and are centred at around 2000m, so snow reliability is not as good as in Risoul, but snowmaking is widespread.

Experts There is little of challenge for experts, though the Crête de Chabrières top section accesses some off-piste, an unpisted route and a tricky couloir at Col de Crevoux. The Olympic red run from the top of La Mayt (2580m) down to Ste-Marie is a respectable 920m vertical.

Intermediates Most of the area is fine for intermediates, with a good mixture of comfortable reds and easy blues, particularly in the main bowl.

Beginners There is a nursery area close to central Vars, with lots of 'graduation' runs throughout the area. Quick learners will be able to get over to Risoul by the end of the week.

Snowboarding There's a fun-park just above Les Claux.

Cross-country There are 25km of trails in Vars itself. Some start at the edge of town, but those above Ste-Marie are more extensive.

Queues Queues are rare outside the French holidays, and even then Vars is not overrun as some family resorts are.

Mountain restaurants There are several in both sectors, but a lot of people head back to the villages for lunch.

Schools and guides Lack of English-speaking has been a problem.

Facilities for children The ski school runs a nursery for children from two years old. There is also a ski kindergarten. A list of babysitters can be obtained from the tourist office.

STAYING THERE

How to go There are a few small hotels, but Les Claux is dominated by apartment accommodation.

Hotels Le Caribou (0492 465043) is the smartest of the hotels and has a pool. L'Ecureuil (0492 465072) is an attractive, modern chalet (no restaurant). There are more hotels in the lower villages, including Ste-Marie.

Eating out The range of restaurants is impressive, with good-value pizzerias, crêperies and fondue places. Chez Plumot does proper French cuisine.

Après-ski Après-ski is animated at tea-time, less so after dinner – except at weekends when the discos warm up.

Off the slopes The amenities are rather disappointing, given the size of Vars – there are 35km of walking paths and an ice rink, but that's about it.

La Rosière 1850m

Pop over to Italy from the sunniest slopes in the Tarentaise

WHAT IT COSTS

4

HOW IT RATES

The slopes

Snow	***
Extent	***
Experts	**
Intermediates	***
Beginners	*****
Convenience	***
Queues	***
Restaurants	*

The rest

Scenery	***
Resort charm	***
Off-slope	*

What's new

For 2000/01 a new accommodation booking centre was opened, a hands-free ski pass was introduced, and improvements to the resort's traffic system were made.

MOUNTAIN FACTS

Covers combined La Rosière and La Thuile area

Altitude	1175m-2640m
Lifts	35
Pistes	150km
Green	11%
Blue	37%
Red	34%
Black	18%
Artificial snow	22km

Recco detectors used

- + Attractive purpose-built resort
- + Fair-sized area of slopes linked with La Thuile in Italy
- + Sunny home slopes with good snowfall record
- + Heli-skiing over the border in Italy
- + Good nursery slopes
- − Links to Italy prone to closure from high winds
- − Snow affected by sun in late season
- − Few on-piste challenges for experts
- − Limited après-ski
- − Few off-slope diversions

Like Montgenèvre a long way to the south, La Rosière enjoys a position on the watershed with Italy that brings the twin attractions of big dumps of snow and access to cheap Chianti. The former is crucial: given the very unusual sunny orientation of the slopes, average snowfalls wouldn't do the trick. The Chianti is less significant, because La Thuile lacks attractive restaurants.

THE RESORT

La Rosière has been built in traditional chalet style beside the road that zigzags its way up from Bourg-St-Maurice to the Petit-St-Bernard pass to Italy (a piste in winter). All the buildings are attractive, and many are dotted around discreetly in the woods. But there isn't much here except accommodation and a few shops. Expect peace, quiet and friendly locals, but not lively nightlife. The most convenient accommodation is in the main village near the lifts, or just below, in Le Gollet or Vieux Village. There is also accommodation by the other main lift up, in Les Eucherts.

THE MOUNTAINS

The link with Italy means La Rosière has a big area of slopes. Its sunny home slopes are south-facing and offer great views over the valley to Les Arcs and La Plagne.

Slopes The chair and drag out of the village take you into the heart of the slopes, from where a series of drags and chairs, spread across the mountain, takes you up to Col de la Traversette (2385m). From there, you can get over the ridge and to the lifts which link with Italy at Belvedere (2640m).

Snowboarding There is a fun-park and a half-pipe.

Snow reliability Snow reliability is surprisingly good despite its south-facing direction; most of the slopes are between 1850m and 2400m. Most of the area's artificial snow is on the Italian side. The top lifts that link with the Italian slopes are prone to closure because of high winds or heavy snow.

Experts Other than heli-skiing from just over the Italian border (it is banned in France) and guided off-piste, there is little excitement for experts. The steepest terrain is on the lowest slopes, down the Marcassin run to Le Vaz (1500m) and down the Ecudets and Eterlou runs to Les Ecudets (1175m) – though these last two runs are reported to be prone to closure.

Intermediates La Rosière would be nothing special on its own, but there's lots to explore if you take into account its links to La Thuile. Apart from the lowest runs down to below the main village, the bottom half of La Rosière's slopes are mainly gentle, open, blue and green runs, ideal for early intermediates to brush up their technique. The top half of the mountain, however, below Le Roc Noir and Col de la Traversette, boasts steeper and more interesting red runs.

The red over the ridge from Col de la Traversette has good snow and views, but is narrow along its top section. Weaker intermediates can avoid it by taking a chair down.

Beginners La Rosière has good nursery slopes and short lifts at the main slopes above the village and at the altiport.

Cross-country La Rosière has four trails totalling 12km, set around the tree line in the altiport area.

Queues Queues are not usually a problem – apart from early in the day on the chair out of the village – but it is much busier here than over in Italy.

Phone numbers
From abroad use the prefix +33 and omit the initial 'o' of the phone number.

TOURIST OFFICE

Postcode 73700
t +33 479 068051
f 479 068320
info@larosiere.net
www.larosiere.net

Mountain restaurants There are two mountain restaurants, both with big, sunny terraces. A reporter recommends the self-service Plan du Repos for its 'friendly staff, huge pasta portions and lovely salads', but found the table-service at La Traversette was 'understaffed and unable to cope with lunchtime crowds'. There are a couple of bars near the top, which are fine for picnics. Many people prefer to take lunch back in the village, which is perfectly convenient. Two of our reporters recommend the Relais du Petit St Bernard at the base of the pistes: 'Good value, wide menu choice,' comments one. Another recommends Le P'tit Relais: 'Self-service and lots of choice.'

Schools and guides There are two schools. Recent reporters praise the Evolution 2 school for its 'good tuition, sympathetic instructors and small groups', but reports of the ESF school are less favourable: 'large groups' and 'insufficient supervision of small children' are two recent comments.

Facilities for children The Village des Enfants has a snow garden, and British tour operator Ski Esprit runs a crèche.

STAYING THERE

How to go A number of British tour operators now offer packages here.

Hotels There are a few 2-star hotels in the village, and more in the valley.

Chalets Of the chalets available we have reports of Chalethotel Roc Noir ('well placed but noisy', 'good food', 'welcoming staff') and of Chalet Ferme d'Elisa ('lovely accommodation but a 150m hike up to the lifts').

Self-catering There is a range of options available through UK tour operators or the resort's central booking service.

Après-ski Après-ski is limited to a couple of bars in town.

Eating out There's a fair choice of restaurants. Le Chalet ('good atmosphere and food okay'), La Terrasse du Yéti and L'Ancolie have all been recommended.

Off the slopes There is little entertainment, apart from scenic flights and walks, and a cinema. The ski schools offer paragliding and organise various non-skiing expeditions on foot.

Serre-Chevalier 1350m-1500m

Surprise! Big, French, but full of character

WHAT IT COSTS

HOW IT RATES

The slopes

Snow	****
Extent	****
Experts	***
Intermediates	****
Beginners	****
Convenience	***
Queues	***
Restaurants	***

The rest

Scenery	****
Resort charm	***
Off-slope	**

What's new

For 2001/02 a new fast six-seater chair will replace the parallel Prorel drag-lifts, linking the Chantmerle section to the Briançon slopes.

Other developments include floodlighting on the beginners' slopes at the Briançon gondola mid-station, a new fun-park with a super-pipe at Alpage, above Villeneuve, and a new children's snow park at Bachas.

Snowmaking is being doubled – 300 guns will cover 30km of pistes for 2001/02 – the Vallons, Casse du Boeuf, Eychauda and Aya runs will all benefit from new artificial cover.

A new Club Med in Villeneuve is also planned for next season.

A free guest card – available at hotels and from the tourist office – gives access to a number of resort amenities.

- ⊕ Big, varied mountain, with something for everyone
- ⊕ Interesting mixture of wooded runs (ideal for blizzards) and open bowls (with acres of off-piste)
- ⊕ One of the few big French areas based on old villages with character
- ⊕ Good-value and atmospheric old hotels, restaurants and chalets
- ⊕ Lift pass covers days elsewhere
- ⊕ Spectacular drive from Grenoble

- ⊖ A lot of indiscriminate new building, which looks awful from the slopes
- ⊖ Still lots of slow, old lifts, including many drags – some of them vicious
- ⊖ Serious queues in French holidays
- ⊖ Busy road runs through the resort villages, with traffic jams at times
- ⊖ Limited nightlife
- ⊖ Inadequate piste map
- ⊖ Few off-slope diversions

Serre-Chevalier is a big-league resort, but isn't as well known outside France as many of its rivals to the north and west. Maybe that's because it doesn't lend itself to marketing hype – the slopes are not super-high, the lifts are not super-efficient, the hotels are far from super-smooth. But we like it a lot: it's one of the few French resorts where you can find the ambience you might look for on a summer holiday – a sort of Provence in the snow, with lots of small, family-run hotels and restaurants housed in old stone buildings.

The slopes are equally likeable. Although there are runs on only one side of the long valley they are split into different segments, so you get a real sensation of travel. In good snow conditions there are excellent off-piste opportunities to keep experts happy, as well as intermediates. What really sets the area apart from the French norm is the woodland runs, making Serre-Chevalier one of the best places to be when snow is falling – though there are plenty of open runs, too.

The resort

The resort is made up of a string of 13 villages set on a valley floor running roughly north-west to south-east, below the north-east-facing slopes of the mountain range that gives the resort its name. From the north-west – coming over the Col du Lautaret from Grenoble – the three main villages are Le Monêtier (or Serre-Che 1500), Villeneuve (1400) and Chantemerle (1350), spread over a distance of 5km. Finally, at the extreme south-eastern end of the mountain, is Briançon (1200) – not a village but a town (the highest in France). Nine smaller villages can be identified, and some give their names to the communes: Villeneuve is in the commune of La Salle les Alpes, for example. Confusing.

Serre-Chevalier is not a smart resort, in any sense. Although each of its parts is based on a simple old village, there is a lot of modern development, which ranges from brash to brutal, and even the older parts are roughly rustic rather than chocolate-box pretty. (A ban on corrugated iron roofs would help.) Because the resort is so spread out, cars and buses are difficult to escape – indeed, in parts the place puts us in mind of some American resorts. But when blanketed by snow the older villages and hamlets do have an unpretentious charm, and we find the place as a whole easy to like.

There are no luxury hotels or swanky restaurants; on the other hand, there are more hotels in the Logis de France 'club' here than in any other ski resort. This is a family resort, which fills up (even more than most others) with French children in the February high season. You have been warned.

The heart of the resort is **Villeneuve,** which has two gondolas and a fast quad chair going up to widely separated points at mid-mountain. The central area of new development near the lifts is brutal and charmless. But not far away is the peaceful and traditional hamlet of

MOUNTAIN FACTS

Altitude	1350m-2780m
Lifts	76
Pistes	250km
Green	19%
Blue	19%
Red	49%
Black	13%
Artificial snow	30km
Recco detectors used	

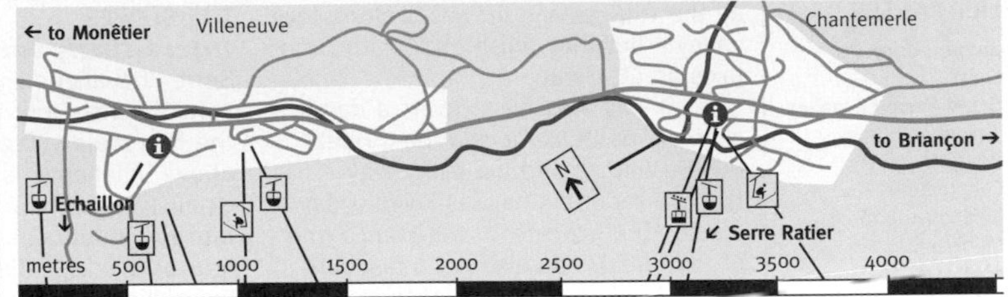

Le Bez, which has a third gondola, and across the main road and river is the old stone village of Villeneuve with its quiet main street lined by cosy bars, hotels and restaurants.

Not far down the valley **Chantemerle** gives access to opposite ends of the mid-mountain plateau of Serre Ratier via a gondola and a cable-car, both with second stages above. (The planned fast chair link from the village up to Prorel has been abandoned.) Chantemerle has some tasteless modern buildings in the centre and along the main road. The old sector is a couple of minutes' walk from the lifts, with a lovely church and most of the restaurants, bars and small hotels.

At the top of the valley, **Le Monêtier** has one main access lift – a fast quad chair to mid-mountain, reached from the village by bus or a long and steepish walk, tricky when ice is around. Le Monêtier is the smallest, quietest and most unspoilt of the main villages, with a pronounced Provençal feel to its narrow streets and little squares, and new building mostly in sympathetic style. Sadly, the through-road to Grenoble, which skirts the other villages, bisects Le Monêtier; pedestrians stroll about bravely blocking the road, hoping the cars will avoid them.

Briançon has a gondola from right in the town to mid-mountain and on almost to the top. The area around the lift station has a wide selection of modern shops, bars, hotels and restaurants, but no character. In contrast, the lovely 17th-century upper quarter is a delight, complete with impressive fortifications, narrow cobbled streets and traditional restaurants, auberges and patisseries. Great views from the top, too.

Regular and reliable ski buses (covered on the free guest card) link

SNOWPIX.COM / CHRIS GILL

Le Monêtier is no Tirolean picture postcard, but it does still look like a mountain village ↓

LIFT PASSES

2001/02 prices in euros

Grand Serre-Chevalier
Covers all lifts in Briançon, Chantemerle, Villeneuve and Le Monêtier.

Main pass
1-day pass 30
6-day pass 150

Senior citizens
Over 60: 6-day pass 107
Over 70: free pass

Children
Under 12: 6-day pass 107
Under 6: free pass

Notes Passes of 6 days or more give one day in each of Les Deux-Alpes, Alpe-d'Huez, Puy-St-Vincent and Voie Lactée (Milky Way). Reductions for families.

Alternative passes
Passes covering individual areas of Serre-Chevalier. Adult 6-day pass: Briançon, 95, Le Monêtier 109, Chantemerle / Villeneuve 129
Morning and afternoon passes. Night-skiing pass. Beginner's pass. Non-skier's pass.

all the villages and lift bases along the valley – but they finish quite early, and taxis aren't cheap.

A six-day area pass covers a day in each of Les Deux-Alpes, Alpe-d'Huez, Puy-St-Vincent and the Milky Way (several reporters have enjoyed a day out to Montgenèvre, at the French end of that area). You also get a discount on a day at La Grave. All of these outings are possible by public transport, but are much more attractive to those with a car. If driving, you are likely to approach over the high Col du Lautaret, which is usually kept clear of snow but is occasionally closed by avalanche danger.

Air travellers are much better off using Turin airport than Lyon.

The mountains

Trees cover almost two-thirds of the mountain, providing some of France's best bad-weather terrain. The Serre-Chevalier massif is not particularly dramatic, but from the peaks and some other points there are fine views of the Ecrins massif, the highest within France (ie not shared with Italy).

The trail map is supposed to have been improved, but it remains infuriatingly unclear and imprecise in places. Readers have found navigation is made even more challenging by 'particularly poor' signposting and the tendency of runs to 'change colour halfway down'. And last winter we found that the signposting at altitude is not up to the job when a storm socks in; take great care.

Piste grading is inclined to exaggerate difficulty – many reds, in particular, could be graded blue.

THE SLOPES
Interestingly varied and pretty

Serre-Chevalier's 250km of pistes are spread across four main sectors above the four main villages. The sector above Villeneuve is the most extensive, reaching back a good way into the mountains and spreading over four or five identifiable bowls. The main mid-station is Fréjus at 2100m. This sector is reliably linked to the slightly smaller Chantemerle sector at quite a low level – well below the tree line. The link from here to Briançon is over a high, exposed col and is now via a new six-pack. The link between Villeneuve and Le Monêtier is liable to closure by high winds or avalanche danger.

SNOW RELIABILITY
Good – especially upper slopes

Most slopes face north or north-east and so hold snow well, especially high up (there are lots of lifts starting above 2000m). The weather pattern is different from that of the northern Alps and even that of Les Deux-Alpes or Alpe-d'Huez, only a few miles to the west. It can get good snow when there is a shortage elsewhere (as it did in the early part of 2001) and vice versa. There is snowmaking on long runs down to each village, and this is being doubled for next season – taking the snow-gun tally up to 300 for 30km of pistes.

FOR EXPERTS
Deep, not notably steep

There is plenty to amuse experts – except those wanting extreme steeps.

The broad black runs down to Villeneuve and Chantemerle are only just black in steepness, but they are

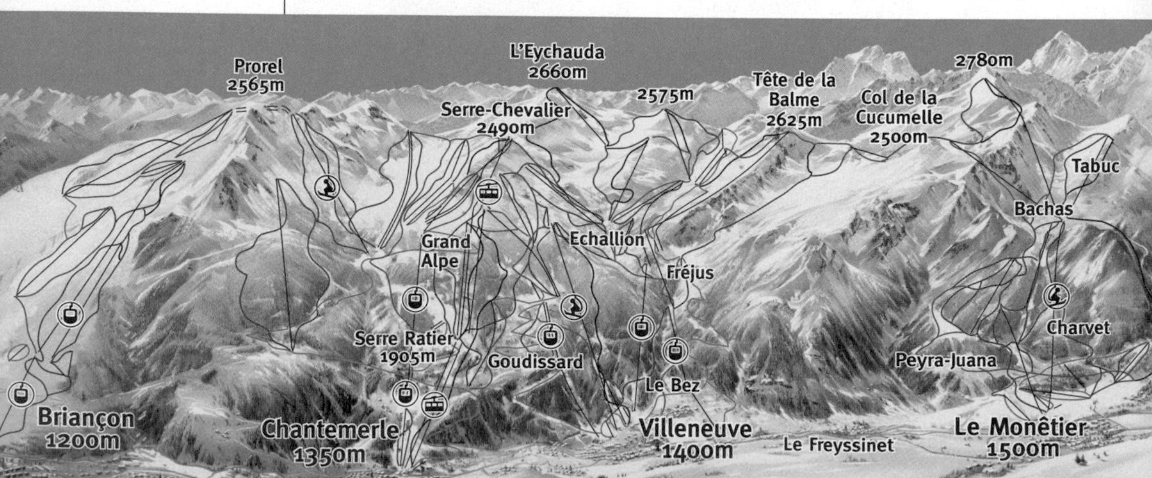

fine runs with their gradient sustained over an impressive vertical of around 800m. One or the other may be closed for days on end for racing or training. The rather neglected Tabuc run, sweeping around the mountain away from the lifts to Le Monêtier, has a couple of genuinely steep pitches but is mainly a cruise; it makes a fine end to the day. For moguls, look higher up the mountain to the steeper slopes served by the two top lifts above Le Monêtier and the three above Villeneuve. The runs beside these lifts – on and off-piste – form a great playground in good snow. The more roundabout Isolée black is a readers' favourite – 'scenic and challenging'.

There are also plenty of more serious off-piste expeditions to be done. Highlights include: Tête de Grand Pré to Villeneuve (a climb from Cucumelle); off the back of L'Eychauda to Puy-St-André (isolated, beautiful, taxi-ride home); L'Yret to Le Monêtier via Vallon de la Montagnolle; Tabuc (steep at the start, very beautiful) – and the Mecca of La Grave is nearby.

FOR INTERMEDIATES
Ski wherever you like

Serre-Chevalier's slopes ideally suit intermediates, who can buzz around without worrying about nasty surprises on the way. On the trail map red runs far outnumber blues – but most reds are at the easy end of the scale and the grooming is usually good, so even nervous intermediates shouldn't have problems with them.

There's plenty for more adventurous intermediates, though. Many runs are wide enough for a fast pace. Cucumelle in the Villeneuve sector is a favourite – a beautiful long red away from the lifts, with a challenging initial section. The red runs off the little-used Aiguillette chair in the Chantemerle sector are worth seeking out – quiet, enjoyable fast cruises.

If the reds are starting to seem a bit tame, there is plenty more to progress to. Unless ice towards the bottom is a problem, the blacks on the lower mountain should be first on the agenda, and the bumpier ones higher up can be tackled if snow is good.

FOR BEGINNERS
Best at Villeneuve

All three main villages have nursery areas (at Chantemerle it's small, and you generally go up to Serre Ratier or Grand Alpe). Villeneuve has excellent green runs to progress to above Fréjus. The Chantemerle sector is less suitable for confidence-building, but has some easy high runs, at Grand Alpe for instance. Both sectors have green paths winding down from mid-mountain. But they are narrow, and not enjoyable when the runs become rutted and others are speeding along. Le Monêtier's easy runs are at resort level, next to excellent nursery slopes, and the area has been recommended by beginners for 'better snow and fewer people'.

FOR CROSS-COUNTRY
Excellent if the snow is good

There are 45km of tracks along the valley floor, mainly following the gurgling river between Le Monêtier and Villeneuve and going on up towards the Col du Lautaret.

QUEUES
Avoid French school holidays

More than most resorts, Serre-Chevalier seems to fill up with French families in the February holidays, producing serious queues all over the place. The Aiguillette chair in the Chantemerle sector is a good place to escape to.

At other times a range of big lifts means there are few problems getting out of the valley. But old, slow lifts still cause queues at altitude. The Prorel double drag from Chantemerle towards Briançon – a regular bottleneck – will be replaced by a six-pack for next season.

boarding *Serre-Che is a snowboarding hot-spot, popular mainly with advanced boarders because of the off-piste powder and because the resort has invested in loads of fun features. There's big air in Briançon, boarder-cross in Villeneuve and Chantemerle and a half-pipe in Villeneuve, all with sound-systems. The diverse pistes with open and tree-lined runs also suit intermediates, though there are annoying flat sections between some lifts and several tracks the less confident might find tricky. The main lifts are chairs and gondolas but there are a lot of difficult-to-avoid and violent drag-lifts. Evenings are fairly quiet but there's at least one lively bar in each centre.*

Chantemerle may have been a mountain village originally, but it sure doesn't look like one any longer →

SNOWPIX.COM / CHRIS GILL

SCHOOLS/GUIDES

2001/02 prices in euros

ESF In all centres
Classes 6 days, 5hr: 3hr am and 2hr pm; half-day am or pm
6 full days: 170
Children's classes
Ages: up to 12
6 full days: 166
Private lessons
Hourly: 29

Ecole de Ski Buissonnière
Classes am or pm
6 mornings: 92
Children's classes
Ages: up to 12
6 mornings: 90
Private lessons
Hourly: 29

Génération Snow
6 mornings: 110
1½hr: 42

Montagne Adventure
Off-piste, ski-touring

Compagnie des Guides de l'Oisans
Off-piste, ski tours, ice-climbing, snow-shoes

Montagne à la carte
Off-piste, ski-touring, heli-skiing, climbing, snow-shoes

Montagne et Ski
Off-piste, ski-touring, heli-skiing, snow-shoes

David Legendre
Snow-shoes

GETTING THERE

Air Turin, transfer 2½hr. Grenoble, transfer 2½hr. Lyon, transfer 4hr.

Rail Briançon (6km); regular buses from station.

MOUNTAIN RESTAURANTS
Not a highlight

Mountain restaurants are quite well distributed, but the few good ones are mostly concentrated in the central sectors. If lunch is an important part of your day, plan it carefully; if it's a very important part, go elsewhere.

For a serious lunch, we head for Pi Maï in the hamlet of Fréjus, a little way below the Fréjus lift station. Its table-service meals are not cheap, but the food is good and the spacious, rustic restaurant with log fire is a fine place to retreat to on a bad day. Service may be charming, or not. Also in the Villeneuve sector is L'Echaillon, a lofty building with table-service food that we and some others have enjoyed; finding it is a bit of a challenge.

At Serre Ratier, above Chantemerle, is a big, popular and noisy self-service, with live entertainment. Higher up, the big Grand Alpe restaurant offers good value and good views but reportedly no longer offers table service.

In the Briançon sector, the little chalet just down from the top of Prorel, has great views of the Ecrins and is reasonably priced.

Above Le Monêtier the choice is between the unremarkable self-service Bachas at mid-mountain and the cosy Peyra Juana much lower down, where we and readers alike have enjoyed excellent service, food and value.

SCHOOLS AND GUIDES
Nothing but praise

We have received a number of reports on the Ecole de Ski Buissonnière over the years – all of them full of praise. For example: 'We thoroughly enjoyed a two-hour introductory snowboarding class. Instructors speak good English and classes are small.' This year we also have an enthusiastic report on an ESF class in Le Monêtier that was 'almost like a private lesson'.

FACILITIES FOR CHILDREN
Facilities at each village

We have had no very recent reports, but the Ecole de Ski Buissonnière (see above) also teaches children and has been praised in the past, as has Les Schtroumpfs in Villeneuve.

Staying there

HOW TO GO
A good choice of packages

There's a wide choice of packages from UK tour operators, offering all kinds of accommodation.

Chalets Several operators offer chalets in the different parts of the resort. Handmade's chalet Pyrene and chalet-hotel Le Rif Blanc have both been approved by readers this year.

CHILDCARE

Each of the main villages has its own non-ski nursery that takes children all day (9am to 5pm). At Villeneuve, Les Schtroumpfs (0492 247095) caters for kids from age 6 months; meals not provided. At Chantemerle, Les Poussins (0492 240343) takes them from age 8 months; meals provided. At Le Monêtier, Garderie de Pré-Chabert (0492 244575) takes them from age 18 months (6 months out of school holiday times); meals not provided.

Phone numbers
From abroad use the prefix +33 and omit the initial '0' of the phone number.

ACTIVITIES

Indoor Swimming pool, sauna, fitness centres, cinemas, bridge
Outdoor At Chantemerle: skating rink, paragliding, cleared paths, snow-shoe walks, snowmobiling. At Villeneuve: ice-driving circuit, skating rink, horse-riding, sleigh rides, cleared paths, paragliding, snow-shoe walks, snowmobiling. At Le Monêtier: skating rink, cleared paths, hang-gliding, hot springs, snow-shoe walks, ski-joring.

TOURIST OFFICE

Postcode 05240
t +33 492 249898
f 492 249884
contact@ot-serrechevalier.fr
www.serre-chevalier.com

Hotels One of the features of this string of little villages is the range of attractive family-run hotels – many of them part of the Logis de France marketing consortium.
In Le Monêtier:
(((3) **Auberge du Choucas** (0492 244273) Smart wood-clad rooms, and good food in stone-vaulted restaurant.
((2) **Europe** (0492 244003) Simple but well run Logis in heart of old village, with pleasant bar and decent food.
((2) **Alliey** (0492 244002) Our favourite place to eat (see Eating out).
In Villeneuve:
((2) **Lièvre Blanc** (0492 247405) Former coaching inn, with a large, busy stone-vaulted bar. British-owned, with its own guide and hire shop.
((2) **Christiania** (0492 247633) Traditional hotel on main road, crammed with ornaments.
((2) **Vieille Ferme** (0492 247644) Stylish conversion on the edge of the village.
((2) **Cimotel** (0492 247822) Modern and charmless, with good-sized rooms and 'excellent' food.
(1) **Chatelas** (0492 247474) Prettily decorated simple chalet by river.
In Chantemerle:
((2) **Plein Sud** (0492 241701) Modern; pool and sauna.
((2) **Boule de Neige** (0492 240016) Comfortable, friendly, in the old centre.
(1) **Ricelle** (0492 240019) Charming, but across the valley from the slopes in Villard-Laté. Good food.
Self-catering There are plenty of modern apartment blocks in Villeneuve, Briançon and Chantemerle. Few have charm.

STAYING UP THE MOUNTAIN
Worth considering

Chalet-hotel Serre Ratier (0492 241581), at the mid-station of the Chantemerle cable-car, does full board at reasonable rates. A more seductive possibility is to stay at Pi Maï (0492 248363) in Fréjus, above Villeneuve (see Mountain restaurants).

EATING OUT
Unpretentious and traditional

In Le Monêtier, there are several good hotel-based options. Our favourite is the panelled restaurant of the Alliey, which offers excellent food at astoundingly moderate prices and an impressive wine list. The Auberge du Choucas considers itself best in town and is certainly the most expensive. The Europe has reliable French cooking at reasonable prices. The Boîte à Fromages does a 'magnificent' fondue.

In the old part of Villeneuve, La Pastorale is a busy, cramped vault with a warm welcome, an open-fire grill and good-value menu. The Marotte, a tiny stone building with classic French cuisine, has been highly praised. The Noctambule and Le Refuge specialise in fondue and raclette. And there are good crêperies – try the Petit Duc, or La Manouille. Over in Le Bez, Le Bidule is said to have 'first-class food and service, at good value', while the Siyou in the old village of La Salle is good for 'local specialities at very reasonable prices'.

In Chantemerle, Le Couch'où is good value for fondue and raclette, and has a pizzeria upstairs. The candlelit Crystal is the smartest, most expensive place in town. The Kandahar is a charming pizzeria and the rustic Ricelle offers amazing value.

APRES-SKI
Quiet streets and few bars

Nightlife seems to revolve around bars, scattered through the various villages.

In Le Monêtier the Alpen is a proper skiers' bar with Tirol-style U-shaped bench seats, a happy hour, free nibbles and welcoming staff. The British-run Rif Blanc bar is dreary but now rivals the Pub in popularity. If you want to forget you're in a ski resort (and see French smoking laws at their least effective), hit the Cibouit.

In Villeneuve the bar of the Lièvre Blanc is popular with Brits; the Iceberg is a pub-style bar frequented by teenagers. The Frog is cramped, but has 'good atmosphere'. In Chantemerle the Yeti and the Underground beneath it are focal. The Kitzbühel has a good atmosphere, particularly when sporting events are shown, and is 'not too full of fellow Brits'. After everything else has closed, a karaoke bar with 'an erratic door policy' may still let you in.

OFF THE SLOPES
Try the hot baths

Serre-Chevalier doesn't hold many off-slope attractions, and it's certainly not for avid shoppers, but the old town of Briançon is well worth a visit. Visitors have enjoyed walking in the valley on 'well-prepared trails', and the indoor-outdoor thermal bath in Le Monêtier (re-opened in 1999) makes a great place to watch the sun go down. The swimming pool in the hotel Sporting in Villeneuve is open to non-residents.

Ste-Foy-Tarentaise 1550m

Secret off-piste haven for those in the know

WHAT IT COSTS

4

HOW IT RATES

The slopes

Snow	***
Extent	*
Experts	****
Intermediates	***
Beginners	**
Convenience	***
Queues	*****
Restaurants	*

The rest

Scenery	***
Resort charm	***
Off-slope	*

MOUNTAIN FACTS

Altitude 1550m-2620m	
Lifts	5
Pistes	25km
Green	8%
Blue	15%
Red	54%
Black	23%
Artificial snow	0km

What's new

Further development in keeping with the character of the resort is under way at the ski station, thanks to a new mayor with a commitment to expansion. Handsome new chalets are being built at the station for the coming season and there will be improvements to a couple of runs. More facilities and even more lifts are on the cards in the long run.

- + No crowds
- + Lots of excellent off-piste and untracked powder
- + Cheap lift pass and good value lodging
- + Tarentaise mega-resorts nearby for a change of scene

- − Tiny mountain hamlet offers few off-slope diversions
- − Very limited piste network for high-mileage piste-bashers
- − Few off-slope diversions
- − Limited après-ski

This small area in the Tarentaise has been developed only since 1990. The millions who flock to the nearby mega-resorts of Val-d'Isère and Les Arcs never give it a thought. But those in the know are well rewarded. It's an uncrowded gem with some wonderful off-piste slopes for experts and intermediates.

THE RESORT

There isn't much of one; that's part of the charm of this place – it's ideal for getting away from the crowds. The ski station of Ste-Foy, also known as Bonconseil, is a tiny mountain hamlet set 8km off the main road between Val-d'Isère and Bourg-St-Maurice: turn off at La Thuile, just after the village of Ste-Foy. The largest building at the station houses the ticket office, a cafe/bar and the only equipment shop (Zigzags, which readers roundly condemn for its shocking service).

THE MOUNTAIN

Off-piste guides from Val regularly impress clients by bringing them to Ste-Foy's deserted slopes, accessed by three quad chairs, rising one above the other to the Col de l'Aiguille.

Impressive as the off-piste can be, you may want to spread your wings from the tiny resort during a week's stay, particularly if the snow is unkind. Luckily Val d'Isère, Tignes, Les Arcs (via Villaroger) and La Rosière are all within easy reach (with a car). You're entitled to a free day in La Rosière, and reduced tariffs in all the rest, with a current Ste-Foy six-day pass – which at 82 euros last season was half the price of neighbouring Val d'Isère. A day pass was a bargain 15 euros.

Slopes The top lift accesses almost 600m of vertical above the tree line and superb, long off-piste routes on the back of the mountain. The two lower chairs serve pleasant green, blue and red runs through trees and back to

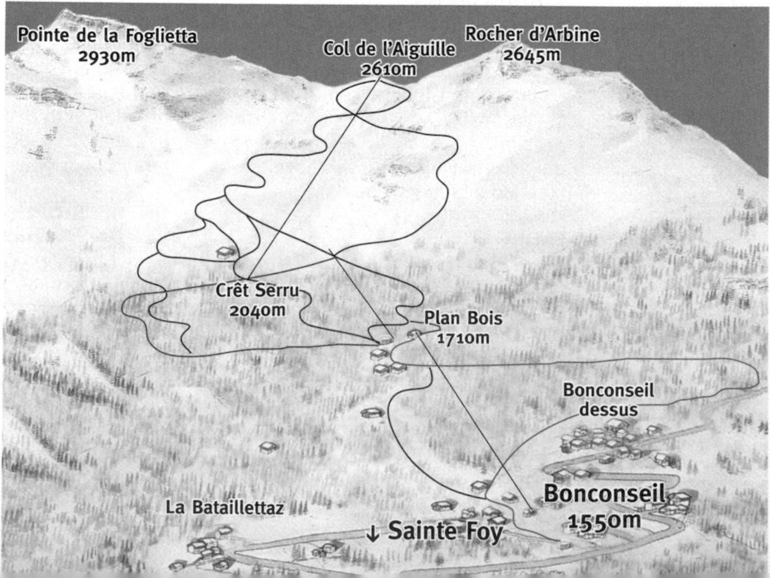

Phone numbers
From abroad use the prefix +33 and omit the initial '0' of the phone number.

TOURIST OFFICE

Postcode 73640
t +33 479 069519
f 479 069509
www.sainte-foy-tarentaise.com

the base station. Don't come here for quality grooming or modern lifts, but this reporter didn't care: 'Most of my ski career I've been in Verbier, Zermatt and Vail. Skiing in Ste-Foy is better.'
Snow reliability The slopes face north or west. Snow reliability is good on the former but can suffer on the latter. But the lack of crowds means you can still make fresh tracks days after a storm.
Snowboarding Great free-riding terrain. A fun-park was built last year too.
Experts Experts can pass happy times on and off the sides of Ste-Foy's black and red runs, but it's the more serious off-piste you come for, for which you need a guide. There are wonderful runs down through deserted old villages to the road between Ste-Foy and Val-d'Isère and a splendid route off to the left which starts with a hike and takes you through trees and over a stream down to the tiny village of Le Crot. The ESF runs group off-piste trips, and arranges transport back to the station. There are three refuges in the area if you fancy an overnight adventure.
Intermediates Intermediates can enjoy 1000m vertical of uncrowded reds – ideal for confidence building and sharpening technique. The higher slopes are the more difficult – the red L'Aiguille is a superb test for confident intermediates, who should also try the off-piste (with a guide). Anyone who doesn't fancy experimenting with off-piste will tire of the limited runs in a day or so and be champing at the bit to get to Val d'Isère or Les Arcs.
Beginners Not the best place, but there is a small nursery drag at the base. After that you can progress to a green run off the first chair – a pleasant, gentle track through trees – and a gentle blue off the second.
Cross-country No prepared trails, but ask the tourist office about marked itinerary routes such as Planay dessus.
Queues You have more chance of winning the lottery than finding a lift queue at Ste-Foy.
Mountain restaurants There are two rustic mountain restaurants at the top of the first chair, Les Brevettes and Chez Léon. Recent reporters enjoyed the plat du jour at the latter but have been less complimentary about the former. La Ruelle, at the bottom of the first chair, is a good, rustic bar-restaurant, and La Maison à Colonnes, also at the base, gets good write-ups: 'Friendly, interesting menu, nice atmosphere.' There's also the Pitchouli for drinks and snacks in the main base building.
Schools and guides We've had good reports of ski school, especially for children (accepted from age four), There's a good chance classes will not be large.
Facilities for children There is a crèche, Les P'tits Trappeurs, which takes children from age three.

STAYING THERE

Drivers have most choice. If you don't have a car it's most convenient to stay at the ski station, since buses to and from Ste-Foy village run only every one to two hours (taking 20 minutes).
How to go Ste-Foy is hardly on the UK market, so most people organise their own trip. Ste-Foy village is only about 20 minutes from the Eurostar terminal at Bourg St Maurice.
Hotels Auberge sur la Montagne (069583), just above the turn-off at La Thuile, sleeps 20, has excellent food and atmosphere and is run by an English couple. Yellow Stone Chalet (069606) is a Gîte de France at the station, run by an American and highly recommended by a recent reporter: 'Beautifully appointed, modern with good food.' Hotel Monal (069007), in Ste-Foy village, is a basic auberge.
Chalets Chalet Number One (UK number: 01572 717259), in the village of La Masure, is run by Brit snowboarder Lloyd Rogers, serving good food in comfortable, rustic surroundings. Skiers are welcome. too!
Self-catering There are quite a few apartments and chalets to rent in the area, and there should be more at the station from this coming season – the tourist office has a list or there are rental agencies in Bourg St Maurice.
Après-ski Pretty quiet. There may be a short-lived après-ski scene in one of the bars at the station, and the bar of the Monal can get lively.
Eating out Book the excellent Chez Mérie, in the village of Le Miroir, well in advance. In La Thuile, book the Auberge sur la Montagne. In Ste-Foy village, the Monal does 'good food' and a reporter tells us that, at the station, La Ruelle opens in the evenings by arrangement.
Off the slopes Not a lot – snowshoeing and dog sledding.

St-Martin-de-Belleville 1400m

Explore the Three Valleys from a traditional old village

WHAT IT COSTS

4

HOW IT RATES

The slopes

Snow	***
Extent	*****
Experts	****
Intermediates	*****
Beginners	***
Convenience	***
Queues	****
Restaurants	****

The rest

Scenery	***
Resort charm	****
Off-slope	*

What's new

There are plans to build a gondola to replace the chair out of the village for the 2002/03 season. The drag-lift on the slope up from the church will be moved to the side of the slope and made less vicious.

MOUNTAIN FACTS

for the Three Valleys – see Les Menuires chapter for piste map

Altitude	1300m-3200m
Lifts	200
Pistes	600km
Green	17%
Blue	34%
Red	37%
Black	12%
Artificial snow	90km
Recco detectors used	

- ⊕ Attractively developed traditional village with pretty church
- ⊕ Easy access to the whole of the extensive Three Valleys network; very quick to get to Méribel and Les Menuires
- ⊕ Long easy intermediate runs on rolling local slopes
- ⊖ Snow reliability worse than in most other Three Valleys bases
- ⊖ No green runs for beginners to progress to
- ⊖ Limited après-ski
- ⊖ Few off-slope diversions

St-Martin is a traditional Savoyard village, with old church (prettily lit at night), small square and wood and stone buildings, a few miles down the valley from Les Menuires. As a quiet, inexpensive, attractive base for exploration of the Three Valleys, it's unbeatable. All our reporters who stayed there have loved it. And it's a great spot to stop for lunch if you are cruising the slopes.

THE RESORT

In 1950 St-Martin didn't even have running water or electricity. Later, while new resorts were developed nearby, St-Martin was a bit of a backwater, though it remained the administrative centre for the Belleville valley (which includes the resorts of Val-Thorens and Les Menuires). But in the 1980s chair-lifts were built, linking it to the slopes of Méribel and Les Menuires. The old village has been developed, of course, but the architecture of the new buildings fits in well with the old, and you can walk around it in a few minutes. The main feature of the centre remains the lovely old 16th-century church – prettily floodlit at night. There are some good local shops and few 'touristy' ones.

THE MOUNTAINS

The whole of the Three Valleys can be easily explored from here.

Slopes Two chair-lifts – the upper one a fast quad – take you to a ridge from which you can access Méribel on one side and Les Menuires on the other.

Snow reliability Natural snow reliability is not the best in the Three Valleys – the local slopes face west and get the full force of the afternoon sun. But there is now snowmaking from top to bottom of the main run.

Experts Locally there are large areas of gentle and often deserted off-piste. And access to La Masse for steep north-facing slopes is just one run away from the top of the local chairs.

Intermediates The local slopes are pleasant blues and reds, mainly of interest to intermediates – including

OT LES MENUIRES / PIERRE EXANDIER

→ New buildings blend in with old in picturesque St-Martin

LIFT PASSES

2001/02 prices in euros

Three Valleys
See Méribel chapter.

Alternative passes
Vallée des Belleville pass covers 72 lifts and 300km piste in Val-Thorens, Les Menuires and St-Martin (adult 6-day 170). Les Menuires and St-Martin pass covers 43 lifts and 160km of piste (adult 6-day 147).

Phone numbers
From abroad use the prefix +33 and omit the initial '0' of the phone number.

one of our favourite runs in the Three Valleys: the long, rolling, wide Jerusalem red. The Verdet blue from the top of the Méribel lifts is a wonderful easy cruise with great views and is usually very quiet. The whole of the Three Valleys is, of course, an intermediate's paradise.

Beginners St-Martin is not ideal – there's a nursery slope but no easy green runs to progress to.

Queues Queues are not usually much of a problem – the local lifts can easily cope with the morning rush from the guest beds the village has. But we had a report in the past of a 20-minute queue and 'queue rage' from some 'embarrassingly pompous Brits'.

Cross-country There are 33km of trails in the Belleville valley.

Snowboarding Some great local off-piste free-riding.

Mountain restaurants There are three atmospheric old mountain restaurants on the main run down to the village. Chardon Bleu and Corbelleys near the second chair-lift are good for lunch and La Loe, lower down, is popular as the lifts close. Brewski's (on the left, halfway down the local village slope with the drag-lift – watch for the signs) does good-value pub grub (pies are a speciality) and has sunny terraces with views down the valley – it attracts customers from all over the Three Valleys. La Bouitte in St-Marcel (an off-piste run away) is one of the best restaurants in the Three Valleys and features in the Gault-Millau gourmet guidebook – a traditional, welcoming, rustic French auberge (but not cheap).

Schools and guides The ski school is said to have instructors with good English. But a reporter said, 'They were kind and considerate to our children but my son struggled with French on his snowboard lesson.'

Facilities for children We've had good reports of the kindergarten, which is housed in a new purpose-built building and takes children from three months.

STAYING THERE

How to go For such a small village there's a good variety of accommodation.

Hotels The Alp'Hôtel (0479 089282), at the foot of the slope by the main lift, got a rave review from a recent reporter: 'Second year there, good food and wine list, comfortable rooms; I've recommended it to *The Good Hotel Guide*.' Saint Martin (0479 008800) is right on the slope, and Edelweiss (0479 089667) is in the village itself. All are 3-stars. But the best value accommodation is the B&B offered at Brewski's (0479 006234), again right on the slope with well furnished en suite rooms of various sizes. This also gives you the chance to try some of the excellent local restaurants.

Chalets Les Chalets de St Martin has been the main British chalet operator in town – and has operated there ever since the first lift was built. It has catered chalets, all with en suite facilities, employs professional chefs and serves a variety of quality wines to match the food (the owner is a wine merchant). This season two of its chalets are being run by Ski Total.

The centre of the village is delightfully old and rustic →

OT LES MENUIRES / J F LEPAGE

TOURIST OFFICE

Postcode 73440
t +33 479 089309
f 479 089171
lesmenuires@lesmenuires.com
www.st-martin-belleville.com

Self-catering Les Chalets de St Martin has a variety of self-catered chalets and apartments to rent and plenty of others are available.

Après-ski Après ski centres around two bars. The Pourquoi Pas? piano bar is delightfully cosy with a roaring log fire and comfortable easy chairs and sofas (it was up for sale at the time we went to press). Brewski's has wooden chairs and tables, a pool table, activities such as karaoke, sumo wrestling or live bands most nights and photos of old pop stars – such as Frank Zappa, Cream, the Beatles, Tina Turner and the Sex Pistols – on the walls. One of the fun-loving Kiwi owners may do his Elvis impersonation if you buy him enough drinks.

Eating out For such a small village there is a good variety of restaurants nearby. Le Montagnard is in a rustic old building and has been highly recommended by a recent reporter: 'Very friendly, massive helpings of excellent traditional Savoyard specialities.' La Voute has reasonable prices and does good pizza. Brewski's does 'good pub grub and specialises in unusual pies (even lamb curry pie)'. Etoile de Neige is a smart traditional French restaurant. Le Lachenal is cosy with intimate small rooms, open fire and good French food. Just down the road in St-Marcel is La Bouitte, the best restaurant in the valley – see Mountain Restaurants. A bit further at Les Granges is the rustic Chez Bidou, popular with locals for its traditional Savoyard food.

Off the slopes If you don't use the slopes, there are better places to base yourself. There are pleasant walks and a sports hall, but not much else.

La Tania 1400m

Small, family-friendly base for exploring the Three Valleys

WHAT IT COSTS

(4)

HOW IT RATES

The slopes

Snow	***
Extent	*****
Experts	****
Intermediates	*****
Beginners	**
Convenience	****
Queues	****
Restaurants	****

The rest

Scenery	***
Resort charm	***
Off-slope	*

- ⊕ Part of the Three Valleys – the world's biggest linked ski area
- ⊕ Quick access to Courchevel and Méribel
- ⊕ Long, rolling, intermediate, wooded runs back to the village
- ⊕ Good local nursery slopes
- ⊕ Attractively developed, small, traffic-free village

- ⊖ Small development without much choice of après-ski
- ⊖ Runs home can suffer when snow is poor, though new snowmaking should help
- ⊖ Runs home too steep for beginners

La Tania does not try to compete with its more upmarket neighbours, Courchevel and Méribel. It has carved out its own niche as a good-value, small, quiet, family-friendly base from which to hit the snowsure slopes of Courchevel and to explore the whole of the Three Valleys. It is prettily set in the trees and the wood-clad buildings make it one of the more attractive French purpose-built resorts (it was started ten years ago, by which time lessons had been learned from the horrendous architecture of resorts that were developed in the 1960s and 70s). Though it has grown, it remains small. If you want lots of shops and varied après-ski you should choose another Three Valleys resort.

What's new

For the 2001/02 season 38 snow-guns are to be installed on the blue piste back to La Tania. So when it is cold enough to make snow you'll be assured of being able to ski or ride all the way into the village.

THE RESORT

La Tania is set just off the small road linking Courchevel Le Praz to Méribel (and, for those with a car, is much nearer to Méribel than Courchevel 1850, if you want to hit the shopping or nightlife). It was built for the 1992 Olympics and has grown into a quiet, attractive, car-free collection of mainly ski-in, ski-out chalets and apartments set among the trees, most with good views. There are few shops other than food and sports shops and not much choice of bars and restaurants. You can walk around the place in a couple of minutes.

A gondola leads to the slopes, and there are two wonderful sweeping intermediate runs down. These aren't ideal for progressing beginners, but the nursery slope is on your doorstep, and visitors say that La Tania is 'very child friendly'. Hourly buses go to Courchevel in the daytime.

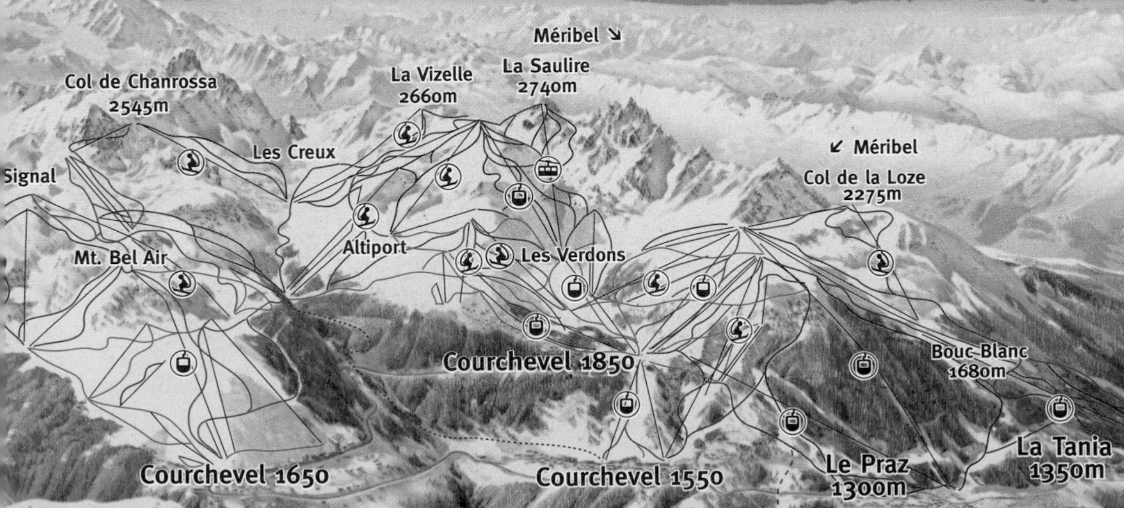

MOUNTAIN FACTS

For the Three Valleys

Altitude	1300m-3200m
Lifts	200
Pistes	600km
Green	17%
Blue	34%
Red	37%
Black	12%
Artificial snow	90km
Recco detectors used	

THE MOUNTAINS

As well as good, though limited, local slopes, the whole of the Three Valleys can be explored easily from here, with just two lifts needed to get to either the Courchevel or Méribel slopes.

Slopes The gondola out of the village goes to Bouc Blanc. From here a drag-lift takes you to Chenus and the slopes above Courchevel 1850 and a high-speed quad goes to the link with Méribel via Col de la Loze. An alternative way to the slopes above 1850 is to take two successive drag-lifts from the village to Loze. From all these points, varied, interesting intermediate runs take you back into the La Tania sector.

Snow reliability Good snow-cover down to Bouc Blanc is usual all season. Below that the snow is less assured – you had to ride the gondola down for much of last season's poor snow. But things should be improved for 2001/02 by extra snowmaking covering the whole of the blue run back to the village.

Experts No local challenges but there's the whole of the Three Valleys to explore and some tough runs and good off-piste are close by in the Courchevel sector.

Intermediates There are two lovely, long, undulating intermediate runs back to La Tania. And the quick access to the rest of the Three Valleys' 600km of well-groomed pistes makes the area an intermediate's paradise.

Beginners There is a good beginner area and lift right in the village and beginner children, in particular, are well catered for. But there are no very easy, long, local slopes to progress to; the intermediate runs back to the village are quite challenging.

Queues A queue can build up for the village gondola but it is quick-moving. Elsewhere in the Three Valleys there are a few remaining bottlenecks – and those that do exist can easily be avoided by taking an alternative route.

Cross-country There are trails at altitude with links to Méribel and Courchevel.

Snowboarding There is no local fun-

park or half-pipe, but Courchevel's are easy to get to. There's a cheap place to stay that might appeal to boarders on a tight budget – see Staying there, below – and one lively local bar.

Mountain restaurants Bouc Blanc, near the top of the gondola, has friendly table-service, good food and a big terrace. Roc Tania at Col de la Loze is tiny but very pretty inside and has table-service.

Schools and guides Magic in Motion was 'absolutely wonderful' for the five children in a recent reporter's group.

Facilities for children We have had excellent reports of tour operator Le Ski's crèche here. The local kindergarten takes children from the age of three.

Phone numbers
From abroad use the prefix +33 and omit the initial '0' of the phone number.

TOURIST OFFICE

Postcode 73125
t +33 479 084040
f 479 084571
info@latania.com
www.latania.com

STAYING THERE

How to go Around 30 British tour operators go here.

Hotels Montana (0479 088008) is a slope-side 3-star next to the gondola with a sauna and fitness club. It was said by a reporter to be 'Very good value, with friendly, English-speaking staff and excellent food.' The Mountain Centre opened last season (www.themountaincentre.com or 01273 897525 in the UK) and has 'cheap backpacker-style accommodation' from £17 a night B&B, with dinner costing £6 and bedding and a towel a few pence more.

Chalets Several tour operators have splendid newish ski-in, ski-out chalets with fine views, though reporters have complained of 'poor soundproofing' in some. Le Ski has a crèche that we have had glowing reports of in one of its chalets.

Self-catering There are lots of apartments. We had a report in 2001 of the Pierre & Vacances apartments having 'incredibly cramped bedrooms and looking tired'. But the views and cleanliness were praised.

Après-ski Pub Le Ski Lodge is by far the liveliest place, with Murpheys on draught and frequent live bands and theme nights ('James Bond night was a good laugh,' said a reporter). L'Arbatt (a bar-tabac) and La Taïga (a bar-pizzeria) are quieter. But if you want a lively varied nightlife, go elsewhere – La Tania is too small.

Eating out La Ferme de la Tania and Le Farçon get generally good reviews for their Savoyard fare. Pub Le Ski Lodge has 'damn good chilli burgers'. La Taïga does 'very good pizzas and is friendly and quite cheap'.

Off the slopes Unless you have a car to travel around, La Tania will be deadly dull for anyone not intending to hit the slopes.

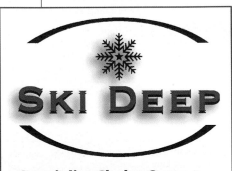

Tignes 2100m

Great skiing and ... er, that's it

WHAT IT COSTS

6

HOW IT RATES

The slopes

Snow	*****
Extent	*****
Experts	*****
Intermediates	*****
Beginners	**
Convenience	****
Queues	****
Restaurants	**

The rest

Scenery	***
Resort charm	**
Off-slope	*

What's new

In 2000/01 the village centres became traffic-free and many hotels and apartments were renovated.

For 2001/02 there are plans for a tunnel under the road between the Chaudannes and the Paquis slopes and for a new restaurant at the top of the Chaudannes chair.

The slow Tommeuses lifts are due to be replaced by an eight-seater detachable chair, but no date has yet been specified.

- ⊕ Good snow guaranteed for a long season – about the best Alpine bet
- ⊕ One of the best areas in the world for lift-served off-piste runs
- ⊕ Huge amount of terrain for all standards, shared with Val-d'Isère
- ⊕ Lots of accommodation close to the slopes (though there is also quite a bit that involves some walking)
- ⊕ Swift access to Val-d'Isère slopes

- ⊖ Resort buildings spoil the views from the slopes
- ⊖ Bleak, treeless setting – no woodland runs, and many slopes liable to closure after heavy snow
- ⊖ Still lots of long, slow chair-lifts
- ⊖ Poor mountain restaurants
- ⊖ Near-beginners have to go over to Val-d'Isère to find long green runs
- ⊖ Limited après-ski

The appeal of Tignes is simple: good snow, spread over a wide area of varied terrain. Tignes and Val-d'Isère together form the enormous Espace Killy – a Mecca for experts, and ideal for adventurous intermediates. And in many ways Tignes makes the better base: appreciably higher, more convenient, surrounded by better intermediate terrain, with quick access to the Grande Motte glacier.

We prefer to stay in Val, which is a more human place. But the case for Tignes gets stronger as results flow from the resort's campaign to reinvent itself in a more cuddly form. Cars are being pushed underground, new buildings are being designed in traditional styles and old ones are getting a facelift. It all helps.

Although Tignes has invested in some impressive lifts in recent years, enjoyment of the expansive western side of the Tignes bowl – and large areas of the Val sector, too – is limited by the time you spend riding slow chair-lifts.

The resort

Tignes was created before the French discovered the benefits of making purpose-built resorts look acceptable. Later than most of its contemporaries, it has now woken up to the demand for traditional Alpine ambience. Traffic is now under control, with pedestrian-only centres, and the villages are certainly more pleasant as a result. The downside is that your transfer bus may not be able to get close to your hotel.

The original and main village – Tignes-le-Lac – is still the hub of the lift system. Some of the smaller buildings in the central part, Le Rosset, are being successfully revamped in chalet style. But the place as a whole is dreary, and the blocks overlooking the lake from the quarter called Le Bec-Rouge will always be monstrous. Some attractive new buildings are being added on the fringes, in a suburb known as Les Almes. Recently added lifts have improved mountain access from here, and from the other suburb of Le Lavachet – a slightly more inviting area than Le Rosset.

Val-Claret (a couple of km up the valley, beyond the lake) was mainly developed after Le Rosset, and is a bit more stylish (though not at all traditional). There are major lifts up to the Grande Motte glacier here, as well as lifts accessing the sides of the bowl and the slopes of Val-d'Isère.

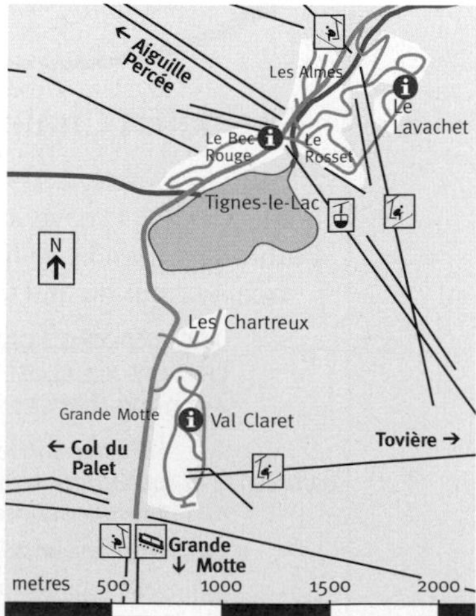

MOUNTAIN FACTS

For entire Espace Killy area

Altitude 1550m-3455m
Lifts 97
Pistes 300km
Green 15%
Blue 46%
Red 28%
Black 11%
Artificial snow 24km
Recco detectors used

LIFT PASSES

2001/02 prices in euros

L'Espace Killy
Covers all lifts in Tignes and Val-d'Isère.

Beginners Free lifts on all main nursery slopes; special beginners' half-day pass.

Main pass
1-day pass 35
6-day pass 167

Senior citizens
Over 60: 6-day pass 142
Over 75: free pass

Children
Under 13: 6-day pass 117
Under 5: free pass

Short-term passes
Half-day pass from 12.30 (adult 25).

Alternative periods
14 non-consecutive days pass available.

Notes 6-day pass and over valid for one day each in the Three Valleys, Pralognan-la-Vanoise, Les Saisies and Valmorel. On 3- to 15-day passes, pass reimbursed if all lifts are shut due to bad weather. Discount on new passes on presentation of previous season's pass. Extra discount for senior citizens aged 70 to 74.

Alternative passes
Super Tignes ski pass covers the lifts on the Tignes side of the Espace Killy only (adult 6-day 142).

The Grande Motte casts a long shadow over Val-Claret in January →

SNOWPIX.COM / CHRIS GILL

Below the high valley of the main resort villages are two smaller settlements. Tignes-les-Boisses, quietly set in the trees beside the road up to the main Tignes villages, consists of a barracks and a couple of simple hotels. Lower Tignes-les-Brévières is a renovated old village at the lowest point of the slopes – a favourite lunch spot, and a friendly place to stay.

Location isn't crucial, as a regular and efficient free bus service connects all the villages until midnight – though in the daytime the route runs along the bottom of Val-Claret, leaving residents of central Val-Claret with some hiking.

A six-day pass covers a day in some other resorts, including Les Arcs or La Plagne and the Three Valleys, all most easily reached with the aid of a car. Preserve your pass and you'll get a loyalty discount off next year's.

The mountains

The area's great weakness is that it can become unusable in bad weather. There are no woodland runs except immediately above Tignes-les-Boisses and Tignes-les-Brévières, heavy snow produces widespread avalanche risk and wind closes the higher chairs.

THE SLOPES
High, snowsure and varied

Tignes' biggest asset is the **Grande Motte** – and the runs from, as well as on, the glacier. The underground funicular from Val-Claret whizzes you up to over 3000m in six minutes. There are chairs and drags to play on, as well as beautiful long runs back to the resort and a link over to Val-d'Isère.

The main lifts towards Val-d'Isère are efficient: a high-capacity gondola from Le Lac to **Tovière**, and a fast 'bubble' chair from Val-Claret to **Col de Fresse**. You can head back to Tignes from either: the return from Tovière to Tignes-le-Lac is via a steep black run (not so difficult now the moguls are regularly smoothed out), but there are easier runs to Val-Claret.

Going up the opposite side of the valley takes you to a quieter area where a series of drags and chair-lifts serve predominantly east-facing slopes split into two main sectors, linked in both directions – **Col du Palet** and **L'Aiguille Percée**. From the latter, you can descend to Tignes-les-Brévières, on blue, red or black runs (but beware the Chardons blue, which should be graded red); there's an efficient gondola back.

The Col des Ves chair-lift, at the south end of the Col du Palet sector, is not normally opened until high season and several recent reporters have commented that some lifts started later in the day than advertised.

SNOW RELIABILITY
Difficult to beat

Tignes has all-year-round runs (barring brief closures in spring or autumn) on its 3455m Grande Motte glacier. And the resort height of 2100m generally means good snow-cover right back to base for most of the long season. The whole region, not just the glacier area, usually has good cover from November to May. The west-facing runs (especially those from Tovière to Val-Claret) and the Bleuets run down to Le Lac suffer from the sun, although they now have serious snowmaking.

FOR EXPERTS
An excellent choice

It is the off-piste possibilities that make Tignes such a draw for experts. Go with one of the off-piste groups

that the schools organise and you'll have a great time (snow permitting).

One of the big adventures is to head for Champagny (linked to the La Plagne area) or Peisey-Nancroix (linked to the Les Arcs area) – very beautiful runs, and not too difficult. Your guide will organise return transport.

Another favourite of ours is the Tour de Pramecou, from the Grande Motte glacier. After some walking and beautiful isolated runs, you end up on a steep, smooth north-facing slope that takes you back to Val-Claret. There are other descents across the glacier to the Leisse chair-lift.

The whole western side of the bowl has lots of off-piste possibilities. The terrain served by the Col des Ves chair is often excellent. To the left (looking up) there are wonderfully secluded, scenic and challenging descents. On the right, lower down, is a less heavily used and gentler area, ideal for off-piste initiation. To the north, there are excellent variants on the Sache run to Les Brévières (see below).

The schools and guides offer the bizarre French form of heli-skiing: mountaintop drops are forbidden, but from Tovière you can ski down towards the Lac du Chevril to be retrieved by chopper. Or you can be dropped over the border in Italy.

The only serious challenge within the piste network is the long black run from Tovière to Tignes-le-Lac, with steep, usually heavily mogulled sections – though no longer so difficult at the bottom, according to this year's reporters. Parts of this run get a lot of afternoon sun. Our favourite black run is the Sache, from Aiguille Percée down a secluded valley to Tignes-les-Brévières, which can become very heavily mogulled at the bottom.

A reporter recommends the black 'Silene' piste: 'big moguls – very challenging and enjoyable'.

FOR INTERMEDIATES

One of the best

For the keen intermediate piste-basher the Espace Killy is one of the top three or four areas in France, or the world.

Tignes' local slopes are ideal intermediate terrain. The red and blue runs on the Grande Motte glacier

La Grande Motte
3455m
Col de la Leisse
3015m
Col des Ves
2840m
Col du Palet
2695m
Col de Fresse
Tovière
2705m
L'Aiguille Percée
2705m
Val-Claret
Tignes-le-Lac
Le Lavachet
Tignes
2100m
Tignes-les-Boisses
1850m
Tignes-les-Brévières
1550m

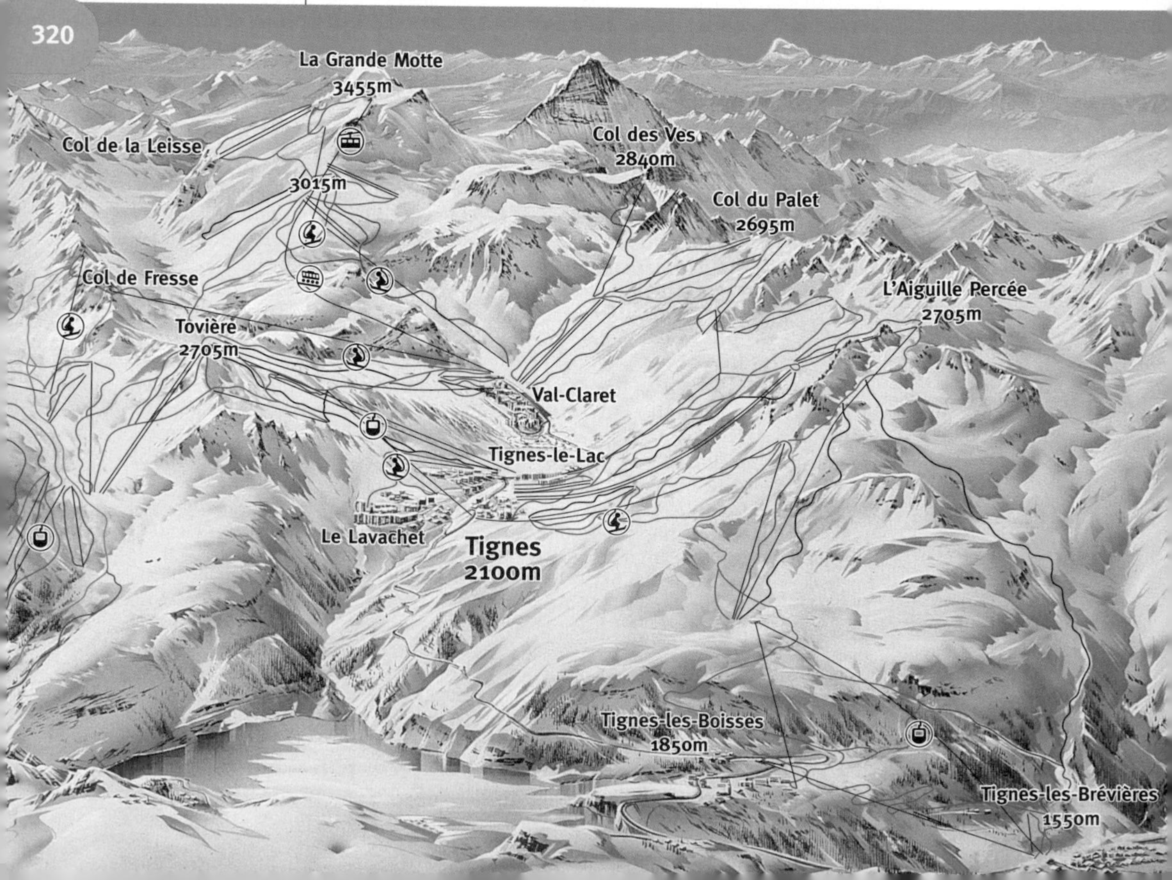

SCHOOLS/GUIDES

2001/02 prices in euros

ESF

Classes 5 days
5 half-days: 105

Children's classes
Ages: 5 to 14
5 half days: 105

Private lessons
Hourly or daily
30 for 1hr

Evolution 2

Classes 5 days
am or pm
5 half days: 122

Children's classes
Ages: 5 to 14
5 half days: 105

Private lessons
Hourly or daily
30 for 1hr

OTHER SCHOOLS

Tignes International
Snow Fun
Snocool
Kebra Surfing
Surf Feeling

nearly always have superb snow. The glacier run from the top of the cable-car is a gentle blue. The Leisse run down to the chair-lift is now graded black and can get very mogulled but has good snow. The long red run all the way back to town is a delightful long cruise – though often crowded.

From Tovière, the blue 'H' run to Val-Claret is an enjoyable cruise and generally well groomed. But again, it can get very crowded.

There is lots to do on the other side of the valley. We particularly like the uncrowded Ves red run reached by the low-capacity Col des Ves chair – the highest point of Tignes' non-glacier runs at 2840m. After an initial mogul field (sometimes quite testing) the run becomes an interesting undulating and curvy cruise, usually with good snow and a few moguls. The runs down from Aiguille Percée to Tignes-les-Boisses and Tignes-les-Brévières are also scenic and enjoyable. There are red and blue options as well as the beautiful Sache black run – adventurous intermediates shouldn't miss it. The runs down from Aiguille Percée to Le Lac are gentle, wide blues. The Bleuets blue from the top of the Aiguille Rouge chair is a more challenging alternative.

FOR BEGINNERS

Good nursery slopes, but ...

The nursery slopes of Tignes-le-Lac and Le Lavachet (which meet at the top) are excellent – convenient, snowsure, gentle, free of through-traffic and served by a slow chair and a drag (free). The ones at Val-Claret are much less appealing – steep and served by a free drag. You can also ride the first stage of the Bollin chair for free.

For long green runs you have to go over to the Val-d'Isère sector – easy enough, but you need an Espace Killy pass to use them, and you have to ride the gondola back down from Tovière. And in poor weather, the high Tignes valley is an intimidatingly bleak place – enough to make any wavering beginner retreat to a bar with a book.

FOR CROSS-COUNTRY

Interesting variety

The Espace Killy has 40km of cross-country trails. There are tracks on the frozen Lac de Tignes, along the valley between Val-Claret and Tignes-le-Lac, at Les Boisses and Les Brévières and up the mountain on the Grande Motte.

QUEUES

Very few

The queues here depend on snow conditions. If snow low down is poor, the Grande Motte funicular generates queues; the parallel high-speed chairs are often quicker. These lifts jointly shift a lot of people, with the result that the run down to Val-Claret can be seriously unpleasant. The worst queues now are for the cable-car on the glacier – half-hour waits are common.

Of course, if higher lifts are closed by heavy snow or high winds, the lifts on the lower slopes have big queues.

Queues can build up late in the day for the slow Tommeuses chairs (due for replacement, but no date as yet), bringing Tignes residents back from the Val slopes to Tovière – the Borsat fast quad to Col de Fresse is quicker.

MOUNTAIN RESTAURANTS

Head out of the bowl

Tignes' mountain restaurants are inadequate, especially on the west side of the bowl. Here there is one cafeteria – Le Palet – 'friendly, not as expensive as some and a good choice of food' – at the Col du Palet mid-mountain lift junction, and one pricey and crowded old hut, now being upgraded and rebuilt – the Savouna – just above Tignes-le-Lac.

The opposite side of the bowl is slightly better equipped, with the atmospheric chalet at the top of Tovière ('very good portions') and the newish but pleasantly woody Chalet du Bollin – just qualifying as a mountain

---

boarding *This is a big area, with a big boarder reputation. Snowsure (if a bit flat) boarding on the glacier gives way to steep tree-hopping above the lowest part, Tignes-les-Brévières. In between, the lift system relies more on chairs and gondolas than drags, and long, wide pistes to blast down, with acres of powder between them to play in. The glacier is a good place for near-beginners to practise. And there are a couple of specialist snowboard schools/shops. You can buy a specific pass for the fun-park and half-pipe. Hiring a guide and exploring the off-piste is recommended for good free-riders.*

Phone numbers
From abroad use the prefix +33 and omit the initial '0' of the phone number.

GETTING THERE

Air Geneva, transfer 3½hr. Lyon, transfer 3½hr. Chambéry, transfer 2½hr.

Rail Bourg-St-Maurice (30km); regular buses or taxi from station.

CHILDCARE

The hotel Diva in Val-Claret (0479 067000) has a nursery taking children from age 18 months.

The Marmottons kindergarten in Le Lac (0479 065167) takes children from 2 to 8, with skiing with Evolution 2 instructors for those aged 3½ or more.

restaurant, a few metres above Val-Claret. Both offer table and self-service.

The big restaurant at the top of the Grande Motte funicular has great panoramic views from its huge terrace, but it is traversed every few minutes by the next funicular-full of people. The new Alpage restaurant at the top of the Chaudannes lift is highly recommended for its 'good, if limited, food and friendly staff'.

There are lots of easily accessible places for lunch in the resorts. One ski-to-the-door favourite of ours is the ground-floor restaurant of the hotel Montana, on the left as you descend from the Aiguille Percée. La Place is reported to be 'a genuine delight with good food and real family hospitality' and a new bar in Val-Claret, the Fish Tank, is described as 'very good value'. In Les Brévières, a short walk round the corner into the village brings you to places much cheaper than the two by the piste.

SCHOOLS AND GUIDES
Enormous choice

There are half a dozen schools, plus various independent instructors. The ESF and Evolution 2 are the main ones, with sections in the main resort centres. Evolution 2 has received good reports with class sizes of eight and standards of English good – the chaos on registration days is also mentioned. The ESF also receives praise apart from the class sizes – sometimes as large as 12. A reporter praises the Ski Company's teaching.

FACILITIES FOR CHILDREN
Mixed reports

In the past, we have had good reports on the Marmottons kindergartens, and on the 'experienced minders' of the Evolution 2 school in Le Lac. A reporter on the ESF considered the classes for five-year-olds too large.

HOW TO GO
Unremarkable range of options

Although all three main styles of accommodation are available through tour operators, there isn't a lot of choice in any category, especially for those who like their creature comforts.

Chalets The choice of catered chalets is limited by comparison with other major French resorts, and there are few notable ones. Ski Olympic's Chalet Rosset has been recommended by a reporter as an exception: 'Superb, with a lovely lounge with views, but a bit of an uphill plod at the end of the day.' Their Chardon is also rated 'excellent'. Crystal's hotel-style Curling, plumb in the centre of Val Claret, has neat public areas and spacious bedrooms.

Hotels The few hotels are small and concentrated in Le Lac. Most are simple – there's nothing really swanky.

(((3 **Campanules** (0479 063436) Smartly rustic chalet (since its makeover) in upper Le Lac, with well equipped rooms and a good restaurant, run by the friendly Reymond brothers.

(((3 **Village Montana** (0479 400144) New, stylishly woody complex on the east-facing slopes above Le Lac, with suites and apartments as well as rooms. Outdoor pool, and spa treatments available. One reporter enthuses about the food but felt the accommodation was fairly 'ordinary'.

((2 **Arbina** (0479 063478) Well-run place close to the lifts in Le Lac, with lunchtime terrace, busy après-ski bar and one of the best restaurants.

((2 **Terril Blanc** (0479 063287) Well run place next to the lake.

((2 **Neige et Soleil** (0479 063294) Excellent family-run place in Le Lac – central, clean, cosy, comfortable, with good food.

↑ Val Claret is no less obtrusive than the older parts, but a bit more stylish

SNOWPIX.COM / CHRIS GILL

ACTIVITIES

Indoor 'Vitatignes' in Le Lac (balneotherapy centre with spa baths, sauna etc), 'Espace Forme' in Le Lac, 'Les Bains du Montana' in Le Lac, Fitness Club in Val-Claret (body-building, aerobics, squash, golf practice and simulation, sauna, hammam, Californian baths, hot-tub, swimming pool, massage), cinemas, covered tennis court, bowling, climbing wall
Outdoor Natural skating-rink, hang-gliding, paragliding, helicopter rides, snow-mobiles, husky dog-sleigh rides, diving beneath ice on lake, heli-skiing, 'La Banquise' for children (ice skating, snow sliding, solarium, snow activities, climbing activities, ski-joring)

TOURIST OFFICE

Postcode 73321
t +33 479 400440
f 479 400315
information@tignes.net
www.tignes.net

ⓒ② **Marais** (0479 064006) Prettily furnished, simple little hotel in Tignes-les-Boisses.
Self-catering In upper Val-Claret, close to the Tovière chair, the Maeva 'Residence Le Borsat' apartments are about the best – not too cramped, reasonably well equipped and with a communal lounge. The Chalet Club in Val-Claret is a collection of simple studios, but has the benefit of free indoor pool, sauna and in-house restaurant and bar. The supermarket at Tignes-le-Lac is reported to be 'comprehensive but very expensive'.

EATING OUT
Good places dotted about

Each of the main centres has a range of restaurants, although the options in Le Lavachet are rather limited. Advance booking is recommended for many restaurants. Finding anywhere with some atmosphere is difficult in Le Lac, though the food in some of the better hotels is good. We and readers have been impressed by the Arbina and the Campanules – 'a meal of the highest quality, excellent service and attention to detail'. In Val-Claret the Bouf'Mich is a favourite ('terrific food, reasonable prices, helpful service, pretty interior'). The Cavern in Val Claret is recommended: 'Superb and there's entertainment – have to book.' Pizza 2000, also in Val-Claret, is recommended for 'reasonable prices, helpful staff, especially with large parties'. The Ski d'Or is a swanky Relais & Châteaux hotel. Les Terrasses du Claret is recommended for large groups. Those on a budget should try the Italian at the Pignatta. The Cordée in Les Boisses is recommended – unpretentious surroundings, great traditional French food, modest prices.

APRES-SKI
Early to bed

Tignes is rather quiet at night, though there is no shortage of bars, some doing food as well. Val-Claret has some early-evening atmosphere and happy hours are popular – the 'pub-like' Crowded House under Crystal's chalet hotel Curling gets most mentions, followed by the Wobbly Rabbit. Other recommendations include the Fish Tank, a new bar above the ski school meeting area – 'excellent audio visual system and satellite TV'.

Le Lac is a natural focus for immediate après-ski drinks, but don't expect anything too riotous. The bar of the hotel Arbina is our kind of spot – adequately cosy, spacious enough to absorb some groups, friendly service.

The most animated bar in Le Lavachet is Harri's – 'good atmosphere and ambience', 'always lively' are this year's verdicts. The satellite TV here is popular. The Alpaka Lodge is recommended as 'a relaxed place, great for conversation and cocktails'.

Les Caves du Lac, Café de la Poste and Jack's are popular late haunts.

OFF THE SLOPES
Forget it

Despite the range of alternative activities, Tignes is a resort for those who want to use the slopes, where anyone who doesn't is liable to feel like a fish out of water.

STAYING DOWN THE VALLEY
Only for visiting other resorts

See the Val-d'Isère chapter; the same considerations apply broadly here. But bear in mind that there are rooms to be had in simple hotels in Tignes-les-Boisses and Tignes-les-Brévières.

Les Trois Vallées

The biggest lift-linked ski area in the world

Despite competing claims, notably from the Portes du Soleil, with 200 lifts and 600km of pistes the sheer quantity of lift-served terrain in Les Trois Vallées cannot be beaten. There is nowhere like it for a keen skier or boarder who wants to cover as much mileage as possible while rarely taking the same run repeatedly. And it has a lot to offer everyone, from beginner to expert.

The runs of Les Trois Vallées and their resorts are dealt with in six chapters. The four major resorts are Courchevel, page 234, Méribel, page 267, Les Menuires, page 264, and Val-Thorens, page 341. St-Martin-de-Belleville, a small village along the mountainside from Les Menuires, gets its own chapter on page 312. And La Tania, a relatively new development on the slopes between Courchevel and Méribel, is covered on page 315.

None of the resorts is cheap. **Les Menuires** is the cheapest but it is also the ugliest (though new developments around the original one are now being built in a much more acceptable style). The slopes around the village get too much sun for comfort, but close by across the valley are some of the best (and quietest) challenging pistes in les Trois Vallées on its north-facing La Masse. Down the valley from Les Menuires is **St-Martin-de-Belleville**, a charming traditional Savoyard village which has been expanded in a sympathetic style. It has good-value accommodation and chair-lift links into the rest of the area.

Up rather than down the Belleville valley from Les Menuires, at 2300m **Val-Thorens** is the highest resort in the Alps, and at 3200m the top of its slopes is the high point of the Trois Vallées. The snow in this area is almost always good, and it includes

two glaciers where good snow is guaranteed. But the setting is bleak and the lifts are vulnerable to closure in bad weather. The purpose-built resort is very convenient. Visually it is not comparable to Les Menuires, thanks to the smaller-scale design and more thorough use of wood cladding, but it still isn't to everyone's taste.

Méribel is a two-part resort. The higher component, **Méribel–Mottaret**, is the best placed of all the resorts for getting to any part of the Trois Vallées system in the shortest possible time. It's now quite a spread-out place, with some of the accommodation a long way up the hillsides – great for access to the slopes, less so for access to nightlife. **Méribel** itself is 200m lower and has long been a British favourite, especially for chalet holidays. It is the most attractive of the main Trois Vallées resorts, built in chalet style beside a long winding road up the hillside. Parts of the resort are very convenient for the slopes and the village centre; parts are very far from either. The new development of Méribel-Village has its own chair-lift into the system but is very isolated and quiet. A gondola leads up to Méribel from the old spa town of **Brides-Les-Bains** which has cheap accommodation but no piste back to it.

Courchevel has four parts. 1850 is the most fashionable resort in France, and can be the most expensive resort in the Alps (though it doesn't have to cost a fortune to stay there). The less expensive parts are Le Praz (aka 1300), 1550 and 1650. They don't have the same choice of nightlife and restaurants, and only 1550 enjoys the same central location in the lift system. Many people rate the slopes around Courchevel the best in the Trois Vallées, with runs to suit all standards. The snow tends to be better than in neighbouring Méribel, because many of the slopes are north-facing. And the piste grooming is the best in the Trois Vallées, if not the best in Europe.

La Tania was built for the 1992 Olympics, just off the small road linking Le Praz to Méribel. It has now grown into a quiet, attractive, car-free collection of chalets and chalet-style apartments set among the trees and is popular with families. It has a good nursery slope and lovely long intermediate runs, but there are no very easy runs back to it.

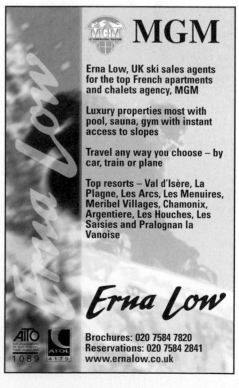

Val-d'Isère 1850m

On- and off-piste playground with reliable snow

WHAT IT COSTS

6

HOW IT RATES

The slopes

Snow	*****
Extent	*****
Experts	*****
Intermediates	*****
Beginners	***
Convenience	***
Queues	****
Restaurants	**

The rest

Scenery	***
Resort charm	***
Off-slope	**

What's new

2000/01 saw a new high-speed chair-lift replace the defunct Cascade and Pissaillas chairs on the Pissaillas glacier.

For 2001/02 the old Bellevarde cable car is being replaced by a giant gondola – each cabin seats 24 passengers. And the Glacier chair, an essential link from Solaise towards the Col de L'Iseran and the Pissaillas glacier is being upgraded to a six-pack.

The slow Tommeuses lifts are due to be replaced by an eight-seater detachable chair, but no date has yet been specified.

- ⊕ Huge area linked with Tignes, with lots of runs for all standards
- ⊕ One of the great resorts for lift-served off-piste runs
- ⊕ High altitude of most slopes means snow is more or less guaranteed
- ⊕ Wide choice of schools, especially for off-piste lessons and guiding
- ⊕ For a high resort, the town is attractive, very lively at night, and offers a good range of restaurants
- ⊕ Wide range of package holidays and accommodation
- ⊕ Piste grooming and staff attitudes have improved noticeably

- ⊖ Piste grading understates the difficulty of many runs – though moguls on greens now uncommon
- ⊖ You're quite likely to need the bus at the start or end of the day
- ⊖ Most lifts and slopes are liable to close when the weather is bad
- ⊖ Runs to valley level often tricky
- ⊖ Nursery slopes not ideal
- ⊖ High-season crowds on some runs
- ⊖ Still some lifts in need of upgrading
- ⊖ Main off-piste slopes get tracked out very quickly
- ⊖ Seems at times more British than French – especially in low season
- ⊖ Few good mountain restaurants

Val-d'Isère is one of the world's best resorts for experts – attracted by the extent of lift-served off-piste – and for confident, mileage-hungry intermediates. But you don't have to be particularly adventurous to enjoy the resort, and the village ambience has improved greatly in recent years.

The list of drawbacks above looks long, but they are mainly petty complaints, whereas the plus-points are mainly things that weigh heavily in the balance, both for us and for the many enthusiastic reporters we hear from. The last of the plus-points – the clear recent improvements in piste grooming and lift staff attitudes – is as welcome as it is surprising. If the lift company would make a serious attempt to grade its runs sensibly, Val would make more friends than it does at present among nervous intermediates who panic on mogul fields.

Despite the unremarkable mountain restaurants, this is, in the end, simply one of our favourite resorts in the world.

The resort 

Val-d'Isère spreads along a remote valley, which is a dead end in winter. The road in from Bourg-St-Maurice brings you dramatically through a rocky defile to the satellite mini-resort of La Daille – a convenient but hideous slope-side apartment complex and the base of lifts into the major Bellevarde sector of the slopes. The outskirts of Val proper are dreary, but as you approach the centre the legacy of the 1992 Olympics becomes more evident: new wood- and stone-cladding, culminating in the tasteful pedestrian-only Val Village complex. The few remnants of the original old village are tucked away behind this.

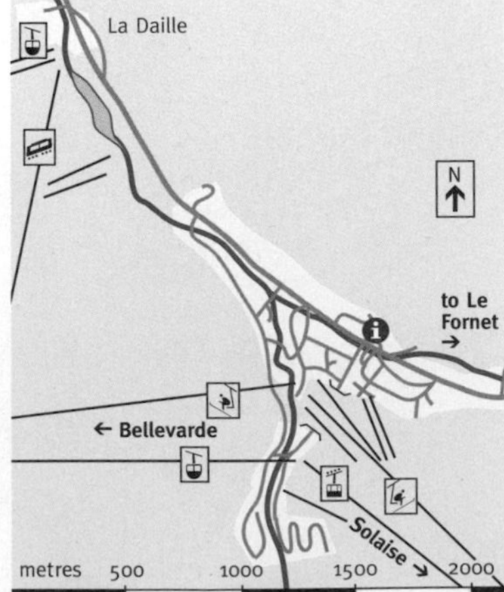

For a quiet time in a rustic setting, head up the valley to Le Fornet →

OT VAL-D'ISERE / MARIO COLONEL

MOUNTAIN FACTS

For entire Espace Killy area

Altitude	1550m-3455m
Lifts	97
Pistes	300km
Green	15%
Blue	46%
Red	28%
Black	11%
Artificial snow	24km
Recco detectors used	

Many first-time visitors find the resort much 'prettier' than they expect a big-name high resort to be, and returning visitors generally find things improving.

Turn right at the centre and you drive under the nursery slopes to Val's big lifts up to Bellevarde and Solaise; there is now a lot of development here, most of it beyond the lifts. Carry on up the main valley instead, and you come to Le Fornet – an old village and the third major lift station.

There is a lot of traffic around, but the resort is working to get cars under control to make the centre more pedestrian-friendly.

The location of your accommodation isn't crucial. Free shuttle-buses run along the main street linking the main lift stations. It is one of the most efficient bus services we've come across; even in peak periods, you never have to wait more than a few minutes. But in the evening frequency plummets and dedicated après-skiers will want to be within walking distance of the centre. The development up the side valley beyond the main lift station is mainly attractive; some places are a pleasant stroll from the centre, but the farthest-flung are a long slog – unless you're happy to pay for taxis, you need a car or a tour operator that provides transport. La Daille and Le Fornet have their (quite different) attractions for those less concerned about nightlife.

A car is of no great value around the resort, but simplifies outings to other resorts. A six-day lift pass gives a day in Les Arcs or La Plagne, plus the Trois Vallées. Other resorts nearby are Ste-Foy and La Rosière.

The mountains

Although there are wooded slopes above the village on all sectors, in practice most of the runs here are on open slopes above the tree line.

Last year's reporters thought that piste grooming had improved – this year's are mixed, ranging from 'no comparison to Méribel' to 'very good even after heavy snow'. A couple of readers complain about poor signing.

The local radio carries good weather reports in English as well as French.

THE SLOPES
Vast and varied

Val-d'Isère's slopes divide into three main sectors. **Bellevarde** is the mountain that is home to Val-d'Isère's famous downhill course – the OK piste, which opens each season's World Cup Alpine circus in early December. You can reach Bellevarde by funicular from La Daille; up to now this has been the favoured route, and even people based in central Val have taken the bus to La Daille at the start of the day. But for the coming season a powerful new gondola will replace the old cable-car from Val. From the top you can get back down to the main lifts, play on a variety of drags and chairs at altitude or take a choice of lifts to the Tignes slopes.

Solaise is the other mountain accessible directly from Val-d'Isère. The Solaise Express fast quad chair-lift takes you a few metres higher than the parallel cable-car. Once up, a short drag takes you over a plateau and down to a variety of chairs that serve

LIFT PASSES

2001/02 prices in euros

L'Espace Killy
Covers all lifts in Tignes and Val-d'Isère.

Beginners 7 free beginners' lifts on main nursery slopes.

Main pass
1-day pass 35
6-day pass 167

Senior citizens
Over 60: 6-day pass 142
Over 75: free pass

Children
Under 13: 6-day pass 117
Under 5: free pass

Short-term passes
Half-day pass from 12.30 (adult 25).

Alternative periods
14 non-consecutive days pass available.

Notes 6-day pass and over valid for one day each in the Three Valleys, Pralognan-la-Vanoise and Les Saisies. On 3- to 15-day passes, pass reimbursed if all lifts are shut due to bad weather. Discount on new passes on presentation of your lift pass for any one of the previous three seasons. Extra discount for senior citizens aged 70 to 74.

boarding *Val-d'Isère is good for boarders, though Tignes is a more popular boarder destination. Most of the main lifts are cable-cars, chair-lifts and gondolas, with very few drag-lifts. But there are a few flat areas where you'll need to scoot or walk. Experts will revel in the off-piste. There's a fun-park with a half-pipe on Bellevarde, under the Mont Blanc chair-lift, and another at La Daille. There are several specialist snowboard shops and schools. The village nursery area is ideal for trying boarding for the first time and Le Fornet is good to progress to. Val's nightlife – with its huge selection of bars – is difficult to beat.*

this very sunny area of predominantly gentle pistes.

From near the top of this area you can catch a chair over to the third main area, above and below the **Col de l'Iseran**, which can also be reached by cable-car from Le Fornet in the valley. The chair-lift ride is spectacular or scary, depending on your head for heights: it climbs over a steep ridge and then drops suddenly down the other side. There is an alternative way over: a short and steep drag-lift takes you to a narrow tunnel through the ridge, leading to an awkward black run which is often closed. The runs at Col de l'Iseran are predominantly easy, with spectacular views and access to the region's most beautiful off-piste sections. The defunct Cascade chair-lift has finally been replaced by a fast quad giving access to the runs on the Pissaillas glacier beyond the col.

SNOW RELIABILITY
Difficult to beat

In years when lower resorts have suffered, Val-d'Isère has rarely been short of snow. Its height means you can almost always get back to the village, especially because of the snowmaking facilities on the lower slopes of all the main routes home. But even more important is that in each sector there are lots of lifts and runs above mid-mountain, between about 2300m and 2900m. Many of the slopes face roughly north. And there is access to glaciers at Pissaillas or over in Tignes, although both take a while to get to.

FOR EXPERTS
One of the world's best

Val-d'Isère is one of the top resorts in the world for experts. The main attraction is the huge range of beautiful off-piste possibilities – see feature panel. There may be better resorts for really steep pistes – there are certainly lots in North America – but there is plenty to amuse the expert here, despite the small number of blacks on the piste map. Many of the red and blue runs are steep enough to get mogulled.

On Bellevarde the famous Face run is the main attraction – often mogulled from top to bottom, but not worryingly steep. Epaule is the sector's other black run – where the moguls are hit by long exposure to sun and can be slushy or rock-hard too often for our liking. There are several challenging

3300m
Glacier de Pissaillas
Col Pers
Col de l'Iseran 2765m
2950m
2900m
Tignes
Col de Fresse 2770m
Tour Charvet
2325m
Le Manchet 1940m
Bellevarde 2705m
Solaise 2560m
Le Châtelard
Le Fornet 1930m
Le Laisinant
Val d'Isère 1850m
La Daille 1785m

ways down from Solaise to the village: all steep, though none fearsomely so. This has traditionally been classic bumps territory, but one of our regular reporters ruefully notes that the resort's new enthusiasm for grooming has extended even to these slopes: 'Solaise bumps the size of small cars are nothing now but a fond memory.'

FOR INTERMEDIATES
Quantity and quality

Val-d'Isère has even more to offer intermediates than experts. There's enough here to keep you interested for several visits – though there are complaints about crowded high-season pistes, and the less experienced should be aware that many runs are under-graded. This remains a regular reporter complaint.

In the Solaise sector is a network of gentle blue runs ideal for building confidence. And there are a couple of beautiful runs from here through the woods to Le Laisinant, from where you catch the bus – these are ideal for bad weather, though prone to closure in times of avalanche danger.

Most of the runs in the Col de l'Iseran sector are even easier – ideal for early and hesitant intermediates. Those marked blue at the top of the glacier could really be graded green.

Bellevarde has a huge variety of runs ideally suited to intermediates of all standards. From Bellevarde itself there is a choice of green, blue and red runs of varying pitch. And the wide runs from Tovière normally give you the choice of groomed piste or moguls.

A snag for early intermediates is that runs back to the valley can be testing. The easiest way is to head down to La Daille, where there is a green run – but it should be graded blue (in some resorts it would be red), and it gets very crowded and mogulled at the end of the day. None of the runs from Bellevarde and Solaise back to Val itself is really easy. The blue Santons run from Bellevarde takes you through a long, narrow gun barrel which often has people standing around plucking up courage, making things even trickier. On Solaise there isn't much to choose between the blue and red ways down – and they're both

OFF-PISTE PARADISE

L'Espace Killy has some of the most extensive lift-served off-piste skiing in the world. There are dozens of classic off-piste runs waiting to be discovered, and all with endless variations. They are best explored with a professional guide because of the avalanche and other hidden dangers, such as cliffs to fall off and rivers to fall in. But many of the more popular runs are skied into an almost piste-like state soon after a fresh snowfall – here, again, a guide will be able to take you on less heavily skied routes. Our favourite off-piste routes include:

– Col Pers, from the top of the glacier above Le Fornet. You traverse over to a big, wide, fairly gentle bowl with glorious views. There are endless variants on the way down. Most bring you down via the very beautiful, narrow Gorges du Malpasset and the frozen river Isère back to the Le Fornet cable-car. This is a good area for spotting chamois grazing in the sun on the rocky outcrops above you.

– Tour de Charvet, from the top of the Grand Pré chair-lift in the Bellevarde sector. The easiest route starts with a long traverse in a huge bowl, before dropping into a narrow gorge which you ski along before the long run-out to the Manchet fast chair up to the Solaise sector.

– Tour de Pramecou, from the Grand Motte area in Tignes. After a long, flat section at the top and a couple of short climbs between downhill sections, you end up at the top of a long, steep, wide, north-facing slope (where the snow is usually excellent) and swoop down to the Carline piste back to the bottom of the Motte.

A seasoned reporter this year recommends the run from the back of Cugnai chair on Solaise: 'Good, steep slopes, excellent snow and a pretty run out by a stream through to the bottom of the Manchet fast chair.'

We recommend the Alpine Experience and Top Ski guided groups: you can join a group of your standard for off-piste skiing every morning (normally 9am until 1pm). Afternoons tend to be more conventional lessons to improve technique.

Most of the slopes are above the tree line, but there are some below – this is the blue Mangard down to Le Fornet ➔

OT VAL-D'ISERE / MARIO COLONEL

narrow in places. At the top, there's no option other than the red run in full view of the lifts. Many early intermediates sensibly choose to ride the lifts down – take the chair for a spectacular view.

FOR BEGINNERS
OK if you know where to go
The nursery slope right by the centre of town is 95 per cent perfect; it's just a pity that the top is unpleasantly steep. The lifts serving it are free.

Once off the nursery slopes, you have to know where to find easy runs; many of the greens should be blue, or even red. One local instructor admits: 'We have to have green runs on the map, even if we don't have so many green slopes – otherwise beginners wouldn't come to Val-d'Isère.'

A good place for your first real runs off the nursery slopes is the Madeleine green run on Solaise – now served by a fast six-pack. The Col de l'Iseran runs are also gentle and wide, and not over-busy. There is good progression terrain on Bellevarde, too, but no genuinely easy way back to the valley.

FOR CROSS-COUNTRY
Limited
There are a couple of loops towards La Daille and another out past Le Laisinant. More picturesque is the one going from Le Châtelard (on the road past the main cable-car station) to the Manchet chair. But keen cross-country enthusiasts should go elsewhere.

QUEUES
Few problems
Queues to get out of the resort have been kept in check by new lifts – first the funicular at La Daille, then fast chair-lifts as alternatives to the two main cable-cars, and now the replacement of the Bellevard cable-car by a big new gondola.

To get to Tignes, it's quicker to take the fast quad to Col de Fresse than the slow and often busy Tommeuses chairs to Tovière. Coming back from Val-Claret at the end of the day is now much quicker thanks to a fast, dual-loading, six-person chair-lift direct to Col de Fresse, with a run down to Bellevarde. Make sure you get into the correct queue: half the chairs stop

SCHOOLS/GUIDES

2000/01 prices in euros

ESF
Classes 6 days
5½hr: 3hr am, 2½hr pm
6 full days: 180
Children's classes
Ages: from 4
6 full days: 165
Private lessons
1hr, mornings, afternoons, or whole day
31 for 1hr

Snow Fun
Classes 6 days
3hr am and 2½hr pm
5 mornings: 90
Children's classes
Ages: up to 13
6 full days: 158
Private lessons
Hourly or daily
29 for 1hr

Top Ski
Specialises in slalom, mogul and off-piste courses for small groups (max 6)
Classes 4 days
4hr: 9am-1pm; 2hr: 2pm-4pm
4 full days: 158
Private lessons
am (8.45-1pm), pm (2pm-4.30) or full day (8.45-4.30) 70 for 2 hours

Alpine Expérience
Specialises in off-piste guiding and teaching for small groups (max 6)

Other schools
Evolution 2
Ski Prestige
Mountain Masters
Altimanya

part-way up the hill, serving runs back into Val-Claret.

The number of slow chair-lifts scattered about the area, particularly in Tignes, is a common complaint. Crowded pistes is another.

At the end of the day, there's usually a wait for the chair back from Col de l'Iseran to Solaise (though you can always descend to Le Fornet instead). A reporter regularly found a queue for the slow Lac chair that links the bottom of the Madeleine up to the Tête Solaise.

If you plan a return visit, keep your lift pass – those with a week's pass bought in the last three years are entitled to a 'loyal customer' reduction.

MOUNTAIN RESTAURANTS
Getting better

The mountain restaurants mainly consist of big self-service places with vast terraces at the top of major lifts.

La Fruitière at the top of La Daille gondola, kitted out with stuff rescued from a dairy in the valley, continues to get good reports: 'Lovely food and friendly service. Very easy to rack up a large lunch bill here!' says one. La Folie Douce is a functional self-service place at the same spot – popular, though this year a visitor comments on the lack of variety. Other recommendations: Solaise ('great pizza bar, good crêpes'), Le Trifollet, about halfway down the OK run – 'efficient table-service, great pizzas', 'excellent'; Marmottes, in the middle of the Bellevarde bowl – big sunny terrace, self-service – 'a good coffee stop'; Le Signal at the top of the Le Fornet cable-car – 'excellent service and value, huge portions'; the 'small and friendly' Bar de L'Ouillette, at the base of the Madeleine chair-lift – 'good selection of snack meals'; the Datcha, at the bottom of the Cugnai lift – 'excellent salads, if expensive'; and La Tanière, a new restaurant between the two chairs going up Face de Bellevard – 'food well priced and service friendly, popular with lifties and pisteurs'.

There are restaurants on the lower slopes at La Daille that are reachable on snow and by pedestrians. Les Tufs is 'a busy, friendly place that does rather a good pizza', and the Toit du Monde (formerly the Crêch'ouna), just across the slope from the funicular station at La Daille offers 'excellent service'. And of course there are lots of places actually in the resort villages.

Our favourite in Val-d'Isère is the big terrace of the Brussels, overlooking the nursery slopes. When at Col de l'Iseran, one possible plan for lunch on a wintry day is to descend to the rustic Arolay at Le Fornet – good food, but 'rude service'. Lunch over in Tignes-les-Brévières is a popular option for those on a high-mileage mission.

SCHOOLS AND GUIDES
A very wide choice

There is a huge choice of schools and private instructors to choose from. We don't get many reports on the ESF adult classes. We've heard from lots of satisfied Snow Fun pupils: their guides seem to 'know their snow'. Reporters are also full of praise for Evolution 2: 'really good, with very encouraging instructors', 'excellent teachers'.

Several small outfits specialise in organising small groups to go off-piste – an excellent way to get off-piste safely without the cost of hiring a guide as an individual. Recent reports describe Evolution 2 as 'top class', Alpine Expérience as providing 'excellent off-piste tuition'. We have also had good reports on Ski Prestige and Top Ski. We've had great days ourselves with both Alpine Expérience and Top Ski. In peak periods it's best to book in advance. Mountain Masters offers private on- and off-piste lessons.

All the schools have teachers who speak good English – in many cases it's their native language. Heli-trips can be arranged – you are dropped over the border in Italy because heli-drops are banned in France.

FACILITIES FOR CHILDREN
Good tour op possibilities

Many people prefer to use the facilities of UK tour operators such as Mark Warner or Ski Beat. But there's a 'children's village' for 3- to 13-year-olds, with supervised indoor and outdoor activities on the village nursery slopes. It's open daily from 8.30 to 6.30. A reporter last season was 'very pleased' with the childcare there: 'The staff speak English, and are very organised, in particular about the children's safety.'

We have personal experience of the indifference of the ESF's handling of children, reinforced by a more recent report from the father of two children who were placed in classes of French pupils and subsequently 'abandoned in mid-class' by their instructors.

CHILDCARE

The new children's village, in the centre of town by the nursery slopes, takes children from 3 to 13, from 8.30 to 6.30.

The Petit Poucet (0479 061397) in the Residence les Hameaux at Val takes children from age 2, from 9am to 5.30.

Both provide indoor and outdoor activities and delivery to and collection from ski school.

Snowfun's Club Nounours takes children aged 3 to 6 for lessons of 1hr 30 min, 2hr or 3hr. Older children can be left in classes all day.

The ESF runs a ski nursery for age 4 up, with rope tows and a heated chalet.

A list of babysitters is available at the tourist office.

Phone numbers
From abroad use the prefix +33 and omit the initial '0' of the phone number.

Staying there 

HOW TO GO

Lots of choice

More British tour operators go to Val-d'Isère than to any other resort. The choice of chalets and chalet-hotels is vast. There is a Club Med 'village'.

Chalets There is everything from budget chalets to the most luxurious you could demand. The resort has a fair number of chalet operators who don't go anywhere else, including YSE and Val d'Isère Properties. Both of these include some luxury places in their portfolios, as do Scott Dunn Ski, Finlays, Supertravel and The Ski Company Limited, which has a group of luxury chalets out beyond the lift stations with fabulous views up the Manchet valley. Le Ski has four splendid new all-en-suite chalets on the edge of town, not far from YSE's lovely old Mountain Lodges.

There are lots of chalet hotels. Mark Warner has four, including the family-friendly, 'very good-value' Cygnaski, the nightlife hot spot Moris – 'basic rooms but ideal location and helpful staff' – and the Val d'Isère, which enjoys free use of the adjoining village swimming pool – 'excellent location, spacious rooms but a touch tired'.

The best-value chalets tend to be away from the centre, at Le Châtelard, Le Laisinant and Le Fornet.

Hotels There are about 40 to choose from, mostly 2- and 3-star, but for such a big international resort surprisingly few are notably attractive.

((((4 **Christiania** (0479 060825) Recently renovated big chalet, probably best in town. Chic, with friendly staff. Sauna.

((((4 **Latitudes** (0479 061888) Modern, stylish. Piano bar, nightclub. Leisure centre: sauna, steam room, whirlpool, massage.

((((4 **Blizzard** (0479 060207) Renovated for Olympics. Indoor-outdoor pool. Convenient. A non-resident praises the food very highly.

(((3 **Grand Paradis** (0479 061173) Excellent position. Good food.

(((3 **Savoyarde** (0479 060155) Rustic decor. Leisure centre. Good food. Rooms a bit small.

(((3 **Kandahar** (0479 060239) Smart,

GETTING THERE

Air Geneva, transfer 4hr. Lyon, transfer 4hr. Chambéry, transfer 3hr.

Rail Bourg-St-Maurice (33km); regular buses from station.

newish building above Taverne d'Alsace on main street.

(3) **Sorbiers** (0479 062377) Modern but cosy B&B hotel, not far from centre. Due to be completely renovated in summer 2001.

(3) **Samovar** (0479 061351) In La Daille. Traditional, with good food.

Self-catering There are thousands of properties to choose from. UK operators offer lots of them, but they tend to get booked up early. Local agency Val-d'Isère Agence has a good brochure. The local supermarkets are said to be well stocked to meet the needs of self-caterers.

EATING OUT

Plenty of good, affordable places

Restaurant standards are generally high. The 70-odd restaurants include Italian, Alsatian, Tex-Mex, even Japanese ones, but most offer good French dishes. High-season visitors have found that it is essential to book ahead – especially on Wednesday when UK chalet staff get the night off.

There are plenty of pleasant mid-priced places. The Perdrix Blanche is popular, offering 'brilliant' fish dishes in particular, but reporters also comment that it is 'impersonal', 'too busy and noisy'. Better, perhaps, to head for the Taverne d'Alsace, another old favourite, with 'plenty of magnificent traditional food in a calm atmosphere'. The Tufs, a little way up the slopes at La Daille, is recommended, and will provide transport for groups. The Toit du Monde nearby (formerly the Crêch'ouna) offers Tibetan cuisine and is praised for 'making a real effort to be a bit different'. Le Canyon is recommended for 'great food with choice of traditional fare as well as pizza, pasta etc', 'very noisy and busy'.

But our favourite – and that of many reporters – for a special night out is the Chalet du Crêt, off the road on the northern edge of downtown Val. Set in a 300-year-old stone farmhouse, beautifully renovated by the Franco-British couple who run it, this place serves a fixed-price menu starting with a magnificent hors-d'oeuvres spread. It's not cheap, but it's highly satisfying.

Those on tight budgets should try Chez Nano (next to Dick's Tea Bar) – 'fantastic pizza and profiteroles'. The Melting Pot also gets good reviews for its interesting menu, which includes

OT VAL-D'ISERE / AGENCE NUTS

As far as the eye can see, there are skiable slopes – the main mountain here is Bellevarde, seen from above Le Fornet ↓

ACTIVITIES

Indoor Swimming pool, sports hall (basketball, volleyball, table tennis, badminton, trampoline and gymnastics), library, bridge, health centres in the hotels Christiania, Brussels and Le Val d'Isère (sauna, hammam, hot-tub, body building, massages, solarium etc), cinema
Outdoor Walks in Le Manchet valley and Le Fornet, natural skating rink, hang-gliding, quad bikes, all-terrain karts, ice driving, snow-mobiles, paragliding, snow-shoe outings, heli-skiing, microlight trips, ice-climbing

TOURIST OFFICE

Postcode 73155
t +33 479 060660
f 479 060456
info@valdisere.com
www.valdisere.com

Thai dishes and 'a good selection of veggie options'. La Corniche and L'Olympique are recommended for being 'more French and less touristy'.

APRES-SKI

Very lively

Nightlife is surprisingly energetic, given that most people have spent a hard day on the slopes. There are lots of bars, many with happy hours followed by music and dancing later on.

La Folie Douce, at the top of the La Daille gondola, has become an Austrian-style tea-time rave, with music and dancing; normally you can ride the gondola down, but it can be closed by the weather, so it pays to keep the consumption of vin chaud within bounds. At La Daille the bar at the Samovar hotel is 'a good spot for a beer after skiing'. In downtown Val, Bananas (lively, busy, heated terrace, good happy hour prices), Café Face (very lively, excellent) and the Moris pub (in the Mark Warner chalet) fill up as the slopes close, and Bar Jacques (also mentioned for its food) and the Perdrix Blanche bar are popular with locals. L'Aventure, next to Killy Sports, has household decor, including a fridge, a bath and a bed – it serves good food in a separate eating area. Victor's bar is popular before it turns into a restaurant later on – black-and-white decor and stainless steel loos. The basement Taverne d'Alsace is quiet and relaxing. The famous Dick's Tea Bar (now 21 years old) was judged 'overpriced and overrated' by two of our reporters this year.

For those who like a quieter time, there are hotel bars, piano bars and cocktail lounges.

OFF THE SLOPES

Not much

Val is primarily a resort for those keen to get on to the slopes – though one non-skier this year was 'very satisfied' with the facilities. The swimming pool has been renovated, but the other sports facilities are not particularly impressive. The range of shops is better than in most high French resorts. Lunchtime meetings present problems: the easily accessible mountain restaurants are few, and your friends may prefer lunching miles away in places like Les Brévières.

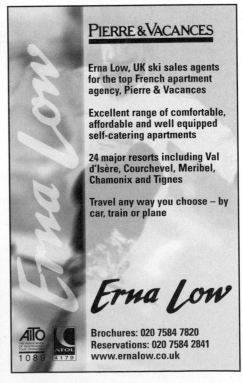

Valmorel 1400m

Under-rated purpose-built resort where they got it right

WHAT IT COSTS

HOW IT RATES

The slopes

Snow	***
Extent	***
Experts	**
Intermediates	****
Beginners	*****
Convenience	*****
Queues	****
Restaurants	**

The rest

Scenery	***
Resort charm	****
Off-slope	**

What's new

For 2000/01 a new quad chair-lift, Le Roset, was built from the bottom of the Madeleine chair-lift in the Col de Madeleine area up to link with the Beaudin sector. This was supposed to speed up the return journey from Longchamp but we have reports of it going 'inexplicably slowly'.

The Prariond chair in the Mottet section was also new last year, with its blue run of the same name.

A new snow-park with a half-pipe and boarder cross course was built by the Crève Coeur chair.

- ➕ Fairly extensive slopes provide something for everyone
- ➕ The most sympathetically designed French purpose-built resort
- ➕ Largely slope-side accommodation
- ➕ Beginners and children particularly well catered for
- ➕ One of the most accessible of the Tarentaise resorts
- ➕ Relatively cheap package holidays

- ➖ Few challenging pistes
- ➖ Fairly low in altitude, so good snow not guaranteed
- ➖ Little variety in accommodation and in restaurants and bars
- ➖ A few fast quads have improved the lift system, but there are still a lot of slow lifts

Built from scratch in the mid-1970s, Valmorel was intended to look and feel like a mountain village: a traffic-free main street with low-rise hamlets grouped around it and along the lower slopes, and traditional Savoie stone and wood materials throughout. The end result is an attractive, friendly sort of place.

The slopes are extensive by most standards – though Valmorel can't rival its huge neighbours, the Three Valleys or Val-d'Isère–Tignes. But with good snow conditions and the whole system open, there's enough here to keep everyone except real experts happy. As the snow conditions deteriorate, the variety of available runs reduces rapidly. Unashamedly aimed at the middle ground (intermediates, families and mixed-ability groups), Valmorel has considerable appeal because it has been so well put together.

The resort

Valmorel, a short drive from Moûtiers and the mega-resorts of the Three Valleys and La Plagne, is the main resort in 'Le Grand Domaine' – a ski area that links the Tarentaise with the Maurienne, by way of the Col de la Madeleine.

Bourg-Morel is the heart of the resort – a traffic-free street where you'll find most of the shops, the restaurants, visitor information – just about everything – in a 200m stretch. It's pleasant and usually lively, with a distinctly family feel. And the slopes are right at hand, with the main pistes back to the resort and the chair-lift out meeting at the end of the street. Nearby is an information board showing lift and piste status and what's on locally.

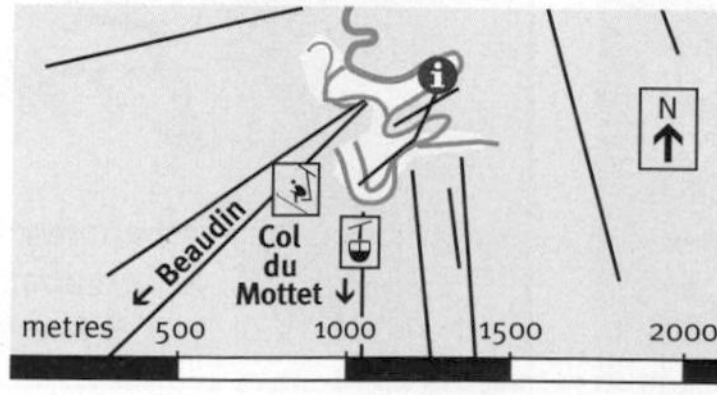

Dotted around the hillside, but not very far from the centre, are the six 'hameaux' with most of the accommodation. Most is self-catering and of a reasonably high standard. Valmorel is a traffic-free resort, with drop-off points for the accommodation. At the bottom end of Bourg-Morel is the base station of the Télébourg, a cross-village lift providing access to the 'Hameau-du-Mottet'.

Walking between the other hameaux and Bourg-Morel doesn't take long – but some of the pathways can be icy. Hameau-du-Mottet is convenient – it is at the top of the Télébourg, with good access to the main lifts and from the return runs. Hameau-du-Crève-Coeur was highly recommended by a reporter this year: 'Convenient for slopes (especially the beginner area) and with own supermarket and boulangerie.

A car is of no use in the resort but very handy for trips to other resorts. All the mega-ski areas of the Tarentaise are within reasonable driving distance – the Trois Vallées, La

Plagne, Les Arcs and even Val-d'Isère–Tignes. An off-piste tour through a number of these resorts starts from the Col du Mottet above Valmorel.

The mountains

MOUNTAIN FACTS

Altitude	1200m-2550m
Lifts	56
Pistes	153km
Green	33%
Blue	39%
Red	19%
Black	9%
Artificial snow	9km
Recco detectors used	

Beginners and intermediates will take to Valmorel. Those looking for more of a challenge will find it more limited. Variety is provided by sectors of quite distinctive character, and the system is big enough to provide interesting, if hardly epic, exploratory trips to its farthest boundaries. There are still a few long, awkward drag-lifts where you can become airborne at the start, but most can be avoided. Piste grooming is said to be better in Valmorel than in neighbouring Longchamp.

THE SLOPES
A big system in miniature

The 56 lifts and 153km of piste are spread out in an interesting arrangement over a number of minor valleys and ridges either side of the Col de la Madeleine, with Valmorel at the eastern extremity of the system and runs coming down into the village on three sides.

The most heavily used route out of the village is via the high-speed Altispace covered quad, which takes you over the main pistes down to the resort. From the top a network of lifts and pistes takes you over to the **Col de la Madeleine** and beyond that to Lauzière (the highest point of the ski area) or the slopes of **St-François** and **Longchamp** at the far western end of the area.

The Pierrafort gondola for the **Mottet** sector and the Crève-Cœur chair for the **Gollet** area take off from Hameau-du-Mottet at the top end of the village. Both have their own runs back towards the village, or you can work your way over to the Beaudin and Madeleine sectors. There's an easy link in the other direction.

Adjacent to the village there are nursery areas with good easy runs.

SNOW RELIABILITY
Sort of average

With a top station of 2550m and many of the runs below 2000m, good snow

boarding *Valmorel is a good place to try boarding for the first time – there's a separate beginners' slope and gentle runs to progress to served by chairs and gondolas. There's a basic fun-park, gentle boarder cross-type course and half-pipe and decent intermediate runs – but inexperienced boarders will find some of the many drag lifts tricky. The main attraction for advanced boarders is the little-used off-piste, where you can still find fresh powder several days after a snowfall. Nightlife is far from throbbing in this family-oriented resort.*

JEANNE CATTINI

Valmorel is the prettiest French purpose-built resort we've seen →

LIFT PASSES

2001/02 prices in euros

Le Grand Domaine
Covers all lifts in Valmorel and St-François-Longchamp.
Beginners Limited area lift pass covers beginner lifts and runs.

Main pass
1-day pass 30
6-day pass 155
(low season 141)

Senior citizens
Over 60: 6-day pass 132

Children
8-13: 6-day pass 132
5-7: 101
Under 5: free pass

Short-term passes
Half-day from 11.30 (26) and 12.45 (22).
Discount on Saturday ski pass throughout season for adults and children.

Alternative passes
Valmorel Domaine covers 37 lifts in Valmorel only (6 days 148 for adults in high season, 126 for children aged 8-13, 96 for ages 5-7).

conditions are not guaranteed. Low runs are often closed, and even Lauzière, which has the system's high point but faces south, can suffer during sunny spells. Mottet is north-facing and usually has the best snow.

Artificial snowmaking covers the nursery slopes and runs under the Altispace chair and the Pierrafort gondola down to village level.

FOR EXPERTS
Deserted off-piste

There are a few challenging pistes. But it is the off-piste that is attractive – because the resort does not attract experts, off-piste powder can lie untracked for days after a snowfall.

Gollet is usually a good place for moguls – plenty of them, but not too big and not too hard. We've done a great off-piste run from here with a guide, which started with a long traverse from the top of the drag-lift and ended right down in the village of Les Avanchers, way below Valmorel, passing through forests and over streams on the way. The off-piste between Gollet and Mottet has lots of couloirs and jumps to attempt.

There are steep black runs below the top section of the Mottet chair and some interesting off-piste variants. From the Riondet drag-lift (often closed) to the north of here, there are a couple of fine runs (one off-piste) which generally have good snow down towards the Madeleine sector.

The Lauzière chair can seem a bit of a trek, but once there you'll probably find the area underused and a lot of fun, provided it hasn't suffered too much sun. There are three marked runs and plenty of acreage in which to pick your own route – there are some steep pitches and often some big bumps. You can also explore a lovely deserted north-facing off-piste run here if you hire a guide – we found long stretches of great powder over a week after the last snowfall.

Touring is a popular activity in the region, and trips such as the Nine-Valley safari can be organised.

FOR INTERMEDIATES
Plenty to keep you busy

Pretty much the whole area except the steepest black runs is ideal for intermediates. A lot of people seem to mill around Beaudin and the Arenouillaz drag and Biollène chair – the adjacent runs are quite friendly. The runs into the Celliers valley are a little more challenging and advanced intermediates will enjoy the red and the black served by the Madeleine chair and the Grande Combe quad.

For a day out, the slopes down to St-François–Longchamp are within easy striking distance, and form a big area of mainly broad, flattering runs.

The main thoroughfare back to the village – from Beaudin along the line of the snow-guns – is graded blue then red, and the red stretch can be quite

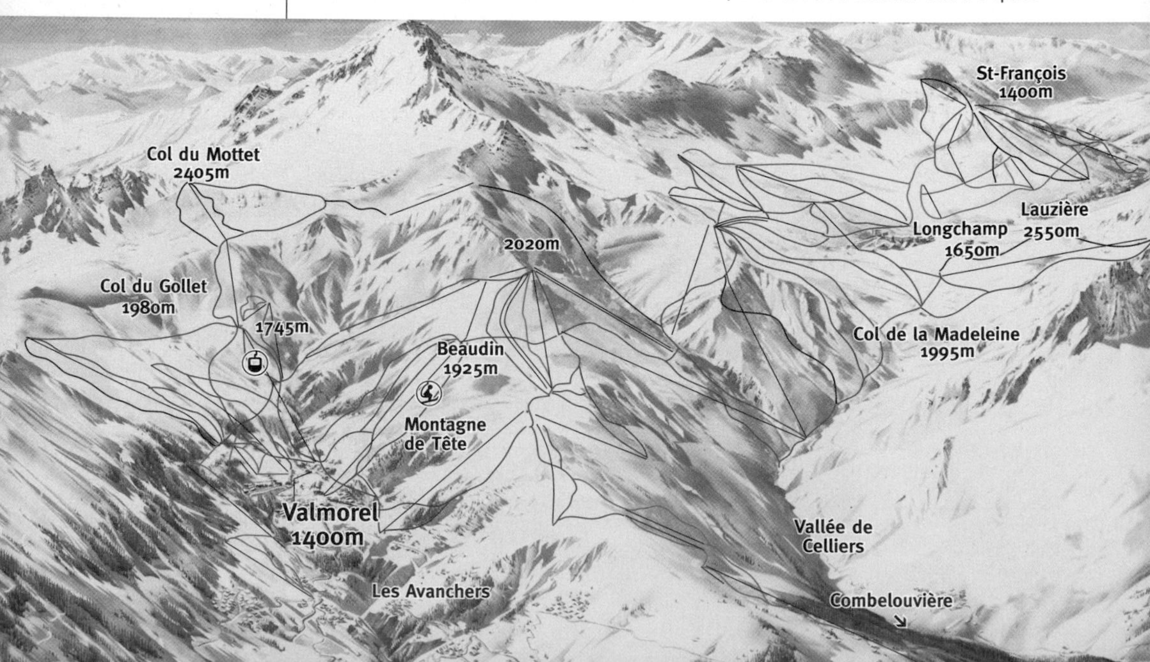

daunting at the end of the day. The artificial snow tends to pile up in surprisingly large heaps, as do tired beginners. After much use even the blue Les Traverses is not easy.

The red route from the top of Mottet is outstandingly boring on the upper half – more push-and-walk than anything else – but the views are some compensation, and the lower half is much better.

The runs back to the village served by the Pierrafort gondola are graded blue but are long, interesting and in parts tricky. The adjacent Gollet slopes also provide plenty of scope for good intermediates to amuse themselves.

FOR BEGINNERS
An excellent choice

Valmorel suits beginners – there are dedicated learning areas right by the village for both adults (at Bois de la Croix) and children (in the snow garden of the children's club), and lots of expertise among the instructors.

The terrain does not allow extensive nursery areas in the valley, so progress from novice to beginner usually sees the children heading for the top of the Pierrafort gondola and adults for the Beaudin sector. The lifts up to these areas can also be ridden down back into the village.

If the snow-cover is complete, there is a very pleasant green run through the trees down to Combelouvière.

FOR CROSS-COUNTRY
Inconvenient and not extensive

Valmorel is not for aficionados – more for those giving it a try. Trails adding up to 23km, at a number of locations in the valley (and so likely to have a limited season only), can be reached by special bus from Valmorel itself.

QUEUES
Much improved in recent years

Two main bottlenecks have been addressed by the Altispace and Grande Combe chairs, so getting on to the slopes in the morning and over to the St-François and Lauzière side now presents fewer problems. But there can still be 10-minute waits. The new Roset quad apparently goes so slowly that there are queues at peak periods. The Frêne drags can't cope when everyone is returning to Valmorel. Lauzière, on the other hand, can be positively lonely, says a reporter.

MOUNTAIN RESTAURANTS
Fair to middling

There are half a dozen or so mountain restaurants in the area, none of them either appalling or wonderful. The Altipano at the top of the gondola has been recommended for good food and value for money and a sunny, peaceful terrace. Prariond, lower down, is livelier but more expensive, with good food and loud music. L'Arbet at the top of Lanchettes is reasonable value. The Banquise has been suggested as a good stopping point after a visit to the views and more challenging runs off Lauzière. Grolla at Combelouvière has 'good service and view'.

SCHOOLS AND GUIDES
Good, especially for first-timers

We've had some good reports about the school over the years. Instructors generally speak good English and are enthusiastic and imaginative. Teaching for first-timers is a speciality of the resort, and likely to produce good results. A reporter told us of a visitor who had never skied before: 'He had one private lesson with the ESF, which he said was fine, and then managed to ski with his friends quite satisfactorily.'

FACILITIES FOR CHILDREN
Comprehensive, but book early

Saperlipopette is a comprehensive childcare facility, though past reports have varied from children loving it to being bored or distraught. We have no very recent reports. Children aged between four and eight taking ski lessons at the ski-school can also have lunch at Saperlipopette, being brought from or taken to their lesson by the staff. Advance booking is essential except for very quiet times.

SCHOOLS/GUIDES

2001/02 prices in euros

ESF
Classes 6 days
2½hr am or pm
6 half days: 98
Children's classes
Ages: 4 to 13
6 half days: 91
Private lessons
Hourly
29 for 1 or 2 people

CHILDCARE

Saperlipopette (0479 098445) provides care for children aged from 6 months to 7 years, from 9am to 5.30. Those aged 18 months to 3 are given 'a gentle and amusing first experience with the snow'. Those aged 3 to 7 have indoor activities as well as ski classes (divided into three levels), and there is a snow play area for those who do not wish to ski.

GETTING THERE

Air Geneva, transfer 3½hr. Lyon, transfer 3½hr. Chambéry, transfer 2½hr.

Rail Moûtiers (18km); regular buses from station.

Phone numbers
From abroad use the prefix +33 and omit the initial '0' of the phone number.

ACTIVITIES

Indoor Cinema
Outdoor Snow-shoe outings, 12km of prepared walks, paragliding, horse-drawn carriage rides

TOURIST OFFICE

Postcode 73260
t +33 479 098555
f 479 098529
info@valmorel.com
www.valmorel.com

Staying there

HOW TO GO
Take a package for value

Self-catering packages are the norm. Beginners may prefer staying at the Bois de la Croix end of the village to avoid having to walk with ski gear.
Chalets There are some run by UK tour operators, but they tend to be catered apartments.
Hotels There are only three hotels.
((3 **Planchamp** (0479 099700) Best in town, family run, with a good French restaurant. Right on the piste.
(2 **Hotel du Bourg** (0479 098666) Simple place in the middle of Bourg-Morel.
(2 **La Fontaine** (0479 098777) Across the piste from the Planchamp. 'Good food, very good value, large rooms (for France),' says a reporter this year.
Self-catering Most people do – 8,500 apartment beds are distributed throughout the six hamlets and they are generally well equipped. While it's great having a view over the piste, the downside of certain locations in Mottet and Planchamp is the proximity of some very noisy snow-guns: the soundproofing is not quite good enough for light sleepers.

EATING OUT
Good enough but rarely thrilling

You can check out the menus of most of Valmorel's restaurants in 15 minutes of wandering up and down the main street. A pattern soon emerges – pizza, pasta, fondues and a smattering of Savoie fare. Couscous and galettes are also available. Not a huge variety but enough, and you're likely to get decent food and fair value. Many of the places need to be booked for any chance of a seat at a reasonable time.

The restaurant of hotel Planchamp is relatively upmarket with prices to match. The Petit Savoyarde is a mid-range place recommended by reporters. The refurbished Ski Roc is now a 'trendy wine bar'. La Marmite in the Hotel du Bourg has been recommended but 'isn't cheap'. The Grenier in Mottet offers a bit of everything, is in a slightly different location and is highly recommended by a reporter who 'ate there every night but one' (and regretted their night off). Locals also recommend La Grange, the Perce Neige, La Cordee and Tex-Mex at Jimbololo. A pizza or fondue in the popular Pizzeria Chez Albert or Pizzeria du Bourg or a takeaway (they deliver) from the Casa Pizz' are good value.

APRES-SKI
Unexciting

Immediate après-ski is centred on the outdoor cafes at the end of Bourg-Morel and Le Grenier. Both are lively spots. The after-dark activities are, like everything else, concentrated around that main street. Café de la Gare has live music but can be full of ESF staff and 'cliquey'. Petit Prince and La Casbah are popular with locals, while the Perce-Neige frequently gets packed and boisterous. Cocktails can be enjoyed in more polished surroundings at the Shaker in hotel La Fontaine. There's one disco, Jeans, which is often neglected but occasionally buzzes.

You may catch an occasional musical event at the village hall, or a street parade (there's a Mardi Gras with medieval costumes and fireworks). A two-screen cinema and a wine-tasting evening are other possibilities.

OFF THE SLOPES
Pleasant but boring

It's a very pretty little place, friendly and traffic-free. But it's not a great place to hang around if you're not using the slopes – unless you are happy spending time in cafes. There are some cleared walks around the village and at the top of all the main lifts and there's a pretty baroque church in Les Avanchers. Several mid-mountain restaurants are accessible to pedestrians, and it's also quite practical for friends using the slopes to return to the village for a lunchtime meet.

Snow-shoe treks and dog-sleigh trips can be organised – you can even learn to 'mush' the dogs.

STAYING DOWN THE VALLEY
Less than appealing

We have stayed at the Edelweiss down at Les Avanchers, which had decent French food, a rustic atmosphere and an eccentric patron. But there is little else there. A regular reporter stays at Combelouvière, and finds it 'has almost as much ski convenience as Valmorel, with a pleasanter run home at the end of the day'. However, it's quiet in the evenings.

Val-Thorens 2300m

Europe's highest resort, with guaranteed good snow

WHAT IT COSTS

5

HOW IT RATES

The slopes

Snow	*****
Extent	*****
Experts	****
Intermediates	*****
Beginners	****
Convenience	*****
Queues	***
Restaurants	****

The rest

Scenery	***
Resort charm	**
Off-slope	**

What's new

For 2001/02 a new jumbo gondola (the Fond 2 Funitel) will start from the bottom of the gondola towards Caron and take you to near the Col de la Montée du Fond, ending the need to walk to the Maurienne side (the Fourth Valley). A new black and a new red run will be built from the top on the Val Thorens side.

Two new successive quad chair-lifts in the Fourth Valley will take you from Plan Bouchet at the top of the gondola up from the Maurienne valley to Pointe du Bouchet, up a valley previously having only an itinéraire run. Three new runs will result – a blue from the lower chair, a red beneath the upper chair and a black where the itinéraire was.

A 120-metre-long moving carpet will be built on the beginner Marmottons piste. The exit of the Caron cable-car will have a rubber walkway.

- ➕ Extensive local slopes to suit all standards, and good access to the rest of the vast Three Valleys
- ➕ The highest resort in the Alps and one of the most snowsure, with north-facing slopes guaranteeing good snow for a long season, even off the glacier
- ➕ Not as much of an eyesore as most high, purpose-built resorts
- ➕ Compact village with direct slope access from most accommodation

- ➖ Can be bleak in bad weather – not a tree in sight
- ➖ Parts of the village are much less attractive to walk through in the evening than to ski past in the day
- ➖ Not much to do off the slopes
- ➖ Some very busy piste intersections
- ➖ Still some queues – especially for the Cîme de Caron cable-car.

For the enthusiast looking for the best snow in the Alps, it's difficult to beat Val-Thorens – especially given that it's also one of the least unpleasant purpose-built resorts. But we still prefer a cosier base elsewhere in the Three Valleys. That way, if a storm socks in, we can play in the woods around Méribel or Courchevel; if the sun is scorching, we have the option of setting off for Val-Thorens. The formula doesn't work the other way round.

The resort 

Val-Thorens is built high above the tree line on a sunny, west-facing mountainside at the head of the Belleville valley, surrounded by peaks, slopes and lifts. The village streets are supposedly traffic-free. Practically all visitors' cars are banished to car parks, except on Saturday. But workers' cars still generate a fair amount of traffic, and weekends can be mayhem with people entering and leaving the resort. One reporter recommends you leave 2½ hours to get to Moûtiers on a Saturday. Many parts of the resort are designed with their 'fronts' facing the slopes, and their relatively dreary backs facing the streets. There are quite extensive shopping arcades, a fair choice of bars and restaurants, and a good sports centre.

It is a classic purpose-built resort – compact, with lots of convenient slope-side accommodation. It's quite a complicated little village; but since it's quite compact, it doesn't matter much where you stay. At its heart is the snowy Place de Caron, where pedestrians mix with skiers and

OT VAL-THORENS / BASILE, MARK BUSCAIL

Snow wherever you look ↓

MOUNTAIN FACTS

for the Three Valleys

Altitude	1300m-3200m
Lifts	200
Pistes	600km
Green	17%
Blue	34%
Red	37%
Black	12%
Artificial snow	90km
Recco detectors used	

boarders. Many of the shops and restaurants are clustered here, along with the best hotels, and the sports centre is nearby. The village is basically divided in two by a little slope (with a drag-lift) that leads down to the main slope running the length of the village. The upper half of the village is centred on the Place de Péclet. A road runs across the hillside from here to the new chalet-style Balcons development. The lower half of the village is more diffuse, with the Rue du Soleil winding down from the dreary bus station to the big Temples du Soleil apartments.

Seen from the slopes, it is not as hideous as many of its rivals. The buildings are mainly medium-rise and wood-clad; some are distinctly stylish.

The mountains

Take account of the height, the extent of its local slopes and the easy access to the rest of the Three Valleys, and the attraction of Val-Thorens becomes clear. The main disadvantage is the lack of trees. Heavy snowfalls or high wind can shut practically all the lifts and slopes, and even if they don't close, poor visibility can be a problem.

THE SLOPES

High and snowsure

The resort has a wide piste going right down the front of it, leading down to a number of different lifts. The big **Péclet**

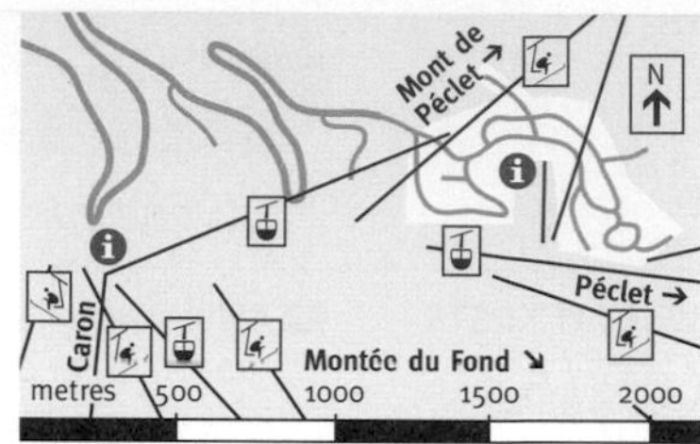

gondola, with 25-person cabins, rises 700m to the Péclet glacier, with three red runs down. One links across to a wide area of intermediate runs served by lifts to cols either side of the **Pointe de Thorens**. From one of these, the **Col de la Montée du Fond,** you can descend into the 'Fourth Valley', the **Maurienne**; for the 2001/02 season you will also be able to reach this point on a new jumbo gondola starting below the village. In the Maurienne valley a chair brings you back and serves red and blue slopes of 660m vertical and two new chairs and three new runs will be built for 2001/02.

The **Cîme de Caron** cable-car can be reached from the Pointe de Thorens area or by taking a gondola or fast chair from the same point as the new jumbo gondola. It rises 900m to the highest lift-served point in the Three Valleys, with red and black pistes down the front of the mountain.

The two Boismint chairs from the lowest part of the domain serve an underused area of intermediate runs.

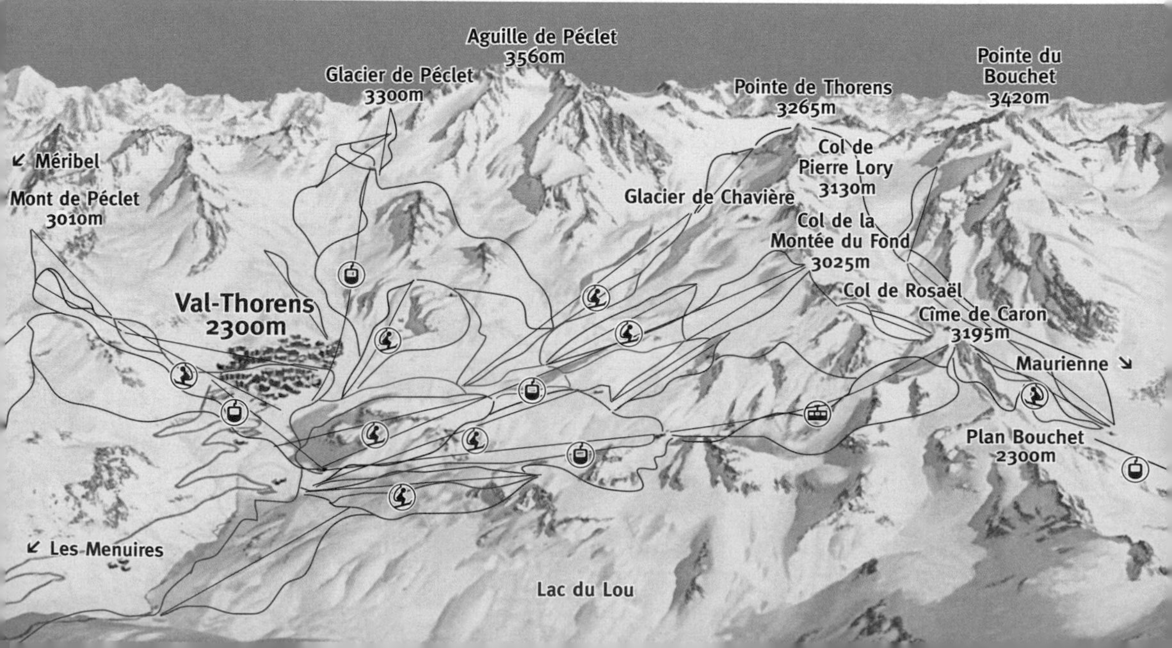

LIFT PASSES

2001/02 prices in euros

Three Valleys
Covers all lifts in Courchevel, La Tania, Méribel, Val-Thorens, Les Menuires and St-Martin-de-Belleville.

Beginners 4 free lifts in Val-Thorens.

Main pass
1-day pass 37
6-day pass 182
6-day low-season pass 109

Senior citizens
Over 60: 6-day pass 146
Over 70 6-day pass 91
Over 75: free pass

Children
Under 17: 6-day pass 137
Under 10: 118
Under 5: free pass

Short-term passes
Half-day passes (from 12.30) available for Val-Thorens lifts (adult 22) and the Three Valleys (adult 28).

Notes 6-day pass and over valid for one day each in Tignes-Val-d'Isère, La Plagne-Les Arcs, Pralognan-la-Vanoise and Les Saisies. Reductions for families.

Alternative passes
Vallée des Belleville pass covers 72 lifts and 300km piste in Val-Thorens, Les Menuires and St-Martin (adult 6-day 170). Val-Thorens-only pass covers 30 lifts and 140km of piste: adult 6-day 138.

Chair-lifts heading north from the resort serve sunny slopes above the village and also lead to the Méribel valley. Les Menuires can also be reached via these lifts; the alternative Boulevard Cumin along the valley floor is nearly flat, and can be hard work.

SNOW RELIABILITY
Difficult to beat

Few resorts can rival Val-Thorens for reliably good snow-cover, thanks to its altitude and generally north-facing slopes. Snowmaking now covers 20% of the pistes, including the busy south- and west-facing runs on the way back from the Méribel valley.

FOR EXPERTS
Lots to do off-piste

Val-Thorens' local pistes are primarily intermediate terrain. The runs down from the Cîme de Caron cable-car are the most challenging. The fast Cascades chair serves a good steep run that quickly gets mogulled but is not currently on the piste map. The sunny Marielle run is one of the easiest blacks we've come across.

The long Lac du Lou itinéraire goes from the Cîme de Caron to the lower Boismint chair. There is also a great deal of unmarked off-piste terrain to explore with a guide, particularly on the north-facing slopes reached from the Col, Fond, Deux Lacs and Boismint chairs. It is rocky terrain with serious hazards. You can also climb up from the top of the Péclet lifts and take a long off-piste run towards Méribel – a guide and high level of fitness are essential.

FOR INTERMEDIATES
Unbeatable quality and quantity

The scope for intermediates throughout the Three Valleys is enormous. It will take a decent intermediate only 90 minutes or so to get to Courchevel at the far end, if not distracted by the endless runs on the way.

The local slopes in Val-Thorens are some of the best intermediate terrain in the region. Most of the pistes are easy reds and blues, made even more enjoyable by the excellent snow.

The snow on the red Col run is always some of the best around. The blue Moraine below it is gentle and popular with the schools. The runs on the top half of the mountain are steeper than those back into the resort. The Fond lifts serve a good variety of red runs. The Pluviometre from the Trois Vallées chair is a glorious varied red, away from the lifts. Adventurous intermediates shouldn't miss the Combe du Caron runs. The black run is not intimidating – it's very wide and usually has good snow.

FOR BEGINNERS
Good late-season choice

The slopes at the foot of the resort are very gentle and provide convenient, snowsure nursery slopes. There are no long green runs to progress to, but the blues immediately above the village are easy. The resort's height and bleakness make it cold in midwinter, and intimidating in bad weather.

FOR CROSS-COUNTRY
Try elsewhere

Val-Thorens is a poor base for cross-country, with only 4km of local trails.

QUEUES
Persistent at the Cîme de Caron

Recent reports suggest few problems. But it is still common to wait 10 or 15 minutes for the Cîme de Caron cable-car, despite a scheme designed to speed up loading, and a March visitor found 40-minute-plus queues.

The Plein Sud six-pack chair-lift does a good job of getting the crowds back towards Méribel and Courchevel in the afternoon. The Côte Brune chair, on the Mottaret side, is a bottleneck for returning Val-Thorens residents.

When snow is in short supply

boarding *The best resort-level snow in Europe appeals to boarders as well as skiers – and pulls in considerable numbers. There are pistes to suit all abilities, and the good snow is great for beginners and carvers. There's plenty of off-piste choice for free-riders, though if you want trees you'll have to travel. The lifts are now mainly chairs and gondolas, though one or two drags remain. The fun-park towards the bottom of the Caron sector, served by a fast chair, has a half-pipe and a sound-system, and hosts weekly competitions. Nightlife centres around bars and a couple of discos that, because of all the young people in the resort (especially Scandinavians and Dutch), are usually noisy and entertaining.*

SCHOOLS/GUIDES

2001/02 prices in euros

ESF

Classes 6 days
3hr am or 2½hr pm
6 mornings 119

Children's classes
Ages: 4 to 12
6 mornings: 105

Private lessons
Hourly from 29 for 1 or 2 people

Ski Cool
2000/01 prices

Classes 6 days
3hr, am or pm
6 mornings: 107

Children's classes
5 days for 3 hours: 86

Private lessons
Hourly or daily
52 for 2hr, for 1 or 2 people

OTHER SCHOOLS

Pros Neige International

CHILDCARE

The ESF can provide all-day care and offers classes for children from age 2½. It also runs Mini Club crèches in two locations, at the top and bottom of the resort, taking children from age 3 months to 4 years.

Phone numbers

From abroad use the prefix +33 and omit the initial '0' of the phone number.

elsewhere the pressure on the Val-Thorens lifts can of course increase.

MOUNTAIN RESTAURANTS
Lots of choice

For a high, modern resort, the choice of restaurants is good. We like the Chalet de Génépi, on the run down from the Moraine chair – great views, an open fire and a wide range of good dishes. The Bar de la Marine, on the Dalles piste, does excellent food, but service can be stretched. The Moutière, near the top of the chair of the same name, is one of the more reasonably priced of Val-Thorens' mountain huts (which are generally expensive). The Plan Bouchet refuge in the Maurienne valley is very popular and welcoming, but bar service can be slow. You can stay the night there, too. Chalet Plein Sud, below the chair of the same name, has excellent views but a 'rather limited menu'. The big Chalet de Thorens has been praised for its food and reasonable prices. Lots of people lunch in the village.

SCHOOLS AND GUIDES
A mixed bag

Like so many branches of the ESF, this one is incompetently run. One reporter speaks of two classes saddled with 'rude, unhelpful and unsympathetic' instructors. More alarmingly, we have yet another report of an ESF instructor losing a child – an incident about which the ESF 'could not have been more arrogant and unconcerned'. In contrast, a reporter found Pros Neige classes 'really excellent – my wife's skiing changed dramatically'.

We've had good reports of private lessons with the ESF and other schools. The ESF have a Trois Vallées group for those who want to cover a lot of ground while receiving tuition – available by the day or the week, and can include off-piste. Ski Cool class sizes are guaranteed not to exceed 10. They also have off-piste courses. But according to one reporter, they took someone with two days' experience down a mogulled black run, causing him to injure his knee. There are several specialist guiding outfits.

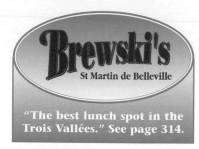

FACILITIES FOR CHILDREN
Not up to much

We have conflicting reports of the ESF Mini-Club crèche. Some reporters are happy with it; others describe it as 'complete chaos' and report having to rescue children abandoned on the slopes. Thomson's 'Kids Club' has been recommended.

Staying there

HOW TO GO
Surprisingly high level of comfort

Accommodation is of a higher standard than in many purpose-built resorts.

Chalets These are catered apartments, and many are quite comfortable.

Hotels There are plenty of hotels, mainly 3-stars.

((((5) **Fitz Roy** (0479 000478) Swanky but charming Relais & Châteaux place with lovely rooms. Pool. Well placed.

((((4) **Val Thorens** (0479 000433) Welcoming and comfortable; next door

OT VAL-THORENS / YVES BONTOUX

The new chalet-style Balcons development in the upper part of the village is very attractive and has great views →

You can slide to and from the door of virtually all Val-Thorens' accommodation →

OT VAL-THORENS / BASILE, MARK BUSCAIL

GETTING THERE

Air Geneva, transfer 3½hr. Lyon, transfer 3½hr. Chambéry, transfer 2½hr.

Rail Moûtiers (37km); regular buses from station.

ACTIVITIES

Indoor Sports centre (tennis, squash, climbing wall, roller skating, golf simulator, swimming pool, saunas, hot-tub, volleyball, weight training, table tennis, fitness, badminton, football), games rooms, music recitals, cinema, beauty centre.

Outdoor Walks, snow-mobiles, paragliding, snowshoe excursions, toboggan run.

TOURIST OFFICE

Postcode 73440
t +33 479 000808
f 479 000004
valtho@valthorens.com
www.valthorens.com

to Fitz Roy.

(((3) **Sherpa** (0479 000070) Highly recommended for atmosphere and food. Less-than-ideal position at the top of the resort.

(((3) **Bel Horizon** (0479 000477) Friendly, family-run 3-star, popular with reporters – 'cuisine wonderful'.

Self-catering The options include apartments of a higher standard than usual in France. The Temples du Soleil are recommended for good facilities.

EATING OUT
Surprisingly wide range

Val-Thorens has something for most tastes. The Fitz Roy and the Val Thorens hotels do classic French food. For something more regional, the best bets are the 'excellent' Vieux Chalet and the Chaumière. The Scapin is cosily done out in wood and stone, with 'good' food. Other reporters' recommendations include the Montana ('good food and service'), El Gringo's ('excellent but cramped Mexican'), Auberge des Balcons ('wonderful raclette'). The Galoubet has been praised for its steaks. The Blanchot is an unusually stylish wine bar with a simple but varied carte and of course an excellent range of wines. Several pizzerias are recommended, including that in the Temples du Soleil.

APRES-SKI
Livelier than you'd imagine

Val-Thorens is surprisingly lively at night. The Red Fox up at Balcons is busy at close of play, with karaoke. At the opposite extreme the Sherlock Holmes in the Temples du Soleil is 'always lively'. The Frog and Roast Beef at the top of the village is a cheerful British ghetto with a live band at tea-time and half-price beer while it plays. It claims to be the highest pub in Europe. Le Monde, Friends and the Viking pub are all lively bars on the same block. The Underground nightclub in Place de Péclet has an extended happy hour but 'descends into europop' when its disco gets going. Bloopers is another popular Scan-oriented bar-disco. The Malaysia cellar bar is recommended for good live bands, and gets very busy after 11pm. Quieter bars include O'Connells (run by a Dane, of course), the cosy Rhum (aka Mitch's) and the St Pierre.

OFF THE SLOPES
Forget it

There's a good sports centre, but the small pool can get crowded. You can get to some mountain restaurants by lift, and the 360° panorama from the top of the Cîme de Caron cable-car is not to be missed. But it is a pretty bleak place for non-slope-users.

The French Pyrenees

Decent skiing and boarding at half the price of the Alps

It took us a long time to get round to visiting the resorts of the French Pyrenees – mainly because we had the idea that they were second-rate compared with the Alps. Well, it is certainly true that they can't compete in terms of size of ski area with the mega-resorts of the Trois Vallées and La Plagne. But don't dismiss them: they have considerable attractions, including price – hotels cost half as much as in the Alps, and meals and drinks are cheap.

We went with several preconceived ideas, not least that the Pyrenees are hills compared with the mountains of the Alps. Not true: the Pyrenees are serious mountains, and have dramatic picturesque scenery too. They are also attractively French. Unlike the big plastic mega resorts, many Pyrenean bases have a rustic, rural Gallic charm.

The biggest ski area is shared by **Barèges** and **La Mongie**. Between them they have 100km of runs and 47 lifts. The runs are best suited to intermediates, with good tree-lined runs above Barèges and open bowl skiing above La Mongie. The best bet for an expert is to try off-piste with a guide – one beautiful run away from all the lifts starts with a scramble through a hole in the rocks. There are atmospheric mountain huts dotted around the slopes. And when we were there, locals dressed in traditional costume were having a fun race near one of the nicest.

Barèges is a spa village set in a narrow, steep-sided valley, which gets little sun in midwinter. It's also the second oldest ski resort in France and the pioneer of skiing in the Pyrenees. Accommodation is mainly in basic 1-star and 2-star hotels. Its rather drab buildings and one main street grow on you, though there's little to do in the evenings other than visit the thermal spa and a restaurant (of which there are a good number serving solid local fare). La Mongie, on the other hand, is a modern, purpose-built resort reminiscent of the Alps.

Cauterets is another spa town but a complete contrast to Barèges. It is much bigger (18,000 beds compared with 3,500) and set in a wide, sunny valley. It is a popular summer destination, and even in March we were able to sit at a pavement cafe with a drink after dinner. It feels more like a town in Provence than a ski resort. Indeed, it wasn't until 1964 that skiing started here, when the cable-car to the slopes 850m above the town was built – you have to ride down as well as up. There are only 30km of slopes, set in an open, semi-circular bowl that can be cold and windy. A decent intermediate could cover all the runs in a day and there's little to challenge an expert. But Cauterets' jewel is its cross-country, set a long drive or bus-ride from town at Pont d'Espagne and served by a gondola. It is the start of the Pyrenees National Park and the old smugglers' route over the mountains between France and Spain. The 36km of snowsure cross-country tracks run up this beautiful deserted valley, beside a rushing stream and a stunning waterfall.

Font-Romeu has about 45km of pistes and 29 lifts, serving mainly easy and intermediate pistes (15 of its 40 pistes are green) and is popular with families. The slopes get a lot of sun and the snow can suffer as a result. But it has 460 snow-guns – the biggest snowmaking set-up in the Pyrenees – and so cover is assured so long as it is cold enough at night to make snow. Weekend crowds arrive from nearby Perpignan and over the border in Spain and both lifts and pistes can get busy. The village is a bus-ride from the slopes and the hotels are mainly 2- and 3-star.

The other major Pyrenean resort is **St-Lary-Soulan**, a traditional village with houses built of stone, with a cable-car at the edge going up to the slopes, of which there are 80km, suiting mainly intermediates. There's a satellite called **St-Lary-Espiaube**, which is purpose-built and right at the heart of the slopes.

All the areas welcome snowboarders – but Cauterets provides the most facilities and is the Pyrenees' leading boarding resort.

In the 1990s, Italy was the boom destination of the Alps. While the French franc, Austrian schilling and Swiss franc soared, the lira plummeted – so Italy became cheaper while other Alpine countries were finding themselves priced out of the international market. Such variations are now supposed to be a thing of the past, since the lira has a fixed rate to the euro and will in due course disappear altogether. And it's clear that Italy isn't as cheap as it was – partly because Italian lift companies, hoteliers and restaurateurs cashed in on the boom. So Italy must now compete with the other Alpine countries on the quality of the holidays it offers, not just their price (although it does still have a small price advantage).

Italy has some enduring attractions. Food and wine always were satisfying, the atmosphere always was jolly, the scenery always was splendid – in the Dolomites, simply stunning. But 10 or 20 years ago Italian lift companies had the reputation of being a bit of a joke.

Not any more. Now, lift systems are modern; snowmaking – which the Italians were early to catch on to – is very widespread, especially in the Dolomites; piste grooming is of a consistently high standard. The value side of the value-for-money equation is one you need not worry about.

Although there aren't huge numbers of them (on the international market, at least), Italian resorts vary as widely in characteristics as they do in location – and they are spread along the length of the Italian border, from Sauze d'Oulx and neighbours (just across the French border from Montgenèvre) all along the Swiss border to the Dolomites, an area that used to be part of Austria. There are high, snowsure ski-stations and charming valley villages, and mountains that range from one-run wonders to some of the most extensive lift networks in the world.

A lot of Italian runs, particularly in the north-west, seem flatteringly easy. This is partly because the piste grooming is immaculate, and also because piste grading seems to overstate difficulty. Nowhere is this clearer than in La Thuile (located in Italy, despite its French name). Its mountain connects (just) with that of La Rosière (across the valley from Les Arcs), and venturing from the Italian side to the French side is like moving from the shelter of harbour to the open sea. Red runs on the La Thuile side are virtually motorways; at La Rosière, they offer challenging moguls – as indeed do some of the blues at times.

We have also been struck by the way Italian resorts continue to be weekend-oriented. Except in the Dolomites (which depend largely on German visitors driving down for a week), resorts can be quiet as the grave during the week, especially in low season, but come to life on Friday night or Saturday morning when the weekenders from Italy's affluent northern plain arrive. If, like us, you quite like having the pistes and perhaps even the hotel bar to yourself, this is a real advantage.

In general, Italians don't take their skiing or boarding too seriously. Some lifts may still close for lunch, and mountain restaurants are generally welcoming places serving satisfying food and wine, encouraging leisurely lunching. Pasta – even in the most modest establishment – is delicious. And eating and drinking on the mountain is still cheaper than in other Alpine resorts, whatever the European Union is doing to harmonise our lives.

DRIVING IN THE ITALIAN ALPS

There are four main geographical groupings of Italian resorts, widely separated. Getting to some of these resorts is a very long haul, and moving from one area to another can involve very long drives.

The handful of resorts to the west of Turin – Bardonecchia, Sauze d'Oulx, Sestriere and neighbours in the Milky Way region – are easily reached from France via two major routes: the Fréjus tunnel from Modane, or via the good road over the pass that the resort of Montgenèvre sits on.

Further north, and about equidistant from Milan and Turin, are the resorts of the Aosta valley – Courmayeur, Cervinia and La Thuile the best known among them. Since the construction of the Mont Blanc road tunnel from Chamonix in France, Courmayeur has been the easiest of all Italian resorts to reach from Britain. But as we go to press in mid-2001 it is still unclear when the tunnel will reopen following the disastrous fire in 1999; the best estimate is not this winter but the next. The Aosta valley can also be reached from Switzerland via the Grand St Bernard tunnel. The approach is high, and may require chains. The road down the Aosta valley is a major thoroughfare, but the roads up to some of the other resorts are quite long, winding and (in the case of Cervinia) high.

To the east is a string of scattered resorts, most close to the Swiss border, many in isolated and remote valleys involving long drives up from the nearest Italian cities, or high-altitude drives from Switzerland. The links between Switzerland and Italy are more clearly shown on our larger-scale Switzerland map at the beginning of that

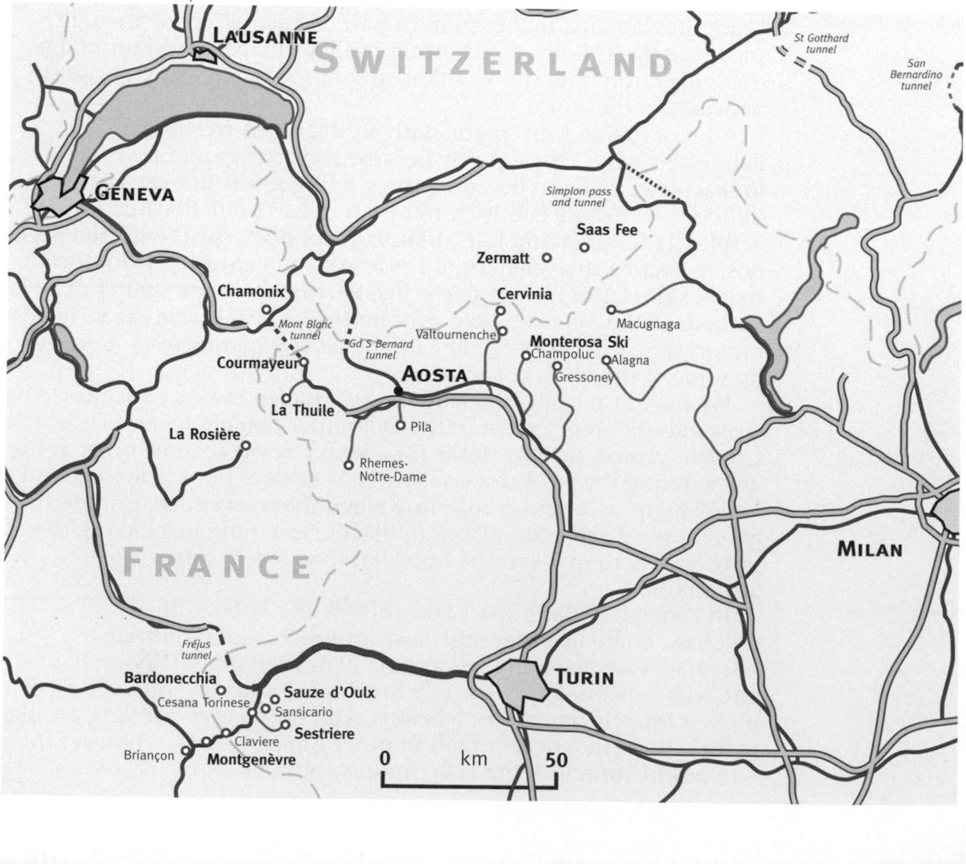

LAUSANNE
SWITZERLAND
St Gotthard tunnel
San Bernardino tunnel
GENEVA
Simplon pass and tunnel
Saas Fee
Zermatt
Chamonix
Cervinia
Macugnaga
Mont Blanc tunnel
Gd S Bernard tunnel
Valtournenche
Monterosa Ski
Champoluc
Alagna
Gressoney
Courmayeur
AOSTA
La Thuile
Pila
La Rosière
Rhemes-Notre-Dame
MILAN
FRANCE
Fréjus tunnel
Bardonecchia
Cesana Torinese
Sauze d'Oulx
Sansicario
Sestriere
Claviere
Briançon
Montgenèvre
TURIN
0 km 50

section. The major routes are the St Gotthard tunnel between Göschenen (near Andermatt) and Airolo – the main route between Basel and Milan – and the San Bernardino tunnel reached via Chur.

Finally, further east still are the resorts of the Dolomites. Getting there from Austria is easy, over the Brenner motorway pass from Innsbruck. But getting there from Britain is a very long drive indeed – allow at least a day and a half. We drove to Cortina for a week's holiday a few years back, and doubt that we'd want to do it again. Even though we believe driving is the best way of getting to the mountains, we wouldn't lightly drive there and back except as part of a longer tour. It's also worth bearing in mind that once you arrive in the Dolomites, getting around the intricate network of valleys linked by narrow, winding roads can be a slow business – not helped by impatient Italian driving.

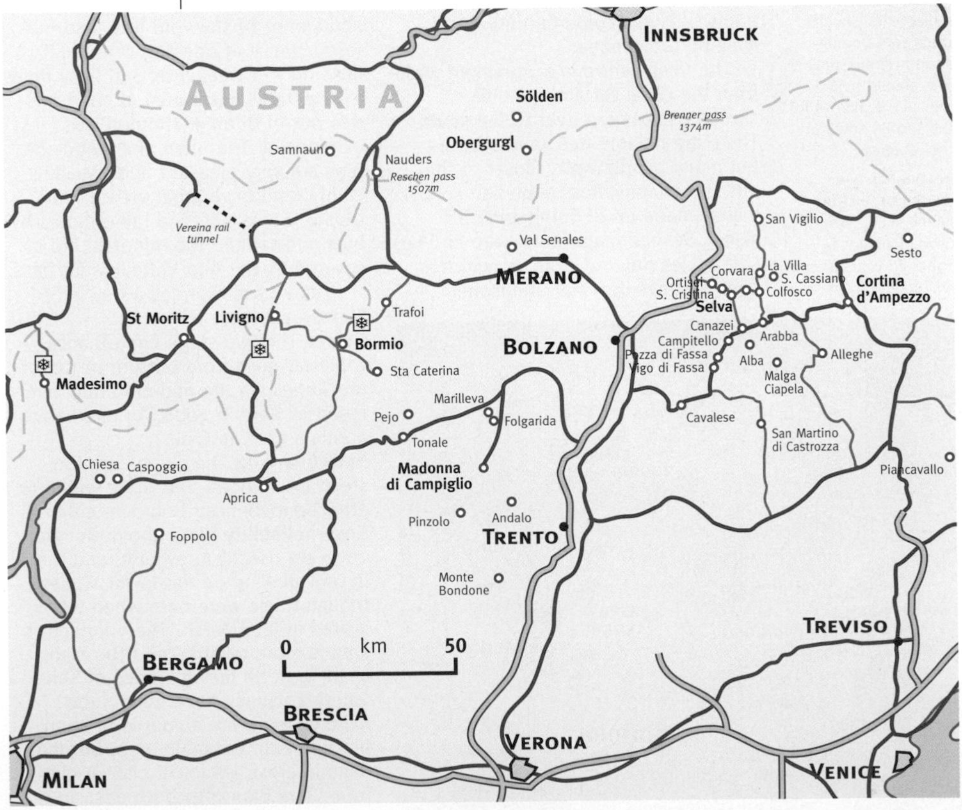

Innsbruck
Austria
Sölden
Brenner pass 1374m
Samnaun
Nauders
Reschen pass 1507m
Obergurgl
Vereina rail tunnel
San Vigilio
Val Senales
Sesto
Merano
Corvara
La Villa
S. Cassiano
Cortina d'Ampezzo
Ortisei
S. Cristina
Colfosco
Selva
St Moritz
Livigno
Trafoi
Canazei
Arabba
Campitello
Bormio
Bolzano
Pozza di Fassa
Vigo di Fassa
Alba
Alleghe
Madesimo
Sta Caterina
Malga Ciapela
Marilleva
Pejo
Folgarida
Cavalese
Tonale
San Martino di Castrozza
Chiesa
Caspoggio
Madonna di Campiglio
Piancavallo
Aprica
Andalo
Pinzolo
Foppolo
Trento
Monte Bondone
Treviso
0 km 50
Bergamo
Brescia
Verona
Milan
Venice

Bormio 1225m

A tall, narrow mountain with a rather narrow appeal

WHAT IT COSTS

(2)

HOW IT RATES

The slopes

Snow	***
Extent	**
Experts	*
Intermediates	***
Beginners	**
Convenience	***
Queues	***
Restaurants	****

The rest

Scenery	***
Resort charm	****
Off-slope	****

What's new

A new fast quad is to replace the Isabella chair from Bormio 2000 next season. This should help reduce the queues for the second stage of the cable-car.

Bormio has been chosen to host the Alpine skiing World Championships in 2005, 20 years after it first staged them.

- ⊕ Good mix of high, open pistes and woodland runs adding up to some good long runs
- ⊕ Worthwhile neighbouring resorts
- ⊕ Attractive medieval town centre – quite unlike any other winter resort
- ⊕ Good mountain restaurants

- ⊖ Slopes all of medium steepness
- ⊖ Rather confined main mountain, with second area some way distant
- ⊖ Still many slow old lifts
- ⊖ Long airport transfers
- ⊖ Crowds and queues on Sundays
- ⊖ Central hotels inconvenient

If you like cobbled medieval Italian towns and don't mind a lack of Alpine resort atmosphere, you'll find the centre of Bormio very appealing – though you're unlikely to be staying there. We'd plan on taking the free bus out to the Valdidentro area and perhaps make longer outings, to Santa Caterina at least.

THE RESORT

Bormio is in a remote spot, close to the Swiss and Austrian borders (we're glad to hear that road improvements have cut the airport transfer to 3 hours). The 17th-century town centre is splendid, with narrow cobbled streets and old stone façades. It began life as a Roman spa, and still has thermal baths. It's very colourful during the evening promenade.

The town centre is a 15-minute walk from the cable-car and gondola stations across the river to the south. There are reliable free shuttle-buses, but many people walk. Closer to the lifts is a characterless suburban sprawl mainly made up of hotels built for skiers. Several major hotels are on Via Milano, leading out of town, which is neither convenient nor atmospheric.

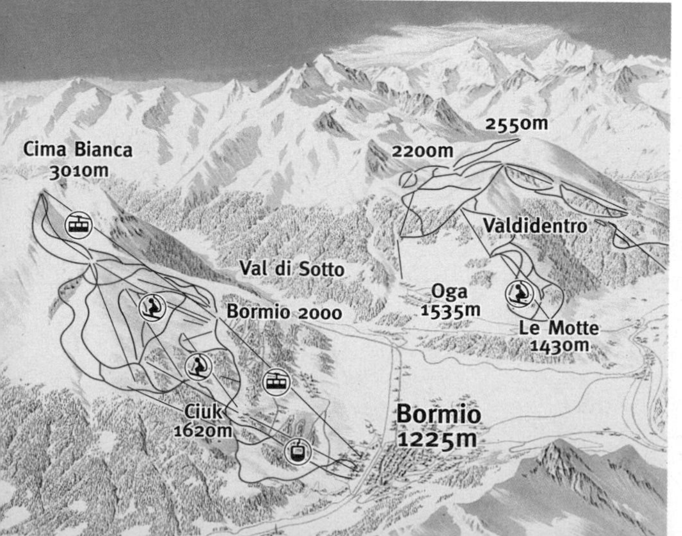

THE MOUNTAINS

There's a nice mix of high, snowsure pistes and lower wooded slopes. The main slopes are tall (vertical drop 1800m) and narrow. Most pistes face north-west and head to town.

Both the piste map and the piste marking need substantial improvement. Reporters have complained about the abundance of slow old lifts, and the resort policy of opening certain lift links only at weekends and busy times.

The Valdidentro area, a short bus-ride out of Bormio, shouldn't be overlooked. The open and woodland runs are very pleasant and usually empty (and have great views). Day trips to Santa Caterina (20 minutes by bus) and Livigno (90 minutes) are covered by the Alta Valtellina lift pass. A six-day pass includes a day in St Moritz (3 hours).

Slopes The two-stage Cima Bianca cable-car goes from bottom to top of the slopes via the mid-mountain mini-resort of Bormio 2000. An alternative gondola goes to Ciuk.

Snowboarding The slopes are too steep for novices, and there's little to attract experienced boarders either.

Snow reliability Runs above Bormio 2000 are usually snowsure, and there is snowmaking on the lower slopes, though these were bare when we visited in late March. The Valdidentro area is more reliable, and the high, shaded, north-facing slopes of Santa Caterina usually have good snow.

Experts There are a couple of short black runs in the main area, but the main interest lies in off-piste routes from Cima Bianca to both east and

↑ A mix of open and wooded slopes

MALCOLM RIDDOCH

MOUNTAIN FACTS

Figures relate to the Bormio, Valdidentro and Santa Caterina areas only

Altitude	1225m-3010m
Lifts	36
Pistes	120km
Blue	36%
Red	48%
Black	16%
Artificial snow	47km
Recco detectors used	

Phone numbers
From abroad use the prefix +39 (and do **not** omit the initial '0' of the phone number).

TOURIST OFFICE

Postcode 23032
t +39 (0342) 903300
f 904696
aptbormio@provincia.so.it
www.valtellinaonline.it

west of the piste area.
Intermediates The men's downhill course starts with a steep plunge, but otherwise is just a tough red, ideal for strong intermediates. Stella Alpina, down to 2000, is also fairly steep. Many runs are less tough – ideal for most intermediates. The longest is a superb top-to-bottom cruise. The outlying mountains are also suitable for early intermediates.
Beginners The nursery slopes at Bormio 2000 offer good snow, but there are no very flattering longer pistes to move on to. Novices are better off at nearby Santa Caterina.
Cross-country There are some trails either side of Bormio, towards Piatta and beneath Le Motte and Valdidentro, but cross-country skiers are better off at snowsure Santa Caterina.
Queues Both sections of the cable-car suffer delays in the morning peak period and on Sundays. A new fast quad from Bormio 2000 should help to relieve the pressure here for 2001/02. When the lower slopes are incomplete, queues form to ride down. Otherwise there are few problems outside carnival week.
Mountain restaurants The mountain restaurants are generally good. Even the efficient self-service at Bormio 2000 has a good choice of dishes. At La Rocca, above Ciuk, there is a welcoming chalet and a smart, modern place with table- or self-service. Cedrone, at Bormio 2000, has a good terrace and a play area for children. The very welcoming table-service Baita de Mario, at Ciuk, is a great place for a long lunch. The new San Colombano in Valdidentro is recommended.
Schools and guides We have received good reports of both the Alta Valtellina and Nazionale schools.
Facilities for children The Bormio 2000 school has a roped-off snow garden at mid-mountain with moving carpet lift.

STAYING THERE

How to go There are plenty of apartments, but hotels dominate the package market.
Hotels Most of Bormio's 40-plus hotels are 2- and 3-star places. The 4-star Palace (0342 903131) is the most luxurious in town. The Posta (0342 904753) is in the centre of the old town – rooms range from adequate to very good. The Baita dei Pinti (0342 904346) is the best placed of the top hotels – on the river, between the lifts and centre. The Ambassador (0342 904625) is close to the gondola.
Self-catering The modern Cristallo apartments have been recommended.
Eating out There's a wide selection of restaurants. The atmospheric Taulà does excellent modern food with great service. The Kuerc and the Vecchia Combo are also popular. There are excellent pizzerias, including the Jap.
Après-ski The après-ski scene starts on the mountain at La Rocca, and there are popular bars around the bottom lift stations. The Clem Pub, Gordy's, Cafe Mozart and the Aurora piano bar are popular spots. Shangri-La is a friendly bar. The King's Club is the best disco.
Off the slopes Diversions include thermal baths, riding and walks in the Stelvio National Park. There is also an excellent sports centre, ice rink and 'superb' swimming pool. St Moritz and duty-free Livigno are popular excursions.
Staying up the mountain The modern Girasole, at Bormio 2000, is simple but well run by an Anglo-Italian couple, with lots of events.

Cervinia 2050m

Mile after mile of high-altitude, snowsure cruising

WHAT IT COSTS

4

HOW IT RATES

The slopes

Snow	*****
Extent	***
Experts	*
Intermediates	****
Beginners	*****
Convenience	***
Queues	***
Restaurants	***

The rest

Scenery	****
Resort charm	**
Off-slope	*

What's new

There's a new piste down into Zermatt from the top of the fast chair-lifts to the Swiss border. And there is new snowmaking on the pistes back down under the fast chairs to Plan Maison. A new morning-only pass, valid until 1pm, has been introduced, and you can now buy your ski pass at your hotel.

- ⊕ Extensive mountain with miles of long, consistently gentle runs – ideal for early intermediates and anyone wary of steep slopes or bumps
- ⊕ High, sunny and snowsure slopes amid impressive scenery
- ⊕ Link with Zermatt in Switzerland provides even more spectacular views and good lunches

- ⊖ Very little to interest good or aggressive intermediates and above
- ⊖ Almost entirely treeless, with little to do in bad weather
- ⊖ Lifts prone to closure by wind, particularly early in the season
- ⊖ Link with Zermatt isn't quite as valuable as you might expect
- ⊖ Village spoils some of the views
- ⊖ Steep uphill walk to main lifts, followed by lots of steps in station
- ⊖ Few off-slope amenities

What brings people to Breuil Cervinia (as the resort now styles itself) in winter in the 20th century is what brought climbers to the original village of Breuil in the 19th century: altitude. For climbers it was a launch pad for assaults on the nearby Matterhorn (Monte Cervino). For winter sports, it offers an unusual combination: slopes that are gentle and extensive, sunny and snowsure.

For cruisers who like to cover the miles on flattering slopes with no worries about unexpected challenges, there is nowhere like it. But the more adventurous should steer clear: they'll find the slopes tame and the link with Zermatt disappointing because it doesn't access Zermatt's best slopes directly.

The resort

Cervinia is at the head of a long valley leading off the Aosta valley on the Italian side of the Matterhorn. The old climbing village developed into a winter resort in a rather haphazard way, and it has no consistent style of architecture. It's an uncomfortable hotchpotch, neither pleasing to the eye nor as offensive as the worst of the French purpose-built resorts. The centre is pleasant, compact and traffic-free. But ugly surrounding apartment blocks and hotels make the whole place feel less friendly and welcoming.

A lot of people stay near the village centre, at the foot of the nursery slopes. You can take a series of drags from here to the slopes. But the main gondola and cable-car to Plan Maison at mid-mountain start an awkward uphill walk away, above the village. To avoid the walk to these lifts, choose a hotel with its own shuttle-bus. There is more accommodation further out at the Cieloalto complex and on the road up to it – but some of these buildings are among the worst eyesores.

As well as the usual souvenir shops there are some smart clothes shops and jewellers. At peak periods, the resort fills up with day trippers and weekenders from Milan and Turin who bring cars and mobile phones, making parts of the village traffic- and fume-ridden at times, and the hills alive with the sound of ringing tones.

The resort is relatively expensive by Italian standards, but reporters have found it good value recently because of the strong pound/weak euro. There are surprisingly few off-slope amenities, such as kindergartens,

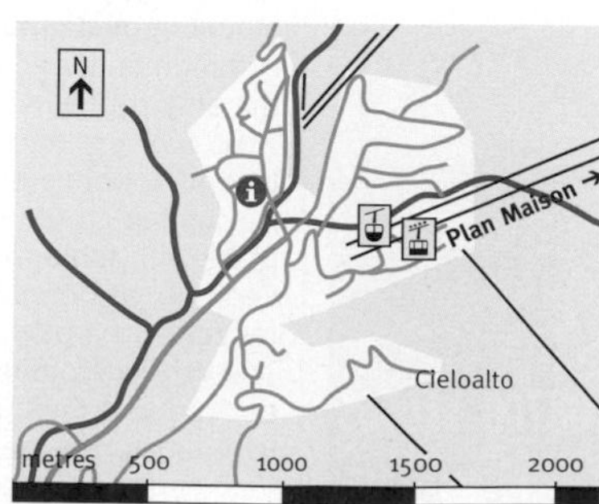

MOUNTAIN FACTS

Altitude	1525m-3480m
Lifts	31
Pistes	200km
Blue	28%
Red	60%
Black	12%
Artificial snow	17km

Recco detectors used

LIFT PASSES

2001/02 prices in euros

Breuil-Cervinia
Covers all lifts on the Italian side of the border including Valtournenche.

Beginners 'First bends' passes available.

Main pass
1-day pass 29
6-day pass 152
(low season 122)

Senior citizens
Over 65: 6-day pass 115

Children
Under 12: 6-day pass 115
Under 8: free pass

Short-term passes
Half-day from noon for Cervinia. Single and return tickets on some lifts.

Notes Daily extension for Zermatt lifts at Klein Matterhorn and Schwarzsee (19) or for all areas (25).

Alternative passes
The International Matterhorn pass includes Zermatt's Klein Matterhorn and Schwarzsee lifts: 6-day pass 178. The International Zermatt pass covers all of Zermatt: 6-day pass 191. Limited area passes for Carosello (four lifts) and Carosello/ Cretaz (seven lifts). Valle d'Aosta ski pass covers all lifts in Courmayeur, La Thuile, Gressoney, Alagna, Champoluc, Pila, Cervinia and Valtournenche (adult 6-day 155).

marked walks and spa facilities.

The slopes link to Valtournenche further down the valley (covered by the lift pass) and Zermatt over in Switzerland (covered by a daily supplement, or a more expensive weekly pass). More about this later in the chapter.

Day trips by car are possible to Courmayeur, La Thuile and the Monterosa Ski resorts of Champoluc and Gressoney.

The mountains

Cervinia's main slopes are on a high, large, open and sunny west-facing bowl. It has Italy's highest pistes and some of its longest (13km from Plateau Rosa to Valtournenche – with only a short drag-lift part-way). Nearly all the runs are accessible to intermediates. The weather is more of a problem than steepness. If it's bad, the top lifts often close because of high winds. And even the lower slopes may be unusable because of poor visibility. There are few woodland pistes.

THE SLOPES

Very easy

Cervinia has the biggest, highest, most snowsure area of easy, well groomed pistes we've come across – though we're very sceptical of the recent hike in the claimed total to 200km. The high proportion of red runs on the piste map is misleading: most of them would be graded blue elsewhere. The slopes just above the village are floodlit some evenings.

The main lifts take you to the mid-mountain base of **Plan Maison** (2555m). From there a further gondola then a giant cable-car go up to **Plateau Rosa** (3480m) and a link with Zermatt. Three successive fast quads (all with windshields) from Plan Maison go up to a slightly lower point on the border, where there is now a piste for Zermatt.

From the top you can ski back on

There is no better way to pack in the miles on-piste than to ride Cervinia's top cable-car repeatedly to Plateau Rosa at 3480m ↑

SNOWPIX.COM / CHRIS GILL

some of Cervinia's easiest slopes to Plan Maison or down to the village. If instead you turn right at Plateau Rosa you take the splendid wide Ventina run. You can use the cable-car to do the top part repeatedly, or go all the way down to Cervinia (8km and over 1400m vertical). Or you can branch off left down towards **Valtournenche** (1525m). The slopes here are served by a number of slow old lifts above the initial gondola from Valtournenche to Salette at 2245m. You can't get back to Plan Maison from this sector except by riding down the gondola.

There is also the small, little-used **Cieloalto** area, served by three lifts to the south of the cable-car at the

boarding *Cervinia has great slopes for learning to snowboard – gentle, wide and usually with good snow. And the main lifts around the area are chairs, gondolas and cable-cars, but beware, there are a lot of drag-lifts (especially difficult to negotiate in high winds) and some long flat bits as well. There's not much to interest better boarders – just as there's not much to interest better skiers. The snowboarder-only piste and fun-park in the Cieloalto sector is open only at weekends during the peak season (the one in Zermatt is better but beware of long T-bars to get back if the Klein Matterhorn cable-car is closed. Nightlife is fairly limited.*

SCHOOLS/GUIDES

2000/01 prices in euros

Cervino
Classes 6 days
2hr 45min: 10am-12.45
6 days: 119
Children's classes
Ages: 5 to 7
Private lessons
Hourly
28 for 1 person; 31 for 2 people

bottom of the Ventina run. This has some of Cervinia's steeper pistes and can be very useful in bad weather as it has the only trees in the area.

Several reporters have criticised the fact that old lift stations and pylons have been left on the slopes as eyesores after the lifts have been scrapped. The piste map is another cause for complaint.

SNOW RELIABILITY
Superb

The mountain is one of the highest in Europe and, despite getting a lot of afternoon sun, can usually be relied on to have good snow conditions. Lift closures due to wind is a bigger worry. Several reporters have complained about the biting winds and one claims that every lift stopped due to high winds at some point in his holiday.

The village nursery slopes and the bottom half of the Ventina run have snowmaking facilities. But the run below the top of the gondola to lower-lying Valtournenche doesn't – and is often closed later in the season.

FOR EXPERTS
Forget it

This is not a resort for experts. There are several black runs dotted about,

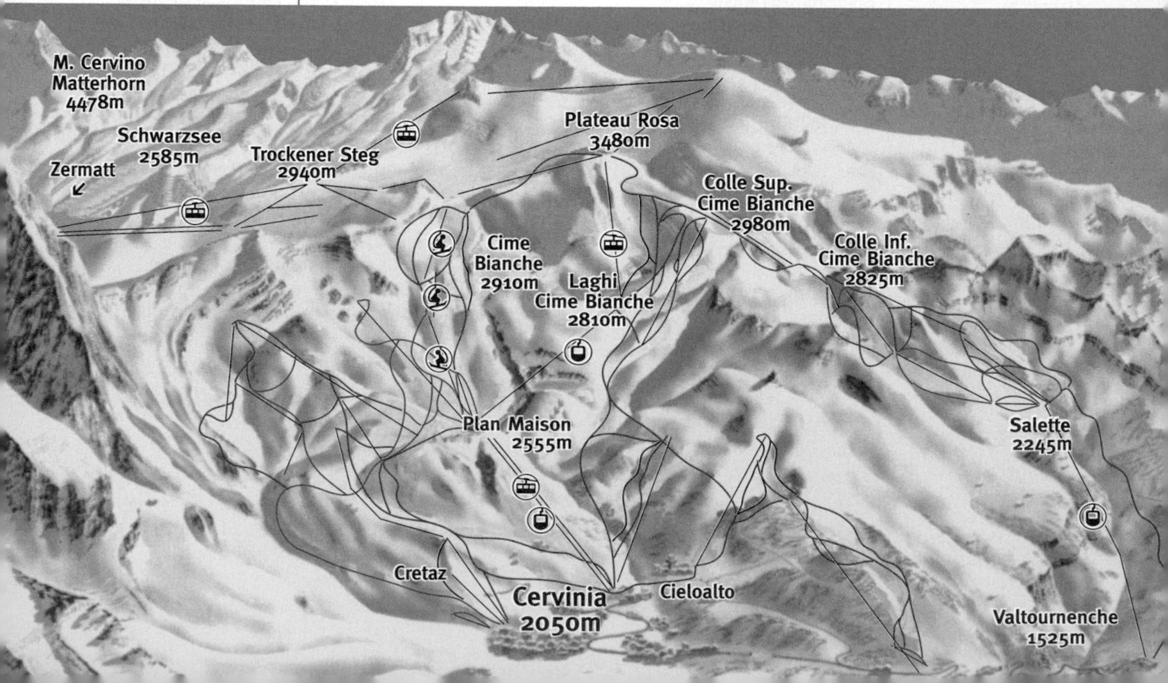

The Matterhorn looks more spectacular from Zermatt, but Cervinia's setting is impressive →

SNOWPIX.COM / CHRIS GILL

M. Cervino
Matterhorn
4478m
Schwarzsee
2585m
Zermatt ↙
Trockener Steg
2940m
Plateau Rosa
3480m
Colle Sup.
Cime Bianche
2980m
Cime
Bianche
2910m
Laghi
Cime Bianche
2810m
Colle Inf.
Cime Bianche
2825m
Plan Maison
2555m
Salette
2245m
Cretaz
Cervinia
2050m
Cieloalto
Valtournenche
1525m

THE ZERMATT CONNECTION

If the weather is good, you're bound to be tempted to go over to Zermatt. And quite right – the restaurants are simply the best, and it's only from the Swiss side that you get the classic view of the Matterhorn. But there are snags.

For a start, the two lift companies can't even convey clearly where you can cross over. Testa Grigia on one side of the joint map becomes Plateau Rosa on the other; Theodulpass becomes nameless. Pathetic.

Then there's the runs. You come first of all to even gentler glacier motorways than on the Cervinia side. There are more challenging pistes once you get down to Schwarzsee. But there is no way to get to Zermatt's classic terrain on Stockhorn and Rothorn without making the long descent to the village, and bussing or walking its length to other lifts.

You could do this, but you couldn't do it enjoyably – partly because you have to set off back early on account of the lift links back to the border. Recent reporters tell of long afternoon queues for the Trockener Steg-Klein Matterhorn cable-car. And if this link is closed by high winds – as is often the case – there may be horrendous queues in grim conditions for the alternative route via two long, slow and very exposed T-bars.

You can get a taste of Zermatt from Cervinia, but you're unlikely to get your fill.

but most of them would be graded red elsewhere. Many reporters head over to Zermatt for more challenging slopes but don't necessarily find them – more about this in the margin on this page.

FOR INTERMEDIATES
Miles of long, flattering runs

Virtually the whole area can be covered comfortably by average intermediates. And if you like wide, easy, motorway pistes, you'll love Cervinia: it has more long, flattering runs than any other resort. The easiest slopes are on the left as you look at the mountain. From top to bottom here there are gentle blue runs and almost equally gentle reds in the beautiful scenery at the foot of the south face of the Matterhorn.

The area on the right as you look at the mountain is best for adventurous intermediates. The Ventina run is a particularly good fast cruise. The long run down to Valtournenche is easy for most of its length. Good intermediates will be capable of the black runs.

FOR BEGINNERS
Pretty much ideal

Complete beginners will start on the good village nursery slope, and should graduate quickly to the fine flat area around Plan Maison and its gentle blue runs. Fast learners will be going all the way from the top to the bottom of the mountain by the end of the week.

FOR CROSS-COUNTRY
Hardly any

There are a couple of short trails, but this is not a cross-country resort.

QUEUES
Can still be problems

Although much improved recently, there are still some antiquated lifts, and the system still has drawbacks. The two main access lifts to Plan Maison can get crowded (twenty minute queues at peak times) and the alternative series of drags and chairs need upgrading. The series of slow lifts back up from Valtournenche are another source of complaint. There can be queues for many lower lifts when upper lifts are shut due to high wind.

MOUNTAIN RESTAURANTS
Disappointing for Italy

The mountain restaurants are not as appealing as you might expect in an Italian resort (and the toilet facilities can be primitive), so some reporters prefer to head over to Zermatt's wonderful huts for lunch. However, the Châlet Etoile, beneath the Rocce Nerre chair-lift at Plan Maison, is highly praised by reporters – 'The best mountain restaurant I've been to,' says one – and it has a '1st class toilet'. Booking in advance is recommended. The Rocce Nere is also recommended. The British-run Igloo, at the top of the Bardoney chair just off the Ventina piste, serves huge burgers and has 'a UK-style loo'. Baita Cretaz, near the bottom of the Cretaz pistes, is good value, but disappointed a recent visitor. The Bontadini, Teodulo, Pousset and Les Clochards are also recommended.

The restaurants are cheaper and less crowded on the Valtournenche side. The Motta, at the top of the drag-lift of the same name, does excellent food including goulaschsuppe that is 'out of this world'.

SCHOOLS AND GUIDES
Getting better

Cervinia has two main schools, Cervino and Breuil. Reports on both are fairly positive.

CHILDCARE

The ski school runs a snow garden with mini-lift at the foot of the Cretaz slopes and one mini-lift in Plan Maison. Care arrangements 10am to 1pm. There is no non-ski kindergarten.

GETTING THERE

Air Turin, transfer 2½hr. Geneva, transfer 2½hr.

Rail Châtillon (27km); regular buses from station.

Phone numbers
From abroad use the prefix +39 (and do **not** omit the initial '0' of the phone number).

ACTIVITIES

Indoor Hotels with swimming pools and saunas, fitness centre, bowling
Outdoor Natural skating rink (until March), paragliding, hang-gliding, mountaineering, skidoos, heli-skiing

TOURIST OFFICE

Postcode 11021
t +39 (0166) 949136
f 949731
breuil-cervinia@netvallee.it
www.montecervino.it

FACILITIES FOR CHILDREN
Could be better

The Cervino ski school runs a ski kindergarten. And there's a babysitting and kindergarten area at Plan Maison. The slopes, with their long gentle runs, should suit families.

Staying there

HOW TO GO
Plenty of hotel packages

Most of the big tour operators come here, providing between them a wide selection of hotels, though other types of accommodation are rather thin on the ground.

Hotels There are almost 50 hotels, mostly 2- or 3-star, with a few 4-stars.

((((5) **Cristallo** (0116 943411) Luxury 4-star quite a way from town with pool, sauna, massage, great views. Free bus to lifts. A change of ownership is apparently imminent.

(((4) **Hermitage** (0166 948998) Small, luxurious Relais et Château just out of the village on the road up to Cieloalto. Great views, pool, free bus to lifts.

(((4) **Punta Maquignaz** (0166 949145) Captivating chalet-style 4-star, in centre near Cretaz lifts.

((3) **Sporthotel Sertorelli** (0166 949797) Excellent food, sauna and hot-tub. Ten minutes from lifts.

((3) **Europa** (0166 948660) Friendly and family run; near Cretaz lifts. Pool.

(2) **Astoria** (0116 940062) Right by main lift station. Family run and simple. 'Comfortable but that's all,' says a reporter this year.

(2) **Marmore** (0166 949057) Friendly, family run, with 'quite good food'; on main street – an easy walk to the lifts.

Self-catering There are many apartments in the resort, but few are available through British tour operators. The Cristallino apartments are fairly simple, but guests have use of the fine facilities of the Cristallo next door, including the free bus.

EATING OUT
Plenty to choose from

Cervinia's 50 or so restaurants allow plenty of choice. The Chamois and Matterhorn are excellent, but quite pricey. The Grotta belies its name with good food. Casse Croute serves probably the biggest, and best, pizzas. The Copa Pan has a lively atmosphere and is again recommended by several reporters. La Bricole, Il Rustico and La Nicchia have also been recommended. The Maison de Saussure does 'very good local specialities'. An evening out at the Baita Cretaz mountain hut makes a change.

APRES-SKI
Disappoints many Brits

Plenty of Brits come here looking for action but find there isn't much to do except tour the mostly fairly ordinary bars. The Copa Pan (see Eating out) is lively, good value and serves generous measures. The Dragon Bar is popular with Brits and Scandinavians and has satellite TV and videos. Lino's (by the ice rink), the Yeti, Labatt and Café des Guides (with mementos of the owner's Himalayan mountaineering trips) are all recommended by reporters. The discos liven up at weekends – the Garage is reputedly the best. There are tour-rep-organised events such as snow-mobiling on the old bob-sled run, quiz nights, bowling and fondue nights.

OFF THE SLOPES
Little attraction

There is little to do. The pleasant town of Aosta is reached easily enough, but it's a four-hour round trip. Village amenities include hotel pools, a fitness centre and a natural ice rink. The walks are disappointing. The mountain restaurants that are reachable by gondola or cable-car are not special.

STAYING UP THE MOUNTAIN
To beat the queues

Up at Plan Maison, the major lift junction 500m vertical above the resort, Lo Stambecco is a 50-room 3-star hotel ideally placed for early nights and early starts. Less radically, the Cime Bianche is a rustic 3-star chalet on the upper fringes of the resort (in the area known as La Vieille).

STAYING DOWN THE VALLEY
Great home run

Valtournenche, 9km down the road, is cheaper than Cervinia, has a genuine Italian atmosphere and a fair selection of simple hotels, of which the 3-star Bijou (0166 92109) is the best.

The new gondola that opened in 1998 has cut the weekend waits. But the slow lifts above it mean it takes quite a time to reach Cervinia. The exceptionally long run back down, however, is a nice way to end the day – when it is all open. The main street through the village is very busy with cars going to and from Cervinia.

Cortina d'Ampezzo 1225m

Simply the world's most beautiful winter playground

WHAT IT COSTS

(5)

HOW IT RATES

The slopes

Snow	***
Extent	***
Experts	**
Intermediates	***
Beginners	*****
Convenience	*
Queues	***
Restaurants	****

The rest

Scenery	*****
Resort charm	****
Off-slope	*****

What's new

Cortina has worked hard on much-needed snowmaking and now tells us that all pistes below 2300m (which is most of the pistes) are covered by snow-guns. But it still has to be cold enough for the guns to be able to work.

The Marmolada glacier lifts are now included in the Dolomiti Superski pass.

Last season also saw the installation of a new two-seater chair-lift on the Socrepes nursery slopes. A new board-park was created in Faloria and a second is planned at Cinque Torri for 2001/02.

- ⊕ Magnificent Dolomite scenery – perhaps the most dramatic of any winter resort
- ⊕ Marvellous nursery slopes and good long cruising runs, ideal for nervous intermediates
- ⊕ Access to the vast area covered by the Dolomiti Superski pass
- ⊕ Attractive, although rather towny, resort, with lots of upmarket shops
- ⊕ Good off-slope facilities
- ⊕ Remarkably uncrowded slopes

- ⊖ Several separate areas of slopes, which are inconveniently spread around all sides of the resort and linked by buses
- ⊖ Erratic snow record
- ⊖ Expensive by Italian standards
- ⊖ Gets very crowded during Italian holidays
- ⊖ Very little to entertain experts
- ⊖ Mobile phones and fur coats may drive you nuts

Nowhere is more picturesque than chic Cortina, the most upmarket of Italian resorts. Dramatic pink-tinged cliffs and peaks rise vertically from the top of the slopes, giving picture-postcard views from wherever you are.

Cortina's slopes are fine for its regular upmarket visitors from Rome and Milan, many of whom have second homes here and enjoy the strolling, shopping, people-watching and lunching as much as the odd leisurely excursion on to the slopes. For beginners and leisurely intermediates, the splendid nursery slopes and long, easy, well-groomed runs are ideal. For keen piste-bashers, Cortina's fragmented areas can be frustrating, especially if snow is scarce and the area is fragmented even more; but the access to the Sella Ronda and other Dolomiti Superski resorts, though time-consuming, is some compensation – having a car is best for exploring. For experts, there are few tough runs, and the best of those are liable to poor snow conditions and closure because they face south.

The resort 

In winter, more people come to Cortina for the clear mountain air, the stunning views, the shopping, the cafes and to pose and be seen than for the winter sports – 70% of all Italian visitors don't bother taking to the slopes. Cortina attracts the rich and famous from the big Italian cities. Fur coats and glitzy jewellery are everywhere.

The resort itself is a widely spread town rather than a village, with exclusive chalets scattered around the woods and the roads leading off into the countryside. The centre is the traffic-free Corso Italia, full of chic designer clothes and jewellery shops, art galleries and furriers – finding a ski shop can seem tricky. The cobbles and picturesque church bell tower add to the Italian atmosphere. In early evening, the street is a hive of activity, with everyone parading up and down in their finery, window-shopping,

CORTINA TURISMO / D G BANDION

Wherever you look there are towering cliffs and peaks →

MOUNTAIN FACTS

Altitude	1225m-2930m
Lifts	51
Pistes	140km
Blue	33%
Red	62%
Black	5%
Artificial snow	133km
Recco detectors used	

people-watching and finalising their clubbing arrangements on mobile phones. Seeing anyone dressed for the slopes at 5pm is a rarity. But all this glamour doesn't mean Cortina has to be expensive.

Unlike the rest of the Dolomites, Cortina is pure Italy. It has none of the Germanic traditions of Selva and the Sud Tirol, and doesn't attract many German visitors.

Surrounding the centre is a horrendous one-way system, often traffic-clogged and stinking of fumes – a nasty contrast to the stunning scenery everywhere else you look. The lifts to the two main areas of slopes are a fair way from the centre, and at opposite sides of town. Other lifts are a lengthy bus-ride away. There's a wide range of hotels in the centre and scattered in the outskirts. To get the most out of the town, staying centrally is the best bet – though you could plump for one of the main cable-cars and base yourself near that. The local bus service is good (though it could do with being more frequent). A car can be useful, especially for getting to the outlying areas – and certainly helps to make the most of other areas on the Dolomiti Superski pass. San Cassiano is not far to the west, with links from there to Corvara and the other Sella Ronda resorts.

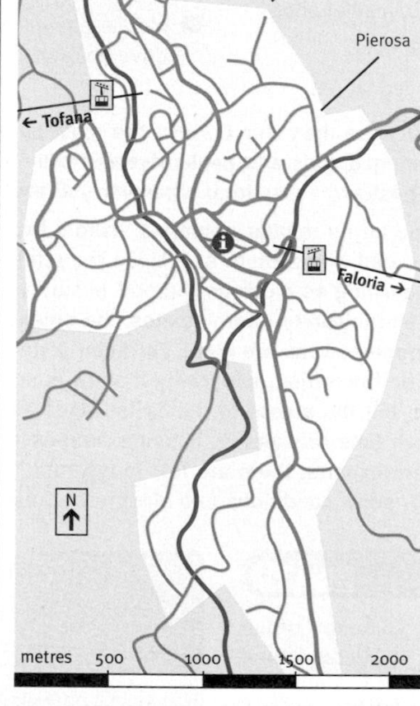

The mountains

Cortina first leapt to fame as host of the 1956 Winter Olympics. At the time, it was very modern; now its facilities feel dated. There is a good mixture of slopes above and below the tree line.

THE SLOPES

Inconveniently fragmented

All Cortina's smallish separate areas are a fair trek from the town centre. The largest is **Socrepes**, accessed by chair- and drag-lifts a bus-ride away. It links with **Tofana**, Cortina's highest area, also reached by two-stage cable-car from near the Olympic ice rink.

On the opposite side of the valley is the tiny **Mietres** area. Another cable-car from the east side of town leads to the **Faloria** area, from where you can head down to the chairs that lead up into the limited but dramatic runs beneath

the **Cristallo** peak.

Other areas are reachable by road. The cable-car from Passo Falzarego (2150m) up to Lagazuoi (2750m) accesses a beautiful red run to Armenterola which takes you away from all lifts and signs of civilisation and is called the Hidden Valley. On the way to Passo Falzarego is the tiny but spectacular Cinque Torri area. Its excellent, north facing slopes are now accessed by a high-speed quad.

Reporters praise the excellent grooming and quiet slopes with few queues, but complain about the piste map not showing some runs, poor piste marking, and World Cup races disrupting January skiing. (Many of the red runs on the map seem to have been regraded blue recently.)

SNOW RELIABILITY
Lots of artificial help
The snowfall record is erratic – it can be good here when it's poor on the north side of the Alps (and vice versa). But the resort has invested heavily in artificial snow and over 90 per cent of the pistes are now covered, so cover should generally be good if it is cold enough to make snow. But last time we visited, the link between Tofana and Socrepes was closed because of lack of snow on a key south-facing slope – which made the areas even more fragmented.

FOR EXPERTS
Limited
The run down from the second stage of the Tofana cable-car at Ra Valles goes through a gap in the rocks, and a steep, narrow, south-facing section gives wonderful views of Cortina, deep down in the valley. It's often tricky because of poor snow conditions.

Cortina's other steep run goes from the top of the Cristallo area at Forcella Staunies. A chair-lift takes you to a steep, south-facing couloir, often shut due to avalanche danger or poor snow.

Other than these two runs (both shut on our last visit) there's little to keep experts happy for a week.

Heli-skiing is available.

FOR INTERMEDIATES
Fragmented and not extensive
If you like cruising in beautiful scenery and don't mind repeating runs, you'll get the most out of Cortina.

The runs at the top of Tofana are short but normally have the best snow. The highest are at over 2800m and mainly face north. But be warned: the only way back down is by the tricky black run described above or cable-car. The reds from the linked Pomedes area are longer and offer good cruising.

Faloria has a string of fairly short north-facing runs – we loved Vitelli, around the back away from all signs of lifts. And the Cristallo area has a long blue (formerly red), served by a fast quad.

It is well worth making the trip to Cinque Torri for wonderful, deserted fast cruising on usually excellent north-facing snow. The 'hidden valley' run from Lagazuoi at the top of the Passo Falzerego cable-car to Armenterola is a must – a very easy red and one of the most beautiful runs we've come across. It offers isolation amid sheer pink-tinged Dolomite peaks and frozen waterfalls. Make time to stop at the atmospheric Scotoni rifugio near the end, then it's a long pole, skate or walk to the welcome sight of a horse-drawn sled (with ropes attached) which tows the weary to Armenterola. Shared taxis take you back to Passo Falzerego (if you've time, try the slopes of Alta Badia, accessed from Armenterola).

FOR BEGINNERS
Wonderful nursery slopes
The Socrepes area has some of the biggest nursery slopes and best progression runs we have seen. Some of the blue forest paths can be icy and intimidating. But you'll find ideal gentle terrain on the main pistes.

boarding *Despite its upmarket chic, Cortina is a good resort for learning to board. The Socrepes nursery slopes are wide, gentle and served by a fast chair-lift. And progress on to the resort's other easy slopes is simple because you can get around in all areas using just chairs and cable-cars – though there are drags, they can be avoided. There's a new half-pipe at Faloria and another is planned at Cinque Torri but there's little off-piste to interest experienced boarders.*

LIFT PASSES
2000/01 prices in euros
Dolomiti Superski
Covers 460 lifts and 1200km of piste in the Dolomites, including all Cortina areas.
Main pass
1-day pass 33
6-day pass 162
(low season 142)
Senior citizens
Over 60: 6-day pass 119
Children
Under 16: 6-day pass 100

Alternative pass
Cortina d'Ampezzo
Covers all lifts in Cortina, San Vito di Cadore, Auronzo and Misurina, and ski-buses.
Main pass
1-day pass 30
6-day pass 148
(low season 130)
Senior citizens
Over 60: 6-day pass 119
Children
Under 16: 6-day pass 91
Under 8: free pass

SCHOOLS/GUIDES

2000/01 prices in euros

Cortina
Classes 6 days
2½hr: 9.30-noon; 2hr: noon-2pm
6 2½hr days: 163
Private lessons
Hourly
35 for 1hr; each additional person 10

Azzurra Cortina
Classes 6 days
3½hr: 9.15-1pm; 6½hr: 9.15-4pm
6 3½hr days: 387
Private lessons
Hourly
39 for 1hr; each additional person 12

CHILDCARE

There is non-skiing childcare, and schools offer all-day classes for children.

GETTING THERE

Air Venice, transfer 2½hr (free transfer available for hotel guests; advance booking required).

Rail Calalzo (35km) or Dobbiaco (32km); frequent buses from station.

Phone numbers
From abroad use the prefix +39 (and do **not** omit the initial '0' of the phone number).

FOR CROSS-COUNTRY
One of the best

Cortina has around 75km of trails, mainly in the woods towards Dobbiaco. There are also trails below the Cristallo area.

QUEUES
No problem

Most Cortina holidaymakers rise late, lunch lengthily and leave the slopes early – if they get on them at all. That means few lift queues and generally uncrowded pistes – a different world to the crowded Sella Ronda circuit. 'Lack of queues was one of the highlights of our holiday,' said one reporter.

MOUNTAIN RESTAURANTS
Good, but get in early

Lunch is a major event for many Cortina visitors. At weekends you often need to book or turn up very early to be sure of a table. Many restaurants can be reached by road or lift, and pedestrians arrive as early as 10am to sunbathe, admire the views and idle the time away on their mobile phones.

Although prices are high in the swishest establishments, we've found plenty of reasonably priced places, serving generally excellent food. In the Socrepes area, the Col Taron is highly recommended and the Piè de Tofana, Rifugio Pomedes and El Faral are also good. The Socrepes sector also has several hotels along the road at its edge – including the best restaurant in the resort, the Michelin-starred Tivoli.

At Cristallo the Rio Gere at the base of the quad chair and Son Forca, with fabulous views at the top of it, are both worth a visit.

The restaurants at Cinque Torri, the Scoiattoli and the Rifugio Averau, offer fantastic views as well as good food, and, unusually, are non-smoking. Rifugio Lagazuoi, a hike up from the top of the Passo Falzerego cable-car, also has great views and no smoking.

SCHOOLS AND GUIDES
Mixed reports

Of the four ski schools, we've had mixed reports of the 'Cortina' school. One couple had good classes in English-speaking groups. But there were other reports of a group that included six Brits being taught mainly in Italian, and a tired intermediate asking for a short rest and being left stranded at the top of the mountain. The Gruppo Guide Alpine offers off-piste and touring.

FACILITIES FOR CHILDREN
Better than average

By Italian standards childcare facilities are outstanding, with a choice of all-day care arrangements for children of practically any age. This is one resort where Mamma gets a break. Given the small number of British visitors, you can't count on good spoken English. And the fragmented area can make travelling around with children difficult.

Staying there

HOW TO GO
Now with more packages

Hotels dominate the market but there are some catered chalets.

Hotels There's a big choice, from 5-star luxury to 1-star and 2-star pensions.

(5) **Miramonti** (0436 4201) Spectacularly grand hotel, 2km south of town. Pool.

(4) **Poste** (0436 4271) Reliable 4-star, at the heart of the town.

(4) **Ancora** (0436 3261) Elegant public rooms. On the traffic-free Corso Italia.

(4) **Parc Victoria** (0436 3246) Rustic 4-star with small rooms but good food, at the Faloria end of the town centre.

(4) **Faloria** (0436 2959) Newish, near ski jump, splendid pool, good food.

(3) **Olimpia** (0436 3256) Comfortable B&B hotel in centre, near Faloria lift.

(3) **Menardi** (0436 2400) Welcoming

ACTIVITIES

Indoor Swimming pool, saunas, museums, art gallery, cinema, indoor tennis court, public library
Outdoor Rides on Olympic bob run, snow rafting down Olympic ski jump, crazy sledge for moonlit excursions, snow-shoe tours, all at Adrenalin centre; Olympic ice-stadium (2 rinks), curling, ice hockey, sleigh rides, horse-riding school, 6km walking paths, toboggan run, heli-skiing

TOURIST OFFICE

Postcode 32043
t +39 (0436) 866252
f 867448
cortina@dolomiti.org
www.cortina.dolomiti.org

roadside inn, a long walk from centre and lifts.
(((3) **Villa Resy** (0436 3303) Small and welcoming, just outside centre, with British owner.
Self-catering There are some chalets and apartments – usually out of town – available for independent travellers.

EATING OUT
Huge choice

There's an enormous selection, both in town and a little way out, doing mainly Italian food. The very smart and pricey El Toulà is in a beautiful old barn, just on the edge of town. Many of the best restaurants are further out – such as the Michelin-starred Tivoli, Meloncino, Leone e Anna, Rio Gere and Baita Fraina. Reasonably priced central restaurants include the Cinque Torri and Al Passetto for pizza and pasta.

APRES-SKI
Lively in high season

Cortina is a lively social whirl in high season, with lots of well-heeled Italians staying up very late. Don't go on the early evening walkabout if fur coats and mobile phones annoy you.

Bar Lovat is one of several popular, high-calorie tea-time spots. There are three good wine bars: Enoteca has 700 different wines and good cheese and meats; Osteria has good wines and local ham; and Febar is a wine bar with good decor and is also busy later. The liveliest bar is the Clipper, with a bob-sleigh in the door, and lots of designer beer. Discos liven up after 11pm.

OFF THE SLOPES
A classic resort

Along with St Moritz, Cortina rates as one of the leading resorts if you're happier off the slopes. The setting is stunning, the town attractive, the shopping extensive, the mountain restaurants easily accessible by road (a car is handy). And there's plenty more to do, including swimming, ice skating and dog-sledding. You can have a run (with driver!) down the Olympic bob-sleigh run. There's horse jumping and polo on the snow occasionally. There are several museums and art galleries.

Trips to Venice are easily and inexpensively organised.

CORTINA TURISMO

If there is a more beautifully set ski town, we haven't found it ↓

Courmayeur 1225m

A seductive village on the sunny side of Mont Blanc

WHAT IT COSTS

4

HOW IT RATES

The slopes

Snow	****
Extent	**
Experts	***
Intermediates	****
Beginners	**
Convenience	*
Queues	****
Restaurants	****

The rest

Scenery	****
Resort charm	****
Off-slope	***

MOUNTAIN FACTS

Altitude	1210m-2755m
Lifts	23
Pistes	100km
Blue	20%
Red	70%
Black	10%
Artificial snow	18km
Recco detectors used	

- ⊕ Charming, traditional village, with car-free centre and stylish shops
- ⊕ Stunning views of Mont Blanc massif
- ⊕ Pleasant range of intermediate runs
- ⊕ Comprehensive snowmaking
- ⊕ Good mountain restaurants
- ⊕ Lively, but not rowdy, après-ski
- ⊕ Good base for heli-skiing

- ⊖ Lack of nursery slopes and easy runs for beginners to progress to
- ⊖ No tough pistes
- ⊖ Relatively small area, with mainly short runs; high-mileage piste bashers will get bored in a week
- ⊖ Slopes very crowded on Sundays
- ⊖ Tiresome walk and cable-car journey between village and slopes

Courmayeur is very popular, especially at weekends, with the smart Italian set from Milan and Turin. It's easy to see why: it's very easy to get to and certainly the most captivating of the Val d'Aosta resorts.

The scenery, the charm of the village, the stylish bars and restaurants and the nightlife are big draws. The main slopes are fine but nothing special given their limited range of difficulty, inconvenient location across the valley from the village and their limited size; a keen piste-basher will cover Courmayeur in a day. It is hoped that the Mont Blanc tunnel will re-open for this season, making the option of a quick trip to Chamonix feasible again. But don't bank on it until it has actually happened.

The resort could make a jolly week for those who want to party as much as hit the slopes. It also appeals to those with quite different ambitions, who want to explore the spectacular Mont Blanc massif with the aid of a guide and other local peaks with the aid of a helicopter.

The resort

Courmayeur is a traditional old Italian mountaineering village that, despite the nearby Mont Blanc tunnel road (currently deserted) and modern hotels, has retained much of its old-world feel.

The village has a charming traffic-free centre of attractive shops, cobbled streets and well-preserved buildings. An Alpine museum and a statue of a long-dead mountain rescue hero add to the historical feel.

The centre has a great atmosphere, focused around the Via Roma. As the lifts close, people pile into the many bars, some of which are very civilised. Others wander in and out of the many small shops, which include a salami specialist and a good bookshop. At weekends people-watching is part of the evening scene, when the fur coats of the Milanese and Torinese take over.

The village is quite large and its huge cable-car is right on the edge.

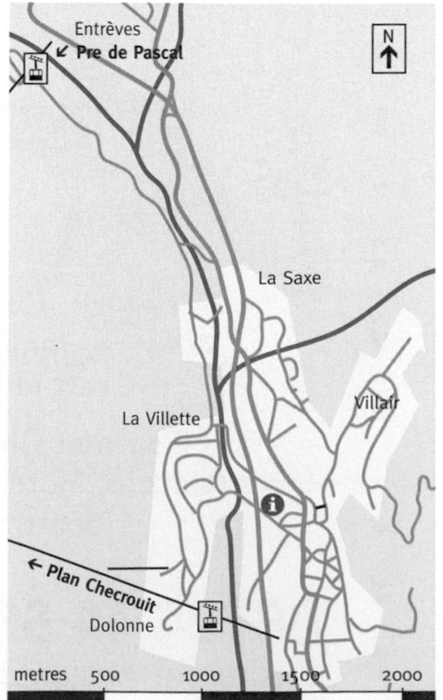

What's new

As we went to press the Mont Blanc tunnel was officially due to open in the autumn, after the tragic fire in 1999. But the project has been delayed several times and locals were predicting that it wouldn't open until December at the earliest and maybe not until after the 2001/02 season. Until it does re-open access will be quickest from Turin or Milan airports. From Geneva, the best route is via the Grand St Bernard tunnel.

The Cresta d'Arp cable-car can now be taken without a guide, to access the off-piste runs. And a heli-operation started where you can get picked up from right by the piste – from £70 a drop, including guide.

The annual Momentum City Ski Championships are now run here. Teams of four compete, with prizes for all standards – great fun and free champagne! This season's dates are 31 Jan to 3 Feb 2002. To enter, call Momentum Ski on 020 7371 9111.

The mountains

The pistes suit intermediates, but are surprisingly limited for such a well-known, large resort. They are varied in character, if not gradient. Piste marking could be improved.

THE SLOPES
Small but interestingly varied

The slopes are separate from the village: you have to ride a cable-car to them and either take it down or take a bus from Dolonne at the end of the day. The cable-car arrives at the bottom of the slopes at Plan Checrouit (where you can store your equipment).

There are two distinct sections, both almost entirely intermediate. The north-east-facing **Checrouit** area accessed by the Checrouit gondola catches morning sun, and has open, above-the-tree-line pistes. The 25-person, infrequently running Youla cable-car goes to the top of Courmayeur's pistes. There is a further tiny cable-car to Cresta d'Arp. This serves only long off-piste runs but it is no longer compulsory to have a guide with you to go up it.

Most people follow the sun over to the north-west-facing slopes towards **Val Veny** in the afternoon. These are interesting, varied and tree-lined, with great views of Mont Blanc and its glaciers. Connections between the two areas are good, with many alternative routes. The Val Veny slopes are also accessible by cable-car from Entrèves, a few miles outside Courmayeur.

A little way beyond Entrèves is La Palud, where a cable-car goes up in three stages to Punta Helbronner, at the shoulder of **Mont Blanc**. There are no pistes from the top, but you can do the famous Vallée Blanche run to Chamonix from here without the horrific initial ridge walk on the Chamonix side. But it's a long way back if the Mont Blanc tunnel is closed. Or you can tackle the tougher off-piste runs on the Italian side of Mont Blanc. None of these glacier runs should be done without a guide.

La Thuile and Pila are an easy drive to the south, and Cervinia is reachable.

SNOW RELIABILITY
Good for most of the season

Courmayeur's slopes are not high – mostly between 1700m and 2250m. Those above Val Veny face north or

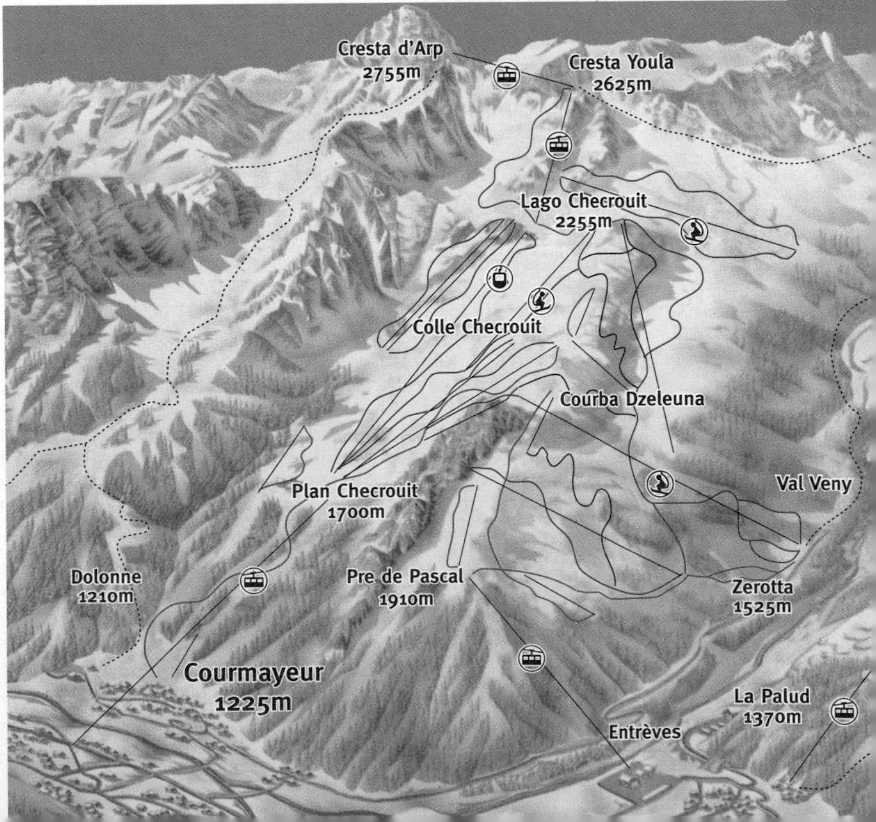

LIFT PASSES

2001/02 prices in euros

Courmayeur Mont Blanc
Covers all lifts in Val Veny and Checrouit, and the lifts on Mont Blanc up to Punta Helbronner.

Beginners Free nursery lifts at Plan Checrouit and top of Val Veny cable-car (which can be paid for by the ride).

Main pass
1-day pass 30 (2000/01 price)
6-day pass 161 (low season 145)

Short-term passes
Single ascent on some lifts and half-day pass (afternoon) available.

Children
Under 12: 6-day pass 121
Under 8: free pass with accompanying adult

Notes Passes of two or more days are valid on the Mt Blanc lift. Passes of three or more days cover all lifts in the Aosta Valley. Passes of six or more days are valid for one day at Pila and Verbier and for two days in the resorts of the Mont Blanc region ski pass (including Chamonix, Les Contamines, St Gervais, Mégève).

Alternative passes
Mont-Blanc ski region pass covers all lifts in 13 resorts around Mont Blanc.

north-west, so keep their snow well, but the Plan Checrouit side is rather too sunny for comfort in late season. There is snowmaking on most of the main runs, so good coverage in midwinter is virtually assured.

FOR EXPERTS
Off-piste is the only challenge

Courmayeur has few challenging pistes. The only black – the Competizione, on the Val Veny side – is not hard, and few moguls form elsewhere. But if you're lucky enough to find fresh powder – as we have been several times – you can have fantastic fun among the trees.

Classic off-piste runs go from Cresta d'Arp, at the top of the lift network, in three directions – a clockwise loop via Arp Vieille to Val Veny, with close-up views of the Miage glacier; east down a deserted valley to Dolonne or Pré St Didier; or south through the Youla gorge to La Thuile.

On Mont Blanc, the Vallée Blanche is not a challenge (though there are more difficult variations), but the Toula glacier route on the Italian side from Punta Helbronner to Pavillon most certainly is, often to the point of being dangerous. There are also heli-drops available on a wide range of terrain.

FOR INTERMEDIATES
Ideal gradient but limited extent

The whole area is suitable for most intermediates, but it is small. The avid piste-basher will find it very limited.

The open Checrouit section is pretty much go-anywhere territory, where you can choose your own route and make it as easy or difficult as you like. The blue runs here are about Courmayeur's gentlest. In Val Veny, the reds running the length of the Bertolini chair are more challenging and very enjoyable. They link in with the pretty, wooded slopes heading down to Zerotta.

The Zerotta chair dominates Val Veny, with lots of alternatives from the top – good for mixed abilities since runs of varying difficulty meet up at several places on the way down.

The Vallée Blanche, although off-piste, is easy enough for adventurous, fit intermediates to try. So is the local heli-skiing, where you are picked up on the piste so there's no wasted time.

FOR BEGINNERS
Consistently too steep

Courmayeur is not well suited to beginners. There are several nursery slopes, none ideal. The area at Plan Checrouit gets crowded, and there are few easy runs for the near-beginner to progress to. The small area served by the short Tzaly drag, just above the Entrèves cable-car top station, is the most suitable beginner terrain, and it tends to have good snow.

FOR CROSS-COUNTRY
Beautiful trails

There are 35km of trails dotted around Courmayeur. The best are the four covering 20km at Val Ferret, to which there is a bus service. Dolonne has a couple of short trails.

QUEUES
Sunday crowds pour in

The lift system is generally excellent. The Checrouit and Val Veny cable-cars suffer queues only on Sundays, and even these can be beaten with an early start. Patience is needed when waiting for the infrequent Youla cable-car – 'Not sure it's worth waiting more than 15 minutes for the one steep red,' said a reporter. Overcrowded slopes on Sundays, particularly down to Zerotta, can also be a problem.

MOUNTAIN RESTAURANTS
Lots – some of them good

The area is lavishly endowed with 27 establishments ranging from rustic on-piste huts to larger self-service places. Most huts do table-service of delicious pizza and pasta and it is best to book. But there are also snack bars selling more basic fare and relying on views and sun to fill their terraces.

Several restaurants are excellent. Maison Vieille, at the top of the chair

boarding *Courmayeur's pistes suit intermediates, and most areas are easily accessible by novices as the main lifts are cable-cars, chairs and gondolas – but it's all a bit steep for beginners. The biggest draws for the more experienced are the off-piste routes to be done with a guide. Like a lot of Italian resorts, Courmayeur has no fun-park or half-pipe; but it still manages to attract quite a few boarders, and you shouldn't find yourself in too much of a minority. Nightlife is lively in a stylish way, and there's plenty of diversity in the bars.*

Many of the mountain huts on the Zerotta side have stunning views like this →

SNOWPIX.COM / CHRIS GILL

SCHOOLS/GUIDES

2000/01 prices in euros

Monte Bianco
Classes 6 days
3hr: 10am-1pm
6 half-days: 129
(106 low season)
Children's classes
Ages: from 4
6 full days incl snack lunch: 258
(232 low season)
Private lessons
Hourly
36 for 1 person (26 low season); each additional person 3

CHILDCARE

The Kinderheim at Plan Checrouit (0165 842477) takes children from the age of 6 months, from 9.30 to 4pm. Children taking lessons can be deposited at the ski school in Courmayeur at 9am, and they will be looked after for the whole day (lesson am, play pm). The Kinderheim at the Sports Centre takes children from the age of 9 months.

GETTING THERE

Air Turin, transfer 2hr.

Rail Pré-St-Didier (5km); regular buses from station.

Phone numbers
From abroad use the prefix +39 (and do **not** omit the initial '0' of the phone number).

of the same name and run by the charming mountain man Giacomo, is our favourite – a welcoming rustic place with superb home-made pastas. Chiecco, next to the drag-lift with the same name at Plan Checrouit, is recommended for good food, atmosphere, friendly service and good views of struggling beginners. The pick of the bunch at Plan Checrouit is the Christiania – book a table downstairs, where you can savour the superb food (especially excellent pizzas) in peace.

On the other side of the mountain in Val Veny is another clutch of places worth noting – La Zerotta, at the foot of the eponymous chair has a sunny terrace and good food; the nearby Petit Mont Blanc, the atmospheric Monte Bianco climbing refuge, along the mountainside, and the jolly Grolla, further along still are also recommended. One of the better snack bars is Courba Dzeleuna, with incredible views, at the top of Dzeleuna chair.

SCHOOLS AND GUIDES
Good reports

We had a very enthusiastic report on the Monte Bianco ski school last year: 'We had the best instructor for ages – possibly ever.' There is a thriving guides' association ready to help you explore the area's off-piste; it has produced a helpful booklet showing the main possibilities.

FACILITIES FOR CHILDREN
Good care by Italian standards

Childcare facilities are well ahead of the Italian norm, but Courmayeur is far from an ideal resort for a young family.

Staying there

The cable-car station is on the southern edge of town, a fair distance from much of the accommodation. There is no shuttle-bus alternative to walking, but you can leave your skis, boards and boots in lockers at the top – highly recommended by most reporters. There is another short walk from the top to the other lifts before you can get on the slopes.

Having accommodation close to the village cable-car is handy. Parking at the cable-car is very limited, but drivers can go to Entrèves, a few kilometres away, where there is a large car park at the Val Veny cable-car. Buses, infrequent but timetabled, link Courmayeur with La Palud, just beyond Entrèves, for the Punta Helbronner-Vallée Blanche cable-car.

HOW TO GO
Plenty of hotels

Courmayeur's long-standing popularity ensures a wide range of packages (including some excellent weekend deals), mainly in hotels. Tour op Interski has cheap hotels out of town and buses people in. One or two UK operators have catered chalets.

Hotels There are nearly 50 hotels, spanning the star ratings.

(((4 **Gallia Gran Baita** (0165 844040) Luxury place with antique furnishings, panoramic views and 'superb food'. Pool. Shuttle-bus to cable-car.

(((4 **Pavillon** (0165 846120) Comfortable 4-star near cable-car, with a pool. Friendly staff.

((3 **Auberge de la Maison** (0165 869811) Small 3-star in Entrèves under same ownership as Maison de Filippo (see Eating Out).

((3 **Bouton d'Or** (0165 846729) Small, friendly B&B near main square.

((3 **Berthod** (0165 842835) Friendly, family-run hotel near centre.

((3 **La Grange** (869733) Rustic, stone-and-wood farmhouse in Entrèves.

((3 **Triolet** (0165 846822) 'Excellent location 100m from lift. Comfy, well furnished.'

ACTIVITIES

Indoor Swimming pool and sauna at Pré-St-Didier (5km), Alpine museum, cinema, library. Sports centre with climbing, skating rink, curling, fitness centre, indoor golf, squash, tennis, basketball, volley ball, sauna and turkish bath
Outdoor Walking paths in Val Ferret, paragliding, snow-biking, dog-sledding

TOURIST OFFICE

Postcode 11013
t +39 (0165) 842060
f 842072
apt.montebianco@psw.it
www.courmayeur.net

(2) **Edelweiss** (0165 841590) Friendly, cosy, good-value; close to the centre.
(2) **Lo Scoiattolo** (0165 846721) Good rooms, good food, shame it's at the opposite end of town to the cable-car.
Self-catering There is quite a lot available to independent bookers.

EATING OUT
Jolly Italian evenings

There is a great choice, both in downtown Courmayeur and within taxi-range; there's a handy promotional booklet describing many of them (in English as well as Italian). The touristy but very jolly Maison de Filippo in Entrèves is famous for its fixed-price, 36-dish feast. We've been impressed by the traditional Italian cuisine of both Pierre Alexis ('good value') and Cadran Solaire. La Terrazza ('excellent pasta and very friendly, jolly service') is a rising star and has just been renovated. The Tunnel pizzeria and Mont-Frety ('good value', 'its antipasti is a must') have been recommended by reporters. Restaurants tend to be busy, so book well in advance.

SNOWPIX.COM / CHRIS GILL

Courmayeur is full of well-groomed intermediate trails like this ↓

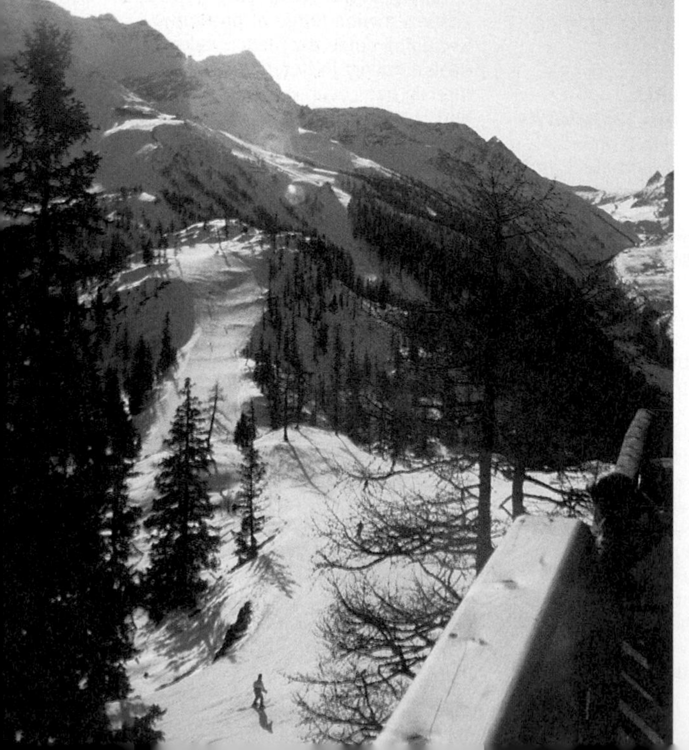

APRES-SKI
Stylish bar-hopping

Courmayeur has a lively evening scene, centred on stylish bars with comfy sofas or armchairs to collapse in. Our favourites are the Roma (reporters have been very taken with the free canapés), the back room of the Caffe della Posta and the Bar delle Guide. The Cadran Solaire is where the big money from Milan and Turin hangs out. The American Bar has good music and an excellent selection of wines. The Red Lion is worth a visit if you're missing English pubs, though a recent reporter found it 'sadly empty'. Ziggy's is an internet cafe popular with local teenagers. There is a disco or two.

OFF THE SLOPES
Much improved for sporty types

If you're not interested in hitting the snow you'll find the village pleasant. You can go by cable-car up to Punta Helbronner, by bus to Aosta, or up the main cable-car to Plan Checrouit to meet friends for lunch. The large sports centre is good but has no pool.

STAYING UP THE MOUNTAIN
Why would you want to?

Visiting Courmayeur and not staying in the charming village seems perverse – if you're that keen to get on the slopes in the morning, this is probably the wrong resort. But the Christiania at Plan Checrouit (see Mountain restaurants) has simple rooms; you need to book way in advance.

Livigno 1815m

Lowish prices and highish altitude – a tempting combination

WHAT IT COSTS

HOW IT RATES

The slopes

Snow	****
Extent	**
Experts	**
Intermediates	***
Beginners	****
Convenience	**
Queues	****
Restaurants	***

The rest

Scenery	***
Resort charm	***
Off-slope	**

- ➕ High altitude plus snowmaking ensures a long season and a good chance of snow to resort level
- ➕ Large choice of beginners' slopes
- ➕ Modern and improving lift system
- ➕ Cheap by the standards of high resorts, with the bonus of duty-free shopping – a great place to treat yourself to new equipment
- ➕ Cosmopolitan, friendly village with some Alpine atmosphere
- ➕ Long, snowsure cross-country trails

- ➖ No difficult pistes
- ➖ Long airport transfers
- ➖ Slopes split into two quite widely separated areas
- ➖ Village is very long and straggling, and a bit rough round the edges
- ➖ Few off-slope amenities
- ➖ Bleak, windy setting – often resulting in upper lifts being shut
- ➖ Not many really comfortable hotels bookable through UK tour operators
- ➖ Nightlife can disappoint

Livigno offers the unusual combination of a fair-sized mountain, high altitude and fairly low prices. Despite its vaunted duty-free status, hotels, bars and restaurants are not much cheaper than in other Italian resorts, but shopping is – there are countless camera and clothes shops. As a relatively snowsure alternative to the Pyrenees or to the smallest, cheapest resorts in Austria, Livigno seems attractive. But don't overlook the long list of drawbacks.

What's new

A new six-pack from Valfin on the Mottolino slopes to the top of Monte Della Neve has opened up a couple of new black runs.

MOUNTAIN FACTS

Altitude	1815m-2800m
Lifts	31
Pistes	115km
Blue	35%
Red	48%
Black	17%
Artificial snow	70km
Recco detectors used	

The resort

Livigno is an amalgam of three villages in a wide, remote valley near the Swiss border – basically a string of hotels, bars, specialist shops and supermarkets lining a single long street. The buildings are small in scale and mainly traditional in style, giving the village a pleasant atmosphere. The original hamlet of San Antonio is the nearest thing Livigno has to a centre. Here, the main street and those at right angles linking it to the busy bypass road are nominally traffic-free. The road that skirts the 'traffic-free' area is constantly busy, and becomes intrusive in the hamlets of Santa Maria, 1km to the north, and San Rocco, a bit further away to the south.

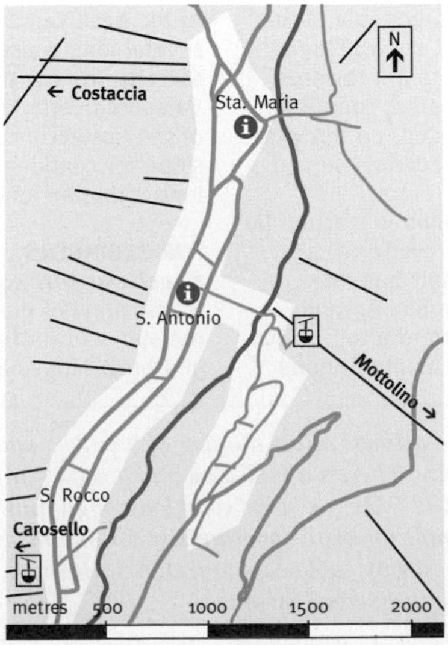

Lifts dotted along the length of the village access the western slopes of the valley. The main lift to the eastern slopes is directly across the flat valley floor from the centre.

In such a long, strung out village, with fragmented slopes, the location of accommodation can be important. San Antonio is the best all-round location. San Rocco is a tiring uphill walk from the centre. The bus services, on three colour-coded routes, are free and fairly frequent, but can get overcrowded at peak times and stop early in the evening.

The lift pass covers Bormio and Santa Caterina, an easy drive or free bus-ride if the high pass is open, and a six-day pass entitles you to a discounted rate on a one-day pass in St Moritz – reached via a road tunnel.

The airport transfer from Bergamo is long – five hours with a snack stop.

↑ There are woods, but most of the slopes are above or below them

APT LIVIGNO / L MARTINELLI

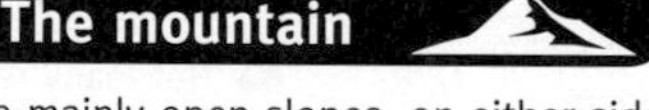

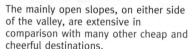

The mountain

The mainly open slopes, on either side of the valley, are extensive in comparison with many other cheap and cheerful destinations.

THE SLOPES
Improved links

There are three sectors, all of them suitable for moderate and leisurely intermediates, and two of them are reasonably well linked.

A two-seater chair from the nursery slopes at the north end of the village take you up to **Costaccia** (2360m), where a long fast quad chair-lift goes along the ridge towards the **Carosello** sector. The blue linking run back from Carosello to the top of Costaccia is flat in places and may involve energetic poling if the snow conditions and the wind are against you. Carosello is more usually accessed by the optimistically named Carosello 3000 gondola at San Rocco, which goes up, in two stages, to 2750m. Most runs return towards the village, but there are a couple on the back of the mountain, on the west-facing slopes of Val Federia – served by a double drag-lift.

The ridge of **Mottolino** is reached by an efficient gondola from Teola, a tiresome walk or a short bus-ride across the valley from San Antonio. A slow antique chair from the top of the Mottolino gondola at Monte Sponda takes you to the top of Monte Della Neve. North-west-facing runs back towards Livigno are served by two fast chairs, and a couple of east-facing pistes above Trepalle and Passo d'Eira on the road to Bormio are served by a third – an efficient setup.

Signposting is patchy and the piste map isn't always entirely accurate.

SNOW RELIABILITY
Very good, despite no glacier

Livigno's slopes are high (you can spend most of your time around 2500m), and with snow-guns on the lower slopes of Mottolino and Costaccia, the season is long.

FOR EXPERTS
Not recommended

The piste map shows a few black runs but these are not particularly steep. Even the all-black terrain served by the new six-pack on Monte Della Neve is really no more than stiff red in gradient. There is off-piste to be done, but guidance would be needed.

FOR INTERMEDIATES
Flattering slopes

Good intermediates will be able to tackle all of the blacks without worry. The woodland black run down from Carosello past Tea da Borch is narrow in places and can get mogulled and icy at the end of the day. The runs on the back of Carosello down to Federia are challenging, and bumpy. Moderate intermediates have virtually the whole area at their disposal. The long run beneath the Mottolino gondola is one of the best. Leisurely types have several long cruises available in all sectors. The run beneath the Valandrea-Vetta fast chair, at the top of the Costaccia sector, is a splendid slope for confidence-building – 1.5km long, dropping only 260m.

FOR BEGINNERS
Excellent but scattered slopes

A vast array of nursery slopes along the sunny lower flanks of Costaccia, and other slopes around the valley,

boarding *Livigno attracts a fair number of boarders and young people generally. There's a half-pipe and a good fun-park/boarder-cross in the Mottolino area. And there are some good long, high runs for free-riders and carvers, as well as ample off-piste opportunities for intermediate riders. Most of the resort can be accessed by cable-cars and chairs. However, the excellent beginner slopes are mainly served by drags.*

LIFT PASSES

2001/02 prices in euros

Alta Valtellina
Covers all lifts in Livigno, Bormio (40km away), Valdidentro (30km away) and Santa Caterina (50km away).

Main pass
1-day pass 28
6-day pass 142
(low season 121)

Senior citizens
Over 60: 6-day pass 99

Children
Under 13: 6-day pass 99
Free pass under 8

Short-term passes
Morning and afternoon passes for Livigno only.

Notes Day pass price is for Livigno lifts only. 6-day pass and over entitles you to a one-day pass at a discounted rate in St Moritz and Engadine.

Alternative passes
Livigno-only pass for up to two days (adult 2-day 41).

SCHOOLS/GUIDES

2000/01 prices in euros

Livigno Inverno/Estate
Classes 6 days
2hr: 9am-11am or 11am-1pm
6 2hr days: 70
Children's classes
Ages: from 3
6 2hr lessons and 2hr nursery
Private lessons
Hourly
26 for 1hr; each additional person 5

Azzurra Livigno
Classes 6 days
2½hr: 10am-12.30pm
6 2½hr days: 88
Private lessons
Hourly
26 for 1hr

OTHER SCHOOLS

Livigno Italy
Livigno Soc Coop
Top Club Mottolino

CHILDCARE

The Livigno school runs the Alì Babà kindergarten for children aged 3 and over. Lessons and lunches available. The staff speak English.

make Livigno excellent for novices – although some of the slopes at the northern end are on the steep side. There are lots of longer runs suitable for fast learners and near-beginners.

CROSS-COUNTRY

Good snow, bleak setting

Long snowsure trails (40km in total) follow the valley floor, making Livigno a good choice, though the scenery is bleak. There is a specialist cross-country school, and the resort organises major cross-country races.

QUEUES

Few problems these days

Lift queues are not usually a problem apart from short delays for the Carosello gondola in peak season. Investment in fast new chairs at Carosello and Mottolino has rid the area of any long queues. A bigger problem is that strong winds often close the upper lifts, causing overcrowding lower down.
The slow old chair along the ridge to Monte Della Neve can be fiercely cold.

MOUNTAIN RESTAURANTS

More than adequate

Mottolino is the best bet for serious lunchers. The recently renovated refuge at the top of Mottolino is impressive with smart self- and table-service sections, a solarium and a crèche. And there are some more charming places lower down. The welcoming Tea del Vidal is at the base of the same sector. Costaccia's Tea del Plan is pleasantly rustic and sunny, with good food and a great atmosphere. The self-service place at the top of Carosello is acceptable and Tea da Borch, in the trees lower down, serves great food in a Tirolean-style atmosphere, though the run down can be tricky. The rustic restaurants at Passo d'Eira and Trepalle are a good option for a quiet stop. Lunch in the valley at the hotel Sporting (near the Carosello gondola station) is popular. The terrace at the hotel Möta, at the base of the Costaccia lifts, is also recommended.

SCHOOLS AND GUIDES

Watch out for short classes

There are several schools. English is widely spoken, but recent reports are mixed. A common complaint is that most of the schools only offer short (two-hour) classes. Another complaint is that beginners spend too long on the nursery slopes before progressing up the mountain. It also seems to be the case that the schools on the Costaccia–Carosello side avoid the Mottolino sector altogether.

FACILITIES FOR CHILDREN

Bring your own

The schools run children's classes, and the Livigno school's Alì-Babà nursery offers all-day care.

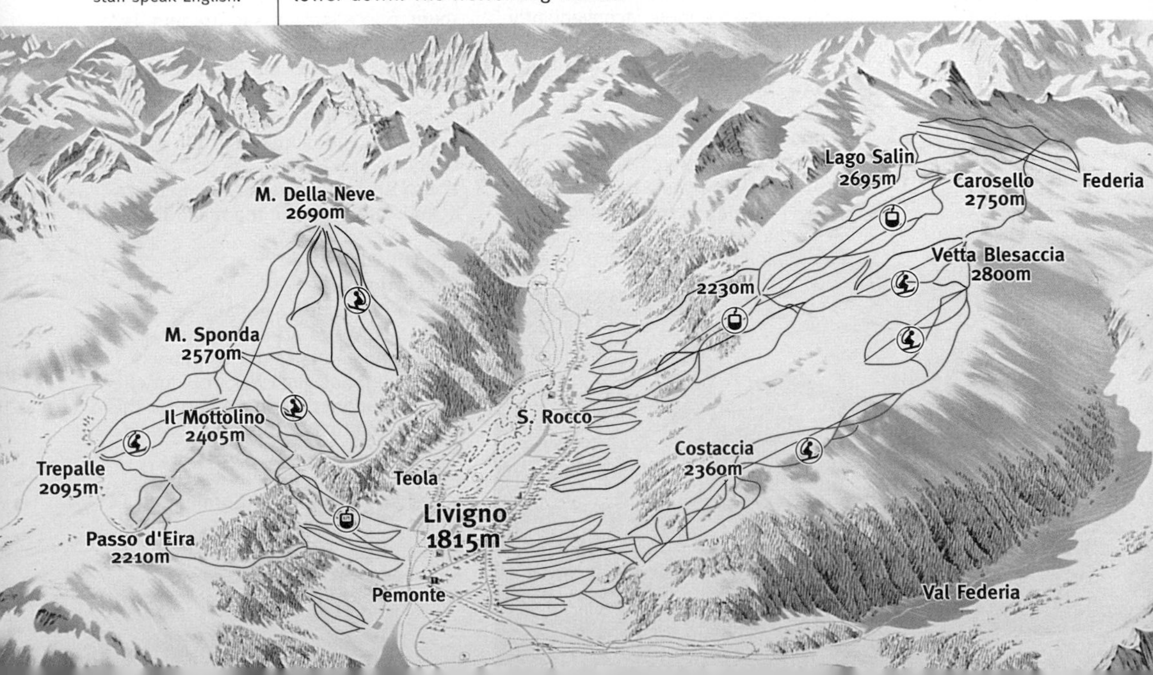

Phone numbers
From abroad use the prefix +39 (and do **not** omit the initial '0' of the phone number).

GETTING THERE

Air Bergamo, transfer 5hr.

Rail Tirano (48km), Zernez (Switzerland, 28km); regular buses from station.

ACTIVITIES

Indoor Sauna, gym, body-building, games room, bowling, cinema
Outdoor Cleared paths, skating rink, snow-mobiles, horse-drawn sleigh rides, paragliding, mountaineering

TOURIST OFFICE

Postcode 23030
t +39 (0342) 996379
f 996881
info@aptlivigno.it
www.aptlivigno.it

Staying there

HOW TO GO
Lots of hotels, some apartments

Livigno has an enormous range of hotels and a number of apartments. There are some attractively priced catered chalets from UK operators.

Hotels Most of the hotels are small 2- and 3-star places, with a couple of 4-stars out of the centre.

(3) **Intermonti** (0342 972100) Modern 4-star with all mod cons (including a pool); some way from the centre, on the Mottolino side of the valley.

(2) **Bivio** (0342 996137) The only hotel in central Livigno with a pool.

(2) **Steinbock** (0342 970520) Nice little place, far from major lifts but a short walk from some nursery slopes.

(2) **Teola** (0342 996324) Quiet place, on the Mottolino side; recommended (despite small bedrooms) for good food and friendly staff.

(2) **Larice** (0342 996184) Stylish little 3-star B&B well placed for Costaccia lifts and slopes.

(2) **Montanina** (0342 996060) Good central 2-star.

(2) **Gimea** (0342 997669) Quiet B&B 300m from Carosello gondola.

(2) **Camana Veglia** (0342 996310) Charming old wooden chalet. Popular restaurant, well placed in Santa Maria.

Self-catering All the big tour operators that come here have apartment options. Most are cheap and cheerful though some are more inconveniently situated than others.

EATING OUT
Value for money

Livigno has lots of traditional, unpretentious restaurants, many hotel-based. Hotel Concordia has some of the best cooking in town. Mario's has one of the largest menus, serving seafood, fondue and steaks in addition to the ubiquitous pizza and pasta. Bait dal Ghet and the Bivio restaurant are popular with the locals, and the Rusticana does wholesome, cheap food. Pesce d'Oro is good for seafood and Italian cuisine. The Bellavista, Ambassador, Mirage, Grolla and the Garden are also recommended.

APRES-SKI
Lively, but disappoints some

It's not that there isn't action in Livigno, but simply that the scene is quieter than some people expect in a duty-free resort. Also, the best places are dotted about, so the village lacks evening buzz. At tea-time many people return to their hotels for a quiet drink. But Tea del Vidal, at the bottom of Mottolino, gets lively, as does the Stalet bar at the base of the Carosselo gondola. The Caffé della Posta umbrella bar, near the centre, is also popular. Nightlife only gets going after 10pm. Galli's pub, in San Antonio, is 'a full-on party pub', popular with Brits. The Kuhstall under the Bivio hotel is an excellent cellar bar with live music, as is the Helvetia, over the road. The San Rocco end is quietest, but Daphne's and Marco's are popular. The stylish Art bar is also recommended. Kokodi and Cielo are the main discos.

OFF THE SLOPES
Go shopping

Livigno does not have many off-slope amenities. Walks are uninspiring and there is no sports centre or public swimming pool. However, the duty-free shopping more than makes up for this – it's a great place to equip yourself with some new ski kit as well as picking up some designer labels at bargain prices. Trips to Bormio and St Moritz are popular.

SNOWPIX.COM / CHRIS GILL

← It may not look much like a pedestrian zone, but a least there's no through-traffic

ITALY

Madonna di Campiglio 1520m

Extensive, easy slopes amid stunning scenery

WHAT IT COSTS

HOW IT RATES

The slopes

Snow	***
Extent	***
Experts	**
Intermediates	****
Beginners	****
Convenience	**
Queues	***
Restaurants	****

The rest

Scenery	****
Resort charm	***
Off-slope	***

What's new

A new fast quad from the valley floor to Pradalago replaced two old chair-lifts last season. And a new bridge was built, linking Grostè to Pradalago with a 140-metre magic carpet conveyor belt. Snowmaking has been extended.

More village parking has been created.

APT MADONNA DI CAMPIGLIO

Gentle slopes amid prettily wooded scenery are the norm ↓

- ⊕ Pleasant traditional-style town with car-free centre
- ⊕ Fairly extensive network of slopes, best for beginners and intermediates
- ⊕ Excellent mountain restaurants

- ⊖ Spread-out resort and poor shuttle bus service
- ⊖ Quiet après ski

Like Cortina, Madonna is a pleasant Dolomite town with an affluent, almost exclusively Italian, clientele – though the scenery isn't in quite the same league. Folgarida and Marilleva, with which Madonna shares its slopes, are quite different, attracting a lot of British groups, including schools.

THE RESORT

Madonna is a spread-out, modern, but traditional-style town with a pedestrian-only centre, set in a prettily wooded valley beneath the impressive Brenta Dolomites. There is more development about 1km south, and a frozen lake between the two.

Madonna attracts an affluent, young, Italian clientele. It has almost as many 4-star hotels as 3-stars, and lots of smart shops. Many visitors potter about the village in the day, and promenading is an early evening ritual.

It's worth staying near a lift base. There's a free bus service, and some hotels run courtesy buses, but morning traffic jams can occur.

THE MOUNTAINS

There are three areas of linked slopes around Madonna: Pancugolo to the west, Pradalago to the north, and Passo Grostè (the highest area) to the east. Pradalago is also linked by lift and piste to Monte Vigo, where the slopes of Folgarida and Marilleva also meet. There are plans for a link between Pancugolo and the separate resort of Pinzolo, but its modest area of slopes remains separate at present.

Slopes The terrain is mainly intermediate, both above and below the tree line. Reporters recommend skiing the Marilleva and Folgarida slopes in the afternoon to avoid busy ski school classes.

Snow reliability Although many of the runs are sunny, they are at a fair altitude, and there has been hefty investment in snowmakers. As a result, snow reliability is reasonable.

Experts Experts should plan on heading off-piste. But the 3-Tre race course and the Spinale Direttissima are steep. Pista Nera, above Folgarida, can be a challenging mogul field.

Intermediates Pancugolo, Madonna's racing mountain, is ideal: early or timid intermediates will love the area and have no difficulty exploring most of the network, though the connection to Folgarida is a bit trickier. Grostè and Pradalago have long, easy runs, though the former can get crowded.

Beginners It's a good resort for beginners, if you don't mind using the erratic bus service out to the excellent nursery slopes at Campo Carlo Magno.

Snowboarding There's a fun-park and half-pipe at Grostè. The resort was included on the FIS World Snowboard Championship circuit last season.

Cross-country There are 30km of pretty trails through the woods.

Queues The links with Marilleva are the main black spot – a recent visitor reported an hour-long wait for the chair back. The new magic carpet link from Grostè to Pradalago is a bottleneck at midday. One reporter tells of pushy queues for the Pradalago chair at the start of ski school classes.

MOUNTAIN FACTS

Altitude	1550m-2505m
Lifts	50
Pistes	150km
Blue	44%
Red	40%
Black	16%
Artificial snow	72km
Recco detectors used	

Phone numbers
From abroad use the prefix +39 (and do **not** omit the initial '0' of the phone number).

TOURIST OFFICE

Postcode 38084
t +39 (0465) 442000
f 440404
info@campiglio.net
www.campiglio.net

Mountain restaurants The mountain restaurants are a highlight: good food, atmosphere and views. Cascina Zeledria, a little off-piste, will tow you back to the piste by snowcat and is recommended by a reporter, as are Bosh and 5 Laghi.

Schools and guides There are several ski schools, but some instructors don't speak English. The Nazionale and Rainalter have been recommended.

Facilities for children Madonna doesn't seem to cater much for children but there are plans for a village nursery.

STAYING THERE

How to go There is a wide choice of hotels, and some self-catering is sold by tour operators.

Hotels The 4-star Spinale (0465 441116) is convenient. The luxury 4-star Lorenzetti (0465 441404) is on the edge of town but with free transport (reportedly 'insufficient at peak times'). The central 3-star Milano (0465 441210) is also recommended. The Christiania (0465 441470) is a convenient B&B. You can also stay at one of the mountain refuges.

Eating out There are around 20 restaurants to choose from. Belvedere, Le Roi and Stube Diana have all been recommended. Some of the mountain huts are also open in the evening.

Après-ski Après-ski is quiet. Franz-Joseph Stube, Bar Suisse and Cantina del Suisse are recommended – and Des Alpes is perhaps the smartest club.

Off the slopes Window-shopping, skating and walking are popular.

Passo Grostè 2505m
Monte Spinale 2110m
Val d'Agola
Malga Grual
Doss del Sabion 2100m
1540m
Pinzolo 770m
800m
Pancugolo 2150m
Madonna di Campiglio 1520m
Pradalago 2145m
Doss della Pesa 2230m
Monte Vigo 2180m
Campo Carlo Magno 1860m
Monte Spolverino 2090m
1880m
Orti
1860m
Folgarida 1400m
1300m
Marilleva 1400m
Marilleva 900m
Mezzana

Monterosa Ski 1640m

Europe's best kept secret – an undiscovered gem

WHAT IT COSTS

HOW IT RATES

The slopes

Snow	***
Extent	****
Experts	***
Intermediates	****
Beginners	**
Convenience	****
Queues	****
Restaurants	**

The rest

Scenery	****
Resort charm	***
Off-slope	*

- ⊕ Fairly extensive network of pistes
- ⊕ Fabulous intermediate and advanced off-piste, including heli-skiing
- ⊕ Beautiful scenery
- ⊕ Good snow reliability and grooming
- ⊕ Quiet, pretty, unspoilt, small villages

- ⊖ Fragmented slopes
- ⊖ Links to and from Alagna currently off-piste only
- ⊖ Few off-slope diversions
- ⊖ Limited après-ski

Monterosa Ski is Italy's little-known and less extensive answer to France's Trois Vallées and has a good lift system which is set for further big development over the next few years. Yet it is hardly heard of on the international market. It is popular with Italians at weekends, when they drive up for the day from Milan and Turin. But during the week it is deserted. The pistes are mostly intermediate and they offer the same feeling of travelling around as the Three Valleys does, amid impressive scenery. And the off-piste is fabulous (and usually deserted). It is the only major ski area we have come across in Europe where there is no real well-developed resort to stay in. The villages that access the slopes have avoided commercialisation and still retain a friendly, small-scale, local ambience. Our advice is to get there soon before all this changes.

THE RESORTS

The main resorts are Champoluc in the western valley, Gressoney, in the central valley, and Alagna to the east. While Champoluc and Alagna have a very Italian ambience, Gressoney shows more Swiss-German influence, even having some signs in German.

Champoluc is towards the end of a long, winding road up from the Aosta valley motorway. It is strung out along the road for quite a distance but retains a certain quiet charm and very Italian feel. The first part you come to is the attractive old village centre with the church and a fast-running river.

Small shops and hotels line the road (part of a one-way traffic system) between here and the gondola station, several minutes' walk away. You can store boots and skis/board there overnight. More accommodation is on the road to Frachey, where there is a chair-lift into the slopes.

MOUNTAIN FACTS

Altitude	1200m-3350m
Lifts	40
Pistes	200km
Blue	33%
Red	62%
Black	5%
Artificial snow	50km
Recco detectors used	

What's new

The area is in the middle of an ambitious programme to link Alagna properly by lifts and piste to Gressoney. For 2000/01 the ancient cable-car out of Alagna was replaced by a new gondola to Pianalunga, followed by a new chair-lift, which takes you to the top cable-car (still tiny and ancient) up to Punta Indren.

The next stage is to build a new cable-car followed by an eight-seater gondola from Pianalunga to Passo dei Salati and another cable-car from there to the Punta Indren area. The off-piste route from Passo dei Salati to Pianalunga will be converted into an official piste. The earliest all this is expected to happen is for 2002/03.

2000/01 also saw new high-speed chairs and more snowmaking at Antagnod and Orsia.

Gressoney La Trinité is a quiet, neat little village, with cobbled streets, wooden buildings and an old church. It is about 800m from the chair-lift into the slopes, where there are a few convenient hotels. It is a bus-ride from the outpost of Stafal at the head of the valley, which is the link between the Gressoney and Champoluc slopes and has a few rather soulless blocks. Gressoney St Jean, a bigger village, is 5km down the valley and has its own separate slopes. Local buses are covered by the lift pass.

The main resort in the east valley is Alagna, a strange place with some large, deserted and dilapidated buildings as well as smaller charming wooden buildings and church.

Trips to Cervinia, La Thuile and Courmayeur (covered by the Aosta Valley pass) are possible by car.

THE MOUNTAINS

The slopes of Monterosa Ski are relatively extensive, and very scenic. The pistes are almost all intermediate (and well groomed), and the lifts are mainly chairs and gondolas, with few drag-lifts. The terrain is undulating and fragmented; runs are attractively varied and long, but many lifts serve only one or two pistes. The piste map is poor: 'Woefully inadequate,' said a reporter.

Slopes A gondola from Champoluc followed by a couple of slow chairs takes you up to the steep, narrow, bumpy link with the rest of the slopes. Taking the bus to the Frachey chair is a quicker way into the main cruising runs and the link via Colle Bettaforca with Stafal in the Gressoney valley.

At Stafal a cable-car followed by a high-speed chair take you back to the Champoluc slopes and a two-stage 12-person gondola opposite takes you up to Passo dei Salati. From there runs lead back down to Stafal and to Gressoney La Trinité and Orsia, both served by more chair-lifts. Or you can head down towards Alagna on an easy, popular off-piste run (due to become a piste in the next couple of years).

From Alagna a new gondola goes to Pianalunga at mid-mountain, where a new two-person chair-lift carries you up to a tiny, ancient cable-car, which accesses the high slopes around Punta Indren. There are a couple of drag-lifts and short pistes up here but the only ways back to Gressoney are off-piste. On the Alagna side there is lots of off-piste and an ungroomed black run that

leads to an old bucket lift that you jump into while it is still moving (it takes you back to the cable-car).

Gressoney St Jean and Antagnod near Champoluc have their own small areas of slopes.

Snowboarding There is no fun-park or half-pipe but great off-piste free-riding.

Snow reliability Good, thanks to the high altitude, extensive snowmaking and good grooming.

Experts The attraction is the off-piste, with great runs from the high-points of the lift system in all three valleys and some excellent heli-drops.

A mountain guide is essential for getting the best out of the area. We had a fabulous day last season with Claudio from Gressoney (all the younger guides speak good English) skiing down to Alagna and then exploring the amazing, deserted off-piste bowls above Gressoney. Snow can lie untracked for days here. Alagna is a cult area for expert off-piste, with couloirs, cornices and cliffs you have to be roped down. There is an epic run down to the Champoluc valley from the top of the Cervinia–Zermatt area.

There are a few black pistes but none of them really deserve their grading. And many of the reds would be blue in other resorts.

Intermediates For those who like to travel on easy, undemanding pistes, the area is great, with long cruising runs from the ridges down into the valleys. There isn't much on-piste challenge for more demanding intermediates, but those willing to take a guide and explore some of the gentler off-piste will have a great time. If you stick to the pistes, a weekend rather than a full week might be worth trying: 'It's great for a short break,' said a recent reporter.

Beginners The high nursery slopes at the top of the gondola at Champoluc are better than the lower ones at La

Phone numbers
From abroad use the prefix +39 (and do **not** omit the initial '0' of the phone number).

TOURIST OFFICE

Postcode 11020
t +39 (0125) 303111
f 303145
kikesly@tin.it
www.monterosa-ski.com

Trinité. But easy runs to progress to are best accessed by the Frachey chair or going to Antagnod.

Cross-country There are long trails around St Jean, and shorter ones up the valley; Brusson, in the Champoluc valley, has the best trails in the area.

Queues Only at weekends, when the hordes from Turin and Milan arrive, are there any queues. The worst bottleneck is the tiny top cable-car on the Alagna side, where waits of over an hour are possible. Pistes can get crowded at weekends, too, but the off-piste is still delightfully quiet.

Mountain restaurants The mountain restaurants are good and cheap. The Chamois at Punta Jolanda, Bedemie on the way to Gressoney from Gabiet, Del Ponte above Gabiet, Vieux Crest and Belvedere, above Champoluc, and the Guglielmina, Lys and Gabiet refuges are recommended.

Schools and guides We have had decent reports on the ski schools and excellent ones of the Gressoney and Alagna mountain guides.

Facilities for children There is a special kids' ski school and snow park at Antagnod near Champoluc and a mini-club at Gressoney St Jean.

STAYING THERE

How to go We've had good reports of Monterosa specialist tour operator Ski 2.

Hotels At Champoluc the Castor (0125 307117) in the old centre is 'an absolute gem' and is managed by a British guy. At the amazing Hotel California (0125 307977 – the owners speak no English) – every room is dedicated to a pop star or group (eg The Byrds, Bob Dylan, Joan Baez, the Doors) and their music plays whenever you turn on the light. It's quite a way out of the centre. The new Relais des Glaciers (0125 308721) near the centre has a spa complex, but a reporter had 'a chilly room, very slow service'.

At Gressoney La Trinité reporters recommend the Jolanda Sport (0125 366140) and Dufour (0125 366139); in Alagna, the Monterosa (0163 923209) and Cristallo (0163 91285).

Eating out Both Gressoney and Champoluc have a few stand alone restaurants, but most are in hotels.

Après-ski Après-ski is quiet. At weekends, the disco beneath Hotel California in Champoluc gets going. The bar of the Hotel Castor is cosy.

Off the slopes There is little to amuse those who don't head for the slopes.

SNOWPIX.COM / CHRIS GILL

Monterosa's easy intermediate pistes and fabulous off-piste are set among spectacular scenery ↓

Sauze d'Oulx 1510m

'Suzy does it' still, but with more dignity than in the past

WHAT IT COSTS

3

HOW IT RATES

The slopes	
Snow	**
Extent	*****
Experts	**
Intermediates	****
Beginners	**
Convenience	**
Queues	***
Restaurants	***
The rest	
Scenery	***
Resort charm	**
Off-slope	*

What's new

Turin has been chosen to host the 2006 Olympic Winter Games; most of the Alpine events will be held at Sansicario and Sestriere, and freestyle competitions at Sauze d'Oulx.

Snowmaking has been improved on the Clotes run and more is planned.

MOUNTAIN FACTS

Figures relate to the whole Milky Way area

Altitude	1390m-2825m
Lifts	92
Pistes	400km
Blue	12%
Red	67%
Black	21%
Artificial snow	75km

- ➕ Extensive and uncrowded slopes, great intermediate cruising
- ➕ Linked into Milky Way network
- ➕ Mix of open and tree-lined runs is good for all weather conditions
- ➕ Entertaining nightlife
- ➕ Some scope for off-piste adventures
- ➕ One of the cheapest major resorts there is – and more attractive than its reputation suggests

- ➖ Still lots of ancient lifts, making progress around the slopes slow
- ➖ Erratic snow record – and still far from comprehensive snowmaking
- ➖ Crowds at weekends
- ➖ Brashness and Britishness of resort will not suit everyone
- ➖ Very few challenging pistes
- ➖ Mornings-only classes, and the best nursery slopes are at mid-mountain
- ➖ Steep walks around the village, and an inadequate shuttle-bus service

If you're looking for a cheap holiday in a resort with extensive slopes, put Sauze on your shortlist. In the 1980s it became known as prime lager-lout territory; but it always was a resort of two halves – young Brits on a budget alongside mature second-home owners from Turin – and these days the two halves seem to be much more in balance, especially at weekends. It still has lively bars and shops festooned in English signs, but sober Brits like you and us need not stay away. We like it more than we expect to – as do many reporters.

We are slightly haunted, though, by the memory of the bare slopes of our first visit, in the mid-1980s. Thin cover two seasons ago brought it all back: Sauze is a resort that needs comprehensive snowmaking, and doesn't yet have it.

The resort

Sauze d'Oulx sits on a sloping mountain shelf facing north-west across the Valle di Susa, with impressive views of the towering mountains forming the border with France. Most of the resort is modern and undistinguished, made up of block-like hotels relieved by the occasional chalet, spreading down the steep hillside from the foot of the slopes to the village centre and beyond. Despite the shift in clientele described above, the centre is still lively at night; the late-closing bars are usually quite full, and the handful of discos do brisk business at the weekend, at least.

It's not immediately obvious, but Sauze also has an attractive old core, with narrow, twisting streets, the occasional carved stone fountain and houses with huge stone slabs serving as roof slates.

Traffic roams freely through the village, which can be congested morning and evening as cars vie for convenient parking spaces or the quickest way out of town. The roads become slushy during the day and icy and treacherous at night – hazardous, as there are few pavements.

Out of the bustle of the centre, where most of the bars and nightclubs are located, there are quiet, wooded residential areas full of secluded apartment blocks, and a number of good restaurants are also tucked out of the way of the front line. Chair-lifts go from the top of the village and from two points on its fringes. There's also a chair from nearby Jouvenceaux.

Most of the hotels are reasonably central, but the Clotes lift is at the top of the village, up a short but steep hill, and the Sportinia chair is an irritatingly long walk beyond that. Buses (not covered by the lift pass) run around the resort, but the service is infrequent and can't cope with high-season crowds. The service around lunch-time is particularly poor, signposting of stops is unclear; and the service to Jouvenceaux stops inconveniently early, at 5pm.

LIFT PASSES

2000/01 prices in euros

La Via Lattea
Covers all lifts in Sauze d'Oulx, Sestriere, Sansicario, Cesana and Clavière.

Beginners Points book (80 points 72), with lifts costing from 1 to 12 points.

Main pass
1-day pass 25
6-day pass 137
(low season 111)

Senior citizens
Over 60: 6-day pass 126

Children
Under 12: 6-day pass 126
Under 8: free pass

Short-term passes
Some single ascent passes and afternoon pass.

Notes Includes one free day in each of: Alpe-d'Huez, Les Deux Alpes, Serre-Chevalier and Puy-St-Vincent. One day extension for Montgenèvre (12). One day extension for Pragelato and Bardonecchia available.

Alternative passes
La Via Lattea VIP card also covers Montgenèvre and Pragelato.

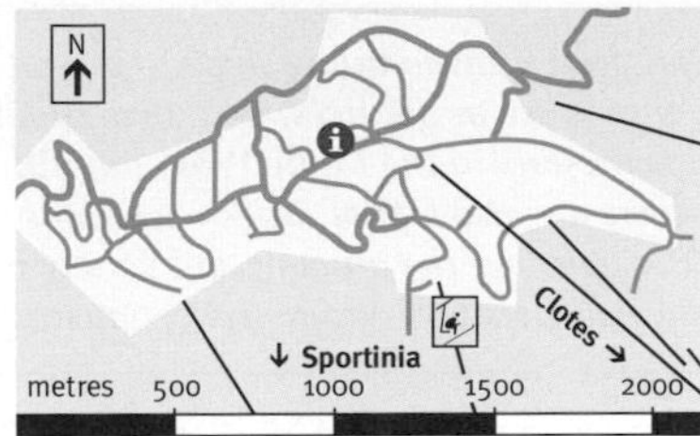

The mountains

Sauze's mountains provide excellent intermediate terrain. The piste grading fluctuates from year to year, if you believe the resort's map – and we're never sure we've caught up with the latest changes from blue to red and red to blue. But most reporters agree that many runs graded red or even black should really be graded blue; challenges are few and far between. (The same might be said of the whole extensive Milky Way area, of which Sauze is one extreme.)

THE SLOPES
Big and varied enough for most

Sauze's local slopes are spread across a broad wooded bowl above the resort, ranging from west- to north-facing. The main lifts are chairs, from the top of the village up to **Clotes** and from the western fringes to **Sportinia** – a sunny mid-mountain clearing in the woods, with a ring of restaurants and hotels (see Staying up the mountain) and a small nursery area.

The high point of the system is **Monte Fraiteve**. From here you can travel west on splendid broad, long runs to **Sansicario** – and on to chair-lifts near **Cesana Torinese** that link with **Clavière** and then **Montgenèvre**, in France, the far end of the Milky Way (both are reached more quickly by car).

You normally get to **Sestriere** from the lower point of Col Basset, on the shoulder of M Fraiteve. The alternative of descending the sunny slope from M Fraiteve itself has been reinstated after a few years of closure; but snow here is not reliable, which we're told is why the old lift from Sestriere up this slope was removed some years ago. You can make the link via the gondola but this is prone to closure in bad weather.

As in so many Italian resorts, piste marking, direction signing and piste map design are not taken particularly seriously.

The slopes of Montgenèvre and Sestriere are dealt with in separate chapters. If you have a car, you can go beyond Montgenèvre to Briançon, Serre-Chevalier and Bardonecchia.

SNOW RELIABILITY
Can be poor, affecting the links

The area is notorious for erratic snowfalls – though it did fairly well last year, it received very little snow two seasons ago. Another problem is that many of the slopes get a lot of afternoon sun. At these modest altitudes, late-season conditions are far from reliable. Reporters have found icy, bare slopes at vital link points earlier in the season, too – particularly from

LAPRESSE

The ideal base for exploration of the whole Milky Way – not Sauze but Sansicario →

boarding *Sauze has good snowboarding slopes – it's got local tree-lined slopes (with space in the trees, too), high, undulating, open terrain, and links to other resorts in the Milky Way. But although it has a fair number of chair-lifts, there are also lots of drags – a serious drawback for novice riders. There's no park or pipe, but the amount and variety of terrain makes up for this. Sauze's mainly young visitors ensure lively, entertaining nightlife.*

M Fraiteve. There's snowmaking on a couple of slopes, notably the key home run from P Rocca via Clotes to the village.

FOR EXPERTS
Head off-piste
Very few of the pistes are challenging. The best slopes are at virtually opposite ends of Sauze's local area – a high, north-facing run from the shoulder of M Fraiteve, and the sunny slopes below M Moncrons.

The main interest is in going off-piste. There are plenty of minor opportunities within the piste network, but the highlights are long, top-to-bottom descents of up to 1300m vertical from M Fraiteve, ending (snow permitting) at villages dotted along the valleys. The best-known of these runs (which used to be marked on the piste map but is no longer) is the Rio Nero, down to the road near Oulx. When snow low down is poor, some of these runs can be cut short at Jouvenceaux or Sansicario.

FOR INTERMEDIATES
Splendid cruising terrain
The whole area is ideal for confident intermediates who want to clock up the kilometres. For the less confident, the piste map doesn't help because it picks out only the very easiest runs in blue – there are many others they could manage. The Belvedere and Moncrons sectors at the east of the area are served only by drags but offer some wonderful, uncrowded high cruising, some of it above the tree line.

The long runs down to Sansicario and down to Jouvenceaux are splendid, confidence-boosting intermediate terrain. Getting back to Sauze involves tackling some of the steepest terrain in the area – the black run from M Fraiteve to the Col Basset lifts at Malafosse. This presents a problem for many intermediates and is a serious shortcoming in the circuit. The run down to Sestriere gets a lot of sun but is worth it for the somewhat more challenging intermediate terrain on the opposite side of the valley. If

SCHOOLS/GUIDES

2000/01 prices in euros

Sauze Sportinia
Classes 6 days
3hr: 10am-1pm
6 3hr days: 108
Children's classes
Ages: from 6
6 3hr days: 108
Private lessons
Hourly
26 for 1hr

Sauze d'Oulx
Classes 6 days
3hr: 10am-1pm
6 3hr days: 103
Children's classes
Ages: from 6
6 3hr days: 103
Private lessons
Hourly
27 for 1hr

Sauze Project
Italian-speaking only school.

CHILDCARE

The village kindergarten, Little Dumbo, has English and Italian staff and takes children up to 6 years, from 9am to 5pm. You have to provide lunch, but it can be heated up.

Phone numbers
From abroad use the prefix +39 (and do **not** omit the initial '0' of the phone number).

GETTING THERE

Air Turin, transfer 2hr.

Rail Oulx (5km); frequent buses.

conditions are too poor, you can always ride the gondola down.

At the higher levels, where the slopes are above the tree line, the terrain often allows a choice of route. Lower down are pretty runs through the woods, where the main complication can be route-finding. The mountainside is broken up by gullies, and pistes that appear to be quite close together may in fact have no easy connections between them.

FOR BEGINNERS
There are better choices
Sauze is not ideal for beginners: its village-level slopes are a bit on the steep side and the main nursery area is up the mountain, at Sportinia. Equally importantly, the mornings-only classes don't suit everyone.

FOR CROSS-COUNTRY
Severely limited, even with snow
There is very little cross-country skiing, and it isn't reliable for snow.

QUEUES
Slow lifts the biggest problem
There can be 10-minute waits at Sportinia when school classes are setting off or immediately after lunch, but otherwise the system has few bottlenecks. The main problem with the network is that, despite the recent introduction of three high-speed quads, most of the lifts are ancient and terribly slow. Amazingly, they haven't yet replaced the museum-piece chair-lift from the village to Clotes which requires you to carry your skis in your lap and hit the ground running at the top. Although it links to a fast quad which takes you the rest of the way to the top, this lift is still hugely inadequate for such an important link; it can create long bottlenecks and makes the uplift seem interminable. Breakdowns on elderly drag-lifts may also be a nuisance.

MOUNTAIN RESTAURANTS
Some pleasant possibilities
Restaurants are numerous and generally pleasant, though few are particularly special. One place that's certainly worth picking out is the hotel Capricorno, at Clotes – one of the most civilised and appealing lunch-spots in the Alps. It is not cheap, though. There are more modest mid-mountain restaurants across the mountainside, with the main concentration at Sportinia. The Capannina and the Belvedere are popular. And the Ciao Pais, at the top of the Clotes chair-lift, the Chalet Pian della Rocca and the Chalet Clot Bourget have been recommended.

SCHOOLS AND GUIDES
Tuition variable, large classes
Recent reporters have found a lack of good English spoken and large classes. Some found the tuition satisfactory, others were disappointed. Classes are only half a day, but last three hours. Reporters on the school in Sansicario have found the instruction enthusiastic and useful, with good spoken English.

FACILITIES FOR CHILDREN
Tour operator alternatives
Although there is a resort kindergarten, you might want to look in to the crèche facilities offered by some of the major UK tour operators in the chalets and chalet-hotels that they run here – Crystal and Neilson, for example.

Staying there

HOW TO GO
Packaged hotels dominate
All the major mainstream operators offer hotel packages here, but there are also a few chalets.

Hotels Simple 2-star and 3-star hotels form the core of the holiday accommodation, with a couple of 4-stars and some more basic places.

(((3) **La Torre** (0122 850020) Cylindrical landmark 200m below centre. Excellent rooms; mini-buses to lifts.

((2) **Hermitage** (0122 850385) Neat chalet-style hotel in about the best spot for the slopes – beside the home piste from Clotes.

((2) **Gran Baita** (0122 850183) Comfortable place in quiet, central backstreet, with excellent food and good rooms, some with spectacular sunset views from their balconies.

((2) **Biancaneve** (0122 850021) Pleasant, with smallish rooms. Near the centre.

((2) **Des Amis** (0122 858488) Down in Jouvenceaux, but near bus stop; simple hotel run by Anglo-Italian couple.

Self-catering There are apartments and chalets available, some through UK tour operators.

EATING OUT
Caters for all tastes and pockets
Typical Italian banquets of five or six courses can be had in the upmarket

ACTIVITIES

Indoor Bowling, cinema, sauna, massage
Outdoor Artificial skating rink, torchlit descents, heli-skiing, ice-climbing, snow-shoeing

Don Vincenzo and Il Cantun restaurants. The Del Falco does a particularly good three-course 'skiers' menu'. In the old town, the Del Borgo and La Griglia are popular pizzerias. Il Lampione is the place to go for 'pub grub' – good-value Chinese, Mexican and Indian food. Sugo's spaghetteria provides delicious, filling and economic fare. Le Pecore Nere also gets good reviews. A number of reporters have suggested booking restaurants in advance to avoid disappointment.

APRES-SKI

Suzy does it with more dignity

Once favoured almost solely by large groups of youngsters, some of whom were very rowdy, the number and atmosphere of Sauze's bars now impress reporters young and old.

The Assietta terrace is popular for catching the last rays of the sun at the end of the day. The excellent New Scotch bar is also recommended. As is Il Lampione, in the old town.

After dinner, more places warm up. One of the best is the smart, atmospheric cocktail bar Moncrons, which holds regular quiz nights. We also like the late-night Village Café (aka Osteria da Gigi), which is popular with Italians and workers. The Cotton Club provides good service, directors' chairs, video screen and draught cider. The Rock Café has as many Italian clients as Brits. Paddy McGinty's is especially popular with resort staff and has a lively atmosphere. Gran Trün has live music and reminded us of a Majorcan barbecue venue, with bottles on the wall and white stucco decor. The Derby is nice for a quiet drink in a relaxed setting. Of the discos, Il Bandito is a walk away, and popular with Italians. Schuss runs theme nights and drink promotions – entrance is normally free.

Tour reps organise activities, including torchlit descents, bowling and 'broomball' on the ice rink.

OFF THE SLOPES

Go elsewhere

Sauze is not a particularly pleasant place in which to while away the days if you don't want to hit the slopes. Shopping is limited, there are no gondolas or cable-cars for pedestrians and there are few off-slope activities. Turin or Briançon are worth a visit.

STAYING UP THE MOUNTAIN

'You pays your money ... '

In most resorts, staying up the mountain is an amusing thing to do and is often economical – but usually you pay the price of accepting simple accommodation. Here, the reverse applies. The 4-star Capricorno (0122 850273), up at Clotes, is one of the most comfortable hotels in Sauze, certainly the most attractive and by a wide margin the most expensive. It's a charming little chalet beside the piste, with a smart restaurant and terrace (a very popular spot for a good lunch on the mountain) and only eight bedrooms.

Not quite in the same league are the places up at Sportinia. Crystal is running a couple of them now as jumbo chalets. The company also has a smaller chalet here. Reporters who stayed here enjoyed the isolation and easy access to the slopes – but you can't get down to town after 4pm, making it more suitable for groups providing their own entertainment or those for whom nightlife matters little.

Sansicario 1700m

If any resort is ideally placed for exploration of the whole Milky Way, it is Sansicario. It is a modern, purpose-built, self-contained but rather soulless little resort, mainly consisting of apartments linked by monorail to the small shopping precinct. The 45-room Rio Envers (0122 811333) is a reasonably comfortable, pricey hotel. Visitors recommend the Chalmettes for its views and food at lunch-time, and the Enoteca in the evening for fondue and grappa. The whole place will doubtless get a bit of a boost from the 2006 Olympics – downhill and super G races will be held here.

TOURIST OFFICE

Postcode 10050
t +39 (0122) 858009
f 850700
sauze@montagnedoc.it
www.montagnedoc.it

Selva/Sella Ronda 1565m

Spectacular Dolomite resort ideal for intermediates

WHAT IT COSTS

4

HOW IT RATES

The slopes

Snow	****
Extent	*****
Experts	***
Intermediates	*****
Beginners	****
Convenience	***
Queues	***
Restaurants	****

The rest

Scenery	*****
Resort charm	***
Off-slope	***

What's new

For 2000/01 a new fast quad replaced the drag from Piz Seteur, in Plan de Gralba, up to Passo Sella. And in Canazei, two chairs on Belvedere were upgraded – to a six-pack and a quad.

Other developments in the area include a new gondola up to Col Pradat in Colfosco's local area, and a new quad chair at Bufaure di Sotto in Val di Fassa.

The Marmolada glacier lifts are now included in the Dolomiti Superski pass.

- ⊕ Vast network of connected slopes – suits intermediates particularly well
- ⊕ Stunning, unique Dolomite scenery
- ⊕ Superb snowmaking and grooming
- ⊕ Jolly mountain huts with good food
- ⊕ Many new lifts have cut out all but a few bad bottlenecks on the famous Sella Ronda circuit
- ⊕ Good nursery slopes
- ⊕ Excellent value

- ⊖ Small proportion of tough runs
- ⊖ Lifts and slopes can be crowded, especially on Sella Ronda circuit
- ⊖ High proportion of short runs, not so many long ones
- ⊖ Selva is not a particularly attractive village, nor especially convenient
- ⊖ Erratic snow record; slopes vulnerable to warm weather

This is an area unlike any other. The Sella Ronda is an amazing circular network of lifts and pistes taking you around the spectacular Gruppo Sella – a mighty limestone massif with villages dotted around it, the biggest of them being Selva (or Selva Val Gardena / Wolkenstein, to give the resort its Sunday name and alternative German form). As well as this impressive main circuit, there are major lift systems leading off it at four main points. In overall scale, the network rivals the famed Trois Vallées in France. And the Superski lift pass covers dozens of other resorts reachable by road. So there's plenty to keep you busy.

The scenery is fabulous – almost a match for nearby Cortina. But the Dolomite landscape that provides the visual drama also dictates the nature of the slopes. Sheer limestone cliffs rise out of gentle pastureland; you spend your time on the latter, gazing at the former. There is scarcely a black run to be seen, and runs of more than 500m vertical are rare. Runs of under 300m vertical are not.

Although we hinge this chapter on Selva, you certainly shouldn't overlook the several alternative bases around the circuit. For experts, in particular, Arabba has clear attractions. It's here that the classic Dolomite landscape gives way to a more familiar kind of terrain, with longer, steeper slopes. For nervous intermediates, on the other hand, the obvious alternative to Selva is Corvara.

VAL GARDENA TOURIST OFFICE

Selva sits at the foot of the towering Sassolungo →

The resort

Selva is a long roadside village, almost merged with the next village of Santa Cristina. It suffers from traffic but has traditional-style architecture and an attractive church. The area is famed for wood carvings – you'll see them all over.

The village enjoys a lovely setting under the impressive pink-tinged walls of Sassolungo and the Gruppo Sella – a fortress-like massif about 6km across that lies at the hub of the Sella Ronda circuit (see the feature box later in the chapter). Despite its World Cup fame (as Val Gardena, the name of the valley) and animated atmosphere, Selva is neither upmarket nor brash. It's a good-value, civilised family resort – and is undoubtedly the biggest and liveliest of the places to stay right on the Sella Ronda circuit.

For many years the area was under Austrian rule, and reporters admire the Tirolean charm of the resort. German is the main language, not Italian, and most visitors are German, too. Selva is also known as Wolkenstein and the Gardena valley as Gröden. The local dialect is Ladino, which has resisted being absorbed into German or Italian.

Ortisei is the administrative centre of Val Gardena – pretty, and more of a complete community – but it is not so convenient for the Sella Ronda slopes. For a brief description of the other villages on or near the circuit, see the end of this chapter.

From Selva, gondolas rise in two directions. One goes east from the top of the nursery slopes towards Colfosco and Corvara and the clockwise Sella Ronda route. The other takes you south from the village to Ciampinoi and the anti-clockwise route. The most convenient position is near one of these gondolas. There is a free, regular bus service throughout the valley until early evening, but reporters say this can get very oversubscribed. Some prefer to share cheap taxis. Others suggest a beer or two before heading for home, to avoid the rush.

The Dolomiti Superski pass covers not only the Sella Ronda resorts but dozens of others. It's an easy road trip to Cortina – worth it for the fabulous scenery alone. But many other drives in this area are very tortuous and slow – it's often quicker on skis.

MOUNTAIN FACTS

Altitude	1235m-2520m
Lifts	81
Pistes	175km
Blue	30%
Red	60%
Black	10%
Artificial snow	140km
Recco detectors used	

The mountain

The slopes cover a vast area, all amid stunning scenery and practically all ideally suited to intermediates who don't mind shortish runs. There are different piste maps for different areas, and a common complaint is that they are inadequate. Piste marking and signing also come in for criticism.

THE SLOPES

High mileage piste excursions

A gondola and parallel-running chair go up from Selva to **Ciampinoi**, from where several pistes, including the famous World Cup Downhill run, spread out across the mountain and lead back down to Selva, **Santa Cristina** and **Plan de Gralba**. From Plan de Gralba, you can head off towards **Passo Sella**, **Canazei** and the rest of the Sella Ronda.

Across the valley from the Ciampinoi gondola is a chair that links with the Dantercëpies gondola. This accesses the Sella Ronda in the opposite direction or you can return to Selva on the Ladies Downhill. From the top you head down to **Colfosco**, then lifts link with **Corvara**, and you go on to **Arabba** and the rest of the Sella Ronda.

At Passo Pordoi between Canazei and Arabba is the one breach in the defences of the Gruppo Sella: a cable-car goes up to Sass Pordoi at 2950m, giving access to off-piste routes as well as spectacular views.

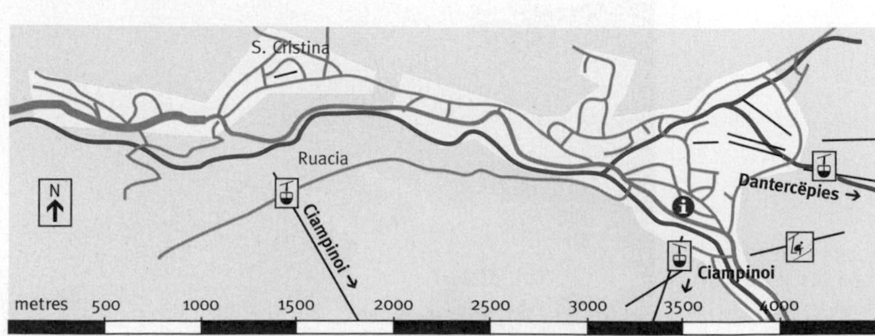

LIFT PASSES

2000/01 prices in euros

Dolomiti Superski
Covers 460 lifts and 1200km of piste in the Dolomites, including all Sella Ronda resorts.

Main pass
1-day pass 33
6-day pass 162
(low season 142)

Senior citizens
Over 60: 6-day pass 129

Children
Under 16: 6-day pass 113

Alternative pass
Val Gardena pass covers all lifts in Selva Gardena, S Cristina, Ortisei and Alpe di Siusi.

There are several linked areas that are not directly on the Sella Ronda circuit that are worth exploring. The biggest is the **Alta Badia** area to the west of Corvara, from which you can get down to **San Cassiano** and **La Villa**.

Local to Selva is the **Seceda** area, accessed by a gondola, a bus-ride from town and on the outskirts of Santa Cristina. You can head back down to the bottom or go on to **Ortisei**. And from Ortisei a cable-car goes up the other side of the valley to **Alpe di Siusi** – a gentle elevated area of quiet, easy runs, cross-country and walks.

The Marmolada glacier near Arabba is open most of the winter and is now included on the main lift pass. One reader recommends it 'for the spectacular views rather than for the typically boring glacier slopes.'

SNOW RELIABILITY

Excellent when it's cold

The slopes are not high – there are few above 2200m and most are between 1500m and 2000m. And natural snowfalls are erratic. But we have experienced excellent pistes here in times of severe natural snow shortage – the area has invested heavily in snowmaking and now has one of the largest capacities in Europe, covering 140km of runs. Most areas have snow-guns on the main runs to the resorts, and almost all Selva's local pistes are well endowed. Good piste grooming adds to the effect.

Problems arise only in poor snow years when temperatures are too high to make snow.

FOR EXPERTS

A few good runs

In general, experts may find the region too tame, especially if they're looking for lots of steep challenges or moguls.

Arabba has the best steep slopes (and snow). North-facing blacks and reds from Porta Vescovo back to Arabba are served by an efficient high-capacity gondola and are great fun. The Val Gardena World Cup piste, the 'Saslonch', is one of several steepish

runs between Ciampinoi and both Selva and Santa Cristina. Unlike many World Cup pistes it is kept in racing condition for Italian team practices, but it is open to the public much of the time. It's especially good in January, when it's not too crowded. The unpisted trail down to Santa Cristina, accessed from the Florian chair on Alpe di Siusi, is not difficult, but pleasantly lonely.

Overall, off-piste is limited because of the sheer-drop nature of the tops of the mountains in the Dolomites, but for the daring there is excitement to be found with a guide. The itinerary from Sass Pordoi back to the cable-car station is not too difficult; the much longer route to Colfosco ends in a spectacular narrow descent through the Val de Mesdi.

FOR INTERMEDIATES
A huge network of ideal runs

The Sella Ronda region is famed for easy slopes. For early or timid intermediates, the runs from Dantercëpies to Colfosco and Corvara, and over the valley from there in the Alta Badia, are superb for cruising and confidence-boosting. They're easy to reach from Selva, but returning from Dantercëpies may be a little daunting. Riding the gondola down is an option.

Nearer to Selva, the runs in the Plan de Gralba area are gentle. The Alpe di Siusi runs above Ortisei are rather flat, but a recent visitor found this area 'a much underrated winter wonderland. It took our breath away for scenery and quiet, good blue runs'.

Average intermediates have a very large network of suitable pistes, though there are few long runs. The beautiful swoop down the far side of the Seceda massif from Cuca to Ortisei is a favourite with recent reporters. The Plan de Gralba area, the runs on either side of the Florian chair on Alpe di Siusi, and the main pistes to San Cassiano and La Villa in the Alta Badia area are other recommended cruises.

Several reporters also enjoyed the area above Canazei, below the Belvedere: 'Well served with efficient lifts, and good snow. The red to Lupo Bianco is an especially beautiful run through the trees.'

The runs back down to the valley direct from Ciampinoi are a bit more challenging, as are the descents from Dantercëpies to Selva. And, of course, most intermediates will want to do the Sella Ronda circuit at least once during a week – see feature panel. The spectacular 'Hidden Valley' is also worth a visit. It's reached via a cable-car at Lagazuoi, which you get to via a bus or shared taxi from Armentarola. See the Cortina chapter for details.

FOR BEGINNERS
Great slopes, but ...

Near-beginners have numerous runs, and the village nursery slopes are excellent – spacious, convenient, and kept in good condition. There are splendid gentle runs to progress to. Visiting beginners have thoroughly recommended the area in the past. However, we have varying reports about the school – see 'Schools and Guides' section.

FOR CROSS-COUNTRY
Beautiful trails

There are over 70km of trails, all enjoying wonderful scenery. The 12km trail up the Vallunga–Langental valley is particularly attractive, with neck-craning views all around. The largest section of trails (40km) has the advantage of being at altitude, running between Monte Pana and Seiseralm, and across Alpe di Siusi.

QUEUES
Much improved: a few problems

New lifts have vastly improved the area and bottlenecks are no longer as common, except in peak periods. That said, we still get complaints about parts of the Sella Ronda circuit. And you may find the crowds on the pistes worse than the queues for the lifts. One recent peak-period visitor was appalled by pushy queues.

---

boarding *Snowboarding is not particularly big in the area. There was a small park at Piz Sella last season, but this was made by the local riders and may not be there for next season. The main lifts out of Selva are all gondolas or chairs and you can do the Sella Ronda clockwise using only one drag – the anti-clockwise route has more. Either way, there are some frustratingly flat sections where you have to scoot or walk. There are enough lively bars to have a good time in the evenings.*

In busy periods the chair-lifts from Arabba in both directions have been a problem, as have the long, cold drag-lifts from Colfosco to Selva.

MOUNTAIN RESTAURANTS

One of the area's highlights

Our reporters are unanimous in their praise for the mountain huts – there are lots of them all over the area, and virtually all of them are lively, offer good food, atmosphere and value for money.

In Val Gardena the Panorama is a small, cosy, rustic suntrap at the foot of the Dantercëpies drag. On the way down to Plan de Gralba from Ciampinoi, the Vallongia Rolandhütte is tucked away on a corner of the piste. In the Plan de Gralba area the top station of the cable-car does excellent pizza slices; the Comici is atmospheric with a big sun terrace. Further west the Sanon, above Col Raiser, 'has bags of atmosphere. It's cosy on bad days, and it's lovely to sit out on the terrace in the sun'.

The trio of little huts in the Colfosco area – Forcelles, Edelweiss and Pradat – are all very pleasant.

At Alta Badia the Piz Sorega above San Cassiano gets very busy. Pride of place must go to Trappers' Home – a Wild West mountain hut with totem pole, teepee, country music and a Harley Davidson in the basement. Cherz above Passo di Campolongo has great views of Marmolada.

Around Arabba, Bec de Roces and Col de Burz are both suntraps. The rifugio at the top of the Porta Vescovo

THE SELLA RONDA

The Sella Ronda is one of the world's classic intermediate circuits. The journey around the Sella massif is easily managed in a day by even an early intermediate. The slopes you descend are almost all easy, and take you through Selva, Colfosco, Corvara, Arabba and Canazei. You can do the circuit in either direction by following very clear coloured signs. We prefer the clockwise route; it is slightly quicker, avoids a tedious series of drag lifts from Colfosco towards Selva, and offers more interesting slopes. But why not do both? There are two free maps of the circuit available; for map-literate people, the better bet is the proper topographical one with contour lines.

The runs total around 23km and the lifts around 14km. We've done it in just three and a half hours plus some diversions and hut stops, though five or six hours may be more realistic during busy periods. The lifts take a total of about two hours (plus any queuing). On busy days it can be crowded (both on the pistes and on the lifts). If possible, choose low season or a Saturday, and set out early.

Not everyone likes it. 'It's a bit of a slog,' said one reporter. Others have found the circuit 'boring', and 'a bit of a rat race' but agree that 'it is a good way to get to other areas'. To make the journey more enjoyable we suggest experts take time out for some diversions. Among the most entertaining segments are the long runs down from Ciampinoi to Santa Cristina and Selva, from Dantercëpies to Selva, from the top of the Boe gondola back down to Corvara and from the top of the Arabba gondola. Take in all those in a day doing the circuit and you'll have had a good day.

Intermediates could take time out to explore the off-the-circuit Alta Badia area from Corvara. Groups of different standards can do the circuit and arrange to meet along the way. There are plenty of welcoming rifugios at which to take a break.

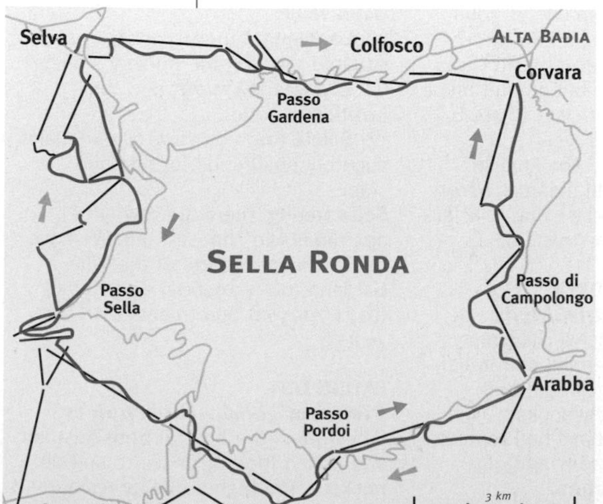

The Gruppo Sella is an almost impregnable rock fortress →

VAL GARDENA TOURIST OFFICE

SCHOOLS/GUIDES

2000/01 prices in euros

Selva Gardena
Classes 6 days
6 4hr days: 132
Children's classes
Ages: 4 to 12
6 6hr days: 201 (includes lunch)
Private lessons
Hourly
29 for 1hr for 1 person

Ortisei
Classes 5 days
2 half-days (3hr) and 3 full days (6½hr): 132
Children's classes
Ages: from 3
5 6½hr days: 188
Private lessons
Hourly
29 for 1hr for 1 person

S Cristina
Classes 6 3½hr days: 127
Children's classes
Ages: from 2½
1 day: 119
Private lessons
Hourly
29 for 1hr for 1 person

CHILDCARE

The ski schools run a kindergarten for children aged 1 to 4, with skiing available for the older children. Those attending proper ski school classes can be looked after all day.

lifts has been recommended as 'modern, clean, bright, efficient and with excellent food'. Capanna Bill, on the long run down to Malga Ciapela, has stunning views of the Marmolada glacier.

On Alpe di Siusi the rustic Sanon Refuge gets a good review, particularly since 'the barman came out to serenade us with his Tirolean accordion'. And the Wilhelms Hutte at the top of the Florian chair has 'superb views under Sassopiatto'.

Above Canazei there are at least six huts dotted around the Belvedere bowl. Lower down, Lupo Bianco is a notable rendezvous point and suntrap. As well as restaurants, there are lots of little snow bars for a quick grappa.

SCHOOLS AND GUIDES
Mixed views

The Selva school is capable of good tuition, provided you get into a suitable group. One recent visitor was very pleased with her tuition and made 'good progress' in her class of six. However, another was 'very unimpressed' when all the English speakers, of varying standards, were lumped in the same class due to a lack of English speaking instructors.

FACILITIES FOR CHILDREN
Good by Italian standards

There are comprehensive childcare arrangements, but German and Italian are the main languages here and English is not routinely spoken. That said, in the past we have had reports of very enjoyable lessons and of children longing to return.

Staying there

HOW TO GO
A reasonable choice

Selva and its neighbours now feature in quite a few tour operator brochures.
Chalets There is a fair choice of catered chalets, and some of the properties are good quality, with en suite bathrooms.
Hotels There are a dozen 4-stars, over 30 3-stars and numerous lesser hotels. Few of the best are well positioned.
((3 **Gran Baita** (0471 795210) Large, luxurious sporthotel, with lots of mod cons including indoor pool. A few minutes' walk from centre and lifts.
((3 **Aaritz** (0471 795011) Best-placed 4-star, opposite the Ciampinoi gondola, and with an open fire.
(2 **Astor** (0471 795207) Family-run chalet in centre, below nursery slopes. Good value.
(2 **Continental** (0471 795411) 3-star situated right on the nursery slopes.
(2 **Olympia** (0471 795145) Well positioned 3-star.
(2 **Solaia** (0471 795104) 3-star chalet, superbly positioned for lifts and slopes.
Self-catering There are plenty of apartments to choose from. We have had excellent reports of the Villa Gardena (0471 794602) and Isabell (0471 794562) apartments over the years.

EATING OUT
Plenty of good-value choices

Selva offers the best of both Austrian and Italian food at prices to suit all pockets. The higher-quality restaurants are mainly hotel-based. The Antares

GETTING THERE

Air Verona, transfer 3hr; Bolzano, transfer 45min; Innsbruck, transfer 3hr.

Rail Chiusa (27km), Bressanone (35km), Bolzano (40km); frequent buses from station.

ACTIVITIES

Indoor Swimming, sauna, solaria, bowling alley, squash, artificial skating rink, ice hockey, museum, concerts, cinema, billiards, tennis, climbing wall, fitness centre

Outdoor Sleigh rides, torch-light descents, snow-shoeing, toboggan runs, paragliding, horse-riding, extensive cleared paths around Selva Gardena and above S Cristina and Ortisei

Phone numbers

From abroad use the prefix +39 (and do **not** omit the initial '0' of the phone number).

TOURIST OFFICE

Postcode 39048
t +39 (0471) 795122
f 794245
selva@val-gardena.com
www.valgardena.it

and Laurin have especially good menus. The Bellavista is recommended for good pasta and Doug and Dagi's Costabella for Tirolean specialities. Rino's has 'excellent pizza'.

APRES-SKI

Above average for a family resort

Nightlife is lively and informal, though the village is so scattered there is little on-street atmosphere. La Stua is an après-ski bar on the Sella Ronda route, with accordion music later on. The Igloo at Plan de Gralba is also 'good fun for those first few beers before heading back to Selva in virtual darkness'. For a civilised early drink try the good value ski-school bar at the base of the Dantercëpies piste. Or the Costabella is cosy, serving good gluwein. Café Mozart on the main street is highly recommended for ice cream and cakes.

Ardent après-skiers should visit the Posta Zirm in Corvara. 'The ski-boot tea dance was excellent,' recommends one reporter. Tour operators often organise transport back to other resorts.

For thigh-slapping in Selva later on, the Laurinkeller has good atmosphere though it's 'quite expensive', while the Luislkeller gets 'a very rowdy German and Scandinavian clientele'.

La Bula 'has live music every night, and gets quite lively later'. The disco of the hotel Stella next door has a 'good crowd and is well used by Brits'.

OFF THE SLOPES

Good variety

There's a sports centre, lovely walks and sleigh rides on Alpe di Siusi; and snow-shoeing around Chertz is reputed to be good. The charming town of Ortisei is well worth a visit for its large hot-spring swimming pool, shops, restaurants and lovely old buildings.

Pedestrians can reach numerous good restaurants, nicely scattered around the mountains, by gondola or cable-car. Car drivers have Bolzano and Innsbruck within reach and tour operators do trips to Cortina.

Ortisei 1235m

Ortisei is a market town with a life of its own, and its local slopes aren't on the main Sella Ronda circuit. It's full of lovely buildings, pretty churches and pleasant shops. The lift to the south-facing slopes is very central, and the north-facing Alpe di Siusi lifts are only slightly further out. The nursery area, school and kindergarten are at the foot of these slopes, but there's a fair range of family accommodation on the piste side of the road. The fine public indoor pool and ice rink are also here.

There are hotels and self-catering to suit all tastes and pockets and many good restaurants, mainly specialising in local dishes. Après-ski is quite jolly, and many bars keep going till late.

Corvara 1570m

Corvara is the most animated Sella Ronda village east of Selva, with plenty of hotels, restaurants, bars and sports facilities.

It's well positioned, with village lifts heading off to reasonably equidistant Selva, Arabba and San Cassiano. The main shops and some hotels cluster around a small piazza, but the rest of the place sprawls along the valley floor.

Colfosco 1645m

Colfosco is a smaller, quieter version of Corvara, 2km away. It has a fairly compact centre with a sprawl of large hotels along the road towards Selva. It's connected to Corvara by a horizontal-running chair-lift. In the opposite direction, a series of drag-lifts head off to the Passo Gardena and on to Selva.

Several large hotels between them provide plenty of services.

San Cassiano 1530m

San Cassiano is a pretty little village, set in an attractive, tree-filled valley. It's a quiet, slightly upmarket resort, full of well-heeled Italian families and comfortable hotels. The local slopes, the Alta Badia, though sizeable and fully linked, are something of a spur of the main Sella Ronda. Adventurers who want to do the circuit will find it a tiresome business.

Phone numbers
From abroad use the prefix +39 (and do **not** omit the initial '0' of the phone number).

The best hotel in town is the 4-star Rosa Alpina (0471 849500). The tea dance in Corvara's Posta Zirm is a must if you want something lively. Stop there at the end of the day, taxi home afterwards. Later nightlife is very limited: the Rosa Alpina has dancing and there's a bowling alley. Walking in the pretty scenery is the main off-slope activity; swimming is the other. There is no nursery or ski kindergarten.

La Villa 1435m

La Villa is similar to neighbouring San Cassiano in most respects – small, quiet, pretty, unspoilt – but it is slightly closer to Corvara, making it rather better placed for the main Sella Ronda circuit. There is a home piste that features on the World Cup circuit, and village amenities include a pool, bowling and skating on a frozen lake.

Canazei 1440m

Canazei is a sizeable, bustling, pretty, roadside village of narrow streets, rustic old buildings, traditional style hotels and nice little shops, set in the Sella Ronda's most heavily wooded section of mountains. There's plenty going on generally – and it has been recommended by many reporters.

A 12-person gondola is the only mountain access point, but it shifts the queues (which can be long) quickly.

A single piste back to the village is linked to runs returning from both Selva and Arabba, but it is often closed. The local Belvedere slopes are uniformly easy and dotted with mountain restaurants. The village nursery slope is good but inconveniently located and is unlikely to be used after day one. The Bella Vista at the top of the gondola has a lovely sun terrace and is recommended for 'excellent food and wine'.

Lack of spoken English in the school can be a problem. Children have an all-day nursery and ski kindergarten. But again the lack of spoken English could pose problems.

There are no really luxurious hotels, but the grand 3-star Dolomiti (0462 601106) in the middle of town is one of the original resort hotels. The chalet-style Diana (0462 601477) is charming and five minutes from the village centre. The 4-star Astoria (0462 601302) has a pool and minibus transfers to and from the gondola.

There are numerous restaurants. The Stala, Melester and Te Cevana are all worth a try. And après-ski is reasonably animated. La Stua dei Ladins serves good local wines. The Husky and Roxy bars are worth a visit.

Off-slope entertainment consists of beautiful walks and shopping. There's also a pool, sauna, Turkish baths and skating in neighbouring Alba.

Campitello 1445m

Campitello is smaller and quieter than next-door Canazei and still unspoilt. By Sella Ronda standards, the village is nothing special, particularly when there's little snow – which is much of the time – but it's still pleasant.

It's remarkably quiet during the day, having no slopes to the village. A cable-car takes you up into the Sella Ronda circuit. If you don't wish to return by lift, take the piste to Canazei and catch a bus.

The Rubino (0462 750225) is an elegant 4-star with a pool and close to the cable-car. The 4-star Park Diamant (0462 750440) next door is under the same management. Campitello is quite lively – we've had trouble getting near the bar of the throbbing Da Giulio in the early evening. Neighbouring Pozza has ice skating and floodlit slopes. There are no children's facilities.

Arabba 1600m

Arabba is a small, traditional, still uncommercialised village. But the lifts into the Sella Ronda in both directions make it very convenient. The high north-facing slopes have the best natural snow and steepest pistes in the Dolomites. The 4-star Sport (0436 79321) is the best hotel, and reporters recommend the large, 3-star Portavescovo (0436 79139): 'Excellent hotel, wonderful food, nicely furnished rooms and a well-equipped fitness centre'. It has the only pool in town. Apartment-conversion chalets and self-catering accommodation are available.

Venues for eating out are limited. 7 Sass and Ru De Mont are cheap and cheerful pizzerias. The après-ski is also limited – but cheap. The atmospheric Rifugio Plan Boe is good for a last drink on the pistes before heading back to the village. Bar Peter and hotel bars are the focal points. The Delmonego family's bar-caravan, at the bottom of the piste, is the tea-time rendezvous.

Sestriere 2000m

Modern resort with access to the Milky Way

WHAT IT COSTS

HOW IT RATES

The slopes

Snow	***
Extent	****
Experts	***
Intermediates	****
Beginners	***
Convenience	****
Queues	***
Restaurants	**

The rest

Scenery	***
Resort charm	*
Off-slope	*

What's new

Turin has been chosen to host the 2006 Olympic Winter Games; Sestriere will host many of the Alpine events.

The fun-park is being improved and expanded for 2001/02. And the village nursery lifts are being improved.

MOUNTAIN FACTS

Figures relate to the whole Milky Way area

Altitude	1390m-2825m
Lifts	92
Pistes	400km
Blue	12%
Red	67%
Black	21%
Artificial snow	75km
Recco detectors used	

PISTE MAP

Sestriere is covered on the Sauze d'Oulx map on page 378.

- ⊕ Part of the extensive Franco-Italian Milky Way area
- ⊕ Snow reliability is usually good, with extensive artificial backup
- ⊕ Local slopes suitable for most levels, with some tougher runs than most neighbouring resorts
- ⊖ Much of the purpose-built village is scruffy, though likely to improve for the 2006 Winter Olympics
- ⊖ Situated at one extreme of the Milky Way area – so inconvenient for exploration of the whole network
- ⊖ Weekend and peak-period queues
- ⊖ Little après-ski during the week

Sestriere was built for snow – high, with north-west-facing slopes – and it has very extensive snowmaking, too. So even if you are let down by the notoriously erratic snowfalls in this corner of Italy, you should be fairly safe here – certainly safer than in Sauze d'Oulx, over the hill.

THE RESORT

Sestriere was the Alps' first purpose-built resort. It sits on a broad, sunny and windy col at 2000m. Neither the site nor the village, with its large apartment blocks, looks very hospitable, though the buildings have benefited from recent investment, and they'll doubtless get more in the run-up to the Olympics. There are some interesting buildings, but much of the village still seems rather scruffy.

This is not the most convenient of purpose-built resorts, but location is not crucial. Borgata is less convenient for nightlife and the shops and a recent report suggests that buses to and from Sestriere are infrequent.

THE MOUNTAINS

Sestriere is at one extreme of the big Franco-Italian Milky Way area. The local slopes have two main sectors: Sises, directly in front of the village, and more varied Motta, above Borgata – to the north-east and 225m higher.

Slopes There are mainly drag- and chair-lifts on the local north-west-facing slopes. Access to Sansicario and the rest of the Milky Way is via gondola from Borgata to Col Basset, at the top of the Sauze d'Oulx area, and a drag-lift back up to Monte Fraiteve. Snow permitting, the return to Sestriere is via a long red from the top of the gondola at Col Basset – or the newly restored red run down from Monte Fraiteve. But it more often depends on riding the gondola down. Signposting and the piste map are poor.

Snow reliability WIth most of the local slopes facing north-west and ranging from 1840m to 2820m, and an extensive snowmaking network covering most of the Sises sector and half of Motta, snow-cover is usually reliable for most of the season. The notoriously erratic snowfalls in the

LAPRESSE

Club Med: Distinctive? Yes. Attractive? Well ... →

Phone numbers
From abroad use the prefix +39 (and do **not** omit the initial '0' of the phone number).

TOURIST OFFICE

Postcode 10058
t +39 (0122) 755444
f 755171
sestriere@montagnedoc.it
www.sestriere.it
www.vialattea.it

Milky Way often leave the rest of the area seriously short of snow while the extensive snowmaking in Sestriere provides fairly reliable cover. The sunny runs down from Sauze suffer from poor snow and do not benefit from any artificial backup.

Experts There is a fair amount to amuse experts – steep pistes served by the drags at the top of both sectors, and off-piste slopes in several directions from here and Monte Fraiteve.

Intermediates Both sectors also offer plenty for confident intermediates, who can explore practically all of the Milky Way areas, conditions permitting.

Beginners The terrain is good for beginners, with several nursery areas and the gentlest of easy runs down to Borgata. However, one reporter points out that there is a lack of easy intermediate runs to progress to.

Cross-country There are two loops covering a total of 10km.

Snowboarding The fun-park next to the Cit Roc chair on Sises is being improved and expanded for 2001/02.

Queues The lifts are mainly modern though there are still some inadequate old ones. But queues for the main lifts occur at the weekends and holidays. The lifts from Borgata to Sestriere can be a bottleneck at the end of the day. Queues occur when poor weather closes the gondola link to Sauze. A recent visitor reported a large proportion of lift closures at the end of March, despite good snow.

Mountain restaurants The local ones could only be described as 'fair' – the one at Sises is best – but there are better ones further afield.

Schools and guides Lack of spoken English can be a problem.

Facilities for children There are no special facilities for children.

STAYING THERE

How to go Most accommodation is in apartments.

Hotels There are a dozen hotels, mostly of 3-star or 4-star status. Just out of the village (but not far from a lift) is the luxurious Principi di Piemonte (0122 7941). The Savoy Edelweiss (0122 77040) is a central, attractive 3-star. The distinctive round towers in the centre are the Club Med quarters.

Eating out There are plenty of options. Try Lu Peirol for home-made ravioli and atmosphere. Tre Rubineti has been highly recommended for 'outstanding Italian cooking' and an enormous wine list. Last Tango and La Baita are also well regarded.

Après-ski Après-ski is quiet during the week but becomes lively at weekends: the Black Sun pub-cum-disco and the Tabatà club are great fun, and the Prestige and Palace are two of the many little bars that liven up. The Pinky is one of the best of the bars that double as eateries, with lots of low sofas in the classic Italian casual-chic style.

Off the slopes There's quite a bit to do, but it isn't a very attractive place, despite some smart shops.

SNOWPIX.COM / CHRIS GILL

M Sises provides world-class slalom slopes directly facing the village ↓

La Thuile 1450m

Little-known resort with extensive slopes and link with France

WHAT IT COSTS

3

HOW IT RATES

The slopes	
Snow	****
Extent	***
Experts	**
Intermediates	****
Beginners	****
Convenience	***
Queues	****
Restaurants	*
The rest	
Scenery	***
Resort charm	***
Off-slope	**

What's new

For 2000/01 a hands-free ski pass was introduced.

MOUNTAIN FACTS

Covers combined La Rosière and La Thuile area

Altitude	1175m-2640m
Lifts	35
Pistes	150km
Green	11%
Blue	37%
Red	34%
Black	18%
Artificial snow	22km
Recco detectors used	

SNOWPIX.COM / CHRIS GILL

The slopes down to the village are shady, and cold in winter ↓

- ⊕ Fair-sized area with good lift system linked to La Rosière in France
- ⊕ Free of crowds and queues
- ⊕ Excellent beginner and easy intermediate slopes
- ⊕ Some very handy accommodation

- ⊖ All the seriously tough pistes are low down, and most of the low, woodland runs are tough
- ⊖ Mountain restaurants are generally disappointing
- ⊖ Not the place for lively après-ski

La Thuile deserves to be better known internationally. The slopes best suit beginners and intermediates not seeking challenges, but are not devoid of interest for experts, particularly if the snow conditions are good.

You'll doubtless want to venture over the border to La Rosière. These days, Italian grooming is better than French, and Italian piste grading often overstates difficulty. Moving from smooth red runs to bumpy blues can be a shock.

The resort

La Thuile is a resort of parts. At the foot of the lifts is the modern Planibel complex, with places to stay, a leisure centre, bars, shops and restaurants – like a typical French purpose-built resort, but with a distinctly Italian atmosphere (and on a much smaller scale). But many people find this rather soulless and prefer to stay in the old town across the river (served by a regular free bus service). La Thuile was a mining town that largely fell into disrepair until the slopes were developed. Much of the old town has been restored and new buildings tastefully added, but parts are still in ruins, with a 'ghost town' feel to them. There are reasonable restaurants and bars but not many entertaining shops.

The slopes link with La Rosière, over the border in France. Courmayeur is easily reached by car, and Cervinia is about an hour away. A car isn't a great help around the resort, especially if staying in the Planibel complex.

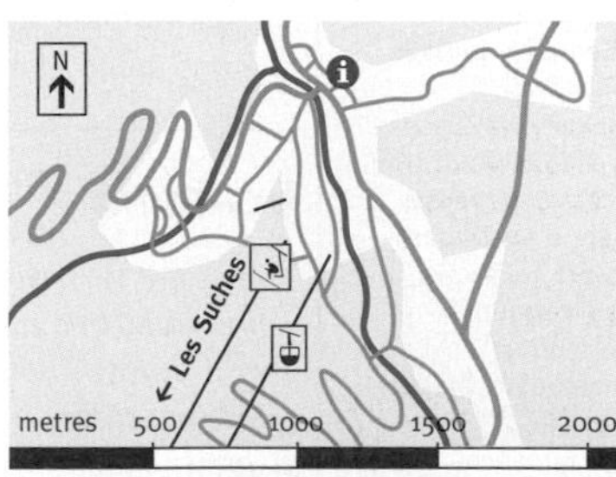

The mountains

La Thuile has quite extensive slopes, with the great attraction that they are normally very uncrowded. Many runs are marked red, but deserve no more than a blue rating. The lift system is excellent in general: a fast chair or gondola takes you up the mountain, and there are high-speed chairs to the top. However, more than one reporter comments that the open chair linking La Thuile and La Rosière (the Belvedere) is very slow and cold.

THE SLOPES
Big and gentle

The lifts out of the village take you to **Les Suches**, with shady black runs going back down directly to the village through the trees, and reds taking a more roundabout route. From here chairs and drags take you to **Chaz Dura** for access to a variety of gentle bowls facing east. You can go off westwards from here to the Petit St Bernard road. From both sides there are lifts back to the ridge, the high-point of Belvedere being the launch pad for excursions via

LIFT PASSES

2000/01 prices in euros

Dominio Internazionale
Covers all lifts in La Rosière and La Thuile.

Beginners One baby-lift in village. Points tickets (50 points 40).

Main pass
1-day pass 28
6-day pass 134
(low season 121)

Children
Under 12: 6-day pass 104
(low season 93)
Under 6: free pass with every purchase of an adult pass of the same length

Short-term passes
Half-day pass (adult 20).

Alternative periods
6-day (non-consecutive) pass available (adult 163).

Alternative passes
Valle d'Aosta pass covers La Thuile, Courmayeur, Gressoney, Champoluc, Alagna, Cervinia, Valtournenche and Pila (adult 6-day 155).

the Col de la Traversette to La Rosière in France. What is not clear from the map is that the French slopes are largely south-facing. They also tend to be steeper than those in La Thuile.

SNOW RELIABILITY
Good

Most of La Thuile's slopes are north- or east-facing and above 2000m, so the snow generally keeps well. There's also a decent amount of snowmaking. You can check the conditions at Les Suches via a camera and screens in the resort.

FOR EXPERTS
Rather limited

The only steep pistes are those down through the trees from Les Suches back to the resort. The steepest of these, the Diretta, is serious stuff.

The best of the rest is the area above the Petit St Bernard road, where there is some genuinely black terrain and plenty of off-piste. You'll find many red runs overgraded.

Heli-lifts are available. One of the best, to the Ruitor glacier, has a 20km run into France ending at La Rosière.

FOR INTERMEDIATES
Something different

La Thuile has some good intermediate runs, and its link with La Rosière adds adventure. But timid intermediates are best off staying on home ground: the start of the route back from La Rosière is a short but tricky red, and most of La Rosière – particularly the top half of the mountain – is fairly challenging.

The bowls above Les Suches have many gentle blue and red runs, ideal for cruising and practising. There are also long reds through the trees back to the resort. The red runs on the other side of the top ridge, down towards the Petit St Bernard road, offer a greater challenge.

boarding *These are great slopes for learning to board. You can confine yourself to riding chair-lifts and the gondola, and most of the slopes are very easy with good snow. For more experienced boarders there are some great tree runs, and the link with France offers some good off-piste possibilities. Though there are no specific facilities for boarders, there is a lot of good free-riding to be had, as well as some good long carving runs. The nightlife is pretty quiet during the week.*

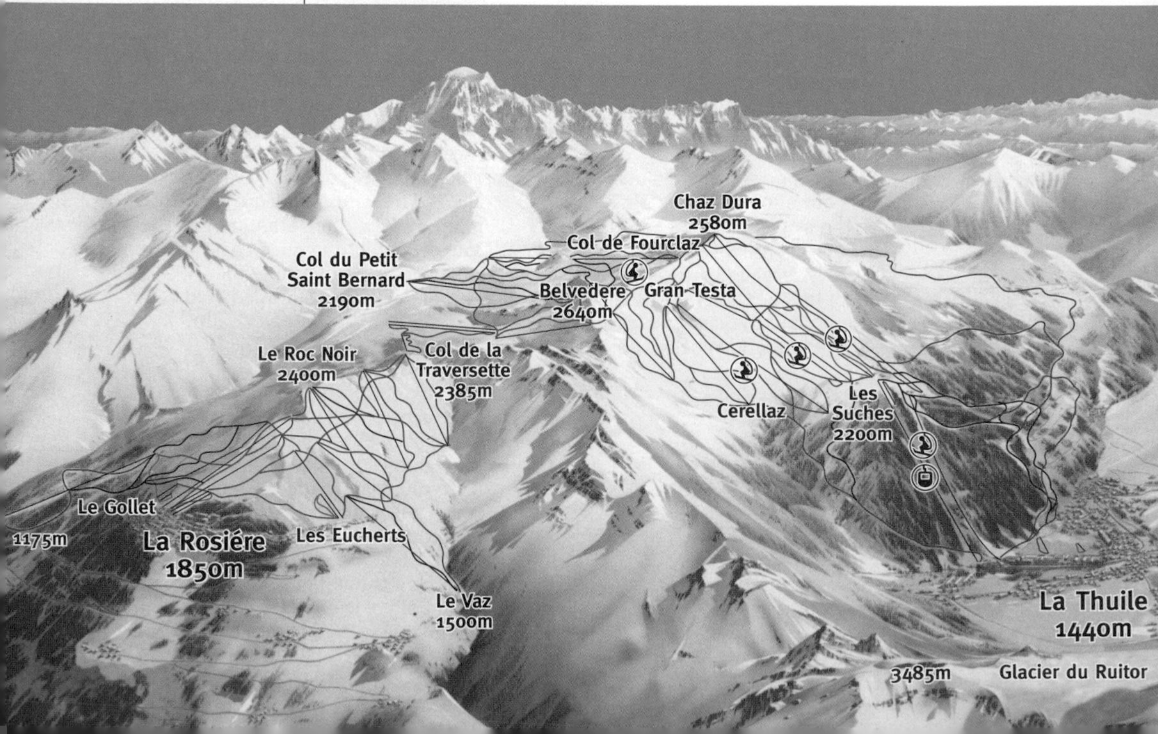

SCHOOLS/GUIDES

2000/01 prices in euros

La Thuile
Classes
6 2hr days: 102
Children's classes
Ages: from 5
6 2½hr days: 102
Private lessons
1hr
29 for 1 person

CHILDCARE

There is a free non-skiing kindergarten for children from 4 to 12 years.

GETTING THERE

Air Geneva, transfer 2½hr, transfer, 2½hr, Turin.

Rail Pré-St-Didier (10km); regular buses to resort.

ACTIVITIES

Indoor Two swimming pools, amusement arcade, gymnasium, solarium, sauna, squash
Outdoor heli-skiing

Phone numbers
From abroad use the prefix +39 (and do **not** omit the initial '0' of the phone number).

TOURIST OFFICE

Postcode 11016
t +39 (0165) 884179
f 885196
lathuile@lathuile.net
www.lathuile.net

FOR BEGINNERS
Good, but slopes can be crowded

There are nursery slopes at village level and up at Les Suches. There's a good gentle green run above Les Suches, and some shallow blues, but nothing is segregated from the main slopes. The slopes above the Belvedere lift are a possibility, but the runs down to the resort are red and black – so taking the gondola back down is the only real option.

FOR CROSS-COUNTRY
Varied choice

La Thuile has four loops of varying difficulty on the valley floor, adding up to 20km of track.

QUEUES
Very rare

The resort has a very effective lift system for the number of visitors, and all our reporters comment that they never had to queue.

MOUNTAIN RESTAURANTS
Disappointing

Our reporters continue to voice their disappointment with the mountain restaurants, with the exception of the Riondet (on Chaz Dura) where a reporter found 'genuinely good food and hospitality'.

SCHOOLS AND GUIDES
Good instruction

Once again our reporters this year praise the school for its reasonably sized classes and fair instruction.

FACILITIES FOR CHILDREN
OK when they're older

There's a Miniclub, and children over the age of 5 can join adult ski classes. One reporter found a registered childminder to look after his daughter.

Staying there

HOW TO GO
Some choice of packages

The number of tour operators going to La Thuile is increasing.
Hotels Choice is between the swanky but characterless 4-star Planibel, a few 3-stars and simpler places.
((((4) **Planibel** (0165 884541) American-style 'resort hotel' with all mod cons, including a pool and underground parking. Right at the base of the lifts.
(((3) **Eden** (0165 885050) Comfortable modern hotel in traditional wood and stone style. Very close to lifts.
((2) **Chalet Alpina** (0165 884187) Simple place with the atmosphere of a catered chalet, on the outskirts of the resort.
Self-catering The Planibel apartments are praised for their proximity to the slopes and great value. Some have been refurbished recently – others are said to be 'showing signs of wear'.

EATING OUT
Limited, but consistently good

La Thuile doesn't have a lot of restaurants, but we've received positive reports on most of them. La Fordze is recommended for its good mix of French/Italian local dishes and the Brasserie du Bathieu for its 'huge' portions. Lo Créton and La Grotta offer good-value pizza and pasta, and the restaurant in the Eden is mentioned for its 'excellent' buffet table.

APRES-SKI
Early to bed

Après-ski and nightlife are limited. La Cage aux Folles (formerly the Rendezvous bar) is popular after the lifts close and on into the evening (it's also recommended for its food). La Bricole bar – with big-screen television and disco – is considered 'easily the busiest and liveliest bar in La Thuile' by one reporter. The Fantasia disco warms up well after midnight.

OFF THE SLOPES
Limited options

The Planibel complex has decent leisure facilities and a good pool, but there are few attractive walks or shops. Excursions to Courmayeur can be organised. It's easy for pedestrians to ride up the gondola for lunch.

Switzerland is home to some of our favourite resorts. For sheer charm and spectacular scenery, the 'traffic-free' villages of Wengen, Mürren, Saas-Fee and Zermatt take some beating. Many resorts have impressive slopes too – including some of the biggest, highest and toughest runs in the Alps, as well as a lot of reassuring intermediate terrain. For fast, efficient, queue-free lift networks, Swiss resorts rarely match French standards – but the real black spots are gradually disappearing. And there are compensations: the world's best mountain restaurants, for example. People always seem to associate Switzerland with high prices. Barring some catastrophic accident to the Swiss franc, prices are never going to be low, but usually they are not greatly different from prices in major French resorts; and what you get for your money is first class.

While France is the home of the purpose-built resort, Switzerland is the home of the traditional mountain village that has transformed itself from farming community into year-round holiday centre. Many of Switzerland's most famous mountain resorts are as popular in the summer as in the winter, or more so. This creates places with a much more lived-in feel to them, and a much more stable local community. Many are still run and dominated by a handful of families who were lucky or shrewd enough to get involved in the early development of the area.

This has its downside as well as advantages. The ruling families are able to stifle competition and prevent newcomers from taking a slice of their action. Alternative ski schools, competing with the traditional school and pushing up standards, are much less common than in other countries, for example.

Switzerland is associated with high living, and the swanky grand hotels of St Moritz, Gstaad, Zermatt and Davos are beyond the dreams of most ordinary holidaymakers. And even in more modest resorts, nothing is cheap. But the quality of the service you get for your money is generally high. Swiss hotels are some of the best in the world. The trains run like clockwork to the advertised timetable (and often they run to the top of the mountain, doubling as ski-lifts). The food is almost universally of good quality and much less stodgy

than in neighbouring Austria. In Switzerland you get what you pay for: even the cheapest wine, for example, is not cheap; but it is reliable – duff bottles are very rare.

Perhaps surprisingly for such a long-established, traditional, rather staid skiing country, Switzerland has gone out of its way to attract snowboarders by developing the facilities they look for. Even staid resorts like Davos cater for boarders thoroughly.

GETTING AROUND THE SWISS ALPS

Access to practically all Swiss resorts is fairly straightforward when approaching from the north – just pick your motorway. Many of the high passes that are perfectly sensible ways to get around the country in summer are closed in winter, which can be inconvenient if you are moving around from one area to another. There are car-carrying trains linking the Valais (Crans-Montana, Zermatt etc) to Andermatt

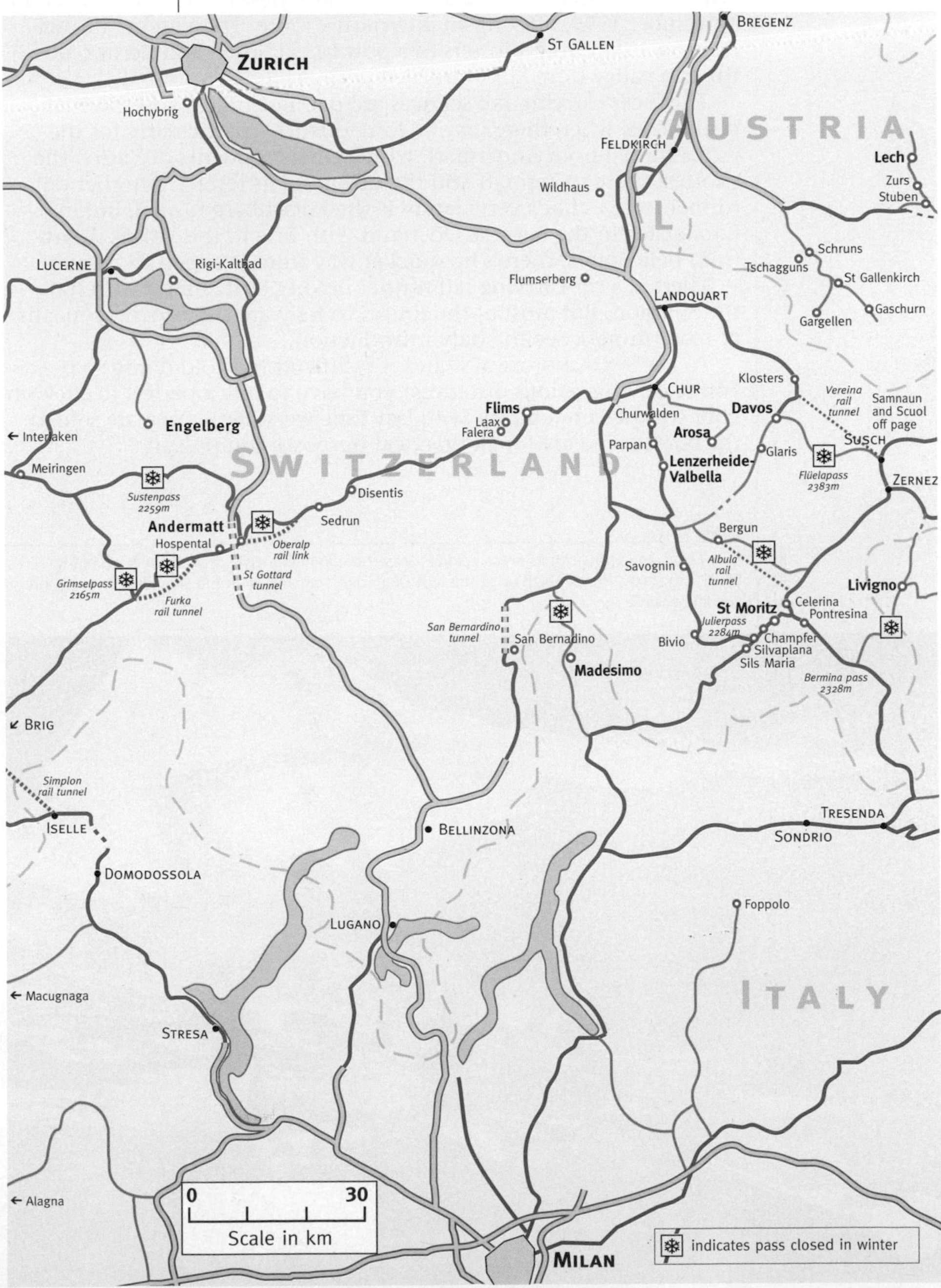

Introduction

via the Furka tunnel and Andermatt to the Grisons (Flims, Davos etc) via the Oberalp pass – closed to road traffic in winter but open to trains except after very heavy snowfalls.

St Moritz is more awkward to get to than other resorts, as well as being further away. The main road route is over the Julier pass. This is normally kept open, but at 2284m it is naturally prone to heavy snowfalls that can shut it for a time. The fallback is the car-carrying rail tunnel under the Albula pass. A major new rail tunnel opened in November 1999, offering an alternative route. The Vereina tunnel runs for 19km from Klosters to a point near Susch and Zernez, down the Inn valley from St Moritz.

These car-carrying rail services are painless unless you travel at peak times, when there may be long queues – particularly for the Furka tunnel from Andermatt, which offers residents of Zürich the shortest route to Zermatt and the other Valais resorts. Another rail tunnel service that's very handy is the Lötschberg tunnel, linking Kandersteg in the Bernese Oberland with Brig in the Valais. Apart from helicopters, there's no quicker way from Wengen to Zermatt.

There is a car-carrying rail tunnel linking Switzerland with Italy – the Simplon. But most of the routes to Italy are kept open by means of road tunnels. See the Italy introduction.

To use Swiss motorways (and it's difficult to avoid doing so if you're driving serious distances) you have to buy a permit to stick on your windscreen (costing SF40 last time we asked). They are sold at the border, and are for all practical purposes compulsory.

SNOWPIX.COM / CHRIS GILL

Saas-Fee is one of the classic Swiss resorts – cosily traditional in style, free of traffic except for a few electric taxis, and set high up at the foot of glaciers tumbling from the shoulders of a ring of 4000m peaks ↓

Adelboden 1355m

Chocolate-box village with fragmented slopes

WHAT IT COSTS

HOW IT RATES

The slopes

Snow	**
Extent	***
Experts	**
Intermediates	***
Beginners	****
Convenience	***
Queues	***
Restaurants	**

The rest

Scenery	***
Resort charm	****
Off-slope	****

MOUNTAIN FACTS

Altitude	1070m-2355m
Lifts	55
Pistes	166km
Blue	48%
Red	44%
Black	8%
Artificial snow	8km
Recco detectors used	

- ⊕ Traditional chocolate-box-pretty mountain village
- ⊕ Extensive slopes to suit all standards, linked to Lenk
- ⊕ Several other worthwhile resorts within day-trip range
- ⊕ Good off-slope facilities

- ⊖ Fragmented slopes – two sectors are a bus-ride away
- ⊖ Unreliable snow cover
- ⊖ Few challenges unless you look off-piste

Adelboden is unjustly neglected by the international market: for intermediates who find relaxing, pretty surroundings more important than convenience for the slopes it has a lot of appeal. The slopes are extensive, and investment in lifts over recent years has meant great improvements.

THE RESORT

Adelboden fits the traditional image of a Swiss mountain village: old chalets with overhanging roofs line the quiet main street (cars are discouraged), and 3000m peaks make an impressive backdrop. Adelboden is in the Bernese Oberland, to the west of the much better-known Jungfrau resorts (Wengen etc). These resorts are within day-trip range, as is Gstaad to the west.

The village is compact, and there are efficient buses to the outlying areas (covered on the lift pass); the ideal location for most people is close to the main street.

THE MOUNTAINS

Adelboden's slopes are split into five sectors (no longer six) – two of them unlinked and a bus-ride from the village. The rest of the sectors are linked, by piste if not by lift, and the ski area stretches across to the village of Lenk, with its own local slopes a bus-ride across the valley from the main body of slopes shared with Adelboden.

Slopes Lifts near the main street access three of the sectors. Schwandfeldspitz (aka Tschenten), just above the village, is reached by a cable-car/gondola hybrid. The main gondola to nearby Höchsthorn and then on to more remote Geils-Sillerenbühl starts below the village at Oey (where there is a car park), but a connecting mini-gondola starts from close to the main street. This is much the biggest sector, with long, gentle runs (and some short, sharp ones) from 2200m down to 1350m – back to

ADELBODEN TOURIST OFFICE

The valley is as scenic as the village is cosy and traditional →

the village and over to Lenk.

Engstligenalp, a flat-bottomed high-altitude bowl is reached by a cable-car 4km south of the resort; Elsigenalp is even more remote, but more extensive.

Snow reliability Most pistes are below 2000m – so snow reliability is not a strong point. But most slopes are above 1500m and north-facing. There is little snowmaking.

Snowboarding There's a good snowboard fun-park and half-pipe at Hahnenmoos, and a natural playground at Engstligenalp. Two specialist schools offer tuition. Beginners may find the high proportion of drag-lifts off-putting.

Experts There are some genuine black pistes at Geils, and a less genuine one on Höchsthorn. Off-piste possibilities are good and remain untracked for much longer than in other, more macho resorts. The Laveygrat and Chummi chairs in the Geils bowl access routes down to both Adelboden and Lenk (though there are protected forest areas to avoid). Engstligenalp has off-piste potential too – and is a launching point for tours around the Wildstrubel.

Intermediates All five areas deserve exploration by intermediates. At Geils there is a lot of ground to be covered – and trips across to Lenk's gentle Betelberg area (covered by the lift pass) are possible.

Beginners There are good nursery slopes in the village and at the foot of nearby sectors. At Geils there are glorious long, easy runs to progress to.

Cross-country The trails along the valleys towards Engstligenalp and Geils are extensive, varied and scenic.

Queues The main gondola isn't entirely free of queues. And the old Hahnenmoos gondola is a bottleneck and is due for replacement. If snow low down is poor, the Engstligenalp cable-car can't cope.

Mountain restaurants There are pleasant mountain restaurants with terraces in the Geils sector. Aebi is particularly charming. A reporter recommends the Metschstand: 'Sunny, small, simple, but good.'

Schools and guides Past reports on the Adelboden ski school have been mixed – 'caring, good English', but 'mix of abilities within group'.

Facilities for children There is a 'very good' ski nursery and kindergarten (taking children from three to six years). And several hotels have child-minding facilities.

STAYING THERE

How to go The choice of how to go is wide. Several UK operators go there, and there are locally bookable chalets and apartments and some 30 pensions and hotels (mainly 3- and 4-star).

Hotels The 4-star Park Hotel Bellevue (673 8000) is pricey, but we have received good reports of its food and facilities (pool and sauna). The central 3-star Adler Sporthotel (673 4141) is pretty and recommended. The little Bären (673 2151) is a simple but captivating wooden chalet.

Eating out The possibilities are varied, and include one or two mountain restaurants – Aebi, for example. Guests on a half-board arrangement can dine at other affiliated hotels twice a week.

Après-ski The après-ski is traditional, based on bars and tea rooms – the Iglu and Time Out are recommended.

Off the slopes There is a fair amount to do, and easy access for pedestrians to a couple of mountain restaurants. There are hotel pools open to the public, indoor and outdoor curling and skating rinks, and a couple of toboggan runs.

Phone numbers
From elsewhere in Switzerland add the prefix 033.
From abroad use the prefix +41 33.

TOURIST OFFICE

Postcode CH-3715
t +41 (33) 673 8080
f 673 8092
info@adelboden.ch
www.adelboden.ch

Andermatt 1445m

An old-fashioned resort with some great off-piste

WHAT IT COSTS

3

HOW IT RATES

The slopes

Snow	****
Extent	*
Experts	****
Intermediates	**
Beginners	*
Convenience	***
Queues	**
Restaurants	*

The rest

Scenery	***
Resort charm	****
Off-slope	**

MOUNTAIN FACTS

Altitude	1445m-2965m
Lifts	13
Pistes	56km
Blue	29%
Red	42%
Black	29%
Artificial snow	0km
Recco detectors used	

- ⊕ Attractive, traditional village
- ⊕ Excellent snow record
- ⊕ Great off-piste terrain. Heli-skiing is also available

- ⊖ Three separate areas of slopes are all fairly limited
- ⊖ Unsuitable for beginners
- ⊖ Limited off-slope diversions and après-ski
- ⊖ Cable-car queues at peak times

Little old Andermatt was rather left behind in the mega-resort boom of the 1960s and 70s. But its attractions have not faded for those who like their mountains tall, steep and covered in deep powder.

THE RESORT

Andermatt is quite busy in summer and gets weekend winter business, but at other times seems deserted apart from the soldiers whose barracks are here. It is quietly attractive, with wooden houses lining the dog-leg main street that runs between railway and cable-car stations. The railway is the only link in winter with the Grisons to the east and the Valais to the west – trains carry cars. The village is small and location is not much of an issue.

THE MOUNTAINS

Andermatt's skiing is split over three separate, unlinked mountains. The slopes are almost entirely above the trees, and the individual areas are all limited in extent. The Gotthard–Oberalp lift pass also covers the nearby resorts of Sedrun and Disentis – reached by train over the Oberalp pass.

Slopes A two-stage cable-car from the edge of the village serves magnificent, varied slopes on the open, steep and usually empty slopes of Gemsstock. Across town is the gentler Nätschen/ Gütsch area. And a bus- or train-ride along the valley is Winterhorn (above Hospental). There is also an isolated nursery slope further along at Realp.

Snow reliability The area has a justified reputation for reliable snow.

Experts It is most definitely a resort for experts. The top Gemsstock cable-car serves two main slopes: the north-facing bowl beneath it is a glorious, long black slope (about 800m vertical), usually with excellent snow, in which

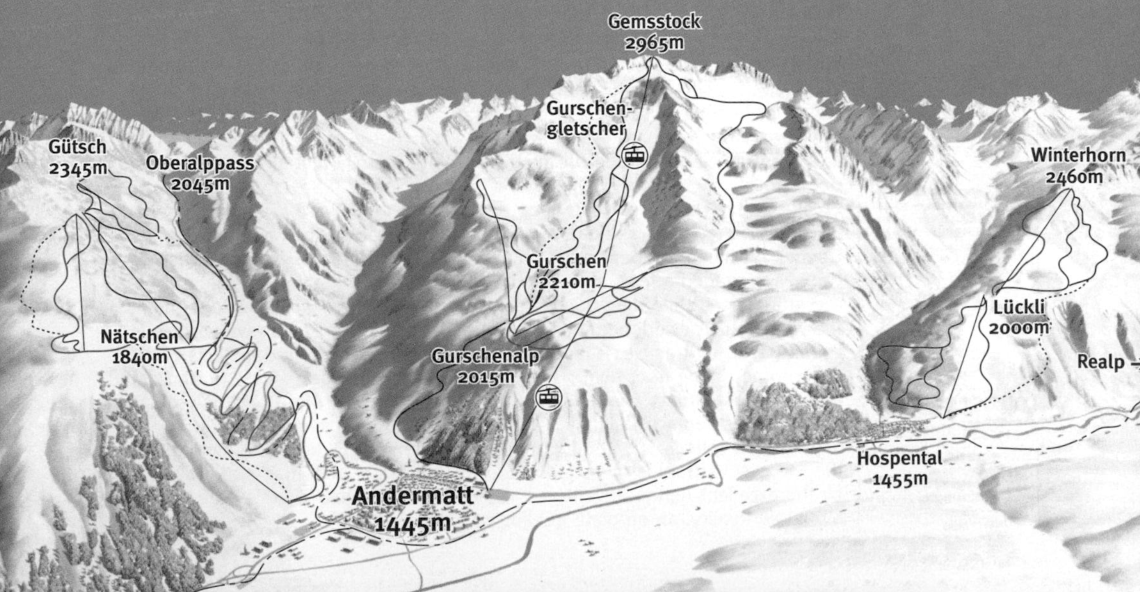

It's a towny little resort – especially when there's no snow on the roofs →

ANDERMATT TOURIST OFFICE

Phone numbers
From elsewhere in Switzerland add the prefix 041.
From abroad use the prefix +41 41.

TOURIST OFFICE

Postcode CH-6490
t +41 (41) 887 1454
f 887 0185
info@andermatt.ch
www.andermatt.ch

there is usually one marked run down, and countless off-piste routes; the Sonnenpiste, once again properly graded red after a spell as a black, is a fine open run curling around the back of the mountain to the mid-station. From mid-mountain to the village there is a black run, not too steep but heavily mogulled. There are guides for off-piste adventure, and heli-trips. Both Nätschen and Winterhorn have black pistes and off-piste areas.

Intermediates Intermediates needn't be put off the Gemsstock: the Sonnenpiste can be tackled, and there is a pleasant red run at mid-mountain, served by a drag-lift. Winterhorn's modest lift system offers all standards of piste down the 1000m vertical, while Nätschen's south and west-facing mountain is perfect for confidence-building.

Beginners The lower half of Nätschen has a good, long, easy run back to the village. But essentially this is not a resort for beginners.

Snowboarding There are facilities (park and pipe) on Nätschen and on the Gemsstock.

Cross-country There is a 20km loop along the valley towards Realp.

Queues Although the Gemsstock cable-car was upgraded a few years ago, it can still generate morning queues in the village and at mid-mountain when conditions are attractive. It takes a while to get going after heavy snow.

Mountain restaurants The few mountain restaurants are basic.

Schools and guides The good work of the Swiss ski school is overshadowed by the excellent Alpine Adventures Mountain Reality, an off-piste guiding

outfit run by the famous Alex Clapasson (who also happens to run the lift company).

Facilities for children There are no special facilities; but there are slopes they can handle at Nätschen and the Swiss school takes children's classes.

STAYING THERE

How to go Andermatt's accommodation is in cosy 2- and 3-star hotels.

Hotels Gasthaus Sternen (887 1130), in the centre, is an attractive old chalet with a lively restaurant and bar. The 3-star Sonne (887 1226), between the centre and the lift, is welcoming and comfortable. The neighbouring 2-star Bergidyll (887 1455) is a British favourite. Alpenhotel Schlüssel (888 7088) is new, with spacious rooms.

Après-ski Après-ski revolves around cosy local bars, and finishes early during the week – Café Gotthard and the terrace at the Drei Könige & Post hotel are recommended.

Eating out Options are limited to a handful of restaurants and bars.

Off the slopes There's little to do off the slopes.

Arosa 1800m

Classic all-round winter holiday resort

WHAT IT COSTS

HOW IT RATES

The slopes

Snow	***
Extent	**
Experts	*
Intermediates	***
Beginners	****
Convenience	***
Queues	****
Restaurants	****

The rest

Scenery	***
Resort charm	**
Off-slope	****

What's new

For 2000/01 the new Carmenna fast quad replaced two old lifts from mid-mountain to near the top of the Weisshorn. There are plans to replace the Plattenhorn T-bar (an important link from Tschuggen to Hörnli) with a quad chair for 2001/03.

MOUNTAIN FACTS

Altitude 1800m-2655m	
Lifts	14
Pistes	70km
Blue	38%
Red	57%
Black	5%
Artificial snow	9km
Recco detectors used	

- ⊕ Classic winter sports resort ambience
- ⊕ Some of the best cross-country loops in the Alps
- ⊕ Few queues
- ⊕ Relatively good snow reliability
- ⊕ Plenty to do off the slopes
- ⊕ Several other worthwhile resorts within day-trip range

- ⊖ Spread-out village means some inconveniently situated accommodation
- ⊖ Limited slopes for mileage-hungry intermediates
- ⊖ Few challenges for experts
- ⊖ Some very dreary buildings in main village

The classic image of a winter sports resort is perhaps an isolated, snow-covered Swiss village, surrounded by big, beautiful mountains, with skating on a frozen lake, horse-drawn sleighs jingling through the streets and people in fur coats strolling on mountain paths. Arosa is just that. It's a pity that many of its comfortable hotels date from the time when pitched roofs were out of fashion.

THE RESORT

High and remote, Arosa is in a sheltered basin at the head of a beautiful wooded valley, in contrast to the open slopes. It's a long, winding road or splendid rail journey from Chur. Obersee, at the centre, is not a pretty sight because of its block-like buildings, though its lakeside setting adds charm. The rest of Arosa is scattered, with a hill separating Obersee from the older, prettier Inner-Arosa – which has a chair, a drag and (away from the village) a gondola. Arosa is quiet; its relaxed ambience attracts an unpretentiously wealthy clientele of families and older people, with very few Brits.

The village is a spread-out place and some accommodation is a long walk from the lifts, but where you stay is not very important as there is an excellent free shuttle-bus. Inner-Arosa has the advantage of lifts into both sectors of the slopes.

You can get to Davos–Klosters, Flims and Lenzerheide by road, though it's quite a drive down to Chur.

THE MOUNTAINS

Arosa's slopes are situated in a wide open bowl, with all the runs returning eventually to the village at the bottom.

Slopes Arosa's slopes are modest and lack challenges. The slopes are spread widely over two main sectors. The Weisshorn sector faces mainly south and south-east. Tschuggen, halfway to the Weisshorn peak, is the major lift junction, reachable from both Obersee and Inner-Arosa. An inconveniently sited gondola below Inner-Arosa is the

AROSA TOURIST OFFICE

The occasional chalet shape has crept in alongside the many rectangular blocks →

main access to the east and north-east-facing slopes of the second sector, Hörnli. Drags and chair-lifts allow you to travel either way between the two sectors. One reporter commented on the abundance of walking paths crossing pistes, and points out the need for caution at these intersections.

Snowboarding There is a park and a half-pipe and a specialist school.

Snow reliability Arosa has relatively good snow reliability. The best south-facing pistes are above 2000m, and the shadier Hörnli slopes hold their snow well.

Experts Arosa isn't the resort for a keen expert. The two black runs don't deserve their grading, but you can ski off-piste to and from Lenzerheide – with a guide.

Intermediates This is a good area for intermediates who want to take it easy and aren't looking for high mileage or much challenge. The home run from the Carmenna middle-station to Obersee (the last section through woodland) is 'a delight'.

Beginners The Tschuggen nursery slopes are excellent and usually have good snow, but they get a lot of through traffic. Inner-Arosa has a quieter but more limited area usually reserved for children.

Cross-country Though it lacks the sheer length of trails of many resorts, Arosa (with 27km) has some of the best and varied cross-country loops in the Alps.

Queues Arosa does not suffer from serious queues. There can be waits for the Weisshorn cable-car, though recent reporters had no problems.

Mountain restaurants The mountain restaurants can get crowded in peak season, despite what seems a reasonable number dotted around. Carmennahütte is the best, while Tschuggenhütte is a rustic little refuge with a nice sun terrace. Alpenblick does 'very good food' and Hörnli is a 'welcoming hut in a dramatic position' at the top of the gondola.

Schools and guides The Swiss and ABC schools are the main ski-schools There's a lot of demand for private lessons from the affluent Arosa guests.

Facilities for children Arosa seems a good choice for a family holiday, and several hotels have kindergartens for the children.

STAYING THERE

How to go Arosa is a hotel resort, with a high proportion of 3- and 4-stars.

Hotels The 4-star Waldhotel National (378 5555) with 'really special food' is recommended. The Belvédère (377 1335) is 'very friendly and handy for the cable-car'.

Eating out Most restaurants are hotel-based, some with a very high reputation. The Kachelofa-Stübli at the Waldhotel National is excellent.

Après-ski Après-ski is quite lively. The Carmenna hotel by the ice rink has a popular piano bar. Later the popular bar of the Eden hotel has live music.

Off the slopes There are plenty of alternatives. You can get a pedestrian's lift pass, and many mountain restaurants are reachable via 40km of cleared, marked walks. Sleigh rides in the mountains are beautiful, and there's a popular outdoor ice rink.

Phone numbers
From elsewhere in Switzerland add the prefix 081.
From abroad use the prefix +41 81.

TOURIST OFFICE

Postcode CH-7050
t +41 (81) 378 7020
f 378 7021
arosa@arosa.ch
www.arosa.ch

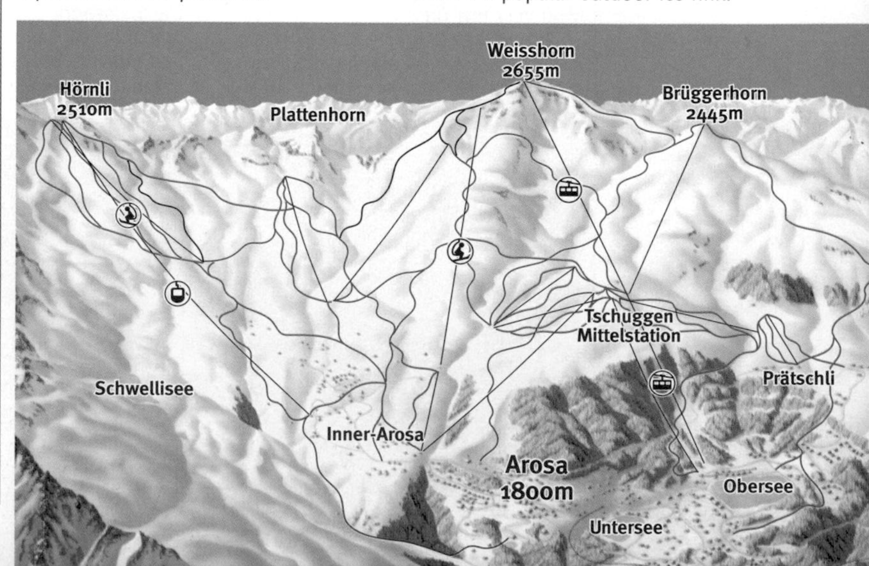

Champéry 1050m

Picture-postcard village, with access to the Portes du Soleil

WHAT IT COSTS

HOW IT RATES

The slopes

Snow	**
Extent	*****
Experts	***
Intermediates	****
Beginners	**
Convenience	*
Queues	****
Restaurants	***

The rest

Scenery	****
Resort charm	****
Off-slope	***

What's new

There are plans to replace old double chair-lifts from Grand Paradis and at Planachaux by fast six-packs. But when we went to press it had not been confirmed if this would happen for 2001/02 or 2002/03.

- ➕ Charmingly rustic mountain village
- ➕ Cable-car takes you into very extensive Portes du Soleil slopes
- ➕ Quiet, relaxed – yet plenty to do off the slopes
- ➕ Easy access for independent travellers

- ➖ Local slopes suffer from the sun
- ➖ No runs back to the village – and sometimes none back to the valley
- ➖ Beginner slopes not easy to get to and not that gentle
- ➖ Not many tough slopes nearby

With good transport links and sports facilities, Champéry is great for anyone looking for a quiet time in a lovely place, especially if they have a car – but not if they're beginners. Not bad access to the Portes du Soleil: Avoriaz is fairly easy to get to – and there may be fresh powder there when Champéry is suffering.

THE RESORT

Set beneath the dramatic Dents du Midi, Champéry is a village of old wooden chalets. Friendly and relaxed, it would be ideal for families if it wasn't separated from its slopes by a steep, fragmented mountainside.

Down a steepish hill, away from the main street, are the cable-car, sports centre and a convenient terminus for the narrow-gauge railway.

THE MOUNTAINS

Champéry's local slopes are as friendly and relaxing as the village, at least for intermediates. There's an electronic lift pass that you can keep in your pocket.

Slopes Champéry's sunny slopes are part of the extensive Portes du Soleil circuit. The bowl of **Planachaux** is way above the village, with a couple of runs leading to the valley at **Grand Paradis**, a short bus-ride from Champéry.

There are no pistes to Champéry itself, though on rare occasions local conditions allow off-piste trips. Explore the Portes du Soleil by heading west towards Avoriaz or north-east to Champoussin, Morgins and Châtel.

For more on the Portes du Soleil, see the chapters on Avoriaz, Châtel and Morzine in France.

Snow reliability The snow on the north-facing French side of the area is usually better than on the sunnier Swiss side to the south. The area would benefit from more snowmaking.

Snowboarding Not ideal for beginners, and everyone else needs to have mastered drag-lifts to access the Portes du Soleil and tougher terrain. There are a couple of fun-parks and half-pipes nearby, but the daddy of all fun-parks, is in Avoriaz – definitely worth a look.

Experts Few local challenges unless the off-piste down to Champéry is skiable, and badly placed for most of the tough Portes du Soleil runs. The Swiss Wall, on the Champéry side of Chavanette, is intimidatingly long and steep, but not that terrifying. There's scope for off-piste at Chavanette and on the broad

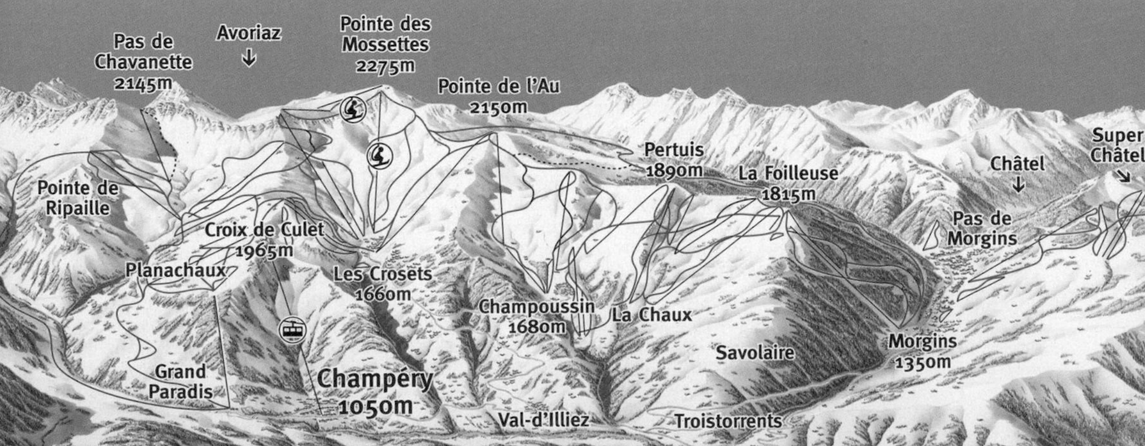

MOUNTAIN FACTS

Altitude	975m-2350m
Lifts	219
Pistes	650km
Blue	51%
Red	40%
Black	9%
Art. snow	522 acres

Recco detectors used

slopes of Les Crosets and Champoussin.

Intermediates Confident intermediates have the whole Portes du Soleil at their disposal. Locally, the runs home to Grand Paradis are good when the snow conditions allow and Les Crosets is a junction of several fine runs.

Also worth trying are the slightly tougher pistes down from Mossette and Grand Conche, the runs back from Pointe de l'Au, Champoussin's leisurely cruising and runs to Morgins – delightful tree-lined meanders.

Beginners Go elsewhere if you can. Despite a good school, Champéry is far from ideal – even the Planachaux runs, where lessons are held, are steepish.

Cross-country Advertised, but very unreliable snow.

Queues Few local problems. If snow is good, avoid end-of-the-day queues for the cable-car down by taking the Grand Paradis run to the valley floor and getting the free bus back to town.

Mountain restaurants Chez Coquoz at Planachaux and Chez Gaby above Champoussin are recommended. The tiny Lapisa on the way to Grand Paradis is delightfully rustic. Further afield, try the Les Lindarets refuges (see Avoriaz).

Schools and guides The few reports that we've had are free of criticism.

Facilities for children The tourist office has a list of child minders. The Swiss ski school takes three- to seven-year-olds.

STAYING THERE

Although it's a small village, most hotels are some way from the cable-car.

How to go Limited packages available. Easy access for independent travellers.

Chalets Tour op Piste Artiste has some.

Hotels Wide choice from 3-star down. Prices low compared with smarter Swiss resorts. The Champéry (479 1071) is the best – a comfy chalet on the main street. Beau Séjour (479 1701) is at the southern end. The National (479 1130) has 'friendly staff, lovely breakfast'.

Self-catering Some apartments are available to independent travellers.

Eating out A fair choice. Two of the best for local specialities are just outside the village: Cantines des Rives is a beautiful traditional chalet; the Grand Paradis is excellent, if pricey, and decorated with stuffed animals.

Locally, try the the Farinet or the 'excellent' restaurant in the Hotel du Nord. Mitchell's bar also has a good restaurant and the Café du Centre will serve Asian food this season. Two evenings a week, when the slopes are floodlit, the restaurant at the top of the cable-car opens.

Après-ski Mitchell's has big sofas, fireplace and a great atmosphere till late. Below the 'rather seedy' Pub, the Crevasse disco is one of the liveliest places in town. The underground Mines d'Or nightclub has 'ridiculously high' drink prices. The Café du Centre will be run by a Scot and have its own micro brewery. Other suggestions are the bars in the hotel Suisse Golden Tulip, the Bar des Guides and the Farinet's spacious cellar nightclub – fun when there are enough people to give it atmosphere, mostly at weekends.

Off the slopes Walks, particularly along to Val d'Illiez, are pleasant, and the narrow-gauge railway allows excursions to Montreux, Lausanne and Sion. There's a decent sports centre.

Les Crosets 1660m

A good base for a quiet time and slopes on the doorstep. Good snow and a prime position on the Portes du Soleil. Not much here, but the Hotel Télécabine (479 1421) is homely, serving great food in a lovely rustic dining room.

Champoussin 1680m

Champoussin is, theoretically, a good family choice – no through traffic, convenient for the slopes, no noisy late-night revellers and the comfortable Royal Alpage Club hotel – pool, gym, disco, two restaurants (476 8300).

Morgins 1350m

A fairly scattered but attractive resort with some nightlife. Suits those with a car, who can easily get to the higher slopes and bars of Châtel. The Hotel Bellevue (477 8171) and the Pension de Morgins (477 1143) are well thought of. Ski Morgins has catered chalets.

Phone numbers
From elsewhere in Switzerland add the prefix 024.
From abroad use the prefix +41 24.

TOURIST OFFICE

Postcode CH-1874
t +41 (24) 479 2020
f 479 2021
champery-ch@portesdusoleil.com
www.champery.ch

Crans-Montana 1500m

Sun-soaked slopes with stunning views and big town base

WHAT IT COSTS

HOW IT RATES

The slopes

Snow	**
Extent	***
Experts	**
Intermediates	****
Beginners	***
Convenience	**
Queues	***
Restaurants	***

The rest

Scenery	****
Resort charm	**
Off-slope	****

What's new

The separate lift companies have merged, and there is now a single lift ticket for the whole area – including the glacier.

- + Large piste area suitable for all, except if you prefer black runs
- + Splendid wooded setting with magnificent panoramic views
- + Fair number of woodland slopes – good in bad weather
- + Modern, well-designed lift system, with few queues
- + Golf course provides excellent, gentle nursery slopes
- + Very sunny slopes (but see right)
- + Excellent cross-country trails

- − Snow badly affected by sun except in early season
- − Large town (rather than village) composed partly of big chalet-style blocks but mainly of dreary cubic blocks – and therefore entirely without Alpine atmosphere
- − Bus or car rides to lifts from much of the accommodation
- − Not many challenging pistes

When conditions are right – clear skies above fresh, deep snow – Crans-Montana takes some beating. The mountains you bounce down with the midday sun full on your face are charmingly scenic, the slopes broken up by rock outcrops and forest. The mountains you gaze at – Zermatt's Matterhorn just discernible among them – are mind-blowing. When conditions are right, mountain-lovers may forgive Crans-Montana anything – in particular, its inconvenient, linear layout and the plain, towny style of its twin resort centres.

Sadly, conditions are more often wrong than right. Except in the depths of winter, the strong midday sun quickly bakes the pistes. For someone booking six months ahead, this is enough to keep Crans-Montana off the shortlist. For those who can time a visit according to the weather – and are more interested in impressive distant views than cosy immediate surroundings – the resort is worth serious consideration.

The resort

Crans-Montana celebrated 100 years as a resort in 1993, but is far from being a picturesque Swiss chocolate-box village. Set on a broad shelf facing south to the great mountains across the Rhône valley, it is really two villages, their centres a mile apart and their fringes now merging. Strung along a busy road, the resort's many hotels, villas, apartments and smart shops are mainly dull blocks with little traditional Alpine character.

Fortunately, the resort's many trees help to screen the buildings, and they make some areas positively attractive. And its wonderful setting means you get a lot of sun as well as superb views. There are several lakes and two golf courses, one home to the Swiss Open.

The resort is reached by good roads, and by a fast funicular railway up from Sierre to Montana. It depends heavily on summer conference business, which sets the tone even in winter. Hotels tend to be comfortable and fairly formal, village facilities varied but daytime-oriented, and visitors middle-aged and dignified. In the evenings there's little Alpine-village atmosphere.

Gondolas go up to the main slopes from both villages. Crans is the more upmarket, with expensive jewellery shops, a casino, and a high fur-coat count. It is well situated for the pretty golf course area, which has baby lifts for complete beginners, a cross-country trail and lovely walks. Montana has somewhat cheaper restaurants and bars.

There are other gondola base stations and places to stay further east: at Violettes in Les Barzettes (the lift from here connects directly to the top glacier lift and is the fastest way to the top) and at Aminona.

MOUNTAIN FACTS

Altitude	1500m-3000m
Lifts	35
Pistes	160km
Blue	38%
Red	50%
Black	12%
Artificial snow	17km
Recco detectors used	

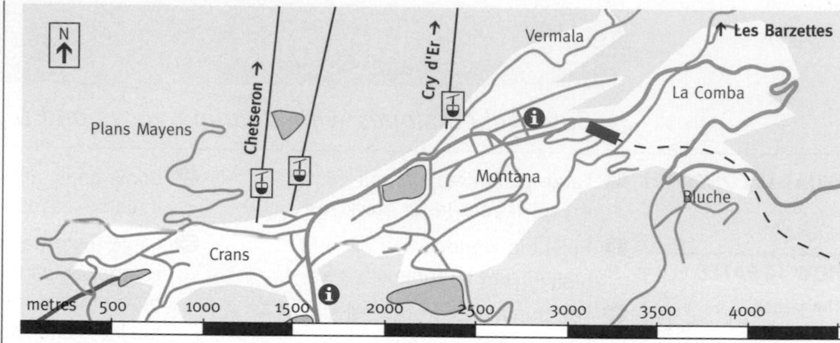

The mountains

Although it has achieved some prominence in ski-racing, Crans-Montana has slopes that suit intermediates well, with few challenges and no nasty surprises. Beginners are well catered for.

THE SLOPES
Interestingly fragmented

Crans-Montana's 160km of piste are spread over three well-linked areas, all equally suitable for intermediates of varying abilities and persuasions. The upper runs are wide and good but many of those down to the valley are narrow woodland paths.

Cry d'Er is the largest sector – an open bowl descending into patchy forest, directly above Montana. Cry d'Er itself is the meeting point of many lifts and the starting point of the cable-car up to the sector high point of Bella-Lui (2545m). Cry d'Er is served directly by two gondolas – a newish eight-person one from just above Crans, and another from just above central Montana, which has a useful mid-station where beginners can get off and access high-altitude nursery slopes. A third gondola goes from the west side of Crans to Chetseron, with a drag above going on to Cry d'Er.

The next sector, reached by another powerful gondola directly from Les Barzettes (labelled 'Violettes' on the resort piste map), is focused on Les Violettes, starting point of the jumbo gondola up to the Plaine Morte glacier. There are three linking routes from Cry d'Er to the **Violettes–Plaine Morte** sector. The highest, starting at Bella-Lui (or, strictly, at Col du Pochet, a short run and drag beyond) used to be off-piste but is now an official red run. Bella-Lui is also the start of the Men's Downhill course (Piste Nationale) that goes past Cry d'Er to Les Barzettes.

The third **Petit Bonvin** sector is served by a gondola up from Aminona at the eastern end of the area. This is linked to Les Violettes by red and blue runs passing the drag and chair-lift at La Toula.

Reporters complain of confusion caused by poor signing.

Anzère is nearby to the west, though the slopes aren't linked. You can make expeditions to Zermatt, Saas Fee and Verbier by road or rail.

SNOW RELIABILITY
The resort's main drawback

Crans-Montana's slopes go up to glacier level at 3000m, but this is misleading; the runs on the Plaine Morte glacier are very limited and,

LIFT PASSES

2001/02 prices in Swiss francs

Crans-Montana-Aminona
Covers all lifts in Crans-Montana and Aminona and the ski-bus.

Beginners Points card

Main pass
1-day pass 54
6-day pass 253

Senior citizens
Over 65 (men), 62 (women) 6-day pass 215)

Children
Under 15: 6-day pass 152
Under 6: free pass

Short-term passes
Half day from 11 (adult 45) or 12.30 (adult 36).

Alternative periods
6 non-consecutive days (adult 292).

boarding *Despite Crans-Montana's staid, middle-aged image, boarding is very popular. There are plenty of broad, smooth pistes, lots of underexploited off-piste, and good specialist facilities. Aminona is a good area for experienced boarders and has a fun-park, and there's a half-pipe in the more central Cry-d'Er area. There are a number of specialist shops and the Stoked snowboard school. The main lifts are chairs and gondolas, and the drag-lifts are usually avoidable with good planning. It is a good place for beginner and intermediate boarders – and, of course, slush is not such a problem for novice boarders to navigate as it is for novice skiers! But avoid the ice first thing in the morning. Nightlife tends to be a fairly civilised affair, though; the George & Dragon can get quite lively and has a 'typical' pub atmosphere.*

excellent though it is, the solitary run down from there does not make this a snowsure area as a whole. Few of the other slopes are above 2250m, and practically all get a lot of direct sun. Late in the season, at least, this makes for slush in the afternoons, rock-hard ice in the mornings, and a tendency for snow to disappear. There is now snowmaking on the main runs down from both Violettes and Cry d'Er to Montana, from Cry d'Er to Crans and the bottom part of the run from Chetseron. We applaud these efforts; but it is a losing battle. We have never experienced good snow on the runs down to the valley.

FOR EXPERTS

Lacks challenging pistes

There are few steep pistes and the only decent moguls are on the short slopes at La Toula. There's plenty of off-piste in all sectors, but particularly beneath Chetseron and La Tza; guides are usually easy to book. The off-piste tour from Plaine Morte to Aminona is recommended.

The Piste Nationale course is far from daunting taken at 'normal' speed, but has some enormous jumps just above Les Marolires. The direct run from La Tza to Plumachit is fairly testing in places, especially when icy.

FOR INTERMEDIATES

Lots of attractive, flattering runs

Crans-Montana is very well suited to intermediates. Pistes are mostly wide, and many of the red runs don't justify the grading. They tend to be uniform in difficulty from top to bottom, with few nasty surprises for the nervous. Avid piste-bashers enjoy the length of many runs, plus the fast lifts and good links that allow a lot of varied mileage.

The 11km run from Plaine Morte to Les Barzettes starts with superb top-of-the-world views and powder snow, and finishes among pretty woods. But many people love the top half so much ('my favourite run in Europe') they do it repeatedly, curtailing their descent halfway down at either the Barmaz or Cabane de Bois chair-lifts to Les Violettes, for quicker access to the top gondola. Because of the gondola's high capacity the run can get crowded.

The short runs from Bella-Lui to just

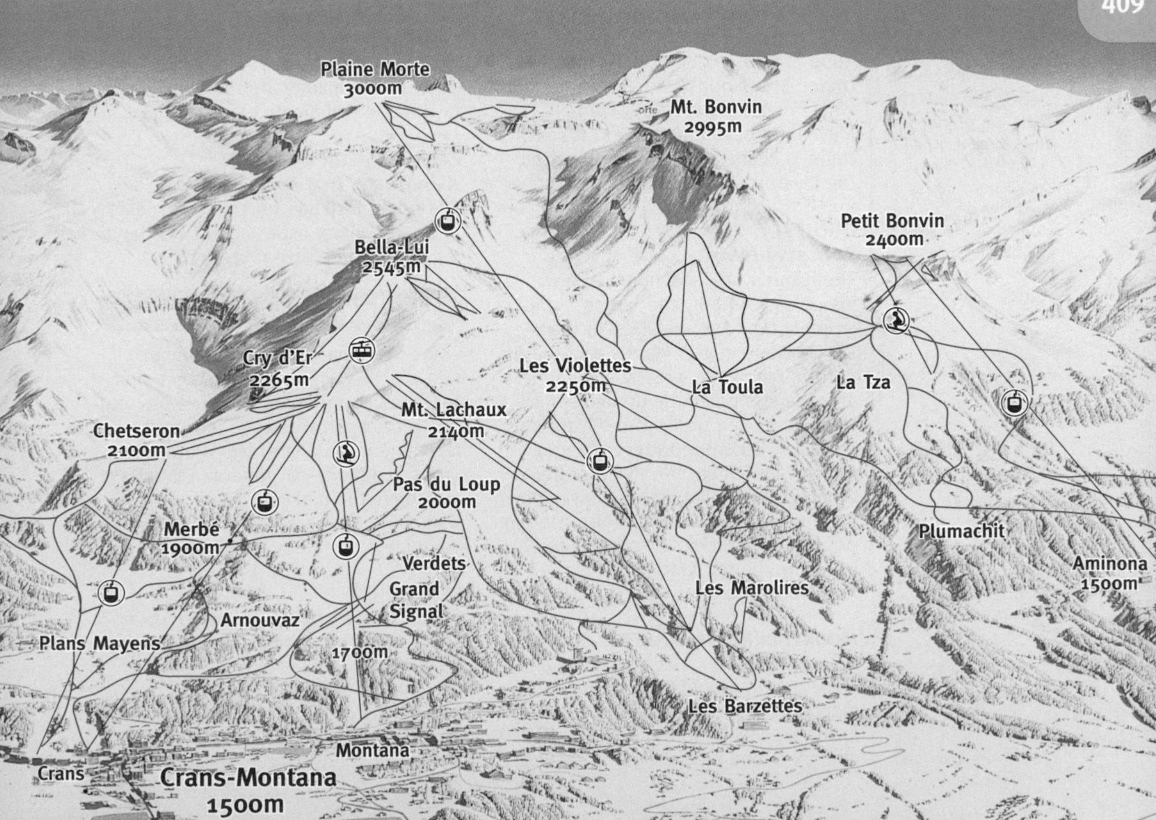

SCHOOLS/GUIDES

2000/01 prices in Swiss francs

Swiss
Classes 6 days
3hr: 9.30-12.30
6 days: 170
Children's classes
Ages: from 3
9.30-12.30 or 9.30-4pm
Half day 45
1 day with meal 80
Private lessons
Hourly
60 for 1hr

Ski & Sky
Private lessons
Hourly
60 for 1hr

Stoked Snowboard
Classes Half day: 50

CHILDCARE

The Montana ski school runs a kindergarten with skiing available up at Signal and the Crans school on the golf course for children aged 3 to 6, from 9.30 to 4.30.

There are several other kindergartens. In Montana, Fleurs des Champs takes children aged 3 months to 7 years; and Zig-Zag takes children from 2 to 6 years.

GETTING THERE

Air Sion, transfer 30min. Geneva, transfer 3hr.

Rail Sierre (15km), Sion (22km); regular buses to resort.

below Cry d'Er have some of the best snow and quietest slopes in the area, and provide fine views of awesome Montagne de Raul. The Piste Nationale is a good test of technique, with plenty of bumps but also lots of room. The quietest area, and good for groups of varying intermediate standards, is the Petit Bonvin sector.

FOR BEGINNERS
Plenty to offer the first-timer
There are three excellent nursery areas, with slopes of varying difficulty. Complete beginners have very gentle slopes on the golf course next to Crans. Cry d'Er has an area of relatively long, easy runs, with up-the-mountain views and atmosphere as well as better snow. But the runs aren't just for beginners, and you do need a full lift pass. The Verdets–Grand Signal run is steeper, and the drag-lift can get terribly icy. Near-beginners can try the little run up at Plaine Morte.

FOR CROSS-COUNTRY
Excellent high-level trails
There are 40km of cross-country trails altogether. There are some pretty, easy trails (skating-style as well as classic) on and around the golf course. But what makes Crans-Montana particularly good for cross-country is its high-level route, in and out of woods, across the whole mountainside from Plans Mayens to beyond Aminona. 10km of trails at Plaine Morte are open when the lower trails are closed.

QUEUES
Few problems
The resort's big investment in new gondolas – notably the jumbo 'Funitel' gondola from Les Violettes to the Plaine Morte glacier slopes and the lift out of Crans – has greatly alleviated any queue problems – though bottlenecks can occur at the Nationale drag-lifts. Recent reporters say you rarely wait longer than five minutes – except occasionally if snow lower down is in poor condition. More of a problem can be bottlenecks on some pistes, including the top glacier run. The resort does not get weekend crowds.

MOUNTAIN RESTAURANTS
A good choice
There are 20 mountain restaurants, many offering table-service. The Merbé, at the Crans–Cry d'Er gondola mid-station, is one of the most attractive,

with good food in a pleasant setting just above the tree line. Advance bookings are recommended because it does get busy. Bella-Lui's terrace (with service) offers good views. The Chetseron eatery has fine views.

Petit Bonvin, at the top of the Aminona sector, has self-service and table-service sections, with superb views. There is not much choice in the Violettes sector, but we had a good meal on the table-service terrace of the main restaurant. And the small self-service Cabane des Violettes, 50m below this, gets rave reviews for food and views (be there early for a seat).

SCHOOLS AND GUIDES
Good reports
Both local branches of the Swiss school have mainly attracted favourable comments over the years.

FACILITIES FOR CHILDREN
Adequate, but few reports
The resort facilities for children seem to be adequate, especially in Montana, but we have no recent reports.

Staying there

Crans-Montana is quite sprawling. A free shuttle-bus links the villages and satellite lift stations during the day but can get very crowded – one reporter recommends taking a car. The main Crans and Montana gondola stations are above the main road and a tiring walk away. Many people store their equipment at lift stations overnight.

HOW TO GO
Much more choice on your own
There is a wide choice of hotels and apartments, and some are available through UK tour operators.
Hotels This conference resort has over 50 mainly large, comfy, expensive hotels. Most have three or more stars.

Phone numbers
From elsewhere in Switzerland add the prefix 027.
From abroad use the prefix +41 27.

ACTIVITIES

Indoor Hotel swimming pools, tennis, bowling, bridge, chess, golf simulator, squash, concerts, cinemas, casino, curling, ice skating, galleries
Outdoor Toboggan run, ski-bob, horse-riding, ice skating, paragliding, balloon flights

TOURIST OFFICE

Postcode CH-3962
t +41 (27) 485 0404
f 485 0460
info@crans-montana.ch
www.crans-montana.ch

((((5) **Crans-Ambassador** (485 4848) Health spa, with some rooms a bit shabby for its 5-star rating. Excellent treatments such as plant baths, mud packs. Just above Montana gondola.
((((5) **Pas du l'Ours** (485 9333) Our favourite. Chic, attractive, wood and stone Relais & Chateaux place with nine individually designed suites.
(((4) **Aïda Castel** (485 4111) Beautifully furnished in chic rustic style. Between the two resort centres. Outdoor pool.
((3) **La Forêt** (480 2131) Highly recommended. Almost at Les Barzettes, with minibus to lifts. Pool, good views.
((3) **National** (481 2681) Perfectly placed for the Crans-Cry d'Er gondola; 'quiet, comfortable, good food'.
((3) **Curling** (481 1242) Comfortable, near centre of Montana.
((3) **Robinson** (481 1353) B&B only; well placed near the National, in Crans.
Self-catering There are many apartments available.

EATING OUT
Plenty of alternatives

There is a good variety of restaurants from French to Lebanese. The best is the Michelin-starred Bistrot in the Pas de l'Ours hotel. Almost all the cheaper places are in Montana. The Dent Blanche is recommended for fondues. We had a good, simple Italian meal at Il Padrino in Crans. La Nouvelle Rotisserie is reputed to be excellent. The Gréni is a welcoming restaurant on the western fringe of Montana. Cervin up at Vermala is unusually rustic.

APRES-SKI
Can be ritzy, but otherwise quiet

Crans-Montana visitors tend to prefer quiet meals and drinks to raucous nightlife. Amadeus 2006 and Chez Nanette are tents on Cry d'Er serving close-of-play vin chaud. The George & Dragon in Crans is one of the liveliest, most crowded bars with 'the cheapest beer in town'. Reporters recommend Bar 1900, La Grange, Le Constellation and Indiana Café. The outdoor ice rink in Montana is 'fun'. The cinema has films in English. Bridge is played in the hotels Royal and Aïda.

OFF THE SLOPES
Excellent, but little charm

There are plenty of off-slope activities including lovely walks. Swimming is available in several hotels.

Sierre is easily reached for shopping, and the larger Sion is only a few minutes further. Montreux is within reach. Mountain restaurants are mainly at gondola and cable-car stations.

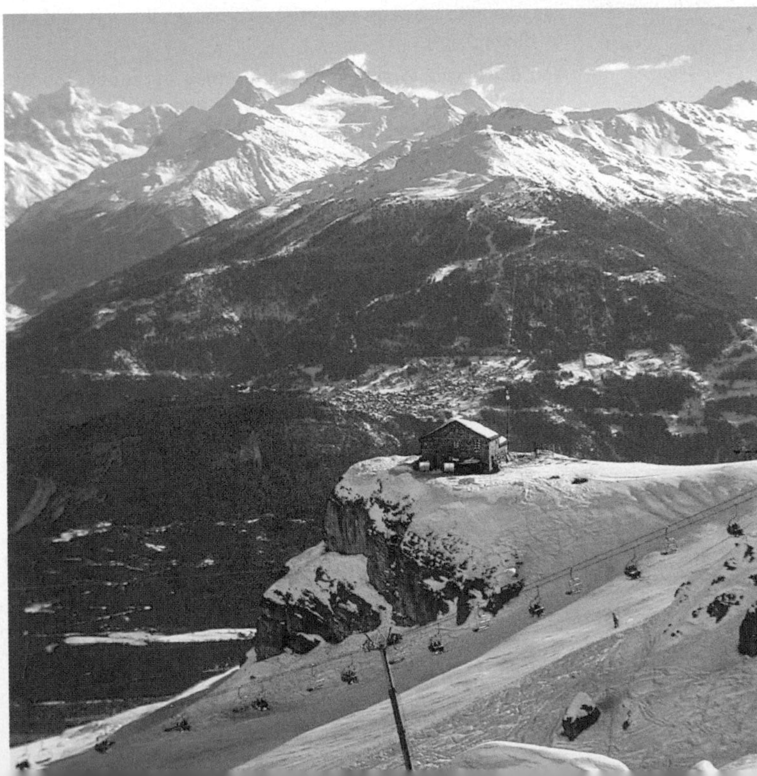

SNOWPIX.COM / CHRIS GILL

One of the chair-lifts back to Violettes from the end of the glacier run – and the ever-present view over the Rhône valley →

Davos 1550m

A big town surrounded by a great Alpine playground

WHAT IT COSTS

5

HOW IT RATES

The slopes

Snow	****
Extent	*****
Experts	****
Intermediates	*****
Beginners	**
Convenience	**
Queues	**
Restaurants	***

The rest

Scenery	****
Resort charm	**
Off-slope	*****

What's new

For 2000/01 the Dorftälli drag up to Weissfluhjoch was replaced by a six-seater chair-lift, starting at the mid-station of the Parsennbahn railway. Plans to replace the railway have been abandoned.

- ⊕ Very extensive slopes
- ⊕ Some superb, long and mostly easy runs away from the lifts
- ⊕ Lots of accessible off-piste terrain, with many marked itineraries and some short tours
- ⊕ Good cross-country trails
- ⊕ Plenty to do off the slopes – excellent sports facilities, pretty walks, good range of shopping
- ⊕ Some captivating mountain restaurants above Klosters
- ⊕ Klosters is an attractively villagey alternative base

- ⊖ Dreary block-style buildings of Davos spoil the views
- ⊖ Davos is a huge, city-like resort, rather plagued by traffic and lacking Alpine atmosphere
- ⊖ The slopes are spread over five or six essentially separate areas
- ⊖ Some access lifts are old and out-of-date, with long queues – especially the main funicular from Davos Dorf
- ⊖ Only one piste (black) back to Davos Dorf, which finishes 500m from town

Davos was one of the original mega-resorts, with slopes on a scale that few resorts can better, even today. But it's a difficult resort to like. It's easy to put up with slopes spread over separate mountains and relatively ancient, queue-prone lifts if that's the price of staying in a captivating Alpine village. But Davos is far from that.

Whether you forgive the flaws and fall for the resort depends on how highly you value three plus-points: the distinctive, super-long intermediate runs of the Parsenn area; being able to visit a different sector every day; and the considerable off-piste potential. We value all three, and we always look forward to visiting.

You don't have to stay in Davos to enjoy its slopes: Klosters offers a much more captivating alternative. Despite royal connections, it is not exclusive – on the contrary, it has exceptionally welcoming places to stay. But it is less well placed than Davos for exploring all the mountains.

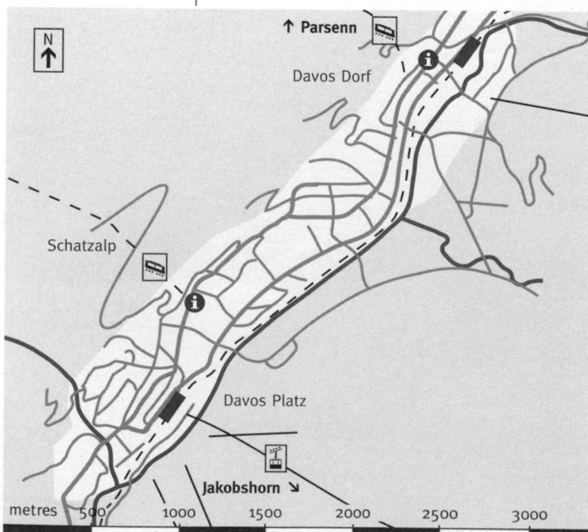

The resort

Davos is set in a high, broad, flat-bottomed valley, with its lifts and slopes either side. Arguably it was the very first place in the Alps to develop its slopes. The railway up the Parsenn was one of the first built for skiers (in 1931), and the first drag-lift was built on the Bolgen nursery slopes in 1934. But Davos was already a health resort; many of its luxury hotels used to be sanatoriums.

Sadly, that's just what they look like. There are still several specialist clinics and these, along with major conferences (including the World Economic Forum) and top international sporting events, are what the town of

↑ For ice skating, there is nowhere to beat Davos

SWISS-IMAGE / DAVOS TOURISMUS

Davos has become well known for. It is also a popular destination for athletes wanting to train at high altitude.

It has two main centres, Dorf and Platz, about 2km apart. Although transport is good, with buses around the town as well as the railway linking Dorf and Platz to Klosters and other villages, location is important. Easiest access to the slopes is from Dorf to the main Parsenn area, via the funicular railway; Platz is better placed for the Strela and Jakobshorn areas, the big sports facilities, the smarter shopping and evening action.

Davos shares its slopes with the famously royal resort of Klosters, down the valley – an attractive village with good links into the Parsenn area and its own separate sector, the sunny Madrisa. Klosters is described in more detail at the end of this chapter.

Trips are possible by car or rail to St Moritz (the Vereina rail tunnel offers access to the Engadine area without having to negotiate the snowy Flüelapass) and Arosa, and by car to Flims-Laax and Lenzerheide.

The mountains

The slopes here have something for everyone, though experts and nervous intermediates need to choose their territory with care. You could hit a different mountain in Davos every day for a week. In practice, the minor areas tend to be neglected by most visitors – and so are much quieter.

MOUNTAIN FACTS

Altitude	810m-2845m
Lifts	54
Pistes	320km
Blue	30%
Red	50%
Black	20%
Artificial snow	18km
Recco detectors used	

THE SLOPES
Vast and varied

The ancient Parsennbahn funicular from Davos Dorf takes you to the major lift junction of Weissfluhjoch, at one end of the **Parsenn**. At the other end is Gotschnagrat, reached by cable-car from Klosters. Between the two is the wide, open Parsenn bowl. From Davos Platz, a funicular takes you up to Schatzalp, at the base of the **Strela** area. Follow this with a long, two-person chair, a cable-car and finally a T-bar, and you will eventually gain access to the Weissfluhjoch.

Across the valley, **Jakobshorn** is reached by cable-car from Davos Platz; this is the main snowboarders' hill. **Rinerhorn** and **Pischa** are reached by bus or (in the case of Rinerhorn) train.

Beyond the main part of Klosters, a gondola goes up from Klosters Dorf to the sunny, scenic **Madrisa** area.

There is a small floodlit slope area at the Jakobshorn.

SNOW RELIABILITY
Good, but not the best

Davos is high by Swiss standards. Its mountains go respectably high too – though not to glacial heights. Not many of the slopes face directly south, but not many face directly north either. Snow reliability is generally good higher up but can be poor lower down – you may have to take the lifts down after using the Parsenn slopes. Snowmaking has been added on some lower runs.

FOR EXPERTS
Plenty to do, on- and off-piste

A glance at the piste map may give the misleading impression that this is an intermediate's resort – there aren't many black runs. But there are some excellent runs among them – the Meierhofer Tälli run to Wolfgang is a favourite – and there are also nine or ten off-piste itineraries (marked on the map and on the ground, but not prepared or patrolled). These are a key feature, adding up to a lot of expert terrain that can be tackled without expensive guidance. Some are on the open upper slopes, some in the woods lower down, some from the peaks right to the valley. Two of the steepest runs go from Gotschnagrat directly towards Klosters – around the infamous Gotschnawang slope. The Wang run is a seriously steep ski route (and rarely open, in our experience). Drostobel is less scary, though the overall gradient is little different.

There is also excellent 'proper' off-piste terrain for which guidance is needed, and some short tours. Arosa can be reached much more quickly on snow than by road or rail, but requires a return by rail via Chur. From Madrisa you can make tours to Gargellen in

LIFT PASSES

2001/02 prices in Swiss francs

Top Card
Covers all Davos and Klosters, the railway in the whole region and buses between the resorts.

Beginners Single and return tickets on main lifts in each area.

Main pass
1-day pass 57
6-day pass 279

Children
6-16: 6-day pass 168
Under 6 (with adult): free pass

Notes
A confusing array of passes are available for individual areas (Parsenn, Gotschna, Schatzalp, Jakobshorn, Rinerhorn, Gotschna and Madrisa) and combined areas, from a half day to 17 days. Several reporters have complained that not all passes are available at each base station.

boarding *Although the nursery slopes are not ideal, the long easy runs of the Parsenn are good for near-beginner boarders and you can avoid drags if you plan your runs. But intermediate and advanced boarders will get the most out of Davos's vast terrain and off-piste potential. The established boarder mountain is the Jakobshorn, with its half-pipe, fun-park, boarder-cross course and funky Jatz Bar nearby. The Rinerhorn and Pischa each have a fun-park. There are several cheap and cheerful hotels specially for boarders, including the 180-bed Bolgenhof hotel near the Jakobshorn, the Snowboardhotel Bolgenschanze and the Snowboarder's Palace.*

Austria's Montafontal. This means an exhausting one-hour walk on skins on the way back.

FOR INTERMEDIATES
A splendid variety of runs

For intermediates of any temperament, this is a great area. There are good cruising runs on all five mountains, so you would never get bored in a week. This variety of different slopes taken together with the wonderful long runs to the valleys makes it a compelling area with a unique character.

The epic runs to Klosters and other places (described in the feature box) pose few difficulties for a confident intermediate or even an ambitious near-beginner (one of your editors did the run to Klosters on his third day on skis, and we have heard from reporters who did the run to Küblis on their second holiday). And there are one or two other notable away-from-the-lifts runs to the valley. In particular, you can travel from the top of Madrisa back to Klosters Dorf via the beautiful Schlappin valley.

FOR BEGINNERS
Platz is the more convenient

The Bolgen nursery slope is adequately spacious and gentle, and a bearable walk from the centre of Platz. But Dorf-based beginners face more of a trek out to Bünda – unless staying out at the hotel of the same name.

There is no shortage of easy runs to progress to, spread around all the sectors. The Parsenn sector probably has the edge, with long, early intermediate runs in the main Parsenn bowl, as well as in the valleys down from Weissfluhjoch.

FOR CROSS-COUNTRY
Long, scenic valley trails

Davos has a total of 75km of trails running in both directions along the main valley and reaching well up into Sertigtal, Dischmatal and Flüelatal. There is a cross-country ski centre and special ski school on the outskirts of town.

QUEUES
Still a problem in the valley

The ancient Parsennbahn railway – the only way out of Davos Dorf – is a relic that generates some of the longest queues remaining in the Alps: a reporter this year tells us of waiting 90 minutes. And when snow on the lower slopes is poor you have to queue to come down at the end of the day as well. So we are very disappointed that its planned replacement has been cancelled. We assume that the six-pack built in parallel with the top section last season will be followed by another chair on the lower mountain.

The Parsenn's super-runs

The runs from Weissfluhjoch that head north, on the back of the mountain, make this area special for many visitors. The pistes that go down to Schifer and then to Küblis, Saas and Serneus, and the one that curls around the mountain to Klosters, are graded red but are not normally difficult – though a reporter this year found the latter parts testing because they were not groomed. What marks them out is their sheer length (10–12km) and the sensation of travel they offer.

Until the late 1980s, only the very top 2.5km and 400m vertical of this enormous snowfield was served by a lift; once below Kreuzweg, you had to go down to the valley and catch the train home. Usually, you did it towards the end of the day, dawdling in the rustic restaurants in the woods on the lower reaches. The long Schiferbahn gondola changed all that – you can now descend the 1100m vertical to Schifer as often as you like. Some long-standing visitors regret the change, but there is the added advantage that the lower runs, below Schifer, are quieter – especially if you do them early in the day rather than as your last run.

There are even longer marked but unpatrolled routes to Fideris and Jenaz, the latter being 18km from Weissfluhjoch, according to official figures. But these are not continuous runs: they require skins or snow-shoes for a couple of short ascents, and payment for the use of the lifts at Fideriser Heuberge on the way. And they are often closed because of shortage of snow low down.

MOUNTAIN RESTAURANTS
Stay low down

The main high-altitude restaurants are dreary self-service affairs, but the Strelapass hut is recommended as particularly enjoyable on a warm sunny day, with good views and 'excellent' food (although it's a five-minute climb). There are other compelling places lower down – notably the rustic Conterser Schwendi ('excellent choice of rösti') and Serneuser Schwendi in the woods on the way down to the Klosters valley from the Parsenn. These are fun places to end up as darkness falls – Klosters Schwendi, at least, sells wax torches to illuminate your final descent to the village. The Skilife, down from Totalp, is self-service, has very loud pop music and is popular with hordes of school children. The Jatzhütte near the boarders' fun-park on Jakobshorn is wild – with changing scenery such as mock palm trees, parrots and pirates. A reporter this year recommends the restaurant at Weissfluhjoch for 'Indian/Chinese food freshly cooked to order on Sunday afternoons – a great treat'. The restaurant Gotschnastübli at the base of the Gotschna cable-car was criticised by a reporter for its 'officious waiter service and confusing menu options'. Both restaurants on the Madrisa slopes were pronounced 'disappointing' in terms of food choice and quality. On the Rinerhorn, the Hubelhütte at the top of the drag-lift was preferred by one reporter to the main restaurant on the Rinerhorn. The Erika at Schlappin below Madrisa is noted for cheese fondue at lunchtime.

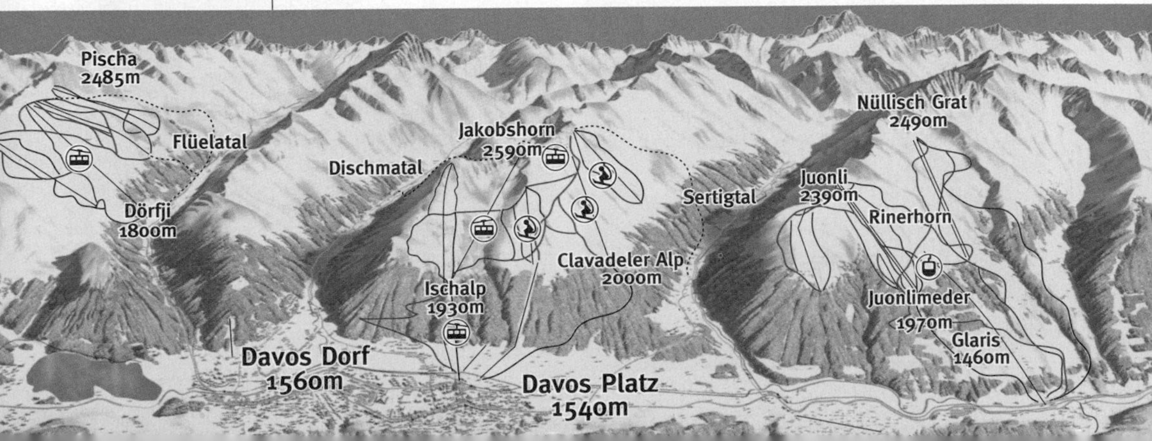

SCHOOLS/GUIDES

2001/02 prices in Swiss francs

Classes

4hr: 2hr am and pm

5 full days: 210

Children's classes

Ages: 4 to 16

5 full days: 210

Private lessons

Half day or full day

175 for half day or 280 for full day

CHILDCARE

The Bobo-Club (formerly Pinocchio nursery) at Bünda takes children aged between 4 and 7 from 10am to noon and from 2pm to 4pm, and offers a 'playful approach to snow and skiing'. Lunch supervision possible.

The day nursery Kinderhotel Muchetta at Wiesen takes children from 3 years. There is also a day nursery for babies from 6 months.

SCHOOLS AND GUIDES

Don't count on English

The Davos Swiss ski school has been renamed the Swiss Snowsportschool to emphasise the variety of instruction available. Given the small number of English-speaking visitors that Davos attracts these days, it's not surprising to find that classes are often German-dominated. A Davos regular tells us that the school is well organised, but that the instructors vary widely. A reporter this year was very happy with the school – 'friendly instructors (who will drop you off at your hotel), good English spoken'. There is an alternative ski school called New Trend and a choice of three schools for snowboarding.

FACILITIES FOR CHILDREN

Not ideal

Davos is a rather spread-out place in which to handle a family – and indeed the school's nursery is in a slightly isolated spot, at Dorf's Bünda nursery slope, inconvenient for dropping off and picking up. A recent reporter tells us the school is 'well organised, but even good instructors forget at times that your child doesn't speak German'.

Staying there

HOW TO GO

Hotels dominate the packages

Although most bed space in Davos is in apartments, hotels dominate the UK package holiday market.

Hotels A dozen 4-star places and about 30 3-stars form the core of the Davos hotel trade, though there are a couple of 5-stars and quite a few cheaper places, including B&Bs. You can book any hotel by phoning the central booking service number (415 2121).

(((((5) **Flüela** (410 1717) The more atmospheric of the two 5-star hotels, in central Dorf, and quite well placed to beat the Parsenn queues. Pool.

((((4) **Golfhotel Waldhuus** (416 8131) As convenient for winter langlaufers as for summer golfers. Quiet, modern, tasteful. Pool.

((((4) **Davoserhof** (415 6666) Best in town. Small, old, beautifully furnished, with excellent food; well placed in Platz. But will be under new management for 2001.

SWISS-IMAGE / DAVOS TOURISMUS

Davos is a big town, but you can quickly escape its streets on to paths and trails ↓

Phone numbers
From elsewhere in Switzerland add the prefix 081.
From abroad use the prefix +41 81.

GETTING THERE

Air Zürich, transfer 2hr by car, 3hr by rail or bus.

Rail Stations in Davos Dorf and Platz. 20 minutes from Davos to Klosters.

ACTIVITIES

Indoor Artificial skating rink, fitness centre, tennis, squash, swimming, sauna, cinema, museums, galleries, libraries, massage, badminton, golf-driving range
Outdoor Over 80km of cleared paths (mostly at valley level), snow-shoe trekking, full-moon skiing, toboggan run, snow volleyball, natural skating rink, curling, horse-riding, mule-trekking, sleigh rides, hang-gliding, paragliding

TOURIST OFFICE

Postcode CH-7270
t +41 (81) 415 2121
f 415 2100
davos@davos.ch
www.davos.ch

(4) **Sunstar Park** (413 1414) At far end of Davos platz. Pool, sauna, games room. Recommended for 'excellent' food.
(3) **Parsenn** (416 3232) Right opposite the Parsenn railway in Dorf. An attractive chalet marred by the big McDonald's on the ground floor.
(3) **Bahnhof Terminus** (413 2525) Friendly, three restaurants including a great Chinese, good sauna, right by bus stop in Platz.
(3) **Berghotel Schatzalp** (415 5151) Converted sanatorium on the tree line 300m above Platz and reached by funicular (free to guests).
(2) **Alte Post** (413 5403) Traditional and cosy; in central Platz. Popular with boarders.
(2) **Hubli's Landhaus** (417 1010) 5km out at Laret, towards Klosters. Quiet country inn with sophisticated, expensive food.
(1) **Snowboarder's Palace** Close to Schatzalp lift, offers good-value dormitory accommodation.

EATING OUT
Wide choice, mostly in hotels
Most of the better restaurants are in hotels. The Davoserhof's two restaurants are among the best in town, both for food and ambience. There is a choice of two good Chinese restaurants – the lavish Zauberberg in the Europe and the Goldener Drachen in the Bahnhof Terminus.

Good-value places include the Pizzeria Al Ponte, La Carretta (good for home-made pasta) and the small and cosy Gentiana (with an upstairs stübli). An evening excursion for dinner out of town is popular. Schatzalp (reached by a funicular), the Schneider and Landhaus in Frauenkirch have also been recommended.

APRES-SKI
Lots on offer, but quiet clientele
There are plenty of bars, discos and nightclubs, and a large casino in the hotel Europe. But we're not sure how some of them make a living – Davos guests tend to want the quiet life. At tea-time, mega-calories are consumed at the Weber, and Scala has a popular outside terrace.

The liveliest place in town is the rustic little Chämi bar (popular with locals); it has 'the best atmosphere later in the evening', according to one of this year's reporters. The Ex Bar is a smart mixture of Parisienne Brasserie with a touch of Pancho Villa and attracts a mixed age group.

Nightclubs tend to be sophisticated, expensive and lacking atmosphere during the week. The most popular are the Cabanna (in the hotel Europe), the Rotliechtli, Cava Grischa, Millennium! Bar Senn and for live music Grand-Café.

Bolgenschanze and Bolgen are popular boarder hang-outs.

OFF THE SLOPES
Great apart from the buildings
Provided you're not fussy about building style, Davos can be unreservedly recommended for off-slope fun. The towny resort has shops and other diversions, and transport along the valley and up onto the slopes is good – though the best of the mountain restaurants are well out of range for pedestrians. The sports facilities are excellent; the natural ice rink is said to be Europe's biggest, and is supplemented by artificial rinks, both indoor and outdoor.

Spectator sports include speed skating as well as hockey (most noteworthy is the Spengler Cup held in December). And there are lots of walks up on the slopes as well as around the lake and along the valleys.

Klosters 1190m

In a word association game, Klosters might trigger 'Prince of Wales'. The world's TV screens have shown him skiing there countless times. In 1988 he was almost killed there in an off-piste avalanche on the Gotschnawang slope that did kill one of his companions, and now the enlarged cable-car to Gotschna – which takes you to the Parsenn area shared with Davos – is named after him.

Don't be put off. We don't know why HRH likes to ski in Klosters particularly, but it is certainly not because the place is the exclusive

Phone numbers
From elsewhere in Switzerland add the prefix 081.
From abroad use the prefix +41 81.

territory of royalty. Most of the really smart socialising goes on behind closed doors, in private chalets.

THE RESORT

Klosters is a comfortable, quiet village with a much more appealing Alpine flavour than Davos, despite its lower altitude. Klosters Platz is the main focus – a collection of upmarket, traditional-style hotels around the railway station, at the foot of the steep, wooded slopes of Gotschna. The road to Davos passes through, and traffic is a problem (although they are building a bypass).

The village spreads along the valley road for quite a way before fading into the countryside; there's then a second concentration of building in the even quieter village of Klosters Dorf.

THE MOUNTAIN

Slopes A cable-car takes you to the Gotschnagrat end of the Parsenn area and a gondola from Klosters Dorf takes you up to the scenic Madrisa area.
Snow reliability It's usually reliable higher up but can be poor lower down – you may have to take the lifts down after using the Parsenn slopes.
Snowboarding Boarders are better off staying in Davos since Jakobshorn is the established boarder mountain.
Experts The off-piste possibilities are the main appeal for experts.
Intermediates There are excellent cruising runs in all five ski areas – see in particular the feature box on the Parsenn's super-runs.
Beginners There are some nursery lifts at valley level, but the wide sunny slopes of Madrisa are more appealing.
Cross-country There are 35km of trails and a Nordic ski school offers lessons.
Queues Queues for the Gotschna cable-car have been reduced by a doubling of its capacity, but can still be a problem at weekends. A reporter tells of hour-long queues at the beginning of the day.
Mountain restaurants There are a number of atmospheric huts in the woods above the village – the Conterser Schwendi is particularly recommended for its 'excellent' food.
Schools and guides There is a choice of three ski and snowboard schools, and Klosters is well known for excellent mountain guides.
Facilities for children The ski schools offer classes for children from the age of four.

STAYING THERE

How to go There is a wide choice of packages offered by UK tour operators.
Hotels There are some particularly attractive hotels – all bookable on the central reservations phone number, 410 2020. The central Chesa Grischuna (422 2222) is irresistible, combining traditional atmosphere with modern comfort – and a lively après-ski bar. The Cresta (422 2525) is a popular 3-star described as 'very pleasant and friendly' by a reporter this year.

The less central but very cosy Wynegg (422 1340) is popular with British visitors, with good-value bedrooms. The Sport hotel in Dorf (423 3030) has also been recommended.
Eating out Good restaurants abound, but a reporter comments that there is a shortage of the cheap and cheerful variety. Top of the price bracket for eating out is the Walserhof, while Alberto's is the best pizzeria in town. The Chesa Selfranga is 20 minutes' walk from the centre of town, but is noted for fondue, both cheese and Chinoise.
Après-ski In the village, the Chesa Grischuna is a focus of activity from tea-time onwards, with its piano bar, bowling and restaurant. A reporter advises that drinks are much cheaper at the Gotschnastübli. The newly rebuilt hotel Vereina is recommended for its piano bar.

Gaudy's at the foot of the slopes is a popular pit stop after skiing, as is the lively bar at the four-star Alpina and the warmly panelled Wynegg.

In the late evening the bar of the hotel Kaiser is popular. The Casa Antica is a small but popular disco – though a reporter this year found only four people there at 11.30 on a Friday night in February. The Kir Royale, under the hotel Silvretta Park, is bigger and more brash. The Funny Place, under the Piz Buin, is more grown-up and expensive.
Off the slopes Klosters is an attractive base for walking and cross-country skiing. There is a sport and leisure centre, and some hotels have pools – the pool and spa/fitness room at the Vereina were available for use by non-residents at a charge of 60 swiss francs per day in 2000/01. An excursion by train to the spa at Scuol Tarasp is recommended by one reporter.

Flims 1100m

A splendid, spacious area that deserves to be better known

WHAT IT COSTS

HOW IT RATES

The slopes

Snow	***
Extent	****
Experts	***
Intermediates	*****
Beginners	****
Convenience	***
Queues	***
Restaurants	***

The rest

Scenery	***
Resort charm	***
Off-slope	***

What's new

A new Slope System piste map has been introduced which uses a unique piste grading system unlike any other we've seen. It may be okay when you've got used to it. But at first sight it is confusing.

For 2000/01 a Pipe & Park pass and limited area beginners' pass were introduced. The snowboard park on Crap Sogn Gion got a new lift, the children's Dreamlands was extended and a second Riders Palace opened at Murschetg. Another New Technology Centre – see The Resort section – opened in Falera. And you can now view and book rental apartments on the website.

- ➕ Extensive, varied slopes suitable for all but experts
- ➕ Impressive lift system
- ➕ Virtually queue-free on weekdays
- ➕ Fair number of slopes above 2000m, partly offsetting effects of their sunny south-east orientation
- ➕ Lots of wooded runs for bad-weather days
- ➕ Just 90 minutes from Zürich airport

- ➖ Though well intentioned, the unique piste grading system is confusing
- ➖ Sunny orientation can cause icy or slushy pistes and shut lower runs
- ➖ Buses or long walks to lifts from much of the accommodation
- ➖ Very subdued in the evenings
- ➖ Village very spread out, which detracts from its charm
- ➖ Weekend crowds

Flims/Laax has an impressive 220km of mainly intermediate pistes. The resort is very popular with weekenders and has some high-capacity lifts which help it cope. It can be very quiet during the week, and is virtually unknown outside the Swiss and German markets. It deserves better. Don't be put off by the unfortunate (for English-speakers) local name for 'peak', which is 'crap'. All the mountain-tops are called crap, a top après-ski venue is the Crap Bar and the tourist office has used the slogan 'Flims is crap' in promotions.

There are very long runs, ideal for adventurous intermediates, amid stunning scenery. And there's plenty to play around on in all areas. For us there have always been two main drawbacks: a sunny orientation which can spoil the snow on the lower part of the mountain, and the lack of real Alpine charm in the villages. Now there's a third: their new piste map uses a unique grading system unlike any other we have seen. Formerly black and red runs have become green (to signify 'Allround Slope'), red now means 'Freestyle Slope', off-piste areas are shaded yellow, black diamonds have appeared. Confused? We are.

The resort 

Flims is made up of two parts over a kilometre apart on a sunny, wooded mountain terrace. Dorf sprawls along a busy road lined with shops, hotels, restaurants, bars and the main lift station. Waldhaus is a sophisticated, sedate huddle of hotels quietly set in the trees. Both parts look traditional, with wooden chalet-style buildings.

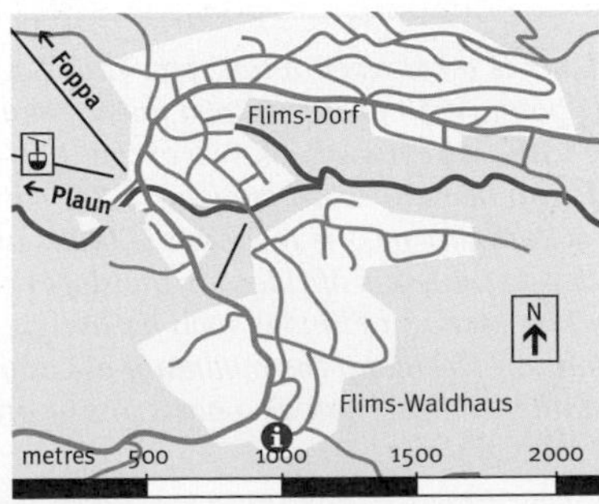

The slopes spread across the mainly south-east-facing mountain to another lift base-station at Murschetg (1.5km from Waldhaus), an outpost of Laax. From here there's an efficient jumbo gondola and a less efficient cable-car – this is the easiest entry point for those with cars. There's also a high-speed quad at Falera, 5km from Waldhaus.

Most hotels are a bus-ride from the slopes but a combination of resort, hotel and post buses works well.

New Technology Centres, now at all three lift bases, offer a package of ski clothing and equipment rental by the day – turn up in city clothes and get all you need from SF115, including lift pass and a shower after you finish.

The mountains

Flims has extensive, underrated, varied slopes: some long runs and some high, exposed peaks (which can be very windswept), including a small glacier.

MOUNTAIN FACTS

Altitude	1100m-3020m
Lifts	28
Pistes	220km
Blue	29%
Red	45%
Black	26%

(% refers to old map and conventional colour gradings – see right for new system)

Artificial snow	13km

Recco detectors used

LIFT PASSES

2000/01 prices in Swiss francs

Alpine Arena
Covers all lifts and buses between Flims, Laax and Falera.

Main pass
1-day pass 59
6-day pass 301

Senior citizens
Over 65 (men) or 62 (women): 6-day pass 241

Children
Under 18: 6-day pass 241
Under 13: 6-day pass 151
Under 6: free pass

Short-term passes
Half day from 12.15 (adult 48).

Alternative passes
One day Pipe & Park pass for Crap Sogn Gion 35.
Beginner passes for limited lifts in Flims, Laax (both 35) and Falera (30).

Notes Free Alpine Arena Clubcards can get you discounts on passes – register on the internet at www.alpenarena.ch/clubcard/eng/register.htm or in resort. You need a Clubcard to claim senior citizen or child lift pass discounts. You get extra points on the Clubcard when you spend money in the Alpine Arena, which can be exchanged for further discounts.

Because of its sunny aspect, lower runs can deteriorate quickly making it difficult to get back to Flims on snow (there is some snowmaking). In poor visibility there are plenty of tree-lined runs. Trips are possible to Lenzerheide, Davos–Klosters and Arosa.

Flims now grades its slopes according to its own innovative system: yellow for 'backcountry' (or off-piste), red for 'freestyle', blue for 'beginner' and green for 'allround'. Difficult slopes are indicated by black diamonds – two for difficult and three for very difficult. So, for instance, the formerly black Sattel run from the Vorab glacier is marked green with two black diamonds. Useful once you understand, but rather open to confusion. One of our reporters certainly had trouble: 'Undoubtedly the most confusing map ever – grading verges on dangerous.' In our map, we have continued to use the conventional grading of the resort's previous piste map.

The new map does, however, show the time it takes to ride each lift – an excellent idea that makes meeting others on time very easy – and marks some flattish pistes as 'traverses'.

THE SLOPES
Impressive and well planned

There are essentially four sectors, each good for all grades but expert. Slopes are well planned, and getting around is easy but can mean a lot of traversing.

The gondola from Flims has two mid-stations, the first at Plaun, where you change cabins or catch a fast six-person chair to **Crap Sogn Gion** at the heart of the Laax slopes. From here you can go towards Murschetg, Laax or Falera or catch a cable-car up to **Crap Masegn**. This is the biggest area.

If, instead, you continue in the gondola there's another mid-station at Scansinas before the top at Nagens – alighting at either will allow you to get over to **La Siala,** from where there's a run to the high **Vorab glacier**.

There is also a link via a two-way, two-stage gondola (which can be closed by wind) between the Vorab glacier and Crap Masegn. And there's a slope linking Crap Masegn with Plaun.

The **Cassons** sector above Flims Dorf is the smallest, particularly when runs to the village are incomplete. It is reached via two chairs and a cable-car and linked to Nagens and Grauberg.

SNOW RELIABILITY
Good higher up

The upper runs are generally snowsure. But due to the sunny aspect, the runs back to Flims itself can suffer. There is snowmaking on three main runs from Crap Sogn Gion, including the splendid black race course run right down to Murschetg. There is also snowmaking from Segnes-Hütte to Flims and on the bottom part of the run to Alp Ruschein.

FOR EXPERTS
Bits and pieces

There is a fair amount to challenge, but it's rather dotted about, with the added frustration that some of it is on short sections of otherwise easy pistes. The toughest run is the steep, unpisted Cassons run to the bottom of its cable car, reached by a steep climb from the top of the cable-car. Other off-piste trips from this summit might look tempting, but we'd recommend hiring a guide (they get three black diamonds on the new piste map). Throughout the area the off-piste is generally between pistes (and is now marked in yellow on the piste map).

One of the great pleasures of the area is the men's World Cup Downhill course (formerly a black run, now marked green on the piste map) from Crap Sogn Gion to Murschetg. It's so long (1000m vertical) and pretty that doing it repeatedly using the Murschetg cable-car doesn't get boring.

boarding *Flims/Laax is a snowboard hot spot. Crap Sogn Gion is a popular meeting point, with plenty of loud music from the outdoor Rock Bar and the No-Name Café, which overlook two of four half-pipes on the mountain – their walls can be built to an amazing 6.7m with the worldbeating Pipe Monster. A Pipe & Park day pass is available if that's all you're into, but the slopes are well suited to all levels of rider. As the slopes close, the Crap Bar at Murschetg is popular. The Arena in Flims is good for live gigs. The Riders Palaces in Murschetg and Mountain Hostel up the mountain at Crap Sogn Gion have great value accommodation. Flims/Laax also hosts lots of international snowboarding events.*

And the Sattel piste from Vorab – see For Intermediates – is long and beautiful. The Nagens–Startgels run is short but steep.

FOR INTERMEDIATES
Paradise for all

In general this is a superb area for all intermediates. When conditions allow, the area just above Flims is splendid for easy cruising. But a real highlight for early intermediates is a trip to the Vorab glacier and back on easy intermediate runs. On the way back you can take the cable-car down from Grauberg to Startgels to avoid steeper slopes.

For more adventurous intermediates there's a wonderful descent of over 1700m vertical if you start at La Siala and go all the way down to Flims. One of the two unpisted runs from Cassons is a lovely trip along the shoulder of the mountain into a valley and on to Startgels – but check snow conditions first and be warned, there's a hike to get to it. The run from Crap Sogn Gion to Larnags via Curnius is also great fun.

Good intermediates will enjoy the superb, long and beautiful Sattel run from the glacier to Ruschein at the extreme west of the area. It starts with a challenging mogul field but develops into a fast cruise.

The Crap Sogn Gion to Plaun routes are interesting, being quite steep and sheltered – and are some of the few runs not to directly face the sun.

Less confident intermediates should note that some easy runs have short steep sections. The links from Nagens towards Flims can be intimidating.

FOR BEGINNERS
Plenty of options

There's a good nursery area in Dorf, and alternatives at Startgels and Nagens if snow is poor. The Foppa and Naraus areas have good confidence-building runs to move on to. Getting the bus to the lovely easy runs above Falera is another option for those just off the nursery slopes. There's plenty of tuition in English.

FOR CROSS-COUNTRY
One of the best

An excellent choice. There are 70km of beautiful, well marked, mainly forest trails. Loops range from 3km to 20km. Another fine 60km network starts near Laax. The ski school, centred at Waldhaus, has a good reputation and organises group classes. 3km of trail are floodlit. The only drawback is the possibility of poor snow.

QUEUES
Some delays

There is generally little queuing during the week, but we have had a report of long waits for the Cassons, Crap Sogn Gion and Crap Masegn cable-cars. At weekends, with coach loads of day visitors arriving at Murschetg, the lifts there get busy. But delays out of Flims in the morning are rare. The chair towards La Siala can generate queues, as can the slow two-person Alp

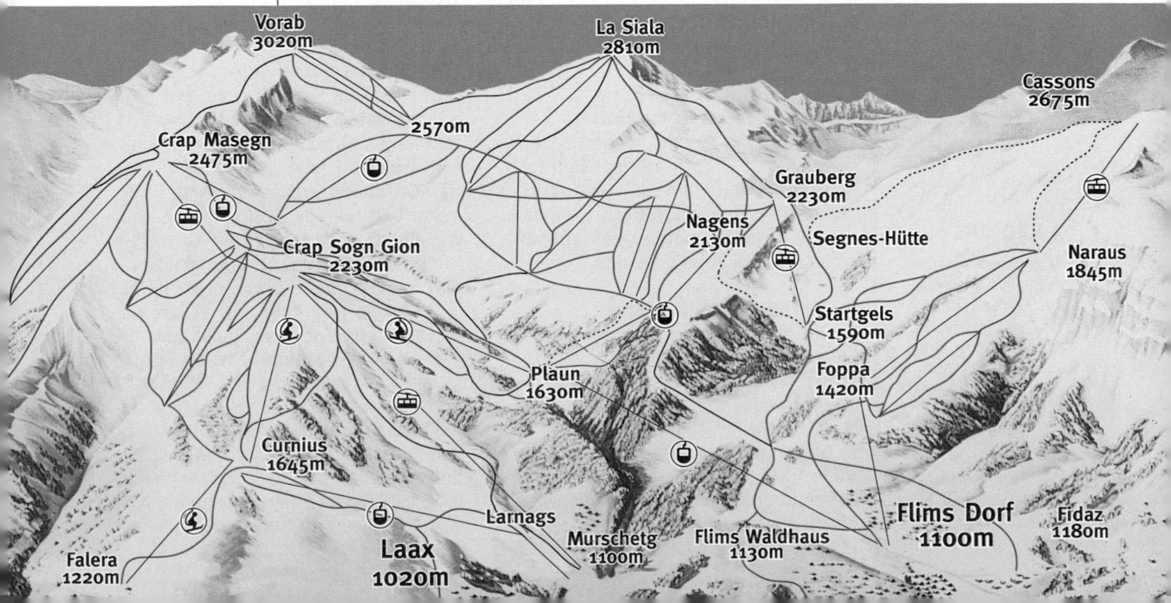

Trust snowboarders to try to ruin your photo of one of the bars outside Crap Sogn Gion →

SWISS-IMAGE / MOUNTAIN MARKETING AG

GETTING THERE

Air Zürich, transfer 1½hr.

Rail Chur (22km); regular buses to resort.

SCHOOLS/GUIDES

2000/01 prices in Swiss francs

Swiss
Classes 5 days 4hr
5 full days: 350
Children's classes
Ages: up to 12
5 full days: 350 with lunch
Private lessons
Full day 320

CHILDCARE

The ski school runs ski kindergartens (Dreamlands) taking children from age 4 – in Flims, Laax and Falera from 9.30 to 11.30 and 1.30 to 3.30.

Several hotels claim special facilities for children – the Park Hotel Waldhaus has its own crèche.

Ruschein chair and some T-bars. Lifts closing because of wind (especially up to Cassons) has been a common complaint among reporters.

MOUNTAIN RESTAURANTS
Good, wide selection

Mountain restaurants are numerous and generally good. The large cafeterias at Curnius, Sogn Gion and Vorab are clean, efficient and serve good wholesome food. Nagens has a place with great views, a sun terrace and live music, but the nicest refuges are lower down, such as The Spaligna below Foppa and the Startgels Hütte above Foppa. We had a great lunch (with electronic ordering) in the rustic Tegia by the Murschetg gondola mid-station at Larnags. The Runcahöhe, where the Stretg piste flattens out and crosses the path down from Startgels, is another good cosy cabin. For a more expensive menu the restaurant at Crap Masegn is highly recommended.

SCHOOLS AND GUIDES
Plenty of English tuition

The school has a good reputation and standards of English are reported to be good too. They offer Early Bird specials on empty pistes followed by breakfast – a great North American concept not generally available in Europe.

FACILITIES FOR CHILDREN
Good Dreamland centres

Children aged three and over (skiers or not) can be looked after at one of three Dreamland centres in Dorf, Murschetg and Falera. The facilities are to be extended for 2001/02, but there were no details as we went to press. For children under three the resort can recommend qualified nannies.

Staying there

It may seem best to stay near the lifts in Dorf, but in practice the better hotels in Waldhaus (and remote bits of Dorf) run efficient courtesy buses to and from the slopes. These satisfy most guests, especially as there's not much to tempt you into town after dinner.

HOW TO GO
Few tour operators

Only a handful of tour operators feature Flims.

Hotels The majority are either 3-star or simple B&B places. Of six top hotels, five are in Waldhaus.

(((((5) **Park** (928 4848) Enormous and very comfortable, but rather institutional, 5-star in wooded grounds at Waldhaus. Efficient courtesy bus. Pool.

((((4) **Adula** (928 2828) Big 4-star in Waldhaus, highly recommended by recent reporters. Good pool. 'Superb food and service,' says reporter.

((((4) **Sunstar Surselva** (911 1121) Part of the reliable Sunstar chain but run in a rather more institutionalised way than most. Quiet situation in Waldhaus with excellent new spa facilities.

(((3) **Grischuna** (911 1139) Pretty little 3-star just outside Dorf, close to lifts.

(((3) **Cresta** (911 3535) Rave review: 'Helpful staff, fabulous spa facilities and food, unpretentious family hotel.'

(((3) **Curtgin** (911 3566) Attractive, quiet place on edge of town, quite near lifts.

(((3) **Albana Sporthotel** (911 2333) Modern 3-star beside lifts, with focal après-ski bar.

(((3) **Waldeck** (911 1228) Neat 3-star in Waldhaus, with pleasant restaurant.

Self-catering The tourist office has a long list of available apartments, which you can view and book on the website.

EATING OUT
Varied options
Most Flims restaurants are in hotels. The National, by the bus station, has good fish dishes. The Meiler hotel restaurant also has a good reputation. For something a bit different, go up to the Spaligna mountain restaurant and use the toboggan run to get home. Little China is a good Chinese, and the Alpina Garni (Waldhaus) is very good value, does good pizzas and is 'busy and fun', says a recent reporter.

APRES-SKI
Not a strong point
Flims is very quiet après-ski. The Spaligna trip mentioned under Eating Out is the highlight of the week. The Iglou bar at the base of the Flims gondola is packed when the slopes close, as is the Stenna-Bar, opposite, which has a tea dance. Just across the road the Albana Pub is popular with a young crowd. Later, the focal spot is also in Dorf, at the hotel Bellevue's Caverna, an atmospheric old wine vault. The Angel is a late-night club. The Park hotel is the centre of limited action in Waldhaus, having an old cellar with entertainer, and the Chadafo bar with dancing to live music. At Murschetg, the Crap Bar is lively when the slopes close and Casa Veglia has live bands and dancing.

OFF THE SLOPES
Lots to do
There are plenty of things to do. The enormous sports centre has a huge range of activities, including shooting – and 'guest cards' from hotels and the tourist office provide a discount. Flims also has some of the best and most extensive (60km) marked walks of any winter resort, some into and through the ski areas. Historic Chur is a short bus-ride away. Other good trips are to the impressive church at Zillis, and to the Rhine canyon, which is nature at its best. The Glacier Express train from Chur to Andermatt takes you through some wonderful scenery.

STAYING UP THE MOUNTAIN
Hostel St John
The Crap Sogn Gion Mountain Hostel, 1100m above Murschetg in the centre of the slopes, has budget 4-bedded rooms as well as single and double. You can also stay above Flims in the more traditional Berghaus Nagens.

Laax 1020m

Laax is a quiet, spacious old farming community which has retained a lot of its original character. Most of its modern development has taken place a short bus-ride away at Murschetg, a modern, functional complex at the base of the lifts. The oldest house in Laax dates from 1615, and the setting is pleasant enough, but the old village is no more than routinely charming.

Laax has its own school and ski kindergarten.

The Laaxerhof (920 8200) and Signina (927 9000) are Murschetg 4-stars. The 4-star Arena Alva (927 2727) is a more attractive building in the old village, with transport to the lifts. The charming, central old Posta Veglia (921 4466) has a lively stubli and piano bar. A good central B&B is the Cathomen (921 4545). The two Riders Palaces (927 9000) offer dorm accommodation at a bargain price at the base station.

Restaurants and bars are mostly hotel-based. The Laaxer Bündnerstuben in the Posta Veglia is best for a meal in traditional surroundings. The limited nightlife centres around the Bistro Bar in the Capricorn hotel, live music in the Vallarosa Bar or Laaxerhof, and, again, the Posta Veglia. At Murschetg the Crap Bar gets packed when the lifts close – popular with snowboarders.

Falera 1220m

Along the road from Flims, beyond Laax, lies the tiny village of Falera, a quiet traffic-free place, with two old churches. Sitting on a sunny plateau, it has good views over three valleys. Two successive fast quad chairs take you to the heart of the slopes.

Accommodation is mostly in apartments, but La Siala (927 2222) is a large 3-star hotel with pool. Its Spielkeller is the only real nightspot.

Phone numbers
From elsewhere in Switzerland add the prefix 081.
From abroad use the prefix +41 81.

ACTIVITIES

Indoor Large public swimming pool and over 20 hotel pools (many open to the public), saunas, 4 indoor tennis courts, covered hall with ice skating and 4 curling rinks, fitness centres (including Prau La Selva), table tennis, whirlpool, solarium
Outdoor 60km of cleared paths, riding, natural skating rinks, curling, sleigh rides, toboggan runs, ski-bob, paragliding, hot-air ballooning, hang-gliding, snow-shoeing, helicopter flights and night skiing

TOURIST OFFICE

Postcode CH-7017
t +41 (81) 920 9200
f 920 9201
tourismus@alpenarena.ch
www.alpenarena.ch

Grindelwald 1035m

Traditional mountain town in spectacular scenery

WHAT IT COSTS

3

HOW IT RATES

The slopes

Snow	**
Extent	***
Experts	**
Intermediates	*****
Beginners	***
Convenience	**
Queues	**
Restaurants	***

The rest

Scenery	*****
Resort charm	****
Off-slope	****

- ➕ Dramatically set in magnificent scenery directly beneath the towering north face of the Eiger
- ➕ Lots of long, gentle runs, ideal for intermediates, with links to Wengen
- ➕ Pleasant old village with long mountaineering history, though the tourist trade now sets the tone
- ➕ Fair amount to do off the slopes, including splendid walks and recently expanded toboggan runs

- ➖ Village gets very little midwinter sun
- ➖ Few challenging pistes for experts
- ➖ Inconvenient for visiting Mürren
- ➖ Snow-cover unreliable
- ➖ Major area accessed by a slow gondola, queue-prone especially at weekends, and by very slow and infrequent trains – life revolves around timetables

For stunning views from your hotel window and from the pistes, there are few places to rival Grindelwald, and two of them are just over the hill. The village is nowhere near as special as Wengen or Mürren, but staying here does give you direct access to Grindelwald's own First area. But you can spend hours queueing for, waiting for or sitting in the gondola or trains up into the Kleine Scheidegg area shared with Wengen. (The gondola ride takes over half an hour.) Grindelwald regulars accept all this as part of the scene, and some elderly skiers even find it adds to the holiday by enforcing a slow pace.

The resort 

Grindelwald is set either side of the road along the foot of a narrow valley. Buildings are primarily traditional Swiss-chalet style. Towering mountains rise steeply from the valley floor, and the resort and main slopes get very little sun in January.

Grindelwald can feel very jolly at times, such as during the ice-carving festival in January, when large and beautiful tableaux are on display along the main street. The village is livelier at night than the other Jungfrau resorts of Wengen and Mürren. There's live music in several bars and hotels, but it isn't a place for bopping until dawn.

The major lifts into the slopes shared with Wengen are at Grund, right at the bottom of the sloping village. Near the opposite end of the village, a gondola goes up to the separate First area. There are trains between the centre and Grund, and shuttle-buses linking the lift stations – but these get congested at times.

The most convenient place to stay for the slopes is at Grund. But this is out of the centre and rather charmless. There's a wide range of hotels in the heart of the village, handy enough for everything else, including the First area, at the foot of which are nursery

MOUNTAIN FACTS

Altitude	945m-2970m
Lifts	45
Pistes	205km
Blue	30%
Red	50%
Black	20%
Artificial snow	30km
Recco detectors used	

GRINDELWALD TOURIST OFFICE

For close-up views of dramatic peaks, it's difficult to beat Grindelwald →

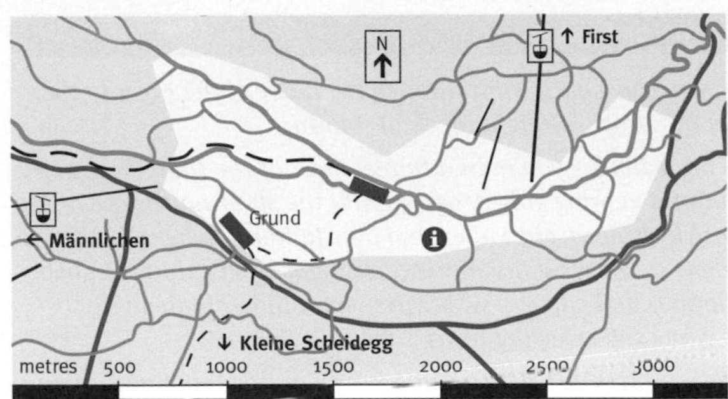

LIFT PASSES

2000/01 prices in Swiss francs

Jungfrau Top Ski Region
Covers all lifts in Wengen, Mürren and Grindelwald, trains between them and Grindelwald ski-bus.

Beginners Points card (adult 100 points 48, lifts cost 4 to 10 points).

Main pass
1-day pass 52
6-day pass 254

Senior citizens
Over 62: 6-day pass 229

Children
16 to 19: 6-day pass 203
Under 16: 6-day pass 127
Under 6: 6-day pass 25

Short-term passes
Single ascent tickets for most lifts. Half-day pass available for each of First, Kleine Scheidegg-Männlichen and Mürren-Schilthorn (adult 40).

Alternative periods
3 days in 7 pass is available (156).

Notes Day pass price is for Kleine Scheidegg-Männlichen area only (102km of piste, 21 lifts), as Jungfrau Top Ski Region pass is only available for 2 days or over.

Alternative passes
1- and 2-day passes available for each of First, Mürren-Schilthorn and Kleine Scheidegg-Männlichen (adult 2-day 95).

slopes, ski school and kindergarten.

Trips to other resorts are not very easy, but you can drive to Adelboden. Getting to the tougher, higher slopes of Mürren is a lengthy business unless you go to Lauterbrunnen by car.

The mountains

The major area shared with Wengen offers a mix of wooded slopes and open slopes higher up. The smaller First area is mainly open, though there are wooded runs to the village.

THE SLOPES
Broad and mainly gentle

From Grund, near the western end of town, you can get to **Männlichen** by an appallingly slow two-stage gondola or to **Kleine Scheidegg** by an even slower cog railway. The slopes of the separate south-facing First area are reached by a long, slow three-stage gondola starting a bus-ride east of the centre. From all over the slopes there are superb views, not only of the Eiger but also of the Wetterhorn and other peaks. Piste marking is poor, and one reporter complains that from First it is difficult to determine which run you are on and therefore easy to end up at the wrong point in the valley, a bus-ride from where you want to be.

SNOW RELIABILITY
Poor

Grindelwald's low altitude (the slopes go down to below 1000m and few are above 2000m) and the lack of many snowmakers mean this is not a resort to book up months in advance. And it's not the place for a late-season holiday. First is sunny, and so even less snowsure than the main area.

FOR EXPERTS
Very limited

The area is quite limited for experts. The black run on First beneath the gondola back to town is quite tough, especially when the snow has suffered from too much sun – late in the season, the run is one of the first to close. See also the Wengen chapter.

Heli-trips with mountain guides are organised if there are enough takers.

FOR INTERMEDIATES
Ideal intermediate terrain

In good snow, First makes a splendid intermediate playground, though the general lack of trees makes the area less friendly than the larger Kleine Scheidegg–Männlichen area, and many of the lifts are T-bars. The runs to the valley are great fun, but naturally popular in the afternoon. Nearly all the runs from Kleine Scheidegg are long blues or gentle reds. On the Männlichen there's a choice of gentle runs down to the mid-station of the gondola up from Grindelwald Grund. In good snow, you can get right down to the bottom on easy red runs – 'barely deserving the grade', says a reporter (and one of these runs used to be marked black).

For tougher pistes, head for the top of the Lauberhorn lift and the runs to Kleine Scheidegg, or to Wixi (following the start of the downhill course). You could also try the north-facing run from Eigergletscher to Salzegg, which often has the best snow late in the season.

FOR BEGINNERS
In good snow, wonderful

The nursery slope is friendly and scenic, just above the village, but in late season it can suffer from the sun and low altitude. There are splendid longer runs served by the railway to Kleine Scheidegg, notably the easy scenic blue Mettlen-Grund run, right from the top to the bottom.

boarding *This isn't prime boarder territory though there is a fun-park and a half-pipe at Oberjoch on First. Intermediates will enjoy the area most – the beginners' slopes can be bare, while experts will hanker for the steep, off-piste slopes of Mürren. Nightlife caters mainly for the more affluent, middle-aged visitors.*

SCHOOLS/GUIDES

2000/01 prices in Swiss francs

Swiss
Classes 5 days
4hr: 10am-noon and 2pm-4pm
5 full days: 214
Children's classes
Ages: 3 to 14
5 full days: 214
Private lessons
2½hr or 5hr
170 for 2½hr
288 for 5hr

CHILDCARE

The ski school takes children from age 3, and they can be looked after at lunchtime in the Children's Club kindergarten at the Bodmi nursery slopes. This takes children from age 3, from 9.30 to 4pm. It apparently ceases to function if snow shortage closes the nursery slopes.

The Sunshine nursery on First takes children from 1 month from 8.30-5pm.

THE JOURNEY TO THE TOP OF EUROPE

From Kleine Scheidegg you can take a train through the heart of the Eiger to the highest railway station in Europe – Jungfraujoch at 3454m.

The journey itself is a bit tedious – you're in a tunnel most of the time. You stop part way up to look out of a viewing gallery carved into the sheer north face of the Eiger, with magnificent views down the valley and over to Männlichen. At the top is a big restaurant complex. There's a fascinating 'ice palace' carved in the glacier with beautiful ice sculptures and slippery walkways, an outdoor 'plateau' to wander around and a panoramic viewing tower called the Sphinx.

The return trip cost SF48 in 2000/01 if you had a Jungfrau lift pass for three days or more, but around three times that if you didn't. So it's much more attractive to skiers and boarders. Watch out for the altitude. At almost 3500m the air is thin, and we met people having breathing and balance problems.

FOR CROSS-COUNTRY
Good but shady

There are over 25km of prepared tracks. Almost all of this is on the valley floor at around 1000m, so it's very shady in midwinter and may have poor snow later in the season.

QUEUES
Can be dreadful at peak times

The queues for the gondola and train at Grund can be very bad in high season, especially when weekend visitors pour in. One Christmas week reporter experienced half-hour waits for the Männlichen gondola last season. The popular Oberjoch chair-lift is a bottleneck. Queues for the rest of the upper lifts build up only when snow is short lower down. (The same Christmas visitor experienced 15-minute queues higher up and also reported long waits for the gondola back down from First as all the lower runs were closed.)

MOUNTAIN RESTAURANTS
Wide choice

See the Wengen chapter for restaurants around Kleine Scheidegg and down towards Wengen. Brandegg, on the railway, is recommended for its 'wonderful' apple fritters. Berghaus Bort does very good rösti, but the 'best rösti anywhere' is at the Jägerstubli, 500m up the road from the Aspen, off the Rennstrecke piste.

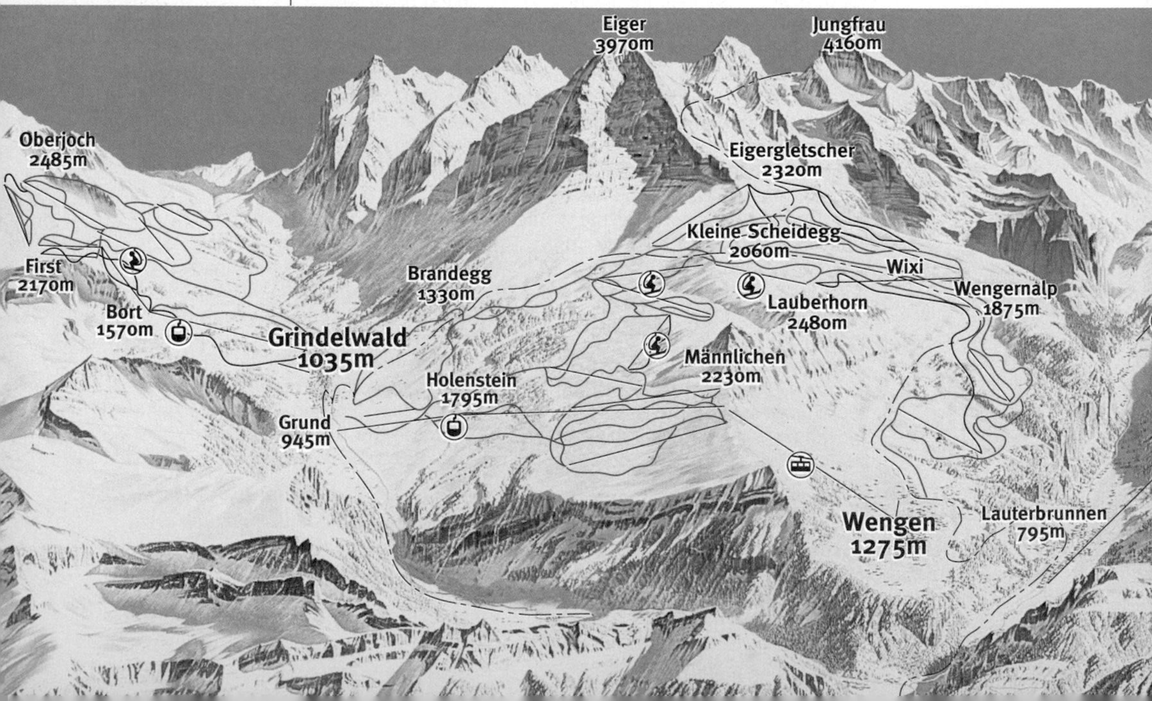

GETTING THERE

Air Zürich, transfer 3hr. Bern, transfer 1½hr.

Rail Station in resort.

Phone numbers
From elsewhere in Switzerland add the prefix 033.
From abroad use the prefix +41 33.

ACTIVITIES

Indoor Sports centre (swimming pool, sauna, solarium, table tennis, fitness room, climbing room, games room), indoor skating rink, curling, bowling, cinema
Outdoor 80km of cleared paths, train rides to Jungfraujoch, tobogganing, snow-shoe excursions, sleigh rides, paragliding, heli-skiing and boarding, open-air ice skating, snowrafting, glacier tours, devalkarts

TOURIST OFFICE

Postcode CH-3818
t +41 (33) 854 1212
f 854 1210
touristcenter@grindelwald.ch
www.grindelwald.ch

SCHOOLS AND GUIDES
One of the better Swiss schools
A recent report declares the Swiss school 'very good'; spoken English is normally excellent. It now has some competition in the form of private lessons from the Buri Sport school.

FACILITIES FOR CHILDREN
Good reputation
A past reporter who put four children through the Grindelwald mill praised caring and effective instructors, and a recent reporter rates them 'brilliant'. The First mountain restaurant runs a day nursery, which is a neat idea.

Staying there

HOW TO GO
Limited range of packages
The hotels UK tour operators offer are mainly at the upper end of the market, but traditional little B&B pensions and self-catering apartments are widely available to independent bookers.
Hotels One 5-star, a dozen 4-stars, and a good range of more modest places are available.
((((5) **Regina** (854 8600) The one 5-star. Big and imposing; right next to the railway station. Nightly music in the bar. Pool.
(((4) **Belvedere** (854 5454) Family-run, recently renovated, close to station and with a 'wonderful' pool.
(((4) **Schweizerhof** (853 2202) Beautifully decorated 4-star chalet at west end of centre, close to station. Pool.
(((4) **Bodmi** (853 1220) Little chalet right on the village nursery slopes.
((3) **Hirschen** (854 8484) Family-run 3-star in central position at foot of nursery slopes. Good food. Security can be a problem – one recent visitor had skis stolen from the ski room.
((3) **Fiescherblick** (854 5353) Hospitable chalet on eastern fringe of village, five minutes from the First gondola.
((3) **Derby** (854 5461) Popular, modern 3-star next to station, with 'first-class' service, good food and great views.
(2) **Tschuggen** (853 1781) Modest chalet in central position below nursery slopes.
① **Hotel Wetterhorn** (853 1218) Cosy, simple chalet way beyond the village, with great views of the glacier.
Self-catering One independent reporter recommended the apartments of the hotel Hirschen for comfort and space.

EATING OUT
Hotel based
There's a wide choice of good hotel restaurants, but cheaper pizzeria-style places are in short supply. The Latino does home-made Italian cooking. Among the more attractively traditional places are: the Swiss Chalet in the Eiger; Schmitte in the Schweizerhof; Challi-Stübli in the Kreuz; and the Alte Post. The Fiescherblick's Swiss Bistro is repeatedly recommended – 'brilliant but expensive'. The Kirchbühl and Oberland are good for vegetarians, the Bahnhof in the Derby for fondue and raclette. Hotel Spinne has many options: Italian, Mexican, Chinese and the candlelit Rôtisserie for a special romantic meal. There's even a Japanese restaurant, the Samurai.

APRES-SKI
Relaxed
A jolly way to end the day is to have a drink or two at Kleine Scheidegg before skiing home. Nightlife is not the special subject of our reporters, but we can say that there are at least three discos and a handful of bars that aim to keep going late. There's also a cinema, plus ice hockey and curling matches to watch. There's an excellent sports centre with pool. Tobogganing and tubing are organised on First, and Thursday to Friday a 'Sledge Express' train takes people up to Brandegg/Alpiglen for fondues and tobogganing.

OFF THE SLOPES
Plenty to do, easy to get around
There are many cleared paths with magnificent views, especially around the First area – and there's a special (though expensive) pedestrian bus/lift pass. A trip to Jungfraujoch is spectacular (see previous page), and excursions by train are easy to Interlaken and possible to Bern. Tobogganing has recently undergone a bit of a renaissance, with runs up 15km on First (Europe's longest) and 70km of runs in total. Helicopter flights from Männlichen are recommended.

STAYING UP THE MOUNTAIN
Several possibilities
See the Wengen chapter for details of rooms at Kleine Scheidegg. The Berghaus Bort (853 1762), at the gondola station in the middle of the First area (1570m), is an attractive alternative.

Gstaad 1050m

Surprisingly unpretentious, with extensive, pretty slopes

WHAT IT COSTS

5

HOW IT RATES

The slopes	
Snow	*
Extent	****
Experts	**
Intermediates	***
Beginners	***
Convenience	*
Queues	***
Restaurants	***
The rest	
Scenery	***
Resort charm	****
Off-slope	****

What's new

Last season saw further improvements to the glacier lifts – the Mazot-Meilleret and Scex-Rouge chair-lifts are the latest lifts to have been upgraded.

MOUNTAIN FACTS

Altitude	950m-3000m
Lifts	67
Pistes	250km
Blue	48%
Red	36%
Black	16%
Artificial snow	12km

- ⊕ Traditional village, traffic-free in centre, without the towny feel of other fashionable Swiss resorts
- ⊕ Lift pass covers large area of slopes
- ⊕ Good long runs for intermediates
- ⊕ Lively après-ski scene
- ⊕ Wide range of off-slope diversions, including swanky shops

- ⊖ Fragmented slopes, none convenient for central hotels – so you are always using buses and trains
- ⊖ Unreliable snow-cover, except on the limited (and distant) Diablerets glacier slopes
- ⊖ No budget accommodation
- ⊖ Few challenges for experts

Gstaad is renowned as a jet-set resort, but for 'ordinary' holidaymakers, too, it has attractions – especially for those with a relaxed outlook, who can happily spend time on trains looking at the landscape without feeling it's precious piste time wasted.

THE RESORT

Gstaad is a traditional, year-round resort in a spacious, sunny setting surrounded by a horseshoe of wooded mountains. The main street, lined with hotels, smart shops and cafes, has a pleasant and relaxed feel now that it's traffic-free. The Montreux–Oberland–Bernois (MOB) railway station is only yards away, and accesses the numerous surrounding villages. These are smaller (and cheaper), and with their own lifts form good alternative bases to Gstaad itself. Three areas of slopes are accessed via lifts dotted around the fringes of Gstaad and served by a regular shuttle-bus service.

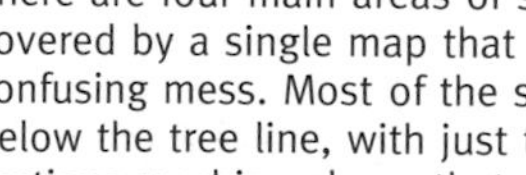

THE MOUNTAINS

There are four main areas of slopes, covered by a single map that is a confusing mess. Most of the slopes are below the tree line, with just the top sections reaching above that.

Slopes Wasserngrat (to the east of the village) and Wispile (to the south) are both small areas with one or two main lifts and runs alongside them. Eggli (to the west) is more complex, and leads via the valley of Chalberhöni to the crags of Videmanette, also accessible by gondola from the rustic village of Rougemont, just over the border into French-speaking Switzerland.

The fourth and largest sector is accessed from the lift stations at Saanenmöser and Schönried. The slopes here have for years been linked with those above St Stephan, over the mountain, and more recently have been linked to those above Zweisimmen. Saanenmöser and Schönried are no more inconvenient than Gstaad's local lift stations, given a train timetable. Schönried also has a separate sunny area of slopes on the opposite side of the valley.

The Glacier des Diablerets is covered by the local area pass but is 15km away to the south, with lifts at Reusch and Col du Pillon. There are excellent runs below glacier level, but the glacier itself is limited. Slightly further afield, past Rougemont, but

SNOWPIX.COM / CHRIS GILL

Gummfluh and La Videmanette (on the right) introduce a bit of drama into the landscape ↓

included on the map and connected by rail, are Château d'Oex and Les Moulins – both with their own small ski areas.

Snowboarding There's a fun-park at Eggli and a half-pipe at Zweisimmen.

Snow reliability A lack of altitude means that snow-cover can be unreliable except on the glacier, but most of the slopes are roughly north-facing and there is now quite a lot of artificial snowmaking.

Experts Few runs challenge experts. Black runs rarely exceed red difficulty, and some should be blue. There are off-piste possibilities – steep ones on the wooded flanks of Wispile and Eggli.

Intermediates Given good snow, this is a superb area for intermediates, with long, easy descents in the major area to the villages dotted around its edges – that to St Stephan being rather more testing than most. The run to Rougemont from the top of the Eggli sector is lovely, with no lifts in view. The adventurous should take a trip to the Diablerets glacier for the splendid shady red run down the lift-free Combe d'Audon – an Alpine classic.

Beginners The nursery slopes at the bottom of Wispile are adequate, and there are plenty of runs to progress to.

Cross-country The 60km of trails are very pretty, and there are some epic journeys to be done given the stamina. Most loops are low down and can suffer from poor snow; but there are higher loops, notably at the special langlauf centre at Sparenmoos.

Queues Time lost on buses or trains is more of a problem than queues, except at peak times and weekends.

Mountain restaurants Mountain restaurants are plentiful, and most are attractive, although pricey.

Schools and guides English is more widely spoken by the ski school than in many other Brit-free zones. It has a good reputation, too.

Facilities for children The kindergarten offers limited hours.

STAYING THERE

How to go Gstaad is certainly exclusive, with over three-quarters of its accommodation in private chalets and apartments. The remainder of the beds are in 3-star hotels and above.

Hotels The 5-star Palace (748 5000) is extravagantly swish, in secluded grounds. The Bernerhof (748 8844) and Christiana (744 5121) are recommended 4-stars. The Olden (744 3444) is a charming, central, chalet-style building.

Self-catering There is a wide choice of self-catering accommodation locally.

Eating out Restaurants are mainly hotel-based, and pricey. The rustic Chlösterli – a massive 350-seat establishment a short drive out – is a popular place to eat and dance. Hotel Rössli is reasonably priced and the locals' bar in the Olden has filling, value-for-money meals.

Après-ski In season nightlife is lively both at tea-time and later on.

Off the slopes Gstaad's activities are wide-ranging. The tennis centre and swimming pool complex are impressive, and there are 50km of pretty cleared walks. Getting around is easy, and excursions by rail to Montreux and Interlaken or even further afield are possible.

Phone numbers
From elsewhere in Switzerland add the prefix 033.
From abroad use the prefix +41 33.

TOURIST OFFICE

Postcode CH-3780
t +41 (33) 748 8181
f 748 8183
gst@gstaad.ch
www.gstaad.ch

SNOWPIX.COM / CHRIS GILL

And La Videmanette gives a grand view over the gentler mountains east of Gstaad →

Mürren 1650m

Stupendous views, an epic run, and a chocolate-box village

WHAT IT COSTS

3

HOW IT RATES

The slopes

Snow	***
Extent	*
Experts	***
Intermediates	***
Beginners	**
Convenience	***
Queues	***
Restaurants	**

The rest

Scenery	*****
Resort charm	*****
Off-slope	***

- ⊕ Tiny, charming, traditional 'traffic-free' village, all snowy paths and chocolate-box chalets
- ⊕ Stupendous scenery, best enjoyed on the challenging run from the panoramic Schilthorn
- ⊕ Good sports centre
- ⊕ Good snow high up, even when the rest of the region is suffering

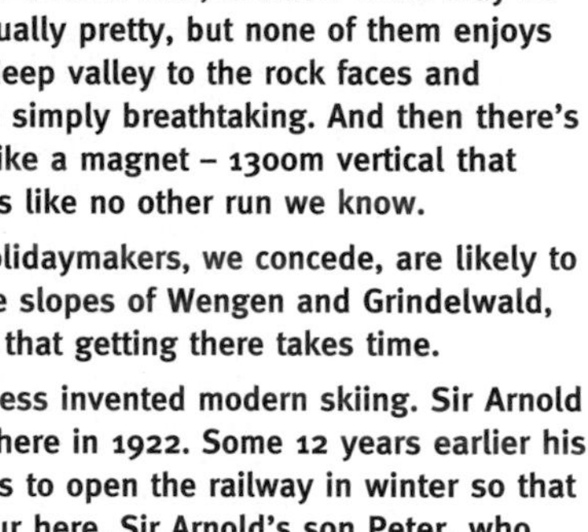

- ⊖ Extent of local pistes very limited no matter what your level of expertise
- ⊖ Lower slopes can be in poor condition and are served by some awkward T-bars
- ⊖ Quiet, limited nightlife
- ⊖ Like all other Swiss 'traffic-free' villages, Mürren is gradually admitting more service vehicles

Mürren is one of our favourite resorts – for a short visit, at least. There may be other Swiss mountain villages that are equally pretty, but none of them enjoys views like those from Mürren across the deep valley to the rock faces and glaciers of the Eiger, Mönch and Jungfrau: simply breathtaking. And then there's the Schilthorn run, which draws us back like a magnet – 1300m vertical that combines varied terrain and glorious views like no other run we know.

Our visits are normally one-day affairs; holidaymakers, we concede, are likely to want to explore the extensive intermediate slopes of Wengen and Grindelwald, across the valley. And you have to accept that getting there takes time.

It was in Mürren that the British more or less invented modern skiing. Sir Arnold Lunn organised the first ever slalom race here in 1922. Some 12 years earlier his father, Sir Henry, had persuaded the locals to open the railway in winter so that he could bring the first winter package tour here. Sir Arnold's son Peter, who first skied here in November 1916, now skis here with his children and grandchildren. Mürren's that kind of place.

The resort

Mürren is set on a shelf 800m above the Lauterbrunnen valley floor, across from Wengen, and can be reached only by cable-car from Stechelberg (via Gimmelwald) or funicular and then railway from Lauterbrunnen. Once you get there you can't fail to be struck by Mürren's tranquillity and beauty. The tiny village is made up of paths and narrow lanes weaving between tiny wooden chalets and a handful of bigger hotel buildings. The roofs and paths are normally snow-covered.

Two further stages of the cable-car take you up to the high slopes of Birg and the Schilthorn, nearby lifts go to the main lower slopes, and a newly modernised funicular halfway along the

KVV MÜRREN

The views of the Eiger, Mönch and Jungfrau are quite amazing →

MOUNTAIN FACTS

Altitude	945m-2970m
Lifts	45
Pistes	205km
Blue	30%
Red	50%
Black	20%
Artificial snow	30km
Recco detectors used	

SCHOOLS/GUIDES

2000/01 prices in Swiss francs

Swiss
Classes 6 days
2hr: 9.45-11.45
6 days 135
Children's classes
Ages: from 4
2hr: 6 days 135
Private lessons
Half day (2hr) or full day (5hr)
from 110 for 2hr

village accesses the other slopes.

Although in our summary above we protest against the gradual 'traffic' increase, Mürren still isn't plagued by electric carts and taxis as most other traditional 'traffic-free' resorts now are.

It's not the place to go for lively nightlife, shopping or showing off your latest gear to admiring hordes. It is the place to go if you want tranquillity and stunning views.

The village is so small that location is not a concern. Nothing is more than a few minutes' walk.

The mountain

Mürren's slopes aren't extensive (53km in total). But it has something for everyone, including one of our favourite runs, and a vertical of some 1300m. And those happy to take the time to cross the valley to Wengen–Grindelwald will find plenty of options. These resorts are covered by the Jungfrau lift pass.

THE SLOPES
Small but interesting

There are three connected areas around the village, reaching no higher than 2145m. The biggest is **Schiltgrat**, served by a fast quad chair behind the cable-car station. You can also get there from the top of the modernised funicular that goes from the middle of the village to the nursery slope at **Allmendhubel** – from where a run and a drag-lift take you to the slightly higher **Maulerhubel**. Runs go down from here to the Winteregg stop on the railway, too. These lower slopes take you up to around 2000m.

Much more interesting are the higher slopes reached by cable-car. The first stage takes you to Birg and the **Engetal** area, where an old T-bar serves short, steep, shady slopes. Two chair-lifts below the Engetal now serve some snowsure intermediate slopes. But plans for a third chair, back up to Birg, have been shelved. To get back to the Birg cable-car station and avoid the tricky black run down to the village, you face an annoying walk up from these chairs to the old T-bar.

The final stage of the cable-car takes you up to the 2970m summit of the **Schilthorn** and the Piz Gloria revolving restaurant, made famous by the James Bond film *On Her Majesty's Secret Service*. In good snow you can go all the way from here (via the Engetal and the Maulerhubel drag-lift) to Lauterbrunnen at 795m – a distance of almost 16km and a vertical drop of

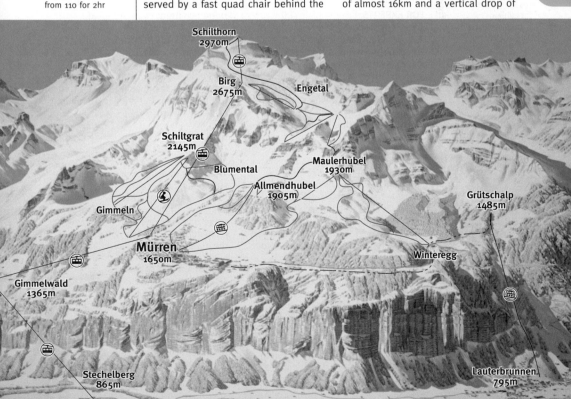

Schilthorn 2970m
Birg 2675m
Engetal
Schiltgrat 2145m
Blumental
Maulerhubel 1930m
Allmendhubel 1905m
Grütschalp 1485m
Gimmeln
Mürren 1650m
Winteregg
Gimmelwald 1365m
Stechelberg 865m
Lauterbrunnen 795m

boarding *Like other Swiss resorts, Mürren has a traditional image, but it is trying to move with the times and offer a more snowboard-friendly attitude. This may be at odds with the resort's usual clientele, but they build a half-pipe every season, and the major lifts are cable-cars and chair-lifts (though there are some key drag-lifts too). The terrain above Mürren is suitable mainly for good free-riders – it's steep, with a lot of off-piste routes. Intermediates will find the area tough and limited, but nearby Wengen is ideal and is much better for beginners. At night, Mürren is quiet, with not much scope for raving.*

LIFT PASSES

2000/01 prices in Swiss francs

Jungfrau Top Ski Region
Covers all lifts in Wengen, Mürren and Grindelwald, trains between them and Grindelwald ski-bus.

Beginners Points card (adult 100 points 48, lifts cost 4 to 10 points).

Main pass
1-day pass 52
6-day pass 254

Senior citizens
Over 62: 6-day pass 229

Children
16 to 19: 6-day 203
Under 16: 6-day pass 127
Under 6: 6-day pass 25

Short-term passes
Single ascent tickets for most lifts. Half-day pass for Mürren-Schilthorn (adult 40).

Alternative periods
3 days in 7 pass is available (156).

Notes Day pass price is for Mürren-Schilthorn area only (53km of piste, 12 lifts), as Jungfrau Top Ski Region pass is only available for 2 days or over.

Alternative passes
1- and 2-day passes available for Mürren-Schilthorn (adult 2-day 95) and Kleine Scheidegg-Männlichen (adult 2-day 95).
4-, 5- and 6-day passes available for non-skiers (adult 6-day 189).

2175m. The Inferno race (see box opposite) takes place over this course, conditions permitting. But below Winteregg it's all boring paths.

The Jungfrau piste map doesn't deal with Mürren's slopes at all well. The one used in the Mürren brochures (on which our own is based) is better.

SNOW RELIABILITY
Good on the upper slopes

The Jungfrau region does not have a good snow record – but Mürren always has the best snow in the area. When Wengen–Grindelwald (and Mürren's lower slopes) have problems, the Schilthorn and Engetal often have packed powder snow because of their height orientation – north-east to east. A recent reporter confirms that piste grooming and marking are poor.

FOR EXPERTS
One wonderful piste

The run from the top of the Schilthorn starts with a steep but not terrifying slope, in the past generally mogulled but now often groomed. It flattens into a schuss to Engetal, below Birg. Then there's a wonderful, wide run with stunning views over the valley to the Eiger, Mönch and Jungfrau. Since the chair-lifts were built here you can play on these upper runs for as long as you like. Below the lifts you hit the Kanonenrohr (gun barrel). This is a very narrow shelf with solid rock on one side and a steep drop on the other – protected by nets. After an open slope and scrappy zig-zag path, you arrive at the 'hog's back' and can descend towards the village on either side of Allmendhubel.

From Schiltgrat a short, serious mogul run – the Kandahar – descends towards the village, but experts are more likely to be interested in the off-piste runs into the Blumental – both from here (the north-facing Blumenlucke run) and from Birg (the sunnier Tschingelchrachen) – or the adventurous runs from the Schilthorn.

FOR INTERMEDIATES
Limited, but Wengen nearby

Keen piste-bashers will want to make a few trips to the long cruising runs of Wengen–Grindelwald. The best easy cruising run in Mürren is the north-facing blue down to Winteregg. The reds on the other low slopes can get mogulled, and snow conditions can be poor. The area below the Engetal normally has good snow, and you can choose your gradient.

FOR BEGINNERS
Not ideal, but adequate

The nursery slopes at Allmendhubel, at the top of the funicular, are on the steep side. And there are not many easy runs to graduate to – though the blue down the Winteregg chair is easy, and the Schilt-Apollo blue served by the long Gimmeln drag and the less tiring Schiltgrat chair are ideal.

FOR CROSS-COUNTRY
Forget it

There is one small loop above the village in the Blumental, and more extensive loops down at Lauterbrunnen or Stechelberg. But snow is unreliable at valley height.

QUEUES
Generally not a problem

Mürren doesn't get as crowded as Wengen and Grindelwald, except on sunny Sundays. There can be queues for the cable-cars – usually when snow shortages bring in refugees. The top stage has only one cabin. The new Allmendhubel funicular goes at twice the speed of the old one.

MOUNTAIN RESTAURANTS
Disappointing at altitude

Piz Gloria revolves once an hour, displaying a fabulous 360° panorama of peaks and lakes. Don't expect particularly good food, or a small bill. By the 'new' Engetal chair-lifts, the Schilthorn Hutte is small and rustic.

Lower down, the Suppenalp in the

CHILDCARE

The ski school takes children from age 4.

For the last few years there has been non-skiing childcare in the sports centre. But lack of demand has meant that it may not be available in the coming seasons. The tourist office staff suggest you contact them for the latest situation.

GETTING THERE

Air Zürich, transfer 3½hr. Bern, transfer 1½hr.

Rail Lauterbrunnen; transfer by mountain railway and tram.

ACTIVITIES

Indoor 'Alpine Sports Centre Mürren' swimming pool, whirlpool and children's pool, library, children's playroom, gymnasium, squash, sauna, solarium, steam bath, massage, fitness room

Outdoor Artificial skating rink (curling, skating), toboggan run to Gimmelwald, 15km cleared paths

Phone numbers
From elsewhere in Switzerland add the prefix 033.
From abroad use the prefix +41 33.

TOURIST OFFICE

Postcode CH-3825
t +41 (33) 856 8686
f 856 8696
info@muerren.ch
www.wengen-muerren.ch

Blumental is rustic and quietly set, does 'excellent food' but gets no sun in January. Sonnenburg is sunnier. Gimmelen is a self-service place with a large terrace, famous for its apple cake. Winteregg does something similar, as well as 'the best burger east of the Rockies'. Both have little playgrounds to amuse kids.

SCHOOLS AND GUIDES
Small, not perfectly formed

Recent reports speak of good progress for beginners, but also of one English speaker who had a rather lonely week in a group with six Germans – the kind of thing that happens in a small resort.

FACILITIES FOR CHILDREN
Adequate

There is a baby slope with rope tow. There may be a children's club at the sports centre but the tourist office staff suggest you contact them in advance to see if it will be open. The ski school takes children from four years.

Staying there

HOW TO GO
Mainly hotels, packaged or not

A handful of operators offer packages to Mürren.

Hotels There are fewer than a dozen hotels, ranging widely in style.

((((4 **Palace** (855 2424) Victorian pile near station – recently renovated.

((((4 **Eiger** (856 5454) Plain-looking 'chalet' blocks next to railway station, widely recommended; good blend of efficiency and charm; good food; pool.

(((3 **Alpenruh** (856 8800) Attractively renovated chalet next to the cable-car.

(((3 **Edelweiss** (855 1312) Block-like but friendly; good food and facilities.

(((3 **Jungfrau** (856 4545) Perfectly placed for families, in front of the baby slope and close to the funicular.

((2 **Alpenblick** (855 1327) Simple, small, modern chalet near station.

Self-catering There are plenty of chalets and apartments in the village for independent travellers to rent.

EATING OUT
Mainly in hotels

The main alternative to hotels is the rustic Stägerstübli – a bar as well as restaurant. The locals eat in the little diner at the back. The food at the Eiger hotel is good, and the Bellevue and Alpenruh get good reports.

APRES-SKI
Not devoid of life

The Eiger Bar (in the Eiger guest house, not the hotel) is the Brits' meeting place. The tiny Stägerstübli is cosy, and the place to meet locals. Other activities are hotel-based. The Palace's Balloon bar is an attempt at a trendy cocktail bar; it also has a weekend disco, the Inferno. The Bliemli Challer disco in the Blumental caters for kids, the nightly Tachi disco in the Eiger for a more mixed crowd.

OFF THE SLOPES
Tranquillity but not much else

There isn't a lot to amuse people who don't want to hit the slopes. But there is a very good sports centre, with an outdoor ice rink. Excursions by car or train to Interlaken and to Bern are easy to undertake. It's no problem for friends to return to the village for lunch. The only problem with meeting at the top of the cable-car instead is the expense.

STAYING DOWN THE VALLEY
A cheaper option

Lauterbrunnen is a good budget place to stay. It has a resort atmosphere and access to and from both Wengen and Mürren until late.

THE INFERNO RACE

Every January 1,800 amateurs compete in the spectacular Inferno race. Conditions permitting, and they usually don't, the race goes from the top of the Schilthorn at 2970m right down to Lauterbrunnen at 795m – a vertical drop of 2175m and a distance of almost 16km, incorporating a short climb at Maulerhubel. The racers start in pairs at 30-second intervals and the fastest finish the course in around 15 minutes, but anything under half an hour is very respectable.

The race was started by Sir Arnold Lunn in 1928 when he and his friends climbed to the top of the Schilthorn, spent the night in a mountain hut and then raced down in the morning. For many years the race was organised by the British-run Kandahar Club, and there is still a strong British presence among the competitors.

Saas-Fee 1800m

Beautiful, car-free village with slopes on top of the world

WHAT IT COSTS

(4)

HOW IT RATES

The slopes

Snow	*****
Extent	**
Experts	***
Intermediates	****
Beginners	*****
Convenience	***
Queues	***
Restaurants	***

The rest

Scenery	****
Resort charm	*****
Off-slope	****

What's new

A new family offer was introduced for 2000/01 – children aged up to 16 ski for free if two adults buy a 6-day or 5-days-in-7 pass.

- ⊕ Spectacular setting amid peaks and glaciers – slopes open year-round
- ⊕ Traditional, 'traffic-free' village
- ⊕ Good percentage of high-altitude, snowsure slopes
- ⊕ Powerful lift access to highest slopes for year-round skiing
- ⊕ Good off-slope facilities are banned

- ⊖ Disappointingly small area of slopes, with mainly easy runs
- ⊖ Glacier stops off-piste exploration
- ⊖ Much of the area is in shadow in midwinter – cold and dark
- ⊖ Bad weather can shut the slopes
- ⊖ Long village can mean quite a bit of walking to and from the slopes

Saas-Fee is one of our favourite places. It oozes Swiss charm, and the setting is stunning – spectacular glaciers and 4000m peaks surround the place. And good snow is guaranteed, even late in the season: the altitude you spend most of your time at – between 2500m and 3500m – is unrivalled in the Alps.

But we tend to drop in for a couple of days at a time, so the limited extent of the slopes never becomes a problem; for a week's holiday, it would. Top to bottom there is an impressive 1800m vertical – but there aren't many alternative ways down. Keen, mileage-hungry intermediates should look elsewhere, as should experts (except those prepared to go touring). For the rest, it's a question of priorities and expectations. Over to you.

The resort

Like nearby Zermatt, Saas-Fee is a high-altitude mountain village centred on narrow streets lined by attractive old chalets and free of cars (there are car parks at the resort entrance) but not free of electric milk floats posing as taxis. On most other counts, Saas-Fee and its more exalted neighbour are a long way apart in style.

There are some very smart hotels (plus many more modest ones) and plenty of good eating and drinking places. But there's little of the glamour and greed that, for some, spoil Zermatt – and even the electric taxis here are driven at a more considerate pace. Saas-Fee still feels like a village, with its cow sheds more obviously still containing cows. The village may be chilly in January, but when the spring sun is beating down, Saas-Fee is a quite beautiful place in which to just stroll around and relax, admiring the impressive view.

Depending on where you're staying and which way you want to go up the mountain, you may do more marching than strolling. It's a long walk from one end of the spread-out village to the other, though your hotel may run a courtesy bus to and from the lifts. Three major lifts start from the southern end of the village, at the foot of the slopes, and lots of the hotels and apartments are 1km or more away. The modern Alpin Express starts below the centre, though, quite near the entrance to the resort.

The village centre has the school and guides' office, the church and a few more shops than elsewhere, but doesn't add up to much. On a sunny day, though, the restaurant terraces fronting the nursery slopes at the far end of the village are a magnet, with breathtaking views up to the ring of 4000m peaks – you can see why the village is called 'The Pearl of the Alps'.

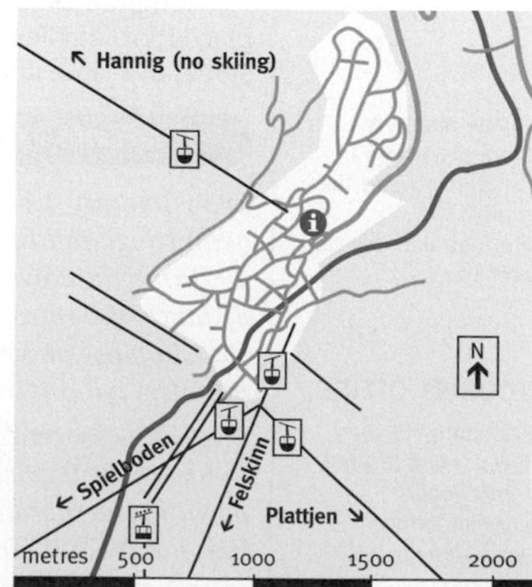

Saas-Fee's highest slopes are on and around the glaciers →

SNOWPIX.COM / CHRIS GILL

Staying near a main lift makes most sense. If you do end up at the wrong (north) end of the village – and most budget accommodation is there – ease the pain by storing kit near the lifts.

The modest slopes of Saas-Almagell and more extensive ones of Saas-Grund are not far away, and you can buy a lift pass that covers all four resorts and buses between them. Day trips to Zermatt, Grächen and Crans-Montana are also realistic options for those itching for a change.

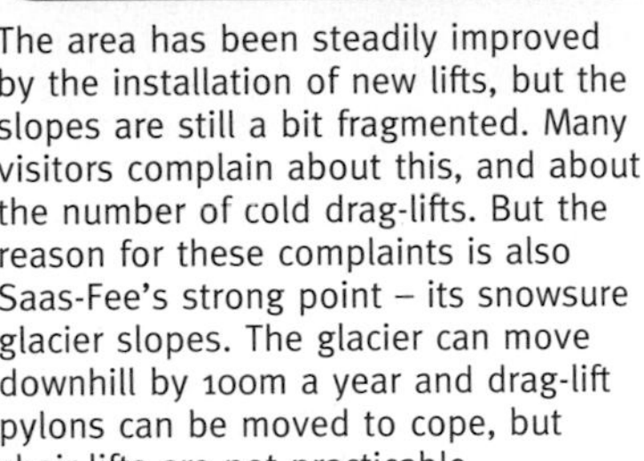

The mountain

MOUNTAIN FACTS

Altitude	1800m-3620m
Lifts	27
Pistes	100km
Blue	25%
Red	50%
Black	25%
Artificial snow	10km
Recco detectors used	

The area has been steadily improved by the installation of new lifts, but the slopes are still a bit fragmented. Many visitors complain about this, and about the number of cold drag-lifts. But the reason for these complaints is also Saas-Fee's strong point – its snowsure glacier slopes. The glacier can move downhill by 100m a year and drag-lift pylons can be moved to cope, but chair-lifts are not practicable.

The upper slopes are largely gentle, while the lower mountain, below the glacier, is steeper and rockier.

Saas-Fee is one of the leading resorts for mountaineering and ski-touring. Several nearby peaks can be climbed, and the extended Haute Route from Chamonix ends here.

LIFT PASSES

2000/01 prices in Swiss francs

Saas-Fee area
Covers all lifts in Saas-Fee only.

Beginners Village area pass covers 5 beginners' lifts. 1-day 20, 6 days 90

Main pass
1-day pass 58
6-day pass 270

Children
Under 16: 6-day pass 162
Under 6: free pass

Short-term passes
Single and return tickets on most main lifts. Half-day pass from noon (adult 46).

Notes Discount for groups of 20 or more.

Alternative passes
Separate passes for each of the other ski areas in the Saastal (Saas-Grund, Saas-Almagell, Saas-Balen). Pass for all four villages in the Saastal also available, and includes ski-bus between them. 6-day pass, 294.

THE SLOPES
A glacier runs through it

The main **Felskinn** area can be reached in three ways. The efficient 30-person Alpin Express jumbo gondola takes you to Felskinn at 3000m, starting across the river from the main village. It has a mid-station at Maste 4 (where you have to change cabins).

The Felskinn cable-car, starting a short drag-lift away from the foot of the main pistes and nursery slopes at the southern end of the village, also takes you to Felskinn.

From Felskinn, the Metro Alpin (an underground funicular) hurtles to the thin air at Mittelallalin (3500m). From below here the top two drag-lifts access the high point of 3620m.

Also from the south end of the village, a gondola leaves for Spielboden. This is met by a cable-car which takes you up to **Längfluh**.

Between Felskinn and Längfluh is an off-limits glacier area. A very long drag-lift from Längfluh takes you to a point where you can get down to the Felskinn area. These two sectors are served mainly by drag-lifts, and you can get down to the village from both.

Another gondola from the south end of the village goes up to Saas-Fee's smallest area, **Plattjen**.

SNOW RELIABILITY
Good at the highest altitudes

Most of Saas-Fee's slopes face north and many are above 2500m, making this one of the most reliable resorts for snow in the Alps. The glacier is open most of the year. Visitors tell us that the substantial recent investment in

boarding *Saas-Fee encourages boarding in a big way. In summer, in particular, its glacier slopes are dominated by boarders. Facilities include a half-pipe, a fun-park and a boarder-cross. The nearby Maste 4 snow-bar is the place for a break. While the gentle glacier slopes are ideal for learning, only main access lifts are boarder-friendly (gondolas, cable-cars and a funicular); nearly all the rest are drags. There are a couple of specialist schools. Expert free-riders may be frustrated by the limits imposed on off-piste riding by the glacier. But nightlife doesn't disappoint – the Popcorn board shop and bar is popular.*

snow-guns still doesn't completely ensure good coverage on the rocky lower slopes below glacier level, though piste grooming is 'excellent'. Conversely, after heavy snowfalls you may find yourself limited to the nursery area for a while.

FOR EXPERTS
Not a lot to keep your interest
There is not much steep stuff, except on the bottom half of the mountain where the snow tends not to be as good. The highest drag-lift on the left near Felskinn serves two short, steep blacks and one easy one. The slopes around the top of Längfluh often provide good powder and there are usually moguls above Spielboden. The blacks and trees on Plattjen are worth exploring. The glacier puts limits on the local off-piste even with a guide – crevasse danger is extreme. But there are extensive touring possibilities, especially late in the season.

FOR INTERMEDIATES
Great for gentle cruising
Saas-Fee is ideal for early intermediates and those not looking for much of a challenge. For long cruises, head for Mittelallalin. The top of the mountain, down as far Längfluh in one direction, and as far as Maste 4 in the other, is ideal, with usually excellent snow. Gradients range from gentle blues to slightly steeper reds which can build up smallish bumps.

Recent visitors loved the 'beautiful, wide blue and red cruising runs accessed by the drag between Maste 4 and Felskinn'.

The 1800m vertical descent from Mittelallalin (via Felskinn or Längfluh) to the village is a great test of stamina – or, if you choose, an enjoyable long cruise with plenty of view stops. The lower runs have steepish, tricky sections and can have poor snow, especially if it isn't cold enough to make snow – timid intermediates might prefer to take a lift down from mid-mountain.

Plattjen has a variety of runs, all of them fine for ambitious intermediates and often underused.

FOR BEGINNERS
Usually a nice place to start
There's a good, large, out-of-the-way nursery area at the edge of the village. Those ready to progress can head for the gentle blues on Felskinn just above Maste 4 – it's best to return by the Alpin Express. There are also gentle

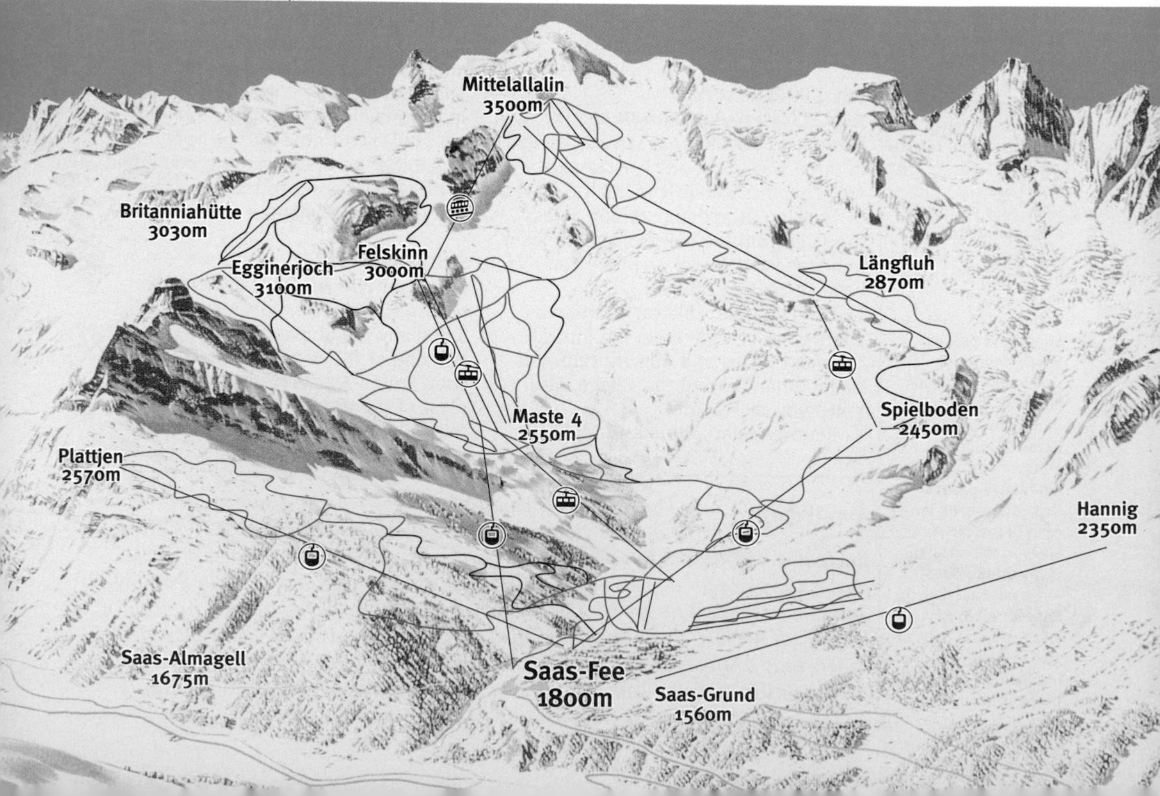

Sadly, the sun terrace doesn't revolve. They're working on a system of mirrors so that the view moves but you never have to turn away from the sun →

SNOWPIX.COM / CHRIS GILL

EUROPE'S HIGHEST LUNCH?

There is something beautifully Swiss about the idea of a revolving restaurant – and all three pivoting pubs in the Alps are in Switzerland. 'Customers not getting a share of the views? Can't have that. Only one thing for it: spin the whole restaurant about once an hour.' Actually, they spin only the bit of floor with the tables on it; the stairs stay put (along with the windows – watch your gloves).

Two years after Saas-Fee built the Alps' highest funicular railway in 1984, it crowned that with the world's highest revolving restaurant – a good 500m higher than the famous original on Mürren's Schilthorn. We don't rate the views from Mittelallalin so highly. But it's an amusing novelty that most visitors enjoy. To reserve a table next to the windows phone 957 1771. And the third spinning speisesaal? At Leysin.

blues at the top of the mountain, from where you can head down to Längfluh. Again, use the lifts to return to base.

A useful beginners' pass covers all the short lifts at the village edge, for those not ready to go higher.

FOR CROSS-COUNTRY
Good local trail and lots nearby
There is one short (8km) pleasant trail at the edge of the village. It snakes up through the woods, providing about 150m of climb and nice views. There are more options in the valley.

QUEUES
Only if snow is poor elsewhere
Lift improvements seem to have done their job and queues are now rare: 'Considering it was half-term, and the weather wonderful with excellent snow, we were relieved at how little we had to queue.' But things change if snow is poor elsewhere, not an uncommon thing late in the season – as one recent Easter visitor found: 'The worst I'd seen for years – half-hour waits for the Felskinn cable-car and 25-minute waits for the Alpin Express – and it got worse as the week went on.'

MOUNTAIN RESTAURANTS
Fair choice, but not like Zermatt
The restaurants at the main lift stations are functional. The best places are slightly off the beaten track: the Berghaus Plattjen (just down from Plattjen) and the Gletschergrotte, halfway down from Spielboden (watch for the path from the piste). Both have good food in old huts. If you're up for a trek, the Britanniahütte is a real mountain refuge, with atmosphere and views. The new restaurant at the top of Plattjen has 'friendly service and the best rösti in the resort'. At Spielboden there's 'good food', a terrace and views of tricky slopes. At Längfluh the large terrace has views of huge crevasses, and Popcorn Plaza nearby is popular with a 'really good atmosphere'. Maste 4 has 'cheap and very good' pizza. Back in the village, the sunny, piste-side terrace of the

SCHOOLS/GUIDES

2000/01 prices in Swiss francs

Swiss
Classes 5 days
3hr: 10am-1pm, 45
5 days (15hr): 168
Children's classes
5-day ski courses including lunch, from age 3
Private lessons
Hourly or daily
56 for 1hr for 1 or 2 people

CHILDCARE

The Bären-Klub (Bears Club) kindergarten takes infants for full days or half days. From age 3, they can go here in the morning and to ski school in the afternoon. Full junior ski school starts at age 4. Lunchtime care and meals can be provided with all programmes.

There's also a children's day centre for kids aged 2 to 6 in Saas Grund.

GETTING THERE

Air Sion, transfer 1hr. Geneva, transfer 3½hr. Zürich, transfer 4hr. Milan, transfer 3hr.

Rail Brig (38km); regular buses from station.

Phone numbers
From elsewhere in Switzerland add the prefix 027.
From abroad use the prefix +41 27.

ACTIVITIES

Indoor Bielen leisure centre (swimming, hot-tub, steam bath, whirlpool, solarium, sauna, massage, tennis, gym), cinema, museum, concerts, badminton
Outdoor 20km cleared paths, natural skating rink (skating, curling, ice hockey), toboggan run, paragliding

TOURIST OFFICE

Postcode CH-3906
t +41 (27) 958 1858
f 958 1860
to@saas-fee.ch
www.saas-fee.ch

Waldesruh Hotel serves 'wonderful' rösti and the terrace of the Belmont is a popular sunbathing spot.

SCHOOLS AND GUIDES
Good reports

For skiing, it's the Swiss school or nothing. In the past we've received complaints of 'arrogant attitude', but recent reporters seem better pleased: 'excellent' says one, 'had a good private lesson and felt I was skiing better afterwards,' says another.

FACILITIES FOR CHILDREN
Seem adequate

The school takes children from four years old, and the reports we have had have been positive – 'Most classes quite small and English spoken'. One solution for younger ones is to stay at a hotel with an in-house kindergarten – see reports below.

Staying there

HOW TO GO
Check the location

Quite a few UK tour operators sell holidays to Saas-Fee, offering an excellent range of hotels. But there are surprisingly few chalet holidays.

Hotels There are 50-plus hotels, so lots of choice.

((((5 **Fletschhorn** (957 2131) Elegant chalet in woods, with original art and individual rooms, a trek from the village and lifts, but fabulous food.
(((4 **Walliserhof** (958 1900) Excellent 4-star. Superb, friendly welcome and service, delicious dinners, champagne breakfast. Spa.
(((4 **Schweizerhof** (957 5159) Stylish place in quiet position above the centre. 'Fantastic food, friendly staff, excellent kindergarten.' Pool.
((3 **Beau-Site** (958 1560) 'First-rate' but quiet 4-star in central, but not convenient, position. Good food. Pool.
((3 **Saaserhof** (957 3551) Modernised old chalet in good position, over river from nursery slopes. Sauna, whirlpool.
((3 **Ambassador** (957 1420) Modern chalet, close to nursery slopes.
((3 **Alphubel** (957 1112) At the wrong end of town, praised by reporters for its own 'brilliant nursery'.
((3 **Waldesruh** (957 2232) Strongly recommended by a reporter: 'Best situation in Saas-Fee for the Alpin Express.'
((3 **Hohnegg** (957 2268) Small rustic alternative to the Fletschhorn, in a similarly remote spot.
(2 **Belmont** (958 1640) The most appealing of the hotels looking directly on to the nursery slopes.

Self-catering Most apartments featured by UK operators are at the north end of the village, remote from the slopes, but they are generally spacious and well equipped. Independent travellers can choose better situated apartments.

EATING OUT
No shortage – some high class

Gastronomes will want to head for the highly acclaimed Fletschhorn – expensive but excellent. Our favourite is the less formal Bodmen along a path into the woods. It has great food (from rösti to fillet steak) and rustic ambience. We had a delicious Thai meal in one of the Walliserhof's several restaurants. Boccalino is cheap and does pizzas – book or get there early. Alp-Hitta specialises in rustic food and surroundings. The hotel Dom's restaurant specialises in endless varieties of rösti. Arvu-Stuba, Zur Mühle, La Gorge, Feeloch, Skihütte and La Ferme have all been recommended.

APRES-SKI
Excellent and varied

Late afternoon, Nesti's ski-bar, Zur Mühle and the little snow-bars such as Black Bull, near the lifts, are all pretty lively, especially if the sun's shining. Later on, Nesti's and the Underground keep going till 1am. Popcorn is packed and praised for 'lively atmosphere, brilliant music and catering for all ages'. The Art Club is smarter and more sophisticated, with live music. The Metro Bar is like being in a 19th-century mine shaft; Why Not pub is popular; The Metropol has the Crazy Night disco and a couple of other bars.

OFF THE SLOPES
A mountain for pedestrians

The whole of the Hannig mountainside is dedicated to eating, drinking, walking, tobogganing and paragliding – skiers and boarders are banned. In the village, the splendid Bielen leisure centre boasts a 25m pool, indoor tennis courts and a lounging area with sunlamps. There's also the 'interesting' Saas museum and the Bakery Museum, where children can make bread. Don't miss the largest ice pavilion in the world, which is carved out of the glacier at Mittelallalin and includes a wedding chapel.

St Moritz 1770m

Luxury living – on and off the flatteringly easy slopes

WHAT IT COSTS

6

HOW IT RATES

The slopes

Snow	****
Extent	*****
Experts	****
Intermediates	****
Beginners	**
Convenience	**
Queues	**
Restaurants	****

The rest

Scenery	****
Resort charm	*
Off-slope	*****

What's new

The World Alpine Ski Championships are to be held in St Moritz in 2003, and have heralded much improvement in the resort, including road access, lift updating, more snowmaking and recent refurbishment of all the 5-star hotels.

For 2001/02 on Corviglia, the Plateau Nair T-bar from Marguns will be replaced by a high-speed quad chair. For 2002/03 the ancient, tiny Piz Nair cable car will be rebuilt to increase its capacity.

Always a centre for teaching blind skiers, St Moritz is now offering the same to blind snowboarders.

- + Beautiful panoramic scenery
- + Off-slope activities second to none – including the Cresta Run, horse-racing and lots of varied festivals
- + Extensive, largely intermediate slopes
- + Fairly snowsure, thanks to altitude and extensive snowmaking
- + Good après-ski, for all tastes
- + Good mountain restaurants, some with magnificent views
- + Painless rail access via Zürich

- − Some hideous block buildings
- − A sizeable town, with little traditional Alpine character
- − No proper nursery slopes at resort level – except at Celerina
- − Several unlinked mountains, with a bus, train or car needed to most
- − Runs on two main mountains all fairly easy and much the same
- − Expensive

St Moritz is Switzerland's most famous 'exclusive' winter resort: glitzy, pricey, fashionable and, above all, the place to be seen – it's the place for an all-round winter holiday with an unrivalled array of different diversions, including such wacky pursuits as polo, golf and cricket on snow and gourmet and music festivals. The slopes on the two main mountains are almost uniformly easy intermediate – we don't rate it highly for complete beginners, and experts must be prepared to venture off-piste. But for cross-country, it is superb.

The town of St Moritz doesn't have the chocolate-box image of a Swiss mountain resort, all wooden huts and cows with bells round their necks. Many buildings resemble council flats (extremely neat and clean ones – it is Switzerland, after all).

But you may find, as some readers have, that St Moritz's spectacular setting, beside the lowest in a long chain of lakes at the foot of the 4000m Piz Bernina, blinds you to the town's aesthetic faults. This is one of those areas where our progress on the mountain is regularly interrupted by the need to stand and gaze. It may not have quite the drama of the Jungfrau massif, or the Matterhorn, or the Dolomites, but its wide and glorious mountain landscapes are equally special. And the langlauf, walking and other activities on the frozen lake give it a real 'winter wonderland' feel.

The resort

St Moritz has two distinct parts. Dorf is the fashionable main part, on a steep hillside above the lake. It's a busy, compact town with two main streets lined with boutiques selling Rolex watches, Cartier jewellery and Hermes scarves, a few side lanes and a small main square. A funicular takes you from Dorf to the main slopes of Corviglia, also reached by gondola from down the road at Celerina, and by cable-car from Dorf's other half, the spa resort of St Moritz Bad, spread around one end of the lake.

Everything in Bad is less prestigious. Many of the modern buildings are uncompromisingly rectangular and spoil otherwise superb views. In winter the lake is used for eccentric activities including horse and greyhound racing, show jumping, polo, 'ice golf' and even cricket. It also makes a superb setting for walking and cross-country skiing.

Other downhill slopes, at Corvatsch, are reached via lifts at Surlej and Sils Maria. Cross-country skiing is the main activity around the outlying villages of Samedan and Pontresina.

The town clientele is typified by the results of a Cresta Run race we saw on one of our visits. In the top 29 were three Lords, one Count, one Archduke and a Baronet – but the race was won by a Swiss, without a title.

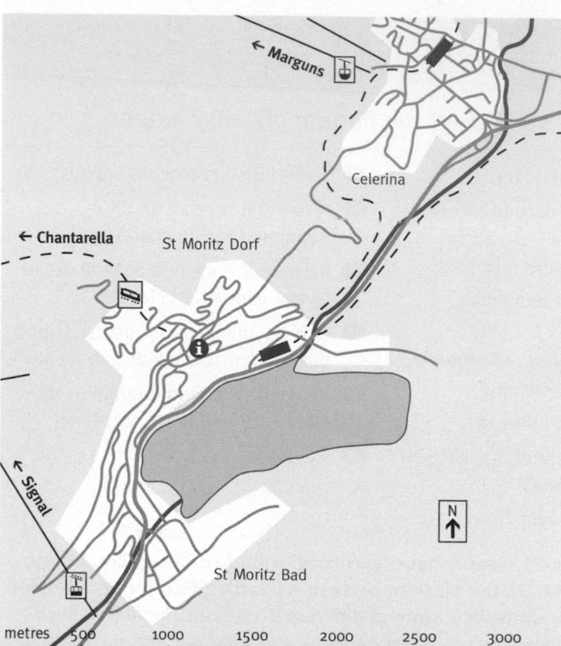

The mountains

MOUNTAIN FACTS

Altitude 1730m-3300m	
Lifts	57
Pistes	350km
Blue	16%
Red	71%
Black	13%
Artificial snow	45km
Recco detectors used	

Like the resort, most of the slopes are made for posing. There are lots of long and generally wide flatteringly well-groomed runs, with varied terrain. There's an occasional black run, but few are seriously steep. But there is tough off-piste, and it doesn't get tracked out as it does in more macho resorts. Beginners' slopes are few and far between. Trips to other resorts such as Klosters, Davos (both around 90 minutes by train or car) and Livigno (an hour by car) are also possible.

THE SLOPES
Big but broken up

The several distinct areas add up to a substantial 350km of pistes. The main slopes, shown on our maps, are nearby Corviglia–Marguns and Corvatsch–Furtschellas, a bus-ride away (although you can get back to Bad on snow). Diavolezza, Piz Lagalb, Alp Languard and a few more distant bits and pieces make up the rest. Some of these are well worth an outing. It helps to have a car, although the free bus service is reported to be fairly efficient.

From St Moritz Dorf a two-stage monorail goes up to **Corviglia**, a fair-sized area with slopes facing east and south. The peak of Piz Nair, reached from here by an ancient cable-car, splits the area – sunny runs towards the main valley, and less sunny ones to the north. From Corviglia you can head down (snow permitting) to Dorf and Bad, and via the lower lift junction of Marguns to Celerina.

From Surlej, a few miles from St Moritz, a two-stage cable-car takes you to the north-facing slopes of **Corvatsch**. From the mid-station at Murtèl you have a choice of reds to Margun-Vegl and Alp Margun. From the latter you can work your way to **Furtschellas**, also reached by cable-car from Sils Maria, and to Bad.

Diavolezza (2980m) and Lagalb (2960m), the main additional areas, are on opposite sides of the road to the Bernina pass to Italy, less than half an hour away by bus. **Diavolezza** has excellent north-facing pistes of 900m vertical, down under its big 125-person cable-car, and a very popular 'amazing' off-piste route, off the back of the mountain, across a glacier and down a valley beneath Piz Bernina to Morteratsch. **Lagalb** is a smaller area with quite challenging slopes, with an 80-person cable-car serving the west-facing front slope of 850m vertical.

SNOW RELIABILITY
Reasonable

This corner of the Alps has a rather dry climate, but the altitude means that any precipitation is likely to be snowy – several reporters told us how good the snow was throughout the 2000/01 season, when many other resorts were

boarding *Despite the high prices and its glitzy image, the terrain in St Moritz turns out to be quite favourable and the resort produces a special boarders' booklet with recommended 'secret spots', 'natural freestyle' and beginner areas. Above the town on Corviglia there is a fun-park and half-pipe in the Signal area and there are two fun-parks in the Corvatsch/Furtschellas area. The Corvatsch area has links that rely on drags – otherwise, most lifts are chairs, gondolas, cable-cars and trains. The extent of well-groomed cruising runs should appeal to any hard-booter, and there are several specialist snowboard shops. At night, there are a few places you don't have to wear a dinner jacket to get in.*

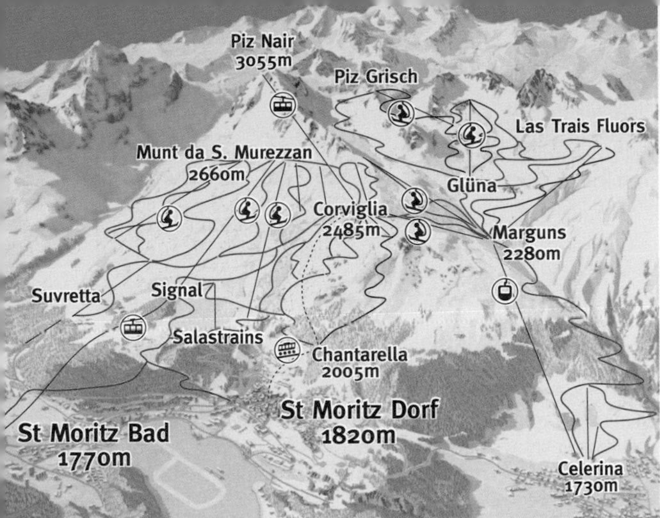

suffering warm weather and rain. There is snowmaking in every sector: several easy slopes around Corviglia are covered, as is an excellent 800m vertical red run on Corvatsch (Murtèl to Surlej), much of the 900m vertical face of Diavolezza and part of Lagalb.

FOR EXPERTS

Dispersed challenges

If you're looking for challenges, you're liable to find St Moritz disappointing on-piste. Red runs (many of which should really be graded blue) far outnumber the black, and mogul fields are few and far between. The few serious black runs are dotted about different sectors.

The blacks at Lagalb and Diavolezza are the most testing pistes. The direct Minor run down the Lagalb cable-car has 850m vertical of non-stop moguls.

There are plenty of opportunities to venture a little way off-piste in search of challenges – there is an excellent north-facing slope immediately above the Marguns lift junction, for example. Experts often head for the tough off-piste runs on Piz Nair or the Corvatsch summit. More serious expeditions can be undertaken – such as down the splendid Roseg valley from Corvatsch. The off-piste potential is all the better for being relatively little exploited.

FOR INTERMEDIATES

Good but flattering

St Moritz is great for intermediates. Most pistes are easyish reds that could well have been graded blue. Reporters enjoyed 'marvellous GS ground' around Corviglia and Murezzan, for example.

One of the finest runs is Hahnensee, from the northern limit of the Corvatsch lift system at Giand'Alva down to St Moritz Bad – a black-graded run that is of red difficulty for most of its 6km length and 900m vertical drop. It's a five-minute walk from the end of the run to the cable-car up to Corviglia.

Diavolezza is mostly intermediate. There is an easy open slope at the top, served by a fast quad, and a splendid long intermediate run back down under the lift. The popular off-piste run to Morteratsch requires a bit of energy and nerve. After a gentle climb, you cross the glacier on a narrow ledge, with crevasses waiting to gobble you up on the right. When we last did it, there were ice-picks and shovels at intervals along the path, put there by

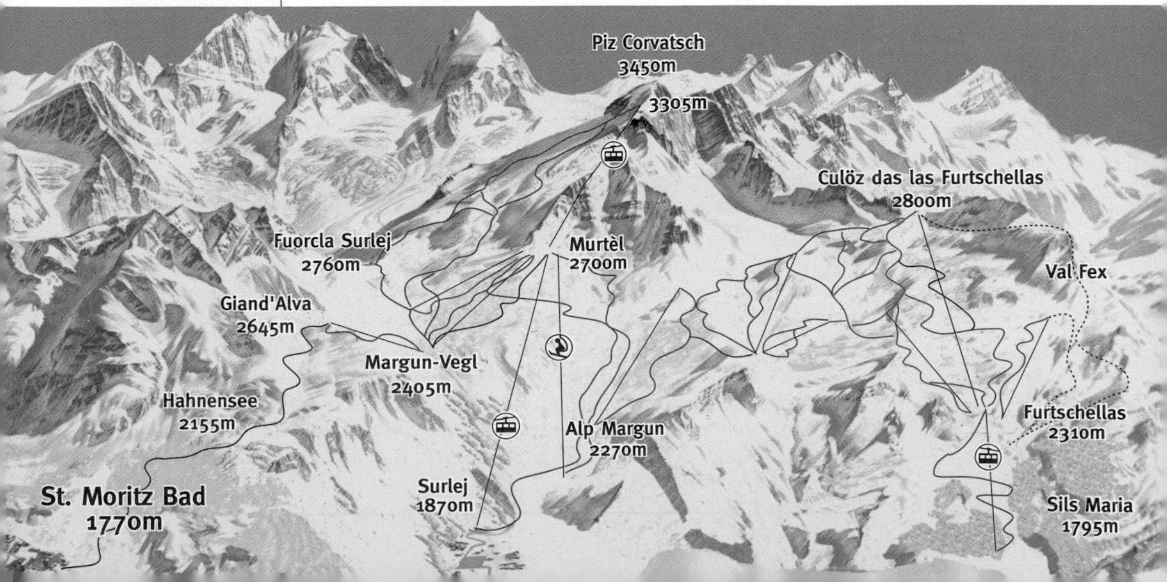

LIFT PASSES

2001/02 prices in Swiss francs

Upper Engadine
Covers all lifts in St Moritz, Celerina, Surlej, Sils Maria, Maloja, Lagalb, Diavolezza, Pontresina, Punt Muragl, Samedan, Müsella and Zuoz, and the swimming pools in St Moritz and Pontresina.

Main pass
1-day pass 65
6-day pass 305

Children/teenagers
Age 16-20: 6-day pass 275
Under 16: 6-day pass 153
Under 6: free pass

Short-term passes
Half-day pass from 11.45 (adult 53).

Notes Prices are for high season. Mid-season adult 6-day pass 290; low season 261. Child reductions too. Deposit of SF5 gets you a hands-free pass. Six-day pass gives one day's skiing in Livigno.

Alternative passes
Half-day and day passes for individual areas within the Upper Engadine.

SCHOOLS/GUIDES

2000/01 prices in Swiss francs

St Moritz

Classes 6 days
4hr: 10am-noon and 1.30-3.30
1 half day 45
6 full days: 250

Children's classes
Ages: from 5
6 full days 250

Private lessons
Half-day (2hr) or full-day (5hr)
160 for half-day

Suvretta
Small groups of 4 to 6 people

Classes 6 days
2hr, 3hr, 4hr or full-day (5hr)
Half day: 42
6 full days 250-310

the enterprising proprietors of the beautifully laid out, welcoming ice bar which greets you at the end of the 30-minute slog. After that, it's downhill through the glacier, with splendid views. Lagalb has more challenging pistes.

FOR BEGINNERS
Not much to offer

St Moritz is not ideal for beginners. It sits in a deep, steep-sided valley, with very little space for nursery slopes at the lower levels. Beginners start up at Salastrains or Corviglia, or slightly out of town, at Suvretta. Celerina has good, broad nursery slopes at village level. Progression from the nursery slopes to intermediate runs is rather awkward – these always include a difficult section.

FOR CROSS-COUNTRY
Excellent; go to Pontresina

The Engadine is one of the premier regions in the Alps for cross-country, with 150km of trails of all levels, including floodlit loops, amid splendid scenery and with pretty reliable snow. The famous Engadine Ski Marathon is held here every March – over 12,000 racers take part. Pontresina makes a great base, with lots of other activities.

QUEUES
Crowds can be a problem

St Moritz has invested heavily in new lifts lately. High-speed quad chairs are common on Corviglia and there are some six-seaters. But the area as a whole is over-dependent on cable-cars – many not huge – both for getting up the mountain from the resort and for access to peaks from mid-mountain. Queues can result, though reporters have had good experiences lately – the enlarged cable-car from Surlej to Murtèl is a big improvement, as will be the one to Piz Nair when it happens. Happy reporters comment that St

Moritz's visitors are often late risers, and that lunch can signal the end of skiing – leaving the slopes pretty clear at the start and end of the day.

MOUNTAIN RESTAURANTS
Some special places

Mountain restaurants are plentiful, and include some of the most glamourous in Europe. Prices can be high, and reservations are advisable. But there are plenty of cheaper places too.

On Corviglia, the gourmet highlight is the Marmite; but it is outrageously expensive. And it is housed in the Corviglia lift station, known locally as the highest post office in Switzerland because of its bright yellow paint. Much better for charm is the Paradiso, with glorious panoramic views from the terrace, and the Lej de la Pesch behind Piz Nair. A reader recommends Mathis for 'first-class food and wine'.

On the Corvatsch side, we've heard good reports about the self-service place at the top and the sunny Sternbar, with live music, at the bottom of Rabguisa. Fuorcla Surlej is delightfully secluded, as is Hahnensee, on the lift-free run of the same name down to Bad – a splendid place to pause in the sun on the way home. On stormy days, most captivating is the rustic Alpetta, at Alp Margun (table-service inside).

THE CRESTA RUN

No trip to St Moritz is really complete without a visit to the Cresta Run. It's the last bastion of Britishness (until recently, payment had to be made in sterling) and male chauvinism (women have been banned since 1929 – unless you can secure an invitation from a club member for the last day of their season).

Any adult male can pay around £200 for five rides on the famous run (helmet and lunch at the Kulm hotel included). Watch out for the Shuttlecock corner – that's where most people come off, and the ambulances ply for trade. You lie on a toboggan (aptly called a 'skeleton') and hurtle head-first down a sheet ice gully from St Moritz to Celerina. David Gower, Sandy Gall and many others are addicts. Fancy giving it a go?

GETTING THERE

Air Zürich, transfer 3hr (or fly into small Upper Engadine airport 5km away).

Rail Mainline station in resort.

CHILDCARE

The St Moritz ski school operates a pick-up service for children. St Moritz and Suvretta schools provide all-day care.

Children aged 3 or more can be looked after in hotels – there are nurseries in the Carlton, the Parkhotel Kurhaus and the Schweizerhof, open from 9am to 4.30 or 5.30.

ACTIVITIES

Indoor Curling, swimming, sauna, solarium, tennis, squash, museum, health spa, cinema (with English films), aerobics, beauty farm, health centre, Rotary International club

Outdoor Ice skating, sleigh rides, ski jumping, toboggan run, hang-gliding, golf on frozen lake, Cresta run, 150km cleared paths, greyhound racing, horse-riding and racing, polo tournaments, cricket tournaments, ski-bob run, paragliding, skydiving, curling

Phone numbers
From elsewhere in Switzerland add the prefix 081.
From abroad use the prefix +41 81.

The hotel-restaurant up at Muottas Muragl, between Celerina and Pontresina, is well worth a visit. It has truly spectacular views overlooking the valley, as well as good food.

Morteratsch restaurant (at the end of the off-piste run from Diavolezza) is splendid – sunny, by the cross-country area and tiny railway station, and with excellent, good-value food.

SCHOOLS AND GUIDES
Internal competition

As well as the St Moritz and Suvretta schools, there is The Wave snowboarding school and The St Moritz Experience, for heli-trips. A free 'ski safari' is offered on Thursdays, something we've only seen in North America before. Some hotels have their own instructors for private lessons.

FACILITIES FOR CHILDREN
Hotel-based nurseries

Children wanting lessons have a choice of schools, but others must be deposited at one of the hotel nurseries: the Parkhotel Kurhaus near the cable-car in Bad, or the Schweizerhof in Dorf. Club Med has its usual good facilities.

Staying there

For high society and a better choice of bars and restaurants, stay in Dorf. Bad has the advantage that you can get back to it from Corvatsch and Corviglia. Celerina is another option.

HOW TO GO
Several packaged options

Packages are available, but many people make their own arrangements. There is a Club Med – its all-inclusive deal cuts the impact of high prices. The tourist office can provide a list of apartments.

Hotels Over half the hotels are 4-stars and 5-stars – the highest concentration of high-quality hotels in Switzerland.

We don't like any of the famous 5-stars or their jacket-and-tie policies. If made to choose we'd prefer the glossy, secluded Carlton or even more secluded Suvretta House to the staid Kulm or Gothic Badrutt's Palace.

((((4) **Crystal** (836 2626) Big 4-star in Dorf, as close to the Corviglia lift as any. Recently renovated and now part of the 'Small Luxury Hotels' group.

((((4) **Schweizerhof** (837 0707) 'Relaxed' 4-star in central Dorf, five minutes from the Corviglia lift, with 'excellent food and very helpful staff'.

((((4) **Albana** (833 3121) 4-star in Dorf, with walls adorned with big game trophies bagged by proprietor's family.

(((3) **Monopol** (837 0404) Good value (for St Moritz) 4-star in centre of Dorf. Excellent buffet breakfasts. Pool, sauna.

(((3) **Nolda** (833 0575) One of the few chalet-style buildings, close to the cable-car in St Moritz Bad.

((2) **Bellaval** (833 3245) A two-star between the station and the lake, offering bargain double rooms from SF60 per person per night last season.

EATING OUT
Mostly chic and expensive

It's easy to spend £50 a head eating out in St Moritz – without wine – but you can eat more cheaply, as reporters love to tell us. We liked the excellent Italian food at the down-to-earth, atmospheric Cascade in Dorf and the three restaurants in the Chesa Veglia. Hauses and the Veltlinerkeller are recommended by locals. But the best food is supposed to be out at Champfer, at Jöhri's Talvo.

Try an evening up at Muottas Muragl for a splendid sunset and dinner in the hotel's unpretentious restaurant.

APRES-SKI
Caters for all ages

There's a big variety of après-skiing age groups here. The fur coat count is high – people come to St Moritz to be seen.

At tea-time, if you can tear yourself away from the mountain bars, the key venue is the famous Hanselmann's, for 'fabulous tea and strudels'. We've also heard good things about Café Hauser.

The pub-style Bobby's Bar, which has internet connection, keeps the younger crowd happy, as do the Prince, with a 'disco/lounge', and the loud music of the Stübli, one of three bars in the Schweizerhof: the others are the Muli, with a country and western theme and live music, and the chic Piano Bar. The Cresta, at the Steffani, is popular with the British, while the Cava below it is louder, livelier and younger. It is also amusing to put on a jacket and tie and explore bars in Badrutt's Palace and the Kulm.

The two most popular discos are Vivai (expensive) at the Steffani, and King's at Badrutt's Palace (even more expensive; jackets and ties required). And if they don't part you with enough cash, try the St Moritz Casino.

TOURIST OFFICE

Postcode CH-7500
t +41 (81) 837 3333
f 837 3377
information@
stmoritz.ch
www.stmoritz.ch

OFF THE SLOPES
Excellent variety of pastimes
Even if you lack the bravado or masculinity for the Cresta Run, there is lots to do. In midwinter the snow-covered lake provides a playground for bizarre events (see earlier in chapter) but in March the lake starts to thaw. There's an annual 'gourmet festival', with chefs from all over the world, a new library with some English books and a couple of museums.

Some hotels run special activities, such as a curling week, health spa week or even rock and roll courses.

Other options are hang-gliding, indoor tennis and even trips to Italy (Milan is four hours away by car). The public pool in Bad is worth a visit.

St Moritz gets a lot of sun – 322 sunny days a year, they claim – so lounging on sunny terraces is popular.

STAYING UP THE MOUNTAIN
Excellent possibilities
Next door to each other at Salastrains are two chalet-style hotels, the 3-star Salastrains (833 3867), with 60 comfy beds, and the slightly simpler and much smaller Zauberhütte (833 3355). Great views, and no queues.

Celerina 1730m

At the bottom end of the Cresta Run, Celerina is unpretentious and villagey, if quiet, with good access to Corviglia. It is sizeable, with a lot of second homes, many owned by Italians (the upper part is known as Piccolo Milano). There are some appealing small hotels (reporters suggest Chesa Rosatsch 837 0101) and a couple of bigger 4-stars.

Pontresina 1805m

Pontresina is small and sedate and an excellent base for the extensive cross-country skiing on its doorstep.

It's a sheltered, sunny village with one main street, spoilt by the usual sanatorium-style architecture. All downhill slopes are a bus-ride away. Towards Celerina is Muottas Muragl, where a funicular serves a tiny mountain-top area with one long run to the bottom. Pontresina's own hill, Languard, has a single long piste.

Much is made of Pontresina being cheaper to stay in than St Moritz, but cheaper doesn't mean cheap. There is a Club Med here. Dining is mostly hotel-based and nightlife is quiet.

SNOWPIX.COM / CHRIS GILL

The popular glacier run from Diavolezza to Morteratsch goes through spectacular scenery ↓

Verbier 1500m

Paradise for nightlife-loving powder hounds with cash

WHAT IT COSTS

HOW IT RATES

The slopes	
Snow	***
Extent	*****
Experts	*****
Intermediates	***
Beginners	**
Convenience	**
Queues	***
Restaurants	***
The rest	
Scenery	****
Resort charm	***
Off-slope	***

What's new

For 2001/02 the first two stages of the gondola from Le Châble to Les Attelas, via Verbier and Les Ruinettes, will be upgraded – though the capacity will still be modest.

- ⊕ Extensive, challenging slopes with a lot of off-piste potential and some good bump runs
- ⊕ Lively, varied nightlife
- ⊕ Sunny, panoramic setting, and great views from the highest slopes
- ⊕ Wide range of chalet holidays
- ⊕ Hardly any drag-lifts in Verbier (though still lots in linked resorts)
- ⊕ Fewer queues than there used to be
- ⊕ Good advanced-level tuition
- ⊕ Much improved piste grooming in recent seasons

- ⊖ Overcrowded pistes in certain areas
- ⊖ Sunny lower slopes will always be a problem, even with snowmaking
- ⊖ Easily accessed off-piste slopes get tracked out very quickly
- ⊖ Still some serious queues, particularly on 4 Valleys links
- ⊖ Piste map and direction signposting still hopelessly inadequate
- ⊖ Busy traffic (and fumes) in centre
- ⊖ Some long walks/rides to lifts
- ⊖ The 4 Valleys network is no rival for the Three Valleys
- ⊖ Pretty expensive

There is no doubt that Verbier is trying hard to retain its international visitors, improving over the last few years its grooming, snowmaking, ski school and lifts – most notably with the overdue replacement three years ago of the Tortin gondola. But major grouses remain. Some are down to the organisation of the resort – the kind of piste signposting shown later in the chapter would be comical if it were not infuriating – but others are down to the lie of the land. 445

For experts prepared to hire a guide in order to explore off-piste, Verbier is one of the big names. With its 4 Valleys lift network and a claimed 400km of pistes, Verbier also seems at first sight to rank alongside the French mega-resorts such as Courchevel or La Plagne for piste skiers. But it doesn't; the 4 Valleys is an inconveniently sprawling affair, while Verbier's local pistes are surprisingly confined. Of course, piste skiers can have a satisfying holiday here – but you can do that in scores of modest resorts from Alpbach to Zell am See. Whether they can match Verbier's famously vibrant nightlife is another question.

The resort

Verbier is an amorphous sprawl of chalet-style buildings, without too much concrete in evidence, and with an impressive setting on a wide, sunny balcony facing spectacular peaks. It's a fashionable, but informal, very lively place that teems with a youngish, cosmopolitan clientele. But it's no longer exclusive. The resort attracts a broad range of British holidaymakers, and there are plenty of Scans too.

Most of the smart shops and hotels (but not chalets) are set around the Place Centrale and along the sloping streets stretching down the hill in one direction and up it in the other to the main lift station at Medran 500m away. Much of the nightlife is here, too, though bars are rather scattered. These

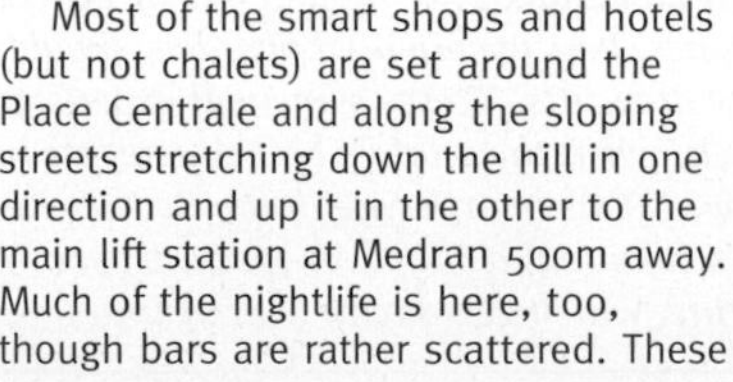

SNOWPIX.COM / CHRIS GILL

The views from the top lifts (this is from Mont-Fort at the very top) are superb →

central areas get unpleasantly packed with cars at busy times, especially weekends.

More chalets and apartments are built each year – which means building sites spoil the views in places – with newer properties inconveniently situated along the road to the lift base for the secondary Savoleyres area, about a mile from Medran.

Staying at the top of the resort, close to the Medran lift station, is convenient for the slopes and sufficiently distant from nightlife to avoid late evening noise. If nightlife is not a priority, staying somewhere near the upper (north-east) fringes of the village may mean that you can almost ski to your door – and there is a piste linking the upper nursery slopes to the one in the middle of the village.

But in practice most people just get used to using the free buses, which run efficiently on several routes until 7pm. Some areas have quite an infrequent service. We are told that from 7pm to 8.30 there is a special taxi service that will drop you at any of the usual bus stops within the resort for five francs per person.

Verbier is at one end of a long, strung-out series of interconnected slopes, optimistically branded the 4 Valleys and linking Verbier to the resorts of Nendaz (described at the end of this chapter), Thyon and Veysonnaz. Other small areas reached by bus are covered by the lift pass, including Bruson – also reached by riding a gondola down to Le Châble and taking a bus from there. Chamonix and Champéry are within reach by car. But a car can be a bit of a nuisance in Verbier itself. Parking is tightly controlled; your chalet or hotel may not have any or may not have enough, which means a hike from the free parking at the sports centre or paying for garage space.

MOUNTAIN FACTS

Altitude	1500m-3330m
Lifts	100
Pistes	410km
Blue	32%
Red	42%
Black	26%
Artificial snow	50km
Recco detectors used	

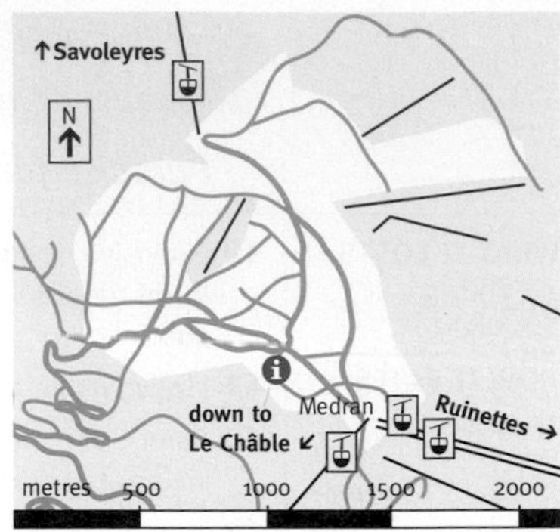

The mountains

Essentially this is high-mountain terrain. There are wooded slopes directly above the village, but the runs here are either bumpy itinéraires or winding paths. There is more sheltered skiing in other sectors – particularly above Veysonnaz.

THE SLOPES

Very spread out

Savoleyres is the smaller area, mainly suited to intermediates and reached by a gondola from the north-west end of town. This area is underrated and generally underused. It has open, sunny slopes on the front side, and long, pleasantly wooded, shadier runs on the back. When conditions are good you can get back to Verbier on south-facing slopes, but in sunny weather these deteriorate quickly.

You can take a catwalk across from Savoleyres to the foot of Verbier's main slopes. These are served by lifts from Medran, at the opposite end of town. Two gondolas rise to **Les Ruinettes** and then on to **Les Attelas**. From Les Attelas a small cable-car goes up to Mont Gelé, for steep off-piste runs only. Heading down instead, you can go back westwards to Les

boarding *As with its skiing, Verbier is one of Europe's best off-piste and extreme boarding resorts for those able and willing to pay for a guide or join a group. The main area is served by gondolas, cable-cars and chairs, with no drag-lifts at all. There are two fun-parks (the Swatch-sponsored boarder-cross course at La Chaux and another one at La Tournelle) and a half-pipe at Col des Gentianes. Less experienced boarders should try Savoleyres, though there are a few drag-lifts. To see some real experts in action, hang around the resort in late March, when the world's best congregate here for the Red Bull Xtreme contest, on the cliff-like north face of the Bec des Rosses. There is a specialist snowboard school and a couple of specialist snowboard shops. And then there's the nightlife, which gets pretty wild at times.*

LIFT PASSES

2000/01 prices in Swiss francs

4 Valleys/Mont-Fort Covers all lifts and ski-buses in Verbier, Mont-Fort, Bruson, Champex-Lac, La Tzoumaz, Nendaz, Veysonnaz and Thyon.

Beginners Station pass covers five beginner lifts.

Main pass
1-day pass 58
6-day pass 294

Senior citizens
Over 65: 6-day pass 176

Children
Under 16: 6-day pass 176
Under 6: free pass

Short-term passes
Half-day pass from 11am (adult 53) or 12.30 (adult 46).

Notes Reductions for families and groups.

Alternative passes
Limited passes for Savoleyres-La Tzoumaz, Bruson, and Verbier only.

Ruinettes, south to La Chaux or north to Lac des Vaux. From here chairs go back to Les Attelas and on to Chassoure, the top of a wide, steep and shady off-piste mogul field leading down to **Tortin**, with a gondola back.

La Chaux is served by two slow chair-lifts and is the departure point of a jumbo cable-car up to Col des Gentianes and the glacier area. A second, much smaller cable car then goes up to **Mont-Fort,** the high point of the 4 Valleys at 3330m. From the glacier is another off-piste route down to Tortin, a north-facing run of almost 1300m vertical. A cable-car returns to Col des Gentianes.

Tortin is the gateway to the rest of the 4 Valleys. From there you head down to **Siviez**, where one chair goes off into the long, thin **Nendaz** sector and another heads for the **Thyon** and **Veysonnaz** sectors, reached by a couple of lifts and a lot of catwalk skiing. Both these sectors suit intermediates best.

Allow plenty of time to get to and from these remote corners – you don't want to be stranded in the wrong valley. It's an expensive taxi-ride.

SNOW RELIABILITY
Improved snowmaking

The slopes of the Mont-Fort glacier always have good snow. The runs to Tortin are normally snowsure too. But nearly all of this is steep, and much of it is formally off-piste. Most of Verbier's main local slopes face south or west and are below 2500m – so they can be in poor condition at times. Snowmaking on the lower slopes has improved a lot in recent years. The north-facing slopes of Savoleyres and Lac des Vaux are normally much better.

FOR EXPERTS
The main attraction

Verbier has some superb tough slopes, many of them off-piste and needing a guide. The very extreme couloirs between Mont Gelé and Les Attelas and below the Attelas gondola are some of the toughest. There are safer, more satisfying off-piste routes from Mont Gelé to Tortin and La Chaux.

There are hardly any conventional black pistes – most of the runs that should have this designation are now defined as itinéraires, which means in theory means they are not patrolled. The blacks that do exist are mostly indistinguishable from nearby reds.

The front face of Mont-Fort is a conspicuous exception: a wonderful tough mogul field, all of black steepness but with a choice of gradient from seriously steep to intimidatingly steep. Occasionally you can get from Mont-Fort all the way to Le Châble off-piste. You can also head off-piste down to Siviez via one of two spectacular couloirs off the back of Mont-Fort. The North Face of Mont-Fort

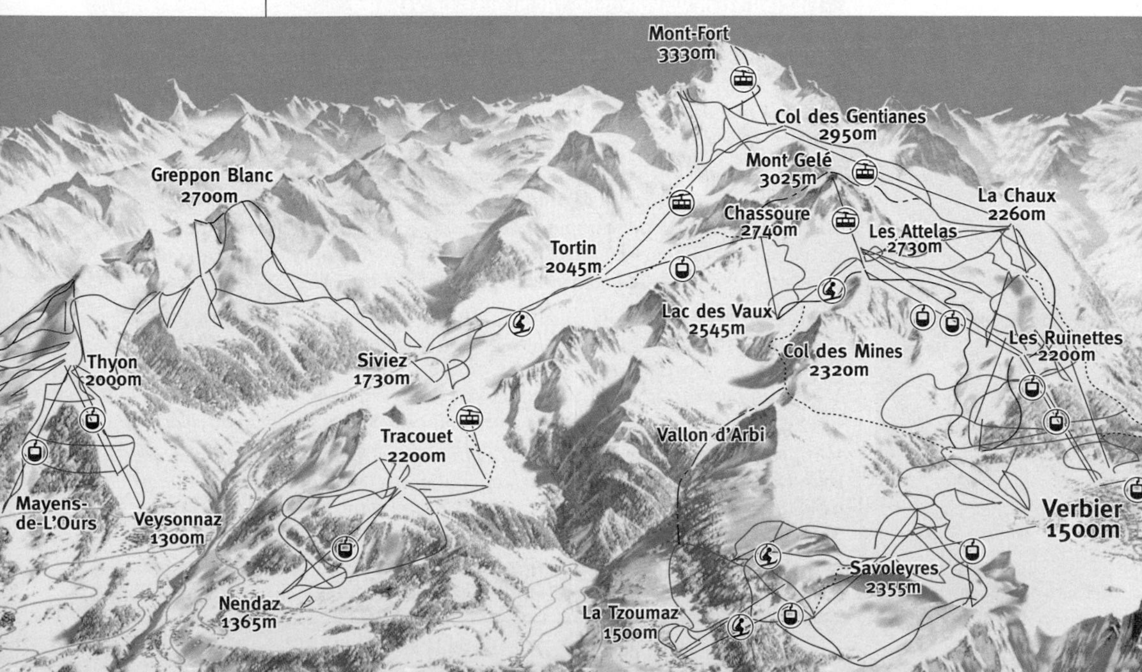

is one of the hottest of expert runs.

The two itinéraires to Tortin are both excellent in their different ways. The one from Chaussoure is just one steep slope, normally a huge mogul field. The north-facing itinéraire from Gentianes is longer, less steep, but feels much more of an adventure. Those willing to walk up a steep slope near the start (known as the Highway to Heaven) are rewarded by usually good powder in a quiet valley parallel to the main run. Les Attelas is the start of shorter runs towards the village.

A couple of long, but easy, off-piste routes go from Lac des Vaux via Col des Mines. One is a popular route back to Verbier, the other a very beautiful run through Vallon d'Arbi to La Tzoumaz. They are not always open: a piste-basher needs to form a ledge across a steep slope to the Col – otherwise the traverse is scary.

The World Cup run at Veysonnaz is a steepish, often icy, red, ideal for really speeding down. There is also an entertaining off-piste run from Greppon Blanc at the top of the Siviez–Thyon sector down to Leteygeon. There are 'memorable' heli-trips.

FOR INTERMEDIATES

Go to Savoleyres

Many mileage-hungry intermediates find Verbier disappointing. The intermediate slopes in the main area are concentrated between Les Attelas and the village, above and below Les Ruinettes, plus the little bowl at Lac des Vaux and the sunny slopes served by the chairs at La Chaux. This is all excellent and varied intermediate territory, but there isn't much of it – to put it in perspective, this whole area is no bigger than the slopes of tiny Alpbach – and it is used by the bulk of the visitors staying in one of Switzerland's largest resorts. So it is often very crowded, especially the otherwise wonderful sweeping red from Les Attelas to Les Ruinettes served by the big gondola. Even early intermediates should taste the perfect snow on the glacier (provided you don't mind T-bars). The red run from Col des Gentianes to La Chaux is not too difficult, but its high-mountain feel can be unnerving and it's no disgrace to ride the cable-car down instead.

Intermediates should make much more use of the Savoleyres area. This has good intermediate pistes, usually better snow and far fewer people (especially on Sundays). It is also a good hill for mixed abilities, with variations of many runs to suit most standards of intermediate.

The area as a whole presents some difficulties for early intermediates, as the editorial daughter, Laura (then aged 8), found a couple of seasons back. There is excellent easy blue-run

FINDING YOUR WAY AROUND THE SLOPES OF VERBIER

It isn't easy. The main area is complicated, and difficult to represent on a single map. A couple of years back the lift company, Téléverbier, dropped its hopeless map and produced a booklet of maps dealing separately with each sector. This, too, was hopeless. Now we seem to be back with one hopeless map.

Direction signposting on the mountain is equally frustrating. There are two problems. One is a strange faith in the kind of 'motorway' signs shown here. We and our readers find these impossible to relate to the real choices of route. The second is that although the signs religiously use piste numbers there are no such numbers on the piste map. So how do you connect the two?

Navigation is further complicated by confusion over where it is prudent to go. For years now, runs that once were black pistes have been defined as 'itinéraires à ski' (eg both runs down to Tortin) or 'itinéraires de haute-montagne' (eg the Col des Mines run home from Lac des Vaux). We've long campaigned for these runs to be restored to piste status, but at least their non-piste status needs to be clear.

With patience, you can work out that neither is patrolled, and possibly deduce that 'itinéraires de haute-montagne' are 'not protected against mountain dangers' (ie avalanches) and should be tackled only in the company of an experienced mountaineer or a guide. But it is far from clear.

No other resort finds all this so difficult to resolve. All it takes is a modest budget, some awareness of visitors' needs and half a brain. Which does Téléverbier lack?

↑ Verbier's lift system now gives few causes for complaint, at least once you are up the mountain (this is Lac des Vaux)

VERBIER OT / MARK SHAPIRO

skiing at La Chaux, but there is no easy way back to Les Ruinettes from there. From Savoleyres there is an easy way across to Medran but there may be no easy way down to that link from the top of Savoleyres. In both cases, we had to take quite testing red runs. Laura managed it, but in a properly run resort the difficulties would have been foreseen and sorted out.

FOR BEGINNERS

Progression is the problem

There are sunny nursery slopes close to the middle of the village and at Les Esserts, at the top of it. These are fine provided they have snow (they have a lot of snowmakers, which helps). The problem is what you do after the nursery slopes. There are easy blues on the back side of Savoleyres, and at La Chaux, but they are not easy to get back from (see above).

FOR CROSS-COUNTRY

Surprisingly little on offer

Verbier is limited for cross-country. There's a 4km circuit in Verbier, 4km at Les Ruinettes–La Chaux and 30km down at Le Châble/Val de Bagnes.

QUEUES

Not the problem they were

It's clear that Verbier's queue problems have been greatly eased by recent investment. The jumbo gondola to Les Attelas has virtually eliminated queues at Les Ruinettes, but it has increased the overcrowding on the pistes back down. The mega-queues at Tortin for Chassoure are a thing of the past, thanks to the new eight-seater gondola. The new fast chair at Lac des Vaux has greatly eased the bottleneck there. But the cable-car from Tortin to Col des Gentianes can produce queues, and the Mont-Fort cable-car above it can still generate very long ones.

Queues at the main village lift station at Medran persist, especially when day visitors are filling one of the gondolas by boarding down in the valley at Le Châble. The upgrade of this gondola for the coming season will help – but it is getting only a 50% boost to its present tiny capacity.

But the main complaints from this year's reporters are of queues for inadequate drag-lifts in the outlying 4 Valleys resorts – and a La Chaux when crowds descend from the glacier.

MOUNTAIN RESTAURANTS

Disappointing in main area

There are not enough huts, which means queues and overcrowding in high season. Savoleyres is the best area. The hotel by the Tzoumaz chair takes some beating for value and lack of crowds. Also worth trying are Chez Simon ('simple and cheap'), Le Mayen (beneath the Combe 1 chair) and the

SCHOOLS/GUIDES

2000/01 prices in Swiss francs

Swiss Ski School
Classes 6 days
2½hr: 9.15-11.45
5 half days: 148
Children's classes
Ages: 3 to 12
5 half days: 136
Private lessons
Hourly, half or full day
120 for 2hr for 1 or 2 people

OTHER SCHOOLS

Fantastique
Adrénaline

rustic Marmotte ('wicked, excellent rösti'), just below the Sud drag. Le Sonalon, on the fringe of the village beneath the gondola, is 'excellent, with great views', but reached off-piste.

In the main area, the rustic Chez Dany at Clambin, on the off-piste run down from the Chaux area, is about the best, and gets packed despite being a bit tricky to get to at times. Carrefour is popular and well situated at the top of the village, above the golf course. The restaurants at Les Ruinettes – table-service upstairs – have big terraces with splendid views. L'Olympique at Les Attelas is a good table-service restaurant.

Everyone loves the Cabane Mont Fort – a proper mountain refuge off the run to La Chaux from Col des Gentianes); great views, but very busy – get there early.

SCHOOLS AND GUIDES
Good reports
Verbier is an excellent place for advanced skiers, in particular, to get tuition. Several reporters have been complimentary about the off-piste lessons with the Swiss ski school. More than 20 guides are available for heli-trips, which include trips to Zermatt and the Aosta valley. The Vallée Blanche at Chamonix and a trip to Zinal are cheaper excursions. Verbier is also quite big on snowboard and telemark tuition. The consensus is that the Swiss school's standards have improved generally, partly thanks to the replacement of some old-timers by keen new recruits. Of the others, the Adrénaline international school gets rave reviews, particularly for its private lessons.

FACILITIES FOR CHILDREN
Wide range of options
The Swiss school's facilities in the resort are good, and the resort attracts quite a lot of families. The playground up at La Chaux has also received favourable reports. Space on the bus back is limited, and priority is given to school groups. The possibility of leaving very young babies at the Stroumpfs nursery is valuable. British families have the option of travelling with family-oriented chalet operators – Ski Esprit and Mark Warner both have crèches, and Simply Ski has a nanny service you can arrange in advance.

There are considerable reductions on the lift pass price for families on production of your passports.

Staying there

HOW TO GO
Plenty of options
Verbier is the chalet-party capital of the Alps. Given the size of the place there are surprisingly few apartments and pensions available, though those on a budget have inexpensive B&B options in Le Châble. Hotels are expensive in relation to their grading. Given a sleeping bag you can bed down at the sports centre for about £10 a night – and that includes the use of the pool.

Chalets There are chalets available for most tastes. Small ones, of the kind that you might take over for a family or small group of friends, are particularly common. There are also large chalets good for groups, places handy for the slopes, and others slap bang in the centre of Verbier's lively nightlife. There are not many luxury options on the UK package market – but this season Descent is introducing a very swish 12-bed place with hotel-style service that sounds irresistible.

CHILDCARE

The ski school's Kids Club kindergarten (771 6333), on the slope at Les Moulins, has its own drag-lift and takes children from aged 3 from 8.30 to 5pm.

The Schtroumpfs non-ski kindergarten (771 6585), close to the middle of the resort, takes children of any age up to 4 years (older ones by arrangement), from 8.30 to 5.30.

GETTING THERE

Air Geneva, transfer 2hr.

Rail Le Châble (7km); regular buses to resort or gondola.

Phone numbers
From elsewhere in Switzerland add the prefix 027.
From abroad use the prefix +41 27.

ACTIVITIES

Indoor Sports centre (swimming, skating, curling, squash, sauna, solarium, steam bath, hot-tub), cinema, ice hockey, indoor golf
Outdoor Ski-bob, 25km cleared walking paths, paragliding, hang-gliding, mountaineering, sledging

Hotels There are half a dozen 4-star places, a dozen 3-star and a handful of simpler places.

((((4) **Rosalp** (771 6323) The place to stay if you can afford it, not least for the food in Roland Pierroz's Michelin-starred restaurant, which is the best you'll find in a Swiss resort. Good position midway between centre and lifts.

((((4) **Montpelier** (771 6131) Very comfortable 4-star, but out of town (a courtesy bus is provided).

((((4) **Vanessa** (775 2800) Central 4-star with spacious apartments as well as rooms; 'excellent' food.

(((3) **Rotonde** (771 6525) Much cheaper, well positioned 3-star between centre and lifts; some budget rooms.

(((3) **Chamois** (771 6402) 3-star close to lifts.

(((3) **Poste** (771 6681) Well placed 3-star midway between centre and lifts; the only hotel pool. Some rooms rather small.

(((3) **de Verbier** (771 6688) Central 3-star, popular with tour operators and their clientele; renowned for good food; atmospheric and traditional, with helpful owners and staff.

((2) **Farinet** (771 6626) Central 3-star hotel, now British-owned, with a focal après-ski bar on its elevated terrace.

Self-catering Apartments bookable through tour operators are very thin on the ground. Self-caterers usually book direct. The comfortable Richemont and Troika apartments are close to the nursery slopes, a trek from the main lifts. The similar standard Blizzard is midway between Place Centrale and lifts.

EATING OUT

Very big choice

There is a very wide range of restaurants. Hotel Rosalp is clearly the best (and most expensive) in town, and among the best in Switzerland, with an awesome wine cellar to match its excellent Michelin-starred food – splash out on the seven-course Menu Gastronomique if you can afford it. The Pinte bistro in the hotel basement is a less pricey option – worth trying out.

The Grotte à Max does a vast variety of rösti plus unusual meats such as ostrich and kangaroo. The popular King's bar developed a restaurant a couple of years back, and its innovative food ('not a fondue in sight') quickly gained favour. An equally refreshing newcomer is the

stylish Millénium, above the Toro Negro steak-house.

The Farinet restaurant is atmospheric and has good food at affordable prices. For Swiss specialities, try the Relais des Neiges, Le Robinson, Le Caveau, Au Vieux-Verbier by the Medran lifts or Les Esserts by the nursery slopes. Le Fer à Cheval is a very popular and lively place for pizza and other simple dishes. Arguably the best-value Italian food in town is at Al Capone's out near the Savoleyres gondola. The Hacienda Café is another inexpensive place. Harold's is Verbier's burger joint.

You can snowmobile up to Chez Dany or La Marmotte for an evening meal, followed by a torchlit descent.

APRES-SKI

Throbbing but expensive

It starts with a 4pm visit to the Offshore Café at Medran, for people-watching. The nearby Big Ben is 'great and lively on a sunny afternoon'. Au Mignon at the bottom of the golf course has become popular since it was given a large sun deck.

Then if you're young, loud and British it's on to the Pub Mont Fort – there's a widescreen TV for live sporting events. The Nelson is popular with locals. The Farinet is particularly good in spring, its live band playing to the audience on a huge, sunny terrace – there's now a conservatory-type cover over it when it's cold. Au Fer à Cheval is a fun place full of locals and regular Verbier-ites.

After dinner the Pub Mont Fort is a very lively pick-up joint, popular with Brits and locals alike (the shots bar in the cellar is worth a visit). Crok No Name has good live bands or a DJ and is entertaining for its cosmopolitan crowd. Murphy's Irish pub in the Garbo hotel is popular, with a good resident DJ. The much-loved King's is a quiet candlelit cellar bar with 60s decor – 'hip crowd, good music'. Bar New Club is a sophisticated piano bar, with comfortable seating and a more discerning clientele. Jacky's is a classy piano bar frequented by big spenders on their way to the Farm Club – an outrageously expensive nightclub which inexplicably is very popular, especially with balding geriatrics with much younger girls in tow (tables are difficult to book). It's packed with rich Swiss paying SF220 for bottles of spirits on Fridays and Saturdays and has more Brits on Tuesdays (chalet girls' day off on Wednesdays!).

More within the pocket of most Brits is the noisy, glitzy Marshalls Club, which sometimes has live music. Taratata is a friendly club that seems to be growing in popularity. Scotch is the cheapest disco in town and popular with teenagers and snowboarders. Big Ben is another cheaper, young place.

The nursery slope at Les Esserts is floodlit for tubing etc on Saturday and Sunday evenings.

OFF THE SLOPES
No great attraction

Verbier has an excellent sports centre and some nice walks, but otherwise very little to offer if you don't want to hit the slopes. Montreux is an enjoyable train excursion from Le Châble, and Martigny is worth a visit for the Roman arena and museums. Various mountain restaurants are accessible to pedestrians. Both toboggan runs – on the shady side of Savoleyres and from Les Ruinettes – are an impressive 10km long.

STAYING IN OTHER RESORTS
A lot going for them

There are advantages to staying in the other resorts of the 4 Valleys. For a start, you can avoid the worst of the morning queues if you set off early, spend the day in the Verbier area and wave to the crowds on your way home.

TOURIST OFFICE

Postcode CH-1936
t +41 (27) 775 3888
f 775 3889
info@verbier.ch
www.verbier.ch

Secondly, they are substantially cheaper for both accommodation and incidentals. What you lose is the Verbier ambience and its range of restaurants, bars and nightlife.

Nendaz is a sizeable and quite rounded resort, described below.

Veysonnaz and Thyon are both small resorts, with mainly apartment accommodation. Veysonnaz is by far the more attractive – an old village complete with church. It has adequate bars, cafes and restaurants, a disco, sports centre with swimming pool, and school and guides. Thyon is a functional, ugly, purpose-built place.

Le Châble is a village a gondola-ride below Verbier. As changing gondola cars is not necessary for moving on to Les Ruinettes and Les Attelas, access to the slopes can be just as quick (or even quicker) from the queue-free valley. Le Châble is particularly convenient for those travelling by train, and for drivers who want to visit other resorts.

Nendaz 1365m

Nendaz is a big resort with over 17,000 beds and handily placed for exploring all of the 4 Valleys. It deserves more attention, especially if you want a cheaper base from which to use Verbier's slopes – but avoid the Sloanes and other Brits it attracts. Airport transfers are quick.

THE RESORT

Nendaz itself is a large place on a shelf above and with great views of the Rhône valley. Most of the resort is modern but built in traditional chalet-style and the original old village of Haute-Nendaz is still there, with its narrow streets, old houses and barns, and baroque chapel dating from 1499.

THE MOUNTAIN

Nendaz has a central and convenient location in the 4 Valleys and allows you to avoid some of the worst queues.

Slopes There's a 12-person gondola straight to the top of the local north-facing slopes at Tracouet (2200m). Here there are good, snowsure nursery slopes plus blue and red intermediate runs back to town through the trees.

Intermediate and better skiers and boarders can head off down the back of Tracouet to a cable-car which takes you to Plan de Fou at 2430m. From there you can go down to Siviez and the links to Tortin, Mont Fort and the local Verbier slopes in one direction and Thyon and Veysonnaz in the other.

Snow reliability Nendaz sits on a north-facing shelf so its local slopes don't get the sun that affects Verbier.

Snowboarding There is also a snowboard fun-park.

Experts Access to the tough stuff is a bit slower from here than from Verbier.

Intermediates Nendaz makes an excellent base for 4 Valleys exploration. Coming back to Nendaz you have to use an unpisted ski route but intermediates can take the Plan de Fou cable-car down instead. Or you can take a shuttle-bus between Nendaz and Siviez.

Beginners There are good nursery slopes at Tracouet.

Cross-country There are 17km of cross-country tracks.

Queues There may be queues at Siviez at the end of the day.

Mountain restaurants The most compelling are in the Verbier area.

Schools and guides A reporter tells us that families seemed pleased with the school.

Facilities for children The school has a nursery area at Tracouet.

STAYING THERE

Accommodation is mainly in apartments but there are a few friendly and traditional hotels.

How to go The resort is virtually unheard of on the British market.

Hotels Reporters recommend the Sourire – 'simple, but good food'.

Self-catering There is no shortage of apartments bookable locally or through Interhome.

Eating out There are several good restaurants; readers recommend the hotel Sourire and the nearby Mont Rouge restaurant.

Après-ski There are plenty of bars and four discos; a 17-year-old reporter recommends the Cactus and the Bodega as the liveliest spots.

Off the slopes Nendaz has 70km of winter walks, an open-air ice rink, a fitness centre and squash courts.

Villars 1300m

Let the train take the strain

WHAT IT COSTS

HOW IT RATES

The slopes	
Snow	**
Extent	**
Experts	**
Intermediates	***
Beginners	****
Convenience	***
Queues	***
Restaurants	***
The rest	
Scenery	***
Resort charm	****
Off-slope	****

What's new

For 2001/02 a six-seater chair will link from La Rasse to Chaux Ronde, replacing a drag and slow chair.

- ⊕ Pleasant, relaxing year-round resort
- ⊕ Fairly extensive intermediate slopes linked to Les Diablerets
- ⊕ Good nursery slopes
- ⊕ Quite close to Geneva airport
- ⊕ Good range of off-slope diversions

- ⊖ Unreliable snow cover
- ⊖ Overcrowded mountain restaurants
- ⊖ Main lift a bus-ride from the town centre

With its mountain railway and gentle low-altitude slopes, Villars is the kind of place that has been overshadowed by modern mega-resorts. But for a relaxing and varied family holiday the attractions are clear – and improved lifts and links with Les Diablerets have added to the appeal.

THE RESORT

Villars sits on a sunny shelf at 1300m, looking across the Rhône valley to the mountains of the Portes du Soleil. A busy high street lined with all sorts of shops gives Villars the air of a pleasant small town; all around are chalet-style buildings, with just two or three block-like large hotels. You can reach Villars by a cog railway from the valley, and it goes on up into the slopes from a station at one end of the town. But a gondola at the other end is the main lift; it's worth staying nearby if possible – there are reliable shuttle-buses, but they get crowded at the peaks. There is an alternative way into the lift system via a gondola at Barboleuse, near Gryon (so you'll see the resort marketed as Villars-Gryon).

The lift system links with Les Diablerets (much more conveniently than it once did), and outings to Leysin and Champéry are possible by rail or road. Many other resorts (such as Verbier) are within driving distance.

Floriettaz 2120m
Gstaad Reusch
Cabane 2525m
Scex Rouge 2970m
Iseneau 1760m
Col du Pillon 1545m
Le Meilleret 1950m
Les Diablerets 1200m
Croix des Chaux 2020m
Petit Chamossaire 2035m
Laouissalet
Chaux de Conches
Grand Chamossaire 2120m
Les Chaux 1750m
Alpe des Chaux
Chaux Ronde 1985m
Les Fracherets 1515m
Roc d'Orsay 2000m
Bretaye 1805m
Sodoleuvre
Col-de-Soud 1525m
La Rasse 1350m
Villars 1300m
Barboleuse 1200m
Gryon

Bretaye is the main on-mountain junction, at the top of the railway →

SNOWPIX.COM / CHRIS GILL

MOUNTAIN FACTS

Altitude	1130m-3000m
Lifts	46
Pistes	125km
Blue	40%
Red	50%
Black	10%
Artificial snow	17km
Recco detectors used	

Phone numbers
From elsewhere in Switzerland add the prefix 024.
From abroad use the prefix +41 24.

TOURIST OFFICE

Postcode CH-1884
t +41 (24) 495 3232
f 495 2794
information@villars.ch
www.villars.ch

THE MOUNTAINS

There's a good mix of open and wooded slopes throughout the area.

Slopes The railway goes up to the col of Bretaye, which has intermediate slopes on either side, with a maximum vertical of 300m back to the col and much longer runs back to the village. To the east, easier open slopes (very susceptible to sun) go to La Rasse (1350m) and the link to the otherwise separate Les Chaux sector. Beyond Les Diablerets the village is Les Diablerets the glacier-equipped mountain, covered by the lift pass. The main interest is the slopes descending from the glacier (see 'Intermediates').

Snow reliability Low altitude and sunny orientation mean that Villars' snow reliability is not good, though new mobile snowmakers have helped.

Experts The main interest for experts is in exploring off-piste. There is plenty of worthwhile terrain reachable from the Chaux de Conches, for example.

Intermediates The local slopes offer a good range of variety, and with the slopes of Les Diablerets there is a fair amount of terrain to explore. The adventurous should take a trip to the Diablerets glacier for the splendid red run down the Combe d'Audon.

Beginners Beginners will feel comfortable on the village nursery slopes, and riding the train to Bretaye. There are gentle slopes here, too, but also lots of people charging about a crowded area.

Snowboarding There are fun-parks at both Bretaye and Les Chaux.

Cross-country The trails up the valley past La Rasse are long and pretty, and there are more in the depression beyond Bretaye (44km in all).

Queues Queues appear for the lifts at Bretaye mainly at weekends.

Mountain Restaurants The mountain restaurants are often over-busy. The Golf Club is pricey but gets excellent reports, as does the Col de Soud ('best rösti ever'); Lac des Chavonnes (open weekends and peak periods) is worth the walk involved. Les Vioz in Les Diablerets is also recommended.

Schools and guides Villars' Ecole Moderne (still using the ski évolutif method) and the Swiss ski school both get positive reports. Riderschool is a specialist snowboard outfit. The Bureau des Guides organises heli-trips.

Facilities for children Both ski schools run children's classes. There is also a non-ski nursery for children up to six.

STAYING THERE

How to go Several tour operators offer packages here. And accommodation can be booked via the resort website.

Hotels The hotel du Golf (495 2477) is popular and has recently been upgraded to a 4-star ('great, family tries hard'). The 4-star Eurotel Victoria (495 3131) lacks character but not space – it has huge rooms.

Eating out Many of the restaurants are hotel-based. The neo-rustic Vieux-Villars is popular for local specialities.

Après-ski Charlie's, the Central and the Mini-Pub are popular bars. El Gringo and Fox are the discos.

Off the slopes There's plenty to keep you active: tennis courts, walks, swimming, skating and curling; or trips on the train – to Lausanne for instance.

Wengen 1275m

Charm, stunning views and extensive intermediate terrain

WHAT IT COSTS

HOW IT RATES

The slopes

Snow	**
Extent	***
Experts	**
Intermediates	****
Beginners	***
Convenience	***
Queues	***
Restaurants	****

The rest

Scenery	*****
Resort charm	*****
Off-slope	****

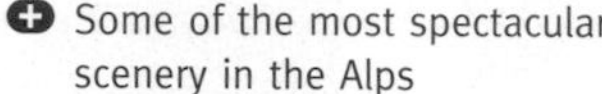

- ⊕ Some of the most spectacular scenery in the Alps
- ⊕ Traditional, 'traffic-free' Alpine village, reached only by cog railway
- ⊕ Lots of long, gentle runs, ideal for intermediates, leading down to Grindelwald
- ⊕ Rebuilt cable-car now an attractive alternative to trains up to the slopes
- ⊕ Nursery slopes in heart of village
- ⊕ Calm, unhurried atmosphere

- ⊖ Limited terrain for experts
- ⊖ Despite some artificial help, snow conditions are unreliable – especially on the sunny home run and village nursery slope
- ⊖ Trains to slopes from here and from Grindelwald are slow and infrequent – you have to plan your movements with the aid of timetables
- ⊖ Getting to Grindelwald's First area can take hours
- ⊖ Subdued in the evening, with little variety of nightlife

Given the charm of the village, the friendliness of the locals and the drama of the scenery, it's easy to see why some people – including numbers of middle-aged British people who have been going for decades – love Wengen. But non-devotees should think carefully about the lack of challenge, the unreliable snow and the dependence on cog railways before signing up.

The last of these drawbacks is slightly less serious than it was. The Männlichen cable-car station, destroyed in the devastating avalanches of 1999, was rebuilt in the heart of the village, where it is not only less vulnerable to avalanche but also much more convenient. Of course, the cable-car is now more popular, and gets queues. So those willing to gear their holiday activities to timetables – or to accept half-hour waits for trains – will still mainly rely on the railway. The rest of us will go probably conclude that life is too short, and go elsewhere.

What's new

A new restaurant next to the Allmend station should be ready for 2001/02.

The hotel Victoria Lauberhorn has been rebuilt, with a new swimming pool – though officially a club hotel (Club Med style) for Swisscom employees only, vacant rooms are available to the public as well.

The resort

Wengen is set on a shelf high above the Lauterbrunnen valley, opposite Mürren, and reached only by a cog railway, which carries on up the mountain as the main lift. Wengen was a farming community long before skiing arrived; it is still tiny, but it is dominated by sizeable hotels, mostly of Victorian origin. So it is not exactly pretty, but it is charming and relaxed, and almost traffic-free. The only traffic is electric hotel taxi-trucks, which gather at the station to pick up guests, and a few ordinary petrol-engined taxis. (Why, we wonder?)

The short main street is the hub of the village. Lined with chalet-style shops and hotels, it also has the ice rink and village nursery slopes right next to it. The nursery slopes double as the venue for floodlit ski-jumping and parallel slalom races.

The views across the valley are stunning. They get even better higher up, when the famous trio of peaks comes fully into view – the Mönch (Monk) protecting the Jungfrau (Maiden) from the Eiger (Ogre).

The main way up the mountain is the regular, usually punctual trains from the southern end of the street to Kleine Scheidegg, where the slopes of Wengen meet those of Grindelwald. The cable-car is a much quicker way to the Grindelwald slopes, and now starts conveniently close to the main street.

Wengen is small, so location isn't as crucial as in many other resorts. The main street is ideally placed for the station. There are hotels on the home piste, convenient for the slopes. Those who don't fancy a steepish morning climb should avoid places down the hill below the station.

You can get to Mürren by taking the train down to Lauterbrunnen, and a funicular and connecting train up the other side. The Jungfrau lift pass covers all of this. Outings further afield aren't really worth the effort.

The mountains

MOUNTAIN FACTS

Altitude	945m-2970m
Lifts	45
Pistes	205km
Blue	30%
Red	50%
Black	20%
Artificial snow	30km
Recco detectors used	

Although it is famous for the fearsome Lauberhorn Downhill course – the longest and one of the toughest on the World Cup circuit – Wengen's slopes are best suited to early intermediates. There are no seriously steep pistes and the scariest part of the Downhill course, the Hundschopf jump, is shut to holidaymakers. Most runs are gentle blues and reds, ideal for cruising.

THE SLOPES
Picturesque playground

Most of the slopes are on the Grindelwald side of the mountain. From the railway station at Kleine Scheidegg you can head straight down to Grindelwald or work your way across the mountain with the help of a couple of lifts to the top of the Männlichen. This area is served by drag- and chair-lifts, and can be reached directly from Wengen by the improved cable-car.

There are a few runs back down towards Wengen from the top of the **Lauberhorn** (2480m), but below Kleine Scheidegg there's really only one.

SNOWPIX.COM / CHRIS GILL

It's not surprising that sightseeing helicopter tours around the Jungfrau massif are in great demand →

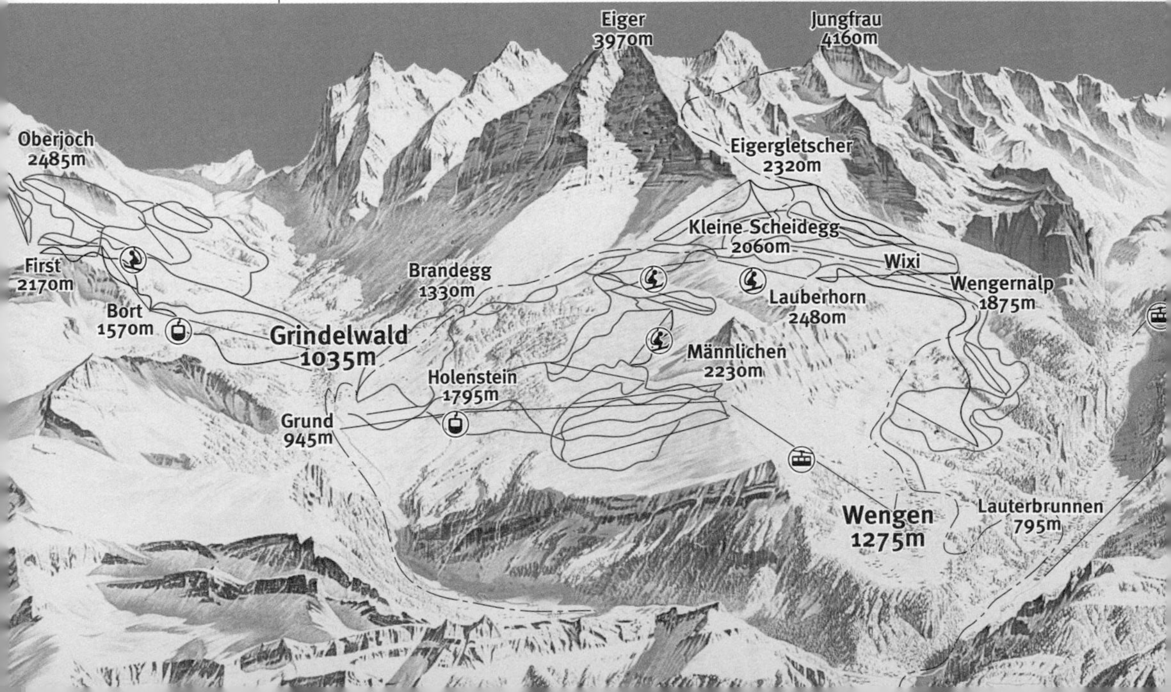

Eiger 3970m
Jungfrau 4160m
Oberjoch 2485m
Eigergletscher 2320m
Kleine Scheidegg 2060m
Wixi
First 2170m
Brandegg 1330m
Wengernalp 1875m
Lauberhorn 2480m
Bort 1570m
Grindelwald 1035m
Männlichen 2230m
Holenstein 1795m
Grund 945m
Wengen 1275m
Lauterbrunnen 795m

LIFT PASSES

2000/01 prices in Swiss francs

Jungfrau Top Ski Region

Covers all lifts in Wengen, Mürren and Grindelwald, trains between them and Grindelwald ski-bus.

Beginners Points card (adult 100 points 48, lifts cost 4 to 10 points).

Main pass

1-day pass 52
6-day pass 254

Senior citizens

Over 62: 6-day pass 229

Children

16 to 19: 6-day 203
Under 16: 6-day pass 127
Under 6: 10

Short-term passes

Single ascent tickets for most lifts. Half-day pass for First (adult 40), Kleine Scheidegg-Männlichen (adult 40) and Mürren-Schilthorn (adult 40).

Alternative periods

3 days in 7 pass available (156).

Notes

Day pass price is for Kleine Scheidegg-Männlichen area only (102km of piste, 21 lifts), as Jungfrau Top Ski Region pass is only available for 2 days or over. Discounts for groups.

Alternative passes

1- and 2-day passes available for First (adult 2-day 95), Mürren-Schilthorn (adult 2-day 95) and Kleine Scheidegg-Männlichen (adult 2-day 95).
4-, 5- and 6-day passes available for non-skiers (adult 6-day 189).

SNOW RELIABILITY
Why not use the guns?

Most slopes are below 2000m, and at Grindelwald they go down to less than 1000m. Very few slopes face north and Wengen's snowmaking facilities are not up to protecting them. The real shame is that the snowmaking that exists isn't always used when it's needed.

All this can mean problems, and while we've found wonderful snow a couple of times in late March, we've also struggled to find decent snow to ski on in January.

FOR EXPERTS
Few challenges

Wengen is quite limited for experts. The one genuine black run in the area takes you from Eigergletscher to Wixi. For most of its length, the Lauberhorn Downhill course is merely of intermediate red run gradient.

The main challenges are off-piste runs such as Oh God from near Eigergletscher to Wixi (and even that is now classified as a 'free-ride piste') and White Hare from under the north face of the Eiger. There are a number of more adventurous off-piste runs from the Jungfraujoch late in the season. For more challenges it's well worth going to nearby Mürren, an hour away by train and funicular. Heli-trips with mountain guides are organised if there are enough takers.

FOR INTERMEDIATES
Wonderful if the snow is good

Wengen and Grindelwald share superb intermediate slopes. Nearly all are long blue or gentle red runs – see Grindelwald chapter. The run back to Wengen is a relaxing end to the day, as long as it's not too crowded.

For tougher pistes, head for the top of the Lauberhorn lift and then the runs to Kleine Scheidegg, or to Wixi (following the start of the Downhill course). You could also try the north-facing run from Eigergletscher to Salzegg, which often has the best snow late in the season.

FOR BEGINNERS
Not ideal

There's a nursery slope in the centre of the village – it's convenient and gentle, but the snow is unreliable. A small part of it is now served by a moving carpet lift, ideal for children. There's a beginners' area at Wengernalp, but to get back to Wengen you either have to climb up to the train or tackle the run down, which can be tricky. There are plenty of good, long, gentle slopes to progress to.

FOR CROSS-COUNTRY
There is none

There's no cross-country skiing in Wengen itself. There are tracks down in the Lauterbrunnen valley, but the snow there is unreliable.

QUEUES
Improving, but a long way to go

The new Männlichen cable-car has helped cut the queues for the trains but both can still suffer from horrific bottlenecks in peak periods, as well as daily scrums to board the trains that the school uses. Weekend invasions can increase the crowds on the Grindelwald side, especially. Queues up the mountain have been alleviated a lot in the last few years by the installation of fast quad chairs on the Grindelwald side – though plenty of old lifts remain.

MOUNTAIN RESTAURANTS
Plenty of variety

A popular but expensive place for lunch is Wengernalp, where the rösti is excellent and the views of the Jungfrau are superb. The highest restaurant is at Eigergletscher. If you get there early on a sunny day, you can nab a table on the narrow outside balcony and enjoy magnificent views of the glacier. The station buffet at Kleine Scheidegg gets repeated rave reviews, so it's not surprising that it also gets packed – the take-away rösti and sausage are a popular option. The Grindelwaldenblick is a worthwhile trudge uphill from Kleine Scheidegg, with great food and

boarding *Wengen is not a bad place for gentle boarding – the nursery area is not ideal, but beginners have plenty of slopes to progress to, with lots of long blue and red runs served by the train and chair-lifts. Getting from Kleine Scheidegg to Männlichen means an unavoidable drag-lift though. There's a fun-park at Wengernalp but experts will tire quickly of the area, and hanker after the steeper slopes of Mürren.*

The cog railway remains the main way up the mountain for Wengen residents →

SNOWPIX.COM / CHRIS GILL

SCHOOLS/GUIDES

2000/01 prices in Swiss francs

Swiss
Classes 6 days
3hr: am
6 half days: 219
Children's classes
Ages: 4 to 12
6 half days: 219
Private lessons
2hr, 3hr or 5hr
135 for 2hr

CHILDCARE

The kindergarten on the first floor of the Sport Pavilion takes children from 18 months from 8.30 to 5pm, Sunday to Friday. Children can be taken to and from lessons with the ski school, which starts at age 4.

A couple of 4-star hotels have their own kindergartens.

GETTING THERE

Air Zürich, transfer 3½hr. Bern, transfer 1½hr.

Rail Station in resort.

views of the Eiger. In the village, the Gruebi cafe, a short walk from the cable-car station, is highly recommended. For restaurants down towards Grindelwald, see the Grindelwald chapter.

SCHOOLS AND GUIDES
Healthy competition

A reporter says, 'The Swiss school is definitely trying harder than a few years ago.' The tuition and the standard of English are usually good. The independent Privat school has been recommended for private lessons.

Snowboarders are well served. And guides are available for heli-trips and powder excursions.

FACILITIES FOR CHILDREN
Apparently satisfactory

Our reports on children's facilities are from observers rather than participants, but are all favourable. It is an attractive village for families, with the baby slope in the centre.

The train gives easy access to higher slopes.

Staying there

HOW TO GO
Wide range of hotels

Most accommodation is in hotels. There is only a handful of catered chalets (and no especially luxurious ones). Self-catering apartments are few, too. There is a Club Med.

Hotels There are about two dozen hotels, mostly 4-star and 3-star, with a handful of simpler places.

((((4) **Wengener Hof** (855 2855) No prizes for style or convenience, but recommended for peace, helpful staff and spacious, spotless rooms with good views.

((((4) **Sunstar** (856 5111) Modern hotel on main street. Comfortable rooms; lounge has a log fire. Live music some nights. Pool with views. Food very good. Friendly.

((((4) **Regina** (855 1512) Quite central. Smart, traditional atmosphere. 'Best food in Wengen.' Carousel nightclub.

((((4) **Silberhorn** (856 5131) Comfortable, modern 4-star in excellent central position, with choice of restaurants.

The British in Wengen

There's a very strong British presence at Wengen. Many Brits have been returning to the same rooms in the same hotels in the same week, year after year, and treat the resort as a sort of second home. There is an English church with weekly services, and a British-run club, the DHO (Downhill Only) – so named when the first Brits persuaded the locals to keep the summer railway running up the mountain in winter so they would no longer have to climb up in order to ski down again. That greatly amused the locals, who until then had regarded skiing in winter as a necessity rather than a pastime to be done for fun. The DHO is still going strong and organises regular events throughout the season.

Phone numbers
From elsewhere in Switzerland add the prefix 033.
From abroad use the prefix +41 33.

ACTIVITIES

Indoor Swimming pool (in Beausite Park and Sunstar hotels), sauna, solarium, whirlpool, massage (in hotels), cinema (with English films), billiards
Outdoor Skating, curling, 50km cleared paths, toboggan runs, paragliding, glacier flights, sledging excursions, hang-gliding

TOURIST OFFICE

Postcode CH-3823
t +41 (33) 855 1414
f 855 3060
info@wengen.ch
www.wengen-muerren.ch

((((4 **Caprice** (855 4141) Small, smartly furnished chalet-style hotel across the tracks from the Regina. Kindergarten. 'Comfortable and friendly' according to a recent guest.
(((3 **Bellevue** (855 1121) Some way out, but does have the best views as well as 'friendly staff and excellent food'.
(((3 **Alpenrose** (855 3216) Long-standing British favourite; eight minutes' climb to the station. Small, simple rooms, but good views; 'first-class' food; friendly staff.
(((3 **Eiger** (855 1131) Very conveniently sited, right next to the station. Focal après-ski bar. Rebuilt with comfy modern rooms.
(((3 **Falken** (856 5121) Further up the hill. Another British favourite, known affectionately as 'Fawlty Towers'.
Self-catering The hotel Bernerhof's decent Résidence apartments (855 2721) are well positioned just off the main street, and hotel facilities are available to guests.

EATING OUT

Lots of choice

Most restaurants in the village are in the hotels. They offer good food and service, and are open to non-residents. Recent recommendations include the Eiger, with a traditional restaurant and a stube with Swiss and French cuisine, the Sunstar ('high quality, not such high prices') and the Bernerhof ('good-value honest cooking'). The little hotel Hirschen has 'the best steaks'. There's no shortage of fondues in the village. Several bars do casual food, including good-value pizza at Sina's. You could eat at Wengernalp's excellent restaurant – but you have to get back on skis or on a toboggan.

APRES-SKI

It depends on what you want

People's reactions to the après-ski scene in Wengen vary widely, according to their expectations and appetites. If you're used to raving in Kitzbühel or Les Deux Alpes, you'll rate Wengen dead, especially for young people. If you've heard it's dead, you may be pleasantly surprised to find that there is a handful of bars that do good business both early and late in the evening. But it is only a handful of small places. The Schnee-Bar, at the Bumps section of the home run, is a popular final run stop-off. And the stube at the Eiger and the tiny, 'always welcoming' Eiger Bar are popular at the end of the day, especially with Germans and Scans. The traditional Tanne and the funky Chilli's are almost opposite on the main street, and generally lively. Sina's, a little way out by Club Med, usually has live music. The Caprice bar is also recommended as is the new Mister Mac bar and disco. There are discos and live music in some hotels. The cinema often shows English-language films.

OFF THE SLOPES

Good for a relaxing time

Wengen is a superb resort for those who want a completely relaxing holiday, with its unbeatable scenery and pedestrian-friendly trains and cable-car (there's a special, though expensive, five-day pass). There are some lovely walks, ice skating and a curling club. Several hotels have health spas. Excursions to Interlaken and Bern are possible by train, as is the trip up to the Jungfraujoch (see the Grindelwald chapter). Helicopter flights from Männlichen are recommended.

STAYING UP THE MOUNTAIN

Great views

You can stay at two points up the mountain reached by the railway: the pricey Jungfrau (855 1622) at Wengernalp and at Kleine Scheidegg, where there's a choice of rooms in the big Scheidegg-Hotels (855 1212) or dormitory space above the Grindelwaldblick restaurant and the station buffet. The big restaurant at Männlichen also has rooms.

STAYING DOWN THE VALLEY

The budget option

Staying in a 3-star hotel like the Schützen (855 2032) or Oberland (855 1241) in Lauterbrunnen will cost about half as much as similar accommodation in Wengen. The train from Wengen runs until 11.30pm and is included in your lift pass. Staying in Lauterbrunnen also improves your chances of getting a seat on the train to Kleine Scheidegg rather than joining the scrum at Wengen – though of course it also means a longer journey time. Lauterbrunnen is also much better placed for Mürren.

You can save even more by staying in Interlaken. Choose a hotel near Interlaken Ost station, from which you can catch a train to Lauterbrunnen (22 minutes) or Grindelwald (36 minutes). Driving can take longer at weekends.

Zermatt 1620m

Magical in many respects – both on and off the slopes

WHAT IT COSTS

5

HOW IT RATES

The slopes

Snow	****
Extent	****
Experts	*****
Intermediates	****
Beginners	*
Convenience	*
Queues	***
Restaurants	*****

The rest

Scenery	*****
Resort charm	*****
Off-slope	****

What's new

For the 2000/01 season moving carpets were installed from the tunnel at Sunnegga to the Eisfluh T-bar and in the snowboard training area at Blauherd.

A fabulous new fun-park and half-pipe were built near Riffelberg, an ice cave opened on Klein Matterhorn and winter hiking along a 2.5km trail made possible on Gornergrat.

The extended and refurbished 5-star Riffelalp resort hotel reopened at 2222m.

A much-needed new ski school (now called StokedAG-The Ski-School Zermatt) opened to compete with the existing school, which has a poor reputation.

- + Wonderful, high and extensive slopes for experts and intermediates, with three separate and interestingly different areas
- + Spectacular high-mountain scenery, dominated by the Matterhorn
- + Charming, if rather sprawling, old mountain village, largely traffic-free
- + Reliable snow at altitude
- + World's best mountain restaurants
- + Extensive helicopter operation
- + Nightlife to suit most tastes
- + Smart shops
- + Linked to Cervinia in Italy

- − Getting to main lift stations may involve a long walk, crowded (but free) bus or expensive taxi-ride
- − Main ski school has poor reputation (but new rival school just started)
- − Beginners should go elsewhere
- − One-way link only between Klein Matterhorn and the other two areas
- − Getting up the mountain and around the different areas can be slow
- − Annoying electric taxis detract from the otherwise relaxed, car-free village ambience

You must try Zermatt before you die. Few places can match its combination of excellent advanced and intermediate slopes, reliable snow, magnificent scenery, Alpine charm and mountain restaurants with superb food and stunning views.

Many people complain that the car-free village is spoiled by intrusive electric carts and taxis; some complain about the time it takes to get to the top of the mountain; others say that the atmosphere is of Swiss efficiency and international tourism rather than mountain-village friendliness. But friendliness and service have definitely improved – we had fewer complaints about lift queues this year and there's a magical feel to both the village and the mountains.

Zermatt's flaws are minor compared to its attractions, which come close to matching perfectly our notion of the ideal winter resort. It's one of our favourites.

The resort

Zermatt started life as a traditional mountain village, developed as a mountaineering centre in the 19th century, then became a winter resort too. Summer is still as important as winter here.

Be warned: Zermatt is big business and most restaurants and hotels are owned by a handful of families. Many of the workers are brought in from outside Switzerland – but that is probably one of the reasons many reporters have remarked on the increased friendliness and improved service in recent years.

The village sprawls along either side of a river, mountains rising steeply on each side. It is a mixture of chocolate-box chalets and modern buildings, most in traditional style. You arrive by rail or taxi from Täsch, where cars have to be left, for a fee. They can be left for free at more distant Visp, from where you can also get a train. The main street runs past the station, lined with luxury hotels and shops.

Zermatt doesn't have the relaxed, quaint feel of other car-free resorts, such as Wengen and Saas-Fee. That's partly because the electric vehicles are

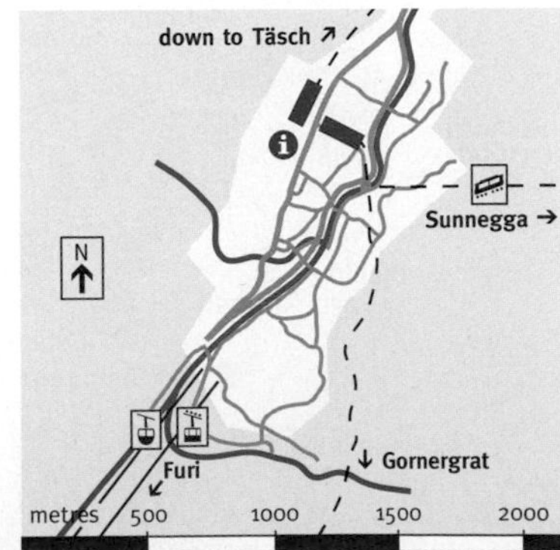

LIFT PASSES

2000/01 prices in Swiss francs

Area Pass

Covers all lifts on the Swiss side of the border.

Main pass

1-day pass 64

6-day pass 318

Senior citizens

Over 65 (male), 62 (female): 6-day pass 239

Children

Under 16: 6-day pass 159

Under 9: free pass

Short-term passes

Single ascent tickets for most lifts.

Notes Daily supplement available to cover all lifts in Cervinia and Valtournenche (33).

Alternative passes

Passes for any period available for each area of Zermatt (Gornergrat-Stockhorn, Sunnegga-Rothorn, Trockener Steg-Klein Matterhorn-Schwarzsee), and combinations of areas. Pass available for Zermatt, Cervinia and Valtournenche (1-day: 64; 6-day: 366).

more intrusive and aggressive, and partly because the clientele is more overtly part of the jet set, with large contingents from the US and Japan.

For a resort with such good and extensive slopes, there's a remarkably high age profile. Most visitors seem to be over 40, and there's little of the youthful atmosphere you get in rival resorts with comparable slopes, such as Val-d'Isère, St Anton and Chamonix.

The main street, with the station square near one end, is the focal point of village life. The cog railway to the Gornergrat area leaves from opposite the main station, and the underground funicular to the Sunnegga area is a few minutes' walk away. From here the gondola to the Klein Matterhorn area (and the link to Cervinia) is a 15-minute trek, busy bus-ride or expensive taxi ('The best daily SF20 investment of the trip,' said a reader).

The school and guides office, the tourist office and many hotels, shops, restaurants, bars and nightspots are on or near the main street. Another main street runs along the river. To each side are narrow streets and paths; many are hilly and treacherous when icy.

Bill Baker in Julen Sport is one of the best boot fitters in the world – pay him a visit if your boots are giving you problems.

The mountains

There are slopes to suit all standards except absolute beginners, for whom we don't recommend the resort. For intermediates and experts Zermatt has few rivals, with marvellously groomed cruising trails, some of the best moguls around, long, beautiful scenic runs out of view of the lift system, exciting heli-trips and off-piste possibilities, as well as the opportunity to get down into Italy for the day and lunch on pasta and chianti. The hands-free, electronic lift pass system means you never have to get it out of your pocket.

THE SLOPES
Beautiful and varied

Zermatt consists of three separate areas, two of which are now well linked. The **Sunnegga–Blauherd–Rothorn** area is reached by the underground funicular starting about five minutes' walk from the station. This shifts large numbers rapidly but can lead to queues for the subsequent gondola – you can take a run down to a high-speed quad alternative.

From the top of this area you can make your way – via south-facing slopes served by snowmakers – to Gant in the valley between Sunnegga and the second main area, **Gornergrat–Hohtälli–Stockhorn**. A new 125-person cable-car opened a few seasons ago linking Gant to Hohtälli in just seven minutes – a vast improvement on the two gruelling steep T-bars that were the only links before. A gondola makes the link back from Gant to Sunnegga. Gornergrat can be reached direct from Zermatt by cog railway trains which leave every 24 minutes and take 30 or 40 minutes to get to the top – arrive at

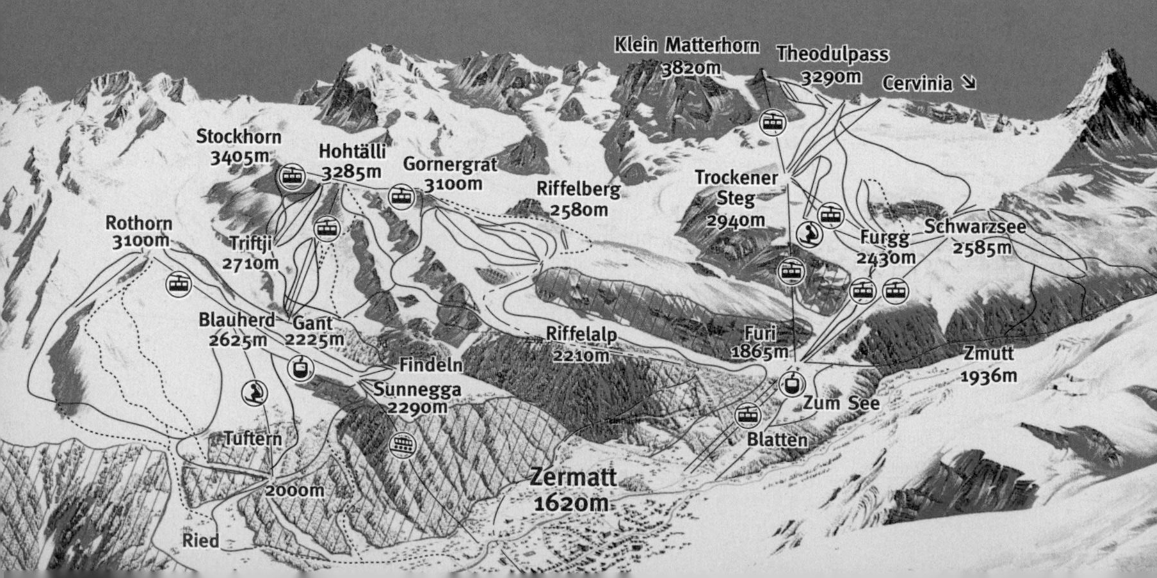

A great view of the Klein Matterhorn (top right) and the slopes between Trockener Steg and Furgg →

SNOWPIX.COM / CHRIS GILL

MOUNTAIN FACTS

Altitude	1620m-3820m
Lifts	71
Pistes	250km
Blue	22%
Red	50%
Black	28%
Artificial snow	43km
Recco detectors used	

the station early to get a seat on the right-hand side and enjoy the stupendous views.

From Gornergrat, there's a piste, followed by a short walk, to Furi to link up with the third and highest area, **Klein Matterhorn–Trockener Steg-Schwarzsee**. But you can't do the journey in the opposite direction: once on the Klein Matterhorn, moving to a different mountain means heading down and getting from one end of the village to the other to catch a lift up. The Klein Matterhorn gives access to Cervinia – you need to buy an 'international pass' or pay a daily supplement to your Zermatt lift pass and the high lifts are sometimes shut because of high winds.

There are pistes back to the village from all three areas – though some of them can be closed or tricky due to poor snow conditions at times.

SNOW RELIABILITY
Good high up, poor lower down

Zermatt has rocky terrain and a relatively dry climate. But it also has some of the highest slopes in Europe, and quite a lot of snowmaking.

All three areas go up to over 3000m, and the Klein Matterhorn cable-car is the highest in Europe, ending at over 3800m and serving a summer glacier. There are loads of runs above 2500m, many of which are north-facing, so guaranteeing decent snow except in freak years.

Artificial snowmaking machines serve some of the pistes on all three areas, from around 3000m to under 2000m. The runs back to the village can still be patchy, but we've had noticeably better reports on piste maintenance and marking lately.

FOR EXPERTS
Good – with superb heli-trips

If you've never been, Zermatt has to be on your shortlist. If you have been, we're pretty sure you'll want to return.

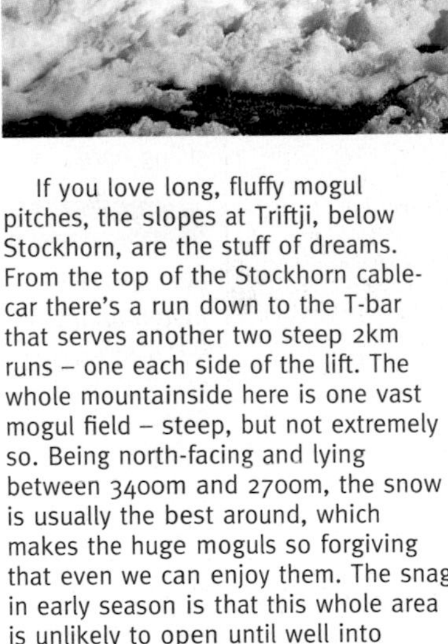

If you love long, fluffy mogul pitches, the slopes at Triftji, below Stockhorn, are the stuff of dreams. From the top of the Stockhorn cable-car there's a run down to the T-bar that serves another two steep 2km runs – one each side of the lift. The whole mountainside here is one vast mogul field – steep, but not extremely so. Being north-facing and lying between 3400m and 2700m, the snow is usually the best around, which makes the huge moguls so forgiving that even we can enjoy them. The snag in early season is that this whole area is unlikely to open until well into January, and possibly later.

You can continue down from here to Gant and catch the gondola up to Blauherd. On that mountain there are a couple of wonderful off-piste 'downhill

boarding *Boarders in soft boots have one big advantage over skiers in Zermatt – they have much more comfortable walks to and from the lift stations! Even so, there aren't many around. The slopes are best for experienced free-riders, because tough piste and off-piste action is what Zermatt is really about. There are acres of underused powder to ride, plus a world-class new fun-park and half-pipe near Riffelberg and another park and pipe on Klein Matterhorn. The main lifts are boarder-friendly: train, funicular, gondolas and cable-cars, but there are T-bars too. The resort is not ideal for learning, just as it isn't ideal for first-time skiers. Evenings have something for all.*

routes' from Rothorn, which have spectacular views down towards the village and over to the Matterhorn.

On the Klein Matterhorn, the best area for experts is Schwarzsee, from where there are several steep north-facing gullies through the woods. Unfortunately, you can't try these repeatedly without taking the beautiful, but slightly boring, track down to Furi and catching the cable-car up again.

There are marvellous off-piste possibilities from the top lifts in each sector, but they aren't immediately obvious to those without local knowledge. They are also dangerous because of rocky and glacial terrain.

We don't recommend anyone going off-piste without a guide. You can join daily ski touring groups but there aren't standard off-piste groups as there are in resorts such as Val-d'Isère and Méribel. Unless you join The Ski School Zermatt off-piste free-ride classes, you have to hire a guide privately for a full day, and that's expensive unless you have a fair-sized group. The Ski Club of Great Britain usually hires a guide for off-piste skiing once a week – we joined that on our last visit and had a great day.

Zermatt is the Alps' biggest heli-trip centre; the helipad resembles a bus station at times, with choppers taking off every few minutes. There are only three main drop-off points, so this can mean encountering one or two other groups on the mountain, even though there are multiple ways down. From all three points there are routes that don't require great expertise. The epic is from Monte Rosa, at over 4000m, down through wonderful glacier scenery to Furi. If there isn't much snow you may need the help of a rope that's fixed at the almost vertical, icy end of the glacier to get down.

FOR INTERMEDIATES

Mile after mile of beautiful runs

Zermatt is ideal for adventurous intermediates. Many of the blue and red runs tend to be at the difficult end of their grading. There are very beautiful reds down lift-free valleys from both Gornergrat and Hohtälli to Gant – we love these first thing in the morning, before anyone else is on them. A variant to Riffelalp ends up on a narrow wooded path with a sheer

THE WORLD'S BEST MOUNTAIN RESTAURANTS

We once met a man who had been coming here for 20 years simply because of the mountain restaurants. The choice is enormous (the tourist information says 38, but it seems more). Most have table-service, nearly all of those we've tried have excellent food and many are in spectacular settings. It is impossible to list here all those worth a visit – so don't limit yourself to those we mention. It is best to book – and check the prices are within your budget when you do so!

The restaurants at Fluhalp (live music and 'great glühwein and chocolate mit rum') and Grünsee have beautiful isolated situations and good food. The large terrace at Sunnegga has decent food and great views. Up at Rothorn, the restaurant has excellent food – we had wonderful lamb – and views. Down at Findeln are several attractive, busy, rustic restaurants, including Findlerhof (aka Franz & Heidy's), Chez Vrony ('this year's must'), Paradies and Enzian ('less busy than others'). And the restaurant at Tuftern sells good Heida white wine from the highest vineyard in Europe – just down the valley at 1200m.

At Furi, the Restaurant Furi, Aroleid above it and Simi's on the road below all have large sun terraces and good food. The hotel at Schwarzsee is right at the foot of the Matterhorn, with staggering views and endless variations of rösti. Round the back from here Stafelalp is simple but charmingly situated. Up above Trockener Steg Gandegghütte has stunning views of the glacier and 'good polenta'. On the way back to the village below Furi, Zum See is a charming old hut serving the best mountain food in Zermatt (which means it is world-class: we had delicious beef, lamb and raspberry tart here last season). Blatten is good too.

The Kulmhotel, at 3100m at Gornergrat, has both self-service and table-service restaurants with amazing views of lift-free mountains and glaciers.

Wherever you go, don't miss the local alcoholic coffee – in its many varieties!

cliff and magnificent views to the right.

On Sunnegga, the 5km Kumme run, from Rothorn to the bottom of the Patrullarve chair, also gets away from the lift system and has an interesting mix of straight-running and mogul pitches. On Klein Matterhorn, the reds served by the Hörnli and Garten drags and the fast four-person chair from Furgg are all long and gloriously set at the foot of the Matterhorn.

For less adventurous intermediates, the blues on Sunnegga and above Riffelberg on Gornergrat and the runs between Klein Matterhorn and Trockener Steg are best. Of these, the Riffelberg area often has the best combination of good snow and easy cruising, and is popular with the school. Sunnegga gets a lot of sun, but the artificial snow means that the problem is more often a foot or more of heavy snow near the bottom than bare patches.

On the Klein Matterhorn, most of the runs, though marked red on the piste map, are very flat and represent the easiest slopes Zermatt has to offer, as well as the best snow. The problem here is the possibility of bad weather because of the height – high winds, extreme cold and poor visibility can make life very unpleasant. To get to Cervinia, you set off from Testa Grigia with a choice of two routes – even an early intermediate should find the easier 10km route (on the left as you look at the Cervinia piste map) down to the village manageable. The red Ventina run is a delightful cruise for better intermediates.

Beware of the run from Furgg to Furi at the end of the day, when it can be tricky and very crowded.

FOR BEGINNERS
Learn elsewhere

Zermatt is to be avoided by beginners. The easiest slopes are outlined above. And there's no decent nursery slope area. Unless you have a compelling reason to start in Zermatt, don't.

FOR EVERYONE
A spectacular cable-car ride

The Klein Matterhorn cable-car is an experience not to miss if the weather is good. The views down to the glacier

SNOWPIX.COM / CHRIS GILL

Zermatt has rustic old buildings in its lanes – amazingly there's no electric taxi racing down this one ↓

CHILDCARE

There are nurseries in two upmarket hotels. The one in the Nicoletta (966 0777) takes children aged 2 to 8, from 9am to 5pm. The Kinderclub Pumuckel at the Ginabelle (966 5000) takes children from 30 months, from 9am to 5pm, and ski tuition is available on the spot. The Kinderparadies (967 7252) takes children from 3 months from 9am to 5pm. Private babysitters are available, too.

Ski school lessons start at age 4.

SCHOOLS/GUIDES

2000/01 prices in Swiss francs

Swiss
Classes 5 days
6hr: 3hr am and pm
5 full days: 280
Children's classes
Ages: 4-6 and 6-12
5 full days including lunch: 270-330
Private lessons
1hr, 2hr or full-day
full day: 330 for 1 or 2 people; each additional person 15

The Ski School
Classes 5hr: 9.3-12 and 1-3.30
5 full days: 410
Children's classes 5 full days including lunch: 485
Private lessons
half or full-day
full day: 360 for 1; each additional person 25

and its crevasses, as the car swings steeply into its hole blasted out of the mountain at the top, are stupendous. When you arrive, you walk through a long tunnel, to emerge on top of the world for the highest piste in Europe – walk slowly, the air is thin here and some people have altitude problems. The top drag-lifts here are open in the summer.

FOR CROSS-COUNTRY
Fairly limited

There's a 4km loop at Furi, 3km near the bottom of the gondola to Furi, and 12 to 15km down at Täsch (don't count on there being snow). There are also some 'ski walking trails' – best tackled as part of an organised group.

QUEUES
Some bottlenecks, and slow lifts

Zermatt used to have one of the worst reputations for queues in the Alps. Many major problems have now been eliminated but there can still be a lengthy scrum for the gondola out of town towards Klein Matterhorn at the start of the day, followed by long waits for the two successive cable-cars to the top – one reporter complained the whole journey took two and a half hours. Buses back to town from Klein Matterhorn at the end of the day are also oversubscribed: 'We scrummed down for 30 minutes one day,' said the same disgruntled reporter. The other problem is the Gornergrat train – you may find there's only standing room.

But some reporters had largely queue-free stays, even in mid-February, and raved about the empty runs. And one thing we love about Zermatt is that the lifts start at 8am. Get out early and you can enjoy deserted slopes for at least two hours.

SCHOOLS AND GUIDES
Welcome competition at last

The main Swiss school has a poor reputation and one reporter said: 'Awful – in three days, the instructor taught our early intermediate no technique, spoke no English and used the follow-me method the whole time.' But another praised the half-day private lessons his wife had: 'Excellent English and her skiing improved dramatically.'

There's a separate Stoked snowboard school, which we have good reports of. This has now combined with a new ski school which started last season and is made up of talented young instructors, some of whom are British and all of whom speak good English. They were called 4Synergies last season and a reporter who took a private instructor highly recommends them. Next season they will be called the The Ski School Zermatt and have 25 full-time instructors. Their programme includes off-piste free-ride classes and freestyle classes (learning tricks in the fun-park) as well as standard lessons.

FACILITIES FOR CHILDREN
Good hotel nurseries

The Nicoletta and Ginabelle hotels have obvious attractions for families who can afford them (though their nurseries are open to others). Despite our fat file of reports on Zermatt, we have no first-hand reports on them.

Staying there 

Choosing where to stay is very important in Zermatt. The solar-powered shuttle-buses are crowded, but at least they are now large, free to lift-pass holders and more frequent than they used to be. Walking from one end of the village to the furthest lifts can take 15 to 20 minutes and can be unpleasant because of treacherous icy paths.

The best spot for most people is near the Gornergrat and Sunnegga railways, near the end of the main street. Some accommodation is up the steep hill across the river from the centre in Winkelmatten. This is less isolated than it appears say reporters – you can ski back to it from all areas and the bus to town is reliable.

Getting up to the village from Täsch is no problem. The trains run on time and have automatically descending ramps that allow you to wheel luggage trolleys on and off. You are met at the other end by electric and horse-drawn taxis and hotel shuttles.

HOW TO GO
A wide choice, packaged or not

Chalets Several operators have places here, many of the most comfortable contained in large apartment blocks.
Hotels There are over 100 hotels, mostly comfortable and traditional-style 3-stars and 4-stars, but taking in the whole range.
((((5) **Mont Cervin** (966 8888) Biggest in town. Elegantly traditional. Good pool.

GETTING THERE

Air Geneva, rail transfer 4hr. Zürich, rail transfer 5hr. Sion, transfer 1 1/2hr.

Rail Station in resort.

Phone numbers
From elsewhere in Switzerland add the prefix 027.
From abroad use the prefix +41 27.

(5) **Zermatterhof** (966 6600) Traditional 'grand hotel' style with piano bar and pool.
(5) **Riffelalp Resort** (966 0555) Up the mountain, newly refurbished and extended, pool and spa, own evening trains.
(4) **Alex** (966 7070) Close to station. Good facilities, including a pool. Reporters love it.
(4) **Ambassador** (966 2611) Peaceful position near Gornergrat station. Large pool; sauna.
(4) **Monte Rosa** (966 0333) Well-modernised original Zermatt hotel, near southern end of village – full of climbing pictures and mementos.
(4) **Ginabelle** (966 5000) Smart pair of chalets not far from Sunnegga lift; great for families – on-the-spot ski nursery as well as day care.
(4) **Nicoletta** (966 0777) Modern chalet quite close to centre, with nursery.
(4) **Sonne** (966 2066) Traditionally decorated, in quiet setting away from main street; 'Roman Bath' complex.
(3) **Butterfly** (966 4166) 'Small, friendly, close to and as well furnished as the Alex, but much better food,' says a recent reporter.
(3) **Julen** (966 7600) Charming, modern-rustic chalet over the river, with Matterhorn views from some rooms.
(2) **Atlanta** (966 3535) No frills, but good food; close to centre, with Matterhorn views from some rooms.
(2) **Alpina** (967 1050) Modest but very friendly, and close to centre.
Self-catering There is a lot of apartment accommodation, but not much finds its way to the UK package market, so it sells out early. But the tourist office can provide a list of apartments and tell you availability.

STAYING UP THE MOUNTAIN
Comfortable seclusion

There are several hotels at altitude, of which the pick is the Riffelalp Resort at the first stop on the Gornergrat railway (see Hotels above), which re-opened as a luxury hotel last season – but you might find its limited evening train

ACTIVITIES

Indoor Sauna, tennis, hotel swimming pools (some open to public), salt water pool, keep-fit centre, squash, billiards, curling, bowling, gallery, excellent Alpine museum, cinema, indoor golf
Outdoor Skating, curling, sleigh rides, 30km cleared paths, helicopter flights, paragliding, cycling, ice-diving

TOURIST OFFICE

Postcode CH-3920
t +41 (27) 966 8100
f 966 8101
zermatt@wallis.ch
www.zermatt.ch

service a bit restricting. At the top of the railway, at 3100m, is the Kulmhotel Gornergrat – a rather austere building with basic accommodation.

STAYING DOWN THE VALLEY
Attractive for drivers

In Täsch, where visitors must leave their cars, there are five 3-star hotels, costing less than half the price of the equivalent in Zermatt. The Täscherhof (967 1818) is next to the station; the City (967 3606) close by. It's a 13-minute ride from Zermatt, with trains every 20 minutes for most of the day; the last train down is 11.10.

EATING OUT
Huge choice at all price levels

There are over 100 restaurants to choose from, ranging from top-quality haute cuisine, through traditional Swiss food, Chinese, Japanese and Thai to egg and chips and even a McDonald's.

'Enzo, Vrony' has superb food and unique decor (combining new with old), with the kitchen in full view in the centre. Booking is essential.

The Mazot is highly rated and highly priced. All the top hotels have classy restaurants open to non-residents. At the other end of the scale, Café du Pont has good-value pasta and rösti.

The Schwyzer Stübli has local specialities and usually live Swiss music and dancing. The Bahnhof Buffet has been rebuilt and serves reasonable food in a dining room built like a panoramic railway carriage.

Da Mario, Casa Rustica, Baku (see Après-ski) and the Spaghetti Factory (in the Hotel Post complex) have all been recommended by readers.

APRES-SKI
Lively and varied

A good mix of sophisticated and informal fun, though it helps if you have deep pockets. On the way back from the Klein Matterhorn there are lots of restaurants below Furi for a last drink and sunbathe – and delicious fruit tarts at Zum See. Recent visitors rave about the new Baku, on the way back to Winkelmatten. It's got a wigwam outside so you can't miss it: 'The staff are friendly, some of the food is exceptional and there is a great atmosphere.' On the way back from Sunnegga, Othmar's Hutte is popular and the Olympia Stübli often has live music. Near the church at Winkelmatten, the Sonnenblick is 'a great place to watch the sun set'. In town the Papperla is one of the few popular early places (it's busy after dinner, too). Elsie's bar is atmospheric and gets packed with an older crowd both early and late. The North Wall is frequented by seasonal workers and Murphy's Irish pub is the place if you're interested in 'loud music and beer'. Promenading the main street checking out expensive shoes and watches is popular.

Later on, the remarkable Hotel Post complex has something for everyone, from a quiet, comfortable bar (David's Boathouse) to a lively disco (Le Broken); Pink Elephant has live music (jazz, Irish etc) and a selection of restaurants.

Grampi's has dancing and is worth a visit. Z'Alt Hischi and the Little Bar are good for a quiet drink. The Hexenbar is cosy too. The hotel Alex draws a mature clientele for eating, drinking and dancing, with 'middle-of-the-road music and candlelit tables'.

The Vernissage is our favourite bar in town for a quiet evening drink. It is an unusual and stylish modern place, with the projection room for the cinema built into the upstairs bar and displays of art elsewhere.

OFF THE SLOPES
Considerable attractions

Zermatt is an easy place to spend time (and money). And, if lunch up the mountain appeals, this is a great resort for pedestrians. The Alpine museum is recommended – as is a helicopter trip around the Matterhorn. There is an 'excellent' cinema, and a reader tells us the free village guided tour is 'well worth doing'. You can also try ice-diving (wetsuit provided) at Trockener Steg.

Until two years ago, virtually all the reports we received on US resorts had one thing in common: wholehearted praise for the US skiing experience. In general, people are captivated by it and by the contrasts with European resorts. Nearly everyone is struck by the high standards of service and courtesy you receive, by the relatively deserted pistes, by the immaculate piste grooming and by the top-quality accommodation. Depending on the resort, you may also be struck by the superb quality of the snow, the cute Wild West ambience and how easy it is to visit other nearby areas. But don't fall into the trap of lumping all US resorts together – they differ enormously. There are distinct disadvantages of US skiing, too. And in the last couple of years we have picked up early signs that America may be losing its edge on service (perhaps because ski resorts are having difficulty recruiting enough staff).

It was snow that first took the British to America in large numbers, during the Alpine snow droughts of the late 1980s. The super-high Rockies had the reputation of getting limitless quantities of super-light snow. The reputation went slightly beyond the reality, but in practice it doesn't matter; most American resorts receive serious amounts of snow (25ft in a season is perfectly normal). And most resorts have serious snowmaking facilities too. What's more, they use them well – they lay down a base of artificial snow early in the season, rather than patching up shortages later on. This is partly a reaction to the pattern of natural snowfall: a lot of the Rockies' snow arrives relatively late in the season – something that seems to be increasingly true in the Alps. In January, or even February, you may encounter signs saying: 'Caution: Early Season Conditions Apply'. What they mean is that you may occasionally encounter a rock.

Piste grooming is taken very seriously – most American resorts set standards that Alpine resorts are only now beginning to attempt to match. Every morning you can expect to step out on to perfect 'corduroy' pistes. But this doesn't mean that there aren't moguls – far from it. It's just that you get moguls where the resort says you can expect moguls, not where you're expecting an easy cruise. Indeed many resorts have now taken to grooming half the width of some runs and leaving the other half mogulled – so you can choose your terrain. Most runs are delightfully deserted compared with Europe.

American resorts are well organised in lots of other respects, too. Many offer free guided tours of the area. Lift queues are short, partly because they are highly disciplined, and spare seats on chair-lifts are religiously filled, with the aid of cheerful, conscientious attendants. Piste maps and boxes of tissues are freely available at the bottom of most lifts. Mountain 'hosts' are on hand to advise you about the best possible routes to take. School standards are uniformly high – with the added advantage of English being the native language. And facilities for children are impressive too – our reporters are universally glowing in their praise about children's ski school classes.

US resorts have the reputation of not providing opportunities for off-piste, but this seriously misrepresents the position. It's true that areas practically always have a boundary, and that venturing beyond it is discouraged or forbidden. But within the area there is often challenging terrain that is very much like being off-piste in an Alpine resort – with the important advantage that it is much safer because it's patrolled and avalanche-controlled. Many resorts are adding areas that you have to hike to – or perhaps get a tow behind a snowcat part of the way. The reward is delightful isolation and untracked snow.

↑ Plenty of cruisers, plenty of bumps – and plenty of trees. That's skiing in the States. (And this is Vail.)

SNOWPIX.COM / CHRIS GILL

There are drawbacks to the US as well, though. One is that many resorts (including big names) have areas that are very modest in extent compared with major Alpine areas. But many US resorts are very close to each other – so if you are prepared to travel a bit, you won't get bored. A more serious problem as far as we (and many of our reporters) are concerned is that the day is ridiculously short. The lifts often shut at 3pm or 3.30. That may explain another drawback for those who like a good lunch on the mountain – the dearth of decent mountain restaurants. Monster self-service cafeterias doing pizza, burgers and other fast foods are the norm – so that people can spend as much time on the slopes and as little time eating as possible. Small atmospheric restaurants with table-service and decent food are rare – but growing in number as resorts try to attract more European guests.

It's also true that much of the terrain and many of the runs are monotonous. You don't get the spectacular mountain scenery and the distinctive high-mountain runs of the Alps – most are below the tree line (the upside of this is the good visibility the trees give when it's snowing). And because most of the mountains have been developed specifically for the skiing, they can feel rather artificial.

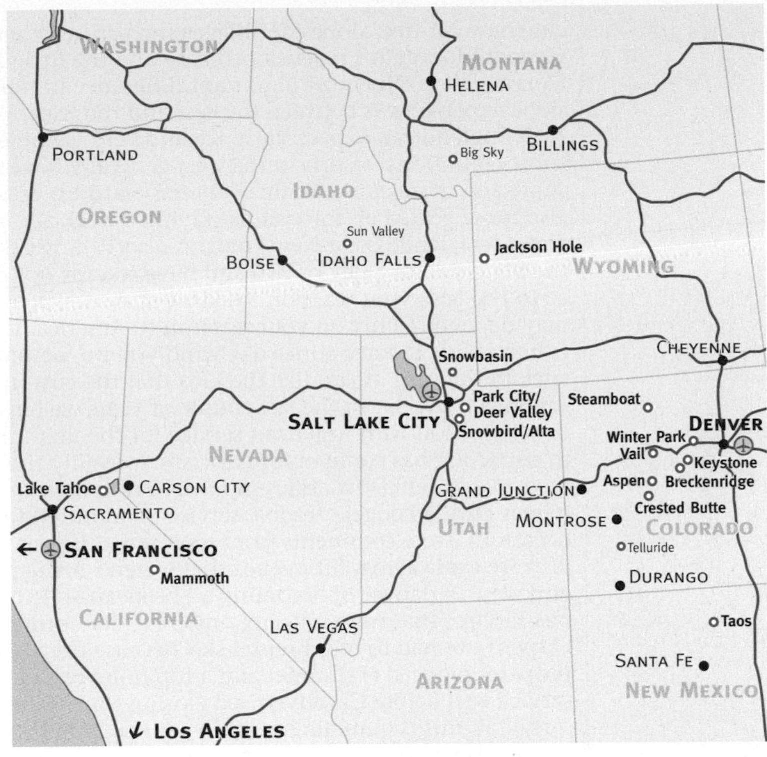

The grading of pistes (or trails, to use the local term) is different from Europe. Red runs don't exist. The colours used are combined with shapes: green circles, blue squares, black diamonds (single and double). Greens correspond fairly closely to greens in Europe (that is, in France, where they are mainly found). American blues largely correspond to blues in Europe, but also include tougher intermediate runs that would be red in the Alps; these are sometimes labelled as double-blue squares, although in some resorts a hybrid blue-black grading is used instead. Single-black-diamond runs correspond to steeper European reds and easier European blacks. Double-black-diamond runs are seriously steep – often steeper than the steepest pistes in the Alps and including high, open bowls. A few resorts have started to class their very steepest runs as triple-black-diamonds.

US resorts vary widely in style and convenience. But two important things that they all have in common are good-value, spacious accommodation and good, reasonably priced restaurants. There are old restored Wild West towns such as Telluride, Crested Butte and Aspen, genuine cowboy towns such as Jackson Hole, purpose-built monstrosities such as Snowbird, and even skyscraping gambling dens such as Heavenly. There is an increasing number of cute new car-free, slopeside villages such as Keystone's River Run, Copper Mountain's redeveloped base and the fledgling village at Squaw Valley. The most important difference in terms of the on-slope experience is between the east and the west. While resorts in New England can expect slush, ice and very variable weather and snow conditions, resorts in the west generally have much better snow and more consistently cold temperatures. Western resorts are also more geared up for visitors staying a week and generally have a resort feel, while most New England resorts target skiers coming from the big cities for a day or two and have less (or no) resort ambience.

In the end, your reaction to skiing and snowboarding in America may depend mainly on your reaction to America. If repeated cheerful exhortations to have a nice day wind you up, perhaps you'd better stick to the Alps. If you like the idea that the customer is king, give America a try. But in the last couple of years we have picked up dissatisfaction with American service for the first time. Breckenridge in particular has come in for criticism: 'possibly the worst burger I have ever eaten' (Vista Haus mountain restaurant), 'dirty rooms' (Great Divide Lodge), 'terrible service ... admitted to not caring on occasions' were comments from reporters this year. On our last US visit we came across lift queues that weren't being properly organised and were in danger of becoming a European-style free-for-all (Vail), bus services that were running only half the normal schedule (Aspen), we had to reject rental skis because they had not been properly serviced (Telluride) and a top hotel restaurant tried to refuse service well before the advertised closing time (Keystone).

But all this is quibbling a bit. In general, you'll still find American service streets ahead of European. We love skiing in America.

California

California? It means surfing, beaches, wine, Hollywood, Disneyland and San Francisco cable-cars. But it also has the highest mountains in continental USA and some of America's biggest winter resorts, usually reliable for snow from November to May (one sometimes remains open until the Independence Day holiday, the 4th of July). What's more, winter holidays in California are tremendous value for money.

Holidays here are cheap because winter is low season for much of the accommodation and for scheduled flights from Britain into Los Angeles and San Francisco. There is huge capacity available for the massive summer tourist trade and hotel owners and airlines are happy to offer cut-price deals to keep a contribution coming in towards their overheads. A few years back we met a British family who had been on four holidays in bargain-basement Bulgaria. They had decided to try California because it wasn't much more expensive. Not surprisingly, they loved it.

California's mountains get a lot of snow. In several recent seasons, Californian resorts have recorded the deepest snow-cover in North America. A common allegation is that the snow that falls in California is wet 'Sierra Cement'. Our fat file of reports from visitors has some complaints about that – especially late in the season – but most people have found the snow just fine, as we have.

Heavenly, Squaw Valley and Mammoth, in particular, are impressive mountains, with something for all standards of skier or boarder. Our main reservation has been the character of the resorts themselves; they don't have the traditional mountain-town ambience that we look for in the States. That's partly because this is California, the automobile state: the resorts were not designed with walking in mind, and this has made them rather soulless. In compensation, Heavenly, at least, offers uniquely big-time entertainment in its casinos. And the scenery, particularly around Lake Tahoe, is simply stunning – much more spectacular than you find in most US winter resorts.

But things are changing, with several new 'pedestrian villages' being developed. Last season in Heavenly there was a new gondola from the centre of town right into the heart of the slopes – and work on the new car-free 'village' at the gondola base has now started. The first stage of the new village at Squaw Valley will be open at the base of the slopes for the 2001/02 season. A couple of smaller Lake Tahoe resorts – Kirkwood and Northstar-at-Tahoe – have small, attractive slope-side villages. Mammoth has new slope-side accommodation, and redevelopment has started on part of Mammoth Lakes to form a 'village' that will eventually be linked to the slopes by gondola.

If you go to California, consider a two-centre trip – taking in Lake Tahoe and Mammoth. Or just go to Tahoe and rent a car. The area has several ski and snowboard areas that are well worth visiting. And the views as you drive round the lake are superb.

HEAVENLY SKI RESORT / CHACO MAHLER

The views in the Lake Tahoe region are stunning→

Heavenly 1995m

Knockout lake views, and gambling until dawn

WHAT IT COSTS

5

HOW IT RATES

The slopes	
Snow	****
Extent	***
Experts	***
Intermediates	****
Beginners	****
Convenience	*
Queues	****
Restaurants	*
The rest	
Scenery	****
Resort charm	*
Off-slope	**

What's new

In December 2000 the long-awaited eight-person gondola from the centre of South Lake Tahoe into the middle of Heavenly's slopes opened. This means that anyone staying downtown no longer has to drive or catch a bus to and from the slopes.

Work on a 34-acre pedestrian village around the new gondola base is under way, with two new hotels, an ice rink and shopping village planned.

There's a new tubing hill at the top of the gondola, and 10-15km of scenic cross-country and snow-shoe trails here should be ready for 2001/02. Two new gladed runs are opening for 2001/02 in the upper Nevada area off Skyline Trail.

Two more new lifts from the top of the gondola, three new runs and a new restaurant are planned but not until 2002/03 at the earliest.

- ⊕ Amazing views across Lake Tahoe and arid Nevada
- ⊕ Fair sized mountain which offers a sensation of travelling around – common in the Alps, not in the US
- ⊕ Lots of easy off-piste among trees
- ⊕ Some serious challenges for experts
- ⊕ Numerous other worthwhile areas within driving distance
- ⊕ Very good value package deals
- ⊕ A unique après-ski scene
- ⊕ Impressive snowmaking facilities

- ⊖ The base-town of South Lake Tahoe is quite unlike a traditional resort, and not attractive – though things are changing with the construction of a new resort village near the existing downtown area
- ⊖ Very little traditional après-ski activity – though this may soon change as well
- ⊖ If natural snow is in short supply, most of the challenging terrain is likely to be closed

A resort called Heavenly invites an obvious question: just how close to heaven does it take you? Physically, close enough: with a top height of 3060m and vertical of 1065m, it's the highest and biggest of the resorts clustered around scenic Lake Tahoe (see Lake Tahoe chapter). Metaphorically, it's not quite so close. The slopes have something for all standards, and having another dozen resorts within easy reach by car means that an interestingly varied holiday is assured. But anyone who (like us) is drawn to the place by its amazing views across the lake is likely to be dismayed by the appearance and atmosphere of the town of South Lake Tahoe, at the foot of the slopes, dominated as it is by a handful of high-rise hotel-casinos and a straggle of rather tacky motels.

But things are changing: the shabby Park Avenue area has been flattened to make way for a new 34-acre resort village with luxury accommodation, shops, restaurants, bars and an ice-rink – all built in a more sympathetic style. And an eight-seat gondola, new last season, runs the two-and-a-half miles from here to the centre of the slopes.

The resort

Heavenly is at the south end of Lake Tahoe, on the borders of California and Nevada, east of San Francisco. Heavenly's base-town – South Lake Tahoe – is unlike any other resort we know. The Stateline area at its centre is dominated by a handful of monstrous hotel-casinos (located just inches on the Nevada side of the line). These brash but comfortable hotels offer good-value accommodation (subsidised by the gambling) and big-name entertainment as well as slot machines, roulette wheels, craps and endless card games. They are a conspicuous part of the amazing lake views from the lower slopes (though not from above mid-mountain, nor on the Nevada side). The area around the casinos is currently strangely devoid of 'downtown' atmosphere (never mind mountain resort atmosphere); there are few bars or shops, and the centre is bisected by US Highway 50. The rest of the town consists of low-rise motels, stores, wedding chapels and so on, spreading for miles along this busy, pedestrian-hostile highway; many are rather shabby, though this is partly camouflaged by the tall trees that surround most of them. The Heavenly Village project – a new, sympathetically designed resort village just on the California side of the stateline – will greatly improve the town's appeal as a base for a holiday.

The new gondola direct from Heavenly Village to the slopes means you no longer need a car or bus to get to the slopes if you stay downtown. But much of South Lake Tahoe's accommodation is more than walking

MOUNTAIN FACTS

Altitude	1995m-3060m
Lifts	29
Pistes	4800 acres
Green	20%
Blue	45%
Black	35%
Art. snow	500 acres

LIFT PASSES

2000/01 prices in dollars

Heavenly
Covers all lifts on Heavenly mountain.

Beginners 3-day learn to ski packages include lift pass and rental (adult 233).

Main pass
1-day pass 57
6-day pass 306

Senior citizens
Over 65: 6-day pass 144

Children
13 to 18: 6-day pass 246
Under 13: 6-day pass 144
Under 5: free pass

Short-term passes
Half-day passes available from 12.30 to 4pm (adult 42)

Notes Passes of three days or more allow one non-skiing day; 6-day pass valid for 7 days, with one non-skiing day.

distance away and having a car is still handy to explore the other resorts around Lake Tahoe and to get to many of the best bars and restaurants, which are tucked out of the way.

South Lake Tahoe is surprisingly downmarket. The casinos have some swanky restaurants, but basically exist to allow gambling-starved Americans to feed their quarters into slot machines. The accommodation away from the centre is not particularly smart. But most of it conforms to American norms, and (except at weekends) all of it is under-used in winter, which is one reason why you can get cheap deals.

You reach the slopes from the new downtown gondola or from any of the base lodges, which can easily be reached by road. The new Heavenly Village will ultimately be the main base area. But California Lodge, up a heavily wooded slope a mile out of South Lake Tahoe, beside a huge car park, will remain the main base for people staying outside the downtown area. Boulder and Stagecoach base lodges lie around the mountain in Nevada. There is an 'excellent' free shuttle-bus service to the three out-of-town bases.

The mountain

Most of Heavenly's slopes suit intermediates down to the ground but there are also good beginner slopes at the California base, and some splendid easy runs to progress to. Experts can find genuine challenges at the two extremes of the area – as well as lots of fun in acre upon acre of easy off-piste wooded terrain. Keep in mind that there are other worthwhile areas within easy reach by car or bus (or paddle steamer!). You'll want to try at least a couple during your stay – see the Lake Tahoe chapter.

The Hornblower boat shuttle across the lake to Squaw Valley and Alpine Meadows is a pleasant alternative to driving. It costs $87 including lift pass and there's a good live band on the way back. But you lose two hours on the slopes – you don't arrive at Squaw until 11am.

THE SLOPES
Interestingly complex

Heavenly's mountain is quite complicated, and getting from A to B requires more careful navigation than is usual on American mountains.

There is a fairly clear division between the California side (the lifts and runs directly above South Lake Tahoe) and the Nevada side (above Stagecoach Lodge and Boulder Lodge).

From the top of the new gondola it's short walk to the Tamerack Express six-seater chair, which allows you to access either side. Or slide down to the Sky high-speed quad: this goes to the top of the California side and the tedious Skyline Trail traverse takes you to the top of the Nevada side. Near the border you can see beautiful views over Lake Tahoe in one direction and the arid Nevada 'desert' in the other.

From the top of the Sky chair you can play on greens, blues and blacks on the top half of the mountain on the Californian side – served by four other lifts as well. The lower half of the Californian side has unrelenting steep

HEAVENLY / SCOTT MARKEWITZ

The locals get blasé about the lake views after a while; but visitors can't take their eyes off them →

black runs down the front face, often heavily mogulled, with the alternative of the narrow, blue Roundabout trail snaking its way down the mountain. Right at the California Lodge base is a great beginner area. From here uplift is by a mid-sized cable-car and the recently upgraded Gunbarrel fast quad.

On the Nevada side there are three main bowls. The central one, above East Peak Lodge, is an excellent intermediate area served by two fast quad chairs, with a downhill extension of the bowl served by the Galaxy chair. On one side of this central bowl is the steeper, open terrain of Milky Way Bowl, leading to the seriously steep Mott and Killebrew canyons, served by the Mott Canyon chair. On the other side is the North Bowl, with lifts up from Nevada's two base lodges.

There are no really easy runs on the Nevada side, apart from limited nursery slopes at the base.

SNOW RELIABILITY
No worries

Heavenly suffered from drought in the early 90s. That, no doubt, prompted it to install a very impressive snowmaking system that now covers around 70% of the trails and ensures that most sections are open most of the time. In recent years Californian resorts have consistently recorded some of the deepest snow cover of any North American resorts; and when we last visited most of the snow-guns were invisible – entirely buried underneath natural snow.

FOR EXPERTS
Some specific challenges

Although the area as a whole suits intermediates better, there are genuine challenges for the more advanced. The runs under the California base lifts – including The Face and Gunbarrel (often used for mogul competitions) – are of proper black steepness, and very testing when the snow is hard. Ellie's, at the top of the mountain, may offer continuous moguls too.

The really steep stuff is on the Nevada side. Milky Way Bowl offers a fairly gentle introduction to this terrain. At the extremity of the bowl the seriously steep Mott and Killebrew canyons have roped gateways. The less expert are steered to lower gates.

All over the mountain, there is excellent off-piste terrain among widely spaced trees, which offers tremendous fun when the conditions are right.

SCHOOLS/GUIDES

2000/01 prices in dollars

Perfect Turn Clinics 7 days

2¾hr: from 10am or 1pm

5 half days: 185

Children's clinics

Ages: 4 to 13

5 5hr days including pass, rental and lunch: 493

Private clinics

1hr, 2hr, 4hr and 6hr

85 for 1hr

CHILDCARE

Heavenly's state-of-the-art Day Care Center opens at 8.30 to care for children between the ages of 2 months and 4 years. Book ahead.

Children between 4 and 13 can enrol in the Perfect Kids programme. It offers skiing from age 4 and a snowboarding option from 8 upwards. It is an all-inclusive day of supervision, lessons, lunch, lift access, equipment and snacks. The programme is based at California Lodge (which includes an indoor play area) or at Boulder Lodge. There are also 'Tag-along' private lessons where a parent can observe their child's progress.

FOR INTERMEDIATES

Lots to do

Heavenly is excellent for intermediates, who are made to feel welcome and secure by excellent piste grooming and signposting. The California side offers a progression from the relaxed cruising of the long Ridge Run, starting right at the top of the mountain, to more testing blues dropping off the ridge towards the Sky Deck restaurant. The confident intermediate may want to spend more time on the Nevada side, where there is more variety of terrain. Recent visitors enjoyed 'fast blues off the Dipper Express chair'. You should also head for some of the long, quite testing runs down to the base stations and to the Galaxy chair.

FOR BEGINNERS

An excellent place to learn

The California side is more suited to beginners, with gentle green runs served by the Pioneer drag-lift and the Powderbowl chair-lift at the top of the cable-car. There are good nursery slopes at base lodge level.

FOR CROSS-COUNTRY

A separate world

The Spooner Lake Cross Country Area located close to Tahoe is an extensive meadow area of over 100km in 21 prepared trails. There are ample facilities for both instruction and rental.

Organised moonlit tours are a popular alternative to the noise and bright lights of the casinos.

QUEUES

Some at weekends

Lift lines are generally not a problem, except during some weekends and public holidays when the entire Tahoe area is swamped with weekenders and day trippers. Thanks to the new gondola, the key lifts moving people out from the base lodges are now under less pressure on busy days.

MOUNTAIN RESTAURANTS

Several options, none exciting

Two restaurants can be recommended on the California side. At The Top of the Tram is a table-service restaurant which makes up for its simple food with a calm atmosphere and the famous lake view (reservations necessary). The Sky Deck at the heart of the California slopes has a good barbecue, where Californian rock music blasts and cool dudes hang out.

In Nevada, East Peak Lodge has a terrace and barbie, plus interesting views over arid Nevada, but it gets hideously overcrowded when the weather drives people indoors. There's an Italian-themed place at Stagecoach Lodge, and a Tex-Mex at Boulder.

SCHOOLS AND GUIDES

Good system

The Perfect Turn ski and ride programmes build on your strengths rather than focusing on your weaknesses and are highly regarded.

FACILITIES FOR CHILDREN

Comprehensive

The Perfect Kids learning centre in the California Base Lodge is expanded by 30% for 2001/02. It attracted particular praise from one reporter: 'This was an excellent facility – very convenient and very professionally run. I would thoroughly recommend it.'

boarding *Lake Tahoe is quickly becoming known as the snowboarding hub of North America and, as you would expect, boarders are very well catered for at Heavenly. There are good fun-parks and half-pipes on both the California and Nevada sides. The off-piste in trees and double-black-diamond bowls make a great playground for good free-riders. Beginners and intermediates will enjoy great cruising runs and the easy-to-ride chair-lifts. There are a couple of specialist board shops in South Lake Tahoe, but quite an absence of lively boarder-friendly bars.*

Heavenly's slopes, seen from across the lake →

HEAVENLY

Staying there 

Give careful consideration to your plans for evenings as well as daytime. If you have a car, your options are numerous; for example, you could base yourself out at one of the Nevada lift stations, and drive when you want entertainment. Night owls can scarcely do better than to stay in a casino.

HOW TO GO

Hotel or motel?

Accommodation in the South Lake Tahoe area is abundant and ranges from the glossy casinos to small, rather ramshackle motels. Hotel and motel rooms are easy to find midweek, but can be sold out at busy weekends.

Chalets UK tour operators run some good catered chalets, including some lakeside ones.

Hotels Caesars (775 558 3515), Harrah's (558 6611), Horizon (775 558 6211), (775 558 2411) and Harveys are the main casino hotels. Rooms booked on the spot are expensive; packages are good value.

((((4) **Embassy Suites** (530 544 5400) Luxury suites in a new, traditional-style building next to the casinos.

((2) **Tahoe Chalet Inn** (530 544 3311) Clean, friendly, near casinos. Back rooms (away from highway) preferable.

((2) **Best Western Timber Cove Lodge** (530 541 6722) Bland but well run, with lake views from some rooms.

Self-catering Plenty of choice. Some are available from tour operators. We've had a rave report about The Ridge Tahoe condos near Stagecoach Lodge: 'Luxury accommodation. The bathroom was big enough for waltzing.' There's an indoor–outdoor pool, hot-tub and a private gondola to whisk you to the slopes.

EATING OUT

Good value

The casino hotels offer fantastic value in their buffet-style all-you-can-eat dining. They have some more ambitious 'gourmet' restaurants too – some high enough up their tower blocks to give superb lake views (try Harrah's 18th floor). The sprawling resort area offers a great choice of international dining, from cosy little pizza houses to large, traditional American diners, Mexican tequila-and-tacos joints, and English and Irish pubs. Visitors' suggestions include Paul Kennedy's steakhouse, and Fresh Ketch at Tahoe Keys Marina for 'wonderful fresh fish and harbour views – though don't expect snazzy presentation'. The Riva Grill is also recommended, as are Bandanas and the Driftwood Café for breakfast. The Tudor Pub is better than it sounds.

APRES-SKI

Extraordinary

What makes the area unique is the casinos on the Nevada side of the stateline. These aren't simply opportunities to throw money away on roulette or slot machines: top-name entertainers, pop and jazz stars, cabarets and Broadway revues are also to be found in them – designed to give gamblers another reason to stay. We saw a great show by acrobats and trapeze-artists on our last visit.

You can dance and dine your way across the lake aboard an authentic paddle steamer.

OFF THE SLOPES

Luck be a lady

You're in luck if gambling is your weakness. Or then again, perhaps not. If you want to get away from the bright lights, try a boat trip on Lake Tahoe, snowmobiling a short drive from South Lake Tahoe, or a hot-air balloon ride.

Pedestrians can use the existing cable-car or the new gondola to view the lake and mountains below.

GETTING THERE

Air San Francisco, transfer 3½hr. Reno, transfer 75 min. South Lake Tahoe, transfer 15 min.

Phone numbers

The state line runs through Heavenly, so two different area codes are used. For this chapter only, therefore, the area code is included with the hotel's number.

From distant parts of the US, add the prefix 1.

From abroad, add the prefix +1.

ACTIVITIES

Indoor 6 casinos, 6 cinemas, cheap factory shops, ice skating, bowling, gyms, spas, Western museum

Outdoor Boat cruises, snowmobiling, horse-drawn sleigh rides, horse riding, ice skating, hot springs, ghost town tours

TOURIST OFFICE

Postcode NV 89449
t +1 (775) 586 7000
f 588 5517
info@skiheavenly.com
www.skiheavenly.com

Lake Tahoe 1890m

Slopes everywhere you look – and magnificent lake views

WHAT IT COSTS

5

What's new

At Squaw, work on a new base village is progressing. For the 2001/02 season the first phase of accommodation, shops, restaurants and underground parking should be in use. Over the next few years, the size of the village will quadruple.

At Kirkwood, the small base village will see a new ice rink and recreation centre.

MOUNTAIN FACTS

Alpine Meadows

Altitude	2085m-2630m
Lifts	12
Pistes	2000 acres
Green	25%
Blue	40%
Black	35%
Art. snow	185 acres

Recco detectors used

Kirkwood

Altitude	2375m-2985m
Lifts	12
Pistes	2300 acres
Green	15%
Blue	50%
Black	35%
Art. snow	55 acres

Recco detectors used

Squaw Valley

Altitude	1890m-2760m
Lifts	30
Pistes	4000 acres
Green	25%
Blue	45%
Black	30%
Art. snow	360 acres

Recco detectors used

Northstar-at-Tahoe

Altitude	1930m-2625m
Lifts	12
Pistes	2420 acres
Green	25%
Blue	50%
Black	25%
Art. snow	1200 acres

Set high in the mountains 200 miles east of San Francisco, on the borders of California and Nevada, Lake Tahoe has the highest concentration of resorts in the US, with 14 downhill and seven cross-country centres. It is a very beautiful region, ideal for driving around on a tour, visiting a different area each day – though the major mountains are worth devoting a few days each to.

THE RESORTS

The resorts of the Lake Tahoe region are mostly not fully fledged resorts in the European sense. Some have no accommodation, others a little. Most of the areas attract weekend or day trippers. There are lots of B&Bs and motels dotted around the lake, and a couple of quite pleasant small towns.

Then there is South Lake Tahoe, at the foot of the Heavenly slopes (the biggest resort in the area), which is a small town unlike any other ski resort we have seen (see Heavenly chapter). It has boomed on the back of gambling, which is a big industry on the Nevada side of the stateline that cuts through the region. (The impact on Tahoe City, on the stateline at the north end of the lake, has been much less pronounced.)

The next biggest resort is Squaw Valley, about a 90-minute drive from South Lake Tahoe. It has had some accommodation for years but now a real resort village is being built – the first phase of which is due to open for the 2001/02 season.

THE MOUNTAINS

The choice of **slopes** around the lake is enormous, with more than enough to keep even the keenest skier or boarder happy for a couple of weeks. With a car you can make the best of the weather, heading for sheltered areas when a storm socks in, for example.

Snow reliability hasn't been a problem in the last few years – which have seen massive falls. The area also has huge amounts of artificial snowmaking capacity.

Heavenly, at the southern end of the lake, has the greatest vertical drop of the region, with slopes to suit all standards and splendid lake views. See the Heavenly chapter for details.

Nearby **Sierra-at-Tahoe** is a smaller, tree-lined area – sheltered, so useful in bad weather, mainly easy cruising plus a few mogul fields. Unusually, it offers some free lessons (or did last season) – two instructors am and pm.

Kirkwood, also at the south end of the lake, is renowned for its powder, steep runs and uncrowded slopes. It also has fine intermediate groomed trails and a small new mountain village with ski-in, ski-out accommodation. A new ice rink and a recreation centre with outdoor heated pool, spa and sun deck will be ready for 2001/02. The lift system is also being developed – the new high-speed quad, Cornice Express, takes you to the top of the mountain in four minutes. Adventurous intermediates can tackle some of the great off-piste – Thunder Saddle to Eagle Bowl is a must.

The major resort at the north end of the lake is **Squaw Valley**, with 4,000 acres of open, above-the-tree-line bowls on six linked mountains. It is unusual in having no trails marked on its piste map. Instead it has green, blue and black graded lifts. The possibilities for experts here are phenomenal, with lots of steep slopes, chutes and big mogul fields – many extreme skiing and boarding movies are made here. But it is good for intermediates, with lovely long groomed runs including a top-to-bottom three-mile cruise, and a superb beginner area at altitude. Squaw is a big snowboarding centre and at night a fun-park, half-pipe and run (for skiers too) down from mid-mountain is floodlit. Massive recent investment has resulted in a very slick lift system, including North America's first twin-cable jumbo Funitel gondola (as in Verbier and Crans-Montana) and high-speed six-seater chairs. For 2001/2, the first phase of the new car-free village will open at the base of the mountain – with accommodation, shops, restaurants and underground parking. When this is completed, it will be a compelling place to stay – it is being developed by Intrawest, owners of Whistler and several other resorts.

Alpine Meadows has the longest season and some of the most varied terrain in the Tahoe region – snow conditions can still be good in July some years. This area is excellent for all standards, with green runs and nursery slopes at the bottom, top-to-bottom blues and some varied blacks, including high bowls and tree-covered terrain. The mountain has slopes facing in all directions, giving good conditions whatever the weather. There is a new fun-park and half-pipe.

Northstar-at-Tahoe is a fairly small, largely easy-to-intermediate mountain close to Squaw. The nine or so black runs on the back-side (served by a single fast quad) vary little in character and are really good long advanced intermediate cruises. A new chair-lift for 2000/01 opened up another five black runs on Lookout Mountain. Previously, this area had been accessible only by snowcat. The whole area is very sheltered and good for bad-weather days. For 2001/02 there will be even more snowmaking, covering over 50% of the mountain. There's some accommodation and a pleasant shopping, restaurant and bar area at the bottom of the mountain.

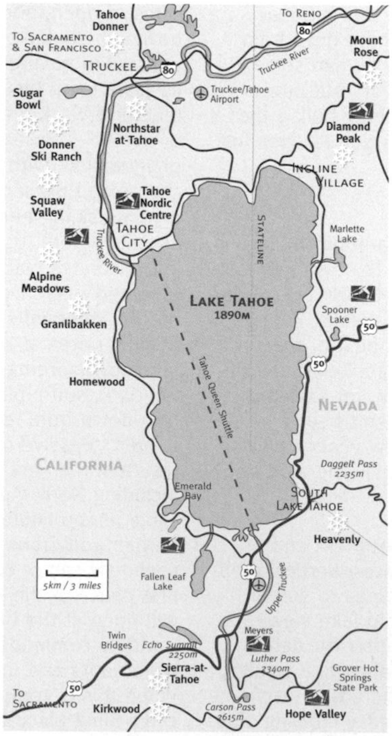

Those are the six areas we'd most recommend visiting. But there are eight other areas in the Tahoe region in case you get bored, most of which are marked on our map. A regular visitor to the region who is particularly keen on the north shore recommends Diamond Peak for its 'breathtaking views and fab restaurant', Mount Rose for its 'great snow always and carving runs', and both for quiet slopes and zero lift queues. There are also **cross-country** possibilities at most of the downhill areas as well as in dedicated cross-country areas.

Queues are rare in all the areas, except at peak weekends when people pour in from San Francisco and Los Angeles. We have few reports of the **schools** or facilities for **children**, but doubtless they are up to the usual high US standards.

STAYING THERE

We'd recommend spending a few days at each end of the lake.

At the southern end the main options are the brash and rather tacky town of South Lake Tahoe (see the chapter on Heavenly), or the quiet mountain village at Kirkwood.

At the northern end there's more choice. Squaw Valley has a handful of hotels and the first phase of a new village. Squaw's cable-car runs in the evenings to serve the floodlit slopes and the dining facilities at High Camp. This is an incredible mid-mountain complex, with several restaurants and bars, outdoor pool, ice skating, tennis and bungee jumping. The new resort village at the base will massively increase Squaw's attraction for a week's stay.

Northstar has very convenient hotel rooms and condominiums. It would be a good family choice for a quiet stay.

An alternative is to stay in the small town of Tahoe City, right on the lake, a short drive from both the Squaw Valley and Alpine Meadows areas and a little bit further from Northstar. It has a fair number of hotels and bars, and some good restaurants.

Our regular Tahoe reporter suggests Incline Village (which comes a close second to Tahoe City for choice of bars and restaurants) for its 'country charm and ambience, and friendly people'. Incline Village is handy for Diamond Peak and Mount Rose, a bit of a drive from Squaw and Alpine Meadows, but under an hour from Heavenly.

TOURIST OFFICE

Alpine Meadows

Postcode CA 96145
t +1 (530) 583 4232
f 583 0963
info@skialpine.com
www.skialpine.com

Kirkwood

Postcode CA 95646
t +1 (877) 547 5966
f (209) 258 8899
kwd-info@ski-kirkwood.com
www.kirkwood.com

Squaw Valley

Postcode CA 96146
t +1 (530) 583 6985
f 581 7106
squaw@squaw.com
www.squaw.com

Northstar-at-Tahoe

Postcode CA 96160
t +1 (530) 562 1010
f 562 2215
northstar@boothcreek.com
www.skinorthstar.com

Mammoth Mountain 2430m

Californian sun and snow with extensive, varied terrain

WHAT IT COSTS

5

HOW IT RATES

The slopes	
Snow	****
Extent	***
Experts	****
Intermediates	****
Beginners	****
Convenience	**
Queues	****
Restaurants	*
The rest	
Scenery	***
Resort charm	**
Off-slope	*

What's new

Work has started on a new car-free village at the core of Mammoth Lakes, eventually with a gondola link to the slopes.

The restaurant at the top of the Panorama gondola will be open for table-service dining for 2001/2.

For 2000/01 the two lifts up from Juniper Springs were replaced by the Mammoth's first fast six-seater.

MAMMOTH MOUNTAIN

You can ski and board all over Mammoth's mammoth mountain ↓

- ⊕ One of North America's biggest and best mountains, with steep bowls at the top and easy/intermediate cruises lower down, in the trees
- ⊕ Can get a lot of snow – and there's extensive snowmaking
- ⊕ Deserted slopes during the week
- ⊕ Good children's facilities
- ⊕ Excellent daytime bus service
- ⊕ Lots of recent resort improvements

- ⊖ Mammoth Lakes is a rather straggling place with no focus, where it helps to have a car
- ⊖ Most accommodation is miles from the slopes – though this is changing
- ⊖ Weekend crowds from Los Angeles
- ⊖ Runs not clearly marked on map or mountain, especially high up
- ⊖ Wind can close high lifts, and upper runs can be icy and windblown

Mammoth lives up to its name, more or less. It may not be giant in Alpine terms, but it is much bigger than most resorts in the US, and big enough to provide a week's amusement for most people. It has everything from steep, high, experts-only chutes and bowls (with magnificent views) to long, easy cruising runs in the trees. What it lacks, more than anything else, is a real village at the base.

Enter Intrawest, owner of Whistler and now of various key plots of land here, plus a majority share in Mammoth Mountain. Intrawest is investing heavily in transforming the resort infrastructure and plans to create 10,000 more guest beds over the next decade. It opened the first stage of a new slope-side development at Juniper Springs a couple of years ago. But plans for a new pedestrian village centre in the town of Mammoth Lakes, to be linked to the mountain by gondola, will take longer to realise. For now, the mountain is the attraction. But it is quite a mountain.

The resort 

Most people stay in Mammoth Lakes, a small year-round resort town four miles from the main lift base. There is no 'downtown' area yet, though one is under construction: hotels, bars, restaurants and little shopping centres are dotted along Main Street, the very wide highway running through the resort, and Old Mammoth Road at right angles to it. The buildings are generally rustic in style, and are set among trees, so although Mammoth Lakes may be short on resort ambience it has a pleasant enough appearance. Even McDonald's has been tastefully designed. The 'village' is usually under a blanket of snow, which also helps.

There is also accommodation at the main base area at the Mammoth Mountain Inn complex, along with some restaurants. And along the road up to the slopes lie several hotels and condos. Shuttle-buses run efficiently on several routes serving the lift bases, but they are limited after 5.30pm and a car is useful, especially for getting to June Mountain for a change of scenery.

The five- or six-hour drive up from Los Angeles, along a very good road, is spectacular. You pass through the San Bernardino mountains and Mojave Desert before reaching the Sierra Nevada range, of which Mammoth is part. Light aircraft can fly into Mammoth Lakes' own airport.

The mountain 

MOUNTAIN FACTS

Altitude	2430m-3370m
Lifts	27
Pistes	3500 acres
Green	30%
Blue	40%
Black	30%
Art. snow	450 acres

Recco detectors used

LIFT PASSES

2001/02 prices in dollars

Mammoth Mountain Covers all lifts at Mammoth.

Beginners 69 a day learn-to-ski packages include pass, lessons and rental.

Main pass
1-day pass 56
6-day pass 293

Senior citizens
Over 65: 6-day pass 145
Over 80: free pass

Children
13-18: six day pass: 218
Under 13: 6-day pass 145
Under 6: free pass

Short-term passes
Scenic Mammoth Gondola ride (adult 16); afternoon pass (adult 45)

Notes Main pass also covers the eight lifts at June Mountain. Passes of over 2 days allow for one non-skiing day – 5-day pass is valid for 6 days, with one non-skiing day, and passes over five days allow for 2 non-skiing days.

Although Mammoth is one of the US's largest areas, its claim to have 150 trails should not be taken too seriously. The slightest variant of a run is given a separate name. Nevertheless, the 27 lifts access an impressive area suitable for all standards. The highest runs are almost exclusively steep bowls and chutes for experts. In general, the lower down you go the easier the terrain.

Finding your way around is something else. The lifts are mainly known by numbers, allocated as they were built, so the system has no geographic logic: chair 17 is between chairs 7 and 8 and below chair 22, and so on. New lifts are now being given names, though, which is starting to make things easier. However, the trail map still shows trails by means of symbols and names, not continuous lines, so it's difficult to see where a particular run takes you. On the lower part of the mountain this doesn't matter a lot: head downhill, and you'll eventually come to a lift. But higher up there are real dangers, especially in poor visibility.

Though Intrawest is now the majority owner, Dave McCoy, who built the first lift here in the 1940s, still has the final say about mountain development. People told him it was too high, too remote and too stormy here to make it as a resort, so he is naturally proud that he has seen it developed into a top American resort.

THE SLOPES
It's all here

There are three major lift-stations along the foot of the slopes, which mainly face north-east. An isolated fourth base – Juniper Springs – is growing in importance.

Main Lodge has the biggest choice of lifts. The newly upgraded two-stage Panorama gondola goes via Mid Chalet, the site of a huge restaurant, right to the top. The views are great, with Nevada to the north-east and the jagged Minarets to the west.

From the top, there are essentially three ways down. The first, on which there are countless variations, is down the front of the mountain, which ranges from steep to very steep – or vertical if the wind has created a cornice, as it often does. The second is off the back, down to **Chair 14 Outpost**, whence chairs 14 or 13 bring you back to lower points on the ridge. The third is to follow the way down to the Main Lodge area. This route brings you past an easy area served by chair 12, and a very easy area by the Discovery fast quad. But finding the way you intend from the top is tricky because of poor signposting and the amazingly unhelpful trail map.

Mid Chalet can also be reached using the Stump Alley fast chair from **The Mill Cafe**, on the road up from town. Other lifts from here, including the fast Gold Rush quad, take you into the more heavily wooded eastern half of the area. This has long, gentle runs served by lifts up from **Canyon Lodge** and the new **Juniper Springs Lodge** and seriously steep stuff as well as some intermediate terrain on the subsidiary peak (nameless, of course) served by lifts 25 and 22.

A separate ski area called **June Mountain** is 30 minutes' drive away and is covered by the lift pass.

SNOW RELIABILITY
A long season

Mammoth has an impressive snow record – an annual average of 380in, which puts it in the second rank, ahead of major Colorado resorts and about on a par with Jackson Hole (but a long way behind Alta and Snowbird). Thanks to both its height and an ever-expanding array of snow-guns, it enjoys a long season – opening as late as 4 July in many years. But the upper mountain can get icy and windswept.

boarding *Mammoth initially set out to attract boarders to its sister mountain June, where there's a good fun-park and half-pipe. But Mammoth itself now has three impressive 'Unbound' terrain parks and half-pipes for different standards. The main one is served by the high-speed Thunder Bound Express lift, with the Quarter Pipe Cafe half-way up the slope. The rest of Mammoth's slopes are ideal for all standards, with some excellent free-riding in the high bowls and perfect beginner and intermediate runs below. All but one tiny lift are chairs or gondolas. There are some good bars in town, lively at weekends.*

SCHOOLS/GUIDES

2000/01 prices in dollars

Mammoth Mountain
Classes 7 days
3hr: 10am-1pm 52
5 full days: 180
Children's classes
Ages: 4 to 14
5 full days including lunch: 380
Private lessons
1hr, 3hr or 6hr
110 for 1hr; each additional person 12

FOR EXPERTS
Some very challenging terrain

The steep bowls that run the width of the mountain top provide wonderful opportunities for experts. There are one or two single-diamond slopes, but most are emphatically double-diamond runs requiring a lot of bottle. The snow up here can suffer from high winds and it can be difficult to find your way – marking is virtually non-existent, so take great care.

The steep chutes either side of lift 22 are also very challenging, and being relatively sheltered are often open in bad weather when the top is firmly shut. Above Main Lodge is another steep area ideal for advanced skiers.

Many of the lower trails are short, but you can go virtually from top to bottom all day entirely on black runs.

FOR INTERMEDIATES
Lots of great cruising

Mammoth's piste maintenance is generally good, and many slopes that might become intimidatingly mogulled are kept easily skiable. And there is plenty for all standards of intermediate.

Some of the mountain's longest runs, served by chairs 9 and 25, are ideal for good intermediates. And a couple of lovely, fairly steep, tree-lined pistes run from the top of the Goldrush chair down to The Mill Cafe.

The tree-lined runs above Juniper Springs Lodge are flattering, and there are several easy cruises – notably the slopes converging on The Mill Cafe.

A reporter recommends the quiet little Santiago bowl at the western extremity of the slopes down to Chair 14 Outpost: 'The whole group enjoyed runs like Arriba, Surprise and Oops.'

The less adventurous have some good, wide runs through trees in the triangle between Main Lodge, The Mill Cafe and Mid Chalet.

June mountain is great for a leisurely day out. Most of its runs are overgraded. Blues are easy cruisers, single blacks groomed and double blacks advanced rather than expert.

FOR BEGINNERS
Good tuition

'Excellent for beginners,' says one visitor. 'Good nursery slopes and lots of marvellous improving slopes, such as Sesame Street West, Lower Road Runner and Bridges.' Excellent tuition, fine piste grooming and snow quality usually make progress speedy.

FOR CROSS-COUNTRY
Very popular

Two specialist centres, Tamarack and Sierra Meadows, provide tuition and tours (the Sierra Meadows trails aren't groomed). There are 70km of trails in all, including some through the pretty Lakes Basin area, and lots of scenic ungroomed tracks through woods.

QUEUES
Weekend invasions

During the week the lifts and slopes are usually very quiet, with no queues. But even the efficient lift system can struggle when 15,000 visitors arrive from LA on fine weekends. That's the time to try June Mountain – it is remarkably uncrowded. Mind you, as one reporter put it, 'The weekend rush was like a quiet day in the Alps.'

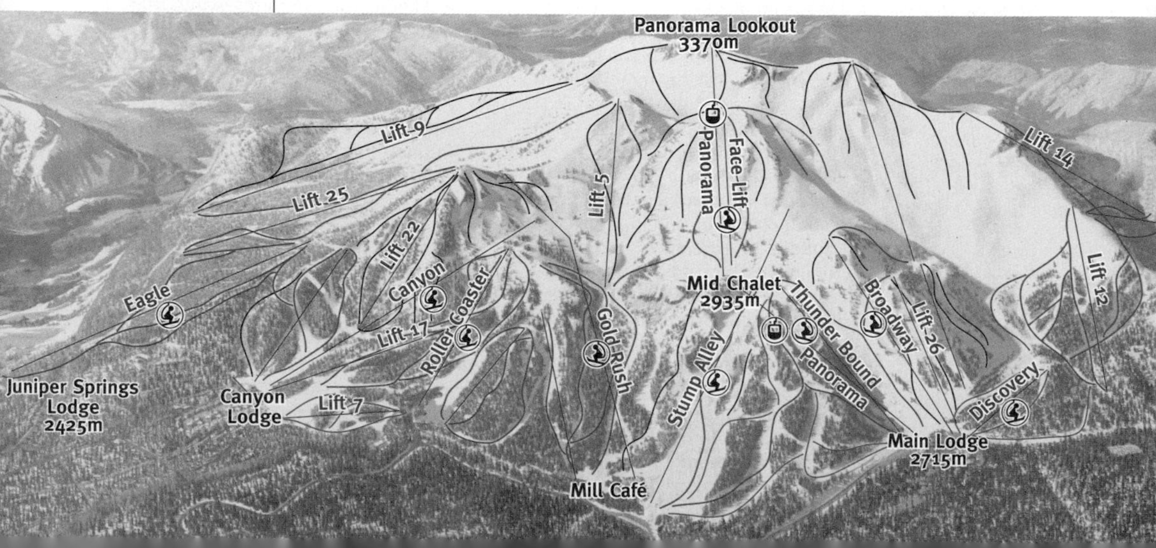

CHILDCARE

Children's classes are handled by the Woollywood Ski and Snowboard School in the Panorama gondola building, which 'interfaces' with Small World Child Care (934 0646) based at the nearby Mammoth Mountain Inn. Small World Child Care takes children from newborn to age 12, from 8am to 5pm.

GETTING THERE

Air Los Angeles, transfer 5hr. Reno, transfer 3hr. Mammoth Lakes, transfer 20 minutes.

ACTIVITIES

Indoor Mammoth museum, art galleries, theatre, mini golf
Outdoor Snowmobiling, ski touring, bob-sleigh, dog-sledding, ice skating, tobogganing, sleigh rides, hot air balloon rides, snow-shoe tours

Phone numbers
From distant parts of the US, add the prefix 1 760.
From abroad, add the prefix +1 760.

TOURIST OFFICE

Postcode CA 93546
t +1 (760) 934 0745
f 934 0616
woolly@mammoth-mtn.com
www.mammothmountain.com

MOUNTAIN RESTAURANTS
Lots of new venues

The giant functional cafeteria at Mid Chalet used to be the only on-mountain option. But for 2001/02 the new Top of the World restaurant, at the top gondola station, will offer table-service and views at Mammoth's highest point. Many people eat at the bases, where there are several options. The Mill Cafe boasts 'gourmet sandwiches'. Or choose from Mexican, Italian, Asian and more at the revamped Canyon Lodge. Sun decks and music are the norm. There are outdoor BBQs at Juniper Springs Lodge and Chair 14 Outpost. There's also a sun deck at the Yodler at Main Lodge.

SCHOOLS AND GUIDES
Excellent reports

Mammoth has a high reputation for tuition. Our most recent reporter rated his three-hour advanced class 'excellent'. And we have reports of beginners making 'excellent progress' as well. There are also some special camps (eg steep terrain and racing) for experts, and for seniors and women.

FACILITIES FOR CHILDREN
Family favourite

Mammoth is keen to attract families. The children's Woollywood school, now based in the new Panorama gondola station, works closely with the nearby Small World childcare centre. We've had glowing reports; one reporter noted the 'family feel of the resort'.

Staying there

Staying near Main Lodge or at the new condo complexes at Canyon Lodge or Juniper Springs Lodge is convenient for the slopes but not much else. The efficient bus service from Mammoth Lakes means staying in town and getting to the slopes is easy.

HOW TO GO
Good value packages

A good choice of hotels (none very luxurious or expensive) and condos. The condos tend to be out of town, near the lifts or on the road to them.
((((4) **Mammoth Mountain Inn** (934 2581) Motel/hotel/condo complex at Main Lodge. Comfortable, spacious bedrooms. Rather gloomy public rooms.
(((3) **Quality Inn** (934 5114) Good main street hotel with a big hot-tub.
(((3) **Alpenhof Lodge** (934 6330) Comfortable and friendly, in central location. Shuttle-bus stop and plenty of restaurants nearby.
(((3) **Austria Hof** (934 2764) Ski-out location near Canyon Lodge, recommended by a reporter despite modest-sized rooms.
(((3) **Sierra Nevada Inn** (934 2515) Central, good value, 'excellent spa'.
Self-catering The new Juniper Springs Lodge opened for 1999/2000. Close to the Canyon Lodge base-station, the 1849 Condominiums are spacious and well equipped. The Mammoth Ski and Racquet Club, a 10-minute walk from the same lifts, is very comfortable.

EATING OUT
Outstanding choice

There are over 50 restaurants in town, dotted around over a wide area, catering for most tastes and pockets. We've had delicious dinners at Nevados and Skadi (both 'modern American' food). Other good places are the atmospheric Slocums and lively Whiskey Creek. The Yodler does good hearty food at the Main Lodge area. Roberto's offers Mexican food; the Shogun Japanese (and karaoke). The Mogul, Alpenrose, Giovanni's, Berger's, Mountainside Grill, Angel's, Ocean Harvest and Grumpy's have all been recommended. For delicious breakfasts and pastries try Schat's Bakery.

APRES-SKI
Lively at weekends

The liveliest immediate après-ski spot is the Yodler, at the Main Lodge base – a chalet transported from Switzerland (so they say). Nightlife in town is essentially bars, which come to life at weekends (one reporter warns that during the week they'll be pushing you out at 12.30am). Whiskey Creek is the liveliest. It has live bands and gets packed. Slocums is popular with locals while Gringo's does great margaritas. Grumpy's is a good typically American sports bar (big screen TVs etc).

OFF THE SLOPES
Mainly sightseeing

The main diversion is sightseeing by car (preferably 4WD), which can be spectacular. Sights include the pretty Mono Lake, the beautiful Yosemite and other National Parks and the gold-mining ghost-town of Bodie. There are some diverting clothes shops (including factory stores). The town of Bishop, 40 minutes' drive south, is a good day out.

Colorado

Colorado was the first US state to market its resorts internationally and is still the most popular American destination for UK visitors. And justifiably so: it has the most alluring combination of attractive resorts, slopes to suit all standards and excellent, reliable snow – dry enough to justify its 'champagne powder' label. It also has direct flights from London to Denver.

Colorado has amazingly dry snow. Even when the snow melts and refreezes, the moisture seems to be magically whisked away, leaving it in soft powdery condition. The snow is good even in times of unusual snow shortage; in December a few years ago, when very little snow had fallen so far that season, we had a great week cruising on magical man-made snow in Breckenridge and Keystone.

Colorado resorts vary enormously, both in the extent and variety of slopes and in the character of the villages themselves. If you want beautifully restored buildings from the mining boom days of the late 1800s, try the dinky old towns of Telluride or Crested Butte (but beware: both these have separate, modern mountain villages too) or the much grander and larger-scale Aspen (which also has its modern outpost at Snowmass).

Some resorts have easy access to other major mountains nearby (eg Breckenridge, Keystone and Copper Mountain). Others, such as Steamboat, Crested Butte and Telluride are rather isolated.

The two biggest Colorado resorts of Vail and Aspen both have substantial amounts of terrain suitable for every standard of skier and boarder. And both have been developing their exciting ungroomed terrain in recent years – Vail has opened up Blue Sky Basin with wonderful skiing and riding in usually excellent snow in the trees, while Aspen has extended its high, steep, open bowls at the top of Aspen Highlands.

The clientele varies as well. You are much less likely to bump into fellow Brits in Telluride or Copper Mountain than Breckenridge and Vail. And while Aspen attracts an arty bohemian crowd, Vail is the destination of choice for the Wall Street dealers and money-men – who can keep in touch with the markets between runs at the mountain-top Communications Center, which has internet access and video-conferencing facilities.

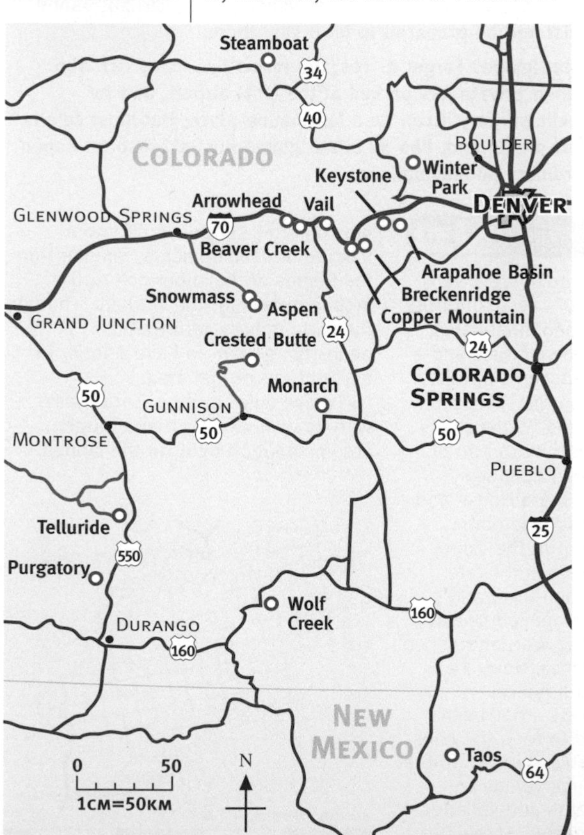

Aspen 2420m

Don't be put off by its ritzy image – it's America's best resort

WHAT IT COSTS

6

HOW IT RATES

The slopes

Snow	*****
Extent	****
Experts	*****
Intermediates	*****
Beginners	*****
Convenience	**
Queues	****
Restaurants	****

The rest

Scenery	***
Resort charm	****
Off-slope	****

What's new

Snowboarders can rejoice as boarding is now allowed on Aspen Mountain, after 54 years of being a skiers-only mountain.

At Highlands, even more steep terrain is to be added in Highland Bowl near the Y, B and recently opened G zones.

The base lodge at Highlands Village is ready. It will house a new bar and restaurant, and Ritz Carlton club.

For 2000/01, Snowmass got a new children's training area with its own lift, kids' trails, snowcat sculpted moguls, a race area, a picnic area, and a video analysis centre.

Buttermilk built a two-mile long fun-park for 2000/01 with numerous hits and jumps, a boardercross course and a 400-foot long superpipe.

- ⊕ Endless slopes to suit all standards, with a vertical drop at Snowmass of 1342m – biggest in the US
- ⊕ Notably uncrowded slopes, even by American standards
- ⊕ Attractive, characterful, old mining town, with lots of smart shops
- ⊕ Lively, varied nightlife and a great range of restaurants in the town
- ⊕ Some of the best 'gourmet' mountain restaurants in the States
- ⊕ Large amounts of slope-side accommodation at Snowmass

- ⊖ Four mountains are widely separated (though there's efficient, free transport between them)
- ⊖ Some accommodation in Aspen town is a long walk or a bus-ride from the local lifts
- ⊖ Can be very expensive (although certainly doesn't have to be)

Aspen is our favourite American resort. We reached that view three editions back, and another tour of Colorado by both editors in March 2000 simply confirmed it. Convenience-freaks will find it a bit of a nightmare, but that really is the only serious drawback, and nowhere else comes close to matching the combination of plus-points listed above. If you're thinking America, put Aspen at the top of your shortlist and be prepared to let it stay there.

Worried by the film-star image? Forget it. Yes, the resort has many rich and famous guests, with their private jets parked at the local airport, and for connoisseurs of cosmetic surgery it can be a fascinating place. But most celebs are keen to keep a low profile and, like all other 'glamorous' ski resorts, Aspen is actually filled by ordinary holidaymakers.

The resort

In 1892 Aspen was a booming silver-mining town, source of one-sixth of the USA's silver, with 12,000 inhabitants, six newspapers, an opera house and a red-light district. But Aspen's fortunes took a nose-dive when the silver price plummeted in 1893, and by the 1930s the population had shrunk to 700 or so. Handsome Victorian buildings – such as the Wheeler Opera House and the Hotel Jerome – had fallen into disrepair. Development of the skiing started on a small scale in the late 1930s. The first lift (then the world's longest chair-lift) was opened shortly after the Second World War, and Aspen hasn't looked back since. Now, the historic centre – with a typical American grid of streets – has been beautifully renovated to form the core of the most fashionable ski town in the Rockies. There's a huge variety of shops, bars, restaurants and galleries – some amazingly upmarket. Spreading out from this centre, you'll find a mixture of developments, ranging from the homes of the super-rich to the mobile homes for the workers. Though the town is busy with traffic, pedestrians seem to have priority in much of the central area.

Twelve miles away is Snowmass, with its own mountain and modern accommodation right on the slopes.

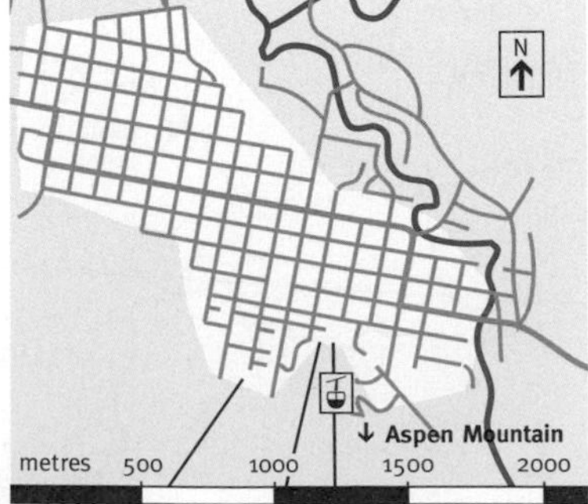

Some of Aspen Highlands' steep terrain, seen from Aspen Mountain →

SNOWPIX.COM / CHRIS GILL

The mountains

Aspen has lots for every standard; you just have to pick the right mountain. All of them have regular free guided tours, given by excellent amateur ambassadors, and other guest services on the slopes such as free suncream, drinks and biscuits. The ratio of acres to visitor beds is high, and the slopes are usually blissfully uncrowded.

MOUNTAIN FACTS

Altitude	2400m-3815m
Lifts	44
Pistes	4780 acres
Green	13%
Blue	44%
Black	43%
Art. snow	566 acres
Recco detectors used	

THE SLOPES
Widely dispersed

There are four mountains, only one accessible directly from Aspen town. Each is big enough to keep you amused for a full day or more, but Snowmass is in a league of its own – almost five miles across, with over 60% of Aspen's total skiable acreage and the biggest vertical in the US. Getting around between the areas by free bus is easy, and for $3 you can have your equipment ferried from one mountain to another overnight.

The Silver Queen gondola takes you from the edge of town to the top of **Aspen Mountain** in 14 minutes. A series of chairs serves the different ridges – Gentleman's Ridge along the eastern edge, the Bell in the centre, and Ruthie's to the west – with gulches in between. In general, there are long cruising blue runs along the valley floors and short steep blacks down from the ridges. There are no greens.

Snowmass is a separate resort some 12 miles west of Aspen, opened in 1967. Chair-lifts fan out from the purpose-built village at the base towards four linked sectors – Elk Camp, High Alpine, Big Burn and Sam's Knob. Since 1995 there has also been access to the Elk Camp sector via the Two Creeks lift base, which is much nearer to Aspen, and has free slope-side parking. There are free shuttle-buses between here and Aspen, as there are between all four mountains. Many of the Snowmass runs are wide, sweeping cruisers. But it also has some of the toughest terrain.

Buttermilk is the least challenging mountain. The runs fan out from the top in three directions. The West Buttermilk and Main Buttermilk areas are almost all gentle; Tiehack, to the east, is a bit more demanding – ideal for an intermediate keen to progress.

Aspen Highlands was, until 1993, separately owned. Since then, Aspen Skiing Company has transformed the

GET THE BEST OF THE SNOW, ON- AND OFF-PISTE

Aspen offers several special experiences for small numbers of skiers or riders.

Fresh Tracks *The first eight skiers to sign up each day get to ride the gondola up Aspen Mountain at 8am the next morning, and to get first tracks on perfect corduroy or fresh powder. Free!*

Off-piste Tours *On Wednesdays and Fridays, backcountry guides lead expert skiers and riders around the famous double-black terrain of Highlands (eg the Y and B Zones) and Snowmass (eg Hanging Valley). 9am–2.30pm, $99 (2000/01).*

Powder Tours *Spend the day exploring the backcountry beyond Aspen Mountain, with a 10-passenger heated snowcat as your personal lift. Away from the lifts and other people, your two guides search out untracked snow – there's 1,500 acres to choose from. You're likely to squeeze in about 10 runs in all. At midday, you break for lunch at an old mountain cabin. Full day, $275 (2000/01).*

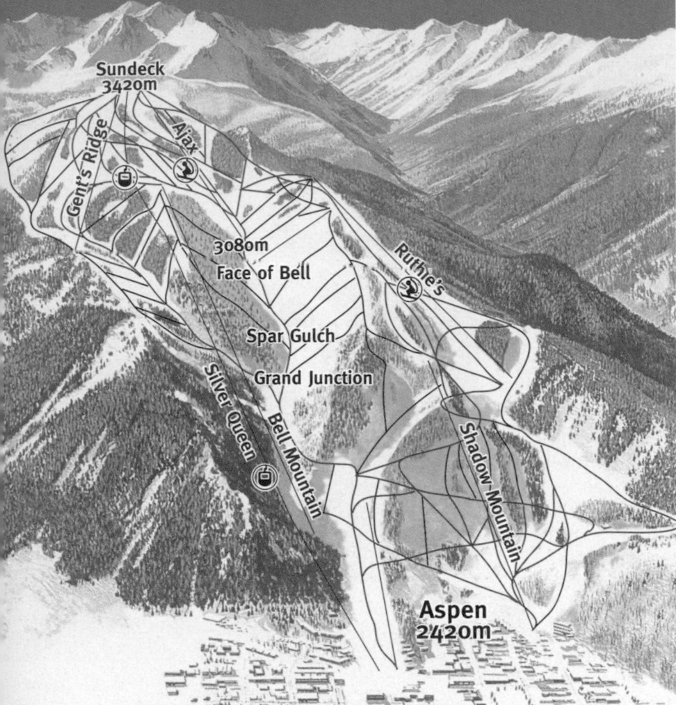

mountain, replacing a network of slow lifts with three fast quad chairs. Broadly, the mountain consists of a single ridge, with easy and intermediate slopes along the ridge itself and steep black runs on the flanks – very steep ones at the top. And beyond the lift network is the Highland Bowl, where gates give access to a splendid open bowl of entirely double-black gradient and the Y, B and G zones. The views from the upper part of Highlands are the best that Aspen has to offer – the famous Maroon Bells that appear on countless postcards. A new base lodge with underground parking and a Ritz-Carlton aparthotel is now finished.

SNOW RELIABILITY
Rarely a problem

Aspen's mountains get an annual average of 300in of snow – not in the front rank, but not far behind. In addition, all areas have substantial snowmaking. Immaculate grooming adds to the quality of the pistes.

FOR EXPERTS
Buttermilk is the only soft stuff

There's plenty to choose from – all the mountains except Buttermilk offer lots of challenges. Consider joining a guided group as an introduction to the best of Snowmass or Highlands.

Aspen Mountain has a formidable array of double-black-diamond runs. From the top of the gondola, Walsh's, Hyrup's and Kristi are double-diamonds on a lightly wooded slope that link up with Gentleman's Ridge and Jackpot to form the longest black run on the mountain. A series of steep glades drop down from Gentleman's Ridge. The central Bell ridge has less extreme single-diamonds on both its flanks. On the opposite side of Spar Gulch are another row of proper double-blacks collectively called the Dumps, because waste was dumped here in the silver-mining days.

At Snowmass, our favourite area is around the Hanging Valley Wall and Glades – beautiful scenery and wonderful tree-covered slopes, and steep enough everywhere to satisfy the keenest – well worth the short hike. The other seriously steep area is the Cirque. The Cirque drag-lift takes you well above the tree-line to Aspen's top altitude of almost 3815m. The Headwall is open and not terrifyingly steep, but there are also narrow, often rocky, chutes – Gowdy's is one of the steepest in the whole area. All these runs funnel into a pretty, lightly wooded valley.

At Highlands there are challenging runs from top to bottom of the mountain. Highland Bowl, beyond the top lift, is superb in the right conditions: a big open bowl with pitches from a serious 38° to a terrifying 48° – facts you can check in the very informative Highlands Extreme

LIFT PASSES

2000/01 prices in dollars

Four Mountain Pass
Covers Aspen Mountain, Aspen Highlands, Buttermilk and Snowmass, and shuttle-bus between the areas.

Beginners Included in price of beginners' lessons; 219 for 3-day learn-to-ski or snowboard lessons and rental.

Main pass
1-day pass approx 65 (depends on season and snow conditions)
6-day pass 342

Senior citizens
Over 65: 6-day pass 312
Over 70: season pass 149.

Children
Under 12: 6-day pass 231
Under 7: free pass

Advance purchase
Big savings can be made if you buy lift passes well in advance or through certain tour operators. Book by 1 December for an adult 6-day ticket from $294, over 70s 6-day from 119, under 14 6-day 234, under 12 six-day 186.

Skiing Guide leaflet. If you're lucky, the ski patrol may be running free snowcat rides from Lodge Meadow to the first access gate of Highland Bowl; otherwise, it's a 20-minute hike. More of this terrain – the furthest-out G Zone – opened for 2000/01. Within the lift system, the Steeplechase area consists of a number of parallel natural avalanche chutes, and their elevation means the snow stays light and dry. The Olympic Bowl area on the opposite flank of the mountain has great views of the Maroon Bells peaks and some serious moguls. The Thunderbowl chair from the base serves a nice varied area that's often underused.

FOR INTERMEDIATES

Grooming to die for

Snowmass is the best mountain for intermediates and the Big Burn is definitely the first place to head for. The huge lightly wooded area is a cruising paradise. The runs merge into each other, though there's a satisfying variety of terrain and some trees to add interest – and the tempting Powerline Glades for the adventurous. The easiest intermediate slopes are reached from the Elk Camp lift. There's a choice of runs from the top, through spruce trees, and long runs all the way down to Two Creeks. Long Shot is a glorious, ungroomed, three-mile run, lost in the forest, and well worth the short hike up to get to the start. In the centre of the area, the two chair-lifts below High Alpine serve yet more intermediate slopes – a little trickier and more varied. The Sam's Knob sector offers slightly more advanced challenges, including some regularly groomed single-black runs. Finally, Green Cabin, at the top of the High Alpine lift, is a magical intermediate run cruising from top to bottom of the mountain, with spectacular views.

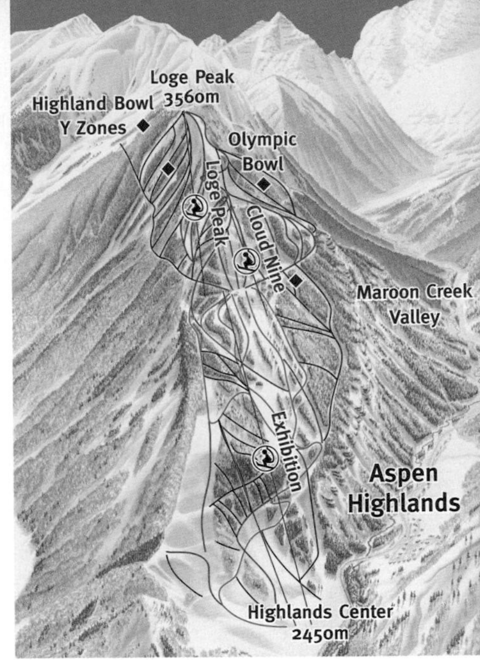

Most intermediate runs on Highlands are concentrated above the mid-mountain Merry-Go-Round restaurant, many (including the very popular Scarlet's Run) served by the Cloud Nine fast quad chair. But there

SCHOOLS/GUIDES

2000/01 prices in dollars

Aspen Skiing Company
Snowmass and Buttermilk for all abilities; Aspen Mountain and Aspen Highlands for intermediate and advanced only
Mountain Explorers
4 days
5hr: 10am-3pm;
4 full days: 339
Private lessons
449 for full day
309 for half day
(up to 5 people)
Other options
Beginner's Magic
1 full day: 99
3 full days incl lift pass: 249
Small group lessons
Approx four skiers
99 for full day
Off-piste tours
Full day 99
Children's classes
Ages: 18 months to 19
Age: 18 months
1 hr private lesson 99
Beginners
Ages: 7-19
One day 79

are good slopes higher up and lower down – don't miss the vast, neglected expanses of Golden Horn, on the eastern limit of the area.

Aspen Mountain has its fair share of intermediate slopes, but they tend to be tougher than on the other mountains. Copper Bowl and Spar Gulch, running between the ridges, are great cruises early in the morning but can get crowded later. Upper Aspen Mountain, at the top of the gondola, has a dense network of well-groomed blues. The unusual Ruthie's chair – a fast double, apparently installed to rekindle the romance that quads have destroyed – serves more cruising runs and the popular Snow Bowl, a wide, open area with moguls on the left but groomed on the right and centre.

The Main Buttermilk runs offer good, easy slopes to practise on. And good intermediates should be able to handle the relatively easy black runs in the Tiehack area.

FOR BEGINNERS
Can be a great place to learn

Buttermilk is a great mountain for beginners. West Buttermilk has beautifully groomed, gentle runs. The easiest slopes of all, though, are at the base of the Main Buttermilk sector – on Panda Hill. The easiest beginner slope at Snowmass is the wide Assay Hill, at the bottom of the Elk Camp area. Right next to Snowmass Village Mall is the Fanny Hill fast quad and beginners' run. Further up, from Sam's Knob, there are long, gentle cruises.

Despite its macho image, Highlands boasts the highest concentration of green runs in Aspen.

FOR CROSS-COUNTRY
Backcountry bonanza

There are 80km of groomed trails between Aspen and Snowmass in the Roaring Fork valley – the most extensive maintained cross-country system in the US. And the Ashcroft Ski Touring Centre maintains around 30km of trails around Ashcroft, a mining ghost-town. Take the opportunity of eating at the Pine Creek Cookhouse: excellent food and accessible by ski, board or sledge only. In addition, there are limitless miles of ungroomed trails. Aspen is at one end of the famous Tenth Mountain Division Trail, heading 230 miles north-east almost to Vail, with 13 huts for overnight stops.

QUEUES
Few problems

There are rarely major queues on any of the mountains. At Aspen Mountain, the gondola can have delays at peak times, but you have alternative lifts to the top. Snowmass has so many alternative lifts and runs that you can normally avoid any problems. But some long, slow chairs can be cold in mid-winter, and the home slope gets very busy. Aspen Highlands is almost always queue-free, even at peak times. The two lifts out of Main Buttermilk sometimes get congested.

MOUNTAIN RESTAURANTS
Good by American standards

On Aspen Mountain the new Sundeck at the top has quite a stylish self-service section with a good range of food, but the table-service Benedict's restaurant is unappealing (unless the terrace is in operation). Sadly the swanky lunch club that shares the new building is strictly for members. The mid-mountain restaurant formerly called Ruthie's is now Gwyn's; as well as a self-service section it has an exceptionally civilised table-service restaurant with excellent food and good views over Aspen.

At Snowmass, Gwyn's High Alpine is an elegant restaurant serving excellent food. The best views are from Sam's Knob, where there is a self-service and a new and impressive Italian table-service restaurant, Finestra.

At Highlands the Cloud Nine 'Alpine

boarding *Aspen has great snowboarding for every standard. And at last the ban on snowboarders on Aspen Mountain was lifted from 1 April 2001. It bowed to pressure after becoming one of just five major areas in the world open to skiers only. All four mountains are served almost entirely by chairs or gondolas and there are lots of special boarder facilities – Aspen Mountain will even have a special Spring Jam fun-park on Little Nell in the spring. Buttermilk has a new two-mile long fun-park with numerous hits and jumps, a boardercross course and a 400-foot long superpipe. Snowmass has two fun-parks and a half-pipe. Some of the bars can be quite entertaining at night.*

Phone numbers
From distant parts of the US, add the prefix 1 970.
From abroad, add the prefix +1 970.

CHILDCARE

The childcare possibilities are too numerous to list in detail.

There's a children's 'learning center' at Buttermilk with a special children's shuttle-bus from Aspen. The Powder Pandas classes there take children aged 3 to 6. At Snowmass, the Big Burn Bears ski kindergarten takes children from age 3½, and children aged 6 weeks to 3½ have the Snow Cubs playschool. The Nighthawks programme looks after children aged 3 to 10 from 4pm to 11pm.

There are several all-day non-skiing crèches.

ASPEN / KEN MISSBRENNER

Highland Bowl has fabulous open terrain with pitches from a serious 38° to a terrifying 48° →

bistro' is the nearest thing you will find in the States to an Alpine chalet with Alpine views and excellent food – thanks to an Austrian chef. The Merry-Go-Round has the biggest terrace in the valley.

On Buttermilk the mountaintop Cliffhouse is known for its 'Mongolian Barbecue' stir-fry bar and great views.

SCHOOLS AND GUIDES
Special programmes

There's a wide variety of specialised instruction – bumps, powder, mountain exploration groups, backcountry groups, and so on. A reporter raves about the semi-private lessons, with maximum four pupils per group. On Snowmass and Aspen Mountain there are performance centres where your alignment is tested and adjusted, and you can test any number of skis. A new addition is the Wizard Ski Deck – an indoor ski and snowboard simulator. It claims to be 'Safe, enjoyable and comfortable'.

FACILITIES FOR CHILDREN
Choice of crèches

There is no shortage of advertised childcare arrangements. We have no recent first-hand reports, but reporters' observations were that, as usual in the US, all the kids were having the time of their lives. And past reports have always been first class. Young children based in Aspen town are taken from the gondola building each morning around 9am by the Max the Moose bus to Buttermilk's very impressive Fort Frog – a wooden frontier-style fort, with lookout towers, flags, old wagons, a jail, a saloon and a native American teepee village – and delivered back at 4pm. Snowmass has its own facilities. The Kids' Trail Map is a great way to get them used to finding their way around using maps.

Staying there 

Aspen town is the liveliest place to stay, and near the gondola is the most convenient location. Buses for the other areas also leave from nearby. Snowmass offers ski-out convenience at 95% of its properties, and buses from Aspen run until 1am or later.

HOW TO GO
Accommodation for all pockets

There's a mixture of hotels, inns, B&Bs, lodges and condos.

Chalets Several UK tour operators have chalets here – some very luxurious.

Hotels There are places for all budgets.

(((((5) **St Regis** (920 3300) Opulent city-type hotel, near gondola. Fitness centre, outdoor pool, hot-tubs, sauna.

(((((5) **Little Nell** (920 4600) Stylish, modern hotel right by the gondola with popular bar. Fireplaces in every room, outdoor pool, hot-tub, sauna.

GETTING THERE

Air Aspen, transfer ½hr. Eagle, transfer 1½hr. Denver, transfer 4hr.

Rail Glenwood Springs (70km).

Phone numbers
From distant parts of the US, add the prefix 1 970.
From abroad, add the prefix +1 970.

ACTIVITIES

Indoor Aspen Athletic Club (racquetball, swimming, free weights, aerobics classes, sauna, steam, hot-tubs), skating, museum.

Outdoor Ballooning, paragliding, snowcat tours, snow-shoe tours, sleigh rides, dog-sledding, snow-tubing, snowmobiles, tours of mines

TOURIST OFFICE

Postcode CO 81612
t +1 (970) 925 1220
f 920 0771
intlres@skiaspen.com
www.aspensnowmass.com

ASPEN / DOUG CHILD

The atmospheric old mining town sits right at the foot of Aspen Mountain's slopes ↓

((((5) **Jerome** (920 1000) Step back a century: Victorian authenticity combined with modern-day luxury. Several blocks from the gondola.
(((4) **Sardy House** (920 2525) Elegantly furnished, intimate little hotel 10 minutes from the gondola. Small outdoor pool, hot-tub.
(((4) **Lenado** (925 6246) Smart modern B&B place with open-fire lounge, individually designed rooms.
(((4) **Silvertree** (923 3520) Large slope-side hotel at Snowmass. Pools.
((3) **Innsbruck Inn** (925 2980) Consistently liked by reporters. Tirolean-style hotel, 10 mins from lifts.
((3) **Stonebridge Inn** (923 2420) Good-value hotel close to Snowmass slopes; nice restaurant, pool, hot-tub.
((3) **Hotel Aspen** (925 3441) Best 'moderate' place in town, 10 minutes from the gondola; comfortable motel-style rooms, pool, hot-tubs.
(2) **Skier's Chalet** (920 2037) Closest 'economy' lodging to the lifts.
Self-catering The standards here are high, even in US terms. Many of the smarter developments have their own free shuttle-buses. The Gant is luxurious and close to the gondola. Chateau Roaring Fork and Eau Claire, four blocks from the gondola, are spacious and well-furnished. A reader says the two small supermarkets are are 'exceptionally well stocked'.

EATING OUT
Dining dilemma

You can dine in whatever style you like in Aspen town. As you'd expect, there are excellent upmarket places, but also plenty of cheaper options.

Piñons serves innovative American food in South-Western surroundings. Syzygy is a suave upstairs place with live jazz from 10pm. On our last visit we particularly enjoyed the 'fierce American food' at Jimmy's. Conundrum (modern American food, expensive) and Pacific (seafood) are top-notch. Poppie's Bistro Cafe is famous for its breads and puddings. L'Hostaria, The Mother Lode, Campo de Fiori and Farfalla are good Italians. Cache Cache does good-value Provençal. Ute City is in the upmarket surroundings of an old bank and good for local game.

Cheaper recommendations include: Boogie's (a 50s-style diner, great for families), Hard Rock Cafe, Main Street Bakery, Mezzaluna, O'Leary's, Red Onion, Rusty's Hickory House and the Skier's Chalet steak house. At Snowmass, the choice is adequate.

APRES-SKI
Party time (later)

As the lifts shut, a few bars at the bases do reasonable business. At Snowmass, the slope-side Cirque Cafe has live bands most days. In Aspen a the Ajax Tavern is popular. But it's after dinner that Aspen town livens up.

Many of the restaurants are also bars – Ajax, Jimmy's (spectacular stock of tequila), Mezzaluna, O'Leary's, Red Onion, and Ute City, for example. The J-bar of the Jerome hotel still has a traditional feel. Shooters is a splendid country-and-western dive with pool and line-dancing. Maxfield's is a popular pool bar. For pool in more suave circumstances, there's Aspen Billiards adjoining the fashionable Cigar Bar, with its comfortable sofas (and smoking permitted!). The Double Diamond has live bands most nights (from 11pm). Popcorn Wagon is the place for munchies after the bars close at 2am. You can get a week's membership of 426, a club appealing to 30-somethings. Old timers like us prefer to get an evening's use of the Caribou club for the price of dinner.

OFF THE SLOPES
Silver service

Aspen has lots to offer, especially if you've got a high credit card limit. There are literally dozens of galleries, as well as the predictable clothes and jewellery shops. Just wandering around town is pleasant. It's a shame that all the best mountain restaurants are awkward for pedestrians to get to. Most hotels have excellent spa facilities. There's tubing at Snowmass.

Beaver Creek 2470m

Smoother than Vail, and in many respects more attractive

WHAT IT COSTS

6

HOW IT RATES

The slopes

Snow	*****
Extent	***
Experts	****
Intermediates	****
Beginners	*****
Convenience	****
Queues	*****
Restaurants	**
The rest	
Scenery	***
Resort charm	***
Off-slope	***

What's new

An extra 30 acres of snowmaking was installed for 2000/01.

Village development projects in Arrowhead and Bachelor Gulch continue – a new Ritz-Carlton hotel in Bachelor Gulch will be ready in 2002.

- ⊕ Blissfully quiet slopes, in sharp contrast to nearby Vail
- ⊕ Mountain has it all, from superb novice runs through fast cruisers to long, daunting mogul fields
- ⊕ Compact, largely traffic-free village centre (though with spacious suburbs beyond it)
- ⊕ Some very convenient lodgings

- ⊖ Rather urban feel to the village core – far from the Wild West atmosphere Europeans might look for
- ⊖ Expensive
- ⊖ Disappointing mountain restaurants – the best ones are exclusive members-only affairs

In contrast to its better-known neighbour, Vail, Beaver Creek is a haven of peace – both on and off the slopes. It gets rather overshadowed by big sister, but we wouldn't dream of making a trip to Vail without spending a day or two in Beaver, and there's a lot to be said for doing it the other way round – if you can live with the prices in this most exclusive of Colorado resorts.

THE RESORT

Beaver Creek, ten miles to the west of Vail, was developed by Vail Resorts in the 1980s. It is unashamedly exclusive, with a choice of top-quality hotels and condos right by the slopes. It centres on a large pedestrian square featuring escalators to the slopes, exclusive shops, exquisite bronze statues and an open-air ice rink. Lifts go up to the slopes from three points around the village, so choice of location isn't of great importance.

The lift system spreads across the mountains to Arrowhead – a secluded area of luxurious chalets 'nearing completion'. And Bachelor Gulch, half-way to Arrowhead, is also being developed into a village base – a hotel will be open here next year.

Nightlife and choice of bars and restaurants is much more limited than in Vail, a 25-minute bus-ride away. The complimentary resort shuttle-bus and taxi service is excellent.

THE MOUNTAINS

Beaver Creek, Bachelor Gulch and Arrowhead offer a small-scale version of the linked lift networks of the Alps. Free mountain tours are available four days a week. British guests can ski the Beaver Creek area once a week with Martin Bell, Britain's best-ever downhiller.

Slopes The slopes immediately above Beaver Creek (where the men's downhill and super-G were held in the 1999 World Championships) divide into two sectors, each accessed by a fast quad chair. The major sector is centred on Spruce Saddle, with lifts above it reaching 3490m. The other is lower and smaller, but forms the link with **Bachelor Gulch** and **Arrowhead**. Up the valley a little, and between these two sectors, is Grouse Mountain.

Resorts within a two-hour drive include Breckenridge and Keystone (owned by Vail Resorts and covered by multi-day lift passes), Aspen, Steamboat and Copper Mountain.

Snow reliability As well as an exceptional natural snow record, Beaver Creek has extensive snowmaking facilities, normally needed only in early season. The Grouse Mountain slopes can suffer from thin snow cover (some locals call it Gravel Mountain). Grooming is excellent.

Snowboarding Good riders will love the excellent gladed runs, perfect carving slopes and three terrain parks. The resort is great for beginners too.

Experts There is quite a bit of intimidatingly steep double-diamond terrain. In the Birds of Prey area and Grouse Mountain areas most runs are long, steep and mogulled from top to bottom. The Larkspur Bowl area has three short steep mogul runs.

Intermediates There are marvellous long, quiet, cruising blues almost everywhere you look, including top to bottom runs with a vertical of 1000m. The Larkspur chair and the chairs going west from the village serve further cruising runs – and lead to yet more

MOUNTAIN FACTS

Altitude	2255m-3490m
Lifts	13
Pistes	1625 acres
Green	34%
Blue	39%
Black	27%
Art. snow	605 acres

Phone numbers
From distant parts of the US, add the prefix 1 970.
From abroad, add the prefix +1 970.

TOURIST OFFICE

PO Box 7, Vail, CO 81658
t +1 (970) 845 5745
bcinfo@vailresorts.com
www.beavercreek.com

ideal terrain served by the Bachelor Gulch and Arrowhead fast chairs.
Beginners There are excellent nursery slopes at resort level and at altitude. And there are plenty of easy longer runs to progress to, including runs from top to bottom of the mountains.
Cross-country There's a splendid, extensive, mountain-top network of tracks at McCoy Park (over 32km), reached via the Strawberry Park lift.
Queues The slopes are delightfully deserted and virtually queue-free, even at peak times – it is amazing that more skiers don't come here from Vail.
Mountain restaurants There's not much choice. Spruce Saddle at mid-mountain is the main place – a food court in a spectacular log and glass building. Redtail Camp does decent barbecues. Rendezvous Bar and Grill at the foot of the main slope is very civilised, with good food. The Broken Arrow at Arrowhead is recommended.
Schools and guides The school has an excellent reputation.
Facilities for children The facilities for young children look excellent, and we've had good reports on the children's school. There are splendid children's areas with adventure trails and themed play areas.

STAYING THERE
How to go There's a reasonable choice of packages.
Hotels There are lots of upmarket places. The luxury Inn at Beaver Creek (845 7800) has ski-in/ski-out convenience and a pool. And the Hyatt Regency (949 1234) has impeccable service, a lively bar and one of the major spas.
Self-catering There's a wide choice of condos available. However, one recent reporter complained that grocery shopping is very limited – a drive to Avon to stock up is advised.
Staying up the mountain Trappers Cabin is a luxurious private enclave up the mountain, which a group can rent (for a small fortune) by the night.
Staying along the valley Avon, a mile away at the foot of the approach road, has budget motels. The Minturn Inn in Minturn is a stylish B&B.
Eating out The SaddleRidge is a luxurious wooden building packed with photos and Wild West artefacts. The Mirabelle, at the bottom of the access road, is also rather special. The sleigh ride to Beano's Cabin makes a good evening out – like Allie's, a beautifully built cabin that is a members-only club at lunchtime but open for dinner. Toscanini's, the Golden Eagle, Dusty Boot, and Blue Moose are all recommended.
Après-ski There is a handful of bars – Rendezvous is recommended – but otherwise it's fairly quiet. Vail is the place to head to for a lively time.
Off the slopes Smart boutiques and art galleries are good for window shopping. There's an impressive ice rink, and some great shows and concerts at the 500-seat Vilar Center. Hot-air balloon rides are popular. There are three seriously indulgent spas.

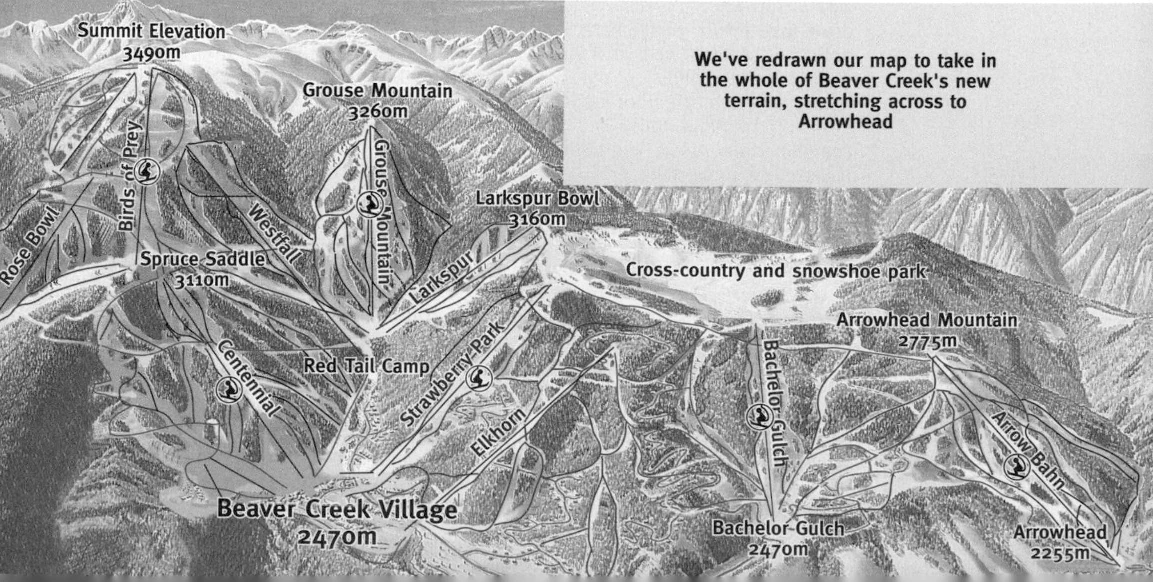

Breckenridge 2925m

Popular introduction to Colorado

WHAT IT COSTS

6

HOW IT RATES

The slopes

Snow	*****
Extent	**
Experts	****
Intermediates	****
Beginners	****
Convenience	***
Queues	****
Restaurants	**

The rest

Scenery	***
Resort charm	***
Off-slope	***

What's new

The Bell Tower Mall at the foot of Peak 9 has been replaced by a Hyatt timeshare complex.

A vast new indoor ice skating rink opened for 2000/01.

In the longer term there are proposals to build new villages at both Peak 7 and Peak 8 and to link them to town by gondola.

BOB WINSETT / VAIL RESORTS, INC

Peak 8 in the centre and Peak 7 on the right have good advanced bowls high up accessed by a T-bar and a hike or traverse ↓

- ⊕ Varied local mountains, with something for all standards
- ⊕ Good snow record and lots of artificial help
- ⊕ Shared lift pass with nearby Keystone and Arapahoe Basin and not-so-nearby Vail and Beaver Creek
- ⊕ Efficient lifts mean few queues
- ⊕ Lively bars, restaurants and nightlife by US standards
- ⊕ Based on restored Victorian mining town, with many new buildings in attractive 19th-century style
- ⊕ One of the nearest major resorts to Denver, so relatively short transfer

- ⊖ The local area is rather small, with few long runs
- ⊖ Best advanced slopes can be windy
- ⊖ At this extreme altitude there is an appreciable risk of sickness for visitors coming straight from lower altitudes (the village is situated at 3000m and the highest lift-accessed terrain is around 4000m)
- ⊖ The pseudo-Victorian style gets a bit overblown in places, and there are some out-of-place modern buildings that detract from its charm
- ⊖ Main Street is just that – always busy with traffic

Breckenridge is very popular with first-time visitors to Colorado. It's easy to see why: it is one of the closest resorts to Denver Airport, has slopes for all standards, usually excellent dry snow, good facilities for families, relatively lively nightlife and good-value slope-side accommodation. Add to that the image of a restored Wild West mining town and you have a very compelling package.

It is true that the slopes do not cover a huge area and that the town is rather spoiled by out-of-style buildings in parts and a rather Disneyesque feel to other parts. But it has skiing and boarding for all standards, and there are lots of other areas to try on day trips, some covered by a shared lift pass (Vail, Beaver Creek, Keystone and Arapahoe Basin), some not (such as Copper Mountain) – much more than you could cover in a week or 10 days. But take heed of the altitude warnings; drink plenty of water and stay well hydrated.

The resort

Breckenridge was founded in 1859 and became a booming gold-mining town. The old clapboard buildings have been well renovated and form the bottom part of Main Street. New shopping malls and buildings have been added in similar style – though they are obvious modern additions.

The town centre is lively in the evening, with over 100 restaurants and bars. Christmas lights and decorations remain throughout the season, giving the town an air of non-stop winter festivity. This is enhanced by a number of real winter festivals such as Ullr Fest – a carnival honouring the Norse God of Winter – and Ice Sculpture championships, which leave sculptures for weeks afterwards.

Hotels and condominiums are spread over a wide, wooded area and are linked by regular free shuttle-buses. If you stay in a condo and don't have a car shopping at the local supermarket can be hard work – it is not in the centre of town. Breckenridge boasts more slope-side lodging than any other Colorado resort.

MOUNTAIN FACTS

Altitude	2925m-3960m
Lifts	23
Pistes	2043 acres
Green	14%
Blue	26%
Black	60%
Art. snow	516 acres

Recco detectors used

The mountains

There are four separate peaks, linked by lift and piste. Boringly, they are named Peaks 7, 8, 9 and 10 – going from right to left as you look at the mountain. Though there's something for all standards, the keen piste-basher will want to explore other resorts too. Breckenridge and Keystone were bought in 1996 by the owners of Vail and Beaver Creek (around an hour away); a multi-day lift ticket covers these four resorts and Arapahoe Basin, also nearby. Copper Mountain is not covered by the same ticket. All six of these resorts are linked by regular buses (free except for a $10 return fare for Vail and Beaver Creek). Steamboat and Winter Park are both less than two hours' drive away.

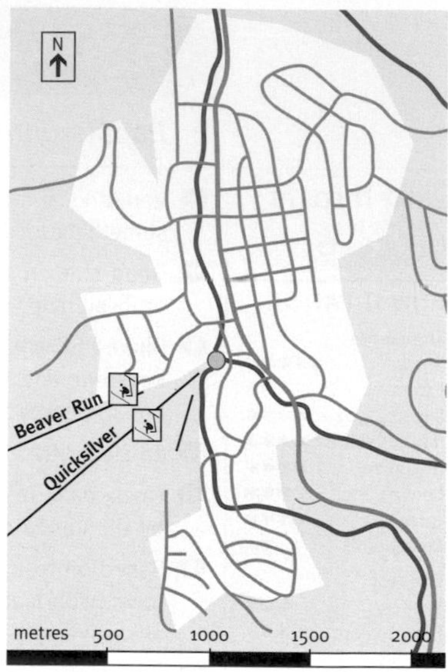

THE SLOPES
Small but fragmented

Two high-speed chair-lifts go from the top end of town up to **Peak 9**, one accessing mainly green runs on the lower half of the hill, the other mainly blues higher up. From there you can get to **Peak 10**, which has a large number of blue and black runs served by one high-speed quad.

The other flank of Peak 9 takes you to a lift up into the **Peak 8** area – tough stuff at the top, easier lower down. The base lifts of Peak 8 at the Bergenhof can also be reached by the town shuttle-bus or the Snowflake lift from the edge of town. From the top T-bar of Peak 8, you can traverse to the all-black **Peak 7** slopes and back bowls which have no lifts of their own – you go back to the base of Peak 8.

For the end of the day three trails lead back to town from Peak 8. A regular free shuttle runs around the resort to the Peak 9 and Peak 8 lifts. The grooming is excellent and the signposting very clear.

SNOW RELIABILITY
Excellent

With the village at almost 3000m (the highest of the main North American resorts), the slopes going up to almost 4000m and a lot of east and north-east-facing slopes, Breckenridge boasts an excellent natural snow record. That is supplemented by substantial artificial snowmaking.

FOR EXPERTS
Quite a few short but tough runs

A remarkable 60% of Breckenridge's runs are classified as 'most difficult' (single-black-diamond) or 'expert' (double-black-diamond) terrain. That's a higher proportion than the famous 'macho' resorts, such as Jackson Hole, Taos and Snowbird. But remember that Breckenridge is not a big area by European standards, so most experts there for a week or more will want to spend some of their time exploring the other nearby resorts.

Peak 7 is an entirely black-run area,

boarding *Breckenridge is pretty much ideal for all standards of boarder and plays host to several major US snowboarding events. Beginners have ideal nursery slopes and easy greens to progress to, and intermediates have great cruising runs, all served by chairs. For good boarders there's one of the best fun-parks in the US on Peak 9, with a series of great jumps, obstacles and an enormous championship half-pipe on Peak 8, which one reporter described as 'massive, steep, well kept and awesome'. The powder bowls at the top of Peaks 7 and 8 make for great riding – unfortunately accessed only by an awkward T-bar, which does not. Nearby Arapahoe Basin is another area for hardcore boarding in steep bowls and chutes.*

LIFT PASSES

2001/02 prices in dollars
Breckenridge-Keystone
Covers all lifts in Breckenridge, Keystone and Arapahoe Basin. Multi-day passes also cover Vail and Beaver Creek.
Beginners
3 beginners' lifts. Beginners and novices have a reduced area pass in ski school.
Main pass
1-day pass 59
6-day pass 240
Senior citizens
Over 64: 1-day pass 42 6-day pass 222
Over 70: 1-day 35 or 99 for a season pass
Children
Under 13: 6-day pass 150
Under 5: free pass
Alternative periods
Passes of 2 days and over allow one non-skiing day, eg 6-day pass valid for a 7-day period, with one non-skiing day.
Notes Prices given are for buying a lift pass in advance through a UK tour operator.

which is reached by traversing or hiking up from the top of the T-bar. It has great steep runs with good snow on north-east-facing slopes. Peak 8 has some good open terrain in Horseshoe and Contest bowls, where the snow normally remains good; and you can hike up to the steepest slopes in Imperial Bowl and Lake Chutes.

We particularly liked the back bowls of Peak 8. This is basically terrain among a thin covering of trees and bushes. Lots of runs, such as Lobo, Hombre, Amen and Adios, are marked on the trail map. But in practice you can easily skip between them and invent your own way down. It's picturesque and not too steep. Steep black mogul fields lead down under chair 4 to the junction with Peak 9.

Peak 9 itself has nothing to offer experts except very steep blacks from the top down under chair E.

Peak 10 offers much more interest. Off to the right of the chair, at the edge of the area, is a network of interlinking black mogul runs by the side of the downhill course – consistently steep and bumpy. To the left of the chair is a lovely, lightly wooded off-piste area called The Burn.

FOR INTERMEDIATES

Nice cruising, limited extent

Breckenridge has some good blue cruising runs for all standards of intermediate. But dedicated piste-bashers will find it limited and will want to visit the other nearby resorts.

Peak 9 has the easiest terrain. It is nearly all gentle, wide, blue runs at the top and almost flat, wide, green runs at the bottom. Timid intermediates will find it reassuring to see the ski patrol enforcing slow-speed skiing in narrow and busy areas. Peak 10 has a couple of more challenging runs graded blue-black, such as Crystal and Centennial, which make for good fast cruising.

Peak 8 has a choice of blues down through trails cut close together in the trees. More adventurous intermediates

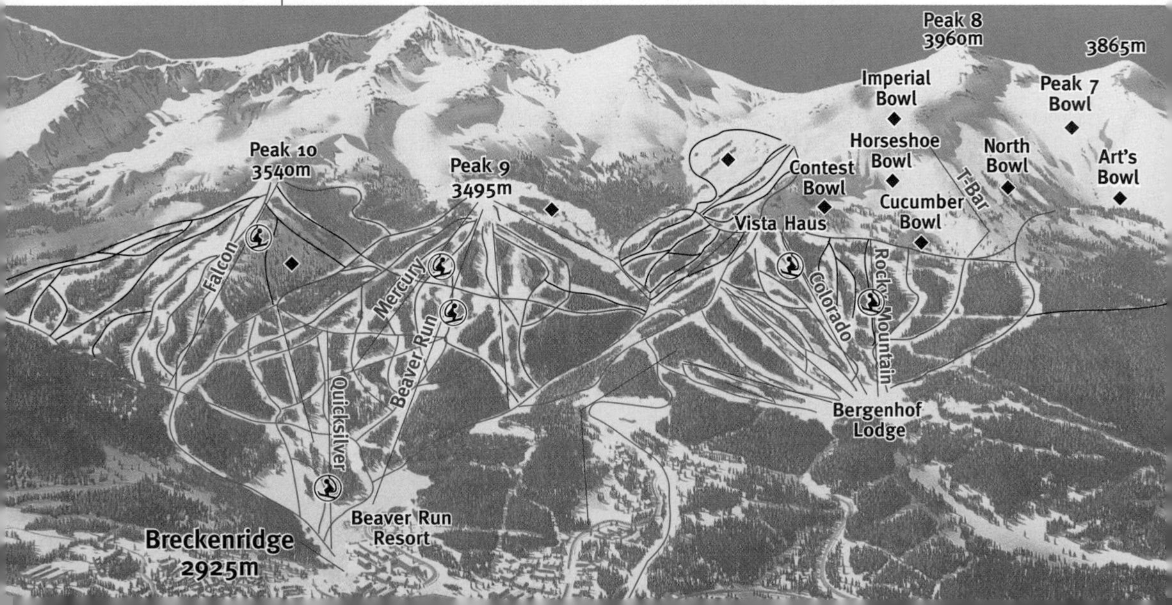

Peak 8
3960m
3865m
Imperial Bowl
Peak 7 Bowl
Peak 10
3540m
Peak 9
3495m
Horseshoe Bowl
North Bowl
Art's Bowl
Contest Bowl
T-Bar
Cucumber Bowl
Vista Haus
Falcon
Mercury
Colorado
Rocky Mountain
Beaver Run
Quicksilver
Bergenhof Lodge
Beaver Run Resort
Breckenridge
2925m

Ten Mile Station with its heated deck is the newest and best of Breck's mountain restaurants →

VAIL RESORTS, INC / TODD POWELL

SCHOOLS/GUIDES

2000/01 prices in dollars

Breckenridge
Classes 7 days
5hr: 9.45-12.15 and 1.30-4pm; 2½hr: am or pm
2 full days: 130
Children's classes
Ages: 3 to 12
6 full days 378 (including lunch for 3 to 5 year-olds)
Private lessons
1hr, 3hr or 6hr – prices are per instructor regardless of 1 to 6 persons.
1hr: 115; 3hr: 260
6hr: 425.

CHILDCARE

At each major lift base there is a resort-run Children's Center (453 3258), with a complex array of options for all-day care from 8.30 to 4.30. Children aged 6 to 14 go into ordinary children's school, but all-day care is available at Kid's Castle meeting areas at each lift base.

At Beaver Run there is also an independent childcare option called Kinderhut for ages six weeks to six years (453 0379). Their hours are 8.15 to 4pm and from Tuesday to Friday they are also open from 6pm to 10pm.

will also like to try some of the high bowl runs (see 'For Experts'). And Keystone, Vail, Beaver Creek and Copper Mountain all offer miles of excellent intermediate terrain.

FOR BEGINNERS
Excellent

The bottom of Peak 9 has a big, virtually flat area and some good gentle nursery slopes. There's then a good choice of green runs to move on to. Beginners can try Peak 8 too, with another selection of green runs and a choice of trails back to town. Reporters praise the good-value beginner package which includes lessons, equipment rental and lift pass.

FOR CROSS-COUNTRY
Specialist centre in woods

Breckenridge's Nordic Center is prettily set in the woods between the town and Peak 8 (and is served by the shuttle-bus). It has 38km of trails.

QUEUES
Not normally a problem

Breckenridge's six high-speed chair-lifts (three on Peak 9, two on Peak 8 and one on Peak 10) make light work of peak-time crowds. We've never come across serious queues, and neither have our reporters, except at exceptional times, such as President's Day weekend and on powder days – when the T-bar at Peak 8 can get busy.

MOUNTAIN RESTAURANTS
Varied but nothing special

Breckenridge is making an effort to improve on the standard US cafeterias.

Ten Mile Station, situated between Peaks 9 and 10, is the newest and best, with a heated outdoor deck as well as indoors. Border Burritos is in the Bergenhof at the base of Peak 8. Spencer's at Beaver Run does an all-you-can-eat breakfast and lunch menu. Vista Haus, at the top of Peak 8, has a couple of restaurants.

SCHOOLS AND GUIDES
Excellent reports

Our reporters are unanimous in their praise for the school: classes of five to eight; doing what the class, not the instructor, wants. Special clinics include bumps, telemark and powder.

FACILITIES FOR CHILDREN
Excellent facilities

Every report on the children's school and crèche bubbles with praise. Typical comments: 'nothing but praise for the children's ski school', 'excellent, combining serious coaching with lots of fun', 'our boys loved it', 'so much more positive than in Europe'.

Staying there

Breckenridge is quite spread out. Although there is a lot of slope-side accommodation, there is also a fair amount away from Main Street and the lift base-stations. Free shuttle-buses serve most of the area well, but less reliably in the evening than the day.

HOW TO GO
Lots of choice

A lot of tour operators feature Breckenridge and it's easy to arrange your own holiday there too. There are frequent bus transfers from Denver Airport. But for a group of four for a week it can be cheaper to hire a car.
Chalets Several tour operators have very comfortable chalets – there is more choice than in any other US resort. We were very impressed by a stay at Chalet

Phone numbers
From distant parts of the US, add the prefix 1 970.
From abroad, add the prefix +1 970.

GETTING THERE

Air Denver, transfer $2\frac{1}{2}$hr.
BA has direct flights from London to Denver.

ACTIVITIES

Indoor Sports clubs, swimming, sauna, massage, hot-tubs, cinema, theatre, art gallery, library, indoor miniature golf course, ice skating, good leisure centre (pool, tubs, gym, climbing wall) on the outskirts of town – accessible by bus
Outdoor Horse- and dog-sleigh rides, fishing, snow-mobiles, toboggans, scooters, mountain biking, snow-shoeing, ice skating, hot-air balloon rides

TOURIST OFFICE

Postcode CO 80424
t +1 (970) 453 5000
f 453 3202
international@vailresorts.com
www.breckenridge.com

Whispering Pines (run by Kokopelli chalets, sold through American Dream) – and it continues to receive rave reviews.
Hotels There's a good choice of style and price range.
(((④ **Great Divide** (453 4500) Used to be the Hilton but is now owned by Vail Resorts. Prime location, vast rooms and recently renovated – although a recent report complains of 'terrible service, poor cleaning and dirty hallways'. Pool, tubs.
(((④ **Lodge at Breckenridge** (453 9300) Stylish luxury spa resort set out of town among 32 acres, with great views. Private shuttle-bus. Pool, tubs.
(((④ **Little Mountain Lodge** (453 1969) Luxury B&B near ice rink.
((③ **Beaver Run** (453 6000) Huge, resort complex with 520 spacious rooms. Great location, by one of the main lifts up Peak 9. Pool, hot-tubs.
((③ **Williams House** (453 2975) Beautifully restored, charmingly furnished four-room B&B on Main St.
(② **Fireside Inn** (453 6465) Dormitory-style rooms. Historic part of town. Tub.
① **Breckenridge Wayside Inn** (453 5540) Friendly budget place out of town. Tub.
Self-catering There is a huge choice of condominiums, many set conveniently off the aptly named Four O'Clock run.

STAYING DOWN THE VALLEY

Good for exploring the area

Staying in Frisco makes sense for those touring around or on a tight budget. It's a small town with decent bars and restaurants. There are cheap motels, a couple of small hotels and some B&Bs (Hotel Frisco is recommended (668 5009).

EATING OUT

Over 100 restaurants

There's a very wide range of eating places, with pretty much everything you'd expect, from typical American food to 'fine-dining'. Pick up a copy of Breckenridge Dining Guide which lists a full menu of most places.

The Brewery is famous for its enormous portions of appetisers such as Buffalo Wings – as well as its splendid brewed-on-the-spot beers. We particularly liked the Avalanche beer.

We also liked Poirier's Cajun Café and the sophisticated food at both Café Alpine and Pierre's Riverwalk Café. Sushi Breck and Mi Casa (Mexican) have had good reviews. The Hearthstone has been recommended for 'lovely food in good surroundings'. And Michael's Italian is recommended for 'good food, extensive menu, large portions and reasonable prices'.

APRES-SKI

The best in the area

The Breckenridge Brewery, Shamus O'Toole's and Tiffany's are popular hangouts. The Gold Pan saloon dates from gold rush days, and is reputedly the oldest bar west of the Mississippi. Cecelia's has good cocktails and The Liquid Lounge and Sherpa & Yetti's are also popular. The Underworld is a trendy disco bar. But one of the locals' best kept secrets is Mount Java – a relaxed cafe-cum-bookshop with Internet access. More unusually, The O2 Lounge is an Oxygen bar, where you can snort different flavours of oxygen – the trick is to 'have a few beers beforehand and you'll leave sober'.

OFF THE SLOPES

Pleasant enough

Breckenridge is a pleasant place to wander around with plenty of souvenir and gift shops. Silverthorne (about 30 minutes away and connected by a free bus service) has excellent bargain factory outlet stores such as Levi, Gap and Ralph Lauren. It is easy to get around and visit other resorts.

Copper Mountain 2960m

Great all-rounder above a born-again resort

WHAT IT COSTS

HOW IT RATES

The slopes

Snow	*****
Extent	**
Experts	****
Intermediates	****
Beginners	****
Convenience	****
Queues	****
Restaurants	*

The rest

Scenery	***
Resort charm	**
Off-slope	*

What's new

Intrawest's new car-free 'Village at Copper' was opened for last season.

Passage Point, a fifth building in the new village complex, will be ready for 2001/02. The new development will house some new restaurants and more lodgings.

Copper's snowmaking capacity is being doubled for next season.

MOUNTAIN FACTS

Altitude	2925m-3765m
Lifts	23
Pistes	2450 acres
Green	21%
Blue	25%
Black	54%
Art. snow	400 acres

- ➕ Convenient purpose-built resort undergoing exciting renaissance
- ➕ Fair-sized mountain, with good runs for all abilities
- ➕ Excellent snow reliability
- ➕ Efficient lift system – few queues
- ➕ Several other good resorts nearby

- ➖ One fast-food mountain restaurant
- ➖ Limited vertical on black-diamond bowls at the top
- ➖ Village still rather limited when compared with established resorts
- ➖ Appreciable risk of altitude sickness for visitors arriving directly from much lower altitudes

Copper's slopes are some of Colorado's best, and last season saw the birth of the all-new slopeside resort centre – 'The new village at Copper' – to match the quality of the slopes. As a result, Copper now makes a much more attractive destination – but watch out for that altitude sickness.

THE RESORT

Copper Mountain was originally built rather like the French resorts of the 1960s – high on convenience, low on charm. Because of that it never took off on the international market. But it has always had one of Colorado's best ski areas. And the resort has now been transformed by its new owners, Intrawest. Last season saw the opening of 'The new village at Copper' – four new impressive wood-and-stone-clad buildings with shops, restaurants and car-free walkways and squares, forming the new heart of the resort. The new village is based at the foot of the main intermediate area, with two fast quads up to the heart of the skiing. This follows the opening, two seasons ago, of the new base lodge and accommodation at East Village – with easy access to the resort's expert and intermediate terrain. A regular free shuttle-bus runs between the two main bases and the family skiing and beginners' area at Union Creek.

Keystone, Breckenridge and Arapahoe Basin are all nearby, and Vail, Steamboat and Winter Park are within an hour or two.

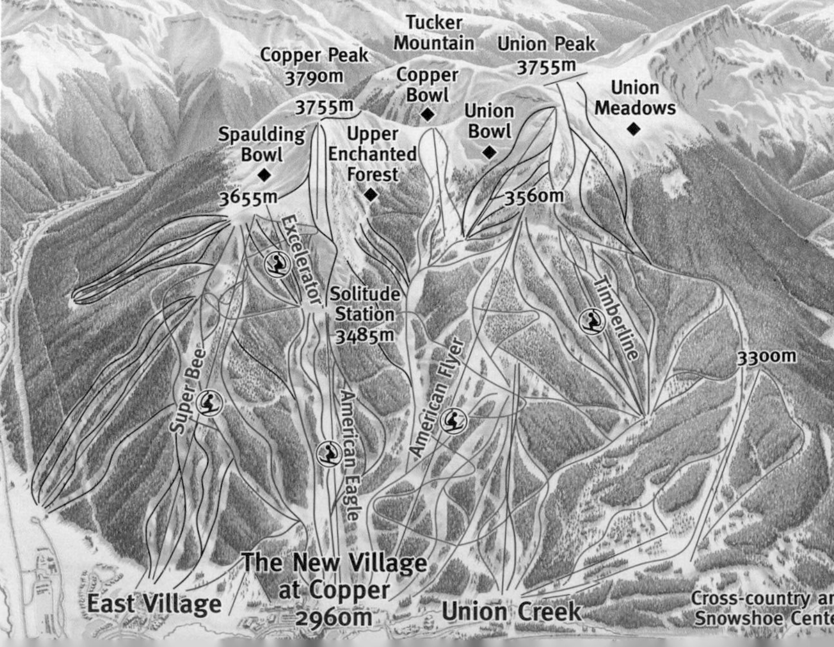

↑ There is some great terrain in the high bowls

COPPER MOUNTAIN / BEN BLANKENBURG

Central reservations
Call 968 2882 (from distant parts of the US, add the prefix 1 970; from abroad, add the prefix +1 970)

Toll-free number (from within the US) 1 888 219 2441.

TOURIST OFFICE

Postcode CO 80443
t +1 (970) 968 2882
f 968 2711
international@ski-copper.com
www.ski-copper.com

THE MOUNTAIN

The area is quite sizeable by American standards, and has great runs for all ability levels. Mountain tours with a Copper guide are available daily.
Slopes As you look up at the mountain, the easiest runs are on the right-hand side and the forested terrain gradually gets steeper and more challenging the further left you go. Above the forest, a series of steeper open bowls is served by two chairs and a drag on the front of the mountain and two further chairs on the back side.
Snow reliability Height and an extensive snowmaking operation give Copper an early opening date each season and excellent snow reliability. Grooming is excellent.
Experts There is a lot of good expert terrain, especially in the steep and wild Copper Bowl on the back side of Copper's mountain and in the bump runs through the trees below Spaulding Bowl.
Intermediates Good intermediates will find long steep runs in the Copper Peak section on the left of the mountain. The slightly less proficient can enjoy gentler runs on the middle section of mountain, while early intermediates have gentle cruisers in the Union Peak area on the right.
Beginners The nursery slopes are excellent, and there are plenty of very easy green runs to graduate to.
Snowboarding There is excellent terrain for all standards and there's also a terrain park and two half-pipes.
Cross-country There are 25km of trails through the White River forest.
Queues Copper is popular with day visitors from Denver but queues are rare because of the efficient lift system.
Mountain restaurants Grim. The main place is a fast food court at Solitude Station. The alternatives are outdoors – a soup shack and a burger bar.
Schools and guides The school offers a wide variety of courses and has a fine reputation, especially for teaching children.
Facilities for children The Belly Button childcare facility, at the Schoolhouse at Union Creek, takes children from two months old and ski school starts from age three.

STAYING THERE

How to go A number of tour operators offer packages to Copper.
Hotels There are no identifiable hotels, but some of the condo buildings are hotel-like in style and look splendidly luxurious, with outdoor hot-tubs, etc.
Après-ski In the past – because the resort mainly catered for day trippers – après-ski was lively at lift closing time, but quiet later on. However, the new resort developments mean that many visitors will now stay overnight. Endo's Adrenaline cafe in the main village, and Molly B's, in the East village, are popular new venues.
Eating out Beachside pizza and pasta is new in the main village. Endo's and Molly B's are also popular. Evening sleigh rides take people out to Western-style dinners in tents.
Off the slopes Facilities include a fine sports club, with a huge pool and indoor tennis, and an ice rink. There's also a multi-screen cinema nearby.

Crested Butte 2855m

Surprises galore in a Jekyll and Hyde resort

WHAT IT COSTS

6

HOW IT RATES

The slopes

Snow	****
Extent	**
Experts	****
Intermediates	***
Beginners	****
Convenience	***
Queues	*****
Restaurants	*

The rest

Scenery	***
Resort charm	****
Off-slope	**

What's new

The Teocalli Bowl debate is still ongoing but should be resolved this year. This 274 acres of expert terrain at the top of the Extreme Limits area has been closed for several years due to patrolling problems and ski boundary discrepancies.

The Crested Butte Marriot Resort hotel at the foot of the slopes was reopened as a Club Med 'village' last season.

MOUNTAIN FACTS

Altitude	2775m-3620m
Lifts	14
Pistes	1058 acres
Green	14%
Blue	32%
Black	54%
Art. snow	300 acres
Recco detectors used	

- ⊕ Lots of 'extreme' and expert terrain
- ⊕ Excellent for beginners and for near-beginners, with long easy runs
- ⊕ Charming, tiny, restored Victorian mining town with good restaurants
- ⊕ Convenient 'village' at lift base
- ⊕ Excellent school
- ⊕ Attractive scenery, for Colorado

- ⊖ Limited for confident intermediate piste-bashers
- ⊖ Old town is 10 minutes from resort village by shuttle-bus
- ⊖ Out on a limb, away from mainstream Colorado resorts
- ⊖ Only one satisfactory mountain restaurant

Among experts who are at home on steep, unprepared runs – and 'extremists' who like their mountains as steep as possible – Crested Butte enjoys cult status. Meanwhile, the commercial success of the place depends on beginners and timid intermediates, who love the long, gentle slopes of the main area. These two groups can safely include Crested Butte on their shortlists. But keen, mileage-hungry intermediates will find there isn't enough suitable terrain.

THE RESORT

Crested Butte is a small resort in a remote corner of Colorado. It takes its name from the local mountain – an isolated peak (a butte, pronounced 'beaut') with a distinctive shape. It started life as a coal-mining town in the late 1800s and is now one of the most attractive resorts in the Rockies – a few narrow streets with beautifully restored wooden buildings and sidewalks, a tiny town jail and a classic general store – straight out of a Western movie.

The town is a couple of miles from the mountain, linked by regular free shuttle-bus. But at the foot of it is the resort 'village' of Mount Crested Butte – modern and characterless, with a cluster of bars and restaurants at the foot of the slopes, a couple of big hotels and a sprawling area of houses and condos. There is some accommodation in the town, but most is at the resort village. You can stroll to the lifts from some of it; but from many condos you need the bus.

THE MOUNTAIN

It's a small area, but it packs in an astonishing mixture of perfect beginner slopes, easy cruising runs and expert terrain. There are free daily mountain tours for intermediates or better.

Slopes Two fast quad chairs leave the base. The Silver Queen takes experts to black runs and links with lifts to the steepest runs. The Keystone lift takes you to the easiest runs. Intermediates can access cruising blue runs from either of these two lifts.

Snow reliability The resort apparently benefits from snowstorms from several directions, and has a substantial snowmaking installation.

Snowboarding There's lots of extreme terrain and a fun-park for good riders. Beginners have a large section of long, wide green runs to the base station.

Experts For those who like steep, ungroomed terrain, Crested Butte is

Phone numbers
From distant parts of the US, add the prefix 1 970.
From abroad, add the prefix +1 970.

idyllic – the 448 acres of the Extreme Limits at the top of the mountain offer seriously steep but prettily wooded and safe terrain. But the area needs a lot of snow cover – it is not unusual for it to be closed until late January. Guided tours of the North Face are available. Though there are also some 'ordinary' black runs, these are few.

Irwin Lodge, a few miles away, runs a snowcat skiing and riding operation on its secluded slopes (details below).

Intermediates Good intermediates are likely to find the area limited. For early intermediates, there are lots of wide, fairly gentle, well groomed and normally uncrowded cruising runs.

Beginners There are excellent nursery slopes near the village and lots of good long runs to progress to.

Cross-country There are 30km of cross-country trails near the old town of Crested Butte, and backcountry tours are available in Elk Mountain and the Gunnison National Forest.

Queues Queues are virtually non-existent.

Mountain restaurants Most people go back to the base for lunch. The restaurant at the base of the Paradise lift is fairly civilised, though, with a table-service restaurant as well as a cafeteria and barbecue.

Schools and guides The school has an excellent reputation.

Facilities for children Parents praise the teaching and separate kids' area.

STAYING THERE

How to go Most tour operators with serious US programmes include Crested Butte. Right at the foot of the slopes is a Club Med.

Hotels You have a broad range of options, from international-style comfort to homely character. In the resort village, the Sheraton Crested Butte Resort (349 2333) is one of the smartest options, with a pool and outdoor hot-tub and great views. The Nordic Inn B&B (349 5542) is a short walk from the lifts: 'Full of character, charming hosts', outdoor hot-tub and large rooms. On the outskirts of the old town, the 'Scandinavian-style' Inn at Crested Butte (349 1225) is a non-smoking hotel with an outdoor hot-tub. Elk Mountain Lodge B&B (349 7533) is a renovated miners' hotel.

Self-catering There are thousands of apartments available in the village.

Eating out Top of the pile is Soupçon, a tiny place in an old log cabin just off the main street in the old town, serving refined French food. Le Bosquet and Timberline run it close, and Bacchanale is a good Italian. The Idle Spur micro-brewery is popular. In the resort village, the WoodStone Grille is recommended. Bubba's and Twister, on the mountain, are open at night.

Après-ski Kochevar's, in the old town, is an amusing Wild West saloon. The Wooden Nickel and The Powerhouse are recommend. At the resort village, Rafters and Casey's are popular.

Off the slopes Activities are limited, though there are some galleries, a theatre and a cinema.

Staying up the mountain Irwin Lodge (349 2773) is a great wooden barn in a remote backcountry area, reached in winter only by snowcat or snowmobile. It has an outdoor hot-tub, great views and simple rooms above a huge communal sitting room with open fire.

TOURIST OFFICE

Postcode CO 81225
t +1 (970) 349 2286
f 349 2250
info@cbmr.com
www.crestedbutte resort.com

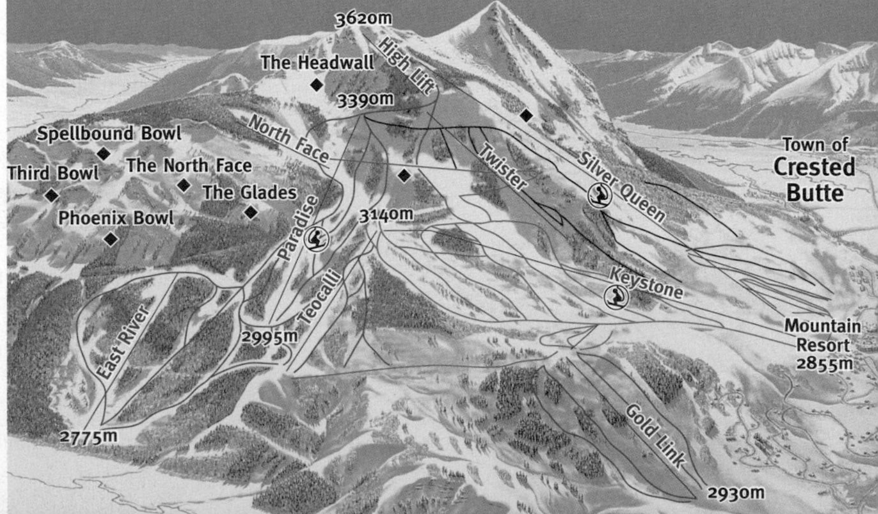

SNOWPIX.COM / CHRIS GILL
← Condos spread widely around the valley from the lift base

Keystone 2835m

Pampered cruising in the trees

WHAT IT COSTS

6

HOW IT RATES

The slopes

Snow	*****
Extent	**
Experts	***
Intermediates	****
Beginners	****
Convenience	**
Queues	****
Restaurants	***

The rest

Scenery	***
Resort charm	**
Off-slope	**

What's new

For 2001/02 two new hotel-condominium buildings will open in River Run, including the ski-in, ski-out Lone Eagle next to the gondola.

Everyone staying at a resort-owned property receives a free mountain passport with over $500-worth of free activities (such as tubing, ice skating, yoga classes and wine tastings).

2000/01 saw a new six-pack, Ruby Express, on the back of Keystone Mountain – speeding up the return from North Peak.

- ➕ Good mountain for everyone but the double-diamond diehard; extensive, immaculately groomed intermediate slopes are a particular strength
- ➕ Huge night-skiing operation – almost half the runs are floodlit and open until 8pm
- ➕ Lots of other nearby resorts, and a shared lift pass with Breckenridge, Vail and A-Basin
- ➕ Efficient lift system – few queues
- ➕ Luxurious condominiums set in woods (with good-value rates)
- ➕ Very impressive childcare facilities

- ➖ Very quiet in the evenings
- ➖ Very high – altitude sickness can be a problem for some visitors
- ➖ Few slope-side properties, and most involve bus-rides to and from lifts
- ➖ Resort lacks village atmosphere except in the newish River Run development
- ➖ Poor shops for self-catering
- ➖ Limited choice of restaurants by usual US resort standards

Keystone's slopes are impressive from many points of view. If there was a village at the foot of them like Vail or Breckenridge, Keystone's stable-mates, it would be easily recommendable. But what Keystone offers at present is less compelling. River Run – a joint venture with Whistler's Canadian owner, Intrawest – is developing into something like a recognisable resort village, but it still has some way to go before a week of evenings spent there could be called an attractive prospect. And the appeal of Keystone's other 'neighborhoods' – all less entertaining, all but one further from the lifts – is difficult to see.

Perhaps it is price: you may find some of Keystone's lodgings offer exceptional value. Hire a car to simplify shopping, and plan on eating in more than out.

The resort

Keystone is a sprawling resort of condominiums spread over wooded countryside at the foot of Keystone Mountain, beside Snake River and the highway to Loveland Pass. As yet it has no clear centre, but is notionally divided into seven 'neighborhoods', with regular buses between them (although one reporter says 'the routes can be very round the houses'). Some consist of little more than groups of condos, while others have shops, restaurants and bars (though no supermarkets or liquor stores – they are out on the main highway).

At River Run, at the base of the main gondola, an attractively designed, car-free development is taking shape that is destined to become the new focal point of the resort. A second lift base area half a mile to the west, Mountain House, is much less of a village. Another mile west is Keystone Village, set around the picturesque lake – a huge natural ice rink in winter. These and some other 'neighborhoods' are shown on our resort plan; Ski Tip (with famous Lodge) is off to the east.

The mountains

Keystone's terrain has expanded rapidly in the last few years and by US standards now offers extensive intermediate slopes and some challenging steeper stuff.

Keystone is owned by Vail Resorts, who also own Vail, Beaver Creek and Breckenridge. Lift tickets between the four resorts are interchangeable, and

↑ Keystone is best-known for its groomed cruising, but it has excellent advanced terrain too

KEYSTONE / DAVE NAGEL

there is bus transport between them. Copper Mountain is nearby and Arapahoe Basin (or A-Basin as it is known locally) a few minutes by road, but both are separately owned. Your lift ticket covers a trip to A-Basin, but not to Copper. In contrast to Keystone's superb modern lifts, A-Basin is still served by a series of slow old chairs.

MOUNTAIN FACTS

Altitude	2835m-3720m
Lifts	22
Pistes	1861 acres
Green	12%
Blue	34%
Black	54%
Art. snow	956 acres

THE SLOPES
A keen intermediate's dream

Three tree-lined, interlinked mountains form Keystone's local slopes. The only one directly accessible from the resort is **Keystone Mountain**, to which lifts depart from Mountain House or River Run. The front face of the mountain has Keystone's biggest network of lifts and runs by far, mainly of easy and intermediate gradient. From the top you can drop over the back down to Keystone Gulch, where there are lifts back up to Keystone Mountain and on to the next hill, **North Peak.** Or you can ride the Outpost gondola directly to the top of North Peak. From North Peak you can get back to the bases of both Keystone Mountain and the third peak, known as **The Outback**. This area is served by another high-speed quad.

SNOW RELIABILITY
Not a natural strength

Keystone's annual snowfall is low by Colorado standards – 230in, whereas many other resorts get 300in or more. But shortage of snow is rarely a problem, not least because Keystone has one of the world's biggest snowmaking systems as back-up.

One of the main reasons for the snowmaking is to help form an early-season base. Keystone traditionally vies with Killington to be the first US resort to open its runs for the season – normally in October.

A-Basin has no need for artificial snow. It has the highest lift-served terrain in the US, at almost 4000m, and the base-station is at an impressive 3290m. The slopes are normally open well into June.

FOR EXPERTS
Some steeps, no super-steeps

Keystone has a reputation for great groomers, but it also has a lot of steeper ungroomed terrain (though none of it gets a double-diamond grading).

Windows is a 60-acre area of experts-only glade runs on Keystone Mountain's back side, opened in 1998. The trail map identifies around 10, but on the ground they are not clearly defined. All three mountains have some good mogul runs, such as Ambush and Geronimo, and there are splendid glade runs on both North Peak and The Outback. Traversing from the top of the lift on The Outback takes you to open and glade runs in the North Bowl and the South Bowls, which are basically ski-anywhere areas.

Arapahoe Basin, down the road, is a good place for those looking for more of a challenge. The East Wall here has some splendid steep chutes. And the opposite side of the bowl is riddled with steep bump runs – although none of the runs is particularly long.

boarding *Until five years ago, snowboarding was banned at Keystone. Then they invested $2.5 million in facilities – these include the 20-acre Jawhacker terrain-park and adjoining Area 51 half-pipe, on the front side of Keystone Mountain – floodlit to make the biggest night-snowboarding operation in Colorado (you can actually ride from 8.30am to 8pm – if you've got superhuman stamina and are mad enough, that is). Keystone as a whole is ideal for beginners and intermediates, with mainly chair-lifts and gondolas, good beginner areas (there are a couple of easily avoidable drag-lifts here) and superb cruising runs. Experienced riders will love The Outback and the bowls and chutes of nearby A-Basin, a favourite area with hardcore boarders. Evenings are quiet.*

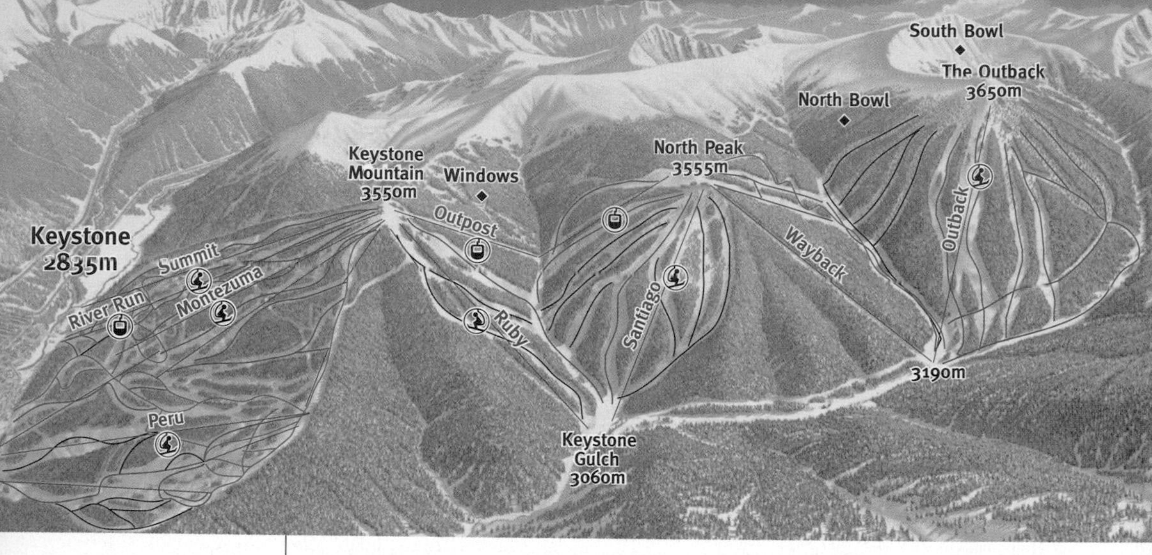

LIFT PASSES

2001/02 prices in dollars

Vail Resorts
1- or 2-day pass valid in Breckenridge and A-Basin as well as Keystone. Passes for 3 days or more also valid for Vail and Beaver Creek.

Beginners Beginners and novices have a reduced area pass in ski school.

Main pass
1-day pass 59
6-day pass 240

Senior citizens
Over 65: 1-day pass 42
Over 70: 1-day 35 or 99 for a season pass

Children
Under 13: 6-day pass 150
Under 5: free pass

Alternative periods
Passes of 2 days and over allow one non-skiing day, eg 6-day pass valid for a 7-day period, with one non-skiing day.

Copper Mountain, Breckenridge, Vail and Beaver Creek have some good challenging terrain, for those prepared to travel around.

FOR INTERMEDIATES
A cruiser's paradise

Keystone is ideal for intermediates. The front face of Keystone Mountain itself is a network of beautifully groomed blue and green runs through the trees. Enthusiastic piste-bashers will love it.

The Outback and North Peak also have easy cruising blues, and The Outback has some of the steepest blue runs, including a couple of blue-blacks through the trees that are pretty much off-piste and unmarked.

On top of that, Vail, Beaver Creek and Copper Mountain all have some great intermediate terrain.

FOR BEGINNERS
Nice gentle greens

There are good nursery slopes (floodlit in the evening) at the top and bottom of Keystone Mountain, which also has some excellent long green runs to progress to – one of them, Schoolmarm, goes right from top to bottom of the mountain. There's another long green on North Peak, accessible by gondola.

FOR CROSS-COUNTRY
Extensive facilities

The special Cross-Country and Touring Centre between Keystone and A-Basin is served by a shuttle-bus. There are 29km of groomed trails. And 57km of unprepared trails take you through spectacular scenery in the Montezuma area, with great views of the Continental Divide. Some trails lead to old mining ghost-towns. The Cross-Country and Touring Centre runs guided tours, including a Full Moon evening tour.

QUEUES
Not a problem

Keystone has an efficient, modern lift system, and, except at the morning peak, there are few queuing problems. Last time we tried the night skiing the River Run gondola stopped running and the parallel high-speed chair made for a mind-numbingly cold ride. The trails are usually beautifully quiet, except for Mozart, the only blue run down from Keystone Mountain to North Peak and The Outback.

MOUNTAIN RESTAURANTS
A resort of extremes

There are two mountain restaurant complexes. Summit House at the top of Keystone Mountain has a food court, a pizza place and a bar, all inclined to get over-busy – 'Eat at the base,' says a reporter. The Outpost Lodge at the top of North Peak is beautifully designed in wood, with high ceilings, picture windows and a big terrace. Its Timber Ridge food court is strictly for refuelling, but the table-service Alpenglow Stube is something else. It has a luxury atmosphere rarely found in mountain restaurants, even in Europe – but it is, of course, expensive. There's a simple cabin and outdoor grill at Keystone Gulch, at the foot of North Peak.

There are lots of luxurious condos set in the trees with use of pool or hot-tub ➔

KEYSTONE / BOB WINSETT

SCHOOLS/GUIDES

2000/01 prices in dollars

Keystone
Classes 7 days
2½hr: 10.30-1pm or 1.30-4pm; 2hr evening: 4.30-6.30
half-day 40
Children's classes
Ages: 3 to 14
Full day including lunch, equipment rental and ski-pass: 84
Private lessons
1½hr, 2hr, half- or full-day
130 for 1½hr

Phone numbers
From distant parts of the US, add the prefix 1 970.
From abroad, add the prefix +1 970.

CHILDCARE

The Children's Centre at the base of the mountain caters for children aged 2 months to 12 years and is open from 8am to 9pm. They can also provide evening babysitting in your own room. From age 3, children can join in the Snowplay programmes.

The school's Mini Minor's Camp takes children aged 3 to 4, the Minor's Camp those from 5 to 12.

SCHOOLS AND GUIDES
Advanced classes a bargain

As well as the normal lessons, there are bumps, race, women-only and various other advanced classes. There are also special courses run by Olympic medallists Phil and Steve Mahre, designed specially for experienced adult skiers. Reporters have been very impressed by the school's advanced classes, partly because they found themselves in tiny groups or even receiving one-to-one tuition for the price of a group lesson.

FACILITIES FOR CHILDREN
Excellent

Childcare facilities are excellent, with programmes tailored to specific age groups, and nursery care going on into the evening. Children have their own teaching areas, with 'magic carpet' lifts. Ske-cology classes are designed to teach children about the environment and the resort's ecology while learning to ski.

Staying there

The most convenient places to stay are near the Mountain House or River Run lifts. But all the accommodation is served by free shuttle-buses.

HOW TO GO
As you please

It's easy to fix your own lodgings, and regular shuttles operate from Denver airport, but packages can offer very attractive prices. There are hotels but most accommodation is in condominiums.

Hotels There isn't a great choice but they're all of a high standard.

(((4) **Chateaux d'Mont** (496 4500) Luxury condo-hotel near the lifts; only 15 suites, with private hot-tubs and other luxuries.

(((4) **Keystone Lodge** (496 2316) Large, recently renovated hotel in Keystone Village. All rooms have mountain views. Pool and fitness centre.

((3) **Inn at Keystone** (496 4242) Modern, comfortable, resort-owned hotel. Hot-tubs with great views. Liked by reporters who stayed there.

GOURMET NIGHT SKIING

Keystone has the biggest floodlighting operation in the US, covering Keystone Mountain top to bottom. When the light begins to fade, the floodlights come on and you can carry on skiing or riding up to 8pm. A gondola, high-speed quad and drag-lift serve 17 green and blue runs (longest top-to-bottom trail over three miles long) and a 20-acre terrain park. Cruising through falling snow illuminated by the bright lights can be delightful. On a clear night, though, it can be bitter.

You can combine the action with dinner on the mountain. The Alpenglow Stube, at the top of North Peak (reached by gondola), stays open until 8.15 to serve haute cuisine with a Colorado flavour for pedestrians, skiers and snowboarders. Slippers are provided. A cheaper option is next door's Der Fondue Chessel which features fondue, raclette and 'Bavarian' music and dancing.

GETTING THERE

Air Denver, transfer 2hr.

ACTIVITIES

Indoor Swimming, hot-tubs, tennis
Outdoor Floodlit ice skating, sleigh and stagecoach rides, snowmobiling, horse-riding, tubing, night skiing, snow-shoeing, cross country skiing, winter fly fishing, star gazing workshops, weekly firework display, torch-light descents, dog-sledding, evening gondola trips

TOURIST OFFICE

Postcode CO 80424
t +1 (970) 496 6772
f 453 3202
international@vail resorts.com
www.keystoneresort.com

(3) **Ski Tip Lodge** (496 4202) Former stagecoach halt and home of Keystone's founder, Max Dercum, who restored and extended it and used broken ski tips found on the slopes as door handles – hence the name. Atmospheric old rooms, bar and lounge with log fires. 'Superb food and very attentive service,' reports one visitor.

Self-catering All the condominiums we've seen or heard about are large and luxurious – and we've stayed in some fabulous ones with nice touches, such as log fires and two-storey floor-to-ceiling windows. Most condos have use of a pool and hot-tub. Except for their position, we particularly liked the Lakeside condos (near the lake!). The equally comfortable and well positioned Frostfire condos have fewer amenities, but each unit has an en suite whirlpool bath. Cinnamon Ridge at Mountain View, Slopeside at Mountain House and Flying Dutchman in the Forest 'neighborhood' are other recommended places. There are lots of condos at the River Run development.

STAYING DOWN THE VALLEY

Possible, good for exploring

A few years ago a couple of reporters stayed in **Silverthorne**. The Days Inn was thought comfortable but basic. The Alpen Hutte was friendly and had its own private bus transfer. **Frisco** is a good centre for visiting other nearby resorts – reporters recommend the Alpine Inn, Lake Dillon Lodge and Hotel Frisco.

EATING OUT

Not the widest choice

You can have your evening meal up the mountain. The Summit House, at the top of the gondola on Keystone Mountain, remains busy at the end of the normal day because of the floodlit sessions at night. There's live country and western entertainment and simple food – hamburgers, ribs and so on. The Outpost, on North Peak, is a hive of dining activity including the Alpenglow Stube (see Mountain restaurants).

There are some good upmarket places at valley level too. We've eaten well at the Ski Tip Lodge by the cross-country track (the menu changes daily) – a charming former stagecoach halt. The Keystone Ranch, well outside the resort, serves six-course dinners in a building based on a 19th-century homestead. The Garden Room of Keystone Lodge overlooks the lake and reports are favourable: 'Small menu but good food.'

River Run and Keystone Village each offer half a dozen options, including steak houses and pizza places. But there isn't the range of mid-market restaurants that makes eating out such a pleasure in many American resorts – and it's in the nature of the place that the restaurants are dotted around in different parts of the resort. Paisano's is an 'excellent' Italian at River Run, where there are also two taverns. The cosy Snake River Saloon in the Mountain View neighbourhood is recommended for grills. The Bighorn Steakhouse in Keystone Lodge is well worth avoiding – lousy service in a dreary room.

APRES-SKI

Pretty quiet in the evenings

Immediately after coming off the slopes, it can be quite lively. The Summit House at the top of the gondola has live music and caters for people using the slopes at night as well as après-skiers. The Kickapoo Tavern at River Run has a sunny deck and eight Colorado microbrews on tap and Montezuma has rock 'n roll. Some of the eateries double as bars with live music. The Snake River Saloon has a happy hour, 5–7pm, and is thoroughly recommended by a reporter: 'Brilliant restaurant and lively bar – including a fire-eating barman.' Ida Belle has ragtime music and a miners' tavern decor; and Dillon Inn has Country and Western.

However, places empty out quite early and Keystone isn't really the place for late-night revellers.

The Inxpot is a quiet, laid-back coffee house, cum bar, cum bookstore, with comfy armchairs and a great selection of books. Other popular hangouts with the locals are The Goat and Out of Bounds.

OFF THE SLOPES

OK if you want a peaceful time

Keystone makes it easy for pedestrians to get around the mountain, with both mountain restaurant complexes easily accessible by gondola. It's also easy to get to Breckenridge and Vail.

There are plenty of other activities, including skating on the frozen lake (the largest outdoor maintained rink in the US) and indoor tennis.

Steamboat 2100m

Something for everyone above a cowboy town

WHAT IT COSTS

6

HOW IT RATES

The slopes	
Snow	****
Extent	***
Experts	***
Intermediates	****
Beginners	*****
Convenience	***
Queues	****
Restaurants	***
The rest	
Scenery	***
Resort charm	**
Off-slope	**

What's new

Steamboat's terrain has expanded a lot in recent years – first into Morningside Park and then into the Pioneer Ridge area. Another lift and another 500 acres of terrain are planned to open at some stage.

A new 'Super-Pipe' is planned for the Dude Ranch snowboard area for 2001/02.

And a new Grand Summit condo-hotel at the base of the mountain, opened in time for the 2000/01 season. It is a large complex of rooms, condos and suites with extensive facilities (pool, hot-tubs, fitness room, conference centre, ballrooms and restaurants).

- ⊕ Now a fair-sized mountain, with a decent amount of black-diamond terrain to go with its excellent beginner and early intermediate runs
- ⊕ Famed for its gladed powder terrain
- ⊕ Plenty of slope-side lodging
- ⊕ Town of Steamboat Springs has some Western character – though it's less of a wild cowboy town than the hype leads you to expect
- ⊕ Good snow record combined with modest altitude – sickness problems are very unlikely

- ⊖ Old town is a couple of miles from the slopes, and the resort as a whole sprawls over a large area
- ⊖ Modern resort 'village' at the foot of the slopes is rather a mess, with some big eyesore buildings
- ⊖ Mountain lacks distinctive character
- ⊖ Not enough tough blue/easy black runs to amuse keen intermediates for a week
- ⊖ Not a huge amount of double-black terrain – some of it a hike away
- ⊖ Green runs tend to be winding catwalks rather than proper runs

Steamboat's brochures routinely feature horse-riding, Stetson-wearing, lasso-wielding cowboys. There are working cowboys around, but as Steamboat the ski resort has grown it has rather swamped Steamboat Springs the cattle town – without itself developing much of a village atmosphere.

Steamboat's mountain may not be a match in extent and challenge for some Colorado neighbours – experts and keen piste-bashers going for a week or more might do well to plan a two-centre holiday. But Steamboat is one of the best resorts for powder fun among the trees. Recent expansions have added to its appeal in this respect.

The resort

The resort is a 10-minute bus-ride from the old town of Steamboat Springs – a long drive or short flight from Denver. Near the gondola station there are a couple of shop- and restaurant-lined multi-level squares. Some of the accommodation is up the sides of the piste, but the resort also sprawls across the valley.

The old town can be a bit of a disappointment after the hype of the brochures. It may be a working cattle town – it's certainly a great place to buy a Stetson (at the famous FM Light & Son). But the Wild West isn't much in evidence except in January when the Cowboy Downhill brings cowhands into town from the Denver Rodeo to compete in a fun race, lassoing and saddling competition.

The main (and almost only) street in the old town is very wide, with multiple lanes of traffic each way – it was built that way to allow cattle to be driven through town. It is lined with bars, hotels and shops, built at various

STEAMBOAT

You have to be there at the right time in January to experience the amazing Cowboy Downhill →

MOUNTAIN FACTS

Altitude	2103m-3221m
Lifts	20
Pistes	2939 acres
Green	13%
Blue	56%
Black	31%
Art. snow	438 acres

LIFT PASSES

2000/01 prices in dollars

Steamboat
Covers all lifts at Steamboat only.

Beginners One free lift at base (Preview); day pass for beginners covers two extra lifts (adult 36).

Main pass
1-day pass 59
6-day pass 306
(low season 264)

Senior citizens
Over 65: 6-day pass 210
Over 70: free pass

Children
Under 13: 6-day pass 204 – but can be free, see Notes below
Under 5: free pass

Short-term passes
Afternoon passes from 12.15 (adult 47) and from 2pm (adult 34). Single ascent on Silver Bullet Gondola for non-skiers only (adult 17).

Alternative periods
3-day pass is valid for 4 days with one non-skiing day. Passes of 4 days and over allow two days' non-skiing, so 4 days' skiing in 6, 6 in 8.

Notes Children up to 12 ski free when parents buy full lift pass and stay for 5 days or more (one child per parent). Discounts for groups.

times over the last 120 years, in a wide mixture of styles, from old wooden buildings to modern concrete plazas.

The town got its name in the mid-1800s, when trappers going along by the Yampa river heard a chugging they thought was a steamboat. It turned out to be the bubbling of a hot spring.

The mountain

Located in the Routt National Forest, Steamboat's slopes are prettily set among trees, with views over rolling hills below. On our last late-season visit we even glimpsed a black bear and her cubs ambling across a piste.

It claims to be one of Colorado's biggest areas, and with its recent ongoing expansion, there's now more terrain for better skiers in particular. But even when the expansion is finished it still won't rival places such as Aspen and Vail.

With an Early Bird pass ($11 including breakfast) you can ride the gondola at 8.15am, and get fresh tracks when the slopes open at 8.30 before having a buffet breakfast at Thunderhead when the crowds arrive.

There are various complimentary guiding deals. Mountain hosts do tours of blue and black runs daily at 10.30. Olympic medallist Billy Kidd takes groups down the mountain most days at 1pm. Nelson Carmichael, bronze medallist at the Albertville Olympics, runs a free mogul clinic on Sundays at 1pm. There are nature ski tours three times a week. And five days a week at 9am local guides lead groups of over-50s on a 'mellow cruise' of groomed runs. There are also snow-shoeing tours on Thursdays and Saturdays.

Holiday visitors generally overlook Steamboat Springs' little local hill, Howelsen. As well as a row of ski jumps, it has a modest area of pistes, floodlit most evenings.

If you have a car, Vail, Beaver Creek, Copper Mountain, Keystone, Breckenridge and Winter Park are all less than a two-hour drive.

THE SLOPES
Five different flanks

The slopes divide naturally into five sectors, and most have runs to suit all abilities. The gondola from the village rises to **Thunderhead**. From here you can choose the runs back to the village and a variety of chairs. Or you can go down to the left to catch a chair up to **Storm Peak** or to the new **Pioneer Ridge** area. From Storm Peak you can drop over the back into **Morningside Park** area. If you turn right from Thunderhead you can catch a chair up to **Sunshine Peak**.

SNOW RELIABILITY
Good despite 'low' altitude

Steamboat is relatively low by Colorado standards; it goes from 2100m to 3220m. So its highest slopes are below the height of the base of Arapahoe Basin. Despite this it has an excellent snow record, with an annual average of 334in – more than most of the higher resorts. This is where they invented the term Champagne Powder™. There is also snowmaking from top to bottom of the mountain.

FOR EXPERTS
Powder glades are the highlight

The main attraction of Steamboat for experts is the challenging 'off-piste' terrain in the forest glades. The trees are fantastic with fresh powder though, sadly, conditions have never been perfect on our visits.

A great area is on Sunshine Peak below the Sundown Express and Priest Creek lifts. You simply take off through the aspens and choose a route where the trees are spaced as you like them – wide or narrow. Of the marked black runs in this area, the two to the left of the lifts as you go up – Closet and Shadows – are only loosely pistes: the trees have just been thinned out a bit.

boarding *Steamboat is ideal for first-time boarders – there's a special learning area, ideal gentle slopes to progress to and you can get all over the mountain using chair-lifts and the gondola. The snowboard school even offers another lesson free if you can't ride from the top of the beginners' area after the first. Steamboat is also great for experienced boarders, with two fun-parks: The Beehive, especially for kids, and the competition-standard Dude Ranch half-pipe and fun-park (which will have a new superpipe for 2001/02). And riding the glades in fresh powder is unbeatable. There's also a choice of specialist snowboard shops, and benches and tools at the top of lifts.*

On the right of the lift as you go up are some clearer marked black runs.

Morningside Park and Pioneer Ridge also have excellent gladed terrain, without any scary gradients.

The scary gradients are reached via the lift back from Morningside – the three numbered chutes are easily accessed, and a short hike gets you to the tree skiing of Christmas Tree Bowl.

Most other marked blacks are easy for good intermediates and make great fast runs if they've been groomed. For bumps, try the series of runs off Four Points – including Nelson's, named after local hero Nelson Carmichael.

Steamboat Powder Cats (aka Blue Sky West) run snowcat skiing tours over 15 square miles of backcountry.

FOR INTERMEDIATES

Some long cruises

Much of the mountain is ideal intermediate territory, with long cruising blue runs such as Buddy's Run, Rainbow and Ego on Storm Peak and High Noon and One O'Clock on Sunshine Peak. Some black runs, such as West Side and Lower Valley View, also make good, challenging intermediate runs when the bumps have been groomed out of them.

Morningside Park is a great area for easy black as well as blue slopes. And don't ignore Thunderhead – there are lots of good runs that are easy to miss if you always head straight to the top. The runs on Sunshine at the far right-hand side of the area are very gentle – Tomahawk and Quickdraw are marked blue but are perfectly possible for those who normally stick to green.

For keen intermediates the area is limited – not really enough to keep you interested for a week unless you enjoy repeating the same runs.

FOR BEGINNERS

Excellent learning terrain

There's a big, gentle nursery area at the base of the mountain served by several lifts. You progress from this to the Christie chairs to a variety of gentle green runs such as Yoo Hoo and Giggle Gulch. A green run winds all the way down from Thunderhead, but there is rather a shortage of 'proper' green runs up the mountain for those not ready for the psychological leap to the easy blues on Sunshine.

FOR CROSS-COUNTRY

Plenty out of town

There's no cross-country in Steamboat itself but a free shuttle service takes you to the Touring Center, where there

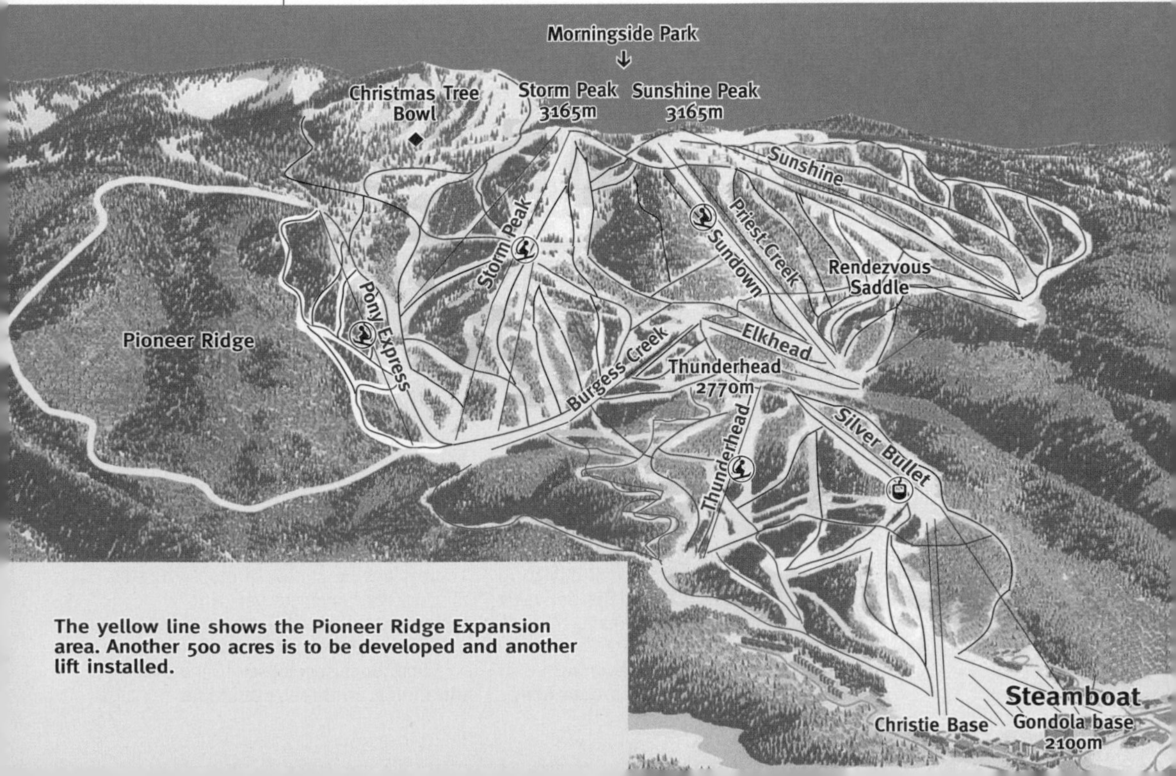

The yellow line shows the Pioneer Ridge Expansion area. Another 500 acres is to be developed and another lift installed.

SCHOOLS/GUIDES

2000/01 prices in dollars

Steamboat
Classes 5 days
2hr 30min: 11.15am-1.45pm
5 half days: 197
Children's classes
Ages: 6 to 15
5 5hr days including lunch: 325
Private lessons
1hr, 2hr, 3hr or full-day
100 for 1hr

Phone numbers
From distant parts of the US, add the prefix 1 970.
From abroad, add the prefix +1 970.

CHILDCARE

The Kids' Vacation Center is run by the resort in the lower gondola station. The Kiddie Coral nursery takes children aged 6 months to 6 years, all day. Those aged 2 can opt for the Buckaroos programme with a one-hour private lesson (ski rental not included). Older children go on to the Mavericks and Sundance Kids group classes.

The school has Rough Rider and Desperados programmes for children up to 15, with their own skiing skills area and lunchtime supervision.

The Adventure Club at Night offers evening childcare in the Vacation Center for ages 4 to 12, from 6pm to 10pm. Reservations necessary.

The Steamboat Grand has child care facilities.

are 30km of groomed tracks and lessons available. There are also Forest Service trails around Rabbit Ears Pass – many quite testing, apparently.

QUEUES
A problem in the morning
Queues can form for the gondola at the start of the day; at least they are well organised. New fast quad chairs have cut out the worst bottlenecks up the mountain, though the slow Sunshine lift serving the easiest top-of-the-mountain runs can be busy.

MOUNTAIN RESTAURANTS
Good by US standards
There are two main restaurant complexes on the mountain, both of which include excellent table-service restaurants. At Thunderhead there's a choice of the big BK Corral self-service food court, a barbecue on the sun deck, or table-service in the pub-style Stoker bar or more elegant Hazie's restaurant. At Rendezvous Saddle there's a slightly smaller alternative, which has a two-floor self-service section including a pizza bar, another sun deck and barbecue and Ragnar's table-service Scandinavian restaurant. You can book for Ragnar's and Hazie's. There's also a snack bar and sun deck at Four Points.

SCHOOLS AND GUIDES
Lots of variety
The programme includes special workshops such as powder, bumps and style clinics. Reports on the school are very positive: 'A fantastic tree skiing lesson.' There's a First Tracks option at 8am for $35 for 90 minutes – great on a powder day. The Guided Demo Center at the top of the gondola provides not only the latest skis to test but instructors to help you get the best out of them, for $10/hr.

FACILITIES FOR CHILDREN
Kids Go Free
Steamboat has a Kids Go Free scheme – free lift pass for one child of up to age 12 per parent buying a pass for at least five days. The school has a variety of courses for different standards and age groups. Recent comments include 'Louis (aged four) pleaded with us to up his half day to a full day,' and 'the camaraderie between instructors and pupils is great'. Childcare arrangements are comprehensive, including evening entertainment or excursions from 6pm.

Staying there

Our preference is to stay on the slopes and make occasional excursions to Steamboat Springs. The free shuttle-buses are very efficient.

HOW TO GO
Plenty of packages
A fair number of UK tour operators have Steamboat in their programme. There's accommodation for all tastes.
Chalets There are some catered chalets run by UK tour operators.
Hotels The smarter hotels out at the resort have less character than some of the in-town options.
(4) **Steamboat Grand** (871 5500) New 330-room resort-owned condo-hotel close to the lifts, with pool, hot-tubs and child care.
(4) **Best Western Ptarmigan Inn** (879 1730) Ideally situated just above the gondola station and right on the piste, with an outdoor pool and hot-tub, a sauna and good après-ski bar.
(4) **Sheraton** (879 2220) Big, comfortable but impersonal hotel near the gondola, with a pool and hot-tub.
(3) **Harbor** (879 1522) The oldest hotel in the old town. Rooms vary in size and style; sauna, steam room and two hot-tubs.
(2) **Bristol** (879 3083) Traditional little hotel on main street of old town, with 'small but fairly priced' rooms.
(2) **Alpiner Lodge** (879 1430) Bavarian style economy in old town.
(2) **Rabbit Ears Motel** (879 1150) Recommended by reporter: 'Excellent. Family run, comfortable rooms.'
Self-catering There are countless apartment developments, many with good pool/tub facilities and shuttle-buses. Recommendations include Bear Claw condos at the top of the nursery slope; Timber Run, a short shuttle-ride from the centre with multiple hot-tubs; The Lodge at Steamboat, close to the gondola station; Thunderhead Lodge & Condominiums; and the aptly named Ski Inn. Storm Meadows condos at Christie Base are 'wonderful'.

EATING OUT
Huge variety
There's a wide choice of places to suit all pockets – over 70 bars and restaurants. Pick up a dining guide booklet to check out menus.

Steamboat specialises in mountain-top dining, in three restaurants

GETTING THERE

Air Yampa Valley regional airport, transfer ¾hr. Denver, transfer 3½hr.

ACTIVITIES

Indoor Ice skating, hot-tubbing, swimming pools, tennis, gym, weights room, climbing wall, museum
Outdoor Ice driving school, dog-sledding, snowmobiling, ballooning, hot springs, dinner sleigh rides, horse-riding, skating, ice and rock climbing, fly-fishing, snowcat skiing, snow-shoeing, cross-country skiing, tubing

TOURIST OFFICE

Postcode CO 80487
t +1 (970) 879 6111
f 879 7844
steamboat-info@steamboat-ski.com
www.steamboat-ski.com

accessed via the gondola to Thunderhead. Five nights a week the Western BBQ does an all-you-can-eat buffet, with country and western music and dancing. Or you can have a gourmet treat at Hazie's, where the menu goes somewhat upmarket from lunchtime. Three nights a week you can take a sleigh hauled by a snowcat to Ragnar's at Rendezvous Saddle for a Scandinavian meal with live music.

In the resort, the Slopeside Grill has a good selection of pizza and pasta dishes and doubles as a bar, with live music some nights. The plush Steamboat Grand has two options: Chaps, a popular cowboy-style bar and grill and The Cabin, which 'does seriously good food'.

In downtown Steamboat Springs try L'Apogee for fine French-style food, or the cheaper Harwig's Grill on the same premises. The Steamboat Yacht Club on the river bank is recommended for seafood and views of ski-jumping. Antares is deservedly popular for its excellent international cuisine. The Steamboat Brewery has a wide-ranging menu as well as its own beers. For more traditional American fare try the popular Old West Steakhouse – 'very charming, reasonably priced, great food' – or the Ore House at the Pine Grove. Cantina is recommended for Tex-Mex and Cugino's for Italian. The Cottonwood Grill offers 'superb' Pacific Rim Cuisine. For a real budget buy, head for the barbecue food at the Double Z, popular with locals.

APRES-SKI
Fairly lively

Restaurants apart, the old town is quiet in the evening. The Old Town Pub has live music at weekends. The Tap House is 'a must for Brits missing their soccer', with 30 TVs as well as the best draft beer choice in town.

The base lodge area is livelier. Popular places at close of play are the Slopeside Grill and the Inferno, in the gondola square, both with live music and a happy hour. The mountain hosts regularly serve up free hot apple cider and hot chocolate at the base of the gondola in the afternoons. The Inferno is the place for dancing to loud live music – and on Sundays it has a very popular 'Disco Inferno' night. Dos Amigos and the Tugboat Tavern are popular bars for drinks by the pitcher. The Ptarmigan Inn offers a rather more sophisticated atmosphere. While The Stoker Comedy Club up at Thunderhead has live stand-up comedy from 7 until 10pm.

Evening activities include watching floodlit ski-jumping in the old town and tubing on the floodlit nursery slope at the main ski area.

OFF THE SLOPES
Lots to do

Getting up to Thunderhead restaurant complex is easy for pedestrians. Visiting town is, too. And you can go and relax in outdoor Strawberry Park Hot Springs six miles from town. The snowmobiling terrain around Rabbit Ears Pass looks great to our untutored eye. The ice rink is Olympic size.

STEAMBOAT / LARRY PIERCE

Steamboat has great skiing among the trees as well as on the open pistes →

Telluride 2660m

Cute old town, massive expansion of slopes for 2001/02

WHAT IT COSTS

6

HOW IT RATES

The slopes

Snow	****
Extent	**
Experts	****
Intermediates	***
Beginners	*****
Convenience	****
Queues	*****
Restaurants	*

The rest

Scenery	****
Resort charm	****
Off-slope	**

What's new

For 2001/02 three new high-speed chair-lifts (Prospect Bowl, Gold Hill and Ute Park) will give access to an additional 733 acres of terrain in Prospect Bowl – this is a 70% increase and includes 20 new runs.

Two further lifts are planned for 2002/03.

A new mountain restaurant with a Ute Indian theme (teepees etc) is planned for 2001/02.

Telluride ski area was sold in March 2001 and the new owner is Hideo 'Joe' Morita (son of Sony founder Akio Morita).

- ⊕ Charming restored Victorian silver-mining town with a real Wild West atmosphere
- ⊕ Skiing for all standards, including long, serious mogul slopes
- ⊕ Dramatic, craggy mountain scenery – unusual for Colorado
- ⊖ Isolated location
- ⊖ Remains to be seen whether the new terrain merits a week's stay
- ⊖ Mountain Village a bit of an eyesore
- ⊖ Limited mountain restaurants (but another planned)

We have always loved the old town of Telluride – it has lots of character, lovely old buildings, good restaurants and shops and dramatic views of the San Juan mountains. Our only criticism has been the limited extent of the lift-served slopes. But all that will change for 2001/02, with a 70% expansion of the slopes and new intermediate and advanced runs. We can't wait to go and try them!.

THE RESORT

Telluride is an isolated resort in south-west Colorado. The town first boomed when gold was found – some say its name is a shortened version of 'To hell you ride', but in fact it's more probably due to the presence of tellurium in the rock. The old wooden buildings and sidewalks have been well-restored and it has more Wild West charm than any other US resort. The shops and restaurants have gone decidedly up-market since its 'hippy' days of a few years ago. But it is still small-scale and friendly. Up on the slopes, Mountain Village is a model American leisure resort with modern buildings. A free gondola (running in the evenings as well as in the day) links the two.

THE MOUNTAINS

There is some fearsomely steep terrain, and also ideal beginner and intermediate areas.

Slopes Chair-lifts and a gondola serve the steep wooded slopes directly above the town, and give access to the bowl beyond which leads down to Mountain Village. This has steep slopes at the top from the Giuseppe's area, intermediate terrain in the middle and ideal, gentle beginner slopes beyond the village down to Big Billie's and the long runs served by the Sunshine Express lift. The new terrain for 2001/02 will be great steep runs on Gold Hill (previously accessed by a 20-minute hike) and intermediate and advanced terrain in Prospect Bowl.

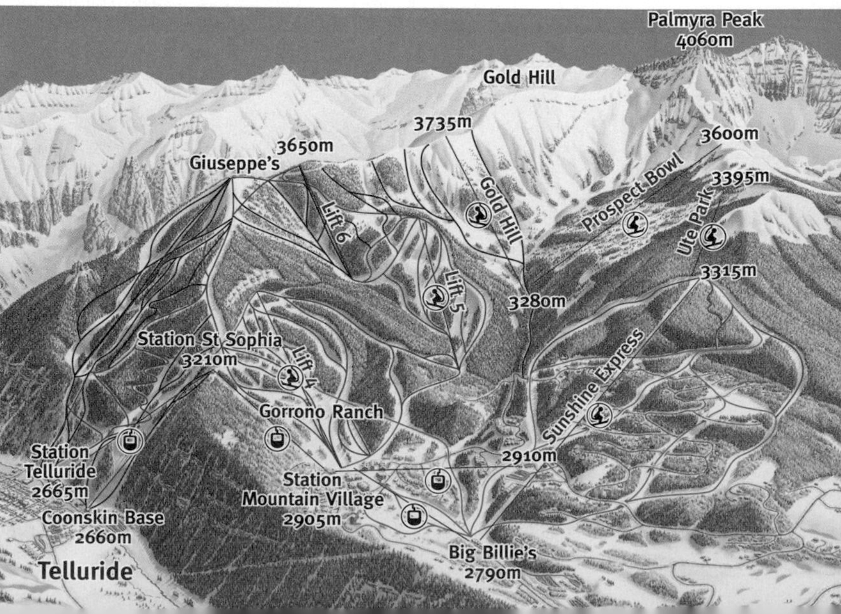

↑ Runs down the front lead right back into the cute old town of Telluride

TELLURIDE SKI & GOLF CO / GUS GUSCIORA

MOUNTAIN FACTS

Altitude	2660m-3625m
Lifts	16
Pistes	1700 acres
Green	22%
Blue	38%
Black	40%
Art. snow	204 acres

Recco detectors used

Central reservations phone number
For all resort accommodation ring 728 7507 (from distant parts of the US, add the prefix 1 970; from abroad, add the prefix +1 970)

Toll-free number (from within the US) 1 888 827 8050.

TOURIST OFFICE

Postcode CO 81435
t +1 (970) 728 3041
f 728 6475
skitelluride@telski.com
www.telski.com

Snowboarding The Surge Air Garden Terrain Park, located next to Gorrono Ranch, is the largest terrain park in the southwest. Its 13 acres include 23 hits, a 'rail garden' and a 12ft half-pipe.
Snow reliability With a high average snowfall and lots of well-placed snowmaking, snow reliability is good.
Experts The double-black bump runs directly above the town are what has given the area its expert reputation and there are steep gladed runs from all along the ridge between Giuseppe's and Gold Hill – no longer a hike away. You can also go heli- and snowcat skiing or boarding.
Intermediates There are ideal blue cruising runs with awesome views right from the top down to Mountain Village (including the aptly-named See Forever). But keen piste-bashers could get bored with their limited extent after a couple of days. The new terrain in the Prospect Bowl area should mean more to keep you interested. The main easy way back down the front to town is the winding Telluride Trail.
Beginners There are ideal runs in the Meadows below Mountain Village, and splendid long greens and blues served by the Sunshine Express chair.
Cross-country The scenic beauty of the area makes it splendid for cross-country – the Telluride Nordic Centre runs over 40km of trails.
Queues These are rarely a problem – there are no weekend crowds, and the lift system is increasingly impressive.
Mountain restaurants Gorrono Ranch is the main on-mountain restaurant, with a big terrace, live music and a BBQ. Another at the top of the Sunshine Express lift with a Ute Indian Village theme (teepees etc) will open for 2001/02.
Schools and guides As well as the usual, the ski school offers day-long outback adventures by snowcat and a biomechanical private lesson where your equipment is adjusted to suit you.
Facilities for children The Adventure Club provides indoor and outdoor play before and after lessons.

STAYING THERE

Thanks to the gondola link between the town and Mountain Village, it doesn't much matter where you stay.
How to go The resort is offered by only a few US specialist operators.
Hotels The 4-star Hotel Telluride, in the old town, promises to be the most luxurious in the resort. The New Sheridan is one of the town's oldest hotels. Skyline Guest Ranch is a lovely old ranch-house with excellent food, a few minutes' drive from Mountain Village. The big Peaks hotel in the Mountain Village is a bit anonymous but has good spa facilities.
Self-catering There are also plenty of self-catering condos and houses.
Eating out There is a cosmopolitan choice of restaurants, from Sushi to French to Tex-Mex. Harmon's (in the old station) is one of the best. Allred's at the top of the gondola is a private club for lunch but offers gourmet dining in the evenings.
Après-ski There's a lively bar-based après-ski scene. Leimgruber's is popular in the early evening, but closes early. The New Sheridan has a lovely old bar. The Swede Finn and the Last Dollar have been recommended by locals. The Fly Me to the Moon Saloon has live music and stays open late.
Off the slopes There's quite a lot to do around town if you are not skiing or boarding, such as dog sledding, horse riding, ice skating and glider rides.

Vail 2500m

Luxury living and the US's biggest and ever-improving area

WHAT IT COSTS

6

HOW IT RATES

The slopes

Snow	*****
Extent	****
Experts	****
Intermediates	*****
Beginners	*****
Convenience	***
Queues	**
Restaurants	**

The rest

Scenery	***
Resort charm	***
Off-slope	***

What's new

The 2000/01 season saw another high-speed quad and another 125 acres of terrain open in Blue Sky Basin.

The snowmaking network has been upgraded.

Several prime hotels have been renovated. The Vail Village Inn and Chateau Vail will remain closed for the 2001/02 season.

- ⊕ Biggest area in the US – great for confident intermediates
- ⊕ The Back Bowls are big areas of treeless terrain – unusual in the US
- ⊕ Fabulous new area of ungroomed, wooded slopes recently opened at Blue Sky Basin
- ⊕ Largely traffic-free resort village, with great bus service

- ⊖ Slopes can be crowded by American standards, with some lift queues even in low season
- ⊖ The famous Back Bowls may be closed in early season – and can suffer from the sun
- ⊖ Inadequate mountain restaurants
- ⊖ Tirolean-style Vail Village doesn't impress Europeans
- ⊖ Expensive

Blue Sky Basin, Vail's new area of shady, wooded, largely ungroomed slopes, has transformed Vail's attraction for good skiers and riders. Not only does it bring a much-needed bit of spice to the resort, but it gets you away from the crowds that are Vail's most serious drawback.

Vail's slopes are now undeniably compelling, especially when you take account of nearby sister-resort Beaver Creek (now given a separate chapter). What continues to push Vail down our American shortlist is its style and atmosphere – a curious mixture of pseudo-Tirol and anonymous suburbs. The resort works well, largely thanks to the efficient buses. But if you hope to be captivated, Vail can't compete with the distinctive Rockies resorts based on old mining towns or cowboy towns. If we're going that far West, we like it to be a bit Wild.

The resort

Standing in the centre of Vail Village, surrounded by chalets and bierkellers, you could be forgiven for thinking you were in the Tirol – which is what Vail's founder, Pete Seibert, intended back in the 1950s. But Vail Village is now just part of an enormous resort, mostly built in anonymous modern style, stretching for miles beside the I-70 freeway – the main route westwards through the Rockies from Denver.

The vast village benefits from a free and efficient bus service, which makes choice of location less than crucial. But there's no denying that the most convenient – and expensive – places to stay are in mock-Tirolean Vail Village, near the Vista Bahn fast chair, or in functional Lionshead, near the gondola. There is a lot of accommodation further out – the cheapest tends to be across the I-70.

Beaver Creek, ten miles away, is covered by the lift pass and is easily reached by bus (see separate chapter). Other resorts within a two-hour drive include Breckenridge and Keystone (both owned by Vail Resorts and covered by the lift pass), Aspen, Steamboat and Copper Mountain.

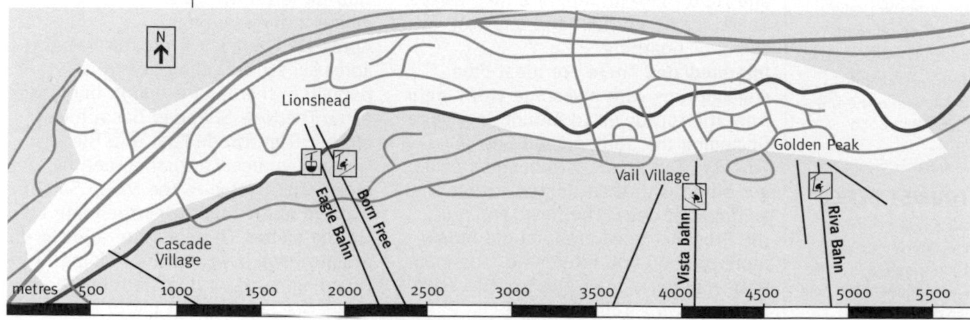

It doesn't look much, but Blue Sky Basin has lots to offer the expert and the adventurous intermediate ➔

VAIL RESORTS, INC / JACK AFFLECK

MOUNTAIN FACTS

Altitude	2475m-3525m
Lifts	33
Pistes	5289 acres
Green	18%
Blue	29%
Black	53%
Art. snow	380 acres
Recco detectors used	

The mountains

Vail has the biggest area of slopes in the US, with immaculately groomed trails and ungroomed powder skiing in open bowls and among the trees. There are runs to suit every taste. The main criticism is that some of the runs (especially blacks) are overgraded.

THE SLOPES

Something for everyone

The slopes above **Vail** can be accessed via three main lifts. From right next to Vail Village, the Vista Bahn fast chair goes up to the major mid-mountain focal point, Mid-Vail; from Lionshead, the Eagle Bahn gondola goes up to the Eagle's Nest complex; and from the Golden Peak base area just to the east of Vail Village, the Riva Bahn fast chair goes up towards the Two Elk area.

The front face of the mountain is largely north-facing, with well-groomed trails cut through the trees. At altitude the mountainside divides into three bowls – Mid-Vail in the centre, with Game Creek to the south-west and Northeast Bowl to the, er, north-east. Lifts reach the ridge at three points, all giving access to the **Back Bowls** (mostly ungroomed and treeless) and through them to the new **Blue Sky Basin** area (mostly ungroomed and wooded or gladed).

The slopes are patrolled by yellow-jacketed 'speed patrollers' who stop slope users skiing or riding recklessly quickly. There's a 'new technology center' at mid-mountain where you can test the latest equipment. British guests may get the opportunity to ski the area with Martin Bell, Britain's best-ever downhiller.

SNOW RELIABILITY

Excellent, except in the Bowls

As well as an exceptional natural snow record, Vail and Beaver Creek both have extensive snowmaking facilities, normally needed only in early season. Although snow in the Back Bowls is often poor because of its largely south-facing aspect, Blue Sky Basin is largely north-facing and sheltered from sun by trees – so the snow quality can be expected to be excellent, with powder lasting for days after the latest fall.

FOR EXPERTS

Transformed by Blue Sky Basin

Vail's Back Bowls are vast areas, served by three chair-lifts and a couple of short drag-lifts. You can go virtually anywhere you like in the half-dozen identifiable bowls, trying the gradient and terrain of your choice. There are interesting lightly wooded areas as well as the open slopes that dominate the area. The Bowls are practically all graded black but are not particularly steep, and they have disappointed some of our more confident reporters.

Blue Sky Basin has some great adventure runs in the trees – see feature panel.

On the front face there are some genuinely steep double-black-diamond runs which usually have great snow; they are often mogulled but sometimes groomed to make wonderful fast cruising. The Highline lift on the extreme east of the area serves three. And Prima Cornice, served by the Northwoods Express, is one of the steepest runs on the front side.

If the snow is good, try the backcountry Minturn Mile – you leave the ski area through a gate in the

Two Elk Lodge
3420m
Summit
3430m
Wildwood
3435m
Game Creek Bowl
Northeast Bowl
Northwoods
Mountaintop
Wildwood
Game Creek
Highline
Mid-Vail
3095m
Avanti
Eagle's Nest
3155m
Riva Bahn
Vista Bahn
Pride
Born Free
Eagle Bahn
Golden Peak
Vail Village
2500m
Cascade
Village
Lionshead
2475m

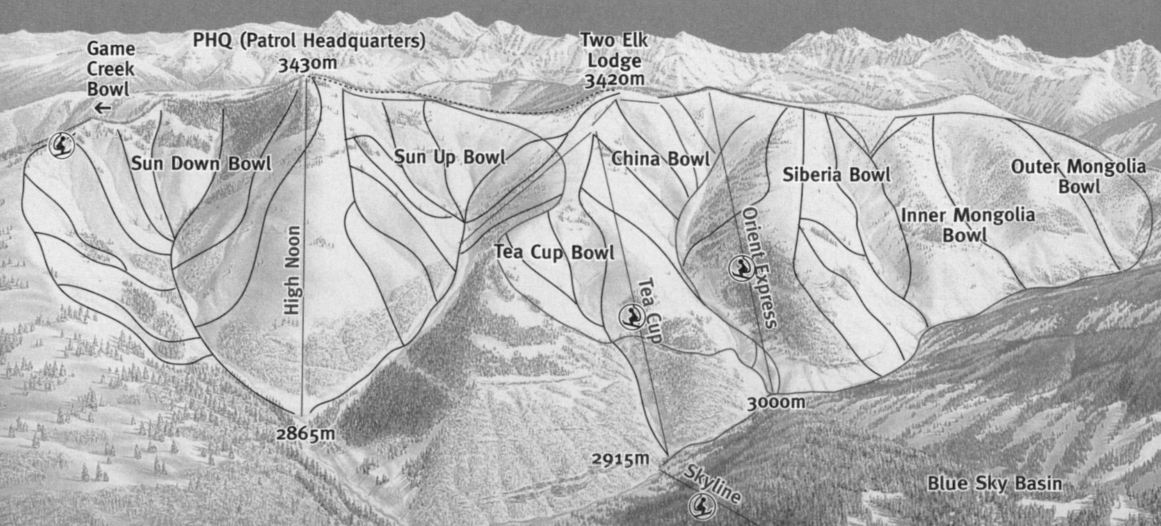
Game
Creek
Bowl
←
PHQ (Patrol Headquarters)
3430m
Two Elk
Lodge
3420m
Sun Down Bowl
Sun Up Bowl
China Bowl
Siberia Bowl
Outer Mongolia
Bowl
Inner Mongolia
Bowl
Tea Cup Bowl
High Noon
Orient Express
Tea Cup
3000m
2865m
2915m
Skyline
Blue Sky Basin

A sense of adventure combined with safety is what Blue Sky Basin provides →

VAIL RESORTS, INC / JACK AFFLECK

LIFT PASSES

2000/01 prices in dollars

Vail and Beaver Creek
Covers all Vail and Beaver Creek lifts, and ski-bus around resort. Multi-day passes also cover Breckenridge, Keystone and Arapahoe Basin.

Main pass
1-day pass 57
6-day pass 342

Senior citizens
Over 65: 6-day pass 330
Over 70: season pass 99

Children
Under 13: 1-day pass 21
Under 5: free pass

Short-term passes
Half-day pass from noon available.

Notes
Discounts may be available if you buy a lift pass in advance through certain UK tour operators. Return trips available on some lifts for foot passengers only. A 10-day pass, entitles you to an extra 4 days free. Full-day lesson and lift pass 109.

Blue Sky Basin

This is the biggest new development in any Colorado ski area for years – and the prospect of it caused outrage among environmental groups; protesters burned down the Two Elk mountain restaurant, the ski patrol HQ and some lift stations in protest. The first 520 acres of it, served by two high-speed quads, opened in January 2000. Last season saw the addition of Pete's Express (named after Vail's founder Pete Seibert), another fast quad, accessing a further 125 acres of gentler terrain – making up 645 acres in total, 80% of the entire 885-acre project.

We skied the Basin two months after opening and loved it. The area is almost entirely ungroomed and the runs are among the trees – some widely spaced, some very tight. Few of the runs are very steep, but because you are basically finding your own way much of the time, there is a great feeling of adventure. The snow will generally be much better than in the Back Bowls because of the shelter given by the trees and the generally north-facing aspect. We had hoped the slightly adventurous nature of the area would mean that the Vail crowds would stay away, but reports suggest that we were wrong.

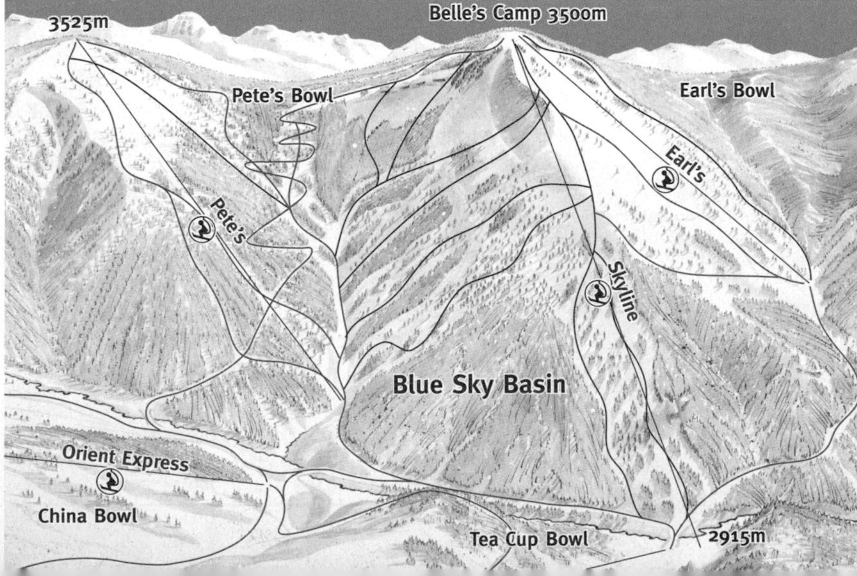

SCHOOLS/GUIDES

2000/01 prices in dollars

Classes 7 days
Full day: 5hr 45 min: 9.45-3.30 with lunch break
Half day: 3hr: am or pm
1 full day: 82

Children's classes
Ages: 3 to 14
Full day: 5hr 45 min including lift pass, lunch
1 full-day: 93

Private lessons
1hr, 2hr, half and full day
1hr: 120, for 1 to 6 people
Half day: 335, for 1 to 6 people

CHILDCARE

School tuition is based at Children's Ski Centers located at Golden Peak and Lionshead. There are separate programmes to suit children of different ages and competence – Mini-Mice for children aged three, Mogul Mice and Superstars for those aged four to six.

Small World Play School, located at Golden Peak, provides day care for children aged two months to six years, from 8am to 4.30.

boarding *Vail has been wooing boarders with excellent facilities and a positive attitude for years. With beautifully groomed, gentle slopes and lots of high-speed chairs, this is a great area for beginners, and there's plenty for experts too including some wonderful gladed runs and an excellent fun-park and super-pipe on Golden Peak. There are specialist board shops and good tuition and a Burton test centre at the top of Vail mountain. The lively bars and nightlife are another draw.*

Game Creek area for a European-style off-piste run starting with a powder bowl and finishing on a path by a river – ending up in the atmospheric Saloon (see Après-ski).

FOR INTERMEDIATES
Ideal territory

The majority of Vail's front face is great intermediate territory, with easy cruising runs. On the western side of the area, especially, there are excellent long, relatively quiet blues – Born Free and Simba both go from top to bottom. Game Creek Bowl, nearby, is excellent, too.

As well as tackling some of the easier front-face blacks, intermediates will find plenty of interest in the Back Bowls. Some runs are groomed. Several of the runs are graded blue, including Silk Road, which loops around the eastern edge of the domain, with wonderful views. Some of the unpisted slopes make the ideal introduction to powder. Confident intermediates will also enjoy Blue Sky Basin – choose the clearly marked blue runs to start with.

FOR BEGINNERS
Difficult to beat

There are excellent nursery slopes at resort level and at altitude. And there are plenty of easy longer runs to progress to – not only winding catwalk runs but also proper green runs that go from top to bottom.

FOR CROSS-COUNTRY
Some of the best

Vail's cross-country areas are at the foot of Golden Peak and at the Nordic Center on the golf course.

QUEUES
Can be bad

Vail has some of the longest lift queues we've hit in the US, especially at weekends because of the influx from Denver. Most queues move quickly. But at Mid-Vail waits of 15 minutes are common and we have reports of 45-minute waits.

MOUNTAIN RESTAURANTS
Surprisingly poor

As other major American resorts are gradually improving their mountain restaurants, Vail's are slipping further behind: demand is increasing to the point where the major self-service restaurants can be unpleasantly crowded from 11am to 2pm. There's table-service (with limited menu) at Eagle's Nest – book ahead.

SCHOOLS AND GUIDES
Among the best in the world

The Vail-Beaver Creek school has an excellent reputation. All the reports we've had of it have again been glowing. Class sizes are usually small – as few as four is not uncommon. Having tried three different instructors, we can vouch for the high standard. There are specialist half-day workshops in, for example, bumps and powder and adventure tours of Blue Sky Basin. You can sign up on the mountain.

FACILITIES FOR CHILDREN
Excellent

The comprehensive arrangements for young children look excellent, and we've had good reports on the children's school. There are splendid children's areas with adventure trails and themed play areas.

Central reservations phone number
For all resort accommodation call 1 800 270 4870 (toll-free from within the US).

GETTING THERE

Air Eagle, transfer 1hr. Denver, transfer 2½hr.

ACTIVITIES

Indoor Athletic clubs and spas, massage, museum, cinema, theatre, tennis courts, artificial skating rink, library, galleries
Outdoor Hot-air ballooning, skating, ice hockey, sleigh rides, fishing, mountaineering, snowmobiles, snow-shoe excursions, snowcat tours, dog-sledding, paragliding, tubing hill, ski biking, thrill sledding, laser tag

TOURIST OFFICE

PO Box 7, Vail, CO 81658
t +1 (970) 496 9090
international@vailresorts.com
www.vail.com

Staying there 

HOW TO GO
Package or independent

There's a big choice of packages to Vail. It's easy to organise your own visit, with regular airport shuttles.
Chalets Vail offers the widest choice of catered chalets in the US, via a range of UK tour operators. Many chalets are out of the centre at East Vail or West Vail or across the busy freeway.
Hotels Vail has a fair choice of hotels, ranging from luxurious to budget. The Vail Village Inn and Chateau Vail are currently closed for renovation.
((((5) **Vail Cascade** One of the best in town. A resort within a resort – lots of facilities and a chair-lift right outside.
((((5) **Sonnenalp Bavaria Haus** Very smart and central. Large spa and splendid piano bar-lounge.
((((5) **Lodge at Vail** Owned by Vail Resorts, right by the Vista Bahn in Vail Village. Some standard rooms small. Huge buffet breakfast. Outdoor pool.
Self-catering For those who want lots of in-house amenities, the Racquet Club at East Vail is superb. The Mountain Haus has high-quality condos in the centre of town. There are plenty of cheaper options, and several tour operators have allocations conveniently close to the Lionshead gondola.

STAYING UP THE MOUNTAIN
Great if you can afford it

Game Creek chalet above Vail (like Trappers Cabin at Beaver Creek) is a luxurious private enclave up the mountain, which a group can rent by the night (for a small fortune). You ski in at the end of the day to a champagne welcome, soak in an outdoor hot-tub and enjoy a gourmet dinner. The cabin-keeper then leaves, returning in the morning to prepare breakfast.

STAYING ALONG THE VALLEY
Cheaper but quiet

Staying out of central Vail is certainly cheaper but not so lively. If you rent a car, staying out of town and visiting nearby resorts makes for an interesting holiday. East Vail and West Vail both have reasonably priced lodging.

EATING OUT
Endless choice

Whatever kind of food you want, Vail has it – but most of it is not cheap. 'All restaurants require a fat wallet' and 'high standards but at New York prices' are typical comments from reporters. Booking in advance is essential.

Recommended fine-dining options include the Wildflower, in the Lodge, Ludwig's, in the Sonnenalp Bavaria Haus, and La Tour.

For a budget option we liked the Hubcap Brewery in Vail Village, with local ales and filling American food.

Recommendations from readers include May Palace (Chinese) in West Vail, Blu's (good value), Montauk (seafood) at Lionshead, the Bistro at the Racquet Club, Los Amigos, Russell's, La Bottega and Vendetta's.

APRES-SKI
Fairly lively

Gravity at Lionshead is convenient for the end of the day and has live music. Garfinkel's has a DJ and happy hour. The Red Lion in the village centre is popular, with big-screen TVs and huge portions of food. The George tries to be an English-style pub. The Ore House serves 'mean margaritas and very hot chicken wings'.

The Swiss Chalet attempts to recreate European 'gemütlichkeit'; King's Club is the place to go for high-calorie cakes, and becomes a piano bar later; and Los Amigos and the Hubcap Brewery are other lively places at four o'clock.

You can have a good night out at Adventure Ridge at the top of the Eagle Bahn gondola. As well as bars and restaurants, there's ice skating, tubing, snowmobiling, snow-shoeing and snowbiking – though a reporter reckons the tubing hill is boring and badly run compared with Keystone's.

Later on, Club Chelsea is a popular disco. 8150 is also good, with a suspended floor that moves with the dancing; the Bully Ranch at the Sonnenalp is famous for its 'mudslide' drinks; Nick's is a snowboard hangout; Vendetta's does good pizza and beer.

Out of town in Minturn, the Saloon is worth a trip – genuine old-west style with photos of famous skier patrons on the wall.

OFF THE SLOPES
A lot to do

Getting around on the free bus is easy, and there are lots of activities to try. Balloon rides are popular. The factory outlets at Silverthorne are a must for shopaholics who can't resist a bargain.

Winter Park 2745m

Good value, great terrain, huge snowfalls, unpretentious town

WHAT IT COSTS

5

HOW IT RATES

The slopes

Snow	*****
Extent	***
Experts	****
Intermediates	****
Beginners	*****
Convenience	***
Queues	****
Restaurants	***

The rest

Scenery	***
Resort charm	**
Off-slope	*

- ⊕ The best snowfall record of all Colorado's major resorts
- ⊕ Slopes to suit all standards, from superb beginner terrain to countless testing mogul slopes
- ⊕ Great expert terrain and great untracked snow at Berthoud Pass
- ⊕ Quiet on weekdays, and impressive lift system copes with weekends
- ⊕ Leading resort for teaching people with disabilities to ski and ride
- ⊕ Good views by US standards
- ⊕ Largely free of the inflated prices and glitz you expect in a resort

- ⊖ Also largely free of the the range of restaurants and shops you expect in a big international resort
- ⊖ Town is a bus-ride away from the slopes – though there is now the option of staying in the new development at the main lift base
- ⊖ The nearest big resort to Denver, so can get crowded at weekends – mainly a problem on runs close to the base, and in hire shops

What's new

The first phase of Winter Park's new slope-side village is now complete. The Zephyr Mountain Lodge condos at the base of the slopes have Slopeside and Riverside buildings, with lodging, shopping and dining.

Land has been purchased to build a gondola from the town to the slopes, but it's still in the planning stages and won't be ready for a few years yet.

Winter Park was developed to amuse the residents of Denver, only a 90-minute drive away, and still belongs to the city. So we were slightly surprised by what we found when we first visited a few years ago: a mountain (if not a resort) of world class. If variety of shops and restaurants is not important to you, and value for money and snow are more important than glamour, the place should be high up on your Colorado shortlist. Especially now that the the first stage of a new pedestrian village at the foot of the slopes is complete.

For good skiers and riders, Winter Park's secret weapon is actually another 'resort' a few miles away – Berthoud Pass. It has no lodgings and only two chair-lifts, but they serve large amounts of wild terrain, the snow approaches Utah's exalted standards and is mostly untracked. It's unreal.

The resort

Winter Park started life around the turn of the century as a railway town, when Rio Grande railway workers climbed the slopes to ski down. One of the resort's mountains, Mary Jane, is named after a legendary 'lady of pleasure' who is said to have received the land as payment for her favours.

The railway still plays an important part in Winter Park's existence, with a station right at the foot of the slopes where trains deposit day trippers from Denver every Saturday and Sunday.

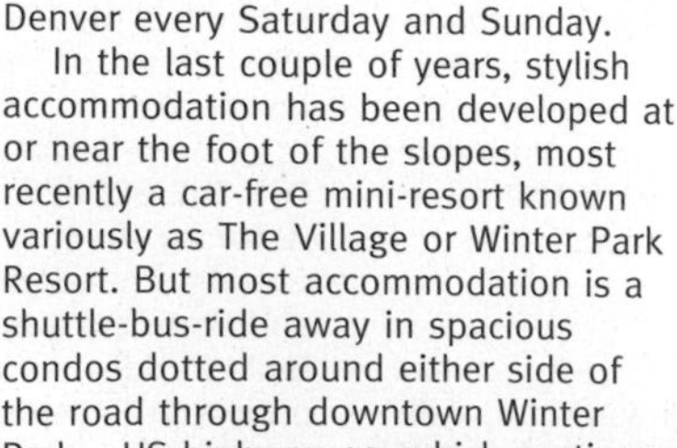

In the last couple of years, stylish accommodation has been developed at or near the foot of the slopes, most recently a car-free mini-resort known variously as The Village or Winter Park Resort. But most accommodation is a shuttle-bus-ride away in spacious condos dotted around either side of the road through downtown Winter Park – US highway 40, which continues

WINTER PARK RESORT

Winter Park's new Zephyr Mountain Lodge condos are pretty convenient for the slopes! →

boarding *The great boarder facilities on Winter Park Mountain make it a favourite with many riders. The half-pipe, just above Snoasis, is great for both experts and novices. The Big Air Park and The Rolls fun-parks have enough jumps, ramps, winding gullies and tabletops to satisfy any big-air thrill seeker. Special 'Terrain Park Ambassadors' are often available to demonstrate tricks. There is some great advanced and extreme boarding terrain. Winter Park is also an ideal beginner and intermediate boarder area, with excellent terrain for first steps on a board, a good school and a network of lifts that is entirely chairs. Though there's no longer a ride guide to the mountain, signposts indicate the most boarder-friendly routes to take. The bars get crowded and lively at weekends – and boarders tend to hang out at Slade's Underground downtown.*

MOUNTAIN FACTS

Altitude	2740m-3675m
Lifts	22
Pistes	2886 acres
Green	9%
Blue	34%
Black	57%
Art. snow	294 acres

LIFT PASSES

2001/02 prices in US dollars

Winter Park Resort
Covers all lifts in Winter Park.

Main pass
1-day pass 55
6-day pass 252
(low season 210)

Senior citizens
Over 61: 6-day pass 180
Over 70: free pass

Children
Under 14: 6-day pass 90
Under 6: free pass

Short-term passes
Half-day passes
up to 12.45: 25
from 12.00 35

Alternative periods
Passes of 2 days and over allow one non-skiing day, eg 6-day pass valid for 7 days with one day off. 8- and 9- day passes allow 2 non-skiing days.

Notes Special rates for disabled skiers. Reduction for all skiing before Dec 3 and after April 2.

to the nearby town of Fraser. There are also motels, bars and restaurants along the road, and at night Winter Park resembles an established ski resort town – but in the daytime it's clear that the place doesn't amount to much. Reporters complain there's no real 'town centre'. Confusingly, an area between the mountain and the town is known as Old Town.

Shuttle-buses run regularly between the town and the lift base, and the hotels and condos also provide shuttle services. But a car does simplify day trips to Denver or to other resorts – within a two-hour drive are Steamboat, Breckenridge, Copper Mountain, Keystone and Vail, and experts should not miss Berthoud Pass (see later in this chapter).

The locals are very friendly and helpful – typical small-town America.

The mountains

Winter Park has a mountain that's big by US standards, and an excellent mix of terrain that suits all standards. 'I would recommend it to anyone visiting Colorado for the first time,' says a reporter; we're inclined to agree, so long as you don't want a swish village.

THE SLOPES
Interestingly divided

There are five very distinct, but well-linked, areas. From the main base, a high-speed quad takes you up the original **Winter Park** mountain to the Sunspot restaurant area at 3260m. From there, you can descend in all directions. Runs lead back towards the main base and over to the **Vasquez Ridge** area on the far right. This is served by a high-speed quad which allows you to use that area continuously or get back to the Winter Park mountain. Both areas are mainly beginner and intermediate terrain.

From the top of Winter Park mountain you can get to **Mary Jane** mountain, which has much tougher runs. Mary Jane is served by six lifts, including four from its own separate base area. From the top you can head up to **Parsenn Bowl** via the slow double Timberline chair, which has intermediate terrain above and in the trees. From here, conditions permitting, you can now get a tow by snowmobile (the 'Ridge Ride') for $5 (or hike for up to half an hour) to access the advanced and extreme slopes of **Vasquez Cirque**. A long ski-out takes you to the bottom of Vasquez Ridge and the Pioneer lift.

SNOW RELIABILITY
Among Colorado's best

'Copious amounts of beautiful, dry powder,' enthuses a reporter. Winter Park's position, close to the watershed of the Continental Divide, gives it an average yearly snowfall of over 350in – the highest of any major Colorado resort. As a back-up, artificial snowmaking covers a high proportion of the runs on Winter Park mountain.

FOR EXPERTS
Some hair-raising challenges

Mary Jane has some of the steepest mogul fields, chutes and hair-raising challenges in the US. The fearsome runs of Mary Jane's back side are accessed by a control gate off a long black run called Derailer. Hole in the Wall, Awe Chute, Baldy's Chute and Jeff's Chute are all steep, narrow and bordered by rocks. More manageable are the wider black mogul fields such as Derailer, Long Haul and Brakeman. There are good blue/black runs on Mary Jane's front side and some good challenges on Winter Park Mountain.

National Sports Center for the Disabled

If you are able-bodied, the most striking and humbling thing you'll notice as you ride your first chair-lift is the number of people with disabilities hurtling down the mountain faster than many of us could ever hope to. There are blind skiers, skiers with one leg, no legs, paralysis – whatever their problem, they've cracked it.

That's because Winter Park is home to the US National Sports Center for the Disabled (NSCD) – the world's leading centre for teaching skiing and snowboarding to people with disabilities. As well as full-time instructors, there are 1,000 trained volunteers who help in the programme. People are placed with instructors trained to teach people with their particular disability – more than 40 disabilities are specially catered for.

If you are disabled and want to learn to ski or snowboard, there's no better place to go. It's important to book ahead so that a suitable instructor is available. The NSCD can help with travel and accommodation arrangements:

NSCD, PO Box 36, Winter Park, CO 80482, USA. Tel: 726 1540.

Phone numbers
From distant parts of the US, add the prefix 1 970.
From abroad, add the prefix +1 970.

When it's open, Vasquez Cirque has excellent ungroomed expert terrain with extensive views. To get to the best of it you no longer have to earn your turns with a 20- to 30-minute hike around the cirque: if you part with $5, you can get a pull from a snowmobile. You don't get much vertical before you hit the forest, though. One way to explore the area is on the Improvement Center's three-hour Cirque Adventure Tour.

FOR INTERMEDIATES

Choose your challenge

From pretty much wherever you are on Winter Park mountain and Vasquez Ridge you can choose a run to suit your ability. Most are well groomed every night giving you perfect early morning cruising on the famous Colorado 'corduroy' pistes.

For bumps try Mary Jane's front side, where 'the blue/blacks are particularly enjoyable'. Parsenn Bowl

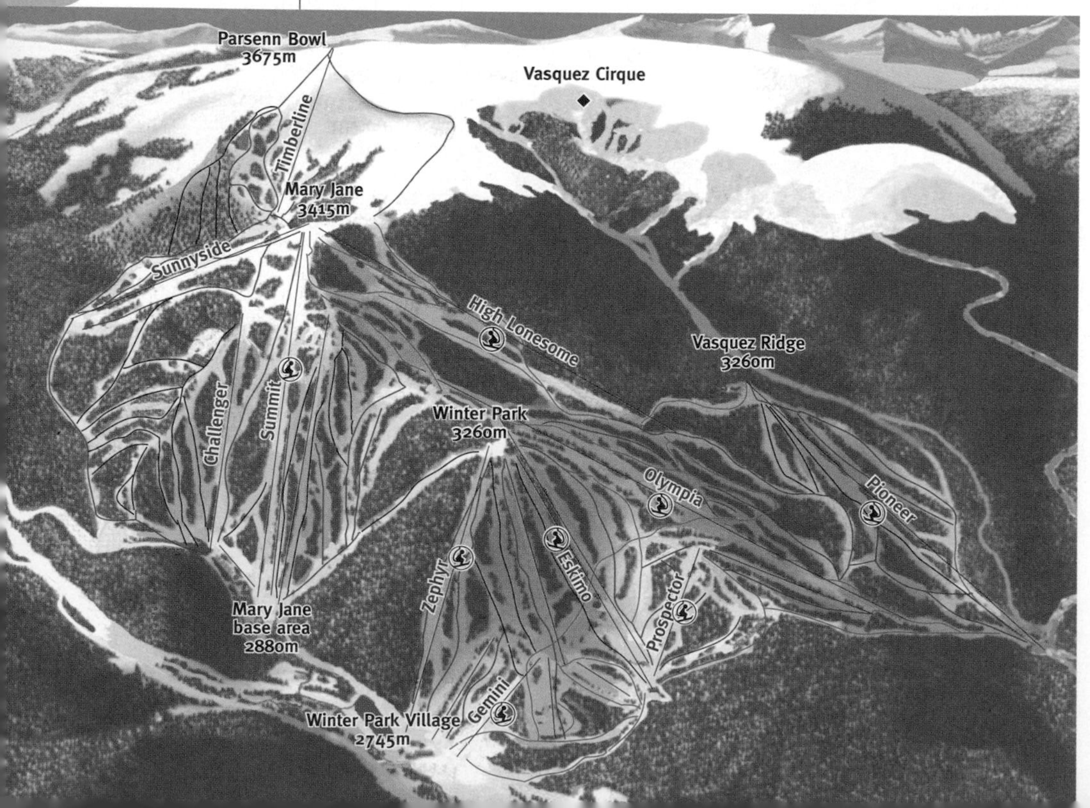

SCHOOLS/GUIDES

2000/01 prices in dollars

Intermediate and advanced classes
6 days
2½hr: from 9.30 or 12.45
6 2½hr days: 234

Beginner classes
6 days
2½hr: from 9.30 or 12.45
6 2½hr days: 150

Children's classes
Ages: 3 to 13
6 full days including pass and lunch: 425

Private lessons
1½hr, 3hr or 6hr
100 for 1½hr, for 1 or 2 people

National Sports Center for the Disabled
Special programme for disabled skiers and snowboarders

Private lessons
3hr or 6hr, with pass and special equipment
40 for 3hr; 80 for 6hr

CHILDCARE

The ski school runs special classes for children aged 3 to 13 and provides lunch. The Children's Center has a popular non-skiing programme for children aged 2 months to 5 years. You can rent out bleepers to keep in touch. Book early to ensure a place.
The Children's Center is open 8am to 4pm. Lessons are 10am to 3pm.

has grand views and some gentle cruising pistes as well as more challenging ungroomed terrain. It's an intermediate paradise and an ideal place to try your hand off-piste.

FOR BEGINNERS
The best we've seen

Discovery Park is a 25-acre dedicated area for beginners, reached by a high-speed quad and served by two more chairs. As well as a nursery area and longer green runs, it has an adventure trail through trees and a special terrain park. Once out of the Park, there are easy runs back to base.

FOR CROSS-COUNTRY
Lots of it

There are several different areas, all with generally excellent snow, adding up to well over 200km of groomed trails, as well as backcountry tours.

QUEUES
Rarely a problem

During the week the mountain is generally quiet, though there may be a crowd waiting for the opening of the Zephyr Express from the main base and there can be queues on the old double Timberline chair. At weekends the Denver crowds arrive – even then

DON'T PASS ON BERTHOUD PASS

The drive to Winter Park from Denver – unusually for an American resort – involves a winding climb. It takes you to the summit of Berthoud Pass (3450m), where there is a small car park – usually near-empty – and a couple of chair-lifts. Press on over the pass to your destination, right? Wrong. Well, wrong if you press on and don't come back during your stay. And if you like deep untracked snow.

You've heard of heli-skiing and cat-skiing. Well, Berthoud offers something damn-near as good: bus-skiing. The chair-lifts – a triple and a quad – lift you a modest 200m vertical above the pass, but you descend to much lower points on highway 40, where beaten-up buses (with classic 60s pop playing) pick you up.

There are runs of every standard, but in practice this is a mountain for good skiers and riders. The slopes down to the road are steep, and sometimes very steep. The runs back to the summit of the pass are easier, but hardly any of them are groomed, and they can be quite tricky if there is a substantial snowfall. And there often is: Berthoud is on the Continental Divide, and claims for its annual snowfall range from 400in to 500in a year. This is Jackson Hole/Alta territory.

The terrain and the snowfall are two key elements. The third is the lack of people. There is a limit of 400 day passes, and there are about 200 season pass holders. In practice, it's normal to have between 100 and 200 people on the slopes, which cover 1,100 acres. That's something in the order of 10 acres each. Enough?

In the base lodge, as well as a ski shop there is the highest pub in North America and a pleasant table-service restaurant – so a day here can be quite a civilised affair. And it won't cost a lot: the price of a day pass is low, and depends on the snow – $34 if there's 4in of fresh powder, $30 if there's no fresh for two days (2000/01 prices). Winter Park's passes are flexible (eg 5 days out of 6) so it's easy to slot in a day at Berthoud. But you may want to make it more than one.

There are easier ways into Vasquez Cirque than this, thank goodness →

WINTER PARK RESORT

ACTIVITIES

Indoor Cinema, swimming pool, roller skating, amusement arcade, health club, comedy club, aerobics, racquetball

Outdoor Dog-sledding, sight-seeing flights, snow-shoe, sleigh rides, 'tubing', ice skating, snowmobiling, snowbiking, snowcat tours, ice fishing, hot springs

GETTING THERE

Air Denver, transfer 1½ hr.

Rail Leaves Denver Sat and Sun at 7.15am and returns at 4.15pm. Journey time 2 hr.

Phone numbers

From distant parts of the US, add the prefix 1 970.

From abroad, add the prefix +1 970.

TOURIST OFFICE

Postcode CO 80482
t +1 (970) 726 5514
f 726 1572
wpinfo@mail.skiwinterpark.com
www.winterparkresort.com

the network of more than twenty lifts (including eight fast quads) makes light work of the crowds.

MOUNTAIN RESTAURANTS
Some good facilities

The highlight is the Lodge at Sunspot, at the top of Winter Park mountain. This wood and glass building has a welcoming bar with a roaring log fire, a table-service restaurant and very good self-service. The Club Car at the bottom of Mary Jane is good and Snoasis is self-service. Lunch Rock Cafe at the top of Mary Jane does quick snacks.

SCHOOLS AND GUIDES
A good reputation

Recent visitors have been 'impressed by the standard of instructors'. As well as standard classes there are ideas such as Family Private, for different standards to learn together; themed lessons such as Mogul Mania; and Quick Tips, a 'quick fix' video analysis with suggestions for improvement (only $5).

FACILITIES FOR CHILDREN
Some of the best

The Children's Center at Winter Park base area houses day-care facilities and is the meeting point for children's classes, which have their own areas, including 'magic carpet' lifts. A recent reporter was very impressed with the lessons and said there's even a 'warming tent' – what a great idea.

Staying there

Most accommodation is down in town, but the choice at or near the base has improved a lot.

HOW TO GO
Fair choice

Several UK operators offer Winter Park.
Chalets Several operators offer them.
Hotels There are a couple of outstanding hotel/condo complexes.
(((④ **Iron Horse Resort** (726 8851) Slope-side, comfortable, condo-style.
(((④ **Vintage** (726 8801) Near resort entrance; good facilities but some poor recent reports of it.
((③ **Mountain Lodge** (726 4211) Across the valley from the lifts; micro-brewery above the bar; good atmosphere.
Self-catering There are a lot of comfortable condo complexes, including the new slope-side Zephyr Mountain Lodge.

EATING OUT
A fair choice

Reporters are keen on the long-established Deno's – seafood, steaks etc. Try the Crooked Creek Saloon at Fraser for atmosphere and typical American food; Smokin' Moe's for ribs, New Hong Kong for Chinese, the Divide Grill for pasta, seafood and grills are all in the new Cooper Creek Square area; The Shed for Mexican and Fontenot's for Cajun. Hernandos is a 'fairly rustic but busy' Italian. Rome on the Range is good for steaks, seafood and pasta plus 20 beers on tap. Gasthaus Eichler does German food.

APRES-SKI
If you know where to go ...

Use the Black Diamond Nightlife Tour Map, which also gets you two-for-one drink deals. At close of play, there's action at the Derailer Bar at the main lift base and the Club Car at the base of Mary Jane. Later on, try The Slope (in Old Town) for live music and dancing or Adolph's, just across the road. Try downtown Rome on the Range for country and western. The Shed can be lively. The Crooked Creek is popular with locals. Randi's Irish Saloon is 'a pleasant and lively bar'.

OFF THE SLOPES
Mainly the great outdoors

Most diversions involve getting about on snow in different ways. If you like shopping, visit Silverthorne's factory outlet stores (90 min away on I70).

Utah

The massive snowfalls and the world's best lift-served powder skiing and riding are the main reasons for taking a holiday in Utah. But the region will get massive publicity this winter for a different reason: Salt Lake City and the Utah resorts will host the 2002 Winter Olympics from 8 to 24 February. The Paralympics will follow from 7 to 16 March.

'The Greatest Snow on Earth' – that's what Utah claims. (Until recently it made the claim on every car number plate, but it now seems to be targeting broader markets.) It's a debatable claim: the Colorado resorts say that their famous powder is drier, and have figures to prove it. What they can't dispute is that some Utah resorts do get huge dumps of snow – up to twice the amount, over the season, that falls on some big-name Colorado resorts. In any case, by Alpine standards the snow here is wonderful stuff. If you like the steep and deep, you should make the pilgrimage to Utah.

There are differences in snowfall though. The biggest dumps are reserved for Snowbird and Alta (an average of 500 inches a year), close together in Little Cottonwood Canyon. The snow record of these small resorts makes them the powder capitals of the world. And the big news for the 2001/02 season is that their slopes will be linked and they will offer a shared lift pass for the first time. They are not holding any Olympic events because of access problems with their avalanche-prone road and their lack of suitable infrastructure.

Park City, the main 'destination' resort of the area, and neighbouring Deer Valley will host the lion's share of the Olympic events. These and the nearby Canyons are only a few miles, as the crow flies, from Alta and Snowbird, but they get 'only' 300 to 350 inches (still more than most Colorado resorts). But it's unknown Snowbasin (400 inches) that gets the prestige downhill and super-G Olympic events. Separate chapters follow on these six resorts.

But there are other Utah resorts that are well worth visiting too. If you enjoy seeing different resorts renting a car, staying in Park City (by far the liveliest

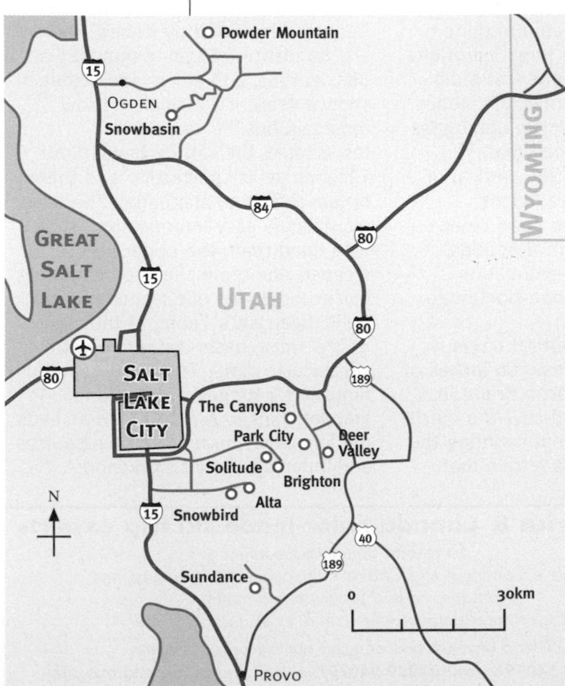

SNOWPIX.COM / CHRIS GILL

One of four fast six-packs that whizz you around the mountain at Park City ↘

The Utah Interconnect is a not-to-be-missed off-piste day tour between Park City and Snowbird (see Park City chapter). This is the Highway to Heaven traverse from Solitude to Alta →

SNOWPIX.COM / CHRIS GILL

resort) or Salt Lake City (with a big city rather than a ski resort ambience), and driving to a different resort each day makes a compelling holiday. The roads are generally good.

Brighton (2670m, vertical 530m, 7 lifts, 64 runs, 850 acres, 500 inches of snow a year), right at the end of the end of Big Cottonwood Canyon (the next one along from Little Cottonwood Canyon), gets as much snow as Alta and Snowbird – which may help to explain why Utah's first ski-lift was built here, in 1936. But the snow gets tracked out less quickly because the resort attracts far fewer visitors. There are a lot of trails packed into quite a small area. Two of the three major lifts – including the area's one fast quad – serve mostly easy-intermediate slopes, but the Great Western slow quad goes over a more testing slope that represents the resort's full vertical of 530m, and the separate Mount Millicent area has some good steep slopes, both in and out of bounds. There are several accommodation options, including a slope-side lodge, cabins and chalets.

Solitude (2435m, vertical 625m, 7 lifts, 63 runs, 1600 acres, 500 inches of snow a year), next door to Brighton, gets as much snow and covers a much bigger area, even without counting the excellent out-of-bounds terrain that you can get to from the top lift. Basically, the slopes here get steeper as you go up the mountain – except that the area's one fast quad, Eagle, serves a slightly separate ridge that is almost entirely blue in gradient, and starts slightly down the valley from the main base. We haven't yet had a chance to explore the entirely black 400 acres of Honeycomb canyon, reached from the top lift. There is one hotel – the 46-room Inn at Solitude (536 5700) – a few small condo developments and some houses.

The other Utah resort that gets a bit of international attention – not least because it's owned by Robert Redford – is **Sundance** (1860m, 655m vertical, 4 lifts, 41 runs, 450 acres, 320 inches of snow a year). It's a small, narrow mountain but the vertical is respectable, the setting beneath Mt Timpanogos is spectacular and there is terrain to suit all standards. The lower mountain is easy-intermediate, served by a quad chair, the upper part steeper: one triple chair serves purely black slopes, the other blue and black trails. Bearclaw's Cabin, at the top of it, is a small, basic restaurant with spectacular views. There are beautifully furnished 'cottages' to rent, and grander chalets. A reporter commends the 'emphasis on renewable resources' and 'interesting craft workshops'.

Solitude phone number
From distant parts of the US, add the prefix 1 801.
From abroad, add the prefix +1 801.

Alta 2605m

Cult resort with fabulous powder and new link with Snowbird

WHAT IT COSTS

(6)

HOW IT RATES

The slopes	
Snow	*****
Extent	***
Experts	*****
Intermediates	***
Beginners	***
Convenience	****
Queues	***
Restaurants	**
The rest	
Scenery	****
Resort charm	**
Off-slope	*

What's new

For 2001/02, Alta is at last emerging from its time-warp. It is installing its first high-speed quad to replace the slow triple Sugarloaf lift.

From the top of this lift you will be able to ski down into Snowbird's Mineral Basin to access the whole of Snowbird's terrain as well as Alta's on a joint area lift pass. A new quad the other side will bring you back. The terrain available will be more than doubled to 4,700 acres, making it the biggest lift-linked area in Utah and one of the biggest in the US. The resorts will keep separate ownership and operation, and Alta is still refusing to allow snowboarding.

The double chair to Point Supreme will become a triple.

- ⊕ Phenomenal snow record
- ⊕ Cult status among powderhounds
- ⊕ New link to Snowbird making one of the largest ski areas in the US
- ⊕ Very cheap local lift pass
- ⊕ Ski-almost-to-the-door convenience
- ⊕ Easy to get to Salt Lake City and other Utah resorts (so long as access road open)

- ⊖ No resort village as such – a handful of scattered lodges
- ⊖ No snowboarding allowed
- ⊖ Old-fashioned lift network
- ⊖ Limited groomed runs for intermediates, though the new link with Snowbird doubles the terrain
- ⊖ Not much après-ski atmosphere
- ⊖ Few off-slope diversions

Alta is famous for remarkable amounts of powder snow arriving with great regularity, for a stubborn refusal to develop or modernise the area and for one of the cheapest lift passes around. This year sees a new lift and piste link with neighbouring Snowbird which also gets phenomenal powder and makes the joint area one of the top powder-pig paradises in the world and one of the US's biggest lift-linked areas. But snowboarders will still be banned from Alta's slopes.

THE RESORT

Alta sits at the craggy head of Little Cottonwood Canyon, 2km beyond Snowbird and less than an hour's drive from downtown Salt Lake City. The peaceful location was once the scene of a bustling and bawdy mining town. The 'new' Alta is a strung-out handful of lodges and parking areas, and nothing more; life revolves around the two separate lift base areas – Albion and Wildcat – linked by a bi-directional rope tow along the flat valley floor.

THE MOUNTAINS

Alta's slopes haven't changed much in the last 20 years and are served by mainly slow double and triple chairs. As Alta's mayor explained to us: 'Alta's philosophy is old-fashioned quality. Keeping slow, old chair-lifts means you never have too many people on the slopes, so you have a quality skiing environment.' It will be interesting to see how that philosophy and environment changes now they have agreed to a high-speed quad and the link with Snowbird.

Slopes The dominant feature of Alta's terrain is the steep end of a ridge that separates the area's two basins. To the left, above Albion Base, the slopes stretch away over easy green terrain towards the black runs of Point Supreme and Devil's Castle; to the right is a more concentrated bowl with blue runs down the middle and blacks either side. These two sectors are linked at altitude, and by a flat rope tow along the valley floor.

Snowboarding Boarding is banned.

Snow reliability The quantity and quality of snow that falls here, and the northerly orientation of the slopes, put Alta among the world's best.

Experts Even without a link with Snowbird, Alta had cult status among

ALTA

Powder is what Alta is all about (but not if you are on a snowboard) →

MOUNTAIN FACTS

For Alta and Snowbird combined area

Altitude	2410m-3355m
Lifts	26
Pistes	4700 acres
Green	25%
Blue	37%
Black	38%
Art. snow	150 acres
Recco detectors used	

Phone numbers

From distant parts of the US, add the prefix 1 801.

From abroad, add the prefix +1 801.

TOURIST OFFICE

Postcode UT 84092
t +1 (801) 359 1078
f 799 2340
info@alta.com
www.alta.com

local experts, who flocked to the high ridges after a fresh snowfall. There are dozens of steep slopes and chutes throughout the area. The new link will mean the area will be the world's best for powderhounds.

Intermediates Adventurous intermediates who are happy to try ungroomed slopes and learn to love powder should like Alta, too. There are good blue bowls in both Alta and Snowbird and not so tough blacks to progress too. But if it is miles of perfectly groomed piste you are after there are plenty of better resorts.

Beginners Timid intermediates and beginners will be happy on the Albion side, where the lower runs are broad, gentle and well groomed.

Cross-country There's little provision for cross-country skiing; but the surrounding backcountry offers adventures for those with guidance.

Queues Bottlenecks are not unknown at Alta – the snow record, easy access from Salt Lake City and the slow, old chair-lifts see to that – especially in spring and on sunny weekends. It will be interesting to see what effect the new link with Snowbird has.

Mountain restaurants There's a mountain restaurant in each sector of the slopes – Collins Grill on the Wildcat side has table-service – and several places in the valley are open for lunch.

Schools and guides The famous Alf Engen ski school naturally specialises in powder lessons – though all the regular classes and clinics are also available. The ski school organises children's lessons.

Facilities for children Day care for those over 3 months old is available at the Children's Center at Albion Base.

STAYING THERE

There are about a dozen places to stay – simple hotels and apartments.

How to go None of the hotels is luxurious in US terms. Most get booked up well in advance by repeat visitors. Unusually for America, most lodges (as they call themselves) are half-board deals with dinner included.

Hotels The Alta Lodge (742 3500) is one of Alta's oldest, and feels rather like an over-crowded chalet-hotel in the Alps. Rustler Lodge (742 2200) is more luxurious, with a big outdoor pool, but impersonal. The comfortable, modern Goldminer's Daughter (742 2300) and the basic Peruvian Lodge (742 3000) are cheaper.

Eating out Eating in is the routine.

Après-ski This rarely goes beyond a few drinks and possibly a sports film in the lodges. The Goldminer's Daughter has the main après-ski bar.

Off the slopes There are few options other than a trip to Salt Lake City.

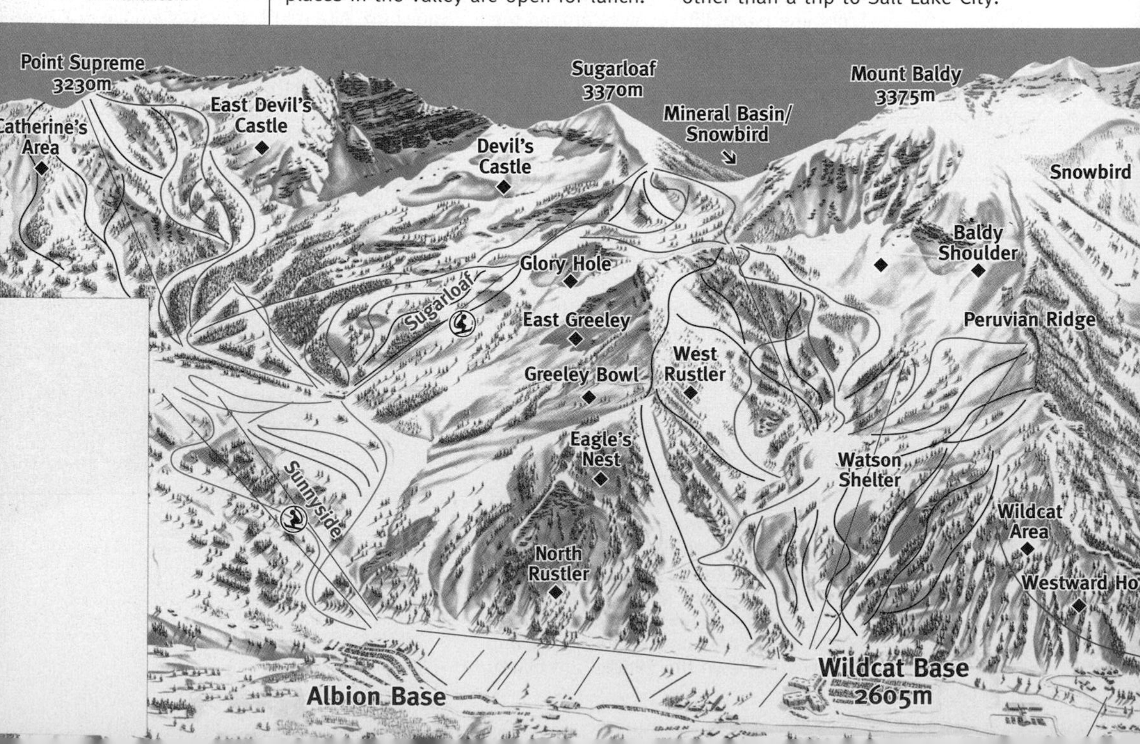

The Canyons 2075m

Potentially the biggest mountain in the US

WHAT IT COSTS

6

HOW IT RATES

The slopes

Snow	****
Extent	***
Experts	***
Intermediates	***
Beginners	***
Convenience	****
Queues	****
Restaurants	***

The rest

Scenery	***
Resort charm	**
Off-slope	**

What's new

For 2001/2 there will be a new fixed-grip three-person chair between Dreamscape and Peak 5, with five new intermediate trails as well as tree runs.

A new terrain park will be built near the Red Hawk lift at the base area.

A new beginners-only area has been made behind Red Pine Lodge.

New snowmaking will be on the main run from Dreamscape to Tombstone.

For 2000/01 an open-air gondola opened to take you from the parking area to the resort village in three minutes.

- ⊕ Extensive ski area with slopes for all abilities – potentially the biggest in the US
- ⊕ Brand new lift system
- ⊕ Convenient new purpose-built resort village
- ⊕ Excellent snow reliability
- ⊕ Few queues
- ⊕ Nearby Park City is an entertaining alternative base
- ⊕ Park City and Deer Valley slopes only a short drive away
- ⊕ Easy access to Salt Lake City and other Utah resorts

- ⊖ Snow often not up to usual Utah standards on the many south-facing slopes
- ⊖ Because the area is a series of canyons (valleys) many runs are short and the area is a bit disjointed
- ⊖ Resort village is still being built – though the first part is finished
- ⊖ Limited après-ski and dining possibilities at resort village
- ⊖ Few off-slope diversions at resort village

The Canyons is the new kid on the Park City block. Formerly a small locals' area known as Park West and then Wolf Mountain, it was taken over and renamed by the American Skiing Company in 1997. (The company itself has been taken over since.) But ambitious plans remain to make the slopes the biggest in the US, and the area has already more than doubled in size and benefited from a virtually new lift system. The first part of a new slope-side resort village is open.

THE RESORT

When we visited in March 1999 there wasn't a resort – just a muddy car park and building site. On our return in March 2000, the car-free village was really taking shape. But a reporter this year still describes it as 'a muddy mess'. Most people visit The Canyons from a base in Park City.

THE MOUNTAINS

The Canyons gets its name from the valleys between the various mountains (now eight of them) that make up the ski area.

Slopes Red Pine Lodge, at the heart of the slopes, is reached by an eight-person gondola from the village base. From here you can move in either direction across a series of ridges – and the valleys between them. These ridges range from Dreamscape to the south (closest to Park City) to Murdock Peak to the north. Runs come off both sides of each ridge, meaning that they generally face north or south (see Snow reliability section). Most runs finish in the valley floors with some long, relatively flat run-outs. Five of the major lifts are high-speed quads, all put in – along with the gondola – since

THE CANYONS / MARK MAZIARZ

One of the green runs leading down to Red Pine Lodge that can get crowded →

MOUNTAIN FACTS

Altitude	2075m-3045m
Lifts	15
Pistes	3650 acres
Green	14%
Blue	44%
Black	42%
Art. snow	150 acres

Recco detectors used

Central reservations phone number
For all resort accommodation call 1 800 472 6309 (toll-free from within the US)

TOURIST OFFICE

Postcode UT 84098
t +1 435 649 5400
f 649 7374
info@thecanyons.com
www.thecanyons.com

1997. Complimentary mountain tours are offered twice daily.

Snowboarding It's a great area to snowboard in, with lots of natural hits, five natural half-pipes and a great terrain-park and half-pipe. Canis Lupis (aka James Bond trail) is a mile-long, tight, winding natural gulley with high banked walls and numerous obstacles – like riding a bob-sleigh course. For beginners and intermediates there's easy cruising served by chair-lifts.

Snow reliability Snow reliability is not the best in Utah. The Canyons gets as much snow on average as next-door Park City and Deer Valley. But although the north-facing slopes are normally in good condition, the south-facing ones suffer in sunny late-season conditions.

Experts There is steep terrain all over the mountain. We particularly liked the north-facing runs off Ninety-Nine-90, with steep double-black-diamond runs plunging down through the trees to a pretty but almost flat run-out trail. Go south at the top of the lift and (when the gate is open) you can legally enter the backcountry – with the right kit and guidance, of course.

Intermediates There are lots of groomed blue runs for intermediates on all the main sectors except Ninety-Nine-90. Some are quite short, but you can switch from valley to valley easily for added interest, and you can contrive some longer runs.

Beginners There's a new area just for beginners behind Red Pine Lodge. But the run you progress to gets very crowded with through-traffic.

Cross-country There are prepared trails on the Park City golf course and the Homestead Resort course. There is also lots of scope for backcountry trips.

Queues We've heard of no problems.

Mountain restaurants The central Red Pine Lodge is a large, new, attractive log-and-glass building with a busy self-service cafeteria and a table-service restaurant. The Lookout Cabin has wonderful views, and we've had excellent table-service food there. Sun Lodge, with decks, is another option.

Schools and guides The ski school uses the American Skiing Company's Perfect Turn formula, which focuses on an individual's strengths and builds on them (rather than correcting faults).

Facilities for children There's day care for children from 18 months.

STAYING THERE

Although there is now some convenient accommodation at the resort village, staying in Park City is a more attractive option – regular shuttle-buses run to the resort.

How to go Accommodation at the resort village is still fairly limited, but you do have the choice of hotel or self-catering.

Hotels The luxurious Grand Summit is right at the base of the gondola.

Self-catering The new Sundial Lodge condos are part of the resort village.

Après-ski The Grand Summit contains several bars, and there are many more in Park City.

Eating out The Cabin restaurant, in the Grand Summit hotel, serves eclectic American cuisine. And there are many more options in Park City.

Off the slopes There's a fair bit going on in Park City – shops, galleries etc – and Salt Lake City has some good concerts, shopping and sights. Balloon rides and snowmobiling are popular activities.

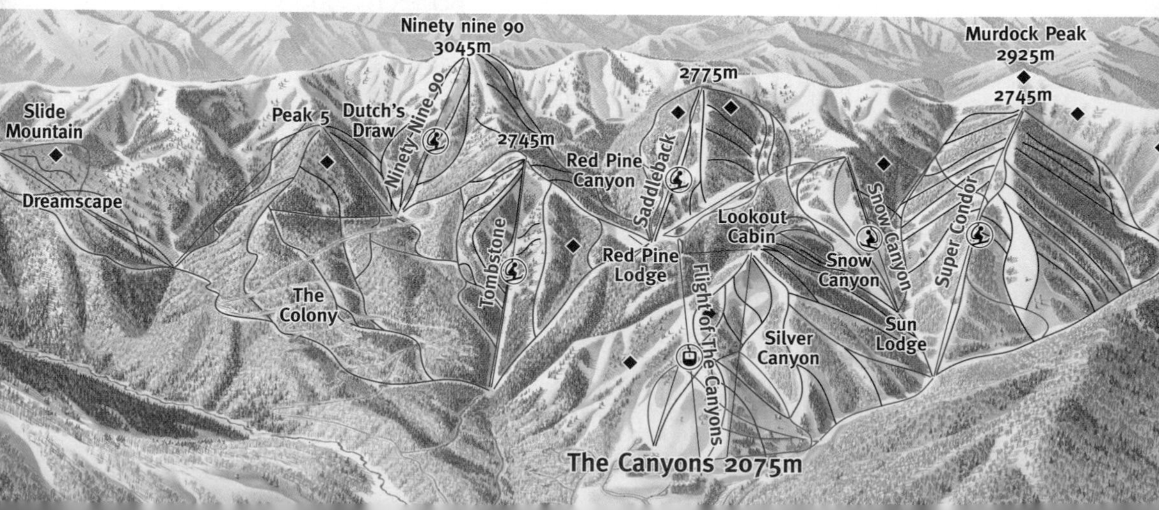

Deer Valley 2195m

The ultimate upmarket ski resort

WHAT IT COSTS

6

HOW IT RATES

The slopes

Snow	****
Extent	**
Experts	***
Intermediates	****
Beginners	****
Convenience	****
Queues	****
Restaurants	****

The rest

Scenery	***
Resort charm	***
Off-slope	**

What's new

A much-needed new day lodge and restaurant at the bottom of the Empire and Ruby lifts will be open for 2001/02.

The Quincy triple chair will be replaced by a high-speed quad.

There will be increased snowmaking.

And a 10,000-seat stadium will be built for viewing the Olympic events.

MOUNTAIN FACTS

Altitude	2000m-2920m
Lifts	19
Pistes	1750 acres
Green	15%
Blue	50%
Black	35%
Art. snow	500 acres
Recco detectors used	

- ⊕ Highly convenient, upmarket luxury resort with superb skier services
- ⊕ Immaculate piste grooming, good snow record and lots of snow-guns
- ⊕ Good tree skiing
- ⊕ No queues
- ⊕ Slopes of Park City and The Canyons very close and access to Salt Lake City and other Utah resorts is easy

- ⊖ No snowboarding allowed
- ⊖ Relatively expensive
- ⊖ Deer Valley itself is quiet at night

Deer Valley prides itself on pampering its guests. Free valet ski storage, gourmet dining, immaculately groomed slopes, limits on numbers of skiers on the mountain, no snowboarding. But there's more to it than that – it has some remarkably good slopes, with interesting terrain for all standards. It will be hosting the freestyle and slalom competitions in the 2002 Olympics.

THE RESORT

Just a mile from the end of Park City's Main Street, Deer Valley is unashamedly upmarket and famed for the care and attention lavished on both slopes and guests. Valets will unload your equipment before you park your car – it's very obviously aimed at people who are used to being pampered and can pay for it. Luxurious private chalets are dotted around the slopes. The hotels are particularly luxurious.

There is not much of a village to stroll around. There are a few shops, hotels and restaurants at Silver Lake Lodge (mid-mountain but accessible by road), but for any real animation you need to head for Park City's Main Street – easily reached by free buses.

THE MOUNTAINS

The slopes are varied and interesting. Deer Valley's reputation for immaculate grooming is justified, but there is also a lot of exciting tree skiing (great when it is snowing) – and some steep mogul runs too. There is a special experts' trail map with extra information on the chutes, bowls and glades.

Slopes Two high-speed quads take you up to Bald Eagle Mountain, just beyond which is the mid-mountain focus of Silver Lake Lodge. You can ski from here to the isolated Little Baldy Peak, served by a gondola and a quad chair-lift, with mainly easy blue and green runs to serve property being developed there. But the main skiing is on three linked mountains above Silver Lake Lodge. From left to right these are Bald Mountain, Flagstaff Mountain and Empire Canyon. Empire is serviced by a fast quad – the top of which is just a few metres from the runs of the Park City ski area and could easily be linked. Empire also has a family area with a three-seater chair.

Snowboarding Boarding is banned.

Snow reliability As you'd expect in Utah, snow reliability is excellent, and there's plenty of snowmaking too.

DEER VALLEY

Although Deer Valley prides itself on its grooming, it has good bump, bowl and tree skiing too →

Central reservations phone number
For all resort accommodation call 645 6528 (from distant parts of the US, add the prefix 1 435; from abroad, add the prefix +1 435)

TOURIST OFFICE

Postcode UT 84060
t +1 (435) 649 1000
f 645 6939
patti@deervalley.com
www.deervalley.com

Experts Despite its image of pampered luxury there is excellent expert terrain on all three main mountains, including fabulous glade skiing as well as bumps, defined chutes and open bowl slopes. And because the place doesn't attract many hotshots the snow doesn't get skied out quickly.
Intermediates There are lots of immaculately groomed blue runs all over the mountains.
Beginners There are nursery slopes at Silver Lake Lodge as well as the base, and gentle green runs to progress to on all the mountains.
Cross-country There are prepared trails on the Park City golf course and the Homestead Resort course, just out of town. There is also lots of scope for backcountry trips.
Queues Waiting in lift lines is not something that Deer Valley wants its guests to experience, so it limits the number of lift tickets sold.
Mountain restaurants There are attractive wood-and-glass self-service places run by the resort at both Silver Lake Lodge and the base lodge, with free valet ski storage. The food is fine (though pricey). There will be a much-needed new restaurant at Empire Canyon for 2001/02 – which should relieve the overcrowding at Silver Lake We recommend you pamper yourself by taking table-service at the Stein Eriksen Lodge or the Goldener Hirsch.
Schools and guides The ski school is doubtless excellent.
Facilities for children Deer Valley's Children's Center gives parents complimentary pagers.

STAYING THERE

Many visitors prefer to stay in livelier Park City. But if it's plush hotels and pampering you want, it's worth staying in Deer Valley itself.
How to go A car is useful for visiting the other nearby Utah resorts, though Deer Valley, Park City and The Canyons are all linked by regular shuttle-buses.
Hotels The Stein Eriksen Lodge and Goldener Hirsch at Silver Lake Village are two of the plushest hotels in any ski resort.
Self-catering There are many luxury apartments and houses to rent.
Après-ski The Lounge of the Snow Park Lodge at the base area is the main après-ski venue, with live music. There are lively bars and restaurants around Main Street, in Park City.
Eating out Of the gourmet restaurants, the Mariposa is the best. The Seafood Buffet and McHenry's grill are also recommended. Park City has a number of good restaurants.
Off the slopes Park City has lots of shops, galleries etc. Salt Lake City has good concerts, sights and shopping. Balloon rides and snowmobiling are popular.

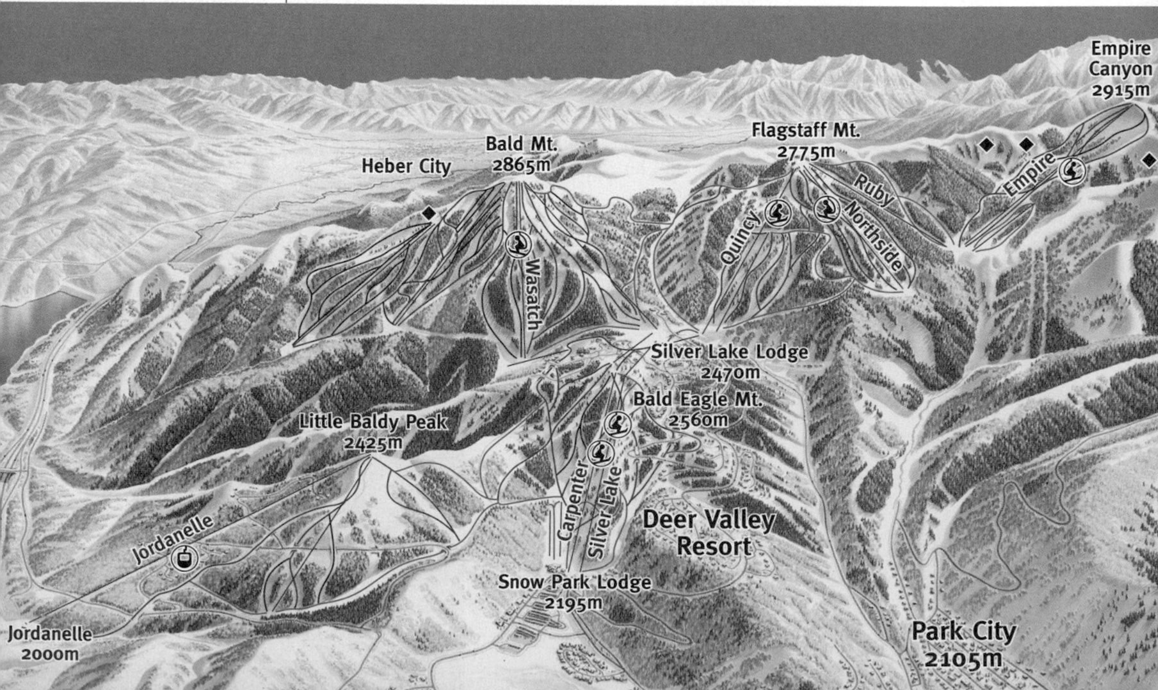

Park City 2105m

An entertaining base for excursions into Utah's deep powder

WHAT IT COSTS

6

HOW IT RATES

The slopes	
Snow	****
Extent	***
Experts	****
Intermediates	****
Beginners	****
Convenience	***
Queues	****
Restaurants	**
The rest	
Scenery	***
Resort charm	***
Off-slope	***

What's new

For 2000/01 a new base lodge – Legacy Lodge – opened. The building reflects the area's mining history and houses a food court restaurant, pub, ski and board rental facilities and shops.

An Olympic half-pipe has been added, making a total of two terrain parks and two half-pipes. Snowmaking facilities have also been recently extended.

- ⊕ Increasingly touristy Wild West-style main street, convenient for slopes
- ⊕ Lots of bars and restaurants make nonsense of Utah's image as a puritanical Mormon state
- ⊕ Well maintained slopes, good snow record, and lots of snowmaking
- ⊕ Good lift system including four fast six-packs
- ⊕ Good base for visiting other major Utah resorts – Deer Valley and The Canyons are effectively suburbs and other resorts less than an hour away

- ⊖ Rest of town doesn't have same charm as main street – lots of recent building has created an enormous sprawl (and building continues)
- ⊖ The blue and black runs tend to be rather short – most lifts give a vertical of around 400m
- ⊖ Although the snowfall record is impressive by normal standards, it comes nowhere near that of Alta and Snowbird, a few miles away
- ⊖ Lack of spectacular scenery

You'll be hearing a lot about Park City this season. For the 2002 Olympics, it is hosting the giant slalom and the snowboarding events, and next-door Deer Valley is hosting the slalom and freestyle events. The bob-sleigh, luge and Nordic events will take place down the road in the new winter sports park.

For a holiday, Park City has clear attractions, particularly if you ignore its sprawling suburbs and stay near the centre to make the most of the lively bars and restaurants in its beautifully restored and developed main street. But the place really comes into its own as a base for touring other resorts as well. Deer Valley is separated from Park City's slopes by a fence between the tops of two lifts, and by separate ownership with quite different objectives. All that is required to link them is to remove the fence – a bizarre situation. The Canyons is only a little further, on the outskirts of town, and reached by free buses. Both are excellent mountains, well worth exploring. And then there are the famously powdery resorts of Snowbird and Alta, less than an hour away by car or bus. All four are covered in separate chapters. If that's not enough, the quiet resorts of Brighton, Solitude and Sundance and the Olympic downhill slopes of Snowbasin (see separate chapter) are within easy reach if you have a car.

PARK CITY / LORI ADAMSKI-PEEK

Though not usually this deserted, Park City has a lot of easy runs like this →

MOUNTAIN FACTS

Altitude	2100m-3050m
Lifts	14
Pistes	3300 acres
Green	18%
Blue	44%
Black	38%
Art. snow	475 acres
Recco detectors used	

The resort 

Park City is in Utah's Wasatch Mountains, about 45 minutes by road from Salt Lake City. It was born with the discovery of silver in 1872. By the turn of the century it boasted a population of 10,000, a red-light district, a Chinese quarter and 27 saloons. Careful restoration has left the town with a splendid historic centre-piece in Main Street.

The old wooden sidewalks and clapboard buildings are now filled with a colourful selection of art galleries, shops, boutiques, bars and restaurants – though it is getting rather touristy, with some tacky shops selling T-shirts and souvenirs. New buildings have been tastefully designed to blend in smoothly. But away from the centre the resort lacks charm, sprawls over a wide area and is still expanding.

There is a lift up to the slopes from the heart of the town, but the main lift base area is Resort Center, on the fringes with modern buildings and its own bars, restaurants and lodgings.

Deer Valley and The Canyons are almost suburbs of Park City, but all three retain quite separate identities. They are linked by free shuttle-buses, which also go around town and run until late. A trolley-bus runs along Main Street. A car is useful for visiting other ski areas on the good roads.

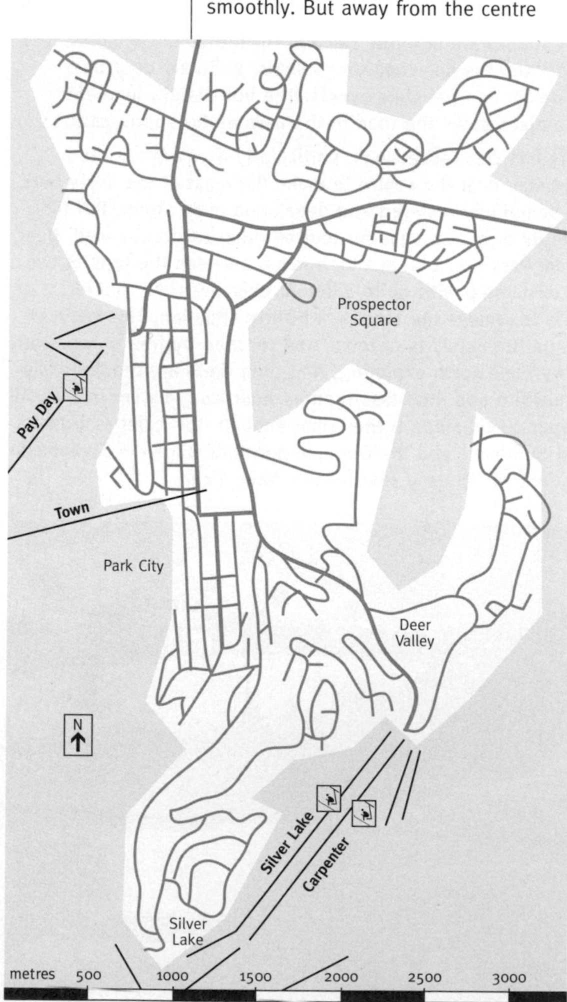

The mountain 

Mostly the area consists of blue and black trails cut through the trees on the flanks of rounded mountain ridges, with easier runs running along the ridges and the gulleys between. The bite in the system is in the lightly wooded bowls and ridges at the top of the resort's slopes.

THE SLOPES
Bowls above the woods

A fast six-seat chair-lift whisks you up from Resort Center, and another beyond that up to Summit House, the main mountain restaurant.

Most of the easy and intermediate runs lie between the Summit House and the base area, and spread along the sides of a series of interconnecting ridges. Virtually all the steep terrain is above Summit House in a series of ungroomed bowls, and accessed by the new McConkey's six-pack and the old Jupiter double chair.

There are a few old wooden mine buildings left dotted around the slopes, which add extra atmosphere. Daily mountain tours of the historical sites are offered free of charge – as are the twice a week black-diamond tours for advanced skiers.

A floodlit run – the longest in the Rockies – is available until 9pm, together with a floodlit half-pipe.

SNOW RELIABILITY
Not quite the Greatest on Earth

Utah resorts make a lot of fuss about the quality and quantity of their snow. Park City's record doesn't match those of Alta and Snowbird, but an annual average of 350in is still impressive, and ahead of most Colorado figures. And there's snowmaking on about 15% of the terrain.

LIFT PASSES

2000/01 prices in dollars

Park City
Covers all lifts in Park City Mountain Resort, with free ski-bus.

Main pass
1-day pass 60
6-day pass 282

Senior citizens
Over 65: 1-day 30
Over 70: free pass

Children
Age 7-12: 6-day pass 126
6 and under: free

Short-term passes
Half-day passes from 1pm to 4pm (adult 44). Twilight skiing pass 1pm-9pm (50). Night pass 4pm-9pm 24.

Notes All multi-day passes are good for one week, allowing for days off. Reductions for groups but not students.

Alternative passes
Multi-area passport is available through UK tour operators.

boarding *Boarding was banned on Park City's slopes until a few years ago. But now the Olympic boarding events are being held here and the resort has fully embraced boarding, with two fun-parks and half-pipes – one floodlit at night. It has wonderful free-ride terrain, its higher lifts giving access to some great powder bowls. Beginners have their own excellent area, good easy cruising and a lift system which is entirely chair-lifts. Intermediates have to put up with fairly short cruising runs. The town has plenty of bars to keep you going.*

FOR EXPERTS
Lots of variety

There is a lot of excellent advanced and expert terrain at the top of the lift system. It is now all marked as double-diamond on the trail map but there are many runs that deserve only a single-diamond rating – so don't be put off. We particularly like the prettily wooded McConkey's Bowl, served by a six-pack and offering a range of open pitches and gladed terrain. The old Jupiter lift accesses the highest bowls, which include some serious terrain – with narrow couloirs, cliffs and cornices – as well as easier wide-open slopes. The Jupiter bowl runs are under the chair, but there is a lot more terrain accessible by traversing and hiking – turn left for West Face, Pioneer Ridge and Puma Bowl, right for Scotts Bowl and the vast expanse of Pinecone Ridge, stretching literally for miles down the side of Thaynes Canyon.

Lower down, the side of Summit House ridge, serviced by the Thaynes and Motherlode chairs, has some little-used black runs, plus a few satisfying trails in the trees. There's a zone of steep runs towards town from further round the ridge. And don't miss Blueslip Bowl near Summit House – so called because ski company employees who skied it in the past when it was out of bounds were handed a blue slip which meant they were fired.

Good skiers (no snowboarders, due to some long flat run-outs and hikes) should not miss the Utah Interconnect (see feature panel). For bigger budgets, Park City Powder Guides offers heli-skiing on 20,000 acres of private backcountry land.

FOR INTERMEDIATES
Many better places

There are blue runs served by all the main lifts, apart from Jupiter. The areas around the King Con high-speed quad and Silverlode high-speed six-pack

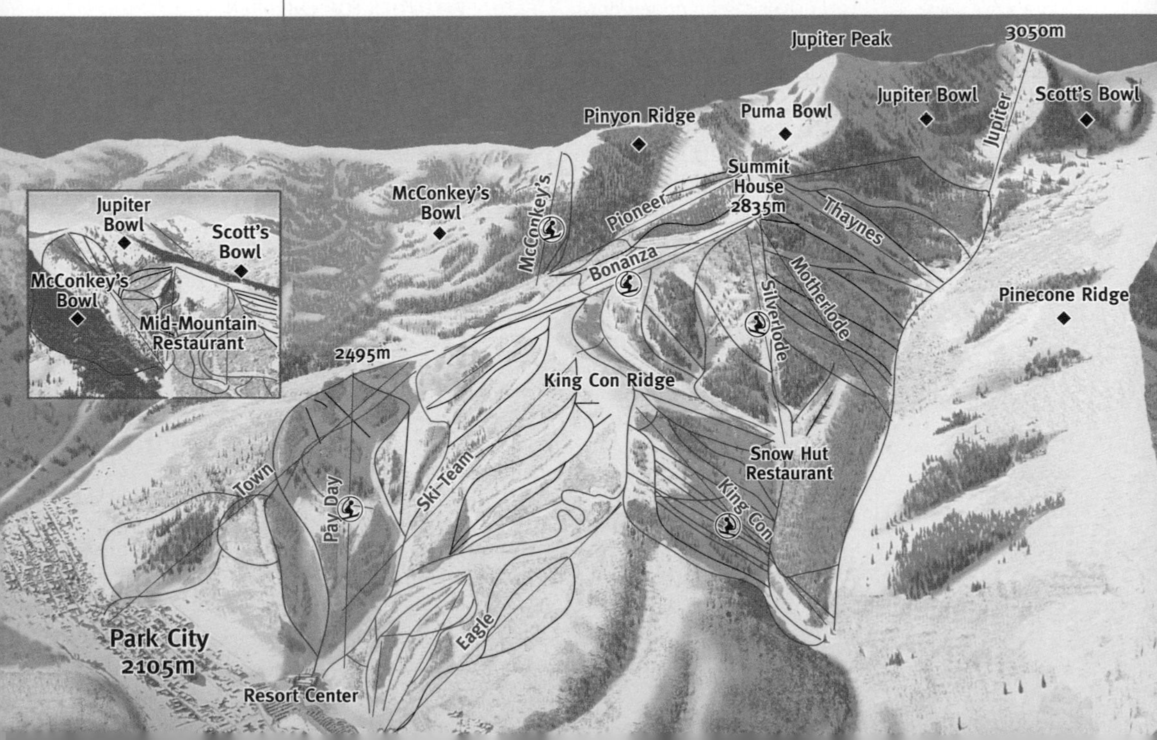

SCHOOLS/GUIDES

2000/01 prices in dollars

Park City
Classes 5 days
3hr: 9.30-12.30 or 1pm-4pm 290; 3 3hr days: 175
Children's classes
Ages: 7 to 12
Full day 105 (incl lunch)
Private lessons
1hr, 2hr, half- or full-day
95 for 1hr; 450 for full day; additional cost for more than one person

CHILDCARE

The ski school's Mountain School takes children aged from 3 to 6, from 8.30 or 9.30 to 4.30, mixing skiing instruction with other indoor and outdoor activities. $115 per day or $330 for three days. There are several different nurseries in the town.

have a dense network of great (but fairly short) cruising runs. There are also more difficult trails close by, for those looking for a challenge.

But the keen intermediate piste-basher who might be happy at Vail or Snowmass won't be so happy here. There are few long, fast cruising runs – most trails are in the 1km to 2km region and many have long, flat run-outs. The Pioneer and McConkey's chair-lifts are off the main drag and serve some very pleasant, often quiet runs. One reporter complains of too many ungroomed mogul runs, 'leaving a choice of ultra-easy cruising or bump-running, with little in between'.

Intermediates will certainly want to visit The Canyons and Deer Valley for a day or two (see separate chapters) and may be tempted further to try the famous Alta/Snowbird powder.

FOR BEGINNERS
A good chance for fast progress

Novices get started on short lifts and a dedicated beginners' area near the base lodge. The beginners' classes graduate up the hill quite quickly, and there's a good, very gentle and wide 'easiest way down' – the three-and a half-mile Home Run – clearly marked all the way from Summit House. It's easy enough for most beginners to manage after only a few lessons. The Town chair can be ridden down.

FOR CROSS-COUNTRY
Some trails; lots of backcountry

There are prepared trails on both the Park City golf course, next to the downhill area, and the Homestead Resort course, just out of town. There is lots of scope for backcountry trips.

QUEUES
Peak period problems only

Lift queues aren't normally a problem with all the high-speed six-seat chairs in the area. But it can get pretty crowded (on some trails as well as the lifts) on busy weekends.

MOUNTAIN RESTAURANTS
Standard self-service stuff

The Mid-Mountain Lodge is a 19th-century mine building which was heaved up the mountain to its present location near the bottom of Pioneer chair. The food is standard self-service fare but most reporters prefer it to the alternatives. The Summit House is cafe-style – serving chilli, pizza, soup etc. The Snow Hut is a smaller log building and usually has an outdoor grill. The Skiosk is an on-mountain yurt (a tent) serving snacks, halfway down the Bonanza chair-lift. There's quite a choice of restaurants back at the base area including the food court at the new Legacy Lodge.

SCHOOLS AND GUIDES
Thorough, full of enthusiasm

The school offers performance workshops (Dealng with the Diamonds, Moguls and Beyond) and Power Clinics (for strong intermediates) as well as beginner and private lessons.

FACILITIES FOR CHILDREN
Well organised; ideal terrain

There are a number of licensed carers who operate either at their own premises or at visitors' lodgings. The ski school takes children from the age of 3. Book in advance.

THE UTAH INTERCONNECT

Good skiers should not miss this excellent guided backcountry tour that runs four days a week from Park City to Snowbird. (Three days a week it runs from Snowbird, but only as far as Solitude.) When we did it we got fresh tracks in knee-deep powder practically all day. After a warm-up run to weed out weak skiers, you head up to the top of the Jupiter chair, go through a 'closed' gate in the area boundary and ski down a deserted, prettily wooded valley to Solitude. After taking the lifts to the top of Solitude we did a short traverse, then down more virgin powder towards Brighton. After more powder runs and lunch back in Solitude, it was up the lifts and a 30-minute hike up the Highway to Heaven to north-facing, tree-lined slopes and a great little gulley down into Alta. How much of Alta and Snowbird you get to ski depends on how much time is left.

The price ($150) includes two guides – one leading, another at the rear – lunch, lift tickets for all five resorts you pass through and transport home.

GETTING THERE

Air Salt Lake City, transfer ½hr.

Phone numbers
From distant parts of the US, add the prefix 1 435.
From abroad, add the prefix +1 435.

ACTIVITIES

Indoor Park City Racquet Club (4 indoor tennis courts, 2 racquetball courts, heated pool, hot-tub, sauna, gym, aerobics, basketball), Silver Mountain Spa (racquetball courts, weights room, swimming pool, aerobics, spa, massage and physical therapy, whirlpool, sauna), art galleries, concerts, theatre, martial arts studio, bowling
Outdoor Snowmobiles, ballooning, sleigh rides, ski jumping, ice skating, bob-sleigh and luge track, snow tubing, sports and recreation opportunities for disabled children and adults

TOURIST OFFICE

Postcode UT 84060
t +1 (435) 649 8111
f 647 5374
info@pcski.com
www.parkcitymountain.com

Staying there

If you're not hiring a car, pick a location that's handy for Main Street and the Town chair or the free bus.

HOW TO GO
Packaged independence
Park City is the busiest and most atmospheric of the Utah resorts, and a good base for visiting the others.
Hotels There's a wide variety, from typical chains to individual little B&Bs.
((((4) **Silver King** (649 5500) Deluxe hotel/condo complex at base of the slopes, with indoor-outdoor pool.
((((4) **Radisson Inn Park City** (649 5000) Excellent rooms and indoor-outdoor pool, but poorly placed for nightlife (out of town on main road).
((((4) **Yarrow** (649 7000) Recently renovated with big welcoming lobby, outdoor pool and hot-tub. Free shuttle.
((((4) **Washington School Inn** (649 3800) 'Absolutely excellent' historic inn in a great location near Main Street, with free wine and snacks creating a thriving après-ski social scene.
(((3) **Best Western Landmark Inn** (649 7300) Way out of town near The Canyons and factory outlet mall. Swimming pool. 'Good place to stay with car to visit other resorts.'
(((3) **Old Miners' Lodge** (645 8068) 100-year-old building next to Town lift, restored and furnished with antiques.
((2) **Chateau Apres Lodge** (649 9372) Close to the slopes: comfortable, faded, cheap.
((2) **1904 Imperial Inn** (649 1904) Quaint B&B at the top of Main Street.
Self-catering There's a big range available. The Townlift studios near Main Street and Park Avenue condos are both modern and comfortable and the latter have outdoor pool and hot-tubs. Silver Cliff Village is adjacent to the slopes and has spacious units and access to the facilities of the Silver King Hotel. Blue Church Lodge is a well-converted 19th-century Mormon church with luxury condos and rooms.

EATING OUT
Book in advance
There are over 100 restaurants but they all get busy, so book in advance. Zoom is the old Union Pacific train depot, now a trendy restaurant owned by Robert Redford. The Riverhorse is in a beautiful, high-ceilinged first-floor room with live music. Chimayo has great south-west cuisine. The Juniper at the Snowed Inn has won awards. Chez Betty is small and has perhaps the best food in town – pricey though. Cheaper places include the US Prime Steakhouse ('best steak ever'), the Grub Steak Restaurant at Prospector Square, Cisero's and Grappa (Italian), Jambalaya (Cajun), Wasatch Brew Pub (good value and an interesting range of beers) and Baja Cantina (Mexican).

APRES-SKI
Better than you might think
Although there are still some arcane liquor laws in Utah, provided you're over-21 and have your ID handy the laws are never a serious barrier to getting a drink. At the bars and clubs that are more dedicated to drinking (ie don't feature food but do serve spirits) membership of some kind is required. This may involve handing over $5 or more – one member can introduce numerous 'guests' – or else there'll be some old guy at the bar already organised to 'sponsor' you (sign you in) for the price of a beer. But a recent reporter points out that the system can be very expensive if you visit different resorts most days and just want a quick beer before hitting the road.

As the slopes close, the Pig Pen in the new lodge is the place to head for at the Resort Center – but you can of course make directly for Main Street. The Wasatch Brew Pub makes its own ale. The Claimjumper, JB Mulligans and the scruffy Alamo are lively places and there's usually live music and dancing at weekends. Harry O's and Cisero's nightclub are good too.

OFF THE SLOPES
Should be interesting
There's a factory outlet mall near The Canyons. Scenic balloon flights and excursions to Nevada for gambling are both popular. Snowmobiling is big. In January there's Robert Redford's Sundance Film Festival.

There are lots of shops and galleries and the museum and old jail house are worth a visit. Salt Lake City has some good concerts and shopping and a few points of interest, many connected with its Mormon heritage. The Capitol Building is open until 8pm and gives 'an interesting perspective on the State' and good views of the city.

You might like to learn to ski-jump or try the Olympic bob track at the Winter Sports Park down the road.

Snowbasin 1785m

Coming shortly to a screen near you

WHAT IT COSTS

5

HOW IT RATES

The slopes

Snow	*****
Extent	***
Experts	****
Intermediates	****
Beginners	**
Convenience	*
Queues	*****
Restaurants	*

The rest

Scenery	****
Resort charm	**
Off-slope	*

What's new

Before the Olympics, the new base lodge will be complete, built in the same plush wood and glass-style as the River Run lodge at Sun Valley. It will include restaurants, bars and a ski school desk. There will also be a skier services lodge nearby for tickets, rentals, children's ski school and, they hope, a daycare centre.

There will be two new on-mountain restaurants with sun decks – at the top of the Middle Bowl gondola and at John Paul chair-lift – also in plush Sun Valley-style.

A new access road has been built, reducing the journey time from Salt Lake City.

- ⊕ Fair-sized ski area
- ⊕ Impressive new lift system
- ⊕ Under an hour from Salt Lake City and other Utah resorts

- ⊖ No resort village as yet
- ⊖ The nearest accommodation is down in nearby Ogden or Huntsville
- ⊖ Not really suitable for beginners

Snowbasin? If you haven't heard of it you soon will. The four Olympic downhill events (men's and women's downhills, plus the downhill elements of the combined) and the two super giant slaloms will be held here in February 2002. It's a great hill, and it gets great snow (usually). All it needs is a great village.

THE RESORT

There is no resort, in the European sense of a village with accommodation. There will be one day: the mountain is in the same ownership as Sun Valley, and big investment in hotels and other accommodation is expected over the next few years. But for now you have to stay elsewhere. Ogden is the closest big town. It's also possible to stay nearer the mountain in (or close to) the backwater town of Huntsville. But we'd recommend staying in another Utah resort and making a day trip to Snowbasin in a rental car. A reporter made the 60-mile trip from Park City in less than an hour. It is 40 miles from Salt Lake City.

THE MOUNTAINS

Snowbasin's slopes cover a lot of pleasantly varied terrain and are served by nine lifts including a fast quad chair and two gondolas, all three installed in 1998. And there are other attractions. Not the least is the amazing view over the ridge at the top of the Strawberry Express gondola across the Great Salt Lake and surrounding plain. Another is the excursion to cutely named Powder Mountain, a few miles away across the other side of the Huntsville basin. This has (as you might hope) a reputation for powder and has an extensive snowcat skiing operation.

Slopes A new base lodge in the plush style of those at Sun Valley will be ready 'before the Olympics'. From this main base, the Middle Bowl gondola goes up to the area's central core, which has lots of different slopes and gulleys presenting different challenges. The John Paul fast quad chair goes up to the right from the base and serves great black slopes, on- and off-piste, with just one blue alternative way down. Above it, a small cable-car goes up to Allen's Peak and the dramatic start of the Olympic men's downhill course. The Strawberry gondola serves good blue runs at the opposite end of the ski area.

Snow reliability At 400in the average snowfall is in the usual Utah class. And there's lots of snowmaking.

SNOWPIX.COM / CHRIS GILL

The Strawberry gondola serves easy blue runs – but you can also hike from the top to the line of chutes seen in the background here →

MOUNTAIN FACTS

Altitude	1785m-2850m
Lifts	9
Pistes	3200 acres
Green	13%
Blue	49%
Black	38%
Art. snow	580 acres

Recco detectors used

Accommodation phone number

For accommodation information call the Ogden Chamber of Commerce on 627 8228 (from distant parts of the US, add the prefix 1 801; from abroad, add the prefix +1 801).

TOURIST OFFICE

Postcode UT 84317
t +1 (801) 399 1135
f 399 1138
info@snowbasin.com
www.snowbasin.com

Experts This is a great mountain for experts. All the lifts serve worthwhile terrain – even Strawberry has some severe chutes reached by hiking from the top, but most of the steep stuff is at the other end of the area. The cable-car serves a short black slope that was mogulled when we were there but will be glass-smooth when it serves as the start of the Olympic downhill race course. The course has been designed by Bernhard Russi – who else? It drops 844 metres and is already claimed to be a modern classic. The parts of it that were open when we visited were certainly impressive. Between the race course and the area boundary is a splendid area of off-piste wooded glades and gulleys. This is where most good skiers and riders will want to spend their time, riding the fast chair.

Intermediates It's also a good mountain for intermediates. Strawberry accesses mainly long open blue runs but also leads to a lightly wooded steeper slope at the extremity of the area. Middle Bowl is great terrain for the adventurous.

Beginners A place like this can't seriously be recommended for beginners from afar, but there is a nursery slope, and a few green runs.

Snowboarding Although there are no specific facilities for boarders, there is some excellent free-ride terrain.

Cross-country Nordic Valley is nearby.

Queues Queues are unlikely.

Mountain restaurants For 2001/02, there will be two – see What's New.

Schools and guides The school has special women's clinics as well as the normal offerings.

Facilities for children The plans for the new base include a daycare centre.

STAYING THERE

Ogden and Huntsville are the two closest towns to Snowbasin.

Hotels Ogden has various standard-issue hotels and motels. Huntsville has a small hotel, a couple of small B&Bs and Utah's oldest tavern (opened in 1879), the Shooting Star – a splendid scruffy relic of times past. On the walls are not only stuffed moose and elk but a stuffed St Bernard dog – apparently a beast of record-breaking enormity.

Après-ski The new base lodge will have a couple of bars and eating places. Otherwise it's back into town for evening entertainment.

Eating out The Shooting Star, in Huntsville, is famous for its huge Starburgers, which come with sausage as well as multiple burger patties etc.

Off the slopes Visits to Ogden, Park City or Salt Lake City are the options – you'll probably stay in one of them!

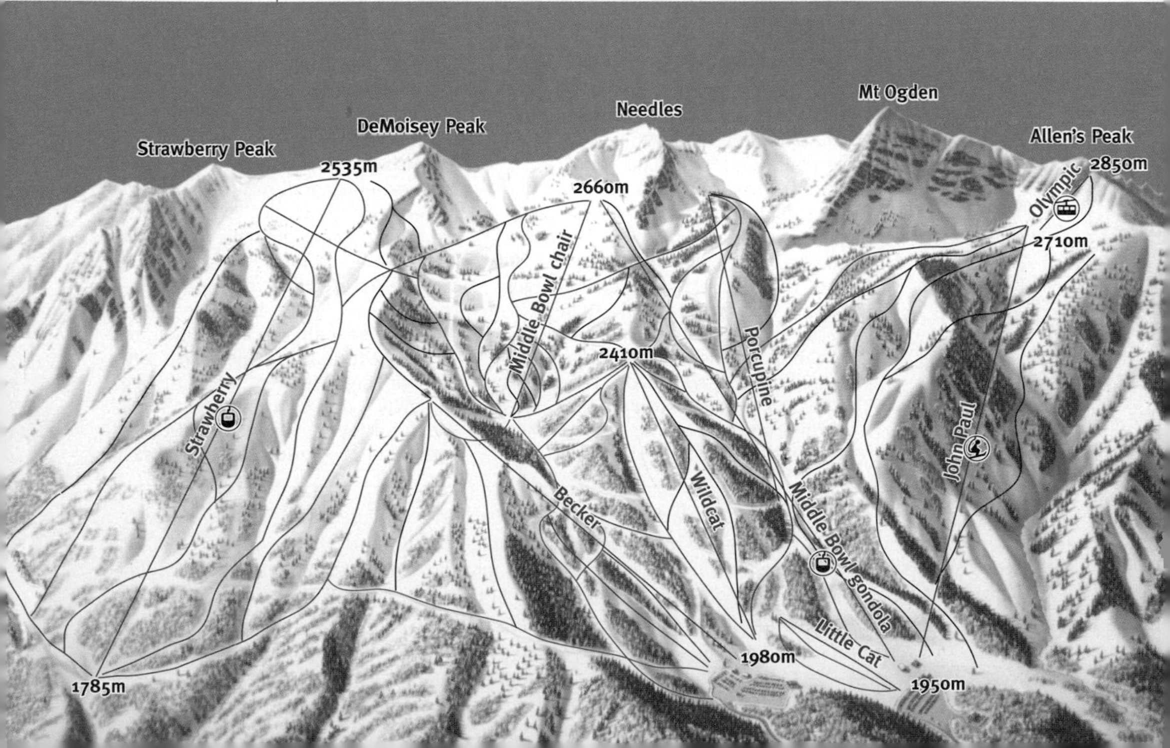

Snowbird 2470m

One of the world's top places for powderhounds

WHAT IT COSTS

(6)

HOW IT RATES

The slopes

Snow	*****
Extent	***
Experts	*****
Intermediates	***
Beginners	**
Convenience	*****
Queues	**
Restaurants	*

The rest

Scenery	***
Resort charm	*
Off-slope	*

What's new

For 2001/02, the Alta and Snowbird areas will be officially linked for the first time. A second high-speed quad in Mineral Basin will take you to the Sugarloaf saddle area above Alta's Albion Base. The return will be from the same area, reached by Alta's new Sugarloaf high-speed quad. A joint Snowbird-Alta lift pass will be available to skiers (but not boarders, as Alta bans them). The joint area will cover 4,700 acres.

There are plans for a new restaurant at the top of the Tram on Hidden Peak, but these are the subject of an ongoing court battle with anti-development groups.

MOUNTAIN FACTS

for Snowbird and Alta combined area

Altitude	2410m-3355m
Lifts	26
Pistes	4700 acres
Green	25%
Blue	37%
Black	38%
Art. snow	150 acres
Recco detectors used	

- ⊕ Quantity and quality of powder snow unrivalled except by next-door Alta
- ⊕ New link to Alta for 2001/02 makes one of the largest ski areas in the US
- ⊕ Fabulous ungroomed slopes, with steep and not-so-steep options
- ⊕ Luxurious accommodation with excellent facilities
- ⊕ Slopes-at-the-door convenience
- ⊕ Easy to get to Salt Lake City and other Utah resorts (so long as access road open)

- ⊖ Limited groomed runs for intermediates, though the new link with Alta doubles the terrain
- ⊖ Tiny, claustrophobic resort 'village'
- ⊖ Uncompromising modern architecture
- ⊖ Frequent queues for main cable-car
- ⊖ Area is very prone to avalanches, which can close the road as well as the slopes and keep you indoors
- ⊖ Very quiet at night

There can be few places where nature has combined the steep with the deep better than at Snowbird and neighbouring Alta, and even fewer places where there are also lifts to give you access. At long last the two resorts have agreed to a shared lift pass – and lifts and pistes to link the two have been built. The combined area will be one of the top powder-pig paradises in the world (with an average snowfall of 500 inches a year) and one of the US's biggest lift-linked ski areas. So it is a shame that Snowbird's concrete, purpose-built 'base village' is so lacking in charm and animation. If you are planning on a week's stay, you may prefer the more traditional (but equally quiet) Alta next door. Snowboarders are banned from Alta's slopes so cannot take advantage of the joint lift pass.

The resort

Snowbird lies 40km south-east of Salt Lake City in the Wasatch mountains, some 10km up Little Cottonwood Canyon – just before Alta. The setting is rugged and rather Alpine – and both the resort and (particularly) the approach road are prone to avalanches and closure: visitors are sometimes confined indoors for safety. The resort buildings are mainly block-like and dull – but they provide high-quality lodging and are convenient for the slopes.

The resort area and the slopes are spread along the road on the south side of the narrow canyon. The focal Snowbird Center is towards the eastern, up-canyon end; much of the rest consists of car-parking areas.

The mountain

Snowbird's new link with Alta (see separate Alta chapter) forms one of the largest ski areas in the US.

THE SLOPES

Looming above the resort

The north-facing slopes rear up from the edge of the resort. Five access lifts are ranged along the valley floor, the main one being the 125-person cable-car (the Aerial Tram) to Hidden Peak. The toughest terrain is on the flanks of the ridge beneath the line of the Tram. To the west, in Gad Valley, there are runs ranging from very tough to nice and easy – and six chair-lifts. Mineral Basin, on the back of Hidden Peak, opened in 1999/2000 with a new fast

boarding *Unfortunately for snowboarders, the joint Alta-Snowbird pass is not available for them as Alta still bans boards. But ask any Utah boarder where the best place to ride is and you'll get the same answer, 'the Bird's the word'. Competent free-riders will have a wild time in Snowbird's legendary powder and there is a terrain park and half-pipe. However, Snowbird's attractions would be wasted on beginners. And the nightlife's deadly dull.*

LIFT PASSES

2001/02 prices in dollars

Snowbird

Covers lifts and Aerial Tram in Snowbird.

Beginners Chickadee chair pass (11 per day).

Main pass

1-day pass 56

6-day pass 258

Senior citizens

Over 65:

1-day pass 43

Children

Under 12: free (chair-lifts only, up to 2 children per adult; upgrade to Tram is 9)

Short-term passes

Half-day (am or pm) pass available (adult 48)

Alternative passes

Joint Snowboard-Alta pass prices had not been agreed at the time of going to press.

Day and half-day passes for Snowbird chair-lifts only (47 per day for adults, 35 for seniors, free for two children under 12 with an adult)

SCHOOLS/GUIDES

2001/02 prices in dollars

Snowbird

Classes 5 days

Half- (pm only) or full-day. 5 full days: 360

Children's classes

Ages: 3 to 15

5 full days including lunch: 400

Private lessons

1hr, 3hr or 6hr

75 for 1hr, for 1 or 2 people, 100 for 3-6 people

CHILDCARE

The Camp Snowbird day camp, in the Cliff Lodge, takes children from 3 to 12, from 8.30 to 4.30. The nursery takes infants from 6 weeks to 3 years.

The Chickadees ski classes start at age 3. Evening babysitting is available.

quad and 500 acres of terrain for all standards. Another new quad there for 2001/02 will form the link with Alta.

The First Tracks programme allows you to ride the Tram to the top at 8am so as to be first up on the mountain. Numbers limited: book ahead ($20).

SNOW RELIABILITY
Exceptional

With Little Cottonwood Canyon's huge snowfalls, north-facing slopes and all runs above 2400m, snow reliability is very good. Snowbird and Alta typically average 500 inches of snowfall a year – twice as much as some Colorado resorts and around 50% more than the nearby Park City area.

FOR EXPERTS
Steep and deep – superb

Snowbird was created for experts, with a lot of tough terrain. The trail map is liberally sprinkled with double-black-diamonds, and some of the gulleys off the Cirque ridge – Silver Fox and Great Scott, for example, are exceptionally steep and frequently neck-deep in powder. Lower down lurk the bump runs, including Mach Schnell – a great run straight down the fall line through trees. There is some wonderful ski-anywhere terrain in the bowl beneath the high Little Cloud chair, and the Gad 2 lift opens up some attractive tree runs. Mineral Basin has added more expert terrain. Backcountry tours are available, and Wasatch Powderbird Guides offer heli-skiing and boarding. And now there's the whole of Alta's slopes to enjoy if you are a skier.

FOR INTERMEDIATES
Quality, not quantity

The winding Chip's Run on the east side of the Cirque ridge provides the only comfortable route down from the top for intermediates – at 5km, it's Snowbird's longest run. For adventurous intermediates wanting to try powder skiing, the bowl below the Little Cloud lift is a must – you'll rarely find better powder than this. There are some testing runs through the trees off the Gad 2 lift. There are also some nice long cruises in Mineral Basin and from the new link with Alta. But if it is miles of perfectly groomed piste you are after, there are plenty of better resorts.

FOR BEGINNERS
Better than you'd expect

Beginners have the Chickadee lift right down in the resort – and then there's a small network of trails to progress to.

FOR CROSS-COUNTRY
Go elsewhere

There are no prepared cross-country trails at Snowbird. All-terrain skiers can hike into the backcountry, but for loops you need to go elsewhere.

QUEUES
Avoid the Tram

For much of the season queues of up to 40 minutes for the Tram are common. The Gadzoom fast quad and the Little Cloud chair above it – sadly, also rather queue-prone – get you almost as high as the Tram. The lift back from Mineral Basin arrives at the same height as the Tram.

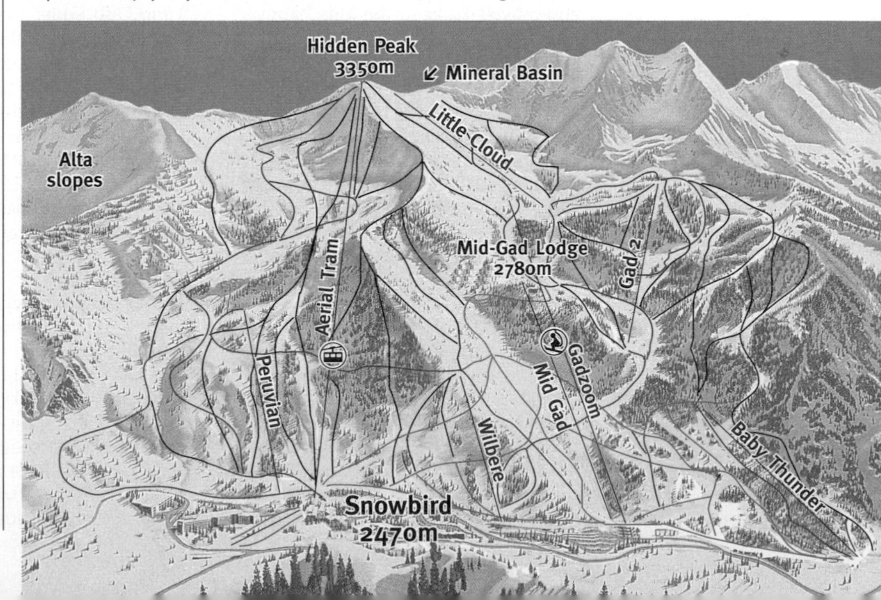

↑ The Cliff Lodge is not pretty – but it has great facilities and is right on the slopes

SNOWBIRD / DEREK SMITH

Central reservations phone number
For all resort accommodation call 1 800 640 2002 (toll-free from within the US)

GETTING THERE

Air Salt Lake City, transfer ½hr.

ACTIVITIES

Indoor Snowbird Canyon Racquet Club (tennis, racquetball, squash, climbing wall, aerobics, weight training, fitness room), hot-tubs, The Cliff Spa (fitness room, aerobics, beauty centre, sauna, steam room, solarium), conference centre, art gallery
Outdoor Swimming pools, hot-tubs, ice skating, tubing, snow-shoeing

TOURIST OFFICE

UT 84092-9000
t +1 (801) 742 2222
f 933 2298
info@snowbird.com
www.snowbird.com

MOUNTAIN RESTAURANT
Note the use of the singular

It's the Mid Gad self-service cafeteria – or 'fuel stop', to use the resort's own description – or else it's back to base. One reporter complains that even at the base it's crowded and limited.

SCHOOLS AND GUIDES
Something for everyone

The ski school offers a progressive range of lessons and speciality clinics – such as women-only clinics, over-50s lessons, bumps and diamonds lessons, and experts-only programmes ('A life-altering experience,' said a reporter).

FACILITIES FOR CHILDREN
All ages well cared-for

The 'kids ski free' programme allows two children (12 and under) to ski for free ($9 a day extra for use of the Tram) with each adult buying an all-day lift ticket. There are occasional evening distractions like parties, games and movies to keep the kids happy.

Staying there 

All the lodgings and restaurants are within walking distance of each other. The Tram station is central and the Gad lifts can be reached on snow. There are shuttle-bus services linking the lodgings, the lifts and the car parks, and a regular service up to Alta.

HOW TO GO
Package or independent

Salt Lake City airport is close, and well set up to handle independent travellers. There are several companies offering frequent transfers. If you plan to visit several other resorts, you'll want to hire a car, and it's worth considering Salt Lake City as a base – not least because avalanche danger can close Little Cottonwood Canyon after heavy snowfalls, in which case you won't be able to tour around.

A few UK tour operators feature accommodation in Snowbird. A number of UK holidaymakers combine a stay in Snowbird with a stay in Park City.

Hotels There are several lodges, and smaller condominium blocks.

Cliff Lodge (800 640 2002 for Snowbird Central Reservations). The main place: a huge luxury hotel and restaurant complex just up the nursery slopes from the Snowbird Center. There's a rooftop pool and hot-tub, sauna, steam room and gym. Prices here are understandably high, but if you can bear to share a four-bed 'dorm' room they're great value, considering the facilities you can use.

EATING OUT
A reasonable choice

Generally eating out revolves around Cliff Lodge and Snowbird Center – both house a number of restaurants. It's advisable for at least one member of a party to pay a few dollars to join the Club at Snowbird (guests at the Cliff Lodge are automatically registered) as most of the better restaurants are classed as private clubs. The Aerie and the Wildflower are quite upmarket venues, the Mexican Keyhole Junction and the Forklift are easier on the pocket and better for families.

APRES-SKI
Very quiet weekdays

Après-ski in Snowbird tends to be a bit muted, especially during the week The Tram Club under the Tram itself was rocking with live music as the slopes closed when we were there. The Keyhole Cantina also has a good atmosphere at end-of-play. A sunset swim and a few cocktails at the rooftop pool in Cliff Lodge is relaxing. It's quite feasible to head into Salt Lake City for the occasional night out – lots of live bands and so on.

OFF THE SLOPES
Head down-canyon

People not using the slopes will be bored at Snowbird once they've tried the Cliff Spa and its treatments. You could head towards the city – the Racquet Club down the valley is owned by Snowbird and has superb tennis facilities, and there are some attractions downtown, particularly around Temple Square.

The Rest of the West

This section covers a varied group of isolated resorts in different parts of the great Rocky Mountain chain that stretches the length of the United States from Montana and Idaho down through Wyoming and Colorado to New Mexico. Each has its own unique character – and each is well worth knowing about.

Sun Valley, Idaho, was America's first purpose-built resort, developed in the 1930s by the president of the Union Pacific Railway. It quickly became popular with the Hollywood jet set and has managed to retain its stylish image and ambience over the years. It hasn't become a big international destination, because of its rather isolated location, limited hotel accommodation and poor reputation for snow – although this has largely been rectified by the huge snowmaking installation. But if you want to indulge yourself a little and be pampered, bear it in mind – it has one of our favourite luxury hotels.

If you don't mind a bit of a cross-state drive, you might combine a visit to Sun Valley with a visit to the famously snowy resorts of Utah or to Jackson Hole in Wyoming – another resort with an impressive snow record. Jackson is the nearest there is to a resort with a genuine Wild West cowboy atmosphere. The old town is lined with wooden sidewalks and there are lively saloons, where modern-day working cowboys drink, play pool and dance to country music. The mountain is a 15-minute drive away and offers some of America's most extreme terrain, with steeps, jumps and bumps to suit all – a sharp contrast to the tame, immaculately groomed runs typical of many US resorts. It does have easier runs, but that's not why most people go there.

A little way north of both Sun Valley and Jackson, just inside Montana, is Big Sky, not to be confused with Big Mountain at the far northern end of the state, or indeed Big White, over the Canadian border in British Columbia. Big Sky has one of the biggest verticals in America (1275m) thanks to its Lone Peak cable-car, going way above the tree line to 3400m. Its extensive slopes have something for everyone, from extreme steeps at the top to countless gentle cruises at the bottom. But there's not much to do here except ski and board.

Taos, New Mexico, is the most southerly major resort in America, and because of its isolation is relatively unknown on the international market. There's a tiny resort development at the foot of the slopes, which are set high above the traditional adobe town of Taos, 18 miles away in the arid valley. The area was developed in the 1950s by a European and is still family-run, with a friendly feel to it. It is one of the few resorts still to ban snowboarders from its slopes, which have many very challenging runs, including some major mogul fields.

JACKSON HOLE / GORAN ASSNER

In many ways the Best of the West – Jackson Hole →

Big Sky 2285m

Vast and empty slopes for all standards

WHAT IT COSTS

6

HOW IT RATES

The slopes

Snow	****
Extent	***
Experts	*****
Intermediates	****
Beginners	****
Convenience	****
Queues	*****
Restaurants	*

The rest

Scenery	***
Resort charm	**
Off-slope	**

MOUNTAIN FACTS

Altitude	2070m-3400m
Lifts	18
Pistes	3600 acres
Green	10%
Blue	47%
Black	43%
Art. snow	350 acres
Recco detectors used	

- + Extensive ski area with runs for all abilities
- + Excellent snow reliability
- + Big vertical by US standards
- + No queues, empty slopes
- + Some slope-side accommodation

- − No real resort village as yet
- − Inadequate on-mountain dining facilities
- − Quite a few slow, old chair-lifts

Big Sky is renowned for its powder, steeps and big vertical, and has lots of blissfully empty gentler slopes. At present, there's no real village, just a very small collection of shops, restaurants and accommodation units – and nightlife is limited to say the least. If that's what you like, go soon – the owners have big expansion plans which include a complete village overhaul and enough extra terrain to put Big Sky in the first division.

THE RESORT

Big Sky, now over 25 years old, has started to attract a few international visitors who have heard of its huge snowfalls and deserted slopes.

The resort is set amid the wide open spaces of Montana, one hour's drive from the airport town of Bozeman. At the foot of the slopes is Mountain Village – the obvious base, with some slope-side condominiums and lodges. Despite efficient free buses, condos dotted around a golf course 10km east at Meadow Village hold little appeal. Hiring a car is recommended.

Bridger Bowl is less than two hours' drive away, and makes a worthwhile outing – a broad, lightly wooded mountain of 600m vertical.

THE MOUNTAINS

The slopes cover a big area spread over two linked mountains, with long runs for all standards. Lone Mountain, with steep open upper slopes and a wooded base, dominates. Andesite mountain is a much more modest

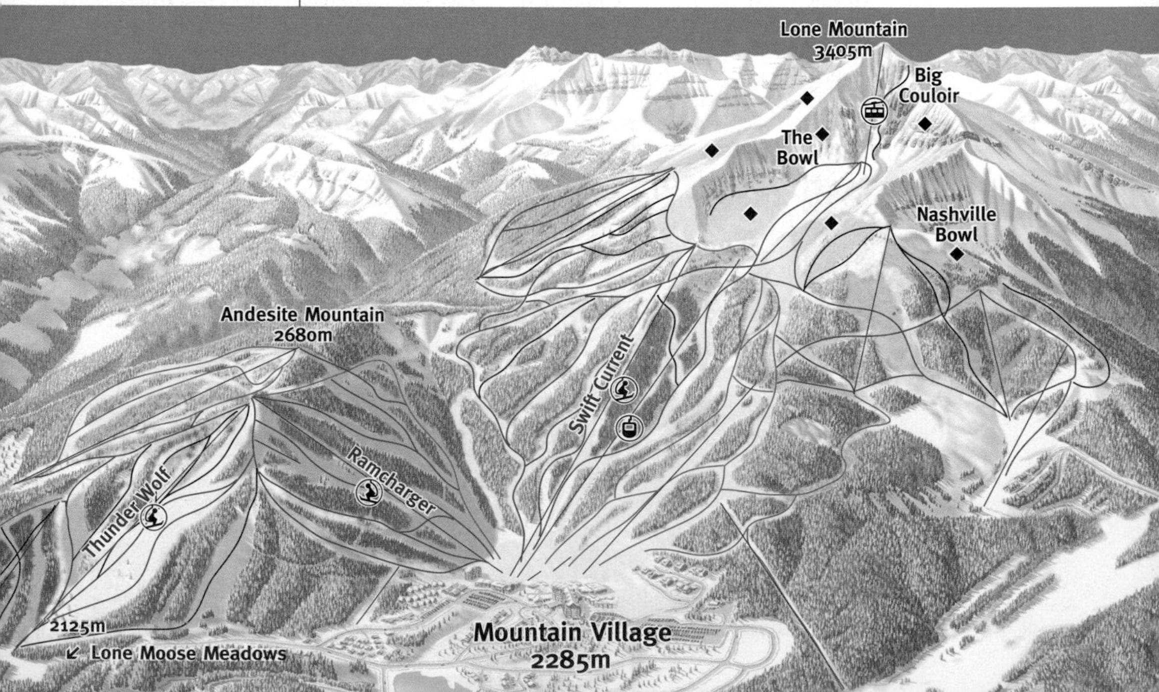

See why they call it Lone Mountain? →

BIG SKY

What's new

A new 80-room Mountain Inn hotel in the Mountain Village will be ready for 2001/02. Four new gladed runs will be created on Andesite.

A 10-year expansion plan has now been approved – developments will include an enhanced mountain village with over 100 shops and restaurants, a spa, conference facilities, 1,800 acres of new terrain and an extra six fast lifts.

Central reservations phone number
For all resort accommodation call 1 800 548 4486 (toll-free from within the US).

TOURIST OFFICE

Postcode MT 59716
t +1 (406) 995 5000
f 995 5001
info@bigskyresort.com
www.bigskyresort.com

wooded hill of 400m vertical. Although there are free fast quads, most of the chair-lifts are old triples and doubles. There are daily free mountain tours.
Slopes Half-a-dozen chairs and a gondola serve the wooded lower half of Lone Mountain (with a vertical of about 500m). The Lone Peak chair accesses a few blue slopes at the bottom of the main bowl and leads to the Lone Peak Tram – a tiny 15-person cable-car to the top, which serves great experts-only terrain all around the top bowl. The longest run – from the top of the Tram, down through Liberty Bowl round the back of the mountain, to the village – is about six miles long.
Snowboarding There is a good terrain park and half-pipe on Andesite and a gentler one on Lone Mountain.
Snow reliability Snowfall averages 400+ inches, which puts Big Sky ahead of most Colorado resorts and alongside Jackson Hole. Grooming is good, too.
Experts The terrain accessed from the Tram is great, including narrow couloirs and wide powder fields. Castro's Shoulder is the steepest route at 50°. There are good black slopes lower down, around the tree line.
Intermediates There is lots of cruising terrain – the shady runs on Andesite from the Ramcharger chair are splendid, but practically all the lower lifts serve worthwhile blue runs.
Beginners It's excellent, with a nursery area at the base and long greens on both mountains.
Cross-country There are 65km of trails at Lone Mountain Ranch. There are also trails at West Yellowstone.
Queues Waiting in queues is unheard of unless high winds close the upper lifts, and the runs seem deserted. There are 3,600 skiable acres, and on an average day they sell 2,000 lift tickets; do the sums.
Mountain restaurants The Dug-Out, on Andesite, is the only mountain restaurant – fast food and barbecues. You can head back to base to eat.
School and guides The ski school receives excellent reviews. A recent reporter described his children's lessons as a '100% success'.
Facilities for children Handprints nursery in the slope-side Snowcrest lodge takes children from age six months ('It was perfection – four to an adult,' says a reporter). Children under 10 years ski for free.

STAYING THERE

How to go Condos are the norm at the slope-side Mountain Village.
Hotels In Mountain Village, Huntley Lodge (highly recommended by a reporter), Shoshone and the new slope-side Summit are the most convenient hotels, with good facilities. Mountain Inn will be open for 2001/02.
Self-catering There are lots of self-catering condos available for rent – the well-equipped Stillwater condos in the resort village are 'excellent'.
Après-ski Chet's bar has live music, pool and poker games. The Carabinier lounge in the Summit, Roosters and Scissorbill's are also popular.
Eating out In Mountain Village, Huntley Lodge has a smart restaurant, The Peaks and Dante's Inferno are popular. You can take a shuttle-bus or a restaurant courtesy car to Meadow Village: Buck's T-4, First Place, Café Edelweiss and Rocco's get good reports. 320 Guest Ranch at Gallatin Canyon is also recommended.
Off the slopes The main things to do are snowmobiling, horse riding, sleigh riding, visiting Yellowstone national park and shopping in Bozeman.

Jackson Hole 1925m

Wild West cowboy town close to wild, exciting slopes

WHAT IT COSTS

6

HOW IT RATES

The slopes	
Snow	****
Extent	***
Experts	*****
Intermediates	**
Beginners	***
Convenience	***
Queues	***
Restaurants	*
The rest	
Scenery	***
Resort charm	****
Off-slope	***

MOUNTAIN FACTS

Altitude	1925m-3185m
Lifts	11
Pistes	2500 acres
Green	10%
Blue	40%
Black	50%
Art. snow	160 acres
Recco detectors used	

- ⊕ Big, steep mountain, with some real expert-only terrain and one of the US's biggest verticals (1260m)
- ⊕ Jackson town has an entertaining Wild West ambience
- ⊕ Unspoilt, remote location with some impressive scenery nearby
- ⊕ Excellent snow record
- ⊕ Even more snow (and astonishingly empty slopes) 90 minutes away at Grand Targhee – with snowcats
- ⊕ Low altitude, so no altitude sickness
- ⊕ Cheap lodgings (winter is off-peak)
- ⊕ Plenty to do off the slopes
- ⊕ Airport is only minutes from town

- ⊖ Intermediates lacking the confidence to tackle black runs (often with deep snow) will be more-or-less confined to the minor Apres Vous mountain
- ⊖ Inadequate mountain restaurants
- ⊖ The cable-car serving the top runs still generates long queues
- ⊖ Low altitude, and slopes face roughly south-east, so snow can be poor on the lower slopes
- ⊖ Jackson town is 15 minutes from the mountain, although Teton Village offers accommodation at the base
- ⊖ Getting there from the UK involves two or three flights

For those who like the idea of steep slopes smothered in deep powder or plastered with big bumps, Jackson Hole is Mecca. Like many American mountains, Jackson has double-diamond steeps that you can't find in Europe except by going off-piste with a guide. What marks it out from the rest is the sheer quantity of black-graded terrain, and the scale of the mountain.

Utah devotees will tell you that the snow here isn't as light as at Alta/Snowbird; but it's light enough, and falls in quantities somewhere between those found in Colorado and those famously found in Alta – the average annual total is around 400in, but in recent seasons it has often been around or above the 500in mark.

With its wooden sidewalks, country-music saloons and pool halls, tiny Jackson is a determinedly Western town – great fun, if you like that kind of thing. We do.

The resort

The town of Jackson sits at the south-eastern edge of Jackson Hole – a high, flat valley surrounded by mountain ranges, in the north-west corner of Wyoming. This is real 'cowboy' territory, and the town strives to maintain its Wild West flavour, with traditional-style wooden buildings and sidewalks, and a couple of 'cowboy' saloons. Jackson gets many more visitors in summer than winter (thanks to the nearby national parks), which accounts for the many clothing and souvenir shops, alongside the more upmarket galleries appealing to affluent second-home owners. But in winter it's basically a ski town with a Western feel.

The slopes, a 15-minute drive north-east, rise abruptly from the flat valley floor. At the base is Teton Village – a small purpose-built collection of lodgings, shops and restaurants in a pleasantly woody setting, some neo-Alpine but increasingly in local style. The public bus service to the mountain ($2 single) is reported to be irregular and slow.

JACKSON HOLE / BOB WOODALL / FPI

The Million Dollar Cowboy Bar in the centre of Jackson has saddles as bar stools and a stuffed grizzly bear staring at drinkers ↓

What's new

A couple of seasons ago Jackson Hole opened gates into the wild backcountry of Grand Teton and Bridger Teton National Parks, making it an even more compelling destination for expert skiers and riders. But don't dream of trying this without a guide.

For 2000/01, the old Union Pass surface lift that brought you back to the base area after doing the Hobacks was replaced by a fixed-grip quad chair. Another quad was built from the Moose Creek condo area of Teton Village to give guests access to the Union Pass chair rather than having to walk to the base area

The big news for 2001/02 is in the nearby resort of Grand Targhee. 500 acres of what was formerly snowcat skiing will now be served by a high-speed quad, opening great ungroomed powder as well as new groomed runs. That will still leave 1000 acres for snowcat guests only.

The mountains

Jackson Hole has long been recognised as one of the world's most compelling resorts for advanced and expert skiers. With recent improvements to the lifts and some of the buildings at Teton Village, the resort may seem less of a cult destination for hard-core experts and more of a conventional resort, with something for everyone. Don't be fooled: the beginner slopes are fine, but intermediates wanting to build up confidence should look elsewhere.

THE SLOPES

One big mountain, one small one

Trail gradings are accurate at Jackson: our own small map doesn't distinguish black from double-black-diamond runs, but the distinction matters once you are there – 'expert only' tends to mean just that. Some of the double-black runs are simply steep; but there are also cliffs, bumps, jumps and couloirs, including the infamous Corbet's.

One big mountain makes Jackson Hole famous – **Rendezvous**. The summit, accessed by a mid-sized cable-car (the Tram), provides a 1260m vertical drop – exceptional for the US. And the vertical is usable: conditions and thighs permitting, you can go from top to almost bottom on black slopes. From the top of the Tram you can now access the backcountry of Cody Bowl.

To the right looking up is **Apres Vous** mountain, with half the vertical and mostly much gentler runs, accessed by the short Teewinot and the longer Apres Vous fast quads.

Between these two peaks is a broad mountainside split by gulleys, accessed since 1997 by the **Bridger gondola**. This opened up new terrain, and gives speedy access to the Thunder and Sublette quad chairs serving some of the steepest terrain on Rendezvous.

Hosts offer complimentary tours of the mountains, starting from the Host building at 9.30. And at 1.30 on weekdays you can usually take a tour with Olympic gold medallist Pepi Stiegler – Jackson's director of skiing.

Snow King is a separate area right next to Jackson town. Locals use it in their lunch-hour and in the evening (it's partly floodlit).

Grand Targhee, famous for its powder snow, is just 90 minutes' drive from Jackson Hole – buses run daily. See end of chapter.

SNOW RELIABILITY

Steep lower slopes can suffer

The claimed average of 402in of 'mostly dry powder' snow is much more than most Colorado resorts claim – and for a core three-month season conditions are likely to be reasonable. But the base elevation here is relatively low for the Rockies, and the slopes are quite sunny – they basically face south-east. If you're unlucky, you may find the steep lower slopes like the Hobacks in poor shape, or even shut. Happily, much of the best expert terrain is relatively shady. And snowmaking covers top-to-bottom runs from the gondola and on Apres Vous.

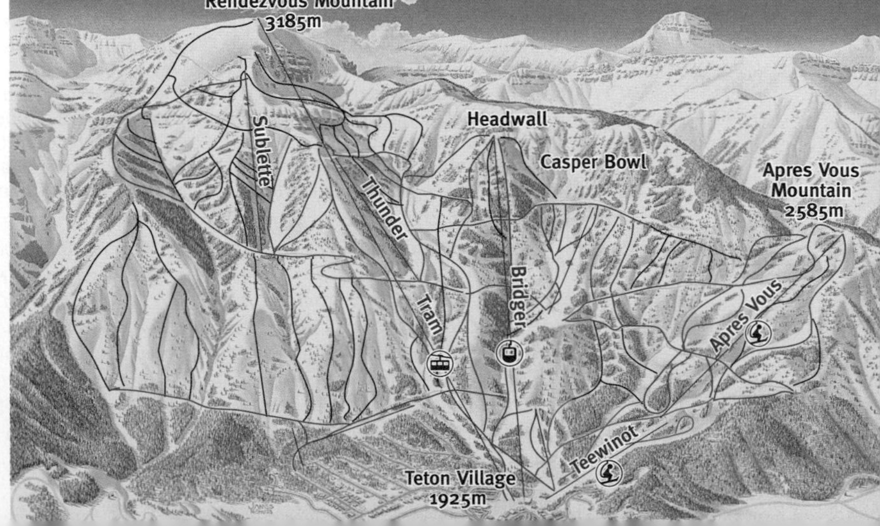

↑ The infamous Corbet's Couloir – leap in and impress the cable-car crowd by surviving to brag about it

JACKSON HOLE / JONATHAN SELKOWITZ

LIFT PASSES

2001/02 prices in dollars

Jackson Hole
Covers all lifts and includes 'Tram'.

Main pass
1-day pass 59
7-day pass 343

Senior citizens
Over 65: 7-day pass 172

Children
15 to 21: 7-day pass 257
Under 15: 7-day pass 172

Short-term passes
Afternoon pass from 12.30 (adult 44)

Notes 5-year-olds and under have free use of some lifts.

FOR EXPERTS
Best for the brave

For the good skier or boarder who wants challenges without the expense of hiring a guide to go off-piste, Jackson is one of the world's best resorts – maybe even the best.

Rendezvous mountain offers virtually nothing but black and very black slopes.

The routes down the main Rendezvous Bowl are not particularly fearsome; but some of the alternatives are. Go down the East Ridge at least once to stare over the edge of the notorious Corbet's Couloir. The Tram passes right above it, providing a great view of people throwing themselves off the lip. It's the jump in that's special; the word is that the slope you land on is a mere 50° to the horizontal.

Below Rendezvous Bowl, the wooded flanks of Cheyenne Bowl offer serious challenges, at the extreme end of the single-black-diamond spectrum. If instead you take the ridge run that skirts this bowl to the right, you get to the Hobacks – a huge area of open and lightly wooded slopes, gentler than those higher up, but still black.

Corbet's aside, most of the seriously steep slopes are more easily reached from the slightly lower quad chairs. From Sublette, you have direct access to the short but seriously steep Alta chutes, and to the less severe Laramie Bowl beside them. Or you can track over to Tensleep Bowl – pausing to inspect Corbet's from below – and on to the less extreme (and less chute-like) Expert Chutes, and the single black Cirque and Headwall areas). Casper Bowl – accessed through gates only – is recommended for untracked powder. Thunder chair serves further steep, narrow, north-facing chutes.

Again, the lower part of the mountain here offers lightly wooded single-black slopes.

The gondola serves terrain not without interest for experts. In particular, Moran Woods is a splendid under-utilised area. And even Apres Vous itself has an area of serious single blacks in Saratoga bowl.

The gates into the backcountry access over 3,000 acres of amazing terrain and you should hire a guide to take you there. There are some heli-ski and heli-board operations.

FOR INTERMEDIATES
Exciting for some

There are great cruising runs on the front face of Apres Vous, and top-to-bottom blues from the new gondola also offer quite gentle runs. But they don't add up to a great deal of mileage, and you shouldn't consider Jackson unless you want to tackle the blacks. It's then important to get guidance on steepness and snow conditions. The steepest single blacks are steep; intimidating when mogulled and fearsome when hard. The daily grooming map is worth consulting.

FOR BEGINNERS
Fine, up to a point

There are a few broad, gentle runs: fine for getting started. The progression to the blue Werner run off the Apres Vous chair is gradual enough – but what then? Most of the blues are traverses and the exceptions will not help build a novice's confidence.

boarding *Jackson Hole is a cult resort for expert snowboarders, just as it is for expert skiers. The steeps, cliffs and chutes make for a lot of high-adrenalin thrills for competent free-riders. There's a fun-park and a half-pipe, and Dick's Ditch is a natural pipe. It's not a bad resort for novices either, with the beginner slopes served by a high-speed quad. Intermediates not wishing to venture off the groomed runs will find the resort a bit limited. There are some good snowboard shops, including the Hole-in-the-Wall at Teton Village. The nightlife in the bars around the town square is reasonably lively.*

SCHOOLS/GUIDES

2000/01 prices in dollars

Jackson Hole
Classes Full day: 65
Half-day: 50
First Tracks (8.30am)
4 hours: 85
Children's classes
Ages: 3 to 6 (inc lunch and lift ticket):
Full day 75
Half day 50
Ages: 7 to 17 (inc lunch and lift ticket):
Full day: 95
Private lessons
1-5 people
Early tram (8.30), Full day (7 hr): 415
Half day (4 hr): 310
All day from 9am 395
Backcountry Guiding
1-5 people
Full day 415
Half day am 310
Half day pm 225

Phone numbers
From distant parts of the US, add the prefix 1 307.
From abroad, add the prefix +1 307.

CHILDCARE

The Kids' Ranch (739 2691) in the Cody House at Teton Village takes children aged 2 months to 6 years, from 8.30 to 4.30, with indoor and outdoor games and one-to-one ski lessons from age 3. Kids use the Fort Wyoming snow-garden, with 'magic carpet' lift.

FOR CROSS-COUNTRY
Lots of possibilities

There are three centres in the valley, offering trails of various lengths and difficulty. The Spring Creek Nordic Center has some good beginner terrain and offers moonlight tours. The Nordic Center at Teton has 17km of trails and organises trips into the National Parks.

QUEUES
Always queues for the Tram

The Bridger gondola has relieved some of the pressure on the 30-year-old Tram. But the Tram is still the quickest way up Rendezvous, still the only way to the very top and still not able to keep up with demand; there may be queues all day.

MOUNTAIN RESTAURANTS
Head back to base

There's only one real restaurant on the mountain – at the base of the Casper chair-lift; it does a good range of self-service food, but gets very crowded. There are simple snack-bars at four other points on the mountain. At the base, Nick Wilson's in the Clocktower, the Alpenhof restaurant and the Mangy Moose are favourites.

SCHOOLS AND GUIDES
Learn to tackle the steeps

As well as the usual lessons, there are also First Tracks classes on steep and deep slopes. On certain dates, special steep skiing and boarding, freestyle and backcountry camps are held. Backcountry guides can be hired.

FACILITIES FOR CHILDREN
Just fine

The area may not seem to be one ideally suited to children, but in fact there are enough easy runs and the 'Kids' Ranch' care facilities are good.

Staying there

HOW TO GO
In town or by the mountain

Teton Village is convenient. But stay in Jackson for cowboy atmosphere.
Hotels There's something to suit most tastes. Because winter is low season, prices are low.
(5) **Amangani Resort** (734 7333) Hedonistic (expensive) luxury in isolated position way above the valley.
(4) **Alpenhof** (733 3242) Our favourite (and our readers') in Teton Village. Tirolean-style, with rooms of varying standard and price. Good food. Pool, sauna, hot-tub.
(4) **Wort** (733 2190) Brick-built hotel right in the centre of town, above the lively Silver Dollar Bar. 'Very comfortable.' Hot-tub.
(4) **Rusty Parrot Lodge** (733 2000) A stylish place in Jackson town, with a rustic feel and handcrafted furniture. Hot-tub.
(4) **Snake River Lodge & Spa** (733 3657) At Teton Village. Smartly welcoming as well as comfortable and convenient, with fine new spa facilities.
(4) **Spring Creek Ranch** (733 8833) Exclusive retreat midway between town and slopes; cross-country on-hand. Hot-tub.
(4) **Huff House Inn** (733 4164) Charming old inn – the best of Jackson's many luxury B&B places.
(4) **Painted Porch** (733 1981) Gorgeous B&B full of antiques.
(3) **Lodge at Jackson Hole** (733 2992) Western-style place on fringe of Jackson town. Comfortable mini-suite rooms, and free breakfast/après-ski munchies. Pool, sauna, hot-tubs.
(3) **Parkway Inn** (733 3143) Friendly, family-run place in Jackson town; nice pool.
(2) **Trapper Inn** (733 2648) Friendly, good value, a block or two from Town Square. Hot-tubs.
Self-catering There is lots of choice at Teton Village, within and around Jackson and at more isolated locations.

EATING OUT
It's a pleasure in Jackson

Teton Village has pizza, Mexican, a steakhouse and a number of hotel restaurants. Most people favour the Mangy Moose – good value, good fun. In Jackson there are lots of places to try (but book ahead). The cool art-deco Cadillac Grille does good food – in the attached bar as well as the restaurant. The Range is excellent for trendy American regional cuisine. The Blue Lion is small, cosy and casually stylish. The 'saloons' do hearty meals, and a reporter reckons the Million Dollar does 'the best steaks and ribs in town'. A good budget place is the Snake River brew-pub – not to be confused with the pricey, over-rated Snake River Grill. The 'Greek-inspired' food at the cute log-cabin Sweetwater is recommended. There's also Italian, Cajun, Chinese (Lame Duck), Indian, Tex-Mex and sushi (Masa Sushi).

GETTING THERE

Air Jackson, transfer ½hr.

ACTIVITIES

Indoor Art galleries, ice skating, cinemas, swimming, theatre, concerts, wildlife art museum

Outdoor Snowmobiles, mountaineering, horse riding, snow-shoe hikes, snowcat tours, floodlit skiing, heli-skiing, sleigh rides, dog-sledding, walks, wildlife safaris and tours of Yellowstone National Park

TOURIST OFFICE

Postcode WY 83001
t +1 (307) 733 7182
f 733 1286
info@jacksonhole.com
www.jacksonhole.com

APRES-SKI

Amusing saloons

For immediate après-ski festivities at Teton Village, the biggest draw is the Mangy Moose – a big, happy, noisy place, often with good live music. In sharp contrast is the calmly welcoming Dietrich's bar, at the Alpenhof.

In Jackson there are two famous 'saloons'. The Million Dollar Cowboy Bar features saddles as bar stools and a stuffed grizzly bear, and is usually the liveliest place in town, with good food and live music some nights (and sometimes line-dancing, with classes, too). The Silver Dollar around the corner is more subdued; there may be ragtime playing as you count the 2032 silver dollars inlaid into the counter. The Rancher is a huge pool-hall. The Shady Lady saloon at Snow King sometimes has live music – country and western of course. The Virginian saloon is a quieter watering hole.

For a night out of town, join the local ravers at the Stagecoach Inn at Wilson, especially on Sundays.

OFF THE SLOPES

'Great' outdoor diversions

The famous Yellowstone National Park is 100km to the north. You can tour the park by snowcat or snowmobile,

but you'll be roaring along the snowy roads in the company of several hundred other snowmobiles – 'more like a Grand Prix than a wilderness', as a recent reporter puts it. There is much more rewarding snowmobiling to be done elsewhere, eg at Goosewing Ranch and along the Gros Ventre river – much quieter and more wildlife.

The National Elk Refuge, next to Jackson and across the road from the National Museum of Wildlife Art, has the largest elk herd in the US. In town there are some 40 galleries and museums and a number of outlets for Indian and Western arts and crafts. There is, believe it or not, a branch of Ripley's Believe It or Not®.

A DAY OUT IN GRAND TARGHEE 2440M

We'd recommend any adventurous visitor to make the hour-and-a-half trip over the Teton pass to sample Grand Targhee's fabled powder. The average snowfall here is over 500in – 25% greater than Jackson, and on a par with Utah's best. Locals call it Grand Foggee, because there is often low cloud even when it's not snowing. This may be just as well, because the slopes generally face south-west, which is about the worst orientation in the book for sun damage.

On the main Fred's Mountain, the 1,500 acres of slopes are blissfully empty. A central fast quad serves a wide area of open and lightly wooded blue and black runs with a respectable 670m vertical. Off to the left, a slow quad chair serves an excellent area of short green runs, and beyond that a longer slow double serves another splendid area of tough blues and easy blacks – deserted when we visited.

Next-door Peaked Mountain offers slopes that are similar in extent, but were previously only accessible by snowcat. For 2001/02 it will be accessed by a new high-speed detachable quad. About a third of the new terrain will be groomed, but pristine glade skiing and open bowls will be left untouched. For those (like us) who loved the Targhee snowcat trips, there are still over 1,000 acres kept just for this. On Peaked Mountain, the vertical is slightly greater, at 860m, than on Fred's; and the lower part of the mountain is more heavily wooded.

Daily buses to Targhee pick up at various points around town and Teton Village. A combined bus/lift ticket costs $56. The snowcat operation costs $240 a day, $175 a half-day. You can take an instructor along, for a premium. You can also stay at Grand Targhee – there's a small, quiet, modern village right at the base.

Sun Valley 1755m

Stylish resort with slopes to flatter its rich and famous guests

WHAT IT COSTS

(6)

HOW IT RATES

The slopes

Snow	***
Extent	***
Experts	***
Intermediates	****
Beginners	***
Convenience	**
Queues	****
Restaurants	****

The rest

Scenery	***
Resort charm	***
Off-slope	***

MOUNTAIN FACTS

Altitude	1755m-2790m
Lifts	13
Pistes	2067 acres
Green	38%
Blue	45%
Black	17%
Art. snow	600 acres

- ⊕ Luxury resort built around the atmospheric old mining town of Ketchum
- ⊕ Ideal intermediate terrain
- ⊕ Wonderful luxurious mountain restaurants and base lodges
- ⊕ Great restaurants and atmospheric bars for dining out, après-ski, and star-spotting
- ⊕ Lots of off-slope diversions

- ⊖ Expensive
- ⊖ Erratic snow record though extensive artificial back-up
- ⊖ Shuttle-buses between two separate mountains and from most accommodation

Millions of dollars have been spent in recent years building new facilities – high-speed chair-lifts, a huge computerised snowmaking system, splendid base lodges and mountain restaurants – to maintain Sun Valley's reputation as the US's original luxury purpose-built winter sports resort. For a peaceful, relaxing time, it's hard to beat. For skiing and boarding alone, there are better resorts.

THE RESORT

Sun Valley is based around the old mining village of Ketchum. It was built in the 1930s by Averell Harriman, President of the Union Pacific Railway, and became a favourite with stars such as Clark Gable and Judy Garland. Its current owner, Earl Holding, has pumped millions of dollars into the mountain to restore it to state-of-the-art luxury and Sun Valley now attracts stars like Clint Eastwood and Arnie Schwarzenegger. The town of Ketchum retains its old-world charm and has atmospheric bars, restaurants and shops. But it's not cheap: 'More expensive than Aspen. I didn't buy, but I enjoyed looking in the high-quality shops,' says a reporter.

SUN VALLEY RESORT

There are three luxury lodges like River Run on Bald Mountain ↓

THE MOUNTAINS

There are two separate mountains – Bald Mountain, with the main body of runs, and the smaller Dollar Mountain.

Slopes The main slopes of Bald Mountain (known locally as Baldy) are accessed from one of two luxurious base lodge complexes at River Run and Warm Springs, a shuttle-bus-ride from most accommodation. Of the 13 lifts, seven are high-speed quads. One reporter complained of 'dangerous icy pistes that should have been closed, and pistes crossing each other, causing more collisions than I have seen anywhere'. The separate Dollar Mountain has good beginner terrain.

Snowboarding Snowboarders are now allowed and the chair-lifts make getting about easy.

Snow reliability The resort has an erratic natural snow record, so it has installed 600 acres of snowmaking, covering over 70% of the groomable runs.

Experts There are a few tough runs and bowls for experts, but nothing beyond single-black-diamond pitch, including the two most famous mogul runs, Exhibition and Limelight. Heli-skiing is available locally.

Intermediates Most of the terrain is ideal, with lots of runs at a similar consistent pitch. There are good blue bowl runs with great views from the top ridge as well as groomed cruisers through the trees.

What's new

Sun Valley's owner Earl Holding has invested millions in high-speed lifts, new runs, a huge computer-controlled snowmaking system and plush on-slope restaurant complexes and base lodges. Currently he is ploughing money into his new baby, Snowbasin in Utah, which will host the downhill events in the 2002 Olympics. So development in Sun Valley on hold.

Central reservations phone number
For all resort accommodation call 1 800 634 3347 (toll-free from within the US).

TOURIST OFFICE

Postcode ID 83340
t +1 (208) 726 3423
f 726 4533
ski@sunvalley.com
www.sunvalley.com

Beginners Dollar is the place to be, with gentle, long green runs to progress to. Baldy's greens are tougher.
Cross-country 40km of prepared trails start at the Nordic Center, with more along the valley.
Queues These are rarely a problem, with Sun Valley's network of high-speed quads whisking people around.
Mountain restaurants The mountain restaurants and base lodges have to be seen to be believed. They are way ahead of most US on-slope facilities, with floor-to-ceiling windows, beautiful wooden decor, heated terraces so snow instantly melts, and marble public restrooms with gold-plated taps. One reporter enjoyed 'the piano and violin players and people-watching at River Run base' at the end of the day.
Schools and guides We have no reason to believe that the tuition is not up to the usual high standards found in most North American resorts.
Facilities for children The ski school takes children from age 3, and under 16s staying with parents in certain lodgings get a free lift pass.

STAYING THERE

Shuttle-buses from most accommodation makes your choice of location less of an issue.
How to go There are some wonderful smart hotels to stay in, and there are plenty of cheaper options as well, including motels and self-catering.
Hotels One of our favourite hotels in any resort is the stylish Sun Valley Lodge. As well as magnificent rooms, there are a big outdoor ice rink and a pool, and the corridors are lined with photos of film-star guests. Ernest Hemingway wrote *For Whom the Bell Tolls* here.
Eating out There are over 80 restaurants and Sun Valley was rated number one in the US by readers of *Gourmet* magazine. We had excellent food at the relaxed Evergreen Bistro and a great breakfast at The Knob Hill Inn. A reporter recommends Chandlers, too.
Après-ski Atmospheric places include the Sawtooth Club (popular with locals), Whiskey Jaques for live music and dancing, and the Pioneer Saloon, popular for its prime rib and Clint Eastwood spotting.
Off the slopes You can have a fine time relaxing off the slopes, including sleigh rides, walking, snowmobiling, ice skating, swimming, fishing, gliding, paragliding and strolling round the galleries and shops. There's a special snow-shoe trail, too.

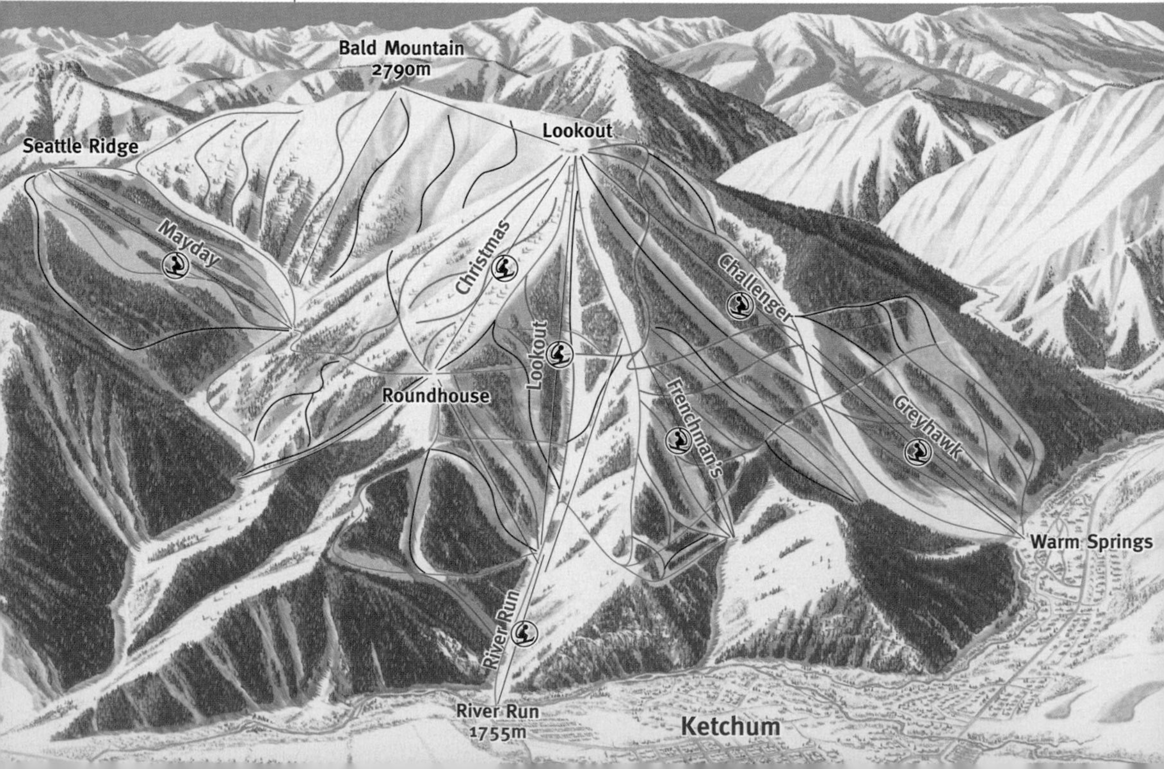

New England

You go to Utah for the deepest snow, to Colorado for the lightest powder and swankiest resorts, to California for the mountains and low prices. You go to New England for ... well, for what? Extreme cold? Rock-hard artificial snow? Mountains too limited to be of interest beyond New Jersey? Yes and no: all of these preconceptions have some basis, but they add up to an incomplete and unfair picture.

Yes, it can be cold: one of our reporters recorded –27°C, with wind chill producing a perceived temperature of –73°C. Early in the season, people wear face masks to prevent frostbite. It can also be warm – another reporter had a whole week of rain that washed away the early-season snow. The thing about New England weather is that it varies. Not as much as in Scotland, maybe, but the locals' favourite expression is: 'If you don't like the weather in New England, wait two minutes.' But we got routine winter weather on both our visits – one in January, one in February.

New England doesn't usually get much super-light powder or deep snow to play in. But the resorts have big snowmaking installations, designed to ensure a long season and to help the slopes to 'recover' after a thaw or spell of rain. They were the pioneers of snowmaking technology; and 'farming' snow, as they put it, is an art form and a way of life – provided the weather is cold enough. And they make and groom their snow to produce a superb surface. Many of the resorts get impressive amounts of natural snow, too – and they did get some huge dumps last season.

Sure, the mountains are not huge in terms of trail mileage. But several have verticals of over 800m (on a par with Colorado resorts such as Keystone) and most have over 600m (matching Breckenridge), and are worth considering for a short stay, or even for a week if you like familiar runs. For more novelty, a two- or three-centre trip is the obvious solution. You won't lack challenge – most of the double-black-diamond runs are seriously steep. And you won't lack space: most Americans visit over weekends, which means deserted slopes on weekdays – except at peak periods such as New Year and during the President's Day holiday, in late February. It also means the resorts are keen to attract long-stay visitors, so UK package prices are low.

But the big weekend and day-trip trade also means that few New England resorts have developed atmospheric resort villages – just a few condos and a hotel, maybe, with places to stay further out geared to suit car drivers who ski, eat, sleep, ski, go home.

But New England is easy to get to

AMERICAN SKIING COMPANY / NATHAN BILOW

Killington is New England's most impressive resort, at least in terms of its terrain and trails →

from Britain – a flight to Boston, then perhaps a three-hour drive to your resort. And there are some pretty towns to visit, with their clapboard houses and big churches. You might also like to consider spending a day or two in Boston – one of America's most charming cities. And you could save a lot of money on normal UK prices by having a shopping spree at the factory outlet stores that abound in New England.

We cover four of the most popular resorts on the UK market in the separate chapters that follow. But there are many other small areas, too. And if you are going for a week or more, we recommend renting a car and visiting a few resorts. In the rest of this introduction, we outline the attractions of the main possibilities.

From Killington (by far the biggest resort), you can go south to a range of smaller resorts. **Okemo** competes with Smugglers' Notch for the family market. Okemo mountain has southern Vermont's biggest vertical (655m) and longest trail (over 7km). The slopes, on several flanks of a single peak, are largely intermediate or easy – though there are a dozen black runs and a couple of short double-black-diamonds. Boarders are well catered for, with an extensive park leading into a half-pipe. There is almost 100% snowmaking cover – and the product is said to be the best in the east.

Mount Snow is another one-peak resort, with a long row of lifts on the front face serving easy and intermediate runs of just over 500m vertical, and a separate area of black runs on the north face – including one short but serious double-black. (The sister resort of **Haystack**, a short drive away, has more steep slopes in its Witches area.) Mount Snow has a huge snowboard park – one of the best in the east.

Stratton offers something like the classic Alpine arrangement of a village at the foot of the lifts. It's a smart, modern development with a pedestrian shopping street. The slopes – mostly easy and intermediate, with some blacks and some short double-black pitches – is spread widely around the flanks of a single peak, served by modern lifts, including a 12-person gondola and a fast six-seat chair.

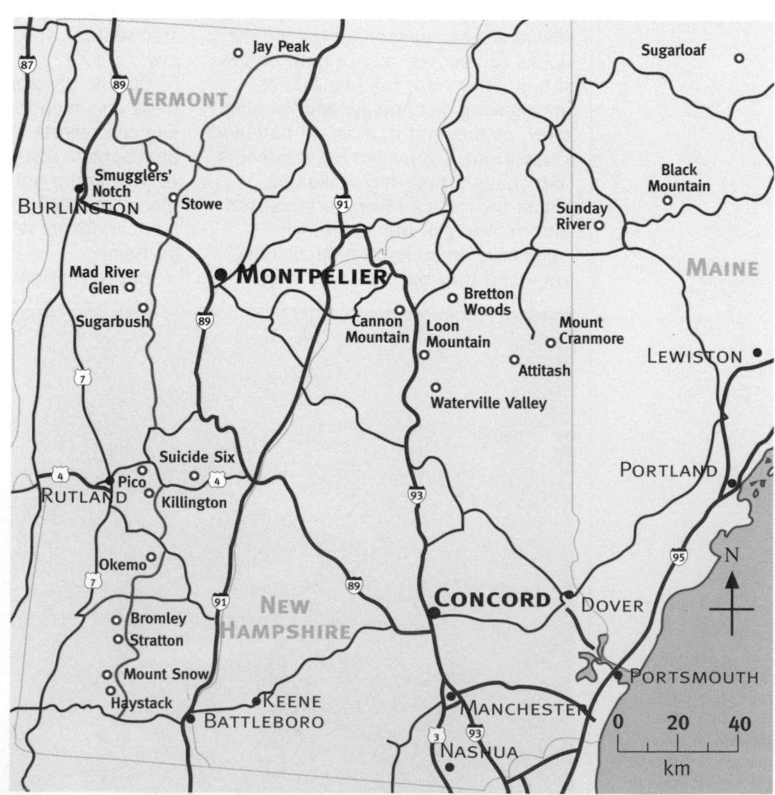

Stratton calls itself the 'snowboarding capital of the east', claiming the best terrain park, half-pipe, instruction and (of course) attitude.

You may find more interest in **Sugarbush**, to the north of Killington on the way to Smugglers' Notch. Sugarbush, midway between Killington and Stowe, is a fast-developing resort with one of the larger ski areas. The main sector is an extensive bowl below Lincoln Peak, with lifts up to six points on the rim; a long up-and-over chair-lift links the Mt Ellen area – smaller, but with more altitude and more vertical (808m). The easy skiing is confined to the lower slopes; higher up, the direct runs are seriously steep. There are snowboard parks in both areas. Most of the accommodation is in the historic village of Waitsfield, but the American Skiing Company is building a village at the base.

Mad River Glen next door is a cult resort with locals, with some tough ungroomed terrain, a few well-groomed intermediate trails and old-fashioned lifts – it still has a single-person chair-lift.

Further north, near the Canadian border, is **Jay Peak**. It gets busy at weekends (with Canadian as well as American visitors) but is quiet in the week. It has Vermont's only cable-car, which takes you to the summit and to views of four US states plus Canada. It gets a lot of snow for New England and has some good runs for advanced skiers and adventurous intermediates.

Sugarloaf in Maine already has a much better developed village than most small New England resorts. But the mountain is small and a keen piste-basher could ski it out in a day or two. Very popular with day and weekend skiers and boarders, it was very noticeable on our visit how safety conscious the local slope-users were. There was a higher proportion of people wearing protective helmets here than any other resort we have visited. We estimate well over 50% were helmeted – and these included all age groups, from children to octogenarians. Even teenage and twenty-something skiers and boarders were comfortable in their helmets – a sign of things to come in Europe perhaps? Sugarloaf is another resort that is now owned by the American Skiing Company (Killington, Mount Snow, Sugarbush, Sunday River and Attitash Bear Peak are its other New England resorts).

New Hampshire has several small resorts dotted along the Interstate 93 highway. **Bretton Woods** is one of the smaller areas, 460m vertical on a single mountain face, but it is highly rated, particularly by families, who relish the top-to-bottom easy trails. There is a good mix of terrain, and snowmaking is comprehensive. Snowboarders have a park and a half-pipe. There are a few places to stay near the base, with more five miles away at Twin Mountain.

Cannon is a ski area and nothing more – lifts from two base areas close to I-93 converge on the summit 650m above, serving mainly intermediate slopes; there are quite a few black runs, but no double-blacks and not much that is genuinely easy. It's only a few minutes' drive to Franconia in one direction and Lincoln in the other.

Loon Mountain Resort is a small, smart, modern resort just outside the sprawling town of Lincoln. The mountain (640m vertical) is mostly of intermediate difficulty, though some fall-line runs merit their black grading. There is a long snowboard park.

Waterville Valley is a compact area with runs dropping either side of a broad, gentle ridge rising 615m above the lift base. There are a couple of short but genuine double-black-diamond mogul fields, but most of the slopes are intermediate. Boarders are well catered for. The village is a Disneyesque affair a couple of miles away down on the flat valley bottom.

Killington 670m

Good slopes, great après-ski, no village (yet)

WHAT IT COSTS

5

HOW IT RATES

The slopes

Snow	***
Extent	**
Experts	***
Intermediates	***
Beginners	****
Convenience	*
Queues	****
Restaurants	*

The rest

Scenery	***
Resort charm	**
Off-slope	*

What's new

Killington has grand plans for a resort village at the Snowshed lift base, where the Grand Resort Hotel and Conference Center were built a couple of years back – work is due to start in summer 2001.

Following a couple of very bad seasons for natural snow, snowmaking was increased by 30% for 2000/01.

- ⊕ The biggest mountain in the east, matching some Colorado resorts, with terrain to suit everyone
- ⊕ Lively après-ski, with lots of bar-restaurants offering happy hours and late-night action
- ⊕ Excellent nursery slopes
- ⊕ Comprehensive and very effective snowmaking
- ⊕ Good childcare, although it's not a notably child-oriented resort

- ⊖ No resort village: hotels, condos and restaurants are widely spread, mostly along the five-mile access road – a car is almost a necessity
- ⊖ New England weather – highly changeable and can be very cold
- ⊖ The trail network is complex, and there are lots of trail-crossings
- ⊖ Terminally tedious for anyone who is not a skier or boarder

It's difficult to ignore Killington. It claims to have the largest mountain in the east (whether gauged in trail length, accessible area, vertical drop or top altitude), the largest number of quad chairs in the east, the world's biggest snowmaking installation and the east's largest grooming fleet. (As a result it claims to have the longest season in the east – it tries to be the first resort in America to open, in October, but often shuts again shortly after.) It also claims to have America's longest lift and longest trail (a winding 16km for a drop of 945m) and New England's steepest mogul slope (Outer Limits – 800m long for a drop of 370m). All impressive by local standards.

A slope-side village is only now starting to take shape at the lift base, but even when it is completed, for most visitors life will continue to revolve around driving. But once you get used to that, it's not an unpleasant place. The vibrant nightspots weigh in the balance, even for us: in the early evening they're jolly places to eat, even if you're visiting with kids.

The main problem, in the end, is the unpredictable New England weather.

The resort

Killington is an extraordinary resort, especially to European eyes. Most of its hotels and restaurants are spread along a five-mile approach road. The nearest thing you'll find to a focus is the occasional set of traffic lights with a cluster of shops, though there is a concentration of buildings along a two-and-a-half mile stretch of the road. The resort caters mainly for day and weekend visitors who drive in from the east-coast cities (including a lot of New Yorkers). The car is king; provided you have one, getting around isn't that much of a hassle. There's also a good free shuttle-bus service during the day – it costs a dollar after 5pm.

A new resort village is slowly taking shape around Snowshed, one of the main lift bases. Practically all the other lodgings are a drive from a lift station – either this one or the Skyeship gondola station on the main highway 100, leading past the resort. Staying near the end of the access road is convenient for this and for outings to Pico, a separate little mountain owned by Killington, to be linked one day to Killington's Ram's Head mountain.

The mountains

Runs spread over a series of wooded peaks, all quite close together but giving the resort a basis for claiming to cover six mountains – or seven if you count Pico. A huge number of runs and impressive number of lifts are crammed into a modest area. The result is a very complex network of runs, and signposting isn't always very clear. To some extent the terrain on its six sectors suits different standards. But there are also areas where a mixed ability group would be quite happy, and there are easy runs from top to

MOUNTAIN FACTS

Altitude	350m-1295m
Lifts	32
Pistes	1182 acres
Green	30%
Blue	39%
Black	31%
Art. snow	752 acres

LIFT PASSES

2001/02 prices in dollars

Killington Mountain Pass
Covers all lifts in the Killington and Pico ski areas.

Beginners See Schools/Guides

Main pass
1-day pass 58
6-day pass 276

Senior citizens
Over 64: 6-day pass 168

Children
Under 6: free
6-12: 6-day pass 168
13-18: 6-day pass 240

bottom of each peak. Some runs of all levels are left to form bumps; there is half-and-half grooming on selected trails; and terrain features – ridges, bumps, quarter-pipes – are created.

Killington has also created areas that are called Fusion Zones – thinned-out forest areas, where you pick your own line. These areas are not groomed or patrolled – and they come in blue and single- and double-black-diamond grades. We found them great fun.

The piste map is one of the largest and most fact-packed we've ever come across. But this makes it unwieldy and awkward to handle.

THE SLOPES
Complicated

The Killington Base area has chairs radiating to three of the six peaks – **Snowdon, Killington** (the high-point of the area) and **Skye** – the last also accessible by gondola starting beside US highway 4. Novices and families head for the other main base area, which has two parts: Snowshed, at the foot of the main beginner slope, served by several parallel chairs; and Rams Head, just across the road up to Killington Base, where there's a Family Center at the foot of the entirely gentle **Rams Head** mountain.

The two remaining peaks are behind Skye Peak; they can be reached by trails from Killington and Skye, but each also has a lift base accessible by road. **Bear Mountain** is the expert's hill, served by two quad chairs from its mid-mountain base area. The sixth 'peak', **Sunrise**, is a slight blip on the mountainside, with a short triple chair up from the Sunrise Village condos area. The area below Sunrise Village is used for snowmobile tours – from the old lift base just off highway 4.

SNOW RELIABILITY
Good if it's cold

Killington has a good snowfall record and a huge snowmaking system. But even that is no good if temperatures are too high to operate it. Bad weather can ruin a holiday even in mid-season. A reporter who had new powder each night in March 1999 went back at the same time in 2000 to find people skiing in shorts and T-shirts on the few runs that were open. A February visitor told of 'everything from frostbite warnings to pouring rain'.

FOR EXPERTS
Some challenges

The main areas that experts head for are Killington Peak, where there is a handful of genuine double-diamond fall-line runs under the two chair-lifts, and Bear Mountain. Most of the slopes here are single blacks but Outer Limits, under the main quad chair, is a double-diamond claimed to be 'the steepest mogul slope in the east'. We suspect there are steeper runs at Stowe and Smugglers' Notch. There are two or three worthwhile blacks on Snowdon, too. The Fusion Zones on Skye and Snowdon are well worth seeking out. But one reporter thought many of the black runs overgraded: 'Some would be red in Europe and comfortably skied by an intermediate.'

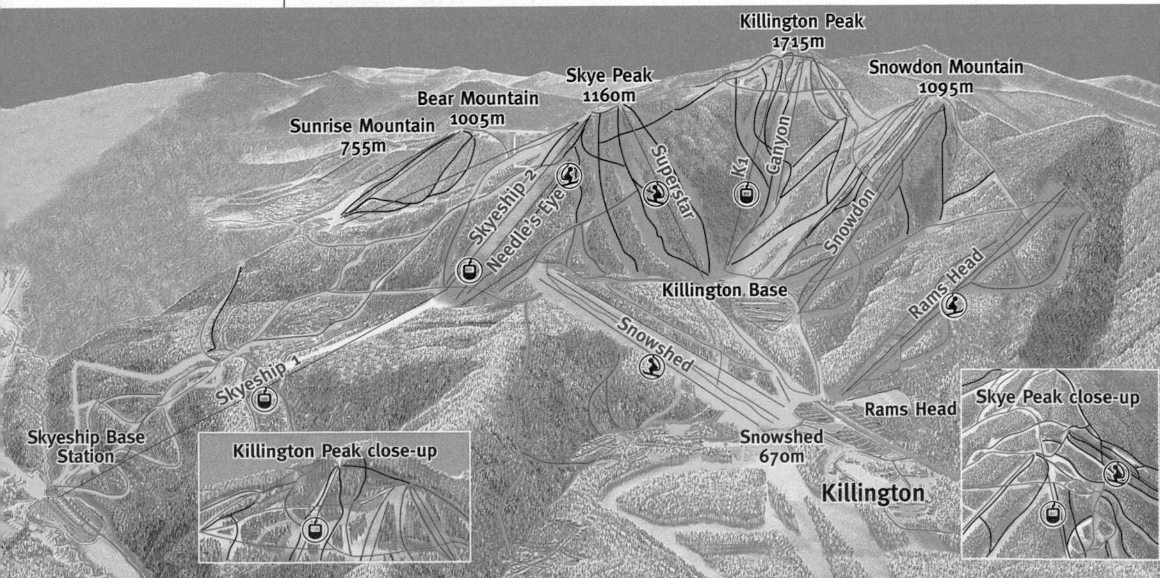

SCHOOLS/GUIDES

2001/02 prices in dollars

Perfect Turn clinics
7 days
2hr: from 9.30, 10.15, or 1.30: 31

Learn to ski clinics
(incl lift pass, equipment and use of Discovery Centre)
1 day: 65
3 days: 150

Children's classes
Ages: 4 to 6 (incl lift pass)
half day: 8.30-12 noon or 12.30-4pm: 59
full day: 89
Ages: 7 to 12 (excl lift pass)
half day: 9.30-11.30 or 1pm-3pm: 71
full day: 101

Private lessons
1hr, 2hr, half or full day
78 for 1hr (115 for 2 people)
202 for half day of 3hr (270 for 2 people)

CHILDCARE

A Family Center at Rams Head was built a few years ago. The Friendly Penguin nursery takes kids from age six weeks to six years – reservations required. Outside the door is the Snow Play Park, with magic carpet lift and handle tow-lift. There are ski classes for several age groups.

FOR INTERMEDIATES
Navigation problems?

There are lots of easy cruising blue and green runs all over the slopes, except on Bear Mountain, where the single blacks present a little more of a challenge for intermediates. Snowdon is a splendid area for those who like to vary their diet. There's a blue-graded Fusion Zone on Rams Head. Finding your way around the complicated network of trails may be tricky, though. One reporter liked Pico a lot but complained that the blue run down was more difficult than some blacks.

FOR BEGINNERS
Splendid

The facilities for complete beginners are excellent. The Snowshed slope is one vast nursery slope served by three chair-lifts and a very slow drag-lift. Rams Head also has excellent gentle slopes. The ski school runs a special, purpose-built Discovery Center just for first-time skiers and boarders – they introduce you to the equipment, show you videos and provide refreshments.

FOR CROSS-COUNTRY
Two main options

Extensive cross-country loops are available at two specialist 'resorts' – Mountain Meadows down on US highway 4, and Mountain Top Ski Touring, a short drive away at Chittenden.

QUEUES
Weekend crowds

Killington gets a lot of weekend and public holiday business, but at other times the slopes and lifts are likely to be quiet. One New Year reporter told of 'a madhouse with overcrowded slopes, and a 20-minute crawl up the access road', and the gondola to Killington Peak and the Rams Head chair can get oversubscribed. Overcrowded slopes are more of a problem than lift queues.

MOUNTAIN RESTAURANTS
Bearable base lodges

There are only two real mountain restaurants. We have mixed reports on the one at the top of Killington Peak, in what was the top station of the old gondola. Max's Place, on Sunrise, has table-service burgers, pasta, salad etc, and is highly recommended by a reporter for 'escaping the squalor of the other on-mountain eating places'. Each of the lift base stations has an eatery, of which the one at Killington Base Lodge is the least dreary and crowded.

SCHOOLS AND GUIDES
In search of the Perfect Turn

The philosophy of the Perfect Turn school is to build on your strengths rather than correct your mistakes, and it seems to work for most people. There is a special Discovery Center for beginners, where you start and finish in a dedicated beginners' building with easy chairs, coffee, videos and help with choosing and fitting your equipment.

FACILITIES FOR CHILDREN
Fine in practice

There is a Family Center at the Rams Head base, which takes kids from six weeks and will introduce them to skiing from age two years. The editorial daughter is a graduate of this institution and approves of it.

Staying there

HOW TO GO
Wide choices

There is a wide choice of places to stay. As well as hotels and condos, there are a few chalets.

Hotels There are a few places near the lifts, but most are a drive or bus-ride away, down Killington Road or on US4.

(((4 **Cortina Inn** 20 minutes away on US4, near Pico; pool, 'excellent food, but poor soundproofing'.

(((4 **Grand Resort** Swanky resort-

---

boarding *A cool resort like Killington has to take boarding seriously, and it does. There are three fun-parks, a super-pipe and a boarder-cross course. And there are terrain features scattered around the area, and parts of the mountain have been reshaped to cut out some of the unpleasant flats on contouring green runs. Several big-name board events are held here. For less competent boarders, there are excellent beginner slopes, and plenty of friendly high-speed (ie slow-loading) chair-lifts – and the Perfect Turn Discovery Center caters just for beginners.*

There is now some accommodation close to the lifts (this is the Rams Head chair), and it is set to increase →

AMERICAN SKIING COMPANY / NATHAN BILOW

Central reservations phone number
For all resort accommodation call 1 800 621 6867 (toll-free from within the US).

GETTING THERE

Air Boston, transfer 2½hr.

ACTIVITIES

Indoor Killington Grand Resort Hotel has massage, fitness centre, outdoor pool, hot-tub, sauna, aerobics. Cinemas and bowling at Rutland

Outdoor Skating, floodlit tubing and snowboarding, sledding, sleigh rides, cross-country, snowshoe tours

TOURIST OFFICE

Postcode VT 05751
t +1 (802) 422 3333
f 422 4391
info@killington.com
www.killington.com

owned place at Snowshed, with outdoor pool and health club.

((((4) **Inn of the Six Mountains** Couple of miles down Killington Road; 'spacious rooms, good pool'.

(((3) **Red Rob Inn** Short drive from slopes – 'good restaurant, a cut above the usual motel style'.

(((3) **North Star Lodge** Well down Killington Road; 'good budget accommodation'.

EATING OUT
You name it

There are all sorts of restaurants spread along the Killington Road, from simple pizza or pasta through to 'fine dining' places. They get very busy at weekends and many don't take reservations. Many of the nightspots mentioned below serve food for at least part of the evening.

The local menu guide is essential reading. Claude's Choices, the Grist Mill, Charity's and the Cortina and Red Rob Inns have been recommended by recent reporters.

APRES-SKI
The beast of the east

Killington has a well-deserved reputation for a vibrant après-ski scene; many of its short-stay visitors are clearly intent on making the most of their few days (or nights) here.

Although there are bars at the base lodges, keen après-skiers head down Killington Road to one of the lively places dotted along its five-mile length. From 3pm it's cheap drinks and free munchies, then in the early evening it's serious dining time, then later on the real action starts (and admission charges kick in). Most of the places mentioned here would also rate a mention in Eating out.

The train-themed Casey's Caboose is said to have the best 'wings' in town. Charity's is another lively bar, with an interior apparently lifted from a turn-of-the-century Parisian brothel. The Wobbly Barn is a famous live-music place that rivals Jackson's Mangy Moose for the position of America's leading après-ski venue. The Pickle Barrel caters for a younger crowd, with theme nights and loud music. The Outback complex has something for everyone, from pizzas and free massages to disco and live bands.

OFF THE SLOPES
Rent a car

If there is a less amusing resort in which to spend time doing things other than skiing or boarding, we have yet to find it. Make sure you have a car, as well as a book.

Smugglers' Notch 315m

Fine fun for families

WHAT IT COSTS

(5)

HOW IT RATES

The slopes

Snow	***
Extent	*
Experts	***
Intermediates	***
Beginners	****
Convenience	*****
Queues	****
Restaurants	*

The rest

Scenery	***
Resort charm	**
Off-slope	*

What's new

Snowmaking was extended by 40% for 2000/01 and a new water reservoir will increase the capacity further for 2001/02.

Four new gladed trails were opened on Sterling Mountain last season and two more are planned for 2001/02.

The construction of new condos goes on.

- ⊕ Excellent children's facilities
- ⊕ Lots of slope-side accommodation
- ⊕ Varied slopes with runs for all abilities
- ⊕ Link to Stowe, over the hill
- ⊕ No queues
- ⊕ Great for beginners, with excellent ski school

- ⊖ Family orientation may be too much for some
- ⊖ New England weather – highly changeable, and can be very cold
- ⊖ Limited local slopes
- ⊖ No proper mountain restaurants
- ⊖ No hotels – condos only
- ⊖ No après-ski atmosphere
- ⊖ Few off-slope diversions

Smuggs hits the family target squarely, with a constant round of early-evening activities, sympathetic instructors, comprehensive childcare, a generally child-friendly layout and some long, quiet, easy runs. There are challenging slopes, too, but mileage-hungry intermediates should go elsewhere.

THE RESORT

Smugglers' Notch is about the nearest thing you'll find in the US to a French-style purpose-built family resort – except that it doesn't look so bad. The village isn't genuinely traffic-free – you may have to tangle with traffic to get to the childcare centre, even – but it comes close, and once installed in your condo you can happily do without a car (much of the accommodation is near to or on the slopes). Those not afflicted with children could find the family orientation of the resort a bit overpowering: you may find it's difficult to get away from Billy Bob Bear and pals.

The resort is energetically managed and produces a constant flow of developments designed to tighten its grip on the market. Yet again it has been voted 'North American family resort of the year' by at least one American skiing publication.

THE MOUNTAIN

Smuggs has varied and satisfying slopes, spread over three hills – Morse, above the village (with the newish Morse Highlands area off to the left), and Madonna and Sterling off to the right, reached by green links.

Slopes There are some real challenges as well as easy cruising, and a worthwhile vertical of 800m. It's blissfully quiet on the mountain except at weekends and holidays. It's undeniably a small area, though. You can get to Stowe's Spruce Peak by an intermediate trail from the top of Sterling, and guests staying two nights or more get a free day in Stowe.

Snow reliability Snow reliability is good, subject to the inherent variability of New England weather. And the snowmaking is being further improved.

Beginners It's a great area for beginners. One of the chair-lifts out of the village runs at half speed, and the

SMUGGLERS' NOTCH

We never saw this many people on one trail when we visited Smuggs →

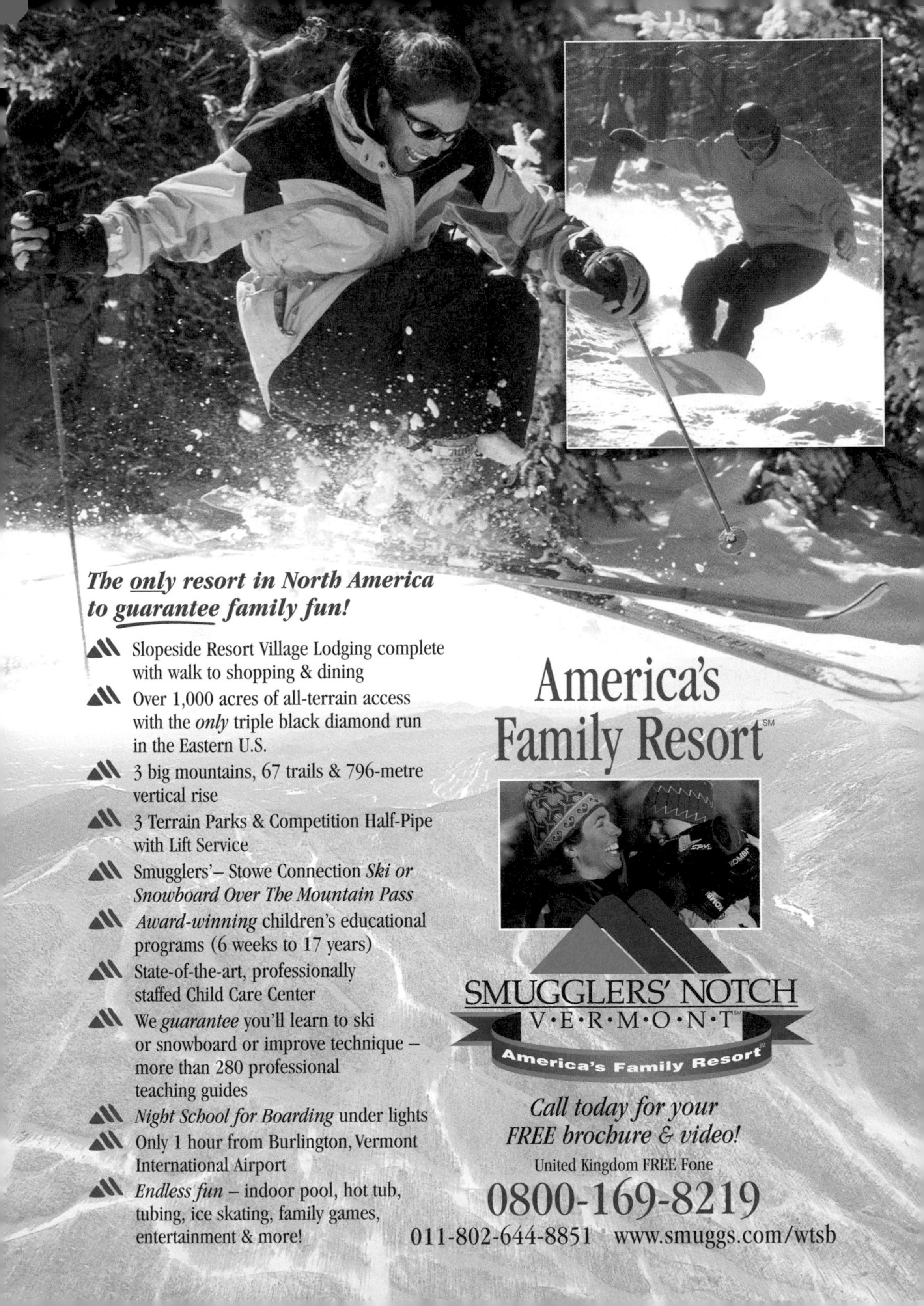
The only resort in North America to guarantee family fun!
Slopeside Resort Village Lodging complete with walk to shopping & dining
Over 1,000 acres of all-terrain access with the only triple black diamond run in the Eastern U.S.
3 big mountains, 67 trails & 796-metre vertical rise
3 Terrain Parks & Competition Half-Pipe with Lift Service
Smugglers'– Stowe Connection Ski or Snowboard Over The Mountain Pass
Award-winning children's educational programs (6 weeks to 17 years)
State-of-the-art, professionally staffed Child Care Center
We guarantee you'll learn to ski or snowboard or improve technique – more than 280 professional teaching guides
Night School for Boarding under lights
Only 1 hour from Burlington, Vermont International Airport
Endless fun – indoor pool, hot tub, tubing, ice skating, family games, entertainment & more!
America's Family Resort SM
SMUGGLERS' NOTCH
V·E·R·M·O·N·T SM
America's Family Resort SM
Call today for your FREE brochure & video!
United Kingdom FREE Fone
0800-169-8219
011-802-644-8851
www.smuggs.com/wtsb

MOUNTAIN FACTS

Altitude	315m-1110m
Lifts	9
Pistes	1000 acres
Green	22%
Blue	53%
Black	25%
Art. snow	159 acres

TOURIST OFFICE

Postcode
VT 05464-9537
t +1 (802) 644 8851
f 644 2713
smuggs@smuggs.com
www.smuggs.com

runs it accesses are of an ideal gradient. Morse Highlands adds another tailor-made novice area. And the higher lifts take you to long easy runs that even 'never-evers' can tackle during their first week.

Intermediates There are intermediate runs of every grade; there just aren't many of them. The link with Stowe adds variety.

Experts There are challenges for experts. We were impressed by the two or three double-diamond runs on Madonna, and they have recently opened The Black Hole – the only triple-diamond run in the east, they say. You can go off through the trees anywhere within the resort boundary – but these areas are not patrolled.

Snowboarding Smuggs encourages snowboarding, and has a couple of impressive fun-parks and a half-pipe.

Cross-country The 23km of trails may be a bit limited for expert skiers.

Queues We encountered no queues, and away from weekends we'd be surprised if anyone else did.

Mountain restaurants There are no real mountain restaurants, but there is a new warming hut with snacks at the top of the Prohibition Park half-pipe and the new lodge at Morse Highlands serves food. Most people go back to base for lunch.

Schools and guides At least one reporter judges the ski school (or 'Snow Sport University') to be 'outstanding', and it has often been voted the best in North America. Among its bright ideas are private lessons for a parent and child, with the idea that the parent learns how to help the child develop while having fun.

Facilities for children Smuggs aims to be simply the best for children. The mountain is child-friendly, offering excitement with safety – with a special jolly kids' trail map. There's a terrain park for kids, and little forest glades where even tinies can be taken 'off-piste'. Alice's Wonderland Child Enrichment Center is a comprehensive nursery. The school arrangements are very good, too, with childcare before and after sessions, and carriage to the kids' chair-lift by horse-drawn sleigh.

STAYING THERE

How to go There are no hotels in the resort itself – though there are some within driving distance.

Self-catering There are lots of comfortable condos on or near the slopes, none very far from the snow.

Eating out There are a couple of restaurants in the resort, including the cosy Hearth and Candle, and others a short drive down the road to the outside world – we and the kids enjoyed an outing to Banditos. Babysitters can be arranged.

Après-ski The adult après-ski possibilities are about the most limited we have come across. We hear good reports of the teen centre.

Off the slopes There is very little to do off the slopes. Organised day trips to Vermont or Montreal are possible.

Stowe 475m

Charming Vermont town, small but serious mountain

WHAT IT COSTS

(5)

HOW IT RATES

The slopes	
Snow	***
Extent	*
Experts	***
Intermediates	****
Beginners	****
Convenience	*
Queues	****
Restaurants	**
The rest	
Scenery	***
Resort charm	****
Off-slope	*

What's new

The new Burton Method Center has created a 'Learn to Ride' programme involving new teaching techniques and special beginner equipment.

MOUNTAIN FACTS

Altitude	390m-1110m
Lifts	11
Pistes	480 acres
Green	16%
Blue	59%
Black	25%
Art. snow	350 acres

- ⊕ Cute tourist town in classic New England style
- ⊕ Some good slopes for all abilities, including serious challenges
- ⊕ Few queues
- ⊕ Link to Smugglers' Notch, over the hill
- ⊕ Excellent cross-country trails
- ⊕ Great children's facilities

- ⊖ Town is a shuttle-bus or short drive from the slopes
- ⊖ One of the mountains is a short shuttle-bus-ride from the other two
- ⊖ New England weather – highly changeable, and can be very cold
- ⊖ Limited local slopes
- ⊖ Weekend queues
- ⊖ No après-ski atmosphere

Stowe is one of New England's cutest little towns, its main street lined with dinky clapboard shops and restaurants; you could find no sharper contrast to the other New England resorts we feature. Its mountain, six miles away, is another New England classic: something for everyone, but not much of it.

THE RESORT

Stowe is a picture-postcard New England town – a real community and a popular spot for tourists year-round, with bijou 'specialty' shops lining its sidewalks and more 3- and 4-diamond hotels and restaurants than any other place in New England except Boston. The slopes of Mount Mansfield, Vermont's snow-capped (though mainly wooded) highest peak, are a 15-minute drive away and much of the resort's accommodation is along the road out to it. There's a good day-time shuttle-bus service but a car is recommended for flexibility.

THE MOUNTAIN

There are three different sectors, two linked by blue runs mid-mountain and green ones at the base, the third (Spruce Peak) a short shuttle-ride away (there are plans for a lift link, but it's not imminent).

Slopes The main sector, served by a trio of chair-lifts from Mansfield Base Lodge, is dominated by the famous Front Four – a row of seriously steep double-black-diamond runs. But there is plenty of easier stuff, too, including long green runs down to the alternative lift base at Toll House.

A fast eight-seat gondola serves the next sector: easy-intermediate runs with one black alternative – plus the short but very steep Waterfall, under the gondola at the top.

The third area, Spruce Peak, has the main nursery area at the bottom, with a slow chair-lift to mid-mountain and another beyond that. 'Possibly the slowest chairs in the world,' says a reporter. The top of this sector links with Smugglers' Notch, over the hill, though the link isn't widely used – it's not particularly easy and involves a walk or scoot across a frozen lake. Guests staying for two nights or more get a free day at Smuggs.

There are free daily mountain tours with a mountain host.

Snowboarding Stowe attracts many snowboarders and has two fun-parks and a half-pipe. Beginners learn on special customised boards at the Burton Method Center on Spruce Peak.

Snow reliability Snow reliability is helped by snowmaking on practically all the blue (and some black) runs of the main sectors, and on lower Spruce Peak.

Experts The Front Four and their variants on the top half of the main sector present a real challenge.

Intermediates The usual New England reservation applies: the terrain is limited in extent; there's also a severe shortage of ordinary black runs (as opposed to double diamonds).

Beginners The nursery slopes and long green runs are great. 'Spruce Peak is one of the best beginner/early skier areas we've seen,' says a report. Progression to longer green runs means moving over to Mount Mansfield, where there are splendid long greens down to Toll House.

Central reservations phone number
For all resort accommodation call 1 877 317 8693 (toll-free from within the US)

From within the UK call 0800 731 9279

TOURIST OFFICE

Postcode VT 05672
t +1 (802) 253 3500
f 253 3406
info@stowe.com
www.stowe.com

Cross-country There are excellent cross-country centres dotted around the landscape (including the musically famous Trapp Family Lodge), with lots of connected trails – 35km of groomed and 40km of back country trails.

Queues The area is largely free of queues mid-week but we've had reports of 25-minute queues at weekends.

Mountain restaurants Cliff House, at the top of the gondola, is a lofty room with table-service and good food and views. Midway Café near the base of the gondola has a BBQ deck and table-service inside. The Octagon Web Café, at the top of the main sector, is a small cafeteria.

Schools and guides A recent reporter was disappointed by the ski school – but this was partly because he had a different instructor every day, which is common in the US.

Facilities for children There are excellent facilities and the nursery takes children from age six months to six years.

STAYING THERE

How to go There are hotels in and around Stowe itself and various points along the road to the slopes, some with Austrian or Scandinavian names and styles.

Hotels 1066 Ye Olde England Inne is recommended by reporters (despite the appalling name). Stowehof Inn and Green Mountain Inn are also recommended. The smart Inn at the Mountain, at the Toll House lift base of Mount Mansfield, is the only slope-side accommodation, with chair-lift access to the main sector of slopes.

Self-catering There is a reasonable range of condos available for rent.

Eating out There are restaurants of every kind. The Cliff House at the top of the gondola is open for dinner.

Après-ski Après-ski is muted – Stowe reportedly goes to bed early. There's a good cinema with new releases.

Off the slopes Stowe is a pleasant town in which to spend time off the slopes – at least if you like shopping. A trip to the Burlington shopping mall is recommended (you need a car).

Sunday River 245m

The biggest snowmaking system in New England

WHAT IT COSTS

5

HOW IT RATES

The slopes	
Snow	***
Extent	**
Experts	**
Intermediates	****
Beginners	****
Convenience	***
Queues	****
Restaurants	***
The rest	
Scenery	***
Resort charm	**
Off-slope	*

What's new

For the 2000/01 season a new terrain-park called Nebula – claimed to be 'the largest in the East'. It is designed for expert skiers and riders looking to catch big air and perform aerial tricks.

For 2001/02 the half-pipe is being made into an 18-feet-deep superpipe. More snowmaking guns are due to be added too.

- ⊕ Some convenient slope-side accommodation
- ⊕ Some good runs for all abilities
- ⊕ Decent natural snow record with extensive artificial back up
- ⊕ Lots of scope for cross-country skiing in the area
- ⊕ No queues

- ⊖ Scattered slope-side developments mean no village atmosphere
- ⊖ Relatively small slopes
- ⊖ No real mountain restaurants
- ⊖ Quiet après-ski scene
- ⊖ Limited off-slope diversions

Sunday River was one of the pioneers of snowmaking, and over 90% of its trails are served by it. So the snow should be as good here as anywhere in the east. The terrain is varied and quite extensive. But it lacks village ambience.

THE RESORT

Sunday River is where the American Skiing Company (which owns eight other US resorts) started and where it still has its HQ. Despite this, there isn't really a slope-side village yet – there are various developments scattered around the slopes – so there isn't much village ambience.

The plan is for the area around the Jordan Grand hotel to become the focus of the resort with shops, bars, restaurants, theatre, nightclub and even a village green and pond. For now, Bethel is the nearest small town, a 10-minute drive away; it's a pleasant place with a few shops and a handful of restaurants and bars. The resort attracts quite a lot of British school groups, especially at half-term and Easter.

THE MOUNTAINS

The slopes range over about 5km from east to west and across eight different peaks. It does feel like a reasonably extensive network of trails and glades – 127 at the last count – and there are numerous base areas, parking lots and accommodation units dotted around.

Slopes The White Cap base marks the eastern extremity of the system and is handy for the Grand Summit hotel, the half-pipe and other evening activities. The peaks around the main base areas are fairly packed with lifts and trails. The Jordan Grand hotel is at the western limit of the system, and in general the western sector (Aurora, Oz and Jordan Bowl) has far fewer lifts and runs and a more remote and backwoods feel.

SUNDAY RIVER / NORM HERSOM

Sunday River's trails spread right along the slopes of eight linked peaks, with lots of car parking for day visitors →

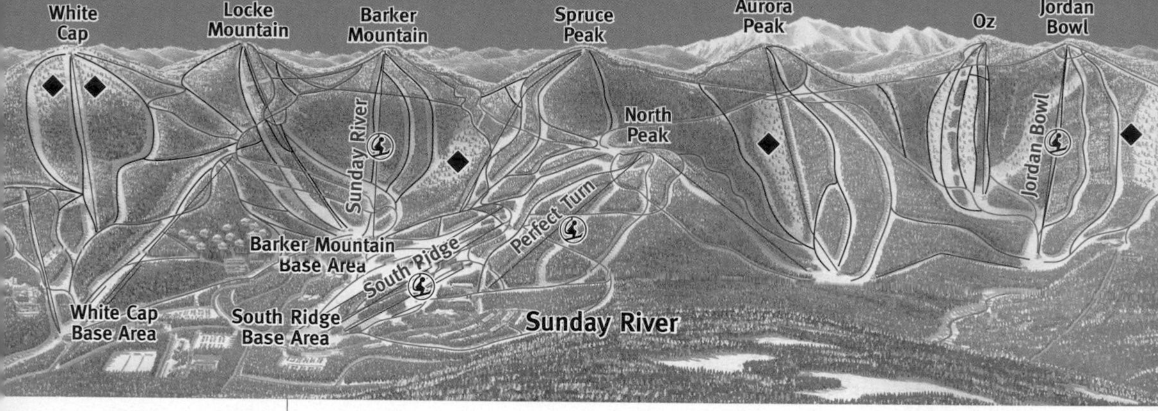

MOUNTAIN FACTS

Altitude	245m-955m
Lifts	18
Pistes	660 acres
Green	25%
Blue	35%
Black	40%
Art. snow	607 acres

Central reservations phone number
For all resort accommodation call 1 800 543 2754 (toll-free from within the US)

TOURIST OFFICE
Postcode ME 04217
t +1 (207) 824 3000
f 824 5110
snowtalk@sundayriver.com
www.sundayriver.com

Snow reliability Snow reliability is good: a decent natural snow record is backed up by a high-capacity, high-tech system for making and grooming man-made stuff. Last season was a vintage one for natural snow.
Experts There are challenging narrow, often mogulled double-blacks on White Cap and Barker Mountain, and there is excellent glade skiing on Aurora, Oz and Jordan Bowl. Indeed, 40% of the trails are graded black.
Intermediates It's generally a good resort for intermediates who will enjoy cruising around on a series of nice rolling blues (often deserted in mid-week). There are some not too fearsome glades to tempt the bold.
Beginners South Ridge is a well-organised area for beginners, with good, easy runs to progress to.
Snowboarding Boarders will find no fewer than five terrain parks (including the largest in the eastern US, called Nebula) and three half-pipes (including a competition standard one, which is floodlit for evening use). For 2001/02 the half-pipe is to be made even bigger and promoted to superpipe status.
Cross-country In and around Bethel there are three cross-country centres with a total of around 140km of trails.
Queues Mid-week queues are non-existent – indeed most lifts and slopes are deserted. Even on busy weekends you should be okay if you stick to the four high-speed quads.
Mountain restaurants There are no real mountain restaurants, but there are good, civilised table-service places at the Jordan Grand and Grand Summit hotels as well as the usual self-service places.
Schools and guides Ski school is not a term they use at Sunday River but there is a series of 'Perfect Turn' clinics available. A reporter who took a group of 40 schoolchildren said the ski instructors were 'overstretched at half-term but still superb, and one even bought his class baseball caps'.
Facilities for children The Grand Summit and South Ridge Centre house the main children's facilities. There's also a family entertainment centre called the White Cap (see Après-ski).

STAYING THERE
There is some slope-side accommodation but many people prefer to stay in Bethel – a 10-minute drive from the ski area.
How to go There are numerous inns, lodges, motels and B&Bs in and around Bethel.
Hotels The main slope-side hotels are the Jordan Grand and the Grand Summit. There's a dorm as well as normal rooms at the Snow Cap Inn.
Self-catering The Brookside condos have been recommended. There are plenty of others too.
Après-ski Après-ski in Sunday River is quiet. Bumps pub often has live bands. A recent reporter recommends the Foggy Goggle bar, which also has live music, and the Matterhorn Steak Bar in Bethel (large steaks, local beers, good atmosphere). There are two brew pubs. The White Cap Fun Center has floodlit tubing, sledding and ice skating. There are guided snow-shoe tours on two evenings a week. And there's a games arcade.
Eating out There's a handful of restaurants in Bethel.
Off the slopes Apart from the likes of snowmobiling, tubing, ice-fishing and swimming, there are a few antique and craft shops.

The winter of 2000/01 was exceptional for Canada. While the eastern resorts in Québec got hammered with frequent snowstorms, the western resorts of Alberta and British Columbia had their worst year for snow in living memory. We took a trip through eight western resorts during the February 2001 snow drought, and the locals were moaning like mad about conditions. But compared with a normal year in the Alps the snow on the groomed runs was just fine in most places. What we missed was gliding through knee-deep powder – something that is normally an everyday experience in western Canada. That's what Canada in a normal season is all about to us: deep, deep, snow and lots of it. That plus the US-style service culture that is missing in Europe. Plus the spectacular mountain scenery that is missing in the US. Plus great value for money because of the weak Canadian dollar.

A few seasons ago we drove from Whistler to Banff, calling in at lots of smaller resorts on the way. The whole trip took two weeks and for eight consecutive days in the middle it snowed. It snowed and snowed and snowed. It made driving from resort to resort tricky as we insisted on driving at night after getting in a full day on the slopes. But the skiing was spectacular – day after day of dry, light powder. That's a normal winter in western Canada.

In an average year Whistler, for example, gets 360 inches of snow and it snows (or rains at resort level!) for half the days in the season. That makes for superb conditions on the slopes. When you reach Banff–Lake Louise you might not get quite the same frequency of snow, but it stays in great condition because it is further inland, the air is drier and temperatures are colder. You get a better chance of blue skies there – but also a higher chance of a day or two of very low temperatures of –20°C or less.

So you go to western Canada for the skiing or boarding, not the sunbathing. If you prefer long lunches on sun-drenched mountain restaurant terraces, stick to March in the Alps. If you want a good chance of hitting powder, put Canada high on your list of possible destinations.

If you really want untracked powder and are feeling flush, there is nothing to beat Canada's amazing heli- and snowcat skiing operations. The main difference is that the former is faster paced and more expensive than the latter. But with both, you are taken to the middle of nowhere in a deserted mountain wilderness and then let loose with a guide who takes you down untracked slopes to another spot in the middle of nowhere, where you are picked up and taken to the top of another mountain and another untracked run. And so it goes on! You can do it by the day, but the hedonistic luxury option is to book a few days or a week in a luxury lodge run by the heli-skiing or snowcat operation, eating gourmet dinners and stepping out of the door each morning straight into the chopper or snowcat.

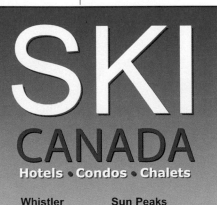

If you can't afford the £3,000 plus a week that this would cost, you can always try a day for £200 plus. But if you resist heli-skiing or snowcat heaven, you'll find a holiday in Canada can be very cheap. Package prices start at around £400 for a week to western Canada and around £350 for a week in the east. These prices are made possible by cheap direct and charter flights to the key airports and the use of accommodation in resorts where winter is low season compared with summer. And once you get there you'll find the cost of eating and drinking out very cheap compared to the Alps.

Another difference you'll notice compared to the Alps is the people. For a start they speak English (very useful, especially for ski or board lessons). But more importantly they are friendly and have the American service culture that 'the customer is king'. You'll find mountain hosts to show you around the slopes, immaculately groomed runs, civilised lift queues, lots of fast quad chair-lifts, piste maps available at the bottom of most lifts, and cheerful, helpful staff.

In the west you'll also find spectacular scenery (when the clouds clear) to rival that of the Alps and far superior to anything you'll find in the US. You'll also find an amazing variety of wildlife, especially in Banff–Lake Louise, Jasper and the interior of British Columbia.

For us, the main attraction of eastern Canada is that the resorts are in the heart of the province of Québec, where the French influence is predominant – language, cuisine and culture are all dominated by French-Canadians and it makes for a unique ambience. Québec is now attracting a fair number of British winter visitors, including school groups. It also has the attraction of a shorter flight time – but it does have the disadvantages of extremes of weather.

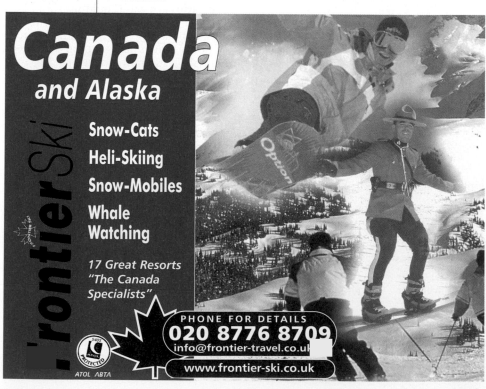

Western Canada

For international visitors to Canada, the main draw is the west. It has fabulous scenery, good snow and a wonderful sense of the great outdoors. The big names of Whistler, Banff and Lake Louise (now dealt with in separate chapters) capture most of the British market at present, but there are lots of worthwhile smaller resorts that more adventurous travellers are now starting to explore. We recommend renting a car and combining two or more of these resorts, perhaps with a couple of days on virgin powder served by helicopters or snowcats as well. You'll have the holiday of a lifetime. Smokers should be warned that BC has banned smoking in all public buildings (ie restaurants etc).

Our map shows the area we're covering in this section.

Five of the smaller resorts where you're most likely to want to stay for a while now get their own chapters. Big White is BC's highest ski area, and second in size to Whistler. It has a reputation for powder, and the small slope-side village is developing fast. Access isn't easy unless you fly into Kelowna airport. Fernie, in the same ownership as Lake Louise, has a deserved reputation for great powder and is fast developing. Jasper is a spectacular three-hour drive from Lake Louise through the Banff and Jasper National Parks; the ski area of Marmot Basin is a 30-minute drive from the tiny town. Panorama, in the same ownership as Whistler, has a big vertical and an attractive village developing at the foot of the slopes. Kicking Horse is the new kid on the block. Formerly known as Whitetooth, the mountain has been transformed by the installation of a single-stage gondola serving a vertical of 1,200m – possibly a world record. With an impressive snow record to boot, this is a coming place. At present you have to stay down in Golden, but not for long.

There are quite a few other resorts that you might want to include in a tour of this area.

Kimberley Alpine Resort is the most accessible – about 90 minutes from Fernie and three hours from Banff. Like Fernie, it's a recent addition to the

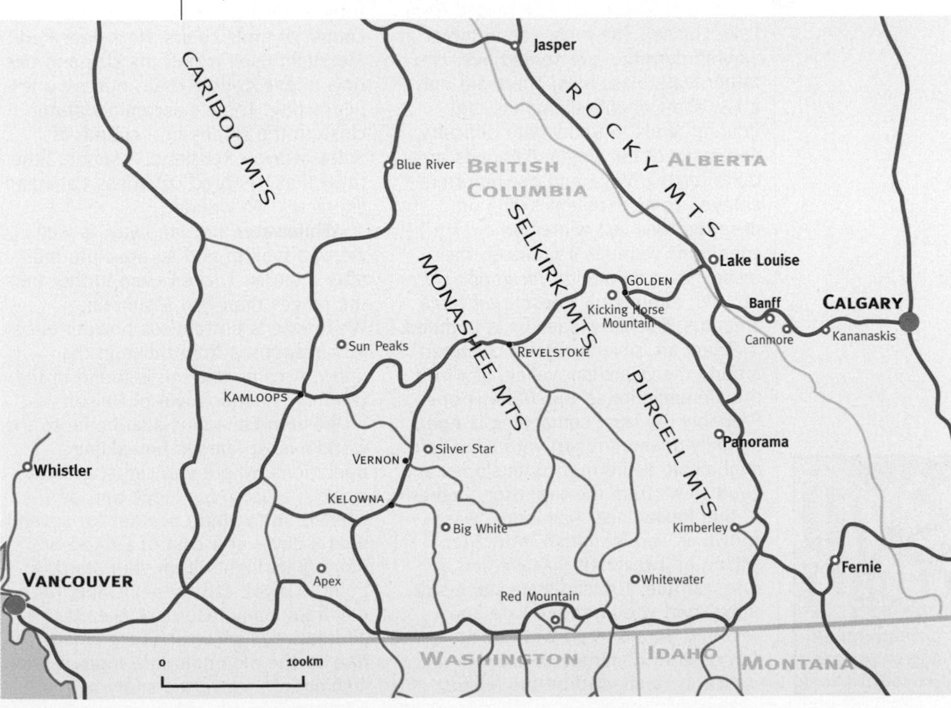

portfolio of Resorts of the Canadian Rockies, owners of Lake Louise.

At the mountain there are in practice two base areas. The original one is not quite at the bottom of the hill; there are two old chairs and a T-bar here (though they are no longer regularly used), and a range of lodgings including the 'lovely' NorthStar Chalets (condos). On the flat ground below this, a new village is being built, served by a new fast quad that is now the resort's staple lift. This set-up may work eventually, but at present it requires everyone using the new chair in order to descend a steep, traffic-polished and congested final slope to the lower level. Not ideal.

The new village is at present very limited, but includes the comfortable and very convenient Trickle Creek Residence Inn by Marriott (catchy, eh?), the 'superb' Polaris condos and a couple of restaurants.

The town of Kimberley, about five minutes' drive away, is known for its synthetic and indescribably naff 'Bavarian theme', but is reported to contain some good restaurants.

Kimberley's terrain offers a mix of blue and black runs (plus the occasional green) and a vertical of 700m. In addition to the lifts up the front there are basically two other slow chairs (one is a double discarded from Lake Louise). The runs – all in forest of varying density – are spread over two rather featureless hills. There are only a few short double-diamonds, but grading tends to understate difficulty, and many of the single-diamonds are quite testing. We – and our reporters – enjoyed some excellent skiing on deserted runs last winter, when conditions were far from ideal; the resort has a reputation for good powder, although it doesn't get huge amounts. Further expansion is planned.

There are several resorts clustered around the Okanagan valley, of which the aforementioned Big White is one. Probably the least compelling is **Apex**, a family-oriented resort with a modern mini-resort at the foot of its slopes and good views from the top, 610m higher.

Sun Peaks, near Kamloops, was known as Tod Mountain. Now $100 million of investment has created a cute, car-free, Tirolean-style slope-side village and good intermediate and beginner terrain to go with the steeps that used to dominate. The 880m vertical is claimed to be the biggest in the BC interior; the mountain, open at the top and densely wooded lower down, has a balance of blue and black runs at top and bottom and a couple of areas of genuinely double-black stuff. Novices are safely tucked away on their own hill.

Silver Star, above the town of Vernon, is a newly developed 'gaslight-era' 1890s-style village right on the slopes. The wooded mountain has two separate but linked faces: the south face around the village has mainly easy and intermediate slopes served by a fast quad of 480m vertical; the back north face is a splendid wooded bowl of easy runs along the rim and black and double-black trails dropping into the middle to meet the 630m-vertical fast quad.

Finally, there are a couple of resorts tucked away in the mountains close to the US border.

Red Mountain is up there with Fernie and other cult powder paradises in our estimation. There are green and red runs, but it's the black and double-black stuff that is the real attraction, coupled with superb powder. We loved the terrain here – mostly in trees, and as steep as you can handle. Granite Mountain is a conical peak with more-or-less separate faces of blue, black and double-black steepness, and a total vertical of 880m – all served by a couple of triple chairs. Next-door Red Mountain itself is half the size and has only a lone double chair, but is no less interesting. There's accommodation close to the slopes or a couple of miles away in Rossland, a simple little town that has bred countless Canadian ski racers. No wonder.

Whitewater, not far away, is well worth a look in and an absolute must after a storm. Tucked even further into the ranges than Red Mountain, Whitewater's bottomless powder elicits rave responses from those in the know. Accommodation is found in the charming historic town of Nelson.

Western Canada is also home to the world's most famous **heli-skiing** operations, where you can stay for a week in a luxurious lodge and be whirled up to virgin powder for several runs a day – at a cost of £2,500 or more (plus flights from your starting point). Or you can try heli-skiing for a day from many resorts. A cheaper alternative is snowcat skiing where you ride up the mountain in a more relaxed fashion in a converted snowcat.

Banff 1340m

A winter wonderland with wildlife

WHAT IT COSTS

4

HOW IT RATES

The slopes

Snow	****
Extent	****
Experts	****
Intermediates	****
Beginners	***
Convenience	*
Queues	****
Restaurants	***

The rest

Scenery	****
Resort charm	***
Off-slope	*****

- ⊕ Spectacular high-mountain scenery – quite unlike the Colorado Rockies
- ⊕ Three widely separated mountains adding up to a lot of terrain
- ⊕ Excellent snow record at Sunshine
- ⊕ Lots of wildlife around the valley
- ⊕ Lots of touristy shops
- ⊕ Good value lodging because winter is the area's low season

- ⊖ You need to drive or take a bus to get to the slopes – between 10 and 45 minutes to the three local areas
- ⊖ Can be very cold – and most lifts offer no protection
- ⊖ Lack of traditional ski resort atmosphere
- ⊖ Can seem over-full of Brits

Huge numbers of British skiers and boarders go to Banff. Price has been a key factor in getting us to make the trip. Winter is low season in the spectacular and unspoilt Banff National Park, so room prices are low; add cheap charter flights to Calgary, and the result is very tempting package prices. But that's only half the story: most visitors are delighted with what they find, and keen to go back.

It's not difficult to see why. The landscape is one of glaciers, jagged peaks and magnificent views, and the valleys are full of wildlife that you'll never see in Europe. The slopes have something for everyone, from steep couloirs to gentle cruising. The snow is some of the coldest, driest and most reliable you'll find anywhere in the world, and there's a lot of it (at Sunshine Village, at least). And there are the standard Canadian assets of people who are friendly and welcoming, and low prices for meals and other on-the-spot expenses.

For us, these factors count for more than the drawbacks. But then we, luckily, have not encountered the extremely low temperatures (–30°C is not unknown) that have left some early-season reporters feeling less convinced.

The resort

Banff is a big summer resort that happens to be within driving distance of three separate ski and snowboard areas. Norquay is a small nearby area overlooking the town. Sunshine Village, 20 minutes away, is a bigger mountain; despite the name, it's not a village (nor is it notably sunny) – it has just one small hotel at mid-mountain. Lake Louise is 45 minutes away (see separate chapter).

Banff is spectacularly set, with several towering peaks rising up around its outskirts. There is lots of wildlife around; don't be surprised to find a herd of elk or long-horned sheep outside your hotel (though we are told that the town is now trying to keep elk away). In spring there may be bears along the highways.

Banff town has grown substantially since 1990, when it became independent of the Banff National Park authority. But it still consists basically

SUNSHINE VILLAGE

Looking down over Sunshine's Delirium Dive (the steep bits are out of shot below the photo!) to Goat's Eye →

What's new

For 2001/02 Sunshine's old access gondola will be replaced by a new eight-seater, almost doubling the capacity and cutting the journey time to Sunshine Village by over 40% to under 13 minutes.

For 2000/01 two new quad chairs were installed. The Wolverine Express high-speed quad has replaced the old Wheeler chair and goes from the bottom of Goat's Eye to a point where you can go back down to Goat's Eye or down to Sunshine Village. The new Jackrabbit quad arrives at the same place and has replaced the Fireweed T-bar. This cuts out a long flat section of the green run back down to the bottom of the gondola.

A couple of seasons ago Sunshine reopened (after 14 years) the Delirium Dive area of extreme terrain.

BANFF-MOUNT NORQUAY

Norquay is the nearest area to Banff town and has short runs for all standards ↓

of one long main street and a small network of side roads built in grid fashion, lined by clothing and souvenir shops (aimed mainly at summer visitors) and a few ski shops. The buildings are low-rise and some are attractively wood-clad. The town is pleasant enough, but it lacks genuine charm; it's a tourist town, not another Aspen or Telluride.

A car can be helpful here, especially in cold weather. The buses to Sunshine, Norquay and Lake Louise (free to Tri-area lift pass holders) are frequent and generally reliable, although a reporter points out that, depending on the number of pickups, the bus-rides can take twice as long as advertised. Buses are also organised to the more distant major resorts of Panorama and Kicking Horse and the small resorts of Nakiska and Fortress, and day-trip heli-skiing and boarding can be organised.

The mountains

The amount of skiing within reach is huge and the views from the slopes are the most spectacular that the Rockies have to offer.

THE SLOPES
Lots of variety

The slopes of **Sunshine Village** are set right on the Continental Divide and as a result get a lot of snow and can be very cold and bleak during a snowfall or cold snap. The main slopes are not visible from the base station: you ride a two-stage gondola, first to the base of the recently developed Goat's Eye Mountain, and then on to Sunshine Village itself. The old slow gondola (the subject of many reporters'

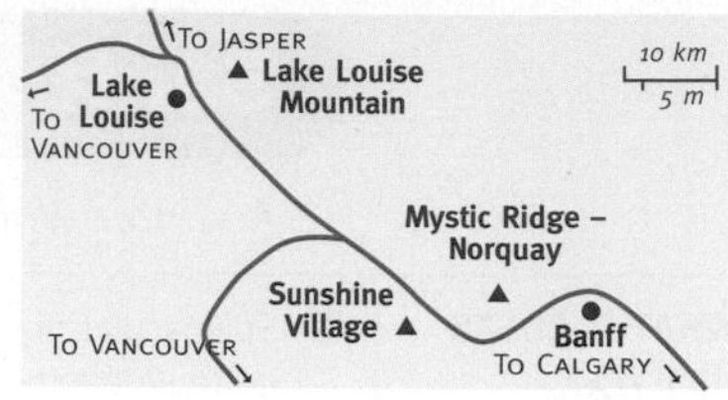

complaints) is due to be replaced by a fast new one for 2001/02. Most of the slopes above the village are above the tree line. Although there is a wooded sector served by the second section of the gondola and a couple of chairs, in bad weather you're better off elsewhere.

Goat's Eye is served by one lift, a fast quad chair rising 580m. Although there are some blue runs, this is basically a black mountain, with some genuine double-blacks at the extremities. There has been talk of building an additional fast quad up the middle of the slopes to a point more or less on the tree line; this would make the area more useful in bad weather, but the plan is still awaiting approval.

Lifts fan out in all directions from Sunshine Village, with short runs back from Mount Standish and longer ones from Lookout Mountain. Lookout is where the Continental Divide is, with the melting snow flowing in one direction to the Pacific and in the other to the Atlantic. From the top of here experts can pass through a gate (you need an avalanche transceiver to get through) and hike up to the extreme terrain of Delirium Dive.

Many people ride the gondola down at the end of the day. But the 2.5km green run to the bottom is a pretty cruise. If you go down while the lifts are running you can take the new Jackrabbit chair to cut out a flat section, but the run gets busy and is much more enjoyable if you delay your descent a bit. The black-diamond Canyon run provides a fun alternative for more advanced skiers and riders.

Norquay is much smaller. But it's worth a visit, especially in bad weather – it has wooded slopes to suit all standards served by a row of five lifts. It is often overlooked by visitors who head for the bigger areas, and so the trails can be delightfully quiet. One trail is floodlit at weekends.

Lake Louise (see separate chapter) is about 45 minutes' drive from Banff.

Banff's Best Snow!

Deeper

Sunshine Village receives an average of 33 feet of dry, Canadian Rockies powder each season.

Bigger

Sunshine offers some of the best skiing and snowboarding in the Canadian Rockies, with three beautiful mountains, offering everything from groomed beginner slopes to steep and deep powder skiing. In addition, snowboarders can enjoy our permanent snowboard half-pipe, boarder–X course and terrain park!

More Convenient

The Sunshine Inn, a remarkable 84 room cozy alpine lodge located right in the middle of the ski area at 7200 feet, offers Banff's only ski-in, ski-out accommodation.

Faster

Sunshines's new state of the art 8 person gondola and recent $4m investment in high speed quads means queues are a thing of the past. Using world-leading technology, the new gondola will cut travel time by 40% and whisk skiers and riders up to the magnificent vistas in much greater comfort.

Airtours 0870 608 1950
Crystal 0870 848 7000
Frontier Ski 020 8776 8709
Neilson 0870 333 3347
Ski the American Dream 020 8552 1201
All Canada Ski 01502 585825
First Choice Ski 0870 754 3477
Inghams 020 8780 4444
Ski Independence 0870 555 0555
Thomson 0870 606 1470

Sunshine Village Ski & Snowboard Resort, Banff, Alberta, Canada. Tel 001 403 762 6500

boarding *Boarders will feel at home in Banff. The nearby mountains have good fun-parks and half-pipes and some excellent free-riding terrain for experienced riders. Norquay offers a snowboard park lift ticket for those wishing to use only the park and pipe. We have had mainly positive reports about the tuition. Beware green trails, however, as they can be really flat and require some walking. Banff is quite lively for nightlife.*

MOUNTAIN FACTS

NORQUAY, SUNSHINE & LAKE LOUISE

Covered by the Tri-area pass

Altitude	1635m-2730m
Lifts	30
Pistes	7558 acres
Green	25%
Blue	45%
Black	30%
Art. snow	1700 acres

NORQUAY

Altitude	1635m-2135m
Lifts	5
Pistes	162 acres
Green	20%
Blue	36%
Black	44%
Art. snow	90%

SUNSHINE

Altitude	1660m-2730m
Lifts	12
Pistes	3168 acres
Green	20%
Blue	50%
Black	30%
Art. snow	none

SNOW RELIABILITY
Excellent

Sunshine Village claims '100% natural snow', a neat reversal of the usual snowmaking hype. Certainly, the lack of snowmaking there has never been a problem in our experience other than in last season's exceptionally poor snow year – when the blues were still fine but the blacks remained rocky during our February visit. 'Three times the snow' is another Sunshine slogan – a cryptic reference to the fact that the average snowfall here is 360 to 400 inches (depending on which figures you believe) – as good as anything in Colorado, and rivalling Jackson Hole – compared with a modest 140 inches at Lake Louise and 120 inches on Norquay. But we're told the Sunshine figures relate to Lookout, and that Goat's Eye gets less. There is snowmaking on 90% of pistes at Norquay. So all in all, lack of snow is unlikely to be a problem.

FOR EXPERTS
Pure pleasure

Both areas have satisfying terrain for good skiers and boarders.

Sunshine has plenty of open runs of genuine black steepness above the tree line on Lookout, but Goat's Eye Mountain makes this area much more compelling. It has opened up a great area of expert double-black-diamond trails and chutes, both above and below the tree line – one reporter enjoyed the area so much that he and his party kept 'going back again and again'. But the slopes are rocky and need good cover, and the top can be windswept. There are short, steep runs on Mount Standish, too. One particular novelty is a pitch, near the mid-station, known as the Waterfall run – because you do actually ski down over a snow-covered frozen fall.

Real experts will want to get to grips with the recently reopened Delirium Dive on Lookout Mountain's north face. You are only allowed to hike up to it if you have a companion, an avalanche transceiver and a shovel – and a guide is recommended. ('Book in advance,' says a disappointed reporter.) But a local expert says: 'The patrol neurotically carpet-bombs the entire cirque and closes Delirium upon sighting the first tiny fog-bank, making Delirium about the safest off-piste on the planet. The mandatory transceiver routine is pure theatre.' The area was closed on our 2001 visit, but we did

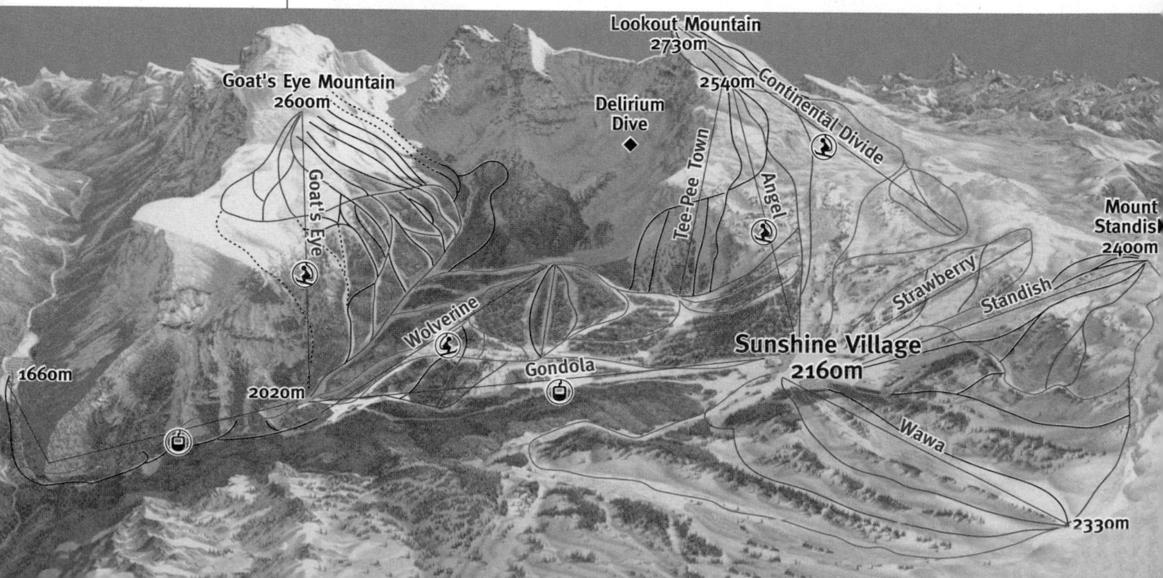

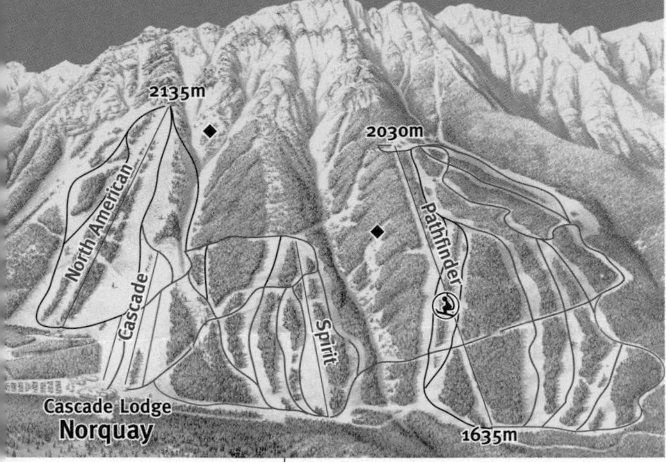

a mixed party of beginners (who may want to stay in one area) and more experienced friends (who are likely to want to visit other places).

FOR CROSS-COUNTRY
High in quality and quantity
It's a good area for cross-country. There are trails near Banff, around the Bow River, and on the Banff Springs golf course. But the best area is around Lake Louise. Altogether, there are around 80km of groomed trails within Banff National Park. Beware of the wildlife though: last season a cross-country skier was killed by a mountain lion.

LIFT PASSES

2001/02 prices in Canadian dollars
Tri-area lift pass
Covers all lifts and transport between Banff, Lake Louise, Norquay and Sunshine Village, available for 3 days or more.
Main pass
3-day pass 175
6-day pass 350
Children
6-12: 6-day pass 128
Beginners First time ski packages including rental, pass and tuition available
Day passes
2000/01 prices
Day passes excluding transport to/from individual areas (10 return)
Sunshine Village: 54
Norquay: 47
with reductions for senior citizens (over 65 at Sunshine, over 55 at Norquay), teenagers (13-17), children (6-12). Kids aged five and under are free.
Short-term passes
Half-day pass for individual areas of Sunshine Village: 43
Mount Norquay: 35 (or hourly rate at any time of day, minimum 2hr: 25). Night skiing also available here on Friday evenings.

take a look at it, and it is suitably impressive, with pitches over 40° and 585m of vertical.

Norquay's two main lifts give only 400m vertical, but both serve black slopes and the North American chair accesses a couple of double-diamond runs that justify their grading.

Heli-skiing is available from bases outside the National Park in British Columbia – roughly two hours' drive.

FOR INTERMEDIATES
Ideal runs
Half the runs on Sunshine are classified as intermediate. Wherever you look there are blues and greens – some of the greens as enjoyable (and pretty much as steep) as the blues.

We particularly like the World Cup Downhill run, from the top of Lookout to the mid-mountain base. Don't ignore the Wawa T-Bar, which gives access to the often quiet Wawa Bowl and Tincan Alley. There's a delightful wooded area under the second stage of the gondola served by Jackrabbit and Wolverine chairs. The blue runs down Goat's Eye are good cruises too.

The Pathfinder fast quad at Norquay serves a handful of quite testing tree-lined blues and a couple of sometimes-groomed blacks – great for a snowy day or a 'first day of the holiday' warm-up.

FOR BEGINNERS
Pretty good terrain
Sunshine has a good area by the mid-mountain base, served by a hand tow. The long Meadow Park Green is a great, long, easy run to progress to.

Norquay has a good small nursery area with a magic carpet and gentle greens served by the Cascade chair.

Banff is not the ideal destination for

QUEUES
Should not be a problem
Half the slope-users come for the day from cities such as Calgary – so it's fairly quiet during the week. The old gondola up to Sunshine was queue-prone in the mornings but the new one should solve that problem.

MOUNTAIN RESTAURANTS
Quite good
Sunshine Village has a choice of eating places at its mid-mountain base. The Day Lodge now has quite a choice of three different styles of food on three floors (table service in the top floor Lookout Lodge, with great views). Mad Trapper's Saloon is a jolly western-style place in Old Sunshine Lodge, serving different food on its two levels (though reporters have criticised its disposable plates). The Sunshine Inn hotel has the best food – table-service snacks in the Chimney Corner Lounge or a full lunch in the Eagle's Nest Dining Room. The Java Hut (actually a tent), at the bottom of Goat's Eye Mountain, has had mixed reports.

At the base of Norquay, the big, stylish, timber-framed Cascade Lodge is excellent – it has great views and a table-service restaurant upstairs as well as a self-service cafeteria.

SCHOOLS AND GUIDES
Some great ideas
Both mountains have their own school. But recognising that visitors wanting lessons won't want to be confined to just one mountain, the resorts have organised an excellent Club Ski and Club Snowboard Program – three-day courses starting on Mondays and Thursdays that take you to Sunshine, Norquay and Lake Louise on different

SCHOOLS/GUIDES

2001/02 prices in Canadian dollars

Club Ski and Club Snowboard
3 days of guided tuition of the three areas

Club Program
4½hr per day
3 full days 169
(incl lunch for Club Junior Program for age 6-12)

CHILDCARE

The nurseries at Sunshine Village and Norquay's Cascade Lodge take children aged 19 months to 6 years, from 9am to 4pm. Children aged 3 or more can take short ski lessons.

days, offering a mixture of guiding and instruction and including free video analysis, a fun race and a group photo. We'd recommend this to anyone who wants to see the whole area while improving their technique. Reporters rave about it: 'absolutely brilliant' and 'improved more in three days than in a week anywhere else'. All standards are catered for, including beginners. We also have a fat file full of praise for the free mountain tours by friendly local volunteer snow hosts.

FACILITIES FOR CHILDREN
Excellent

One reporter who used Sunshine, Norquay and Lake Louise said: 'I'd recommend all three.'

Staying there

Unless you stay mid-mountain on Sunshine, it will be a drive or bus-ride to the slopes. Don't expect resort ambience or too much nightlife. Some of the Banff lodgings (even on the main Banff Avenue) are quite a distance from downtown, but there's a good bus service.

HOW TO GO
Superb-value packages

A huge amount of accommodation is on offer – especially hotels and self-catering, but also a few catered chalets run by British tour operators. We have an enthusiastic report ('wonderful views, excellent food, great hot-tub') on the Timberline Inn, reachable on skis from Norquay and now run as a kind of chalet hotel by Crystal.

Hotels Summer is the peak season here. Prices halve for the winter – so you can stay in luxury at bargain rates.

(4) **Banff Springs** (762 2211) A turn-of-the century, castle-style Canadian Pacific property, well outside town. It's virtually a town within itself – it can sleep 2,000 people, has over 40 shops, numerous restaurants and bars, a nightclub and a superb health club and spa (which costs extra).

(4) **Rimrock** (762 33560) Spectacularly set, out of town, with great views and a smart health club. Luxurious.

(3) **Sunshine Inn** (762 6550) On the slopes at Sunshine Village. Luggage transported for you in the gondola while you hit the slopes. Rooms vary

SUNSHINE VILLAGE
Coming down into Sunshine Village and its beginner area ↘

Phone numbers
From distant parts of the Canada, add the prefix 1 403.
From abroad, add the prefix +1 403.

GETTING THERE

Air Calgary, transfer 1½hr.

ACTIVITIES

Indoor Film theatre, museums, galleries, swimming pools (one with water slides), gym, squash, racquetball, weight training, bowling, hot-tub, sauna, mini-golf, climbing wall
Outdoor Swimming in hot springs, ice skating, heli-skiing, horse-drawn carriage rides, sleigh rides, dog-sled rides, snowmobiles, curling, ice hockey, ice fishing, helicopter tours, night skiing, snow-shoe tours

TOURIST OFFICE

Postcode ToL oCo
t +1 (403) 762 4561
f 762 8185
info@sblls.com
www.sblls.com

in size. Big outdoor hot-pool. Sauna. Good restaurant.
(3) **Inns of Banff** (762 4581) About 20 minutes' walk from town; praised by reporters for large rooms, room service and fitness facilities.
(3) **Banff Park Lodge** (762 4433) Best-quality central hotel, with hot-tub, steam room and indoor pool.
(2) **Banff Caribou Lodge** (762 5887) On the main street, slightly out of town. It has a variety of wood-clad, interestingly and individually designed rooms, a sauna and hot-tub complex and a good restaurant and bar. Repeatedly recommended by reporters.
(2) **Banff King Edward** (762 2202) Right in the town centre, set above shops; large rooms and surprisingly quiet for its position.
Self-catering The Banff Rocky Mountain Resort is set in the woods on the edge of town; facilities include indoor pool, squash and hot-tubs. Reporters have also recommended the Douglas Fir resort for families – though 'a bit out of town' – and Woodland Village.

EATING OUT
Lots of choice

Banff boasts over 100 restaurants, from McDonald's to fine dining in the Banff Springs hotel. Reporters praise lots of places but complain about them being busy and many places not taking bookings. Many places do huge portions that you can share. Regular recommendations include the new Maple Leaf (Canadian, relatively expensive), Earl's (burgers and ethnic dishes, very popular and lively), Magpie and Stump (Mexican, with Wild West decor), Giorgio's (Italian), Rose & Crown (pub grub), the Keg (steaks, two branches – one in town and one in Caribou Lodge), Seoul Country (Korean), Wild Bill's (burgers, grills, Tex Mex, dancing), Grizzlies Fondue House.

APRES-SKI
Livens up later on

One of the drawbacks of the area is that teatime après-ski is limited because the villages are a drive from the slopes. But Mad Trapper's Saloon at the top of the Sunshine Village gondola is popular during the close of play happy hour (with endless free peanuts). In town later in the evening, Wild Bill's has live country and western music and line dancing. The Rose & Crown has live music and gets crowded. The Works and the Barbary Coast nightclubs are popular. And Outabounds attracts a young lively crowd, while Aurora is for more serious clubbing. The St James Gate Irish pub has 'great atmosphere, good-value food and a wide range of beers'.

OFF THE SLOPES
Lots to do

For someone who does not intend to hit the slopes, Banff has to be one of the best resorts there is: there are so many other things to do and lots of wildlife to see. There are lovely walks, including organised ice canyon walks, and you can go snow-shoeing, dog-sledding, skating and tobogganing. You can go on sightseeing tours and visit natural hot springs as well.

There are museums to visit such as Banff Park Museum, the Whyte Museum of the Canadian Rockies, the Natural History Museum, the Canadian Ski Museum West and the Buffalo Nation's Luxton Museum of the Indians of the Northern Plains.

There are hundreds of shops, though most of them are overtly aimed at the tourist trade.

STAYING UP THE MOUNTAIN
Worth considering

At Sunshine Village, the Sunshine Inn is the only slope-side hotel (see Hotels, above).

Big White 1755m

Big by local standards, white by any standard

WHAT IT COSTS

HOW IT RATES

The slopes

Snow	****
Extent	***
Experts	*****
Intermediates	****
Beginners	****
Convenience	****
Queues	*****
Restaurants	*

The rest

Scenery	***
Resort charm	**
Off-slope	**

What's new

Last season saw the opening of the new Happy Valley adventure area, with a huge tubing hill, a skating rink, paths, kids' nursery slope and a day lodge, all linked to the village by a new eight-person gondola. More accommodation was also added.

Much more development is planned, and 2001/02 should see more lodgings as well as new slopes. Four new trails are being cut on the black-graded terrain off the Ridge Rocket chair.

MOUNTAIN FACTS

Altitude	1510m-2285m
Lifts	13
Pistes	2200 acres
Green	18%
Blue	56%
Black	26%
Art. snow	none

- ⊕ BC's highest ski area, with a good snow record
- ⊕ Mainly fast lifts, with few queues
- ⊕ Extensive, varied slopes, deserted except at weekends and holidays
- ⊕ Convenient, purpose-built village with mainly ski-in/ski-out accommodation and car-free centre
- ⊕ Excellent kids' facilities

- ⊖ Few off-slope diversions – and isolated without a car
- ⊖ Upper mountain is very exposed – and is known for freezing fog
- ⊖ No mountain restaurants
- ⊖ Limited après-ski

'It's the snow,' says the Big White slogan. And as slogans go, it's spot on. If all you want to do is ski or ride, with a fair chance of doing it in deep snow, put Big White high on the shortlist. If other things enter into your holiday equation, the attractions are less clear, despite current improvements. That's if you're planning a week-long stay in one place; for anyone planning a tour of BC resorts, Big White should be an automatic choice.

THE RESORT

Big White is a modern, purpose-built resort above the Okanagan valley. It is built on a sloping hillside, slightly above the three main chair-lift bases so that much of the accommodation is ski-in/ski-out. A lot of the resort's business comes from day visitors, who can park near these lift bases or at the more remote base of Westridge, but these days are most likely to park at the newly created Happy Valley activity area, where a powerful new gondola gives access to the village centre. This is a rather piecemeal affair (Intrawest-style urban planning not in evidence) but attractive in wood and stone.

Big White is only 45 minutes from Kelowna airport (but a long drive from bigger gateways). Other candidates for inclusion in a tour along with Big White are Silver Star and Red Mountain (see Western Canada introduction).

THE MOUNTAINS

Much of the terrain is heavily wooded though the trees thin out towards the summits, leading to almost open slopes in the bowls at the top. There's at least one green option from the top of each lift so beginners need not be intimidated by any one sector. Grooming is excellent.

Slopes Fast chairs run from points below village level to above mid-mountain, serving the main area of wooded beginner and intermediate runs above and beside the village. Slower lifts – a T-bar and two chairs – serve the higher slopes. Quite some way across the mountainside is the Gem Lake fast chair, serving a range of long top-to-bottom runs to its base at Westridge; with its 710m vertical, this lift is in a different league from the others. There are free daily mountain tours and floodlit skiing.

BIG WHITE / KLAUS GRETZMACHER

This shot shows only the 'front face' of Big White – the Gem Lake chair and its runs are off to the left →

Central reservations phone number
For all resort accommodation call 765 8888 (from distant parts of Canada, add the prefix 1 250; from abroad, add the prefix +1 250)

Toll-free number (from within Canada) 1 800 663 1772.

TOURIST OFFICE

Postcode V1X 4K5
t +1 (250) 765 8888
f 765 1822
bigwhite@bigwhite.com
www.bigwhite.com

Snowboarding There's some excellent free-riding terrain and three fun-parks and pipes. Novices are well catered for with long, chair-lift-served green runs.
Snow reliability Big White has a reputation for great powder; average snowfall is about 300 inches, which is not quite Alta or even Fernie class, but not far short. There is no snowmaking.
Experts There is lots to do, especially if you get good snow. The main bowl off the side of the T-bar is of serious double-black pitch. The Sun-Rype bowl at the opposite edge of the ski area is more forgiving. There are some superb long blacks off the Gem Lake chair and several shorter ones off the Powder and Ridge Rocket chairs – with more in the latter area for this season. In most of these areas there are extensive glades to explore, too.
Intermediates The resort is excellent for cruisers and families with long blues and greens all over the hill.
Beginners There's a good dedicated nursery area in the village and lots of long easy runs to progress to.
Cross-country There are 25km of trails in total.
Queues With four fast quads and few visitors still, queues are pretty rare. However, the Alpine T-bar can be a bottleneck on sunny days.
Mountain restaurants The nearest thing to a mountain restaurant is the Westridge base warming hut.
School and guides The ski school offers some interesting options.
Facilities for children The excellent 'Kids' Centre' takes children from 18 months. And there's a dedicated nursery slope with a magic carpet lift at the new Happy Valley area. Evening activities are organised.

STAYING THERE

How to go There's an increasing range of packages to Big White.
Hotels The White Crystal Inn, Coast Resort and Chateau Big White are recommended – all are convenient for the slopes.
Self-catering There's a reasonable choice of accommodation. Grocery shopping is very limited.
Eating out The choice of restaurant is gradually widening. Snowshoe Sam's is good for casual dining. Other recommendations include Powder Keg (Greek), Swiss Bear in the Chateau Big White (Swiss!), China White Wok, Loose Moose (steaks and grills), and Coltino's in the Hopfbrauhaus (Italian).
Après-ski The atmospheric Snowshoe Sam's is a focal point, with a DJ and live entertainment. Powder Keg, Loose Moose and Grizzly Bear are also recommended, and Raakel's is good for families.
Off the slopes The brand new Happy Valley adventure park features western Canada's largest tubing hills and ice skating, and is the launch pad for snowmobiling, snow-shoeing and dog-sledding. Helicopter tours and the two health spas are also popular.

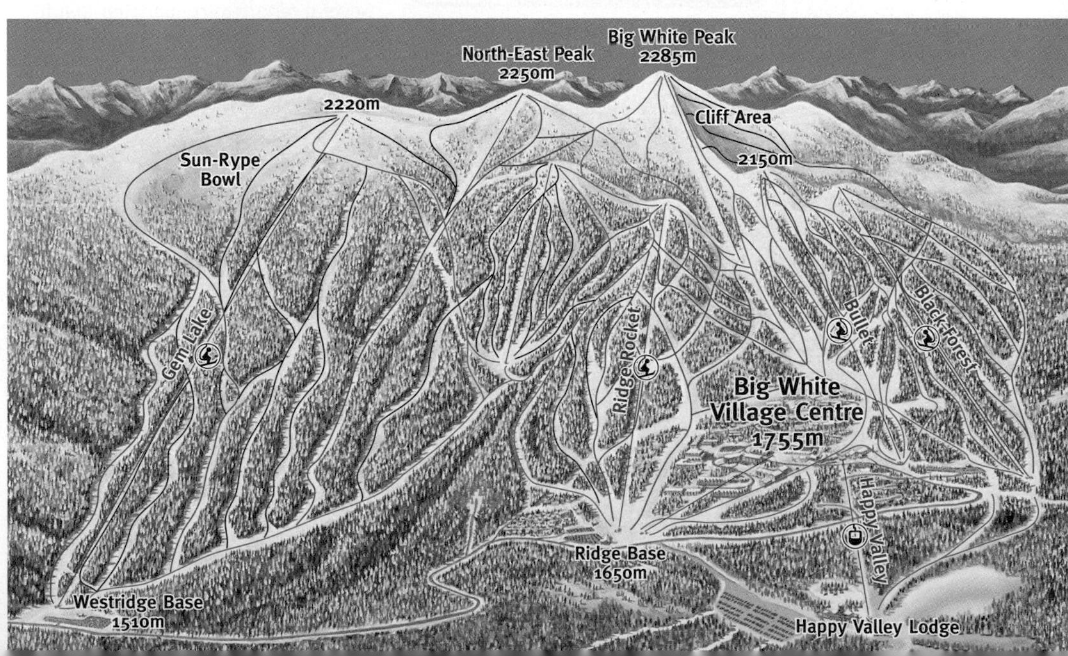

Fernie 1070m

Lots of snow, and lots of steeps

WHAT IT COSTS

5

HOW IT RATES

The slopes

Snow	****
Extent	***
Experts	*****
Intermediates	**
Beginners	****
Convenience	****
Queues	****
Restaurants	*

The rest

Scenery	****
Resort charm	**
Off-slope	**

What's new

The new mountain village has started to take shape with the opening of new condo-hotels, restaurants, a couple of shops and a crèche, and development continues.

The Bear T-bar was replaced by a fast quad for 2000/2001, improving access to both Lizard and Cedar Bowls.

SNOWPIX.COM / CHRIS GILL

The centre of Fernie Alpine Resort with the new Cornerstone Lodge on the right ↓

- ⊕ Good snow record, with less chance of rain than at Whistler, and less chance of Arctic temperatures than at Lake Louise
- ⊕ Great terrain for those who like it steep and deep, with lots for confident intermediates and beginners, too
- ⊕ A couple of snowcat operations nearby
- ⊕ Good on-slope accommodation becoming increasingly available in small, friendly mountain resort

- ⊖ Lift system poor, with a primitive rope tow and hikes and traverses to some of the best terrain
- ⊖ After a dump it can take time to make the black bowls safe
- ⊖ Little groomed cruising for timid or average intermediates
- ⊖ No decent mountain restaurants
- ⊖ Mountain resort is still small and under construction with very limited evening options, and town of Fernie (a short drive away) is not particularly appealing either

Fernie has long had cult status among Alberta and BC skiers for its steep gladed slopes and superb natural snow, and it is now attracting a lot of British visitors. In 1998 the operation was bought by Charlie Locke, owner of Lake Louise. There has since been a lot of investment in the development of the village at the foot of the slopes – though it still remains small without many facilities, and for much of last winter it seemed like a muddy construction site. Some visitors would rather see more investment in the mountain, to speed up the lifts, cut down the amount of hiking and traversing, and to hasten reopening after a serious snowfall. We see their point, but most reports we get are dominated by excitement at Fernie's combination of snow and terrain. 'Just like Jackson Hole', said two reporters independently this year. When we went to press Charlie Locke's company had hit financial problems and further investment was on hold.

The resort 

Fernie Alpine Resort is set at the lift base a little way up the mountainside from the flat Elk Valley floor and a couple of miles from the little town of Fernie. It has grown from nothing in the last two or three years. But there's still not much there other than convenient accommodation and a few places to eat. It is quiet at night. Several reporters commented that it lacked charm and resembled a muddy building site. But we were there when there was snow on the ground and found it okay. Owner Charlie Locke has been good at attracting crowds of Brits to his flagship resort of Lake Louise and is now doing the same in Fernie. It remains to be seen how his financial difficulties affect further development.

The town of Fernie is named after William Fernie – a prospector who discovered coal here and triggered a boom at the turn of the century. Much of the town was destroyed by fire in 1908 but some downtown stone and brick buildings survived and are still there. We thought it a nondescript spot on our first visit three years ago but noticed a few more tourist shops on our 2001 visit. One reporter described it as 'a bit like staying in an industrial estate on the outskirts of Barnsley' – a bit unfair, we thought, but you can't describe it as 'charming'.

The mountains

Fernie's 2,500 acres pack in a lot of variety, from superb green terrain at the bottom to ungroomed chutes (that will be satisfyingly steep to anyone but the extreme specialist) and huge numbers of steep runs in the trees. A lot of the runs have the rare quality of consistently steep pure fall lines.

MOUNTAIN FACTS

Altitude	1070m-1925m
Lifts	10
Pistes	2500 acres
Green	30%
Blue	40%
Black	30%
Art. snow	25 acres
Recco detectors used	

THE SLOPES
Bowl after bowl

What you see when you arrive at the lift base is a trio of impressive mogul slopes towering above you. The Deer chair approaches the foot of these slopes, but goes no further. You get to them by traversing and hiking from the main Lizard Bowl, on the right. This is a broad snowfield reached by a series of lifts: a slow quad (which one reporter found stopped 'on average four times per uplift'); a fast quad (which replaced the old T-bar last season); and finally the short Face Lift, a dreadful rope tow that wasn't working when we were there in February 2001 because lack of snow meant it was high above the ground – it also 'shredded' one reporter's gloves. This is also the main way into lift-free Cedar Bowl (where a reporter came across a moose) and to Snake Ridge beyond it. There is a mini-bowl between Lizard and Cedar, served by the 500m vertical Boomerang chair.

The Timber Bowl fast quad chair gives access to Siberia Bowl and the lower part of Timber. But for access to the higher slopes and to Currie Bowl you must take the White Pass Quad. A long traverse from the top gets you to the steeper slopes on the flanks of Currie (our favourite area), which are otherwise reached by hiking from the main Lizard Bowl. From there you have to go right to the bottom, and it takes quite a while to get back for another go.

There are excellent, free, hosted tours of the area in groups of different abilities for two hours twice a day. These may be a good way to get your bearings, as several readers found the signposting 'minimal', and we found both signs and trail map dangerously inadequate. Indeed, when we tried to find the long, black Diamond Back run from the top of the White Pass quad, we failed and ended up in narrowly spaced trees on a slope of triple-diamond steepness – pretty scary.

Outings to Kimberley are possible; a coach does the trip every Thursday (there's also a helicopter option). Buses back to Fernie town at the end of the day are 'excellent' for $2.50, and a reporter said they were dropped off at their chalet if they asked.

SNOW RELIABILITY
A key part of the appeal

Last year's exceptionally poor year apart, Fernie has an excellent snow record – with an average of 350 inches per year, better than practically all of Colorado. But the altitude is modest – rain is not unknown, and in warmer weather the lower slopes can suffer. There is very little snowmaking, and reporters said piste maintenance was poor in last season's snow drought.

FOR EXPERTS
Wonderful – deep and steep

The combination of heavy snowfalls and abundant steep terrain with the shelter of trees makes this a superb mountain for good skiers. There are about a dozen identifiable faces offering genuine black or double-black slopes, each of them with several alternative ways down. Currie and

Phone numbers
From distant parts of the Canada, add the prefix 1 250.
From abroad, add the prefix +1 250.

RIDE THE SNOWCATS AT ISLAND LAKE LODGE

Any good skier who relishes off-piste should consider treating themselves to three or four days staying at Island Lake Lodge (423 3700). Book as far in advance as you can as we've heard they can be booked up to three years in advance! You can do single days without accommodation, but only on a standby basis; we did this three years ago but could not get in on our 2001 visit. The Lodge is a cosy chalet 10km from Fernie, amid 7,000 acres of spectacular bowls and ridges. It has 36 beds, and four snowcats to act as lifts. In a day you might do eight powder runs averaging 500m vertical, taking in all kinds of terrain from gentle open slopes to some very Alpine adventures – maybe not as exciting as heli-skiing, but in its way just as rewarding. Three-day packages cost around £700. There are other snowcat operations in the region, less well-known and so less likely to be booked solid.

boarding

Fernie is a fine place for boarders (and there are a lot of local experts here). Lots of natural gulleys, hits and endless off-piste opportunities – including some adrenalin-pumping tree-runs and knee-deep powder bowls – will keep free-riders of all standards grinning from ear to ear. There's also a good terrain-park and half-pipe. Snowcat operators can take you to some excellent untouched powder. There are a couple of decent bars in the town, and Frozen Ocean and Board Stiff are the main board shops.

LIFT PASSES

2000/01 prices in Canadian dollars

Main pass

1-day pass 54
6-day pass 300

Senior citizens

Over 65: 6-day pass 228

Children

13-17: 6-day pass 228
Under 13: 6-day pass 90
Under 6: free pass

Short-term passes

Half-day pass from noon (adult 43)

Notes

Mighty Moose lift passes available for beginners: 15

Timber Bowls both have some serious double-diamonds but mainly have single-diamonds. However, one of our regular reporters says, 'The majority of the single blacks are tough. Some of them are so steep that I can't work out how you could get anything harder without falling off the mountain ... just like Jackson Hole but without the cliffs.' Even where the trail map shows trees to be sparse, expect them to be close enough together, and where there aren't any, expect alder bushes unless there's lots of snow.

There are also backcountry routes you can take with guidance and snowcat operations to try. If you can't get in at Island Lake – see feature panel – try Fernie Wilderness Adventures.

FOR INTERMEDIATES
Far from ideal

Although there are intermediate runs both low down and high up, they don't add up to a lot of mileage. Most high runs are not groomed, and one reporter said, 'The blues in all bowls except Timber would be black in most resorts.' Adventurous, strong intermediates willing to give the ungroomed terrain a try will enjoy the area. The blue/green Falling Star run (a short hike up from the top of the Timber Bowl chair) is often completely deserted and has good snow, although near the bottom it is narrow and it gets a bit flat. But if you want miles of groomed cruising, go elsewhere.

FOR BEGINNERS
Excellent

There's a good nursery area and the lower mountain served by the Deer and Elk chairs has lots of wide, smooth trails to gain confidence on. But most runs from the top of the mountain have tough parts to them.

FOR CROSS-COUNTRY
Some possibilities

There are 15km of trails marked out in the forest adjacent to the resort, and the Fernie golf and country club allows enthusiasts on to their white fairways.

QUEUES
Not usually a problem

Unless there is a weekend invasion from Calgary, queues are rare. Last year's poor snow kept numbers down but in a normal year we guess that the new fast Bear quad chair will lead to queues at the inadequate and

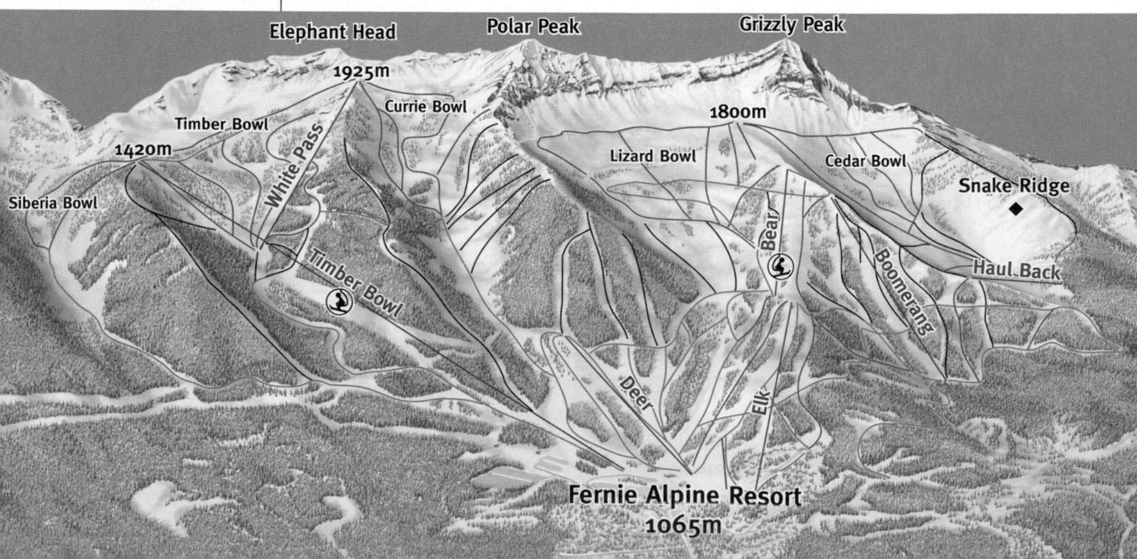

SCHOOLS/GUIDES

2000/01 prices in Canadian dollars

Fernie

Classes

1¾hr: 10am and 1.30
Half day: 27
Multi half days: 23

Children's classes

Ages 3 to 4 years and 5 to 12 years
Multi full day: 38

Private lessons

2 hr: 92 (22 for each additional person)

CHILDCARE

The resort day care centre takes children of all ages. It is open daily from 9am to 4pm.

ACTIVITIES

Indoor Museum, galleries, aquatic centre, saunas, bowling, fitness centre, ice skating, cinema, curling
Outdoor Sleigh rides, snowmobiling, dog-sledding, snow-shoe excursions, ice fishing, cross-country skiing.

GETTING THERE

Air Calgary, transfer 3½hr.

Central reservations phone number
For all resort accommodation call 1 800 258 7669 (toll-free from within Canada).

TOURIST OFFICE

Postcode VoB 1M6
t +1 (250) 423 4655
f 423 6644
info@skifernie.com
www.skifernie.com

atrocious Face Lift tow (if it is working). If heavy snow keeps part of the mountain closed, there can be queues elsewhere.

MOUNTAIN RESTAURANTS
What mountain restaurants?

Bear's Den at the top of the Elk chair is an open-air fast-food kiosk. So it's back to base for lunch – the ancient Day Lodge is grim but cheap and serves good soups and sandwiches to order. Or see Eating Out.

SCHOOLS AND GUIDES
'Lessons for all abilities'

Reporters have praised the ski school and its small classes. One tried telemarking and described the tuition as 'outstanding' and 'best ever', with only two people in the class. 'First Tracks' gets you up the mountain at 8am for two hours, but when we tried it the instructor didn't know which lifts were open and there was a lot of wasted time.

FACILITIES FOR CHILDREN
New day care centre

There's a new day care centre in the Cornerstone Lodge, which a reporter found 'very well run'. There are also 'Kids' Activity Nights'.

Staying there

You're going for the snow, so our advice would be to stay on or close to the hill. A reader warns that if you're self-catering in the village, the only decent food shopping is in the town. It's cheaper to stay in the town, where there is a wider choice of restaurants, bars and other diversions, and a much wider choice of shops.

HOW TO GO
More packages

Fernie is increasingly easy to find in tour operator brochures.
Chalets Some UK tour operators run chalets, and a reporter highly recommends one 10 minutes from the slopes with free guiding bookable on the internet at cdnpowdertours@elkvalley.net.
Hotels and condos
As the resort develops, the choice is widening and shifting upmarket.
((((4 **Lizard Creek Lodge** New luxury ski-in/ski-out condo hotel. Spa, outdoor pool and hot-tub. We stayed there and highly recommend it.
(((3 **Cornerstone Lodge** New condo hotel in the village core.
(((3 **Griz Inn** Condo-hotel with good facilities. Pool.
((2 **Wolf's Den Lodge** 'Adequate but uninspiring' with 'simple' rooms say reporters. Indoor hot-tub, games room and small gym. At base of slope.
((2 **Timberline Village** Very comfortable condos a shuttle-ride from the lifts.
((2 **Cedar Lodge** Motel on road to town. 'Comfortable and clean, but not very welcoming,' said reporters.
((2 **Alpine Lodge** New B&B recommended by reporter.

EATING OUT
Not a highlight

At the base, the Lizard Creek Lodge is expensive but serves the best gourmet food in the district (in small portions). Kelsey's (part of a chain) is more casual and offers good food and large servings, with Asian dishes as well as standard burgers, steaks, pasta, The Powderhorn in the Griz Inn does 'good, reasonably priced' food. Gabriella's Pasta Place is cheap but nothing special.

In Fernie, the restaurants at the Royal and Grand Central hotels are recommended, as is Rip n' Richard's Eatery – south-western food and a lively atmosphere. The Old Elevator is in a converted grain store and does good grills and pasta; Jamocha's is a coffee house that does meals. The Cottage has a 'nice ambience, friendly staff and good food'. Coltraynes is very busy with an interesting menu and international food. The Curry Bowl has recently opened and is very good.

APRES-SKI
Have a beer

The Grizzly bar in the Day Lodge and the Powderhorn, in the nearby Griz Inn, are quite lively when the lifts close – the latter with live bands sometimes. During the week, the bars are pretty quiet later on, but one reporter recommends Kelsey's. In town, the bar of the Royal hotel is popular with locals. Other recommendations are the Park Place Lodge Pub and the bar in the Grand Central hotel.

OFF THE SLOPES
Get out and about

There is a heritage walking tour of historic Fernie. The old railroad station is now the Art Station. The main diversion is the great outdoors.

Jasper 1064m

Small area of slopes set amid glorious scenery and wildlife

WHAT IT COSTS

(4)

HOW IT RATES

The slopes

Snow	****
Extent	*
Experts	**
Intermediates	**
Beginners	****
Convenience	*
Queues	****
Restaurants	**

The rest

Scenery	***
Resort charm	***
Off-slope	***

What's new

A new quad chair-lift will be ready for the 2001/02 season. The new chair, starting just below mid-mountain, will open up twenty new runs on Eagle East and Chalet Slope on either sides of Eagle Ridge – previously accessible only by taking the high traverse from the top of the Knob chair-lift. It will also provide a more direct route to the Knob chair-lift.

MOUNTAIN FACTS

Altitude	1705m-2600m
Lifts	8
Pistes	1000 acres
Green	35%
Blue	35%
Black	30%
Art. snow	10 acres

- ⊕ Lots of lovely walks and drives in National Park land
- ⊕ Spectacular scenery and wildlife
- ⊖ Slopes are a long way from town and limited in size, especially for intermediates
- ⊖ Town rather spread out and lacks charm

Set in the middle of Jasper National Park, the small railroad town is surrounded by spectacular scenery and wildlife. There's a small area of slopes 30 minutes away, but Jasper best suits those looking for an all-round winter holiday. It would be best combined with a stay in Whistler, Banff or Lake Louise.

THE RESORT

Jasper is an unremarkable, growing railway town that started life as a stopover for fur traders. There's little more to it than a couple of main streets. Most accommodation is out of town or on the outskirts and the local slopes are a 30-minute drive away.

Its main attractions are the beautiful scenery and drives and walks in the surrounding unspoiled National Park land. One of the most beautiful drives in the world is the three-hour trip to Lake Louise on the Columbia Icefields Parkway through the Banff and Jasper National Parks – past glaciers, frozen waterfalls and lakes.

This makes Jasper a good place to stay for a couple of days as part of a two-centre holiday. You can travel from Whistler to Jasper by overnight train from Vancouver and wake up to spectacular Rocky Mountains scenery.

Although there are buses to and from the slopes, it would be handy to have a car (to explore the surrounding area as well as reach the slopes).

THE MOUNTAINS

The slopes are at Marmot Basin, in the heart of the unspoiled National Park.

Slopes A high-speed quad takes you to mid-mountain, with three slow chairs above that and a new one to Eagle Ridge for 2001/02. The highest Knob chair ends way below the 2600m peak that the area includes in its claim of almost 900m vertical.

Snow reliability Snow reliability is reputed to be good, but cover has been sparse on both our visits and there is little snowmaking capacity.

Experts There are some decent mogul runs on the top and bottom halves of the mountain, and some entertaining off-piste on the top half. For those willing to hike up from the top of the Knob chair and take the High Traverse, virtually the whole of the left-hand side of the mountain, as you look up, is made up of black-diamond runs. But unless you hit excellent snow the area is very small and limited.

Intermediates Keen piste-bashers will cover all the groomed runs in half a

MARMOT BASIN / HUGH LECKY

Marmot Basin's slopes are quiet but not huge – in either extent or vertical drop →

Phone numbers
From distant parts of Canada, add the prefix 1 780.
From abroad, add the prefix +1 780.

TOURIST OFFICE

Postcode T0E 1E0
t +1 (780) 852 3816
f 852 3533
info@skimarmot.com
www.skimarmot.com

day and find the area very small unless they are prepared to brave the ungroomed blacks. Less adventurous intermediates will be happy to cruise the greens and blues for a day or two.
Beginners The area around the base is very gentle, and there are greens to progress to from a T-bar and the quad.
Snowboarding There's a fun-park below Caribou Ridge.
Cross-country Over 300km of trails make this one of the best areas in Canada, with good trails near Jasper.
Queues These are rarely a problem.
Mountain restaurants At mid-mountain the Paradise Chalet has a big self-service cafe and the connected Eagle Chalet is a cosy table-service place. At the base the rebuilt Caribou Chalet is another option. Catering is run by the Jasper Park Lodge (see Hotels).
Schools and guides These are doubtless up to the usual high Canadian standards.
Facilities for children The Little Rascals nursery takes children from 19 months.

STAYING THERE
Hotels The Jasper Park Lodge (852 3301) is a beautiful collection of luxurious log cabins set 4km out of town around a lake in the middle of 1,000 acres of land rich with wildlife. Room service is delivered on bicycles and you may well have to walk around grazing elk to reach your room or visit the outdoor pool and other facilities. On the edge of town, the Royal Canadian Lodge (852 5644) has some comfortable rooms and indoor pool.
Eating out There's plenty of choice – from fine dining at the Jasper Park Lodge to Cajun, pizza and Japanese. We had good seafood and steak at the Fiddle River on the main road.
Après-ski The bar in the base lodge is busy at the end of the day. In town, try Astoria, O'Shea's and Nick's.
Off the slopes, There is lots to do, including beautiful walks, ice skating and snow-shoeing, and there is a fine aquatic centre and indoor sports complex.

Kicking Horse 1200m

Heli-skiing for the rest of us

WHAT IT COSTS

HOW IT RATES

The slopes

Snow	****
Extent	***
Experts	****
Intermediates	***
Beginners	***
Convenience	*
Queues	*****
Restaurants	**

The rest

Scenery	***
Resort charm	*
Off-slope	*

- ⊕ A good bet for powder snow
- ⊕ Some great terrain for experts and adventurous intermediates
- ⊕ Big vertical served by one fast lift
- ⊕ Splendid mountaintop restaurant

- ⊖ No resort village yet
- ⊖ Golden, the resort substitute, is neither attractive nor convenient
- ⊖ Single-stage gondola suits summer visitors, not skiers and riders
- ⊖ Few groomed intermediate runs

Two years ago, this was Whitetooth, the local ski hill of the nondescript logging town of Golden: two old lifts, open over the weekend, serving modest wooded slopes beneath high bowls used by the local heli-skiing operation. Enter a Dutch–Canadian consortium, bringing with it vision, capital and a cute name. Within months, in go a new access road, a gondola rising 1150m to the heart of the heli-terrain, and smart base and mountaintop restaurants. Soon, in will go a designer mountain village at the lift base, making this a real destination resort. Meanwhile, any competent skier or rider staying in Banff or Lake Louise should give Kicking Horse a shot.

THE RESORT

Eight miles from the small logging town of Golden, Kicking Horse is nothing but a lift base station. When we visited early in 2001, the developers planned to open the first phase of a mountain village in time for the 2001/02 season, but as we went to press in July this was not confirmed.

Golden is a spread-out place beside the transcontinental highway that climbs up into the main Rockies range to the east. It has no real centre – it's the kind of place where you travel from motel to restaurant to shops by car.

THE MOUNTAINS

The lower two-thirds of the hill is wooded, with trails cut in the usual style. The upper third is a mix of open and lightly wooded slopes.

Slopes The only way up to the top of the mountain is by the eight-seater gondola to Eagle's Eye. Despite the serious vertical of 1150m, this lift goes up in a single stage – to give summer sightseeing visitors a quick ascent. In winter, the lack of a mid-station is a real drawback: you have to make the full descent regardless of the conditions and your own preferences. The lift accesses runs on both sides of the central CPR ridge. As well as the marked runs there are literally hundreds of ways down through the bowls, chutes and trees. The plan is that hardly any of the terrain will be groomed – making the area a paradise

From this point at Eagle's Nest, you can descend into Crystal Bowl or spend half an hour hiking up to Blue Heaven to tackle it from there. The descent is less steep than it looks →

SNOWPIX.COM / CHRIS GILL

What's new

The resort started operating last season, 2000/01. As we go to press it is unclear when the chair-lift to Blue Heaven or the first developments at the mountain village will be open.

MOUNTAIN FACTS

Altitude	1200m-2450m
Lifts	4
Pistes	4000 acres
Green	20%
Blue	45%
Black	35%
Art. snow	None

Phone numbers
From distant parts of Canada, add the prefix 1 250.
From abroad, add the prefix +1 250.

TOURIST OFFICE

Postcode VOA 1HO
t +1 (250) 439 5400
f 5401
www.kickinghorse resort.com

for powder pigs. A new chair-lift – shown dotted on our map – is planned to go from the bottom of Crystal Bowl to the slightly higher peak of Blue Heaven – so this part of the higher terrain, at least, will in future be skiable without descending to the base. Two chair-lifts from near the base serve the lower runs that formed the original Whitetooth ski area.

Snow reliability Excellent: until recently the top half of the mountain was heli-skiing terrain, and it gets almost 300 inches of snow a year. We were there in the February 2001 snow drought and had excellent skiing in powder in the bowls even though much of the middle of the mountain was closed.

Experts It's advanced skiers and riders who will get the most out of the area. From the ridge under the gondola, drop off to skier's right through trees or to skier's left through chutes – there are endless options. The lower half of the mountain has fine black runs on cleared trails through the trees, some with serious moguls. Do six or seven laps on the gondola in a day and you'll have had a fine time. If you detect signs of the powder getting tracked out, you can spend 30 minutes hiking up the ridge to Blue Heaven for a different approach to Crystal Bowl. From the top you can also take off (with guidance) into the next bowl, which is still part of the terrain used by Purcell heli-skiing (in Golden).

Intermediates Adventurous intermediates will have a fine time at Kicking Horse, learning to play in the powder up in Crystal Bowl. But don't expect many groomed runs. Piste-bashers and timid intermediates should go elsewhere. The only easy, groomed way down the mountain is a boring winding road.

Beginners There are some excellent nursery slopes and gentle green trails on the lower mountain.

Snowboarding Free-riders will love this powder paradise. But there's no fun-park or half-pipe.

Cross-country There are 12km of trails at Dawn Mountain near the ski area and a 5km loop on the golf course.

Queues No problem at the moment – and you won't see many people on the slopes either.

Mountain restaurants The Eagle's Eye table-service restaurant at the top of the gondola serves excellent food in stylish log cabin surroundings and has fine views. The base lodge is also

newly built with logs and beams; its small self-service restaurant seems likely to prove inadequate before long.

Schools and guides Surprise, surprise: the school specialises in powder lessons and runs two-hour 'powder tune-up' group lessons.

Facilities for children The school teaches children from the age of three.

STAYING THERE

How to go For 2001/02, you'll have to do a day-trip from a nearby resort such as Panorama, Lake Louise or Banff, or stay in Golden – a dull prospect for more than a night or two.

Hotels The Prestige Inn (344 7990), a neat, functional hotel with a small pool just off the Trans Canada Highway, probably the best in town. Sisters and Beans (344 2443) has some well kept rooms – see below.

Eating out There are several restaurants in Golden; we enjoyed the cosy Sisters and Beans (pasta, steaks, Asian dishes) run by sisters of Swiss origin. Eagle's Eye at the top of the gondola opens some nights.

Après-ski The Mad Trapper is the main drinking spot in town – a lively high-ceilinged pub.

Off the slopes There is lots of local snowmobiling and you can go ice-climbing and dog-sledding. But for someone who isn't going to hit the slopes, Golden is a dire place to stay.

Lake Louise 1645m

Knockout scenery and the Banff area's biggest mountain

WHAT IT COSTS

HOW IT RATES

The slopes

Snow	****
Extent	****
Experts	****
Intermediates	****
Beginners	***
Convenience	*
Queues	****
Restaurants	**

The rest

Scenery	*****
Resort charm	***
Off-slope	****

What's new

For 2000/01 the Glacier triple chair from the base was replaced by an additional high-speed quad to eliminate any peak period waits at the bottom of the mountain.

SKI BANFF / LAKE LOUISE

The views from Lake Louise's slopes are the most spectacular of any North American resort ↓

- ⊕ Spectacular high-mountain scenery – the best of any North American resort
- ⊕ Local slopes are the largest area in the Banff region
- ⊕ Lots of wildlife around the valley
- ⊕ Good value for money

- ⊖ Local slopes are a short drive away, other Banff areas further
- ⊖ Can be very cold – and lifts offer no protection
- ⊖ 'Village' little more than a collection of buildings around a road junction with little to offer
- ⊖ Slopes can seem over-full of Brits

Lake Louise's slopes are the biggest of Banff's three local areas and have good terrain for all ability levels. Many week-long visitors will want to spend two or three days there. The views from the slopes are stunning; and those of the lake itself and the Victoria Glacier behind it from the Chateau Lake Louise hotel must be among the most spectacular in the world. Owner Charlie Locke has done a good job marketing his slopes and they tend to be the busiest in the Banff area – and full of British voices. It is a shame that the 'resort' of Lake Louise is basically a collection of disparate buildings around a road junction with no character or resort feeling. It has a couple of characterful hotels, and if you are happy to relax in their pools and hot-tubs, you'll enjoy your stay. But if you want a choice of shops, bars, restaurants and nightlife or some streets to stroll around, you should stay in Banff. Banff is also more convenient for reaching the other two local areas of slopes.

The resort

Lake Louise is a resort of parts. First, there's the lake itself, in a spectacular mountain setting beneath the 3564m Victoria Glacier. Tom Wilson, who discovered it in 1882, declared, 'As God is my judge, I never in all my exploration have seen such a matchless scene.' Neither have we – it is simply stunning. And it can be appreciated from many of the rooms of the monster Chateau Lake Louise hotel on the shore. Then there's Lake Louise 'village' – a shapeless little collection of hotels, condominiums, petrol station, supermarket, liquor store and a few shops, a couple of miles away on a road junction down in the main valley, close to the railway and highway from Banff to Jasper. Finally, a mile or two across the valley is the lift base station (1645m). A car can be helpful especially in cold weather. Buses to the Lake Louise ski area are frequent, but a lot less so to Sunshine and Norquay (free to Tri-area lift pass holders). You can also organise trips to the more distant major resorts of Panorama and Kicking Horse and the small resorts of Nakiska and Fortress. Day-trip heli-skiing and boarding can also be organised.

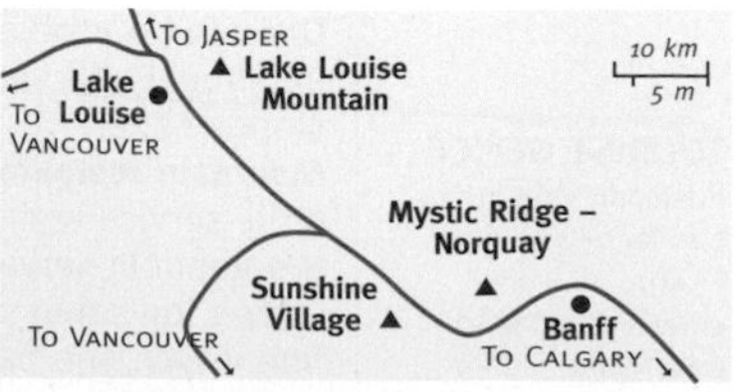

MOUNTAIN FACTS

SUNSHINE, NORQUAY & LAKE LOUISE

Covered by the Tri-area pass

Altitude	1635m-2730m
Lifts	30
Pistes	7558 acres
Green	25%
Blue	45%
Black	30%
Art. snow	1700 acres

LAKE LOUISE

Altitude	1645m-2635m
Lifts	13
Pistes	4200 acres
Green	25%
Blue	45%
Black	30%
Art. snow	40%

Recco detectors used

The mountains

The Lake Louise ski area is big, and the views are the most spectacular that the Rockies have to offer. There are plenty of slopes to suit every level of skill. Reporters are full of praise for the free guided tours of the area given by volunteer 'Ski Friends'.

THE SLOPES

A wide variety

A choice of two high-speed quads (one new for last season) take you up the **Front Face** to mid-mountain and are met by another which goes to the top. From here, as elsewhere, there's a choice of green, blue or black runs to other lifts. The tree line comes about halfway up the top lift, but there are alternative lifts that stop a bit lower, so you can stay in the trees in bad weather. From mid-mountain, a drag-lift takes you to the high-point of the area (2635m), at the shoulder of Mount Whitehorn.

From the top there's a stunning view of the high peaks and glaciers of the Continental Divide, including Canada's uncanny Matterhorn lookalike, Mount Assiniboine.

From either the top chair or the drag you can go over the ridge and into Lake Louise's treeless **Back Bowls**. The bowls are predominantly north-facing and so keep their snow well.

From the bottom of the bowls you can take a lift back to the top again or up to the separate **Larch** area, served by a fast quad chair. With a vertical of 375m it's not huge, but it has pretty wooded runs of all standards. From the

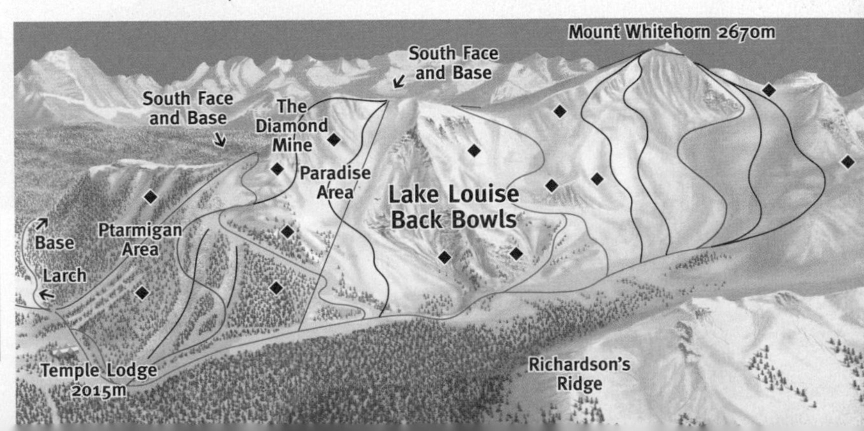

LIFT PASSES

2001/02 prices in Canadian dollars
Tri-area lift pass Covers all lifts and transport between Banff, Lake Louise and Sunshine Village, available for 3 days or more.
Main pass
3-day pass 175
6-day pass 350
Children
6-12: 6-day pass 128
Beginners First time ski packages including rental, pass and tuition available
Day passes
2000/01 prices
A day pass for Lake Louise is 54, with reductions for senior citizens (over 65), teenagers (13-17) and students with ID (13-25).
Short-term passes
Half-day pass for Lake Louise 43

SNOWPIX.COM / CHRIS GILL

Easy green runs at the bottom of the slopes lead to the splendid Lodge of the Ten Peaks amid the scenic grandeur ↓

bottom you can return to the top of the main mountain via the Ptarmigan chair or take a long green path back to the main base area.

SNOW RELIABILITY
Usually excellent

Lake Louise gets around 140 inches a year on the front face, and there is snowmaking on 40% of the pistes. The backside is north-facing, so it holds the snow pretty well. Lack of snow is unlikely to be a problem, except in an exceptionally poor snow year such as 2000/01 (when one reporter was annoyed to have to take his skis off and walk over a bare patch of slope on a piste that was described as open).

FOR EXPERTS
Widespread pleasure

There are plenty of steep slopes. On the front face, as well as a score of marked black-diamond trails in and above the trees, there is the alluring West Bowl, reached from the Summit drag – a wide open expanse of snow outside the area boundary. Because this is National Park territory, you can in theory go anywhere. But outside the boundaries there are no patrols and, of course, no avalanche control. A guide is essential. Inside the boundaries there are also areas permanently closed because of avalanche danger. Going over to the back bowls opens up countless black mogul/powder runs. Try the recently opened avalanche-prone Whitehorn 2 area directly behind the peak (marked 'Occasional Openings' on the trail map). It gave our Ozzie editor what she called 'some of the most exciting in-bounds skiing in North America' – a row of extreme chutes, almost 1km long.

The Top of the World quad takes you to the very popular Paradise Bowl, served by its own triple chair – one run is marked on the map but there are endless variants. From the Summit drag you can access wide open slopes that take you right away from all signs of lifts. Again, there are endless variations. The seriously steep slope served by the Ptarmigan quad chair provided many of the logs for the new base lodge, and offers great glade terrain as a result. The Larch area has some steep double-diamond stuff in the trees, and open snowfields at the top for those with the energy to hike up above the lift. Heli-skiing is available from bases outside the National Park in British Columbia – roughly two hours' drive.

FOR INTERMEDIATES
Some good cruising

Almost half the runs are classified as intermediate. But from the top of the Front Face the blue runs down are little more than paths in places, and there are only two blue and two green routes marked in the Back Bowls. Once

boarding *Lake Louise is a great mountain for free-riders, with all the challenging terrain in the bowls and glades. Unless you are proficient, avoid the one drag-lift, which is a tricky one to ride. The resort claims that its terrain-park is now the biggest in Canada, and it's certainly impressive, as is the half-pipe. The bars at the base are the liveliest at the end of the day of any of the Banff areas, but the village is deadly dull at night.*

SCHOOLS/GUIDES

2001/02 prices in Canadian dollars

Club Ski and Club Snowboard
3 days of guided tuition of the three areas

Club Program
4½hr per day
3 full days 169
(incl lunch for Club Junior Program for age 6-12)

CHILDCARE

The nursery at Lake Louise takes children aged 18 days to six years, from 8am to 4.30. Children aged three or more can take short ski lessons.

you get part way down the Front Face the blues are much more interesting. And when groomed, the Men's and Ladies' Downhill black runs are great fast cruises on the lower half of the mountain. Juniper and Juniper Jungle are wonderful cruising runs in the same area. Meadowlark is a beautiful tree-lined run from the top of the Eagle chair to the base area. The Larch area has some short but ideal intermediate runs. And the adventurous should try the blue-graded Boomerang, which starts with a short hike from the top of the Summit drag and some of the ungroomed Back Bowls terrain.

FOR BEGINNERS
Excellent terrain

Louise has a good nursery area near the base, served by a short T-bar; Progress to the gentle, wide Wiwaxy (designated a slow skiing zone) and the slightly more difficult Deer Run or Eagle Meadows on the upper mountain. There are even greens round the back bowls and in the Larch area – worth taking for the views.

FOR CROSS-COUNTRY
High in quality and quantity

It's a very good area for cross-country, with around 80km of groomed trails within Banff National Park.There are excellent trails in the local area (and on Lake Louise itself). And Emerald Lake Lodge 25 miles away has some lovely peaceful trails and has been highly recommended as a place to stay for a peaceful time.

QUEUES
Not unknown

Half of the area's visitors come for the day from nearby cities such as Calgary – so it's fairly quiet during the week. Lake Louise is so sure of its lift system that it offers vouchers, to be used within the year, if you have to queue for over ten minutes. A new chair on the front side was installed for 2000/01 to be on the safe side. But a recent reporter encountered weekend queues of up to ten minutes on the back of Lake Louise, not the front.

MOUNTAIN RESTAURANTS
Good base facilities

The Lodge of the Ten Peaks at the base is a hugely impressive, spacious, airy, modern, log-built affair with various eating, drinking and lounging options. The neighbouring, refurbished Whiskeyjack building has the good Northface table-service restaurant and buffet. Beavertails, at the Gazebo, is popular with reporters for a quick lunch, though it can get very crowded.

Up the mountain, Temple Lodge, near the bottom of the Larch lift, is built in rustic style with a big terrace. It too can get very crowded, but options include a calm table-service restaurant and a well-priced buffet (buffalo stew a speciality). Whitehorn Lodge, at mid-mountain on the front face, has good views from its balcony.

SCHOOLS AND GUIDES
Excellent reports

'The best tuition we've encountered' is how a reporter described his 'bumps' lesson at Lake Louise. See the Banff chapter for details on the excellent three-day, three-mountain Club Ski and Club Snowboard Program.

FACILITIES FOR CHILDREN
First-class

A reporter who used Lake Louise, Sunshine and Norquay facilities said: 'I'd recommend all three and advise booking in advance at Lake Louise.'

Staying there 

Lake Louise village is handy for the slopes, which are 10 minutes' drive away. But don't expect resort ambience or much nightlife.

GETTING THERE

Air Calgary, transfer 1½hr.

Phone numbers
From distant parts of Canada, add the prefix 1 403.
From abroad, add the prefix +1 403.

ACTIVITIES

Indoor Mainly hotel-based pools, saunas and hot-tubs
Outdoor Ice-skating, walking, cross-country skiing, ice fishing on the lake, swimming in hot springs, heli-skiing, sleigh rides, dog-sled rides, snowmobiles, helicopter tours, snowshoe tours

TOURIST OFFICE

Postcode ToL oCo
t +1 (403) 762 4561
f 762 8185
info@sblls.com
www.sblls.com

HOW TO GO
Superb-value packages

Hotels Summer is the peak season here. Prices halve for the winter – so you can stay in luxury at bargain rates.
((((4) **Chateau Lake Louise** (522 3511) Isolated position with stunning views over frozen Lake Louise, 500 rooms, lots of shops, groups of tourists (lots of Japanese groups), indoor pool, steam room and hot-tub.
((((4) **Post Hotel** (522 3989) Small, comfortable Relais & Châteaux place in village with good restaurant and indoor pool, hot-tub, sauna.
((2) **Lake Louise Inn** (522 3791) The cheaper option in the village, with pool, hot-tub and sauna. 'Comfortable rooms' and an efficient shuttle-bus, but 'disappointing restaurants'.
((2) **Deer Lodge** (522 3747) Charming old hotel next to the Chateau, good restaurant, rooftop hot-tub with amazing views.
Self-catering A limited amount is available.

EATING OUT
Limited choice

The Post hotel has the best cuisine in the Banff region. The Outpost (also in the Post hotel) does good inexpensive pub food. The Station Restaurant is in an atmospheric old station building, but we were disappointed with the food there. The small bakery/coffee shop in the village has had praise from reporters and is good for breakfast.

APRES-SKI
Lively at teatime, quiet later

There are several options at the bottom of the slopes. The Sitzmark Lounge in Whiskeyjack Lodge is a popular – with an open fire and often a live band. The upstairs part of The Lodge of the Ten Peaks has lovely surroundings, an open fire, a couple of bars and a relaxed atmosphere. Beavertails has a good sun terrace. A few times a week there are weekly parties with live music and dancing and an excellent buffet dinner at the mid-mountain Whitehorn Lodge. You ski or ride there as the lifts close and the evening ends with a torchlit descent. It is hugely popular with British visitors and we loved it.

Later on, things are fairly quiet. For most guests, it's a leisurely dinner followed by bed. But the Glacier Saloon, in Chateau Lake Louise, with traditional Wild West decor, often has live music until late. Explorer's Lounge, in the Lake Louise Inn, has nightly entertainment. The Post hotel's Outpost Pub has been recommended.

OFF THE SLOPES
Beautiful scenery

Lake Louise makes a lovely, peaceful place to stay for someone who does not intend to hit the slopes. The lake itself makes a stunning setting for walks, snow-shoeing, cross-country skiing and ice skating. There are plenty of other things to do and lots of wildlife to see. You can go on organised ice canyon walks, sleigh rides and sightseeing tours, and you can go dog-sledding and tobogganing, and visit natural hot springs.

For a more lively day or for shopping you can visit Banff and all its attractions.

Lake Louise is near one end of the Columbia Icefields Parkway, a three-hour drive to Jasper through National Parks, amidst stunningly beautiful scenery of high peaks and glaciers – one of the world's most beautiful drives.

SNOWPIX.COM / CHRIS GILL

Temple Lodge at the bottom of the Larch area, with the Ptarmigan glades on the far side →

Panorama 1160m

Vertically challenging and fast developing

WHAT IT COSTS

(5)

HOW IT RATES

The slopes

Snow	***
Extent	**
Experts	****
Intermediates	***
Beginners	****
Convenience	****
Queues	****
Restaurants	*

The rest

Scenery	***
Resort charm	**
Off-slope	*

What's new

For 2000/01 a new blue trail was cut – Millennium. New expert terrain was opened in Taynton Bowl.

Village developments include a bucket lift up from the lower village.

- ⊕ Increasing amount of slope-side accommodation, and the lower village is now linked by lift
- ⊕ Fairly extensive slopes with big vertical and challenging runs for all standards
- ⊕ Runs are usually deserted
- ⊕ Heli-skiing by the day on hand

- ⊖ May be too challenging for timid intermediates – not many cruisers
- ⊖ Snowfall record not impressive by high local standards
- ⊖ Mainly slow lifts, including T-bars
- ⊖ Some lift queues
- ⊖ No real mountain restaurants
- ⊖ Few off-slope diversions

You can expect to hear more and more about Panorama. Its dynamic owner, Intrawest, has big plans for it, and the mountain has great potential. Its vertical of 1220m is one of the biggest in North America, and less than half of the available terrain is in use at present. Like Fernie's, the slopes are less good for the intermediate piste-basher than for the novice and the expert or the confident intermediate.

THE RESORT

Panorama is a small (but growing) purpose-built resort above the lakeside town of Invermere in eastern BC, about two hours' scenic drive south-west of Banff. Accommodation is concentrated mainly in two car-free areas. Recently, lodges have been built at the foot of the main slopes but a lot of accommodation is in a 'lower village'. This is now linked to the lift base area by a bucket lift. There are also houses spread widely around the hillside.

Outings by car are possible to Kimberley, less than two hours south, or to Lake Louise or Kicking Horse, slightly further away to the north.

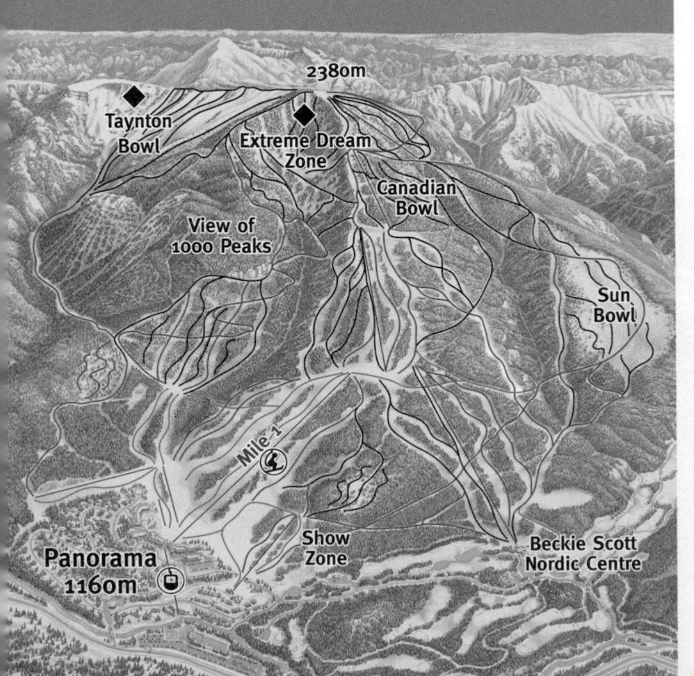

THE MOUNTAIN

The slopes basically follow three ridges, joined at top and bottom. At the top, between the left and central ridges, is the double-black-diamond Extreme Dream Zone. Almost all of the terrain is wooded. Daily mountain tours are available.

Slopes From the upper village, a fast quad goes over gentle slopes to mid-mountain. Above this a double-chair followed by two T-bars opens up intermediate and expert slopes. From the summit there are long runs down the two outer ridges as well as the central one. Those on the right bring you to a triple-chair up to mid-mountain, which also serves its own bunch of runs. Either way, the whole vertical is usable. 2000/01 saw the opening of the new 'Outback' area in Taynton Bowl, off the back of the summit area – 700 acres of lightly wooded expert terrain (previously used for heli-skiing) funnelling down to a single blue run back to the village.

Snowboarding The extensive powder bowls and tree runs are ideal for good riders, and there's also the Show Zone terrain-park and pipe (open in the evening too). Beginners have several

MOUNTAIN FACTS

Altitude	1160m-2380m
Lifts	10
Pistes	2847 acres
Blue	15%
Red	55%
Black	30%
Art. snow	800 acres

Central reservations phone number
Call 1 800 663 2929 (toll-free from within Canada)

TOURIST OFFICE

Postcode V0A 1T0
t +1 (250) 342 6941
f 341 6262
paninfo@panorama resort.com
www.skipanorama.com

INTRAWEST / SCOTT ROWED

From higher up they say you can see 1,000 peaks ↓

good long green runs to practise on, but the two main nursery slopes are served by drag-lifts.

Snow reliability Snow reliability could be better – the annual snowfall is less than half of the Fernie/Whistler figure. But snowmaking covers 40% of the area, and most slopes are not over-sunny. And grooming is excellent.

Experts There are genuine black runs dotted all over the mountain, but also some areas of special interest for experts. At the very top of the mountain and accessed by a gateway is the Extreme Dream Zone – seriously steep trails complicated by cliffs as well as tight trees, said to contain the best snow on the mountain. Off the back of the summit, is the new Taynton Bowl area offering challenging but less extreme expert terrain. There are often good bumps on the blacks at mid-mountain. On the extreme right of the mountain is an area of gentler glades, where you can pick the density of trees and steepness of slope to suit yourself. And RK Heli-Skiing operates from a base right next to the village.

Intermediates For adventurous intermediates the terrain is excellent – there are easy blacks all over the mountain, some of them regularly groomed. The View of 1000 Peaks (now regraded black) and Schober's Dream are beautiful and long for North America (up to 3.5km). But for the less experienced it may be uncomfortably challenging. The blues in the centre of the area are excellent – the new Millennium (black running into blue) is a great roller-coaster – but they don't add up to a lot.

Beginners There are a couple of nursery lifts and access to good, longer runs served by the lower lifts.

Cross-country There are 17km of trails out at the Nordic Centre.

Queues There can be queues for the double-chair from mid-mountain and the T-bars above it, though the trails are usually deserted.

Mountain restaurants There are no real mountain restaurants, just two huts offering basic refreshments. But there's a good coffee shop and the Ski Tip day lodge at the base is an excellent modern affair.

Schools and guides The Bilodeau School of Skiing and Snowboarding (SOS) was 'universally agreed as superb by all who tried it', says one reporter. Another reporter was pleased with his private bumps class.

Facilities for children Wee Wascals is the childcare centre, taking children from 18 months. Evening babysitters are also available.

STAYING THERE

How to go There's an increasing choice of hotels and condos. The better places are the newer ones up on the nursery slope level.

Hotels Ski Tip, Tamarack and the new Panorama Springs have all been recommended. And the new slope-side stone and timber-clad Taynton Lodge looks impressive. The Pine Inn is 'a high standard' budget option.

Self-catering There are plenty of condo blocks and town homes. The store is inadequate, so stock up in Invermere.

Eating out Eating out options are mainly in the lodges – the Toby Creek restaurant is good (though a bit gloomy for some tastes), and the Starbird Steak House does a good buffet breakfast. The Heliplex restaurant offers good value. There's also an evening shuttle-bus to the restaurants down in Invermere.

Après-ski Après-ski revolves around the Kicking Horse bar in the Pine Inn and the Jackpine pub in the Horsethief Lodge. The Ski Tip Lodge terrace is popular on sunny afternoons. The Glacier is the night club.

Off the slopes The new hot pools facility, with different thermal baths, a swimming pool, slides and sauna, is a welcome addition but gets rather taken over by kids.

Whistler 675m

North America's biggest mountain set in Alpine-style scenery

WHAT IT COSTS

6

HOW IT RATES

The slopes

Snow	****
Extent	****
Experts	*****
Intermediates	*****
Beginners	****
Convenience	****
Queues	***
Restaurants	**

The rest

Scenery	***
Resort charm	***
Off-slope	**

What's new

A couple of seasons ago, two much-needed fast quad chairs opened on Whistler mountain, making an alternative route up from the base to the often overcrowded gondola, bringing Whistler's total number of fast lifts to 15. The funky Chic Pea restaurant opened near the top, and additional gladed runs were cut beneath the higher Garbanzo chair-lift. Whistler Mountain's Nintendo 64 terrain-park doubled in size to 26 acres.

Whistler Creek continues to be developed, making it less of an outpost and more a suitable place to stay in its own right.

- ⊕ North America's biggest mountain, both in area and vertical (1610m)
- ⊕ Good slopes for all standards, with an unrivalled combination of high open bowls and woodland trails
- ⊕ Good snow record
- ⊕ Almost Alpine scenery, unlike the rounded Rockies of Colorado
- ⊕ Attractive modern village at the foot of the slopes, car-free in the centre, with lively après-ski
- ⊕ Good range of restaurants and bars (though not enough of them)
- ⊕ Easy access from the UK – non-stop flights to Vancouver, short transfer
- ⊕ Excellent heli-operation nearby

- ⊖ Proximity to the ocean means a lot of cloudy weather and, with the low altitude, when it's snowing on the mountain it's often raining at resort level
- ⊖ Two separate mountains are linked only at resort level
- ⊖ Some runs get very busy
- ⊖ Lift queues are often a problem
- ⊖ Mountain restaurants are mostly functional (and overcrowded)
- ⊖ Whistler is in danger of becoming a victim of its own success – attracting more people than the mountain or the village facilities (restaurants in particular) can cope with

Provided you go to Whistler prepared for cloudy skies and rain at the base, you'll love it. Last season was an unusually poor snow year for the whole of western Canada and meant more blue sky days than usual – we had virtually a whole week of them in a December visit. But Whistler still got more snow than most places and reporters were generally happy with it throughout the season. Whatever the weather, Whistler's combination of wonderful varied and extensive terrain, big vertical, reliable snow and good lifts is unrivalled, and for a purpose-built resort the village is attractive. Most readers love it, though queuing is becoming more of a problem, as are overcrowded runs and restaurants. Extracts from this year's crop of reports: 'Enough terrain to satisfy any expert.' 'Awesome.' 'Charming, pretty and friendly.' But a touch of scepticism has crept in too: 'Just like Disneyland on snow – highly organised, good at extracting money from you and prone to the odd queue for the best attractions!'

The resort

Whistler Village sits at the foot of its two mountains, Whistler and Blackcomb, a scenic 75-mile drive inland from Vancouver on Canada's west coast. Whistler started as a locals' ski area in 1966 with a few ramshackle buildings in what is now Whistler Creek. Whistler Village was developed in the late 1970s, and a village spread up the lower slopes of Blackcomb Mountain in the 1980s. Whistler has now annexed Blackcomb's village, a 10-minute walk away, and it's now called Upper Village.

Both centres are traffic-free. The architecture is varied and, for a purpose-built resort, quite tasteful. There are lots of chalet-style apartments on the hillsides. The centres have individually designed wood and concrete buildings,

INTRAWEST / RANDY LINCKS

From the top of Harmony Express there are bowls in every direction →

MOUNTAIN FACTS

Altitude	650m-2285m
Lifts	33
Pistes	7071 acres
Green	18%
Blue	55%
Black	27%
Art. snow	530 acres
Recco detectors used	

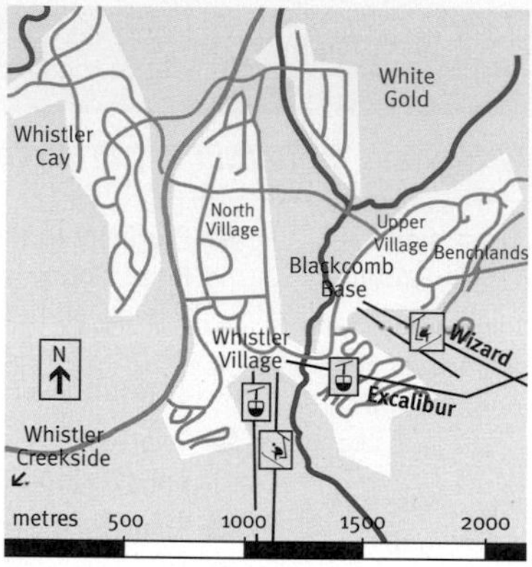

blended together in a master plan around pedestrian streets and squares. There are no monstrous high-rise blocks – but there are a lot of large five- or six-storey hotel and apartment buildings. Whistler Village has most of the bars, restaurants and shops, and the two main gondolas (one to each mountain). Whistler North, further from the lifts, is newer and has virtually merged with the original village, making a huge car-free area of streets lined with shops, condos and restaurants. Upper Village is much smaller and quieter. Its huge Chateau Whistler hotel dominates the views of the village from the mountain.

Whistler Creek, a 10-minute bus-ride from Whistler Village, is rather out on a limb, with limited bars and restaurants. But it's changing fast – a five-year development project is well under way and more readers are staying there.

There is a free bus between Whistler and Upper Village but it's just as quick to walk. Staying further out means paying for buses ($1.50) or taxis – which are inexpensive.

Whistler is very cosmopolitan, with many visitors from Japan and Australia as well as Europe and the US. But it is now getting very busy and reporters have complained of rowdy behaviour (over 100 arrests on New Year's Eve and fights at the taxi rank).

The mountains

The area has acquired a formidable and well-deserved reputation among experts. But both Whistler and Blackcomb also have loads of well-groomed intermediate terrain. Together they have over 200 marked trails, and form the biggest area of slopes, with the longest runs, in North America.

Many reporters are enthusiastic about the mountain host service and the 'go slow' patrol – some find the latter 'over zealous', but busy slopes, especially on the runs home ('a human slalom'), mean they're often needed.

THE SLOPES

The best in North America

Whistler Mountain is accessed from Whistler Village by a two-stage, 10-person gondola that rises over 1100m to the Roundhouse Lodge, the main mid-mountain base at 1850m. There is an alternative of two consecutive fast quads, which take you slightly lower.

Runs back down through the trees fan out from the top of the gondola – cruises to the Emerald and Big Red fast chairs on the flanks, longer runs to the gondola mid-station (1005m).

From Roundhouse you can see the jewel in Whistler's crown – magnificent above-the-tree-line bowls below the peak, served by the fast Peak and Harmony quads. The bowls have some groomed trails, but are mostly go-anywhere terrain for experts.

A six-person gondola from Whistler Creek also accesses Whistler mountain.

Access to **Blackcomb** from Whistler Village is by an eight-seater gondola, followed by a fast quad. From Upper Village you take two consecutive fast quads up to the main Rendezvous restaurant. From the arrival points you can go left for great cruising terrain and the Glacier Express quad up to the Horstman Glacier area, or right for steeper slopes, the terrain park or the 7th Heaven chair. The 1610m vertical

boarding *Both mountains are excellent for every standard of boarder. All the main lifts are chairs and gondolas and terrain ranges from gentle green runs to wide open bowls and heart-stopping cliff drops and chutes. The Whistler terrain-park and half-pipe is a good place to hone your skills before trying the more difficult park on Blackcomb. The resort regularly hosts big snowboard events so it's not uncommon to see pro riders. There are T-bars on the glacier, but they're not vicious and any discomfort is worth it for the powder! It's popular with snowboarders and well known for its summer boarding camps.*

LIFT PASSES

2000/01 prices in Canadian dollars

Whistler/Blackcomb Lift Ticket
Covers all lifts on both Whistler and Blackcomb mountains.

Main pass
1-day pass 61
6-day pass 336

Senior citizens
Over 65: 6-day pass 286

Children
Age 13-18: 6-day pass 286
Age 7-12: 6-day pass 168
Under 7: free pass

Short-term passes
Half-day pass 46

Notes
Whistler/Blackcomb pass of 5 days or over gives one non-skiing day; 6-day pass valid for 7 days with one day non-skiing. Further discounts for groups of over 25.

from the top of this chair to the base is the largest in North America (and big even by Alpine standards). Or you can go into the glacier area. A T-bar from the Horstman Glacier brings you (with a very short hike) to the Blackcomb Glacier in the next valley – a beautiful run which takes you away from all lifts.

Fresh Tracks is a deal that allows you to ride up Whistler mountain (at extra cost) at 7.30, have a buffet breakfast and hit the slopes as soon as they open – very popular with many of our reporters. A good tip is to hit the slopes first and breakfast after – otherwise you may miss the quietest time on the slopes. Blackcomb has floodlit beginner slopes a couple of nights a week. Free guided tours of each mountain are offered twice a day.

SNOW RELIABILITY
Excellent at altitude

Snow conditions at the top are usually excellent – the place gets around 360 inches of snow a year, on average. The 2000/01 season was a surprising exception to the rule, but reporters still had few complaints. Even in a good year, since the resort is low and close to the Pacific, the bottom slopes can be wet, icy or unskiable. People may 'download' from the mid-stations due to poor snow, especially in late season.

FOR EXPERTS
Few can rival it

Whistler Mountain's bowls are enough to keep experts happy for weeks. Each has endless variations, with chutes and gulleys of varied steepness and width. The biggest challenges are around Glacier, Whistler and West Bowls, with runs such as The Cirque and Doom & Gloom – though you can literally go anywhere in this high, wide area.

Blackcomb has challenging slopes too; not as extensive as Whistler's, but some are more testing. From the top of the 7th Heaven lift, traverse to Xhiggy's Meadow, for good sunny bowl runs.

If you're feeling brave, go in the opposite direction and drop into the extremely steep chutes down towards Glacier Creek, including the infamous 41° Couloir Extreme, which had moguls the size of elephants at the top when we last visited. Or try the also serious, but less frequented, steep bowls reached by hiking up Spanky's Ladder, after taking the Glacier Express lift.

Both mountains have challenging trails through the trees. The adventurous can explore the 'Peak to Creek' trails, from below Whistler's West Bowl to Whistler Creek – still outside the area boundary at present, so rescues are costly.

If all this isn't enough, there's also local heli-skiing available by the day.

FOR INTERMEDIATES
Ideal and extensive terrain

Both mountains are an intermediate's paradise. In good weather, good intermediates will enjoy the less extreme variations in the bowls on both mountains.

One of our favourite intermediate runs is the Blackcomb Glacier from the top of the mountain to the bottom of the Excelerator chair about 1200m below. This 5km run away from all lifts starts with a two-minute walk up from the top of the Showcase T-bar. You drop over the ridge into a wide, wide bowl – not too suddenly or you'll get a short, sharp shock in the very steep double-diamond Blowhole. The further you traverse, the shallower the slope.

You are guaranteed good snow on the Horstman Glacier too, and typically gentle runs. Lower down there are lots of perfect cruising runs through the trees – ideal when the weather is bad.

On Whistler Mountain, there are easy blue pistes in Symphony, Harmony and Glacier bowls, which allow even early intermediates to try the bowls, always knowing there's an easy way down. The Saddle run from the top of the Harmony Express lift is a favourite with many of our reporters. The blue path round the back from the top of The Peak chair, which skirts West Bowl, has beautiful views over a steep valley and across to the rather phallic-shaped Black Tusk mountain.

Lower down the mountain there is a vast choice of groomed blue runs with a series of efficient fast chairs to bring you back up to the top of the gondola. It's a cruiser's paradise – especially the aptly named Ego Bowl. A great long run is the fabulous Dave Murray Downhill all the way from mid-mountain to the finish at Whistler Creek. Although marked black on the map, it's a wonderful fast and varied cruise when it has been groomed.

FOR BEGINNERS
Great if the sun shines

Whistler has excellent nursery slopes by the mid-station of the gondola – and Blackcomb down at the base area. Both have facilities higher up too.

On Whistler, after progressing from the nursery slopes, there are some gentle first runs from the top of the gondola, except for other people speeding past. You can return by various chairs or carry on to the base area on greens. Check the latter are in good condition first, and maybe avoid them at the end of the day, when they can get very crowded.

On Blackcomb, Green Line runs from the top of the mountain to the bottom. The top part is particularly gentle, with some steeper pitches lower down.

Our main reservation is – you guessed – the weather. Beginners don't get a lot out of heavy snowfalls, and might be put off by rain.

FOR CROSS-COUNTRY
Picturesque but low

There are over 28km of cross-country tracks, starting in the valley by the river, on the path between Whistler and Blackcomb. But it is low altitude, so conditions can be unreliable. Keen cross-country merchants can catch the train to better areas.

QUEUES
An ever-increasing problem

Whistler is becoming a victim of its own success. Even with 15 fast lifts – more than any other resort in North America – the mountains are queue-prone, especially at weekends when people pour in from Vancouver. There is a cute system for displaying waiting times at strategic points, but most people would prefer shorter queues. Some reporters have signed up with the ski school to get lift priority. Others have visited Vancouver at the

SCHOOLS/GUIDES

2000/01 prices in Canadian dollars

Whistler and Blackcomb
Guided instruction with Ski Esprit course

Classes 3 or 4 days
Full day from 9.45
3 days: 249
4 days: 289

Children's classes
Ages: 3 to 6
5 6hr days including lunch, lift ticket and equipment rental: 445

Private lessons
Half day: 305
Full day: 469

weekend to avoid the crowds. The fast chairs in parallel with the Whistler gondola have helped but queues still form at the base in the morning, especially for the Blackcomb gondola. Whistler Creek is less of a problem. Some of the chairs up the mountain also produce queues (up to 30 minutes) – especially Harmony ('Even the singles queue doesn't make it quicker,' says a reporter) – and several on Blackcomb build queues, too.

MOUNTAIN RESTAURANTS

Overcrowded

The main restaurants sell decent, good-value food but are charmless self-service stops with long queues. They're huge, but not huge enough. 'Seat-seekers' are employed to find spaces, but success is not guaranteed. In previous years, reporters have stressed the need to lunch early. That no longer works – 'they're packed by 11.30'. 'Try a big breakfast followed by a 2.30 lunch instead,' suggests a recent visitor.

Blackcomb has the Rendezvous, mainly a big (850-seat) self-service place but also home to Christine's, a table-service restaurant – the best on either mountain. Glacier Creek Lodge, at the bottom of the Glacier Express, is a better self-service place. But even this (1,496 seats) gets 'incredibly busy'. Whistler has the massive (1,740-seat) Roundhouse Lodge; Steeps Grill is its table-service refuge.

Reporters generally prefer the smaller places – but they're still packed unless you time it right. On Blackcomb Crystal Hut at the top of the Crystal Ridge chair and Horstman Hut at the top of the mountain are tiny Alpine-style huts with great views.

On Whistler Raven's Nest, at the top of the Creekside gondola, is a small and friendly deli/cafe. And the Chic Pea near the top of the Garbanzo chair-lift is 'funky and rustic' for pizza and barbecue. You can of course descend to the base – the table-service Dusty's at Whistler Creek has good sandwiches and soup and doesn't get too busy.

SCHOOLS AND GUIDES

A great formula

Ski Esprit and Ride Esprit programmes run for three or four days and combine instruction with showing you around the mountains – with the same instructor daily. Many of our reporters

INTRAWEST / RANDY LINCKS

There's nowhere better in North America for ungroomed bowl skiing and riding amidst spectacular scenery ↘

↑ Whistler gets a lot of snow – in the village as well as on the mountain if you are lucky

WHISTLER RESORT ASSOCIATION / PAUL MORRISON

have joined these groups (usually small), and all reports are glowing: 'Big improvement in confidence and skill' is typical. There are specialist clinics and snowboard classes, too.

We have rave reviews of Extremely Canadian's challenging free-skiing clinics (938 9656) for experts.

FACILITIES FOR CHILDREN
Impressive

Blackcomb's base area has a special slow-moving Magic Chair to get children part-way up the mountain. Whistler's gondola mid-station has a splendid kids-only area. A reporter found the staff 'friendly and instilled confidence'. The drawback for young children is the risk of bad weather.

Staying there 

The most convenient place to stay is Whistler Village as you can go straight up either mountain by gondola. A lot of accommodation is an inconvenient walk or bus-ride from the villages and slopes. Whistler Creek, though convenient for Whistler's slopes, is less so for Blackcomb and is pretty quiet.

A number of recent visitors have found the central area around Village Square very noisy in the early hours.

HOW TO GO
High quality packages

A lot of British tour operators go to Whistler and some run catered chalets.

Hotels There is a very wide range.

(5) **Chateau Whistler** (938 8000) Modern but in traditional Canadian Pacific château-hotel style, at the foot of Blackcomb mountain. Indoor–outdoor pool and tubs. The Entree Gold floor is expensive and cosseting.

(5) **Westin Resort & Spa** (905 5000) New luxury all-suite hotel at foot of Whistler mountain next to lifts.

(4) **Pan Pacific Lodge** (905 2999) Luxury all-suite place at Whistler Village base. Pool/sauna/tub.

(4) **Lost Lake Lodge** (932 2882) 'Excellent' place: studios and suites, out by the golf course. Pool/tub.

(4) **Crystal Lodge** (932 2221) 'Comfortable, friendly, convenient', in Whistler Village. Pool/sauna/tub.

(3) **Glacier Lodge** (932 2882) In Upper Village. Pool/tub.

Self-catering There are plenty of spacious, comfortable condominiums in both chalet and hotel-style blocks.

EATING OUT
High quality and plenty of choice

Reporters are enthusiastic about the range, quality and value of places to eat, but do book well ahead: there simply aren't enough restaurant seats to meet demand. Some cheaper places won't take bookings for small groups, meaning long waits. Bars serve decent food, too. If you've got kids, as one reporter found, '60% of restaurants don't allow under-19s in, or even to sit outside, and we had to wait up to two hours elsewhere.'

At the top of the market, Umberto's in Whistler Village has classy Italian cuisine. The Rimrock Café at Whistler Creek serves 'the best seafood we have ever eaten'.

Good mid market Whistler Village places include Araxi (Italian/Pacific), the Keg (steak and seafood), Teppan Village (Japanese), Mongolie (Asian) and Kipriaki Norte (Greek). Crab Shack has good-value seafood. In Village North: the good-value Brewhouse has great atmosphere (steaks, burgers),

CHILDCARE

Whistler Kids takes non-skiing children aged 3 months to 3 years, as well as acting as the base for ski tuition.

Whistler Kids offers various skiing and snowboarding programmes to children of all ability levels, aged 3 to 17. The Kids' Adventure Camp is a 5-day camp for 3 to 12 year olds. Ride Tribe is the teen programme for ages 13 to 17.

Après-ski programmes – with a 'Kids' Night Out' – are offered during the season.

GETTING THERE

Air Vancouver, transfer 2hr.

Phone numbers

From distant parts of Canada, add the prefix 1 604.

From abroad, add the prefix +1 604.

ACTIVITIES

Indoor Ice skating, museum, tennis, hot-tubs
Outdoor Flightseeing, heli-skiing, snow-shoe excursions, snowmobiling, paragliding, fishing, horse-riding, sleigh rides, guided tours

TOURIST OFFICE

Postcode VoN 1B4
t +1 (604) 932 3928
f 932 7231
reservations@tourismwhistler.com
www.whistler-blackcomb.com

Caramba has 'good Mediterranean food at reasonable prices' and the Tandoori Grill has 'Indian just like at home'. Hy's Steakhouse has the best steaks. Sushi-Ya, and Quattro (Italian) are good.

There are plenty of budget places, including the bars mentioned under après-ski. Uli's Flipside and The Old Spaghetti Factory have been recommended for pasta.

APRES-SKI
Something for most tastes

With over 50 bars, night-clubs and restaurants, Whistler is very lively. Most of the après bars seem to compete to see who can serve the biggest dustbin lid of nachos. Popular at Whistler are the Longhorn, with a huge terrace, and the Garibaldi Lift Company. The Dubh Linn Gate Irish pub has 'great live music and Guinness'. Black's is good for a quiet drink while Tapley's seems 'the nearest thing to a locals' bar'. Merlin's is the focus at Blackcomb base, and Dusty's at Whistler Creek – good beer, loud music.

Later on, Buffalo Bills is lively and loud and the Amsterdam is worth a look. The Cinnamon Bear in the Delta Resort hotel is a sports bar with some live music. Tommy Africa's vies with the Savage Beagle, Maax Fish and Garfinkel's for the clubbing crowd, and Moe Joe's has been recommended. The bizarre AlpenRock House has all sorts of games (from glow-in-the-dark bowling to virtual reality), restaurants and bars – all in a neo-Swiss setting. ('Excellent for the kids.') Try the Mallard bar in Chateau Whistler and the Crystal Lodge piano bar for a relaxed time.

OFF THE SLOPES
Not ideal

Whistler is a long way to go if you don't ski or ride. Meadow Park Sports Centre has a full range of fitness facilities. There are also several luxurious spas. Excursions to Squamish (famous for its eagles) are easy. A day trip to Vancouver is recommended.

Eastern Canada

For us the main attraction of skiing or riding in eastern Canada is the French culture and language that are predominant in the province of Québec. It really feels like a different country from the rest of Canada – as indeed many of its residents want it to become. It is also only a six-hour flight from the UK, compared with ten for Canada's west. Tremblant is the main destination resort and is one of the cutest purpose-built resorts we've seen. The other main base is Québec city, which dates from the 17th century and is full of atmosphere and Canadian history. The slopes of the main resorts are small both in extent and in vertical drop, and the weather can be perishingly cold in early and mid-winter. But at least this means that the extensive snowmaking systems that all the resorts have can be effective for a long season. Be prepared for variable snow conditions and don't go expecting light, dry powder – if that's what you want, head west.

There are lots of ski and snowboard areas in Ontario – Canada's most populated province – but most of them are tiny and cater just for locals. For people headed on holiday for a week or more, eastern Canada really means the province of Québec. Québec – and its capital, Québec city – are heavily dominated by the French culture and language. Notices, menus, trail maps and so on are usually printed in both French and English. Many ski area workers will be bilingual or just French-speaking. And French cuisine abounds.

The weather is very variable, rather like New England's – but it can get even colder. Hence the snow, though pretty much guaranteed by snowmaking, can vary enormously in quality. When we were there in April we were slush skiing in Tremblant one day and rattling along on a rock hard surface in Mont-Ste-Anne the next. Last season one of our reporters visited Mont-Ste-Anne, Stoneham and Le Massif in late January and experienced mild temperatures and several perfect blue sky days.

The main destination resort is Tremblant (see separate chapter), about 90 minutes' drive from Montreal. Other areas near here popular with locals include **Mont Blanc** (with only 300m of vertical, hardly a competitor to the Franco-Italian version) and the **Saint-Sauveur** valley (five areas, each with around 200m of vertical and with interchangeable lift passes).

The other main place to stay for easy access to several ski resorts is **Québec city**. Old Québec, at the city's heart, is North America's only walled city and is a World Heritage site. Within the city walls are narrow, winding streets and 17th and 18th century houses. It is situated right on the banks of the St Lawrence river. In January/February there is a famous two-week carnival, with an ice castle,

INTRAWEST

One of the best addresses in Tremblant: Chateau Mont Tremblant →

snow sculptures, dog-sled and canoe races, night parades and grand balls. But most of the winter is low season for Québec city, with good-value rooms available in big hotels. Because of this, the area is popular with British school groups, especially in late season.

There are several ski and snowboard areas close to Québec city. There's now a Carte Blanche pass which covers the three main areas: a total of 106 runs and 26 lifts and including Canada's largest night skiing area. A car is handy, but there are buses to some areas.

The biggest and most varied area (though easily skied in a day by a good skier) is **Mont-Ste-Anne**, 30 minutes away and with some accommodation of its own. A gondola takes you to the top, and slopes lead down the front (south) and back (north) sides. There are intermediate cruising runs on both sides and some steep blacks (including World Cup runs) through the trees on the front among its 63km of trails. There are some easy top-to-bottom runs and good nursery slopes at the base. The views from the front over the ice-flows of the St Lawrence are spectacular.

Fourteen trails are floodlit until 10pm five nights a week. Over 80% of the runs are covered by snowmaking. It also has the largest cross-country centre in Canada, with 223km of trails. In the spring you can stop by the Taffi hut and try fresh maple toffee, made to order.

Stoneham is the closest resort to Québec city, around 20 minutes away. It also has its own small village with accommodation and an impressive base lodge with bar, restaurant and big wooden deck. Après-ski in the lodge can be lively, and there is sometimes live music. It is a small area, with only around 30km of runs spread between three faces and a vertical of 420m. But it is very sheltered in a sunny setting protected from wind. It suits families well, with mainly intermediate and beginner terrain. Snowboarders, freestylers and freeskiers are attracted to the area by the resort's impressive terrain-park and 1km long permanent boarder-cross course. A reporter who went there last season raved about how addictive it was. Stoneham also has the biggest night-skiing operation in Canada, with two of the three faces lit top-to-bottom. Some 95% of the area has snowmaking.

Le Massif is around an hour away from Québec city and is a cult area with locals. It is in a UNESCO World Biosphere Reserve, and is just metres from the St Lawrence. The views of the ice-flows are stunning, and you feel you are heading straight down into them when you are on the pretty, tree-lined trails.

The area of slopes, though small, has the largest vertical drop in the east. There are a couple of steep double-black-diamond runs and some good, well-groomed black and blue cruising runs. But it suits experts and good intermediates best – beginners and timid intermediates would be better off elsewhere.

Major new development is due to be complete for the 2001/02 season. Two new quad chair-lifts will supplement the three existing lifts. A new lodge is being built with a 1,500 capacity car park, accessed by a new road. The area of slopes will increase by a third, with up to 10 new trails, including one designed to meet International Ski Federation World Cup standards.

Tremblant 265m

Charming new village below surprisingly small area of slopes

WHAT IT COSTS

HOW IT RATES

The slopes

Snow	****
Extent	**
Experts	***
Intermediates	***
Beginners	****
Convenience	****
Queues	***
Restaurants	**

The rest

Scenery	***
Resort charm	****
Off-slope	***

What's new

For 2001/02 there will be a new two-acre beginner area by the village with two magic carpet lifts of 420ft and 210ft, a heated rest area with washrooms, an observation deck and a fire pit.

Better snowmaking facilities, a new half-pipe grinder and a new rental shop are also planned for 2001/02.

- ⊕ Charming purpose-built village
- ⊕ Slope-side accommodation
- ⊕ Good snow reliability with extensive artificial back-up
- ⊕ Some good runs for all abilities
- ⊕ Good variety of restaurants and bars

- ⊖ Limited area for high-mileage piste-bashers
- ⊖ Can be perishingly cold in early and mid-winter
- ⊖ Weekend queues and overcrowding can be a problem

Tremblant is eastern Canada's main destination resort and attracts quite a lot of Brits. But for keen piste-bashers the limited slopes don't really do justice to the cute and lively little village, which has been built in traditional style.

THE RESORT

Tremblant has been transformed in recent years from a day or weekend ski area for locals to being eastern Canada's leading ski resort and cutest resort village. Intrawest (which also owns Whistler and several other North American resorts) has developed a charming purpose-built village in the same traditional style as the original old village. Buildings in bright, vibrant colours line narrow, cobbled traffic-free streets and squares, with lots of galleries, boutiques, patisseries and cafes. It has a very French feel to it and large ski-in, ski-out hotels and condos blend in unobtrusively, as does a £2 million Acquaclub pool complex built to resemble a lake set in a forest.

THE MOUNTAINS

In its small area, Tremblant has a good variety of terrain.

Slopes A heated gondola takes you to the top, from where there are good views over the village and a 14km lake on the so-called south side and over National Park wilderness on the north side. The north side is really north-east facing and gets the morning sun – a high-speed quad brings you back and there are two other chairs to play on. In 2000/01 a new beginner run was made, stretching from top to bottom of the north side. The Edge lift accesses another summit, serving mainly expert terrain. Back on the south side (really south-west facing and so good for the afternoon sun) you can go right back to town on blue or green runs, or use two high-speed quads to explore the top and bottom halves. The Versant Soleil area is more directly south-facing and has one top-to-bottom blue run with all the rest being black runs and tree runs.

Snow reliability Over 70% of the terrain is covered by snowmaking –

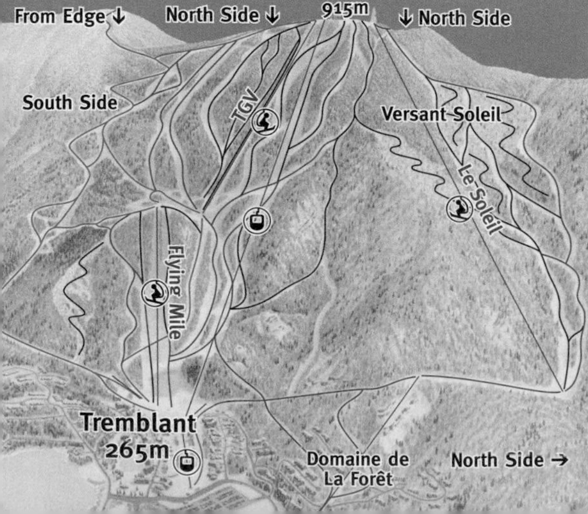

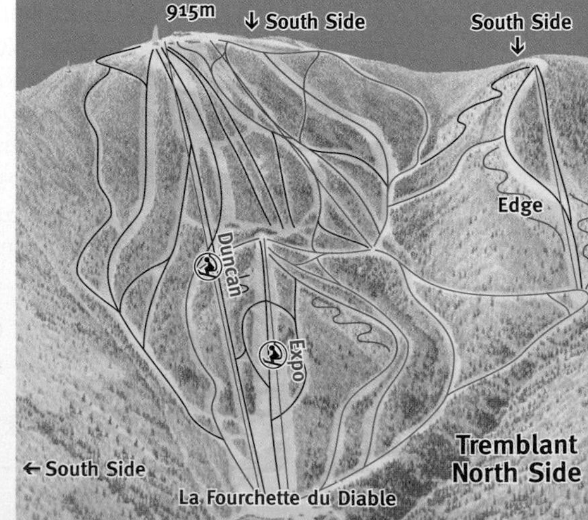

The charming purpose-built village is right next to the slopes →

INTRAWEST

claimed to be 'the most powerful in North America'.

Experts Over half the runs are graded as suitable for advanced skiers and riders. But we found a few of the blacks rather overgraded. There are steep top-to-bottom bump runs on the north side and great tree runs off the Edge lift. The south side has some shorter challenging runs. The Versant Soleil area has more black runs and some tough runs in the trees.

Intermediates Both north and south sides have good cruising and we found the north side rather less crowded. There are blue-graded runs in the trees as well as on groomed trails.

Beginners The new beginner area for 2001/02 will be a huge improvement on the previously inadequate facilities. There are long, easy top-to-bottom green runs to progress to on both north and south sides.

Snowboarding The slopes are good, with mostly chairs, and the excellent gravity fun-park and half-pipe are on the top half of the north side.

Cross-country There are around 100km of trails.

Queues At weekends there can be lines but they tend to move quickly. We found crowds on the main run back to the village more of a problem.

Mountain restaurants The main Grand Manitou restaurant has good views back over town and decent food but can get crowded. Many people go back to town for lunch – La Diable was recommended by a reporter for its own micro-brewed beer and huge portions of poutine (a local speciality: chips, melted cheese and gravy).

Schools and guides There's a wide variety of options and a reporter recommends the 90-minute Super Group 4 (maximum of four people): 'Very impressed with instructors and small group was brilliant.'

Facilities for children Children from age one can be looked after during the day and until 9.30pm.

STAYING THERE

How to go There's no shortage of packages from the UK.

Hotels and condos Many of our reporters stayed at the luxurious Chateau Mont Tremblant and praise it highly. Others stayed at the Plaza condos – 'central', 'comfortable' and 'well equipped' but warned of 'very limited food shopping – best to have a car'.

MOUNTAIN FACTS

Altitude	265m-915m
Lifts	12
Pistes	79km
Green	20%
Blue	25%
Black	55%
Art. snow	440 acres

Central reservations phone number
For all resort accommodation call 425 8681 (from distant parts of Canada, add the prefix 1 819; from abroad, add the prefix +1 819)

TOURIST OFFICE

Postcode JOT 1ZO
t +1 (819) 681 2000
f 5990
info_tremblant@intrawest.com
www.tremblant.ca

Eating out There is a good variety of restaurants.

Après-ski There are several lively bars, and there was live music in the main square when we were there in April. There are floodlit slopes some nights.

Off the slopes You can go ice climbing, horse-riding, snow-shoeing, ice skating, snowmobiling, dog-sledding and swimming – and visit Montreal.

INTRAWEST

The central Place St-Bernard square is usually lively, with a band playing or something going on →

Andorra

- ⊕ Excellent choice for beginners and early intermediates, with good tuition, good piste grooming and plenty of gentle slopes
- ⊕ Lots of efficient, modern lifts
- ⊕ Good combination of altitude and extensive snowmaking with strong southern sunshine
- ⊕ Lively nightlife, with cheap duty-free drinks and generous measures
- ⊕ Cheap packages in some resorts, competing with those offered in inferior resorts in eastern Europe
- ⊕ Resorts close enough to each other – and some are now physically linked – so you can sample at least one other during a week

- ⊖ Most resorts have little in the way of charm, and Soldeu and Pas de la Casa are sited on the busy main road through the country
- ⊖ Nightlife tends to revolve around bars – not much variety, and some places can get rowdy
- ⊖ Potential for a really impressive linked lift network is not exploited – no shared lift pass
- ⊖ Packages to major resorts no longer the bargain they once were
- ⊖ There seems to be no end to the construction work

It's tempting to generalise about a small duty-free country like Andorra, with only a handful of resorts all within an hour's drive of the capital, and the generalisations above should help you decide whether it's the place for you. But there are differences between the resorts that make things a bit more complicated.

These days the major resorts – Soldeu and Pas de la Casa – compete more with middle-market Alpine resorts than with the budget destinations of eastern Europe. They have impressive mountains with efficient lifts, their hotels include some attractively smart places, and package prices are no lower than those in mid-market resorts in the Alps. Not surprisingly, the clientele they attract is not as youthful, impecunious and lager-oriented as it once was.

The less impressive resorts of Arinsal and Pal, and the valley towns of La Massana and Encamp, are considerably less attractive from most points of view. But packages here are appreciably cheaper, and do still compete with Bulgaria, Romania and Slovenia for the business of those on the tightest of budgets.

Soldeu, Pas de la Casa and Arinsal now get their own separate chapters; this introduction includes some comments on the valley towns, and on the excellent out-of-the-way day skiing area of Arcalis.

Andorra attracts many international visitors away from Austrian and Italian resorts partly because of its relatively reliable snow record. Its situation close to both the Atlantic and the Mediterranean oceans, together with the high altitude of its resorts means it usually gets substantial natural snowfalls. It has also invested heavily in snowmaking. This combination means you can book Andorra months in advance with some confidence. And an early reservation is necessary: late bookers can have difficulty finding an Andorra package.

As we've explained, package holiday prices vary between resorts. So, to a degree, do prices once you arrive. But prices for drinks and extras such as tuition and equipment hire are generally lower than in the Alps. Some reporters have been disappointed to find duty-free luxury goods not the super-bargain they had expected.

Duty-free prices and large, unmeasured measures of spirits mean that nightlife can be very lively. If you want to spend your nights in the company of drunken young Brits, you will have no trouble finding places to do it. But in our recent experience you will equally have no trouble avoiding such scenes, and finding more civilised places in which to celebrate your day on the slopes.

The sight of cranes is not uncommon, as the Andorrans continue to build hotels and apartments as fast as they can to keep up with the demand. It is no longer true to say (as it once was) that the resorts resemble giant construction sites, but they all have construction sites within them. Perhaps more irritating is the fact that the Andorrans don't seem to feel any obligation to finish the construction or renovation of a hotel in time for the season. They may still be installing lights, or even staircases, in hotels in mid-season.

Adjacent resorts have begun to link their areas together, meaning bigger ski areas and a bit more variety. Pas de la Casa's and Soldeu's slopes have been physically linked by lift and piste for a couple of seasons. But there seems to be no immediate prospect of a joint lift pass, which is incredibly frustrating for keen intermediates who would relish the chance to explore the two adjacent areas. Arinsal and Pal in the west were linked by a new cable-car for the 2000/01 season – and have had a joint lift pass for some years.

STAYING DOWN THE VALLEY

Several valley towns can be used as bases either to use the slopes of one resort or to explore several resorts in the course of a week.

The obviously strong candidate here is **Encamp**, which now has a powerful gondola giving a quick way into the Pas de la Casa slopes. From the top of it you can actually ski into the Soldeu area as well, but you would need to have a day ticket for that area before you set off. Encamp seemed to us the least attractive of the towns, but we can't claim to have examined it closely.

La Massana is a more appealing town, and has the considerable attraction of being quite well placed for access to Arcalis – an excellent but accommodation-free ski area directly to the north, described later in this chapter. La Massana is more often used as a base for Pal and Arinsal, which are much closer – and the hotel-owning mayor is apparently planning a gondola link directly into the Pal slopes. **Ordino** is slightly nearer Arcalis, and pleasantly rustic.

The capital of **Andorra la Vella** is not far down the valley from Encamp (and the gondola into Pas de la Casa slopes) but is a much more attractive

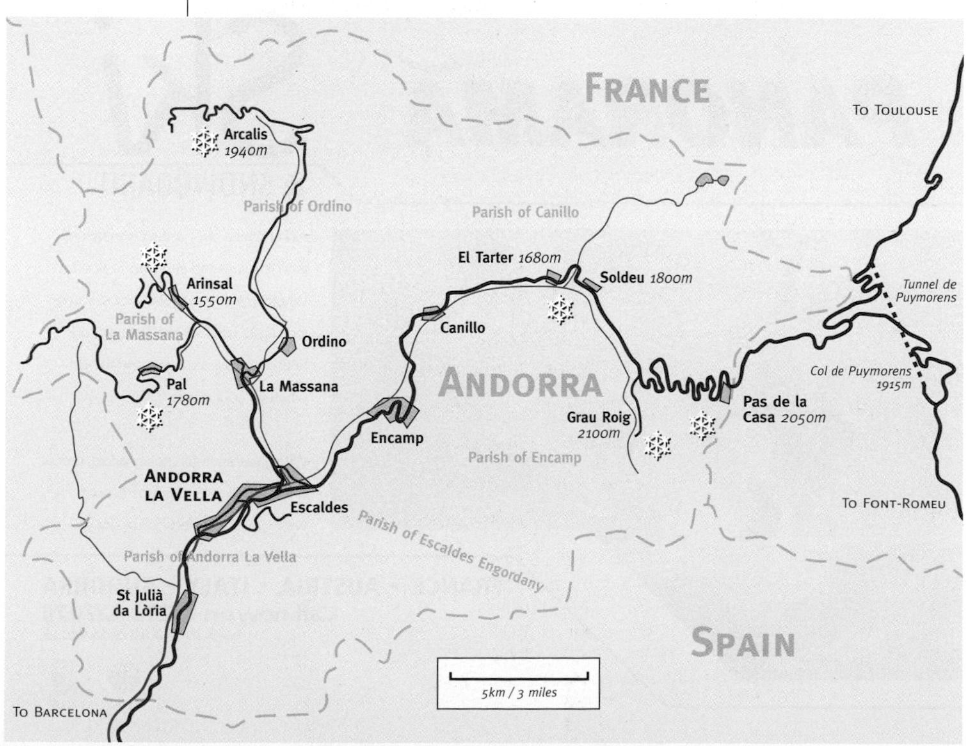

We've never seen anything quite as daft as this: a single piste splits into two, one way leading to the Soldeu lifts and the other to the Pas de la Casa lifts – and no lift-pass sharing arrangements ➔

SNOWPIX.COM / CHRIS GILL

base, especially for someone wanting a more rounded holiday. The duty-free shopping could fill a page, but probably the most interesting place is Caldea spa. The interior is laid out in a 'Hanging Gardens of Babylon' style, and the facilities are very impressive – indoor–outdoor pools, with fountains and waterfalls, saunas, hot-tubs, Turkish baths, hydrotherapy, sunbeds, massage ... even a grapefruit bath!

There are plenty of high-quality, if relatively expensive, hotels. Andorra la Vella is not a big place, and most hotels are within easy walking distance of the centre of the town.

There is plenty of choice when it comes to dining out. Andorrans love seafood, and the traditional Catalan restaurants delight in providing it, which seems odd in the mountains; it is delivered fresh from the coast daily.

Nightlife is also well catered for – there are plenty of bars and nightclubs, and most stay open until 4am. However, the clientele is generally a more sophisticated bunch, mainly Andorrans and Spaniards, and the 'drink-until-you-drop' attitude of the mountain resorts is rare.

What's new

2000/01 saw the extension of the snowmaking network and new signposting was installed around the mountain.

A new magic carpet conveyor belt has replaced the old rope tow in the children's snow playground.

MOUNTAIN FACTS

Altitude 1940m-2640m	
Lifts	14
Pistes	26km
Green	24%
Blue	24%
Red	44%
Black	8%
Art. snow	10km

Recco detectors used – helicopter based

TOURIST OFFICE

t +376 850121
f 850440
ito@andorra.ad
www.andorra.ad/comuns/ordino

SNOWPIX.COM / CHRIS GILL

There are some excellent testing runs from the central ridge back down into the Cercle d'Arcalis →

Arcalis 1940m

Arcalis is the most remote resort in Andorra, tucked away at the head of a long valley. But it makes a very worthwhile day trip – the variety of the terrain is better than most of the other resorts, and the snow is usually the best you will find. There is no accommodation at the mountain, but increasing amounts along the Vall d'Ordino leading up to it.

THE RESORT

Arcalis resembles some of the smaller New World resorts in having nothing at the lift base apart from a day lodge buildings and a lot of car parking – the resort is very popular with weekenders, both from Andorra and Spain. There are actually two lift bases: Els Planells is up the hill from Arcalis itself, reached by a winding road that provides additional parking.

THE MOUNTAIN

The slopes are made up of two bowls, with lifts meeting at the ridge that separates them. The lower slopes of the main bowl, above the the resort base, are lightly wooded, but all the higher slopes are open.

Slopes Chair-lifts from both bases – a fast one from the lower base – cross the main bowl, the Cercle d'Arcalis, to reach the central ridge at 2550m. Long red and black runs come back down. On the left-hand side of this bowl, red and blue runs are served by a chair and several drags. From the dividing ridge, blue and red runs descend into the bowl, the Cercle de la Coma, which is entirely tree-free (its floor is at 2200m). On the far side of this second bowl, a recently added chair-lift goes up to the area high point at 2640m, with just one red piste back down. From the Cercle de la Coma, there are three ways back to the base: a long red to Arcalis, a long green to Els Planells, or off-piste itineraries off the shoulder of the dividing ridge, reached by a short drag-lift.

Snow reliability This is good. Artificial snow covers the base area and some pistes leading into it. The height of the area, which starts a good 400m higher than Arinsal, also adds to the length of the season.

Snowboarding We're not aware of any special facilities. Beware flat sections on the easy pistes in the Cercle de la Coma.

Experts Of all the resorts in Andorra, Arcalis has the most to offer experts. The black run that leads from the ridge back down towards the base is steep, and often mogulled, while the red run it connects to starts from the top of the main chair, going through a spectacular gulley before widening out. There is also plenty of space between runs for off-piste forays, especially in the Cercle de la Coma. There must be some good routes down from the new chair on the far side of it. Arcalis is well known for heli-skiing; the mountains facing the area are favoured by the guides.

Intermediates You are well catered for here, with smooth, long blues and reds being the main feature of the slopes in both bowls.

Beginners The beginners' slopes are conveniently located near the upper base lodge, with a couple of drag-lifts leading to some longer blue runs.

Queues There are no problems with queues midweek, when you can explore the resort and see hardly anyone. At the weekend the area is much busier, especially in good weather, and you may encounter a long wait at the bottom in the morning, especially if racers take over one of the lifts.

Mountain restaurants The base stations have a restaurant and bar. Up the mountain choices are limited; there is a snack bar at the top of the main lift, and a self-service restaurant in the Cercle de la Coma.

Schools and guides We have no reports on the ski school, but it seems well run, with a good range of options.

Facilities for children There is a day nursery for children aged 1 to 5, and a ski kindergarten for 5- to 12-year-olds.

Arinsal 1470m

Andorra's bargain basement just got better

WHAT IT COSTS

HOW IT RATES

The slopes

Snow	***
Extent	*
Experts	*
Intermediates	**
Beginners	***
Convenience	***
Queues	***
Restaurants	**

The rest

Scenery	***
Resort charm	*
Off-slope	*

What's new

2000/01 saw the separate resorts of Pal and Arinsal link and finally become one. The new link is via a 50-person cable-car from Coll de la Botella in Pal's Setúria sector to Port Negre at the top of the Arinsal slopes. The new link has increased the area's appeal hugely. Snowmaking was also extended and now covers 17km of slopes.

MOUNTAIN FACTS

Altitude	1550m-2560m
Lifts	30
Pistes	63km
Green	10%
Blue	39%
Red	39%
Black	12%
Artificial snow	17km

- ⊕ Good value – package prices competitive with eastern Europe
- ⊕ Plenty of lively bars
- ⊕ Ski school geared to British needs
- ⊕ New cable-car link with Pal is very good news for non-beginners
- ⊕ Newish gondola from village centre gives easy access to the slopes

- ⊖ Very confined local slopes
- ⊖ Runs to village need good snow to be open, and don't lead to gondola station
- ⊖ Long, linear and rather dour village, with no focus
- ⊖ Obtrusive construction sites

Arinsal is the most British-dominated resort in Andorra, despite the fact that it is the least attractive. This may be partly because the Spanish and French set their sights higher; but it is also because British tour operators offer packages here at prices that are very tempting, especially for beginners on a budget. Whatever reservations we have, the place is way ahead of Borovets and Poiana Brasov.

Lots of young people come here for the alcohol-fuelled nightlife, and Arinsal does not disappoint. But the village doesn't have many other attractions.

THE RESORT

Arinsal is a long, narrow village of grey, stone-clad buildings, near the head of a steep-sided valley north of Andorra la Vella. Development in recent years has been rapid, and it continues, giving the place a building-site appearance.

There is some accommodation at Pal, but it is a bus-ride from the lift base. Staying in Arinsal (preferably close to the gondola station) and accessing the Pal slopes via the new cable-car link makes better sense for most visitors. Since 1998/99 a gondola from the village centre has given access to the slopes; for most guests, the alternative chair-lift a kilometre out of town is now happily irrelevant – though you can stay next to it and ski to the door in good conditions.

There is attractive accommodation in the lower town of La Massana (see the introductory chapter to Andorra). A gondola link from here to the Pal slopes is planned, possibly for 2002/03; La Caubella is 700m above the town.

THE MOUNTAIN

The very small local area above Arinsal's gondola is a narrow, east-facing bowl of open slopes. Pal's slopes, in contrast, are the most densely wooded of the Andorran resorts, calling to mind American resorts. They mainly face east, those down to the link with Arinsal north.

Slopes Arinsal's slopes consist essentially of a single, long, narrow bowl above the upper gondola station at Comallenpla, with runs leading straight back towards that point served by a complex network of chairs and drags. Almost at the top is the cable-car station for the link to Pal. Again, these slopes present a sharp contrast – the runs are widely spread around the mountain with four main lift bases, all reachable by road. The main one, La Caubella, is at the opposite extreme from the linking cable-car.

Snow reliability With most runs above 1950m, north-easterly orientation and an impressive 350 snow-guns, snow is relatively assured.

Snowboarding It's possible to get around much of the area without using drags. Arinsal has a new fun-park.

Experts These aren't great mountains for experts, but there are short, sharp black slopes at Arinsal, and quite long and testing reds (and one black) at Pal – where there is also some off-piste scope.

Intermediates Arinsal offers a reasonable range of difficulty, but any confident intermediate is going to want to explore the Pal slopes, which are much more interesting, varied and extensive. There are easy cruises, and a variety of challenges in the central and Seturia sections.

Beginners Almost half the guests here are beginners. Arinsal and Pal both have gentle nursery slopes apart from the main runs; they can get very crowded at peak times. There are long easy runs to progress to.
Cross-country There isn't any.
Queues Although there is only one lift out of the centre, queues are not a problem on weekdays; however, Spanish weekenders and local children can hit the slopes en masse at times. Most of the higher lifts are drags, keeping the mountain open when it's windy – the new cable-car link can easily be closed by wind.
Mountain restaurants These are not a highlight. They are mainly functional self-service places, doing routine snack food, and are often crowded.
Schools and guides Arinsal's ski school is its pride and joy. It offers technically sound, patient instruction, and is geared to the British market – over half the instructors are native English-speakers. Class sizes can, however, be very large in peak season. English speaking is not so widespread in the Pal school.
Facilities for children There is a ski kindergarten and a non-skiing crèche for younger children.

Phone numbers
From abroad use the prefix +376.

STAYING THERE

How to go There is a wide choice of packages, using hotel and self-catering accommodation.
Hotels Rooms in the hotel Arinsal (835640) are not large, but it is well run, ideally placed and has a pleasant bar. The Princesa Parc (836699) is a big new glossy 4-star place, also close to the gondola, with a swanky spa. The Xalet Verdu (737140) is a smooth little 4-star, a little further from the gondola. The Micolau (835052) is a characterful stone house, close to the centre, with simple rooms and a jolly beamed restaurant. If there is snow to the valley, the Crest (835866), up at the old chair-lift station, has the attraction that you can ski to the door.
Self-catering There is a reasonable choice of places. Aparthotel Sant Andreu (836164) offers simple but comfortable apartments, with a relaxed bar-restaurant on site. There are also apartments attached to the new Princesa Parc hotel.
Eating out There is a fair range of restaurants for a small resort. The Surf disco-pub is a lively spot doing open-fire grills. Cisco's is a central Tex-Mex place in a lovely wood and stone building serving Mexican food. The Rocky Mountain, up at the top of the village, is popular for steaks. The Micolau does very satisfying meals. Borda Callisa does Indian.
Après-ski Arinsal has plenty of animated bars and discos. The Surf, Cisco's and Rocky Mountain, mentioned above, all have lively bars. The liveliest places when we visited are only a short stagger apart – the Quo Vadis (a pub) and El Cau (big, noisy, with disco lights, full of kids). El Derbi was also heaving on karaoke night. If, like us, you prefer something quieter, head for Borda Callisa – out of the way and pleasantly relaxed – or the bar of the hotel Arinsal.
Off the slopes Arinsal has few facilities off the slopes. The main thing to do is to shop in Andorra la Vella, half an hour away by infrequent bus.

TOURIST OFFICE

Pal
t +376 737000
f 835904
Arinsal
t +376 737020
f 836242
pal@arinsal.ad
www.palarinsal.com

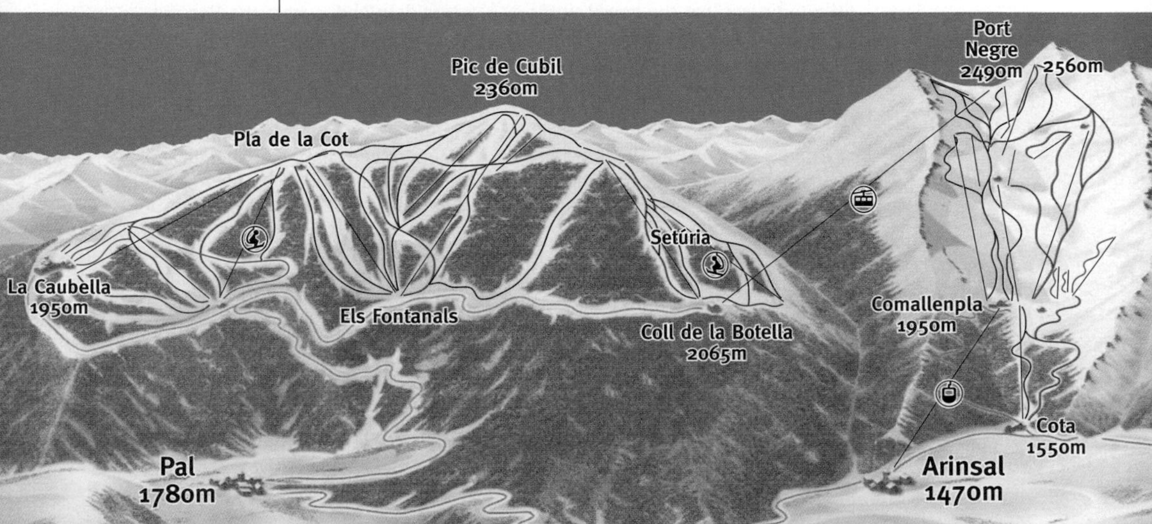

Pas de la Casa 2100m

Andorra's biggest ski mountain

WHAT IT COSTS

HOW IT RATES

The slopes

Snow	***
Extent	***
Experts	*
Intermediates	***
Beginners	****
Convenience	****
Queues	***
Restaurants	***

The rest

Scenery	**
Resort charm	*
Off-slope	*

What's new

For 2000/01 the Font Negre drag above Pas de la Casa was replaced by a six-pack – the new lift now extends up towards the top of the Pic Blanc ridge. And two of the three Llac del Cubill drags to the Grau Roig area from the Encamp side have also been upgraded to a six-pack.

Next season's developments include the expansion of the Pas de la Casa beginners' area, extra snowmaking and improvements to the fun-park and boarder-cross.

MOUNTAIN FACTS

Altitude	2050m-2640m
Lifts	31
Pistes	100km
Blue	25%
Red	55%
Black	20%
Artificial snow	23km
Recco detectors used	

- ⊕ Slopes to match many mid-sized resorts in the Alps
- ⊕ High altitude means relatively reliable snow
- ⊕ Andorra's liveliest nightlife
- ⊕ Encamp (linked by gondola) is a cheaper but even more dreary base
- ⊕ Grau Roig is a more attractive, quiet base (if you can afford it)
- ⊕ Equally worthwhile Soldeu area is physically linked, but ...

- ⊖ No shared lift pass with Soldeu, although runs overlap
- ⊖ Pas is an eyesore – an uncompromisingly commercial frontier town – and the centre suffers from traffic (and fumes)
- ⊖ Very few woodland slopes, and none directly above the village – unpleasant in bad weather

The tour op brochures (and the few readers' reports we get) all say that Pas is Andorra's wildest party resort, and we don't doubt it. Having driven through it and skied down to it, we are quite happy to stay over the hill in Soldeu – or, for ideal access to the Pas slopes, secluded Grau Roig.

THE RESORT

Sited right on the border between Andorra and France, Pas de la Casa owes its development as much to duty-free sales to the French as to skiing. It is a sizeable collection of concrete-box-style apartment blocks and hotels, a product of the rapid development Andorra saw in the late 1960s and early 1970s. Some thought has gone into its layout, if not its appearance, with most accommodation conveniently placed near the lift base and slopes. The town centre boasts plenty of cheap shops and bars, as well as a sports centre. Reporters complain that it's starting to look a little tatty and that the heavy traffic generates fumes.

The resort attracts a lot of French visitors (so beware the February school holidays) and Spanish families, with only a smattering of Brits.

The lift system spreads from Pas over three adjacent valleys. The furthest from Pas has nothing but a lift station, but in the attractively wooded middle one is Grau Roig ('Rosh'). This is a mini-resort that acts as the access point for day visitors arriving by road from central Andorra and Spain, but it also makes a good base.

The road through from France goes on over the Port d'Envalira towards Soldeu and central Andorra. There is accommodation at the pass, which we suggest you avoid.

THE MOUNTAINS

Pas de la Casa boasts the most extensive slopes in Andorra, and has the Soldeu slopes right next door. With the exception of a couple of attractively wooded slopes in the central valley, the slopes are all open, and vulnerable to bad weather. There's floodlit skiing every Wednesday night.

Slopes The treeless local slopes, facing north-east, descend from a high, north–south ridge; lifts go up to it at four points. Runs on the far side of the ridge converge on Grau Roig, where there is some wooded terrain at the head of the valley. And a single lift goes on further west to the bowl of Llac del Cubill, where the Pas area adjoins the Soldeu one. On the far side of this bowl is the arrival station of the new 6km gondola up from Encamp.

Snow reliability Heavy investment in artificial snowmaking equipment, coupled with the area's height, means a good snow reliability record and a season that often reaches late April.

Snowboarding Boarding is popular with the young crowd that Pas de la Casa attracts, and there is a small, lift-served board-park and half-pipe on the Grau Roig side of the mountain.

Experts There are few challenges on-piste – the black runs are rarely of serious steepness, and moguls are rare. But there seem to be plenty of off-piste slopes inviting exploration when fresh snow arrives.

Intermediates The slopes cater for confident intermediates far better, with plenty of top-to-bottom reds and blues on the main ridge, though they do rather lack variety.
Beginners There are beginner slopes in both Pas and Grau Roig. The Pas area is a short but inconvenient bus-ride out of town. Progression to longer runs is easier in Grau Roig, too.
Snowboarders There's a terrain park with half-pipe and boarder-cross at Grau Roig. Drags are usually avoidable.
Cross-country Although they get very little attention, there are loops totalling 12km below Grau Roig.
Queues Queues are rarely serious, now that there are two fast chairs out of Pas – one of them a six-pack. But during French school holidays some bottlenecks can develop.
Mountain restaurants There are routine places at the ridge above Pas and the top of the gondola from Encamp, but the Rifugi dels Llacs dels Pessons at the head of the Grau Roig bowl is far from routine: as well as a bar it has a cosy beamed table-service restaurant with excellent food.
Schools and guides The ski school has an excellent reputation, with good English spoken.
Facilities for children There are ski kindergartens at Pas and Grau Roig, and a non-ski one at the latter.

STAYING THERE

How to go There's a wide choice of apartments and hotels on offer through tour operators, and even a few chalets and chalet hotels.
Hotels We don't have any special recommendations in Pas. The Grau Roig hotel is in a league of its own for comfort and seclusion. (Beware: some operators list it under Soldeu, presumably because it seems a bit out of place alongside brash Pal.)
Self-catering We have no particular recommendations.
Eating out There are doubtless various possibilities, but we rarely get reports on them. 'There are no really good restaurants,' says a reporter.
Après-ski 'The après-ski is very lively' and 'Nightspots get very crowded' say reporters. British tour operators take over one bar (the Marselles). The Billboard is 'by far the best club', and the Milwaukee is one of the most popular bars. The Safari bar is 'a good place to chill out'.
Off the slopes Off-slope activity is limited to shopping ('Electrical goods and perfume are good buys,' says one reporter), visiting the leisure centre or taking a trip to Andorra la Vella for more of the same.

Central reservations phone number
For all resort accommodation call 801060.
From abroad, add the prefix +376.

TOURIST OFFICE
t +376 801060
f 801070
info.reserves@pasgrau.com
www.pasgrau.com

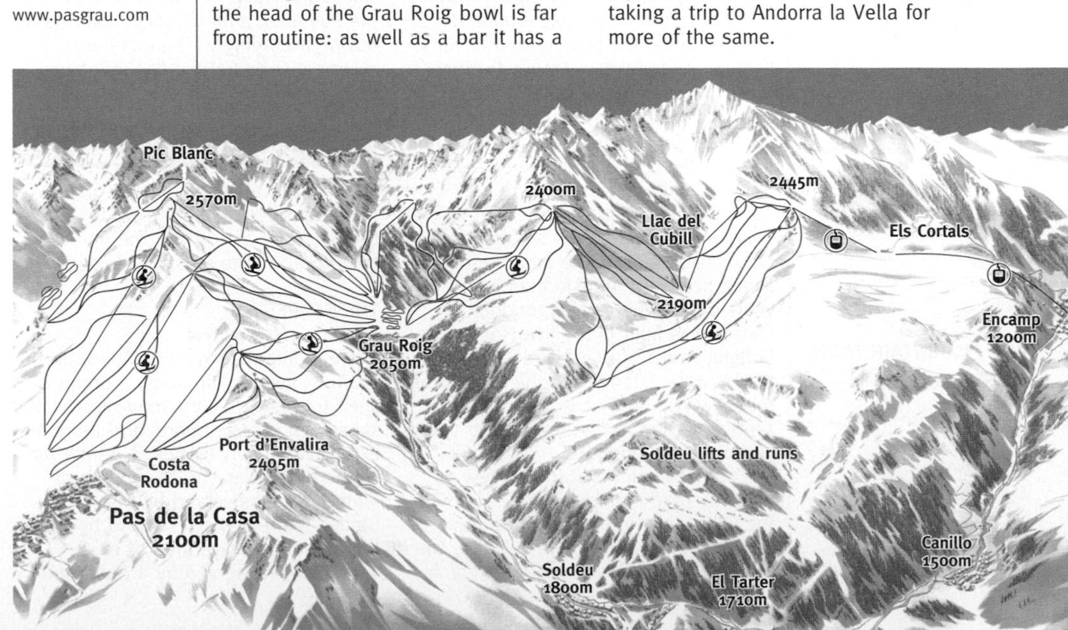

Soldeu 1800m

Andorra's best all-rounder

WHAT IT COSTS

HOW IT RATES

The slopes

Snow	***
Extent	**
Experts	*
Intermediates	***
Beginners	****
Convenience	***
Queues	***
Restaurants	*

The rest

Scenery	***
Resort charm	*
Off-slope	*

What's new

The slopes above El Forn were developed for last season.

For 2001/02, the Riba Escorxada beginners' area is being improved – a new quad is being added. There will also be a couple of new runs.

The Espiolets beginner area is being further improved and a new drag-lift installed.

A new black run is planned for the Canillo slopes.

The El Tarter terrain park is being improved. New piste signing and information boards are also planned.

MOUNTAIN FACTS

Altitude	1710m-2560m
Lifts	28
Pistes	88km
Green	24%
Blue	32%
Red	36%
Black	8%
Artificial snow	25km

Recco detectors used – helicopter based

- ⊕ Slopes to match many mid-sized resorts in the Alps
- ⊕ Impressively efficient lift system
- ⊕ Not at all the rowdy resort it once was
- ⊕ Ski school has excellent British-run section for English-speaking visitors
- ⊕ Equally worthwhile Pas de la Casa area is physically linked, but ...

- ⊖ No shared lift pass with Pas de la Casa, although runs overlap
- ⊖ Village is over-run by traffic on main road through from France to Andorra la Vella
- ⊖ Packages not particularly cheap
- ⊖ Not much to do off the slopes

If we were planning a holiday in Andorra, it would be in Soldeu (unless it was in the isolated hotel at Grau Roig, up the road – covered in the Pas de la Casa chapter). Despite the traffic, it is the least unattractive village, and its slopes are the most interestingly varied. Mind you, we would make expeditions to the Pas de la Casa slopes, too, even if it meant spending more on lift passes. Bear in mind the alternative bases of El Tarter and Canillo, which may be cheaper.

For many people the trickier question is whether to come here or to go somewhere completely different. Soldeu no longer competes on price with the bargain basements of eastern Europe, so the alternatives are more likely to be in Austria or Italy. It's easy to find villages there that are a lot prettier than Soldeu, scenery that is more impressive, and off-slope diversions that are more, well, diverting. But you would often have to settle for less extensive and interesting slopes, and less carefully organised ski tuition.

The resort

The village is a small, though ever-growing, ribbon of modern buildings – not pretty, but mainly given a stone veneer in traditional style – on a steep hillside, lining the busy road that runs through Andorra from France to Spain. Most of them are hotels, apartments or bars, with the occasional shop; for serious shopping – or for any other off-slope diversions – you have to head down to Andorra la Vella.

The steep hillside leads down to the river, and the ski slopes are on the opposite side of it. The practicalities of skiing here were transformed a few years back, when a new gondola station was built in the heart of Soldeu, next to the main road, and the slopes were extended to the bottom of this new station by a wide bridge across the river, with elevators to take you up to the gondola.

For many years El Tarter, a few miles by road and 200m vertical down the valley, has offered an alternative way into the slopes. From last year the same is true of Canillo, another 200m lower – though there is no proper shared lift pass. Nor is there one with Pas de la Casa, whose piste network actually overlaps that of Soldeu. Keen skiers and riders will want to explore the Pas area, and will tailor their pass buying accordingly. There is easy access at Grau Roig, a few miles up the valley.

The mountain

The main local slopes are on open mountainsides above the woods, though there are runs in the woods back to all of the resort lift bases.

THE SLOPES
Pleasantly varied

The gondola rises over wooded, north-facing slopes to Espiolets, a broad shelf that is virtually a mini-resort – the ski school is based here, and there are extensive nursery slopes. A gentle run to the east takes you to an area of long, easy runs served by one of Soldeu's three six-packs. And beyond that is an extensive area of more varied slopes, served by a quad and

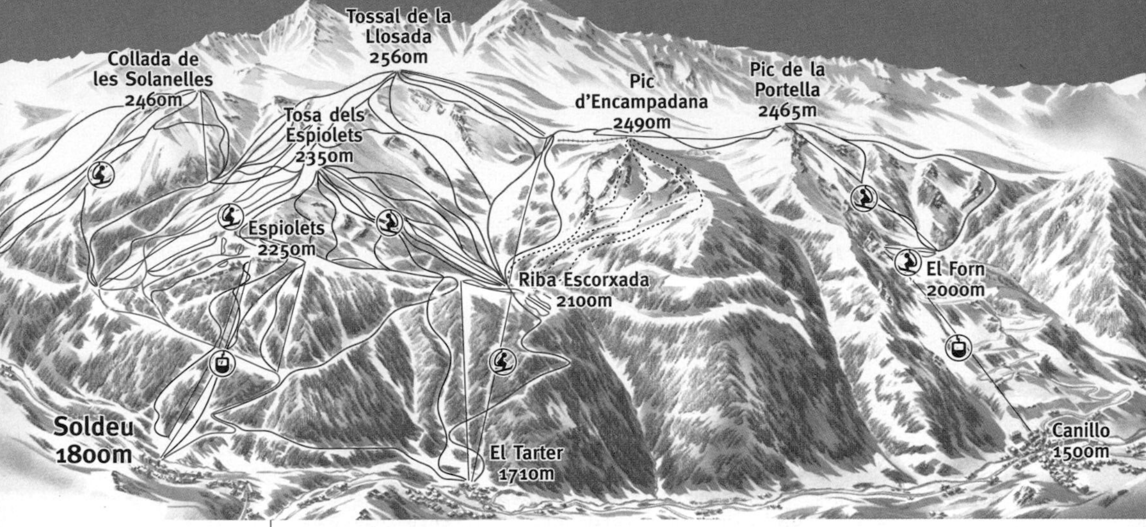

LIFT PASSES

2000/01 prices in euros

Soldeu El Tarter
Covers all lifts in Soldeu El Tarter.

Main pass
1-day pass 26
6-day pass 123
Over 65: 10 (1 day)
Over 75: free pass

Children
Under 12: 6-day pass 98
Under 6: free pass

Short-term passes
Half-day pass 19

Notes
A supplement is charged for the El Forn area: 3 euros for 1 day or 15 euros for 6 days.

Alternative passes
The 5-day Ski Andorra pass covers all five resorts and costs around 115 euros.

another six-pack, that overlaps with the Pas de la Casa area – hence the extraordinary signs shown in our introduction to Andorra. Going west from Espiolets takes you to the open bowl of Riba Escorxada and the arrival point of the lift up from El Tarter. From here, the third six-pack serves sunny slopes on Tosa dels Espiolets, while a slow quad leads off southwards towards drags serving the high-point of Tossal de la Llosada and the little-used link with the slopes above Canillo.

SNOW RELIABILITY
Not at all bad

Soldeu enjoys fairly reliable snow. Most slopes are north-facing, with artificial snow on the descents to Soldeu. The snowmaking is expanded each year, but even if runs to the village are incomplete, the area as a whole is not unduly affected.

EXPERTS
Hope the snowcat's going

It's a limited area for experts, at least on-piste. The black runs down to Soldeu and El Tarter more or less justify their grading, and the one at the top of the Canillo sector looked like fun but was short of snow when we visited. The blacks on Tosa dels Espiolets are indistinguishable from the neighbouring (and more direct) red and blue. One intriguing possibility that we were not able to explore last winter is that when conditions permit a snowcat takes people up to Pic d'Encampadana whence a range of off-piste routes (shown dotted on our map) descend to Riba Escorxada. There is plenty of other off-piste potential, given the necessary guidance – notably in the bowl above Riba Escorxada, in the area where Soldeu meets Pas, and above El Forn.

SNOWPIX.COM / CHRIS GILL

Espiolets is a regular little mini-resort, though there is no accommodation up here →

boarding *There's a well-equipped fun-park and half-pipe for snowboarders, which is easier to get to due to a new six-seater chair. Competent free-riders should be among the first in line for the snowcat service when it's running (see Experts).*

SCHOOLS/GUIDES

2000/01 prices in euros

Soldeu El Tarter school

Classes 5 or 6 days 15 hours: 79

Children's classes 15 hours: 67

Private lessons Hourly: 26 for 1 or 2 people, 32 for 3 or 4 people.

CHILDCARE

The three nurseries, at Espiolets, Riba Escorxada and El Forn, take children from 3 to 10.

INTERMEDIATES
Pity about the pass position

There is plenty to amuse all but the keenest intermediates. The area east of Espiolets is splendid for building confidence, while those who already have it will be able to explore the whole mountain. Riba Escorxada is a fine section for mixed ability groups, and the new link to Canillo/El Forn and newly created runs there allow for more cruising mileage completely free of crowds. The great frustration for mileage-hungry intermediates is the lack of a joint Soldeu/Pas pass.

BEGINNERS
One of the best

This is a good resort for beginners. It is relatively snowsure, and there are numerous easy pistes to move on to. The Espiolets nursery area and playground has recently been expanded by 50%, and two new rope tows have been added. A bar, cafeteria, and nursery are soon to be located inside a new building there.

CROSS-COUNTRY
Er, what cross-country?

If there is any cross country here we've neither seen it nor heard about it. There is some not far away at Grau Roig (covered in the Pas de la Casa chapter), but Andorra's serious cross-country resort is at La Rabassa, some distance away in the south-west corner of the country, close to Spain – 20km of loops at an altitude of 2000m.

QUEUES
Weekends only

The lift system is a mixture of the old and the impressively new and powerful – there aren't many resorts in the Alps with three six-packs – which seems to be able to cope with those staying locally. When there is an influx at weekends, there can be waits up the mountain.

MOUNTAIN RESTAURANTS
Not a highlight

The mountain restaurants are crowded, not because they stimulate trade but because there aren't enough of them. There is a choice of places at Espiolets, including a restaurant doing service at crowded refectory-style tables. Reporters favour descending to El Tarter, particularly to the snack bar El Clos.

SCHOOLS AND GUIDES
One of the best for Brits

The ski school is effectively run as two units, the one dealing with English-speaking clients headed by an Englishman and largely staffed by native-English-speaking instructors. 40% of the pupils are beginners, and the school has devised a special 'team teaching' scheme to cope with the challenge of helping this number of beginners to find their feet and sorting them into aptitude groups. The school has an excellent reputation for quality of tuition and friendliness.

FACILITIES FOR CHILDREN
With altitude

Children are looked after at the mid-mountain stations. We lack recent reports, but given the way the ski school is run we would expect the child-care to be competent too.

Staying there 

HOW TO GO
Some comfortable hotels

A wide range of UK tour operators offer packages here, mainly in hotels but with occasional apartments and catered chalets.

Hotels The best hotels are very civilised, and far removed from the standards of a decade ago.

((((4) **Sport Hotel Village** Clearly best in town, with a style and spaciousness to the public areas that is rare. Directly over the gondola station. But no ski room – you share with the Sport.

(((3) **Sport** Comfortable and pleasant, with good lounge areas, a lively bar and a popular basement disco-bar used for ski school presentations. Over the road from the gondola.

(((3) **Piolets** Pleasant enough, with a pool and other amenities. Central.

((2) **Himalaia** Recently refurbished, central.

GETTING THERE

Air Toulouse, transfer $3\frac{1}{2}$hr.

Rail L'Hospitalet-Près-L'Andorre (25km); buses and taxis to Soldeu

ACTIVITIES

Indoor Ice skating, swimming, gym, squash, tennis
Outdoor Thermal spas, snowmobiling, tobogganing

Central reservations phone number
For all resort accommodation call 890501.

From abroad, add the prefix +376.

TOURIST OFFICE

t +376 890500
f 890509
soldeu@soldeu.ad
www.soldeu.ad

Self-catering The Edelweiss apartments are spacious and generally pleasant, and well placed opposite the Sport hotel, the facilities of which are available.

EATING OUT
Some gourmand delights

Last winter we enjoyed excellent, satisfying meals at two cute rustic restaurants – Fat Albert's in downtown Soldeu and 'Snails and Quails', 3km up the road in Bordes d'Envalira. The Pussycat and El Squirol (Indian) are recommended by readers.

APRES-SKI
Lively

Although après-ski is lively, it consists mainly of bars and rep-organised outings. The bar at Fat Albert's (see above) has a great atmosphere, with videos shot on the mountain and often a live band. The long-established Pussycat is a good late-night place, with changing party themes. The Piccadilly under the Sport hotel is popular. Aspen is the main snowboard hang-out. The Naudi has a quieter locals' bar. The El Duc is the best disco. Expect noise from late-night revellers on the streets.

OFF THE SLOPES
Head downhill

There is little to amuse non-skiers in Soldeu itself. Down the valley in Canillo is the smart Palau de Gel (see below), and in Escaldes (effectively Andorra la Vella) there are other diversions including the impressive Caldea spa, and some very serious shopping opportunities. There are several small museums dotted around the country. Some of the bigger hotels have excellent sports facilities.

El Tarter 1710m

El Tarter has grown over recent years to the point where it now seems no smaller than Soldeu; but it is quieter. There is no shortage of places to stay here – UK tour operators tend to list it under Soldeu. A recent reporter recommends the resort, the Hotel del Tarter and the local ski school. El Mosquit is a recommended pizzeria; a new British-run bar, Peanuts, beneath it seems set to monopolise the British custom.

Canillo 1500m

If you like the idea of deserted local slopes and don't mind riding a gondola down at the end of the day, consider Canillo, which looked an acceptably pleasant spot as we repeatedly drove through it on a recent tour. (Again, UK operators generally list accommodation here under Soldeu.) It has the attraction of the impressive Palau de Gel – an Olympic ice-rink plus swimming pool, gym and other amenities.

SNOWPIX.COM / CHRIS GILL

El Tarter is an increasingly popular alternative to Soldeu, with equally good access to the shared slopes ↓

Spain

The Spanish Pyrenees were a popular British budget destination a decade ago, but then Andorra and eastern Europe succeeded in capturing much of the Spanish trade. It's easy to see why this happened. The mass-market resorts often struggled for snow and, even when conditions were good, there was a tendency for high winds to close the lifts. Although prices were low, they were lower elsewhere, and these resorts weren't able to compete with the Alps for quality.

But it's dangerous to generalise about Spanish resorts – which is why we don't provide the lists of ⊕ and ⊖ points that we do for other second-division countries. There are now some well equipped Pyrenean resorts with fine, snowsure slopes that compare favourably with mid-sized places in the Alps. Two resorts are certainly not downmarket – Sierra Nevada and Baqueira-Beret are both frequented by the King of Spain. Winter sports are becoming more popular with the prosperous Spanish themselves, and as a result many of the smaller resorts are continually improving.

Furthermore, the general ambience of Spanish resorts is attractive – not unlike that of Italy. There's plenty of animation, with eating, posing and partying taken seriously. Large families often lunch together, creating much merriment while huge amounts of food are consumed. Dinner starts late after such a blowout so, in turn, nightlife doesn't get going before many a British punter has retired, disgruntled at the lack of action.

Sierra Nevada (2100m) – also known as Sol y Nieve – in the extreme south of Spain suffers from extremely unpredictable weather conditions. The much-fêted 1995 World Championships had to be cancelled at the eleventh hour due to a lack of snow-cover, with high temperatures rendering the resort's state-of-the-art snowmaking installation useless (fortunately better conditions permitted the Championships to take place in 1996).

The resort's natural snow arrives via completely different weather patterns from those supplying the Alps and the Pyrenees; in 1990, when the Alps were disastrously snowless, Sierra Nevada had the best conditions in Europe.

The mostly intermediate slopes are very exposed to the elements. When the wind blows, as it does, the slopes close, and the strong sun makes the pistes either icy or soft in late season. On a good day, however, visitors are treated to a fantastic view from the top of the highest point at Veleta, across the Med, all the way to the Atlas mountains in Morocco.

The resort is very ugly but user-friendly, and its restaurants, bars and shops are nicely gathered around a central square. Granada's proximity means good outings but overcrowding at weekends and holidays. Hotels are comfortable and good value, but a recent visitor recommends staying in Granada and driving up each day.

The best of the Pyrenean resorts is Baqueira-Beret, on the northern slope of the range (see next chapter).

There is a group of worthwhile resorts in the western Pyrenees, between Pau and Huesca.

Formigal appears in a couple of tour operator brochures and is working hard to improve its standing as a winter resort. There has been recent expansion and a number of lift improvements but the 56km of pistes are windswept. When the wind blows, retreat to nearby **Panticosa** – a charming old village with sheltered but limited slopes that have recently doubled in size to 34km of pistes. **Candanchu** and nearby **Astún**, with almost 100km of piste between them, are popular on the Spanish market. They offer a wide range of lodging set in some of the Pyrenees' most stunning scenery. Candanchu has a reputation for tough runs.

The other resorts of international interest are just east of Andorra. The 44km of runs at **La Molina** and its purpose-built satellite **Supermolina** (1700m) are now linked to those of **Masella**, over the mountain, via a gondola and six-pack. The whole area, called Alp 2500, now extends over 100km of mainly intermediate skiing.

Baqueira-Beret 1500m

Spain's leading winter resort – fit for their king

WHAT IT COSTS

HOW IT RATES

The slopes	
Snow	***
Extent	***
Experts	***
Intermediates	****
Beginners	**
Convenience	***
Queues	***
Restaurants	**
The rest	
Scenery	***
Resort charm	**
Off-slope	*

What's new

For 2000/01 a new fast chair and drag opened up a new area facing the main Beret slopes. And a new chair in the Bonaigua sector has opened up a couple of new blue runs. Snowmaking has been further extended

Two new hotels opened last season, and another is to follow for the coming season.

MOUNTAIN FACTS

Altitude	1500m-2510m
Lifts	27
Pistes	86km
Green	8%
Blue	8%
Red	37%
Black	47%
Art. snow	35km

- ⊕ Compact modern resort
- ⊕ Efficient lifts with few queues
- ⊕ Reasonable snow reliability
- ⊕ Some good off-piste potential
- ⊕ Lots of good intermediate slopes
- ⊕ Friendly, helpful locals
- ⊕ Good restaurants and bars for après-ski

- ⊖ Drab high-rise blocks dominate the main village, though new developments are more attractive
- ⊖ Resort is not cleverly laid out, and suffers from traffic around the lift base station
- ⊖ Few off-slope diversions other than walks

Baqueira is in a different league from other resorts in the Spanish Pyrenees – a smart family-oriented resort with a wide area of north-facing slopes that gives a real feeling of travel. It attracts an almost entirely Spanish clientele (which regularly includes the royal family), so don't count on English being spoken.

THE RESORT

Baqueira was purpose-built in the 1960s and has its fair share of drab, high-rise blocks; these are clustered below the road that runs through to the high pass of Port de la Bonaigua, while the main lift base is just above it. But up the steep hill from the main base are some newer, smaller-scale stone-clad developments. At the very top is an alternative chair-lift into the slopes. The most convenient base is close to the main chair-lift, but the village is small enough for location not to be too much of an issue. There is a lot of accommodation spread down the valley, and a big car park with road-train shuttle up to the lift base.

Ski Miquel has long been the only UK tour operator here. They cater for non-Spanish-speakers by offering their own chalet hotel and tame instructors.

THE MOUNTAINS

There is an extensive area of long, mainly intermediate, runs, practically all of them on open treeless slopes. There are long-term plans to extend the slopes to the sunny side of the Bonaigua pass.

Slopes The slopes are split into three distinct but well-connected areas – Baqueira, Beret and Bonaigua. From the base station at Baqueira, a fast quad takes you up to the nursery slopes at 1800m. Fast chairs go on up to Cap de Baqueira. From here there is a wide variety of long runs, served by chairs and drags. From several points you can descend into the Argulls valley and the Bonaigua sector, leading over to the summit of the Bonaigua pass. From the opposite extremity at Orri a triple chair takes you off to the Beret sector, where a series of more-or-less parallel chairs serve mainly blue and red runs. A new fast quad and a drag-lift serve a new fourth sector across the valley from the Beret slopes, with new red and blue pistes. Beret, Orri and Bonaigua are accessible by road.

Snowboarding There's a permanent half-pipe at Bonaigua. The nursery slopes are served by drags and some of the blues are a bit tricky for novices.

Snow reliability Mainly north-west-facing slopes above 1800m and extensive snowmaking make the area fairly snowsure. But the latitude means strong sun in late season.

Experts Experts will find few on-piste challenges, but there's plenty of off-

BAQUEIRA TOURIST OFFICE

Baqueira's lift base is just above the village →

piste if you hire a guide. The infamous Escornacrabes itinerary, from the top of Cap de Baqueira, is steep and narrow. Cheap heli-lifts are available.
Intermediates It's excellent for intermediates, with lots of varied blues and some classic long red runs such as Mirador. The excursion to Port de la Bonaigua has a nice air of adventure. Less daring intermediates will enjoy the long blue from the Dossau ridge to Beret, and the Argulls valley runs.
Beginners There are some good nursery runs, but on the main mountain progression is not easy – some of the blues can be a bit tough; there are gentler blue runs at Beret, but you'd need to take a taxi to them.
Cross-country There is 7km of cross-country skiing between Orri and Beret.
Queues The network of modern lifts means few queues most of the time. But at peak times, when French and Spanish holidaymakers flood into the resort, some waits can be 10 minutes.
Mountain restaurants Most are cheap and charmless, but with good-value food and pleasant terraces. You can get table service at Cap del Port, at the Bonaigua pass.
Schools and guides The school gets good reports – some spoken English.
Facilities for children The kindergarten takes children from three months to three years. Lack of spoken English is a problem in the kindergartens. Ski school classes start from age four, and English is less problematic here.

STAYING THERE

How to go There is a reasonable choice of hotels and apartments locally. UK operator Ski Miquel offers packages here. Their chalet-hotel Salana generates good reports, except from people with young children.
Hotels In the main village three hotels have been recommended – the 4-star Montarto (973 639001) and the 3-star Tuc Blanc (973 644350) and Val de Ruda (973 645258). The 5-star Tryp Royal Tanau at the top of the resort looks good (973 644446). There is a Parador (973 640801) down the valley in Arties.
Eating out The more interesting restaurants are down the valley in Salardu and Arties. Reporters have enjoyed the local tapas bars.
Après-ski There are lots of pubs and discos in the valley. Tiffany's and Pacha are in the main village. They get going very late (ie in the early hours).
Off the slopes Pool and spa facilities are available in several hotels, but not much else. Viehla, 15km away, has a good sports centre.

Phone numbers
From abroad use the prefix +34.

TOURIST OFFICE
Postcode 25530
t +34 973 639000
f 973 644488
baqueira@baqueira.es
www.baqueira.es

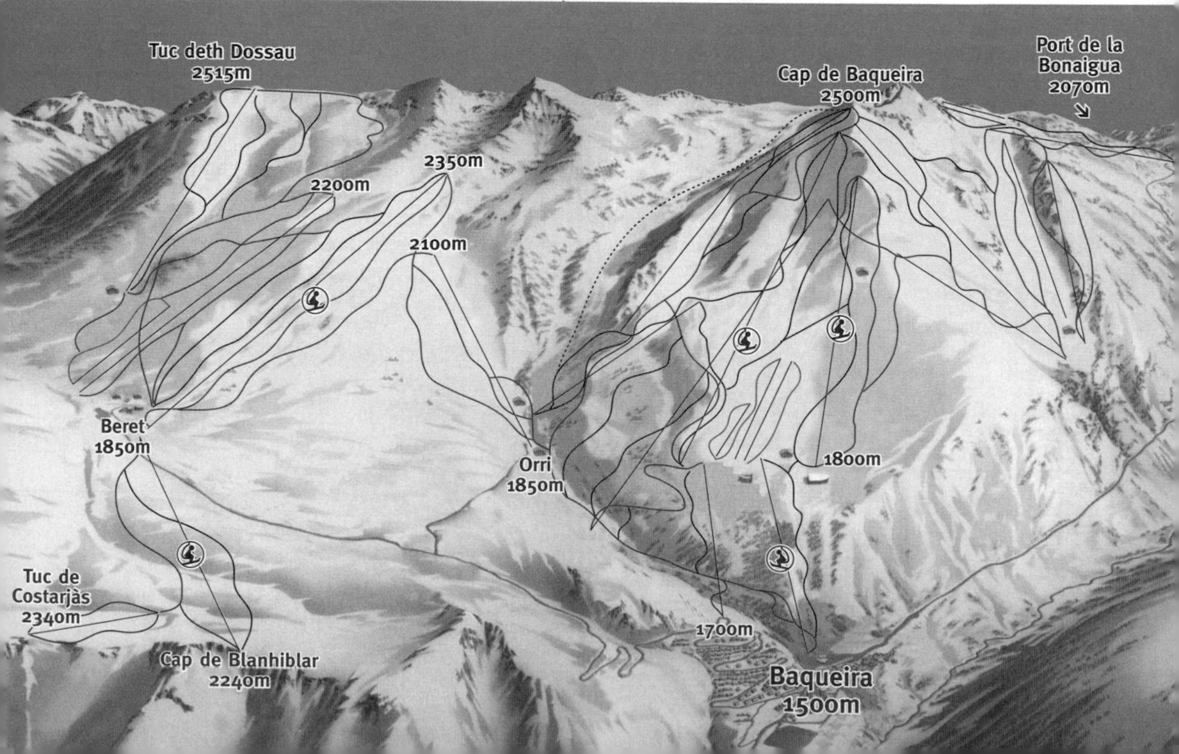

Bulgaria

WHAT IT COSTS

①

- ⊕ Very cheap
- ⊕ A different winter holiday, with the chance to experience a fascinating, although depressed, culture
- ⊕ Very friendly, welcoming people
- ⊕ Good ski schools

- ⊖ Not enough snowmaking
- ⊖ Poor piste and lift maintenance
- ⊖ Problems with theft of equipment
- ⊖ Borovets hotels and food poor
- ⊖ Archaic airports, airline and coaches can cause long travel delays

Bulgaria attracts holidaymakers on a tight budget: the basic flight-and-hotel-package, equipment hire, school and lift pass are all very cheap. Drawbacks include limited slopes, old lifts, and mountain food that can have you reaching for the Mars bars. But there are compensations: reporters are struck by the friendliness of the people, the ski schools are excellent, the tour op-organised nightlife is good fun, and from Borovets an excursion to Sofia is recommended.

But keen piste-bashers, gourmets, posers, and those wanting creature comforts should look elsewhere or be prepared for a shock.

The flow of readers' reports has dried up over the last few seasons, but we have trawled the internet for holiday reports. Most – at least from absolute beginners – are extremely positive, enthusing about the benefits mentioned above, but others tell worrying tales of burgled rooms and stolen ski equipment (mainly in Borovets). And those who have skied elsewhere tend to be more critical.

Bulgaria's two main resorts are some way apart, served by different airports, with similarly short transfer times (less than two hours). They are similar places in that both have good tuition and a poor selection of quality restaurants, but they suit different levels of ability.

Pamporovo 1650m

THE RESORT

Despite the bus-ride to the lifts, families praise Pamporovo. The purpose-built village has 'everything to hand'.

THE MOUNTAIN

Pamporovo is Bulgaria's best bet for beginners and early intermediates, with mostly easy runs. Others are likely to find 17.5km of mainly short runs too limited.

Slopes The slopes are pretty and sheltered, with pistes starting at a high point of 1925m and cutting through pine forest. Getting lost is difficult even in the worst weather.

Snow reliability Late-season snow-cover is unreliable.

Snowboarding The Snow Shack is best for snowboard hire and tuition.

Experts Experts will find little to challenge them in this limited ski area.

Intermediates The slopes are too limited for most intermediates.

Beginners Book a 'learn to ski' package through your tour operator, saving up to 80% on local prices.

Mountain restaurants The best bets are the Lodge and the Spider restaurant.

Schools and guides The ski schools are repeatedly praised by reporters – instructors are patient, enthusiastic and speak good English, and class sizes are usually quite small.

Facilities for children The English-speaking crèche is well regarded.

STAYING THERE

The main hotels are in the centre of the handy purpose-built village.

Hotels Hotel Pamporovo was new for 1999/2000 and offers the best accommodation in the resort. It's close to the village centre, and facilities include an indoor swimming pool, a hot-tub and a gym. More basic are the Perelik (also with a pool) and Mourgavets – both in the centre.

Eating out The food can be poor. You are best off sticking to local Bulgarian stew dishes, gyuvech and kavarma, which can be delicious. The breakfast buffets offer a fair choice.

Après-ski The nightlife is fairly lively, although limited to a handful of bars and discos – BJ's, the White Hart, Dax and the Havana club are popular.

Off the slopes The organised evening events are recommended by reporters.

Borovets 1300m

THE RESORT

Borovets is a collection of large, modern hotels, with bars, restaurants and shops housed within them. There is a ramshackle selection of quirkier bars, shops and eating places. The beautiful wooded setting provides a degree of Alpine-style charm, and trees hide some of the worst architectural excesses. A cluster of large hotels is at the main village lift (a gondola) up to two of the three ski sectors. A couple of minutes' walk takes you to the top of the resort, where an enormous hotel overlooks the remaining village lifts.

THE MOUNTAIN

The 40km of piste are spread over three sectors – two are loosely linked.

Slopes The two largest sectors have fairly steep and awkward slopes. The gondola rises over 1000m to service both the small, high, easy slopes of Markoudjika (up to 2700m), and the mainly long, steepish Yastrebets pistes. A little drag-lift and path connect the two. The third Baraki sector is accessed by several lifts. Runs are short, with a range of just 550m up to a top station at 1850m.

Snow reliability Reliable cover is by no means guaranteed.

Experts There's little of real challenge.

Intermediates The runs are best suited to good intermediates. Less confident skiers may find the mainly tough red runs a bit intimidating.

Beginners The slopes are not particularly suitable for novices. The nursery slopes are inadequate and Markoudjika is good for near beginners, but progress beyond that means going on to reds.

Queues When snow is poor and when the resort is full, queues can be bad – 'unruly and pushy'. Reporters suggest an early start to avoid the worst of the gondola queues – the main bottleneck. Erratic grooming and poor signing are other common complaints.

Mountain restaurants Mountain restaurants are mostly basic little snack bars with limited seating, serving large portions of very simple fare.

Schools and guides 'Brilliant,' says a reporter with children aged 6 and 9.

Facilities for children Reports of the ski kindergarten have been complimentary. The non-ski nursery is in the Rila hotel.

STAYING THERE

Hotels A report says of the Rila: 'Clean, good food, rooms secure.' The Samokov is popular and its pool is a major asset. The Breza and Edelweiss get reasonable reviews.

Eating out Alpin Hotel, Krima, Bulgarian Dish, La Bamba, Ela Tavern and Franco's are better than the rest.

Après-ski The nightlife is very lively, catering well to an 18–30 type crowd. Events organised by tour operator reps include pub crawls, folklore evenings and a visit to a local village for dinner. The Black Tiger pub (with karaoke), the Buzz Bar, Titanic and Bonkers have been recommended.

Off the slopes Excursions to the Rila monastery by coach and to Sofia by coach or helicopter are interesting.

Vitosha 1810m

No more than a few widely scattered hotels with very limited, bland runs and a top height of 2290m. The hotels are fairly dour, and most are a bus-ride from the lifts. The resort is just over 20km from the centre of Sofia, allowing for short transfers and easy excursions, but the slopes get overrun at weekends. The slopes are north-facing and have a decent snow record.

Romania

WHAT IT COSTS

①

- ⊕ Extremely cheap
- ⊕ Interesting excursions and friendly local people
- ⊕ Good standard of affordable tuition

- ⊖ Primitive facilities
- ⊖ Uninspiring food
- ⊖ Limited slopes with few real challenges

Like Bulgaria, Romania sells mainly on price. On-the-spot prices, in particular, are very, very low. Provided you have correspondingly low expectations – and provided you go to Poiana Brasov and not Sinaia – you'll probably come back content. If you have any interest in good living, and particularly good lunching, stay away. It's a place for beginners and near-beginners – the slopes are limited in extent and challenge, but the tuition is good (and cheap, of course).

There is another possible dimension to a holiday here, which is the experience of visiting (and supporting) an interesting and attractive country with a traumatic recent history. Reporters have commented on the friendliness of the people, and most recommend exploring beyond the confines of the resorts. Bucharest is 'not to be missed'.

It's some years since we visited the country. The abiding impression we brought back then was one of resources stretched to their limits. To judge by the few reports we have since received, post-revolutionary Romania has, sadly, not made much progress.

Romania's two main resorts are in the Carpathian mountains, about 120km north-west of the capital and arrival airport, Bucharest. They are very different places, but have one or two things in common apart from low prices: patient tuition, with excellent spoken English, and small classes; and very basic mountain restaurants, with extremely primitive loos that, according to one past reporter, would 'shock the toughest of characters'.

The main resort is **Poiana Brasov** (1030m), near the city of Brasov. It is purpose-built, but not designed for convenience: the hotels are dotted about a pretty, wooded plateau, served by regular buses and cheap taxis. There is nothing resembling a real village – the place has the air of a spacious holiday camp.

The main slopes (approximately 17km of pistes in total) consist of decent intermediate tree-lined runs of about 750m vertical, roughly following the line of the main cable-car and gondola, plus an open nursery area at the top. There are also some nursery lifts at village level. A black run takes a less direct route down the mountain, which means that on average it is less steep than the red run under the lifts; it has one steepish pitch towards the end. The more adventurous would need to seek opportunities to go off-piste. The resort gets weekend business from Brasov and Bucharest, and the main lifts can suffer serious queues as a result.

The recently refurbished Bradul and Sport hotels are handy for the lower nursery slopes and for one of the cable-cars. The Capra Neagra and Tyrol are brand new and the Alpin gets good reports. The Ciucas is a 'good, basic' place with satellite TV. Après-ski revolves around the hotel bars and discos and can be quite lively at times. The nightclub puts on cheap cabarets. Off-slope facilities are limited; there is a good-sized pool, and bowling. A trip to the Carpathian Stag in Brasov for an evening of wine tasting in the wine cellars, dinner and a folklore show is recommended. An excursion to nearby Bran Castle (Count Dracula's home) is also popular.

You may be offered holidays in **Sinaia** – a small town on the busy road from Bucharest to Brasov. When we visited it some years ago we were impressed by the modest intermediate slopes, on largely treeless hills next to the town. The town seemed to us a rather depressing place, and reporters since have been shocked and saddened by the evident poverty. But a new 4-star Holiday Inn hotel and new chalets may help to attract your much-needed cash.

Slovenia

WHAT IT COSTS

(2)

- ⊕ Good value for money
- ⊕ Beautiful scenery
- ⊕ Good beginners' slopes and tuition
- ⊕ Good off-slope diversions and excursions

- ⊖ Limited, easy slopes on the whole
- ⊖ Mainly antiquated lifts
- ⊖ Uninspiring food

Slovenia offers good value for money 'on the sunny side of the Alps'. A handful of UK tour operators run packages to some of the better-known resorts. An alternative would be to arrange an independent trip to the mountains combined with a break in the vibrant city of Ljubljana.

Kranjska Gora and Bohinj are the best-known resorts, popular with economy-minded British and Dutch visitors, and with visitors from neighbouring Italy and Austria, giving quite a cosmopolitan feel to the resorts.

Slovenia is a small country bordering Italy to the west and Austria to the north. It was the first state to break away from former Yugoslavia and has managed to escape the turmoil that engulfed the Balkans. The economy is improving steadily, and there is a positive feel to the resorts – along with a warm and hospitable welcome.

The main resorts are within two and a half hours' bus-ride of the capital, Ljubljana.

The ski areas are generally small, with fairly antiquated lifts but few queues. The mountain restaurants are mainly unappealing, while the ski schools are of a high standard and cheap, with good English encountered by our most recent reporter. Hotel star ratings tend to be a trifle generous, but high standards of service and hygiene are observed. Snow reliability is not particularly good, but some resorts have artificial cover.

Kranjska Gora (810m), a few kilometres from the Austrian and Italian borders, is the best-known resort on the British market. The pretty village is dominated by the majestic Julian Alps. The Lek, Kompass and Larix hotels – with pools – are the best placed for slope-side convenience.

There are 30km of mainly intermediate slopes, rising up to 1623m. The only challenging slopes are a couple of short, demanding runs in the Podkiron area and the World Cup slalom run. For those wanting a change of slopes, trips to Arnoldstein in Austria are available. Snow reliability is not good, despite artificial backup and a northerly exposure. The lift system is rather antiquated (most of the 23 lifts are T-bars), but at least queues are rare. Mountain restaurants are poor and most people choose to lunch in the village. There are 40km of cross-country trails. There is a good selection of bars and discos for Austrian-style après-ski.

Vogel (1540m), in the beautiful **Bohinj** basin, has the best slopes and conditions in the area. The 36km of slopes are reached by a cable-car up from the valley. There's a collection of small hotels and restaurants at the base. Pistes of varying standards run from the high point at 1800m back into a central bowl with a small beginner area. When conditions permit, there is a long run to the bottom cable-car station. For a change of scene, **Kobla**, with 23km of wooded runs, is a short bus-ride away.

Bled, with its beautiful lake and fairly lively nightlife, is an attractive base. Its local slopes are very limited indeed, but there are free buses to Vogel (about 20km) and Kobla (slightly nearer). The Grand Hotel Toplice and the Park are among the best lakeside hotels.

Kanin (2200m), near the village of **Bovec**, 17km from Italy, offers the only high Alpine skiing – 15km of pistes between 980m and 2300m.

Slovenia's second city, **Maribor** (325m), in the north-east, is 6km from its local slopes – the biggest ski area in the country, with 64km of runs and 20 lifts. Accommodation is cheap and there are several atmospheric old inns serving good, Hungarian-influenced food.

Turkey

WHAT IT COSTS

4

- ⊕ Exotic curiosity value
- ⊕ Cultural interest
- ⊕ Very friendly, welcoming people
- ⊕ Turkish baths after skiing
- ⊕ Short transfer (to Palandöken)

- ⊖ Small ski areas
- ⊖ Not as cheap as other fringe destinations

Holidaymakers who have enjoyed the Turkish summer – for its warm welcome and low prices, seasoned with history and haggling to taste – may be tempted to repeat the experience in winter. Of Turkey's 13 ski areas, which are widely spread around the vast country, only two have attracted outside attention.

The most developed of them is Uludag, a fashionable weekend escape from Istanbul above the old city of Bursa, with a small ski area on the upper slopes of Turkey's Mount Olympus, also known as Zirve. More than a thousand kilometres further east, the Anatolian city of Erzurum's local ski area of Palandöken has higher, bigger and better slopes and an airport less than half an hour from them. Recent investment in new lifts and hotels has attracted the interest of the package holiday industry, and the first direct charter flights from Europe are scheduled to arrive for the winter of 2001/02. This will transform the accessibility of a previously ultra-remote destination, and give a boost to Erzurum's down at heel economy. That's the plan, anyway.

Will Palandöken catch on? You could wait and see, and allow time for the inevitable rough edges to smooth; or take the pioneering view that rough edges are part of the fun, and seize the opportunity before Erzurum grows tourist-hardened and cynical. The slopes are good and – as is usually the case in Turkey, but in Alpine ski resorts often isn't – the locals are super-keen to make visitors feel welcome. But this is a Moslem country, so don't expect to find the cheap alcohol that is such an important ingredient of the success of Bulgaria, Romania and Andorra. Perhaps the best comparison is not with eastern Europe, but with that lofty outpost in southern Spain, Sierra Nevada, which offers a similar combination of worthwhile skiing and nearby sightseeing interest in Granada.

Erzurum is a famously cold and windy outpost in winter, and claims an absolute snow guarantee for the treeless slopes of nearby **Palandöken**. These give around 1000 vertical metres of varied skiing from a top lift station (3125m) that overlooks the city and include the longest run in Turkey at about 12km. But on the evidence of last winter, when the first serious snow arrived in late February, Anatolia may not be immune from the effects of global warming.

The ski area is not new, but has been transformed by new lifts and two big hotels. The smart and well-equipped, if somewhat anonymous, 5-star Polat Renaissance is at the foot of the slopes, and has an excellent pool, Turkish spa and all you need for a business conference. The less luxurious 4-star Dedeman has a small pool and sauna at the heart of the ski area (2450m), where the altitude is quite noticeable. These hotels are self contained mini-resorts, each with ski rental and in-house child care. The Dedeman's après ski cafe and night club are popular with the Russian visitors who have made up the bulk of Palandöken's foreign custom until now.

INGHAMS

The Dedeman hotel is in the middle of Palandöken's slopes at 2450m ↓

The seven lifts include a gondola and three new chair lifts, a single-seater chair and a couple of nursery drags outside the Dedeman hotel. Most of the 17 pistes are easy, or would be, if well groomed. Piste marking and mapping are a bit sketchy too. The run down to the Polat is a snow-covered road, but the higher slopes offer steeper terrain: black 18 beneath the top chair-lift is an excellent slope of sustained pitch and the off-piste is quite steep enough to pose an avalanche risk. The Dedeman cafe is convenient for lunch, and the new Café Ejder at the summit has an open fire and overhead electric heaters – much needed on a windy day.

On the not too distant frontier with Armenia and Iran, Mount Ararat (over 5000m) is talked of as a potential heli-ski excursion. But don't count on it.

Erzurum is the biggest city in eastern Turkey and on first impression (shoddy tower blocks on the ring road) may seem less than enchanting. But the centre is rich in historic interest. It is a good place to shop for rugs, so long as you enlist local help and have a few hours to spare for the haggling. The other speciality is jet-black local stone used for bracelets, worry beads and other jewellery. A traditional lie-down lunch or supper at the Erzurum Houses restaurant is not to be missed.

Uludag is 250km from Istanbul and 32km, by long hairpin climb, from Bursa. It is easily – indeed inevitably – combined with a visit to Istanbul and makes an attractive twin-centre proposition for Easter, when the Alpine resorts are overcrowded and Turkish skiers are enjoying sizzling kebab lunches out of doors. Most of its 13 lifts are short drags and chairs serving unremarkable if pleasant intermediate and easy skiing; the vertical range is modest – 1800m to 2250m. The resort is a cluster of modern hotels at the tree line, with several swimming pools between them, at least one ice rink and a backless squash court. Most people eat and spend the evening in their hotels, where the atmosphere is cheerful at weekends, otherwise quiet.

Bursa was the home of the Ottoman dynasty and is well worth a visit, with fine mosques, a splendid public hammam (Turkish bath), and good shopping. Access, if not by car, is by bus from Istanbul, or bus and ferry across the Sea of Marmara.

Norway

WHAT IT COSTS

4

- ⊕ Probably the best terrain and facilities in Europe for serious cross-country skiing
- ⊕ The home of telemark – plenty of opportunities to learn and practise
- ⊕ Complete freedom from the glitziness often associated with downhill resorts, and from the ill-mannered lift queues of the Alps
- ⊕ Quiet atmosphere that suits families and older people
- ⊕ Impressive snowboard parks
- ⊕ Usually reliable snow conditions throughout a long season

- ⊖ Very limited downhill areas – small, and mostly with few challenges
- ⊖ Mountain restaurants are little more than pit stops
- ⊖ Prohibitively high prices (because of high taxes) for alcoholic drinks
- ⊖ Unremarkable scenery – even 'Alpine' Hemsedal resembles the Pennines more than the Alps
- ⊖ Après-ski is either deadly dull or irritatingly rowdy
- ⊖ Short daylight hours in midwinter
- ⊖ Highly changeable weather
- ⊖ Limited off-slope activities

Norway and its resorts are very different from the Alps, or indeed the Rockies. Some people find the place very much to their taste. For cross-country there is nowhere like it; and for downhillers who dislike the usual resort trappings, and prefer a simpler approach to winter holidays, it could be just the place. For families with young children, in particular, the drawbacks are less pronounced than for others; you'll have no trouble finding junk food for the kids to eat – the mountain restaurants serve little else.

Speaking for ourselves, any one of the first three ⊖ points we've listed above would probably be enough to put us off; when these are combined in a single destination – and when you add in the other negative points – you can count us out.

From the 1960s to the 1980s, Norway's popularity with British skiers declined steadily, until the country was attracting only 1,500 or so – about one-tenth of the peak number. So in 1988 the tourist agencies launched an initiative to reverse the trend. Aided by the Alpine snow shortages at the turn of the decade and the award of the 1994 Olympic Winter Games to Lillehammer, the campaign has been a success. Bookings from the UK have grown appreciably.

There is a traditional friendship between Norway and Britain, and we think of Norwegians as welcoming people, well disposed towards British visitors. We have to say that our visits have left us underwhelmed by the warmth of welcome. But at least English is widely spoken – universally spoken, in our experience.

For the Norwegians and Swedes, skiing is a weekend rather than a special holiday activity, and not an occasion for extravagance. So at lunchtime they tend to haul sandwiches out of their backpacks, and in the evening they cook in their apartments. Don't expect a wide choice of restaurants.

The Norwegians have a problem with alcohol. Walk into an après-ski bar at 5pm on a Saturday and you may find young men already inebriated – and by that we mean not merry but incoherent. And this is despite – or, some say, because of – prohibitively high taxes on booze. Restaurant prices for wine are ludicrous, and on our last visit we were unable to check out shop prices because the resort (Hemsedal) had no state-controlled liquor store. Our one attempt at self-catering (well, OK, our one takeaway meal) was an unusually sober affair as a result. Crystal, cutely, offers free wine with dinner in some of its hotels.

Other prices are generally not high by Alpine standards, and those for ski equipment rental and ski school are relatively low.

Cross-country skiing comes as naturally to Norwegians as walking;

and even if you're not that keen, the fact that cross-country is normal, and not a wimp's alternative to 'real' skiing, gives Norway a special appeal. Here, cross-country is both a way of getting about the valleys and a way of exploring the hills. Although you can plod around short valley circuits as you might in an Alpine resort, what distinguishes Norway for the keen cross-country skier is the network of long trails across the gentle uplands, with refuges along the way where backpackers can pause for refreshment or stay overnight. This network of mountain huts offers basic but cheap accommodation which can turn touring into a week-long adventure away from the crowds. Several tour operators now offer ski-touring packages, or they can be arranged on the spot.

More and more Norwegians are taking to telemarking (a bit like cross-country, with a free-heel binding, but with broader skis) for both downhill and backcountry skiing trips.

Snowboarding is very popular, particularly with local youths who swarm on to the slopes and impressive fun-parks at weekends.

For downhill skiing, the country isn't nearly so attractive. Despite the fact that it is able to hold downhill races, and despite the successes of its Alpine racers during the 1990s, Norway's Alpine areas are of limited appeal.

The most rewarding resort for downhillers is Hemsedal, which we cover in detail in the next chapter.

The site of the 1994 Olympics, the little lakeside town of **Lillehammer** (200m), is not actually a downhill resort at all. There is plenty of cross-country terrain around, but the nearest downhill runs are 15km north at Hafjell (230m). This is a worthwhile little area, with a vertical of 830m, 11 lifts, and pistes totalling 25km with a longest run of 4.5km. The Olympic slalom events were held here; but the planned women's downhill and super-G races were moved elsewhere after the racers judged the course too easy. They went to Kvitfjell, about 35km further north, developed specially for the men's downhill and super-G. It's steeper but a bit smaller – 23km of pistes.

Norway's other internationally known resort is **Geilo** (800m) – a small, quiet, unspoilt community on the railway line that links Bergen, on the coast, to Oslo. It provides all the basics of a resort – a handful of cafes and shops clustered around the railway station, 10 hotels more widely spread around the wide valley, children's facilities and a sports centre.

Geilo is a superb cross-country resort. As the Bergen–Oslo railway runs through the town it is possible to go for long tours and then catch the train back at the end of the day.

But Geilo is very limited for downhillers. The 28km of piste are spread over two small hills – one, Vestlia, a bus-ride away from Geilo, with a good, informal hotel and restaurant at its foot – offering a maximum vertical of 380m and a longest run of 2km. None of the runs is really difficult.

Clearly the best hotel, and one of the attractions of staying in Geilo, is the Dr Holms Hotel – smartly white-painted outside, beautifully furnished and spacious inside. This is the centre for après-ski, but prices are steep. All the other hotels we have seen can be safely recommended. The resort is quiet at the end of the day, but the main hotels often provide live entertainment.

A long way north of the other resorts is **Oppdal** (550m), with more downhill runs than any of its rivals (58km). The total vertical is 790m, but this is misleading as most of the runs are short.

There are almost equally extensive slopes at **Trysil** (460m), off to the east on the border with Sweden, and the runs are longer (up to 4km and 685m vertical). The runs here are all around the conical Trysilfjellet, some way from Trysil itself – though there is some accommodation at the hill.

In complete contrast to all of these resorts is **Voss** (50m), a sizeable lakeside town quite close to Bergen and the sea. A cable-car links the town to the slopes on Hangur and Slettafjell, with a total of 40km of pistes. Snow reliability can be poor. There are plenty of excursion possibilities, in particular the spectacular Flåm railway, which plunges down the side of a mountain to fjord (sea) level. From there you can take a boat trip to link up with a bus back to Voss. Nearby Bergen is a pleasant city that is worth a visit.

Hemsedal 650m

Norway's best Alpine resort

WHAT IT COSTS

HOW IT RATES

The slopes

Snow	****
Extent	*
Experts	**
Intermediates	****
Beginners	***
Convenience	**
Queues	****
Restaurants	*

The rest

Scenery	**
Resort charm	**
Off-slope	*

What's new

2000/01 saw 50 new ski-in/ski-out apartments at the mountain base. The children's area and nursery slope have been extended and two new baby lifts have been added. The snowmaking network is being extended for next season. And more ski-in/ski-out accommodation is being built. New facilities will include a new restaurant/bar, nightclub and bowling alley.

SNOWPIX.COM / CHRIS GILL

The mountains hereabouts are more craggy than in most Norwegian resorts →

- ⊕ Impressive snow reliability because of northerly location
- ⊕ Increasing amounts of convenient slope-side accommodation
- ⊕ Extensive cross-country trails compared to the Alps
- ⊕ Some quite challenging slopes, and mountains with a slightly Alpine feel

- ⊖ Not much of a village
- ⊖ Infrequent shuttle-bus service to the slopes
- ⊖ Limited slopes for high-mileage piste-bashers
- ⊖ Exposed upper mountain prone to closure because of bad weather
- ⊖ Weekend queues
- ⊖ Poor mountain restaurants
- ⊖ No liquor store for miles
- ⊖ Après-ski limited during the week and rowdy at weekends

Hemsedal's craggy terrain, 800m vertical, proper black runs and worthwhile off-piste terrain are reminiscent of a small-but-serious Alpine resort. Most people not resident in Scandinavia would be better advised to go for the real thing, but if you like the sound of Norway, Hemsedal is the place for downhill skiing.

THE RESORT

Hemsedal is both an unspoilt valley and a village, also referred to as Trøym and Sentrum ('Centre'), which amounts to very little – a couple of hotel/ apartment buildings, a few shops, a bank and a petrol station. Though there has been talk of a lift from Trøym to the slopes, for now the lift base is a mile or two away, across the valley. There are self-catering apartments beside the slopes and in a separate cluster a walkable distance down the hill from the lifts. A ski-bus links these points, and others in the valley, but the service is inadequate; really, the place is geared to weekend visitors arriving by car or by coach.

THE MOUNTAINS

Hemsedal's slopes pack a lot of variety into a small space.

Slopes With no less than four fast chairs to play on, you can pack a lot of runs into the day. The lift pass also covers smaller Solheisen, a few miles up the valley. A small supplement is required to ski at Geilo, an hour away.

Snow reliability The combination of northerly latitude and reasonable altitude makes for impressive snow reliability. It's a good bet for a late holiday; the season runs until the first weekend in May.

Snowboarding There's a fun-park and two half-pipes.

Experts There is quite a bit to amuse experts – two or three black pistes of 450m vertical served by a fast triple chair from the base, and wide areas of gentler off-piste terrain served by drags above the tree line.

Intermediates Mileage-hungry piste-bashers will find Hemsedal's 42km of runs very limited, but others will find good variety in the blue and red runs, and the easier blacks.

MOUNTAIN FACTS

Altitude	670m-1455m
Lifts	16
Pistes	42km
Green	32%
Blue	47%
Black	21%
Art. snow	12km

Phone numbers
From abroad use the prefix +47.

TOURIST OFFICE

Postcode N-3561
t +47 320 55030
f 320 55031
hemsedal@hemsedal.net
www.hemsedal.com

Beginners There's a gentle new nursery slope for absolute beginners. And there are splendid long green runs (up to 6km), but they get a lot of traffic, some of it irresponsibly fast. Some long blues and reds also suit near-beginners.

Cross-country The steep mountainsides that make this a worthwhile Alpine resort mean that it is not classic Norwegian cross-country skiing terrain. But by Alpine standards there is still lots to do, both in the valley and at altitude, and a few miles down the valley at the Gravset cross-country centre – 90km in all.

Queues Hemsedal is Norway's premier downhill resort, and is only a three-hour drive from Oslo, the capital. Good weekend weather fills the car parks, leading to queues for the main access lifts, and possibly for others. But midweek it is quiet. The upper lifts are very exposed, and are easily closed by bad weather.

Mountain restaurants There's one functional self-service mountain restaurant doing dreary fast food, plus two or three kiosks with benches.

Schools and guides Our most recent reporter on the ski school was not particularly impressed, except by the spoken English.

Facilities for children The facilities at the lift base are good, with day care for children over three months. The kids' nursery slope is admirably gentle but not particularly convenient.

STAYING THERE

How to go Most of the accommodation is in apartments, varying widely in convenience. Catered chalets are available through certain UK operators.

Hotels The best hotel is the Skogstad (320 60333) in central Hemsedal – comfortable, but noisy at weekends. Other hotels along the valley are used by UK tour operators.

Self-catering The Alpin apartments, (320 55700) a walk from the lift base, are satisfactory, provided you don't fill all the beds. The adjacent Tinden (320 55700) ones are quite smart.

Eating out There are half-a-dozen restaurants in the village.

Après-ski It's minimal in the early and middle parts of the week, rowdy at weekends and holidays.

Off the slopes There are some diversions, including sleighs drawn by horses or dogs. The pool at the hotel Skogstad is open to the public.

Sweden

WHAT IT COSTS

4

- ⊕ Snowsure from December to May
- ⊕ Unspoilt, beautiful landscape
- ⊕ Uncrowded pistes and lifts
- ⊕ Vibrant (but regimented) après-ski
- ⊕ Good range of non-skiing activities

- ⊖ Limited challenging downhill terrain
- ⊖ Small areas by Alpine standards
- ⊖ Lacks the dramatic peaks and vista of the Alps
- ⊖ Short days during the early season

Sweden's landscape of forests and lakes and miles of unspoiled wilderness is entirely different from the Alps' grandeur and traffic-choked roads. Standards of accommodation, food and service are good and the people welcoming, lively and friendly. There are plenty of off-slope activities, but most of its downhill areas are limited in size and challenge. Sweden is likely to appeal most to those who want an all-round winter holiday in a different environment and culture. Don't be put off by the myths that Sweden is expensive, dark and cold – see below.

Holidaying in Sweden is a completely different experience, culturally as well as physically, from a holiday in the Alps. The language is generally incomprehensible to us and, although virtually everyone speaks good English, the menus and signs are often written only in Swedish. The food is delightful, especially if you like fish and venison.

One of the myths about Sweden is that it is expensive. Sweden is significantly cheaper than neighbouring Norway, especially for alcohol, and prices are pretty much on a par with the main Alpine countries.

Another myth is that it is dark. It is true that the days are very short in December and early January. But from early February the lifts generally work from 9am to 4.30 and by March it is light until 8.30. And most resorts have floodlit pistes for night skiing.

On the down side, downhill slopes are generally limited in both challenge and extent and the lift systems tend to be dominated by T-bars. But there is lots of cross-country and backcountry skiing. Snowboarding is also popular, with parks and pipes in most resorts.

Après-ski is taken very seriously – with live bands from mid- to late-afternoon. But it all stops suddenly, dinner is served and then the nightlife starts and the bands are back. There is plenty to do off the slopes: snowmobile safaris, ice fishing, ice climbing, dog-sled rides, and saunas galore. You can visit a local Sami (the politically correct name for Lapp) village. And resorts are very family-friendly.

The main resort is Åre (see separate chapter). **Sälen** is Scandinavia's largest winter sports area – and is made up of four separate sets of slopes totalling 144km of piste. Most slopes are very gentle, suiting beginners and early or timid intermediates best, though there are 31 black runs listed, including the locally notorious 'Wall' in Hundfjället. Lindvalen and Högfjallet are vaguely linked by a lift and a long cross-country slog. But you need the unreliable bus service to the others.

Vemdalen has two separate areas of slopes 18km apart by road. **Björnrike** is great for families, beginners and early intermediates, with eight lifts and 15km of mainly gentle pistes. The Country Club hotel is right on the slopes and built in modern Scandinavian style. **Vemdalsskalet** has more advanced intermediate terrain, which is served by 10 lifts and 13km of pistes. The Högfjällshotell at the base is large, dates from 1936 and prides itself on its lively après-ski.

Riksgränsen, 250km north of the Arctic Circle, is an area of jagged mountain peaks and narrow fjords. The season starts in mid-February and ends in June – when you can be on the slopes under the midnight sun. There are only six lifts and 21km of piste. But there is some good off-piste and midnight heli-skiing.

Björkliden, also above the Arctic Circle, is famous for its subterranean skiing inside Scandinavia's largest cave system. You need to go with a guide.

Ramundberget is a good, small, quiet family resort with ski-in, ski-out accommodation. It gets large amounts of snow and its 22km of pistes are mainly easy or intermediate cruising runs. There is a special children's area with its own lift.

Åre 380m

Sweden's best slopes strung out along a frozen lake

WHAT IT COSTS

HOW IT RATES

The slopes

Snow	***
Extent	**
Experts	**
Intermediates	****
Beginners	****
Convenience	***
Queues	****
Restaurants	***

The rest

Scenery	***
Resort charm	***
Off-slope	***

What's new

For 2001/02 there will be two new red and two new blue slopes (all with snowmaking) in the central area above the town.

There are plans for two new high-speed six-seater chair-lifts to replace T-bars and open up some easy off-piste for the following season.

For 2000/01, a new 1.4km boarder- and skier-cross course was built.

- ✚ Cute little town centre
- ✚ Good snow reliability
- ✚ Ideal intermediate and beginner runs
- ✚ Extensive cross-country trails
- ✚ Excellent children's facilities
- ✚ Lively après-ski scene
- ✚ Lots of off-slope diversions

- ▬ Lots of T-bars
- ▬ Exposed upper mountain prone to closure because of bad weather
- ▬ High winds detrimental to snow conditions
- ▬ Few expert challenges
- ▬ High season queues

Åre has the biggest area of linked slopes in Sweden and some of its most challenging terrain. But it suits beginners, intermediates and families best. It has a dinky little town centre and a long area of slopes set along a frozen lake.

THE RESORT

Åre is a small town made up of old, pretty, coloured wooden buildings and some larger, modern additions. When we were there the main square had a roaring open fire to warm up by. As well as accommodation in town, there is lots spread out along the valley, with a concentration in the Duved area. All the slopes and accommodation are set on the shore of a huge, long lake, frozen in the winter months.

THE MOUNTAINS

The terrain is mainly green and blue tree-lined slopes, with a couple of wind-swept bowls above the trees.

Slopes There are two main areas. The largest is accessed by a funicular from the centre of town or a chair or cable-car a short climb above it. This takes you to the hub of a network of runs and T-bars that stretches for 10km from end to end. The cable-car is often shut because it goes to the top of the above-the-tree-line slopes (known as the 'high zone'), which often suffers from howling gales. A gondola also accesses the high zone from a different point. You can get back on-piste right into the town square. A separate area of slopes is above Duved, the other main bed base, now served by a high-speed chair. There are four floodlit slopes, each open on a different night.

Snow reliability Snow reliability is good from November to May. More of a problem is the wind, which can blow fresh snow away. It also means that artificial snow is often deliberately made wet so that it doesn't blow away – it then compacts to a hard, icy surface (and certainly had when we tried the Olympia night skiing area – the top part was sheet ice).

Experts Experts will find Åre's slopes limited, especially if the 'high zone' is closed. If it is open, there is a lot of off-piste available, including an 8km run over the back accessed by a snowcat service in high season. On the main lower area the steepest (and iciest when we were there) pistes are in the Olympia area. There are also

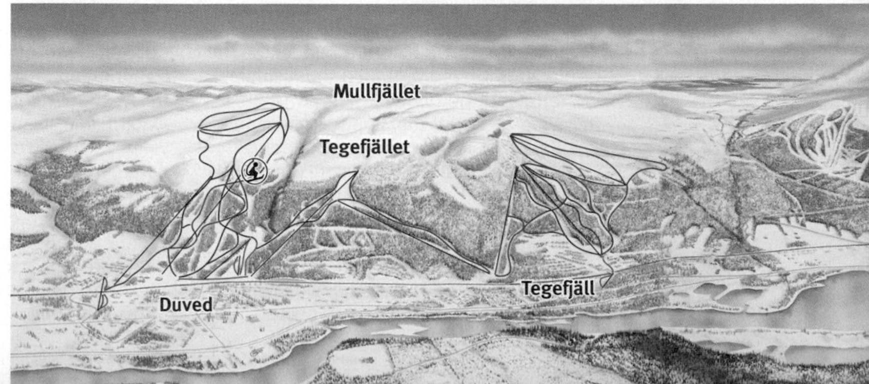

Most of Åre's runs are easy and intermediate and cut through the trees with great views of the frozen lake →

ÅRE RESORT / OLSSON

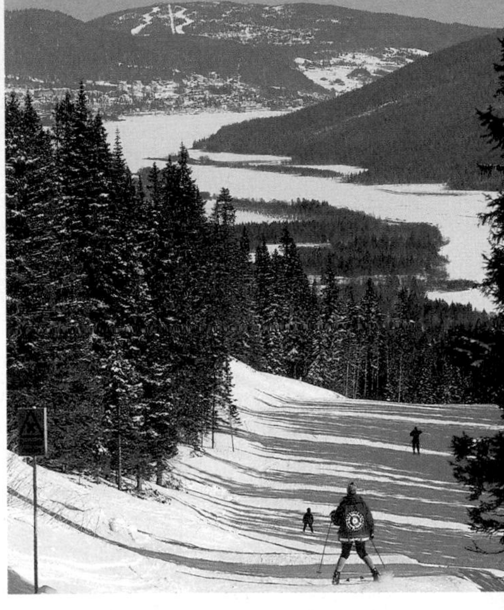

MOUNTAIN FACTS

Altitude	380m-1275m
Lifts	44
Pistes	93km
Green	11%
Blue	43%
Red	36%
Black	5%
Unpatrolled	5%
Recco detectors used	

steep black and red runs back to town.

Intermediates The slopes are ideal for most intermediates with pretty blue runs through the trees. Because they tend to be more sheltered, the blue runs also often have the best snow. You can get a real sense of travelling on the main area – from hill to hill and valley to valley.

Beginners There are good facilities for beginners, both on the main area and at Duved.

Cross-country The area has an amazing 300km of cross-country trails, both on prepared tracks and unprepared trails marked with red crosses. Some trails are floodlit in the evening.

Queues In high season there can be queues for some lifts, especially in the central area immediately above Åre.

Mountain restaurants There are some good mountain restaurants. Our favourite was the rustic Buustamons, tucked away in the woods near Rödkulleomradret.

Schools and guides The ski school has a very good reputation – and this, the easy terrain and excellent childcare facilities make it a good area for families and children.

Facilities for children There are special children's areas and under 11-year-olds get free lift passes if wearing helmets. There's a kindergarten that takes children from the age of two.

STAYING THERE

There are plenty of cabins and apartments as well as some hotels.

How to go A couple of the major UK tour operators offer packages to Åre.

Hotels The main central hotels are the delightful old Åregarden and the simpler Diplomat Ski Lodge. The big Sunwing is right on the slopes, but a bit out of town. The Renen in Duved is very popular with families.

Self-catering There is plenty of choice.

Eating out Our favourite restaurant was Sames, with excellent Swedish food. There are plenty of alternatives.

Après-ski Après-ski is amazingly lively – the Sunwing on the slopes and the Diplomat in town are packed from 3pm onwards (both have live bands). Later on, the Diplomat, the Country Club and Bygget all have live bands and there are plenty of bars for a quiet drink.

Off the slopes Lots to do including dog- and reindeer-sled rides, skating, ice fishing, tobogganing, ice driving, ice climbing and snowmobiling.

Central reservations phone number
For all resort accommodation call 17700.
From elsewhere in Sweden add the prefix 0647.
From abroad use the prefix +46 647 .

TOURIST OFFICE

Postcode 830 13
t +46 (647) 17720
f 17712
info@areresort.se
www.areresort.se

Åreskutan 1275m
Tväråvalvet
Lillskutan
Ullådalen
Sadeln
Förberget 725m
Tötthummeln 825m
Rödkullen
Åre Björnen
Åre
Åresjön 370m

Scotland

- ➕ The resorts are easy to get to from northern Britain
- ➕ It is possible to experience perfect snow and stirring skiing
- ➕ Decent, cheap accommodation and good-value packages are on offer
- ➕ Mid-week it's rarely crowded
- ➕ There are extensive ski-touring and ski-mountaineering possibilities
- ➕ Few travel hassles
- ➕ Lots to do off the slopes

- ➖ Weather is extremely changeable and sometimes vicious
- ➖ Snowfall is erratic
- ➖ Slopes are limited; runs tend to be short
- ➖ Queueing can be a problem – though usually only at peak times and if some lifts are closed
- ➖ Little ski village ambience and few memorable mountain restaurants

Scotland is different. If you want reliable snow, perfect pistes, blue skies, sunshine and charming mountain restaurants, forget it. Conditions in Scotland are unpredictable, to say the least. If you are willing to take a chance, or if you live nearby and can go at short notice when things look good, fine. But don't look on it as a replacement for your usual week in the Alps. If you try it, you'll either love it or hate it; but at least you'll know. And you'll have something to talk about in the pub.

What's new

The long-awaited funicular railway at Cairngorm will be ready for 2001/02. The new Ptarmigan restaurant will also open for the coming season.

Nevis Range's snowboarding facilities are being further extended for next season.

A new three-person chair-lift was installed last season at The Lecht, and there's a new snow-tubing run.

Scotland's five ski areas are surprisingly different from one another, although they do share some characteristics. Snow conditions and the weather can vary dramatically – especially from west to east; up-to-date and accurate information on conditions and the latest weather forecast are particularly important for those contemplating a trip at short notice. Conditions can be testing. Rain, gales, icy slopes, slush, fog, rocks and heather are not unheard of, but those who ski regularly in Scotland tend to finish up as strong, versatile skiers. Some of the resorts have artificial snowmaking and this is being increased in places.

For novices who are really keen to learn – and who are prepared for the possibility of less than ideal conditions – Scotland could make sense, especially if you live nearby. One option is to book instruction via one of the excellent outdoor centres, many of which also provide accommodation and a wide range of other activities. Otherwise, the tuition at the resorts themselves, with BASI and BSA qualified instructors, is also very good.

For intermediates, a tour by car that takes in the five main areas is an amusing way to spend a week if you are lucky with the weather. Most of the slopes in most of the areas fall somewhere around the intermediate level. But all areas, apart from the Lecht, offer the occasional piece of tough or very tough skiing. Much of the terrain is suitable for ski touring and ski mountaineering; Cairngorm especially is something of a centre of expertise for mountain activities.

Snowboarding is popular in Scotland and most of the resorts have some special snowboard-friendly features, but conditions are not always conducive to maintaining these fun-parks and half-pipes in good nick. Fortunately, the natural terrain is very good for free-riding when the conditions are right.

Apart from weather, Scotland's style, ambience and attitude is not to everyone's taste. All these elements are better than they were – the relatively new Nevis Range area has probably had a lot to do with that – but Aviemore is still ugly, Fort William is hard to like, and cosy, charming cafe-bars and restaurants are still too few in number. Licensed restaurants have appeared at the slopes in the last few years, bringing not just alcohol but also much better catering. The limited facilities at the base areas (none has accommodation) mean that après-ski there is poor. By 5pm almost everybody has gone. There is nightlife, of course – there are reasonable pubs

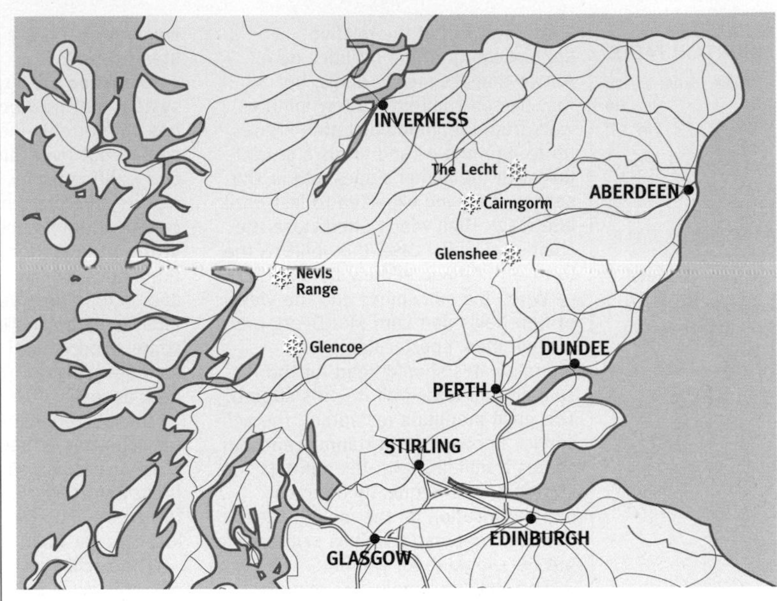

CAIRNGORM MOUNTAIN FACTS

Altitude	550m-1100m
Lifts	16
Pistes	37 km
Green	16%
Blue	32%
Red	47%
Black	5%
Artificial snow	none

Cairngorm Chairlift Company

Postcode PH22 1RB
t +44 (1479) 861261
f 861207
mail@cairngormmountain.com
www.cairngormmountain.com

NEVIS RANGE MOUNTAIN FACTS

Altitude	655m-1220m
Lifts	12
Pistes	35 km
Green	20%
Blue	34%
Red	31%
Black	15%
Artificial snow	none

Tourist Office

Postcode PH33 6SW
t +44 (1397) 705825
f 705854
nevisrange@sol.co.uk
www.nevis-range.co.uk

and bars – but it's like Scotland, not Switzerland.

Cairngorm is the best-known resort in Scotland. Aviemore is the main centre (with a regular shuttle-bus link to the slopes) but a significant amount of Cairngorm business also comes in from other villages in the Spey valley.

The slopes, which lie between 550m and 1100m, are accessed from car parks about a mile apart at the base of two corries – Coire Cas (the main area) and Coire na Ciste (a narrow gulley with the toughest skiing in it). The two sectors come together at the Ptarmigan beginners' area just below the summit of Cairn Gorm. A new funicular from the main car park (655m) up to Ptarmigan at 1100m will replace the Car Park and White Lady chair-lifts for 2001/02, and will mean a warm, swift ride (taking less than five minutes) to the top on bad-weather days, when high winds might well have caused the chair-lifts to close. A series of chair-lifts and drags take you to the top from the Ciste base.

There are mountain restaurants at each of the base areas, at the Shieling (midway up Coire Cas) and at Ptarmigan, at the very top.

There's a fun-park for boarders, the condition of which is heavily dependent on the snow conditions. Free guided tours of the mountain start from the Day Lodge twice daily.

There's no accommodation at the ski area. The Stakis Coylumbridge, the nearest hotel, offers good-value packages. And there are many more attractive options in and around Aviemore. Chalets, cottages, houses and caravans (and even the occasional castle) are available to rent on a self-catering basis – the Highlands of Scotland tourist board provides a comprehensive list. For the après-ski late in the evening, the Anglers, Chevvy's, the Winking Owl and Crofter's Show Bar are the most popular nightspots. A recent reporter recommends the restaurant at the Cairngorm Hotel.

Nevis Range is the highest and newest Scottish resort – it opened in 1989. It occupies the north-facing slopes of Aonach Mor (Gaelic for Great Ridge) – Britain's eighth highest peak, at 1220m – and is in close proximity to the Ben itself. In the mid-1990s the resort invested in three new lifts – two chairs and a T-bar, which have opened up the north-east-facing corries in the Coire Dubh area and doubled the amount of available slopes to 35km. The additional area holds its snow well because of its orientation. The new beginners' area higher up the mountain has more reliable snow than the original, low nursery slopes. There are a couple of fun-parks and snowboard features on the main face of the mountain.

You get up to the slopes by means of a long six-seater gondola, which is something of a novelty in Scotland and

GLENSHEE MOUNTAIN FACTS

Altitude	610m-1070m
Lifts	26
Pistes	40 km
Green	26%
Blue	34%
Red	34%
Black	6%
Artificial snow	6 guns

Glenshee Ski Area

Postcode AB35 5XU
t +44 (1339) 741320
f 741665
info@ski-glenshee.co.uk
www.ski-glenshee.co.uk

GLENCOE MOUNTAIN FACTS

Altitude	305m-1110m
Lifts	7
Pistes	20 km
Green	18%
Blue	35%
Red	35%
Black	12%
Artificial snow	none

Glencoe Ski Centre

Postcode PA39 4HZ
t +44 (1855) 851226
f 851233
info@ski-glencoe.co.uk
www.ski-glencoe.co.uk

THE LECHT MOUNTAIN FACTS

Altitude	610m-825m
Lifts	14
Pistes	20 km
Green	33%
Blue	33%
Red	30%
Black	4%
Artificial snow	6 guns

The Lecht Ski Area

Postcode AB36 8YP
t +44 (1975) 651440
f 651426
info@lecht.co.uk
www.lecht.co.uk

a fair indicator of the relative sophistication of the facilities here. Above that it's mostly drags, but a four-person chair-lift – a few minutes' walk from the gondola station – goes up to 900 metres and forms a crucial link with the higher slopes late in the season (they are expected to last until late May). High winds often close the chair – in which case, the uplift to the top can be made entirely by drag-lifts.

When the sun shines and the views of Ben Nevis and Carn Mor Dearg are at their most spectacular, intermediates should head for the summit and take it all in – it's superb. The main mountain restaurant, the self-service Snowgoose Restaurant and Bar, shares a building with the gondola top station and is frequently the most popular location on the mountain. Gondola trippers as well as skiers hang out here looking for warmth.

Fort William is only a 15-minute drive from the slopes. The town provides everything that the visitor needs; some hotels arrange transport to the slopes. There are many B&Bs and hotels in and around Fort William that offer accommodation – the Milton hotel has great leisure facilities. Self-catering units are plentiful. The Nevisport bar and Chekka's are popular nightspots. The Grog & Gruel is known for good-value pub fare, and the Crannog is recommended for top quality seafood.

Glencoe's slopes lie between 305m and 1110m, on the Meall a' Bhuiridh mountain at the edge of Rannoch Moor and just east of Glen Coe – a moody and magnificent setting if ever there was one. The base area is a car park and a few buildings housing the Log Cabin restaurant, ticket office and a museum. The double Access chair-lift rises to the Plateau tow, which opens up the main nursery area and provides access to the other tows (and one chair) and the bulk of the slopes, including the Fly Paper black run – Scotland's steepest piste. The only on-mountain cafe, the Plateau, is up here. The upper slopes enjoy good snow-cover, often for a season that lasts from December to May.

The area is popular with snowboarders thanks to some good natural terrain full of bumps, jumps and gulleys that make up for the lack of a fun-park.

The only hotel nearby is the isolated Kings House Hotel, a mile away. It also has a bunkhouse and an area for tents.

Glenshee has expanded into a system that now boasts 26 lifts and has comfortably the biggest area – spread out over three minor valleys – and uplift capacity of the Scottish resorts. There are two big on-slope cafe-restaurants and another big cafe at the base station car park. Most of the slopes, which lie between 610m and 1070m, are suitable for intermediates and beginners. There's some good natural snowboard terrain for free-riding and a reasonable fun-park as well.

Glenshee remains primarily a venue for day-trippers because of the lack of a major accommodation centre, though there are hotels, hostels and B&Bs in the area – lists can be provided by the local tourist board.

The Lecht is largely a beginners' area, 32 miles from Aviemore. The slopes are on the gentle east-facing side of a high pass with a series of parallel lifts and runs just above the car parks. The main area includes five beginner tows and five longer button-lifts, each with a run or two back down towards the road – and there is one button lift on the opposite side of the road. The new Snowy Owl triple chair runs up through the centre of the slopes from the main base area. With a maximum vertical of only around 200m, runs are short. There is a floodlit dry ski slope on the mountainside which ensures some evening skiing and a bit of summer business. There's also a fun-park with a half-pipe for snowboarders (with its own tow lift), and a new tubing area. Refreshments are supplied by the Day Lodge at the base station, and a snack bar.

The nearest place to stay, Tomintoul, is six miles away from the slopes. It is a typical Highland village with a few hotels and B&Bs, but the nearest accommodation is at the Allargue Arms in Corgarff, three miles from the slopes.

Australia

- ➕ Offers skiing and boarding during the European summer
- ➕ In one holiday you can also take in a visit to tropical northern Australia
- ➕ Some of the resorts are year-round destinations offering sophisticated upmarket accommodation

- ➖ It's a long way from anywhere except New Zealand and south-east Asia
- ➖ Mountains are rather low, and lift/trail networks are small by Alpine standards

Even more than New Zealand, Australia offers resorts that are basically of local interest, but which might amuse people with other reasons to travel there – catching up with those long-lost relatives, say. The mountains are certainly more entertaining than most of the glacier areas that snow-starved Europeans must normally rely on in the summer. Skiing among the snow-laden gum trees is also a unique experience for northern hemisphere skiers, plus there is often the chance to see kangaroos, emus and wombats. The resorts mainly offer some accommodation close to the slopes (unlike those in New Zealand), and ski schools are sizeable and professional.

The major resorts are concentrated in the populous south-east corner of the country, between Sydney and Melbourne, with the largest in New South Wales (NSW) – in the National Park centred on Australia's highest mountain, Mt Kosciusko (2230m), about six hours' drive from Sydney. Skiing has been going on here since the early years of the century – as in the next-door state of Victoria, where there are several resorts within three or four hours' drive of Melbourne. Visitors to Tasmania may want to check out the possibilities there, too.

The season generally runs from early June to mid-October, but may be extended at either end if snow conditions allow.

Last year's big news was the construction of a commercial airport just 20 minutes' drive from Mount Hotham in Victoria. Qantas started twice-weekly flights in 2000, effectively making the resort the closest to a major city: 90 minutes from Sydney, under an hour from Melbourne. Mount Hotham doubled its terrain three years ago, putting it on a par with NSW's Thredbo.

Thredbo is a long-established and relatively upmarket alpine village in NSW. It hosted the only World Cup race event held in Australia thanks to its size and vertical of 670m.

Thredbo is rather like a small and quite smart French purpose-built resort – user-friendly, and mostly made up of modern apartments (and lodges run by clubs). But there are many more bars than you would find in the French equivalent. There is an Austrian flavour to some of the lodges and bars, due to the early influx of Europeans. It's a steep little place, with stiff climbs to get around from one part to another. Road access is easy, but the toll is high. It costs A$60 just to enter the park. Once you're there it's A$75 a day to ski, the same as its long-standing rival Perisher Blue.

The slopes, prettily wooded with gum trees, rise up across the valley from the village, served by a regular shuttle-bus through the resort. The runs are well laid out, with better connections between slopes than in many areas – and the resort as a whole gives the impression of good organisation. The dozen lifts include four fast quad chairs, and the trails include Australia's highest (2035m) and longest (6km). While the blacks are not difficult, they offer some variety, and on the higher lifts there are off-piste variants.

Since 1987 A$100 million has been poured into Thredbo by its owners. The result is an abundance of luxurious apartments, an attractive pedestrian mall with good shopping and some high-class restaurants both on and off the mountain. There is also an impressive four-year-old Australian

Institute of Sport training complex open to the public, with an Olympic-size pool, waterslide, traverse climbing wall, squash and tennis courts, gym, and basketball courts. On the hill a 700m bob-sleigh track for the public is popular all year round. You can take the Crackenback gondola to the mountain top for dinner.

On the other side of the mountain range is the **Perisher Blue** resort complex, with a pass covering 51 lifts – more than anywhere else in Australia – but a vertical of less than 400m. The main area is **Perisher/Smiggins**, where lifts and runs – practically all easy or intermediate – range over three lightly wooded sectors. The resort is reachable by road, but is also served by the Skitube, a rack railway that tunnels its way up from Bullocks Flat and goes on to the second area, **Blue Cow/Guthega**, where the slopes offer more challenges.

Perisher Blue has been doing its best to catch up with Thredbo by upgrading hotels and building more facilities, but it remains spread out and does not have the cosy village atmosphere that Thredbo fans adore. On the other hand, Perisher Blue has more ski-in ski-out accommodation. Its main advantage over Thredbo is its snow, thanks to its position further within the mountain ranges and its altitude: Perisher Blue's lifts start at about the same elevation as Thredbo's mid-station.

Many people also stay in apartments or hotels in the lakeside town of Jindabyne, a half-hour drive from both Thredbo and Perisher, or in cosy chalets along the Alpine Way, which leads to Thredbo.

From Perisher, a snowcat can take you on an 8km ride to the isolated chalets of Australia's highest resort, **Charlotte Pass** (1760m), with five lifts but only 200m vertical. People visit the Pass more for its charm than the skiing, although it is a favourite with families. The major hotel is the historic and turreted Kosciusko Chalet, a good spot for romantic weekends.

In Victoria, resorts are not as high as in NSW but many have good snow since they are set well within the ranges. The aforementioned **Mount Hotham** has a reputation for powder snow. The 11 lifts serve a complete range of runs with plenty of variety. The longest run is 2.5km and there is more consistently steep terrain here than at any other area in Australia.

Mount Hotham is unique among the Australian fields in that the village is built along the top of a ridge, with the slopes below it. The focus of the village is Mount Hotham Central, comprising apartments, shops and a choice of eateries, including several excellent restaurants catering to the rising champagne factor in the village. Mount Hotham skiers can also stay 15 minutes' drive away at Dinner Plain, a settlement of architect-designed chalets set prettily among gum trees. There are a few restaurants and bars here, and many cross-country trails.

There is also a 10-minute helicopter link from Mount Hotham to another resort nearby (and covered by the same lift pass), **Falls Creek**, that costs all of A$59. Falls Creek is the most alpine of Australia's resort, completely snow-bound in winter. Guests not arriving by chopper are taken by snowcat to their ski-in ski-out lodge. There are 18 lifts, though the area is smaller than Mount Hotham's.

The other Victorian resort of note is **Mt Buller**. This place is to Melbourne what Cape Cod is to Manhattan – a magnet for old money and a place to be seen. Drive time from Melbourne is just three hours. Big-time entrepreneurs have poured millions into infrastructure surrounding Mt Buller's isolated peak, creating a proper resort village with a luxury hotel, and even a university campus. Draped around the mountain are 25 lifts – the largest network in Victoria, including 13 chair-lifts. There's also a tubing hill, snow-shoeing, cross-country, telemarking lessons and tobogganing.

2000 brought snowcat skiing on Australia's steepest accessed mountain, **Mt McKay**, and in 2001 the mountain's true expert terrain hosted the country's first real extreme skiing contest. Snowmobiling and dog-sleigh rides are also possible.

Mt Buffalo is worth visiting mainly to stay in the historic Mt Buffalo Chalet, with its dramatic views over the craggy Victorian alps. The slopes, a short drive away, are in an alpine basin surrounded by boulders, with five lifts almost purely for beginners.

New Zealand

- ⊕ For Europeans, good for a combined holiday to the southern hemisphere and more interesting than summer skiing on glaciers
- ⊕ For Australians, conveniently close, with flights from Sydney
- ⊕ Huge areas of off-piste terrain accessible by helicopter on the South Island
- ⊕ Some spectacular views

- ⊖ It's a long way from anywhere except Australia
- ⊖ Limited mountain facilities – mountain restaurants are mostly basic pit stops
- ⊖ Generally long drives from accommodation up to the ski areas
- ⊖ Highly changeable weather
- ⊖ No trees, so skiing in bad weather is virtually impossible

The number of keen skiers and boarders from New Zealand found kicking around the Alps gives a clue that there must be some decent slopes back home – and indeed there are. The resorts are rather different from those of the Alps or the Rockies, and the networks of lifts and runs are rather limited by those exalted standards. However desperate you are for snow during the northern summer, we wouldn't advise travelling halfway round the world from Europe or the US just to get access to the likes of Coronet Peak, Mount Hutt or Whakapapa. But the heli-skiing around the Mt Cook region on the South Island is definitely worth writing home about. For Europeans already spending a lot to travel to New Zealand, the extra cost of a day or two's heli-drops is well worth while. New Zealand's ski resorts could make an interesting part of a wider-ranging visit to the country, and may be the best option you have if you're starting from somewhere nearer.

The big news is that Whakapapa and Turao have joined forces to offer a shared lift pass. A linking lift is being planned, creating arguably the most impressive network in the southern hemisphere.

There are exceptions but, broadly speaking, the system in New Zealand is that you stay in towns at fairly low altitude – usually below the snow line – and drive up each day to a base lodge where there will be a simple restaurant, equipment hire and one or two shops as well as the main lifts, but usually no accommodation.

There are resorts on both North Island and South Island. The main concentration on South Island is around the lakeside town (and year-round resort) of Queenstown, covered in detail in a separate chapter after this one. Queenstown has become known as the adrenalin capital of New Zealand – and probably the world – by offering a range of dangerous (or at least thrilling) activities, of which the best known is bungee jumping. Most of these are available in winter as well as summer.

In what follows, we describe the most prominent resorts (apart from Queenstown and its two local mountains), but there are a number of other possibilities. The main commercial ones are described briefly in our directory at the back of the book, but there are also other ski-fields run by clubs. By all means enquire about what's available on the club field front, but don't expect groomed trails or other luxuries: club fields are pretty primitive, involving stiff walks to get to the base and crude rope tows when you get there. You even have to bring your own food and drink. If you must visit any club field, Craigieburn on the South Island, near Mt Hutt, wins the vote for the most impressive terrain out of the selection.

Any of the major resorts is worth a day or two of your time if you're in the area and the conditions are right. But if your credit card is also in good condition, don't miss the heli-skiing; even if you're no expert off-piste, with powder skis it's a doddle, and tremendously satisfying. There are several companies operating on South Island, based in Queenstown, Wanaka

WHAKAPAPA MOUNTAIN FACTS

Altitude	1625m-2300m
Lifts	20
Pistes	1360 acres
Blue	25%
Red	50%
Black	25%
Art. snow	some

TOURIST OFFICE

t +64 (7) 892 3738
f 892 3732
snow@whakapapa.co.nz
www.whakapapa.co.nz

and Methven. Methven Heli Ski arguably has the most impressive terrain on offer, operating in steep and spectacular ranges surrounding New Zealand's highest peak Mt Cook. Harris Mts Heli-Ski, operating out of Queenstown and Wanaka, caters mainly for the large Japanese market, and the three-run days are generally very easy skiing with long waits in between lifts. The other major Queenstown operation, Southern Lakes Heli-Ski, is more amenable to exciting skiing. Try to leave the arrangements loose, to cope with the highly changeable weather. A heli-ski day NZ-style usually starts with a 7.30 phone call to let you know if the weather's suitable.

An alternative adventure is to fly by plane to ski 10km down the length of the Tasman Glacier. Be aware that this is quite a costly venture for a gentle schuss down a very mild slope, with few areas to lay real turns. The main drawcard of the Tasman is the immense grandeur of the place, along with the ski-plane flights over stunning blue ice-flows and the close proximity of Mt Cook. The Tasman is also one of the few glaciers in the world where it is possible to walk through the eery ice-blue glacial caves – quite a surreal experience.

As in the northern hemisphere, the season doesn't really get under way until about midwinter – mid or late June; it runs until some time in October. Mount Hutt aims to open first, in mid-May, and disputes the longest-season title with Whakapapa, which generally stays open until mid-November.

Snowboarding is very popular in New Zealand, and most of the major resorts have special terrain parks including half-pipes, as well as boarding classes and hire equipment.

Whakapapa (pronounced Fukapapa) is on the slopes of the active volcano Mt Ruapehu, which has occasionally erupted in recent years, leaving the slopes black with volcanic ash. Until the late 1990s the volcano had not caused havoc since the 1950s, when an eruption carried away a bridge.

Mt Ruapehu is in the middle of the North Island and within four hours' drive of both Auckland and Wellington. Whakapapa, New Zealand's largest ski field, is located on the north-facing slopes with a top height of 2300m and a vertical of 675m served by 20 lifts including one fast quad. Terrain is typified by large, wide open cruisers plus challenging off-piste. Next to the base lodge is an extensive beginner's area, Happy Valley, with half a dozen rope tows and snowmaking that allow this particular section to open early in the season. The resort's lifts and runs range across craggy terrain made especially interesting because of the unpredictable twists, turns and drops of the solidified lava on which it sits. There is a mix of deep gulleys, superb natural half-pipes for snow boarders and narrow chutes. There is a handful of mountain restaurants.

Accommodation is 6km away at Whakapapa village, with the best middle-of-the-road property being a

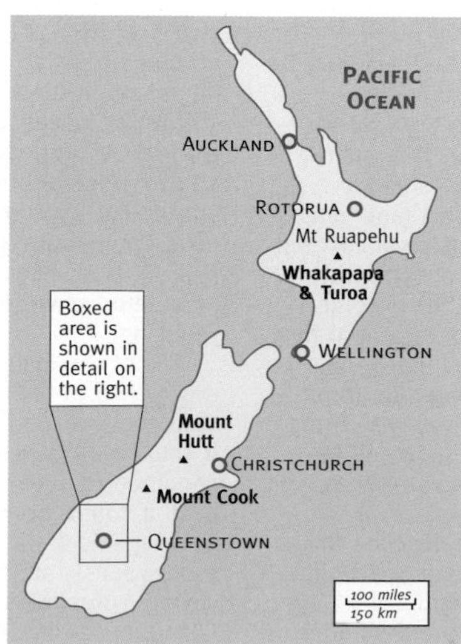

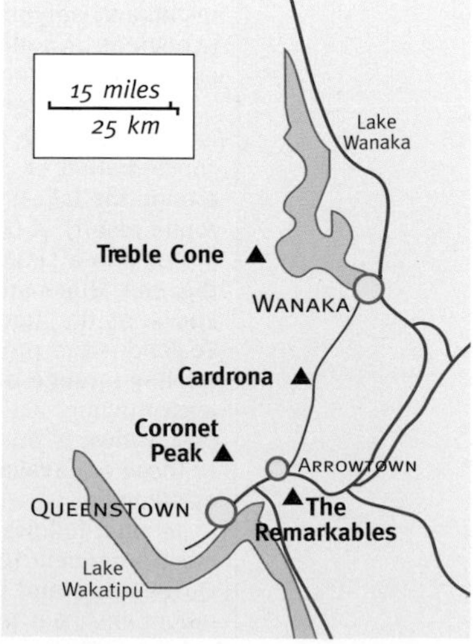

TREBLE CONE MOUNTAIN FACTS

Altitude	1200m-1860m
Lifts	5
Pistes	1359 acres
Green	15%
Blue	45%
Black	40%
Art. snow	125 acres

TOURIST OFFICE

t +64 (3) 443 7443
f 443 8401
tcinfo@treblecone.co.nz
www.treblecone.co.nz

CARDRONA MOUNTAIN FACTS

Altitude	1505m-1895m
Lifts	7
Pistes	790 acres
Green	20%
Blue	55%
Black	25%
Art. snow	none

TOURIST OFFICE

t +64 (3) 443 7411
f 443 8818
info@cardrona.com
www.cardrona.com

MOUNT HUTT MOUNTAIN FACTS

Altitude	1420m-2075m
Lifts	10
Pistes	902 acres
Green	25%
Blue	50%
Black	25%
Art. snow	103 acres

TOURIST OFFICE

t +64 (3) 308 5074
f 308 5076
marketing@nzski.com
www.nzski.com

motel named the Skotel. A complete anomaly in this area of rustic lodges is the Chateau, a hotel in the grand style of the 1920s, with overly high ceilings, sweeping drapes over picture windows, a marble foyer and formal dining room with grand piano.

Worth knowing about is the hike to Mt Ruapehu's fizzing Crater Lake. Ask ski patrol for directions or better still talk them into taking you on a guided trip. This involves about a half-hour hike up from the top of the highest T-bar, and then a long traverse across a large flat tundra-like area. A few lefts and rights and you are staring into the mouth of a volcano. Awesome views and neighbouring volcanos give this area an other-worldly feel.

On the south-western slope of Mt Ruapehu is **Turoa** – now under the same ownership as Whakapapa and soon to be joined by lift and piste. (At present it is reachable on snow by going off-piste from Whakapapa after a stiff climb.) Turoa is smaller, but with an impressive 720m vertical – the biggest in Australasia. The longest run is 4km. There's plenty of scope off-piste away from the gentle intermediate runs, plus the chance to ski on the Mangaehuehu Glacier. Accommodation is 20 minutes away in Ohakune.

The South Island has 15 ski areas, including five club fields. **Mt Hutt**, an hour west of Christchurch in the northern part of the island, has a 670m vertical and some of the country's most impressive, consistently steep, wide-open terrain – all within view of the Pacific Ocean. On a clear day you can even see the sandy beaches in the distance beyond the patchwork Canterbury plains. The lift system is half the size of Whakapapa's and a few more fast chair-lifts would not go amiss. The main area is an open bowl with gentle terrain in the centre served by chairs and drags and steeper terrain around the outside, some of which requires a short hike to the top. A large new base lodge was built for the 2000 season, including a big carpeted cafe and brasserie, plus a well stocked hire shop. Mt Hutt Helicopters offers six-run days in the mountains beyond for $NZ600. The helicopter departs from the heli-pad right in the car park – just wander up to the heli hut and book in. There is no accommodation on-mountain – most people stay in the quiet little town of Methven, where there are several truly comfortable up-market B&Bs as well as motels and apartments. The very British South Island capital of Christchurch, an hour and a half away, is also an option for accommodation.

About six hours' drive south of Christchurch is the quiet lakeside town of Wanaka, which is also 90 minutes from Queenstown, and there are two resorts accessible from here.

Treble Cone, 20km from Wanaka, has more advanced slopes than any other NZ ski area, plus the advantage of a better lift system including the first six-seater chair-lift in the southern hemisphere. There are two well maintained intermediate trails, one 3.5km, the other 2km. Both on the main flank and off to the side in Saddle Basin there are long natural half-pipes which are great fun when snow is good, as well as smooth, wide runs for cruising. Treble Cone is reached by a long and winding dirt track that adds to the excitement. The ski field offers stunning views across Lake Wanaka, its shores usually free of snow, with snowcapped Alpine-style peaks in the distance. There's an adequate cafe at the lift base.

Cardrona, 34km from Wanaka, is famous for its dry snow. The terrain is noted for its well-groomed, flattering cruisers. But there are some serious if short chutes, and the middle basin, Arcadia, hosts the New Zealand Extreme Skiing Championships. The total vertical is a modest 390m. Millions have been poured into the resort by its family owners over the past few years, resulting in a large base area focused around an impressive, if odd, clock tower. There's a bar and brasserie-style restaurant, large hire facility and a licensed childcare centre, plus several neat and modern self-contained apartments at the base (but bring all your own supplies). There are four half-pipes for boarders. Learners are looked after well, with three magic carpet lifts.

Queenstown 310m

A lively base for sampling a range of resorts

HOW IT RATES

The slopes

Snow	**
Extent	*
Experts	***
Intermediates	***
Beginners	***
Convenience	*
Queues	***
Restaurants	*

The rest

Scenery	****
Resort charm	**
Off-slope	*****

What's new

A magic carpet conveyor-belt now connects the car park at The Remarkables with the main lift stations.

- ⊕ For Europeans, more interesting than summer skiing on glaciers
- ⊕ For Australians, conveniently close, with flights from Sydney
- ⊕ Huge areas of off-piste terrain accessible by helicopters, with excellent snow at the right time
- ⊕ Lots to do off the slopes, especially for adrenalin junkies
- ⊕ Lively town, with lots going on and good restaurants
- ⊕ Grand views locally, and the spectacular 'fjord' country nearby

- ⊖ Slopes (in two separate areas locally) are a drive from town
- ⊖ Limited lift-served slopes in each area
- ⊖ It's a long way from anywhere except Australia
- ⊖ No real mountain restaurants – just pit stops at the lift bases
- ⊖ Highly changeable weather
- ⊖ No trees, so skiing in bad weather virtually impossible

If you want a single destination in New Zealand – as opposed to visiting a few different mountains on your travels – Queenstown is probably it, especially if you can cope with the cost of a few heli-drops. Although the resorts of North Island are impressive, the Southern Alps are, in the end, more compelling – and their resorts are free of volcanic interruptions. Mount Hutt may be a slightly more impressive area than either of Queenstown's local fields – Coronet Peak and The Remarkables – but it's a rather isolated field. From Queenstown you have a choice of the two local fields plus the option of an outing to Treble Cone and Cardrona. The best way to take them in would be to plan on a night or two in Wanaka, an hour or two away (see Introduction to New Zealand).

The resort

Queenstown is a winter-and-summer resort on the shore of Lake Wakatipu. (There is a map of the area in the introductory chapter.) Although the setting is splendid, with views to the peaks of the aptly named Remarkables range beyond the lake, the town itself is no beauty – it has grown up to meet tourists' needs, and has a very commercial feel. In recent years much effort has been put into smartening up the town, with such additions as the classy new Steamer Wharf complex by the lake and luxury accommodation. It has a lively, relaxed feel, and makes a satisfactory base, with some good restaurants, plenty of entertaining bars and lots of touristy clothes shops.

The mountains

There are four lift-served mountains – all small by Alpine standards – that you can get to from Queenstown. The two described here – Coronet Peak and The Remarkables – are close by. The others – Cardrona and Treble Cone – are a more serious drive away, near Wanaka. At each base area you'll find a mini-resort – a ski school, a ski rental shop, a functional self-service restaurant, but no accommodation except at Cardrona.

All these areas have something for all standards of skier or boarder, with off-piste opportunities as well as prepared and patrolled trails. These areas use the American green/blue/black convention for run gradings, not the European blue/red/black.

THE SLOPES
Not the height of convenience

The Remarkables, true to their name, are a dramatic range of craggy peaks visible across the lake from some parts of Queenstown. The slopes are tucked in a bowl behind the peaks, a 40-minute drive from town.

Two chairs go up from the base. The slow Alta lift serves easy runs and accesses the higher Sugar Bowl chair, which serves mainly long, easy runs plus a couple of black chutes. The

THE REMARKABLES MOUNTAIN FACTS

Altitude	1620m-1980m
Lifts	5
Pistes	543 acres
Green	30%
Blue	40%
Black	30%
Art. snow	25 acres

TOURIST OFFICE

t +64 (3) 442 4615
f 442 4619
admin@theremarkables.co.nz
www.nzski.com

CORONET PEAK MOUNTAIN FACTS

Altitude	1210m-1650m
Lifts	7
Pistes	690 acres
Green	20%
Blue	45%
Black	35%
Art. snow	200 acres

TOURIST OFFICE

t +64 (3) 442 4620
f 442 4624
admin@coronetpeak.co.nz
www.nzski.com

boarding *Boarding is popular in New Zealand, and although the two mountains close to Queenstown don't seem to have quite such a hold on the boarding market as Cardrona (see New Zealand introduction), they have everything you need, including equipment, tuition and new terrain-parks and half-pipes. You needn't go anywhere near a drag-lift, and there are no flats to worry about except on the lowest green run at The Remarkables.*

Shadow Basin chair accesses steeper terrain, including three hike-accessed, expert-only chutes that drop down to Lake Alta, and the Homeward Run – a broad, fairly gentle, unprepared slope down to the resort access road, where a shuttle-truck takes you back to the base. The Remarkables is also home to New Zealand's first snowcat operation in the bowls behind the main slopes.

Coronet Peak, about 25 minutes' drive from Queenstown, is a far more satisfying resort, especially for intermediates and above. Again, there are three main chair-lifts, one a fast quad that accesses practically all the runs. The main mountainside is a pleasantly varied intermediate slope, full of highly enjoyable rolling terrain that snowboarders adore, though it steepens near the bottom. A fourth lift, a T-bar, serves another mainly intermediate area to one side. There are also drags for beginners. Night skiing runs from July to September on Fridays and Saturdays.

SNOW RELIABILITY
Good at Coronet

The New Zealand weather is highly variable, so it's difficult to be confident about snow conditions. Coronet tends to receive sleet and/or rain even when it's snowing in The Remarkables. But Coronet Peak has snowmaking on practically all its intermediate terrain, and boosted the system's capacity by 30% last season.

FOR EXPERTS
Challenges exist

Both areas have quite a choice of genuinely black slopes. Coronet's Back Bowls is an experts-only area, and there are other black slopes dotted around the mountain. The main enjoyment comes from venturing off-piste all over the place. The Remarkables' Shadow Basin chair serves some excellent slopes.

FOR INTERMEDIATES
Fine, within limits

There's some very enjoyable intermediate skiing in both areas – appreciably more at Coronet, where there are also easy blacks to go on to. But remember: these are very small areas by Alpine standards.

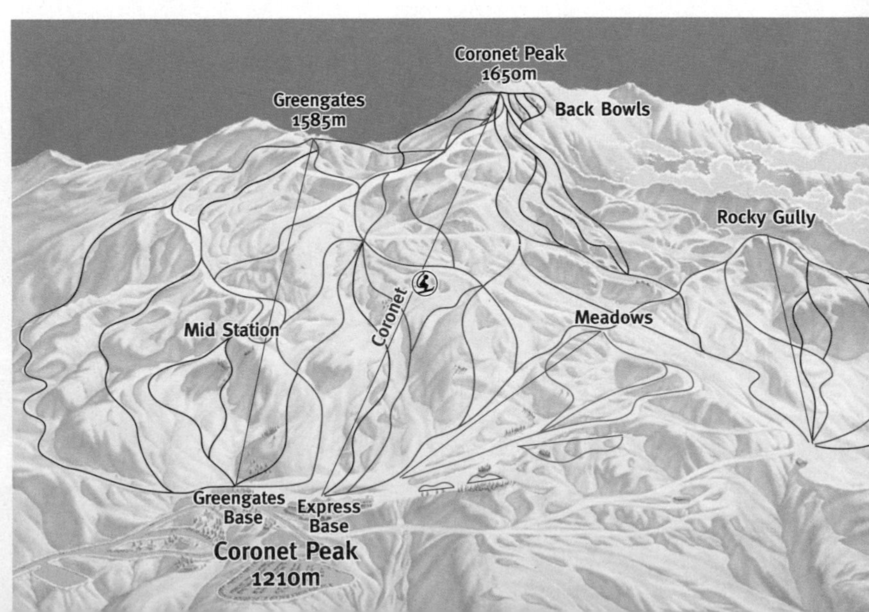

CHILDCARE

At both areas there is a Skiwiland Club for children aged 4 to 6 with morning and afternoon sessions. The Queenstown Crèche can take younger children all day. There is a licensed crèche at the Remarkables, taking children from 2 to 4.

FOR BEGINNERS
Excellent
There are gentle slopes at both areas served by rope tows, and longer green runs served by chairs. And many other diversions if you decide it's a drag.

FOR CROSS-COUNTRY
Unremarkable
There is a short loop around a lake in the middle of The Remarkables area, but the only serious cross-country area is the elevated plateau of Waiorau Snow Farm, near Cardrona.

QUEUES
It depends
Coronet and The Remarkables can suffer a little from high-season crowds – there are certainly enough beds locally to lead to queues at peak times. But they aren't a major worry.

MOUNTAIN RESTAURANTS
Er, what mountain restaurants?
Both areas have a simple cafeteria at the base, and Coronet has a brasserie, but nothing up the mountain.

SCHOOLS AND GUIDES
All the usual classes
The schools are well organised, with a wide range of options, including 'guaranteed' beginner classes.

FACILITIES FOR CHILDREN
Look good
Childcare looked OK to us.

Staying there

Some hotels are quite some way from central Queenstown – inconvenient for après-ski unless there's a shuttle-bus.

HOW TO GO
Stay out of town?
There are lots of big, smart but rather impersonal places built to meet the big summer demand for beds in this popular lakeside resort.
Hotels The hotels range from the very simple to the glossily pretentious Millennium. Aim to get a room with a view across Lake Wakatipu and the mountains – the view is worth the extra dollars. One of the most welcoming places – with more of a 'ski-lodge' atmosphere – is Nugget Point, a few miles out.

EATING OUT
Lots of choice
There are over 100 restaurants – Chinese, Italian, Malaysian, Lebanese ... you name it. The Moa is a particularly stylish bar-restaurant, with live music sometimes. Solero Vino has delicious Mediterranean food and a

SKYLINE QUEENSTOWN

Queenstown has a gondola but it doesn't access slopes – just Remarkable views across Lake Wakatipu ↓

rustic bar, and McNeill's is an excellent brew-pub housed in a stone cottage, with a range of tasty beers. The Bunker does excellent local cuisine such as Bluff oysters and lamb. At the other end of the scale, pizza-lovers crowd into The Cow, a cosy barn-like place where you sit on logs around a fire waiting for tables or takeaways. Lone Star offers big servings of satisfying American-style food.

APRES-SKI
Lively little town

Queenstown has a good range of bars and clubs that stay open late with disco or live music. A small upmarket casino opened in 1999 in the plush Steamer Wharf, which also holds a classy cigar bar and good duty free.

OFF THE SLOPES
Scare yourself silly

There are lots of scary things to do – see below. Just to the west is New Zealand's spectacularly scenic 'fjord country', and you can go on independent or guided walks. By all reports, the Milford Sound sightseeing flights by plane or helicopter are to be preferred to the slow, lumbering bus-ride from Queenstown – but be aware that the weather can ruin your plans. Arrowtown is interesting for a quick visit – a cute, touristy old mining town where you can kit yourself out to go panning for gold. The Winter Festival, held in mid-July, is an annual 'action-packed week of mayhem on the mountain and in the town'.

GET THAT ADRENALIN RUSH

The streets of Queenstown are lined by agencies offering various artificial thrills.

AJ Hackett's bungee jump at Kawarau Bridge is where this crazy activity got off the ground – you plunge towards the icy river, but are pulled up short by your bungee cord and lowered into an inflatable boat.

The Shotover Jet Boat experience is less demanding. You get chauffeured at high speed along the rocky river in a boat that can get along in very shallow water, execute high-speed 360° turns and pass very close to cliffs and trees. It's probably more fun in summer than in temperatures of –10°C.

The whitewater rafting is genuinely thrilling – and not as uncomfortable as you'd expect, thanks to the full wet-suit, helmet, boots and gloves, and to the exertion involved. The rivers have some exciting rapids. One route even passes through a tunnel excavated in the gold-mining days, after which comes a small but steep waterfall where your souvenir shots are snapped.

Reference section

Tour operators

Arranging your own accommodation in a resort is not difficult. But most people still prefer the convenience of a package holiday, which is what most of the companies listed below are set up to provide. Note that we've also included some operators that offer accommodation without travel arrangements.

Absolute Ski
Chalet in Méribel
Tel 01788 860800
Fax 01788 860358
holiday@absoluteski.com
www.absoluteski.com

Airtours
Mainstream operator
Tel 0870 608 1950
Fax 01706 232977
www.airtours.co.uk

All Canada Ski
Holidays in Canada
Tel 01502 585825
Fax 01502 500681
mail@all-canada.com
www.all-canada.com

Alp Active
Holidays in Les Gets
Tel 01223 568220
Fax 01223 519314
info@alpactive.com
www.alpactive.com

Alpine Action
Chalets in Les Trois Vallées
Tel 01903 761986
Fax 01903 766007
sales@alpine-action.co.uk
www.alpine-action.co.uk

Alpine Answers Select
Tailor-made holidays
Tel 020 8871 4657
Fax 020 8871 9676
select@alpineanswers.co.uk
www.alpineanswers.co.uk

Alpine Options
Holidays in the French Alps
Tel 01932 828668
Fax 01932 840005
info@alpine-options.com
www.alpine-options.com

Alpine Tours
Group and schools holidays, mainly in Austria, Italy and Slovenia
Tel 01227 454777
Fax 01227 451177
alpinetoursltd@btinternet.com

Alpine Weekends
Weekends in the Alps
Tel 020 8944 9762
Fax 020 8947 9552
valweekends@btinternet.com
www.val-disere-ski.com

American Ski Classics
Holidays in major North American resorts
Tel 020 8392 6660
Fax 020 8392 6606
sales@holidayworld.ltd.uk
www.americanskiclassics.com

APT Holidays Ltd
Weekend breaks by coach to France
Tel 01268 783878
Fax 01268 782656
apt.holidays@virgin.net
www.apt-holidays.co.uk

Aravis Alpine Retreat
Chalet in St Jean-de-Sixt (La Clusaz)
Tel 00 33 450 023 625
Fax 00 33 450 023 982
info@aravis-retreat.com
www.aravis-retreat.com

Avant-ski
Mainly holidays in France
Tel 0191 212 1173
Fax 0191 239 9459
sales@avant-ski.com
www.avant-ski.com

Balkan Holidays
Holidays in Bulgaria, Slovenia and Romania
Tel 020 7543 5555
Fax 020 7543 5577
res@balkanholidays.co.uk
www.balkanholidays.co.uk

Barrelli Ski
Eclectic selection of French resorts
Tel 0890 220 1500
Fax 0890 230 1501
whiplash@barrelliski.co.uk
www.barrelliski.co.uk

Beaumont Holidays Ltd
Flexible breaks in Chamonix, Megève and Cervinia
Tel 020 8544 0404
Fax 00 33 450 530932
stay@beau-mont.com
www.beau-mont.com

Bigfoot
Variety of holidays in Chamonix
Tel 01491 579601
Fax 01491 576568
ann@bigfoot-travel.co.uk
www.bigfoot-travel.co.uk

Bladon Lines
Chalet arm of Inghams
Tel 020 8780 8800
Fax 020 8780 8805
bladonlines@inghams.com
www.inghams.com

Board and Lodge
Catered snowboarding holidays in Chamonix
Tel 020 7916 2275
Fax 020 7916 8953
info@boardnlodge.com
www.boardnlodge.com

Bonne Neige Ski Holidays
Catered chalets in Méribel
Tel 01270 256966
Fax 01270 251033
ukoffice@bonne-neige-ski.com
www.bonne-neige-ski.com

Borderline
Specialist in Barèges
Tel 00 33 562 92 68 95
Fax 00 33 562 92 83 43
sorbiers@sudfr.com
www.borderlinehols.com

The Chalet Company
Catered chalets in Morzine and Ardent (Avoriaz)
Tel 00 33 450 79 68 40
Fax 00 33 450 74 84 81
moran@thechaletco.com
www.thechaletco.com

Chalet Kiana
Chalet in Les Contamines
Tel 00 33 450 915518 / 01689 838558
Fax 00 33 450 915538
chaletkiana@aol.com
www.alpesactives.com

Chalets de St Martin
Chalets in St-Martin
Tel 01202 473255
Fax 01202 480042
les.chalets@virgin.net
www.leschalets.co.uk

Chalet Snowboard
Snowboard holidays in France and US
Tel 01235 767575
Fax 01235 767576
info@chalet-snowboard.co.uk
www.chalet-snowboard.co.uk

Chalets 'Unlimited'
Chalets worldwide
Tel 0191 212 1173
Fax 0191 239 9459
sales@avant-ski.com
www.avant-ski.com

Chalet World
Chalets in big-name resorts
Tel 01952 840462 / 020 7373 2096
Fax 01952 840463 / 020 7244 8764
sales@chaletworld.co.uk
www.chaletworld.co.uk

Challenge Activ
Chalets and apartments in Morzine
Tel 0800 328 0513
Fax 0800 328 0513
challenge_activ_morzine@compuserve.com
www.challenge-activ.com

Chez Jay Ski
Chalet in Les Arcs
Tel 01843 298030
Fax 0845 3344356
ski@chezjayski.com
www.chezjayski.com

Classic Ski Limited
Holidays for 'mature' skiers/beginners
Tel 01590 623400
Fax 01590 624387
info@classicski.co.uk
www.classicski.co.uk

Club Europe
Schools trips to Austria, France and Italy
Tel 020 8699 7788
Fax 020 8699 7770
ski@club-europe.co.uk
www.club-europe.co.uk

Club Med
All-inclusive holidays in 'ski villages'
Tel 0700 258 2633
Fax 020 7536 5414
admin.uk@clubmed.com
www.clubmed.co.uk

Club Pavilion
Budget holidays
Tel 0870 241 0427
Fax 0870 241 0426
sales@paviliontours.co.uk
www.clubpavilion.com

Collineige
Chamonix valley specialist
Tel 01276 24262
Fax 01276 27282
info@collineige.com
www.collineige.com

Connick Ski
Chalet in Châtel
Tel 00 33 450 73 22 12
Fax 00 33 450 81 30 45
nick@connickski.com
www.connickski.com

Contiki
Coach-travel holidays for 18-35s
Tel 020 8290 6422
Fax 020 8225 4246
travel@contiki.co.uk
www.contiki.com

Cooltip Mountain Holidays
Chalets in Méribel
Tel 01964 563563
ski@cooltip.com
www.cooltip.com

The Corporate Ski Company
Corporate specialists
Tel 020 7627 5500
Fax 020 7622 6701
ski@vantagepoint.co.uk
www.vantagepoint.co.uk

Crystal
Major mainstream operator
Tel 0870 848 7000
Fax 0870 848 7032
skires@crystalholidays.co.uk
www.crystalski.co.uk

Crystal Schools
Schools arm of major mainstream operator
Tel 0870 848 7007
schools@crystalholidays.co.uk
www.crystalholidays.co.uk

Descent International
Chalets in Méribel and Verbier
Tel 020 7989 8989
Fax 020 7989 8990
ski@descent.co.uk
www.descent.co.uk

Elegant Resorts
Luxury ski holidays
Tel 0870 333 3330
Fax 0870 333 3331
enquiries@elegantresorts.co.uk
www.elegantresorts.co.uk

Equity School Ski
School group holidays
Tel 01273 299299
Fax 01273 203212
schoolski@equity.co.uk
www.equity.co.uk

Equity Total Ski
All-in holidays
Tel 01273 298298
Fax 01273 203212
travel@equity.co.uk
www.equity.co.uk

Erna Low
Hotel and self-catering holidays, mostly in France and Switzerland
Tel 020 7584 2841
Fax 020 7589 9531
info@ernalow.co.uk
www.ernalow.co.uk

Esprit Ski
Families specialist in Europe and North America
Tel 01252 618300
Fax 01252 618328
travel@esprit-holidays.co.uk
www.esprit-holidays.co.uk

Eurotunnel Motoring Holidays
Self-drive holidays to France
Tel 0870 333 2001
Fax 0870 333 2002
ethols@crestahols.co.uk

Fairhand Holidays
Ski-drive holidays to France
Tel 01959 540796
Fax 01959 540797
sunshine@fairhandholidays.com
www.fairhandholidays.com

Fantiski
Chalet holidays in France and USA
Tel 01622 844302
Fax 01622 842458
fctravel@dircon.co.uk
www.fantiski.co.uk

Finlays
Mainly chalets in France
Tel 01835 830562
Fax 01835 830550
finlayski@aol.com
www.finlayski.com

First Choice Ski
Major mainstream operator
Tel 0870 754 3477
Fax 0870 333 0329
sales@fcski.co.uk
www.fcski.co.uk

FlexiSki
Specialists in flexible breaks
Tel 0870 909 0754
Fax 0870 909 0329
reservations@flexiski.co.uk
www.flexiski.co.uk

Freedom Holidays
Weekends and 'flexible duration' holidays in Switzerland
Tel 01798 342034
Fax 01798 343320
freedomhols@hotmail.com
www.freedomholidays.co.uk

Frontier Ski
Holidays in Canada
Tel 020 8776 8709
Fax 020 8778 0149
info@frontier-travel.co.uk
www.frontier-ski.co.uk

Frosty's Ski and Snowboard Holidays
Chalet in St-Jean-de-Sixt
Tel 00 33 450 02 37 28
info@frostys.co.uk
www.frostys.co.uk

Haig Ski
Hotels with guiding and nanny service in Châtel
Tel 00 33 450 811947
Fax 00 33 450 811947
haigski@compuserve.com
www.haigski.com

Handmade Holidays
Tailor-made specialists
Tel 01285 642555
Fax 01285 651685
travel@handmade-holidays.co.uk
www.handmade-holidays.co.uk

Hannibals
Holidays in Serre-Chevalier
Tel 01233 813105
Fax 01233 813432
sales@hannibals.co.uk
www.hannibals.co.uk

Headwater Holidays
Cross-country skiing holidays
Tel 01606 813333
Fax 01606 813334
info@headwater.com

High Mountain Holidays
Catered chalet in Les Praz (Chamonix)
Tel 01993 775540
Fax 01993 772388
info@highmountain.co.uk
www.highmountain.co.uk

Huski
Holidays in Chamonix
Tel 020 7938 4844
Fax 020 7504 3776
sales@huski.com
www.huski.com

Iglu.com
Accommodation online
Tel 0870 870 5787
Fax 020 8542 9223
enquiries@iglu.com
www.iglu.com

Independent Ski Links
Tailormade holidays mainly in France
Tel 01964 533905
Fax 01964 536006
info@ski-links.com
www.ski-links.com

Inghams
Major mainstream operator
Tel 020 8780 4444
Fax 020 8780 4405
reservations @inghams.co.uk
www.inghams.co.uk

Inntravel
Cross-country skiing holidays
Tel 01653 629002
Fax 01653 628741
winter@inntravel.co.uk
www.inntravel.co.uk

Interhome
Apartments and chalets in Europe
Tel 020 8891 1294
Fax 020 8891 5331
info@interhome.co.uk
www.interhome.co.uk

Interski
Group holidays with tuition in Italy
Tel 01623 456333
Fax 01623 456353
email@interski.co.uk
www.interski.co.uk

Kuoni
Holidays in Switzerland and Canada
Tel 01306 747000
Fax 01306 744222
switzerland.sales@kuoni.co.uk
www.kuoni.co.uk

La Source
Luxury chalet in Villard-Reculas (Alpe-d'Huez)
Tel 01707 655988
Fax 01707 655988
lasourcefrance@cs.com
www.lasource.f9.co.uk

Lagrange Holidays
Self-catering holidays in France
Tel 020 7371 6111
Fax 020 7371 2990
info@lagrange-holidays.com
www.lagrange-holidays.com

The Last Resort
Chalet in St Jean de Sixt
Tel 0800 652 3977
Fax 00 33 450 023671
info@lastresorthols.co.uk
www.lastresorthols.co.uk

Le Ski
Chalets in Courchevel, Val d'Isère and La Tania
Tel 0870 754 4444
Fax 0870 754 3333
mail@leski.com
www.leski.com

Les Deux Chalets
Chalets in Méribel
Tel 01303 246966
Fax 01303 246966
anjid@ukonline.co.uk
www.chalet-de-launey.demon.co.uk

Lotus Supertravel
European and North American holidays
Tel 020 7962 9933
Fax 020 7962 9965
donald@lotusgroup.co.uk
www.supertravel.co.uk

Made to Measure
Wide variety of tailor-made holidays
Tel 01243 533333
Fax 01243 778431
madetomeasure.holidays@which.net
www.madetomeasureholidays.com

Mark Warner
Chalet hotel holidays in big-name resorts
Tel 08708 480 482
Fax 020 7761 7001
www.markwarner.co.uk

MasterSki
Christian holidays
Tel 020 8942 9442
Fax 020 8949 4396
holidays@mastersun.co.uk
www.mastersun.co.uk

McNab Mountain Sports
Chalets in Argentière
Tel 01546 830243
Fax 01546 830243
inf@www.mcnab.co.uk
www.mcnab.co.uk

Meriski
Chalet specialist in Méribel
Tel 01451 843100
Fax 01451 844799
sales@meriski.co.uk
www.meriski.co.uk

Momentum Ski
Tailor-made specialists
Tel 020 7371 9111
Fax 020 7610 6287
sales@momentumski.com
www.momentumski.com

Moswin Tours
Small German programme
Tel 0116 271 9922
Fax 0116 271 6016
germany@moswin.com
www.moswin.com

Motours
French ski-drive operation
Tel 01892 677777
Fax 01892 677711
sales@motours.com
www.motours.com

Mountain Highs
Chalet specialist in Morzine
Tel 0121 550 9321
Fax 0121 550 9321
mhighs@dircon.co.uk
www.mhighs.dircon.co.uk

Neilson
Major mainstream operator
Tel 0870 333 3347
Fax 01273 626285
sales@neilson.com
www.neilson.com

Optimum Ski
Chalet in Les Arcs
Tel 01992 561085
Fax 00 33 479 169356
info@optimumski.com
www.optimumski.com

The Oxford Ski Company
Chalets in Crans-Montana
Tel 07000 785349
Fax 07000 785340
info@oxfordski.com
www.oxfordski.com

Panorama
Budget-oriented holidays in Italy, Andorra and Spain
Tel 01273 427070
Fax 01273 427111
panoramaski@phg.co.uk
www.panoramaholidays.co.uk

Peak Ski
Chalets in Verbier
Tel 01442 832629
Fax 01442 834303
peakski@which.net
www.peak-ski.co.uk

PGL Ski Europe
Specialist in school group holidays
Tel 01989 768168
Fax 01989 768376
ski@pgl.co.uk
www.pgl.co.uk

PGL Teenski
Holidays for teenagers
Tel 01989 767767
Fax 01989 766306
holidays@pgl.co.uk
www.pgl.co.uk

Piste Artiste
Holidays in Champéry and heli-skiing in India
Tel 020 7436 0100
Fax 00 41 24 479 3490
ski@pisteartiste.com
www.pisteartiste.com

Plus Travel
Specialists in Swiss resorts
Tel 020 7734 0383
Fax 020 7292 1599
plustravel@stlondon.com

Powder Byrne
Small programme of luxury holidays
Tel 020 8246 5300
Fax 020 8246 5322
enquiries@powderbyrne.co.uk
www.powderbyrne.com

Powder Skiing in North America Limited
Heli-skiing holidays in Canada
Tel 020 7736 8191
Fax 020 7384 2592

Ramblers
Cross-country holidays
Tel 01707 331133
Fax 01707 333276
info@ramblersholidays.co.uk

Rocketski
All-in holidays online
Tel 01273 262626
Fax 01273 203212
info@rocketski.com
www.rocketski.com

Rocky Mountain Snowboard Tours
Season holidays in the Rockies
Tel 0151 706 0344
Fax 0151 706 0350
seasons@rockymountain.co.uk
www.rockymountain.co.uk

Scott Dunn Latin America
Tailor-made holidays to South America
Tel 020 8767 8989
Fax 020 8767 2026
latin@scottdunn.com
www.scottdunn.com

Scott Dunn Ski
Upmarket holidays
Tel 020 8767 0202
Fax 020 8767 2026
ski@scottdunn.com
www.scottdunn.com

Silver Ski
Chalet holidays in France
Tel 01622 735544
Fax 01622 738550
karen@silverski.co.uk
www.silverski.co.uk

Simply Ski
Holidays in big-name resorts
Tel 020 8541 2209
Fax 020 8541 2280
ski@simply-travel.com
www.simplyski.co.uk

Ski 2
Monterosa Ski specialists
Tel 01962 713330
Fax 01962 713355
sales@ski-2.com
www.ski-2.com

Ski Activity
Holidays in big-name resorts
Tel 01738 840888
Fax 01738 840079
sales@skiactivity.com
www.skiactivity.com

Ski Addiction
Chalets and hotels in Châtel and St Anton
Tel 01580 819354
Fax 01580 819354
sales@skiaddiction.co.uk
www.skiaddiction.co.uk

Ski Amis
Chalet holidays in the La Plagne area
Tel 020 7692 0850
Fax 020 7692 0851
info@skiamis.com
www.skiamis.com

Ski Arrangements
Chalets/apartments in France. Also Austria and eastern USA
Tel 08700 110565
Fax 01629 826345
info@skiarrangements.com
www.skiarrangements.com

SkiAway Holidays
Holidays in the Pyrenees and French Alps
Tel 01903 824823
Fax 01903 821858
skiaway@tourplaneurope.com
www.tourplaneurope.com

Ski Balkantours
Holidays in Eastern Europe
Tel 028 9024 6795
Fax 028 9023 4581
mail@balkan.co.uk
www.balkan.co.uk

Ski Barrett-Boyce
Chalet in Megève with tuition
Tel 020 8288 0042
Fax 020 8288 0761
kerry@skibb,com
www.skibb.com

Ski Beat
Chalets in La Plagne, Val-d'Isere and La Tania
Tel 01243 780405
Fax 01243 533748
Ski@skibeat.co.uk
www.skibeat.co.uk

Ski Blanc
Chalets in Méribel
Tel 020 8502 9082
Fax 01737 213617
anthonydejode@cs.com
www.skiblanc.co.uk

Ski Bon
Chalets in Méribel
Tel 020 8649 8458
enquiry@skibon.com
www.skibon.com

SkiBound
Schools division of First Choice
Tel 0870 900 3200
Fax 0870 333 0329
sales@fcski.co.uk
www.fcski.co.uk

Ski Chamois
Holidays in Morzine
Tel 01302 369006
Fax 01302 326640
skichamois@morzine1550.freeserve.co.uk

Ski Choice
Mainly hotels and self-catering in Europe
Tel 01491 837607
Fax 01491 833836

Ski Club of GB
Holidays for club members
Tel 020 8410 2022
Fax 020 8410 2001
skiers@skiclub.co.uk
www.skiclub.co.uk

The Ski Company
Holidays in France and US with tuition
Tel 0870 241 2085
Fax 01288 352306
info@theskicompany.co.uk
www.theskicompany.co.uk

The Ski Company Ltd
Luxury chalets in France and Switzerland
Tel 01451 843123
Fax 01451 844799
sales@skicompany.co.uk
www.skicompany.co.uk

Ski Cuisine
Chalets in Méribel
Tel 01702 589543
Fax 01702 588671
skicuisine@dial.pipex.com
www.skicuisine.co.uk

Ski Deep
Chalets in La Tania and Le Praz
Tel 00 33 479 081905
Fax 00 33 479 081905
ski@skideep.com
www.skideep.com

Ski Equipe
Upmarket chalet operator
Tel 08704 445533
Fax 0870 4423355
ski@ski-equipe.co.uk
www.ski-equipe.co.uk

Skiers World
School trips to North America and Europe
Tel 0870 333 3620
Fax 0870 333 3627
info@skiersworld.com
www.skiersworld.com

Ski Etoile
Chalet in Montgenèvre
Tel 01588 640442
Fax 01588 640442
ski-etoile@clun25.freeserve.co.uk
www.skietoile.co.uk

Ski Expectations
Mainly hotels and chalets in Europe
Tel 01799 531888
Fax 01799 531887
skiexpectations@virgin.net
www.skiexpectations.com

Ski Famille
Holidays for families in Les Gets
Tel 01223 363777
Fax 01223 519314
info@skifamille.co.uk
www.skifamille.co.uk

Ski France
Chalets and catered apartments
Tel 020 8313 0690
Fax 020 8466 0653
ski@skifrance.co.uk
www.skifrance.co.uk

SkiGower
School and group trips, mainly Switzerland
Tel 01527 851411
Fax 01527 851417
linda@gowstrav.demon.co.uk
www.skigower.co.uk

Ski Hillwood
Austrian, French and Canadian family holidays
Tel 01923 290700
Fax 01923 290340
sales@hillwood-holidays.co.uk
www.hillwood-holidays.co.uk

Ski Hiver
Chalets in Peisey (Les Arcs)
Tel 023 9242 8586
Fax 023 9242 8904
skihiver@aol.com
www.skihiver.co.uk

Ski Independence
USA and Canada, and self-drive to France / Switzerland
Tel 0870 555 0555 (USA / Canada);
0870 600 1462 (Europe)
Fax 0870 550 2020
ski@ski-independence.co.uk
www.ski-independence.co.uk

Ski La Cote
Chalets in Chapelle d'Abondance
Tel 01482 668357
Fax 01482 668357
adrian@ski-la-cote.karoo.co.uk
www.ski-la-cote.karoo.net

Ski Leisure Direction
Mainly self-catering in France
Tel 020 8324 4042
Fax 020 8324 4030
sales@leisuredirection.co.uk
www.leisuredirection.co.uk

Ski Life
Self-drive holidays to the French Alps
Tel 0113 205 0247
Fax 0113 258 4211
skilife@frenchlife.co.uk
www.skiinglife.co.uk

Ski Line
Holidays in Europe and North America
Tel 020 8650 5900
holidays@skiline.co.uk
www.skiline.co.uk

Ski McNeill
Tailor-made to USA and European weekends
Tel 028 9066 6699
Fax 028 9068 3888
mail@skimcneill.com
www.skimcneill.com

Ski Miquel
Small but eclectic programme
Tel 01457 821200
Fax 01457 821209
ski@miquelhols.co.uk
www.miquelhols.co.uk

Ski Morgins Holidays
Chalet holidays in Morgins
Tel 01568 770681
Fax 01568 770153
info@skimorgins.co.uk
www.skimorgins.co.uk

Ski 'n' Action
Chalets in Le Praz (Courchevel)
Tel 01707 251696
Fax 01707 259874
info@ski-n-action.co.uk
www.ski-n-action.co.uk

Ski Olympic
Chalet holidays in France
Tel 01709 579999
Fax 01709 579898
info@skiolympic.co.uk
www.skiolympic.com

Ski Partners
Schools programme
Tel 0117 925 3545
Fax 0117 929 3697

Ski Peak
Specialist in Vaujany
Tel 01428 741144
Fax 01428 741155
info@skipeak.com
www.skipeak.com

SkiPlan incorporating STS
Schools holidays
Tel 01273 774666
Fax 01273 734042
sales@topstravel.co.uk

Ski Rosie
Holidays in Châtel and Morgins
Tel 00 33 450813100
Fax 00 33 450813100
skirosie@dial.pipex.com

Ski Safari
Canadian specialist
Tel 020 7740 1221
Fax 020 7740 1223
info@skisafari.com
www.skisafari.com

Skisafe Travel
Mainly holidays in Scotland
Tel 0141 812 0925
Fax 0141 812 1544
skisafe@osa-travel.co.uk
www.osa-travel.co.uk

Skisar US
Hotels and B&Bs in North America
Tel 01959 540796
Fax 01959 540797
ian.porter@skiarus.com
www.skiarus.com

Ski Scott James
Chalets in Argentière
Tel 01845 501139
Fax 01845 501139
jamie@skiscottjames.co.uk
www.skiscottjames.co.uk

Ski Solutions
Tailor-made holidays
Tel 020 7471 7777
Fax 020 7471 7771
alc@skisolutions.com
www.skisolutions.com

Ski Success
Group holidays to the USA and Italian Dolomites
Tel 01225 764205
Fax 01225 777520
paul@success-tours.demon.co.uk
www.success-tours.co.uk

Ski Supreme
Coach and self-drive to France
Tel 01355 260547
Fax 01355 229232
roddy@skisupreme.co.uk
www.skisupreme.co.uk

Ski The American Dream
Major operator to North America
Tel 020 8552 1201
Fax 020 8552 7726
holidays@skidream.com
www.skidream.com

Ski Total
European and US holidays
Tel 020 8948 3535
Fax 020 8332 1268
sales@skitotal.com
www.skitotal.com

Ski-Val
Holidays in France and Austria
Tel 01822 611200
Fax 01822 611400
reservations@skival.co.uk
www.skival.co.uk

Ski Verbier
Specialises in Verbier
Tel 020 7385 8050
Fax 020 7385 8002
info@skiverbier.com
www.skiverbier.com

Ski Weekend
Weekend and ten-day holidays
Tel 01367 241636
Fax 01367 243833
sales@skiweekend.com
www.skiweekend.com

Ski Weekends
Coach or self-drive trips to Les 3 Vallées
Tel 01375 396688
Fax 01375 394488
sales@harris-travel.com
www.skiweekends.com

Ski with Julia
Hotels and catered chalets in Switzerland
Tel 01386 584478
Fax 01386 584629
julia@skijulia.co.uk
www.skijulia.co.uk

Skiworld
European and North American programme
Tel 020 7602 4826/7444
Fax 020 7371 1463
sales@skiworld.ltd.uk
www.skiworld.ltd.uk

Ski Yogi
Holidays to the Italian Dolomites
Tel 01799 531886
Fax 01799 531887
ski.expectations@virgin.net

Sloping Off
Schools and tailor-made, by coach
Tel 01725 552247
Fax 01725 552489
victorytours@dial.pipex.com
www.victorytours.co.uk

Snowbizz Vacances
Holidays in Puy-St-Vincent
Tel 01778 341455
Fax 01778 347422
wendy@snowbizz.co.uk
www.snowbizz.co.uk

Snowcoach
Holidays to Andorra, Austria and France
Tel 01727 833141
Fax 01727 843766
info@snowcoach.co.uk
www.snowcoach.co.uk

Snowfocus
Chalet in Châtel with nannies
Tel 01872 553003
action@snowfocus.com
www.snowfocus.com

Snowlife
Holidays in La Clusaz
Tel 01534 863630
Fax 01534 862222
snowlife@psilink.co.uk
www.holiday-rentals.co.uk/snowlife

Snowline
Chalet holidays in France
Tel 020 8870 4807
Fax 020 8875 9236
ski@snowline.co.uk
www.snowline.co.uk

Solo's
Singles' holidays, ages 25–69
Tel 020 8951 2800
Fax 020 8951 1051
travel@solosholidays.co.uk
www.solosholidays.co.uk

St Anton Ski Company
Hotels and chalets in St Anton
Tel 00 43 676 495 3438
jonathanverney@compuserve.com
www.atlas.co.uk/ski

Stanford Skiing
Megève specialist
Tel 01223 477644
Fax 01223 710318
stanskiing@aol.com
www.stanfordskiing.co.uk

Susie Ward Alpine Holidays
Catered and self-catered accommodation in Châtel
Tel 01872 553055
susie@susieward.com
www.susieward.com

Swiss Travel Service
Hotels in Switzerland
Tel 0870 727 5955
Fax 01992 448855
swiss@bridge-travel.co.uk
www.swisstravel.co.uk

Thomson Ski & Snowboarding
Major mainstream operator
Tel 0870 606 1470
Fax 020 8939 0402
reservations@thomson-ski.com
www.thomson-ski.com
www.thomson-snowboarding.co.uk

Top Deck
Lively, informal holidays
Tel 020 7370 4555
Fax 020 7751 1205
res@topdecktravel.co.uk
www.topdeckski.co.uk

Tops Ski Chalets and Club Hotels
Chalets in France
Tel 01273 774666
Fax 01273 734042
sales@topstravel.co.uk
www.topstravel.co.uk

Trail Alpine
Chalet in Morzine
Tel 01745 570106
Fax 01745 570641
trailalpine@cs.com
www.trailalpine.co.uk

United Vacations Ski Freedom USA
US and Canada programme
Tel 0870 606 2222
Fax 020 8313 3547
uvuk@unitedvacations.com
www.unitedvacations.co.uk

Val d'Isère A La Carte
Holidays in Val-d'Isère
Tel 01481 236800
Fax 01481 239804
skialacarte@aol.com
www.skivaldisere.co.uk

Val d'Isère Properties (VIP)
Specialist in Val-d'Isère
Tel 020 8875 1957
Fax 020 8875 9236
ski@valdisere.co.uk
www.valdisere.co.uk

Vanilla Ski
Chalet in Seez (near La Rosière and Les Arcs)
Tel 01932 860696
Fax 01932 860696
sam@vanillaski.com
www.vanillaski.com

Virgin Ski
Holidays to America
Tel 01293 414243
Fax 01293 536957
brochure.requests@virginholidays.co.uk
www.virginholidays.co.uk

Waymark Holidays
Cross-country skiing holidays
Tel 01753 516477
Fax 01753 517016
enquiries@waymarkholidays.com
www.waymarkholidays.com

Weekends in Val d'Isère
Weekends – and not just in Val d'Isère
Tel 020 8944 9762
Fax 020 8947 9552
valweekends@btinternet.com
www.val-disere-ski.com

White Mountain Lodge
Chalets in Argentière
Tel 01403 267769
Fax 01403 267769
skiwml@yahoo.com

White Roc
Weekends and short breaks
Tel 020 7792 1188
Fax 020 7792 1956
ski@whiteroc.co.uk
www.whiteroc.co.uk

YSE
Variety of holidays in Val-d'Isère
Tel 020 8871 5117
Fax 020 8871 5229
sales@yseski.co.uk
www.yseski.co.uk

Black-and-white pages

A classified listing of the names, numbers and addresses you are likely to need.

Airlines

Air Canada
Tel 0870 524 7226
www.aircanada.ca

Air France
Tel 0845 0845 111
www.airfrance.com/uk

Air New Zealand
Tel 020 8741 2299
www.airnewzealand.com

Alitalia
Tel 0870 544 8259
www.alitalia.co.uk

American Airlines
Tel 020 8572 5555
www.aa.com
08547 789789 outside London

Austrian Airlines
Tel 0845 601 0948
www.austrianairlines.co.uk

British Airways
Tel 0845 77 333 77
www.british-airways.com
Flights: 0870 55 111 55;
General: 0845 77 999 77

Buzz
Tel 0870 240 7070
www.buzzaway.com

Continental Airlines
Tel 0800 776464
www.continental.com

Delta Airlines
Tel 0800 414767
www.delta.com

EasyJet
Tel 0870 6 000 000
www.easyjet.com

Go
Tel 0870 607 6543
www.go-fly.co.uk

KLM
Tel 08705 074074
www.klmuk.co.uk

Lauda Air
Tel 020 7434 7310
www.laudaair.com
Freephone 0800 767737

Lufthansa
Tel 0845 773 7747
www.lufthansa.com

Qantas
Tel 0845 7 747 767
www.qantas.com.au

Ryanair
Tel 0870 333 1231
www.ryanair.com

Swissair
Tel 0845 601 0956
info@swissair.com
www.swissair.co.uk

United Airlines
Tel 0845 844 4777
www.unitedairlines.co.uk

Virgin Atlantic Airways
Tel 01293 747 747
www.virgin-atlantic.com

Airports

Aberdeen
Tel 01224 722331
Fax 01224 775845
www.baa.co.uk

Belfast
Tel 028 9448 4848
Fax 028 9448 4849
www.bial.co.uk

Birmingham
Tel 0121 767 5511
Fax 0121 782 8802
info@bhx.co.uk
www.bhx.co.uk

Bournemouth
Tel 01202 364000
Fax 01202 364119
www.flybournemouth.com

Bristol
Tel 0870 121 2747
www.bristolairport.com

Cardiff
Tel 01446 711111
Fax 01446 711675
www.cial.co.uk

Dublin
Tel 00 353 1 814 1111
www.dublin-airport.com

East Midlands
Tel 01332 852852
www.eastmidlandsairport.com

Edinburgh
Tel 0131 333 1000
www.baa.co.uk

Exeter
Tel 01392 367433
Fax 01392 364593
www.exeter-airport.co.uk

Glasgow
Tel 0141 887 1111
www.baa.co.uk

Leeds-Bradford
Tel 0113 250 9696
Fax 0113 250 5426
www.lbia.co.uk

London Gatwick
Tel 0870 000 2468
www.baa.co.uk

London Heathrow
Tel 0870 0000 123
www.baa.co.uk

London Luton
Tel 01582 405100
Fax 01582 395313
info@london-luton.co.uk
www.london-luton.com

London Stansted
Tel 01279 680500
Fax 01279 662066
www.baa.co.uk

Manchester
Tel 0161 489 3000
Fax 0161 489 3813
www.manchesterairport.co.uk

Newcastle
Tel 0191 286 0966
Fax 0191 271 6080
dm@newcastleairport.com
www.newcastleairport.com

Teesside
Tel 01325 332811
Fax 01325 332810
information@teessideairport.com
www.teessideairport.com

Airport Transfers

Airport Transfer Service
Tel 00 33 450 536397
Fax 00 33 450 536397
Geneva transfers to Portes du Soleil, Chamonix and Haute Savoie region.

The Alpine Cab Company
Tel 00 33 450 731938
Fax 00 33 450 731938
info@alpinecabco.com
www.alpinecabco.com

Breakdown Insurance

AA Five Star Service
Tel 0800 085 2840
customer.services@theAA.com
www.theAA.com

Autohome
Tel 01604 232334
Fax 01604 231304

Direct Line Rescue
Tel 0845 246 8702
www.directline.com/rescue

Europ Assistance
Tel 01444 442442
www.europ-assistance.co.uk

First Assist Group
Tel 020 8763 1550
Fax 020 8668 1262
www.firstassist.co.uk

Green Flag
Tel 0800 400638
european-sales@greenflag.com
www.greenflag.com

Leisurecare Insurance Services
Tel 01793 750150
Fax 01793 750661

Mondial Assistance UK
Tel 020 8681 2525
Fax 020 8688 0577
www.mondial-assitance.co.uk

RAC Travel Services
Tel 0800 550055
Fax 01454 208391
www.rac.co.uk

Car Hire

Alamo Rent-a-Car
Tel 0990 994000
Fax 01273 223315
www.alamo.com

Avis Rent A Car
Tel 020 8848 8765
Fax 020 8569 1436
www.avis.co.uk

Budget Car and Van Rental
Tel 08701 565656
Fax 01442 276000
www.go-budget.co.uk

Europcar UK
Tel 0870 607 5005
Fax 01923 811010
www.europcar.co.uk/index

Hertz Europe
Tel 08708 484848
Fax 020 8679 0181
www.hertz.co.uk

Holiday Autos International Ltd
Tel 0870 400 0000
Fax 0870 400 4460
www.holidayautos.com

Suncars
Tel 0870 500 5566
Fax 01293 843368
customerservices@suncars.com
www.suncars.com

Car Winter Equipment

Brindley Chains Ltd
Tel 01925 825555
Fax 01925 825338
www.brindley-chains.co.uk
Pewag snowchains

DAP (Cambridge) Ltd
Tel 01223 323400
Fax 01223 324952
www.skidrive.co.uk
Thule roof systems, Kar Rite boxes, Skandibox, Konig snowchains

GT Towing Ltd
Tel 01707 652118
Fax 01707 644638
www.gttowing.co.uk
Ski boxes and snowchains

Lakeland Roof Box Centre
Tel 01539 732793
Fax 01539 732818
sales@lakeland.sagehost.co.uk
www.roofbox.com

Latchmere Motor Spares
Tel 020 7223 5491
Fax 020 7228 3907
Snowchains, roof bars, ski clamps, boxes

Motor Traveller
Tel 01753 833442
Fax 01753 832495
www.carbox.co.uk
Thule racks and boxes; Milz snowchains

RUD Chains Ltd
Tel 01227 276611
Fax 01227 276586

Snowchains Ltd
Tel 01732 884408
Fax 01732 884564

Spikes Spiders
Tel 0161 834 4153
Fax 0161 839 2941
www.spikesspider.com

The Roof Box Company
Tel 08700 766326
Fax 01539 621886
www.roofbox.co.uk

Thule Ltd
Tel 01275 340404
Fax 01275 340686
www.thule.co.uk

Cross Channel Travel

Brittany Ferries
Tel 08705 360 360
Fax 08709 030 400
www.brittanyferries.co.uk
Portsmouth–Caen

Eurotunnel
Tel 08705 35 35 35
Fax 01303 288784
www.eurotunnel.com
Folkestone–Calais/Coquelles via the Channel Tunnel

Hoverspeed
Tel 0870 524 0241
Fax 01304 865203
www.hoverspeed.com
Dover–Calais; Dover–Ostend; Newhaven–Dieppe

Norfolkline
Tel 0870 870 10 20
Fax 01303 260022
www.norfolkline.com
Dover–Dunkirk

P&O North Sea Ferries
Tel 0870 1296002
Fax 01482 706438
www.ponsf.com
Hull–Zeebrugge; Hull–Rotterdam

P&O Portsmouth
Tel 0870 242 4999
www.poportsmouth.com
Portsmouth–Cherbourg; Portsmouth–Le Havre

P&O Stena Line
Tel 0870 600 0600
Fax 01304 863464
www.posl.com
Dover–Calais

SeaFrance
Tel 08705 711 711
www.seafrance.co.uk
Dover-Calais

Stena Line
Tel 08705 707070
www.stenaline.co.uk
Harwich–Hook of Holland

Dry Ski Slopes

South-West England

Christchurch Ski Centre
Matchams Lane, Hurn, Christchurch, Dorset BH23 6AW
Tel 01202 499155
www.newforest-online.co.uk/christchurch_ski

Exeter and District Ski Club
Belmont Road, Exeter EX1 2DJ
Tel 01392 211422

High Actions' Avon Ski Centre
Lyncombe Drive, Churchill, North Somerset BS19 5PQ
Tel 01934 852335
www.highaction.co.uk

John Nike Leisuresport
Plymouth Ski Centre, Alpine Park, Marsh Mills, Plymouth PL6 8LQ
Tel 01752 600220
www.jnll.co.uk

Torquay Alpine Ski Club
Barton Hall, Kingskerswell Road, Torquay, Devon TQ2 8JY
Tel 01803 313350
www.skitorquay.co.uk

Warmwell Snow Zone
Warmwell, Dorchester, Dorset DT2 8JE
Tel 01305 853245

Wellington Sports Centre
Corams Lane, Wellington, Somerset TA21 8LL
Tel 01823 663010

Yeovil Ski Centre
Addlewell Lane, Nine Springs, Yeovil, Somerset BA20 1QW
Tel 01935 421702

South-East England

Alpine Snowsports Aldershot
Gallwey Road, Aldershot, Hants GU11 2DD
Tel 01252 325889
www.alpinesnowsports.co.uk

Beckton Alpine Centre
Alpine Way, London E6 4LA
Tel 020 7511 0351
www.becktonalps.co.uk

Bishop Reindorp Ski Centre
Larch Avenue, Guildford, Surrey
Tel 01483 504988
www.brski.co.uk

Bowles Outdoor Centre
Eridge Green, Tunbridge Wells TN3 9LW
Tel 01892 665665
www.bowles.ac

Bromley Ski Centre
Sandy Lane, St Paul's Cray, Orpington, Kent BR5 3HY
Tel 01689 876812

Calshot Activities Centre
Calshot Spit, Fawley,
Southampton SO45 1BR
Tel 023 8089 2077
www.hants.gov.uk/calshot

Folkestone Sports Centre
Radnor Park Avenue,
Folkestone, Kent CT19 5HX
Tel 01303 850333
www.folkestoneski.co.uk

Hillingdon Ski Centre
Gatling Way, Park Road,
Uxbridge, Middlesex UB8 1NR
Tel 01895 255183

John Nike Leisuresport
Bracknell Ski Centre, Amen
Corner, Bracknell, Berkshire
RG12 8TN
Tel 01344 789002
www.jnll.co.uk

John Nike Leisuresport
Chatham Ski and Snowboard
Centre, Alpine Park, Capstone
Road, Gillingham, Kent
ME7 3JH
Tel 01634 827979
Fax 01634 814075
www.jnll.co.uk

Sandown Ski Centre
More Lane, Esher, Surrey
KT10 8AN
Tel 01372 467132
www.sandownsports.co.uk

Southampton Ski Centre
The Sports Centre, Bassett,
Southampton SO16 7AY
Tel 023 8079 0970

Wycombe Summit
Abbey Barn Lane, High
Wycombe, Bucks HP10 9QQ
Tel 01494 474711
www.wycombesummit.co.uk

MIDDLE ENGLAND

The Ackers
Golden Hillock Road, Small
Heath, Birmingham B11 2PY
Tel 0121 772 5111
www.theackers.co.uk

Gloucester Ski Centre
Jarvis International Hotel and
Country Club, Robinswood Hill,
Matson Lane, Gloucester
GL4 6EA
Tel 01452 414300
www.gloucesterski.com

John Nike Leisuresport
Swadlincote Ski Centre, Hill
Street, Swadlincote, Derbyshire
DE11 8LP
Tel 01283 217200
www.jnll.co.uk

Kidsgrove Ski Centre
Kidsgrove, Stoke-on-Trent
ST7 4EF
Tel 01782 784908
www.ski-kidsgrove.co.uk

Snozone
Xscape, 602 Marlborough Gate,
Central Milton Keynes MK9 3XS
Tel 01908 230260
www.snozonemk.co.uk

Stoke Ski Centre
Festival Park, Stoke-on-Trent
ST1 5PU
Tel 01782 204159
www.stokeskicentre.co.uk

Tallington Ski Centre
Tallington Lakes Leisure Park,
Barholm Road, Tallington,
Stamford, Lincs PE9 4RJ
Tel 01778 344990
www.waspdirect.com

Tamworth Snowdome
Leisure Island, River Drive,
Tamworth, Staffordshire
B79 7ND
Tel 08705 000011
www.snowdome.co.uk

Telford Ski Centre
Court Street, Madeley, Telford,
Shropshire TF7 5DZ
Tel 01952 586862

EASTERN ENGLAND

Brentwood Park Ski Centre
Warley Gap, Brentwood, Essex
CM13 3LG
Tel 01277 211994

Gosling Ski Centre
Stanborough Road, Welwyn
Garden City, Hertfordshire
AL8 6XE
Tel 01707 384384
www.goslingsports.co.uk

Hemel Ski Centre
St Albans Hill, Hemel
Hempstead, Herts HP3 9NH
Tel 01442 241321
www.hemel-ski.co.uk

Norfolk Ski Club
Whitlingham Lane, Trowse,
Norwich, Norfolk NR14 8TW
Tel 01603 662781

Suffolk Ski Centre
Bourne Terrace, Wherstead,
Ipswich IP2 8NQ
Tel 01473 602347
pst@suffolkski.co.uk

NORTHERN ENGLAND

Alston Adventure Centre
High Plains Lodge, Alston,
Cumbria CA9 3DD
Tel 01434 381886

Halifax Ski Centre
Sportsman Leisure, Bradford
Old Road, Swalesmoor,
Ploughcroft, Halifax HX3 6UG
Tel 01422 340760
www.halifaxsnowsports.com

Kendal Ski Club
Canal Head North, Kendal,
Cumbria LA9 7AL
Tel 01539 732948/733031
www.kendalski.co.uk

The Oval Ski Club
Old Chester Road, Bebington
CH63 7LF
Tel 0151 645 0551

Pendle Ski Club
Clitheroe Road, Sabden,
Clitheroe, Lancs BB7 9HN
Tel 01200 425222

Runcorn Ski Centre
Town Park, Palace Fields,
Runcorn, Cheshire WA7 2PS
Tel 01928 701965
www.runcornskicentre.co.uk

Sheffield Ski Village
Vale Road, Parkwood Springs,
Sheffield S3 9SJ
Tel 0114 276 9459
www.sheffieldskivillage.co.uk

Ski Rossendale
Haslingden Old Road,
Rawtenstall, Rossendale,
Lancashire BB4 8RR
Tel 01706 226457
www.ski-rossendale.co.uk

Whickham Thorns Centre
Market Lane, Dunston
NE11 9NX
Tel 0191 460 1193

WALES

Cardiff Ski Centre
Fairwater Park, Fairwater,
Cardiff CF5 3JR
Tel 029 2056 1793
www.skicardiff.com

Dan-yr-Ogof Ski Slopes
Abercrave, Upper Swansea
Valley, Powys SA9 1GJ
Tel 01639 730284

John Nike Leisuresport
Great Orme, Llandudno
LL30 2QL
Tel 01492 874707
www.jnll.co.uk

Plas y Brenin
Capel Curig, Gwynedd
LL24 0ET
Tel 01690 720214

Pontypool Ski Centre
Pontypool Leisure Park,
Pontypool, Gwent NP4 8AT
Tel 01495 756955

Rhiwgoch Ski Centre
Bronaber, Trawsfynydd,
Gwynedd LL41 4UR
Tel 01766 540578
www.logcabins-skiwales.co.uk

Ski Pembrey
Pembrey Country Park, Llanelli,
Carmarthenshire SA16 0EJ
Tel 01554 834443

SCOTLAND

Alford Ski Centre
Greystone Road, Alford,
Aberdeenshire AB33 8TY
Tel 01975 563024

Ancrum Resource Centre
10 Ancrum Road, Dundee,
Tayside DD2 2HZ
Tel 01382 435911

Bearsden Ski Club
Stockiemuir Road, Bearsden,
Glasgow G61 3RS
Tel 0141 943 1500
www.skibearsden.co.uk

Firpark Ski Centre
Tillycoultry, Clackmannanshire
FK13 6PL
Tel 01259 751772

Glasgow Ski/Snowboard Centre
Bellahouston Park, 16
Dumbreck Road, Glasgow
G41 5BW
Tel 0141 427 4991
www.ski-glasgow.org

Glenmore Lodge
Scottish National Sports
Centre, Aviemore, Inverness-
shire PH22 1QU
Tel 01479 861256
www.glenmorelodge.org.uk

Hilton Craigendarroch Country Club
Braemar Road, Ballater, Royal
Deeside AB35 5XA
Tel 01339 755858

Loch Rannoch Outdoor Centre
Kinloch Rannoch, Perthshire
PH16 5PS
Tel 01882 632201

Lochanhully Woodland Club
Carrbridge, Inverness-shire
PH23 3NA
Tel 01479 841234

Midlothian Ski Centre
Hillend, Near Edinburgh,
Midlothian EH10 7DU
Tel 0131 445 4433
www.midlothian.gov.uk

Newmilns Ski Slope
High Street, Newmilns
KA16 9EB
Tel 01560 322320

Polmonthill Ski Centre
Polmont, Falkirk FK2 0YE
Tel 01324 503835
www.polmonthill.net

NORTHERN IRELAND

Craigavon Golf and Ski Centre
Turmoyra Lane, Silverwood,
Lurgan BT66 6NG
Tel 028 3832 6606

Mount Ober Ski Centre
24 Ballymaconaghy Road,
Knockbracken, Belfast
BT8 6SB
Tel 028 9079 5666

Insurance Companies

ABC Holiday Extras
Tel 0870 844 4358
Fax 0870 844 4310
insurance@abcmail.co.uk
www.abctravelinsurance.co.uk

Aon Suretravel
Tel 01883 834033
Fax 01883 835010
customer.care@aon.co.uk
www.aon.com

Atlas
Tel 020 7609 5000
Fax 020 7609 5011
sales@travel-insurance.co.uk
www.atlasdirect.net

AUL
Tel 01206 577770
Fax 01206 542079
enquiries@aul.co.uk
www.aul.co.uk

Blackwater Travel Indemnity Limited (BTI)
Tel 01621 855553
Fax 01621 858777
mail@blackwater-insurance.co.uk
www.blackwater-insurance.co.uk

British Activity Holiday Insurance Services
Tel 020 7251 6821
Fax 020 7490 0708
ansell@easynet.co.uk
www.ansell.co.uk

BUPA Travel Services
Tel 0870 103 2123
www.bupa.co.uk/travel

CGNU
Tel 0800 121007
www.norwichunion.co.uk

Columbus Travel Insurance Direct
Tel 020 7375 0011
Fax 020 7375 0022

Direct Travel Insurance
Tel 01903 812345
Fax 01903 813555
info@direct-travel.co.uk
www.direct-travel.co.uk

Douglas Cox Tyrie
Tel 01708 385969

Euclidian Insurance Services Ltd
Tel 01784 484601
Fax 01784 484610

Europ Assistance
Tel 01444 442442
Fax 01444 459292
www.europ-assistance.co.uk

Hamilton Barr
Tel 01483 255666
Fax 01483 255660
www.hamiltonbarr.com

Jardine Lloyd Thompson
Tel 0161 957 8000

Ketteridge Group
Tel 01277 630770
Fax 01277 630770

Matthew Gerard Travel Insurance Ltd
Tel 01483 730900
Fax 01483 730969
sales@mgtis.easynet.co.uk
www.mgtis.co.uk

P J Hayman & Company
Tel 023 9241 9010
Fax 023 9230 1425
travel.insurance@pjhayman.com
www.pjhayman.com

Perry Gamble
Tel 020 8542 1122

Preferential
Tel 0990 133723
www.preferential.co.uk

Primary Insurance Group
Tel 0870 200 0012
Fax 0870 200 0013
enquiries@primaryinsurance.co.uk
www.primaryinsurance.co.uk

Select Travel Insurance
Tel 08707 370870

Snowcard Insurance Services Ltd
Tel 01327 262805
Fax 01327 263227
enquiries@snowcard.co.uk
www.snowcard.co.uk

Sportscover Direct Ltd
Tel 0117 922 6222
Fax 0117 922 1666
info@sportscover.co.uk
www.sportscover.co.uk

Sterling Travel Insurance Services plc
Tel 0161 475 6000
Fax 0161 475 6001
csa@sterling-n.co.uk
www.sterlingtvlins.co.uk

Supreme Travel
Tel 01355 260547
Fax 01355 229237
sales@travelinsurance-uk.com
www.travelinsurance-uk.com

Travel Protection Group plc
Tel 028 9032 6585
Fax 028 9033 1387
www.thetravelprotectiongroup.plc.uk

Voyager Insurance Services Ltd
Tel 01483 562662
Fax 01483 569676
enquiries@voyagerins.com

World Ski and Snowboard Association
Tel 0114 279 7300
Fax 0114 276 2348
info@worldski.co.uk
www.worldski.co.uk

WorldCover Direct
Tel 0800 365121
Fax 0180 557 4941
world.cover@gecapital.com
www.worldcover.com

Worldwide Travel Insurance Services Ltd
Tel 01892 833338
Fax 01892 837744
sales@worldwideinsure.com
www.worldwideinsure.com

National Tourist Offices

Andorran Delegation
Tel 020 8874 4806

Argentinian Tourist Board
Tel 020 7318 1340

Australian Tourist Commission
Tel 09068 633235
Fax 020 8780 1496
www.australia.com

Austrian National Tourist Office
Tel 020 7629 0461
Fax 020 7499 6038
info@anto.co.uk
www.austria-tourism.at
Correspondence and phone calls only

Canadian Tourism Commission
Tel 0906 871 5000
visitcanada@dial.pipex.com
www.travelcanada.ca

Chile – Consulate General
Tel 020 7580 1023
Fax 020 7323 4294
cglonduk@congechileuk.demon.co.uk

Czech Republic Tourist Authority
Tel 09063 640641
Fax 020 7436 8300
ctainfo@czechcentre.org.uk
www.visitczech.cz

Finnish Tourist Board
Tel 020 7365 2512
Fax 020 8600 5681

French Government Tourist Office
Tel 09068 244123
Fax 020 7493 6594
info@mdlf.co.uk
www.franceguide.com

German National Tourist Office
Tel 09001 600100
Fax 020 7495 6129
gntolon@d-z-t.com
www.germany-tourism.de

Italian State Tourist Office
Tel 020 7408 1254
Fax 020 7493 6695
enitlond@globalnet.co.uk
www.enit.it
Brochure line: 0891 600280

Japanese Tourist Commission
Tel 020 7734 9638
Fax 020 7734 4290
jntolon@dircon.co.uk
www.jnto.go.jp

Norwegian Tourist Board
Tel 020 7839 6255
Fax 020 7839 6014
infouk@ntr.no
www.visitnorway.com

Romanian Tourist Office
Tel 020 7224 3692
Fax 020 7935 6435
uktouroff@romania.freeserve.co.uk
www.romaniatravel.com

Scottish Tourist Board
Tel 0131 332 2433
Fax 0131 343 1513
www.holiday.scotland.net

Slovenian Tourist Office
Tel 020 7287 7133
Fax 020 7287 5476
www.slovenia-tourism.si

Spanish Tourist Office
Tel 020 7486 8077
Fax 020 7486 8034
londres@tourspain.es
www.tourspain.co.uk

Swedish Travel and Tourism Council
Tel 00800 3080 3080
Fax 020 7724 5872
info@swetourism.org.uk
www.visit-sweden.com

Switzerland Tourism
Tel 020 7851 1700
Fax 020 7851 1720
stlondon@switzerlandtourism.ch
www.MySwitzerland.com

Tourism New Zealand
Tel 09069 10 10 10
Fax 020 7839 8929
www.purenz.com

Turkish Tourist Office
Tel 020 7629 7771
Fax 020 7491 0773

Visit USA Association
Tel 09069 101020

Railways

Deutsche Bahn
Tel 0870 243 5363
sales@deutsche-bahn.co.uk
www.bahn.co.uk

Eurostar
Tel 08705 186186
www.eurostar.com

Rail Europe
Tel 08705 848 848
www.raileurope.co.uk

Swiss Federal Railways
Tel 020 7734 1921
Fax 020 7437 4577
www.rail.ch

Retailers

These retailers of ski/board equipment also stock *Where to Ski and Snowboard.*

South-West England

Apex Sports
24 Mill Street, Bideford, Devon EX39 2JW
Tel 01237 477739

BSB Snowboarding
68 West Street, Old market, Bristol
Tel 0117 955 0779
Fax 0117 941 1744

Christchurch Ski Centre
Matchams Lane, Hurn, Christchurch, Dorset BH23 6AW
Tel 01202 499568
Fax 01202 483564

Devon Ski Centre
Oak Place, Newton Abbot, Devon TQ12 2EX
Tel 01626 351278
Fax 01626 351065

Green Room
53 Park Street, Bristol BS1 5NT
Tel 0117 929 1033

Mission Adventuresport
1 Bank Lane, Brixham, Devon TQ5 8EX
Tel 01803 855796
Fax 01803 855796

Penrose Outdoors
Town Quay, Truro, Cornwall TR1 2HJ
Tel 01872 272116
Fax 01872 240431

Skate and Ski
104 High Street, Staple Hill, Bristol BS16 5HL
Tel 0117 970 1356

Ski Lark
33 Middlehill Rd, Colehill, Wimborne, Dorset BH21 2SB
Tel 01202 886035

Snow & Rock
Units 1-3 Shield Retail Centre, Gloucester Road North, Filton, Bristol BS34 7BQ
Tel 0117 914 3000

Team Ski
37 High East Street, Dorchester, Dorset DT1 1HN
Tel 01305 268035
Fax 01305 268035

Westsports
Market House, Marlborough Rd, Old Town, Swindon SN3 1HQ
Tel 01793 532588
Fax 01793 542371

South-East England

47 Degrees
164 Hurlingham Road, Fulham, London SW6 3NG
Tel 020 7384 1747

Activ (Folkestone)
145 Sandgate Road, Folkestone, Kent CT20 2DA
Tel 01303 240110
Fax 01303 255193

Captain's Cabin
93 High Street, Chatham, Kent ME4 4DL
Tel 01634 819777
Fax 01634 819777

Captain's Cabin
14 St George's Walk, Croydon CR0 1YG
Tel 020 8680 6968

Captain's Cabin
19 Wincheap, Canterbury, Kent CT1 3TB
Tel 01227 457906
Fax 01227 763292

Captain's Cabin Sevenoaks
113-115 St John's Hill, Sevenoaks, Kent TN13 3PE
Tel 01732 464463
Fax 01732 464463

Carters
99-113 Caversham Road, Reading, Berkshire RG1 8AN
Tel 0118 959 9022
Fax 0118 950 0618

Country Trails Limited
39 Mount Pleasant, Tunbridge Wells, Kent TN1 1PN
Tel 01892 539002
Fax 01892 534902

Finches
25-29 Perry Vale, Forest Hill, London SE23 2NE
Tel 020 8699 6768
Fax 020 8699 7295

John Pollock
157 High Road, Loughton, Essex IG10 4LF
Tel 020 8508 6626

John Pollock
119 High Road, East Finchley, London N2 8AG
Tel 020 8883 4364

John Pollock
67 High Street, Barnet EN5 5UR
Tel 020 8440 3994

Lang & Hunter
12 Thames Street, Kingston-upon-Thames, Surrey KT1 1PE
Tel 020 8941 2057
Fax 020 8549 4626

Mountain Bike & Ski Co
18 Gillingham Street, Victoria, London SW1V 1HU
Tel 020 7834 8933
Fax 020 7834 8933

Snow Boats
8-10 The Street, Wrecclesham, Farnham, Surrey GU10 4PR
Tel 01252 715169
Fax 01252 715169

Snow & Rock
188 Kensington High Street, London W8 7RG
Tel 020 7937 0872

Snow & Rock
4 Mercer Street, Covent Garden, London WC2H 9QA
Tel 020 7420 1444

Snow & Rock
150 Holborn, Corner of Grays Inn Road, London EC1N 2LC
Tel 020 7831 6900

Snow & Rock
99 Fordwater Road, Chertsey, Surrey KT16 8HH
Tel 01932 566886

Snowball Ski Company
1 George Street, Richmond, Surrey TW9 1JY
Tel 020 8940 6293
Fax 020 8940 6466

Middle England

Active Outdoor & Ski
28 Castle Centre, Banbury, Oxfordshire OX16 5NG
Tel 01295 273700
Fax 01295 254108

Attwoolls Ski Shop
Bristol Road, Whitminster, Gloucestershire GL2 7LX
Tel 01452 742200
Fax 01452 742244

Beans
86 Sheep Street, Bicester, Oxfordshire OX6 7LP
Tel 01869 246451
Fax 01869 840412

BestBuys
Nene Court, 27-31 The Embankment, Wellingborough, Northamptonshire NN8 1LD
Tel 01933 272699
Fax 01933 441 471

Fox's
1 London Road, Amersham HP7 0HE
Tel 01494 431431
Fax 01494 431838

Lockwoods Ski Shop
125-129 Rugby Road, Leamington Spa CV32 6DJ
Tel 01926 339388
Fax 01926 470408

Ski Force (South West)
9 Draycott Crescent, Cam, Dursley, Glos GL11 5LN
Tel 01453 519084
Fax 01453 519084

Skiforce Ltd
38 Tamworth Street, Lichfield, Staffordshire WS13 6JJ
Tel 01543 411422
Fax 01543 415416

Snow & Rock
14 Priory Queensway, Birmingham B4 6BS
Tel 0121 236 8280

Solihull Ski Centre
100 Widney Rd, Bentley Heath, Solihull B93 9BN
Tel 01564 774176
Fax 01564 770349

Sporting Triangle
18 West Street, Hereford HR4 0BX
Tel 01432 271500

Tracks
22/24 Halford St, Leicester LE1 1JB
Tel 0116 251 7040
Fax 0116 251 8060

Tracks
47 Queen Street, Derby DE1 3DE
Tel 01332 342245
Fax 01332 200650

Two Seasons
39 Pelham Street, Nottingham NG1 2EA
Tel 0115 950 1333

Two Seasons
229-231 Wellingborough Road, Northampton NN1 4EF
Tel 01604 627377

Two Seasons
15 Pump Street, Worcester WR1 2QY
Tel 01905 731144

EASTERN ENGLAND

Eskimowear
The Old Cottages, Market Place, Hockley Rd, Rayleigh, Essex SS6 8EB
Tel 01268 770362

Skee-Tex
The Old Mill, Battlesbridge, Essex SS1 8TR
Tel 01268 768282

Ski Surf 2000
13 Peartree Centre, Stanway, Colchester, CO3 5JN
Tel 01206 502000

Snow & Rock
Hemel Ski Centre, St Albans Hill, Hemel Hempstead HP3 9NH
Tel 01442 235305

SnowFit
2 Cucumber Lane, Brundall, Norwich NR13 5QY
Tel 01603 716655

Two Seasons
34 Chesterton Road, Cambridge CB4 1EN
Tel 01223 356207

NORTHERN ENGLAND

1st Wet & Wild
619 Anlaby Road, Hull HU3 6SU
Tel 01482 354076
Fax 01482 354972

BAC Outdoor Leisure
Central Hall, Coronation Street, Elland, Halifax, West Yorkshire HX5 0DF
Tel 01422 371146
Fax 01422 371146

Endless Summer Ltd
20B Duke Street, Douglas, Isle of Man IM1 2AY
Tel 01624 616987
Fax 01624 833333

Glide & Slide
5/7 Station Road, Otley LS21 3HX
Tel 01943 461136
Fax 01943 461244

LD Mountain Centre Limited
34 Dean Street, Newcastle-upon-Tyne NE1 1PG
Tel 0191 232 3561
Fax 0191 222 0082

Mayhem Surf Snow Skate
7 Jubbergate, York YO1 8RT
Tel 01904 655062

Mountain & Marine
159 London Road South, Poynton, Cheshire SK12 1LQ
Tel 01625 859863
Fax 01625 859878

Sail & Ski
9 Pepper Street, Grosvenor Shopping Centre, Chester, Cheshire CH1 1EA
Tel 01244 344580
Fax 01244 344580

Sayers
66 High Street, Yarm, Cleveland TS15 9AG
Tel 01642 785423

Severn Sports
80 Town Street, Armley, Leeds, West Yorkshire LS12 3AA
Tel 0113 279 1618
Fax 0113 231 0231

Snow & Rock
Sheffield Ski Centre, Vale Road, Parkwood Springs, Sheffield S3 9SJ
Tel 0114 275 1700

SCOTLAND

Summits
36 Moss Street, Paisley PA1 1BA
Tel 0141 887 5536

Summits
5 Bridge Street, Dunfermline KY12 8AQ
Tel 01383 730181
Fax 01383 730184

NORTHERN IRELAND

Macski
140 Lisburn Road, Belfast BT9 6AJ
Tel 028 9066 5525

IRELAND

The Great Outdoors
Chatham Street, Dublin 2, Ireland
Tel 00 353 1679 4293
Fax 00 353 1679 4554

The Lowe Alpine Shop
17-18 Temple Lane, Templebar, Dublin 2, Ireland
Tel 00 353 1672 7088
Fax 00 353 1672 7089

SKI ORGANISATIONS

British Association of Snowsport Instructors (BASI)
Tel 01479 861717
Fax 01479 861718
www.basi.org.uk

British Ski and Snowboard Federation
Tel 0131 445 7676
Fax 0131 445 7722
www.ifyouski.com

British Ski Club for the Disabled
Tel 01895 271104

British Snowboard Association
Tel 07000 360540
Fax 07000 720540
www.isf.net

English Ski Council
Tel 0121 501 2314
Fax 0121 585 6448
www.englishski.org

Ski Club of Great Britain
Tel 020 8410 2000
Fax 020 8410 2001
www.skiclub.co.uk

Snowsport Scotland
Tel 0131 445 4151
Fax 0131 445 4949
www.snsc.demon.co.uk

Snowsport Wales
Tel 029 2056 1904
Fax 029 2056 1924
www.snowsportwales.net

The Uphill Ski Club
Tel 01479 861272
Fax 01479 861272
www.uphillskiclub.co.uk
For people with disabilities

World Ski and Snowboard Association
Tel 0114 279 7300
Fax 0114 276 2348
www.worldski.co.uk

SKI TRAVEL AGENTS

Alpine Answers
Tel 020 8871 4656
Fax 020 8871 9676
www.alpineanswers.co.uk

Avant-ski
Tel 0191 212 1173
Fax 0191 239 9459
sales@avant-ski.com
www.avant-ski.com

Iglu.com
Tel 0870 870 5787
Fax 020 8542 9223
enquiries@iglu.com
www.iglu.com

Independent Ski Links
Tel 01964 533905
Fax 01964 536006
info@ski-links.com
www.ski-links.com

Ski Expectations
Tel 01799 531888
Fax 01799 531887
skiexpectations@virgin.net
www.skiexpectations.com

Ski McNeill
Tel 028 9066 6699
Fax 028 9068 3888
mail@skimcneill.com
www.skimcneill.com

Ski Solutions
Tel 020 7471 7700
Fax 020 7471 7701
www.skisolutions.com

Ski Travel Centre
Tel 0141 649 9696
Fax 0141 649 2273
snow@skitravelcentre.com
www.ski-travel-centre.co.uk

Skiers Travel
Tel 0113 292 0893
www.skiers-travel.co.uk

Snow Finders
Tel 01858 466888
Fax 01858 466788
sales@snowfinders.com
www.snowfinders.com

Snow Line
Tel 01858 828000
Fax 01858 828020
www.snow-line.co.uk

Ski Line
Tel 020 8777 0440
www.skiline.co.uk

Resort index / directory

This is an index to the resort chapters in the book; you'll find page references for about 400 resorts described elsewhere. But you'll also find brief descriptions here of another 700 resorts, most of them much smaller than those we've covered in full, but often still worth a short visit. We also list here the companies offering package holidays to each resort. To get in touch with one of these tour operators, look them up in the list starting on page 650.

Key

Lifts
Pistes
⊠ *UK tour operators*

49 Degrees North USA
Inland area with best snow in Washington State, including 120-acre bowl reserved for powder weekends.
1195m; slopes 1195–1760m
5 780 acres

Abetone Italy
Resort in the exposed Appennines, less than two hours from Florence and Pisa.
1390m; slopes 1390–1900m
25 50km
⊠ *Alpine Tours*

Abtenau Austria
Sizeable village in Dachstein-West region near Salzburg, on large plain ideal for cross-country for which it's known.
710m; slopes 710–1260m
6 10km
⊠ *Thomson*

Achenkirch Austria
Unspoilt, low-altitude Tirolean village close to Niederau and Alpbach, in a beautiful setting overlooking a lake.
930m; slopes 930–1800m
10 25km
⊠ *Ramblers*

Adelboden 399
⊠ *Interhome, Kuoni, Made to Measure, Plus Travel, Swiss Travel Service*

Les Aillons France
Traditional village near Chambéry. Nicely sheltered slopes.
1000m; slopes 1000–1900m
24 40km

Akakura Japan
Old spa of some oriental charm, 150km from Tokyo; modern lift system and easy runs.
770m; slopes 770–1500m
41 85km

Alagna 373
Small resort on the western fringe of Monterosa Ski area, but only linked by off-piste at present.
⊠ *Ski Club of GB, Ski Weekend*

Alba Italy
Picturesque Dolomite village with a small, quiet area; access to the Sella Ronda at Canazei.
1515m; slopes 1515–2440m
5 10km
⊠ *Crystal*

Alleghe Italy
Dolomite village in a pretty lakeside setting close to numerous areas. Cheap base near Cortina.
980m
24 80km
⊠ *Crystal*

Alpbach 95
⊠ *Crystal, Inghams, Interhome, Made to Measure, Thomson*

Alpe-d'Huez 193
⊠ *Airtours, Alpine Options, Chalet World, Chalets 'Unlimited', Club Med, Crystal, Erna Low, Esprit Ski, Eurotunnel Motoring Holidays, Fairhand Holidays, First Choice Ski, Iglu.com, Independent Ski Links, Inghams, Interhome, La Source, Lagrange Holidays, Made to Measure, Motours, Neilson, Panorama, Ski Arrangements, Ski Club of GB, Ski Expectations, Ski France, Ski Independence, Ski Leisure Direction, Ski Life, Ski Line, Ski Miquel, SkiAway Holidays, Skiworld, Thomson, Tops Ski Chalets and Club Hotels*

Alpe-du-Grand-Serre France
Tiny resort near Alpe-d'Huez and Les Deux-Alpes. Good for bad-weather days.
1400m; slopes 1400–2200m
20 55km

Alpendorf
Hamlet-cum-base-station 4km from St Johann im Pongau. Linked to Wagrain and the extensive Salzburger Sportwelt Amadé lift network.

Alpine Meadows 479
⊠ *Virgin Ski*

Alps Korea
Korea's most northerly, snow-reliable resort. An hour from Seoul; 8 slopes; enormous ski-to-the door condo high-rise complex. 5

Alta 529
⊠ *Ski The American Dream*

Altenmarkt Austria
Unspoilt village well placed just off the Salzburg-Villach autobahn for numerous resorts including snowsure Obertauern and Wagrain.
855m; slopes 855–2130m
23 150km
⊠ *Made to Measure, Sloping Off*

Alto Campoo Spain
Barren, desolate place with undistinguished slopes, but single hotel is superb and wilderness views from mountain magnificent.
1700m; slopes 1650–2175m
10

Alt St Johann Switzerland
Old cross-country village with Alpine slopes connecting into Unterwasser area near Liechtenstein.
900m; slopes 900–2260m
21 50km

Alyeska USA
Alaskan area 60km from Anchorage, with luxury hotel. Spring best for weather.
75m; slopes 75–1200m
9 785 acres
⊠ *Inghams*

Aminona 407
Purpose-built resort on the eastern side of the Crans-Montana network.
⊠ *Lagrange Holidays*

Andalo Italy
Atmospheric Dolomite village near Madonna, with low wooded slopes well equipped with snowmakers; best for novices.
1050m; slopes 1035–2125m
17 60km
⊠ *Equity Total Ski, Rocketski, Sloping Off*

Andermatt 401
⊠ *Iglu.com, Made to Measure, Ski Weekend*

Andorra la Vella 608

Angel Fire USA
Intermediate neighbour of Taos, New Mexico. Height usually ensures good snow. Interesting sightseeing.
2620m; slopes 2620–3255m
6 455 acres

Les Angles France
Attractive resort with one of the best ski areas in the Pyrenees. Pretty, tree-lined, mostly easy skiing.
1600m; slopes 1650–2400m
23
⊠ *Lagrange Holidays*

Annaberg-Lungötz Austria
Peaceful village in a pretty setting, sharing a sizeable area with Gosau, close to Filzmoos.
775m; slopes 775–1620m
33 65km

Antagnod Italy
Weekend day-tripper area on way up to Champoluc, above Aosta valley. No village.
1710m; slopes 1710–2000m
4 7km

Anzère Switzerland
Sympathetically designed modern resort on a sunny balcony near Crans-Montana, with slopes suited to leisurely intermediates.
1500m; slopes 1500–2460m
13 40km
⊠ *Interhome, Lagrange Holidays, Made to Measure*

Apex 571
⊠ *Frontier Ski, Made to Measure, Ski Safari, Skisar US*

Aprica Italy
Ugly, straggling village between Lake Como and Brenta Dolomites, with bland slopes and limited facilities.
1180m; slopes 1180–2310m
24 40km
⊠ *Interhome, Thomson*

Arabba 381
Tiny village with the Sella Ronda's highest, steepest skiing on its doorstep.
⊠ *Crystal, Independent Ski Links, Inghams, Momentum Ski, Neilson, Ski Yogi*

Aragnouet-Piau France
Purpose-built mid-mountain satellite of St-Lary, best suited to families, beginners and early intermediates.
1850m; slopes 1420–2500m
32 80km

Arapahoe Basin 504
Small resort with the highest lift-served slopes in the US – Keystone is a few minutes away by road.

Arcalis 608
Isolated ski area (there's no resort), 15km from La Massana, with varied, scenic and, in places, steep terrain, and the best snow around.
⊠ *Snowcoach*

Les Arcs 202
⊠ *Airtours, Avant-ski, Chalets 'Unlimited', Chez Jay Ski, Club Med, Crystal, Erna Low, Esprit Ski, Eurotunnel Motoring Holidays, Fairhand Holidays, First Choice Ski, Iglu.com, Independent Ski Links, Inghams, Interhome, Lagrange Holidays, Made to Measure, Motours, Neilson, Optimum Ski, Ski Activity, Ski Amis, Ski Arrangements, Ski Club of GB,*

Ski France, Ski Independence, Ski Leisure Direction, Ski Line, Ski Olympic, Ski Supreme, SkiAway Holidays, Skiworld, Thomson, Vanilla Ski

Ardent 208
Quiet hamlet with quick access to Avoriaz and, more excitingly, Châtel's Linga sector.
✉ *The Chalet Company*

Åre 634
✉ *Neilson*

Arêches-Beaufort France
Secluded little resort accessible only from Mont Blanc region to the north.
1050m; slopes 1050–2300m
15 50km

Argentière 212
Unremarkable old village beneath a remarkable mountain, Chamonix's Grands Montets.
✉ *Alpine Answers Select, Bigfoot, Board and Lodge, Chalets 'Unlimited', Collineige, Crystal, Fairhand Holidays, Independent Ski Links, Interhome, Lagrange Holidays, McNab Mountain Sports, Motours, Ski Arrangements, Ski Club of GB, Ski Hillwood, Ski Scott James, Ski Weekend, Snowline, White Mountain Lodge, White Roc*

Arinsal 612
✉ *Airtours, Chalets 'Unlimited', Crystal, First Choice Ski, Inghams, Neilson, Panorama, Snowcoach, Thomson, Top Deck*

Arnoldstein/Dreiländereck
Austria
One of several little areas overlooking town of Villach.
680m; slopes 680–1455m
8 12km

Arolla Switzerland
Tiny village in pretty riverside setting south of Sion. Main attraction is heli-skiing. Wonderful descents from 3800m.
2005m; slopes 2005–2890m
5 47km

Arosa 403
✉ *Inghams, Interhome, Kuoni, Made to Measure, Momentum Ski, Plus Travel, Powder Byrne, Ski Choice, Ski Weekend, Swiss Travel Service, White Roc*

Artesina Italy
Purpose-built resort lacking character and atmosphere. Old lifts – nearly all drags.
1350m; slopes 1320–2100m
14 60km

Asiago Italy
Sizeable resort close to Verona, but low altitude and limited vertical.
1000m; slopes 1000–1380m 17
✉ *Headwater Holidays*

Aspen 486
✉ *Alpine Answers Select, American Ski Classics, Chalet World, Chalets 'Unlimited', Crystal, Elegant Resorts, Esprit Ski, Fantiski, Iglu.com, Independent Ski Links, Lotus Supertravel, Made to Measure, Momentum Ski, Ski Activity, Ski Expectations, Ski Independence, Ski Line, Ski Safari, Ski The American Dream, Ski Total, Skisar US, Skiworld, Thomson, United Vacations*

Attitash USA
One of the biggest ski areas in eastern US. Uncrowded slopes. Accommodation in nearby North Conway. Other New Hampshire areas close by.
slopes 180–715m
12 275 acres
✉ *Ski Success, Virgin Ski*

Auffach 181
Unexceptional village in the Wildschönau area.

Auris-en-Oisans 193
Quiet hamlet with local ski area linked across the valley to Alpe-d'Huez.
✉ *Fairhand Holidays, Lagrange Holidays*

Auron France
Pleasant village with varied, sheltered slopes; a stark contrast to nearby Isola 2000.
1600m; slopes 1165–2450m
26 130km

Auronzo di Cadore Italy
Sizeable village that's a cheaper base for visiting Cortina. Own slopes of negligible interest.
865m; slopes 865–1585m
5 7km

Aussois France
One of many rustic working villages near Modane that share Maurienne valley pass.
1500m; slopes 1500–2750m
11 50km

Autrans France
Major cross-country centre with 160km of trails. Pleasant village, close to Grenoble.
1050m; slopes 1050–1710m
15 18km
✉ *Headwater Holidays, Lagrange Holidays*

Avon USA
Small town only a couple of miles from Beaver Creek. Inexpensive base from which to ski Beaver Creek, Vail and Breckenridge.
✉ *Skisar US*

Avoriaz 208
✉ *Airtours, Chalets 'Unlimited', Club Med, Crystal, Erna Low, Eurotunnel Motoring Holidays, Fairhand Holidays, First Choice Ski, Iglu.com, Independent Ski Links, Lagrange Holidays, Made to Measure, Motours, Neilson, Ski Arrangements, Ski Choice, Ski Independence, Ski Leisure Direction, Ski Life, Thomson*

Axamer Lizum 111
✉ *Club Pavilion, Crystal*

Axams 111
Quiet village in Innsbruck area, below Axamer Lizum ski area
✉ *Lagrange Holidays*

Ax-les-Thermes France
Sizeable spa village with own train station near Font-Romeu and Andorra.
1400m; slopes 1400–2400m
17 75km

Bad Gastein 97
✉ *Crystal, Inghams, Made to Measure, Ski Miquel*

Badger Pass USA
Centre for 350 miles of superb backcountry touring in Yosemite National Park. Spectacular views.
2195m; slopes 2195–2435m
5 90 acres

Bad Hofgastein 97
Relaxed and spacious spa resort at the foot of the most attractive ski area in the Gastein Valley.
✉ *Crystal, Inghams, Made to Measure*

Bad Kleinkirchheim Austria
Spacious, sophisticated, quiet spa village in south-east of Austria, with queue-free, intermediate, tree-lined terrain.
1100m; slopes 1100–2055m
29 80km
✉ *Alpine Tours, Crystal, Sloping Off*

Banff-Lake Louise 573
✉ *Airtours, All Canada Ski, Alpine Answers Select, Club Pavilion, Crystal, Elegant Resorts, Equity Total Ski, First Choice Ski, Frontier Ski, Handmade Holidays, Independent Ski Links, Inghams, Kuoni, Lotus Supertravel, Made to Measure, Neilson, Rocketski, Ski Activity, Ski Club of GB, Ski Equipe, Ski Independence, Ski Line, Ski Safari, Ski The American Dream, Skisar US, Skiworld, Thomson, United Vacations*

Bansko Bulgaria
Old traditional cobble-street town. Eastern Europe's most interesting ski resort. Skiing very limited and 12km away.
935m; slopes 1760–2500m
3 5km
✉ *Balkan Holidays*

Baqueira-Beret 621
✉ *Ski Miquel*

Barboleuse 454
Quiet base from which to ski the Villars and Les Diablerets slopes.

Bardonecchia Italy
Traditional market-town near Italian/French border; two separate areas of slopes add up to a big, mainly easy area.
1310m; slopes 1290–2750m
23 140km
✉ *Alpine Answers Select, Crystal, Equity Total Ski, Interhome, Motours, Neilson, Rocketski, Ski Arrangements, Thomson*

Barèges 346
✉ *Borderline, Fairhand Holidays, Lagrange Holidays, SkiAway Holidays*

Les Barzettes 407
Smaller base along the road from Crans-Montana, with a gondola up to the main section of slopes.

Bear Mountain USA
Southern California's main area, in the beautiful San Bernardino National Forest region. Full snowmaking.
slopes 2170–2685m
12 195 acres

Bear's Town Korea
Ugly modern resort with pistes cut out of thick forest; 10 slopes. Only 40 minutes from Seoul, so crowded. 11

Beaulard Italy
Little place just off the road between Sauze d'Oulx and Bardonecchia.
1215m; slopes 1215–2120m
6 20km

Beaver Creek 516
✉ *Crystal, Elegant Resorts, Handmade Holidays, Made to Measure, Ski Equipe, Ski Independence, Ski The American Dream, Ski Total, Skisar US, Thomson, United Vacations*

Beaver Mountain USA
Small Utah area north of Salt Lake City, too far from Park City for day trip.
2195m; slopes 2195–2680m
3 525 acres

Belleayre Mountain USA
State-owned resort near Albany, New York State. Cheap prices but old lifts and short runs.
775m; slopes 775–1015m
7 170 acres

Belle-Plagne 287
High-altitude satellite of La Plagne built in a pleasing neo-Savoyard style.
✉ *Motours*

Berchtesgaden Germany
Pleasant old town close to Salzburg, known for its Nordic skiing but with several little Alpine areas nearby.
550m; slopes 630–1800m
21 50km
✉ *Moswin Tours*

Bergün Switzerland
Traditional, quiet, unspoilt, virtually traffic-free little family resort on the rail route between Davos and St Moritz.
1375m; slopes 1400–2550m
5 25km

Berthoud Pass 522
Powder heaven on the drive to Winter Park.

Berwang Austria
Unspoilt village nestling in a spacious valley, close to Lermoos.
1335m; slopes 1335–1740m
13 40km

Bessans France
Old cross-country village (80km of trails) near Modane. Well placed for touring Maurienne valley resorts such as Val-Cenis.
1710m; slopes 1740–2200m
4 5km

Besse France
Charming old village built out of lava, 6km from purpose-built slope-side satellite Super-Besse. Beautiful extinct-volcano scenery.
1050m; slopes 1350–1800m
21 80km
✉ *Lagrange Holidays*

Bethel USA
Pleasant, historic town very close to premier Maine area, Sunday River. Attractive alternative to staying in characterless slope-side resort.
✉ *Skisar US*

Le Bettex **258**
Small base at the gondola mid-station above St-Gervais, with links to the Megève network.

Bettmeralp Switzerland
Central village of the sizeable Aletsch area near Brig, perched high above the Rhône valley, amid spectacular glacial scenery.
1955m; slopes 1925–2710m
31 90km

Beuil-les-Launes France
Alpes-Maritimes resort closest to Nice. Shares area with Valberg.
1400m; slopes 1400–2100m
26 90km

Bezau Austria
Virtually no slopes of its own but main village in low Bregenzerwald region north-west of Lech.
650m; slopes 1210–1650m 2

Biberwier Austria
Limited little village with a small area, best as a quiet base from which to cover the Zugspitz area.
1000m; slopes 1000–1880m
5 25km

Bichlbach Austria
Smallest of the Zugspitz villages with very limited slopes of its own, suitable as an unspoilt base.
1070m; slopes 1070–1620m
3 7km

Bielmonte Italy
Milanese day-tripper spot. Worthwhile on a bad-weather day.
1200m; slopes 1200–1620m
13 20km

Big Mountain USA
Impressive ski area close to Montana's Glacier National Park, with good snow, fun town and low prices.
1370m; slopes 1370–2135m
10 3000 acres
✉ *Inghams, Ski Independence, Skisar US*

Big Powderhorn USA
Area with most 'resort' facilities in south Lake Superior region – highest lift capacity too. Extensive regional lift pass but areas suffer from winds.
370m; slopes 370–560m
10 250 acres

Big Sky **546**
✉ *Ski Independence, Ski The American Dream, Skisar US*

Big White **571**
✉ *All Canada Ski, Crystal, Frontier Ski, Made to Measure, Ski Activity, Ski Independence, Ski Safari, Ski The American Dream, Skisar US, Solo's*

Bischofshofen Austria
Working town cum mountain resort near St Johann im Pongau with very limited runs on local hill and main slopes starting nearby at Muhlbach.
545m; slopes 545–1000m
2 2km

Bivio Switzerland
Quiet village near St Moritz with easy slopes opened up by a few drag lifts.
1775m; slopes 1780–2600m
4 40km

Bizau Austria
One of two main areas in low Bregenzerwald region north-west of Lech.
680m; slopes 680–1700m
6 24km

Björkliden **633**

Björnrike **633**

Blackcomb **597**
✉ *Frontier Ski*

Blatten-Naters Switzerland
Stunning glacial scenery, immediately above Brig, with larger Aletsch slopes nearby.
675m; slopes 1325–2880m
9 60km

Bled **626**
✉ *Alpine Tours, Balkan Holidays, Crystal, Thomson*

Blue Cow **639**

Blue Mountain Canada
Largest area in Ontario, with glorious views of Lake Huron. High-capacity lift system. 100% snowmaking. Worthwhile excursion from nearby Toronto or Niagara Falls.
230m; slopes 230–450m
15 275 acres
✉ *All Canada Ski*

Blue River Canada
Base of world-famous Mike Wiegele heli-ski operation in Cariboo and Monashee mountains. High standard in-the-mountains retreat with all mod cons.

Bluewood USA
Particularly remote area even by American north-west standards. Worth a visit if you're in Walla Walla.
1355m; slopes 1355–1725m
3 530 acres

Bogus Basin USA
Sizeable area overlooking Idaho's attractive, interesting capital, Boise.
1760m; slopes 1760–2310m
8 2600 acres

Bohinj **626**
✉ *Alpine Tours, Balkan Holidays, Crystal, Thomson*

Bois-d'Amont France
One of four resorts that make up Les Rousses area in Jura region. Useful stopover.
1050m; slopes 1120–1680m
40
✉ *Lagrange Holidays*

Bolognola Italy
Tiny area in Macerata region near Adriatic Riviera.
1070m; slopes 1070–1845m
7 5km

Bolton Valley USA
Neighbour of Stowe. Amtrak run ski train to nearby Waterbury and Burlington. Mostly intermediate slopes.
465m; slopes 465–960m
6 155 acres

Le Bonhomme France
One of several areas near Strasbourg. Snowmakers.
830m; slopes 830–1235m
9 12km

Bonneval-sur-Arc France
Unspoilt, remote old village in the Haute Maurienne valley with many of its slopes above 2500m. Pass to neighbouring Val-d'Isère closed in winter.
1800m; slopes 1800–3000m
18 25km
✉ *Motours*

Bons **242**
Rustic, unspoilt old hamlet linked to Les Deux Alpes' skiing, conveniently placed down the valley for day trips to La Grave, Alpe-d'Huez and Serre-Chevalier.

Boreal USA
Closest area to north Lake Tahoe town, Truckee. Limited slopes, best for novices, but has large snowboard park.
2195m; slopes 2195–2375m
9 380 acres

Bormio **350**
✉ *Airtours, Inghams, Interhome, Ski Arrangements, Sloping Off, Thomson*

Borovets **623**
✉ *Airtours, Balkan Holidays, Crystal, First Choice Ski, Inghams, Neilson, Ski Balkantours, Thomson*

Bosco Chiesanuova Italy
Weekend day tripper's place near Verona. A long drive from any other resort.
1105m; slopes 1105–1805m
18 20km

La Bourboule France
Spa village cum cross-country centre with Alpine slopes of Le Mont-Dore nearby. Amid spectacular extinct-volcano scenery.
850m; slopes 1050–1850m
41 80km
✉ *Lagrange Holidays*

Bourg-d'Oisans France
Pleasant valley town on main Grenoble-Briançon road. Civilised, inexpensive base from which to visit Alpe-d'Huez and Les Deux-Alpes.

Bourg-St-Maurice **202**
French valley town, useful as a base for visiting nearby resorts and with a funicular to Les Arcs.
✉ *Erna Low, Interhome*

Bovec **626**

Boyne Highlands USA
Area with impressive, high-capacity lift system for weekend Detroit crowds. Fierce winds off Lake Michigan a major drawback.
225m; slopes 225–390m
10 240 acres

Boyne Mountain USA
Weekend Detroit crowds. Not as windy as sister Boyne Highlands. Shared lift pass.
190m; slopes 190–340m
12 115 acres

Bramans France
Old cross-country village (50km of trails) near Modane. Well placed for touring numerous nearby resorts such as Val-Cenis and Valloire.
1230m 1

Bramberg Austria
Village near Pass Thurn (Kitzbühel area). Shares odd area with Neukirchen – only valley lift in Neukirchen with best runs to liftless Bramberg.
820m; slopes 820–900m
2 11km

Brand Austria
Old family favourite, unpopular these days, perhaps because it lacks the charm to compensate for its small, low area.
1050m; slopes 1050–1920m
8 30km
✉ *Interhome*

Les Brasses France
Collective name for six traditional hamlets with some of the closest slopes to Geneva, but known for cross-country.
900m; slopes 900–1600m
17 50km

Braunwald Switzerland
Sunny but limited area, a funicular ride above Linthal.
1300m; slopes 1300–1910m 8

Breckenridge **495**
✉ *American Ski Classics, Chalet World, Chalets 'Unlimited', Crystal, Esprit Ski, Handmade Holidays, Iglu.com, Independent Ski Links, Inghams, Made to Measure, Neilson, Rocky Mountain*

Snowboard Tours, Ski Activity, Ski Expectations, Ski Independence, Ski Line, Ski Safari, Ski The American Dream, Ski Total, Skisar US, Skiworld, Thomson, United Vacations

Brentonico Italy
Little resort just off Verona-Trento motorway. Worth half-day visit in conjunction with a look at Lake Garda.
1160m; slopes 1160–1520m
16

La Bresse France
Largest of ski areas near Nancy and Strasbourg. Snowmaking.
900m; slopes 900–1350m
21 62km
✉ *Fairhand Holidays, Lagrange Holidays*

Bretton Woods 555
✉ *Elegant Resorts, Virgin Ski*

Briançon 304
Part of the Grand Serre Chevalier region, but with own ski area.
✉ *Lagrange Holidays, Motours, Ski Leisure Direction*

Brian Head USA
Utah area south of Salt Lake City, too far from Park City for day trip.
2925m; slopes 2925–3445m
10 500 acres
✉ *Virgin Ski*

Brides-les-Bains 267
Quiet, unattractive old spa town with a long gondola connection up to Méribel.
✉ *Avant-ski, Crystal, Erna Low, Eurotunnel Motoring Holidays, First Choice Ski, Inghams, Made to Measure, Motours, Ski Arrangements, Ski France, Ski Leisure Direction, Ski Life, Ski Weekends, SkiAway Holidays, Snowcoach*

Bridger Bowl 546
Montana area near Big Sky. Only a third of area is groomed. Good powder.

Brighton 527
✉ *Skisar US*

Brixen im Thale 162
Best equipped of Grossraum villages, with gondola access to the slopes, shared with Söll and Ellmau.

Brodie Mountain USA
Largest Massachusetts area. 100% snowmaking. Mostly easy slopes.
440m; slopes 440–820m
6 250 acres

Bromley USA
New York City weekend retreat, reputedly the warmest place to ski in chilly Vermont.
595m; slopes 595–1000m
9 300 acres

Bromont Canada
Purpose-built resort an hour east of Montreal, with one of the best small areas in eastern Canada, popular for its night skiing.
slopes 405–575m
6 135 acres

Bruck Austria
Low, two-lift beginners' resort, but might suit intermediates looking for a small, quiet base from which to go to nearby Zell am See.
560m; slopes 560–600m 2

Brundage Mountain USA
Remote, uncrowded Idaho area with glorious views across lake towards Hell's Canyon. Mostly intermediate, plus snowcat operation.
1760m; slopes 1760–2320m
5 1300 acres

Bruson Switzerland
Relaxing respite from Verbier's crowds, on the other side of Le Châble. Well placed for car trips to Chamonix and Champéry.
1080m; slopes 820–2200m
7 15km

Burke Mountain USA
Uncrowded, isolated family resort in Vermont with mostly intermediate slopes. Great views from top.
385m; slopes 385–995m
4 130 acres

Bürserberg Austria
Undistinguished valley town which shares lift pass with neighbour Brand.
900m; slopes 1035–1850m
5 16km

Cairngorm 636
✉ *Skisafe Travel*

Caldirola Italy
Genoese weekend day-tripper spot in remote region off motorway to Turin.
1010m; slopes 1010–1460m
4 5km

Camigliatello Italy
Tiny area way south on foot of Italian 'boot' near Cosenza. Weekend/day-trip spot.
1270m; slopes 1270–1750m
4 6km

Campitello 381
Linked by cable-car to the Sella Ronda, with quick connections to the interesting Arabba section.
✉ *Crystal, Inghams, Neilson, Thomson*

Campitello Matese Italy
Only slopes near Naples. Surprisingly large area when snowcover is complete. Weekend crowds.
1440m; slopes 1440–2100m
8 40km

Campo di Giove Italy
Highest slopes in L'Aquila region east of Rome. Accessed by cable-car.
1070m
6 23km

Campodolcino Italy
Valley town with new funicular up to fringe of Madesimo slopes.
1070m; slopes 1545–2880m
15 45km

Campo Felice Italy
Easiest resort to reach from Rome, off Aquila motorway. One of the better lift systems in the vicinity.
1410m; slopes 1520–2065m
14 40km

Campo Imperatore Italy
One of the best of many little areas east of Rome in L'Aquila region. Accessed by cable-car.
1980m
8 20km

Canazei 381
Sizeable and lively, rustic village in the Sella Ronda's most heavily wooded section of mountain.
✉ *Airtours, Crystal, Equity Total Ski, Inghams, Neilson, Rocketski, Thomson*

Candanchu/Astún 620

Canillo 616
Small, quiet town, with good sports facilities and newly developed lifts and slopes, linked to Soldeu.
✉ *Top Deck*

Canmore Canada
Attractive alternative to staying in neighbouring Banff. Old frontier town on the way to Nakiska/Fortress, well placed for touring region.

Cannon 555
✉ *Elegant Resorts, Virgin Ski*

The Canyons 531
✉ *Crystal, Ski Independence, Ski Safari, Ski The American Dream, United Vacations*

Cardrona 641

Les Carroz 247
An attractive, spacious village on a sunny shelf on the road up to Flaine.
✉ *Fairhand Holidays, Lagrange Holidays, Motours*

Caspoggio Italy
Attractive, unspoilt village north-east of Lake Como, with easy slopes (and more at neighbouring Chiesa).
1100m; slopes 1100–2155m
8 22km

Castel S Angelo Italy
Tiny area in Macerata region near Adriatic Riviera.
805m
4 2km

Cauterets 346
✉ *Fairhand Holidays, Lagrange Holidays, SkiAway Holidays*

Cavalese Italy
Unspoilt medieval town with its own pretty slopes and proximity to the Sella Ronda.
1000m; slopes 975–2265m
9 70km
✉ *Alpine Tours*

Ceillac France
Neighbour of highest village in Europe, St-Veran. Tight cluster of rustic old buildings near Serre-Chevalier.
1600m; slopes 1600–2400m

Celerina 439
Quiet, unpretentious village, with links up to St Moritz's Corviglia sector.
✉ *Made to Measure*

Cerler Spain
Very limited, purpose-built resort with a compact ski area similar to that of nearby Andorra's Arinsal.
1500m; slopes 1500–2630m
14 35km

Le Cernix France
Hamlet near Megève where Les Saisies' slopes link to those of Crest-Voland. Uncrowded retreat.
1250m; slopes 1150–1950m
24 100km

Cerrato Lago Italy
Only area near coastal town La Spezia. Very limited. Exists for weekend day-trip trade.
1270m; slopes 1270–1890m
5 3km

Cerro Castor Argentina
Ski area near Tierra del Fuego. The most southerly ski centre in the world.

Cervinia 352
✉ *Airtours, Alpine Answers Select, Beaumont Holidays Ltd, Club Med, Crystal, Elegant Resorts, Equity Total Ski, Esprit Ski, First Choice Ski, Iglu.com, Independent Ski Links, Inghams, Interhome, Momentum Ski, Neilson, Rocketski, Ski Arrangements, Ski Club of GB, Ski Solutions, Ski Weekend, Thomson*

Cesana Torinese 277
Little Italian village linking the Sauze d'Oulx, Sestriere and Sansicario side of the Milky Way to the Clavière, Montgenèvre side.

Le Châble 445
Small village below Verbier, linked by gondola.

Chacaltaya Bolivia
Highest ski area in the world; altitude headache guaranteed. 4WD from nearby La Paz. Primitive facilities.
5190m; slopes 5220–5420m
1 2km

Chaillol France
Cross-country centre at edge of beautiful Ecrins National Park, near Gap. Small Alpine area, lots of snowmakers.
1600m; slopes 1450–2000m
11

Chamois Italy
Neighbour of Cervinia close to Valtournenche. Good bet when higher areas affected by bad weather.
1815m; slopes 1815–2270m
8 20km

Choice Ski, Iglu.com, Independent Ski Links, Inghams, Interski, Mark Warner, Momentum Ski, Rocketski, Ski Arrangements, Ski Expectations, Ski Line, Ski Solutions, Ski Weekend, Thomson, White Roc

Cranmore USA
Area in New Hampshire with attractive town/resort of North Conway. Easy skiing. Good for families.
150m; slopes 150–515m
8 190 acres
⊠ *Elegant Resorts, Skisar US*

Crans-Montana **407**
⊠ *Alpine Answers Select, Crystal, Elegant Resorts, Erna Low, First Choice Ski, Iglu.com, Independent Ski Links, Inghams, Interhome, Kuoni, Lagrange Holidays, Made to Measure, Momentum Ski, Motours, Plus Travel, Ski Club of GB, Ski Weekend, Swiss Travel Service, The Corporate Ski Company, The Oxford Ski Company, Thomson*

Crested Butte **502**
⊠ *Club Med, Crystal, Made to Measure, Ski Activity, Ski Independence, Ski Safari, Ski The American Dream, Skisar US, United Vacations*

Crest-Voland France
Attractive, traditional village near Megève with uncrowded slopes linked to Les Saisies.
1150m; slopes 1230–1650m
26 45km
⊠ *First Choice Ski, SkiAway Holidays*

Crissolo Italy
Small, remote day-tripper area, south-west of Turin.
1320m; slopes 1745–2340m
30km

La Croix-Fry **225**
Couple of hotels on pass close to La Clusaz.
⊠ *Ski Leisure Direction*

Les Crosets **405**
Isolated and limited mini-resort, in a prime position within the Portes du Soleil circuit, above Champéry.

Crystal Mountain USA
Area in glorious Mt Rainier National Park, near Seattle. Good, varied area given good snow/weather, but both are often wet.
1340m; slopes 1340–2135m
10 2300 acres

Cuchara Valley USA
Quiet little family resort in southern Colorado, some way from any other ski area.
2800m; slopes 2800–3285m
4 250 acres

Cutigliano Italy
Neighbour of Abetone in exposed Appennines. Less than 2 hours from Florence and Pisa. Sizeable village.
1125m; slopes 1125–1850m
9 13km

Cypress Mountain Canada
Vancouver's most challenging area with 40% for experts. 20 minutes from city centre. Good snowfall record but rain is a problem.
910m; slopes 910–1445m 5

Daemyung Korea
One of the less ugly Korean resorts. 13 slopes; impressive lift system – most are high-capacity quads. Usual Korean tree-lined pistes. 2 hours from Seoul. 12

La Daille **326**
Ugly apartment complex at the entrance to Val-d'Isère.

Daisen Japan
Western Honshu's only area, 4 hours from Osaka.
800m; slopes 740–1120m 20

Damüls Austria
Scattered but attractive village in Bregenzerwald area close to the German and Swiss borders.
1430m; slopes 1430–2005m
8 38km

Davos **412**
⊠ *Crystal, Elegant Resorts, FlexiSki, Inghams, Interhome, Kuoni, Made to Measure, Momentum Ski, Plus Travel, Ski Choice, Ski Club of GB, Ski Weekend, SkiGower, Swiss Travel Service, The Corporate Ski Company, White Roc*

Deer Mountain USA
South Dakota area close to 'Old West' town Deadwood and Mount Rushmore.
1825m; slopes 1825–2085m
4 370 acres

Deer Valley **533**
⊠ *Made to Measure, Ski Independence, Ski Safari, Ski The American Dream, Skisar US, United Vacations*

Les Deux-Alpes **242**
⊠ *Airtours, Alpine Options, Avant-ski, Chalet World, Chalets 'Unlimited', Club Med, Crystal, Equity Total Ski, Erna Low, Esprit Ski, Fairhand Holidays, First Choice Ski, Iglu.com, Independent Ski Links, Inghams, Interhome, Lagrange Holidays, Made to Measure, Mark Warner, Motours, Neilson, Panorama, Rocketski, Ski Arrangements, Ski Independence, Ski Leisure Direction, Ski Line, Ski Supreme, Skiworld, Thomson, Tops Ski Chalets and Club Hotels*

Les Diablerets **454**
Spacious chalet resort; modest intermediate skiing linked to Villars.
⊠ *Crystal, Interhome, Lagrange Holidays, Made to Measure, Momentum Ski, Plus Travel, SkiGower*

Diamond Peak USA
Quiet, pleasant alternative to brash South Lake Tahoe.
slopes 2040–2600m
7 755 acres

Dienten Austria
Quiet village at the heart of large, low-altitude area, close to Zell am See.
1070m; slopes 790–1825m
18 150km

Dinner Plain Australia
Australia's most attractive resort, built from stone and wood. Cross-country centre. Shuttle to Mt Hotham for Alpine slopes. 4.5 hours from Melbourne.
1520m

Discovery Ski Area USA
Pleasant intermediate area near Butte, Montana. Fairmont Hot Springs (two huge thermal pools) nearby.
2080m; slopes 2080–2485m
4 380 acres

Disentis Switzerland
Unspoilt old village in a pretty setting on the Glacier Express rail route near Andermatt. Scenic area with long runs.
1135m; slopes 1150–2920m
10 60km
⊠ *Interhome*

Dobbiaco Italy
One of several little resorts near Austrian border. Feasible day out from Sella Ronda.
1250m; slopes 1250–1610m
5 15km
⊠ *Ramblers, Waymark Holidays*

Dodge Ridge USA
Novice/leisurely intermediate area north of Yosemite. Pass from Reno closed in winter, preventing crowds.
2010m; slopes 2010–2500m
12 815 acres

Dolonne **362**
Quiet suburb of Courmayeur – the gondola link is no more, but the off-piste run home is still a classic.

Dorfgastein **97**
Quieter, friendlier alternative to Bad Gastein and Bad Hofgastein, with its own intermediate ski area.

Dundret Sweden
350m vertical. Good resort to learn about Lapland culture. Floodlit slopes open through winter when sun barely rises.
6 15km

Durango Mountain Resort USA
Mountain formerly known as Purgatory, with good slopes now accessed by long six-pack; main base still know as Purgatory. Durango itself, a half hour away, is a fun western town with historic main street.
2680m; slopes 2680–3300m
11 1200 acres
⊠ *Ski Independence, Skisar US*

Eaglecrest USA
Close to famous Yukon gold rush town Skagway. Family resort famous for ski school.
365m; slopes 365–790m
3 640 acres

Eaux-Bonnes-Gourette France
Most snowsure resort in the French Pyrenees. Very popular with local families, best avoided at weekends.
1400m; slopes 1400–2400m
23 30km

Eben im Pongau Austria
Village spoilt by autobahn passing almost straight through it. Part of Salzburger Sportwelt Amadé pass that includes nearby St Johann-Wagrain-Flachau-Zauchensee slopes.
855m; slopes 855–2185m
100 350km

Ehrwald Austria
Friendly, relaxed, pretty village with several nicely varied areas, notably the Zugspitz glacier, nearby. Poor bus services make having a car desirable.
1000m; slopes 1000–3000m
21 25km

Eldora Mountain USA
Varied terrain close to Boulder City and Denver. Crowded at weekends.
2795m; slopes 2805–3230m
12 680 acres

Elk Meadows USA
Area south of Salt Lake City, more than a day trip from Park City.
2775m; slopes 2745–3170m
6 1400 acres

Ellmau **104**
⊠ *Airtours, Crystal, Inghams, Interhome, Motours, Neilson, Thomson*

Encamp **608**
⊠ *First Choice Ski, Thomson*

Enego Italy
Limited weekend day-trippers' area near Vicenza and Trento.
1300m; slopes 1300–1445m
7 30km

Engelberg Switzerland
Traditional, towny resort popular with weekenders from Lucerne; fragmented but varied slopes with snowsure glacier and one of the biggest verticals in the Alps.
1050m; slopes 1050–3020m
23 82km
⊠ *Crystal, Iglu.com, Inntravel, Interhome, Kuoni, Made to Measure, Plus Travel, Ski Weekend, SkiGower, Swiss Travel Service, The Corporate Ski Company*

Entrèves **362**
Characterless cluster of hotels at base of cable-car up to Courmayeur slopes.

Escaldes Andorra
Central valley town, effectively part of Andorra la Vella.

Etna Italy
Scenic, uncrowded, short-season area on the volcano's flank, 20 minutes from Nickolossi, with a couple of fair runs and easy off-piste.
1800m; slopes 1800–2350m
5km

Evolène Switzerland
Charming rustic village in unspoilt, attractive setting south of Sion. Own little area, with Verbier's slopes accessed at nearby Les Masses.
1380m; slopes 1300–3330m
100 400km

Faak am See Austria
Limited area, one of five overlooking town of Villach.
550m; slopes 840–1045m
2 2km

Fairmont Hot Springs Canada
Major luxury spa complex ideal for relaxing holiday with some gentle skiing thrown in.
1280m; slopes 1280–1585m
2 60 acres

Faistenau Austria
Cross-country centre close to Salzburg and St Wolfgang. Limited Alpine area.
785m; slopes 785–1000m
6 3km

Falcade Italy
Largest of many little ski areas close to but not part of Sella Ronda.
1145m; slopes 1145–2170m
11 39km
⊠ *Alpine Tours*

Falera 419
Small, rustic village, with improved access to big ski area shared by Flims and Laax.

Le Falgoux France
One of the most beautiful old villages in France. In very scenic Volcano National Park. Several ski areas nearby.
930m; slopes 930–1350m

Falkertsee Austria
Base area rather than village, with bleak, open slopes in contrast to nearby Badkleinkirchheim.
1690m; slopes 1690–2385m
5 15km

Falls Creek 639

Farellones / El Colorado Chile
Chile's best ski area, an hour from Santiago. Crowded at weekends.
⊠ *Scott Dunn Latin America*

La Feclaz France
One of several little resorts in remote Parc des Bauges. Close to Chambéry by crow flight but miles from anywhere by road.

Fernie 582
⊠ *Airtours, All Canada Ski, Crystal, Frontier Ski, Handmade Holidays, Inghams, Made to Measure, Ski Activity, Ski Independence, Ski Safari, Skisar US, Thomson*

Fieberbrunn Austria
Jolly old traditional village, an inconvenient distance from its small but attractive ski area.
800m; slopes 800–2020m
14 30km

Fiesch Switzerland
Traditional Rhône valley resort close to Brig, with a lift into the beautiful Aletsch area.
1060m; slopes 1050–2870m
10
⊠ *SkiGower*

Filzmoos Austria
Charming, unspoilt, friendly village; leisurely slopes, ideal for novices. Good snow record for its height.
1055m; slopes 1055–1645m
12 32km
⊠ *Inghams*

Finkenberg 134
Between Mayrhofen and Hintertux, with a large area of mainly intermediate skiing
⊠ *Crystal, First Choice Ski*

Fiss Austria
Nicely compact, quiet traditional village with a sun-kissed area well protected by snowmakers and linked to Serfaus.
1435m; slopes 1200–2540m
17 70km
⊠ *Alpine Tours, Interhome*

Flachau Austria
Quiet village in a pretty setting. Linked to Wagrain and extensive Salzburger Sportwelt Amadé lift network.
925m; slopes 925–2185m
100 350km
⊠ *Interhome, Thomson*

Flachauwinkl Austria
Well placed within the Salzburger Sportwelt Amadé area, but with the Salzburg-Villach autobahn carving through it.
930m; slopes 800–2185m
100 350km

Flaine 247
⊠ *Classic Ski Limited, Club Med, Crystal, Erna Low, Eurotunnel Motoring Holidays, Fairhand Holidays, First Choice Ski, Iglu.com, Independent Ski Links, Inghams, Lagrange Holidays, Made to Measure, Motours, Neilson, Ski Arrangements, Ski Choice, Ski Club of GB, Ski Independence, Ski Leisure Direction, Ski Weekend, Skisafe Travel, Thomson*

Flims 419
⊠ *Alpine Answers Select, Freedom Holidays, Interhome, Kuoni, Made to Measure, Momentum Ski, Plus Travel, Powder Byrne, Ski Choice, Ski Weekend, Swiss Travel Service, The Corporate Ski Company, White Roc*

Flumet France
Surprisingly large resort, well placed for whole Mont Blanc area. Cheap big-village alternative to Megève.
1000m; slopes 1000–1600m
10 40km

Flumserberg Switzerland
Collective name for villages sharing a varied area an hour south-east of Zürich.
1220–1400m;
slopes 1220–2220m 17

Folgaria Italy
Largest of several resorts east of Trento. Old lift system.
1165m; slopes 1185–2005m
38 70km
⊠ *Alpine Tours*

Folgarida 371
Pleasant Dolomite village, with links to Madonna di Campiglio's extensive piste network.
⊠ *Equity Total Ski, Rocketski, Sloping Off*

Foncine-le-Haut France
Major cross-country centre with 220km of trails, relatively close to Channel.
⊠ *Headwater Holidays, Lagrange Holidays*

Fonni Gennaragentu Italy
Sardinia's only 'ski area'. Barely exists.
1 5km

Font-Romeu 346
⊠ *Lagrange Holidays, Solo's*

Foppolo Italy
Relatively unattractive but user-friendly village, a short transfer from Bergamo, best for families on a budget.
1510m; slopes 1610–2160m
10 45km
⊠ *Equity Total Ski*

Forca Canapine Italy
Limited area near Adriatic and town of Ascoli Piceno. Weekend day-tripper spot.
1450m; slopes 1450–1690m
11 20km

Formazza Italy
Cross-country centre with some downhill slopes.
1280m; slopes 1275–1755m
8km

Formigal 620

Le Fornet 326
Rustic, old hamlet 3km further down the valley from Val-d'Isère.

Forstau Austria
Secluded hamlet above Radstadt-Schladming road. Very limited area with old lifts, but nice and quiet.
930m; slopes 930–1885m
7 14km

Fortress Mountain Canada
Primitive, wild little mountain between Banff and Calgary, renowned for powder snow, dramatic scenery and uncrowded slopes.
2040m; slopes 2040–2370m
7 325 acres

La Foux-d'Allos France
Purpose-built resort that shares a good intermediate area with Pra-Loup.
1800m; slopes 1800–2600m
53 230km
⊠ *Fairhand Holidays, Lagrange Holidays*

Frabosa Soprana Italy
One of numerous little areas south of Turin, well placed for combining winter sports with Riviera sightseeing.
850m; slopes 860–1740m
40km

Frisco 495
Small town based on a Victorian settlement, down the valley from Breckenridge.

Frontignano Italy
Best lift system in Macerata region near Adriatic Riviera.
1340m; slopes 1340–2000m
8 10km

Fügen Austria
Unspoilt village with limited area best suited to beginners, poorly placed for other Zillertal resorts.
560m; slopes 560–2400m
19 48km
⊠ *Lagrange Holidays*

Fulpmes 111
⊠ *Crystal, Esprit Ski*

Funäsdalen Sweden
Cross-country Mecca. Home of world's longest ski trails, with 600m vertical of Alpine runs. Top-class facilities throughout.
600m; slopes 600–1200m
30 85km

Furano Japan
Small Hokkaido resort. One of the few Japanese areas to get reasonable powder.
235m; slopes 235–1065m 17

Fusch Austria
Across golf course from Kaprun and Schuttdorf. Cheap(er), quiet place to stay when visiting Zell am See.
805m; slopes 805–1050m
2 5km

Fuschl Austria
Attractive, unspoilt, lakeside village close to St Wolfgang and Salzburg, 30 minutes from its slopes. Best suited to part-time skiers-cum-sightseers.
670m

Gala Norway
Centre for downhill and cross-country skiing an hour's drive north of Lillehammer.
930m 7
⊠ *Inntravel*

Gallio Italy
One of several low resorts near Vicenza and Trento. Weekend day-trippers' place.
1100m; slopes 1100–1550m
11 50km

Galtür 115
Charming traditional village near Ischgl, in the news in 1998/99 due to a tragic avalanche disaster.
⊠ *Inghams, Made to Measure, Ski Choice*

Gambarie d'Aspromonte Italy
Italy's second most southerly ski area (after Mt Etna). On toe of Italian 'boot' near Reggio di Calabria.
1310m; slopes 1310–1650m 3

Gantschier Austria
No slopes of its own but particularly well placed at junction of roads for visiting all the Montafon areas.
700m

Gargellen 139
✉ *Interhome, Made to Measure*

Garmisch-Partenkirchen
Germany
Large twin resort; unspoilt, traditional Partenkirchen much the prettier. Superb main area of wooded runs when the unreliable snowcover allows; great glacier views from another section when it doesn't.
700m; slopes 700–2830m
38 118km
✉ *Moswin Tours*

Gaschurn 139

Geilo 629
✉ *Crystal, Inntravel, Neilson, Solo's, Thomson, Waymark Holidays*

Gérardmer France
Closest slopes to Channel, near Strasbourg. Sizeable resort with plenty of amenities. Night skiing, too.
665m; slopes 750–1150m
20 40km
✉ *Fairhand Holidays, Lagrange Holidays*

Gerlitzen Alpe Austria
Modern gondola ride above Villach. Great views. Worthwhile excursion from Badkleinkirchheim.
500m; slopes 1003–1911m
14 20km

Gerlos Austria
One of Austria's few inexpensive but fairly snowsure resorts, now linked to Zell im Zillertal as well as Konigsleiten to form a fair-sized intermediate area.
1250m; slopes 1250–2300m
23 70km
✉ *Esprit Ski, Interhome*

Les Gets 281
Sprawling chalet resort on low pass near Morzine, on the periphery of the Portes du Soleil area.
✉ *Alp Active, Avant-ski, Chalets 'Unlimited', Fairhand Holidays, Fantiski, Iglu.com, Lagrange Holidays, Made to Measure, Motours, Ski Activity, Ski Expectations, Ski Famille, Ski Hillwood, Ski Independence, Ski Total, Ski Weekend, SkiAway Holidays, Tops Ski Chalets and Club Hotels*

La Giettaz France
Small resort between La Clusaz and Megève with no particular attractions.

Gitschtal/Weissbriach Austria
One of many little areas near Hermagor in eastern Austria close to Italian border.
690m; slopes 690–1400m
4 5km

Glaris Switzerland
Hamlet base station for the uncrowded Rinerhorn section of the Davos slopes.
1455m; slopes 1455–2490m
5 30km

Glencoe 636

Glenshee 636
✉ *Skisafe Travel*

Going 104
Small local ski area near Ellmau, linked to the huge Ski Welt area.

Goldegg Austria
Year-round resort famous for its lakeside castle. Limited slopes but Wagrain (Salzburger Sportwelt Amadé) and Grossarl (Gastein valley) are nearby.
825m; slopes 825–1250m
4 12km

Golden Canada
Small logging town, accommodation town for Kicking Horse resort 15 minutes' away. Also launch pad for Purcell heli-skiing.

Gore Mountain USA
One of the better areas in New York State. Near Lake Placid, sufficiently far north to avoid worst weekend crowds. Intermediate terrain.
455m; slopes 455–1095m
9 290 acres

Göriach Austria
Hamlet with trail connecting into one of longest, most snowsure cross-country networks in Europe.
1250m

Gortipohl Austria
Traditional village in pretty Montafontal.
920m; slopes 900–2395m
62 209km

Gosau Austria
Straggling village with plenty of pretty, if low, pistes. Snowsure Obertauern and Schladming are within reach.
765m; slopes 765–1800m
37 65km

Göstling Austria
One of Austria's easternmost resorts, between Salzburg and Vienna. A traditional village in wooded setting.
530m; slopes 530–1800m
12 20km

Götzens Austria
Valley village base for Axamer Lizum area.
870m

Grächen Switzerland
Uncommercialised, quiet little family village with a scenic but small intermediate area. Tricky access road.
1615m; slopes 1615–2890m
13 50km
✉ *Interhome*

Le Grand-Bornand 225
✉ *Fairhand Holidays, Lagrange Holidays*

Grand Targhee 548
Powder skiing paradise an hour from Jackson Hole.
✉ *Lotus Supertravel, Ski The American Dream, Skisar US*

Grangesises Italy
Small satellite of Sestriere, with lifts up to the main slopes.

Grau Roig 614
Mini-resort at foot of Pas de la Casa's only woodland runs, with one smart hotel and abundant day-tripper parking.
✉ *Inghams*

La Grave 253
✉ *Alpine Answers Select, Interhome, Lagrange Holidays, Motours, Ski Arrangements, Ski Club of GB, Ski Weekend*

Gray Rocks Canada
Very popular family resort, 130km north of Montreal, renowned for its ski school.
250m; slopes 250–440m
4 200 acres

Great Divide USA
Area near Helena, Montana, best for experts. Mostly bowls; plus near-extreme Rawhide Gulch.
1765m; slopes 1765–2195m
6 720 acres

Gresse-en-Vercors France
Resort south of Grenoble. Sheltered slopes worth noting for bad-weather days.
1250m; slopes 1250–1800m
16
✉ *Interhome, Lagrange Holidays*

Gressoney-la-Trinité 373
Smaller and higher of the two villages in the central valley of the Monterosa Ski area.
✉ *Crystal, Motours, The Ski Company*

Gressoney-St-Jean 373
Larger and lower of the two villages in the central valley of the Monterosa Ski area.

Grimentz Switzerland
Captivating, unspoilt rustic village with high, varied pistes served by modern lifts; near Valais town of Sierre.
1570m; slopes 1570–3000m
12 50km

Grindelwald 424
✉ *Crystal, Elegant Resorts, Iglu.com, Independent Ski Links, Inghams, Interhome, Kuoni, Made to Measure, Momentum Ski, Plus Travel, Powder Byrne, Ski Club of GB, SkiGower, Swiss Travel Service, The Corporate Ski Company, Thomson, White Roc*

Grossarl 97
Secluded village linked to Dorfgastein in the Gastein valley.

Grosskirchheim Austria
Very limited neighbour of Heiligenblut.
1025m; slopes 1025–1400m
2 3km

Grouse Mountain Canada
Vancouver area with largest lift capacity. Superb city views. Mostly easy slopes, night skiing.
880m; slopes 880–1245m
11 120 acres

Grünau Austria
Attractive, spacious riverside village in a lovely lake-filled part of eastern Austria. Nicely varied area, but very low.
525m; slopes 600–1600m
14 40km

Gryon 454
Village below Villars, with which it shares a ski area.

Gstaad 428
✉ *Alpine Answers Select, Crystal, Elegant Resorts, Interhome, Made to Measure, Momentum Ski, Plus Travel, Ski Weekend, SkiGower, The Corporate Ski Company, White Roc*

Gunstock USA
One of closest New Hampshire resorts to Boston, popular with families. Primarily easy slopes. Gorgeous Lake Winnisquam views. 98% snowmaking.
275m; slopes 275–700m
8 220 acres

Guthega 639

Hallanrinteet Finland
Collective name for twin ski areas 20 minutes apart. Good lake views. Short intermediate runs. *14*

Happo One Japan
Pseudo-European resort in same vicinity as Nagano (Shiga Heights). One of Japan's more challenging areas.
750m; slopes 750–1830m 34

Harrachov Czech Republic
Closest resort to Prague, with enough terrain to justify a day trip. No nursery area.
685m; slopes 650–1020m
4 8km

Hasliberg Switzerland
Four rustic hamlets on sunny plateau overlooking Meiringen and Lake Brienz, 2 of them bottom stations of varied intermediate area.
1055m; slopes 600–2435m
16 60km

Haus in Ennstal 156
Real village next to Schladming, with good local slopes connected to the rest of the network.

Haystack 555

Heavenly 474
✉ *American Ski Classics, Crystal, Esprit Ski, Independent Ski Links, Inghams, Neilson, Ski Activity, Ski Independence, Ski Line, Ski Safari, Ski Success, Ski The American Dream, Skisar US, Skiworld, United Vacations, Virgin Ski*

Hebalm Austria
One of many small areas in Austria's easternmost ski region near Slovenian border. No major resorts in vicinity.
1350m; slopes 1350–1400m
6 11km

Heiligenblut Austria
Picturesque village in beautiful surroundings with mostly high terrain. Its remote position west of Bad Gastein ensures crowds don't invade.
1300m; slopes 1300–2900m
14 55km

Hemlock Resort Canada
Area 55 miles east of Vancouver on way to Sun Peaks, with snowfall of 600 inches a year. Mostly intermediate terrain. Lodging at base area.
1000m; slopes 1000–1375m
4 350 acres

Hemsedal **631**
✉ *Crystal, Neilson, Thomson*

Heremence Switzerland
Quiet village in unspoilt attractive setting south of Sion. Verbier slopes accessed a few minutes' drive away at Les Masses.
1250m; slopes 1300–3330m
100 400km

Hermagor Austria
Carinthian village below the Sonnenalpe ski area. Franz Klammer rates this one of the best areas in Austria.
600m; slopes 1210–2005m
29 101km

Himos Finland
Varied Alpine skiing, half-pipes and snowboard park, cross-country.
80m; slopes 80–220m 10

Hintersee Austria
Very close to Salzburg. Several long top-to-bottom pistes and lifts, so size of area greatly reduced if snowline high. Easy slopes.
745m; slopes 750–1470m
9 40km

Hinterstoder Austria
Quiet, unspoilt traditional village, 80km east of Salzburg, with a good snow record for its height.
600m; slopes 600–1860m
14 35km

Hintertux **107**
✉ *Alpine Tours, Esprit Ski, Lagrange Holidays*

Hippach **134**
Hamlet near a queue-free lift into Mayrhofen's main area.

Hochgurgl **142**
Quiet, upmarket, mountain-side hotel-village with a gondola connection to Obergurgl's slopes.
✉ *Airtours, Inghams, Ski Expectations*

Hochpillberg Austria
Peaceful hamlet with fabulous views towards Innsbruck. Varied terrain. Safe for children since virtually no traffic.
1330m
5 10km

Hochsölden **160**
Quieter mountain-side satellite above lively, sprawling Sölden, with links to the whole network.

Hochybrig Switzerland
Purpose-built complex only 64km south of Zürich, with facilities for families.
1050m; slopes 1050–2200m
16 50km

Hohuanshan Taiwan
Limited ski area with short season in high wild inaccessible Miitaku mountains.
3275m 1

Hollersbach Austria
Pass Thurn hamlet near Mittersill. Uncrowded base from which to visit Kitzbühel if snowline low; Kaprun, Gerlos, Matrei and Uttendorf if high.
805m; slopes 805–1000m
2 5km

Homewood USA
Area with unsurpassed Lake Tahoe views, near accommodation centre Tahoe City. Most sheltered slopes in vicinity so a good choice in bad weather.
1895m; slopes 1895–2400m
10 1260 acres

Hoodoo Ski Bowl USA
Typical Oregon area – sizeable but short runs. Snow record isn't as good as competitors near Portland.
1420m; slopes 1420–1740m
5 800 acres

Hopfgarten **162**
Small chalet village with lift link into extensive Ski Welt area shared with Söll and neighbours.
✉ *Contiki, First Choice Ski*

Horseshoe Resort Canada
Toronto region resort with high-capacity lift system, 100% snowmaking. Second mountain – The Heights – doubles size of area but is open to members only.
310m; slopes 310–405m
7 60 acres

Hospental **401**
Small village with local slopes included on the Andermatt lift pass – connected by road and rail.

Les Houches **212**
Varied, tree-lined area above spread-out village at the entrance to the Chamonix valley.
✉ *Avant-ski, Barrelli Ski, Bigfoot, Chalets 'Unlimited', Lagrange Holidays, Motours, Ski Expectations*

Hovden Norway
Big lakeside hotel in wilderness midway between Oslo and Bergen. Cross-country centre with Alpine slopes as sideline.
760m; slopes 760–1205m 2

Huez **193**
Charming old hamlet on the road up to Alpe d'Huez with lift into ski area.

Hunter Mountain USA
New Yorkers' favourite area so it gets very crowded at weekends – and also Wednesdays.
485m; slopes 485–975m
14 230 acres

Hüttschlag Austria
Hamlet in dead-end valley with lifts into Gastein area at neighbouring Grossarl.
1020m; slopes 840–1220m
2 5km

Hyundai Sungwoo Korea
Massive high-rise monstrosity with plans for future expansion, 2 hours from Seoul. 21 slopes.
8

Idre Sweden
Collective name for four areas whose lifts and buses are on one pass. Snowsure but only 305m vertical.
710m; slopes 710–890m
30 28km

Igls **111**
✉ *Inghams, Lagrange Holidays, Made to Measure*

Iizuna Japan
Tiny area one hour from Nagano, 4 hours from Tokyo.
5

Incline Village **479**
Large village on northern edge of Lake Tahoe – reasonable stop-off if touring.

Indianhead USA
South Lake Superior area with the most snowfall in region. Winds are a problem.
395m; slopes 395–585m
12 195 acres

Inneralpbach **95**
Small satellite 3km up the valley from Alpbach.

Innerarosa **403**
The prettiest part of Arosa.

Innsbruck **111**
✉ *Made to Measure, Ramblers*

Interlaken **456**
Large lakeside summer resort at entrance to the valleys leading to Wengen, Grindelwald and Mürren.
✉ *Kuoni, Made to Measure, SkiGower, Swiss Travel Service*

Ischgl **115**
✉ *Fairhand Holidays, Inghams, Made to Measure, Momentum Ski, Ski Solutions*

Ishiuchi Maruyama-Yuzawa Kogen Japan
Sizeable resorts that share lift pass, offering largest area in central Honshu region.
255m; slopes 255–920m 36

Isola 2000 France
Small purpose-built family resort 90km from Nice, with a compact ski area and an improving range of accommodation.
2000m; slopes 1840–2610m
24 120km
✉ *Avant-ski, Club Pavilion, Erna Low, Fairhand Holidays, Lagrange Holidays, Made to Measure, Ski Arrangements, Ski Life*

Isoyöte Finland
Southernmost downhill skiing in Finland. Finnish championship venue, but mostly easy skiing. Main hotel at top of mountain.
430m; slopes 240–430m
11 21km

Itter **162**
Next to Söll, skiing linked to Hopfgarten and Brixen, and to the whole of the Ski Welt region.
✉ *Neilson, Panorama*

Jackson USA
Classic New England village, and major cross-country centre. Lovely base from which to ski New Hampshire's Alpine areas.

Jackson Hole **548**
✉ *Alpine Answers Select, American Ski Classics, Crystal, Elegant Resorts, Inghams, Lotus Supertravel, Made to Measure, Momentum Ski, Neilson, Ski Activity, Ski Independence, Ski Line, Ski Safari, Ski Success, Ski The American Dream, Skisar US, Skiworld, United Vacations*

Jasper **571**
✉ *All Canada Ski, Crystal, Elegant Resorts, Frontier Ski, Inghams, Made to Measure, Neilson, Ski Activity, Ski Independence, Ski Safari, Ski The American Dream, Skisar US, Thomson*

Jay Peak **555**

Jochberg **120**
Straggling village, 8km from Kitzbühel. Shares its varied, snowsure ski area with Pass Thurn.

La Joue-du-Loup France
Purpose-built little ski-in/ski-out family resort. Shares sizeable intermediate area with Superdévoluy. High proportion of drags.
1500m; slopes 1500–2510m
31 100km
✉ *Lagrange Holidays, Motours, Ski France, Ski Life*

Jouvenceaux **376**
Less boisterous base from which to ski Sauze d'Oulx's splendid cruising terrain.

Jukkasjärvi Sweden
Centuries-old resort with unique ice hotel – rebuilt every December out of 3,000 tons of snow and ice.

June Mountain USA
Well liked by day-visitors from nearby Mammoth (shared lift pass). Quiet slopes and superb school.
2300m; slopes 2300–3090m
8 500 acres

Juns 107
Small, spread out village between Lanersbach and Hintertux, with its own tiny beginners' area.
⊠ *Alpine Tours*

Kals am Grossglockner Austria
Village in remote valley north of Lienz.
1325m; slopes 1325–2305m
7 15km

Kaltenbach Austria
Village with one of the larger, quieter Zillertal areas, with plenty of slopes above 1800m.
560m; slopes 560–2300m
16 60km

Kananaskis Canada
Small area near Calgary, nicely set in woods, with slopes at Nakiska and Fortress Mountain.
slopes 1525–2465m
12 605 acres
⊠ *All Canada Ski, Frontier Ski, Made to Measure*

Kandersteg Switzerland
Good cross-country base amid beautiful scenery near Interlaken.
1175m; slopes 1175–2000m
7 13km
⊠ *Headwater Holidays, Inntravel, Kuoni, Made to Measure, Waymark Holidays*

Kanin 626

Kaprun 184
Classic Austrian charmer of a village. Extensive sheltered slopes at nearby Zell am See.
⊠ *Crystal, First Choice Ski, Made to Measure, Ski Club of GB*

Les Karellis France
Resort with slopes that offer more scenic, challenging and snowsure pistes than better-known Valloire, nearby.
1600m; slopes 1600–2550m
19 60km

Kastelruth Italy
Charming picture-book village in the south Tirolean Italian Dolomites with good cross-country trails. Near the Sella Ronda circuit.
⊠ *Inntravel*

Kasurila Finland
Siilinjarvi area ski centre popular with boarders.
5

Katschberg Austria
Lovely hamlet above St Michael in southern Austria.
1140m; slopes 1650–2220m
15 80km
⊠ *Alpine Tours*

Keystone 504
⊠ *Crystal, Handmade Holidays, Made to Measure, Ski Independence, Ski Safari, Ski The American Dream, Ski Total, Skisar US, Thomson, United Vacations*

Kicking Horse Mountain 571
⊠ *Crystal, Ski Safari, Skisar US, Thomson*

Killington 558
⊠ *Chalets 'Unlimited', Crystal, Equity Total Ski, Esprit Ski, First Choice Ski, Iglu.com, Independent Ski Links, Inghams, Made to Measure, Neilson, Rocketski, Ski Activity, Ski Arrangements, Ski Independence, Ski Line, Ski Safari, Ski Success, Ski The American Dream, Solo's, Thomson, United Vacations, Virgin Ski*

Kimberley 571
⊠ *Crystal, Frontier Ski, Inghams, Made to Measure, Ski Safari, Skisar US, Thomson*

Kirchberg 120
Lively little town which shares its slopes with Kitzbühel.
⊠ *First Choice Ski, Interhome, Lagrange Holidays, Top Deck*

Kirchdorf 177
Attractive village near St Johann in Tirol.
⊠ *Crystal, Snowcoach, Thomson*

Kirkwood 479
⊠ *Skisar US*

Kitzbühel 120
⊠ *Airtours, Avant-ski, Bladon Lines, Chalets 'Unlimited', Crystal, Elegant Resorts, Esprit Ski, First Choice Ski, Iglu.com, Independent Ski Links, Inghams, Interhome, Lagrange Holidays, Made to Measure, Neilson, Panorama, Ski Arrangements, Ski Club of GB, Ski Solutions, The Corporate Ski Company, Thomson*

Kleinarl Austria
Secluded traditional village up a pretty side valley from Wagrain, with lifts into the Flachau section of the Salzburger Sportwelt Amadé.
1015m; slopes 800–2185m
100 350km

Klippitztorl Austria
One of many little areas in Austria's easternmost ski region near Slovenian border.
1460m; slopes 1460–1820m
6 25km

Klosters 412
Quiet, affluent chalet village that shares a huge ski area with Davos.
⊠ *Alpine Answers Select, Elegant Resorts, Inghams, Kuoni, Made to Measure, Momentum Ski, Plus Travel, Powder Byrne, Ski Club of GB, Ski Solutions, Ski Weekend, Ski with Julia, SkiGower, The Ski Company Ltd, White Roc*

Kobla 626

Kolsass-Weer Austria
Dated resort; low, inconvenient, limited slopes; now loses out to cheaper, more snowsure Andorra.
555m; slopes 555–1010m
3 14km
⊠ *Crystal*

Königsleiten
Quiet, high resort sharing fairly snowsure area with Gerlos, now also linked to Zell im Zillertal to form a fair-sized area.

Kopaonik Serbia
Modern, sympathetically designed family resort in a pretty setting.
1770m; slopes 1110–2015m
21 57km

Koralpe Austria
Largest and steepest of many gentle little areas in Austria's easternmost ski region near Slovenian border.
1550m; slopes 1550–2050m
10 25km

Korea Condo Korea
Odd resort – a single condo complex built some away from the 3 slopes. 2

Kössen Austria
British schools destination near St Johann in Tirol with little to attract others; very low, scattered, limited slopes.
600m; slopes 600–1700m
11 25km

Kötschach-Mauthen Austria
One of many little areas near Hermagor in eastern Austria close to Italian border.
710m; slopes 710–1300m
4 6km

Kranjska Gora 626
⊠ *Alpine Tours, Balkan Holidays, Crystal, First Choice Ski, Solo's, Thomson*

Krimml Austria
Sunny area high enough to usually have good snow. Shares regional pass with Wildkogel resorts (Neukirchen).
1075m; slopes 1640–2040m
8 33km

Krispl-Gaissau Austria
Very close to Salzburg. Several long top-to-bottom lifts, so size of area greatly reduced if snowline high. Easy slopes.
925m; slopes 750–1570m
11 40km

Kühtai Austria
Huddle of good hotels (and little else) with a small, snowsure area suited to intermediates and only 35km from Innsbruck.
2020m; slopes 2010–2520m
11 40km
⊠ *Crystal, Inghams*

Kurumayama Kogen Japan
Remote resort, 6 hours from Osaka. Probably the least crowded slopes in Japan. 11

Kusatsu Onsen Japan
Spa village with attractive hot springs, 3 hours from Tokyo.
15

Laax 419
Old farming community with a lot of character and some new development nearby – linked to Flims.
⊠ *Alpine Answers Select, Made to Measure*

Ladis Austria
Smaller alternative to Serfaus and Fiss, with lifts that connect into the same varied ski area.
1200m; slopes 1200–2540m
4 18km
⊠ *Alpine Tours*

Le Laisinant 326
Tiny hamlet a short bus-ride down the valley from Val-d'Isère.

Lake Louise 573
⊠ *Airtours, All Canada Ski, Alpine Answers Select, Crystal, Elegant Resorts, First Choice Ski, Frontier Ski, Independent Ski Links, Inghams, Kuoni, Lotus Supertravel, Made to Measure, Neilson, Ski Activity, Ski Club of GB, Ski Equipe, Ski Independence, Ski Line, Ski The American Dream, Skisar US, Thomson, United Vacations*

Lake Tahoe 479
⊠ *Equity Total Ski, Independent Ski Links, Rocketski, Ski Activity, Ski Independence, Skisar US, Thomson, United Vacations, Virgin Ski*

Lanersbach 107
Attractive village with charming little ski area of its own, plus Hintertux glacier nearby.

Lans-en-Vercors France
Neighbour of Villard-de-Lans, near Grenoble. Highest slopes in region; few snowmakers.
1020m; slopes 1400–1805m
16 24km

Lauterbrunnen 430
Valley town in the Jungfrau region, with a funicular and train connection up to Mürren.
⊠ *Ski Miquel, Top Deck*

Le Lavancher 212
Quiet village between Chamonix and Argentière, with off-piste runs home for the insane.

Lavarone Italy
One of several areas east of Trento, for weekend day-trip.
1195m; slopes 1075–1555m
13 12km

Leadville USA
Old mining town full of historic buildings. Own easy area (Ski Cooper) plus snowcat operation. Characterful inexpensive base for visiting Copper Mountain, Vail and Beaver Creek.

Lech 126
✉ *Avant-ski, Chalets 'Unlimited', Crystal, Elegant Resorts, Erna Low, Esprit Ski, Fairhand Holidays, FlexiSki, Iglu.com, Inghams, Made to Measure, Momentum Ski, Simply Ski, Ski Choice, Ski Expectations, Ski Solutions, Ski Total, Ski Weekend, White Roc*

The Lecht 636

Lélex France
Family resort with pretty wooded slopes between Dijon and Geneva. Shares lift pass with neighbour Mijoux.
900m; slopes 900–1680m
29 50km
✉ *Lagrange Holidays*

Las Leñas Argentina
Upmarket, Euro-style resort, 3 hours south of Mendoza, with varied, beautiful terrain. Peak season crowds and queues.
2240m; slopes 2240–3430m
12 65km
✉ *Scott Dunn Latin America*

Lenk 399
Traditional village that shares a sizeable area of easy, pretty terrain with Adelboden.
✉ *Made to Measure, Swiss Travel Service*

Lenzerheide Switzerland
Spacious village, separated by a lake from Valbella and sharing a large intermediate area.
1500m; slopes 1230–2865m
35 155km
✉ *Interhome, Made to Measure, Plus Travel, Ski Choice*

Leogang 149
Quiet, spread-out village with over-the-mountain link to Saalbach-Hinterglemm.
✉ *Equity Total Ski, Esprit Ski, Rocketski*

Lermoos Austria
Focal resort of the Zugspitz area, a delightful base for beginners and cross-country enthusiasts.
1005m; slopes 1005–2250m
10 29km

Lessach Austria
Hamlet with trail connecting into one of longest, most snowsure cross-country networks in Europe.
1210m

Leukerbad Switzerland
Major spa resort of Roman origin, with spectacular scenery and high runs including a World Cup downhill course.
1410m; slopes 1410–2700m
17 60km
✉ *SkiGower*

Leutasch Austria
Traditional cross-country village with limited slopes but a pleasant day trip from nearby Seefeld or Innsbruck.
1130m; slopes 1130–1605m
4 9km
✉ *Headwater Holidays, Inntravel*

Levi Finland
Finland's most rapidly developing and most Alpine-like resort. Easy to get to – Kittila airport is 10 minutes. 325m vertical and slope-side village with several hotels.
205m; slopes 205–530m 15
✉ *Inghams*

Leysin Switzerland
Large resort near Aigle, with a good range of facilities, but low, sunny terrain.
1400m; slopes 1400–2300m
19 60km
✉ *Club Med, Crystal, Plus Travel, SkiGower*

Lienz Austria
Pleasant town-cum-resort in pretty surroundings.
675m; slopes 730–2290m
12 55km

Lillehammer 629
✉ *Neilson*

Limone Italy
Pleasant old railway town not far from Turin, with a pretty area, far from snowsure. A taste of the 'real' Italy.
1010m; slopes 1030–2050m
29 80km

Lincoln 555
✉ *Crystal*

Lindvallen-Hogfjallet Sweden
Largest ski area (but two unlinked mountains) in Scandinavia. Start of Vasalopp, world's largest cross-country race. Also has world's first ski-through McDonald's.
800m; slopes 800–1000m
72 85km

Le Lioran France
Auvergne village with purpose-built satellite above. Spectacular volcanic scenery.
1160m; slopes 1160–1850m
24 60km

Livigno 367
✉ *Airtours, Chalets 'Unlimited', Crystal, First Choice Ski, Iglu.com, Inghams, Interhome, Neilson, Panorama, Ski Arrangements, Thomson*

Lizzola Italy
Small base development in remote spot north of Bergamo. Several other little areas nearby.
1250m; slopes 1250–2070m
9 30km

Llaima Chile
Exotic, popular ski touring area (Alpine and Nordic) around and below a mildly active volcano; trails through trees.
1500m

Loch Lomond Canada
Near Thunder Bay on shores of Lake Superior. Shares lift pass with neighbour Candy Mountain. Challenging slopes: steep, narrow, bumpy.
215m; slopes 215–440m
3 90 acres

Lofer Austria
Quiet, traditional, village close to Salzburg with a small area of its own, and Waidring's relatively snowsure Steinplatte nearby.
640m; slopes 640–1745m
13 46km

Longchamp 336
Purpose-built resort that shares its ski area with Valmorel.

Loon Mountain 555
✉ *Equity Total Ski, Rocketski, Virgin Ski*

Lost Trail USA
Remote Montana area, open only Thursday to Sunday and holidays. Mostly intermediate.
2005m; slopes 2005–2370m
6 800 acres

Loveland USA
High, varied slopes, a day trip from Keystone and renowned for snow. Long season, good for all standards.
3220m; slopes 3220–3730m
11 836 acres

Luchon France
Sizeable village with plenty of amenities and train station, with gondola (8 minutes) to its ski area. Superbagnères purpose-built at top.
630m; slopes 1440–2260m
16 35km
✉ *Lagrange Holidays*

Lurisia Italy
Sizeable spa resort. Good base for visits to surrounding little ski areas and Nice.
750m; slopes 850–1800m
30km

Luz-Ardiden France
Spa village below its ski area. Cauterets and Barèges nearby.
710m; slopes 1730–2450m
19 60km

Macugnaga Italy
Pretty, two-part village set amid stunning scenery. Novice and intermediate slopes,
1330–1390m;
slopes 1330–2970m 12
40km
✉ *Interhome, Neilson*

Madesimo Italy
Remote valley village, with limited area of mainly intermediate runs, and a famous itinerary route.
1545m; slopes 1545–2880m
15 45km
✉ *Crystal, Inghams, Ski Arrangements, Thomson*

Madonna di Campiglio 371
✉ *Alpine Tours, Crystal, Equity Total Ski, Inghams, Interhome, Rocketski, Ski Arrangements, Ski Club of GB, Sloping Off, Solo's, Thomson*

Mad River Glen 555

La Magdelaine Italy
Neighbour of Cervinia, good on bad weather days.
1645m; slopes 1645–1870m
4 4km

Maishofen Austria
Cheap(er) place to stay when visiting equidistant Saalbach and Zell am See.
765m

Malbun Liechtenstein
Quaint, civilised, user-friendly little family resort, 16km from the capital, Vaduz. Limited slopes, with short easy runs.
1600m; slopes 1595–2100m
6 16km

Malcesine Italy
Large summer resort on Lake Garda with fair area.
1430m; slopes 1430–1830m
8 12km

Malga Ciapela Italy
Resort at the foot of the Marmolada glacier massif, with a link into the Sella Ronda, and Cortina nearby.
1445m; slopes 1445–3270m
8 18km

Mallnitz Austria
Village in a pretty valley close to Slovenia, with two varied areas providing a fine mix of wooded and open runs and good off-piste.
1200m; slopes 1300–2650m
5 30km
✉ *Crystal*

Mammoth Mountain 481
✉ *Crystal, Independent Ski Links, Ski Activity, Ski Independence, Ski Line, Ski Safari, Ski The American Dream, Skisar US, United Vacations, Virgin Ski*

Manigod France
Small valley village over the Col de la Croix-Fry from La Clusaz.

Marble Mountain Canada
Area near charming Newfoundland town Corner Brook and Gros Morne National Park wilderness. One of highest snowfall records on east coast.
85m; slopes 85–570m
5 126 acres
✉ *Frontier Ski*

Maria Alm Austria
Charming unspoilt village east of Zell am See with a varied area that stretches impressively over five linked mountains.
800m; slopes 800–2000m
36 150km

Mariapfarr Austria
Village at centre of one of the longest, most snow-reliable cross-country networks in Europe. Sizeable Mauterndorf-St Michael Alpine area on doorstep. Obertauern nearby.
1120m
7 30km

Mariazell Austria
Traditional Styria village with an impressive basilica, that has a real antiquated feel to it. Limited slopes.
870m; slopes 870–1265m
5 11km

Mont Ste Anne 604
✉ *All Canada Ski, Frontier Ski, Inghams, Ski Safari*

Mont St Sauveur 604

Mont Sutton Canada
Varied area with perhaps the best glade skiing in eastern Canada, including some for novices. Quaint Sutton village nearby.
9 *175 acres*

Morgins 405
Chalet resort on Portes du Soleil, indirectly linked to Champéry.
✉ *Ski Morgins Holidays, Ski Rosie*

Morillon 247
Valley village with a gondola link up to its purpose-built satellite and the Flaine network.
✉ *Fairhand Holidays, Lagrange Holidays, Motours, Ski Life*

Morin Heights Canada
One of the best areas in the Montreal region. 100% snowmaking. Attractive base lodge. 6

Morzine 281
✉ *Airtours, Alpine Weekends, Avant-ski, Chalet Snowboard, Chalets 'Unlimited', Challenge Activ, Crystal, Esprit Ski, Fairhand Holidays, First Choice Ski, Iglu.com, Independent Ski Links, Inghams, Lagrange Holidays, Made to Measure, Momentum Ski, Motours, Mountain Highs, Ski Activity, Ski Arrangements, Ski Chamois, Ski Choice, Ski Expectations, Ski France, Ski Line, Ski Weekend, SkiAway Holidays, Snowline, Solo's, The Chalet Company, The Corporate Ski Company, Thomson, Trail Alpine, White Roc*

Les Mosses Switzerland
Uninteresting resort and area, best for a day trip.
1500m; slopes 1500–2200m
13 *25km*

Mottaret 267
Purpose-built but reasonably attractive component of Méribel.
✉ *First Choice Ski, Ski Club of GB, Ski Leisure Direction, Skiworld, Thomson*

Mottarone Italy
Closest slopes to Lake Maggiore. No village – just a base area.
1200m; slopes 1200–1490m *25km*

Mount Abram USA
Small, pretty, tree-lined area in Maine, renowned for its immaculately groomed easy runs.
295m; slopes 295–610m
5 *170 acres*

Mountain High USA
Best snowfall record and highest lift capacity in Los Angeles vicinity – plus 95% snowmaking. Mostly intermediate cruising.
2010m; slopes 2010–2500m
12 *220 acres*

Mount Ashland USA
Arty town in Oregon renowned for Shakespeare. Mountain includes glaciated bowl rimmed with steeps. Best for experts.
1935m; slopes 1935–2285m
4 *200 acres*

Mount Bachelor USA
Extinct volcano in Oregon offering deserted runs on every side served by many fast chairs. Gets a lot of rain. Accommodation in Bend, 25 miles away.
1740m; slopes 1740–2765m
13 *3680 acres*

Mount Baker USA
Almost on the coast near Seattle, yet one of the top resorts for snow (averages 600 inches a year). Plenty of challenging slopes. Known for spectacular avalanches.
1115m; slopes 1115–1540m
9 *1000 acres*

Mount Baldy Canada
Tiny area, but worthwhile excursion from Big White. Gets ultra light snow – great glades/powder chutes.
slopes 1705–2150m
2 *150 acres*

Mount Baldy USA
Some of the longest and steepest runs in California. Near Los Angeles, but 20% snowmaking and antiquated lifts are a major drawback.
1980m; slopes 1980–2620m
4 *400 acres*

Mount Baw Baw Australia
Small but entertaining intermediate area in attractive woodland, with great views. Closest area to Melbourne. Nearest town – Noojee.
1480m; slopes 1340–1565m
8 *61 acres*

Mount Buffalo 639

Mount Buller 639

Mount Dobson New Zealand
Best of smaller Kiwi areas. Mt Cook and Pacific views. Wide treeless basin with long runs by NZ standards. Good snowcover record. Mostly intermediate.
1630m; slopes 1630–2045m
4 *990 acres*

Mount Hood Meadows USA
One of several sizeable areas amid magnificent Oregon scenery. Impressive snowfall record but snow tends to be wet, and weather damp.
1375m; slopes 1375–2535m
12 *2150 acres*

Mount Hood Ski Bowl USA
Sizeable area set amid magnificent Oregon scenery. Weather can be damp.
1095m; slopes 1095–1540m
9 *960 acres*

Mount Hotham 639

Mount Hutt 641

Mount Lemmon USA
Southernmost area in North America. close to famous Old West town Tombstone, Arizona. Reasonable snowfall.
2500m; slopes 2500–2790m
3 *70 acres*

Mount Lyford New Zealand
Limited but developing area close to the superb whale- and seal-watching centre, Kaikoura, 140km north of Christchurch.
1200m; slopes 1200–1640m
6 *395 acres*

Mount McKay 639

Mount Olympus Greece
Ski mountaineering site with chain of huts on both faces. Late winter is best time to visit.

Mount Rose USA
Only 22 miles from Reno. Good slopes of its own and well placed for trips to other Tahoe resorts.
2515m; slopes 2515–2955m
5 *900 acres*

Mount Selwyn Australia
Popular with beginners and families. Surprisingly good lift system. 6 hours from Sydney.
1520m; slopes 1490–1610m
13 *111 acres*

Mount Snow 555
✉ *Ski Success, Virgin Ski*

Mount Spokane USA
Little intermediate area outside Spokane (Washington State) with cheap lift pass.
1160m; slopes 1160–1795m
5 *350 acres*

Mount St Louis / Moonstone Canada
Premier area in Toronto region, spread over three peaks. Very high-capacity lift system and 100% snowmaking.
13 *175 acres*

Mount Washington Resort Canada
Main area in remote part of Vancouver Island; beautiful scenery. Base village has lodging. Impressive snowfall record but rain is a problem.
1110m; slopes 1110–1590m
6 *970 acres*
✉ *Frontier Ski, Ski Safari*

Mount Sunapee USA
Closest area of any size to Boston; primarily intermediate terrain.
375m; slopes 375–835m
10 *210 acres*

Mount Waterman USA
Small Los Angeles area where kids ski free. Little snowmaking is a drawback.
2135m; slopes 2135–2440m
3 *210 acres*

Mühlbach Austria
Village near Bischofshofen, a short bus hop from one end of an impressive five-mountain area
855m; slopes 790–1825m
23 *80km*

Mühltal 181
Small village halfway between Niederau and Auffach in the Wildschönau. No local skiing of its own.

Muhr Austria
Village by Katschberg tunnel well placed for visiting areas that get different weather patterns – St Michael, Badkleinkirchheim, Flachau, Obertauern.
1110m

Muju Korea
Largest area in Korea (30 slopes) and the furthest from Seoul (3.5 hours south). Not as ugly or crowded as most Korean resorts. 13

Mürren 430
✉ *Inghams, Kuoni, Made to Measure, Plus Travel, Ski Club of GB, Ski Solutions, SkiGower, Swiss Travel Service, Thomson, Top Deck*

Mutters 111

Myoko Kogen Japan
Japan's best all-round area. Extensive slopes spread over 5 distinct, interconnected sections with longer, wider runs than Japanese norm. 57

Naeba Japan
North of Tokyo – attracts the fashion conscious.
900m; slopes 900–1800m *34*

Nakiska Canada
Small area of wooded runs between Banff and Calgary, with state-of-the-art snowmaking.
1525m; slopes 1525–2215m
5 *230 acres*

Nasserein 169
Quiet suburb of St Anton, a short bus ride from the centre.

Nauders Austria
Attractive village on Italian border with a high, sunny intermediate area with lots of snowmakers.
1400m; slopes 1400–2750m
16 *65km*
✉ *Waymark Holidays*

Nax Switzerland
Quiet, sunny village in balcony setting overlooking Rhône valley. Own little area and short drive from Veysonnaz.
1300m; slopes 1300–3330m
100 *400km*

Nendaz 445
Enormous apartment development offering quiet alternative to Verbier.
✉ *Interhome*

Neukirchen Austria
Quiet, pretty beginners' resort with a fairly snowsure plateau at the top of its mountain. Intermediates have the Ziller valley nearby.
855m; slopes 855–2150m
14 *35km*

Neustift 111
✉ *Alpine Tours, Esprit Ski, Interhome, Made to Measure*

Nevegal Italy
Weekend day-trippers' place near Belluno, south of Cortina.
1030m; slopes 1030–1650m
14 28km

Nevis Range **636**

Niederau **181**
Amorphous chalet-style village in the Wildschönau region.
⊠ *First Choice Ski, Inghams, Neilson, Thomson*

Niedernsill Austria
Astute choice for crowd-free slopes when snowline high, Kaprun queues long. Tucked behind Kaprun. Also well placed for visiting uncrowded, snowy Gerlos and Matrei.
770m; slopes 770–1000m *3*

Niseko Kogen Japan
Hokkaido's main resort. Very exposed with unpredictable weather, little skied until February. Small area with very short runs. 22

Nockberge Innerkrems Austria
Area just south of Katschberg tunnel. Gets weather from east (Tirol gets it from west).
1500m; slopes 1500–2300m
10 33km

Nordic Valley USA
Utah cross-country area close to Salt Lake City. Powder Mountain and Snowbasin are nearby Alpine areas.

Nordseter Norway
Cluster of hotels in deep forest 14km north of Lillehammer. Basic Alpine facilities but better cross-country centre.
1000m

Norefjell Norway
120km north-west of Oslo. Norway's toughest run, a very steep unpisted 600m drop.
750m; slopes 185–1185m *11*

La Norma France
Traffic-free purpose-built resort near Modane and Val-Cenis, with mostly easy terrain.
1350m; slopes 1350–2750m
18 65km
⊠ *Erna Low, Fairhand Holidays, Interhome, Lagrange Holidays, Motours*

Norquay **573**

North Conway USA
Attractive factory-outlet-shopping town in New Hampshire close to Attitash and Cranmore ski areas.
⊠ *Skisar US, Virgin Ski*

Northstar-at-Tahoe **479**
⊠ *Skisar US, United Vacations, Virgin Ski*

Nosawa Onsen Japan
Shinetsu spa village with good hot springs. Pistes cut out of heavy vegetation.
500m; slopes 500–1650m *27*

Nôtre-Dame-de-Bellecombe **258**
Pleasant village spoilt by the busy Albertville-Megève road. Inexpensive base from which to visit Megève, though it has fair slopes of its own.
⊠ *Barrelli Ski, Motours*

Nova Levante Italy
Little area used mostly by weekend day-trippers.
1180m; slopes 1180–2200m
14 20km

Nub's Nob USA
One of the most sheltered Great Lakes ski areas (many suffer fierce winds). 100% snowmaking; weekend crowds from Detroit. Wooded slopes suitable for all levels.
275m; slopes 275–405m
8 245 acres

Oberau **181**
Very pretty village in the Wildschönau region.
⊠ *First Choice Ski, Inghams, Neilson, Thomson*

Obereggen Italy
Tiny resort used mainly by weekend day-trippers.
1550m; slopes 1550–2200m
6 10km

Obergurgl **142**
⊠ *Airtours, Crystal, Esprit Ski, Independent Ski Links, Inghams, Made to Measure, Ski Club of GB, Ski Expectations, Ski Solutions, Thomson*

Oberlech **126**
Car- and crowd-free family resort alternative to Lech. Snowsure due to height, snow-pocket position and snow-guns.

Oberndorf **177**
Quiet hamlet with beginners' area, and a chair connecting it to St Johann's undemanding ski area.
⊠ *Lagrange Holidays*

Oberstdorf Germany
Attractive winter-sports town near the Austrian border with three small areas. Famous ski-jumping hill.
815m; slopes 800–2220m
31 30km
⊠ *Moswin Tours*

Obertauern **147**
⊠ *Inghams, Made to Measure, Thomson*

Ochapowace Canada
Main area in Saskatchewan, east of Regina. Doesn't get a huge amount of snow but 75% snowmaking helps.
4 100 acres

Ohau New Zealand
Some of NZ's steepest slopes, served by long T-bar. Great views of Lake Ohau. Unusually for NZ, base has accommodation.
1425m; slopes 1425–1825m
3 310 acres

Okemo **555**

Oppdal **629**

Orcières-Merlette France
Good family resort with convenient, snowsure nursery slopes. Longer runs mostly funnel safely back to town.
1850m; slopes 1850–2650m
27 80km
⊠ *Fairhand Holidays, Lagrange Holidays, Motours*

Ordino **608**
Valley village near La Massana, on the way up to Andorra's best snow at Arcalis.

Oropa Italy
Little area just off Aosta-Turin motorway. Easy change of scene from Courmayeur.
1180m; slopes 1200–2390m
15km

Les Orres France
Friendly modern resort with great views and varied intermediate terrain; but snow is unreliable, and it's a long transfer from Lyon.
1550m; slopes 1550–2720m
23 62km
⊠ *Fairhand Holidays, First Choice Ski, Interhome, Lagrange Holidays*

Orsières Switzerland
Traditional, sizeable winter resort near Martigny. Well-positioned base from which to visit equidistant Verbier and Chamonix valley.
900m

Ortisei **381**
Charming, lively, old market town in the Italian Dolomites with indirect links to the Sella Ronda.
⊠ *Inghams*

Oslo Norway
Capital city with cross-country ski trails in its parks. Alpine slopes and lifts in Nordmarka region, just north of city boundaries.

Otre il Colle Italy
Smallest of many little resorts near Bergamo.
1100m; slopes 1100–2000m
7 7km

Oukaimeden Morocco
Slopes 75km from Marrakesh with a surprisingly long season. A few simple hotels and equipment available.
2600m; slopes 2600–3260m
8 15km

Ovindoli Italy
One of smallest areas in L'Aquila region east of Rome, but has higher slopes than most and one of the better lift systems.
1375m; slopes 1375–2220m
9 10km

Ovronnaz Switzerland
Pretty village set on a sunny shelf above the Rhône valley, with a good pool complex. Limited area but Crans-Montana and Anzère close.
1350m; slopes 1350–2080m
10 25km

Owl's Head Canada
Steep mountain rising out of a lake that affords superb views, in a remote spot bordering Vermont, away from weekend crowds.
7 90 acres

Oz-en-Oisans **193**
Attractive old village with higher satellite at base of lifts into Alpe-d'Huez.
⊠ *Lagrange Holidays, Motours, Ski Life*

Pajarito Mountain USA
Los Alamos area laid out by nuclear scientists. Atomic slopes too – steep, ungroomed. Open Fridays, weekends and holidays. Fun day out from Taos.
2685m; slopes 2685–3170m
6 220 acres

Pal **612**
Prettily wooded mountain, now linked with slopes of Arinsal and soon to be accessible from valley town of La Massana.
⊠ *Panorama, Snowcoach*

Palandöken **627**
⊠ *Inghams*

Pamporovo **623**
⊠ *Balkan Holidays, Crystal, First Choice Ski, Neilson, Ski Balkantours, Thomson*

Panarotta Italy
Smallest of resorts east of Trento. Higher altitude than nearby Andalo, so worth a day out from there.
1500m; slopes 1500–2000m
6 7km

Panorama **595**
⊠ *All Canada Ski, Frontier Ski, Inghams, Made to Measure, Ski Safari, Skisar US*

Panticosa **620**

Park City **535**
⊠ *Alpine Answers Select, American Ski Classics, Crystal, Iglu.com, Made to Measure, Momentum Ski, Ski Activity, Ski Independence, Ski Line, Ski Safari, Ski The American Dream, Skisar US, Skiworld, United Vacations*

Parnassus Greece
Biggest and best area in Greece with surprisingly good slopes and lifts, 30km from Delphi. Wonderful sea views.
slopes 1600–2250m *10*

Parpan Switzerland
Pretty village linked to the large intermediate area of Lenzerheide.
1510m; slopes 1230–2865m
35 155km

Partenen 139
Traditional village in pretty setting at end of Montafontal (dead-end in winter). Slopes start at neighbour Gaschurn with lots more in vicinity.

La Parva Chile
Chile's best ski area, an hour from Santiago. Crowded at weekends.
2815m; slopes 2815–3570m ⛫ *14*
⊠ *Scott Dunn Latin America*

Pas de la Casa 614
⊠ *Airtours, Chalets 'Unlimited', Crystal, First Choice Ski, Independent Ski Links, Inghams, Lagrange Holidays, Neilson, Panorama, Thomson, Top Deck*

Passo Lanciano Italy
Closest area to Adriatic. Weekend crowds from nearby Pescara when snow good.
1305m; slopes 1305–2000m ⛫ *13*

Passo Tonale Italy
Ugly resort in a bleak setting with guaranteed snow at a bargain price. Pretty Madonna is nearby.
1885m; slopes 1885–3025m
⛫ *30* ⛷ *80km*
⊠ *Airtours, Alpine Tours, Crystal, Equity Total Ski, First Choice Ski, Inghams, Rocketski, Sloping Off, Thomson*

Pass Thurn 120
Road-side lift base for Kitzbühel's most snowsure, but unconnected, ski area.

Pebble Creek USA
Small area on Utah-Jackson Hole route. Blend of open and wooded slopes.
1920m; slopes 1920–2530m
⛫ *3* ⛷ *600 acres*

Pec Pod Snezkou Czech Republic
Collection of hamlets spread along the valley road leading to the main lifts. Piste skiing very limited. Strictly for ultra-tight budgets.
770m; slopes 710–1190m
⛫ *5* ⛷ *12km*

Peisey-Nancroix 202
Small village linked to the Les Arcs network via a five-minute gondola ride to Plan-Peisey-Vallandry.
⊠ *Ski Hiver*

Pejo Italy
Unspoilt traditional village in a pretty setting, with a limited area. A cheap base for nearby Madonna.
1340m; slopes 1340–2800m
⛫ *6* ⛷ *15km*

Perisher/Smiggins 639

Pescasseroli Italy
One of numerous areas east of Rome in L'Aquila region. Summer camping spot.
1250m; slopes 1250–1945m
⛫ *6* ⛷ *25km*

Pescocostanzo Italy
One of numerous areas east of Rome in L'Aquila region. Summer mountain retreat.
1395m; slopes 1395–1900m
⛫ *4* ⛷ *25km*

Pettneu 169
Snow-sure specialist beginners' resort with an irregular bus link to nearby St Anton.
⊠ *Esprit Ski*

Petzen Austria
One of many little areas in Austria's easternmost ski region near Slovenian border.
600m; slopes 600–1700m
⛫ *6* ⛷ *13km*

Peyragudes-Peyresourde France
Small Pyrenean resort with its ski area starting high above. Better snow record than neighbouring Barèges.
1000m; slopes 1600–2400m
⛫ *15* ⛷ *37km*
⊠ *Lagrange Holidays*

Pfunds Austria
Picturesque valley village close to several resorts in Switzerland and Italy, as well as Ischgl in Austria. Ski school runs safari weeks to explore the possibilities.
970m

Phoenix Park Korea
Characterless golf complex with 12 ski slopes to keep things ticking over in winter. 2 hours from Seoul. ⛫ *7*

Piancavallo Italy
Uninspiring yet curiously trendy purpose-built village, an easy drive from Venice.
1270m; slopes 1270–1830m
⛫ *17* ⛷ *45km*
⊠ *Sloping Off*

Piani delle Betulle Italy
One of several little areas near east coast of Lake Como.
730m; slopes 730–1850m
⛫ *6* ⛷ *10km*

Piani di Artavaggio Italy
Small base complex rather than village. One of several little areas near Lake Como.
875m; slopes 875–1875m
⛫ *7* ⛷ *15km*

Piani di Bobbio Italy
Largest of several tiny resorts above Lake Como.
770m; slopes 770–1855m
⛫ *10* ⛷ *20km*

Piani di Erna Italy
Small base development – no village. One of several little areas above Lake Como.
600m; slopes 600–1635m
⛫ *5* ⛷ *9km*

Piau-Engaly France
User-friendly St-Lary satellite similar in appearance to Les Arcs 1600, in one of the best areas in the Pyrenees.
1850m; slopes 1420–2500m
⛫ *21* ⛷ *40km*
⊠ *Lagrange Holidays*

Piazzatorre Italy
One of many little areas in Bergamo region.
870m; slopes 870–2000m
⛫ *5* ⛷ *25km*

Pico 558
Low-key little family area (no resort) close to Killington in central Vermont.
⊠ *Virgin Ski*

Piesendorf Austria
Cheap(er), quiet place to stay when visiting Zell am See. Tucked behind Kaprun near Niedernsill.
780m; slopes 780–1275m
⛫ *3* ⛷ *3km*

Pievepelago Italy
Much the smallest and most limited of Appennine ski resorts. Less than 2 hours from Florence and Pisa.
1115m; slopes 1115–1410m
⛫ *7* ⛷ *8km*

Pila Italy
Purpose-built mountain resort linked by gondola to historical valley village. Varied, snowsure terrain, and nearby La Thuile, Cervinia and Monterosa ski included on Aosta valley lift pass.
1800m; slopes 1550–2710m
⛫ *13* ⛷ *70km*
⊠ *Crystal, Interhome, Interski, Sloping Off*

Pilion Greece
350m vertical. Pleasant slopes cut out of dense forest, only 15km from holiday resort Portaria above town of Volos. ⛫ 3

Pinzolo Italy
Atmospheric village with slopes well equipped with snowmakers. Cheap base for nearby Madonna.
800m; slopes 780–2100m
⛫ *8* ⛷ *29km*
⊠ *Alpine Tours, Equity Total Ski, Rocketski*

Pitztal Austria
Long valley with good glacier area at its head, accessed by underground funicular.
1250m; slopes 1735–3440m
⛫ *12* ⛷ *40km*

Pla-d'Adet France
Purpose-built complex at foot of St-Lary ski area (original village down at 830m). Limited but has restaurants, childcare, disco.
1680m; slopes 1420–2450m
⛫ *32* ⛷ *80km*
⊠ *Lagrange Holidays, Lagrange Holidays*

La Plagne 287
⊠ *Airtours, Chalet World, Chalets 'Unlimited', Club Med, Crystal, Erna Low, Esprit Ski, Eurotunnel Motoring Holidays, Fairhand Holidays, First Choice Ski, Handmade Holidays, Iglu.com, Independent Ski Links, Inghams, Interhome, Lagrange Holidays, Made to Measure, Mark Warner, Motours, Neilson, Silver Ski, Simply Ski, Ski Activity, Ski Amis, Ski Arrangements, Ski Beat, Ski Club of GB, Ski Expectations, Ski France, Ski Independence, Ski Leisure Direction, Ski Life, Ski Line, Ski Olympic, Ski Supreme, SkiAway Holidays, Skiworld, Solo's, Thomson, Top Deck, Tops Ski Chalets and Club Hotels*

Poiana Brasov 625
⊠ *Balkan Holidays, Inghams, Neilson, Ski Balkantours*

Pomerelle USA
Small area in Idaho on the Utah–Sun Valley route.
2430m; slopes 2430–2735m
⛫ *3* ⛷ *300 acres*

Pontechianale Italy
Highest, largest area in remote region south-west of Turin. Day-tripper place.
1600m; slopes 1600–2680m
⛫ *8* ⛷ *30km*

Ponte di Legno Italy
Attractive sheltered alternative to bleak, ugly neighbour Tonale. Linked by piste and bus.
1255m; slopes 1255–1920m
⛫ *5* ⛷ *15km*

Pontresina 439
Small, sedate base linked to nearby St Moritz by road, with extensive cross-country trails.
⊠ *Club Med, Made to Measure*

Porter Heights New Zealand
Closest skiing to Christchurch (1 hour). Open, sunny bowl; mostly intermediate plus back bowls for powder hounds. Snowmakers.
1300m; slopes 1300–1980m
⛫ *5* ⛷ *200 acres*

Porterillos Argentina
Limited area near Mendoza, just over the border from renowned Chilean resort Portillo.

Portes du Soleil 295

Portillo Chile
Luxury hotel 150km north-east of Santiago, with more snowsure, less crowded pistes than Las Leñas in Argentina.
2880m; slopes 2510–3290m
⛫ *12* ⛷ *25km*
⊠ *Scott Dunn Latin America*

Powderhorn USA
Area in west Colorado perched on world's highest flat-top mountain, Grand Mesa. Sensational views. Day trip from Aspen.
2490m; slopes 2490–2975m
⛫ *4* ⛷ *300 acres*

Powder King Canada
Remote resort in British Columbia, between Prince George and Dawson City. As its name suggest, great powder. Plenty of lodging.
880m; slopes 880–1520m
⛫ *3* ⛷ *160 acres*

Powder Mountain USA
Sizeable Utah area, a feasible day out from Park City. Wonderfully uncrowded locals' secret, renowned for bowls of fluffy virgin powder. Snowcat operation too.
2315m; slopes 2315–2710m
🚡 *6* ⛷ *1600 acres*

Pozza di Fassa Italy
Pretty Dolomite village with its own slopes, three other small areas on its doorstep, and access to the Sella Ronda at nearby Campitello.
1340m; slopes 1340–2155m
🚡 *6* ⛷ *20km*

Pragelato Italy
Inexpensive base short drive east of Sestriere. Own area worth a try for half a day.
1535m; slopes 1535–2580m
⛷ *35km*

Prägraten am Grossvenediger Austria
Traditional mountaineering/ski touring village in lovely setting south of Felbertauern tunnel. Ski slopes at neighbouring Matrei.
1310m; slopes 1310–1490m
🚡 *2* ⛷ *3km*

Prali Italy
Tiny resort east of Sestriere. Worthwhile half-day change of scene from Milky Way.
1455m; slopes 1450–2500m
🚡 *6* ⛷ *25km*

Pralognan-la-Vanoise France
Unspoilt traditional village with pistes overlooked by spectacular peaks. Champagny (La Plagne) and Courchevel are close by.
1410m; slopes 1410–2355m
🚡 *14* ⛷ *25km*
⊠ *Lagrange Holidays, Motours*

Pra-Loup France
Convenient, purpose-built family resort with an extensive, varied intermediate area linked to La Foux-d'Allos.
1500m; slopes 1500–2600m
🚡 *32* ⛷ *73km*
⊠ *Equity Total Ski, Fairhand Holidays, Lagrange Holidays, Rocketski*

Prati di Tivo Italy
Sizeable resort by southern Italy standards. East of Rome near town of Teramo. Weekend day-trip place.
1450m; slopes 1450–1800m
🚡 *6* ⛷ *16km*

Prato Nevoso Italy
Purpose-built resort with rather bland slopes. Novel mountain-top skidoo transfer to/from Artesina.
1500m; slopes 1500–1950m
🚡 *13* ⛷ *30km*
⊠ *Equity Total Ski, Rocketski*

Prato Selva Italy
Tiny base development – no village – way east of Rome near Teramo. Weekend day-trip place.
1370m; slopes 1370–1800m
🚡 *4* ⛷ *10km*

Le Praz 234
The lowest and most attractive of the Courchevel resorts, with direct access to the slopes.
⊠ *Ski Deep, Ski 'n' Action*

Les Praz 212
Quiet hamlet 4km from Chamonix, with convenient cable-car link to the varied Flégère area.
⊠ *High Mountain Holidays*

Praz-de-Lys France
Little known snow-pocket area near Lake Geneva that can have good snow when nearby resorts (eg La Clusaz) do not.
1500m; slopes 1200–2000m
🚡 *23* ⛷ *60km*
⊠ *Lagrange Holidays*

Praz-sur-Arly 258
Traditional village in a pretty, wooded setting just down the road from Megève, with its own varied slopes.
⊠ *Lagrange Holidays, Motours, Ski Life*

Le Pré 202
Charming, rustic hamlet with lifts up to Arc 2000 and excellent runs back down.

Predazzo Italy
Small quiet place between Cavalese and Sella Ronda resorts. Well positioned for touring Dolomites area.
1015m; slopes 995–2205m
🚡 *8* ⛷ *17km*

Premanon France
One of four resorts that make up Les Rousses area in Jura region. Useful stopover en route to resorts beyond Geneva.
1050m; slopes 1120–1680m 🚡 *40*
⊠ *Lagrange Holidays*

La Presolana Italy
Large summer resort near Bergamo. Several other little areas nearby.
1250m; slopes 1250–1650m
🚡 *6* ⛷ *15km*

Punta Arenas Chile
Most southerly organised slope in the world, in Patagonia, near Cape Horn. 🚡 1

Puy-St-Vincent 297
⊠ *Esprit Ski, Fairhand Holidays, Interhome, Lagrange Holidays, Motours, Snowbizz Vacances*

Pyhä Finland
Finland's steep and deep resort (280m vertical), popular with good skiers and boarders. Youthful atmosphere in its only hotel. 🚡 6

Pyrenees, French 346

Pyrenees 2000 France
Tiny resort built in pleasing manner. Shares pretty area of short runs with Font-Romeu. Impressive snowmaking.
2000m; slopes 1750–2250m
🚡 *32* ⛷ *52km*

Québec 604
⊠ *Inghams*

Queenstown 644

Radium Hot Springs Canada
Commercialised summer resort near Panorama offering alternative to purpose-built slope-side resort.
slopes 975–2135m
🚡 *8* ⛷ *300 acres*
⊠ *Skisar US*

Radstadt Austria
Interesting, unspoilt medieval town near Schladming that has its own small area, with the Salzburger Sportwelt Amadè accessed from nearby Zauchensee or Flachau.
855m; slopes 855–2185m
🚡 *100* ⛷ *350km*

Rainbow New Zealand
Northernmost ski area on South Island, 90 minutes from Nelson. Wide, undulating, treeless. Mostly novice and intermediate.
1440m; slopes 1440–1760m
🚡 *4* ⛷ *865 acres*

Ramsau am Dachstein Austria
Charming village overlooked by the Dachstein glacier. Renowned for cross-country, it also has Alpine slopes locally, on the glacier and at Schladming.
1200m; slopes 1100–2700m
🚡 *18* ⛷ *30km*

Ramundberget 633

Rauris Austria
Old roadside village close to Kaprun and Zell am See, with a long narrow area that has snowmakers on lower slopes.
950m; slopes 950–2200m
🚡 *10* ⛷ *30km*
⊠ *Crystal*

Ravascletto Italy
Resort close to Austria in a pretty wooded setting, with most of its terrain high above on open plateau.
920m; slopes 920–1735m
🚡 *12* ⛷ *40km*
⊠ *Sloping Off*

Reallon France
Traditional-style village, with splendid views from above Lac de Serre-Ponçon.
1560m; slopes 1560–2115m
🚡 *6* ⛷ *20km*
⊠ *Lagrange Holidays*

Red Lodge USA
Characterful Old West Montana town. Ideal for two-centre trip with Big Sky or Jackson Hole.
1800m; slopes 2155–2860m
🚡 *8* ⛷ *1600 acres*
⊠ *Skisar US*

Red Mountain 571
⊠ *Frontier Ski, Ski Safari, Skisar US*

Red River USA
New Mexico western town – complete with stetsons and saloons – with slopes above. Intermediate neighbour of Taos.
2665m; slopes 2665–3155m
🚡 *7* ⛷ *270 acres*

Reichenfels Austria
One of many small areas in Austria's easternmost ski region near Slovenian border. Only resort not in regional lift pass share arrangement.
810m; slopes 810–1400m

The Remarkables 644

Rencurel-les-Coulumes France
One of seven little resorts just west of Grenoble totalling 200km of piste. Unspoilt, inexpensive place to tour. Villard-de-Lans is main resort.

Reutte Austria
500-year old market town with many suitably traditional hotels, and rail links to nearby Lermoos.
855m; slopes 855–1900m
🚡 *9* ⛷ *18km*

Revelstoke Canada
Town from which you can heli-ski in Monashees or cat-ski locally at more reasonable cost than most places.
460m
⊠ *Powder Skiing in North America Limited*

Rhêmes-Notre-Dame Italy
Unspoilt village in the beautiful Rhêmes valley, south of Aosta. Courmayeur and La Thuile within reach.
🚡 *2* ⛷ *5km*

Riederalp Switzerland
Pretty, car-free village perched high above the Rhône valley amid the glorious scenery of the Aletsch area. Access by cable-car from near Brig.
1900m; slopes 1900–2710m
🚡 *32* ⛷ *90km*

Rigi-Kaltbad Switzerland
Resort on a mountain rising out of Lake Lucerne, with superb all-round views, accessed by the world's first mountain railway.
1440m; slopes 1195–1795m
🚡 *9* ⛷ *30km*

Riihivouri Finland
Unusual in having its 'base' area at the top of the mountain. 20km from city of Jyvaskyla. 🚡 4

Riksgränsen 633

Riscone Italy
Dolomite village sharing pretty area with San Vigilio. Good snowmaking. Short easy runs.
1200m; slopes 1200–2275m
🚡 *35* ⛷ *40km*

Risoul 299
⊠ *Crystal, Erna Low, Fairhand Holidays, First Choice Ski, Iglu.com, Interhome, Lagrange Holidays, Made to Measure, Motours, Neilson, Ski Arrangements, Ski Independence, Thomson*

Rivisondoli Italy
Sizeable summer mountain retreat east of Rome, with one of the better lift systems in vicinity.
1350m; slopes 1350–2050m
🚡 *7* ⛷ *16km*

Rjukan Norway
Gateway to ultimate cross-country region – Hardanger Vidda. Trails to Voss take a week.
300m

Roccaraso Italy
Largest of the resorts east of Rome, at least when snowcover is complete.
1280m; slopes 1280–2200m
12 56km

Rohrmoos 156
Situated below small mountain in Dachstein-Tauern region, next to Schladming.

La Rosière 302
✉ *Crystal, Erna Low, Esprit Ski, Iglu.com, Interhome, Lagrange Holidays, Motours, Ski Arrangements, Ski Life, Ski Olympic, Vanilla Ski*

Rossland Canada
Main town with excellent range of restaurants; the place to stay when skiing Red Mountain, 5km away.

Rougemont 428
Only 7km from Gstaad, and part of the Gstaad super ski region.

Ruka Finland
Finland's best-known ski resort. Most slopes have snow guns – season starts October. Spacious area by Finnish standards. 18

Russbach Austria
Secluded village tucked up side valley, linked into Gosau-Annaberg-Lungotz area. Slopes spread over wide area.
815m; slopes 780–1620m
33 65km

Saalbach-Hinterglemm 149
✉ *Airtours, Crystal, Equity Total Ski, First Choice Ski, Iglu.com, Inghams, Interhome, Made to Measure, Neilson, Panorama, Rocketski, Sloping Off, Thomson*

Saalfelden Austria
Ideally placed for touring eastern Tirol. Maria Alm, Saalbach nearby.
745m; slopes 745–1550m
3 3km

Saanen Switzerland
Cheaper and more convenient alternative to staying in Gstaad – but much less going on.
slopes 950–3000m
69 250km
✉ *SkiGower*

Saanenmöser 428
Small village with local slopes and rail/road links to the rest of Gstaad's neighbours.
✉ *SkiGower*

Saas-Almagell Switzerland
Compact village up the valley from Saas-Grund, with good cross-country trails and walks, and limited Alpine area.
1670m 6

Saas-Fee 434
✉ *Avant-ski, Crystal, Erna Low, First Choice Ski, Independent Ski Links, Inghams, Interhome, Kuoni, Made to Measure, Momentum Ski, Plus Travel, Powder Byrne, Ski Choice, Ski Club of GB, Ski Independence, Ski Solutions, SkiGower, Swiss Travel Service, Thomson*

Saas-Grund Switzerland
Sprawling valley village below Saas-Fee, with separate, small but high Alpine area.
1560m; slopes 1560–3100m
7 45km
✉ *SkiGower*

Saddleback USA
Small area between Maine's premier resorts. High slopes by local standards.
695m; slopes 695–1255m
5 100 acres

Sahoro Japan
Ugly, purpose-built complex on Hokkaido island. Limited area, but one of the most exotic package destinations.
400m; slopes 400–1100m
9 15km
✉ *Club Med*

Les Saisies France
Traditional-style cross-country venue in a pretty setting, surrounded by varied four-mountain Alpine slopes.
1650m; slopes 1150–2000m
24 40km
✉ *Classic Ski Limited, Inntravel, Lagrange Holidays, Motours, Ski Life, SkiAway Holidays*

Sälen 633

Salt Lake City USA
Underrated base from which to ski Utah. 30 minutes from Park City, Deer Valley, The Canyons, Snowbird, Alta, Snowbasin. Cheaper and livelier than the resorts.
✉ *Club Pavilion, Skisar US*

Salzburg-Stadt Austria
Single long challenging run off back of Salzburg's local mountain, accessed by spectacular cable-car ride from suburb of Grodig.
425m

Samedan Switzerland
Valley town, just down the road from St Moritz.
1720m; slopes 1740–2570m
3 7km

Samnaun 115
Shares large ski area with Ischgl.

Samoëns 247
Beautiful rural valley village, a bus-ride from lifts into Flaine's skiing.
✉ *Fairhand Holidays, Inntravel, Interhome, Lagrange Holidays, Motours, Ski Life*

San Bernardino Switzerland
Pretty resort south of the road tunnel, close to Madesimo.
1625m; slopes 1600–2595m
8 35km

San Candido Italy
Austrian border resort on road to Lienz.
1175m; slopes 1175–1580m
4 15km

San Carlos de Bariloche Argentina
South America's only year-round resort, with five areas nearby.
790m; slopes 1050–2300m
29 26km
✉ *Scott Dunn Latin America*

San Cassiano 381
Pretty village linked to the Sella Ronda.

Sandia Peak USA
World's longest cable-car trip ascends from Albuquerque. Mostly gentle slopes; kids ski free.
slopes 2645–3165m
7 100 acres

San Grée di Viola Italy
Easternmost of resorts south of Turin, surprisingly close to Italian Riviera.
1100m; slopes 1100–1800m
30km

San Martin de los Andes Argentina
Limited area on the slopes of Cerro Chapelco. Neighbour to main resort Bariloche. 6
✉ *Scott Dunn Latin America*

San Martino di Castrozza Italy
Plain village in the southernmost Dolomites with varied slopes in four disjointed areas, none very extensive.
1465m; slopes 1465–2610m
20 50km
✉ *Equity Total Ski, Interhome, Rocketski*

Sansicario 376
Small, stylish, modern resort, centrally placed in the Milky Way near to Sauze d'Oulx.
✉ *Equity Total Ski, Rocketski*

San Simone Italy
Tiny development north of Bergamo. Lift pass shared with unappealing Foppolo area, 10 minutes' drive away.
2000m; slopes 1105–2300m
9 45km

Santa Caterina Italy
Pretty, user-friendly village near Bormio, with a snowsure novice and intermediate area.
1740m; slopes 1740–2725m
8 25km
✉ *Airtours, Thomson*

Santa Cristina 381
Quiet village on the periphery of the Sella Ronda.
✉ *Crystal, Inghams*

Santa Fe USA
One of America's most attractive and interesting towns. Varied slopes – glades, bowls, cruiser pistes, desert views. Great excursion from Taos.
3145m; slopes 3145–3645m
7 600 acres

Santa Maria Maggiore Italy
South of Simplon Pass from Rhône valley, near Lake Maggiore.
820m; slopes 820–1890m
5 10km

San Vigilio Italy
Charming, atmospheric Dolomite village with a delightful, sizeable area well covered by snow-guns.
1200m; slopes 1200–2275m
33 40km

San Vito di Cadore Italy
Sizeable, alternative place to stay to Cortina. Own slopes of negligible interest.
1010m; slopes 1010–1380m
9 12km

Sappada Italy
Isolated resort close to the Austrian border below Lienz.
1215m; slopes 1215–2050m
17 50km

Sappee Finland
Southern resort within easy reach of Helsinki. Popular with telemarkers and boarders. Lake views. 4

Sarnano Italy
Main resort in Macerata region near Adriatic Riviera. Valley village with ski slopes accessed by cable-car.
540m 9 11km

Le Sauze France
Fine area near Barcelonnette, sadly remote from airports.
1400m; slopes 1400–2440m
23 65km

Sauze d'Oulx 376
✉ *Airtours, Chalets 'Unlimited', Crystal, Equity Total Ski, First Choice Ski, Independent Ski Links, Inghams, Neilson, Panorama, Rocketski, Ski Arrangements, Thomson*

Savognin Switzerland
Pretty village with a good mid-sized area; a good base for top nearby resorts – St Moritz, Davos/Klosters, Flims.
1200m; slopes 1200–2715m
17 80km

Scheffau 162
Rustic beauty a few kilometres from Söll.
✉ *Airtours, Crystal, First Choice Ski, Thomson*

Schia Italy
Only area near Parma. No village. Very limited – short runs served by drags.
1245m; slopes 1245–1415m
7 15km

Schilpario Italy
Only one of many little areas near Bergamo.
1125m; slopes 1125–1635m
5 15km

Schladming 156
✉ *Crystal, Equity Total Ski, Interhome, Made to Measure, Rocketski, Sloping Off*

Schönried 428
A cheaper and quieter resort alternative to staying in Gstaad.
✉ *Interhome*

Schoppernau Austria
Scattered farming community, one of two main areas in Bregenzerwald north-west of Lech.
860m; slopes 860–2050m
8 37km

Schröcken Austria
Bregenzerwald area village close to the German border.
1260m; slopes 1260–2100m
16 60km

Schruns 139
✉ *Interhome*

Schüttdorf 184
Characterless dormitory satellite of Zell am See, with easy access to the shared ski area.

Schwarzach im Pongau Austria
Riverside village with railway station. Limited slopes nearby at Goldegg. Wagrain (Salzburg Sportwelt) and Grossarl (Gastein valley) also nearby.
600m

Schweitzer USA
In Idaho but near Spokane (Washington State). Good snowfall record; uncrowded, varied slopes.
1215m; slopes 1215–1945m
6 2350 acres
✉ *Skisar US*

Scopello Italy
Low area close to Aosta valley, worth considering for day trip in bad weather.
slopes 690–1740m
9 26km

Scuol Switzerland
Year-round spa resort close to Austria and Italy, with an impressive range of pistes.
1250m; slopes 1250–2785m
15 80km

Searchmont Resort Canada
Modern lift system and 95% snowmaking draws Americans across border away from limited Michigan areas. Fine Lake Superior views.
275m; slopes 275–485m
4 65 acres

Sedrun Switzerland
Charming, unspoilt old village on the Glacier Express rail route close to Andermatt, with fine on- and off-piste terrain amid glorious scenery.
1440m; slopes 1450–2350m
12 50km

Seefeld 111
✉ *Airtours, Crystal, Inghams, Interhome, Lagrange Holidays, Made to Measure, Thomson*

Le Seignus-d'Allos France
Neighbour of La Foux-d'Allos (shares large area with Pra-Loup). Own little area too. Lift pass share arrangement.
1400m; slopes 1400–2425m
13

Sella Nevea Italy
Limited but developing resort in a beautiful setting on the Slovenian border. Summer glacier nearby.
1140m; slopes 1190–1800m
11 8km
✉ *Sloping Off*

Selva/Sella Ronda 381
✉ *Bladon Lines, Chalets 'Unlimited', Crystal, Independent Ski Links, Inghams, Momentum Ski, Ski Arrangements, Thomson*

Selvino Italy
Closest resort to Bergamo.
960m; slopes 960–1400m
6 20km

Semmering Austria
Long established, civilised winter-sports resort amid pretty scenery, 100km from Vienna, towards Graz. Mostly intermediate terrain.
1000m; slopes 1000–1340m
5 14km

Seoul Korea
Small, unattractive, barren area 25 minutes from the capital. 3 very crowded slopes; short season. 3

Les Sept-Laux France
Ugly, user-friendly family resort near Grenoble, like a small Avoriaz. Pretty slopes for all grades.
1350m; slopes 1350–2400m
25 100km
✉ *Lagrange Holidays*

Serfaus Austria
Charming traffic-free village (with underground people-mover) at foot of long, narrow ski area, mainly easy and intermediate. Linked to Fiss.
1425m; slopes 1200–2700m
19 80km
✉ *Alpine Tours, Interhome, Made to Measure*

Serrada Italy
Very limited area near Trento.
slopes 1250–1605m 5
✉ *Alpine Tours, Equity Total Ski, Rocketski*

Serre-Chevalier 304
✉ *Airtours, Alpine Answers Select, Bladon Lines, Chalets 'Unlimited', Club Med, Crystal, Equity Total Ski, Erna Low, Fairhand Holidays, First Choice Ski, Handmade Holidays, Hannibals, Iglu.com, Independent Ski Links, Inghams, Interhome, Lagrange Holidays, Made to Measure, MasterSki, Motours, Neilson, Rocketski, Ski Arrangements, Ski Expectations, Ski France, Ski Independence, Ski Leisure Direction, Ski Life, Ski Miquel, Skiworld, Sloping Off, Solo's, Thomson, Tops Ski Chalets and Club Hotels*

Sesto Italy
Dolomite village on the road to Cortina, surrounded by pretty little areas.
1310m
31 50km

Sestola Italy
Appennine village a short drive from Pisa and Florence with its pistes, some way above, almost completely equipped with snowmakers.
900m; slopes 1280–1975m
23 50km

Sestriere 389
✉ *Alpine Answers Select, Club Med, Crystal, Equity Total Ski, Interhome, Momentum Ski, Motours, Neilson, Rocketski, Ski Arrangements, Ski Weekend, Thomson*

Shames Mountain Canada
Remote spot inland from coastal town Prince Rupert. Impressive snowfall record and gets deep powder.
670m; slopes 670–1195m
3 183 acres

Shawnee Peak USA
Small area near Bethel and Sunday River renowned for its night skiing. Spectacular views. Mostly groomed cruising.
185m; slopes 185–580m
5 225 acres

Shemshak Iran
Most popular of the three mountain resorts within 65km of Teheran. Packed at weekends, though few go to ski.

Shiga Heights Japan
Largest area in Japan, site of Nagano's 1998 Olympic skiing events, 150km from Tokyo. Happo One is nearby.
930m; slopes 1220–2305m
73 130km

Showdown USA
Intermediate area in Montana cut out of forest north of Bozeman. 50km to nearest hotel.
2065m; slopes 2065–2490m
4 640 acres

Sierra-at-Tahoe 479
✉ *Skisar US, Virgin Ski*

Sierra Nevada 620
✉ *First Choice Ski, Independent Ski Links, Neilson, Solo's, Thomson*

Sierra Summit USA
Sierra Nevada area accessible only from the west. 100% snowmaking.
2160m; slopes 2160–2645m
8 250 acres

Silbertal 139
Low secluded village in the Montafon area, linked to Schruns. Good base for touring numerous areas.

Sils Maria 439
Pretty lakeside village, linked to the St Moritz Corvatsch slopes via a cable-car to Furtschellas.
✉ *Interhome, Made to Measure*

Silvaplana 439
Pretty lakeside village near St Moritz, a short drive from the lift connections.
✉ *Interhome, Made to Measure*

Silver Creek USA
Winter Park's little neighbour. Very child-oriented. Low snowfall record for Colorado.
2490m; slopes 2490–2795m
5 250 acres

Silver Mountain USA
Up and coming northern Idaho area, near delightful resort town Coeur d'Alene. Best for experts, but plenty for intermediates too.
1215m; slopes 1215–1915m
6 1500 acres

Silver Star 571
✉ *All Canada Ski, Crystal, Frontier Ski, Made to Measure, Ski Independence, Ski Safari, Ski The American Dream, Skisar US*

Silverthorne USA
Factory outlet town on main road close to Keystone and Breckenridge. Good budget place for the five resorts on the Vail resorts lift pass.

Sinaia 625

Sipapu USA
Great little New Mexico area that would be better known if it had more reliable snow-cover. Mostly tree-lined runs. Nice day out from Taos when conditions are good.
slopes 2500–2765m
3 40 acres

Siviez 445
A quieter and cheaper base for skiing Verbier's Four Valleys circuit.
✉ *Interhome*

Sixt 247
Traditional village near Samoëns, at foot of new piste down from Flaine area. Own little area across valley, too.

Sjusjoen Norway
Cluster of hotels in deep forest close to Lillehammer. Basic Alpine facilities but better cross-country centre.
885m
✉ *Headwater Holidays, Inntravel, Waymark Holidays*

Ski Apache USA
Apache-owned area south of Albuquerque noted for groomed steeps. Panoramic views. Nearest lodging in charming Ruidoso.
2925m; slopes 2925–3505m
11 750 acres

Ski Cooper USA
Small area close to historic Old West town of Leadville. Good ski/sightseeing day out from nearby Vail, Beaver Creek and Copper Mountain.
slopes 3200–3565m 4

Ski Windham USA
2 hours from New York City and second only to Hunter for weekend crowds. Decent slopes by eastern standards.
485m; slopes 485–940m
7 230 acres

Smokovec Slovakia
Spa town near Poprad, with 3 small areas on its doorstep, known collectively as High Tatras.
1000m; slopes 1000–1500m 5

Smugglers' Notch 562
✉ *Esprit Ski, Ski The American Dream*

Snowbasin 540
✉ *Skisar US*

Snowbird 542
✉ *Crystal, Made to Measure, Ski Independence, Ski The American Dream, Skisar US, United Vacations*

Snowbowl (Arizona) USA
One of America's oldest areas, near Flagstaff, Arizona, atop extinct volcano and with stunning desert views. Good snowfall record.
2805m; slopes 2805–3505m
5 135 acres

Snowbowl (Montana) USA
Montana area renowned for powder, outside lively town of Missoula. Intermediate pistes plus 700 acres of extreme slopes. Grizzly Chute is the ultimate challenge.
1520m; slopes 1520–2315m
4 1400 acres

Snowmass 486
Purpose-built village with big mountain near Aspen.
✉ *Fantiski, Lotus Supertravel, Made to Measure, Ski Independence, Ski The American Dream, Ski Total, Skisar US, United Vacations*

Snow Summit USA
San Bernardino National Forest ski area near Palm Springs. Lovely lake views. 100% snowmaking. High-capacity lift system for weekend crowds.
2135m; slopes 2135–2500m
12 230 acres

Snow Valley USA
Area quite near Palm Springs. Fine desert views. High-capacity lift system copes with weekend crowds better than nearby Big Bear.
2040m; slopes 2040–2390m
11 230 acres

Solda Italy
Other side of Stelvio Pass from Bormio. Very long airport transfers.
1905m; slopes 1905–2625m
19 25km
✉ *Inghams*

Sölden 160
✉ *Esprit Ski, Made to Measure*

Soldeu 616
✉ *Airtours, Chalets 'Unlimited', Club Pavilion, Crystal, First Choice Ski, Independent Ski Links, Inghams, Lagrange Holidays, Neilson, Panorama, Ski Club of GB, Thomson, Top Deck*

Solfonn Norway
Tiny development 2 hours west of Geilo with some of Norway's most challenging Alpine slopes. Extensive, interesting cross-country trails too.
550m; slopes 550–760m 2

Solitude 527
✉ *Skisar US*

Söll 162
✉ *Airtours, Crystal, First Choice Ski, Inghams, Interhome, Neilson, Panorama, Ski Club of GB, Ski Hillwood, Thomson*

Sommand France
Purpose-built base that shares area with Praz-de-Lys.
1420m; slopes 1200–1800m
22 50km

Sorenberg Switzerland
Popular weekend retreat between Berne and Lucerne, with a high proportion of steep, low pistes.
1165m; slopes 1165–2350m
18 50km

South Lake Tahoe 479
Downmarket and tacky base for skiing Heavenly, with cheap accommodation, traffic and gambling.

South Tatras Slovakia
An area (there's no resort) covering both sides of Mount Chopok near Poprad.
slopes 1240–2005m
19 20km

Spindleruv Mlyn Czech Republic
Largest Giant Mountains region resort but few facilities. Several scattered little low areas.
750m; slopes 750–1300m
9 25km

Spital am Pyhrn Austria
Limited village east of Schladming, 4km from its easy intermediate slopes. Nearby Hinterstoder is more interesting.
650m; slopes 810–1885m
10 18km

Spittal/Drau Austria
Historic Carinthian town with a limited area starting a cable-car ride above it. A good day-trip from Bad Kleinkirchheim or Slovenia.
555m; slopes 1650–2140m
12 22km

Sportgastein 97
Characterless mountain village with some of the more interesting skiing in the Badgastein valley.

Squaw Valley 479
✉ *Crystal, Ski Activity, Ski Independence, Ski Safari, Ski The American Dream, Skisar US, United Vacations, Virgin Ski*

Srinagar India
Himalayan resort in Kashmir, with a small pisted area but excellent heli-skiing.
2720m; slopes 2645–3645m
7 5km

Stafal 373
Isolated village, with access to the Monterosa Ski area.

St Andrä im Lungau Austria
Valley-junction village ideally placed for one of the longest cross-country networks in Europe. Close to Tauern pass.
1045m

St Anton 169
✉ *Airtours, Alpine Answers Select, Alpine Tours, Avant-ski, Bladon Lines, Chalet World, Chalets 'Unlimited', Crystal, Elegant Resorts, Esprit Ski, First Choice Ski, FlexiSki, Iglu.com, Independent Ski Links, Inghams, Lotus Supertravel, Made to Measure, Mark Warner, Momentum Ski, Neilson, Simply Ski, Ski Addiction, Ski Arrangements, Ski Equipe, Ski Expectations, Ski Line, Ski Solutions, Ski Total, Ski-Val, Skiworld, St Anton Ski Company, The Corporate Ski Company, Thomson, White Roc*

St Cergue Switzerland
Limited resort less than an hour from Geneva, good for families with young children.
1045m; slopes 1045–1700m
9 20km

St Christoph 169
Small village on Arlberg pass above St Anton.
✉ *Elegant Resorts, Made to Measure*

St-Colomban-des-Villards France
Small resort in next side valley to La Toussuire. Good base for visiting largest areas in vicinity (Valloire and Val-Cenis).

Steamboat 509
✉ *Alpine Answers Select, American Ski Classics, Chalets 'Unlimited', Crystal, Inghams, Lotus Supertravel, Made to Measure, Neilson, Ski Activity, Ski Independence, Ski Line, Ski Safari, Ski The American Dream, Ski Total, Skiworld, Thomson, United Vacations*

Sainte-Foy-Tarentaise 310
✉ *Alpine Weekends, Independent Ski Links, Ski Arrangements, Ski Weekend*

Steinach Austria
Pleasant village in picturesque surroundings, an easy outing from Innsbruck.
1050m; slopes 1050–2205m
6 16km
✉ *Alpine Tours*

Stevens Pass USA
A day trip from Seattle, and accommodation 60km away in Bavarian-style town Leavenworth. Low snowfall and no snowmakers. Mostly intermediate slopes,
1235m; slopes 1235–1785m
14 1125 acres

St-François-Longchamp 336
Sunny, gentle slopes, with a couple of harder runs. Linked to Valmorel.
✉ *Lagrange Holidays, Motours, Ski Life*

St Gallenkirch 139

St-Gervais 258
Small town sharing its ski area with Megève.
✉ *APT Holidays Ltd, Fairhand Holidays, Interhome, Lagrange Holidays, Snowcoach*

St Jakob in Defereggen Austria
Unspoilt traditional village in a pretty, sunny valley close to Lienz and Heiligenblut, and with a good proportion of its slopes above 2000m.
1390m; slopes 1390–2520m
9 35km

St Jakob in Haus Austria
Snowpocket village with its own slopes, and a shared lift pass with nearby Fieberbrunn, Waidring and St Johann.
855m; slopes 855–1500m
7 22km

St-Jean-de-Sixt 225
Traditional hamlet, a cheap base for La Clusaz and Le Grand-Bornand (3km to both).

St-Jean-Montclar France
Small village at foot of thickly forested slopes. Good day out from nearby Pra-Loup.
1300m; slopes 1300–2500m
18 50km
✉ *Lagrange Holidays*

St Johann im Pongau Austria
Bustling, lively town with a small area of its own, but the impressive Salzburger Sportwelt Amadé area starts only 4km away at Alpendorf.
650m; slopes 800–2285m
100 350km

St Johann in Tirol 177
✉ *Crystal, Esprit Ski, Thomson*

St Lary-Espiaube 346

St-Lary-Soulan 346
✉ *Fairhand Holidays, Lagrange Holidays*

St Leonhard in Pitztal Austria
Village beneath a fine glacier in the Oetz area, accessed by underground funicular.
1250m; slopes 1735–3440m
12 40km

St Luc Switzerland
Quiet, unspoilt rustic village on the south side of the Rhône valley, with plenty of high, easy pistes.
1650m; slopes 1650–3025m
15 75km
✉ *Iglu.com, Inntravel*

St Margarethen Austria
Village near Obertauern in remarkable snow pocket.
1065m; slopes 1075–2210m
14 *50km*

St Martin bei Lofer Austria
Traditional village in lovely setting beneath impressive Loferer Steinberge massif. Cross-country centre with Alpine slopes at Lofer.
635m

Saint-Martin-de-Belleville 312
⊠ *Chalets de St Martin, Equity Total Ski, Independent Ski Links, Made to Measure, Motours, Rocketski, Ski Total, Thomson*

St Martin in Tennengebirge Austria
Highest village in Dachstein-West region near Salzburg. Limited slopes of its own but close to Annaberg which has an interesting area.
1000m; slopes 1000–1350m
5 *4km*

St-Maurice-sur-Moselle France
One of several areas near Strasbourg relatively close to the Channel. No snowmakers.
550m; slopes 900–1250m
8 *24km*

St Michael im Lungau Austria
Quiet, unspoilt village in the Tauern pass snowpocket with an uncrowded but disjointed intermediate area. Close to Obertauern and Wagrain.
1075m; slopes 1075–2360m
25 *60km*
⊠ *Alpine Tours, Equity Total Ski, Rocketski*

St Moritz 439
⊠ *Alpine Weekends, Club Med, Crystal, Elegant Resorts, FlexiSki, Iglu.com, Independent Ski Links, Inghams, Interhome, Kuoni, Made to Measure, Momentum Ski, Plus Travel, Ski Club of GB, Ski Solutions, Ski Weekend, Ski with Julia, SkiGower, Swiss Travel Service, The Corporate Ski Company*

St-Nicolas-de-Véroce 258
Small hamlet with a handful of simple hotels on the northern fringes of the Megève network.

St-Nizier-du-Moucherotte France
One of seven little resorts just west of Grenoble totalling 200km of piste. Unspoilt, inexpensive place to tour. Villard-de-Lans is main resort.

Stoneham 604
⊠ *Frontier Ski, Inghams, Ski Safari*

Stoos Switzerland
Small, unspoilt village an hour from Zurich. Overcrowded at weekends. Amazing views of Lake Lucerne from summits.
1300m; slopes 570–1920m 7

Storlien Sweden
Small family resort amid magnificent wilderness scenery, 1 hour from Trondheim, 30 mins from Sweden's top Alpine resort, Åre.
600m; slopes 600–790m
7 *15km*

Stowe 565
⊠ *Chalets 'Unlimited', Crystal, Elegant Resorts, Esprit Ski, Inghams, Made to Measure, Neilson, Ski Arrangements, Ski Independence, Ski Line, Ski The American Dream, Thomson, United Vacations, Virgin Ski*

St-Pierre-de-Chartreuse France
Locals' weekend place near Grenoble. Second oldest French ski resort (after Chamonix). Unreliable snow.
900m; slopes 900–1800m
14 *35km*

Stratton 555

Strobl Austria
Neighbour of St Wolfgang in beautiful lakeside setting. Slopes at nearby St Gilgen and Postalm, but best for relaxing winter holiday.
545m; slopes 545–1510m
9 *12km*

St Stephan Switzerland
Unspoilt old farming village at the foot of the largest area in the Gstaad Super Ski region.
995m; slopes 950–2155m
69 *250km*

Stuben 126
Small, unspoilt village linked to St Anton.

St Veit im Pongau Austria
Spa resort with limited slopes at neighbouring Goldegg but Wagrain (Salzburg Sportwelt Amadé) and Grossarl (Gastein valley) are nearby.
765m

St-Veran France
Highest 'real' village in Europe, full of character. Close to Serre-Chevalier and Milky Way. Uncommonly snow-reliable cross-country skiing.
2040m; slopes 2040–2800m
15 *30km*

St Wolfgang Austria
Charming lakeside resort near Salzburg, some way from any slopes, best for a relaxing winter holiday with one or two days on the slopes.
540m; slopes 665–1350m
9 *17km*
⊠ *Airtours, Crystal, Inghams, Thomson*

Sugar Bowl USA
Exposed area north of Lake Tahoe with highest snowfall in California, best for experts. Accommodation in Truckee but Squaw Valley nearby. Weekend queues.
2095m; slopes 2095–2555m
8 *1500 acres*

Sugarbush 555
⊠ *Made to Measure, Ski Arrangements, Ski Success, Solo's*

Sugarloaf 555
⊠ *First Choice Ski, Ski Success*

Summit at Snoqualmie USA
Four neighbouring areas – Summit East, Summit Central, Summit West and Alpental – with interlinked lifts, European-style. Damp weather and wet snow are major drawbacks.
slopes 915–1645m
24 *2000 acres*

Sun Alpina Japan
Collective name for 3 tiny neighbouring areas that share lift pass. 4 hours from Tokyo, 3 hours from Osaka. 23

Sundance 527
⊠ *Skisar US*

Sunday River 567
⊠ *Crystal, First Choice Ski, Made to Measure, Neilson, Ski Independence, Ski Safari, Ski Success, Skisar US, Virgin Ski*

Sunlight Mountain Resort USA
Quiet little area worth the easy trip from Vail to get away from its crowds for a day. Varied terrain. Good snowboard park.
2405m; slopes 2405–3015m
4 *460 acres*

Sun Peaks 571
⊠ *All Canada Ski, Frontier Ski, Made to Measure, Ski Independence, Ski Safari, Ski The American Dream, Skisar US*

Sunrise Park USA
Arizona's largest area, operated by Apaches. Slopes spread over 3 mountains; best for novices and leisurely intermediates.
2805m; slopes 2805–3500m
12 *800 acres*

Sunshine Village 573
⊠ *Airtours*

Sun Valley 553
⊠ *Crystal, Ski Activity, Skisar US*

Suommu Finland
No village – just a lodge right on the Arctic Circle. A few pistes but mostly ski-touring centre. 60km from Rovaniemi.
140m; slopes 140–410m

Superbagnères France
Little more than a particularly French-dominated Club Med, best for a low-cost, low-effort family trip to the Pyrenees.
1880m; slopes 1440–2260m
16 *35km*
⊠ *Lagrange Holidays*

Super-Besse France
Purpose-built resort amid spectacular extinct-volcano scenery. Shares area with Mont-Dore. Limited village.
1350m; slopes 1300–1850m
22 *45km*
⊠ *Lagrange Holidays, Ski Life*

Superdévoluy France
Ugly, purpose-built, user-friendly family resort, an hour south-east of Grenoble, with a sizeable intermediate area.
1500m; slopes 1500–2510m
32 *100km*
⊠ *Fairhand Holidays, Lagrange Holidays, Motours*

Supermolina 620

Tahko Finland
Largest resort within 500km of Helsinki. Plenty of intermediate slopes. Snowboard championships venue. Attractive, wooded, frozen-lake setting. 8

Tahoe City 479
Small lakeside accommodation base for visiting nearby Alpine Meadows and Squaw Valley.

Talisman Mountain Resort Canada
One of best areas in Toronto region, but relatively low lift capacity suggests long weekend queues inevitable. 100% snowmaking.
235m; slopes 235–420m 8

Tamsweg Austria
Large village with railway station in ultra snowy region close to Tauern Pass and St Michael. Cross-country centre.
1025m

La Tania 234
⊠ *Airtours, Alpine Action, Alpine Options, Avant-ski, Chalet World, Chalets 'Unlimited', Crystal, Erna Low, Eurotunnel Motoring Holidays, Fairhand Holidays, First Choice Ski, Independent Ski Links, Lagrange Holidays, Le Ski, Made to Measure, Motours, Neilson, Silver Ski, Ski Amis, Ski Arrangements, Ski Beat, Ski Club of GB, Ski Deep, Ski France, Ski Independence, Ski Leisure Direction, Ski Life, Ski Weekends, Snowline, Thomson*

Taos 545
⊠ *Made to Measure, Ski Independence, Ski The American Dream, Skisar US*

Tärnaby-Hemavan Sweden
Twin resorts where Stenmark learned his trade. Only Swedish area with its own airport. Snowsure.
slopes 265–830m
7 *44km*

El Tarter 616
Relatively quiet, convenient alternative to Soldeu, with which it shares its slopes.
⊠ *Panorama, Thomson, Top Deck*

Tarvisio Italy
Interesting, animated old town bordering Austria and Slovenia. A major cross-country centre with fairly limited Alpine slopes.
750m; slopes 750–1860m
12 *15km*

Täsch 461
The final base accessible by road on the way to car-free Zermatt – you take the train the rest of the way.
✉ *Interhome*

Tauplitz Austria
Traditional village at the foot of an interestingly varied area north of Schladming.
900m; slopes 900–2000m
18 *25km*

Tazawako Japan
Small area 4 hours from Tokyo. One of the few Japanese areas to get reasonable powder. 10

Telluride 514
✉ *Alpine Answers Select, American Ski Classics, Elegant Resorts, Iglu.com, Made to Measure, Ski Independence, Ski Safari, Ski The American Dream, Skisar US, Skiworld, United Vacations*

Temu Italy
Sheltered hamlet near Passo Tonale. Worth a visit in bad weather.
1155m; slopes 1155–1955m
4 *5km*

Tengendai Japan
Tiny area 3 hours from Tokyo with one of Japan's best snow records, including occasional powder. 5

Termignon France
Traditional rustic village. Good slopes of its own, and good base for touring Maurienne valley resorts – Valloire, Val-Cenis etc.
1300m; slopes 1300–2500m
6 *35km*
✉ *Fairhand Holidays, Lagrange Holidays*

Terminillo Italy
Purpose-built resort 100km from Rome with a worthwhile area when its lower runs have snowcover.
1500m; slopes 1500–2210m
15 *40km*

Cedars Lebanon
Largest of Lebanon's ski areas, 80 miles inland from Beirut. Good, open, go-anywhere slopes with surprisingly long season. Fully mechanised.
1850m; slopes 2100–2700m 5

Thollon-les-Mémises France
Attractive base for relaxed holiday. Own little area and close to Portes du Soleil.
1000m; slopes 1600–2000m
19 *50km*
✉ *Alpine Weekends, Lagrange Holidays*

Thredbo 639

La Thuile 391
✉ *Chalets 'Unlimited', Crystal, Equity Total Ski, First Choice Ski, Independent Ski Links, Inghams, Interski, Neilson, Rocketski, Ski Arrangements, Thomson*

Thyon 2000 445
Extremely limited ski-from-the-door mid-mountain resort above Veysonnaz in the Verbier ski area.

Tignes 318
✉ *Airtours, Avant-ski, Chalet World, Chalets 'Unlimited', Club Med, Crystal, Erna Low, Fairhand Holidays, First Choice Ski, Iglu.com, Independent Ski Links, Inghams, Interhome, Lagrange Holidays, Made to Measure, MasterSki, Motours, Neilson, Silver Ski, Ski Activity, Ski Amis, Ski Arrangements, Ski Choice, Ski Club of GB, Ski Expectations, Ski France, Ski Independence, Ski Leisure Direction, Ski Life, Ski Line, Ski Olympic, Ski Solutions, Ski Supreme, Ski Weekend, Skiworld, The Ski Company, Thomson*

Timberline (Palmer Snowfield) USA
East of Portland, Oregon, and the only lift-served summer skiing in the US: winter snow maintained by spreading vast amounts of salt to harden it.
slopes 1830–2600m
6 *2500 acres*

Togari Japan
One of several areas close (one hour) to 1998 Olympic site Nagano. 16

Torgnon Italy
Neighbour of Cervinia, good for bad weather.
1500m; slopes 1500–1965m
4 *6km*

Torgon Switzerland
Old village in a pretty wooded setting, with a lift connection to the Portes du Soleil.
1150m; slopes 975–2275m
219 *650km*
✉ *Interhome*

Le Tour France
Charming, unspoilt hamlet at the head of the Chamonix valley with much easier terrain than neighbours.
1465m; slopes 1465–2185m
9 *40km*

La Toussuire France
Dreary, downmarket, modern resort off Maurienne valley with a large, uncrowded intermediate area.
1800m; slopes 1400–2225m
19 *45km*
✉ *Fairhand Holidays, Interhome, Lagrange Holidays*

Trafoi Italy
Quiet, traditional (Austrian-style) village near Bormio, worth a day-trip if snow is good at low levels.
1570m; slopes 1570–2550m
6 *10km*

Treble Cone 641

Tremblant 606
✉ *All Canada Ski, Club Pavilion, Crystal, Elegant Resorts, Esprit Ski, First Choice Ski, Frontier Ski, Iglu.com, Inghams, Made to Measure, Neilson, Ski Independence, Ski Safari, Ski The American Dream, Thomson*

Les Trois Vallées 324

Troodos Cyprus
A good outing from Greek-sector coastal resorts, with interesting old villages en route. Pretty, wooded pistes and fine views.
1920m *4* *5km*

Trysil 629

Tschagguns 139
Village with a varied little area of its own but part of Montafon valley area.

Tsugaike Kogen Japan
Sizeable resort four hours from Tokyo, 3 hours from Osaka. Helicopter service to top station March to May.
800m; slopes 800–1700m 28

La Tuca Spain
Purpose-built development near Viella with lift to slopes. Worthwhile excursion from nearby Baqueira-Beret, especially in bad weather.
1050m; slopes 1270–2250m 7

Tulfes 111

Turoa 641

Turracherhöhe Austria
Tiny, unspoilt resort on a mountain shelf, with varied intermediate slopes above and below it. A good outing from Bad Kleinkirchheim.
1765m; slopes 1400–2200m
11 *30km*
✉ *Alpine Tours*

Tyax Mountain Lake Resort Canada
Heli-skiing operation in Chilcotin mountains. Transfers from Whistler or Vancouver. High-standard in-the-mountains retreat.

Uludag 627

Unken Austria
Traditional village with closest slopes to Salzburg, hidden in side valley.
565m; slopes 1000–1500m
4 *8km*

Untergurgl 142
Valley-floor alternative to staying in more expensive Hochgurgl or Obergurgl.

Unternberg Austria
Riverside village with trail connecting into one of longest, most snowsure cross-country networks in Europe. Large St Margarethen Alpine area on doorstep.
1030m

Unterwasser Switzerland
Old but not especially attractive resort 90 minutes from Zurich. Fabulous lake and mountain views. More challenging half of area shared with Wildhaus.
910m; slopes 900–2260m
21 *50km*

Uttendorf-Weiss-See Austria
Astute choice for crowd-free slopes when snowline high and Kaprun queues long. Tucked behind Kaprun.
805m; slopes 1485–2600m
9 *20km*

Vail-Beaver Creek 516
✉ *American Ski Classics, Chalet World, Crystal, Elegant Resorts, Erna Low, Esprit Ski, Handmade Holidays, Iglu.com, Independent Ski Links, Inghams, Lotus Supertravel, Made to Measure, Momentum Ski, Neilson, Ski Activity, Ski Club of GB, Ski Equipe, Ski Expectations, Ski Independence, Ski Line, Ski Safari, Ski The American Dream, Ski Total, Skisar US, Skiworld, Thomson, United Vacations*

Valbella Switzerland
Convenient but characterless village sharing large intermediate Lenzerheide area.
1540m; slopes 1470–2865m
35 *155km*
✉ *Club Med, Kuoni, Made to Measure*

Valberg France
Surprisingly large Alpes-Maritimes resort (bigger than better-known Isola 2000) close to Nice.
1650m; slopes 1430–2100m
26 *90km*

Val-Cenis 255
✉ *Erna Low, Inghams, Lagrange Holidays, Motours, Ski France, Ski Life, Snowcoach*

Val d'Illiez Switzerland
Peaceful, unspoilt village a few minutes below Champoussin. Nice open-air thermal baths. Good views of impressive Dents du Midi.
950m; slopes 1050–2280m
228 *650km*

Val-d'Isère 326
✉ *Airtours, Alpine Answers Select, Avant-ski, Bladon Lines, Chalet World, Chalets 'Unlimited', Club Med, Crystal, Elegant Resorts, Erna Low, Eurotunnel Motoring Holidays, Fairhand Holidays, Fantiski, Finlays, First Choice Ski, Handmade Holidays, Iglu.com, Independent Ski Links, Inghams, Interhome, Lagrange Holidays, Le Ski, Lotus Supertravel, Made to Measure, Mark Warner, Momentum Ski, Motours, Neilson, Scott Dunn Ski, Silver Ski, Simply Ski, Ski Activity, Ski Amis, Ski Arrangements, Ski Beat, Ski Choice, Ski Club of GB, Ski Expectations, Ski France, Ski Independence, Ski Leisure Direction, Ski Life, Ski Line, Ski Solutions, Ski Supreme, Ski Total, Ski Weekend, Ski-Val, SkiAway Holidays, Skiworld, Snowline, The Corporate Ski Company, The Ski Company, The Ski Company Ltd,*

Thomson, Val d'Isère A La Carte, Val d'Isère Properties (VIP), Weekends in Val d'Isère, White Roc, YSE

Val Ferret Switzerland
Old climbing village near Martigny, with spectacular views. Own tiny area.
1600m 4

Valfrejus 255
⊠ *Fairhand Holidays, Lagrange Holidays, Made to Measure, Motours*

Val Gardena 381
Valley area of Selva, Ortisei and Santa Cristina – part of the Sella Ronda circuit.
⊠ *Waymark Holidays*

Vallandry 202
Family-friendly satellite of Les Arcs with direct access to the main slopes.
⊠ *Independent Ski Links, Motours*

Valloire 255
⊠ *Fairhand Holidays, First Choice Ski, Lagrange Holidays, Snowcoach*

Valmeinier 255
Spread out resort, with links over a ridge to Valloire.
⊠ *Club Med, Erna Low, Fairhand Holidays, Lagrange Holidays, Motours, Ski Leisure Direction, Ski Life, Snowcoach*

Valmorel 336
⊠ *Airtours, Chalets 'Unlimited', Crystal, Erna Low, Fairhand Holidays, Iglu.com, Independent Ski Links, Lagrange Holidays, Made to Measure, Motours, Neilson, Ski Arrangements, Ski Independence, Ski Leisure Direction, Ski Supreme, Thomson*

Val Senales Italy
In the Dolomites near Merano; not so much a resort as a top-of-the-mountain hotel, the highest in the Alps.
3250m; slopes 2005–3250m
10 *24km*

Val-Thorens 341
⊠ *Airtours, Chalet World, Chalets 'Unlimited', Club Med, Crystal, Equity Total Ski, Erna Low, Eurotunnel Motoring Holidays, Fairhand Holidays, First Choice Ski, Iglu.com, Independent Ski Links, Inghams, Interhome, Lagrange Holidays, Made to Measure, Motours, Neilson, Panorama, Rocketski, Silver Ski, Ski Amis, Ski Arrangements, Ski Choice, Ski Club of GB, Ski Expectations, Ski France, Ski Independence, Ski Leisure Direction, Ski Life, Ski Line, Ski Supreme, Ski Weekend, Skisafe Travel, Skiworld, Thomson*

Valtournenche 352
Cheaper alternative to Cervinia, with genuine Italian atmosphere, and access to the extensive area.

Vandans 139
Sizeable working village well placed for visiting all the Montafon areas.

Vars 299
Large, convenient purpose-built resort linked to neighbouring Risoul.
⊠ *Fairhand Holidays, Iglu.com, Interhome, Lagrange Holidays, Tops Ski Chalets and Club Hotels*

Vaujany 193
Tiny, rustic village with huge cable-car, accessing the heart of the Alpe-d'Huez ski area.
⊠ *Erna Low, Lagrange Holidays, Motours, Ski Independence, Ski Life, Ski Peak*

Las Vegas Resort USA
Area formerly known as Lee Canyon, cut from forest only 50 minutes' drive from Las Vegas. Height and snowmaking gives fairly reliable snow. Night skiing too.
2590m; slopes 2590–2840m
3 *200 acres*
⊠ *Virgin Ski*

Vemdalen 633

Vemdalsskalet 633

Vent Austria
High, remote Oztal village with just enough pistes to warrant a day trip from nearby Obergurgl.
1900m; slopes 1900–2680m
4 *15km*

Ventron France
One of several areas near Strasbourg. No snowmakers.
630m; slopes 900–1110m
8 *15km*

Verbier 445
⊠ *Airtours, Alpine Answers Select, Alpine Weekends, Avant-ski, Bladon Lines, Chalet World, Chalets 'Unlimited', Crystal, Descent International, Elegant Resorts, Erna Low, Esprit Ski, First Choice Ski, FlexiSki, Freedom Holidays, Iglu.com, Independent Ski Links, Inghams, Interhome, Made to Measure, Momentum Ski, Motours, Neilson, Peak Ski, Plus Travel, Simply Ski, Ski Activity, Ski Choice, Ski Club of GB, Ski Expectations, Ski Line, Ski Solutions, Ski Verbier, Ski Weekend, Ski with Julia, Skiworld, Swiss Travel Service, The Corporate Ski Company, The Ski Company Ltd, Thomson, White Roc*

Verchaix France
Charming hamlet in lovely surroundings, next to Morillon, at foot of Flaine area.
700m; slopes 700–2560m
80 *260km*

Verditz Austria
One of several small, mostly mountain-top areas overlooking town of Villach.
675m; slopes 675–2165m
5 *17km*
⊠ *Sloping Off*

Vermion Greece
Oldest ski centre in Greece. In central Macedonia 60km from Thessaloniki. Barren but interesting slopes. 5

Vex Switzerland
Major village in unspoilt, attractive setting south of Sion. Verbier slopes accessed nearby at Mayens-de-l'Ours.
900m; slopes 1300–3330m
100 *400km*

Veysonnaz 445
Little, old village within Verbier's Four Valleys network.
⊠ *Iglu.com*

Vic-sur-Mere France
Charming village with fine architecture, beneath Super-Lioran ski area. Beautiful extinct-volcano scenery.
680m; slopes 1250–1850m
24 *60km*

Viehhofen Austria
Cheap(er) place to stay when visiting Saalbach. 3km from Schönleiten gondola, piste back to village from Asitz section.
860m

Vigo di Fassa Italy
Best base for Fassa valley, with Sella Ronda access via nearby Campitello.
1430m; slopes 1465–2060m
8 *25km*

La Villa 381
Quiet Sella Ronda village in pretty setting, surrounded by mostly very easy skiing.

Villacher Alpe-Dobratsch
Austria
One of several small, mostly mountain-top areas overlooking town of Villach.
500m; slopes 980–1700m
8 *12km*

Villar-d'Arêne France
Tiny area on main road between La Grave and Serre-Chevalier. Empty, immaculately groomed, short easy runs, plus a couple of hotels.
1650m

Villard-de-Lans France
Unspoilt, lively, traditional village west of Grenoble. Snowsure, thanks to snowmaking.
1050m; slopes 1160–2170m
29 *130km*
⊠ *Fairhand Holidays, Lagrange Holidays*

Villard-Reculas 193
Rustic village on periphery of Alpe-d'Huez ski area, with few local amenities.

Villaricas Chile
Vies with New Zealand's Mt Ruapehu resorts for the title of most active volcanic ski area in the world.
1200m

Villaroger 202
Rustic hamlet with direct links up to Arc 2000 and excellent runs back down.

Villars 454
⊠ *Club Med, Crystal, Erna Low, Interhome, Kuoni, Made to Measure, Momentum Ski, Plus Travel, Ski Club of GB, Ski Independence, Ski Weekend, Swiss Travel Service, The Corporate Ski Company*

Vipiteno Italy
Well-known year-round bargain-shopping town close to Brenner Pass.
960m; slopes 960–2100m
12 *25km*

Virgen Austria
Traditional village in beautiful valley south of Felbertauern tunnel. Slopes at Matrei.
1200m

Vitosha 623

Vogel 626

Vorderlanersbach 107
Small, satellite village of pretty Lanersbach, with access to Mayrhofen ski area.

Voss 629

Vuokatti Finland
Small mountain in remarkable setting, surrounded on three sides by dozens of little lakes. Good activity centre with plenty of indoor sports. 8

Wagrain Austria
Traditional village at the heart of the intermediate three-valley area linking Flachau and St Johann im Pongau – part of Salzburger Sportwelt Amadé.
900m; slopes 800–2185m
100 *350km*
⊠ *Thomson*

Waidring 177
Quiet, snowpocket resort near St Johann in Tirol, with good nursery slopes. Fine easy skiing area – 4km by ski bus. Unsuited to mixed level groups.
⊠ *Thomson*

Waiorau Nordic New Zealand
Specialist cross-country centre just over an hour from Queenstown. All levels of trails through valley floors, bowls, ridges. Spectacular views. Overnight huts.
1600m *50km*

Wald im Pinzgau Austria
Cross-country centre surrounded by Alpine areas – Gerlos, Krimml and Neukirchen – with Pass Thurn also nearby.
885m

Wanaka 641

Waterville Valley 555
⊠ *Virgin Ski*

Weinebene Austria
One of many gentle little areas in Austria's easternmost ski region near Slovenian border. No major resorts in vicinity.
1560m; slopes 1560–1835m
🚡 5 ⛷ 12km

Weissbach bei Lofer Austria
Traditional resort between Lofer and Saalfelden. No slopes of own but well placed for touring Tirol. Kitzbühel, Saalbach, St Johann, Zell am See nearby.
665m

Weissensee Naggeralm Austria
Famous for Europe's largest frozen lake. Every conceivable ice sport played including ice-golf. One of many little areas in eastern Austria.
930m; slopes 930–1330m
🚡 4 ⛷ 7km

Weisspriach Austria
Hamlet in very snowy pass near Obertauern which shares surprisingly undeveloped area with Mauterndorf and St Michael.
1115m; slopes 1115–2050m
🚡 7 ⛷ 20km

Wengen 456
✉ Club Med, Crystal, Iglu.com, Inghams, Kuoni, Made to Measure, Plus Travel, Ski Club of GB, Ski Solutions, SkiGower, Swiss Travel Service, Thomson

Wentworth Canada
Long-established Nova Scotia area with largest accessible acreage in Maritime Provinces. Harsh climate ensures snow arrives and stays despite low altitude.
55m; slopes 55–300m
🚡 6 ⛷ 150 acres

Werfen Austria
Traditional village spoilt by Tauern autobahn passing between it and slopes. Good touring between peaks to Dachstein West region.
620m

Werfenweng Austria
Hamlet with advantage over main village Werfen of being away from autobahn and by the slopes. Best for novices.
1000m; slopes 1000–1835m
🚡 11 ⛷ 40km

Westendorf 179
✉ Inghams, Thomson

Whakapapa 641

Whistler 597
✉ All Canada Ski, Alpine Answers Select, American Ski Classics, Chalet World, Chalets 'Unlimited', Club Pavilion, Crystal, Elegant Resorts, Esprit Ski, First Choice Ski, Frontier Ski, Handmade Holidays, Iglu.com, Independent Ski Links, Inghams, Kuoni, Lotus Supertravel, Made to Measure, Momentum Ski, Neilson, Rocky Mountain Snowboard Tours, Simply Ski, Ski Activity, Ski Arrangements, Ski Club of GB, Ski Equipe, Ski Expectations, Ski Hillwood, Ski Independence, Ski Line, Ski Miquel, Ski Safari, Ski The American Dream, Ski Total, Skisar US, Skiworld, The Ski Company, Thomson, United Vacations

Whitecap Mountains Resort USA
Largest, snowiest area in Wisconsin, close enough to Lake Superior and Minneapolis to ensure winds and weekend crowds.
435m; slopes 435–555m
🚡 7 ⛷ 500 acres

Whiteface Mountain USA
Varied area in New York State 15km from attractive lakeside resort of Lake Placid. 93% snowmaking ensures good snowcover. Plenty to do off the slopes.
365m; slopes 365–1345m
🚡 10 ⛷ 211 acres

White Pass Village USA
Closest area to Mt St Helens. Remote and uncrowded with a good snowfall record. Mostly intermediate cruising.
1370m; slopes 1370–1825m
🚡 6 ⛷ 635 acres

Whitewater 571
✉ Skisar US

Wildcat Mountain USA
New Hampshire area infamous for bad weather, but one of the best areas on a nice day. Accommodation in nearby Jackson and North Conway.
slopes 600–1250m
🚡 4 ⛷ 225 acres

Wildhaus Switzerland
Undeveloped farming community in stunning scenery, near Liechtenstein, popular with families and serious snowboarders.
1100m; slopes 1100–2075m
🚡 9 ⛷ 50km

Wildschönau 181
✉ Interhome

Wiler Switzerland
Main village in particularly remote, picturesque dead-end valley near Lotschberg rail tunnel north of Rhône valley. Very limited slopes.
1380m; slopes 1380–2700m 🚡 6

Willamette Pass USA
US speed skiing training centre in national forest near beautiful Crater Lake, Oregon. Small but varied piste area popular with weekenders.
1560m; slopes 1560–2035m
🚡 7 ⛷ 550 acres

Williams USA
Tiny area above the main accommodation centre for Grand Canyon.
slopes 2010–2270m
🚡 2 ⛷ 50 acres

Windischgarsten und Umgebung Austria
Large working village on same railway line as Schladming. Slopes at nearby Hinterstoder and Spital. Lacks holiday atmosphere.
600m; slopes 810–1870m
🚡 11 ⛷ 18km

Winter Park 522
✉ Alpine Answers Select, American Ski Classics, Chalets 'Unlimited', Crystal, Lotus Supertravel, Made to Measure, Neilson, Ski Independence, Ski Safari, Ski The American Dream, Skisar US, Skiworld, Thomson, United Vacations

Wolf Creek USA
Remote area with highest snowfall record in Colorado. Uncrowded; wonderful powder. Great stop (accommodation 30km away) en route between Taos and Telluride.
3155m; slopes 3155–3590m
🚡 6 ⛷ 800 acres
✉ Skisar US

Xonrupt France
Cross-country centre only 3km from nearest Alpine slopes to Channel at Gérardmer.
715m; slopes 666–1150m
🚡 20 ⛷ 40km
✉ Lagrange Holidays

Yangji Pine Korea
Modern, ever-growing resort with pistes cut out of dense forest. 8 slopes, 40 minutes south of Seoul. Gets very crowded. *🚡 7*

Ylläs Finland
Largest ski centre in the Arctic area (463m vertical), 170km from Lapland's capital Rovaniemi. Unusually open slopes for Finland, popular with boarders and telemarkers for off-piste.
255m; slopes 255–715m 🚡 18
✉ Inghams, Inntravel

Yong Pyeong Korea
Largest resort in Korea, 200km east of Seoul, with snowmakers on all 18 of its exclusively short runs.
750m; slopes 750–1460m
🚡 16 ⛷ 20km

Zakopane Poland
An interesting old town near charming medieval Cracow and moving Auschwitz. Mostly intermediate pistes.
830m; slopes 1000–1960m
🚡 20 ⛷ 10km

Zao Japan
3 interconnected areas. Unpredictable weather and very cold temperatures. Renowned for 'chouoh' – pines frozen into weird shapes.
780m; slopes 780–1660m 🚡 42

Zauchensee Austria
Purpose-built resort with lifts fanning out into the Salzburger Sportwelt Amadé area that surrounds it.
855m; slopes 800–2185m
🚡 100 ⛷ 350km
✉ Made to Measure, Ski Hillwood, Sloping Off

Zell am See 184
✉ Airtours, Crystal, Equity Total Ski, Esprit Ski, First Choice Ski, Inghams, Interhome, Made to Measure, Neilson, Panorama, Rocketski, Thomson

Zell im Zillertal Austria
Sprawling valley town with pistes on two nearby mountains. now linked to higher Gerlos and Konigsleiten to form a fair-sized area.
580m; slopes 930–2410m
🚡 22 ⛷ 47km
✉ Equity Total Ski, Rocketski, Thomson

Zermatt 461
✉ Alpine Answers Select, Bladon Lines, Chalet World, Chalets 'Unlimited', Crystal, Elegant Resorts, Erna Low, FlexiSki, Iglu.com, Independent Ski Links, Inghams, Interhome, Kuoni, Lotus Supertravel, Made to Measure, Momentum Ski, Plus Travel, Powder Byrne, Scott Dunn Ski, Ski Choice, Ski Club of GB, Ski Expectations, Ski Independence, Ski Solutions, Ski Total, Ski with Julia, SkiGower, Swiss Travel Service, The Corporate Ski Company, Thomson, White Roc

Zinal Switzerland
Pretty, rustic village with high slopes. For some, the modern buildings are incongruous.
1680m; slopes 1680–2895m
🚡 9 ⛷ 70km
✉ Interhome

Zug 126
Tiny village in scenic location with Lech's toughest skiing on its doorstep.

Zürs 126
High, smart but soulless village on road to Lech, with which it shares extensive skiing.
✉ Crystal, Elegant Resorts, Erna Low, Esprit Ski, Iglu.com, Made to Measure, The Corporate Ski Company

Zweisimmen 428
Limited but inexpensive base for slopes around Gstaad, with its own delightful little easy area too.

MONEY BACK VOUCHER – PART 1

To be sent to
SKI SOLUTIONS, 84 Pembroke Road, London W8 6NX
along with your booking form

Name ______________________________

Address ______________________________

____

E-mail address ______________________________

Daytime phone number ______________________________

Tour operator (if applicable) ______________________________

Departure date _______________ **Number in party** _______________

I have bought a copy of Where to Ski and Snowboard 2002 and claim a refund of the £15.99 cover price. I understand this amount will be deducted from the cost of the holiday I am booking through Ski Solutions. Offer valid for bookings for 2001/02 and 2002/03 seasons holidays made before 30 April 2003.

Signature _______________ **Date** _______________

MONEY BACK VOUCHER – PART 2

To be sent to
WHERE TO SKI AND SNOWBOARD,
The Old Forge, Norton St Philip, Bath BA2 7LW

Name ______________________________

Address ______________________________

____

E-mail address ______________________________

Daytime phone number ______________________________

Resort(s) to be visited ______________________________

Departure date _______________ **Number in party** _______________

I have booked a ski holiday through Ski Solutions and claimed a refund of the £15.99 cover price of Where to Ski and Snowboard 2002.

Signature _______________ **Date** _______________

Have you booked any other holiday through Ski Solutions in the last two seasons? ☐ **Yes** ☐ **No**

WHERE to SKI AND Snowboard 2002

WHERE to SKI AND Snowboard 2002

WHERE to SKI AND Snowboard 2002

WHERE to SKI AND Snowboard 2002

WHERE to SKI AND Snowboard 2002